PERFORMING ARTS MANAGEMENT AND LAW

by

JOSEPH TAUBMAN
Doctor Juridical Science
Member of New York Bar

Introduction by Jed Harris

VOLUME I

LAW-ARTS PUBLISHERS, INC.
New York, New York
1972

Library of Congress Cataloging in Publication Data

Taubman, Joseph.

Performing arts management and law.

1. Copyright—United States. 2. Performing arts—United States. I. Title.

KF4290.T35 344'.73'097 74-189328

ISBN 0-88238-055-9

Library of Congress Catalog Card No. 74-189328

Printed in the United States of America by
MEILEN PRESS INC., NEW YORK, N. Y.

By Joseph Taubman

Author

Copyright and Antitrust (1960)

The Joint Venture and Tax Classification (1957)

Separate Stations (Poems) with Liffy Taubman (1963)

Editor

Subsidiary Rights and Residuals (1968)

The Business and Law of Music (1965)

Financing A Theatrical Production (1964)

Antitrust Bulletin (1962-1966)

Performing Arts Review (1969—)

To Liffy

With Gratitude

For Encouragement and Assistance

From Perception to Realization

TABLE OF CONTENTS

VOLUME II

Part III. Torts and Crimes

PAGE

FOREWORD

How does one essay to write a treatise on Performing Arts Management and Law, wherein copyright is a major component, in the midst of proposed copyright revision? Admittedly copyright revision, in its current go-about, is generational. That is, studies were sponsored by the Copyright Office with respect to copyright revision in the 1950's and the early 1960's. Granted the first bills of the current series of proposed copyright revision were introduced in 1964 and 1965.

At the outset the writer was faced with a crucial question of judgment. Like Hamlet's soliloquy, "To Be Or Not To Be," the writer had to face the choice of current copyright law which might be buried in the course of writing the treatise by actual, fundamental copyright revision, or, conversely, the preparation of an opus on copyright revision which might never come to life.

The writer decided that generational copyright revision merited an intermediate approach (some might call it squaring the circle). Just as one has only one life to lead, so we have only one Copyright Act in being. To gamble on prospective copyright revision as the focus of attention seemed foolhardy. At the same time, proposed copyright revision merited consideration because if enacted, well, it would have been covered, and—perish the thought—if it died aborning, then it would be most useful to discuss its provisions conceptually to be held as a mirror, so to speak, to current law.

And so the opus considers both current law and proposed copyright revision. But the problem did not quite end there. Congress, in its wisdom, did not see fit to enact fundamental copyright revision during the writing of this work. The pundits have it that by reason of the election campaign of 1972 no overall copyright revision is in sight in 1972. But with the inception of each new Congress, legislation must be introduced anew with new numbers, which cannot be ascertained in advance, even where substantially the same bills are resubmitted excepting only for conforming changes, such as effective dates. Thus, automatically, references to existing bills will eventually require the reader to consider in place thereof the new bills to be submitted in 1973 whose numbers are presently unknown.

Inasmuch as this treatise is intended to be updated periodically, then, in due course, the writer will be able to conform the technical changes accordingly by references therein to bills to be submitted hereafter. Indeed, because actual writing of the work has been preparation over the past two and a half years, the writer also had to meet the same problem in respect of the bills now before the current session of Congress. For example, one could easily have excised all references to S. 543, introduced in the Senate in 1969 and substituted the current bill, S. 644, therefor. But S. 644 is mainly S. 543 with conforming technical changes. Instead, the writer decided to treat the matter as a continuum, particularly since S. 543 was the principal bill before the Senate in substantially its present form.

Hence the references to S. 543 in the text are intended as a convenience to obviate the need for interminable revision by the writer in order to refer to S. 644. However, where pertinent the conforming, technical changes of S. 644 have been alluded to.

In the same context, the writer has given the year of works in looseleaf or periodic revision form, such as "Nimmer on Copyright," as of the date of copyright in such reference, at the date of first referral thereto by the writer even though the writer has had occasion to refer to such works on a continuing basis over the years in preparation of this treatise.

The continuum approach thereby becomes the most feasible way to write a treatise without being overwhelmed by the dichotomy between the desire to be as current as the daily newspaper and the reality of the time lapse entailed in immersion in printer's galley pages, page proofs and publication, let alone writing and revision of the manuscript. In part, this can be overcome by revision, such as inclusion herein of P.L. 92-140, the new anti-piracy amendment to the Copyright Act with respect to sound recordings, in the course of the endless exchange of material between writer and publisher. Where this has not obtained, then the work reflects the decision to cover new matter on a supplementary basis at a later date. Again the approach is by way of the notion of continuum.

In this regard, the appendices have been kept to a minimum because such material will be covered comprehensively at a later date. Consequently, it was felt desirable to leave the fuller exposition thereof to subsequent publication.

On the other hand, references in the text to Volumes of Forms include all forms edited and compiled by the writer, be they volumes which will be published in conjunction with the present text, or such material as will appear later, since the editing and compilation have been completed to the point of enabling cross references to be made in the present text to all such forms.

The text has been divided into three parts: Part I, Scope; Part II, Arts Market Place, Copyright and Contract (comprising together Volume 1 of the text), and Part III, Torts and Crimes, together with appendices, bibliography, table of cases and subject index (comprising Volume 2 of the text). Additional parts will be added in the future as the preparation of further textual material progresses.

For the writing of this opus has been conceived of as long-range. To cover the relationships inherent in performing arts management and law, one must look at both copyright and non-copyright parameters. In the course of further writing, the writer hopes to get into the latter areas in greater detail. This much can be said, however, as one looks back at the copyright parameters, as garnered from the research and conclusions of the writer: when, oh when, will Congress finally give us a modern copyright statute in place of the present law with all its archaisms! One is mindful of the numerous efforts to replace the old Metropolitan Opera House in New York over the course of many years with a new plant. At least there, the efforts eventually succeeded.

The irony, here, is that even resubmission of bills with new numbers in 1973 may do little more than spawn new House hearings, apart from the more immediate question of the annual extension battle as to renewal copyrights to conform with eventual overall copyright revision. This might then defer actual consideration until 1974 with attendant consequences of a cliffhanger fate for comprehensive copyright revision.

That would be most unfortunate. For in many major respects, the performing arts and Congressional and executive recognition thereof have come of age. Federal support for the arts has become a reality on a continuing basis, supplemented, as it were, by the realization of the federal tribute to the performing arts in the guise of the John F.

Kennedy Center for the Performing Arts in the nation's capital. Such support is widespread and bi-partisan and will presumably so continue into the foreseeable future.

In the light of such happy auguries for our cultural growth as a nation, one wonders why we cannot overcome the peccadilloes of the jurisprudence of interests which now inhibit fundamental copyright revision. Consensus by compromise may become the albatross around the neck of the arts in America unless surmounted by a national willingness to acknowledge the imperatives of time and technology. Our statute became law in 1909 at a time when motion pictures, sound recordings and radio were in their infancy and television was non-existent. Wholly new technologies have developed in the interim and further changes in the electronic arts—CATV, video cassettes, computers, xerography, and others—are making and are about to make further transformations. The remarkable growth of the dance in this country merits much more serious consideration than the limited means of protection hitherto accorded under existing laws. The restructuring of educational means—hardware and software—is upon us and requires further attention.

There is the excitement of change in the arts and its technologies that merits continuing consideration, e.g., mixed media production. We need a Commission on Technology of the Arts to be set into being by Congress as part of proposed copyright revision, but one that would not just make a survey, render a report and disband. We need an on-going Commission of this kind on a permanent basis to study the constant changes in technologies and their impact on the arts and concomitant copyright and other protections that might be accorded with respect thereto.

Then, too, the time has come for performing arts management and law to overcome their lag in theory and practice in the forward march of the arts in America. For the contributions of management and law to the arts, as this treatise has endeavored to show, are fundamental to the work and welfare of the artist and creator in the performing arts.

Management and law in the performing arts have an obligation, not only to proffer modern copyright legislation, but to show the way preceptually by every educational means at their command, to the performing artists and creators, as well as to society as a whole, because of the crucial position of management and law as the ball bearings of the performing arts. This can be done by elucidation of the nature and role of management and law in the performing arts by means of research, symposia and publication. Additionally, management and law can play a key role in conjunction with the artist and creator in experimentation and study of avant garde and other forms, productions and techniques in the arts. In this regard, management and law should not have to wait years for the results of litigation as the crucible in which legal doctrines are ultimately elaborated. We should not have to wait for test cases to be finally determined for definitive guidance as to the nature of new forms and media.

In this regard, perhaps management and law should not have to wait years for judicial articulation as to the meaning of what has happened. Possibly management and law should take a leading role in the day-to-day operations of the arts in the quest for definition and meaning. In this regard, fundamental copyright revision is only a part, albeit a giant step forward.

Foreword

In a sense, this treatise is dedicated to the search for meaning in the arts, in the relationship of law to market mechanisms, and of both to the artist and creator. Although the actual writing was done in recent years, nonetheless it is intended to reflect a major part of the writer's studies, whether as practitioner, writer or editor, in the law and management relative to the arts. The starting point has been, throughout several decades of participation in this area, a feeling of healthy respect and appreciation for the artist and creator as such and as members of and pace-setters for humanity as a whole. Yet, with it all, the writer must conclude that all of us, who owe so much of the richness of our lives to the works of the world's artists and creators, have barely repaid them with even a smidgen of return.

Management and law have much of a positive nature with which to repay our artists and creators—past, present and future, for the many satisfactions of a priceless nature which artistry and creation have afforded us. The performing arts are vibrant in America today, and should include major contributions which management and law inherently can and should make thereto.

JOSEPH TAUBMAN

Baldwin, New York
July, 1972

ACKNOWLEDGMENTS

Writing is an individual craft, yet in many respects it is the most social of endeavors because its essence is communication. This is all the more so when one is engaged in preparing an opus of this sort entailing need for access to material of all kinds.

In the course of writing this work, the writer made repeated visits to the Copyright Office and wishes to express his gratitude and thanks for the cooperation accorded. In particular, the writer is grateful to George D. Cary, Abe Goldman, Benjamin Rudd, Wilma S. Davis and Barbara Ringer (who is currently with UNESCO in Paris). Their cooperation cannot be overstated. We are fortunate in having persons so deeply committed to the arts who conceive of their function as being so helpful.

The writer also wishes to express his thanks and appreciation to Irving Moross, Esq. and Samuel Reice, Esq. of Columbia Pictures Industries, Inc. and his former colleague there, Harold S. Klein, Esq., as well as to Stanley Rothenberg, Esq., M. William Krasilovsky, Esq., Alan J. Stein, Esq. and James Mosher, Esq. of the New York Bar. Thanks are in order to Walter Evans of Warner Bros. Music and to John McKellan, Esq. of MCA Music for ferreting out obscure material when contacted.

The writer wishes to thank Bernard Stebel, Esq., and Ronald Greenberg, Esq. for their cooperation in the preparation of this work. The writer wishes to acknowledge his thanks and appreciation to Rubin Wachtel Baum & Levin generally and to his friend, Abraham G. Levin, Esq. for making their facilities available during the writing of this opus.

The writer desires to thank his colleagues, Abraham L. Meilen and Peter M. Meilen of Law-Arts Publishers, Inc. for their unflagging cooperation during the entire period of gestation of the work.

A special thanks to the writer's many friends, acquaintances and colleagues in the arts—be they artists, creators, managers, administrators or lawyers—be they in New York, California, Florida, or elsewhere in the United States or outside this country, for their unsuspecting role in the education of the writer so as to make this work possible.

Finally, the writer wishes to express his unreserved gratitude and thanks to his wife, Liffy, not only for having the patience and endurance to abide the event cheerfully, but for her own substantial contributions to the endless reading of manuscripts, revisions, galley pages, page proofs, etc. As for our children, Dan, Fred and Susan, a word of thanks and appreciation for their understanding and indulgence as to which we can only say that like Jacques Brel, we are alive and well and living in Baldwin!

INTRODUCTION

BY JED HARRIS

It is almost impossible nowadays to find anyone to say a good word for the law. Oddly enough, there is nothing new about this condition. Except among the ancient Hebrews whose basic laws were, of course, handed down by the Almighty Himself, there has never been much respect for the law. More than fifty years ago, James Reed, a salty old senator from Missouri said, "The law—the law! How sinuous in its absurdity, how absurd in its sinuosity!" But long before that, one of Dickens' minor characters said, "The law is a ass." Through the agency of another minor character, Shakespeare said what is probably the last word on the subject: "First let's kill all the lawyers." On the unlikely chance that enough dedicated persons should undertake to carry out this suggestion, I think some of us would exert ourselves to save the small, round, soft-spoken author of this book.

A born philosophical anarchist, I became a convinced one as a direct consequence of my first encounter with the law. I had just produced "Broadway," a great popular success, when I was sued for half the profits by a man called Leonard Blumberg. The grounds upon which he based his action were somewhat curious. He claimed that after seeing a performance of the play during a try-out in Atlantic City, he had agreed to finance the play; that he had the necessary money, ready and available; he was only waiting for word from me to send along his check. His complaint was that I never got in touch with him. Totally ignored was the fact that when Blumberg saw the play, it was already completely financed and almost ready to open in New York.

If all this seems, as it did to me, completely preposterous, "wiser" and more "practical" men assured me that this was a very serious matter. Perhaps as much as a million dollars might be at stake and that I had better get an attorney, and a damned good one, to fight the case. Never having had a lawyer, I had not the faintest idea how to go about getting one. And then somebody mentioned the name of Nathan Burkan.

Burkan was one of the great lawyers of the day. He had brilliantly and successfully defended some rather unscrupulous and even criminal characters. I said that if I were guilty of some crime, Burkan would be my choice. But since I was totally innocent, it did not matter who represented me, because Blumberg was bound to be totally discredited.

In any event "practical" advice prevailed and I engaged Burkan. I put up a hefty fee as a down payment and soon found myself being ferociously cross-examined by my own lawyer. First he went through all my files and learned that Blumberg had financed my first two plays. Blumberg had profited by almost twenty thousand dollars out of them. Although our relations were perfectly amicable, we were not friends but merely business partners. He had driven rather hard bargains with me on those plays and I had decided to turn elsewhere for the money for my third play, "Broadway." And as each one of these ventures was a separate transaction, I was under no obligation of any kind to have further dealings with him.

But Burkan took the position that there *had* to be something that I was concealing from him, some conversation with Blumberg, some written communication which might be missing from my files. I was beginning to be exasperated and finally I said, "If you don't believe me, why not drop out of the case and let me engage someone else?" He smiled and said, "I'm only trying to protect you. You have stood up very well under my 'cross-examination,' as you call it. And when you're called to the witness stand, I think you'll do all right." He paused for a moment. "William Klein, the Shubert's attorney, is going to represent Blumberg. He's a smart lawyer and I find it hard to believe he will be going into court with as poor a case as this. There must be something they've got and I've been doing my best to find out what it might be."

Like his other clients, I grew quite fond of Burkan. Victor Herbert was devoted to him. Indeed, he and Burkan created ASCAP. Upon his death, one of his oldest clients, August Luchow, left him his restaurant. My trust in him was so great that I was shocked when, in the hall outside the court room where the trial was to begin, he hurried over to me and said, "We don't have to go to trial. I can settle this case right now for five thousand dollars." I said, "No, I wouldn't settle the case for a nickel." "You're mad," he said. "A court room is simply an arena. Anything can happen. My advice is to settle right now. Five thousand dollars is peanuts." I refused his advice. "Nathan," I said, "I've paid you a damned good fee. Now it's up to you to go and do your stuff."

He threw up his hands and in a few minutes the trial was under way, and Blumberg was on the stand. Burkan had furnished me with a legal pad and a pencil and asked me to make notes of any mis-statements Blumberg might make. It is only fair to admit that Blumberg gave his name, address, and the nature of his employment (he was general manager for the Shuberts in Philadelphia and the fact that the Shuberts assigned their lawyer to represent him, may not have been entirely coincidental)—quite accurately. Thereafter, he lapsed into a stream of errors and small, tedious lies. I was not accustomed to getting out of bed at seven-thirty. I was drowsy and bored with these proceedings. I stopped making notes and was beginning to doze off when I heard something that startled me.

Blumberg had testified that he had never bothered to read the manuscripts of the plays he had financed for me; he professed absolute faith in my judgment. Then Burkan showed him a letter he had written to an out-of-town theatre manager recommending that he book my first play. "I have read the script," he wrote, "and think it is very good." Blumberg readily acknowledged he had written the letter and that he had read the script. But he added with a patronizing little smile, he had not read the manuscript.

There was a moment of silence in the court room. William Klein raised his hands and clasped his head like a man bereft. The knuckles of Burkan's hands, clasping the rail, turned dead white. I felt sick.

Burkan now asked what the difference was between a script and a manuscript. "Well," said Blumberg after some reflection, "one had dialogue but no stage business, while the other had both." Which, asked Burkan, had which? By the time we recessed for lunch, Blumberg was floundering like a beached whale in a morass of definitions, distinctions, explanations and contradictions. Burkan said, "I will have this fellow in the hospital before the day is out."

After lunch, Burkan continued to question him about scripts and manuscripts. By four-thirty, Blumberg had broken down and was taken to the Polyclinic Hospital and the case was abandoned. And I was out about $7,500 in legal fees.

In England, as I soon discovered, Blumberg would have had to reimburse me for every penny of it. So there are comparatively few of these "nuisance suits." These are, after all, a perfectly legitimate form of litigation, not merely permitted by law, but actively encouraged by it.

After Blumberg's collapse, I became a devout supporter of the American Arbitration Society. Here, at last, was a forum for the settlement of disputes without the absurd and costly shenanigans of the law courts. Or so I thought.

One day, I was asked to appear as an expert witness in an arbitration between the late John C. Wilson and Metro-Goldwyn-Mayer. Again, I was asked to appear at nine in the morning. Again I arrived in a slightly drowsy state, only to find two banks of lawyers arranged at opposite sides of a long table. The arbiter was a very impressive gentleman, the president of the Equitable Life Insurance Company. The arbitration, I was astonished to learn, had already consumed two days' time and the air was foul with cries of "I object!" "Irrelevant!" "Immaterial!" I listened to these bizarre exchanges for fifteen minutes. Then I rose from my chair, got my hat, and started to leave the room.

"Where are you going, Mr. Harris?" said the arbiter.

"Home."

"But we are expecting to call on you in a little while."

"I'm sorry", I said, "but I won't sit here and listen to this guff. I joined this Society under the impression that we were going to rid ourselves of these tiresome legal gambits. I will stay on if you can call on me without further delay. I think I understand what this affair is about and I am ready to say what I have to say and then get the hell out of here."

"Very well," said the arbiter. He turned to the lawyers. "If you gentlemen will agree, we will now call on Mr. Harris."

"First," I said as I took my seat again, "I will take the liberty of stating this case as I see it. Wilson produced this play, "A Day in Spring," in partnership with MGM. The play was presented in New York with indifferent results. While it wasn't a flat failure, it wasn't doing profitable business. There were losses in which the partners shared. Mr. Wilson then moved the production to Chicago where it was a disastrous failure. But while MGM shared the costs and losses in New York, it has refused to pay its share of the losses in Chicago. MGM takes the position that since the play was a failure in New York, it should not have been transferred to Chicago and places the full responsibility for the losses incurred there on Mr. Wilson.

"I will not bore you with accounts of plays that succeeded in New York and failed in Chicago, nor the far more numerous plays that were successful in Chicago with contrary results in New York. I believe that as men reasonably familiar with show business, you will not contest that statement. I will merely add an item from my own experience. I once press-agented a show that cleared about $150,000 during its Chicago engagement, and then died in a week in New York.

"Perhaps MGM has a good argument that the show should not have been sent to Chicago after its failure in N.Y. But that is based entirely on the unfortunate result of the move to that city. And it would seem to me that MGM ought to win this case hands down providing the company can provide convincing evidence that if the play had been successful in Chicago, MGM would have refused to share in the very considerable profits that might have come from a successful engagement in that town. Short of that, I think it is the plain duty of the Arbiter to rule in favor of Mr. Wilson. That is all I have to say."

I then said goodbye and went back to get more sleep. The Arbiter had rendered his decision within ten minutes of my departure. Just before I fell asleep, I had a call from a Mr. Margolies of the Metro legal staff. "You murdered us," he said, "but I would like to congratulate you on the way you did it."

"I must say that I had no intention of murdering MGM. I simply called the shot as I saw it. But thanks just the same."

But since these volumes are prepared for the professional reader, what relevance does my own sour attitude toward the law, toward the courts and the lawyers who practice in them have to do with the laws governing the performing arts? Especially in the light of my avowal of anarchy?

I can furnish only a partial answer. Like the ninety-year old man who was asked how he could bear the painful burdens of extreme old age, I can say when I think of what the alternative is, I can endure them with considerable equanimity.

Anarchy is fine when confined to a colony of one. As soon as you get two or more anarchists together, you have got to have rules and such is the human lot, these rules must, of necessity, be hardened into laws and laws must be enforced. Hence the need for police, lawyers, judges, courts, and the whole staggering and woefully inefficient organization somewhat optimistically called civilized society.

Mr. Taubman's immense labors in collecting and organizing the material in these volumes is a great service to all those concerned with the legal aspects of the performing arts. And their numbers are likely to grow because with the rise of the media, we are all, professionals and laymen alike, destined to be involved more and more in the performing arts. Indeed, politics have already been characterized as a slum area of show business. Should a politician have to pay for his appearances on television or should he join one of the artists' unions and be paid for his work as an accredited performer? It is a nice point and it will surely come up as a legal position before long.

Many of these pages make fascinating reading for people in show business. Some of the laws are poorly written but then that seems to be true of the laws generally. I think that artists, producers, directors, agents and managers might do worse than to keep a set of these books if only to browse through them. As water runs downhill, everything connected with the performing arts tends to gravitate toward the media. And once there, they become objects of international trade, endless repetition and it is doubtful if, in the course of these infinite transactions, the artists and creators get a fair shake. Once, during a film festival in Venice, I found myself more taken with the antics of the Levantine film salesmen who infest these affairs, than with the "prize" pictures that were being shown:

> "Leesten, Alberto, I tell you what I got for you. T'ree Laurel and Hardy for Grriss and Algeria and I tell you what I do. I t'row in Tunisia and Albania—"
>
> "Now, Felici, dawn't tell me anymore before I show you beeyoutiful, ladder suit-case I bought in London and wan dozen made-to-order shirts I got from Tremlett—"
>
> "Aha, where you bought the suitcase, tell me, plizz?"

It is of course a lead-pipe cinch that neither Laurel nor Hardy, neither the writer nor the director got so much as an Irish linen-type handkerchief out of this charming transaction.

Am I then biased in favor of the artists? Yes, absolutely. And I therefore feel strongly that since their work is an international commodity, they might do well to familiarize themselves with all the vagaries, omissions and loop-holes in these laws. By and large, the agents and lawyers, even the unions, tend to accept the status quo, the "common practice," as it is called.

Do I mean that the artist should become his own lawyer? Very definitely not. But he should inform himself and then pick his lawyer very carefully, as he picks his doctor, not for the sake of his ailments but for his complete personal protection. Thus, Victor Herbert, who was a professional musician and a composer, an artist presumed to be feckless and impractical but armed with a sense of outrage, found in Nathan Burkan the means to create ASCAP, an effort which in the beginning at least seemed like a very long shot indeed.

Good men have always been hard to find. In this world a really good lawyer is a priceless asset to a modern performing artist.

As for the lawyers themselves, this work fulfills a vital need. Indeed it is quite indispensable. But then this is something they are bound to discover for themselves.

Part I
SCOPE

Chapter I

PERFORMING ARTS

Sec. 1.1. Treatise and Treatment

The term "treatise" has been defined as a "book or article which treats a subject, esp. in a systematic manner and for an expository or argumentative purpose; a methodical discussion of the facts and principles involved and conclusions reached." [1]

This work is intended as a systematic treatment of the arts, particularly the performing arts, live and electronic, in relation to the principles and practice of law and management. The discussion will deal principally with the United States and, insofar as it may be relevant thereto, also with other countries.

As such principles and practice are set forth and correlated, necessarily the purpose will be expository—to state, explain and systematize. In the course of so doing, points of view perforce will be expressed. In that sense, the work will be argumentative, and unavoidably so, since the very selection, treatment and methodology employed in presenting facts, principles and conclusions will comprehend a certain amount of subjectivity, opinions and observations representing the views of the writer.

Indeed, the choice of subject matter necessitates bringing the application of point of view into the foreground at the inception. At the outset, one is beset with the question of the nature of art and the arts.

---

[1] Webster's New International Dictionary, Second Ed., Unabridged, 1961 at p. 2699.

Sec. 1.2. Art

The term "art" in its broadest sense has a variety of meanings which, in gross, provides a useful overview of its sense in terms of the subject matter and scope of the work. In a generic sense, art is science. Webster defines art[2] as "A branch of learning; a science, esp. a science such as grammar, logic, or mathematics, serving chiefly as a discipline or as an instrument of knowledge." It is also systematization. Webster continues, defining it as "The general principles of any branch of learning or of any developed craft; a system of rules or of organized modes of operation serving to facilitate the performance of certain actions; as, the *art* of building or navigation; the *art* of war; the *art* of engraving". (italics).

Several other dictionary definitions of the term will serve to round out the picture. Webster goes on,[3] "Systematic application of knowledge or skill in effecting a desired result. Also, an occupation or business requiring such knowledge or skill; a craft; as industrial *arts*" (italics). Thus, the practice and application of principles in any general area take on the character of the art of that area, e.g. mechanical arts. In yet another definition, Webster states,[4] "Application of skill and taste to production according to aesthetic principles; an occupation having to do with the theory or practice of taste in the expression of beauty in form, color, sound, speech or movement. . . . That which is produced, as paintings, sculpture, etc. by the application of skill and taste."

Finally, for our purposes, his definition also includes,[5] "Skillful plan; device; also, cunning; artifice; craft." and

---

[2] *Idem* at p. 155.

[3] *Ibid.* at p. 155.

[4] *Ibid.* at p. 155.

[5] *Ibid.* at p. 155.

"Conventional or artificial expression in the fine arts." In short, overemphasis on technique or motivation not in harmony with principled application produces distortion that is also denominated art.

Sec. 1.3. Fine Arts

Webster's definition of fine arts[6] is quite simple. "Painting, drawing, architecture, and sculpture (these four being often called the *arts of design*); poetry, music, dancing, and dramatic art;—sometimes restricted to the first four named." (italics). Thus, in this term we get closer to the subject matter of our treatise than we do in the term "art" as defined above. It becomes clear that we are referring to particular skills or arts as the subject matter of our study and not something embraced by the comprehensive term "art". If one were to use the term "crafts" in the sense of skills, the nature of the scope of our study would become somewhat clearer. This can be seen in the contrasting nature of "mechanical arts". This pertains to the skills employed either manually and/or by the use of tools and machinery. Those utilizing such skills are artisans or craftsmen in mechanics.

Our concern, then, is with those artistic crafts wherein imagination and emotion are applied in the creation of particular forms and contents. The "arts" we are concerned with, at least, as set forth by Webster, are the "fine arts", made up of various categories of types of crafts as opposed to others, such as the mechanical crafts. This does not mean that there may not be skills common to fine arts and mechanical arts or, indeed, fine arts and any other arts. Our concern is with those engaged in the creation of objects of fine arts in the broadest definitional sense.

---

[6] *Idem* at p. 949.

Sec. 1.4. Performing Arts

Significantly, one searches in vain in Webster for a dictionary definition of "performing arts". It is noteworthy that the Webster definition of "fine arts" is stated to sometimes include "music, dance and dramatic art". In that sense the term "fine arts" as defined by Webster, includes some of the performing arts, to wit, music, dance and theatre.

Nor are the encyclopedias particularly helpful as to the term "performing arts". For example, Collier's Encyclopedia[7] does not discuss the term as a separate category. Nor, for that matter, does it set forth separate categories of "arts" [8] or "fine arts".[9] It does, however, contain separate discussions of motion pictures,[10] dance,[11] music,[12] theatre[13] and television.[14] The Index Volume[15] does not even list the term "performing arts" in its index. Interestingly, the Subject Guide to Bibliographies of the Index Volume includes a subject called "art".[16] Then a bibliography is set forth under the term "The Arts" [17] which contains a subheading, "Including Archaeology; Architecture; Painting; Sculpture; Design and Applied Arts; Prints and

---

7 Collier's Encyclopedia, 1960, volume 15, covering PAL through PRI.

8 *Idem* 1960, volume 2, covering APO through BAN. There is, however, a category "Art, Philosophy of" at p. 234.

9 *Idem* 1960, volume 7, covering END through FOR.

10 *Idem* 1960, volume 13, at p. 438.

11 *Idem* 1961, volume 6, at p. 66.

12 *Idem* 1960, volume 13, at p. 566.

13 *Idem* 1960, volume 18, at p. 306.

14 *Idem* 1960, volume 18, at p. 226.

15 *Idem* 1960, volume 20.

16 *Idem* 1960, volume 20, at p. 1.

17 *Idem* 1960, volume 20, at p. 68.

Illustrations; Minor Arts and Crafts; Music; The Dance; The Theatre; Photography and Motion Pictures".

One must therefore turn to the dictionary for the definition of "performance" for guidance. Webster defines the term as "The act of performing, the carrying out or execution in action; execution in set or formal manner or with technical or artistic skill; as the *performance* of a duty, a play, or a piece of music; . . ." [18] Webster goes on, "An act of performing, esp. of performing in a formal or ceremonious manner or of performing the functions required of one; a deed; feat; esp. one executed in public or in a manner to attract attention; hence, a public entertainment or exhibition of skill; a presentation of a play; as, to attend a *performance*." [19]

Sec. 1.5. The Artist

The foregoing consequently does much to explain the term "artist". Webster defines "artist", as, "One who professes and practices an art in which conception and execution are governed by imagination and taste; a person skilled in one of the fine arts." [20] Webster then defines a term which is in vogue in England, but rarely currently used in the United States, "artiste". He defines "artiste" as "A public performer, as a singer, actor or dancer." [21] Thus, by the device of orthography, a variant spelling of the term "artist" is synonymous with the term "performing artist".

It would seem that the term "artist" is currently used in two senses. In the broader sense, it denotes a practitioner of the particular skill or art with not less than

[18] Webster, *op. cit., supra,* at p. 1818.

[19] *Ibid.* (italics).

[20] Webster, *op. cit., supra,* note 1, at p. 157.

[21] *Ibid.*

minimum standards of skillfulness in that art. Generally that minimum consists of professionalism. The performer is sufficiently proficient in the proposed performance so that he will receive some sort of compensation for his services. Very often, concomitantly, a condition of such agreement is the requirement that the artist must join the relevant guild or union having jurisdiction upon entry into his agreement if he is not already a member thereof.[22] In turn the collective bargaining agreement of that union and the employer will specify that each artist employed by the employer must join that union upon entry into the agreement with the employer if he is not already a member thereof.[23] Thus, the concept of the open shop union agreement is predicated on minimum standards of professional artistry. Moreover, if the artist had to be a member of the union or guild, prior to and as a condition of employment, the resultant characterization of artistry would still be based on comparable minimum standards of professionalism even though it were based on a closed shop agreement.

By contrast to the normative approach of describing any performer entering into a record artist's agreement as "artist", whether or not such artist thereafter becomes a member of the union, the term "artist" is also used in a qualitative sense. To refer to someone who performs well as an "artist" is to bestow the highest praise. In that sense, the term takes on the meaning of the second part of the dictionary definition, to wit, "a person skilled in the fine arts", with the word "highly" being implicit before "skilled".

---

[22] See, for example, Recording Artist's Agreements, Form Nos. 5A-1 *et seq.* in Volumes of Forms; and Screen Actor's Agreement, Form No. 1B-1 in Volumes of Forms. See Sec. 18.6, *infra.*

[23] *Idem.*

Thus, the term "artist" takes on two meanings in common usage. The broader meaning is functional. It is used as a means of classification. The more restrictive meaning is intended to be judgmental, critical and an evaluation of the underlying artistry of the performer. Such a determination is very often subjective and ultimately a matter of consensus rather than objective standardization, as in the union agreements, unless surrounded by recognized established emoluments, such as awards for best actor, best actress, participant in a great artist series, and so on. The term, then, is used both in the quantitative and qualitative senses.

Sec. 1.6. Entertainment

By contrast, the meaning of the term "entertainment" does not have this dual meaning. Webster defines the term "That which engages the attention agreeably, amuses, or diverts, whether in private, as by conversation, etc., or in public." [24] The term is broader than art because out of the engagement of the attention agreeably, amusement or diversion need not necessarily come art in its broadest sense. Indeed, one may be entertained by a variety of non-artistic means where the entertainment is based on lack of skill. A competition of inept log-rollers may very well satisfy any of the foregoing criteria of entertainment. The gambling casinos of Las Vegas would appear to qualify as a form of entertainment without necessarily involving artistic performance although both are very often combined there. The basis for professional sports is without any doubt whatever the entertainment of the spectator.

Naturally the arts have been prime forms of entertainment providers, since by definition the arts were applica-

---

[24] Webster, *op. cit., supra,* note 1 at p. 853.

tions of skill and taste in the area of esthetics and emotions. This was true when an opera, mask or dance was performed at court for the amusement and diversion of the courtiers. The pastime aspect of the incidental nature of the use of the arts is best expressed by the musical form *"divertimento"*. The same is true today in the musical comedy on stage, the lavish film extravaganza and the variety type of TV spectacular. The principal purpose of these is to entertain, to provide pleasant diversions and amusement. One difference is that, whereas the courtier was sometimes a participant, as in the mask or dance, the contemporary recipient of the entertainment is seldom a participant. On the one hand, there are the professional performing artists; on the other, the audience, public in the film and theatre, private in TV in the home, with the pure "divertimentee" (to coin a word), the expense account executive, only a relatively small part of the overall audience being entertained.

It would appear that the classification of classical music as "serious" music, in contrast to "popular" music is an acknowledgment that a segment of the arts is not necessarily comprehended by the term "entertainment". If persons are serious about certain types of music, then they are considering other factors than being amused, diverted or agreeably attended to. It would appear that the term is used in a context where other criteria or perhaps additional criteria enter into the composition of the audience. The sideline, incidental use of art for entertainment appears to give way to the central position of art in the response of the listener. The listener takes his music seriously whether or not it diverts, amuses or is agreeable. He or she may nevertheless take it seriously, as in comic opera or theatrical farce, for purposes of emotional, artistic and intellectual attributes of the production, even though he or she may enjoy it as an entertainment. By considering the same more than an entertainment, the listener-viewer is in some degree a participant by reacting critically to the performance.

It would seem, therefore, that the term "performing arts" is intended as something broader than the term "entertainment". In the latter, professionalism will be employed to amuse and divert. Commercial considerations of artistic excellence will very often apply to the accomplishment of that end. In the former, since the purpose may be other than amusement and diversion or purpose, in addition thereto, the effect may be non-commercial. The intent may be to achieve such purpose whether or not there is a market, i.e., audience, that is ready, willing and able to pay for the cost of production. Performing arts in this sense strive to reach their listener-viewers because they respond, whether or not box office receipts alone or advertiser-sponsor equivalent make it feasible. The basis of the non-profit operation of the performing arts is inherent in this factor although status, amusement and *divertimento* factors are far from unknown in such non-profit activities.

Sec. 1.7. Amusement

The term is close in meaning to "entertainment", yet in some respects is broader and in others narrower. Webster defines "amusement" as "Pleasurable diversion; entertainment, esp. when characterized by quiet mirth; hence, the state of being amused, as by something droll or humorous. . . . That which amuses or entertains." [25]

It is broader in that additional areas may be brought within the scope of the person whom it is sought to amuse,

---

[25] *Ibid.* at p. 91.

e.g., pin ball machines and amusement parks. The essence of the entertainment is that the person being entertained is in the position of a recipient although he might also be amused thereby. In amusement, the person being amused is not necessarily responding principally as recipient. In an amusement park or in a pin ball gallery, such person becomes a participant, for it is mainly by going on rides and operating machines and gadgets that he or she is amused.

It is narrower in that the element of diversion may be secondary or even eliminated. Because the element of participation may be stronger, as in an amusement park, there is less of the passive, spectator attribute to it. It is narrower, too, because the intent is to furnish amusement and for the participant to seek amusement. This can be accomplished without engagement of the performing arts. Indeed, one can find amusement parks consisting of assorted rides and skills (riflery, baseball pitching, etc.) without any performing arts or other entertainment whatsoever.

Nevertheless, entertainment has been and remains a prime form of amusement and artistic performances a major method of presentation of both. That is why the pertinent pages of newspapers and periodicals, for example, might variously be entitled, "Amusement", "Entertainment" or "The Arts" and use the expressions interchangeably to refer to what is being offered publicly.

Sec. 1.8. Show Business

The term does not appear to be defined in the dictionary.[26] Of course, the term "show" denotes exposure to

---

[26] See Webster, *op. cit., supra,* note 1, at p. 2324 under word "show" or word combination thereof.

sight, exhibition, display, brought to view, spectacle. Webster also defines it as "A spectacle conducted for entertainment, as in the Roman circus, a pageant, or a masque . . . A theatrical performance . . . Loosely, a display for gatherings of people, whether dramatic, artistic, or social." [27] Webster's definition of "business" is most interesting in this context. He defines it as "That which busies, or engages time, attention, or labor, as a principal *serious* concern or interest. Specif. . . . Constant employment, regular occupation, work . . . Any particular occupation or employment habitually engaged in, esp., for livelihood or gain." [28]

Show business, then, is enterprise involving performance or presentation of some kind in the arts for commercial gain. The most likely means of attracting a profitable audience, as far is the entrepreneur presenting the "show" is concerned, is to make it an "entertainment". Thus, we have a paradox, for the viewer the "show" is principally a means of entertainment, whereby the entrepreneur seeks to agreeably attend to, amuse and divert the viewer, while the same performance represents to the producer of the performance a professional engagement of *serious* concern because it is the principal source of occupation to the presenter. In short, entertainment of the audience is a means of livelihood for the impresario. The term "promoter" a term often applied to impresarios and entrepreneurs of rock and other popular musical festivals or events, connotes someone who assumes the risk of gain or loss, usually from commercial enterprise. The promoter may be local, national or international and may or may not have a managerial interest in his "acts".

---

[27] *Idem* at p. 2324.
[28] *Idem* at p. 362. (emphasis added).

In short, "show business" is the juncture of performing arts and economics where the vehicle for entertainment for gain is one of the performing arts. The standards for accomplishment of the desired dual purpose are professional performance of a quality sufficient to entertain, amuse or divert, attractive enough to assure a satisfactory return to the entrepreneur so that he might continue to devote his time, effort and resources to other presentations that might bring him gain.

It may be seen, therefore, that non-profit presentation by definition cannot be "show business" in the strict etymological sense that performance is for gain. Of course, box office receipts are an indispensable ingredient of non-profit performance, unless the same is without admission charge. However, non-profit presentation may nevertheless be, and often is, a means of livelihood and regular occupation. But it is submitted that the motivation of non-profit performance is the production, whether or not profitability at the box office ensues. In "show business", strictly speaking, the entrepreneur cannot and will not undertake production (other than an occasional non-profit benefit for a worthy cause) unless there is some expectation of gain. Since the most likely way to achieve such gain is by presenting an entertainment, the essence of "show business" becomes entertainment for profit.

Performing arts, on the other hand, very often are presented on a non-profit basis because the likelihood of profit is remote or non-existent. Thus, certain presentations of the performing arts become removed from "show business" because the possibility of profitable presentation is simply not present. Still other presentations become removed from the "show business" arena in terms of performance for gain because the serious purpose underlying the presentation conceivably reduces expectations of audience attendance. Hence the entrepreneur for gain will not run the risk of loss or lack of gain, whereas he might otherwise seek the possibility of gain in an entertainment.

Thus, "show business" and performing arts co-exist. They may at times be one and the same where there is production for profit, while at other times they may be presented under profit and non-profit auspices respectively.

Sec. 1.9. Recreation

Another area in which "show business" and "performing arts" co-exist is in recreation. Webster defines the term "recreation" as "Act of recreating, or state of being recreated; refreshment of the strength and spirits after toil; diversion; play; also a mode or means of getting diversion or refreshment." [29] Here the essence of the relationship is that of renewal, sometimes physically, at other times spiritually, and on occasion, both. The term suggests tacit recognition that mankind does not live by bread and toil alone. Humanity must have stimulation to regain renewal, both of mind and body.

The term seems to suggest participation for renewal. Purely spectator viewing of play—sportively on the athletic field and emotively in the theatre—is not quite the equivalent of refreshment of the strength and spirits after toil. One can argue that this may certainly be true of sports, where participation is essential for refreshment of strength, but that spirits may be refreshed in a purely spectator fashion. Perhaps. It must be borne in mind, however, that psychic recreation is neither a function of the for profit or not for profit syndromes. Recreation is recreation whether or not the promoter of the same does so for com-

[29] *Idem* at p. 2082.

mercial gain or otherwise. Moreover, recreation presupposes a measure of responsiveness by the recipient. He or she must be recreated or restored spiritually in order for it to be said that the recreation was effective. Conceivably recreation can be said to occur in an entertainment, an amusement, a diversion. Then again, it may require some emotional and intellectual participation by the recipient for the occurrence of recreation. It may require a degree of artistry in the qualitative sense on the part of the performer to bring the recipient to the requisite degree of stimulation necessary before it may be said that his or her recreation has occurred.

Sec. 1.10. Leisure

Recreation may be provided as part of one's employment or occupation and often is. Thus, factories may furnish facilities for all kinds of sports—outdoor athletic fields, indoor gymnasia, swimming pools—for employee recreation as an incident of employment. There may also be facilities—auditoria, rehearsal rooms—for films, choral and orchestral groups, and so on. Recreation may indeed be entirely incidental to one's gainful employment.

Leisure, on the other hand, is the antithesis of employment, when one is not unemployed. Webster defines the term "leisure" as "Freedom or opportunity afforded by exemption from occupation or business; time free from employment. Time at one's command, free from engagement; a period of unengaged time; hence, convenience, ease."[30]

Whereas recreation is purposeful—physical or mental activity for purposes of rejuvenation, there is no teleology

---

[30] *Idem* at p. 1414.

of leisure per se. Leisure represents the obliteration of responsibility time-wise, temporary freedom from preoccupation of earning a living where one has leisure time during employment and rather permanent free time during retirement. It would appear that leisure in unemployment is a contradiction in terms since this period hardly signifies a time of convenience, ease, freedom or opportunity.

Leisure imports a wide possibility of choice, within the means of the person enjoying that opportunity of free time. A person with leisure time can choose to be amused, entertained, engage in recreation. or simply abstain completely from sports and the arts. Leisure, then, is a time construct during which a person with free time can participate in a variety of experiences, or be the more or less passive recipient of performances of others. It would seem, however, that any employment during leisure time terminates the leisure period during such employment, even though the same may not be one's principal occupation and may be a form of "moonlighting" in more congenial employment.

Thus, there may be a wide variety of activities offered to those in leisure time which have little or no relationship to the arts. Hiking, picnicking, reading, traveling or carousing can and do fill leisure time for many people.

On the other hand, the availability of leisure time, as the employment work week has shortened and vacation period has lengthened in this century, has permitted the functioning of the performing arts as leisure time industries and facilities. One can speak of the film industry and like industries in the arts where there are aggregations of enterprises involved in production, distribution and exhibition for profit. In the non-profit sector, it would seem that it is not apt to characterize the activities and even organization of symphony orchestras and opera companies, for example, as industries.

Non-profit or profit motivation, therefore, for purveyors of leisure time is not particularly relevant. Any given person in leisure time can fill his or her time with either variant because the notion of free time permits that person to choose any kind of leisure time within the limits of his or her means. Leisure time, then, is not normative as to the types of activities it induces.

Sec. 1.11. Sports

Favorite leisure time and recreational activities are sports. Athletics may be purely spectator sports wherein one's free time is devoted to viewing professional or amateur events, or participatory sports of a recreational nature in which one spends one's leisure time in competing in that particular sport. To the spectator, viewing partakes of entertainment, amusement and agreeable diversion. On occasion the viewer is involved emotionally for extraneous reasons—he has placed a bet on his favorite horse or champion! The participant, on the other hand, generally is involved in some physical activity which, hopefully, will bring him gratifications of muscle tone, bodily development and health. The competition will often induce an emotional response in the participant of the excitement of involvement. The spectator may also become involved emotionally, but only derivatively, as a rooter for his team or side.

Webster has defined the term "sport" as "That which diverts, and makes mirth; pastime; amusement . . . Specif., some particular play, game, or mode of amusement; as (1) A diversion of the field, as fowling, hunting, fishing, racing, games, esp. athletic games, and the like; also, any of various similar games or diversions usually played under cover, as bowling, rackets, basketball, etc., (2) Any game or contest, esp. one involving individual skill and physical prowess, on which money is staked." [31]

It is to be noted that sports and arts have one principal characteristic in common; in both, performances are a predominating method for the occurrence of each. In each, too, it is the skill of the performer which is the attraction. However, the prowess of the athlete elicits a somewhat different response from that of the performing artist. Presumably this is so because the ability of the athlete brings out the admiration of the spectator, the possibility of emotional response, varying in degree and intensity to the excitement of the competition. On the other hand, viewing outstanding artistry in performance may touch a wide range of emotional responses that sometimes fuses into intellectuality. In other words, audience reaction might include not only heart and stomach, but the head.

Having said as much, it should be noted that at various points sport and art appear to shade into each other. For example, free style gymnastics and figure skating partake of many of the forms and characteristics of the dance. Conversely, the dance, as the art of movement, will sometimes choreograph forms that are first cousins to gymnastics. Then, too, the game of chess is classified as a sport even though it is principally a game of intellectuality and not of physical competition. The excitement it generates is virtually wholly intellectual.

Finally, the locus of the particular event often determines its nature as sport or art. For example, a ping pong game among champions in a variety show on stage will constitute an act of a theatrical entertainment while the

---

[31] *Idem* at p. 2437.

marching bands at half time of a football game, even if consummately well played, will be no more than incidental diversion or entertainment at a sporting event.

In sports, in most instances, there is no underlying literary or artistic property, be it play, novel, or musical composition, which is the basis of ownership via copyright, proprietorship and the licensing and transformation of the bundle of rights. In the performing arts, as a result, creativity becomes inextricably entwined with artistry so as to affect the very legal, business, and yes, artistic, matrix of the performing arts thereby making the latter fundamentally different in their parameters from sports.

Sec. 1.12. Communications and Media

Yet another perspective is afforded by the term "communication". Webster defines it to mean, "Intercourse by words, letters, or messages; interchange of thoughts or opinions, by reference or other means; converse; correspondence . . . That which is communicated or imparted; intelligence; news; a verbal or written message . . . Act, power, or means of communicating or passing from place to place; access; a connecting passage; as, open lines of *communication* are of first importance in warfare. Specif., pl.: A system using signals, couriers, telegraphy, radio, or other means for communicating information or orders, as in the armed forces. A system of routes for moving troops, supplies, etc., in military operations."[32]

Interestingly, Webster does not define the term "media". Nor does his definition of the term "medium", which is the singular of "media", refer in so many words to its meaning in communications, except as follows: "That through or

---

[32] *Idem* at p. 541. (italics).

by which anything is accomplished, conveyed or carried on; an intermediate means or channel; instrumentality; as, an advertising *medium*." [33]

At first blush one might wonder how the notion of communications, which is the creature of technology, i.e., the various means of communications, comes into relationship to the arts. For the term connotes a comparison or means of the various forms of communication. No doubt this was the original meaning of the term in its sense of two way staying in touch, both sending or imparting and receiving. Its analogue was transportation, going or shipping goods someplace. Communication was the process of staying in touch without necessarily traveling or sending commodities. Communications were the systems or means employed in the process.

The primary means of communication, of course, is language. In spoken form, this meant speech; in written form, writings. The term "communications" imports a multiplicity of forms or means. Before the advent of the Industrial Revolution, one would have referred to the spoken word and the printed word as communications. It required invention of a multiplicity of means, e.g., telegraphy, telephone and radio, to set into being systems of communications in the sense of sending and receiving messages. These were truly systems of communications in the classic sense of two way interaction. Thus, for a number of years before the advent of radio broadcasting as a means of reaching the general public for pleasure, it operated principally as a system of communications, particularly for maritime and military, especially, naval, purposes.[34]

---

[33] *Idem* at p. 1528. (italics).

[34] See Barnouw, Erik, A Tower in Babel, A History of Broadcasting in the United States to 1933, vol. 1 (1966).

As radio broadcasting and later television became everyday means of reaching masses of people throughout the nation and the world, emphasis shifted to the separate components of "communications". Instead of the two way interaction of receiver and sender in the classical sense, by means of wired or wireless circuitry, with instantaneous or delayed response of receiver to sender in return communication, one had, instead, basically one way communication. There was the sending of the communication, either simultaneously or by delayed transmission, and the more or less passive receipt of the same. Communications, then, became basically a one way process, in terms of technology. This, of course, is also the function of the newspaper, the book and the periodical. But the term "communications" had already taken root in its classic sense of two way interaction. The logical difficulty of connotation was overcome by going back to the original meaning of the term "communication" as speech or language. Speech imports two way intercourse, i.e., speaking and hearing by speaker and listener. The person addressed replies in language.

It becomes an easy elision to carry the literal two way meaning of communications to a figurative one way meaning. The reader of a newspaper understands solely because the means of expression is language. In order for the communication to be effective, the reader uses his grasp of language to understand. Reading is the primary form of responding in this situation. The reader also responds by his acts, whether by letters to the editor or by political, social, economic or recreational activities in response to what he reads, as news, features, advertising or otherwise.

But the communication can include a variety of matters, among them, the cultural. When one goes from the printed to the audio and later to the audio-visual means of communication, one comes into the area of the performing arts, for music, dance and the theatre must be heard and/or seen. The printed word, the drawing or cartoon as communication cannot, without sound, become music. Movement is required for the dance or theatre. Thus, as radio and television became means of imparting entertainment, as well as news or commercial advertisement, they partook of methods of representing the performing arts and, by reason of their technology, of forms of the arts. Just as the play, in relation to film, became the screenplay, so the play, in relation to radio and television, became the radio play and the teleplay.

Once the incorporation of the performing arts in one way communication had been completed, it became evident that other areas of the arts should be deemed aspects of "communications". Thus, feature films could be shown on television. Even though cinema was definitely part of entertainment, yet it, too, was a one way means of communication of language in sight and sound by producer to audience. Ergo, motion pictures were one of the communication arts.

By similar extension, the term "communications" could serve to comprehend all of the arts. For example, the term "communication arts" has been defined as follows: "The many arts which are used in the exchange of messages, ideas, attitudes or feelings, e.g. the art of journalism, of film, of television, of dance, of theater, of folk and popular music, of literature, of public forum, and of graphic and fine arts." [35]

Because of the extensive reach of these means of communication, they have become known as mass media. As one writer has stated, "Not until the middle of the century,

---

[35] Jacobson, Howard Boone, Editor, A Mass Communications Dictionary 67 (1961).

however, has communication been studied in an independent context which first frames these broad and persuasive systems we have come to call the public or mass media . . ." [36] Another writer refers to, "the various media of mass communication." [37]

Indeed, the importance of the means is best expressed in McLuhan's phrase, "The medium is the message." [38] Thus, form or technology of communication provides the context for study of what it comprehends, including the performing arts.

But emphasis on means in due course provides an identification with the variety of content utilizing those means so as to impart the sense of the means to the content. Thus Steinberg correctly refers to television "as the world's largest advertising medium . . . " [39] and "advertising . . . as such" is not " . . . a medium of mass communication." [40]

By extension, because "communications" refers to means of reaching people, they also have reference to the specific means of reaching people. The context may refer to the comparative means of transmission of news on radio, television and the press. Perhaps the most technical form of comparison is provided with respect to advertising in the various "media". This form of usage has become so common that the term "media" has taken on a specific meaning relating to advertising. Thus, the term "medium"

---

[36] Bluem, A. William, at p. ix in Mass Media and Communication, edited by Steinberg, Charles S., (1966).

[37] Steinberg, Charles S., Public Relations and Mass Communication, at p. 401, in Mass Media and Communication, *Ibid.*

[38] McLuhan, Marshall, Understanding Media: The Extension of Man (1964), Preface to Third Printing at p. vii.

[39] Steinberg, *op. cit., supra,* note 37 at p. 239.

[40] *Idem* at p. 375.

has been defined as the "Means used to convey an advertising message such as newspaper, magazine, direct mail, radio, television, billboards, etc. (Plural: media)." [41] The advertising context, moreover, has produced terminology which is even more specifically related to advertising. Thus, for example, the term "media director" is defined as "The person in an agency responsible for the selection and purchasing of all media." [42]

The emphasis on comprehensive means of communication covering the arts as well would appear to lose something in terms of arts classification. Certainly the term "mass communications" by definition would exclude any form that is not mass. Taking the term "communications" in its generic sense, however, the thrust of the approach seems to be on the fact of communication, even if, in its broadest sense, it denotes one way communication. To look at the fact of communication is to look at its *gestalt,* its configuration, its structure. In a sense, the creative process in its various stages is beside the point. It is only the final embodiment in a particular means, radio, television, film, etc., that becomes important from this point of view. The lonely process of writing by the individual author, as he revises and revises until completion, would appear to be peripheral to the scope of communications. The latter is directed more to its own means and technology and the effect thereof on the performing arts, through its transmission, than on the nature of the creative and artistic process or on the creation of literary and artistic property in its broadest sense. Indeed, the sense of common law literary and artistic property is that of creative works which have not been published or offered for sale.

---

[41] Jacobson, *op. cit., supra,* note 35 at p. 210.
[42] *Ibid.* at p. 210.

Excluding communication thereof by performance and even limited publication not tantamount to divestiture of common law copyright, so as to require protection by notice of copyright, deposit and registration in Washington,[43] common law works are uncommunicated works. Nevertheless, as such, they are and can be important parts of the performing arts. Consider, for example, manuscripts of some of our leading writers if such were unpublished and unperformed. If one were to discover a play under common law copyright of a Eugene O'Neill or a novel of an Ernest Hemingway, even if never published, produced or adapted, the same would assume creative importance even though never communicated. Thus, the facets of creativity are not necessarily comprehended by the term "communications".

Finally, it would seem that qualitative, critical evaluations of literary and artistic works and their transformation and transmutation into other forms are comprehended by the arts, performing and creative, and would appear to have little reason for inclusion of the same under the term "communications" unless the same were actually performed or published.

Sec. 1.13. Culture

The term "culture" has two different meanings. The broader notion is sociological and anthropological; the other conception is limited to the fine and performing arts. The effect of the particular state of the arts is the degree of culture in the individual or community induced thereby. In the conception is the idea of cause and effect. Culture results from the prevalence of the arts. In this sense cul-

---

[43] See, Nimmer on Copyright (1969), Sec. 58. Limited Publication: When a Publication is Not a Publication; Sec. 26.4, *infra*.

ture is a kind of inherence or immanence. The fact of the arts begets culture.

Webster differentiates the social science meaning from the esthetic concept. In the broader sense he defines "culture" as "A particular state or stage of advancement in civilization or the characteristic features of such a stage or state; as, primitive, Greek, Germanic *culture*. . . . The complex of distinctive attainments, beliefs, traditions, etc., constituting the background of a racial, religious or social group." In the sense of the arts, he goes on by denominating it as "The state of being cultivated; esp., the enlightenment and refinement of taste acquired by intellectual and aesthetic training; the intellectual content of civilization; refinement in manners, taste, thought, etc. . . . Conversance with and taste in fine arts, humanities, and broad aspects of science;—distinguished from vocational, technical, or professional skill or knowledge." [44]

Culture, as it relates to the arts, denotes catholicity. The refinement of taste is not necessarily synonymous with class or caste sophistication. Otherwise one could not speak of peasant art, peasant culture, folk art, folk music, and folk dancing as cultural phenomena. Rather it is the ability to accept variant art forms, no matter how simple in form or superficially crude in development, that characterizes a cultured person. It is a refinement of liberality of sentiments, of openness to art experience that becomes a characteristic of culture in relation to the arts. Culture, then, is a comprehension of a variety of art forms and contents with an intellectualizing response thereto. Liberality of sentiments can take, however, a more limited form. Culture may be manifested in espousal of a particular cause or sentiment such as the aims and purposes of a Handel Society or a

---

[44] Webster, *op. cit., supra*, note 1, at p. 643 (italics).

Gilbert and Sullivan Society rather than of the all-embracive arts. To the extent any given art form or content is or becomes part of our culture in the broader sociological sense, it is also a manifestation of our art experience. Thus, jazz and rock are perforce cultural elements in the art sense because refinement of taste would comprehend knowledge and experience thereof and response thereto.

Intellectual content is the other prime characteristic of the arts as culture. Esthetic training and professional skill alone are not enough. The artist and creator in the fine and performing arts must convey the particular art form utilized in a manner to elicit a response that is emotive in the listener-spectator, however structured or unstructured the form may be. The mind must effect such catharsis. Concomitantly, thought is induced as emotional responses are realized. Thought is not only the means for effecting this, but in the course of so doing, the mind relates, characterizes and classifies. Thus, intellection is a necessary ingredient of response, just as it is of creativity. For in this respect, talent is the application of the thinking process to emotional elaboration in the particular art form utilized to produce a content which is sought to induce a measured response of acceptance by the listener-viewer. In turn, this means that the latter's emotions have been touched by the performance or exhibition in some coherent response centering in the brain. Thus to state that an artist has ideas or a style is to refer to the transmission of artistic content from performer or exhibitor to listener-viewer.

It is the degree of catholicity of any given art form and content plus the degree of interaction of artist and creator, on the one hand, and their public, on the other, that are the meaning of culture in the art sense.

Sec. 1.14. Arts Common Denominators

By being comprehensive in this sense, the term "culture" nevertheless is not a primary tool for arts classification. One must first determine which forms of human activity properly qualify for inclusion in the generic term "arts". On first inspection, the musician playing at a desk in a symphony orchestra or in an ensemble or combo may have very little in common with the thespian on the boards in a dramatic work without even incidental music.

In short, the happenstance of characterizing art events as entertainment, amusement, show business, recreation or leisure does not necessarily provide a factor for classification. The amateur making music at home or the student studying a musical instrument certainly is not in any sense part of show business. Yet he is participating in the arts and is a part of our musical culture. This is true of millions of persons. Nor is the relationship one of recreation or leisure necessary for the proverbial music teacher and his or her students, since the same may be part of the educational process. Finally, study of art forms and contents may be serious preoccupation for the musicologist or art historian, for example, without regard to entertainment, amusement or diversion.

The starting point is that the arts, both fine and performing, are probably the broadest genus correlative to the term "culture" since there may be entertainments and amusements, such as sports, which are beyond their scope.

The second approach to setting up the categories constituting this genus is that of tradition. Certain disciplines—music, theatre, dance, for example—have traditionally been linked together, partly for historical reasons, partly for practical reasons. In a sense the muses of Greek mythology are the arts. In practice, the various art forms overlap and have overlapped for milennia. The theatre often employs music and the dance. Dance without music is a rarity. Music combines with theatre and the dance in opera, operetta, musical comedy, the revue and many other forms.

A third approach is the means employed—theatres, auditoria, halls, museums, salons, tents and other locations for providing a physical locus for performance and exhibition. What makes the arts is the requirement of a place for presentation, be it public or private. In the case of motion pictures, film may be shot at the studio or on location and except for home viewing, exhibition is almost always public, be it in four-walled theatre, drive-in theatre, non-theatrical institution, or moving vehicle (plane or ship). As for radio and television, performance takes place at one place and viewing at another, as opposed to the live dramatic production, concert or dance recital, where performance and viewing are simultaneous occurrences. However, unlike film, radio and television are usually characterized by private listening or viewing in the home, emanating from production which is largely public, in that large group activity is involved in performance and broadcasting. Phonograph or tape recording is much like radio and television in that playback may be largely private in the home. However, recording in the studio may be a far more private event than either radio or television broadcasting because the equivalent of a station audience is generally not present and fewer technicians are involved in creation of the performance.

A fourth approach is to structure the persons, firms and organizations involved in the arts, e.g., professional, academic, and amateur. To this one would have to add the various governmental agencies on a national, state and local level involved with the arts on a regulatory or other basis.

Finally, one would have to include the pertinent legal, business, management and administrative factors involved in the arts. Inherent in these factors are the economics of arts enterprises.

It is submitted that cognition of arts law and management is a principal ingredient for understanding the phantasmagoria of contemporary arts classification and therefore, our culture, in the sense of status and development of the arts in our society. This is so because the underlying basis for arts activity is the nature of creativity, both in the form of literary and artistic property, and in performances and exhibitions based thereon. Art and law mesh indissolubly in this area. The means of implementation are considered as the business, economics, management and administration thereof. Out of the coalescence of art, law and these factors originate varieties of forms of production, distribution and exhibition. It is this context that provides the environment for the creator and artist and resultant performance and exhibition.

Chapter II

PERFORMING ARTS MANAGEMENT

Sec. 2.1. Manager and Administrator

Webster defines the term "manager" as "One who manages; a conductor or director; as the *manager* of a theater. . . . A person who conducts business or household affairs with economy and frugality." [1] He defines the verb "to manage" [2] as "To control and direct, to handle successfully or cope with, to conduct, guide, administer." The derivation of the term "manage" is from the Latin, *manus*, meaning hand, and in English was influenced by the French word *ménage* meaning housekeeping.[3] Thus, two thoughts are conveyed, one, the Latin notion of handling, derived from *manus* meaning hand, and the French conception of *ménage* with its overtones of husbandry and household.

The term "administrator" by contrast is defined by Webster as "One who administers, . . . manages, executes or dispenses." [4] It is derived from the Latin, *ministrare* meaning "to serve". "To administer" is defined as "To manage or conduct . . . direct or superintend the execution, application or conduct." [5] The term "administration" is given the

---

[1] Webster's New International Dictionary, Second Ed., Unabridged, 1961, at p. 1492. (italics).

[2] *Ibid.* at p. 1492.

[3] *Ibid.* at p. 1492.

[4] *Idem* at p. 34.

[5] *Ibid.* at p. 34.

definition of "The persons collectively who are managing an *institution,* business, or the like . . ."[6]

The manager therefore acts as an intermediary on behalf of creators of literary and artistic material and/or their interpreters, the performing artists. He "handles" artists. He must also be conversant with the norms of business and commerce. As representative of the artistic elements, he must deal with the creative components vis-à-vis production and performance and maximize the artistic contribution thereto. Normatively, at least, this requires the manager to be empathetic to the creative components.

At the same time the manager must husband and cope successfully with the economics of bringing the creative components he represents into production. This is a business, executive function which the manager has in common with any other enterprise.

The combination of these two facets serves to give the manager a creative stance himself, in that he brings to production essential functions which partake of both creative and entrepreneurial elements.

Administration, on the other hand, denotes the acts and effects of those who *serve* in the direction, execution and conduct of affairs of an organization. Very often the administrator serves to implement and carry out organizational policies initiated by the governing board of directors or trustees of an organization. In other instances, the administrator serves as the actual moving spirit of the organization who not only carries out policy but often initiates it.

The terms "manager" and "administrator" overlap in many ways so that neat classification is impossible. Many

---

[6] *Ibid.* at p. 34. (emphasis added).

of the functions of administrators in certain organizations are and will continue to be purely managerial and entrepreneurial. Similarly, the duties of those holding the position of managers in other organizations are often ministerial and are purely in implementation of policies of others in a routine, administrative sense.

Sec. 2.2. The Functions of the Manager

In certain theatrical union agreements the opposite party is designated as "manager". Thus, the form of agreements used by Actors' Equity Association designates the party engaging the services of the "actor" as "manager." [7] Similarly a "designer" of the United Scenic Artists will enter into an agreement for the engagement of his services with a "manager". [8]

On the other hand, the same party designated as "manager" in those contracts is referred to as "producer" in the Minimum Basic Production Contract of the Dramatists Guild.[9] Even though Actors' Equity and the Dramatists Guild were both organized during the second decade of this century, one wonders why such apparently differing terms were used by guilds representing creative and artistic talent in the same sector of the entertainment world, the theatre. Actors' Equity was founded in 1913 and its famous strike took place in 1919.[10] The Authors League of Amer-

---

[7] See Form Nos. 3D-1 and 3D-1.1 in Volumes of Forms.

[8] See Form No. 3D-4.1 in Volumes of Forms.

[9] See Form of Minimum Basic Production Contract of the Dramatists Guild, Form Nos. 3B-1 and 3B-1a in Volumes of Forms. It is to be noted that production-distribution agreements in motion pictures and television likewise often use the term "producer". The term "manager" is not used in those agreements.

[10] Taubman, Howard, The Making of The American Theatre 127 (1965).

ica, Inc. was incorporated December 18, 1912. In September, 1919 an offshoot "Dramatic Committee" was formed, out of which the Dramatists Guild was later born.[11] It should be borne in mind that the term "managers" in this context referred to either theatre managers who produced plays or others who produced plays as "producing managers". George Middleton refers to "the then powerful, tightly controlled Manager's Protective Association".[12] More recently, Jean Dalrymple has written, "The producer then turns over to his general manager some of the chores the old-time producers did themselves. In fact years ago they were called managers, not producers, and Actors' Equity still refers to them in all contracts as "the management".[13]

It is submitted that the term "manager" as so used by Actors' Equity Association is not vestigial even though the term in current parlance does not have the vogue it had when Equity first devised its forms. One reason for this is the changing role of the producer in the theatre. The producer devoting greater attention to financing has shifted the actual handling of details of administration of the theatrical production to others designated variously as company managers and general managers.

The company manager will handle internal matters of administration of the theatrical production, including the books and records, transportation of cast, housing arrangements on previews, and so on. The general manager oversees arrangements for rental of the theatre, hiring of cast, posting of bonds with Equity and other organizations, and

---

[11] Middleton, George, The Dramatists Guild, Fifth Ed. 3-6 (1959).

[12] *Idem* at p. 5.

[13] Dalrymple, Jean, Careers and Opportunities in the Theatre 141 (1969).

the like.[14] The separation of functions and increasing specialization at the producer's end has impelled Jean Dalrymple to observe that "Alfred de Liagre is one of the few present-day producers who still likes to do all 'the management' himself".[15]

It would seem, however, that the Latin derivation of "manager"—*manus* or hand and the French term of *ménage* or household would give us some insight as to the pervasive use of the term "manager" by Equity and other unions.

Sec. 2.3. Historic and Economic Role of the Manager

In the Middle Ages, when the medieval guilds controlled production, arts and crafts were not separated into labor and capital, but rather into masters, journeymen and apprentices.[16] In turn, these were often related to a household economy where production was carried on either in the home or an offshoot or extension of the home.[17] Banking in the Middle Ages, for example, had its origins in family banking such as the Fuggers. Latterly, one thinks of the House of Rothschild.[18] Whether as guild or household economy, there were close personal ties between those directing and those executing production.

It is submitted that the manager in the theatre was associated with his players in the personal relationship of the

---

[14] See Poggi, Jack, Theater In America—The Impact of Economic Forces, 1870-1967 (1968).

[15] Dalrymple, *op. cit., supra,* note 13, at p. 141.

[16] Webster, Hutton, and Wolf, John B., History of Civilization (1947) at p. 499, vol. 1, " . . . the craft guild formed a three-fold hierarchy of apprentices, journeymen, and masters."

[17] Weber, Max, General Economic History, Knight translation, Collier Books, 1961.

[18] Orsingher, Roger, Banks of the World 38 (1967); Wechsberg, The Merchant Bankers 11, 337-338 (1966).

guild. The fraternity of the theatre made the role and function of the manager analogous to that of the head of the household.[19]

Managers and players, then, were not basically entities apart, however disparate the ultimate division of rewards of production might be. They were, so to speak, part of the same production team. Some of this relationship inheres today in the respective roles of the performing artist and his personal manager. In principle the personal manager today directs the career of his artist and controls the economy generated thereby, handling of receipts and disbursements. Indeed, the personal manager handling a group of performing artists is even closer to the construct of manager and players of the Middle Ages.

The agreements of Actors' Equity, then, simply acknowledged the heritage in formal terms, even though the content had changed vis-à-vis the actor. The "manager" in the Equity agreement was now the employer of the actor, the employee. But the employment relationship nevertheless carried with it a recognition of the creative function of the "manager" historically. The "manager" was now the producer, separated from the actor in the historic relationship, and was basically a third party employer in respect of the actor and his union.

Yet, the "manager" in relation to his production continued to handle the business affairs of the show and its

---

[19] The relationship of the players to patron is illuminated in William Shakespeare's Hamlet, Act II, Scene II. See The Complete Works of Shakespeare, The Cambridge Edition Text, Doubleday (1936). Hamlet, p. 731, at pp. 749-751. See also, William Gibson's play "A Cry of Players", which was performed by the Lincoln Center Repertory Theater at the Vivian Beaumont Theater in the 1968-69 season. See Chambers, E. K., The Mediaeval State, 2 volumes, Oxford (1903).

relationship with its cast. The "manager" in this respect was continuing to be the cement and mortar uniting the creative components of production with economics, the business side of the production. In a large sense, the "manager" was still in a personal relationship because the term described either a known individual, the same person functioning as a general partner, or an easily identifiable corporate alter ego for that individual.

This was all the more so, since in the American theatre production was geared to the individual show, rather than a string of seasonal productions of a production or distribution company, such as in motion pictures or television. In the American theatre, except for occasional repertory theatre companies and the more recent incidence of the regional non-profit repertory theatre, production in the main was unitary. Each show was generally a separate production and a separate accounting entity. Management was formed for each show with profits and losses divided for that show. Management in this sense was entrepreneurial. The "manager" was the impresario *par excellence* undertaking a venture in the arts by bringing in the artistic and financing components and, hopefully, launching the production for profit.

Sec. 2.4. The Personal Manager

This continues to be the historic function of the theatrical "manager". Hence the continued use of the term by Actors' Equity and other theatrical unions contractually is justified. The personal manager shares this function vis-à-vis his artist in that the personal manager, like the artist himself, is concerned with a series of separate enterprises.

Conceivably the artist might be involved in long-term employment wherein his manager acts principally as agent entitling him to periodic commissions on his artist's salary. But generally, even where the artist is a member of one or more guilds or unions, there, too, the personal manager is handling the economy of creative endeavors as though the artist were engaged in enterprise.

The artist, in fact, may be hired through the manager for a series of engagements as an employee only. At times he may be engaged as a free-lance independent contractor. At still other times, tax, corporate and other business considerations may induce the use of a complicated business structure as the framework for rendition of the artist's services. Nevertheless, managing the artist is a business and the manager functions as an entrepreneur in directing the affairs of his artist or artists.

Thus, by and large, in the commercial sector of the performing arts, the artist or groups of artists under management function in the environment of the entrepreneur and of the money-making possibilities inherent in each venture. This is also true to a great extent where artists are engaged in subsidy non-profit productions, such as the opera, where the outlets may differ but where the manager's perspective for his performing artist is likewise entrepreneurial.

The two-fold function of the manager, dealing with empathy in respect of the creative and artistic components on the one hand, and with the economics of production on the other, serves to give him a creative stance.

Sec. 2.5. The Producer

But the manager as producer is himself a creative component. Without assembly of the creative components and without organization thereof on business lines, the production could not be undertaken. Without financing and without a theatre for presentation, the production could not be launched.

In the commercial sector of the performing arts, the manager remains the entrepreneur functioning basically on a venture by venture basis. The theatrical production is the prototype of the unitary structure of each venture although the relationship legally of the producer differs considerably from that of the personal manager and agency, and indeed, from producers in motion pictures, television and phonograph recording, i.e., from the other performing arts.

The personal manager acts as agent to his artist, the principal. Likewise, the booking agency serves in the relationship of agent to its artist principal. By contrast, in the theatre, the producer, as general partner of a limited partnership, will act as employer of the actor, his employee.

In motion pictures and television, as in the theatre, the manager's role, in the Actors' Equity sense, is that of producer. However, the individual producer may operate all of his ventures through one production corporation or he may set up one corporation as corporate producer, with limited liability, for a series of ventures and another corporation for another series of ventures, and so on. Thus, an individual producer may have a multi-picture deal under one corporate structure and set up a new company for a later multi-picture deal, depending upon who his associates are in each deal, tax and other business considerations. But the person carrying out production duties and undertaking production responsibilities on behalf of the corporate production company is known as the individual producer.[20] In

---

[20] The fee or salary of the individual producer is an above the line item of the budget. Generally a production budget is divided into costs, or estimated costs if the budget is only an estimated

television such person is very often called the executive producer.

The impresario producing live concerts often functions as a producer of each concert or sometimes a series of concerts in terms of his relationship with the performing artist or artists. To the extent he is also the personal manager of the talent he is in an agency relationship. Sometimes the impresario is producing the concert with artists managed by others. Then the relationship may be one of employer-employee or independent contractor.

The record producer may function like the motion picture producer as independent contractor for a number of ventures. Thus, he may be an independent "a & r" (artists and repertoire) producer. As such, he very often will have his own independent production company acting as corporate independent producer of records for which he will function as independent producer,[21] in effect, manager of the recording sessions and producer of the records embodying performances reproduced at such sessions.

On the other hand, the record producer may be a staff employee of a record manufacturer. To that extent, he will operate as a manager of the recording sessions with limited scope to direct the affairs of the artist. Artistically, he may have final say in respect of the recordings subject to whatever approvals a recording artist of stature can obtain in his recording artist's agreement.[22]

---

budget of creative components (above the line) and the technical components (below the line).

[21] See Form No. 5B-2, in Volumes of Forms, for a form of agreement of independent record producer.

[22] E.g., album cover approval, selection of material to be recorded, prohibition against coupling with other artists unless expressly consented thereto in writing, and so on. See Form Nos. 5A-1 to 5A-2.3, inclusive, in Volumes of Forms for recording artist's agreements.

As a free-lance producer, the "a & r" man generally has the freedom and control to direct the recording session to a conclusion without the risk of being superseded were he an employee. In that sense, he is comparable to the motion picture or television producer. The salaried "a & r" man of a large record company is generally an employee assigned to a particular project in production by that company. The staff executive producer of a large motion picture or television operation is likewise an employee given responsibilities in connection with production of a particular venture. Like the salaried "a & r" man, he may be functioning as manager of that production, but he is also subject to the control of someone else and may be replaced.

Consequently the staff "a & r" man or staff producer in motion pictures and television may function as manager in relation to the artist and indeed is hired for that purpose. At the same time he must complete his record, film or tape production, as the case may be, with an eye to business considerations. Nevertheless, the managerial function is tentative because it is not based on contract between the artist and that manager. The staff "a & r" man or staff producer in films and television is not a principal in the agreement with the artist. As managers, they must exercise managerial control on behalf of their employers who are the principals. Thus, the artist performs as an employee, generally of the production company, while managerial supervision and control are exercised by an "a & r" man or staff producer who is accountable to that production company, also as an employee.

Hence, in the large production organization, there is a separation of managerial functions. Primary relationship with the performing artist is delegated to the staff "a & r" man or staff producer. However, managerial functions facing the business world, for which the production is undertaken, are delegated to still other business executives. Management in this sense represents a separation of production from the sales and distribution functions. The large organization, by means of specialization, has separated the traditional dual position of manager as relator to the artist and as business representative to the public.

Sec. 2.6. The Agent

But managerial norms are vastly more complicated in the 20th Century. In addition to producers and personal managers, there are agencies of all kinds who act as business intermediaries. Thus, an artist may have not only a personal manager but also a large booking agency such as William Morris, International Famous, or Creative Management to represent him.[23]

Their contracts with the artists may refer to "manager's contract" or "agency contract" because the large agency functions as a booking agency and in a managerial capacity in that it also handles and directs the affairs of the artist. At times, such an agency will function in an entrepreneurial capacity as a packager of a show or production, for which it will secure engagements for artists it represents. At other times, it will simply book its talent in productions or shows in which it serves in no production capacity as packager.

The large agency is a multi-faceted operation. Specialization is operative in respect of the particular performing art. Thus, a record agent, a film agent, a book agent, and a television agent may all be called in from time to time to serve

---

[23] See Form Nos. 4C(b)-1 to 4C(b)-4, inclusive, in Volumes of Forms for forms of agreement utilized by a booking agency with talent.

the needs of the same artist. Each of such agents will be an employee of the large agency.

While it is true that the individuals so functioning as managers specializing in particular performing and related arts are no more than employees of the large agency, nevertheless, the agency, in a sense, is a manager by agreement with the artist, with the individual agents serving as representatives of the large agency. Thus, the large agency is closer in conception and function of management to the traditional manager in that it is directed both toward the artist and third parties.

Sec. 2.7. Legal Relationships of Personal Managers, Agents and Producers

In legal contemplation, the personal manager and the booking agency function as agent for the artist who is the principal. Generally the law of principal and agent is applicable. On the other hand, the theatrical manager or producer functions in quite a different capacity. The manager of a stage production is usually the general partner of a limited partnership, which is the production company. The general partner may receive a credit as presenter or producer of the show. But basically the law of the limited partnership governs.[24]

In motion pictures and television, the producer may be the principal stockholder of the production company formed by him to produce the picture, series or show. He may receive a credit as individual producer. But, basically, the

---

[24] See Taubman, Limited Partnerships, 3 Corporate Practice Commentator 15 (1962); Taubman, Theatrical Limited Partnerships, 37 Taxes 979 (1959); Colton, Theatrical Limited Partnerships and Joint Ventures, in Financing A Theatrical Production (edited by Taubman, Joseph) 375 (1964).

law of corporations is applicable with the powers of the manager exercised by him as the principal officer and stockholder of his production company with a board of directors chosen by him.

Sec. 2.8. The Lawyer as Manager

Managerial functions are further complicated by the role of lawyers, accountants and assorted business advisers of the artist. Indeed, the artist may not have a personal manager or booking agent serving him. He may be rendering services to various ventures under advice of counsel and/or his accountant and/or his business adviser. Sometimes the artist may be utilizing the services of all of these—personal manager, booking agency, lawyer, accountant and business adviser.

Counsel very often prepares and negotiates agreements for the artist. Since this is at the heart of the economic and entrepreneurial function, large agencies often employ counsel as their representatives in business affairs to negotiate terms on behalf of the artist. Still other attorneys are employed to draft the agreement. One finds a comparable division in the television networks between business affairs and legal departments. Lawyers, both in the agencies and the networks, are then employed in differing capacities. Some negotiate agreements as part of business affairs. Of course, there are many non-attorneys handling negotiations in business affairs as well. Other lawyers are then employed to draft legal agreements. Non-business details of such agreements, i.e., legal issues therein, may be negotiated with counsel on the other side by either the lawyer engaged in drafting the agreement or, sometimes, by counsel acting as a member of the business affairs department. At times, the distinction between legal and business issues can be rather refined since the problem sometimes has attributes of both.

In addition, lawyers may sometimes be acting in an executive capacity as an officer or otherwise. Generally, counsel is then functioning in an administrative capacity. Such counsel may be acting principally in a business capacity, not so much as a negotiator of deals, as in business affairs, but as a corporate officer or departmental or divisional executive, whatever may be his nominal title. As such, he may be assisted by negotiators in business affairs as well as members of the legal department and/or outside regular or special counsel. Executive officers, nevertheless, quite often are themselves involved in major deal making whether or not they happen to be attorneys. Once the major points of a deal have been so negotiated, then the executive might bring in business affairs and/or legal departments to complete the negotiation, draft and execute the agreements.

Lawyers may be acting in all of these capacities in respect of closely held companies. Counsel may be an executive officer negotiating the deal and also the attorney who drafts and consummates the execution of the agreement. As such, he may be doing all of this physically out of his law offices with his operations as officer of a company and negotiator of a deal as incidental thereto.

Because the managerial function is inextricably bound with problems of law and contracts, sometimes counsel gravitate into the managerial function and, in fact, become managers side by side with law practice. Indeed, they may go exclusively into management full time. This happens because the practice of the law in the entertainment field has become almost quasi-managerial since at every step of the way legal problems are immanent. There is another reason. Principal and agent relationships apply in each instance, although of a somewhat differing nature. The lawyer as legal representative functions as agent for his principal, the client. Where the lawyer also functions as manager, he acts as agent for his principal, the artist. Thus, the law of principal and agent applies in both instances, apart from the differences as to the special nature of the attorney-client relationship, e.g., canons of legal ethics.

On the other hand, one cannot exclude the possibility of corporate structures being set up by the artist in conjunction with counsel and/or accountants and/or business advisers wherein doctrines of the close corporation and corporate norms of officers, directors and stockholders apply. On occasion, counsel and accountant are one and the same person who also acts as business adviser. Whether or not the business adviser also doubles as attorney and/or accountant, the business adviser is closest to the *ménage* or household concept in managing the personal affairs of the artist in the economic sense, i.e., receipts and disbursements, payment of taxes, etc. Yet, the lawyer and/or the accountant often assume this function for the artist without benefit of the title "business adviser". However denominated, the person undertaking this function acts as a business manager, without being called "personal manager", in the relationship of agent for his principal, the artist.

Sec. 2.9. The Administrator

If the term "manager" is the predicate of the commercial sector, it may be said that the term "administrator" is more in vogue in the non-profit sector. Is this a distinction in name only, without fundamental differences in substance? After all, one of the meanings of the verb "to administer" is "to manage" and of the noun "administration" is "one who manages".[25]

Administration denotes the acts and effects of those persons serving an organization by carrying out the conduct of its affairs. It is an executive function because the administrator serves in the execution of policy of the organization.

In respect of the non-profit entity, by its very nature it cannot be a business organization since it is not engaged in business for profit.[26] There must be some other purpose of a continuing nature, generally, which justifies the non-profit status of the organization. In most instances it is accomplished by organization under a statute defining the non-profit purposes or, if unincorporated, by reference to the non-profit purposes in the articles of organization. Very often this is buttressed by tax exemption as a non-profit organization based, in large measure, upon the non-business purposes and activities of the organization.

In most instances, the non-profit organization is of a continuing nature so that duration in point of time is a further characteristic thereof. Such an organization is very often referred to as an "institution".

The combination of continuity and non-profit motivation operates to produce changes in the nature of the organization as compared to the commercial sector. The non-profit organization projects purposes—the aims for which it was set up. Its policies are intended to implement and carry out those aims. Such implementation is the resultant prod-

---

[25] Webster, *op. cit., supra,* at p. 34.

[26] I.R.C. (1954), Sec. 501 (c), See Taubman, Book Review of Baumol and Bowen: Performing Arts: The Economic Dilemma, 43 Tulane L. Rev. 184 (1968).

uct of the activities of those appointed by the organization to serve and carry them out.

It may be seen, therefore, that administration in the non-profit organization is intended to reflect decisions not necessarily made by the administrators themselves. They may be carrying out policy decisions of others. In this sense, the managerial function as found in the commercial sector may be a lesser function of the administrator. Basically, then, the administrator may have other functions and often what he does is quite different from the role of the manager in the traditional, commercial sense.[27]

The administrator may or may not be in a position of making policy in the first instance. He may be only or principally carrying out policy of others, who, to that extent, are performing the managerial function. In business organization relating to the arts, the manager may perform both aspects of the managerial function, that of dealing with the artist as well as with third parties. As such, his role may be quite creative, particularly where he organizes production components as a producer.

By contrast, the administrator may be the creature of continuity. Generally, non-profit organization is not based on unitary production such as a single show or picture, as in the limited partnership in the commercial theatre or the close corporation set up to produce a single picture. Rather non-profit organization is founded upon institutional continuity of productions for seasons, entered into year after year. This long range nature of non-profit organiza-

---

[27] Cf. Smith, George Alan, Arts Administrator Need and Potential in New York State, A Study for the New York State Council on the Arts, 1 Perf. Arts Rev. 127 (1969) at pp. 128-131 under heading, What Is An Arts Administrator?

tion tends to make it institutional. Norms and patterns of functioning are built upon the basis of continuity of production. Thus, the *fact* of production itself ceases to be a managerial function, whereas, by contrast, the manager is primarily concerned with getting his unitary production off the ground and into production as a reality. Problems of finance aside, for the moment, production with long range continuity becomes institutionalized. There will be a season of so many weeks in the year. The season will be followed by another season. Planning on a more or less long range basis can therefore be undertaken because of the fact of continuity.

The institution, as it were, thereby acquires a life of its own. Its administration is handled by those who serve to carry out its policy on a short and/or long range basis. This is not to assert that institutions thereby constitute some sort of group person or collective organism separate and apart from their members.[28] Rather the sense of it is that a non-profit institution, built as it is on a rationale of non-profit purposes, presumably excludes the self-serving motivation of the profit sector. The administrator can therefore look inward for gratification based upon fulfillment of other motives, such as the proclaimed non-profit artistic and/or eleemosynary purposes of the organization.

Because of the requirements of long range continuity, the administrator must constantly look into the workings of his organization as an institution. Looking inward, he runs the risk of becoming or being absorbed into a bureaucratic apparatus, based upon the fact of continuity. This does not mean that commercial organization, which is or

---

[28] See, Taubman, The Joint Venture and Tax Classification (1957), Chap. V, On Conceptions and Classification.

becomes larger than the small group, cannot be or become bureaucratic.[29] But the large commercial organization, geared as it is to profit-making in the arts, even when the managerial function is split between those dealing with the artist and those dealing with the outside world, is accountable in some form to itself by reason of the profit-making imperative.

The term "accountable" as used here is not a reference to its use in a strict accounting or legal sense. What is meant is that there are standards of immediacy that the commercial firm, at least, uses for its own self-evaluation, whether or not these standards are reflected in acceptance of the venture for accounting and legal purposes as well as for shareholders and third parties. This factor of accountability produces an immediacy of valuation which is closer to the managerial function, even though the economic imperatives of profit motivation make it far more difficult to sustain institutional loyalties in commercial organization than in non-profit organization. On the face of it, loyalties to artistic, educational, charitable and scientific purposes are not likely to shift so quickly as in commercial organization, where accountability as well as financial motivation are likely to induce changes and shift of allegiances. This is so because at any given time the factors of accountability and concomitant economic motivation may predominate over non-economic motivations in commercial organization and thereby attenuate institutional loyalties.

The factor of immediacy by reason of accountability at least makes the for profit organization cognizant of an *economic* relationship in the underlying basis of the enter-

---

[29] For a discussion of the small group, see Taubman, Law and Sociology in the Control of Small Groups, 13 U. of Toronto L. J. 23 (1959).

prise, i.e., the performing artists and the relationship of the organization to them, even though the acknowledgment may take a somewhat distorted form, such as equation of artistic excellence with economic excellence by way of box office, ratings, etc. The administrator of a non-profit organization, plagued though he may be by problems of recurring deficits and of finance, functions in the context that somehow these have been overcome in the past and therefore will continue to be overcome in the future.

The administrator may be closer in empathetic relation to the performing artist because the goals or purposes of his institution are non-commercial. But the direct relationship of the manager as entrepreneur, vis-à-vis the performing artist, tends to give way to a more indirect, symbiotic relationship of the administrator. Something is thereby lost in the process, for the administrator is functioning neither as performing artist himself, at least in the capacity of administrator, nor in the direct, policy-making, decision-making position of manager as entrepreneur. The administrator, then, may have lost some of the force of maker, because as doer, he is implementing or carrying out the directives of someone else. Arts administration, in this context, runs the risk, then, of sacrifice of the creative component of the manager as entrepreneur because of the leavening effect of the intermediate position of the administrator.

Sec. 2.10. The Role of Management and Administration

Management and administration in the performing arts are not execrations that have arisen to plague the performing artist and which therefore should be wished away. Indeed, the performing arts can only function in terms of some economic relationship to society, whatever the form, profit or non-profit.[30]

Production is inextricably entwined with the artistic process. Consequently, economic and organizational elements of production are perforce also artistic components. Management and administration are simply means of implementation of production. Problems of management and administration are therefore very close to and entirely relevant to the hopes, aspirations, and inspirations of the artists and creators in the performing arts.

Recognition by management and administration of the stake of the performing artist and creator in the facet of management and administration as an ingredient of artistic exposition and of creation, and not merely the economic results of such exposition, might do much to overcome the inward tendency of administration toward bureaucratization and of management to evaluate artistic ends and achievements in terms of economic equivalents.

The euphoria of an arts orientation in the abstract that characterizes some of the present interest in the arts cannot survive without coming face to face with the realities that the arts represent commitment in one form or another —esthetic, emotional, intellectual and physical. The so-called "cultural explosion", insofar as it generates an interest in the arts generally, can be sustained for only so long. For it is in the very nature of the arts to be passionate, to take sides on one issue or another, regardless of what that may be and to pronounce a point of view, whether implicitly or explicitly. It is this factor that will, in due course,

---

30 Increasingly, as a part of the non-profit sector, colleges and universities have become part of the basic training ground of the performing artist.

fracture the euphoria of the appeal of the performing arts, if it has not already done so.

The problem, then, is relating the performing artist to management and administration so that the performing artist and creator understand this environment in which they function. Alienation proceeds apace when there is no such understanding. Similarly, management should start from the premise that its function is significant only when it becomes meaningful to artist and creator. Any other premise, such as, that the artist is there to serve the manager, reduces the artist to a commodity and, perforce, becomes a contradiction in terms, because, by definition, artistry is unique and does not consist of fungible units of a product. Administration, likewise, should start from the same premise because any orientation other than artist and creator in the non-profit sector is even worse than in the commercial sector in that the institutional purposes of the organization presume some concern for artist and creator. Hence, to the extent non-profit administration veers from such concern, it tends to become more deadening and hypocritical than its commercial counterpart which, in theory, at least, may have no avowed concern for artist and creator.

Just as the performing arts demand commitment of artist and creator as prerequisite of creativity, in a real sense the same is true of those who deal with the business and economics of the arts, management and administration.

Chapter III

PERFORMING ARTS LAW

Sec. 3.1. The American Judicial Process

Sec. 3.1(a). State and Federal

American jurisprudence is extraordinarily complex. This is not stated as a justification of law as some kind of occult mystery known only to the initiated, known as lawyers, but rather that its parameters are so extensive.

The complexity of American jurisprudence arises mainly from its historical antecedents. In theory there is no federal common law in the United States.[1] The English historical experience of the growth and development of the common law there, following the Norman conquest, was carried over to the colonies.[2] Law was a derivative of judge-made processes where judicial doctrine, in a process of induction from the specific to the general principle, carried with it the notion of judicial precedent and the binding nature of a rule previously enunciated. On the other hand, continental European experience was basically deductive. Principles were enunciated in codes, and rulings were then made by deduction.[3] This was the continental heritage going back to Roman Law.[4] American colonial and later

---

[1] See Hall, Readings in Jurisprudence (1938).

[2] Plucknett, A Concise History of the Common Law, Fourth Ed. (1948).

[3] Schlesinger, Comparative Law Cases and Materials (1950); see *Code Civil* of France, Librairie Dalloz (1953) and *Code de Commerce* of France, Librairie Dalloz (1954).

[4] Wolff, Roman Law An Historical Introduction (1951).

state experience was not entirely common law. Dutch, Spanish and French influences were felt in those areas where non-Anglo-Saxon settlement brought with it continental European legal heritage.[5]

American constitutional theory reserved to the states those powers not granted to the federal polity.[6] Federalism therefore meant that powers had to be specifically granted to the federal government. Otherwise they were reserved to the states. In addition to powers granted to the federal government by the Constitution, the warranty for federal power emanated from legislation of Congress and the judicial gloss on the Constitution of the United States and acts passed by Congress.

All other rights were in theory reserved to the respective states. This meant that, in particular, vast areas of private law continued largely to be under the governance of each state. Contract is a good example. Notions of what constitutes a valid contract are largely a matter of state law. Although this has been codified in some states with a heritage of Spanish and French legal background, notably, in the southwest, California and Louisiana, in others, legislative enactments as to contract are not at all comprehensive and are still largely governed by case law.[7]

---

[5] Burdick, Principles of Roman Law and Their Relation to Modern Law (1938), Chap. II, The Civil Law in the United States and Canada, at pp. 35-36.

[6] The Tenth Amendment to the Constitution of the United States provides:

> "The powers not delegated to the United States by the Constitution nor prohibited by it to the States, are reserved to the States respectively, or to the people."

[7] The basic distinction between a "Code" state and a common law state is that in the former the principal rules of contract are purported to be set forth systematically whereas in the common

An overlay on the state judicial system is the federal judicial system. Each state has its judicial structure of lower and appellate courts. The federal judicial structure is also a hierarchy of inferior and superior courts. Jurisdiction arises in the federal pattern if the matter encompasses a federal power, e.g., interstate commerce, or diversity of citizenship.[8] In matters involving constitutional questions, appeals will lie from the highest court of a state to the Supreme Court of the United States. Moreover, in matters involving the binding effect of judicial precedent, if the rule has not been determined by the highest appellate court, in the case of the federal judicial system, if conflicting rules have been enunciated by two or more lower courts of co-ordinate jurisdiction, e.g., two District Courts or two Courts of Appeals, then the decision is binding in the jurisdiction making the decision and other co-ordinate courts are free to decide otherwise. Indeed, the doctrine of *stare decisis* or the binding nature of judicial precedent may be said to be vertical, and not horizontal, in the federal system. Each of the District Courts within the jurisdiction of a Court of Appeals is bound by the decisions of that higher appellate court. There are ten Courts of Appeals in the United States. In the absence of a ruling by the Supreme Court of the United States, which, of course, would be binding on the entire judicial system of the United States, state as well as federal, the rulings of each Court of Appeals are binding only within the judicial Circuit comprising that Court of Appeals. If there is no legal decision in another judicial district, the extant rule of

---

law state, codification, by contrast, purports to cover special situations while major doctrines or rules of law, e.g., in the law of contracts or obligations, are enunciated by means of judicial decisions.

[8] The tests are a minimum amount of $10,000. and citizenship in different states. 28 U.S.C. 1332.

the other Court of Appeals will be accorded weight as judicial precedent. However, a judicial circuit would be free to disregard the rule adumbrated by another circuit and come to the contrary conclusion. In due course, the Supreme Court might grant *certiorari* on the ground that there is a conflict of opinion among two or more circuits. The state judicial system operates in a similar manner in respect of its lower courts in relation to the departments, circuits, or districts of its appellate courts, in relation to its highest court.

Thus, within our constitutional system of checks and balances, where the judiciary can declare legislation unconstitutional, the courts have power to develop common law even further. For, in this sense, common law is seen as a process of the modification as well as the creation of law, case by case, with due respect being accorded to the binding nature of judicial precedent. In this context, decisions of the judiciary, federal as well as state, become effective as the elaboration of our common law of judge made jurisprudence.

Sec. 3.1(b). Equity and Administrative Law

Nor does the interaction stop there. The trend in recent centuries has gone from the development of notions of equity or fairness to cure rigidities of judge made common law by means of what were originally parallel courts of equity. The English Chancellor's equity procedure was domesticated in colonial America and later in American jurisprudence to serve side by side with our courts of law. Whether or not the state structure still carries nominal divisions between courts of law and courts of equity, local law, i.e., state and municipal law, has effectively absorbed law and equity as part of the common law legal system.

In recent decades administrative law has arisen as federal agencies, in particular, and state and local agencies, to a lesser extent, have taken the spotlight in adjudication in areas new to the common law or superseding those theretofore served by the common law. Thus, the Federal Trade Commission was set up by Congress in 1914 to act as a kind of legal intermediary in trade regulation with inquisitive, prosecutorial and judicial functions.[9] So, too, the Federal Communications Commission was formed in the 1930's pursuant to Act of Congress to regulate and control broadcasting.[10]

Administrative law was a further development to meet and resolve pressing problems of modern society. It was necessary for American common law to adjust itself to this intrusion into traditional methods of resolving legal controversies and disputes. Over the course of recent decades, an accommodation has been reached whereby traditional legal safeguards were imparted to administrative law.[11] In the course of such provision, common law notions of judicial gloss of statute and administrative rules and regulations assumed the character of *stare decisis* or binding precedent, subject, from time to time, to the highest court of competence reversing the rule as no longer binding because of change of circumstances, due process, constitutional

---

[9] Public Law 203—63rd Congress, approved Sept. 26, 1914, as amended; 15 U.S.C. 41, *et seq.*

[10] Kohlmeier, Jr., Louis, The Regulators Watchdog Agencies and the Public Interest (1969) Chap. 16, The Master Plan for Television at p. 203, "The Federal Communications Commission, established in 1934, gave consumers a single agency to regulate communications by radio and wire."

[11] Administrative Procedure Act, 5 U.S.C. 551 *et seq.*, 60 Stat. 237.

grounds or otherwise, or to legislative enactment changing the rule.

Even administrative law, when it was brought into particular areas of concern, was not always given exclusive jurisdiction. Thus, the Department of Justice has co-ordinate jurisdiction with the Federal Trade Commission in enforcement of certain aspects of the antitrust laws, such as mergers and acquisitions.[12] Thus, a branch of the executive, the Department of Justice, directly under the authority of a cabinet member, the Attorney General, functions in a common area in co-ordination with an independent federal regulatory agency.

In enforcing the Sherman Act, the Department of Justice acts in a dual capacity. It may bring civil suits or criminal actions.[13] The former are proceedings which will not subject the defendant to imprisonment or criminal sanctions, but the wrong is in the nature of a tort or harm to society susceptible to a variety of drastic penalties ranging from injunction to divorcement and divestiture.[14] In turn, the Sherman and Clayton Acts provide for private treble damage actions[15] to redress private torts and wrongs, such as restraint of trade and monopolization, and to act as a kind of policeman of the antitrust laws on behalf of society generally.[16]

---

[12] See, the Sherman Antitrust Act, 15 U.S.C. 1, *et seq.* and the Clayton Antitrust Act, 15 U.S.C. 12, *et seq.*

[13] See Clabault and Burton, Sherman Act Indictments 1955-1965 A Legal and Economic Analysis (1966).

[14] See, Hoffmann's Antitrust Law and Techniques, 3 volumes (1963), Vol. 1, Part II, entitled Antitrust Enforcement Objectives.

[15] Timberlake, Federal Treble Damage Antitrust Actions (1965).

[16] Hoffmann, *op. cit., supra,* note 14, Part III, entitled Practice, Procedure and Remedy, includes Lee Loevinger's Private Action—The Strongest Pillar of Antitrust at p. 373, vol. 1.

Sec. 3.1(c). Literary and Artistic Property

In addition to the federal and state judicial, statutory and administrative overlay, yet another area of relevance is that relating to literary and artistic property. First, there is an agency set up to handle federal copyright, the Office of the Register of Copyrights in Washington, D.C., which is a division of the Library of Congress.[17] Second, there must be a determination, in most instances, whether or not there is a publication of the work so as to require the affixing of a notice of copyright thereon and registration of the copyright under federal law by reason of the consequent loss of protection under state law.

Indeed, American conceptions are quite complex. Copyright protection in the United States is by no means a simple matter of registration under federal law by the creator or his assigns. Prior to publication, the work is protected under state law which is principally case law and not statutory. Thus, rights and protection thereof are covered under the panoply of local law. After publication, common law protection is lost and the property is protected from falling into the public domain by compliance with statutory provisions of the Copyright Act as to notice, deposit and registration.[18]

In addition to determination as to whether or not there has been a publication sufficient to divest common law jurisdiction, certain categories of unpublished works, e.g., musical compositions, may be protected under federal law by copyright registration and thereby removed from common law protection.[19]

---

[17] See the Copyright Act, 17 U.S.C. 1, *et seq.*

[18] See Nimmer on Copyright (1969) and Warner, Radio and Television Rights (1953); Sec. 26.4, *infra.*

[19] 17 U.S.C. 12.

The ambiguities of what constitutes publication and therefore loss of protection under common law are heightened by doctrines enunciated by the courts that performance, such as the rendition of a play, does not constitute a publication.[20] Consequently, performance without publication enables a work to stay under perpetual common law copyright where not otherwise brought under federal protection as an unpublished work qualifying for copyright protection under federal law. Thus, one must consider whether or not there has been offering of a literary or artistic work for sale or the making of copies thereof available for general distribution in order to ascertain if there has been a publication which causes federal norms to pre-empt state norms. For performance without publication allows a work to retain common law copyright perpetually, whereas federal protection both by the language of the Constitution and by statute is for a limited term or terms.[21]

The effect of this is the operation of two systems of copyright protection, federal and state side by side, depending upon the factor of publication. Proposed legislation now before Congress would subject even common law copyright to federal control and make all copyrights subject to

---

[20] Ferris v. Frohman, 223 U.S. 424 (1912). See Nimmer, *op. cit., supra,* note 18, Sec. 53, at p. 208, "It is firmly established law that the oral dissemination or performance of a literary, dramatic, or musical work does not constitute a publication of that work." See Chap. 15, *infra.*

[21] Art. 1, Sec. 8, Clause 8 grants exclusive rights to authors in their writings "for limited times". The Copyright Act, 17 U.S.C. 24, provides for an original term of 28 years and a renewal term of 28 years. Congress has extended the renewal term of copyrights which would otherwise have expired from year to year recently in expectation of copyright revision. See Nimmer, *op. cit., supra,* note 18, Appendix C, at pp. 932 *et seq.*; Sec. 11.11, *infra.*

statutory limitations of a limited term of protection.[22] Even if federal copyright were to so pre-empt copyrights now under common law, it is submitted that the effects of state jurisprudence will be felt for a long time to come.

Sec. 3.1 (d). Law and Sovereignty

Still another facet of the legal conundrum is the fact that law is basically national and territorial. There is no world law as such, sovereign nations and states each enforcing their own laws. International law is accorded sanction by virtue of treaties, conventions or bilateral pacts.

Thus, in addition to the extraordinary complexities in the federal and state overlay outlined above, there is a further limiting factor of great significance. New rules and guidelines must be sought when the focus shifts to areas of concern that transcend national borders. Thus, questions arise as to what law governs, not only within the federal union, but internationally. In the field of copyright, for example, the United States is a party to the Universal Copyright Convention which came into existence in the 1950's, but has never joined the earlier Berne Convention.[23]

---

[22] See, for example, S. 543, 91st Congress, 1st Session, Sec. 301 (a). "On and after January 1, 1971, all rights in the nature of copyright in works that come within the subject matter of copyright as specified by sections 102 and 103, whether created before or after that date and whether published or unpublished, are governed exclusively by this title. Thereafter, no person is entitled to copyright, literary property rights, or any equivalent or equitable right in any such work under the common law or statutes of any State." Report No. 83, to the House Bill, H.R. 2512, as to Section 303 of the House Bill, states at p. 106, "Its basic purpose is to substitute statutory for common law copyright for everything now protected at common law . . ."

[23] See, Nimmer, *op. cit., supra* note 18, Appendix K, Universal Copyright Convention (Text) at p. 989; Appendix L—List of Ac-

Sec. 3.2. Legal Classification

In this potpourri of historical development, sovereignty and overlay of legal procedures and processes, American legal authorities have created their own schemata of legal classification and authorities. In this context, legal authorities are those who set the framework of consideration of legal phenomena by reason of judicial decision and legislation, as well as by writing of texts, treatises, encyclopedia and law review articles. Usage of terminology and of legal forms arises from day to day legal practice as modified by legislation, judicial decisions and the parlance of assorted commentators claiming expertise in the field.

The upshot of custom and usage in the field is notions that are closer to the encyclopedists in terms of traditional categories of law and their classification, such as contracts, torts, copyrights, trade regulation, and so on. Sometimes further relationships of categories arise for historical reasons, as in our chosen area. For example, the Constitution of the United States combined patent and copyright as follows: "To promote the Progress of Science and useful Arts, by securing for limited Times to Authors and Inventors the Exclusive Right to their respective Writings and Discoveries."[24] Then, since trademark regulation under federal law has come within the purview of the Patent Office,[25] the American Bar Association, for example, has linked patents, trademarks and copyrights in a Section of Patent, Trademark and Copyright Law. This is the norm of

---

cessions and Ratifications at p. 1002; Appendix N for list of bilateral treaties entered into by the United States at p. 1007; Appendix O at p. 1017 for text of Berne Convention.

[24] Art. 1, Sec. 8, Clause 8; See Chap. V, *infra*.

[25] See, Callmann, Unfair Competition Trademarks and Monopolies, Third Edition, Vol. 5, Appendix XV, Trade Mark Laws of the United States, at pp. 187-271.

most other bar associations as well. The common denominator of such sections presumably is to consider these areas as species of intangible, intellectual property with many common aspects or problems. Yet, a prerequisite for practice before the Patent Office is qualification as a member of the Patent Bar, i.e., expertise in patent law. This special licensing by the Patent Office is not available to copyright lawyers who are not also patent lawyers, whereas there are no such restrictions applicable to practice before the Copyright Office. Moreover, a great many members of the copyright bars, so-called, never qualify as patent lawyers. The result is that members of the patent bar may advise the public on the letterhead and business card that they specialize in "patents, trademarks and copyrights" as a speciality, whereas, to this writer's knowledge, experts in copyright law who are not also members of the patent bar do not so hold themselves out publicly on letterhead and business card.[26] Whatever the reasons for historical linking of patents and copyrights, it is clear that with or without the overlap of the two, copyright is a traditional classification of our jurisprudence.

Sec. 3.3. Entertainment and Theatrical Law

In what sense, then, can one speak of an entertainment or theatrical lawyer in the context of American jurisprudence? There is no separate branch of the law known as "Entertainment Law" or "Theatre Law", such as there is with respect to the law of copyright or of contracts. But proponents of the realist theory of jurisprudence have resolved similar dilemmas by formulating categories of clas-

---

[26] For a discussion of differences between patents and copyrights, see Taubman, Copyright and Antitrust 42-50 (1960).

sification in the context of real life problems.[27] Thus, to lawyers practicing in respect of legal problems in the theatre, the sum total of problems relating to the theatre constitutes theatre law. More particularly, those areas of law which have the greatest prevalence in the theatre might be said to make up the category of theatre law. Such areas would include copyright, libel, privacy, contracts, torts and regulation where recurring problems would necessitate their consideration in relation to the theatre. Similarly, motion picture law would comprehend antitrust law because of the large number of motion picture antitrust cases. Trade regulation would be categorized under music law because it is so important to an understanding of the operation of the recording industry, whereas licensing under the Federal Communications Commission would be a significant category of television law.

Specialization may sometimes limit the area of expertise of a particular practitioner, but all lawyers in that particular field would be aware of the main categories of that field even though the specialist is not involved in practice in categories other than his own. For example, motion picture antitrust lawyers may not be involved in problems of copyright in any significant way, other than the antitrust aspects thereof, yet they are aware of the significance of copyright and contracts as categories of motion picture law. So, too, a tax lawyer may be conversant with problems of capital gains insofar as they relate to copyrights without being a theatrical lawyer, while an entertainment lawyer will acknowledge that certain areas of taxation are

---

[27] See, Taubman, Copyright and Antitrust (1960), at p. 26, "The real school of jurisprudence classifies . . ." the bundle of rights constituting the copyright ". . . along the lines of the trade, as they are used in practice, much as negligence cases are referred to as sidewalk cases, bathtub cases, or automobile cases."

within the scope of entertainment law even though he personally may not be involved in these problems to any significant degree. Thus, specialization may cut across the various areas denominated entertainment or theatrical law, whether or not the specialist, strictly speaking, is an entertainment or theatrical lawyer.

Nevertheless, specialization of practice does not detract from the existence of a body of law denominated as theatrical or entertainment law under notions of real jurisprudence. If the industry or industries involved are concerned with certain areas of law and problems recur in those areas, then, under that theory, a classification of the law as theatrical law or entertainment law is in order. For, under that theory, the scope may be different from and larger than that embraced by traditional categories. Although there is a copyright bar, whose members are located principally in New York and California, and whose scope is concern with the principles of copyright, yet theatrical or entertainment law is broader in scope. Each includes many areas of law besides those of interest to the copyright bar. For example, a theatrical lawyer might be involved with antitrust law, securities regulation or many fields other than copyright law, and still be deemed a theatrical lawyer.

One must therefore inquire whether or not the terms "theatrical law" and "entertainment law" are synonymous. If so, then perhaps either term is enough so that legal nomenclature should not be burdened with additional terms, such as performing arts law.

Sec. 3.3(a). Theatrical Law

Basically, theatre law is probably derived from the days when the principal form of performing arts was the theatre or concert hall, apart from home entertainment, such as sheet music played on the piano or sung at home.[28] The term originates from the days before television became a major form of electronic performing art and probably before the emergence of motion pictures, recording and radio as electronic performing media. Theatre law is both specific and generic. It is specific in that it describes the law of the theatre as contrasted with motion picture law, music law or television law. It is generic in that it has been used as a category to describe all kinds of performing arts law.

In that sense it is synonymous with entertainment law. On the other hand, entertainment law is generic only, since it describes all forms of performing arts law and is not limited descriptively to any particular medium or industry engaged in entertainment or the performing arts.

The mixed usage of theatre law, both as species and as genus, would tend to militate against its extension to characterize current phenomena. The growth of motion pictures, music and television has given rise to species denominated motion picture law, music law and television law respectively. The extension of the term "theatre law," to them does not as a generic term quite accurately describe these areas. That is probably why the term "entertainment law" has been in greater vogue in recent years as a generic term.

---

[28] See, Goldin, Milton, The Music Merchants (1969), Chap. III, A Novel Innovation, as to the competition of Steinway, Chickering and others to sell pianos, most of which were manufactured for home use. Herman Finkelstein writes, "At the time of the 1909 Act an author's primary source of income was from sale of sheet music." Public Performance Rights in Music and Performance Rights Societies, from 7 Copyright Problems Analyzed (1951) as reprinted in Copyright Problems Analyzed 69 (1966) at p. 71.

Sec. 3.3(b). Entertainment Law

While entertainment law as a genus continues to describe the commercial sector of the performing arts, it does not quite accurately describe the non-profit and academic sectors, where the basic thrust of those ventures may be more than the entertainment of the audiences. True, the non-profit and academic sectors may serve to amuse and the commercial sectors may do far more than entertain. Yet, inherent in the notion of the former is the factor that centers of performing arts and specialized offshoots, such as regional theatres, may be furnishing something more than entertainment. Factors of intellection, emotion, as well as artistic growth and opportunity may be accorded greater respect therein, in theory at least, than by institutions and facilities considered principally as means of amusement and diversion. Presumably the cultural explosion, so-called, would include entertainment, but probably a greater role would be accorded the performing artist in terms of his creative intention.

Although the term "entertainment law", in turn, may be inadequate to reflect the transformation of the performing arts in America over the past decade, it continues to be used as a means of classification. Nevertheless, the fact of its use, as, indeed, also of the term "theatre law" attests to the application by lawyers of the tools of realist jurisprudence in legal classification.

Sec. 3.4. Law and the Non-Profit and Academic Sectors of the Arts

If the growth of the law arises from adjustment to new situations and, indeed, to reconciliation of new problems and situations to existing legal criteria by invention and adoption of new terminology of classification to meet new needs, then it can be said that such a need exists at the present time.

Two new components of the performing arts, the non-profit and academic sectors, have grown tremendously in recent years, while the remaining sector, the commercial one, has not remained immune from change. The development of the latter has increasingly been affected by the other areas, be it by repertory and regional theatre vis-à-vis Broadway, educational TV in relation to commercial free television, or foreign subsidy in respect of American motion picture production.

The form and style of traditional areas of law relevant thereto also change. Thus, contracts in the non-profit or academic sectors may not be as formal or as settled in style as in the commercial sector because the profit imperatives are not present.[29] Union representation may be inchoate or not as highly developed as in the commercial sector so that highly formalized union approved agreements are not in evidence, or only coming into usage.[30]

Sec. 3.5. Performing Arts Centers and the Law

Before one can set forth the scope and meaning of performing arts law, one must first ascertain the bounds and limits of the performing arts. Two decades ago the term frequently used was "theatre law" to describe the area covered by the arts, while its practitioner was often

---

[29] See, Form Nos. 3D-3.1a and 3D-3.1b in Volumes of Forms relating respectively to repertory and regional theatre.

[30] See also, Lyon, Milton, The Professional Actor at the University, 1 Perf. Arts Rev. 219 (1969) for a discussion of contracts used by Actors' Equity Association for its members employed at colleges and universities.

called a theatrical lawyer.[31] A term probably as much or more in vogue today is "entertainment law" and its practising lawyer is known as an entertainment lawyer. However, new fashions and conventions appear which give rise to still other terms that comprehend the latest trends and become, as it were, almost terms of sex appeal that arouse interest almost instantaneously.

A decade ago such a term was "festival", which denominated something new and exciting in the form of concentration at a given time and place of one or more of the entertainment arts. Today the term "festival" no longer increases the flow of adrenalin; in and of itself the term has become as bland and neutral as the terms "concert" or "performance".

Today, on the other hand, our approbative glandular secretions center responsively around the term "performing arts center" thereby suggesting that perhaps the clue to the rather restrictive and therefore somewhat distorted use of the term "performing arts" is to be found in its architectural derivative. By concentrating in one "center" structures intended to be available all year round, architecture was impressed as the handmaiden to create such centers. Permanent homes would no longer simply be provided for concerts, opera, theatre, ballet, or other live presentations based upon the predilections of the dominant motivators of the particular art form in that community or perhaps of the real estate interests involved. Thereto-

---

[31] See, Jacobs, Milton C., Outline of Theatre Law (1949). It is to be noted that Chap. 3 thereof contains the heading, Musical Compositions, Chap. 4, Motion Pictures, and Chap. 5, Radio Broadcasting. Cf., Theatrical Law, The Legal Right of Managers, Artist, Author and Public, by Brackett, Albert (1907), which is almost entirely a compendium of the law of the theatre.

fore, such facilities either had adorned the theatrical district of a municipality along with assorted legitimate and motion picture theatres and the like, or else found refuge in the sanitized marble of the civic center of the community.

But the new vogue of a performing arts center represented a double transplantation. On the one hand, the center implied a gathering in of various of the performing arts which had led a peripheral, tangential existence in or about the *laissez-faire* theatre districts, even though many of those gathered in had been heavily subsidized in the past, e.g., symphony orchestras and opera companies. Nevertheless, the mainstream of entertainment interest was in commercial presentations of commercial productions in theatres operated for profit.

The gathering in of the performing arts in a center represented a movement away from art through commercial architectural forms to a coagulation of interests in which the non-profit and subsidy elements predominated. In order to do this, the concentration of the festival had to be flattened out to accommodate year round operations or even seasonal operations. For the term "festival" implied the notion of a feast, the excitement of a special occasion. Intensity was achieved by placing a large number of events in sequence over a short period of time, of days or weeks, or at the outside limit, a few months. For intensity cannot be sustained over too long a period of time or in too many places at the same time. Like feasting itself, quantification by concentration eventually turns into overindulgence and surfeit. The embodiment of the center for seasonal or annual presentations of performing art forms is intended to transmogrify quantification into a constant, even sequence of events, with due allowances here and there for the summer hiatus. The concentration of the festival was to be leavened along with periodic performances of series, as well as random, single performances into year long or season long events. By concentration in place in a center embodying permanence, concentration in time assumed a secondary role. It was no longer necessary to highlight the event by concentration in time to attract more of the public interest. The same result could be achieved more effectively architecturally in a permanent center where the in-gathering of the arts could be achieved on a continuous basis. The grind concept of continuous performance of motion pictures in a theatre, of operations of radio and television for hours on end without interruption and the even, year round operations of the art museum were now joined by the notion of continuity in the performing arts centers.[32]

Sec. 3.5(a). Comparison of Performing Arts Centers and Other Forms

Cyclical regularity of center operations differed, however, in several material respects from motion picture and television exhibition. The dominant form of motion picture theatre construction and of exhibition in the United States is private enterprise. Motion picture production may avail itself of subsidy aids under subvention for production in foreign countries, such as England, France, Italy and Spain, and to a negligible extent, of subsidy aid in the United States.[33] Nevertheless, American production and distribution of motion pictures is still almost entirely private enterprise.

---

[32] Indeed, the Lincoln Center for the Performing Arts in New York City not only includes concert halls, theatres and an opera house, but also a Performing Arts Library and Museum.

[33] See, Klein, Harold S., S.O.S., Subsidy for our Screen, An Examination of Subsidy Abroad, 1 Perf. Arts Rev. 19 (1969).

Except for educational television and phenomena, like the Public Broadcasting Laboratory,[34] which are of secondary economic significance, television production, distribution and exhibition are mostly privately owned and operated in the United States, albeit under license for television station operation over public air waves by grant of license and license renewal from the Federal Communications Commission.

Unlike motion pictures and television, the performing arts center, in the main, is not privately owned and operated. The centers required public support in order to acquire the necessary funds for construction, operation and maintenance. Often the center was built and opened because both public and private enterprises, in one or another aspects of construction and operation, collaborated in some form to achieve the desired result. Even in the purest form of public subsidy, federal, state or municipal subvention, or any combination of them, the private enterprise aspect was rarely absent because the persons furnishing talent to the non-profit productions,—managers, agencies and sometimes the incorporated artists themselves—are in business for profit.

Moreover, neither could motion pictures and television continue to operate for long if only the best productions and performances were to be exhibited; there simply would not be enough "product" to go around. By contrast, the

[34] Compare the unflattering account in Levy, Alan, The Culture Vultures (1968) in his chapter on educational television and Public Broadcasting Laboratory with the rather sympathetic account of subsidy for radio and television, as well as the live performing arts, in certain countries of Western Europe in Dorian, Frederick, Commitment to Culture Arts Patronage in Europe Its Significance for America (1964).

center could provide a place for performance where quality might not necessarily be lost by reason of the factor of continuity of presentation as opposed to the shorter span of the festival. Of course, neither could the center achieve such qualitative excellence as the precondition for performance despite this theory and goal even though commercial considerations were secondary.

Sec. 3.5(b). Considerations of Commercial Forms

Side by side with the center, not necessarily in a purely geographic sense, but in a municipal sense, were the legitimate theatres operated for profit, at least in the largest metropolitan centers and, seasonally, in a variety of stock theatres. But in the live commercial theatre, the particular performance predominated. As in motion pictures, the length of the run determined how long each theatre operated each year or season as well as the contents of the productions. Criteria for operation of the legitimate theatre and its offshoots, whether road shows or stock theatre, were as different from the center as could be. Without a measure of success at the box office, commercial theatre could not continue to operate, whereas the center, with the aid of subsidy and non-profit covering of annual deficits, could. Indeed, it has been maintained, with good and sufficient reason, that such forms are inherently liable to incurrence of deficits by the very nature of their economy so that without subsidy they simply could not exist.[35] The theatre for profit was not necessarily motivated by criteria of artistic excellence unless also accompanied by viability at the box office. Critical acclaim

---

[35] See, Baumol, William J. and Bowen, William G., Performing Arts: The Economic Dilemma (1966) and this writer's critique from the legal point of view in his book review of the Baumol and Bowen book in 43 Tulane L. Rev. 184 (1968).

unmatched by public acceptance at the box office could not sustain a production. The successful run and whatever else created continuous operation of the production at the box office were the determinative factors.[36]

Motion picture exhibition in its predominant theatrical form is analogous. Commercial television arrives at a comparable result by a somewhat different route. The popularity of any given production is measured from time to time by periodic samplings by polling agencies as to projected actual audience out of a potential total audience. Sponsor support is then presumed to be attracted because of the value to the advertiser of that program in terms of size of audience in that market in relation to advertising dollar spent. Commercial legitimate theatre and motion pictures are therefore concerned with actual body count (the box office) whereas commercial broadcasting is activated by the economic determinism of the projected body count in relation to sponsor's costs.

Recordings, whether disc, tape or wire, partake of the features of commercial theatre and motion pictures more so than radio and television. Phonograph recording in the United States is mostly private enterprise. There, too, critical success unaccompanied by commercial success cannot continue for long. Unit sales of records, whether singles or albums, are generally the measure of success. To that extent, the situation is analogous to the body count in the theatre. But performance embodied in permanent

---

[36] For example, the shift to an all black cast headed by Pearl Bailey in "Hello Dolly" by David Merrick, after a run of several years, is believed to have extended the run on Broadway for a period of several years. The play was still in its Broadway run when the Twentieth Century-Fox film "Hello Dolly" starring Barbra Streisand opened its run on a hard ticket basis.

form in the mechanical recording takes on some of the aspects of radio and television in that overall sales performance is logged on the "chart".[37] In motion pictures and legitimate theatre, it is specific body count that is important. Success or failure in a commercial sense is of significance in a unitary sense because the welfare of the particular theatre is tied in with the body count of that particular production at that time. Of course, projected body counts are made in estimations of overall box office by the producers in the legitimate theatre and in motion pictures by the distributors. But recording success is measured basically in terms of overall volume, not unlike the best seller charts of book publication.

Sec. 3.5(c). The Nature of the Performing Arts Center

The center, being principally the focus of live performances,[38] is concerned in an accounting sense with body count. Operations are principally on a non-profit basis so that commercial imperatives take on the characteristics

---

[37] Trade periodicals, such as Billboard, Cashbox, Record World and Variety set forth on charts each week which are the top 100, top 40 or other category of sales and acceptance for the various internal groupings of the respective journals. Thus categories may be found in terms of top singles and top albums, respectively. Still other groupings of top tunes are done by type—pop, serious or classical, rhythm and blues, soul, country and western, and even foreign, i.e., acceptance in particular countries, England, France, etc.

[38] This is so even though, for example, the Lincoln Center for the Performing Arts runs an annual film festival and at times performances are telecast. In this context, film and television are not the main functions of the center. For a discussion of the John F. Kennedy Center for the Performing Arts, see 1 Perf. Arts Rev. 341 (1969), including the drawings of its component theatres and halls, at pp. 350-354. Again, it would appear that film, even with the construction of a film theatre as a part of that center, is not central to the scope and purposes of the performing arts there.

of theatre and motion pictures for profit. Nevertheless, body count determines overall house gross and ultimately the size of the deficit. Break even points are of great importance to the center because even in the non-profit operation there is a limit to the size of the deficit that can be countenanced.

The center, then, grew as the embodiment of the non-profit presentation because by gathering in the live performing arts, basically of a non-profit nature, it emphasized the centricity of these arts. Heretofore, peripheral, or at best no more than co-ordinate with the profit-making area, the center, by virtue of architecture and gathering in of the various performing arts, began to occupy a central place in the American cultural scene. To the extent there has been a "cultural explosion" in America it is epitomized by the proliferation of performing arts centers.

But construction was not limited to the municipal center, although that is the predominant form. The center, by providing continuity, transformed the arts in another sense. Continuity begot institutional elaboration, and institutions, as they built centers, begot continuity. Continuity presupposed a measure of planning, of administration, of programming. Professionalism began to take hold in operation of the center as a *sine qua non* of support, both artistic and financial.

Studies began to be made of the new phenomenon, such as the Rockefeller Panel Report[39] and the economic analysis of Baumol and Bowen.[40] These concentrated on the *live* performing arts. Consequently, commercial theatre

---

[39] The Performing Arts: Problems and Proposals. Rockefeller Brothers Fund (1965).

[40] Baumol and Bowen, *op. cit., supra,* note 35.

was included in these studies along with music, opera and the dance as well as the non-profit theatre. By and large, however, electronic performing arts, motion pictures, radio, television and recordings were almost entirely excluded.

Live commercial theatre came within the ambit of these studies because the center very often comprehended live theatre, even though it might be repertory theatre. Consideration of the economics and other problems of the repertory theatre required consideration of those of the commercial theatre.

As a result, by reason of the primary function of the center, these studies denominated the live performing arts as embodied in the center as the performing arts. Then, just as usage by leading writers sets the style and meaning of language, so the function of the performing arts centers, as characterized in these studies, has achieved a popular acceptance of the equation of the performing arts with the live performing arts.

In this respect, the rise of the state and local arts councils, as the aftermath of construction of the centers in major areas and of the jelling of the concept of the center, is geared mainly to the live performing arts rather than the electronic, and live performing arts to the extent the arts councils are not otherwise concerned with the fine arts, such as painting and sculpture.[41] This is not to say that arts councils are unconcerned with electronic performing arts, but rather that their principal focus of interest is in the live performing arts reflecting in the main, the actual and projected construction of centers.

---

[41] See, for example, California Arts Commission Resume of Activities 1965-1968, 1 Perf. Arts Rev. 177 (1969).

Sec. 3.5(d). Academe and Performing Arts

Yet the very institutionalization of the center has given rise to yet another focus of the performing arts which perceives the performing arts in the broadest sense as inclusive of the electronic performing arts as well as the live performing arts. The rise of the municipal center, with its emphasis on in-gathering continuity of the live performing arts has presented the academic world with new perspectives as to the function of college and university in relation to the performing arts.

Prior to the rise of the center, the study of acting was either a matter of apprenticeship or of private actors' workshops, studios or both. Academe had its theatre departments, to be sure, but quite often as an offshoot of the speech department. Presumably this was so because the drama, like speech, was a facet of oral communication.[42] In any event, however denominated, the department was instrumental in making amateur presentations of students available at the school, either directly, through student dramatic clubs or combination of similar means rather than as a primary source of talent and technical skill for the profession of the theatre.

Musical study had a more serious relationship to the professional world of opera and concert in the conservatory of music which was conceived of as a professional school and was either independent or affiliated with a college or university. On the other hand, music departments in the college and university, other than those with a strong music emphasis in professional training, were comparable to the speech and drama departments.

---

[42] See, Sec. 1.12, Communications and Media, *supra,* for a discussion of communication.

The dance occupied the most ephemeral place of all. Like the theatre, one learned either by apprenticeship, private dance schools or both. Dance programs in colleges and universities were either designed in some relation to physical education programs or were a minor phase of arts and science programs, like the theatre and music departments.

The transformation wrought by the center in respect of the performing arts has also affected the function of academe. For one thing, construction of the center was by no means limited to the municipality. The growth of student populations on campus and concomitantly, of the faculty community, provided a concentration of numbers that could serve as audience for a performing arts center. At the same time construction of a campus performing arts center also provided facilities for training future professionals to serve the municipal performing arts centers. In addition, the campus center provided an alternative route to construction and maintenance of performing arts centers, on campus, as opposed to the same in the municipality. Finally, academe could, by the operation of its center and training programs, become a connecting link between the non-profit world of the municipal centers, on the one hand, and the commercial theatre and electronic performing arts worlds, on the other. For the academic center faced in both directions. It shared a non-profit status with the municipal centers and served as a training ground for them. It also prepared future professionals for service in the for profit performing arts, both live and electronic.

Indeed, academe itself was geared to the concept of the center. The campus is in principle a center of learning. Hence, the construction of campus facilities for the performing arts was entirely consistent with the in-gathering notion of the institution of higher learning as an agora of knowledge, experience and wisdom.

At the same time, academe, as a center of the humanities, was never really the tower encased in ivy divorced from the surrounding society. Indeed, training in the arts implies that the skills so acquired might be used outside academe. Education is a process of interaction of the particular with the general, the specialty with the generality. Higher education sensed or saw that the relationship of education to its specific disciplines in the arts had a parallel to the outside world. In the latter, there were the electronic performing arts as well as the live performing arts. Varying degrees of preparation and training had been prevalent in the respective performing arts, live and electronic, from highly competent and professional conservatories and trade schools to substantially complete lack of formal training courses and facilities, in which event service of apprenticeship was a requisite for acquisition of the necessary skills and training.

But over the last decade, the marked shift of academe to a distinct relationship of pedagogue to the performing arts has occurred. In school after school, either new performing arts curricula have been set up or traditional departmental structure evaluated anew and invigorated with new facilities, courses and approaches. Academe has recognized the usefulness of its own center as a means of education for the profusion of new performing arts centers and the electronic media. At the same time it has advanced the broader objective of training future professionals in *both* the live and performing arts.

Sec. 3.5(e). Construction of Specialized Performing Arts Facilities

A *caveat* is in order in respect of specialized facilities that have also been constructed in recent years, such as regional or even national specialized theatres, e.g., The Guthrie Theatre in Minneapolis[43] or the American Shakespeare Theatre in Stratford, Connecticut. The growth of the performing arts has not been entirely or uniformly the story of construction of centers catering to all of the live performing arts, such as the Lincoln Center for the Performing Arts. That prototype has had a parallel growth of specialized facilities of a regional, municipal or even academic nature. The richness and diversity of the American experience in recent years are not susceptible of neat categorization. What has taken place and what continues to materialize contain a texture of many strands and varieties, often reflecting the goals and ambitions of entire communities, their guiding individuals and the degree of interest and financial support.

Yet, it is submitted that focusing attention on the phenomena of the performing arts center furnishes an explanation of the nature and development of the performing arts and performing arts law. The construction of specialized facilities and the movement in support of these are not basically antithetical to the centricity of the live performing arts in American cultural experience today, but underscores that, side by side with the principal forms of architectural growth, other forms have arisen which are part and parcel of the same trend and generally serve one or more functions of the center.

Sec. 3.5(f). The Synthesis of the Performing Arts

If the areas of specialization do not basically denigrate from the performing arts center, but serve to reinforce the new notions of theory and practice of the live perform-

---

[43] See Morison, Bradley and Fliehr, Kay, In Search of An Audience (1968) for a study of the construction of this theatre from conception to completion.

ing arts, then we can see that the function of academe is, in essence, to act as an integrative factor between the live and the electronic performing arts. In academe, performing arts disciplines have gone beyond the rigidities of architecture of the non-profit center, which is substantially a gathering place for performance of the live performing arts. In academe, disciplines become coordinate in theory even if, for whatever reason, facilities may not be available or adequate for particular studies. Thus, failure to construct motion picture, television or recording facilities in the center comparable to first-rate studio and other facilities used professionally makes the likelihood of integration of electronic performing arts with the live performing arts through the center minimal. An occasional film exhibition or even annual film festival at a center does not serve the same purpose as the construction of film theatres, film production, radio, television and recording studios, completely equipped, to carry on all phases of production as well as radio and television broadcasting on a permanent basis. Obviously a telecast, or even a series of telecasts, now and then, emanating from a performing arts center do not convert the center from live performing arts centers into live and electronic performing arts centers with coordinate electronic facilities comparable to those for the live performing arts.

But academe bridges the gap. If schools of communication are not uniformly part of a particular college or university in the performing arts, then, at least, courses in motion pictures and television may be part of the curriculum of existing theatre arts programs. Even where electronic performing arts courses are not yet in being, it is relatively easy for academe to implement its program of instruction in the electronic performing arts. Thus, to an extent, academe has already related itself to the electronic as well as the live performing arts. Where it has not done so already, conceptually it may do so with relative ease compared to the inherent architectural restrictions of the center. Even though, in the present inflationary period,[44] it might be more difficult to fund such a project as contrasted to a few years ago, nevertheless, institution of the necessary courses and the acquisition of the required equipment would not begin to compare in expense to construction of a performing arts center and conceivably would be manageable by the school if it were minded to set up such a program.

Sec. 3.6. Performing Arts Law Classification

Can one speak of performing arts law in this context? Is there in being or coming into being a body of law which is sufficiently generic to the performing arts to merit such analysis and classification? Has the new ferment in the performing arts, the centers, the specialized offshoots, the academic intercession amidst the continuance of conventional commercial activity coalesced into something qualitatively new and different so as to merit coordinate attention in terms of legal classification?

Although the questions are not readily susceptible of easy answers, the growth of the non-profit and academic sectors signifies a shift to areas of public law from private law in that formation and expansion of non-profit institu-

---

[44] The request of President Nixon for the sum of $40 million dollars for the National Endowment for the Arts and Humanities from Congress for its next fiscal year, 1970-1971, and of Governor Rockefeller for some $18 million dollars from the Legislature of the State of New York are indications of official response to the arts to meet urgent needs in a time of economic pinch and also of the abiding importance of the arts to nation, state and community in terms of their growth and development.

tions with large measure of community responsibility are paramount. The shift also represents one from managers to administrators, imbued with many of the attributes of fiduciaries, because of their responsibilities to the communities they serve.

The changes in the social context therefore necessitate a correlative use of a generic term that encompasses the new phenomena, namely, performing arts law. In a comparable period of time, the term "space law" has come into usage to classify developments in the new period of the space exploration era. So, too, the transformation of the performing arts in recent years requires usage of classification that accurately describes and encompasses these developments.

A basic change in the relations, character and thinking in respect of the performing arts has taken place and continues to affect existing traditions and conceptions. In order to translate this cultural transformation, which is so many-sided,—architectural, institutional and thoroughgoing—into legal doctrine, the law itself must develop new tools with which to analyze and give effect to what has happened and what may be expected to materialize. In this sense, it is immaterial whether or not there has been a cultural explosion or something far less than an explosion. The fact is that substantial change has already taken place that is here to stay and that further change will continue to develop in the same direction. The result of all this is that there is now something known as performing arts which requires analysis in terms of performing arts law classification.

We can no longer consider only the entertainment business and industries. The new performing arts sectors compel us to take into consideration, not only business and its management in the entertainment industries, but also the economic imperatives of non-profit arts enterprises, academic as well as non-academic, as new forms of institutions requiring consideration of their administration as well. For these functions the term "performing arts law" should serve as the basic classificatory device, rooted, as it is, in the social context of the realist jurisprudence of our times.

Sec. 3.7. Performing Arts Management, Administration and Law

If management and administration of the performing arts, in order to be meaningful, must relate to the artist and creator, then it follows that performing arts law must be something other than normative. For performing arts law is the expression, through our legal system, of rules and regulations governing the mesh of the business and economic factors of the performing arts with their legal effects. If performing arts law is nothing but normative, applying the law to yet another area of activity, then it adds nothing except certain categories and rules applied to particular activity.

Here, too, performing arts law only becomes meaningful in terms of its utility in enabling artist and creator to relate with fewer impediments their strivings and accomplishments to those who provide the milieu for performance, the managers and administrators. If copyright law, for example, is deemed to apply to the labels on a can of soup but not to choreography except to the limited extent of some filmic, tape or notational representation, such as Labanotation, then performing arts law must concern itself with this problem of copyright protection for the dance. Otherwise, legal forms and norms in this regard will continue to remain inadequate to create legal relationships that will be meaningful for the protection of the work of the choreographer.[45] The legal impediment would serve to prolong the artistic impediment and make the contribution of the manager and administrator in the field of the dance all the more difficult.

If performing arts law is to be meaningful in this context, it must create a milieu for meaningful norms of management and administration, the nature and prerogatives of management, as well as the type of agreement that best serves the interest of artist and creator and of manager and administrator. Consequently, performing arts law must concern itself with much more than traditional copyright law just as performing arts economy itself is broader. Performing arts law perforce must consider the personal, legal and artistic problems of artist and creator—taxation, estate planning, privacy, censorship, etc.—as well as the institutional problems of artist and creator in organization—business organization, regulation, antitrust, financing, as well as production, distribution and exhibition. All of this must be considered in terms of a performing arts that consists of both the live and electronic performing arts. In addition, its scope must include the various facets of creation, the literary and artistic works, their adaptations and transformations on which the performances of the artists are based as well as the artistic emoluments and economic possibilities of protection of the artists' performances (the neighboring rights), subsidiary rights and residuals. Performing arts law, in its scope, then, should correspond to the real problems of artist and creator, arts institutions—commercial, non-profit and academic—manager and administrator in our social context as expressed in legal content.

---

[45] See Sec. 22.13b, *infra*.

Part II

ARTS MARKET PLACE COPYRIGHT AND CONTRACT

Chapter IV

MARKET MECHANISMS

Sec. 4.1. Definition of the Market

Zechariah Chafee, Jr. refers to the sharp conflict of interests between the author and his family, on the one hand, and the public, on the other, with a third group involved in the pattern of conflict falling on both sides of the fence, the marketing agencies.[1] His formulation postulates that the intermediary between the creator and the user is some kind of agent or representative, or possibly a medium for transmission.

One of the principal problems of the creator is the ascertaining of what Chafee calls "marketing agencies". Perhaps a more appropriate term might be "market mechanisms". This refers to the ways and means that the creative works are marketed, i.e., the methods of passing from conception through completion as a creation by creator to the user or consumer.

Before one can ascertain the market and its mechanisms with which the creator must deal, it would be useful to delineate the possible areas open to the creator. A useful starting point is the classification of industries in the United States that depend upon the exploitation of copyrightable material. Such a survey was made by William M. Blaisdell in his study of the size of the copyright indus-

---

[1] Chafee, Zechariah, Jr., Reflections on the Law of Copyright, reprinted in Copyright and Related Topics, Edited by the Los Angeles Copyright Society and the UCLA School of Law 1, 14 (1964).

tries.[2] Table II of his study enumerates the pertinent industries, as follows:

"Newspaper publishing
Periodical publishing
Book publishing
Miscellaneous publishing
Commercial printing
Lithographing
Greeting cards
Bookbinding and related industries
Phonograph record industries
Bookstores
Newsdealers and newsstands
Music stores
Commercial photography
Advertising
News syndicates
Radio broadcasting and television
Motion pictures
Theaters and theatrical producers (except motion pictures)
Bands, orchestras, and entertainers
Amusement and recreation services . . . (operation of automatic coin-operated phonographs)
Miscellaneous copyright industries"[3]

In connection with the last category, Blaisdell states, "In classifying the copyright industries for purposes of this study, about 5 percent of the copyright registrations

[2] Blaisdell, William M., Size of the Copyright Industries, Study No. 2 of General Revision of the Copyright Law of the Copyright Office (1959) reprinted in 1 Studies on Copyright 3 (1963), 2 volumes, Arthur Fisher Memorial Edition.

[3] *Idem* at p. 6.

could not be closely identified with any industrial classification, but were scattered throughout the economy in such a way as to make estimation impossible on an industrial basis." [4] The Foreword of the editors to this study observes, "The study measures the economic 'size-importance' of the segments of the economy which exploit copyrightable material for profit by their contribution to the national income. This is estimated at more than six billion dollars out of a total national income of almost $300 billion." [5]

As the gross national product of the economy approaches the trillion dollar mark, it may be assumed that the dollar income of the copyright industries has correspondingly increased. Of course, not all of the categories contained in Blaisdell's industrial classification comprehend creative works relevant to the performing arts, e.g., bookbinding and related industries. The temptation would be to extract only those industries which are directly involved in the performing arts, i.e., book publishing, radio broadcasting and television, motion pictures, theaters and theatrical producers, bands, orchestras, entertainers, amusement and recreation services. However, Blaisdell's definition of "Miscellaneous Publishing" includes sheet music which very definitely should be considered as part of the creative area covered by the performing arts.[6]

Moreover, the cross over of other categories into the performing arts is a recurring phenomenon. Thus, a newspaper may acquire copyrights of short stories, comic strips, cartoons, feature articles as well as news stories of its staff reporters and others. It may be the copyright proprietor

---

[4] *Idem* at p. 25.

[5] *Idem,* Part I An Economic Foreword, Size of the Copyright Industries, at p. 1.

[6] *Idem* at p. 14.

thereof either as employer for hire or by assignment of the particular item published. As copyright proprietor, it is in the market place of literary and artistic properties for the sale of subsidiary rights emanating therefrom and for the grant of rights of adaptation into some derivative work in the performing arts, such as a feature motion picture or a television special or series. Similarly, periodical publishers have been known to be a source of material for feature motion pictures based upon material owned by the periodical. News syndicates function in a similar capacity.[7]

Nor can it be determined for certain into which of these categories the particular activities of any given participant might be classified. For example, Grove Press, Inc. expanded from publishing into operation of an Off-Broadway theatre "The Evergreen", publication of a periodical, "The Evergreen Review", and distribution of a motion picture, "I Am Curious (Yellow)". It also acted as agent for some of its authors in the licensing of subsidiary rights.[8] To the extent such activities were carried on by a corporate sub-

---

[7] For example, footage for an 8mm. short subject on the assassination of President Kennedy was obtained by a major motion picture distributor for marketing from one of the principal news syndicators. The record subsidiary of the same distributor also obtained other material from the same news syndicator for editing and release of phonograph album based on the same events. The album is entitled "The Actual Voices And Events of FOUR DAYS THAT SHOOK THE WORLD Nov. 22-25, 1963 The Complete Story". It was produced by Colpix Records, CP-2500, then a division of Columbia Pictures Corporation, Inc. in association with United Press International.

[8] For example, Grove Press, Inc. granted an option for Off-Broadway production of Eugene Ionesco's play, "Amédée" which it had published in the United States. The translator of the play was separately represented by a literary agent in a separate and subsequent negotiation.

sidiary, an affiliate or even a corporate division, they might conceivably be included in the pertinent industrial categories other than book publishing. However, to the extent they were undertaken directly as an activity of the parent, presumably such activities might be included in the category of book publishing even though they were not book publishing functions.

Similarly, one can only speculate in what category the Voice of Firestone program, which was self-produced by the Firestone Tire and Rubber Co. for radio and television, might have been placed. The program, which was a musical show featuring outstanding soloists performing with the Voice of Firestone Orchestra as well as the Voice of Firestone Chorus and assorted dance numbers, might have been included in the "miscellaneous copyright industries" category or possibly radio broadcasting and television.

Sec. 4.2. Market of Creation—Laissez-Faire

The market, then, for the creator must be deemed to be pervasive and ill-defined. This is so because the market is *laissez-faire.* For one thing, in general neither creator nor user, nor for that matter their marketing agencies and representatives, are subject to licensing as a condition for creation and acquisition of literary and artistic properties. The author of a literary or artistic property requires no license from any governmental authority in order to create. In theory he or she may create freely subject only to the vagaries of censorship on a federal, state or municipal level in respect of publication and/or performance of the work. Nor, for that matter, is there a closed union or guild licensing the author as a precondition for creation. One need not be a member of the Authors Guild, Inc. in order to have a novel published. Indeed, in recent years that organization has exhorted its members to seek inclusion in contracts with the publishers a clause stipulating provision in the title or other opening pages that the author is a member of the Authors Guild.

Generally, authors of plays on Broadway will use the form of contract of the Dramatists Guild, Inc. of the Authors League of America, Inc.[9] The form of Minimum Basic Production Contract[10] is required by agreement of producers who are members of the League of New York Theatres.[11] Farber states, "If the Author is not a member of the Guild, and you wish to option his play for a Broadway production, then he will become a member of the Guild." [12] No such provision would appear to be applicable with respect to productions Off-Broadway, Off-Off-Broadway or out of New York. Thus, the playwright need not be a member of the Dramatists Guild, Inc. in order to be produced away from Broadway. Nor would there be any requirement for membership upon entering into an agreement with a producer for such production.

Similarly, writers of scripts would be required to become a member of the Writers Guild of America, East or Writers Guild of America, West,[13] as the case may be, if the pro-

---

[9] The Authors League of America, Inc. is the parent body of which the separate components are the Authors Guild, Inc. and the Dramatists Guild, Inc. See Middleton, George, The Dramatists Guild, Fifth Ed. (1966).

[10] See Form Nos. 3B-1 and 3B-1a in Volumes of Forms.

[11] See, Farber, Donald C., Producing on Broadway, A Comprehensive Guide (1969), Chap. 7, League of New York Theatres, at pp. 143-149.

[12] *Idem* at p. 11.

[13] Middleton, *op. cit., supra,* note 9, at p. 19, as a footnote to his discussion of reorganization of the Authors League of America, Inc. into two guilds, The Authors Guild, Inc. and the Dramatists Guild, Inc. as branches of the parent body, states: "For several years prior to 1954 the Screen Writers Guild was an affiliate of

ducer of that particular film or television show were a signatory to an agreement with that guild.

Agreements of this nature generally provide that the author must either be a member of the particular guild or else become a member within thirty (30) days after entering into the individual agreement. The agreement of the author with the particular producer who is a signatory to the guild agreement generally so provides.[14]

From the point of view of the user, except for reciprocal obligations of the producer who is signatory to such a union or guild agreement, there is virtually no restriction of an explicit nature as to the literary or artistic properties which a user may acquire for performance. Censorship restrictions may prevent distribution of a book or periodical as obscene, but despite the recrudescence of censorship at-

---

the League, and the League's members who wrote for radio and television were assigned to its Radio Writers Guild and Television Writers Group. As conflicts and jurisdictional disputes had frequently arisen it was amicably agreed in 1954, by all groups, that the special problems of those who wrote for motion pictures, television and radio, primarly on a salary basis and without control of the copyrights in their work, should be separated from those of author and Dramatist members who retained control of their copyrights."

[14] Farber, *op. cit., supra,* note 11 at p. 148 states as to the League of New York Theatres, Inc., "All of the Agreements state in similar language that an employee doing the kind of work covered by the Union Contract must become a Union Member within a specified time, usually within 30 days after his employment." Farber is referring to actors, wardrobe crew, directors, choreographers, dramatists and scenic artists. Stage hands, for example, must be union members as a condition of employment. Creators and performers, however, generally utilize a form of open shop in terms of membership in union or guilds. Membership is not a precondition of entering into the agreement, but membership is thereafter required of such author or creator.

tempts and battles, here and there, the First Amendment guarantees of freedom of speech, press and assembly prescribe broadest areas of freedom of acquisition and of performance of literary and artistic properties within constitutional protection as interpreted by the Supreme Court of the United States.[15]

Again the powers granted to the Federal Communications Commission in licensing radio and television stations[16] imply a measure of supervision as to obscenity and even taste insofar as it is a measure of programming and license renewal. Nevertheless, these remind one of the morals clause of large users which permit such user to cancel the agreement in the event of a breach of said clause by the other party to the agreement.[17] Note, however, that the right of cancellation refers to action or conduct of the creator which tends to result in moral obloquy rather than the particular literary or artistic property. As to that, pre-

---

[15] In a footnote to a review by this writer of "Movies, Censorship, and the Law," by Ira H. Carmen, in 41 Tulane L. Rev. 976 (1967), this writer stated at pp. 982-3 with respect to certain decisions on censorship handed down by the Supreme Court that year, "The majority extrapolated a new set of standards from existing decisions, indicating that in none of the cases at issue was there a claim that a statute in question reflected concern for juveniles, nor was there any assault upon privacy by publication, nor was there any pandering of the sort found in Ginzburg v. U.S., 383 U.S. 463 (1966)."

[16] Communications Act of 1934, 47 U.S.C. 151 *et seq.,* 48 Stat. 1964.

[17] A typical clause is that contained in 2 Lindey, Entertainment Publishing and the Arts (1963) at p. 595 which provides that Producer of a TV show under employment contract with script writer may terminate the agreement by reason of action or conduct of the writer which " . . . tends to shock or offend the community, public morals or decency, or tends to prejudice the Producer or the television industry in general."

sumably the user has approved of the acquisition of the literary and artistic property from the creator so that the reference to non-utilization of the work refers to conduct dehors the creation of the work or the work itself unless such conduct were unknown to the user.

Comparable restrictions inherent in self-enforcement codes of various sectors of the copyright industries are more in the nature of partial limitations and restrictions rather than prohibition. Thus, the rating system of the Motion Picture Association of America, Inc. is applicable not only to its members but also to non-members who are signatories to and users of its Title Registration Bureau. But even there motion picture classification is not a form of prohibition per se because even pictures with an "X" rating are not prohibited from exhibition. On occasion, too, a major studio will release a picture without prior approval of the Motion Picture Code Administration of the Motion Picture Association of America, Inc. Even events giving rise to claims of a conspiracy and combination in restraint of trade by reason of alleged concerted acts and utterances[18] are basically incidental to the free market interplay of creation and acquisition of literary and artistic properties for the performing arts. The same may be said not only of motion pictures but of television which has its own self-enforcement code.[19]

---

[18] A particular classification or rating may or may not engender difficulties with respect to exhibition and may or may not have antitrust consequences, e.g., the antitrust suit brought by the distributors of "Without a Stitch" as a consequence of certain remarks made by Jack Valenti. See, Variety, February 11, 1970, p. 4, cols. 1-2.

[19] The Television Code of the National Association of Broadcasters.

Thus, for all practical purposes neither licensing of creators, as such, nor of those who acquire literary and artistic properties, as such, is an operative fact of the live and electronic performing arts. True, there may be particular subject matter, such as musicals, westerns, situation comedies, sex novels and the like. Particular prejudices, biases and shibboleths of users may lean to the quest for and acceptance of preferred content and thematic material by users. But tastes and standards change from time to time and relate more to the subject matter that might be acquired rather than any outright restriction upon creation or acquisition thereof. Subjects considered taboo only a few years ago are scarcely considered so at the present time. Thus the freedom of creation and acquisition should not necessarily be equated with the operation of that freedom in the particular choices and selections made. As to these, one must take into consideration subjective factors as to the manner of creation, i.e., form and style, as well as proclivities at any given time of the user as to the desirability of that particular material.

Sec. 4.3. The Distended Market Place

Having posited *laissez-faire* freedom of creator and user in the market place, the writer does not mean that the mechanisms of the market are by reason of that fact necessarily efficacious or efficient. It may be seen from the panoply of users in the market that the very characterization of the market, taken as a whole, is difficult and complex.

A basic effect thereof is the substantial absence of a market in a purely geographic sense. In this regard, the reference is to the users and not to the media where used. Obviously the market of use is fairly precise when one refers to a play written for production on Broadway. Similarly, a TV special created for network production relates to three specific networks—ABC, CBS and NBC.

The fact of the matter is that the places of creation and of acquisition of literary and artistic properties do not have the characteristics of the market in the sense of a place as a geographic meeting center where creative works are marketed. Thus, one cannot speak of the equivalent of a fur market, a garment center or of a jewelry district where members of the same industry are in geographic propinquity of one enterprise to another for purposes of trade.

True, one may characterize New York and Hollywood as entertainment centers or as centers of particular copyright industries. Indeed, New York is deemed the capital of the publishing and theatre industries. The example of the theatre is apt for purposes of illustration. There is a theatre district in the midtown of Manhattan which includes all of the theatres known collectively as Broadway. Yet, this theatre district is by no means co-terminous with the physical market for acquisition of plays for production on Broadway. Here, the location of the producer is critical. For it is the producer who acquires the rights to produce the play on Broadway from the author. Producers may and do have their places of business any place. Authors may likewise create as far from the madding crowd as they can get. Author and producer may negotiate an acquisition thousands of miles from Broadway with regard to a production on Broadway. More likely, producer and author may resort to agents for representation for such purposes. One or more of the agents may be in Hollywood with respect to a New York negotiation. Or, the author may be residing or engaged abroad and may utilize a British agent for such purposes. Then, again, the negotiation may be handled by counsel for the parties who do not necessarily practice in New York, or, if they do, are not necessarily located in the midtown area. A similar observation may be made with respect to creation for other forms of the performing arts and the acquisition of such works.

Sec. 4.4. Market Structure and Marketing Techniques

Sec. 4.4(a). Film

If there was not, strictly speaking, a geographical locus, as market *place,* as between creator and user, there was at least a semblance of structure which served as a marketing mechanism. In the days when film studios were all-powerful, most pictures were produced by the studio rather than by outside producers. Screen writers were therefore employed by the studios as producers. Seven of the eight major companies, prior to the decision on remand in *U.S.* v. *Paramount*[20] in 1949, were engaged in production and distribution and five of the seven, in exhibition as well. Although there were a number of minor studios,[21] the majors were the principal users of creative material. Their

---

[20] Paramount, Fox, Loew's, Warners and R.K.O. were studios which not only produced and distributed but also owned circuits of theatres. They were the "majors", strictly speaking. Columbia and Universal produced and distributed, but did not own theatres. United Artists distributed but did not own theatres. Columbia and Universal owned studios but not United Artists. The reference here is to the period when the companies developed as such into powerful segments of the motion picture industry in the 1920's until divorcement and divestiture following the decision in U.S. v. Paramount, 66 F. Supp. 323 (S.D.N.Y. 1946), *aff'd* in part, 334 U.S. 131 (1948), on remand, 85 F. Supp. 881 (S.D.N.Y. 1949).

[21] Republic Pictures and Allied Artists, among others.

acquisitions came from the principal book publishers, the large agencies or the handful of literary agents. The studios had their corresponding literary departments and readers to screen acceptances of properties on both coasts.

This more or less idealized mechanism at least provided a form of market for acceptance or rejection of literary and artistic properties for ultimate adaptation into screenplays. Of course, individual producers of greater importance to the studio carried greater weight in property selection for adaptation. Properties might also be submitted to them in the first instance. The same would be true of stars, whether actors or directors, under contract to the studio. A property with a juicy part for a star or with great possibilies for the director might start its trek, market-wise, to the star or director in the first instance.

In a sense, the integrated, large scale studios provided a cohesive pattern of marketing because of the structure of the film industry. In a sense the market was defined by the user. The principal instrumentalities of the user, the location of the studios in California and the home offices in New York, gave the market some geographical nexus. The market was principally wherever the users were headquartered for studio production and overall operations. In the broadest sense of location, the market places were the Island of Manhattan and Hollywood, at least in respect of the American film industry. In a secondary sense, the market places were wherever the peripatetic individuals making decisions with respect to particular properties happened to be at any given time, at any place, at the time of decision making.

With divorcement and divestiture, the studios owning theatres could no longer produce a steady stream of "product" for their own theatres. Block-booking prohibitions in the decrees in *Paramount*[22] were further factors transforming the film industry in America. Finally, the competition of television affected the movie-going habits of the populace so that theatrical film exhibition no longer became the principal medium of mass entertainment.

As a result, independent film production, financed, to be sure, by the studios, came into its own as a principal form of film production and continues to be such to this very day. Although the accounting departments of film companies may continue to refer to the independent producers as outside producers, for all practical purposes, they are the producers while the self-produced film of the studio is a rarity. Independent production imports that the individual producer, through his independent production company or through a joint venture with another production company, brings in the literary and artistic property to be filmed. Literary departments of the studios may continue to function. The studio may continue to acquire properties for ultimate production; it may enter into agreements with producers to film such works. But a measure of autonomy has gone to the individual producer in finding the property and in bringing it to the studio for a production-distribution agreement.

The effect of this has been to disperse the market of users. Concomitantly, the independent producer has sought to produce on location. He has also pursued the benefits of foreign subsidy, as has the studio itself.[23] Thus, the producer is not necessarily headquartered in Hollywood or New York. For that matter, studios enter into production agreements with producers through their foreign

---

[22] See, Taubman, Copyright and Antitrust (1960).

[23] See, Klein, S.O.S., Harold S., Subsidy for Our Screen, An Examination of Subsidy Abroad, 1 Perf. Arts Rev. 19 (1969).

production headquarters in England, France, Italy and elsewhere.

The market place of the user has thereby become considerably extended to a great variety of places, the various foreign production offices of the studios and foreign and domestic habitats of the producer. As to the producer, he has also sometimes headquartered his company or companies in various places outside the United States for various tax and other advantages that might accrue thereby. In a sense, the market places of the user become manifold. One must take into consideration the principal production centers of Western Europe—London, Paris, Rome, Munich, Madrid, in addition to New York and Hollywood—to locate the users effectively, for the producers and studios are virtually global in operations. Moreover, even though RKO liquidated its film production and distribution activities more than a decade ago,[24] two of the three networks, CBS and ABC, as well as several of the important exhibition circuits, instituted various types of production activities. In addition, Embassy Pictures, now Avco Embassy,[25] became an important producer and distributor. Disney Pictures continued as an important factor in its specialized production and distribution program. Thus, the overall number of important users has grown in terms of competitive distributors while individual producers and their companies have proliferated globally.

Sec. 4.4(b). Television

Many of the characteristics of the film industry today in terms of user are also apt in respect of television even

---

[24] In 1957, RKO General discontinued its operations in film production and distribution.

[25] After its merger into Avco Industries.

though there are only three major networks. Important individual producers have their own production companies as users of literary and artistic property. Teleplay writers are employed by these companies rather than the networks themselves. Producers and their companies are also dispersed even though, as in the film industry, the principal production centers of the networks and their headquarters are in Hollywood and New York.

In addition to network distribution, various properties are developed for syndication, that is, for market by market distribution, either locally, regionally, or both. A second source of user in television is therefore the syndicator. Among the syndicators are the television affiliates and subsidiaries of the major film companies. Syndicators, in turn, often enter into production agreements with individual producers who set up their independent production companies for this purpose. A third area of television user is educational television. Although the latter is operated on a non-profit basis, which affects production costs and expected returns, the stations, whether taken as an educational TV network, individually or regionally, are nonetheless users. Whereas syndicators are mostly located in Hollywood and New York, their individual producers and the independent production companies of the latter operate globally and may be headquartered anywhere. As for educational television, individual stations as users are spread over the United States, although nationally they may be located in the primary production centers. Also, from time to time, owners of a group of television stations, such as Westinghouse, may engage in varying degrees of production, financing and distribution. Those groups may be considered as users found all over the country.

Thus, in television, as in film, there is a diversity of users even though the reasons therefor may have arisen differently, apparent concentration in the form of three networks, notwithstanding, as indicated above. Whatever controls the studios in film and the networks may have by way of approvals of use of particular literary and artistic properties and of script adaptations thereof, such controls relate to the production process in terms of degree of interrelationships. The fact that selection by the individual producer may have to be approved by studio or network merely amounts to a form of joint selection. Similarly, the various approvals retained contractually by the financing-distributing entity may affect the relative degree of independence of the independent production company. In effect, they modify independent production to a form of production independently, subject to certain important controls of the distributor party to the agreement. They do not thereby transform the production entity into a dummy or corporate shell.[26] Thus, independent production subject to approvals and like controls does not thereby affect the contention made here with respect to the variety and dispersal of users of literary and artistic properties in film and television.

Sec. 4.4(c). Theatre

As for the theatre, when the theatre operator was also the producer, the market was generally where the manager had his principal place of business.[27] The stock system was replaced by the combination system.[28] Bernheim writes, "When the local managers lost their stock companies they

[26] This was the result in Herbert v. Riddell, 103 F. Supp. 369 (S.D. Cal. 1952), a tax case and would seem to be correct as well from the point of view of legal theory generally.

[27] Bernheim, The Business of The Theatre, An Economic History of the American Theatre 1750-1932 (1932).

[28] *Idem* at pp. 1-30.

ceased to be producers and became real estate operators, leasing their houses either for a fixed rental or on sharing terms to the renting combination."[29] Moreover, a chain of legitimate theatres, the Shuberts, was made subject to various restrictions as to production by reason of their ownership and control of large numbers of key theatres on Broadway and elsewhere under an antitrust consent decree after the Supreme Court held their legitimate theatres to be subject to the Sherman Act because they were engaged in interstate commerce.[30] Moreover, the Shuberts had to divest themselves of certain theatres under that decree.[31]

Thus Broadway productions and road tours sent therefrom were principally based on plays selected by a variety of producers. True, the theatre as landlord might wish to protect its position as profit sharing landlord to the producer tenant by exercising some approval of the particular play, its director, stars and the like, but this does not detract from the relative independence of the producer as the primary user of the literary and artistic property. The theatre owner as landlord merely made the selection of the producer subject to a limitation of some degree of control by the possibility of approval in the owner.

The Broadway producer was not necessarily as centralized as the theatres he might use for performance of the play. Indeed, as the function of the producer increasingly became one of arranging for financing through the limited partnership, he might have a theatre manager and company manager handling details for him so that as producer he did not even have to be headquartered in New York.

---

[29] *Idem* at p. 29.

[30] U.S. v. Shubert, 348 U.S. 222 (1955), consent decree (S.D. N.Y.) February 17, 1956, see CCH Trade Cases, Par. 68,272.

[31] *Ibid,* CCH Trade Cases, Par. 68,272.

Moreover, the Off-Broadway and Off-Off-Broadway expansion of theatrical production served to decentralize the geographic place of the producer. He now did not even have to maintain his principal place of business in the midtown area of Manhattan. He could be located anywhere. Indeed, by use of managers, agents and attorneys he could tend to many of the production functions in the pre-production stages without even being physically at hand at all times.

The expansion of the regional theatre in recent years as well as the growth of professionalism in the university theatre[32] have further decentralized and enhanced user possibilities. Producers may now seek properties for primary production in a variety of theatres throughout the United States. Moreover, some of these theatres themselves at times undertake the production function. As users, they are spread all over the country.

Sec. 4.4(d) Music

In music, there have been a variety of users. True, that performing rights societies are limited in numbers—ASCAP, BMI and SESAC.[33] True that these societies are

---

[32] See, Lyon, Milton, The Professional Actor at the University, 1 Perf. Arts Rev. 219 (1969).

[33] The American Society of Composers, Authors and Publishers (ASCAP) is an unincorporated, non-profit organization. Broadcast Music, Inc. (BMI) is a corporation for profit originally organized by the broadcasting companies to counter ASCAP. Formerly called The Society of European Stage Authors and Composers, Inc., Sesac, Inc. (SESAC) is a closely held corporation. ASCAP was formed in 1914; BMI in 1939; SESAC in 1930. See, Warner, Harry P., Radio and Television Rights (1953), Chap. XIII, The Music Industry—The ASCAP Story at pp. 323-455; Arrow, Allen, Performing Rights Societies, in The Business and Law of Music, edited by Taubman, Joseph, at pp. 95-100.

principally located at the entertainment capitals, New York and Hollywood, with headquarters situated in New York. Nevertheless, insofar as radio and television are concerned, the principal sources of revenue of the performing rights societies, the actual users of the music licensed to the performing rights societies are the broadcasters. The societies function as licensing agencies, generally on a blanket basis, to the networks and the stations, with respect to the "small rights", i.e., non-dramatic performing rights, in musical compositions. The advantage to the broadcaster is that the societies, ASCAP and BMI, in particular, can each make available substantial catalogues of musical compositions under the blanket license fee without the expense and time involved in separate licensing and without having to undertake copyright clearance procedures with respect to the music under license because of the representation of the performing rights society that it is the licensee of the performing rights.

Thus, whatever has been indicated above with respect to radio and television as to the pattern of the users applies as well to music. In other words, if television abounds in independent producers, the market of users is widespread because independent producers are many and are to be found all over even though the licensing of music may be simplified. That is, the market for licensing music by the societies to broadcasters may be relatively concentrated, the two large societies principally dealing with the three networks. But the selection of the music to be performed, whether original music especially composed for that show or library music adapted thereto, nevertheless remains that of the production company. Mass licensing by the societies is a means of assurance to the suppliers of music, composers and authors as the creators thereof, on the one hand, and the publishers thereof, on the other, that their music, in gross, will receive overall adequate compensation and will be properly policed. Mass licensing does not thereby dictate which compositions will be selected for performance; nor does it exclude the operative fact that the societies divide the funds received for licensing in gross after deducting administrative expenses, on some basis of actual or presumed performance.

In the main, then, the market continues to be that of the producer as user and the supplier as provider of the music within the context of licensing by performing rights societies. One must therefore consider not only the nature of the market in terms of the producer as user but also that of the suppliers. Immediately one is impressed with the effects generated by Sec. 1(e) of the Copyright Law, the compulsory license provision.[34] Pursuant thereto, the copyright proprietor of music may not restrict recording of music after licensing of first performance thereof subject to payment of a compulsory license of two cents a side by the user. In practice the statute operates as a ceiling both as to rate and formulas; most recording companies negotiate a mechanical license providing for accounting less frequently than monthly, the statutory requirement, and sometimes at a rate less than two cents a side, e.g., a cent and a half, or a cent.

Given further the fact that the creators of the musical composition generally share royalties from mechanicals on a 50-50 basis with the music publisher who licenses the music to the record manufacturer, then at the rate of two cents a side, the creators are entitled to half thereof from their publisher. Performance fees are usually shared on the same 50-50 basis as between creators on the one hand

---

[34] 17 U.S.C. 1(e). See Sec. 16.2, *infra*.

and their publisher. However, creators generally receive their performing rights royalties directly from the performing rights society to which they belong by reason of license of the performing rights in such music to the society in which they are members. The music publisher receives its share directly from the society by reason of its membership therein.

The economic incentives generated by Sec. 1(e) and the royalties derived from performance have had the effect of turning many performing artists to composers of their own music for performance by themselves. Thus, the statute and the division of performance royalties have had the effect of making musical performing artists troubadors, i.e., artists-composers performing works of their own.

As a result, the market not only includes composers and authors who are not also performers but a very large number of performers who also create their own music and lyrics. Thus the creators of musical composition are legion. Moreover, this has had the effect of enlarging the number of publishers of music as well. Many creators seek to enlarge their economic possibilities even further by setting up music publishing companies which they will own in whole or in part. Creators thereby hope to receive all or a share of the music publishing net profits after deduction of operating expenses by reason of such ownership, as well as equity in the catalogue of the publisher either by way of sale of stock or assets of the publishing company.

The effect of all of this has been the proliferation of music publishing companies, particularly since traditional functions of the music publisher such as printing of music can be licensed to third parties, minimized if handled directly, or simply not undertaken, since the principal sources of income of the music publisher are in mechanicals under the compulsory license and in performing rights licensed through the performing rights society.

Thus, in addition to large music publishers set up by film companies and the networks, independent but large music publishers, and those acquired by conglomerates, there are a great many small to medium sized music publishers. The consequence of this diversity is that the suppliers of music are geographically widespread and quite numerous.

Sec. 4.5. Representation by Intermediaries

Nor can it be said that the functioning of the market is carried on directly between principals and principals, i.e., suppliers and users. The panoply of intermediary arrangements is truly staggering.

Thus, in music, the music publisher will very often utilize the Harry Fox Agency as collection and auditing agency vis-à-vis the record companies, on behalf of the National Music Publishers Association. The Harry Fox Agency also negotiates synchronization rights with film users on behalf of its licensees.[35]

The creators of music have set up their own means of policing payments by the publishers, by the agency of a guild, The American Guild of Authors and Composers (AGAC), formerly known as the Songwriters Protective Association. AGAC acts as a collection and auditing agency on behalf of its member composers and lyricists whose musical compositions have been assigned to third party publishers. Creators obviously would not require

---

[35] See, Shemel, Sidney and Krasilovsky, M. William, "This Business of Music" (1964) at pp. 125-127.

such services with respect to their own publishing companies.

Sec. 4.5(a). Literary Agents

Even in book publishing, which is a prime source of literary and artistic properties for the performing arts, generally by adaptation of the underlying work to some other written form suitable for the requirements of that art, intermediaries abound. Authors may and do submit their manuscripts directly to publishers. However, trade publishers, i.e., publishers of novels, stories and literary works generally for sale by the trade as opposed to text and specialized publishers, have consisted of several dozen major and minor book publishing companies, many of them now absorbed into conglomerates. As such they were and are fairly well known to each other. This book fraternity, in the figurative sense, makes it easier for the literary agent to function. The literary agent generally knows his publishers personally. The agent has entrée, a prime advantage to an author when it is still customary to submit manuscripts seriatim, one at a time, publisher by publisher, rather than to circulate copies to a number of publishers at the same time.

However, the above picture is basically oversimplified because the terms of reference have been the hard cover book publisher in the United States, which has centered largely in the New York area while the literary agent has been described in terms of a small or moderate-sized literary agency on a basis of personal relationship both to author and publisher. As in the performing arts, the picture is considerably more complex. In addition to the hard cover book publisher, there are many paperback book publishers. They are not only a derivative means of publication, that is, paperback edition following hard cover edition but a book may be published initially as a paperback without ever going into a hard cover edition. The market for original publication is accordingly enlarged.

Then, too, the variety of types of publishing in America evidences a complexity that may not be apparent on the surface. Thus, there are reprint publishers, publishers of abridgments, the vast potential of book clubs, serialization in newspapers and periodicals, licensing of publication in foreign markets, both in English and in translation, and assorted forms of hot type and cold type reproduction. Then there is the area of publication in anthologies and excerpts under permission from the primary book publisher.[36] The numerous possibilities for reproduction in published form are buttressed by subsidiary rights in other media by reason of adaptation of the basic work.

The economic possibilities of effective packaging of a work, such as that of Truman Capote's "In Cold Blood", bring into play other forms of representation as well, for now the marketing of the basic work may produce over a million dollars by skillful licensing of paperback, book club and film rights. Thus, lawyers become necessary adjuncts of the negotiation on behalf of the author with a known market either upon submission of the manuscript or, more likely, upon negotiation of the agreement for the writing and publishing thereof. The lawyer, however, becomes far more than adjunct in the context. Counsel must be skilled in the law of literary and artistic property so as to know and advise as to the ownership and legal possibilities in the subsidiary rights. Counsel, indepen-

---

[36] See, Wittenberg, Philip, Subsidiary Rights at pp. 9-17 in Subsidiary Rights and Residuals (1968), edited by Taubman, Joseph. The author catalogues both subsidiary publishing and non-publishing rights at pp. 11-12.

dently or in association with other counsel, must also be apprised of the income, gift, and estate tax possibilities inherent in any given transaction. Counsel often guides in terms of business organization considerations if the author is to undertake the adaptation for another medium.

In the area of multi-rights negotiations, one also finds that the large booking agencies also have literary departments. They, too, act as literary agents which are departments along with departmental handling of the media, e.g., film agents, record agents, TV agents, concert agents, and so on. The large agency purports to act as a multi-service agency, not only to accommodate authors but to undertake the many-faceted negotiations required in respect of the commercial possibilities open to an author whose work is in demand.

Sec. 4.5(b). Personal Managers and the Artist—Creators

Although the pattern for the author, as such, is related to agency and counseling, and not directly to being managed, as such, again the picture of representation by intermediaries is not as forthright as depicted above. Many performing artists also write. Whether the artist writes directly or collaborates on an "as told to" basis or has a ghost writer, the artist is primarily a performer whose literary work is in demand because of his or her popularity at the time. Generally, the popular performer has a personal manager. The negotiation of book publication and of literary publication in newspapers and periodicals is then simply another function undertaken by the personal manager on behalf of his client. This does not exclude the role and function of the lawyer in the contract negotiations. The manager and counsel act in tandem on behalf of the performer-author.

Analogously, film studios and the networks often divide the function of negotiation of subsidiary rights between a "business affairs" executive, however denominated internally, and the legal department.

The performer-author may also avail himself or herself of the services of a business adviser or business manager in addition to that of the personal manager and counsel. The business adviser may or may not be the accountant for the artist-author. His concern is the handling of the funds generated by the talent of his client as an artist and the successful negotiations. The business adviser may or may not come directly into the course of negotiations of the creation of the literary and artistic work. But the effects of his advice will, in any event, have some bearing upon the implementation of the negotiations, i.e., where the funds generated are to be utilized and in what manner, the share to be set aside for tax and other needs, and so on.

As for the performer who is also a creator of his own musical compositions, the functions of composer and lyricist are so directly related to his performance that the personal manager directly becomes involved. Thus, the manager will either find suitable outlets for the performer in a music publishing company, whether formed by the performer with the manager or by assignment of the musical compositions to a third party music publisher, as well as a suitable record company to record his artist. The manager also will seek to maximize the potential for his client by performance. Performance automatically will increase the share of the artist as creator of the musical composition not only from the record company through the payment of royalties by the music publisher for mechanical licenses, but also from the performing rights society if the performance has been logged on radio and television. Finally, performance, which is accepted publicly and has resulted in the artist's own recording, will encourage other record companies to bring out "cover" records in expectations of capturing a share of the market by reason of the popularity of the musical composition. The Louis Armstrong recording of "Hello Dolly" is a case in point since the Armstrong single was not the original recording, but certainly was one of the most popular recordings of the tune. In such event, licensing of mechanical rights assures the artist-creator additional mechanical royalties from his music publisher.

The personal manager then acts as a kind of *largo factotum* to make things happen in order to maximize the economic possibilities for his client. This, in turn, is made easier to the extent his artist is not only a performer but also a performer who creates literary and artistic properties.

Sec. 4.6. Commercial Mechanisms and the Non-Profit and Academic Sectors

From the foregoing it may be seen that the principal market mechanisms are commercial and that they are exceedingly diverse and complex. The intent is to maximize economic possibilities with respect to each of the media and the subsidiary rights within each of the media. By contrast, the non-profit and academic sectors operate from a different perspective and necessarily so. One uses the non-profit sector, as differentiated from the academic, to refer to performing arts organizations and centers which are organized on a non-profit basis which are not primarily educational institutions. The academic sector in most instances is also organized on a non-profit basis but its frame of reference is principally education.

From the market point of view, their problems and approaches are similar. They are organized for particular purposes. Most of these organizations are also tax-exempt because they are organized for such non-profit purposes. Consequently, they would lose their tax exemption if they were to abandon these purposes and operate as commercial enterprises.

The aim of such sectors in terms of the market is therefore much more limited even though their function in terms of scope of the performing arts may be indeed comprehensive. Thus, a non-profit performing arts center may contain facilities for music, theatre, the dance and conduct film festivals and television broadcasts from its facilities. Schools, in addition, may serve as places of instruction for all of the performing arts, electronic as well as live.

Basically, however, their approach is other than to maximize economic potential because that would put them into business and might be contrary to their avowed purposes of providing centers for performance and, in the case of the schools, training grounds as well. Moreover, in some respects they must be the poor relation in the market place. Schools putting on amateur performances of plays, for example, cannot afford to pay royalties of commercial producers. These are licensed by the author to various organizations handling "stock and amateur" rights.[37] Amateur rights would be licensed by such organization to the schools for non-profit amateur performance. However, the theatre of the performing arts center, be it the professional theatre of the municipality, or the partly-professional theatre of

[37] See, Weissberger, L. Arnold, Subsidiary Rights in the Theatre, pp. 115-184, at p. 120, in Subsidiary Rights and Residuals, edited by Taubman, Joseph (1968). Amateur rights are licensed by the Dramatists Play Service, Samuel French, Inc. and others to the schools. For a discussion of the Dramatists Play Service, see Middleton, George, The Dramatists Guild, Fifth Ed. (1966), at pp. 26-29.

some of the academic performing arts centers are not amateurs. They may conceivably be licensed as stock companies. On the other hand, they may produce original plays or negotiate for agreements for limited runs as professional theatre. In that event, the author or his representative may be negotiating, rather than agencies to whom stock and amateur rights have been licensed.

Of course, the generalization must yield to the facts of the particular. Opera performance in the United States is mainly non-profit. The most important single market therefor is the Metropolitan Opera. From the point of view of the composer and his music publisher the "Met" is the market and considered for all practical purposes as though it were a commercial operation insofar as royalties materialize therefrom. Here one must differentiate performance for profit, within the meaning of Sec. 1(e) of the Copyright Law[38] in the sense of an admission charge therefor, from the non-profit purposes of the organization generally. Similarly, academe as an outlet for concerts is likewise a lucrative source for the performer because a large student body automatically has the makings of a large audience for the performance.

Nevertheless, the performing arts center and academe are more likely to commission works for exclusive first performance and perhaps a limited run of the work so created while the creator retains all other rights in his creation. The commission may also provide for certain repeat performances at a later date at specified royalties, but in most

---

[38] 17 U.S.C. 1(e) grants exclusive rights as to copyrighted works "To perform the copyrighted work publicly for profit if it be a musical composition . . ." Sec. 1(d) does not contain a for profit limitation as to performance of dramatic works. See Chaps. 23-24, *infra.*

instances the creator reserves control of all other rights. The concept of the non-profit organization is more akin to that of patron than of entrepreneur in relation to the work so created.

Sec. 4.7. Market Mechanisms and the Creator

The upshot of this is that the non-commercial sector as patron cannot provide sustenance by commissions alone to the creator. Nor can the creator, with few exceptions, look to the non-profit sectors for economic succor in any significant sense in terms of the performing arts.

Although the market of the non-profit sectors can be defined with some ease because it is largely geographical—the administrators are mostly located in their respective institutions—economic limitations of this market make it relatively secondary to the creator of literary and artistic works for the performing arts. True, students are consumers in the sense of buying books and being very much interested in the cinema. But in this respect, they serve as ultimate consumers and do not thereby turn the schools into users, as such. Moreover, the university presses exist primarily for scholarly publication rather than for trade publication.

The creator, therefore, must look to the commercial sector and its market mechanisms in the first instance for economic motivation because it is there where the principal possibilities exist. The same would be true of the musical composition which becomes popular even though students buy it in large numbers because the market is only ultimately that of students. The direct market is the user, the record companies, radio and television and the music publishing companies.

The creator is perforce confronted with an array of complex and often indirect market mechanisms criss-crossed in and through the various rights and media. The picture is bewildering. Indeed, the personal relationship that may have existed in the past in respect of a small group, compactly forming one of the copyright industries, which one might denominate as the market, has become considerably attenuated by organic changes in structure and function of those industries.

The possibilities of personal knowledge and relationship of any one of these industries which provided entrée for the creator, have been modified by the growth of independent production, often diversified and geographically scattered, as well as the function of intermediaries as the ball bearings of the market mechanisms.

The market for literary and artistic properties may therefore be said to have three branches, quite apart from ultimate consumer, the creator, the user and the representative who functions as a supplier from the creator. Thus, the creator, even though he or she is, in principle, free to create, functions in a legal system that is complex, with copyright laws that are complicated and marketing systems that reflect both complexities and complications.

Chapter V

COPYRIGHT AND CREATIVITY

Sec. 5.1. Historical Antecedents of American Copyright

In terms of cause and effect, it may be said that the creator's difficulties emanated in the first instance from the complexities of our copyright jurisprudence, which, in turn, set the stage for the nature and operation of our market mechanisms with all their complications within an overall jurisprudence that was far from simple.

American copyright is a direct product of foreign jurisprudence, in this instance, the mother country, England. But English experience itself did not originate full-blown with its first copyright legislation, the Statute of Anne.[1] That act was passed in 1710. Printing had been in effect for several centuries prior thereto. Mankind had been writing for millennia prior to printing and writings in manuscript form had been collected and preserved all over the world.

But copying by hand was a laborious process. Later the copying and preservation of manuscripts became the task of the monasteries. Also, anonymity was not infrequent so that there was not even an author by name to claim authorship of many works.[2] With the advent of printing in the 15th Century, various printers were granted *privilegii* and later, authors.[3]

---

[1] 8 Anne c. 19 (1710).

[2] See Kaplan, Benjamin, An Unhurried View of Copyright (1967), Chap. I, The First 350 Years, at pp. 1-37; Bowker, Richard Rogers, Copyright Its History and Its Laws (1912).

[3] See Messinger, Barry William, A Nice Dilemma: The Protection of Literary Titles, 1 Perf. Arts Rev. 585 (1970) at pp. 588-589.

In England, the pattern took the form of privileges and patents tempered by notions of censorship. Kaplan asserts:

> "Caxton founded his press in Westminster in 1476, and soon afterward the Crown began to take an acute interest in this dangerous art and to assert prerogative rights regarding it. A Royal Printer appeared in 1485, and from 1518 onward came a stream of royal grants of privileges and patents for the exclusive printing of particular books or books of stated kinds. With the religious and political unheaval of the Act of Supremacy of 1534, the prerogative was employed in a negative way to impose a general censorship through official licensing. . . In a later reign, it was thought strategic to enlist in aid of the censorship the covetous self-interest of the very printers and booksellers." [4]

And so the Stationers Company was chartered, with letters patent in 1557. The grant was not to the authors who were usually paid a lump sum for their work. Kaplan refers to it as a "right of copy" which was "the stationer's not the author's." [5]

Finally, the first English copyright statute was passed, the Statute of Anne, which granted the copyright for 21 years to books in print, 14 years to new books with a 14 year right of renewal. Finkelstein avers, "when the concept of copyright was established, authorship was not yet recognized as one of the professions," [6] and that the

---

[4] Kaplan, *op. cit., supra,* note 2, at p. 2. See also, Birrell, Augustine, Seven Lectures on The Law and History of Copyright in Books (1899).

[5] *Idem* at p. 5.

[6] Finkelstein, Herman, The Copyright Law—A Reappraisal, 104 U. Pa. L. Rev. 1025, 1037 (1956).

Statute of Anne established this recognition of authors. Addison and other writers were instrumental in seeking passage of the Statute of Anne.[7] For patronage had declined for the writer while the reading public had grown so that authors had begun to think and act as members of a profession.[8]

Writing in 1847, Curtis felt that from the time of Addison on, " . . . authors as a class, seem to have had little influence in parliament. Upon nearly all occasions, when their claims have been brought to the attention of the legislature, they have been so much entangled with the interests of booksellers and publishers, in whose hands the great mass of literary property, existing at the time, has generally been found, that they have had to encounter all the national prejudice against monopolies." [9]

It is to be borne in mind that what was protected was the exclusive right in copy to make copies. Bowker indicates that the term "copyright" is derived from the Latin, *copia*, meaning plenty and that the term has two senses, right in copy and right to make copies.[10] He further defines the term "property" in the sense of a literary and artistic property, as being derived from the Latin, *proprius*, meaning one's own, and as having the meaning of "creation of the individual brain".[11]

---

[7] Curtis, George Ticknor, Treatise on the Law of Copyright (1847), at p. 72, "Addison is said to have been concerned in procuring the act of Anne to be passed."

[8] Kaplan, *op. cit., supra,* note 2 at pp. 22-23, "With the decline of patronage, writers had to stand on their own feet; and as a reading public grew, writers began to feel themselves members of a professional class, and occasionally to speak out with their own demands for recognition and protection."

[9] Curtis, *op. cit., supra,* note 7, at pp. 72-73.

[10] Bowker, *op. cit., supra,* note 2, at p. 1.

[11] *Idem* at p. 3.

Even before the American Revolution, the Statute of Anne came to be construed in fundamentals by the British courts. This took the form of determining the nature of the copyright and of the protection that flowed therefrom. The question arose in *Millar* v. *Taylor* in 1769.[12] It was whether the common law copyright in Thompson's book of poems "The Seasons" continued after the expiration of the statutory copyright so as to prevent copying. The Court held that it did. But this was reversed in 1774 by the House of Lords in the same case, *sub nomine, Donaldson* v. *Beckett.*[13] According to Curtis, *Donaldson* v. *Beckett,* ". . . decides only that the common law right had been taken away by the statute of Anne." [14]

Sec. 5.2. Origins of American Copyright

Prior to the adoption of the American Constitution, some of the state governments passed copyright legislation.[15] Thus, Connecticut and Massachusetts were among the first states to pass copyright legislation in 1783.[16] Significantly, "In October 1781, the state of Connecticut, by special legislative enactment, gave Andrew Law an 'exclusive *patent*' for 5 years for his COLLECTION OF THE BEST AND MOST APPROVED TUNES AND ANTHEMS KNOWN TO EXIST." [17] Thus, be-

[12] 4 Burr. 2303 (1769).

[13] 1 Eng. Rep. 837; 4 Burr. 2408 (1774). For a discussion of these cases, see Whicher, John F., The Creative Arts & The Judicial Process, Chap. V, The Ghost of *Donaldson* v. *Beckett* at pp. 85 *et seq.* (1965).

[14] Curtis, *op. cit., supra,* note 7, at p. 75.

[15] Dichter, Harry and Shapiro, Elliott, Early American Sheet Music Its Lure and Its Lore 1768-1889 (1941) at p. XXIV; Messinger, *op. cit., supra,* note 3, at p. 594.

[16] Messinger, *Idem,* at p. 594; Curtis, *op.cit., supra,* note 3, at p. 77. See Sec. 20.1, *supra.*

[17] Dichter and Shapiro, *op. cit., supra,* note 15 at p. XXIV (emphasis added).

fore passage of the first copyright legislation of the states, the grant was couched in terms of patent and privilege, hearkening back to the days preceding the Statute of Anne.

Then, in 1789, the Constitution of the United States was adopted. The Constitution as adopted contained a provision as to copyright. Article I, Section 8, Clause 8 thereof provided power in the Congress, "To promote the Progress of Science and useful Arts, by securing for limited Times to Authors and Inventors the exclusive Right to their respective Writings and Discoveries." [18] It is noteworthy that this clause combined patent and copyright. Congress did not hesitate to exercise its powers in relation to copyright. The first Copyright Act was enacted in 1790 to grant protection to books, charts and maps.[19] Music was not mentioned specifically until the Copyright Act of February 8, 1831. Dichter and Shapiro believe that "Prior to that date, music was sometimes registered as 'books'." [20] They come up with an interesting explanation as to sheet music and publication at the time. They state:

"Broadsides and Periodicals

> Under this heading will be found many songs unknown in sheet music form. Broadsides were extremely common in the 18th century, and this may account for the fact that separate publications of music before 1789 are practically unknown in America. Broadsides could be written, published and peddled on the streets a few hours after the news of any local or national event, the verses were usually written to the tune of old English,

---

[18] Section 8 contains an enumeration of the powers granted to Congress.

[19] Act of May 31, 1790, c. 15, 1 Stat. 124.

[20] Dichter and Shapiro, *op. cit., supra,* note 15 at p. XXIV.

> Irish or Scotch songs, and no printed music was necessary.
>
> There are a few references to publication as sheets of music, but such copies are unknown to us." [21]

It should be noted that the language of the constitutional clause may have meant something different from and other than the ordinary meaning of the same words today. Two economists, Stocking and Watkins, observe that "A common mistake is to associate the constitutional authorization to promote the progress of 'Science' with the grant of patents to 'inventors'. *But the branch of knowledge now called science was in the eighteenth century termed natural philosophy. As the men who drafted the Constitution used the term, 'Science' embraced all knowledge.* If the eighth paragraph of Section 8, Article 1, had been divided into two paragraphs, instead of covering both copyright and patents in a single paragraph, these would have read: 8a. To promote the Progress of Science, by securing for limited Times to Authors the exclusive Right to their Writings. 8b. To promote the Progress of useful Arts, by securing for limited Times to Inventors the exclusive Right to their Discoveries." [22]

Credence is given to this by the fact that the Patent Act of 1790, passed in the same year as the first Copyright Act,

---

[21] Dichter and Shapiro, *op. cit., supra,* note 15 at p. XIX. But see Variety Music Cavalcade, by Maltfield, Julius, New and Enlarged Edition (1962), at pp. 1-5, Music of the Pilgrims, American Colonial Period. This lists various works published from 1698 on. In 1721 the first book was published with barred music notes, The Ground & Rules of Musick Explained, or, An Introduction to the Art of Singing by Note. Boston, 1721. By Reverend Thomas Walter, of Roxbury, Mass.

[22] Stocking and Watkins, Monopoly and Free Enterprise, footnote at p. 447 (1951).

granted a patent to persons who ". . . have invented or discovered any *useful art,* manufacture, engine, machine, or device, or any improvements therein not before known or used. . ." [23] Indeed, James Madison, writing in The Federalist, wrote, "The copyright of authors has been solemnly adjudged, in Great Britain, to be a right of common law. The right to *useful inventions* seems with equal reason to belong to the inventors." [24] Thomas Jefferson is quoted as having said that "*In the arts,* and especially in the *mechanical arts,* many ingenious improvements are made in the consequence of the patent right." [25]

On the other hand, Curtis refers to an author as an "inventor" and invention as a synonym of creation.[26] Considering that Curtis wrote in 1847, it would seem that the conceptual distinction between the copyright and the patent either had not been carefully elaborated or else felt to be closely related. After all, the original copyright statute in England stemmed from practices of grant of privileges and patents in literary works.[27] Even as late as 1781, the State of Connecticut had granted a patent for 5 years in a work of music.[28]

Even though in modern terminology the language of the copyright clause represents an involution of terms,[29] the Supreme Court in due course had occasion to construe the

---

[23] 1 Stat. 109-110. As quoted from U.S. v. Line Material Co., 333 U.S. 287 (1948), dissent of Justice Burton, p. 333, footnote 11 (emphasis added).

[24] The Federalist, No. 43 at p. 278 (Modern Library Ed. 1937) (emphasis added).

[25] U.S. v. Line Material Co., note 23, at p. 335 (emphasis added).

[26] Curtis, *op. cit., supra,* note 7, at p. 72.

[27] See Sec. 5.1, *supra.*

[28] Note 17, *supra.*

[29] Taubman, Copyright and Antitrust (1960) at p. 18.

meaning of the clause in copyright terms, thereby setting forth prevailing juridical theory as to the nature of the federal copyright, when it held in *Wheaton* v. *Peters*, "Congress, then, by this act, instead of sanctioning an existing right, as contended for, created it." [30] Thus, the Court reached the same conclusion as in *Donaldson* v. *Beckett*.[31]

Sec. 5.3. Theories of Copyright

What is the nature of copyright? Ladas has written that "There has been no thorough-going juristic analysis of copyright in England or the United States on the basis of present day understanding of legal rights and interests in terms of modern juristic legal interpretations." [32] Chafee appears to agree, stating that "the philosophy of the subject has been somewhat submerged in the statutes and case-law because of the pressure of practical problems of narrow scope which demanded immediate attention." [33]

Drone,[34] on the other hand, had set forth four theories as to the nature of copyright. According to him, copyright was:

1. A species of property which is founded in natural law and which is therefore not lost by publication nor taken away by publication; or

2. An exclusive right before publication; or

---

[30] 8 Peters 591, 660-1 (1834).

[31] 1 Eng. Rep. 837; 4 Burr. 2408 (1774).

[32] Ladas, Stephen P., 1 The International Protection of Literary and Artistic Property 4 (1938).

[33] Chafee, Reflections on the Law of Copyright, 45 Col. L. Rev. 503, 719 (1945) at p. 503.

[34] Drone, Eaton S., The Law of Copyright and Playwright 2 (1879). See also Putnam, George Haven, The Question of Copyright 2d Ed. (1896) at p. 375.

3. A right not lost by publication but destroyed by statute; or

4. A monopoly of limited duration, created and wholly regulated by the legislature.

It would appear that in the view of the Supreme Court of the United States it is an artificial right and has been so regarded for a long time. Following the British decision of *Donaldson* v. *Beckett*[35] of 1774, it held in 1834 that "Congress, then, by this act, instead of sanctioning an existing right, as contended for, created it." [36] In recent years, Justice Reed reiterated this view in his opinion in *Mazer* v. *Stein,* stating, "Congress may after publication protect by copyright any writing of an author. Its statute creates the copyright. It did not exist at common law even though he had a property right in an unpublished work." [37] Justice Douglas has observed, "The copyright law, like the patent statutes, makes the reward to the owner a secondary consideration." [38] Justice Hughes has commented, "The sole interest of the United States and the primary object in conferring the monopoly lie in the general benefits derived by the public from the labors of authors." [39]

But this view must take into consideration the legislative scheme expressed by Congress in Sec. 2 of the Copyright Law which reads:

> "Nothing in this title shall be construed to annul or limit the right of the author or proprietor of an unpublished work, at common law or in equity, to prevent

[35] 1 Eng. Rep. 837; 4 Burr. 2408 (1774).
[36] 8 Peters 591, 660-1 (1834).
[37] 347 U.S. 201, 214 (1954).
[38] U.S. v. Paramount, 334 U.S. 131, 158 (1948).
[39] Fox Film Corp. v. Doyal, 286 U.S. 123, 127 (1932).

the copying, publication, or use of such unpublished work without his consent, and to obtain damages therefor."[40]

In other words, the Supreme Court, in the above opinions, addressed itself to the nature of the statutory copyright. Unpublished works retain their common law copyright under the statute.

Thus it may be seen that items 2 and 3 of Drone's categories are really variants of item 4 of his classification. The common law right ceases to exist upon publication because the new right, the monopoly for a limited term or terms, takes effect. This would appear to be reinforced by the thinking of the Supreme Court in the *Sears*[41] and *Compco*[42] cases where failure to seek patent relief under federal law pre-empted state relief of unfair competition. Justice Black in the latter case stated, "Today, we have held in *Sears, Roebuck & Co.* v. *Stiffel Co., supra,* that when an article is unprotected by a patent or a copyright, state law may not forbid others to copy that article. To forbid copying would interfere with the federal policy, found in Art. I, Sec. 8, cl. 8, of the Constitution and in the implementing federal statutes, of allowing free access to copy whatever the federal patent and copyright laws leave in the public domain."[43]

Of course, Sec. 2 of the Copyright Law is an implementing statute which preserves the common law statute prior to publication. However, Sec. 8 of the Act states in pertinent part, "No copyright shall subsist in the original text of

[40] 17 U.S.C. 2.
[41] Sears, Roebuck & Co. v. Stiffel Co., 376 U.S. 225 (1964).
[42] Compco Corp. v. Day-Brite Lighting, Inc., 376 U.S. 234 (1964).
[43] *Ibid.* at p. 237 (italics).

any work which is in the public domain. . ." [44] Sec. 10 of the statute provided in part that "Any person entitled thereto by this title may secure copyright for his work by publication thereof with the notice of copyright required by this title. . ." [45] The Regulations of the Copyright Office spell out the importance of the copyright notice in the statutory scheme. Sec. 202.2(a)(1) provides that "With respect to a published work, copyright is secured, or the right to secure it is lost, at the date of publication. . ." [46] Sec. 202.2(a)(2) continues, "If publication occurs by distribution of copies or in some other manner, without the statutory notice or with an inadequate notice, the right to secure copyright is lost." [47]

Thus publication for federal statutory purposes destroys the common law copyright. It is really a matter of semantics whether the common law right is lost by publication sufficient to invoke the aforesaid Regulations of the Copyright Office or whether the same is deemed destroyed. Effectively the result is identical. Upon such publication, federal law pre-empts; unless the formalities of the Copyright Law are observed as to notice, there is no longer any protection under state law.

Similarly, whatever the nature of the right at common law, be it an exclusive right as item 2 in the Drone classification, it nonetheless falls upon publication. As soon as the statute takes effect, it is no longer a right. Thus item 2 is a function of item 4; it depends for its existence upon the requirements for item 4 not coming into effect.

---

[44] 17 U.S.C. 8.
[45] 17 U.S.C. 10.
[46] Regulations of the Copyright Office, Sec. 202.2(a)(1).
[47] *Ibid.* Sec. 202.2(a)(2).

But the views of the Court, above, are only partly an explanation of the theory of copyright. Statutory copyright is rationalized as a monopoly of limited duration, created and regulated by statute. But the current Act leaves a residue of rights at all times where federal law does not preempt. The regimen of federal law does not apply to the common law copyright. Warner has characterized it as, ". . . independent of statute." Section 2 of the Copyright Code confirms its existence.

"Common law copyright is thus an absolute incorporeal right which is protected to the same extent by the common law as other personal property." [48]

Drone opted for his first item and concluded, "Literary property, like all property, has its origin in natural law, and not in legislation; and it is therefore, a natural, and not an artificial right." [49] He drew upon the notion of pre-occupancy to explain the origin of property, for pre-occupancy is first possession. Property, in his view, is derived from labor, since what a man produces is his.[50]

Judge Aston in *Millar* v. *Taylor* characterized it as "a personal incorporeal property".[51] The Register of Copyrights discussed various theories of copyright in his Report on copyright revision.[52] He referred to it under various theories as property, which is intangible and incorporeal, as a

---

[48] Warner, Harry P., Radio and Television Rights, Sec. 202, Rights Conferred by Common Law Copyright at p. 857 (1953).

[49] Drone, The Law of Copyright and Playwright 26 (1879).

[50] *Ibid.* at p. 3. See, also, Drone's opening chapter, The Origin and Nature of Literary Property.

[51] 4 Burr. 2303, 2341 (1769).

[52] Report of the Register of Copyrights on the General Revision of the U.S. Copyright Law, reprinted in 2 Studies on Copyright 1199-1346 (1963).

personal right, and as a monopoly.[53] The Register, Abraham L. Kaminstein, remarked, "Copyright is generally regarded as a form of property, but is property of a unique kind. It is intangible and incorporeal. The thing to which the property right attaches—the author's intellectual work—is incapable of possession except as it is embodied in a tangible article such as a manuscript, book, record, or film. The tangible articles containing the work may be in the possession of many persons other than the copyright owner, and they may use the work for their own enjoyment, but copyright restrains them from reproducing the work without the owner's consent." [54] Indeed, the Copyright Law sets forth this distinction. Sec. 27[55] reads in part:

> "The copyright is distinct from the property in the material object copyrighted, and the sale or conveyance, by gift or otherwise, of the material object shall not of itself constitute a transfer of the copyright, nor shall the assignment of the copyright constitute a transfer of the title to the material object;"

The statute characterizes the intangible and incorporeal nature of the copyright well indeed!

Thus, even though characterized as a monopoly in the sense of "exclusive control over the market" [56] for the work, as set forth in Sec. 1 of the Copyright Law for the limited terms provided for in Sec. 24 thereof,[57] it would appear

---

[53] *Idem* at pp. 1203-1205.

[54] *Idem* at p. 1203.

[55] 17 U.S.C. 27.

[56] Report of the Register, *op. cit., supra,* note 52 at p. 1205.

[57] 17 U.S.C. 1 reads in part, "Any person entitled thereto, upon complying with the provisions of this title, shall have the exclusive right:" 17 U.S.C. 24 sets forth the duration of the original and renewal terms of copyright.

that the statute serves to characterize a right of property which may be sold, assigned or otherwise dealt in. This is so, even though the right of renewal passes by way of the statutory scheme of Sec. 24, rather than by operation of the laws of inheritance under local law unless the author survives into the renewal term of the respective copyrights and has assigned his renewal rights.[58] For Sec. 24 relates to a statutory method of devolution of such property intended to give the widow and children, i.e., the family of the creator, a second chance at adequate provision if the author, because of unequal bargaining position, had assigned his original term improvidently.[59]

The Register of Copyrights appeared to conclude that attributes of personal rights are also immanent in copyright. He stated in his Report, "In the United States the moral rights of authors have never been treated as aspects of copyright. But authors have been given much the same protection of personal rights under general principles of the common law such as those relating to implied contracts, unfair competition, misrepresentation, and defamation." [60] This is much the same conclusion as that of William S. Strauss, who prepared a study for the Copyright Office on moral rights. Strauss summed up his study as follows:

---

[58] The copyright renewal creates a new estate, G. Ricordi v. Paramount Pictures, 189 F. 2d 469, 471 (2d Cir. 1951); the author's assignment prior to the 28th year of original term is only an expectancy and falls if he does not survive, Fred Fisher Music Co. v. M. Witmark & Sons, 318 U.S. 643 (1943), Miller Music Corp. v. Charles N. Daniels, Inc., 362 U.S. 373, 377 (1960). See Chaps. VII-VIII, *infra.*

[59] Cf. Sec. 304 of S. 543 (1969) of proposed copyright revision bill providing for termination of interest by author or family in certain circumstances. See discussion in House Report No. 83, 90th Cong., 1st Sess. (1967) at pp. 107-108.

[60] Report of the Register, *op. cit., supra,* note 52 at p. 1204.

"Without using the label 'moral right,' or designations of the components of the moral right, the courts in the United States arrive at much the same results as do European courts. Substantially the same personal rights are upheld, although often under different principles. Also, substantially the same limitations are imposed on these rights, frequently, on the same basis." [61] Strauss summed these up as (1) the right to be given a credit, which he may waive; (2) the right to prevent prejudicial changes, which he may waive; (3) the author cannot be compelled to perform his contract to create a work, even though he must respond in damages for breach of contract; (4) the right to publish or withhold from publication; which right may be assigned or licensed; and (5) the author may prevent defamation of character (excessive criticism) and unfair use or misuse of the work by actions in tort—e.g., by way of defamation, libel, slander or unfair competition.[62]

This is consistent with the view of Warren and Brandeis in their landmark article on privacy ". . . that the protection afforded to thoughts, sentiments and emotions, expressed through the medium of writing or of the arts, so far as it consists in preventing publication, is merely an instance of the enforcement of the more general right of the individual to be let alone." [63]

On the other hand, Stevenson has pointed out, "French writers take the view that the right is *sui generis,* existing independently of the pecuniary rights of the cre-

---

[61] Strauss, William S., The Moral Right of the Author, Study No. 4, in Studies on Copyright, at pp. 963-992 (1963).

[62] *Ibid.* at p. 992.

[63] Warren and Brandeis, The Right to Privacy, 4 Harv. L. Rev. 193, 205 (1890), reproduced in Hofstadter, The Development of the Right of Privacy in New York, 55, 67 (1954).

ator. In Germany, Austria and Italy, however, the moral right is simply a part of a single copyright composed of pecuniary and personal rights."[64]

Justice Thompson speculated in his dissent in *Wheaton* v. *Peters,* "Whether literary property is *sui generis,* or under whatever denomination of rights it may be classed, it seems to have been founded upon the same principle of general utility to society, which is the basis of all other moral rights and obligations."[65]

If Justice Thompson equivocated, later commentators did not. Bergstrom characterized the right as a "property right".[66] Katz asserted that the copyright statute ". . . gives protection to the work, and only indirectly to the individual."[67] Chafee minced no words as to where the emphasis lay. He stated, "For the time being, we had better concentrate our energies on the pecuniary aspects of copyright. We have enough trouble there. After we get the issues of dollars and cents, we can go on to moral rights."[68] Katz lamented this neglect of the author's interest of personality which is part of his creation.[69]

---

[64] Stevenson, Moral Right and the Common Law: A Proposal, Sixth Copyright Law Symposium 89, 108 (1955); see also, Tournier, The French Law of March 11, 1957 on Literary Property and Artistic Property, 6 Bull. Cr. Soc. 1 (1958).

[65] 8 Peters 591, 671 (1834).

[66] The Businessman Deals with Copyright. Third Copyright Law Symposium 249, 251 (1940).

[67] Katz, The Doctrine of Moral Right and American Copyright Law: A Proposal, Fourth Copyright Law Symposium 79, 89 (1952).

[68] Chafee, Reflections on the Law of Copyright, 45 Col. L. Rev. 503, 719 (1945) at p. 729.

[69] Katz, *op. cit., supra,* note 67, at p. 101.

Yet another approach is to resolve the property-moral right syndrome by sweeping it under the rug through pragmatic analysis of interests involved. Ladas would prefer to consider the problem in terms of ". . . interests recognized and delimited for the purpose of securing them by law rather than in the sense of legal rights by which these interests are secured." [70]

Of course, the various interests involved must be identified and evaluated. In connection with current copyright revision, this writer had the following to say about the interests involved and revision:

> "Indeed, if copyright revision is effectuated, it will be because the Register of Copyrights has been so adept in the jurisprudence of interests. For the past year, more or less, periodic meetings have been held in Washington and elsewhere by the Copyright Office, to which the interested copyright public has been invited to discuss and review, seriatim, sections of legislation to be embodied in a new bill to be proposed to Congress by the Copyright Office. Various proposals and alternative proposals indicate that the recommendations in the Register's Report are not rigid and inflexible formulae but were also intended to be exposed to the scrutiny of the copyright public for consideration in advance of submission of a general copyright revision bill to Congress. What may or may not eventuate in the proposed new bill must first be sifted through the sieve of compromise and conciliation of copyright interests, e.g., authors, publishers, motion picture producers, broadcasters, etc." [71]

---

[70] Ladas, *op. cit., supra,* note 32, at p. 10.

[71] Taubman, Review of Studies on Copyright: Arthur Fisher Memorial Edition, 32 Ford. L. Rev. 875, 877 (1964).

One would have concluded that, in the light of hindsight, the "etc." at the end of the quote refers to CATV, jukebox operators and educators, among others.[72]

In a sense, the jurisprudence of interests[73] is a form of instrumentalism; it is a means of understanding of how legislation in copyright is derived. It also provides a searchlight for analysis of trends of legal decisions of the judiciary on copyright. But such an approach, while invaluable for understanding, neatly evades formulation of underlying conceptions.

It is this that Ebenstein deplores when he refers to the lack of a workable, unifying concept of copyright. Ebenstein appears to be seeking the social nature of the creative process when he defines copyright as the ". . . qualified control which the law gives an author over the means by which the original literal and mental content of his work may be communicated to the minds of others." [74]

Sec. 5.4. The Nature of Creativity in Relation to Copyright

Although used in another context, Spring has written that copyrights originate in a fluid concept.[75] There is a flow

---

[72] See Copyright Law Revision—CATV, Hearings before the Subcommittee on Patents, Trademarks and Copyrights of the Committee on the Judiciary, U.S. Senate, 89th Cong., 2nd Sess., August 2, 3, 4 and 25, 1966, and Hearings on Copyright Law Revision of said Subcommittee, 90th Cong., 1st Sess., March 15, 16, 17, 20, 21, 1967 and April 4, 6, 11, 12 and 28, 1967.

[73] Professor Lon L. Fuller in his introduction to the book, The Jurisprudence of Interests, a compilation of selected writings translated and edited by Schoch, M. Magdalena (1948) states in his opening sentence, "The central problem of this book is that of legal method." at p. xvii.

[74] Ebenstein, Morris, Introduction to Rothenberg, Copyright Law Basic and Related Materials (1956) at pp. XXIII-IV.

[75] Spring, Risks and Rights 75 (1952).

from creation to property to creation whereby the author begets literary and artistic property.

Various views were advanced in *Millar* v. *Taylor*.[76] Justice Aston opined: "... though the sentiments and doctrine may be called *ideal*, yet when the same are communicated to the sight and understanding of every man, by the medium of printing, the work becomes a distinguishable subject of property and not merely destitute of corporeal qualities . . . Publication therefore is the necessary act, and only means, to render this confessed property useful to mankind, and profitable to the owner; in this they are jointly concerned."[77]

Justice Yates took a different approach. "Ideas are free. But while the author confines them to his study, they are like birds in a cage, which none but he can have a right to let fly: for, till he thinks proper to emancipate them, they are under his dominion."[78] Drawing upon the analogy of wild animals in the doctrine of *ferae naturae*, he considered it a right of first publication, where the work is laid open.

Lord Mansfield seemed to reflect concern over the author and notions that copyright is a right of personality in opposing the view that the statute creates the right. He observed as to the author, "He is no more the master of the use of his name. He has no controul over the correctness of his own work. He can not prevent additions. He can not retract errors. He can not amend or correct a faulty edition."[79]

---

[76] 4 Burr. 2303 (1769).

[77] *Idem* at p. 2341.

[78] *Idem* at p. 2378.

[79] *Idem* at p. 2397. See Secs. 22.4-5, *infra*.

Basically these views are in accord that creation consists of reducing ideas to a written form. That is why the Constitution refers to writings of the authors.[80]

Perhaps the term "written form" can be understood to mean concrete, tangible form because that is the means of protection of what is otherwise incorporeal. The form identifies the *res* of creation.

It is submitted that the term "writings" has been expanded judicially from a limited category to a broad comprehensive term by a legal fiction.[81] Obviously the framers of the Constitution were not aware of electronic technology and of motion pictures and television. The Supreme Court, in deciding that a statue which was also a lamp base was entitled to copyright protection in *Mazer* v. *Stein,*[82] seemed to give support to this theory. For it permitted a three dimensional work of art which was also utilitarian to be a subject of copyright, even though Justice Douglas would have sent the case back for reargument. He asked, "Is a sculptor an 'author' and is his statue a 'writing' within the meaning of the Constitution? We have never decided the question."[83] It was not obvious to Justice Douglas that a variety of three dimensional objects as works of art by the Copyright Office were "writings" in a constitutional sense.[84] Justice Doug-

---

[80] Art. I, Sec. 8, Clause 8. See, The Meaning of "Writings" in the Copyright Clause of the Constitution, Study No. 3 in Studies on Copyright 43 (1963), also published as Note, Copyright-Study of the Term "Writings" in the Copyright Clause of the Constitution, 31 N.Y.U. L. Rev. 1263 (1956).

[81] Gray, John Chipman, The Nature and Sources of the Law, Second Ed. (1921).

[82] 347 U.S. 201 (1954).

[83] *Idem* at p. 220.

[84] *Idem* at p. 221.

las adverted to the meagerness of the constitutional materials and that much research was needed.[85]

Indeed, the authors of Study No. 3 are impelled to conclude that the term "writings" in the constitutional clause only makes sense because of its broad interpretation. They state:

> "Only by a broad interpretation of the words 'writings' and 'authors' in terms of standards, such as originality and creativity, and in terms of purpose, such as promoting the progress of the arts and sciences, can the action of both the courts and Congress be justified or rationalized in terms of the words contained in section 8.
>
> "It seems resonable to assume that no copyright statute passed by Congress allowing copyright protection to new forms of expression will be declared unconstitutional. This is so, despite the discussion in some cases that certain objects are not 'writings' within the meaning of the Constitution. Congress seems to be free to include in a copyright statute any object, conforming to the requirements of originality and creativity, without fear of judicial interference."[86]

But comprehensiveness of the term "writings" in the constitutional clause as construed by Congress and the courts is only one of the parameters in determining the nature of creativity. The work must be original, fixed in a tangible form and be within the scope of the statute, even if it be a writing.

---

[85] *Idem* at p. 220. Justice Douglas cites Fenning, The Origin of the Patent and Copyright Clause of the Constitution, 17 Geo. L.J. 109 (1929).

[86] Study No. 3, *op. cit., supra,* note 80, at p. 86.

As Judge Frank has stated, "'Original' in reference to a copyrighted work means that the particular work 'owes its origin' to the 'author'. No large measure of novelty is necessary." [87] He points out that legislators familiar with the purpose of the constitutional clause imposed far less exacting standards by statute for copyright than for patent. He observes, "They authorized the copyrighting of a mere map which, patently, calls for no considerable uniqueness. They exacted far more from an inventor. And, while they demanded that an official should be satisfied as to the character of an invention before a patent issued, they made no such demand in respect of a copyright." [88] He concludes that the Constitution recognizes basically different standards for patents and copyrights,[89] and that "All that is needed to satisfy both the Constitution and the statute is that the "author" contributed something more than a 'merely trivial' variation, something recognizably 'his own'. Originality in this context 'means little more than a prohibition of actual copying.' " [90]

In the last analysis, the minimal originality is a matter of degree which sets a floor in legal contemplation for

---

[87] Alfred Bell & Co. v. Catalda Fine Arts, Inc., 191 F. 2d 99 (2d Cir. 1951) at p. 102. Cf., Justice Douglas dissent in Lee v. Runge, 171 U.S.P.Q. 322 (1971), denying certiorari in re the decision below, 441 F.2d 579 (9th Cir. 1971), at p. 323. "No reason can be offered why we should depart from the plain import of this grant of congressional power and apply more lenient constitutional standards to copyrights than to patents." Justice Douglas in his dissenting opinion to denial of certiorari would apply the standard of novelty rather than originality.

[88] *Ibid.* at p. 101.

[89] *Idem* at p. 103.

[90] *Idem* at pp. 102-3.

creativity.[91] The Copyright Office once returned a lead sheet consisting of only a few bars of music as insufficiently original for copyrighting. Copyright was duly obtained thereafter when a substitute lead sheet was submitted with expanded composition. The policy of the Copyright Office is in line with its expression in its Regulations. Thus it will not accept for copyright "Words and short phrases, such as names, titles and slogans . . ." [92]

As a facet of originality, there appears to be a like requirement of minimal creativity, as to which again a judicial floor has been set. The Supreme Court accomplished this by enunciating the esthetic requirement in terms of minima. Thus, when it stated in *Mazer* v. *Stein*, "The dichotomy of protection for the esthetic is not utility and beauty but art for the copyright . . .",[93] it did so within the context of the remarks of Justice Holmes in holding a circus poster copyrightable in *Bleistein* v. *Donaldson Lithographing Co.* There he referred to ". . . a very modest grade of art has in it something irreducible, which is one man's alone. That something he may copyright." [94] Nimmer believes that the nature of the relationship between minimal requirements of originality and of creativity is only semantic. He remarks, "It is of only semantic significance whether originality is defined as embodying such creativity or whether such creativity is regarded as a necessary adjunct to originality. However, a greater clarity of expression is perhaps achieved by regarding originality and creativity as separate elements." [95]

---

[91] See, Nimmer on Copyright (1969), Sec. 10.2 Quantum of Originality.

[92] Regulations of the Copyright Office, Sec. 202.1 (a).

[92] Sec. 202.1(a), Regulations of Copyright Office.

[93] 347 U.S. 201, 218 (1954).

[94] 188 U.S. 239, 250 (1903). See Sec. 21.1, *infra*.

[95] Nimmer, *op. cit., supra,* note 91 at p. 36.

Unfortunately, the minimal standard of originality as expressed by Judge Frank, may be paraphrased as something more than an insignificant variation, recognizably the author's, which has not been copied. Thus, one must ascertain what is a copy before one determines whether the criterion of originality has been met. Here fixation in some form must be considered. Prior to the passage of the present Copyright Law in 1909, the Supreme Court held in *White-Smith Music Corp.* v. *Apollo Co.* that musical notes reproduced on a player piano music roll were not a copy since they were perceived by the ear and not the eye.[96] Therefore, the defendant had not infringed the plaintiff's copyright. Congress purported to remedy the situation by granting the mechanical right to the copyright proprietor but subject to a compulsory license after initial licensing of use in Sec. 1(e) of the Copyright Law.[97]

However, the Copyright Office took the position that a mechanical reproduction of a work in sound was not a copy, and declined to copyright the same. Thus its Regulations stated, "A phonograph record or other sound recording is not considered a 'copy' of the compositions recorded on it, and is not acceptable for copyright registration. Likewise, the Copyright Office does not register claims to exclusive rights in mechanical recordings themselves, or in the performances they reproduce." [98] This also was

---

[96] 209 U.S. 1 (1908).

[97] 17 U.S.C. 1(e).

[98] Regulations of the Copyright Office, Sec. 202.8(b). This did not prohibit the Copyright Office several years ago from requesting copyright deposit of album covers of phonograph records by demand for deposit under Sec. 14 of the Copyright Law. The intent of the Copyright Office was to thereby build the archives of phonograph records of the Library of Congress. Many of the record manufacturers had affixed notice of copyright to their album covers

the view expressed by the Ninth Circuit in *Corcoran* v. *Montgomery Ward & Co., Inc.*[99] which did not believe that Sec. 1(e) of the present act modified the rationale of the *White-Smith* case. *Corcoran* dealt with a claim of copying of poem by reproducing the same on a phonograph record set to music.

In this regard, it is to be noted that although proposed copyright revision of a long range nature extends copyright protection to "sound recordings,"[100] it excludes phonorecords from its definition of "copies".[101] Exclusive rights, however, are granted to "copies or phonorecords" in repro-

---

to protect the same upon release for sale of the albums, but they preferred not to incur the expense of copyright registration of large numbers of such albums. After informal meetings, a compromise arrangement was worked out.

But with the passage of Public Law 92-140, 92nd Cong., S. 646, on October 15, 1971, Congress provided for copyright protection for sound recordings, fixed, published and recorded from and after the effective date—4 months after enactment—i.e., February 15, 1972 and before January 1, 1975. The purpose of passage of S. 646 was to provide interim federal anti-piracy protection in sound recordings by means of copyright in sound recordings and extension of copyright remedies thereto. The Copyright Office has now devised a Form N for registration of sound recordings. See Billboard, Dec. 18, 1971, p. 1, col. 5, Historical Booklet Out On Copyright by Mildred Hall. See notes 104a and b and 127, *infra* and Secs. 6.3, 17.2 and 23.7, *infra*.

[99] 121 F.2d 572 (9th Cir. 1941).

[100] S. 543, 91st Cong., 1st Sess., submitted Jan. 22, 1969, provides copyright protection as to works of authorship in sound recordings in Sec. 102.

[101] Sec. 101 of S. 543 defines "copies" as material objects "other than phonorecords". It defines "Phonorecords" as nonvisual material objects for fixation of sound "by any method now known or later developed". It also defines "Sound Recordings" as the nonvisual fixation of sound regardless of nature, "such as disks, tapes, or other phonorecords".

ducing the copyrighted work and distributing the same,[102] limited in sound recordings to "the actual sounds fixed in the recording".[103] As to sound recordings of the same work that is an independent fixation of other sounds, the right does not extend thereto, " . . . even though such sounds imitate or simulate those in the copyrighted sound recording." [104] Thus, the proposed revision of a long range nature purports to preserve the distinction of *White-Smith* that mechanical aural reproduction is not copying, although copyright is to be granted in sound recordings.

One must, however, differentiate the objectives of proposed revision of a long-range nature and interim legislation. Because of the prevalence of record piracy, Congress enacted a short range act to accord federal protection against this. S. 646 became law as Public Law 92-140 on October 15, 1971.[104a]

The law added: a new Sec. 1(f) to the Copyright Act granting the exclusive right of reproduction and distribution in sound recordings, but not as to imitations or simulations thereof; a new classification subsection as to "sound recordings" by way of Sec. 5(n); notice provisions therefor by means of the letter P in a circle as an addition to Sec. 19; affixation of such notice to label or container by amendment of Sec. 20; a definition of "sound recordings" in Sec. 26; and a revision of Sec. 101(e) providing that sound recordings are *copies* for purposes of damages and infringement.

---

[102] S. 543, Sec. 106.
[103] S. 543, Sec. 114
[104] *Ibid.*
[104a] Public Law 92-140, signed Oct. 15, 1971, which enacted S. 646, 92d Cong., 1st Sess., amending 17 U.S.C. See notes 98, *supra,* 104b and 127, *infra,* Secs. 6.3, 17.2 and 23.7, *infra.*

Sec. 3 of S. 646 as enacted provided that it was to become effective on February 15, 1972,—four months after enactment—as to sound recordings, fixed, published and copyrighted thereafter and prior to January 1, 1975.[104b]

Thereby the prohibition contained in the Regulations of the Copyright Office as to copyrighting phonograph records has been eliminated. Congress has acted to resolve the copyrightability of sound recordings even if only on an interim basis. But long range revision relates its classification scheme to tangibility. The proposed statutory revision of a long range nature departs from the present classification scheme in several material respects. Present Sec. 4 of the Copyright Law includes all the "writings" of an author as to which works copyright may be secured.[105] Sec. 5 of the present Act then proceeds to enumerate classes in which the work to be copyrighted is claimed to belong.[106] The present Act therefore purports to embrace "writings", the very criterion of the constitutional clause, while specifying categories of copyrights for purposes of application for copyright,[107] even though Sec. 5 states that the specifica-

---

[104b] See notes 98 and 104a, *supra,* note 127, *infra,* Secs. 6.3, 17.2 and 23.7, *infra.*

[105] 17 U.S.C. 4.

[106] 17 U.S.C. 5.

[107] Sec. 5 as amended by S. 646 reads as follows:

"The application for registration shall specify to which of the following classes the work in which copyright is claimed belongs:

(a) Books, including composite and cyclopedic works, directories, gazetteers, and other compilations.

(b) Periodicals, including newspapers.

(c) Lectures, sermons, addresses (prepared for oral delivery).

(d) Dramatic or dramatico-musical compositions.

(e) Musical compositions.

tions shall not be deemed a limitation of subject matter of copyright as defined in Sec. 4, which extends the possibility of copyright protection to all the "writings" of an author. Tangibility is achieved through the term "writings" in Sec. 4 and through the specification of classes, all of which are in concrete form in Sec. 5.

Notwithstanding the inclusion of sound recordings as a new classification under Sec. 5(n) by the enactment of S. 646, as part of the interim legislation to cope with record piracy, proposed copyright revision of a long range nature, however, purports to be explicit in this respect. Although it eliminates reference to the term "writings" now contained in Sec. 4, it purports to achieve the same broad scope as to subject matter of copyright by expressly relating the same to tangibility. Thus, Sec. 102 of S. 543 reads as follows:

> "Copyright protection subsists, in accordance with this title, in original works of authorship fixed in any tangible medium of expression, now known or later developed, from which they can be perceived, repro-

---

(f) Maps.
(g) Works of art; models or designs for works of art.
(h) Reproductions of a work of art.
(i) Drawings or plastic works of a scientific or technical character.
(j) Photographs.
(k) Prints and pictorial illustrations including prints or labels used for articles of merchandise.
(l) Motion-picture photoplays.
(m) Motion pictures other than photoplays.
(n) Sound recordings.

The above specifications shall not be held to limit the subject matter of copyright as defined in section 4 of this title, nor shall any error in classification invalidate or impair the copyright protection secured under this title."

duced, or otherwise communicated, either directly or with the aid of a machine or device. Works of authorship include the following categories:

(1) literary works;

(2) musical works, including any accompanying words;

(3) dramatic works, including any accompanying music;

(4) pantomimes and choreographic works;

(5) pictorial, graphic, and sculptural works;

(6) motion pictures and other audiovisual works;

(7) sound recordings." [108]

Thus, the proposed copyright revision of a long range nature purports to reclassify on a systematic basis rather than by accretion of classes under the old statute, e.g., motion pictures added as a separate category in 1912[109] whereas they had been previously classifiable as photographs.[110]

The proposed revision would therefore appear to have heeded the recommendation of the authors of Study No. 3 when they wrote:

"The confusion created by the broad language of section 4 in the present act should be corrected. The courts should no longer be put in the position of

---

[108] S. 543, Sec. 102.

[109] Act of Aug. 24, 1912, c. 356, 37 Stat. 488.

[110] American Mutoscope & Biograph Co. v. Edison Mfg. Co., 137 Fed. 262 (C.C.D. N.J. 1905); Edison v. Lubin, 122 Fed. 240 (3d Cir. 1903).

denying protection to objects because of the practical and policy considerations involved while having to speak in quasi-constitutional terms because the plain language of the statute expends the constitutional grant. Congress should specifically enumerate the subjects it desires to cover and not attempt to project itself too far into the future."[111]

The House Report on H.R. 2512[112] relates tangibility and the classificatory scheme to creation. It states:

"Section 301, one of the bedrock provisions of the bill would accomplish a fundamental and significant change in the present law. Instead of the dual system of 'common law copyright' for unpublished works and statutory copyright for published works, which has been in effect in the United States since the first copyright statute of 1790, the bill adopts a single system of Federal statutory copyright from creation. Under section 301 a work would obtain statutory protection as soon as it is 'created' or, as that term is defined in section 101, when it is 'fixed in a copy or phonorecord for the first time'."[113]

Sec. 101 of S. 543 contains this definition:

"A work is 'created' when it is fixed in a copy or phonorecord for the first time; where a work is prepared over a period of time, the portion of it that has been fixed at any particular time constitutes the work as of that time, and where the work has been

---

[111] Note 80, *op. cit., supra,* at p. 86.

[112] Report No. 83, House of Representatives, 90th Cong., 1st Sess., March 8, 1967, to accompany H.R. 2512.

[113] *Idem* at p. 96.

prepared in different versions, each version constitutes a separate work." [114]

However, the House Report contains a very interesting observation on the role of fixation in the proposed statute. It states: "Under the bill, the concept of fixation is important since it not only determines whether the provisions of the statute apply to a work, but it also represents the dividing line between common law and statutory protection . . . an unfixed work of authorship, such as an improvisation or an unrecorded choreographic work, performance, or broadcast, would continue to be subject to protection under State common law or statute, but would not be eligible for Federal statutory protection under section 102." [115]

The proposed statute, then, would eliminate distinctions between common law copyright and statutory copyright as to works now not protected by the federal statute because they have not been published. This is the purpose of Sec. 301 of the proposed legislation in effecting pre-emption by federal law of the common law copyright. The dual system, now in effect purported to comprehend, as between them, under notions of common law copyright and statutory copyright, virtually the entire range of intellectual creation. Warner opines, "Thus common law copyright comprehends every new and original product of mental labor embodied in writing or some other visible form which remains unpublished."[116] He goes on to say, "In all probability the great bulk of 'live' television programs which will be pre-

---

[114] S. 543, Sec. 101.

[115] Note 112, *op. cit., supra,* at p. 15.

[116] Warner, Harry P., Radio and Television Rights (1953), p. 845.

sented only once or twice will not be copyrighted; common law copyright will afford adequate protection."[117]

Thus, although the proposed statute defines the term "created" it does so in terms of fixation in tangible form. The effect of pre-emption is to convert the common law copyright into statutory copyright at time of such fixation and not, as under present law, at time of publication. Thus, as to such works, the dual system of copyright would be terminated in favor of a single, comprehensive federal system. Yet performance which is unrecorded, such as that of a choreographic work or a broadcast, would continue under common law protection. Being unfixed in form by virtue of being unrecorded, it is not the subject of copyright. Borge Varmer writes that "It is doubtful, at best, whether the Federal statute could extend copyright protection to a work presented only in a performance and not recorded in some tangible form of 'writing' ".[118] Varmer found no case in which literary property rights under common law were accorded to a choreographic work, but saw no reason "why the common law protection accorded to unpublished works of authorship generally would not extend to an unpublished choreographic work". . .[119] But Varmer presumably had in mind a choreographic work recorded in some tangible form of writing since an unrecorded work would not have been reduced to a writing capable of publication.

The proposed copyright revision leaves an area of creativity which is not subject to pre-emption, the unrecorded

---

[117] *Idem* at p. 843.

[118] Varmer, Borge, Copyright in Choreographic Works, Study No. 28, October 1959, in Studies in Copyright, 103 (1963) at pp. 114-115.

[119] *Ibid.* at p. 106.

work or a work which has not been fixed in tangible form. If a *sine qua non* of copyright is tangibility, then unrecorded choreographic works or broadcast "live" performances which are never recorded are beyond the scope of the present statute and the proposed legislation.[120]

To the creator of such an unrecorded choreographic work, it would be a supererogation to tell him that because he is not deemed a creator of the work for copyright purposes, he is not therefore a creator. Add to that the law's minimal concern with quality, esthetically speaking. Thus, the House Report on copyright revision makes this observation, "Use of the term 'literary works' connotes no criterion of literary merit or qualitative value . . . Correspondingly, the definition of 'pictorial, graphic, and sculptural works' carries with it no implied criterion of artistic taste, aesthetic value, or intrinsic quality."[121]

Thus it may be seen that copyright merely sets certain minimal parameters for protection of creativity which do not comprehend creativity in the arts, in the sense of a creative work as opposed to performance thereof and that these parameters are of significance to the performing arts principally in terms of the rights protected and the con-

---

[120] Sec. 202.7 of the Regulations of the Copyright Office provides in part: 'Choreographic works of a dramatic character, whether the story or theme be expressed by music and action combined or by actions alone, are subject to registration in Class D." This refers to works in fixed form, such as Labanotation. Filmed choreographic works might be registered under Classes L or M. The Regulation continues: "However, descriptions of dance steps or choreographic works which do not tell a story, develop a character or emotion, or otherwise convey a dramatic concept idea, are not subject to registration in Class D." The proposed statute would extend copyright to "choreographic works", S. 543, Sec. 102(3).

[121] Note 112, *op. cit., supra,* at p. 17.

comitant possibility of a market therefor by reason of grant of these rights. The rights, in turn, may affect the nature of the structure of the market, but quantitative standards of the copyright system do not thereby transmute creative works into any criteria of the qualitative nature of creativity.

Sec. 5.5. The Creative Process

Creation of literary and artistic works is the evocation of thought in some form which originates from the creator. The form is generally that of a writing, in the literal sense, with respect to a literary work; that of a painting or drawing, of a two-dimensional work; and that of the application of some form of art or craft, e.g., sculpture or molding, of a three-dimensional work. In such forms, the creative work may be appreciated without the intercession of a performer, as in reading or viewing an art exhibition. In other forms, such as a dramatic work, the writing is intended primarily for performance. There are then two facets, creation and performance; creation being the function of authorship, and performance, that of the performing artist. Creator in this sense refers to the originator of the literary and artistic work. Artist here denotes the performer.

In drama there is only a transmission of the same form. That is, the words, as interpreted and rendered by the performer, are the words written by the playwright. Granted that there is an element of tentativeness and plasticity in playwrighting, that lines are "wrought", i.e., molded and revised constantly until eventually fixed in final form for official opening or whatever performance is deemed a fixation in final form by playwright and director.

In music, on the other hand, unimprovised music is a transmutation from notation to sound. The composer creates certain forms of notation in order to have them turned into a particular collocation of sounds by performance. Music is a form of sound; notation is only a form of representation as a writing. Its appreciation takes place by transcription from the visual to the aural. The medium changes form from creator to interpreter, the performing artist.

So far we have considered music as creation in the copyright sense. Music can be created without notation by way of improvisation. It can be created in sound directly without notation. If not recorded the form is not preserved in some tangible manner except in memory.

In this regard, the comments of Alan Rich are illuminating. In a book comparing and tracing the history of music and art, he has this to say about the music of antiquity. "We have very little firsthand knowledge of the music of the ancient world. It did not survive because very little of it was written down. It was an improvised art, governed by intricate rules regarding melody and rhythm, and its practitioners were expected to be able to create the proper song or dance for the proper occasion at the time the music was needed."[122] He goes on, " . . . but the music itself no longer exists . . . In the case of Oriental music we can consider ourselves closer to ancient sources, because these civilizations, isolated from the West until comparatively recent times and relatively self-contained, do show in their current musical styles a remarkable persistence of ancient tendencies . . . in the classical Indian music . . . There are ragas for various times of day, ragas of contemplation and joy, of birth, rebirth, and death. It is an improvised music, as was that of the ancient Western world,

---

[122] Rich, Alan, Music, Mirror of the Arts 14 (1969).

and it seems to have changed little in sound and purpose throughout its existence."[123]

But ragas consist of lyrics as well as music. Oral communication can thus be made without fixation in form of language as well as music. Calypso is a contemporary form where lyrics are improvised to suit the occasion. If neither music nor lyrics is recorded, there is likewise oral communication in calypso. But neither ragas nor calypso need necessarily be improvised. Music and lyrics may never be written but handed down orally from generation to generation. Here there is not improvisation, i.e., making up the music and lyrics by the performers in the course of performance. Rather, memory acts as the means of handing down music and lyrics as part of the culture of the performers, in all likelihood as the traditional way of transmitting song because the performers, being probably illiterate, conveyed their knowledge by performance, rather than writing and notation. Moreover, the composer and lyricist, if one and the same person, created his work in performance and handed it down through performance. Other types of folk music, including that of the United States, were similarly created.[124] Indeed, much of song originated in the bardic tradition, where poetry was sung and author and composer were the same person,[125] and at the same time the creator was anonymous.

---

[123] *Idem* at p. 15.

[124] See Lomax, Alan, Editor, The 111 Best American Ballads, Folk Songs U.S.A., Collected, adapted and Arranged by John A. Lomax and Alan Lomax, 1947 at p. x; Cowboy Songs and Other Frontier Ballads, Collected by John A. Lomax and Alan Lomax (1938) at pp. xxix-xxx; The Indians' Book: Songs and Legends of the American Indians, Recorded and Edited by Natalie Curtis, (1950) at p. vi.

[125] Goldron, Romain, Ancient and Oriental Music (1968), at p. 20, "Nomads have always had a predilection for the temporal arts

Oral tradition was, therefore, antithetical to notions of copyright. If song passed on by memory and in passage could also be embellished, and if authorship was anonymous, there was an absence of something that could be called property. Song, then, was common; it could not be appropriated as one's own. Moreover, if the creator was anonymous, there was nothing in the nature of personality attributable to authorship. Works intended for oral transmission assumed variable melodic and lyrical lines as remembered and/or transmitted by successive performers.

It may be seen, therefore, that copyright, defined as relating to a literary and artistic work of originality reduced to some tangible form, is not necessarily co-terminous with creation of literary and artistic works. However, our system of copyright takes cognizance of traditional works as being within the "public domain". As such they are not subject to the protection of copyright except to the extent they have been modified by new material of a creator or arranger.[125a]

---

and music and we are indebted to them for the creation of the narrative song and epic poem. The nomads of Asia to this day have their bards who travel from one encampment to another, reciting to their own accompaniment the legends and heroic deeds of their ancestors."; Friedman, Albert B., The Viking Book of Folk Ballads of the English-Speaking World (1956), at pp. ix-x. "The folk ballad . . . is an oral phenomenon . . . Originally and naturally ballads were preserved in the memory of peoples whose culture was traditional, word-of-mouth, preserved without benefit of paper and ink . . . ballads alter with every singer, the more popular ones appearing in innumerable versions and variants . . ." See also, Leach, MacEdward, The Ballad Book (1955) at p. 9; Briffault, Robert, The Troubadours (1965), pp. 3-4.

[125a] 17 U.S.C. 8 provides in part: "No copyright shall subsist in the original text of any work which is in the public domain.", while

Thus it is only creation in the copyright sense that is subsumed by notions of copyright. There must be a creator who is not anonymous claiming authorship. His work must have a minimal degree of originality. Hence, a million tourists taking photographs of the Statue of Liberty from the same perspective are all creators, even though many of the pictures might seem identical, because the snapshot originated with that particular tourist and was not a copy or reproduction of another's photograph. Finally, it must be reduced to some tangible form in which the creative work is embodied. That form, if visual, is copyrightable under the present statute.[126] If only aural, such as a tape or disk, it may be subject to copyright under the interim legislation of Public Law 92-140.[127]

Creation, then, in the copyright sense, is the evocation of thought in many drafts, revision following revision, until it has been fixed in some final form as the literary and artistic work of the author. The fixation of form may be rendered final by the author solely, as in the case of the

---

17 U.S.C. 7 states that "Compilations or abridgements, adaptations, arrangements, dramatizations, translations or other versions of works in the public domain . . . shall be regarded as new works subject to copyright under the provisions of this title; but the publication of any such new works shall not . . . be construed to imply an exclusive right to such use of the original works, or to secure . . . copyright in such original works."

[126] 17 U.S.C. 4, permits copyright in all the writings of the author. 17 U.S.C. 5 enumerates classes of writings; the classes so specified are for purposes of application for copyright.

[127] S. 646, 92nd Cong., 1st Sess. became law October 15, 1971 and covers sound recordings fixed, published and copyrighted four months after enactment and prior to January 1, 1975. See notes 98, 104a and b, *supra*, Sec. 5.4, *supra* and Secs. 6.3, 17.2 and 23.7, *infra*. S. 543, Sec. 102(7) includes sound recordings among the subject matter of copyright.

unpublished manuscript, under common law copyright. The author himself has fixed the work in that form. If unpublished and performed, the fixation may have been accomplished by the author as approved by the producer and director of that performance, as in the case of a stage play or broadcast. If published, whether or not approved by editor and publisher, assuming lawful publication, the work has been fixed in the form as published for copyright purposes.

Thus creation generally is like a tape recording of thinking in which images may be changed or erased at will. Creation is fluid. It is a process. The creator may indeed be vitally concerned with the *fact* of creation, that is, the creative process itself, as the outstanding facet of creativity. In this respect, the work is only a manifestation of that process. As a process, creativity goes on. The work is only a projection of the creative process at a point in time. Creativity in this sense is generation, growth of the artist. He not only gives birth to that particular work, but it is merely a stage or stepping stone for his own growth as an artist. To that extent, the creator views his works as an extension of his personality, of his creative growth.

But creation is not only fluid, it is also social, even though it originates in the mind. Creation, in the copyright sense, creates copyright, the right to copyright and the whole concatenation of rights constituting the copyright. It creates copyright in the common law copyright sense because completion of the work automatically invests the creator with the common law copyright.[128] Compliance with for-

---

[128] In the proposed statute, S. 543, statutory copyright would cover unpublished works by pre-emption (Sec. 301). Copyright therein would be given a fixed duration and would subsist from its creation (Sec. 302(a)).

malities is required for statutory copyright, notice of copyright, registration and deposit.[129] In that respect, the creator or his assignee has only a right to copyright under federal law.

Creation is social because it is intended for a reader, viewer or audience to appreciate the same. Creation is a form of transmission in finite form of what the creator had in mind. The end result, the work created, is the *res* communicated from creator to recipient.

Copyright, in turn, is a system for protection of the work of the creator within the context of the marketability of the work. It defines the protections granted the creator, upon origination and thereafter to himself or his assigns as proprietor. In this respect, common law copyright operates *eo instante* to protect the creator upon origination in tangible form. Under the proposed copyright revision, statutory copyright would subsume that function.[130]

The rights protected under common law copyright and thereafter under statutory copyright comprehend the protection granted by the copyright to creator as originator and to him or his assigns as proprietor. The rights comprehended thereby structure the market for the work. These rights in the aggregate are property rights because they can be owned, assigned, licensed and otherwise dealt in as objects of property, subject to certain limitations such as the compulsory license[131] and the statutory system of devolution of the renewal copyright.[132]

---

[129] 17 U.S.C. 10 as to notice; 17 U.S.C. 11 as to registration; and U.S.C. 13 as to deposit. 17 U.S.C. 12 covers registration of certain types of unpublished works not reproduced for sale.

[130] Note 128, *supra*.

[131] 17 U.S.C. 1(e).

[132] 17 U.S.C. 24.

Under statutory copyright these exclusive rights are enumerated.[133] But enumeration under the present Copyright Law represents an accretion, since the first Copyright Act of 1790 was limited to maps, charts and books.[134] Prints were not protected until 1802;[135] photographs were added in 1865.[136] Even after passage of the present Act in 1909 additional categories were added. Motion pictures were included in 1912[137] although protected as photographs prior to such inclusion. While the proposed statute purports to be comprehensive, one cannot exclude the possibility of accretion in the future as new rights and forms are made the subject of copyright.[138]

Copyright, then, is the principal mechanism, provided by our legal system, for the structure of the market in connection with the dissemination of creative works of a literary and artistic nature. Through it, the works and the creators thereof come to the public. The works as works of art can be marketed because of the rights and protections granted to the creator and through him to his assigns. Copyright therefore creates the framework for the market. The creator perforce reaches his audience through the marketing of his work, now an object of property. But the ideas embodied therein in tangible form represent the fruits of his creation. The creator effectively has extended

---

[133] 17 U.S.C. 1(e); in proposed copyright revision see S. 543, Sec. 106, with a somewhat different formulation because of different concepts used, e.g., derivative works.

[134] Act of May 31, 1790, c. 15, 1 Stat. 124.

[135] Act of April 29, 1802, c. 36, 2 Stat. 171.

[136] Act of March 3, 1865, c. 126, 13 Stat. 540.

[137] Act of August 24, 1912, c. 356, 37 Stat. 488.

[138] S. 543, Sec. 102 enumerates the types of works which are the subject of copyright and Sec. 106 sets forth the exclusive rights granted therein.

his thoughts and feelings to the recipient through the fixation of form. The work has therefore acted as a transmission belt of the author's creativity, i.e., the expression of his thoughts, feelings and personality.

But copyright acts as the lowest common denominator for the creator. Copyright invests the creator and his assigns with the same bundle of rights, depending only upon how they are marketed, regardless of the degree of quality of the work from any point of view, so long as the irreducible minima of originality and tangibility are there. Copyright only structures the market; it does not create the market.

Criteria of marketability are created dehors copyright. Qualitative evaluations, such as those of criticism of the artistic merits of the work, tend to create a market. In the performing arts, in particular, professional evaluation, qualitatively, brings the judgment of merit into consideration as a reason for becoming a recipient of the literary or artistic work. One would become a recipient as a purchaser if the work were in printed form. If a performance, one would be in nexus with the work as the person to whom it were communicated by becoming a viewer or listener. Qualitative evaluation tends to relate the particular work to the body of works of the creator. Criticism often considers the development of the author's creativity; criticism is therefore concerned with the personality of the creator as expressed creatively. It is far less involved with the work as property except for taking cognizance of the medium in which it is being communicated.

But the market is principally concerned with the particular work, as such, as property. It is quantitative, seeking to maximize sales, licenses, uses. It is concerned with maximum exploitation of the work and utilizes certain marketing devices and techniques in aid thereof, best-seller charts, box office, ratings, and the like. Even criticism of the work as a creation on the merits is adapted to the market in the form of quotes in advertising.

Copyright, then, is an indispensable adjunct of creativity and of the market. It is the manifestation of creativity which is transmuted into art and commerce by other means. The performing arts and the market for these arts constitute the principal means therefor. Publication, in turn, represents one of the instrumentalities of the bundle of rights in the copyright.

Chapter VI

AUTHORSHIP AND OWNERSHIP

Sec. 6.1. The Right of Copy and the Bundle of Rights

Kaminstein sets forth the traditional theory of accretion of copyright from right of copy to bundle of rights. He states:

> "Copyright began with the protection of books against copying. The first Federal statute in the United States also covered maps and charts, but the protection of all three categories was limited to 'printing, reprinting, publishing, and vending.' The acts of 1802 and 1831 added new materials subject to copyright, but not until 1856 did Congress grant a new type of protection, the right of public performance in dramatic compositions. In 1891 Congress made it unnecessary for authors to reserve the rights of translation or dramatization given to them in 1870. The act of 1897 gave a right of public performance or representation in any copyrighted 'dramatic or musical composition.'
>
> "The turn of the century thus saw copyright, departing from its original concentration on the publishing right; it now included rights of translation, dramatization and of public performance in dramatic and musical compositions. Copyright was no longer a single right, but had become an aggregation or bundle of rights, which might conveniently be referred to as 'copyright' but was in reality, many copyrights. If each new right had acquired and retained a different name, e.g., 'playright' for dramatic rights more

attention might have been given to the necessity of distinguishing between them."[1]

Actually, Brander Matthews made a similar distinction when he characterized the latter as a "stage-right", the sole right to dramatize a play, and distinguished it from a copyright. He wrote, "Copyright and stage-right are wholly different; and a dramatist is entitled to both."[2] He referred to France's grant of the stage-right in 1791 and the U.S. grant thereof in 1856, as to which he stated that the author derived a double profit, ". . . controlling the publication copyright and controlling performance by stage-right."[3]

Kaplan, referring to the right in the hands of the Stationers Company in England, following grant of letters patent of 4 May 1557 by Queen Mary, states that the "Right of copy was the stationer's not the author's."[4] It is this right to control the making and sale of copies that Kaminstein calls a publishing right as to which protection was given to "printing, reprinting, publishing and vending" in the first federal Copyright Act of 1790 in the United States.

On the other hand, in *Millar* v. *Taylor,* Lord Mansfield, alluding to possible loss of control of the author over his work, were there no common law copyright, stated, "He is no more the master of the use of his own name. He has

---

[1] Kaminstein, Abraham L., Divisibility of Copyrights, Study No. 11 in Studies on Copyright (1963) pp. 623-687 at p. 627.

[2] Matthews, Brander, The Evolution of Copyright, reprinted from the Political Science Quarterly (Nov. 1890), in Putnam, George Haven, The Question of Copyright 2d Ed. (1896), p. 324, at p. 342.

[3] *Idem* at p. 343.

[4] Kaplan, Benjamin, An Unhurried View of Copyright (1967) at p. 5.

no controul over the correctness of his own work. He can not prevent additions. He can not retract errors. He can not amend or correct a faulty edition." [5]

Indeed, the role of editor and publisher might well be examined in respect of the copyright as a right of publication. For editor and publisher may suggest changes, edit, revise or delete. They may recommend substantial rearrangement of the work, an index, appendices of all sorts, a preface, or other changes of a substantial nature.

Moreover, the publishing right is no longer the simple right of copy that protection of printing, reprinting, publishing and vending contained in the Act of 1790 might suggest. The typical book publishing contract is also concerned with book club rights and paper back rights as subsidiary rights of hard cover book publishing.[6] Add to this the economic possibilities of first and second serial publication in newspapers and periodicals and the simple hard cover publication of a work and occasional reprint thereof seem transformed into something else again. One might almost conclude that the publishing right itself either comprehended many rights or was in fact a bundle of rights. If the latter, then the accretion of the copyright historically was not from single right to a bundle of rights. Rather the progression was from a smaller number of then known or devised rights, collectively called the publishing right or right of copy, to a far larger number of rights which are called the copyright. Indeed, there was

---

[5] 4 Burr. 2303, 2397 (1769).

[6] See, Form Nos. 7B-1 to 7B-4, inclusive and 7C(a)-2.2 in Volumes of Forms. See also the enumeration of publishing subsidiary rights as part of subsidiary rights generally in Wittenberg, Philip, Subsidiary Rights, Chap. III of Subsidiary Rights and Residuals, edited by Taubman, Joseph (1968), pp. 9-17 at pp. 11-12 and the grant of rights relating thereto at pp. 15-16.

nothing in the technology of publishing from the time of chartering of the Stationers Company in 1557 through the Statute of Anne and thereafter on through the first American federal copyright statute that inhibited per se book club operations, paper back editions, or serialization. One may assume that there were indeed paper back publications and newspaper and periodical serializations in the 18th century. Thus, the concept of subsidiary rights within publication alone was not unimaginable during the early period of copyright. True, methods of transportation and marketing mechanisms may not have reached the point where book club operations might have been economically feasible so that the concept had simply not been devised.[7]

But Kaminstein focussed his attention upon the accretion of copyright in respect of legislative history. It does not necessarily give us the answer with respect to the scope of the common law copyright. *Ferris* v. *Frohman*[8] would seem to indicate that the common law copyright was far broader than the publication right. Although Justice Holmes did not use the phrase "common law copyright", but rather the phrase "common-law right", it would appear that he had the same thing in mind. He stated, "The present case is not one in which the owner of a play has printed and published it and thus, having lost his rights at common law, must depend upon statutory copyright in this country. The play in question has not been printed and published." [9] He concluded, "The public representation of a dramatic composition, not printed and published, does not deprive

[7] Harry Scherman, one of the founders of the Book-of-the-Month Club in the 1920's, is generally considered the originator of the book club concept as an outgrowth of his earlier mail order sales of his "Little Leather Books".

[8] 223 U.S. 424 (1912), *aff'g* 238 Ill. 430 (1909).

[9] 223 U.S. 424 at p. 434.

the owner of his common-law right, save by operation of statute. At common law, the public performance of the play is not an abandonment of it to the public use." [10] Note that the Supreme Court of the United States affirmed the decision of the Supreme Court of Illinois which, in turn, had stated, "At common law the author of a literary composition had an absolute property *right* in his production, . . . Upon the publication of the production the author's common law *rights* ceased, and it became public property unless protected by statute." [11]

Thus, common law copyright appears to be used in two senses, as an absolute right of property and as a bundle of rights. It is the former unitary sense of the right that has given rise to the theory of the indivisibility of copyright.[12] Harry Henn sums it up by writing, "Thus, from a single right applicable to books, copyright grew into an aggregation of several rights covering many types of intellectual creations reduced to concrete form." [13]

The Kaminstein and Henn view may be considered probably the dominant view in American copyright law. Implicit in it is the premise that copyright is a generic term and that by virtue of the Statute of Anne and the Copyright Act of 1790 copyright was also coincident with the species, book. The copyright was primarily one right, the exclusive right to copy. A transfer thereof was an assignment. Anything less than this was not a transfer of the whole and was therefore a license. Indivisibility of copy-

---

[10] *Idem* at p. 435.

[11] 238 Ill. 430 (1909) at pp. 435-436 (emphasis added).

[12] Kaminstein, *op. cit., supra,* note 1.

[13] Henn, Rights Magazine—A Division of Indivisible Copyright. 40 Corn. L. Q. 411, 416 (1955).

right was consistent therewith as the transfer of a single right. But, as the rights proliferated, the theory of indivisibility was strained. This created problems as to the nature of the grant of an author to a periodical in which his work was published.[14] In such instances, the problem arising is substantive. In other instances, the problem may be one of procedure as to the right of a licensee to bring suit for infringement of copyright unless by contract he has been authorized to bring suit in the name of the copyright owner.[15]

Proposed copyright legislation would dispose of the doctrine of indivisibility of copyright. Sec. 201(d)(2) of S. 543 provides:

> "Any of the exclusive rights comprised in a copyright, including any subdivision of any of the rights specified by section 106, may be transferred as provided by clause (1) and owned separately. The owner of any particular exclusive right is entitled, to the extent of the right, to all of the protection and remedies accorded to the copyright owner by this title." [16]

In this regard, the House Report as to the analogous section in the House Bill states, "Clause (2) of subsection (d) contains the first explicit statutory recognition of the principle of divisibility of copyright in our law. This provision, which has long been sought by authors and their representatives, and which has attracted wide support from other groups, means that any of the exclusive rights

---

[14] See, Dam v. Kirke La Shelle Co., 175 Fed. 902 (2d Cir. 1910).

[15] Kaminstein, *op. cit., supra,* note 1, at p. 639 discusses right to sue.

[16] S. 543, 91st Cong., 1st Sess., January 22, 1969.

that go to make up a copyright, including those enumerated in section 106 and any subdivision of them, can be transferred and owned separately."[17]

But the elimination of indivisibility does not, in and of itself, provide us with the taxonomy of the species in the bundle of rights. For example, the synchronization right is not referred to in the present Copyright Law; nor for that matter does it appear to be mentioned in proposed copyright revision.[18] On the other hand, the House Report anticipates proliferation of rights and subdivision of rights ad infinitum. It states, "The five fundamental rights that the bill gives to copyright owners—the exclusive rights of reproduction, adaptation, publication, performance and display—are stated generally in section 106. These exclusive rights, which compromise the so-called 'bundle of rights' that is a copyright, are cumulative and overlap in some cases. Each of the five enumerated rights may be subdivided indefinitely, and . . . each subdivision of an exclusive right may be owned and enforced separately."[19]

The House Report, in effect, constitutes recognition that the copyright, juridically speaking, is a bundle of rights. But this would appear to be the purport of Justice Holmes in *Ferris* v. *Frohman*[20] when he referred to the right of performance as a "common-law right" in the context of its being a common law copyright. Immanent in the theory of common law copyright, then, is the notion that the absolute right of property in the author prior to publication

---

[17] Report No. 83, 90th Cong., 1st Sess., re Copyright Law Revision, March 8, 1967, to accompany H.R. 2512, at p. 89.

[18] See, for example, S. 543, *op. cit., supra.*

[19] Report No. 83, *op. cit., supra,* note 17, at p. 23.

[20] Note 8, *supra.*

consists of the sum of the common law rights comprising the common law copyright.

The notion that the common law copyright consists of a bundle of rights leads to a conclusion that copyright is derived from authorship as a matter of natural law. Ladas has written, "However, the theory of property right has remained in Anglo-American law in respect to the common law copyright in unpublished works, and the right created by statute in published works is commonly considered to be a property right of a limited duration. It is a natural-law theory, based on the idea of creation through labor." [21]

Curtis posited that widespread copyright legislation superseding common law copyright is a recognition of the inherent existence of this right in the author in natural law. He wrote:

> "Every civilized nation, of any literary rank, has some law recognizing the property of authors in their works. This universal legislation is founded in a conviction that such property exists in natural justice; for although the protection thus afforded by positive law is generally temporary, and embodies, as I shall hereafter suggest, a compromise between the strict rights of the author and the demands of society, yet it proves the existence of those rights, by undertaking to reconcile them with the wants and interests of the public at large. There is no other hypothesis to account for the careful legislation of so many countries." [22]

---

[21] Ladas, Stephen P., 1 The International Protection of Literary and Artistic Property 4 (1938).

[22] Curtis, George Ticknor, Treatise on the Law of Copyright 17 (1847).

This writer has written:

> "Suppose Congress were to repeal the Copyright Code? It is submitted that this would be unconstitutional, not only for the reason that the constitutional grant of the copyright is coordinate with the promotion of science and the useful arts, but because it would violate the First and Fifth Amendments. It would abridge freedom of speech and the press if no man could make an utterance or a writing which he could not call his own because immediately upon publication it could be copied. Freedom of speech and press imports a right of recognition of authorship. It would constitute a denial of life, liberty and property if a man's creations were denied value by fiat.
>
> "Therefore, the copyright must be something other than a grant by legislative grace." [23]

It is submitted that since copyright is necessarily an outgrowth of authorship, i.e., creativity, whether conceived of as a single indivisible right or a bundle of rights, that it is at the same time a right of property, and, by virtue of the creation, the literary and artistic work is also an expression of the personality of the author. Moreover, copyright as a bundle of rights by accretion from a single right or as a generic term for a bundle of rights vests in the author as owner, at the instant of creation, with the means of transference by contract of the power to create with respect to the work by assignment or license of rights of ownership or, alternatively, the means of exercise thereof himself as author by retention or reservation thereof.

---

[23] Taubman, Copyright and Antitrust 32-33 (1960).

Sec. 6.2. Authorship—Proprietorship and Transformation Rights

The predicate for operation of the power to create is determination of authorship and ownership, on the one hand, and of proprietorship of the copyright and licensee of the particular right in the bundle of rights comprising the copyright, on the other. The Copyright Law itself sets forth the structure of this interplay.

Sec. 9 thereof provides, "The *author or proprietor* of any work made the subject of copyright by this title, *or his executors, administrators* or *assigns,* shall have copyright for such work under the conditions and for the terms specified in this title: . . ." [24] Sec. 2 thereof provides, "Nothing in this title shall be construed to annul or limit the right of the author or proprietor of an unpublished work, at common law or in equity, to prevent the copying, publication, or use of such unpublished work without his consent, and to obtain damages therefor." [25] Sec. 28 of the statute states that "Copyright secured under this title or previous copyright laws of the United States may be *assigned, granted,* or mortgaged by an instrument in writing signed by the proprietor of the copyright, *or may be bequeathed* by will." [26] Sec. 7 is the basis for the transformation[27] or derivative[28] rights which stem from the grant of exclusive rights "to the person entitled

---

[24] 17 U.S.C. 9 (emphasis added).

[25] 17 U.S.C. 2.

[26] 17 U.S.C. 28 (emphasis added).

[27] Warner, Harry P., Radio and Television Rights, characterizes these rights as "the Right of Transformation", in Chap. XI so entitled, at pp. 283-300.

[28] Nimmer, Melville, Nimmer on Copyright, discusses the same subject matter in Chap. 3 entitled Derivative Works at pp. 165 *et seq.*

thereto, upon complying with the provisions of this title." [29] Publication with notice is required for securing copyright by "any person entitled thereto by this title." [30] Registration of claim to copyright is to be made by "such person." [31] As to certain works not reproduced for sale, copyright is available therein under Sec. 12. That section goes on to state, "But the privilege of registration of copyright secured hereunder shall not exempt the copyright *proprietor* from the deposit of copies, under sections 13 and 14 of this title, where the work is later reproduced in copies for sale." [32] Sec. 24, dealing with duration, renewal and extension of term, provides that in respect of posthumous works or composite works "upon which the copyright was originally secured by the *proprietor* thereof, or a work originally secured by a corporate body (otherwise than as assignee or licensee of the original author) or by an *employer* for whom such work is made *for hire*," . . . the proprietor of such copyright shall be entitled to the renewal . . ." term.[33] In connection with any other work, the statute provides that the renewal shall be in " . . . the *author* . . . , if still living, or the *widow, widower, or children,* of the author, if the author not be living, or if such author, widow, widower, or children be not living, then the author's *executors,* or in the absence of a will, his *next of kin* . . ." [34] Finally, Sec. 26 provides that ". . . the word '*author*' shall include an *employer* in the case of works for hire." [35]

---

[29] 17 U.S.C. 1.
[30] 17 U.S.C. 10.
[31] 17 U.S.C. 11.
[32] 17 U.S.C. 12 (emphasis added).
[33] 17 U.S.C. 24 (emphasis added).
[34] *Ibid.* (emphasis added).
[35] 17 U.S.C. 26 (emphasis added).

Thus, it may be seen that the Copyright Law provides a variegated system of interplay of authorship and ownership which, if one accepts its premises, is internally consistent and systematic. Sec. 2 represents an acknowledgment that the common law copyright is a right of property which may be in the author or may be in the hands of the proprietor. It is submitted that the terms "author" and "proprietor" as used in Sec. 2 have the same meaning as in Sec. 9 which permits the author or proprietor to have copyright under the statute. Both notions are best expressed by the contractual clause providing for a grant of "the right to copyright, the copyright, the right to renew the copyright and the renewal copyright" or some variant expression thereof.[36] The right to copyright is a right to secure copyright. An unpublished work very often is still in the author's possession and control. Not having divested himself of the work by assignment or otherwise, such author, at common law, of course, remains the absolute owner. As author he has the right to obtain statutory copyright upon publication. If he should do so, then the copyright secured by the author would be owned by him as the proprietor thereof. But if the author should have divested himself of the common law copyright, then the right to secure copyright is obtainable by his assignee of the common law copyright who then proceeds to register the copyright under federal law as the proprietor thereof. This is the typical procedure for registration of a copyright in a musical composition. The author assigns his right to copyright to the publishing company which thereafter proceeds to secure copyright therein in its own name as copyright proprietor thereof. Where, however, the composer has registered his musical composi-

---

[36] See Form Nos. 1A-1 and 1A-2 in Volumes of Forms.

tion in his own name as copyright proprietor thereof, then a music publishing company assignee would obtain the rights therein by assignment from the composer as copyright proprietor thereof. Since the renewal term operates as a new estate, the same concept is operative with respect thereto. The author, if living, is entitled to secure the renewal copyright, i.e., the right to renew copyright. If he assigns his right to secure the same, and he survives into the 28th year of original copyright, then the assignee secures copyright as the copyright proprietor, albeit in the name of the author.[37] Likewise, if the author were to secure renewal copyright in his own name, then he might assign the renewal copyright to a third party who would then become the copyright proprietor.

The statutory scheme permits employers for hire, including corporate employers, to have the status of authors. Accordingly, a corporate employer for hire would be deemed an author for purposes of securing copyright and the above interplay as between author and proprietor would be applicable to the employer for hire except for the different patterns of renewal vesting operative in Sec. 24 of the Copyright Law. In any other capacity, the corporation is not deemed an author and would be only an assignee of a copyright. For example, a music publishing company might take a work from a composer and lyricist by assignment. The composer and lyricist are authors of the work. If, on the other hand, the music publishing company paid the composer and lyricist a

[37] Regulations of the Copyright Office, "Sec. 202.17 (a) Claims to renewal copyright must be registered within the last (28th) year of the original copyright term. . . . (b) Renewal claims may be registered only in the names of persons falling within one of the classes of renewal claimants specified in the copyright law. . . ." See Chaps. VII-VIII, *infra*.

salary, then they would be employees for hire for purposes of renewal copyright. The music publishing company could renew the work in the 28th year in its own name without concern about survivorship of the author or which class is in existence to renew were this not an employment for hire relationship. Here, of course, one must differentiate between the legal fiction which gave rise to the relationship of employer for hire as author and the underlying factual reality. In all likelihood, the concept originated to provide the employer the right to secure copyright in situations, as in newspaper copy, where the story was revised by so many persons, that the final story is a group creation. Varmer distinguishes between actual authorship by the employee for hire and the right of first ownership of copyright vested in the employer for hire by reason of the legal fiction.[38] He states, "As long as copyright ownership as between employer and employee can be provided for by contract, it may make little practical difference in most situations whether one or the other is considered to be the initial copyright owner in the absence of a contract." [39] There may be little practical difference as to terms of royalties in the songwriter illustration, above. However, there is considerable difference in the legal effects arising in the free lance songwriter assignment as to the renewal period as opposed to the employment for hire relationship. The latter, however, is an instance where custom and practice in the industry accord the actual author credit on sheet music and other places where credit is customarily given to the author as free lance assignor. The industry, in effect, in such situations where an employment for hire status

---

[38] Varmer, Works Made For Hire And On Commission, Study No. 13, in 1 Studies on Copyright (1963) at p. 717.

[39] *Idem* at p. 732.

exists, acknowledges the rights of personality of the actual author by giving him credit as author, legal fiction for copyright purposes notwithstanding.

Sec. 24 also sets forth various other categories of copyright proprietors, i.e., widow, widower, children, executor, next of kin. None of these is an author, either in fact or in legal fiction. Any renewal by them necessarily is a renewal in the capacity of copyright proprietor. The same would be true of a person, firm or legal entity, or any type of fiduciary who acquires rights in the original term by gift or bequest or in the renewal term, after one of the classes of permitted renewers of copyright has renewed.

Taking the copyright as a whole, it consists of the exclusive rights enumerated in Sec. 1 of the Act. Sec 1 (a) in effect comprises the publishing right, and consists of the exclusive right "To print, reprint, publish, copy and vend the copyrighted work;".[40] Sec. 1(b) comprises the so-called transformation rights which are the basis for derivative works and consists of the exclusive right "To translate the copyrighted work into other languages or dialects, or make any other version thereof, if it be a literary work; to dramatize it if it be a non-dramatic work; to convert it into a novel or other non-dramatic work if it be a drama; to arrange or adapt it if it be a musical work; to complete, execute and finish it if it be a model or design for a work of art;".[41] The balance of Sec. 1 enumerates the various performance and mechanical rights granted exclusively and as to mechanical reproductions, the nature and basis of the compulsory license therein.[42]

---

[40] 17 U.S.C. 1(a).

[41] 17 U.S.C. 1(b).

[42] 17 U.S.C. 1(c)(d) and (e). Subsection (f) according an exclusive right of reproduction and distribution as to sound record-

Sec. 7 sets forth the basis for creation of derivative works by means of operation of the transformation rights. It reads:

> "Compilations or abridgments, adaptations, arrangements, dramatizations, translations, or other versions of works in the public domain or of copyrighted works when produced with the consent of the proprietor of the copyright in such works, or works republished with new matter, shall be regarded as new works subject to copyright under the provisions of this title; but the publication of any such new works shall not affect the force or validity of any subsisting copyright upon the matter employed or any part thereof, or be construed to imply an exclusive right to such use of the original works, or to secure or extend copyright in such original works." [43]

When one reads this section together with Sec. 1 and Sec. 5, the classification section, in conjunction with the statutory scheme of the author-proprietor interplay, as above, the pattern of the power to create emerges. The key to all this is in creation, i.e., the original work in tangible form under common law or statutory copyright. The creator has authored a form of basic work. Transmutation of the form of the work into other art forms into which it can be transmitted implies the embodiment of essential parts of the creative work into other forms. Here the phrase, "can be transmitted" is used advisedly. Music is a non-representational form. A literary work,

---

ings, but not as to simulation and imitation thereof, has been granted by Public Law 92-140, enacting S. 646, 92nd Cong., 1st Sess. for sound recordings fixed, published and copyrighted four months after effective date of October 15, 1971—i.e., from February 15, 1972 and prior to January 1, 1975. See Sec. 5.4, *supra.*

[43] 17 U.S.C. 7.

without adaptation into lyrics or other linguistic accompaniment, cannot be transformed into music. In effect different non-translatable modalities are used. The visual may indeed be attempted to be depicted in music by way of program music, but only because the composer actually describes the effects that he is attempting to achieve in words can it be said that music is so descriptive. Sound may indeed have a physical equivalent in the form of representation of sound waves pursuant to the laws of physics. But music is sound. Notation of music is no more than schematic representation of the sound. If the sound is not a direct transformation of the literary work, then the notation likewise fails to be such. In short, the ideas of the author of the literary work act as inspiration for the music but the tangible expression of the author's ideas as embodied in the literary work are not carried over into the musical work. The element of copying which one can trace in adaptations of novels into plays and scripts where, for example, there is a carry over of characters, themes, lines, story line and means of expression simply is not present. Of course, a visual literary or artistic work may be "inspired" by another without its being an adaptation thereof.

The creator, then, has the exclusive right to transform his work. As long as he retains exclusive rights therein as author and copyright proprietor, he may prevent third parties from making such transformations. Indeed, the author as such proprietor may enjoin the same. Under the Copyright Law, Sec. 101 gives him this right. It reads in part, "If any person shall infringe the copyright in any work protected under the copyright laws of the United States such person shall be liable:

(a)—to an injunction restraining such infringement;". [44]

---

[44] 17 U.S.C. 101. See Chap. XXVI, *infra*.

At common law, too, an injunction will lie preliminarily to restrain infringement. Warner avers, "Common law copyright is governed by the same rules of transfer and succession and may employ the remedies accorded other personal property.[45] . . . Thus an injunction may issue." [46]

Of course, the reference here is to what may be done as a matter of law. An infringer may have the ability to create an adaptation without having first secured the right to do so. But the exercise of this ability does not represent a valid creation in contemplation of law. The complainant prevailing under Sec. 101 in an action for infringement may compel destruction of the infringing copies. Sec. 101 (d) of the Act in such event may require the infringer "To deliver up on oath for destruction all the infringing copies or devices, as well as all plates, molds, matrices, or other means for making such infringing copies as the court may order." [47] Moreover, willful infringement for profit may be prosecuted as a misdemeanor and subject the infringer upon conviction to imprisonment of up to one year, a fine or both in the discretion of the court.[48] Fraudulent notice of copyright or removal or alteration thereof may likewise subject a person to criminal prosecution as a misdemeanor and a fine.[49] Finally, there are prohibitions in the Act as to importation and destruction.[50] This is in addition to provisions for damages and loss of profits provided in Sec. 101 of the Copyright Law.[51] The power "to grant injunctions to prevent and restrain the

---

[45] Warner, *op. cit., supra,* note 27, at p. 859.

[46] *Idem* at p. 859, fn. 15.

[47] 17 U.S.C. 101(d). See Sec. 26.2, *infra.*

[48] 17 U.S.C. 104. See Sec. 21.4, *infra.*

[49] 17 U.S.C. 105. See Sec. 21.6, *infra.*

[50] 17 U.S.C. 107, 108, 109. See Chap. XXI, *infra.*

[51] 17 U.S.C. 101(b) and, as to mechanicals, see 101(e).

violation of any right secured by this title" is accorded to the courts mentioned in Sec. 1338 of Title 28 or a judge thereof by Sec. 112.[52]

What may be validly created are derivative works by the same author without license or contract therefor, assuming that author is also the copyright proprietor. The author of a common law copyright can freely transform his own work where he has never divested himself of any rights in and to the original creation. This flows from the author's right as author to change, modify, transform and in general do what he pleases with his own work. In theory creation by transformation by the same author is an extension of his personality creatively; as creator, he is the absolute controller of his creative work and can determine its forms.

With respect to published basic works, the author-proprietor cannot follow through in precisely that form. As soon as he publishes the derivative work, he must affix a notice of copyright thereto.[53] This is quite apart from the statutory requirement of notice of copyright as to the basic works. As a derivative work, by definition some of the tangible expression of the basic work has been incorporated therein. Thus, in order to protect such material from falling into the public domain, the author must affix a notice of copyright thereto.[54] In addition, the notice of

---

[52] 17 U.S.C. 112. See also Strauss, William S., The Damage Provisions of the Copyright Law, Study No. 22 in Studies on Copyright (1963) at p. 995 and Strauss, William S., Remedies Other Than Damages For Copyright Infringement, at p. 1029, Study No. 24. See Chap. XXVI, *infra*.

[53] 17 U.S.C. 10.

[54] See Nimmer, *op. cit., supra,* note 28, Sec. 41, Scope of Protection for a Derivative Work, at pp. 169-170, "Thus copyright in a derivative work is usually regarded as merely protecting against

copyright protects any new material embodied in the derivative work.

But generally the works of an author enter into commerce through assignment of the copyright or by license of one or more of the bundle of rights comprising the copyright to some other party by the proprietor of the copyright in the basic work.

Sec. 6.3. Creation of Derivative Works

Proposed copyright revision defines a derivative work as, "A work based upon one or more pre-existing works, such as a translation, musical arrangement, dramatization, fictionalization, motion picture version, sound recording, art reproduction, abridgment, condensation, or any other form in which a work may be recast, transformed, or adapted. A work consisting of editorial revisions, annotations, elaborations, or other modifications which, as a whole, represent an original work of authorship, is a 'derivative work'." [55]

Sec. 106 of S. 543 grants the owner of copyright exclusive rights as follows:

> "(1) to reproduce the copyrighted work in copies or phonorecords;
>
> (2) to prepare derivative works based upon the copyrighted work;
>
> (3) to distribute copies or phonorecords of the copyrighted work to the public by sale or other transfer of ownership, or by rental, lease, or lending;

---

copying or otherwise infringing the particular compilation, arrangement or other original contribution contained in the derivative work."

[55] S. 543, Sec. 101.

(4) in the case of literary, musical, dramatic, and choreographic works, pantomimes, and motion pictures and other audio-visual works, and sound recordings, to perform the copyrighted work publicly;

(5) in the case of literary, musical, dramatic and choreographic works, pantomimes, and pictorial, graphic, or sculptural works, including the individual images of a motion picture or other audiovisual work, to display the copyrighted work publicly." [56]

The House Report refers to these exclusive rights as the "five fundamental rights . . . of reproduction, adaptation, publication, performance, and display . . ." [57]

The House Report then proceeds to comment on derivative works:

"*Preparation of derivative works.*—The exclusive right to prepare derivative works, specified separately in clause (2) of section 106, overlaps the exclusive right of reproduction to some extent. It is broader than that right, however, in the sense that reproduction requires fixation in copies or phonorecords, whereas the preparation of a derivative work, such as a ballet, pantomime, or improvised performance, may be an infringement even though nothing is ever fixed in tangible form.

"To be an infringement the 'derivative work' must be 'based upon the copyrighted work', and the definition in section refers to 'a translation, musical arrangement, dramatization, fictionalization, motion picture version, sound recording, art reproduction, abridgment, condensation, or any other form in which a work may be

---

[56] *Idem,* Sec. 106.
[57] Note 17, *supra,* at p. 23.

> recast, transformed, or adapted'. Thus, to constitute a violation of section 106(2), the infringing work must incorporate a portion of the copyrighted work in some form; for example, a detailed commentary on a work or a programmatic musical composition inspired by a novel would not normally constitute infringements under this clause." [58]

In order to analyze the relationship of authorship and proprietorship to derivative works, it is necessary to consider the respective components constituting the transformation rights. As will be seen, the factual context varies, the creative relationship differs and the results are quite different in terms of authorship.

Sec. 6.3(a). Translations

The right to translate the copyrighted work was not one of the original rights in the Copyright Act of 1790. As to it, Kaminstein writes, "In 1891 Congress made it unnecessary for authors to reserve the rights of translation or dramatization given to them in 1870."[59] In testimony presented by Charles S. Burton on June 9, 1906 in connection with the hearings which led to passage of the present act in 1909, Mr. Burton made these comments as to the right of translation:

> "The present bill, however, makes the right of translation not merely one which is conditioned upon the existence of copyright of the original work, but an essential and integral part of that copyright, so that it will pass with the assignment of the copyright without special mention, and the proprietor of the copy-

[58] *Idem* at p. 24.

[59] Kaminstein, Abraham L., Divisibility of Copyrights, Study No. 11, in Studies on Copyright (1963) p. 623 at p. 627.

> right, and not the author, would thereafter have the right of translation. The author could not translate his own work without infringing the copyright which he had sold to the proprietor. *Any translation, however maladroit or misleading, which the copyright owner-publisher—might approve would pass under the author's name* as his work into the foreign language, and he would have no voice to protest against the libel, no power to remedy the injury by putting out a correct translation."[60]

True, from a copyright view the basic work is transformed into a new work derived from a pre-existing work. But what is significant here, is that the translation, whether that of the author of the basic work or another, must show the name of the author of the basic work as that of the creator. The essential ingredient of translation is an aptitude of expression in maintaining the sense of the original work. Fidelity to the author is strived for in linguistic ability. Only the form changes, to that of another language or dialect, but the expression is substantially that of the author as expressed in such other language or dialect. There is a new copyright, to be sure, but the translation merely carries a credit line showing the name of the translator. Thus, authorship is identical with that of the basic work.

Moreover, the right of translation, while technically a transformation of the basic work, is substantially a right of publishing. Historically, it may have been sanctioned at

---

[60] Burton, Charles S., representing Melville Clark Piano Company, Statement before the Committees on Patents of the Senate and House of Representatives Conjointly on the Bills S. 6330 and H.R. 19853, June 9, 1906, pp. 191-202, at pp. 201-202 (emphasis added).

a later date by Congress, but this does not lessen the nature of the right as principally one of publication. That is, translations appear principally in written form and have commercial value as one of the rights of publication. Thus, a book publishing contract might ordinarily give the publisher rights of translation in the work and to license the same and/or to market the work in translation in various countries and territories of the world, unless the author reserves such rights by agreement.[61]

Sec. 6.3(b). Abridgments

Abridgments, which are transformation rights covered by the language of Sec. 1(b) of the present Act which grants the exclusive right to ". . . make any other version thereof, if it be a literary work;"[62] are likewise publishing rights where publication is had in the name of the author of the basic work. Kaplan traces the development of copyright in abridgments in the author of the basic, unabridged work and remarks as to the present statute, ". . . 'books' had already comprehended written material in various forms . . ."[63] Abridgment under the statute may be copyrighted as a new work based upon the basic, unabridged work. The transformation is primarily one of form; the original appears in a shortened version. Presumably, substantially the same language is carried over from the unabridged to the abridged version. Consequently, abridged versions must appear in the name of the author of the basic work as the author of the abridged version. The making of the abridg-

---

[61] See Form Nos. 7C(a)-3 and 7C(a)-4 in Volumes of Forms.

[62] 17 U.S.C. 1 (b).

[63] Kaplan, Benjamin, An Unhurried View of Copyright, 39 (1967), Chap. 1, The First 350 Years, at pp. 1-37, traces the development of the right of abridgement in the original author and copyright proprietor of the basic, unabridged work.

ment is therefore primarily editorial, whether the abridgment is rendered by the author or someone else. If done by a person other than the author, then his or her contribution is entitled to a credit line of abridgment by such person, assuming the publisher may do so under his basic agreement with the original author and the publisher has accorded the person making the abridgment a credit line by agreement with such person.

Sec. 6.3(c). Arrangements

Musical arrangements are in a somewhat different category of transformation rights. Translation is generally written; an oral translation might also constitute a performance of the work, enabling the copyright proprietor of the original work to protect the same under other subdivisions of Sec. 1.[64] Nimmer states that the right of translation ". . . is necessarily infringed by infringement of the exclusive right to copy."[65] As such, a copy cannot be performed without a grant of right therefor. There is even less ground for performance of an abridgment because there the infringement in performance would arise from rendition of the original language of the author without any transformation by way of translation.

As to music one is in a different situation by virtue of the nature of arrangement and by reason of the compulsory license. Until recently, music as a subject of copyright had

---

[64] 17 U.S.C. 1(c) (d) or (e). Sec. 1(c) covers exclusive right to deliver, read or present, etc., a nondramatic work. Sec. 1 (d) covers exclusive dramatic right of performance. Sec. 1 (e) protects the copyrighted work, subject to mechanical license, if it be a musical composition. See also, Chap. XVI, *infra*. New Sec. 1(f) grants interim exclusive rights in sound recordings. See Sec. 5.4, *supra* and Sec. 17.2, *infra*.

[65] Nimmer, *op. cit., supra*, note 28, Sec. 105.2, at p. 393.

to be in written form to be accepted for copyright; the Copyright Office would not accept a recording of the work for copyright prior to enactment of Public Law 92-140 on October 15, 1971.[66] Regulation 202.8 provided that Class E registration must be "in the form of visible notation" and that "a phonograph record or other sound recording is not considered a 'copy' of the compositions recorded on it, and is not acceptable for copyright registration." [67] Thus, only written arrangements were accepted for copyright. Moreover, under Sec. 1 (e), the compulsory license provision, recordings may be made by third parties without direct grant of right from the copyright proprietor after the latter has permitted a first mechanical recording of the work.[68] It has become customary in the music industry to dispense with the formalities of the statute, e.g., monthly accounting, and to obtain a license for mechanical recording from the music publisher.[69] But the effect of such license is comparable. A record producer is authorized to record a particular rendition of the musical work, with or without words, with the rate to be paid under the statutory compulsory license as a ceiling. The license from the publisher may provide for the statutory rate or may provide for a negotiated lesser "rate", such as one and a half cents per side in lieu of the statutory two cents per side.

Obviously, styles in rendition on such recordings differ. Performers may also improvise in the course of perfor-

---

[66] Regulations of the Copyright Office, Sec. 202.8. Public Law 92-140, S. 646, 92nd Cong., 1st Sess. grants an interim right to copyright protection for sound recordings which are fixed, published and copyrighted from and after February 15, 1972 and prior to January 1, 1975. See Secs. 5.4, *supra,* and 17.2 and 23.7, *infra.*

[67] *Ibid.*

[68] 17 U.S.C. 1(e).

[69] See Form Nos. 6C-1.1a-c in Volumes of Forms.

mance of the work. Under the present statute prior to enactment of Public Law 92-140, the recording did not constitute a copy. Not being a copy, aural arrangements embodied therein were likewise not copies of the work. Although under Sec. 3 of Public Law 92-140, sound recordings are deemed copies for purposes of infringement under Sec. 101 of the Copyright Act, Sec. 1 of said Public Law grants the exclusive right of reproduction and distribution of sound recordings subject to the exception that such exclusive grant does not extend to simulation or imitation in an independently fixed sound recording.

Thus, musical arrangements are of a two-fold nature and treatment under the statute. Sec. 1(b) enumerates the right to arrange a musical work as one of the transformation rights. This means that a composer of the basic work controls arrangements thereof in written form under common law copyright. Should the composer copyright the work as an unpublished[70] or published work, then he does so as copyright proprietor and continues to control exclusive right to written arrangement of the original work. It is more likely that the composer will have assigned the copyright to a music publishing company, whether the same be a third party music publisher or a company in which the composer is interested. The music publishing company will then copyright the work under the statute as copyright proprietor. Should the publisher register the copyright in an unpublished work, it would also deposit a "lead sheet" which is a notation of the melodic line or the melodic and harmonic lines of the composition in the simplest form capable of copyright.[71] Thereafter, if the work is published in copies for

---

[70] 17 U.S.C. 12.

[71] The statute, 17 U.S.C. 12, requires deposit of one complete copy of the work with the application for copyright.

sale, deposit of two copies of the work as published is required, under Sec. 13[72] of the Act, subject to the provisions of Sec. 14[73] of the statute, whereunder the Register may demand deposit subject to certain penalties. Thus, if the work is copyrighted in unpublished form, a lead sheet is submitted with the application for copyright. Upon publication, notice of copyright must be affixed to the work as published. As a condition for utilizing the remedies under the Act for protection against infringement, the copyright proprietor must register his published work in Washington. At such time, the proprietor will also submit two complete copies of the published work for deposit. If the lead sheet consists of one page of music and lyrics, it will bear the name of the composer(s) and lyricist(s), in the form of, Music by ————, Lyrics by ————, or Words and Music by ————, or some such form. The publication of the work in the same form, e.g., as sheet music, would bear comparable credits of authorship.

However, the work may not necessarily be published in the same form. There may be a piano arrangement of the original work. If arranged by the author himself, presumably the published piano score would simply indicate his authorship thereof. The application for copyright

---

[72] 17 U.S.C. 13 provides for deposit of two complete copies of the best edition of the work, and that "No action or proceeding shall be maintained for infringement of copyright in any work until the provisions of this title with respect to deposit of copies and registration of such work shall have been complied with."

[73] Under 17 U.S.C. 14, the Register of Copyrights may make a demand for deposit and upon non-compliance within three months from within the United States and six months outside thereof, may subject the copyright proprietor to a fine of $100, a penalty of twice the retail price of the best edition of the work payable to the Library of Congress and voiding of the copyright.

would then refer to the fact that this was a piano arrangement.[74] The piano version might be copyrighted as an unpublished work and later as a published work along the lines of the original work as above.

Where the arranger is a person other than the composer, the piano arrangement will give authorial credit to the composer in the form of, Music by ————————, and then the arranger will receive credit as arranger in some form such as, Arranged by ————————, Arrangement by ————————, or Arr. by ————————. Since the copyright proprietor of the original work controls the right to arrange under Sec. 1(b), any unauthorized *written* arrangement constitutes an infringement of the basic work. Thus, the music publisher as copyright proprietor may proliferate arrangements of the basic work in the form of band arrangements, orchestral arrangements, and a variety of specialized arrangements and control the copyrights therein.

Indeed, the music publishing industry traditionally was structured upon exploitation of the rights in and to the basic work by way of publication in the form of transformation rights until the economic value and incentives of other rights, performance and mechanicals, surpassed that of actual publishing of musical works. Nevertheless, the fact remains that in terms of transformation rights, musical arrangement is basically creation of new forms of that basic copyright in which the credit of the original composer is retained as composer. This is true even where an arrangement is made of works in the public domain except, of course, where the author is unknown or the work is deemed "traditional". Thus, the credit to the composer of a work in the public domain is an acknowledgment by

---

[74] See Forms 6B-3.1a-b in Volumes of Forms.

custom and practice of the industry of the right of personality of the author by way of recognition of his authorship. This is also true where the music publisher acquires the copyright from the composer by assignment or as employer for hire. Again the personality of the composer is accorded recognition as composer even though the agreement between the parties may be silent as to the means and manner of according credit to the composer. Such a provision would be deemed implied as a matter of fact and law.

Sec. 6.3(d). Adaptations

The foregoing rights of transformation are principally extensions of the publishing right into various types of publications. A different set of facts is operative as to authorship with respect to works of adaptation. In an adaptation there has been a revision of the work for another genre or medium. The dictionary defines "adapt" as "to alter so as to fit for a new use; to render fit, by changing." [75] An adaptation is therefore a modification of a literary work for use in another literary form (genre) or for use in another medium of communication (medium). Adaptation refers both to the process of such modification and the resultant literary work constituting the adaptation. Adaptation is thus the means, modification and the end result.

The critical role of the adaptation as a creative market and copyright mechanism can best be understood if its character can be put into proper focus. In this respect, the definition of "literary works" in the proposed copyright revision is confusing. S. 543 defines the term as,

[75] Webster's New International Dictionary, Second Ed. (1961) at p. 29.

"... works ... expressed in words, numbers or other verbal or numerical symbols or indicia, regardless of the nature of the material objects, such as books, periodicals, manuscripts, phonorecords, or film, in which they are embodied."[76] The House Report states that a definition is needed because the meaning of the term is unsettled and because the distinction between the work and the material object requires clarification.[77] The definition, it is submitted, is broader than its commonly accepted meaning as relating to letters or literature. A film is not a literary work. Indeed, S. 543 defines "motion pictures" as audiovisual works.[78] Of course, a literary work, such as a poem or ballad may be embodied in a film if it is recited or sung or superimposed in writing in the picture. Likewise, a film version of a stage play may be an embodiment of the drama in filmic form. Phonorecords might accomplish a similar result.

But an adaptation, more often than not, is not a mere change of form from one medium to another. It goes much further. An adaptation usually is a basic change in the structure of the work, embodying the characters and expression of content of the underlying work in a form which the adaptor, in the first instance, and ultimately the producer, if the work be intended for another medium, deem suitable. Adaptation may follow the form of the basic work closely or it may deviate from it in basic ways. An adaptation of a novel for a film, for example, may focus on a relative handful of incidents in the story line as compared to the original. Here intent at arriving at the essence of the work may be more important than literal faithfulness because of the differing natures of

[76] S. 543, Sec. 101.
[77] Note 17, *supra,* at p. 17.
[78] S. 543, Sec. 101.

literature and film. Ultimately, the key word guiding the adaptor is "selectivity"; it becomes a matter of good judgment for him to be able to select those portions of the novel and characterization therein that, in his opinion, best lend themselves to depiction in cinematic form.

Yet another form of adaptation from one medium of expression to another is the free adaptation. Here elements of imagination come into play importantly. Thus, for example, a classic version may be modified as to time, place and characters to achieve a different effect; the transformation of "Carmen" into "Carmen Jones" would be this type of adaptation.

The reason for the confusion in the definition of "literary works" in S. 543 is that the material objects which embody literary works are not only different in form but serve different functions as to what they embody. Books and periodicals generally will embody the basic literary work, with authorial credit in such books and periodicals being given to the author of the basic work. This is true whether the particular publication embodies a translation, abridgment or serialization of the work. These are not, strictly speaking, adaptations. The publications print or reprint either the original work, translations or edited versions thereof.

Motion pictures, on the other hand, embody *adaptations* of the basic work. Thus, a film derived from an underlying work is not directly based thereon. There is an intermediate process of adaptation, of preparing a literary work, usually not for publication, as the basis for the film. An adaptor might prepare a treatment or outline as the basis for a screenplay. The scenario then becomes the mediate literary form from which the motion picture is derived. The film, then, embodies the shooting script as the literary work from which it is produced.

The function of transformation of basic works into literary works fit for use in other media is better suggested by the language of the present statute. Sec. 1(b) grants exclusive rights as to copyrighted works ". . . to make any other version thereof, if it be a literary work; to dramatize it if it be a nondramatic work; to convert it into a novel or other nondramatic work if it be a drama; . . ." [79] Other versions of a literary work need not necessarily be adaptations, such as abridgments. But treatments and outlines for screenplays, particularly without dialogue, would constitute other versions of a literary work that are clearly adaptations. On the other hand, the remainder of the above quote clearly relates to adaptations. To dramatize a nondramatic work is to adapt a literary work from one genre to another. There is a change of form of the basic work to enable it to be used in some form where drama is intended, whether the stage, motion pictures or television. An adaptation of a work into a stage play is an adaptation of genre, from one literary form, be it from a novel or nonfictional work, into a drama. Where the adaptation is intended for the screen, then it is not a change merely of form of literary work, but also of medium. Indeed, from a non-copyright point of view, the screenplay is not considered as a literary work in itself, such as a stage play is generally deemed. A stage play is presented live in that form, as a presentation of a dramatic work. A scenario, on the other hand, must again be transformed from words to audio-visual depiction. The whole nature of moving pictures is involved in the transformation. Comparably, the nature of television is basic to the making of a teleplay

[79] 17 U.S.C. 1 (b).

from a telescript. In effect, a double or triple transformation takes place. The basic literary work is adapted to a form of literary work. There may, in some instances, be the preparation of a scenario as an adaptation of a nondramatic work, without the intermediate step of a treatment or outline. Or there probably will be an adaptation in the form of a preliminary treatment or outline. Thereafter, the script is prepared from the treatment or outline. This, too, is a form of adaptation, directly from the treatment or outline, which is an adaptation of the basic work, and indirectly from the basic work. The feature film or teleplay resulting from the script is then a transformation of the script into the final form in another medium. Treatments, outlines, scripts are rarely intended for use as literary works per se, to be read as such, as literature, although on occasion some are published. To the extent they are published, they are literary works in another *literary* genre. Of course they are genres of creative works, but they are not, as such, primarily literary works where they are created as instrumentalities as an aid in production of the feature film or teleplay.

The conversion of a drama into a novel or other nondramatic work, referred to in Sec. 1(b), generally has the effect of a transformation of an adaptation of one genre of literary work into another if the adaptation is primarily intended for publication. But if the process is the adaptation of a treatment or outline from a stage play for the purposes of making a feature film or teleplay from a script adapted from such treatment or outline, then the primary purpose of the adaptation is not the creation of another literary work in another genre, but a means for production of a work in audio-visual form. In other words, the intent may be to transform the basic work from words alone into words and pictures.

It is ironic that proposed copyright revision, as aforesaid, thereby ultimately comes back to the generic nature of literary works as writings in the broadest sense even though the term "writings" as now set forth in Sec. 4 of the Copyright Law is avoided. For the definition of "literary works" in Sec. 101 of S. 543 uses the term "literary" in its broadest sense of works " . . . expressed in words, numbers or other verbal or numerical symbols or indicia . . . " [80] True, this is not co-ordinate with the term "writings" in either the constitutional or statutory sense because it is intended to cover only that part of the expression "literary" as is embraced in the phrase "literary and artistic property". The term "literary" then, in proposed copyright revision, is intended as a generic term to cover works in written form, in the lay sense, as opposed to artistic works, which are in non-verbal form. Proposed copyright revision adds a category of "Pictorial, graphic and sculptural works" which ". . . include two-dimensional and three-dimensional works of fine, graphic, and applied art, photographs, prints and art reproductions, maps, globes, charts, plans, diagrams, and models." [81] Presumably the term "motion pictures" when defined as audio-visual works in the proposed statute, includes elements of both literary works and pictorial works since generally a literary work is embodied in the film which consists of a series of related images of pictures.[82] Yet, Sec. 102 of the proposed statute grants exclusive rights in seven categories, the first of which is literary works,

---

[80] S. 543, Sec. 101, definition of "literary works".

[81] *Idem,* definition of "pictorial, graphic, and sculptural works".

[82] *Idem,* definition of "motion pictures", to wit, " 'Motion pictures are audiovisual works consisting of a series of related images which, when shown in succession, impart an impression of motion, together with accompanying sounds, if any."

as differentiated from musical works, dramatic works, pictorial, graphic and sculptural works, and motion pictures and other audio-visual works.[83] The classification scheme of Sec. 102 of S. 543 is therefore closer to Sec. 5 of the present act which enumerates books in Sec. 5(a) and periodicals and newspapers in Sec. 5(b) as categories for registration for copyright. However, the generic definition of literary works in Sec. 101 of S. 543 indicates that Sec. 102 is to have a broader meaning than the market sense of works intended for publication in the form of books, periodicals and newspapers, but all kinds of literary works in whatever form, even if their sole market function is not that of being read as literature, but as means for implementing production of motion pictures and audio-visual works.

In short, both the present statute, Sec. 1(b), and the proposed definition of S. 543 as to "literary works" wrestle with the nature and role of the adaptation in the market without quite coming to grips with its distinctive role. For the Copyright Law and its proposed revision take as predicates the continued authorial function in the transformation. Theoretically, the creator of the basic work is in the position of creating by himself the transformations necessary to bring derivative works into being. As to certain types of transformations, such as translations and abridgments, the author need do nothing in order to continue to receive authorial credit as creator. This is so because he continues to receive credit in a translation because the basic intent there is to reproduce the work in linguistic versions with attribution of authorship to the author of the basic work. The process of abridgment is editorial and the intent is similar, to market the work of the author of the basic work as his work.

---

[83] S. 543, Sec. 102.

Adaptations, on the other hand, conceivably might be created by the author of the basic work. To that extent there is a correlation between the copyright notion of the exclusive right of transformation, being one of the rights in the bundle of rights constituting the copyright and creation of the adaptive literary work. Because the adaptation, by definition, would constitute an infringement of the basic work since sufficient ingredients thereof are embodied therein, it is therefore an exclusive right belonging to the creator of the copyright, in the first instance, and upon copyright of the basic work, to the copyright proprietor thereof.

Thus, whereas translations and abridgments are reproductions of different versions of the original work of the creator, adaptations are putative, and when done, are actually new creations, based on the original work. The copyright creator is invested with the power to create a variety of variations of his basic work in the form of adaptations and also with the power to create further derivative works from either the basic work or the adaptations thereof, so long as he remains the copyright proprietor thereof. At common law, so long as the creator has not encumbered or divested himself of his rights in and to the unpublished work, the power of the creator is absolute. Moreover, the distinction between his capacities as author and proprietor is undifferentiated, generally, and derivative works held by the author at common law are likewise undifferentiated as to his capacities as author and proprietor, unless and until the works come into some legal nexus by way of encumbrance, assignment, devolution or otherwise.

But statutory copyright reflects the differentiation at the time of copyright registration. The application distinguishes authorship from proprietorship as two separate categories.[84] Authorship and ownership may indeed appear as two separate parties therein. Unless there has been a reservation of rights of adaptation to an author in a grant of copyright, or the author's rights as proprietor vest in the creator by reason of the renewal copyright,[85] the creator does not have the right to make adaptations of his own basic work, absent contractual arrangement therefor with the copyright proprietor.

Whether or not the creator has retained the rights to make adaptations as a matter of law, the author does not necessarily conceive of himself, in his role as a creator, as the principal literary means of making the adaptation rights operative. Authors may, from time to time, prepare adaptations of their own works for other media. Some authors prefer to adapt their novels into treatments for films and then to write the scenarios therefor. On occasion, such authors might even go further and prepare the derivative works from their own adaptations, i.e., produce the film or telecast from their scripts, which they have adapted from their basic work. However, just as a novelist does not necessarily dramatize his novel into a stage play, licensing adaptation rights to third parties to do so, such an author may likewise prefer to license adaptation rights to others. Here the assumption is that the author of the basic work is also the copyright proprietor thereof.

But in a great many instances the author is not even the copyright proprietor of his basic work, so that the adaptation rights are in others. Third party copyright proprietors perforce conceive an adaptation as a means to an end, the creation of the ultimate derivative work, the film or teleplay. Indeed, the producer is vitally concerned with the

---

[84] See Sec. 6.2, *supra*.
[85] 17 U.S.C. 24.

fact that, in the United States, it is the producer of the film or television show that is deemed the creator of the work because the creation is generally a group creation and the producer contracts for the creative components as an employer for hire. The producer thereby eliminates problems of right of copyright renewal in the author of the scenario because the latter is employed for hire. Thus, right of renewal automatically vests in the producer as employer for hire in and to the screenplay under Sec. 24 of the Copyright Law.[86] The context here is the authorization of creation of a screenplay by a screen writer as employee for hire pursuant to grant of motion picture rights from the author or other copyright proprietor of the basic work to the producer. This would not be true of an adaptation created by A from an original work by B where the rights in and to A's adaptation are thereafter acquired by producer C. A did not write the adaptation as an employee of C. The latter acquires such rights as to duration that A obtained from B. If A, as a free lance writer, prepares an adaptation and has acquired rights for duration of B's copyright therein, then C might acquire A's rights for the duration of the original copyright term in the adaptation, plus the right of renewal copyright therein if A survives into the 28th year and grants such right of renewal. The foregoing is predicated upon B, as copyright proprietor of the basic work, having granted A the exclusive right to create adaptations for motion pictures and to grant motion picture rights in and to the adaptations for the duration of B's original term of copyright in the basic work and B's surviving into the 28th year of his original term of copyright of the basic work. This, of course, assumes that B is both creator and copyright proprietor of the original work.

---

[86] *Ibid.*

Thus, it may be seen that the exclusive right to create adaptations, even though the statute and the proposed statute, do not spell out this right *in haec verba*, is a principal instrumentality for creation of derivative works and the fundament of the power to create.

Sec. 6.4. Creation: Authorship—Ownership

Creation may thus be deemed versionary. Fixation of form takes place for purposes of identification of authorship and for copyright purposes. Thereby identification of the work also takes place for ownership purposes as well. Formal identification of certain types of versions, such as translations and abridgments, is primarily one of continued authorship of the basic work in the same author whether or not he himself translates the work or makes an abridgment thereof. But inasmuch as the transformation in such forms are changes into new, albeit entirely derivative works, new copyrights may be had therein. In this regard, the copyright is itself versionary. Each translated and abridged version would probably also carry a new notice of copyright thereon and be separately registered for copyright.

By contrast, adaptive versions very often effect new versions created by persons other than the original creator of the basic work under grant of right to make the same from some party, whether the author-proprietor or a third party copyright proprietor. These are also new works, not only in a copyright sense, but particularly in a creative sense. The power to create has been given to such other person or persons by the holder of the right to create the adaptation. Walter Wheeler Cook has defined a power as ". . . one's affirmative 'control' over a given legal relation as against another." [87] Cook goes on,

[87] Hohfeld, Fundamental Legal Conceptions (1927); Introduction of Walter Wheeler Cook at p. 9.

". . . any person who can produce by his acts changes in legal relations has a legal power or powers."[88] From a literary point of view, such other person is a putative author who, by his acts of creation acceptable to the owner of the right of adaptation pursuant to which such other person is creating the work, thereby produces a new literary work which then becomes the basis for the copyright in the derivative work. The power to create is not necessarily co-terminous with the ability to create. A putative author may have been authorized to create an adaptation but he might never exercise his power to create by not making an adaptation or by writing an unsuitable one. He may not have literary ability at all. On the other hand, he may have created an adaptation which was not satisfactory to the owner of the right to create derivative works out of the adaptation. In such event the power to create is deemed unexercised, as much as in situations where nothing is created, because the process of creation has failed to create new legal relationships. This might arise where a producer hires an author to create an adaptation as preliminary for preparation of a screenplay based on an underlying work of another author but as to which the producer either owns the motion picture rights or has an option to acquire the same. If the adaptor creates an unsatisfactory adaptation, his work will not form the basis for production of the derivative work thereon, the motion picture. In the case of an option, the creation of the unsatisfactory adaptation might induce the producer simply not to exercise his option to acquire the motion picture rights in the basic work.

On the other hand, if the adaptor creates a satisfactory treatment, the producer might then proceed to have the

[88] *Idem* at p. 7.

adaptor create a screenplay thereon if he has already acquired the motion picture rights in and to the basic work. Or, he might exercise his option to acquire such rights and then authorize his adaptor to create a screenplay based upon his adaptation in the form of a treatment. Such treatments and screenplays are, in turn, literary works capable of being owned by the producer as copyright proprietor thereof, subject to the term of the underlying grant of motion picture rights in and to the basic work.

Thus, authorship and copyright originate the power to create through which new legal relationships arise. If copyright remains in the author of the basic work, the power to create new versions is vested in him. It may, however, be transferred by the copyright proprietor of the basic work to third parties. The power to create presupposes lawful creation pursuant to valid transference of the right to create, for an invalid creation might be enjoined and destroyed as an infringement of copyright. The right to create puts a party into a stance of lawful authority to designate a putative creator who, by his creative ability, transforms this power to create into literary and artistic property capable of copyright protection as a new work based upon the original work. Such new work then becomes the basis either for further adaptation by the creator thereof by yet another putative creator invested with the power to create, or else the basis for a derivative work by either in another medium.

In this sense, copyright is far more than "... a negative right to prevent the appropriations of an author by another." [89] Copyright is the means of bringing literary

---

[89] Copinger and Skone James, Law of Copyright 2 (8th Ed. 1948).

and artistic properties into commerce. It not only creates the mechanisms of the market to deal with the same, but also acts as a catalyst of creativity insofar as the bundle of rights, particularly the transformation rights of adaptation, infuse the power to create derivative works for different media.

Chapter VII

DERIVATION: DURATION: RENEWALS

Sec. 7.1. The Sequential Roll of Authorship and Ownership

Like the credit roll at the beginning or end of a motion picture or telecast, the factors of original creation, ownership, medium of exploitation, rights granted to create derivative works, power to create and new copyright in the derivative work take on a sequential pattern of elaboration that go to the heart of creation, copyright, the nature of the performing arts and their market mechanisms in the United States.

This can best be shown by summary of the pertinent litigation in several cases. One example is the leading case of *G. Ricordi & Co.* v. *Paramount Pictures, Inc.*[1] There, the original work was a novel entitled "Madame Butterfly" by John Luther Long, published in the Century Magazine and copyrighted by the Century Company. David Belasco then wrote a play in 1900 based thereon with the consent of the copyright proprietor; the play was copyrighted in 1917. Thus there was a grant of rights to create a derivative work, a drama, obtained by the putative creator from the owner of the original work. Belasco exercised his power to create. In 1901 the author of the original work, Long, and the creator of the stage play, Belasco, entered into an agreement with G. Ricordi & Co., the plaintiff, granting it exclusive rights to create a libretto for an opera based upon Belasco's dramatic work, which in turn was derived from the original novel. Ricordi copyrighted the

[1] 189 F. 2d 469 (2d Cir. 1951).

opera in 1904 with music and lyrics by Puccini in collaboration with Giacosa and Illica. Plaintiff Ricordi thereafter acquired the renewal copyright from Puccini's son. Evidently Puccini did not write the opera as an employee for hire, otherwise the renewal copyright would have been directly in Ricordi as employer for hire. This would indicate that the opera was written as a collaborative work by the authors and that Ricordi had acquired the copyright in the opera by assignment. Here we have a classic example of the rights to create an opera having been granted to Ricordi by Long and Belasco. Ricordi then authorized Puccini to create an opera. Puccini then had a power to create. Upon exercise of this power, he brought into effect a chain of legal relations in connection with the opera. Ricordi acquired the copyright proprietorship in the opera pursuant to its assignment from Puccini and by virtue of the grant of rights from Long and Belasco. Thus, by means of contract and the power to create, a stage play and an opera came into existence without the creator of the underlying work, the novel, being involved in the authorship of the derivative works. So, too, the creation of the opera originated in relation to the authorship of the stage play. Stage play and opera were new works, giving rise to new copyrights. Yet at the same time they were derivative works. Moreover, in the case of the opera it was a derivative work based upon the stage play, which, in turn, was a derivative work based upon the novel.

But the sequential roll did not stop there. Plaintiff brought this action for a declaratory judgment to declare it the owner of the exclusive motion picture rights in its renewal copyright in the opera. Defendant, Paramount, claimed ownership of the motion picture rights in the novel and the drama and claimed that Ricordi required Paramount's consent to make the picture. The copyright in the original term of the novel had expired in 1925. Long, as author, had obtained a renewal thereof in 1925. Presumably, the renewal term had not been granted by Long as author to the Century Company when the latter acquired copyright in the novel for the original term, inasmuch as Long renewed and Paramount acquired the motion picture rights in 1932 from Long's administrator. Thus, the renewal by Long in 1925 could not have been effected by the Century Company in the name of Long for the benefit of the latter. In 1932 Paramount also obtained motion picture rights from the trustee under Belasco's will, but the copyright in the play, which expired in 1945, was not renewed.

Paramount contended that the 1901 grant to Ricordi did not convey motion picture rights. Although the court below had concluded that such rights had been conveyed, the Court of Appeals felt that it was not necessary to determine the question and decided the case on other grounds. Justice Swan then stated:

> "The right which Long had to make motion pictures of the story of his copyrighted novel did not extend beyond the term of the copyright; hence, if it be assumed that he assigned to plaintiff any moving picture rights, they were necessarily limited to the term of the copyright, unless the assignment included the right of renewal. It did not; the 1901 agreement made no allusion to renewal of copyright. In Fred Fisher Music Co. v. M. Witmark & Sons, 318 U.S. 643, 63 S. Ct. 773, 87 L. Ed. 1055, which held that an author has power to assign his right of renewal during the term of the original copyright, no one suggested that rights assigned under the original copyright did not end with it, if nothing was said of renewal. We think they do. A copyright renewal creates a new estate,

> and the few cases which have dealt with the subject assert that the new estate is clear of all rights, interests or licenses granted under the original copyright. It is true that the expiration of Long's copyright of the novel did not affect the plaintiff's copyright of so much of the opera as was a 'new work' and entitled to be independently copyrighted as such. But the plaintiff has acquired no rights under Long's renewal of the copyright on his novel and the plaintiff's renewal copyright of the opera gives it rights only in the new matter which it added to the novel and the play. It follows that the plaintiff is not entitled to make general use of the novel for a motion picture version of Long's copyrighted story; it must be restricted to what was copyrightable as new matter in its operatic version."[2]

Thus the sequential roll of authorship and ownership in "Madame Butterfly" had to take into consideration the time factor of duration of copyright in the underlying work and the artistic relationship of the opera to the novel. Ricordi did not acquire renewal rights in the novel. Therefore when the renewal copyright therein became effective, the renewal estate as a new estate was clear of all rights, licenses and interests granted under the original copyright. Query, did rights of Ricordi, insofar as they related to the opera, also fall in the renewal period if Ricordi acquired no rights under Long's renewal copyright? True, this issue was not raised in the opinion; nor were the Long heirs a party to this litigation. But it would seem that if Ricordi acquired no rights as to the renewal copyright in the novel, it might also have had no rights in the opera to the extent the same was based upon the novel. Of course the music in the opera

---

[2] *Idem* at p. 471.

was a new work but the libretto, to the extent it was based upon the theme of the novel, ought to have created problems of rights for Ricordi from the inception of the renewal estate in the copyright in the novel. However, Paramount was not concerned with the opera as such. In addition, some time in 1953 the issue became moot because the renewal copyright in the novel expired and thereafter the novel was in the public domain. Thereafter, the copyright in the opera would have governed until expiration of the renewal copyright.

As to the rights of Ricordi in the Belasco play, the Court indicated that Belasco had received an oral license to write the play. Belasco had common law rights of authorship in the play until 1917, when it was copyrighted. Upon expiration of this copyright in 1945, the play was in the public domain. Thus, the motion picture rights acquired by Paramount in 1932 expired in 1945. Both parties were free thereafter to make film versions of the play.

The Court concluded that since Paramount had motion picture rights in the renewal copyright in the novel, Ricordi could not use the general story of the novel to make a picture version of the opera. Ricordi was not restricted as to new matter in the opera nor from using the play which was in the public domain, while Paramount was free to use the novel and the play in making its picture, but it could not use the opera without Ricordi's consent. The injunction granted below to the plaintiff was accordingly modified.

If the opera were actually based upon the story line and characters of the novel, it is evident that Ricordi would have had great difficulty in creating a motion picture from the opera. While the play was in the public domain and could be used freely by both parties, only new work embodied in the play could be utilized freely. To the extent the play was also based upon the story line and characters of the novel, here, too, the opera would have been deemed a derivative of the novel by virtue of the derivation of the play from the novel and the use of such derivative material in the opera. On the other hand, Paramount could conceivably have made a movie based upon the novel and play but without any use of the music and lyrics of Puccini.

Thus, the *Ricordi* case illustrates the manner of effectuation of creativity and ownership from medium to medium—here from published form, to stage play to opera to consideration of making a motion picture. It also indicates how derivative works are generated and the hazard of perfecting the chain of title within the operative facts of authorship, ownership, a system of statutory copyright alongside a system of common law copyright, and of the laws of contract as affected by the nature of copyright.

A more recent illustration is the case of *Davis* v. *E. I. DuPont de Nemours & Company.*[3] Here the sequential roll is even more complex. Copyright in the novel "Ethan Frome" was first obtained by the publisher, Charles Scribner's Sons in 1911. In June, 1934, Lowell Barrington obtained a copyright in a purported dramatization of the novel under the title of "The Silent Woman". In December of 1934, an agreement was entered into among Edith Wharton, Lowell Barrington, and Owen and Donald Davis stating that the Barrington play was not satisfactory to Edith Wharton and that the Davises had obtained exclusive dramatic rights to dramatize the novel utilizing any portion of the Barrington play. The dramatic rights in the novel, the Barrington play and the dramatization of the Davises were deemed by this agreement an entity and the respective parties would participate in earnings in the proportion

[3] 240 F. Supp. 612 (S.D.N.Y. 1965).

specified, 50% to Edith Wharton, 25% to Barrington, 25% to the Davises. In 1935 the Barrington percentage was reduced to 12½% and the Donald Davis percentage increased to 25%. Copyright under the December, 1934 agreement was to be taken out in the name of the Davises who would hold the same under a deed of trust in the respective proportions. In December, 1934 the Davises obtained a copyright in the play written pursuant to this agreement as an unpublished work. Scribner then published the play in 1936 and copyrighted the same in that year.

Edith Wharton died in 1937. Her executors renewed the copyright in the novel in 1939. In 1942, Scribner conveyed all right, title and interest in the copyright of the novel to the executors and all right, title and interest in the copyright of the play to the Davises. Presumably the rights in the renewal copyright in the novel had vested in the executors as a new estate in 1939 so that what Scribner was assigning by agreement to the executors in 1942 belonged to the executors as a matter of law. Of course, the reference here is to the United States. If Scribner also assigned the copyright in other countries and territories of the world where copyright term was measured by a period of years after death of the author, then in such places the Scribner copyright would have been extant so that the assignment was of a valid and subsisting copyright.

In 1942, the executors transferred all of their right, title and interest in the novel, including all versions and dramatizations thereof to Elisina Tyler, residuary legatee under the Edith Wharton will. A few days later in that year, Tyler, Barrington, the Davises and the producers of the Davises' play granted Warner Bros. Pictures, Inc. the right to create a motion picture based on the novel, the Barrington play, and the Davises' play, including the rights to exhibit the film on television, but not the right to make a telecast with live actors or other television rights therein. Warners paid a consideration of $17,500, 50% thereof to the producers of the play, 50% in proportion to the December, 1934 agreement to Tyler, Barrington and the Davises.

Thereafter, one Helen Deutsch, an employee of Warner Bros., wrote a screenplay, but no motion picture was ever produced under the Warner motion picture rights agreement. Thus, Warners, under its right to create a motion picture version, authorized a screen writer to create a script on an employment for hire basis. The power to create in Deutsch was never exercised because for various reasons Warners decided not to go ahead. Thus, by a legal fiction intended to give the studio the right of renewal as employer for hire, Warners would have derived proprietorship in the screen play as employer for hire because it was deemed to be the author.[4] Technically, the author by operation of the statute, Warners would have been deemed such only by operation of a legal fiction. In fact, authorial credit would have been given by agreement to Helen Deutsch had the film been produced. Moreover, screen credits for writers are also the subject of collective bargaining agreements between the Screen Writers Guild[5] and the studio.

By various mesne conveyances, Columbia Pictures Corporation (Columbia) had succeeded to the rights of Warners by January, 1958. Owen Davis died in 1956 and plaintiff, Donald Davis, qualified as his executor.

---

[4] 17 U.S.C. 26.

[5] The studios have collective bargaining agreements with the Screen Writers Guild (West), operating out of Hollywood and the Screen Writers Guild (East), operating out of New York. See, Form No. 1A-5 in Volumes of Forms as to supplemental form relating to screen credits of writer of screen play which is annexed to agreement between studio and writer of screen play.

In 1959 David Susskind, then executive vice president of Talent Associates, Ltd. (Talent) had secured the approval of Batten, Barton, Durstine & Osborn, Inc., the advertising agency for DuPont and of DuPont to produce "Ethan Frome" on television on "The DuPont Show of the Month". Talent endeavored to obtain television rights to the Davis adaptation from Donald Davis but negotiations broke down because the terms were unacceptable to Davis. Talent obtained rights from the Tyler estate, however.

Plaintiff, Donald Davis, conceded that a teleplay based solely on the novel would have been proper, but maintained that the rights obtained from the Tyler estate did not include the right to use the Davis play. In 1959 and 1960, Talent acquired from Columbia rights to present a single live telecast of "Ethan Frome" and to use and adapt the Deutsch screenplay in preparation thereof. Here, it may be recalled, the Deutsch screenplay had been owned by Warners and presumably assigned to Columbia. Columbia then would have owned the rights as assignee of Warners, i.e., as assignee of the copyright proprietor, Warners, in whom the first copyright had vested as author by reason of the legal fiction of employment for hire. Very likely this was a common law copyright since the screenplay does not appear to have been copyrighted under the statute.[6]

Davis advised defendants in December, 1959 and January, 1960 that performance on television based on the Deutsch screenplay without his consent would constitute

---

[6] Warner, Harry P., Radio and Television Rights, Sec. 41, at p. 93, "Under common-law copyright, and in the absence of a special agreement between the parties, the law presumes in an employer-employee relationship, the employer as the sole proprietor of the common law rights."

a copyright infringement. The performance was telecast in February, 1960 over the CBS network.

The Court held that the telecast had copied the Davis dramatization. In the light of the Davis demand, defendants' efforts to "unDavis" the television script ". . . were too little, too late and too transparent. In almost every instance, their 'changes' amounted to mere paraphrasing, inversion of dialogue, or substitution of one insignificant object for another. But paraphrasing is tantamount to copying in copyright law. Defendants did not successfully remove the original, protectible features of the Davis play from the television script, and defendants are therefore liable for copyright infringement." [7]

The Court at the outset, after detailing the copyright history of this matter, stated, "Proof of copying here is complicated by two factors: four different media of expression are involved (the novel, the theater, moving pictures and television), and the claimed copying is primarily secondhand, not direct. Plaintiff seeks to prove that the allegedly infringing television script was copied from the Deutsch screenplay which, in turn, was copied from the Davis play." [8]

Thus it may be seen that derivation followed derivation from medium to medium. In *Ricordi* v. *Paramount*, the primary question involved use of material in the original work, the novel. There, it is to be noted, that the enduring work from an artistic point of view is, of course, the opera "Madame Butterfly" by Puccini. In *Davis* v. *DuPont,* the enduring work artistically was the underlying work, the novel "Ethan Frome". Yet the

---

[7] Davis v. DuPont, *supra,* note 3, at pp. 621-22.

[8] *Idem* at p. 617.

sponsor, the advertising agency, the producer and the broadcasting network were all held to have infringed the copyright in a derivative work by copying from a work as to which the defendant had certain rights, the Deutsch screenplay, but which, in turn, had copied from the Davis dramatization. Warners originally had only television motion picture rights. That was all Columbia could have acquired from Warners. Thus, for Talent to use the screenplay for a live TV performance constituted copying of the Davis dramatization since the screenplay copied elements of the Davis play.

Thus, artistic excellence is not the criterion for the sequential roll of derivative rights and the power to create. Copyright standards alone govern. Copyright determines authorship and ownership for purposes of the progression of derivative works, originality, copying and the means and manner of acquisition of rights, creation of derivative works, and the protection thereof. But because duration is a function of contract and/or operation of law, i.e., the term of each estate, original term and renewal, the nature of the sequential roll can be quite complex and beset with pitfalls of all kinds.

Sec. 7.2. Duration, Renewals and Ownership

But the sequential roll from creation of original work through grant of rights to create a derivative work, which later gives rise to grant of rights to create a further derivative work, and so on, does not necessarily follow a straight linear sequence in time. Thus, in *Ricordi* there was a collaboration in the creation of the opera "Madame Butterfly." The decision refers to deaths. Long, the author of the novel died, so did Belasco, author of the play. Puccini died during the original term, too. Death may change the configuration of ownership, not only of the original term, but also of the renewal term. Thus, collaboration, death and the renewal term may have the effect of bringing into being joint ownership of the copyright and/or the renewal copyright. Thus, the sequential roll of the chain of title and of rights from original work through one or more derivative works may not be a simple linear configuration in a time sequence. Like the proverbial family tree, joint ownership may have the effect of horizontal linear branches which then take their respective linear projections in time as part of the sequential roll.

Thus, in *Davis* v. *DuPont,* father and son, Owen and Donald Davis, created the Davis dramatization of the novel, "Ethan Frome". When the father died, the son acted as his executor. But as creators of the work, they were collaborators, and in the absence of agreement, presumably each owned an undivided one-half interest in the work. Yet there was a special agreement involving equitable ownership of the work, including interests owned by Edith Wharton, as author of the novel, and Barrington, the author of the aborted Barrington dramatization.

Collaboration, as joint authorship, creates at the instant of creation, co-ownership. Each creator, in the absence of agreement to the contrary, owns an undivided interest in the copyright. Each collaborator at that time becomes an author-proprietor. The collaborators need not necessarily assign their rights to the work to the same third party proprietor who would then own a 100% interest in the work. In such event, the sequential roll commences not in a pure linear manner in time. Each collaborator is a separate line, at the start. But the separate lines converge in the single copyright proprietor assignee from whom rights would be obtained for creation of derivative works in the sequential line. Those obtaining rights for creation of a second derivative work would seek to obtain rights from the owners of the original work and the first derivative work to perfect a chain of title in the second derivative work. Of course, this is not a mechanical process. Each party wishing to perfect title in the later derivative work has to evaluate the nature of the derivation of material from each source and the concomitant necessity for a grant of rights in relation thereto.

Collaboration, however, may, on occasion, proceed in parallel lines in the sequential roll because there is no assignment to a single copyright proprietor. Co-ownership remains. As a consequence, there may be a split copyright in a market sense. Each collaborator may assign his undivided interest to a separate copyright proprietor. The latter proceeds to exploit that undivided interest, subject to an obligation of cross-accounting over to the other proprietor of the split copyright.[9] Thus, each copyright proprietor of the split copyright may set up its own sequential roll in a valid grant of rights subject to such cross-accounting. Thus, the nature of the sequential roll in the chain of derivative works may differ for each proprietor of an undivided interest in the split copyright.

If the copyright is in the author and is in the original term, then a new configuration may commence at his death. The will of the author would determine whether such copyright passed to one party or several A single legatee would have 100% ownership as copyright proprietor. If there were more than one, each would own an undivided equal interest therein unless the will specified some other proportion. In the event of intestacy, multiple heirs would very likely mean joint ownership with the respective interests

---

[9] Shapiro, Bernstein & Co. v. Jerry Vogel Music Co., 73 F. Supp. 165 (S.D.N.Y. 1947).

of the heirs dependent upon the laws of intestate succession of each jurisdiction Thus, death would have the effect of instituting multiple lines of ownership as to derivative works thereafter. As to rights granted prior to death of the author, in respect of derivative works, it is most likely that such grant will have bound the heirs, representatives, successors and assigns of the deceased author.

Moreover, death is domiciliary, whereas copyright is territorial. That is, a decedent dies a resident of a particular place. In most instances, probate or administration of his estate is had in the jurisdiction where the decedent was domiciled. Since copyrights are intangible personal property, they would be assets administered by the fiduciary of the estate where probate or administration was had. There would be no ancillary executors or administrators appointed in another jurisdiction as in the case of real property or tangible personal property.

On the other hand, duration of copyright is determined by the laws of each country or territory having copyright legislation. Only the United States and the Philippines have renewal copyrights.[10] In effect, then, the renewal system here is *sui generis,* even though it was originally a feature of British copyright in the Statute of Anne in 1710.[11] This means that, in respect of an American decedent, the devolution of his copyright would follow his will or the laws of intestacy in the jurisdiction where his estate is administered and not the laws of renewal of Sec. 24 of the Copyright Law,[12] because Sec. 24 relates only to Amer-

---

[10] See the chart prepared by Joseph Dubin, Counsel for Universal Pictures, at Universal City, California, as to duration of copyright in the different countries and territories of the world.

[11] 8 Anne c. 19 (1710).

[12] 17 U.S.C. 24.

ican copyrights and not to foreign copyrights. Thus, if an author of a work dies in the United States, having granted worldwide rights to a third party for the duration of copyright and any renewals and extensions thereof, then apart from the two renewal countries, in all other countries where the work is subject to copyright the grant will be for the life of the single term of copyright, generally the period of life of the author plus a period of years thereafter. Thus, it may be seen that a different sequential roll in respect of derivative works may take place in respect of copyright of the same original work outside the United States.

Duration may also be affected by the nature of the copyright. If the work is under common law copyright, then there is no term of copyright at issue. Ownership continues in perpetuity. This means that the sequential roll of an underlying work owned under common law copyright theoretically may continue ad infinitum insofar as the duration of protection of the basic work is concerned and the measuring period thereof for derivative works based thereon. For example, if Belasco had written a play not based on "Ethan Frome" or any other work and had never published the same nor copyrighted the same as an unpublished work, he would have a common law copyright therein. Performance would not constitute publication.[13] Proprietors of the derivative work based thereon would not be concerned about the duration of copyright in the basic work, the play, as in the *Ricordi* litigation where the original work had a duration in the original term and thereafter in a renewal term as a new estate.

Duration under statutory copyright, however, is a function of ownership of the renewal term as provided by Sec. 24 of the Act unless the grant of rights is for a period

---

[13] Ferris v. Frohman, 223 U.S. 424 (1912).

less than the period embracing the vesting of the renewal terms. Thus, if an author grants rights to make a derivative work from his basic work as copyright proprietor thereof for a term of ten (10) years and the original term of copyright does not expire until twenty (20) years after the date of the grant, the renewal term obviously never becomes operative insofar as the grantee of those rights is concerned. The agreement relates only to a period within the original term. The renewal term comes into effect after the expiration of the grant of rights and therefore does not affect the grantee of those rights. But a grant of rights in the original work for a term of years less than the period of copyright or the period of copyright and any renewals and extensions thereof *ipso facto* becomes a limiting factor of potential major consequence in the sequential roll of derivative rights. If, for example, the grant of rights in the novel, "Madame Butterfly" to Ricordi had been no longer than ten (10) years, it is unlikely that Ricordi would have attempted to have a derivative work, the opera, created based thereon. To the extent the story line and the characters of the novel were essential to the opera, the rights to indispensable parts of the story line of the opera would have to be abandoned after ten (10) years. This would simply be economically impractical and artistically unattractive for creation of an adaptive work.

Duration, then, in respect of a meaningful sequential roll generally is impacted by the fact of the renewal copyright.

Sec. 7.3. Renewals: First Proviso

Sec. 24 of the Copyright Law provides for an original term of 28 years from date of first publication.[14] It is to be noted that Belasco wrote his play in 1900. He did not

---

[14] 17 U.S.C. 24.

copyright the same until 1917. Thus for 17 years it was under common law copyright. Upon copyright registration in 1917, the original term began to run and expired in 1945 when it was not renewed. Thus, the measuring period is not the date of creation but the date of publication, or, in the case of an unpublished work, the date when it is registered for copyright under Sec. 12 of the Act.[15] Thus the derivative work based thereon, to wit, "Madame Butterfly", not only had the period of grant of rights of the original term, but also of the period of the common law copyright prior thereto. Ricordi copyrighted the opera "Madame Butterfly" based in part on the Belasco play, in 1904. Thus, Ricordi had exclusive rights to create a derivative work, the opera, based upon the play for a period from 1901 when it entered into the agreement with the author of the original work, the novel, and Belasco, the author of the derivative play. But assuming completion of the opera in 1904, Ricordi had exclusivity in the rights to create an opera from the play for a period of 44 years, 1901 to 1945, when the original term of copyright in the Belasco play expired without renewal. The opera itself enjoyed such exclusivity from possible new versions of "Madame Butterfly" being based on the Belasco play for a period of 41 years, 1904 to 1945, assuming for this purpose that the Belasco play was the original work, that the opera was validly renewed and that the opera was derived from the play in significant matter.

Sec. 24 has two provisos as to the renewal term of 28 years. The first proviso reads:

> "*Provided*, That in the case of any posthumous work or of any periodical, cyclopedic, or other composite work upon which the copyright was originally secured

---

[15] 17 U.S.C. 12.

by the proprietor thereof, or of any work copyright by a corporate body (otherwise than as assignee or licensee of the individual author) or by an employer for whom such work is made for hire, the proprietor of such copyright shall be entitled to a renewal and extension of the copyright in such work for the further term of twenty-eight years when application for such renewal and extension shall have been made to the copyright office and duly registered therein within one year prior to the expiration of the original term of copyright;" [16]

Judge Learned Hand aptly summarized the nature of the first proviso in *Shapiro, Bernstein & Co., Inc.* v. *Bryan.*[17] He states:

"The first of these covers those cases in which the 'proprietor' of the copyright (obviously there must always have been an original copyright) is not the author of the work, and it is divided into four classes. The first class provides for 'posthumous' works, i.e. those on which the original copyright has been taken out by someone to whom the literary property passed before publication. The second provides for 'composite works', by which we understand those to which a number of authors have contributed distinguishable parts, which they have not however 'separately registered', a situation at that time provided by the second proviso though now changed—but which they have allowed a 'proprietor' to include in one copyright. The third

[16] 17 U.S.C. 24.

[17] 123 F. 2d 697 (2d Cir. 1941). See Donaldson Publishing Co. v. Bregman, Vocco & Conn, Inc., 375 F. 2d 639 (2d Cir. 1967), cert. den. 389 U.S. 1036 (1968) wherein the Court referred to the limited scope of the third class of the first proviso.

> class is not entirely plain and it is not indeed necessary for us to define its scope. Coupled as it is with the fourth—which alone is here important—it may include 'works' which are composed by persons who may be related to a corporation neither as employees 'for hire' nor as assignors or licensors. (Members of a corporation producing a common 'work' by mutual contributions, fused so as to be indistinguishable, may conceivably be one example.) The first proviso merely provides exceptions to the second, which grants the right of renewal in all other cases to the 'author' in the colloquial sense provided he survives the copyright; otherwise to his widow, children, next of kin or executors." [18]

In that case, it is to be noted that Fred Fisher wrote the lyrics, Alfred Bryan, the music, to a musical composition which was copyrighted by Maurice Shapiro, plaintiff's predecessor in title, on October 18, 1910. The copyright would have expired on October 18, 1938 in original term. Plaintiff filed a renewal application on October 19, 1937 and Bryan and Fisher filed separate applications on the same day, one for the music and the other for the words. The Court of Appeals affirmed the decision below. Judge Learned Hand in his opinion stated: "The simple meaning of the words is that when the employer has become the proprietor of the original copyright because it was made by an employee 'for hire', the right of renewal goes with it, unlike an assignment." [19]

Thus, in the employment for hire situation, the fact that the creators of the work were collaborators does not have the effect of converting an employment for hire situation

---

[18] *Idem* at p. 699.

[19] *Idem* at p. 700. Cf. Donaldson, note 17, *supra.*

into a relationship where the creators have the right to renew as authors. Moreover, the attempted separate renewal of music and words respectively is puzzling. A song consisting of words and music is a joint work with an undivided interest of composer and lyricist in the entire work. It is possible for the authors of a joint work, such as a song, to restore the work to its components wherein the music is separated from the lyrics and title (if the title has been supplied by the lyricist). In such event there would be separate literary properties after such separation; there would no longer be a joint work. It is conceivable that a work in renewal copyright might be renewed separately as a composite work under Sec. 3 of the Copyright Law.[20] Thus, a book of text with illustrations may be copyrighted under separate copyright in the text and another in the illustrations. These are separate copyrights. Presumably the separate copyrighting stems from the physical separability of text and illustrations and also from the desire of the illustrator to retain copyright proprietorship in his illustrations for all purposes.

However, the significance of the initial relationships between the parties in terms of its effect on renewal copyright cannot be overemphasized. Just as the employment for hire relationship in *Bryan* at the inception determined that for copyright renewal purposes composer and lyricist collaborating on a song could not renew because they were

---

[20] 17 U.S.C. 3 states: "The copyright provided by this title shall protect all the copyrightable component parts of the work copyrighted, and all matter therein which copyright is already subsisting but without extending the duration or scope of such copyright. The copyright upon composite works or periodicals shall give to the proprietor thereof all the rights in respect thereto which he would have if each part were individually copyrighted under this title."

employees for hire, so, too, the drawing of cartoons and comic strips for newspaper syndication under an employment for hire relationship gives the proprietor protection against copying such cartoons under Sec. 3 of the Act as component parts.[21] Thus, although King Features had not separately copyrighted "Barney Google" and "Spark Plug", it could protect the comic strips against copying in the form of toys.[22] Not only that, as employer for hire, King Features would have the right to renew the copyright therein as copyright proprietor of a composite work. If the comic strips had been separately copyrighted by King Features, it would nevertheless still have the right of renewal therein as employer for hire.

Moreover, Sec. 3 has been construed to cover the component parts of trade catalogs. Against the contention that it was applicable to composite works or periodicals but not to mere compilations, the Court in *Markham* v. *Borden* remarked:

> "There is nothing in the statute to indicate that the protection of component parts is limited to composite works whose parts are separately authored. A broader protection is more consistent with the general purposes of the Copyright Act and is clearly within the language of Section 3. An original achievement in the publication of a trade catalog, such as in this case the authorship of a comprehensive library, concisely describing the function and utility of refrigeration supplies, would have to be protected as to all component parts in order for the protection to be meaningful. Otherwise, if only the whole catalog were protected,

---

[21] King Features Syndicate v. Fleischer, 299 Fed. 533 (2d Cir. 1924).

[22] *Ibid.*

and not each of its parts, then various wholesalers could select just a few items from the copyrighted catalog, according to each wholesaler's particular inventory, or according to each wholesaler's particular preference for certain illustrations or descriptions. If such a selective pirating were allowed by applying the 'material and substantial' test to the whole catalog rather than to each of its parts, then the copyright on the catalog would seem to have very little value." [23]

Barbara Ringer observes that Congressional purpose as to giving the copyright renewal to the proprietor was to cover situations where there were too many authors to join in making the claim for renewal. She takes issue with judicial insistence upon a dichotomy between joint works and composite works and remarks, "In setting up 'composite works' as the only alternative to 'joint works,' the courts seem to have disregarded the criterion of multiple authorship, and have substituted an entirely new criterion: the separability of the contributions. The necessary implications of these decisions is that any work consisting of distinct and separable contributions which do not emerge into a unitary whole is a 'composite work,' regardless of how many authors are involved." [24]

Nimmer sheds light on the nature of the compilation in relation to the composite work. He states, "A compilation is simply a collection of diverse materials and as such may constitute a form of derivative work." [25] He then proceeds to distinguish composite works from other types of compilations.

---

[23] 206 F. 2d 199 (1st Cir. 1953) at pp. 201-202.

[24] Ringer, Barbara A., Renewal of Copyright, Study No. 31, in Studies on Copyright (1963), pp. 503-622 at p. 528.

[25] Nimmer on Copyright, (1969), Sec. 13.3, at p. 54.

in the creator. Nevertheless, the characteristics of each category differ vis-à-vis the creator of the work.

In the case of the posthumous work, as in the case of the composite work and periodicals where distinguishable parts have not been separately copyrighted, contract may play an important role as between the author or his heirs or representative, on the one hand, and the publisher, on the other. Thus, the publisher may have the renewal right as the proprietor under Sec. 24, first proviso, but the agreement originally may have provided that the publisher shall have the publication rights only, or in the case of the periodical, periodical rights only. By contract, only certain of the bundle of rights in the copyright were intended to be vested in the publisher. The remaining rights might have been reserved by agreement or provision for a grant back provided as to other rights even though the copyright might be in the publisher. The contract might not necessarily be express but implied in fact.[29]

On the other hand, corporate works with no distinguishable authorship, or where it is clearly intended that no individual creator thereof should have any right of copyright therein, compilations with no separate parts which might have been copyrighted, such as trade directories, and works of employment for hire where no rights are given contractually to the creator, or authorship is not clearly distinguishable, are categories of the first proviso where the copyright continuity for all purposes continues in the copyright proprietor into the renewal term, assuming renewal thereof.

In such event, the sequential roll vests in the proprietor or its successors and assigns for a duration through the

---

[29] See Henn, "Rights Magazine"—A Division of Indivisible Copyright, 40 Corn. L. Q. 411 (1955); Kaminstein, Abraham L., Divisibility of Copyrights, Study No. 11, in Studies on Copyright (1963) at p. 623.

renewal term as extended. The creators' contributions are not deemed to give them rights of proprietorship at the time of such creation. The corollary follows in the renewal period; neither are such creators vested with any rights in respect of the renewal period.

As to the sequential roll with respect to composite works, very often separate copyright is not taken out in the separate parts. Nimmer suggests that as to the original copyright in the composite work taken out by the copyright proprietor, it may be acting as a trustee for the creator of the individual contribution and that the relationship carries over into the renewal copyright. Therefore, the individual may renew the copyright in the name of the proprietor if the latter fails to request renewal.[30] Nimmer refers to the second proviso, the reversionary renewal in the author and succeeding statutory classes as, "in the nature of a residual clause not modifying anything in the first proviso".[31] This might suggest that if the author were to renew as beneficial owner under the first proviso, then the statutory scheme of the second proviso would not be operative. That is, in such situations the renewal by equitable owner of the copyright vests in the author pursuant to the first proviso only, and therefore the second proviso never comes into effect. To the extent the author is living, it makes no difference under either proviso if he renews. Should the author not be living, then is the right of renewal in the estate or heirs of the author under local law by reason of devolution of the copyright therein under local law, or might the widow and children take under the second proviso because the equitable ownership of the author is deemed to be the equivalent of legal ownership for such purposes? Nimmer's observation of the effect of assign-

[30] Nimmer, *op. cit., supra,* note 25, Sec. 114.2 at pp. 467-468.
[31] *Idem* at p. 467.

ment prior to the time of renewal by the proprietor to the author does not quite meet this point. He states, "If prior to the time for renewal the proprietor has assigned the legal title to the author, then such author (or next succeeding class) may claim the renewal in his or their own name."[32] This would appear to suggest that the form of the renewal determines the category of the renewal. If the rights inure to the author to renew under the first proviso in the name of the proprietor, then the second proviso is simply not applicable. If so, local law controls if the author is not living, and not the second proviso.

Clearly, as to the first proviso in situations where the proprietor copyrights a composite work or a periodical where the separate components are not copyrighted, the intent is to preserve the renewal copyright in that form of compilation in the proprietor. In other words, the proprietor is given the renewal term in the composite work or periodical just as it had it in the original term provided renewal is made. But the intent of such renewal is not to divest the author thereby of any rights he had in the original term. The intent of the second proviso is to give the author and his

---

[32] *Idem* at p. 468. Cf. Davis v. DuPont de Nemours & Co., 240 F. Supp. 612 (S.D.N.Y. 1965). It will be recalled that Edith Wharton, Lowell Barrington and Owen and Donald Davis had entered into a trust agreement as to sharing by all of them in stipulated proportions out of the Davis dramatization because it was based upon the novel by Edith Wharton and the unsatisfactory dramatization thereof by Barrington. The defendants claimed that by obtaining rights from Tyler, Wharton's residuary legatee, they were the licensee or transferee from an equitable co-owner of the Davis copyright. The Court declined to consider the question of the power of an equitable owner of a copyright to license a work when such person was not a joint author because it found that the transfer from Tyler did not transfer or license the equitable interest in the Davis play.

family a second chance to secure rewards from his creation in the event he had made an improvident disposition of his work in the initial period. The renewal copyright may indeed be a new estate for purposes of copyright,[33] for purposes of the second proviso. There the statutory scheme supersedes local law in the devolution of ownership. The Court of Appeals in *Ballentine* v. *De Sylva* stated, "And it is highly important to observe that the 'right' of the renewal never goes into an estate of a decedent. If not acted upon, the right dies. And the possession of the right is provided for in the Act and is not dependent upon or fixed by the law of descent." [34] However, the context of that case was the right of renewal under the second proviso.

The fact remains, however, that Sec. 24 in the instance of the composite work or periodical acts as a factor in time in the sequential roll of the work. If the intent has been to grant the publisher only those particular publishing rights, then that becomes only a facet of the chain of title and clearances in the sequential roll. Suppose, for example, a motion picture is to be made from an author's short story published in a book of short stories or a periodical. The author may not have himself copyrighted the story and copyright in the composite work or periodical will appear as the only copyright. The author will grant motion picture rights to his story, presumably exclusively, either for

---

[33] G. Ricordi & Co. v. Paramount Pictures, 189 F. 2d 469, 471 (2d Cir. 1951) "A copyright renewal creates a new estate . . . the new estate is clear of all rights, interests or licenses granted under the original copyright."

[34] 226 F. 2d 623, 627 (9th Cir. 1955). However, the Supreme Court, in affirming in De Sylva v. Ballentine, 351 U.S. 570 (1956), determined the meaning of "children" in the phrase "widow, widower or children" was to be construed under local law, after affirming the decision below that the word "or" was to be construed as "and" in the statute without regard to local law.

duration of copyright, duration of copyright and renewal and extension thereof, or for a term of years. In any event, the practice is to obtain a quitclaim from the publisher of the motion picture rights.[35] A similar procedure would be employed in respect to television rights in the work.

In short, the renewal copyright might be a factor in the sequential roll as in any other renewal situation, excepting only the question as to who owns the renewal rights if the author is not living in the case of a composite work where the separate part has not been copyrighted. If rights were at issue in the original term, as in the case of making a film, the studio might very well seek to acquire by agreement renewal rights from the widow and children and other heirs and provide that they will agree by will to make provision for transfer of his renewal motion picture rights to the studio. In such event, the question may become moot if all classes covered survive into the renewal period.

In short, the problems of marketing composite works from the point of view of the author thereof are substantially the same as in situations where the work of the author only is the subject of a copyright. Duration is comparable as a factor in the sequential roll, clearances and the chain of title.

---

[35] See Form 1A-2.3a in Volumes of Forms.

Chapter VIII

RENEWALS: THE SECOND PROVISO

Sec. 8.1. Renewals: The Second Proviso: Composite Works

The first proviso sets forth the situations in which the copyright renewal vests in the proprietor. The second proviso is the means for securing renewal copyright in other circumstances and reads as follows:

> "*And provided further,* That in the case of any other copyrighted work, including a contribution by an individual author to a periodical or to a cyclopedic or other composite work, the author of such work, if still living, or the widow, widower, or children of the author, if the author be not living, or if such author, widow, widower, or children be not living, then the author's executors, or in the absence of a will, his next of kin shall be entitled to a renewal and extension of the copyright in such work for a further term of twenty-eight years when application for such renewal and extension shall have been made to the copyright office and duly registered therein within one year prior to the expiration of the original term of copyright." [1]

The final sentence of Sec. 24 provides that in default of renewal under either proviso, the copyright in any work shall terminate at the end of 28 years from first publication.[2]

The second proviso is operative then as to copyright in the name of individual authors, copyright which was as-

[1] 17 U.S.C. 24.

[2] *Ibid.*

signed by individual authors, right to copyright assigned by individual authors, other than posthumous works covered under the first proviso, which were then copyrighted by someone else as proprietor. In addition, an author of a composite work or a work in a periodical or encyclopedia may secure copyright therein under an amendment to Sec. 24 passed in 1940 which deleted from the second proviso the phrase "when such contribution has been separately registered" immediately following "or other composite work".[3] Nimmer and Ringer appear to have reached differing interpretations as to the meaning of the amendment. Nimmer states:

> "Based upon the above construction it appears that the proprietor of a composite work is the one who is entitled to and who must claim the renewal in all material the copyright in which was originally secured by the proprietor. An individual author (and the successor classes) may claim renewal in their own names only if the author originally secured a separate copyright in the contribution".[4]

Nimmer then qualifies this by adding that if the proprietor fails to claim renewal, then the author may do so in the name of the proprietor.

Ringer, on the other hand, states:

> "On the whole, it would seem that justice and the real legislative intent would best be served by the second theory, under which an author may renew sepa-

---

[3] Act of March 15, 1940, 54 Stat. 51; see Nimmer on Copyright, Sec. 114.2 "Composite Works" at p. 465 and Ringer, Barbara A., Renewal of Copyright, Study 31, Studies on Copyright (1963), pp. 503 *et seq.* at pp. 539-545.

[4] Nimmer, *idem* at pp. 467-468.

rately if he wishes, but his beneficial rights are still preserved to him if the periodical or composite work is renewed by the proprietor".[5]

This second theory is posited in reference to contributions not made for hire nor copyrighted separately. As to the latter situation, exclusive rights are in the author.[6]

Thus, Nimmer would not permit the author to renew in the name of the author unless the contribution were separately copyrighted, whereas Ringer would permit the author to renew in the name of the author to save the copyright. Since Nimmer would permit the author to renew in the name of the proprietor, absent a separate copyright in the contribution, it would appear that both would construe the statute to save the contribution from public domain, the difference being only in whose name the renewal may be effected.

Proposed copyright revision eliminates the confusion by eliminating the renewal term, as to new copyrights in favor of a system of life of author plus fifty years,[7] but retains the renewal term for subsisting copyrights for a renewal period of 47 years.[8] The House Report opines, "One of the worst features of the present copyright law is the provision of renewal of copyright. A substantial burden and expense, this unclear and highly technical requirement results in incalculable amounts of unproductive work".[9]

---

[5] Ringer, note 3, *supra,* at p. 545.

[6] *Idem* at p. 543.

[7] S. 543, 91st Cong., 1st Sess., Jan. 22, 1969, Sec. 302.

[8] *Idem,* Sec. 304.

[9] House Report 83, 90th Cong., 1st Sess., to accompany H.R. 2512 (March 8, 1967) at p. 101.

As to the Nimmer and Ringer interpretations, it would appear that the amendment of 1940 would have been unnecessary if the same result is achieved by separate copyright only after the amendment as contended by Nimmer. On the other hand, the statutory scheme of the second proviso's prefatory language "in the case of any other copyrighted work" after the statutory enumeration of applicability of the first proviso, would appear to vest the right of renewal in the proprietor rather than the author in opposition to the Ringer contention. Both Nimmer and Ringer would rely on equitable principles to protect the author. Indeed, the present statute, notwithstanding its confusing construction, would appear to be predicated upon an intent to do equity by the author, in the face of a custom and practice of non-copyrighting by the author of his work in a periodical or composite work. The practical significance is two-fold: (a) acceptance by the Copyright Office of renewal either in the name of the proprietor or in the name of the author and (b) the persons entitled to renew if the author not be living. As to (a), it would seem that the Copyright Office would accept a renewal in the name of the copyright proprietor because the right is vested in the latter under the first proviso. An heir of the author presumably would take this route if he is not claiming as a member of one of the classes of the second proviso. Per contra, the renewal by members of a class is so made only by means of the second proviso. In part, the result hinges upon what the Copyright Office might accept or reject subject to litigation as to the correctness of its decision. In part, the result may rest upon agreement between the contending parties as to some sharing of the renewal proceeds on an equitable basis among the two contending positions. Perhaps the safest resolution is to renew under both provisos pursuant to such an agreement.

Sec. 8.2. Renewals

The Supreme Court has held that authors may assign their renewal interests, stating in *Fred Fisher Music Co.* v. *M. Witmark & Sons,* "We conclude, therefore, that the Copyright Act of 1909 does not nullify agreements by authors to assign their renewal interests".[10] This follows because the renewal right reverts to the author as a new estate[11] and he can by agreement transfer those rights, if living. As stated by the Supreme Court in a later case, "An assignment by an author of his renewal rights made before the original copyright expires is valid against the world, if the author is alive at the commencement of the renewal period".[12] Justice Douglas, writing for the majority in that case, *Miller Music* v. *Daniels,* in a 5-4 decision, stated, "Section 24 reflects, it seems to us, a consistent policy to treat renewal rights as expectancies until the renewal period arrives. When that time arrives, the renewal rights pass to one of the four classes listed in Section 24 according to the then-existing circumstances. Until that time arrives, assignees of renewal rights take the risk that the rights acquired may never vest in their assignors. A purchaser of such an interest is deprived of nothing. Like all purchasers of contingent interests, he takes subject to the possibility that the contingency may not occur".[13]

The requirement of survivorship plus the nature of the renewal term within the statutory scheme make for tre-

[10] 318 U.S. 643, 657 (1943).

[11] White-Smith Music Publishing Co. v. Goff, 187 Fed. 247 (1st Cir. 1911) traces the historical background and concludes that the right of renewal is in the author or the classes named in the statute and not in the administrator.

[12] Miller Music Corp. v. Charles N. Daniels, Inc., 362 U.S. 373, 375 (1960).

[13] *Idem* at pp. 377-8.

mendous practical consequences in respect of the second term of copyright. As stated by Judge Swan in *Ricordi* v. *Paramount Pictures,* "A copyright renewal creates a new estate . . . the new estate is clear of all rights, interests or licenses granted under the original copyright".[14] The renewal right is personal to the author vis-à-vis the copyright proprietor of the original term. But it is a right which vests in the author absolutely so as to become part of his estate. He must survive as a precondition for the right to vest. That does not mean that the right may not vest in his estate ultimately. If the author survives into the renewal period and renews, the renewal term has vested in his estate as an asset thereof if he has not assigned the copyright.

The precondition, however, is survivorship. The copyright may be, in certain instances, renewed so as to achieve a like effect, if there were no assignment, but the like effect is achieved entirely by operation of the statute. Thus, the Supreme Court held in *Fox Film Corp.* v. *Knowles* that an executor was the proper party to renew where the author, widow and children were not living to renew.[15] Where, however, the executor was discharged, it was held that the next of kin as tenants in common were entitled to renew and the renewal of less than all was in trust for all.[16]

The reasons for the renewal scheme of the statute has been set forth by one Court as follows:

> "The initial copyright period is frequently assigned to a publisher with but little gain to the author. If the

[14] 189 F. 2d 469, 471 (2d Cir. 1951).

[15] 261 U.S. 326 (1923).

[16] Silverman v. Sunrise Pictures Corp., 273 Fed. 909 (2d Cir. 1921), modified, 290 Fed. 804 (2d Cir. 1923), cert. den. 262 U.S. 758 (1923).

work proves meritorious and successful, the author may have had but little benefit. The second period is intended, not as an incident of the first for the benefit of the then owner of the expiring copyright, but as a second recognition extended by the law to the author of work that has proven permanently meritorious by giving directly to him, if alive, or, if not, to his widow, children, next of kin, or executor . . . a supplementary copyright . . .".[17]

Sec. 8.3. Renewals: Widow, Widower or Children

It is to be noted that while referred to as a renewal copyright, the renewal is such as to the author only if he survives to renew in the 28th year, or having assigned the copyright, survives and the assignee renews in the name of the author. Strictly speaking, it would not be a renewal copyright in any other situation, except of course under the first proviso in terms of the meaning of the word "renewal" insofar as it relates to the parties involved with the original copyright. Strictly speaking, it is not a renewal at all except in the sense that another copyright in the same work has been taken out to take effect upon the expiration of the original copyright; for the renewal copyright is a new estate. However, one might speak of renewal where the author survives because he either copyrighted in the original term and assigned the copyright or else he assigned the right to secure copyright. In either instance he had a nexus to the original copyright at its inception and can be bound to his obligation of assignment of the renewal copyright if he survives. So, too, the proprietor who secures copyright originally does so under some right to do so under the statute, such as employer for

---

[17] Harris v. Coca-Cola Co., 73 F. 2d 370, 371 (5th Cir. 1934).

hire or other category of the first proviso; there is a nexus upon renewal under the first proviso.

Absent collaboration, renewal by the author if he survives or by his assignee presents few problems in the sequential roll. It is as though there were continuity from original term into renewal term. That continuity is provided by the two factors of survivorship and assignment. Of course, the very fact of survivorship or not creates a problem in practical terms because prior to actual survivorship into the 28th year and renewal, it is only an expectancy. The contingency is real in the event of assignment prior to the 28th year and not merely an actuarial computation as to the possibility of survivorship. The author *must* survive, else the assignment is inchoate and never vests.

Therefore, the next succeeding class under the second proviso is of great importance. Actually, absent collaboration, there are only two pertinent categories in that class. The class may be paraphrased as "widow or widower, as the case may be; children". For if the author is male, the widower category automatically disappears; conversely, if the author is female, *ipso facto* the first category is that of widower.

This being so, the Supreme Court was faced with a construction of the meaning of the term "or" in the class "widow, widower or children". The Court in *De Sylva* v. *Ballentine*[18] unanimously affirmed the Court of Appeals and held that the section was so ambiguous that the word "or" was to be read conjunctively within the meaning of the Act of 1831 which had used "and" in referring to renewals.[19] Thus it decided that widow and children are

---

[18] 351 U.S. 570 (1956), *aff'g*, 226 F. 2d 623 (9th Cir. 1955).

[19] Act of Feb. 3, 1831, c. 16, Sec. 2, 4 Stat. 436.

members of the same class for purposes of renewal; the statute was not to be read disjunctively but surviving spouse and children were to be deemed members of the second class under the second proviso. The determination was made by construction of the statute. When it came to deciding the meaning of the term "children" in that clause, the Court turned to state law—there only California law was involved and illegitimacy was at issue. The Supreme Court left open the question as to the respective shares of the "widow and children", stating, "Finally, there remains the question of what are the respective rights of the widow and child in the copyright renewals, once it is accepted that they both succeed to the renewals as members of the same class. Since the parties have not argued this point, and neither court below has passed on it, we think it should not be decided at this time".[20]

Thus the matter of the nature of the division of the second class of "widow, widower, or children" was not decided by the Court. It is to be noted that this is the only category under the second proviso which is uncertain. In the absence of agreement to share in some other proportion, joint authors share equally. An individual author renewing does so for the entire copyright since the renewal copyright is a new estate which reverts to him. An executor who renews under the third category does so as a representative of the estate of the deceased author. The executor does not qualify in the first instance *qua* executor as a matter of local law; he does so solely by operation of Sec. 24. But once he qualifies under the third class, there being no widow and children and the author, of course, not being alive, then the executor takes the copyright as an asset of the estate. Devolution of the copyright

[20] De Sylva v. Ballentine, note 18, *supra,* at p. 582.

so renewed would take place in accordance with the provisions of the will. Similarly the members of the fourth class, the next of kin, take solely by operation of Sec. 24 under federal law, although their designation arises under local law. The laws of intestate succession of the respective states specify the categories of next of kin. The next of kin who do qualify to take under the fourth class of the statute do so by operation of Sec. 24 and not by the laws of intestacy. However, those who constitute next of kin in any given copyright renewal are determined by reference to local law. Once the next of kin have been ascertained and they renew, they take a renewal as tenants in common, and if fewer than all of the next of kin renew, such renewal is deemed to be in trust for members of the class.[21]

First, as to the meaning of the term "widow" in the second class, one decision has held that a surviving spouse takes the renewal as a widow notwithstanding her subsequent remarriage.[22] The result would appear to be correct. A widow is nonetheless a widow by the fact of remarriage. She at all times was the widow, i.e., the surviving spouse of the deceased author, whether or not she remarries. The statute does not single out as the object of its bounty widows—or widowers—who do not remarry. The purpose of the statute is to provide some reward to the family of the deceased author, not to serve as a censorious agency discriminating against surviving spouses who remarry. Moreover, remarriage, per se, is no assurance of elimination of need for the rewards emanating from the renewal copyright. The statute does not discriminate against children of the deceased author who marry—

[21] Silverman v. Sunrise Pictures Corp., note 16, *supra.*

[22] Edward B. Marks Music Corp. v. Borst Music Pub. Co., 110 F. Supp. 913 (D. N.J. 1953).

or remarry—for like reasons; nor does it, it is submitted, do so against remarrying surviving spouses. Moreover, it is to be noted that renewals are effected seriatim. Each copyright stands on its own in determining which class takes under the statute. That is, the renewal copyrights of an author are themselves in a sequential roll, with the last year of the original copyrights of each being determined by date of publication in respect of a published work and, in the case of an unpublished work, from date of registration. The statute would be operating in an arbitrary and capricious manner if a widow were to become *declassée,* so to speak, that is, eliminated from the second class, after a number of renewals by her, solely because she remarried thereafter and prior to the next renewal. Administrative difficulty, moreover, would be increased manifold in respect of Sec. 24, where, in the event of remarriage, there is an annulment. Thus, if a subsequent remarriage were later declared a nullity, the renewal copyright might have to be unscrambled to protect the interests therein of the newly restored widow, all at the risk of possible loss of the renewal copyright for failure to renew timely if the "widow" were the only member of the second class in our example.

Second, assuming the status of surviving spouse remains inviolate under the statute after death of the author without regard to the matrimonial penchants of the survivor, problems of arithmetic remain to plague us if there are also children. In the absence of statutory guides and decisions as to the manner of sharing as between widow and children, the commentators have had a field day of speculation and none of them may be gainsaid.

Barbara Ringer would opt for local law. She states,

> "In the *De Sylva* case the Supreme Court left open the question of whether the author's widow and children

take the renewal *per capita,* or whether the widow takes half and children divide the other half. In view of the court's holding that the meaning of the word 'child' was to be determined by the State law of descent and distribution, it is possible to infer that the proportion of ownership between the widow and children might be settled on the same basis." [23]

Nimmer, on the other hand, contends that the result of the Ringer view would be lack of uniformity, confusion and would result in shopping for a domicile. Moreover, her view would apply only where there was no will. In *De Sylva,* only California law was at issue, but if the widow and children were to reside in different states, possibly differing local laws of succession might be applicable, unless, as Nimmer avers, "Under the prevailing conflicts rule it would appear that the law of the domicile of the decedent author should control".[24] Nimmer would look, rather, to the 'four corners' of the Copyright Act to determine such division. However, "Since the act fails to indicate any internal division for what has been established as a single class it appears to be most logical to regard all members of the class, widow and children alike, as equally sharing claimants." [25]

One notewriter has stated, "There is much to commend the view that Congress intended the widow and children to share equally and as a class." [26] Kupferman has ex-

[23] Ringer, note 3, *supra,* at p. 568.

[24] Nimmer, note 3, *supra,* fn. 74, at p. 473.

[25] *Idem* at p. 473.

[26] Note: Copyright—Renewals—Rights of Widow and Children of Deceased Author, 31 N.Y.U. L. Rev. 1319, 1320 (1956).

pressed the view " . . . that spouse and children hold together as tenants in common." [27]

However, in a case of co-authorship where Milo A. Sweet wrote the music and he and Glen Grant wrote the lyrics of a musical composition entitled, "Fight On", defendants therefore claimed that they were entitled to three-fourths interest in the renewal copyright, claiming by mesne assignment from Sweet, because he presumably wrote half the words and all the music. The Court held that there was an undivided one-half interest derived by them from Sweet and stated,

> "No facts are in evidence indicating that the ownership was intended as other than an undivided one-half interest for each of the co-authors. The 1939 assignment, providing for advance royalties to be paid to Sweet and Grant, states that these royalties are 'to be divided equally between them'. Moreover, looking to the analogy of tenants-in-common generally, the long-settled rule is that 'if their shares are not fixed in the deed or will creating the cotenancy, they take in equal shares'. 2 American Law of Property Section 6.5 (Casner ed. 1952)." [28]

Sweet Music v. *Melrose Music* involved the relationship of co-authors insofar as characterization of their respective interests in the renewal copyright is concerned. It did not relate to the second class of the second proviso dealing with the method of sharing of widow and children

---

[27] Kupferman, Theodore R., Note: Renewal of Copyright—Section 23 of the Copyright Act of 1909, 44 Col. L. Rev. 712, 717 (1944).

[28] Sweet Music, Inc. v. Melrose Music Corp., 189 F. Supp. 655, 659 (S.D. Cal. 1960).

within the class as such. The determination in *Silverman v. Sunrise Pictures Corp.*[29] that next of kin share as tenants in common also is not directly in point. There the fourth class, next of kin, was at issue. Nimmer avers, "The composition of such next of kin is determined by the intestacy laws of the author's domicile at the time of his death." [30] Thus, the fourth class of the statute is a virtual direction to resort to local law to determine the nature and constitution of the class of next of kin. Once this is done, the renewal by fewer than all the members of the class inures to the benefit of all the members of the class. State law would determine whether next of kin share *per stirpes* or *per capita.* It bears on the nature of the fourth class, but it would be an extension to make it applicable to the second class. Local law is a variant, each state having its own rules of devolution in the event of intestate succession. Because the second class is *sui generis,* that is, a category set up to take effect in spite of the wishes of decedent as expressed in his last will and testament, it would appear to be uniformly operative by some interpretation that is not a function of local law. Otherwise, it is difficult to rationalize its inclusion in the statute since the fourth class, next of kin, would normally comprehend widow and children as the beneficiaries of a deceased author in the event there is no will. Yet, the class of "widow, widower or children" precedes both the executor and next of kin classes in the statutory scheme. It would appear, therefore, that resort to local law for purposes of determination of the method of sharing the renewal was not intended, but that rather some uniform construction was sought by Congress.

---

[29] Note 16, *supra.*

[30] Nimmer, note 3, *supra,* at pp. 478-479.

A number of variants is possible. First, it might be contended that the children share *per stirpes.* That is, there are in effect two categories—surviving spouse and children. Each shares 50% with the share of the children divided *per capita.* Thus, if there were a widow and four children surviving, the widow would receive 50% and each child, 12½%. A second approach is a *per capita* approach. In our example, widow and children each receive an undivided one-fifth of the renewal copyright—i.e., 20% each. A *caveat* is in order here as to the usage of the term *per stirpes* in this context. It is used only in the sense that all the members of that group constitute a single class. It has no relevance whatsoever to any sense of lineal descendants taking by representation. This is so because the members of the class must all be alive in the 28th year to receive an undivided interest in the renewal copyright, if the author not be living. Thus, in our example, if one child should die prior thereto, the children of such child will have no renewal interest whatsoever in that copyright. Widow and children, too, like the author, have only an expectancy until renewal in the 28th year of each copyright. As indicated by one Court, "The rights of adult children of an author to assign their renewal expectancies do not differ from those of the author himself or of his widow who succeeds to the right of renewal only as a member of a class which includes the children." [31] Presumably the reference to adult children relates to the possibility of later disaffirmance in respect of any assignments made by infant children.

The scheme for sharing in respect of termination interests in proposed statutory revision should not be deemed

---

[31] Cresci v. Music Publishing Holding Corp., 210 F. Supp. 253, 258 (S.D.N.Y. 1962).

a yardstick of Congressional intent in prior acts. There is nothing in the bill, S. 543,[32] for example, or in the House Report relating to an analogous bill, H.R. 2512.[33] As to the purpose of the termination interests, the House Report states,

> "After careful consideration, the committee concluded that the reversionary provisions of the present section on copyright renewal (17 U.S.C. sec. 24) should be eliminated, and that the proposed law should substitute for them a provision safeguarding authors against unremunerative transfers. A provision of this sort is needed because of the unequal bargaining position of authors, resulting in part from the impossibility of determining a work's value until it has been exploited." [34]

On its face, the proposed bill, S. 543, does not purport to deal with sharing of copyright renewals in the class of widow, widower and children. Moreover, the intent is to set forth a method of sharing as to termination interests. Therefore, the fact that the proposed bill contains formulae for sharing is not authority for *ex post facto* application thereof, even by analogy, to the present law. In this regard, the proposed bill deviates in material aspects, even apart from the nature of the interest involved, from present law. Proposed copyright revision extends the right to share in a termination interest *per stirpes* to the surviving children of any dead child of the author.[35] Moreover, Sec. 203 of S. 543 provides for a termination interest in the event of a grant by the author in any case other

---

[32] S. 543, note 7, *supra,* Secs. 203 and 304.

[33] House Report 83, note 9, *supra,* pp. 90-95, 107-109.

[34] *Idem* at p. 90.

[35] S. 543, Sec. 203(a)(2)(B) and Sec. 304(c)(2)(B).

than a work made for hire with respect to such grants executed on or after January 1, 1971. Where the author creates such work on or after January 1, 1971, then the duration of the copyright is for life of the author plus fifty years under Sec. 302 of S. 543. (S. 644 having merely changed the cut-off dates of these sections to read January 1, 1973 rather than January 1, 1971).[36] Thus, the present statute would have no relevance whatsoever. On the other hand, Sec. 304 of S. 543 is most interesting in this regard. Sec. 304 relates to subsisting copyrights. Sec. 304(a) repeats the language of Sec. 24 of the present Act except that the renewal term is stated to be forty-seven (47) years rather than twenty-eight (28) years. In other words, the combined term on copyrights in original term and renewal term is seventy-five (75) years as compared to Sec. 24, without extension thereof, of fifty-six (56) years. Indeed, the purpose of the extensions in recent years by Congress has been to prevent renewal copyrights otherwise expiring in the period of extension from falling into the public domain so as to preserve an overall period of seventy-five (75) years for all subsisting copyrights including those subsisting while Congress was considering copyright revision in the 1960's, and 1970-1972.[37] Sec. 304(b) of S. 543 extends renewal term of subsisting copyrights in renewal term to an overall term of seventy-five (75) years. Sec. 304(b) provides a consistent scheme, therefore, with Con-

---

[36] S. 543, Sec. 302(a) provides for a duration of life plus 50 years after death of an author. The term for joint works is set by Sec. 302(b) at life of last surviving author plus 50 years. Note that Secs. 203, 302, 303 and 304 of S. 644, 92nd Cong., 1st Sess., February 8, 1971, refer to a later cut-off date, viz., January 1, 1973.

[37] See, Nimmer, note 3, *supra,* Appendix C., as to various Congressional resolutions extending the renewal term of copyright annually for one additional year.

gressional extension and renewal of original term under Sec. 304(a) for a term of forty-seven (47) years.

Sec. 304(c) then proceeds to set forth a termination interest as to any grants or licenses in respect of the renewal copyright executed prior to January 1, 1971 other than a work made for hire and other than a transfer or license granted by will. Sec. 304(c)(2) is the pertinent provision as to the manner of sharing of the termination interest in the event of the death of the author and reads as follows:

> "Where an author is dead, his termination interest is owned and may be exercised by his widow (or her widower) and children or grandchildren as follows:
>
> (A) The widow owns his entire termination interest unless there are surviving children or grandchildren of the author, in which case the widow owns one half of his interest;
>
> (B) The author's surviving children, and the surviving children of any dead child of the author, own his entire termination interest unless there is a widow (or widower), in which case the ownership of one half of his interest is divided among them;
>
> (C) The rights of the author's children and grandchildren are in all cases divided among them and exercised on a per stirpes basis according to the number of his children represented; the share of the children of a dead child in a termination interest can be exercised only by the action of a majority of them." [38]

The House Report should be dispositive that the proposed statute was not intended to shed any light on the present law. It states:

---

[38] S. 543, Sec. 304(c)(2).

"Section 304(c) adopts the majority principle underlying the amendments of section 203 with respect to the termination rights of a dead author's widow and children. There is much less reason, as a matter of policy, to apply this principle in the case of transfers and licenses of renewal rights executed under the present law by the author's widow, children, executors, or next of kin, and the practical arguments against doing so are conclusive. *It is not clear how the shares of a class of renewal beneficiaries are to be divided under the existing law,* and greater difficulties would be presented if any attempt were made to apply the majority principle to further beneficiaries in cases where one or more of the renewal beneficiaries are dead. The committee has therefore retained the requirement of section 304(c) that, where the grant was executed by a person or persons other than the author, termination can be effected only by the unanimous action of the survivors of those who executed it." [39]

Thus, it would be erroneous to draw any conclusion from proposed copyright revision as to the nature of sharing under the second class as between widow (or widower) and children. This much is clear, however, that as to termination interests to take effect under the proposed legislation, there is an intent to give the widow one-half and the children and surviving children of a deceased child the remaining half *per stirpes.*

Sec. 8.4. Renewal Allocation Agreements

In the absence of legislative and judicial guidelines, allocation must nevertheless somehow be determined, and pref-

---

[39] House Report, note 9, *supra,* at p. 109 (emphasis added).

erably short of litigation. Indeed, it must be assumed that the lack of judicial decision to date evidences that counsel has been adept at fashioning solutions acceptable to their respective clients. Certainly, where there is no possibility of a contest, for example, where the widow is also the mother of all of the children and where widow and children are close to each other, the lack of guidelines need not necessarily be a cause for frustration. For one thing, if the renewal copyrights are of sufficient economic importance, allocation as between widow and children may become a facet of estate planning. The range which should be acceptable to the Internal Revenue Service would appear to be the upper limit of not less than 50% to the widow all the way to the lower limit of per capita division among widow and children. Thus, where there are a widow and four children, her share would be 20%. The *caveat*, in any resolution, it would seem, would be that all children would share the same percentage. That is, all children surviving in respect to each copyright would receive the identical percentage. In our example, assuming an allocation of 20% per child upon an overall allocation of 20% to the widow with regard to all copyright renewals as to which she survives, if one child dies before certain copyright renewals vest in the 28th year, such deceased child would not be entitled to share in further renewals. That child's 20% share as to such future renewals would then be deemed added, to the extent of one-third of 20%, to the share of the surviving three children. Thus the share of each of the three survivors would increase from 20% to 26⅔%.

Factors for consideration in a friendly allocation would be the anticipated earnings from the renewals, the other assets of the widow and aggregate income to be thrown off, the respective ages of widow and children, health and foreseeable needs of each. Thus, if a widow is on in years and has substantial other assets and income and the children are themselves married and raising young children with financial requirements of a corresponding nature, it would seem that the allocation should favor a per capita division where there are two or more children.

Offhand, it would seem that a decedent might not be able to control allocation by will. Sec. 24 supersedes local law in the manner of vesting of renewals. If a decedent by his will could control the matter of allocation as among widow and children, then it would seem that, notwithstanding Sec. 24, pertinent aspects of vesting of renewals would be controlled by local law after all. On the other hand, there is nothing to prevent a knowledgeable decedent from providing in his last will and testament that it is his wish but not his command that allocation proceed in a certain manner.

It might happen that widow and children prefer more precise guidelines. Or, some or all of the children might be offspring of the decedent by a prior marriage. Then again, there might be strained relations among the members of the class or some of them. If so, a negotiated compromise agreement as to allocation might be desirable. Several approaches might be considered in such circumstances: (1) The parties might consider the formula for distribution of the decedent's estate generally among widow and children. The will might provide one-half to the widow or perhaps one-third, as in intestacy. The will might not even be a proper guideline. If the children have been disinherited by will, or left a pittance, then the result would be grossly unjust and the will obviously could not be used as a formula for allocation; (2) The law as to intestacy in that jurisdiction might be proper if the widow and children all lived in the same state where the decedent's estate was being administered. At least it would have uniform application. If, on the one hand, widow and children live in different states with varying rules as to descent and distribution, then they may not agree on which formula to accept; (3) Widow takes as one category; children, as another, *per stirpes*. Widow would then receive 50% and in our example, each child 12½%; (4) Widow and children take *per capita*—20% each; and (5) Using (3) and (4) to obtain a mean average which would give the widow 35% and each child 16.25%.

It would seem that potential conflict might be reduced and possibly eliminated by the parties utilizing some flexible approach within the limits of what might be permissible.[40]

Sec. 8.5. Time of Vesting of Renewals

The statute is silent as to when renewals vest and there are no cases in point. But the renewal copyright term begins immediately after the expiration of the original term.

If the author survives to the 28th year of the original term, having assigned his expectancy prior thereto, the right to renew has accrued and the assignee may renew.[41] The renewal application must be taken in the name of the author, if living, and not in the name of the assignee even if made by the assignee.[42] Assignments of renewal expectancies are deemed assignments under the recording statute[43] and should be recorded within three (3) months after

---

[40] See Form No. 6D-3.1 in Volumes of Forms for a form of compromise agreement as to allocation.

[41] Fred Fisher Music Co. v. M. Witmark & Sons, 318 U.S. 643 (1943).

[42] Regulations of the Copyright Office, Sec. 202.17.

[43] 17 U.S.C. 30.

execution in the United States (or within six (6) months if executed outside the U.S.A.) to defeat the claims of any subsequent purchaser for value without notice who has recorded his assignment.[44]

If the author does not survive into the 28th year, a member of the next succeeding class must survive to the 28th year. The rule as to prior assignment of an expectancy by such a member is the same as in respect of an author. There must be survival to the 28th year in order for the right of renewal under the assignment of the expectancy to be operative.[45] Should a member of a class die in the 28th year, after vesting of the assignment, or at any time thereafter, his undivided interest in the copyright is shared by his legatees or heirs as tenants in common. But if the member of the class dies *before* the copyright vests in the 28th year, that person is not in being at the time of vesting and hence is not deemed to be included as a member of the class in which the copyright vests.

Absent any such assignment whereby the assignee can renew in the name of the assignor, the member of the class who survives into the 28th year must actually file an application before death in the 28th year or the assignee of the right to renew must renew in that year, albeit in the name of the member of the class. Thus, if an author survives to the 28th year without any assignment and dies before renewal in that year, any member of the next succeeding class may renew.[46] It is sufficient compliance if

---

[44] Rossiter v. Vogel, 134 F. 2d 908, 911 (2d Cir. 1943); Bricker, Renewal and Extension of Copyright, 29 So. Cal. L. Rev. 23, 35 (1955).

[45] Cresci v. Music Publishers Holding Corp., 210 F. Supp. 253 (S.D.N.Y. 1962); 17 U.S.C. 24.

[46] Nimmer, note 3, *supra*, at p. 483.

the application for renewal is filed in the 28th year. But application after the 28th year is fatal and the work would fall into the public domain.[47]

[47] 17 U.S.C. 24. Regulations 202.17 of the Regulations of the Copyright Office reads as follows:

"Renewals—(a) Claims to renewal copyright must be registered within the last (28th) year of the original copyright term. The original term for a published work is computed from the date of first publication; the term for a work originally registered in unpublished form is computed from the date of registration in the Copyright Office. Unless the required application and fee are received in the Copyright Office during the prescribed period before the first term of copyright expires, copyright protection is lost permanently and the work enters the public domain. The Copyright Office has no discretion to extend the renewal time limits.

(b) Renewal claims may be registered only in the names of persons falling within one of the classes of renewal claimants specified in the copyright law. If the work was a new version of a previous work, renewal may be claimed only in the new matter.

(c) Whenever a renewal applicant has cause to believe that a formal application for renewal (form R), if sent to the Copyright Office by mail, might not be received in the Copyright Office before the expiration of the time limits provided by 17 U.S.C. section 24, he may apply for renewal registration by means of a telephone call, telegram, or other method of telecommunication. An application made by this method will be accepted if: (1) The message is received in the Copyright Office within the specified time limits; (2) the applicant adequately identifies the work involved, the date of first publication or original registration, the name and address of the renewal claimant, and the statutory basis of the renewal claim; and (3) the fee for renewal registration, if not already on deposit, is received in the Copyright Office before the time for renewal registration has expired."

Sec. 202.17 was added March 27, 1970 and appeared in the Federal Register on April 1, 1970. See 17 Bull. Cr. Soc. 406 (1970).

Renewals: The Second Proviso

As to the necessity of survivorship through the 28th year, Ringer is of the opinion that death in the 28th year after registration vests the renewal notwithstanding failure to survive to the renewal term.[48] Nimmer, on the other hand, believes that the renewal claimant must survive to the expiration of the original copyright term.[49] It would seem that the requirement of survivorship to the renewal term is superfluous and not called for by the statute and that therefore the Ringer view is correct. Words and Phrases gives the following definitions: "The word 'vest' is defined as giving an immediate fixed right of present or future enjoyment. . . . The normal sense of the word 'vest' is to indicate a present and immediate interest as distinguished from one that is contingent." [50] In respect of the original term of copyright, the author may assign the right to copyright and there is no requirement under the statute of survivorship to the actual statutory copyright thereof, i.e., the inception of the original term. As to the renewal term, the renewal claimant has complied with the terms and provisions of the statute "*when* application for such renewal and extension shall have been made to the copyright office and duly registered therein within one year prior to the expiration of the original term of copyright;" [51] immediately preceding the same, Sec. 24 recites that the members of the class " . . . shall be entitled to a renewal and extension of the copyright in such work for a further term of twenty-eight years". [52] The statute is explicit and does not qualify the requirement as to time of filing the application by a further requirement for survival thereafter through

---

[48] Ringer, note 3, *supra,* at p. 582.

[49] Nimmer, note 3, *supra,* at pp. 481-483.

[50] 44 Words and Phrases 254 "vest".

[51] 17 U.S.C. 24 (emphasis added).

[52] *Ibid.*

the 28th year. The effect of the Nimmer view would be to place administration of the renewal copyright in further uncertainties until the commencement of the 28th year to ascertain survivorship of the otherwise qualifying member of the class. The Nimmer view would, in fact, convert the accrual of the expectancy by survivorship into the 28th year into a vesting only at the inception of the 28th year by survivorship to such time. For a vesting with a condition subsequent of survivorship would not be a true fixation of the right and would indeed be merely a continuation of the expectancy. It is submitted that the critical period for vesting is the year prior to the renewal and vesting necessarily must take place then. If the requirements of the Copyright Office are satisfied under the statute, such vesting should not be subject to divestiture by a further requirement of survivorship. It would appear that the language of the statute is consistent with the definitions of the term "vest" as set forth in Words and Phrases.

Chapter IX

JOINT AUTHORSHIP

Sec. 9.1. Collaboration: Common Design

It is strange that the present Copyright Law is silent as to joint authorship because the nature of collaboration provides many insights into the nature of creativity, literary and artistic property, and the market place. This impelled Judge Learned Hand to observe in 1915 that he found ". . . strangely little law regarding the rights of joint authors of books or dramatic compositions." [1] Redleaf noted in 1948, "The present Copyright Act apparently does not contemplate by its terms a dual application by co-owners of a copyright for a work of joint design. There are no specific means provided for the creation of a joint copyright, and no attempt at regulating the rights between the parties." [2]

When faced with the problem in *Maurel* v. *Smith,* Judge Learned Hand adverted to the British rule, stating: "When several collaborators knowingly engage in the production of a piece which is to be presented originally as a whole only, they adopt that common design, mentioned in Levy v. Rutly . . ." [3] The Court in *Levy* v. *Rutly* had stated that "to constitute joint authorship, there must be a common design." [4] Subsequently, the Copyright Act of 1911 in England characterized co-authorship as a collaboration, by providing:

---

[1] Maurel v. Smith, 220 Fed. 195, 199 (S.D. N.Y. 1915).

[2] Redleaf, Co-Ownership of Copyright, 119 N.Y.L.J. 760, 782, 802, 821 (1948), at p. 760, col. 1.

[3] Note 1, *supra,* at p. 200.

[4] L.R. 6 C.P. 523, 529 (1871).

"For the purposes of this Act, 'a work of joint authorship' means a work produced by the collaboration of two or more authors in which a contribution of one author is not distinct from the contribution of the other author or authors." [5]

The Court of Appeals, in affirming in *Maurel* v. *Smith* commented, "What took place thereafter through the efforts of the appellants and also Victor Herbert was a confusion of literary labor contributed by independent efforts. The appellee furnished the scenario, the appellants Smith the libretto and lyrics, and Victor Herbert the music." [6] The Court of Appeals referred to the contract between appellant Robert B. Smith and G. Schirmer, Incorporated, which referred to appellee as co-author of the operetta "Sweethearts" and added, "The result is that there was a joint co-operation in carrying out the effort to complete the opera. It is not essential that the execution of the work should be equally divided; as long as the general design and structure was agreed upon, the parties may divide their parts and work separately." [7]

A different result was obtained in the case of *Herbert* v. *Fields*.[8] There Lee Shubert obtained American rights to the German play "Old Dutch" in 1908. In 1909 he had the play translated and adapted by Edgar Smith for the American stage. He and Lew Fields entered into an agreement to produce it as a musical comedy. Fields engaged Victor Herbert to write the music. The latter declined to collaborate with Smith. George V. Hobart was then engaged to write the lyrics to which Herbert set the music.

---

[5] 1 & 2 Geo. 5, c. 46.

[6] 271 Fed. 211, 214 (2d Cir. 1921).

[7] *Idem* at p. 215.

[8] 152 N.Y. Supp. 487 (Sup. Ct., Spec. T., N.Y. Cty 1915).

The opera "Old Dutch" was produced in 1909. In this action, Herbert sought to enjoin Lew Fields and others from producing motion pictures of the play "Old Dutch". The Court held that the libretto was a separate creation owned by Shubert and Fields independent of any rights of Victor Herbert. The Court distinguished *Maurel* v. *Smith*, stating: "In the case at bar it is quite clear that Smith's production is a complete play, namely, the American adaptation of a German farce. Of course it is quite possible that music might be so composed for use with that play as to make a complete and inseparable whole out of words and music; but the fact that Herbert and Smith did not collaborate, that, on the contrary, Hobart composed additional and separate lyrics, to which alone apparently the music of the plaintiff applies, differentiates this case clearly from the Maurel case." [9]

It took several subsequent decisions to illuminate the nature of collaboration and the place of renewal there. These cases related to musical compositions. Judge Leibell had to determine the nature of the respective contributions of composer and lyricists in original term and renewal period in *Edward B. Marks Music Corporation* v. *Jerry Vogel Music Co., Inc.*[10] with respect to musical compositions "I Wonder Who's Kissing Her Now", "The Bird on Nellie's Hat", and "December and May". It appeared that Joseph E. Howard was engaged by Morton Singer, producer of a musical show, to write music for the show. He sent his lead sheets, upon instructions from Singer, to Will M. Hough and Frank R. Adams, writers of the book and lyrics.

---

[9] *Idem* at p. 489.

[10] 42 F. Supp. 859 (S.D.N.Y. 1942), *aff'd* 140 F. 2d 266 (2d Cir. 1944). See connected cases, 47 F. Supp. 490 (1942), (Lovett, J.) and 49 F. Supp. 135 (1943) (Knox, J.).

"I Wonder Who's Kissing Her Now" was copyrighted in original term in 1909 as a musical composition with Hough and Adams as authors of the lyrics and Howard as author of the music.

Plaintiff, Edward B. Marks Music Corporation, claimed renewal copyright in the music only by an instrument of assignment from the composer. Defendants filed renewal applications in the musical composition. Plaintiff claimed that upon renewal the musical composition disintegrates. The Court stated: "Here the title, music and lyrics were originally copyrighted as a musical composition—one copyright—and I am of the opinion that under Section 24, supra, a renewal of the 'subsisting' copyright is a renewal of the musical composition, comprising both music and lyrics—not the music or lyrics alone." [11] The character of the copyright, i.e., of the literary and artistic property in which copyright is secured, does not change by reason of the termination of the original term and the inception of the new estate in the renewal term. The nature of the copyright remains constant even though ownership of the new estate may differ by reason of the effect of Section 24 of the Copyright Law.[12]

One must therefore look to the factor of creation of the original work to determine its character in renewal. As to this, Judge Leibell stated, "The collaboration that produced the harmony of the two, the words and the music, made the song a musical composition, which was the result of a joint effort. Physical propinquity of the authors and consultations while this was being done, were not essential. They both knew that the lyric and music were to be properly combined in the musical composition to be published

---

[11] *Idem* 42 F. Supp. 859, at p. 863.

[12] See, Chap. VIII, *supra*.

as a unit. This was the common design." [13] Co-authorship thereby resulted and the original unity was not dissolved in renewal. He then proceeded to a determination. "I am of the opinion that the renewal copyright obtained by a co-author of a joint work embraces the whole work, that his interest in the renewal copyright is that of an owner in common, that the renewal copyright enures to the benefit of his co-author or of those entitled to a renewal under the provisions of the Copyright Act, if that co-author be dead." [14]

With respect to "December and May" Edward B. Marks wrote the lyrics and then asked his publisher to obtain someone to write the music for the same. The publisher obtained William Loraine to do so without the knowledge of Marks; a copyright was obtained by Frank Harding, the publisher, as copyright proprietor in the music and lyrics in 1893. Edward B. Marks as plaintiff's assignor secured renewal copyright in the musical composition. Loraine was alive during the 28th year of the original term and failed to obtain a renewal copyright. The Court held that this failure was not fatal since the renewal by Edward B. Marks was as trustee for himself and his assigns and Loraine and his assigns. Here Loraine had assigned his interest to defendant Vogel Co. in 1940. Applying equitable considerations, the Court held, "If a co-author or his statutory successors apply for a renewal of the copyright of a joint work, the renewal should inure to the benefit of those who would be entitled to the renewal as co-authors or as the appropriate successors to the co-authors' renewal rights, in the order prescribed in the Copyright Act." [15]

---

[13] 42 F. Supp. 859 at p. 864.

[14] *Idem* at p. 865.

[15] *Idem* at p. 868.

In the appeal involving "December and May", Judge Learned Hand extended the meaning of common design as elaborated by him in his prior opinion in *Maurel* v. *Smith*.[16] Where there is joint laboring in a common design, " . . . it makes no difference whether the authors work in concert, or even whether they know each other; it is enough that they mean their contributions to be complementary in the sense that they are to be embodied in a single work to be performed as such . . . It is true that each knew that his part could be used separately; the words, as a 'lyric'; the melody, as music. But this was not their purpose; the words and the music were to be enjoyed and performed together; unlike the parts of a 'composite work', each of which is intended to be used separately, and whose only unity is that they are bound together. This comports also with the practical aspects of the situation . . . "[17]

A few years later, the Second Circuit was again called upon to make law in this field. In this case, *Shapiro, Bernstein & Co., Inc.* v. *Jerry Vogel Music Co., Inc.*,[18] in 1911, Ernie Burnett wrote music and his then wife, Maybelle Watson, the lyrics to a song entitled "Melancholy". The work was copyrighted as an unpublished work in 1911. This copyright was renewed by the authors and assigned to the plaintiff, Shapiro, Bernstein & Co., Inc.

In 1912, Burnett offered to sell the unpublished song to Theron C. Bennett, a music publisher. The latter liked the music, but not the lyrics. Bennett, with Burnett's consent, then engaged George A. Norton to write the lyrics. This was published in 1912 under notice of copyright, after Ernie Burnett had transferred to Bennett the 1911 copy-

---

[16] 220 Fed. 195 (S.D.N.Y. 1915).

[17] 140 F. 2d 266, 267 (2d Cir. 1944).

[18] 161 F. 2d 406 (2d Cir. 1946), cert. den. 331 U.S. 820 (1947).

right. That assignment carried the statement "Lyrics now by Geo. A. Norton." A third version which was the 1912 Burnett-Norton song with a chorus in march time was published in 1914 under the title "The Melancholy Baby". Judge Swan stated, in his decision reversing the court below and remanding, that Burnett and Norton were co-authors and collaborators, with respect to the 1912 version. He remarked, "We submit that no court would hold that the fact that when Burnett composed the music he expected his wife to write the words, would make the actual song any less a 'joint work' of Burnett and the lyricist found by Bennett. If that be true, it should make no difference that Burnett's original design to have his music combined with his wife's words was in fact realized. If the words and music of a song constitute a unitary work, as the Marks case held, then the 1912 version, composed of Burnett's music and Norton's lyrics, was a 'new work' separately copyrightable from the 1911 version by the express terms of section 6, 17 U.S.C.A. section 6. It was also, as we have shown, a 'joint work.' Therefore, when Bennett united Burnett's music with Norton's words, either of the joint authors had the statutory privilege of renewal, and if he did renew, he did so for both." [19]

Sec. 9.2. Fusion of Effort by the Copyright Proprietor

A similar result ensued in even later litigation. In *Shapiro, Bernstein & Co., Inc.* v. *Jerry Vogel Music Co., Inc.*,[20] Euday L. Bowman had composed a "12th Street Rag" in 1914. He assigned his rights to the instrumental music to

[19] *Idem* at p. 410.

[20] 221 F. 2d 569 (2d Cir. 1955), modified on rehearing, 223 F. 2d 252 (2d Cir. 1955), reversing 115 F. Supp. 754 (S.D.N.Y. 1953).

J. W. Jenkins Music Co., a music publisher in 1916. In 1918, the latter, without authorization or consent of Bowman, had James S. Sumner write lyrics to the music and copyrighted the song in 1919. Plaintiff acquired its interest through Bowman and Jenkins, including the renewal copyright in the instrumental music. Defendant Vogel obtained from Sumner renewal rights in the song, and thereafter published the same. Plaintiff sued for copyright infringement. Judge Leibell held for the plaintiff on the theory that the song was a composite work because Bowman had written an instrumental work and did not intend to join it with lyrics. If so, only the new matter in the song, i.e., the lyrics, was protected so that defendant Vogel could not publish the song without the permission of the plaintiff.

The Court of Appeals reversed. It held the song to be a joint work and stated, ". . . ordinarily we look to the consent of the first author to see whether or not we have a joint work; when the first author has assigned away all his rights which he can assign, we look to the intent of the assignee . . . That intent should govern. Since that intent was to merge the two contributions into a single work to be performed as a unit for the pleasure of the hearers we should consider the result 'joint' rather than 'composite'. The result reached in the district court would leave one of the authors of the 'new work' with but a barren right in the words of a worthless poem, never intended to be used alone. Such a result is not to be favored." [21]

The decision has been criticized, albeit for different reasons. George D. Cary has remarked:

> "On the basis of this decision, no longer does there seem to be required a preconcerted common design

---

[21] 221 F. 2d 569, at p. 570.

or any active collaboration. It is now sufficient if there be any 'fusion of effort' in the creation of a revision, adaptation or modification of any existing work. The authors of the original work are not required to have any knowledge of the modification, nor do they have to take part in it. Any action on the part of their transferees which utilizes the preexisting work in the creation of a new version thereof is sufficient to make the original creators joint authors with those who later revise their work. Not only does this extension of the joint author concept do violence to the renewal policy of the law, but it would appear to extend, for an indefinite period, the control of the original author over any subsequent revision of the work." [22]

Nimmer characterizes the holding as follows:

"In so holding, the '12th Street Rag' court extended the doctrine of joint authorship in two respects. First it held that the operative intent to create a joint work may be that of the author's assignee rather than of the author himself. Secondly, and more significantly, the court held that even if the intent to contribute to a joint work does not exist at the time the author's contribution is initially created, if such intention is subsequently formed by the author or his assignee this will be sufficient to render the resulting combination a joint work." [23]

---

[22] Cary, George D., Joint Ownership of Copyrights, Study No. 12, in 1 Studies on Copyright 689, 696 (1963).

[23] Nimmer on Copyright, Sec. 69 at p. 275 (1969). See Picture Music, Inc. v. Bourne, Inc., 314 F. Supp. 640 (S.D.N.Y. 1970) where adaptor of song from film into popular song substantially by additional lyrics was held to vest contribution in owner of original material so that, after court review of songwriter indepen-

Nimmer then criticizes the decision stating, "Yet there is nothing in the '12th Street Rag' doctrine which restricts its application to situations where the underlying and derivative works are in the same medium. Moreover, the results are only slightly less incongruous where the two works are in the same medium.

"It is then submitted, that the '12th Street Rag' rule should not be regarded as viable doctrine."[24] Nimmer would prefer to follow the "traditional preconcerted common design rule."[25]

Sec. 9.3. "Joint Work" Defined

Unlike the present Copyright Law, which is silent on joint authorship, proposed copyright revision purports to cover the same. Thus, S. 543 defines a "joint work" as "a work prepared by two or more authors with the intention that their contributions be merged into inseparable or interdependent parts of a unitary whole."[26] Query, would this definition reassert the "traditional preconcerted common design rule" and in effect repeal the "12th Street Rag" rule or would some theory of implied consent on the part of one author enable the rule to be followed even when a publisher as assignee arranges for a later contributor to add elements to a new work? Nimmer does not believe that such an inference is permissible in the absence of a clear expression of such intent.[27]

---

dent contractor and for hire criteria, no renewal interest was held to belong to the writer of the adaptation, there principally additional lyrics.

[24] *Idem* Sec. 73.2 at p. 282.

[25] *Ibid.*

[26] S. 543, 91st Cong., 1st Sess., January 29, 1969. Sec. 101.

[27] Nimmer, *op. cit., supra,* note 23, Sec. 72, at p. 279.

Sec. 9.3(a). Joint Works and Composite Works

It is submitted that the courts, in this entire line of cases, have paid undue attention to formal considerations and also, as in the later cases involving renewals, have been swayed by equitable considerations so as to do justice between the parties rather than by primary considerations of the nature of creativity and creation. The initial thrust has been to distinguish the composite work from the joint work in terms of categorization. In holding in *Harris* v. *Coca-Cola* that the renewal in 1908 by the widow of Joel Chandler Harris of the 1880 copyright in his book on the Uncle Remus stories did not cover illustrations by Frost first included in the 1895 edition, the Court of Appeals stated:

> "Composite works, that is, those composed of the copyrightable work of several persons, are provided for in these sections and are put on a special basis, in that the right of renewal is given to the proprietor of the original copyright rather than to the several contributing authors, except that, when an author has separately registered his several contributions, he may have a renewal of his particular copyright. This history, culminating in the present provisions of law, makes it very plain that the second period, now called a renewal or extension, is afforded to the author or his relatives or his executor for the author's own work and because of its merit. It does not extend to another's work, although associated in the same book. If the association is such as to render the work a composite one within the meaning of the last act, the whole right of additional renewal created by section 24 is given to the copyrighting proprietor. Thus one may as a proprietor sometimes have a right of re-

newal for his own benefit of a copyright which covers the work of others, but as an author one never can."[28]

This decision serves to underscore the first formal consideration, to wit, that juxtaposition per se does not create collaboration. That is, the mere fact of physical combination and propinquity, even in the same book and subject matter, does not create joint authorship. Mere combination by editor or publisher does not in and of itself create a joint work. Disparate contributions remain such thereafter. Legal consequences among the authors *inter sese* remain disparate in the composite work regardless of the position of the proprietor as to copyrighting or renewal and as between the proprietor and each author respectively.

Consequently, claims and defenses are often couched in terms of rights in a work as a composite work because by definition there is no co-author therein unless, of course, any particular contribution to the composite work happened to have more than one author. Legal consequences aside, the nature of the composite work does not tell us much about the nature of the joint work; it merely provides us with a negative concept that one category of literary and artistic property is not jointly created.

In positive terms, as to the nature of the joint work, it is submitted that teleology per se is not enough. The purpose to create a common design is the basis of a true collaboration, i.e., working together and intending to do so. But origination by intent to create jointly, it would appear, may not be the sole and exclusive method of creation of the joint work. Nimmer seems to go far in this direction by suggesting that two authors may choose to regard two

[28] 73 F. 2d 370 (5th Cir. 1934) at pp. 371-2.

separate works as owned in common and treat them as a single work for internal purposes.[29] But even he draws back from the full implications of the logical extension of a doctrine of intent per se. He footnotes his observation by stating: "This is not to say that two authors may convert two separately copyrighted works into a single work for purposes other than internal ownership. That is, the applicable term of copyright, damages for infringement etc. may not be varied simply by agreement of the respective authors." [30] The fact is that under present law not even the authors, or their publishers, can control the situation by agreement as such if one or more of the authors fails to survive into the renewal period and the succeeding classes, e.g., widow or children, under Sec. 24, are not signatories to such agreement.

Sec. 9.3(b). Joint Works and Joint Ownership

Consensual collaboration is, of course, a principal means of creation of a joint work. At this point one must differentiate various meanings of joint work. Nimmer states, "A joint work may be defined as one in which the copyright is owned in undivided shares by two or more persons." [31] On the other hand, S. 543 states, "A 'joint work' is a work prepared by two or more authors with the intention that their contributions be merged into separable or interdependent parts of a unitary whole." [32] The joint work in the Nimmer sense will be herein deemed to be a jointly owned work regardless of the manner in which such joint ownership originates, whether by collabora-

---

[29] Nimmer, *op. cit., supra,* note 23, Sec. 70, at p. 276.

[30] *Idem* fn. 20.

[31] *Ibid.* Sec. 67, p. 271.

[32] Note 26, *supra.*

tion, death, gift, operation of the renewal statutes or otherwise.

Sec. 9.4. The Nature of Joint Creation

Again, one must look outside of copyright for an overview of the nature of joint creation. The oral tradition of balladry enabled songs to be handed down from generation to generation by memory. A facet of performance was the embellishment of the performer with his own contribution by way of additions, deletions and modifications. New versions were thereby created. Songs, in this tradition, were not so much written and composed as wrought; they were molded, fashioned, and reshaped as it suited the performer. Even under copyright, lyrical versions are at times so created. Thus, A might write music and lyrics to a song. Without his knowledge or consent and without the intercession of the publisher in any manner, B proceeds to fashion new lyrics. The publisher, at the behest of A, conceivably might seek to suppress the new lyrics, assuming they are reduced to writing, by an action for infringement. But if the lyrics are good, it is more likely that A and his publisher will prefer to enter into a new songwriter's agreement with B as to the integration of such lyrics into A's version or as to the treatment of B's lyrics as a new lyrical version.

In such circumstances one cannot speak of a common design, whether preconcerted or after the fact by act of the publisher as in the "Melancholy" and "12th Street Rag" situations. As in the case of the oral tradition, if the work created as a joint work by subsequent contribution to material created earlier is all in the public domain, one cannot even speak in terms of copyright or copyright protection.

Joint Authorship

The definition of S. 543 is apt in requiring that the respective contributions of two or more authors "be merged into separable or interdependent parts of a unitary whole."[33] By adding common intention, the definition imports the notion of "fusion of effort" of the common design. But, inseparability of material is functional, and not necessarily exclusively teleological. The song created in the oral tradition is as much an integrated unitary whole as the collaborative work created by common design. Copyright does not create the joint work in the non-Nimmer sense; the preparation of inseparable literary and artistic material accomplishes that, whether or not there are in fact unities of time, place and intent to collaborate as such.

The nature of the work as unitary is determined by practical considerations of art. Logically, words and music of a song can be separated, and, indeed, separately copyrighted. Yet, the fusion of the two has resulted in a song, which is the particular art form that is significant. In the first instance this is so because the public accepts the fusion as a unitary whole. This is the function of art. In the second, the market follows the public acceptance of the art form by providing performers, those who render the songs publicly. Copyright therein is an acknowledgment that they are, as such, literary and artistic property. They are, indeed, joint works because at some point in time the songs have been wrought into inseparable works of more than one creator.

This plasticity is also evident in music without lyrics where composers embellish and build upon the themes of their predecessors with their own variations. Again, this

---

[33] *Ibid.*

may not be a true collaboration where the original composer may be dead. Yet, the latter day composer builds thereon with his own variations. Copyright aside, new works have been created which are not exclusively the work of the later composer but embody essential elements of a prior composer in a new work. It follows that there must be intent but that the intent can be unilateral; it need not be joint or in a common design.

Sec. 9.5. The Theory of Adaptive Joint Creation

The perspective should be that of the ultimate inseparable unitary whole as the basis for elaboration of rights in joint works. Shafter has stated, "scenarists are entitled to consideration as joint authors since they furnish the idea of the play, the framework, the 'bone and flesh' on which lyrists, dramatists and composers build the finished work." [34] Indeed, that would appear to be the rationale for the decision of *Maurel* v. *Smith.*[35] There the plaintiff, a scenarist, had an agreement which denominated her as a co-author. No doubt Judge Learned Hand was concerned about equitable considerations that if she were not deemed a co-author she might not receive her fair share of compensation. Yet the writer is troubled by the characterization. A scenario is only a preliminary written exposition. The book and lyrics of the musical play are derived therefrom as is, in an ultimate sense, the music as well. Protection might have been given to the plaintiff as copyright creator of the scenario thereby making the musical comedy a derivative work. This would be the situation if a musical motion picture were to be made from an original screenplay created independently and

---

[34] Shafter, Musical Copyright 163 (2d Ed. 1939).

[35] Note 1, *supra*.

not as employee for hire. Such a film could not be made based thereon because it would be a derivative work unless rights were obtained from the scenarist as author and owner.

This is different from the situation of William Shakespeare, who derived his plots and themes from historical sources. There was no copyright protection therefor. If there were, many of the background stories would have been in the public domain anyway, because copyright term would have long expired. This also differs from the motion picture company which employs a scenarist as employee for hire. The film company is then deemed the author of the screenplay and of the film produced therefrom so that copyright is vested in the same entity as author and the problem does not arise.

The important consideration is not that plots, characters and theme have been taken from the scenarist and embodied in the musical play. That is also true of the derivative work. Common design as such is not the answer. In effect plaintiff in that case had indicated that it was her underlying property and that she wished to be considered as an author of the play. The writers of book, music and lyrics were aware of this.

Nevertheless, the joint work was the musical play as to which, in fact, she presumably did not contribute book, music or lyrics. In *Maurel,* as it were, her underlying literary form was, almost by osmosis, absorbed into the play and, ergo, she was held to be an author.

The ruling in *Maurel* may therefore be deemed the rationale for a variety of methods of creating authors who may be deemed authors from a legal point of view, but, it is submitted, are not in fact authors from a literary point of view. Thus, for example, where a film studio licenses creation of a musical stage play from an existing motion picture which it owns as proprietor and which it copyrighted as author, the film studio, in its agreement with the producer of the musical stage play, will often be denominated as an author for purposes of sharing in the subsidiary rights. It would seem that this is more than a formal designation for contract purposes. By the logic of the decision in *Maurel*, might not the film studio insist that its existing film is the source of plot, themes, characters and even dialogue so that, like the plaintiff in *Maurel,* it is entitled to be deemed an author for all purposes because its film incepted the musical stage play? It is submitted that what is involved in each instance is the creation of a new collaborative work as a derivative work from an underlying work.

The emphasis on common intent, rather than the fact of creation of the ultimate work as an inseparable unitary whole of two or more authors, also created problems with the rationale of *Herbert* v. *Fields.*[36] Admittedly, Victor Herbert had declined to collaborate with Edgar Smith who translated the play "Old Dutch" from German into English and adapted the same. But such a construction, that Victor Herbert collaborated with George V. Hobart who wrote the lyrics, but not with Edgar Smith, is formalistic and not an accurate picture of the work as a unitary whole. The fact presumably is that Victor Herbert knew that he was writing music to lyrics which, together, would be performed with the Edgar Smith adaptation as the opera "Old Dutch". The fact is that Lew Fields knew that the Edgar Smith adaptation would be utilized with music by Victor Herbert and lyrics by George V. Hobart. Indeed it was so produced as an opera in 1909.

---

[36] Note 8, *supra.*

Perhaps implicit in the decision, denying Victor Herbert the right to enjoin Lew Fields and others from producing motion pictures of the play, was an equitable notion that Victor Herbert, having turned his back on the adaptation, should not thereafter be allowed to assert claims with respect thereto. Since motion pictures being made then were silent films, Victor Herbert's music was not part of the picture. It might be added that if Herbert were held to be a collaborator, it would be difficult to see how he could stop Fields or others from granting rights through a chain of title derived from Edgar Smith as adaptor of the play. They would be able to grant such rights as owners or licensees of an undivided interest of the motion picture rights derived from the co-authors, subject only to a right of accounting to the co-owners.[37] This view is predicated on the theory that the Edgar Smith adaptation is a new work and that the German author is not also a co-author. However, if the work were principally translation rather than adaptation, the original author of the play in German would also be a co-author.

Sec. 9.6. The Limitations of Common Intent

The implications of determination of collaboration by intent of this decision can be seen from the play by Peter Weiss, popularly known in short form as "Marat/Sade".[38] There the Royal Shakespeare Company arranged to have

---

[37] Shapiro, Bernstein & Co., Inc. v. Jerry Vogel Music Co., Inc., 221 F. 2d 569 (2d Cir. 1955), modified on rehearing, 223 F. 2d 252 (2d Cir. 1955). See, Taubman, Joint Authorship and Co-ownership, 31 N.Y.U.L. Rev. 1246 (1956).

[38] The full title is "The Persecution and Assassination of Marat the Direction of the Marquis de Sade."
as Performed by the Inmates of the Asylum of Charenton under

it performed in an English version in England under the direction of Peter Brook. Peter Brook engaged Richard C. Peaslee, an American composer, to write the music with lyrics by Adrian Mitchell.[39] The play was brought to New York by David Merrick through the David Merrick Arts Foundation for a limited engagement which had to be extended because it was a huge success. Subsequently there was another run in New York and numerous stock and amateur performances. United Artists then negotiated the making of a motion picture of the play with Lord Birkett as producer and Peter Brook as director.

It is to be noted that Caedmon records brought out a record of the stage play including music and lyrics as well as dialogue. United Artists Record Corp., the record subsidiary of the parent film company, later released a sound track album of the music and lyrics in the film. The music and lyrics in the film were substantially the same as the music and lyrics in the stage play. There were at least five compositions therein consisting of both music and lyrics; the balance consisted of music.

Rights to the motion picture were negotiated by Lord Birkett as producer with representatives of Peter Weiss. Separate negotiations were had with Peaslee and his music publisher. This was so because the stage play was considered an independent work without the music and lyrics. It is apparent that United Artists Corp. and the producer were proceeding in accordance with the rationale of the *Herbert* v. *Fields* decision. Peter Weiss wrote his play in German long before the production of the work in

---

[39] An interesting and amusing account of this is provided by Peaslee in his article, Notes on Composing the Marat/Sade, 1 Perf. Arts Rev. 113 (1969).

England by the Royal Shakespeare Company. It may be presumed that other music had been composed therefor with German lyrics. Concededly, Peaslee and Mitchell did not collaborate with Weiss as author of the play, but they did with each other, just as Victor Herbert wrote music in collaboration with George V. Hobart.

It is submitted that in the premises the concept of intent to collaborate as the basis for determining co-authorship is inconsistent with what is in fact the literary and artistic property and the intrinsic fact of co-authorship to be derived therefrom. The predicate of this view is that Peaslee's music was not incidental music in the sense of a typical stage play with background incidental music. Music and lyrics were, as far as the audience and the critics were concerned, an integral part of the whole work. Indeed, there was enough music and lyrics therein for United Artists to release a sound track album consisting of the music and lyrics. Moreover, the great public interest in later runs of the play and in stock and amateur performances was precisely that the play was being presented with the Peaslee music and Mitchell lyrics. Indeed, the producer of the film insisted upon incorporating the same in the film and utilized the services of Peaslee in the course of making the picture.

It is submitted that there had been in fact a new work created of the Peter Weiss play, to wit, a dramatico-musical play, and that there had been a merger of book, music and lyrics into a unitary whole. It is this work that was filmed and licensed for stage presentations all over the United States. Objectively, from a non-legal, non-copyright point of view, the play as staged by Peter Brook, was a single work, a dramatico-musical work with three authors who should have been deemed co-authors thereof, just as Lerner and Loewe were considered joint authors of "My Fair Lady". There, too, there was a prior stage play, "Pygmalion" by George Bernard Shaw. But "My Fair Lady" was created in the traditional manner as a collaboration. Therefore, George Bernard Shaw did not get credit as a co-author of the musical play. He received credit that the musical stage play was based upon his stage play. Book and lyrics were credited to Alan Lerner, music to Fritz Loewe.

In "Marat/Sade", however, the original version by Peter Weiss not only served as the book of the Peter Brook production, but it was marketed as an independent work, as a work not written in co-authorship. This was done presumably under the rationale of *Herbert* v. *Fields.*[40] But market users were interested in the version which included the Peaslee music and Mitchell lyrics. The result was that it was Peter Weiss, through his agents, who negotiated the principal deal. The agreement with Peaslee and Mitchell, through their music publisher, became incidental thereto. From a legal point of view, the users such as the film producer, could have new music and lyrics created therefor, subject, presumably, to the approval of Peter Weiss. The net effect was to deprive the copyright proprietor of the music and lyrics of the leverage in such negotiations that it would otherwise have if composer and lyricist were deemed co-authors with Peter Weiss.

Thus, by application of the doctrine of intent to collaborate, co-authorship of "Marat/Sade" in a legal sense was not available to composer and lyricist. Concomitantly, copyright would subsist in the book of the play only and

---

[40] Note 8, *supra*.

not in the book, music and lyrics as a dramatico-musical play. It would appear that legal norms and rewards to the creator envisaged by the Constitution of the United States[41] have travelled in different directions.

Analogies to choreography and other creative components of such a work are not entirely in point. It is conceded that a choreographer of a dramatico-musical play likewise is not deemed a co-author, and hence, from a legal point of view, a collaborator, and that the choreographer is similarly situated in having to negotiate separately for the licensing of film rights to his choreography. There, too, the choreographer runs the risk that the film company might utilize other choreography and that thereby his leverage in negotiations is reduced. But from a copyright point of view, the nature of choreography is such that unless it is somehow embodied in film or notation it is not a writing that is the subject of copyrighting. Hence, there is always the element of fixation in form that is a preliminary concern. Moreover, in the traditional musical stage play, choreography is not yet deemed a collaboration for purposes of co-authorship. It is also doubtful that from a non-legal point of view, i.e., public and critical acceptance of a dramatico-musical play, there is any consideration as yet that a choreographer is a co-author and therefore co-creator of the work. *A fortiori,* there is no such accreditation to a director or set designer, as such, of co-authorship legally and from a non-legal point of view because of the elements of fixation and customary attribution of creation to authorship, even though the set designer conceivably might copyright drawings of his sets separately.

---

[41] Art. I, Sec. 8, Clause 8.

Sec. 9.7. The Copyright in the Joint Work

Indeed, the relationship of copyright to a dramatico-musical play does not take on the incidence of correspondence of copyright to literary and artistic property and of derivative copyright to derivative literary and artistic property in the sense that each such work automatically generates its own copyright. That would be true of a sequential roll where an underlying work is adapted into derivative works. In such event the copyright in the derivative work covers the new material in the derivative work. In the sequential roll it might almost seem axiomatic that each creation, i.e., a work that is not exclusively a copy with the requisite minimum irreducible originality, generates its own copyright.

But copyright and creation are more complex than the simple one copyright to a creation formula. For creation is not simply configurative. One cannot simply carve out the factor of originality and match it with a copyright so that, geometrically speaking, there is an independence of material in the underlying work and/or the succeeding derivative works and the respective matching copyrights. Literary and artistic property is not analogous in this sense to real property where blocks and lots, i.e., units of measurement of parcels of land, are the basis of ownership.

Sec. 9.8. The Copyright and the Collaboration Agreement

To avoid ambiguities as to the nature of the legal relationship, let us posit a true collaboration meeting the intent to work together of two or more authors in creating a unitary whole. Suppose A, B and C collaborate in writing a musical show for Broadway, A writing the book, B, the music and C, the lyrics. They enter into a collaboration agreement governing their collaboration *inter sese.*[42] In his discussion of a collaboration contract, Paul Sherman has written as follows:

> "The agreement should stipulate how the copyright will be held. Quite often the libretto containing the lyrics is copyrighted as a dramatic-musical work jointly in the name of the bookwriter, composer and lyricist. The musical compositions in the show are generally copyrighted separately in the names of the composer and lyricist. Of course, there are many cases where the author of the libretto, particularly one of stature, will insist on copyrighting the book of the Play in his sole name." [43]

Still another variant would be the copyrighting of the book of the play in the name of the bookwriter and lyricist where music is not included. For the basis of such disparate copyrighting is publication. Without publication there is no need for separate copyrighting for the musical play since performance of the play is not a publication and common law copyright might be maintained, in the absence of publication, in perpetuity.[44] Thus, a collaboration agreement often provides in whose name copyright of the book of the play shall subsist in the event of publication. There, actual printing and sale of the book of the play are contemplated.

---

[42] See 1 Lindey, Entertainment Publishing and the Arts, Form 4:E-1.01, Collaboration Agreement 271 (1963). A footnote to this form states that it is adapted from the form recommended by the Dramatists Guild of the Authors League of America, Inc.

[43] Sherman, Paul, Tin Pan Alley to Shubert Alley, Chap. VI of The Business and Law of Music 41, 43 (1965) edited by Taubman, Joseph.

[44] Ferris v. Frohman, 223 U.S. 424 (1912).

Similarly, the collaboration usually will recite that the composer and lyricist, here B and C in our example, can separately copyright the music and lyrics. That is, B and C will, pursuant to this clause in the collaboration agreement, assign the songs written for the show to their own or a third party music publishing company for exploitation.

The theory, in each instance, is separate copyrighting by fewer than all of the collaborators inures to the benefit of the creators of the separate copyrights only as a corollary of the separate, less than common uses. Thus, the composer will not share in the copyright of the publication of the play in book form because his contribution, the music, does not appear in the book, generally. Likewise, the bookwriter does not share in the exploitation of the small rights in the music and lyrics, that is, in the non-dramatic rights, because the book is not involved in the separate exploitation of individual songs from the show.

In other words, the collaboration agreement, in this respect, spells out a functional approach to copyright and ownership. To the extent the work is treated as a unitary whole intended to be created as such by the three authors, the work is a collaboration and the copyright therein is in all three as co-authors. To the extent the work, for certain purposes, is separated into its component parts of combinations thereof of less than the whole, then copyright therein is in fewer than the three collaborators in the musical play. Thus, in respect of book publication, rights therein would be vested in the bookwriter, if the agreement of collaboration provides that only he is to be the copyright proprietor thereof. In respect of music publication, the rights would be granted therein to composer and lyricist as a collaboration and copyright would be vested in them as co-authors who could assign such rights to a music publishing company.

Suppose, in our example, A copyrights the book of the play in his name upon publication thereof. B and C also copyright the music and lyrics of the play, albeit by assignment to a music publishing company which copyrights the same as proprietor thereof and designating B and C as authors of the music and lyrics in the various applications for copyright. What, then, happens to the theretofore existing common law copyright in the musical play? If there were a publication of the show, as such, clearly common law copyright would be lost at the instant of publication and arise under the statute only if the formalities of notice of copyright, etc., were complied with thereunder. In our example, the component parts of the show, in varying degrees, have been separated and copyrighted. Might it be said that common law copyright continues to subsist in the show because the show, as the underlying work, has never been copyrighted as such? Here, it would seem that what is in fact copyrighted are not really derivative works. There is no new element in book, music or lyrics when under separate copyright. Taken together, they correspond to the show as a whole. Yet in no sense, in our example, is there any copyright of the show, as such, by way of statutory copyright.

It would seem, however, that the collaborators would be relegated to protection of their rights under statutory copyright. For Sec. 2 of the Copyright Act provides,

> "Nothing in this title shall be construed to annul or limit the right of the author or proprietor of an unpublished work, at common law or in equity, to prevent the copying, publication, or use of such unpublished work without his consent, and to obtain damages therefor." [45]

---

[45] 17 U.S.C. 2.

Taken together, i.e., book, music and lyrics, the work has been published. It would seem, therefore, that there is nothing left that has not been published and therefore no residue of the work remaining under common law copyright. As stated by Judge Laughlin in *O'Neill* v. *General Film Co.*:

> "It is well settled that an author or an owner of a book or play, by publishing it, which is a condition precedent to obtaining a copyright, waives and abandons his common-law rights therein, and must thenceforth depend upon the statutory rights conferred by the acts of Congress, which give exclusive rights and provide for injunctive relief and damages, . . ." [46]

In this regard, Judge Learned Hand stated, "I think that play right and copyright are quite distinct under the statute, in spite of the fact that printed publication will forfeit both, and that one statutory copyright will protect both." [47]

If there were an infringing performance of the musical play of A, B and C then it would appear that the respective copyright proprietors would have to join as parties plaintiff or be joined as involuntary parties plaintiff.[48] If A were the copyright proprietor of the book of the

---

[46] O'Neill v. General Film Co., 171 App. Div. 854, 867 (1st Dept. 1916) modifying 152 N.Y. Supp. 599 (Sup. Ct., Spec. T., N.Y. Cty. 1915).

[47] Fitch v. Young, 230 Fed. 743, 744 (S.D.N.Y. 1911).

[48] Nimmer, *op. cit., supra,* note 23, Sec. 132, at pp. 581-582, "If the license is exclusive, then regardless of the limitations of the scope of the license, the licensee may sue for infringement if he joins the copyright proprietor as a party plaintiff, or defendant. If the proprietor refuses to voluntarily join in the action after being requested to do so, and if he is outside the jurisdiction he may be joined as an involuntary plaintiff."

play and XYZ Music Publishing Company, the proprietor of the copyrighted music and lyrics, then it would seem that the latter will have been joined so that suit will have been brought by the copyright proprietors. A can validly sue on infringement of the book, but insofar as the stage right or play right is concerned, he does so for the benefit of the three collaborators, so, too, for the music publishing company holding the copyright beneficially for the benefit of the collaborators insofar as the grand or dramatic rights are concerned.

Whatever the complexities of indivisibility of copyright and the theoretical underpinnings for procedural protection of the collaborators, the problem of collaboration in the theatre underscores that there is no simple correspondence of copyright in collaboration and the nature of the unitary work that is the result of collaboration, at least when not embodied in a non-ephemeral form.

Sec. 9.9. The Literary and Artistic Collaborative Work

Thus, Nimmer states that ". . . the express statutory recognition of copyright protection for motion pictures must be deemed to include the vital element of sound as contained therein, . . ." [49] Hence for a work embodied in film or tape, the copyright in such work protects the work as a whole. But a motion picture generally is copyrighted in the name of the producer in the United States. Moreover, the producer is deemed the author of the motion picture. The creative components are contracted for as

---

[49] See Nimmer, *op. cit., supra,* note 23, Sec. 25.2 at p. 111, Form Nos. 1A-4.1, 1B-5-6b, inclusive, in Volumes of Forms. See Jerome v. Twentieth Century-Fox Film Corp., 67 F. Supp. 736 (S.D.N.Y. 1946) *aff'd* 165 F. 2d 784 (2d Cir. 1948).

employees for hire. This is done to give the film production company rights of authorship in the work as a whole without any claim of renewal in that contribution in that creator. Thus, in respect of a musical motion picture, screen writer, composer and lyricist are all provided contractually to be employed by the production company.[50] Of course, a different result obtains as to an existing musical composition under copyright where synchronization and performing rights are licensed. There it is a matter of negotiation as to duration of rights in the licenses, generally with the Harry Fox Agency as agent for the music publisher owning the copyright. There the duration of rights in the licensed music and lyrics may be subject to limitations in that if the music publisher has the copyright in original term, if the authors not be living into the renewal period, the license would automatically terminate with the expiration of the term if the license were for term of copyright unless widow and children were parties to the grant of renewal rights to the same music publisher and survived to the renewal period. In any event, the screen writer would be engaged as an employee for hire.

Sec. 9.10. The Creative and Legal Senses of Collaboration

Thus it may be seen that the terms "collaboration" and "joint authorship" are to be seen in two senses, the legal point of view and the lay perspective. Obviously the motion picture is a product of collaboration of many persons creatively from a non-copyright, non-legal point of view. Moreover, comparable categories of bookwriter, composer and lyricist of the stage musical play are in-

[50] See Form Nos. 1A-4.1, 1B-5-6b, inclusive, in Volumes of Forms.

volved in the screenplay writer, composer and lyricist of the motion picture. Yet, the former are deemed collaborators and co-authors for copyright purposes and as a matter of law, whereas the latter are not for film authorship.[51] A predicate to any determination of collaboration or co-authorship is therefore the form of origination of the work. The persons desirous of collaboration must be free to collaborate, as independent contractors, so that proceeds of their contribution are not otherwise appropriated by a third party as employer for hire.

The nature of collaboration from a legal point of view, i.e., of the incidence of co-authorship, it appears, then, is also a function of the genre or medium involved. In this context, we now examine the music publishing cases referred to above. In "December and May",[52] Edward B. Marks wrote the lyrics and then asked the music publisher to obtain a composer to add music thereto. The publisher had William Loraine do so without the knowledge of Marks. Here there was a consent on the part of the lyricist to the publisher obtaining a composer to convert the lyrics into a song by adding music thereto. Again, in "Melancholy" [53] there is a turning to a publisher for assistance in some form of collaboration, only here one of the co-authors of an existing tune, to wit, the composer, does so and consents to the writing of new lyrics. An important factor there is that composer and original lyricist were husband and wife. The music publisher had insisted

---

[51] Cf. norms of authorship on the continent in Europe where the director, writer, composer and lyricist are deemed the authors of a motion picture. The film producer obtains the necessary rights from such persons contractually.

[52] Note 10, *supra*.

[53] Note 18, *supra*.

upon a new lyrical version and had George A. Norton write the lyrics, with composer Ernie Burnett's consent.

Sec. 9.10(a). The Fused Effort and Creative Credits

Ordinarily one might be troubled by this as a matter of legal theory in terms of the rights of Maybelle Watson, Burnett's then wife and writer of the original lyrics. In theory, the original tune was a unitary whole as to which each co-author was the owner of an undivided one-half interest. But the unitary whole consisted of two parts which were separable into music and lyrics. That is, the song, by its very nature, consists of a fusion of music and lyrics. Music and lyrics are capable of being separately copyrighted. But as a song, all contributors of authorship thereto are deemed to be collaborators, and properly so. However, the fusion of effort denoting collaboration does not necessarily mean that accreditation is also fused. Thus, where A writes the music and B, the lyrics of a tune, the credit thereon might be—Words and Music by A and B. Alternatively, the credits might read —Words by B; Music by A. In either event, the fact that B wrote the lyrics in no real sense makes him the author of the music; B is co-author of the fused new work, the song. This means that separability of the song into its component parts is ever a possibility. For commercial purposes, the music publisher considers the same as a facet of marketability. Thus the music publisher, generally through sub-publishers, might seek to market a tune in foreign language lyrical versions. By agreement with the original lyricist and the composer or by the fact of ownership of the copyright, the music publisher will sometimes undertake to have foreign language lyrical versions made. Generally, the provision there is that as to those foreign lyrical versions, the original lyricist will not share therein, but the composer as co-author thereof will. In effect, the new lyrical versions are treated as new works. It is, of course, advisable to embody provisions relating to the making of foreign language lyrical versions in the songwriters' agreement so that the royalties and rights of the original lyricist relating thereto are specified.[54] So, too, consideration might be given to the sharing of royalties in purely instrumental versions of the work.

Sec. 9.10(b). The Role of the Proprietor of the Joint Work

It is submitted that Maybelle Watson must have known of the music publisher's request for new lyrics to "Melancholy" other than her own and by implication consented thereto.[55] Whether she did or not, her co-author consented to the writing of new lyrics to his music as a new work. In no event would she thereby become the co-author of the song, the new work. Conceivably she might have claimed an undivided one-half of the royalty share of her husband in the new lyrical version on some equitable principle that the share of the proceeds derived by the composer was a derivative of the original song. Thus, while each co-author was entitled to license use of the work or derivative works, such co-author was accountable to his collaborator. Maybelle Watson, in all likelihood, probably waived any such right of accounting from her husband collaborator on the original tune.

As for the "12th Street Rag",[56] again the nature of music publishing is pertinent. Euday L. Bowman wrote an instrumental work and assigned the copyright to a music

---

[54] See Form Nos. 6B-1.1a-b in Volumes of Forms.

[55] Note 18, *supra.*

[56] Note 20, *supra.*

publisher. The latter obtained James S. Sumner, without the authorization or consent of Bowman, to write lyrics thereto. It was held to be a joint work by reason of merger of the contributions of the two and not a composite work. The result is correct because the resultant song represented a fusion of effort, objectively speaking. Intent to fuse may be unilateral. A composer taking lyrics of a long deceased author and writing music thereto nonetheless writes a song. To the world at large this is as much of a song as a similar work written by composer and lyricist working together or intending to collaborate.

Moreover, a composer submitting a piece of music to a music publisher expects it to be exploited. The publisher may publish band versions, orchestral versions, piano versions and so on. Very often the versions are prepared by an arranger employed by the music publisher for this purpose and not necessarily by the original composer. These versions are copyrightable as new, derivative works and indeed the music publisher will hasten to copyright such versions upon publication thereof. This is the bread and butter of music publication in terms of exploitation of a musical composition publishing-wise. This, in fact, has been the historic function of music publishing. The addition of lyrics to instrumental works has similarly proceeded from the ambit of the publishing function by the music publisher as copyright proprietor. Of course, if the music publisher is wise, it will arrange to consult with the composer as to the music publisher's choice of lyricist. Whether the music publisher does so or not, the authorizing of creation of derivative works from the underlying work is the function of the music publisher as copyright proprietor thereof. Presumably Bowman ascertained the fact of a lyrical version in due course, whether or not he was consulted at the time

Sumner's services were engaged by the music publisher. He would have discovered the fact either from publication, common trade knowledge or simply from the periodic royalty accounting.

It must be assumed, therefore, that in music publishing an implied condition of assignment of the copyright in the work is that composer and/or lyricist consent to creation of derivative works therefrom. There may, of course, be a clause requiring express consent thereto in the particular songwriter's agreement. Indeed, knowledgeable composers and lyricists entering into songwriter agreements with third party publishers will often discuss possible means of exploitation of the work, including creation of derivative works therefrom, as a preliminary to entering into such agreement and assignment of the underlying copyright pursuant thereto.

Sec. 9.11. Judicial Doctrines and Industry Practices

Thus the courts have taken a realistic position in relation to the extension of the doctrine of common design in collaboration. The definition of S. 543 of "joint work",[57] if taken literally, or in the sense that the collaborative work cannot arise through the intention of the assignee, would, in effect, repeal existing rules of the "Melancholy"[58] and "12th Street Rag"[59] cases. Such repeal is not in accord with established practices in the various copyright industries involved. Nor, in fact, does it accord with the best interests of the creators themselves, i.e., the original creators, whose primary objective is to maximize the exploitation of their work through the copyright pro-

---

[57] Note 26, *supra*.
[58] Note 18, *supra*.
[59] Note 20, *supra*.

prietor to whom the work is assigned, one whose principal function in this regard is to superintend the creation of derivative works therefrom.

Nor is the theory of mutual intent of co-authors as collaborators in accord with historic methods of creation by later creators incorporating elements of the work of prior creators in a fusion of a new unitary whole. It is interesting to note that many of the legal battles arise long after the creation of the new work and involve renewals as well. Thus, the parties are using legal arguments, any which way that provide a possible legal handle, without generally being concerned about the creative stance of the original collaborators.

As long as creators rely on third parties to exploit the work of the original creators, the scope of such parties in the role of copyright proprietors must be acknowledged. Inherent in the nature of our copyright jurisprudence is a strong measure of reliance on the function of such third parties in creation, i.e., the managerial, administrative function.

The creators have the alternative of protecting their position vis-à-vis putative collaboration induced by the copyright proprietor by means of contract. The creator can set up suitable protections and controls in this manner in the basic agreement assigning the copyright. The music publisher will not lightly disregard a request of a composer of an instrumental version for right of approval of the lyrics or of right of approval of selection of a lyricist by the music publisher.

The nature of collaboration of co-authors appears then to be far more complex than one imagines. It would seem that the judicial trend has been in the right direction, after all, notwithstanding the observations of its critics.

Chapter X

JOINT OWNERSHIP: CO-AUTHORSHIP: RENEWALS

Sec. 10.1. Fusion of Effort; Diffusion of Ownership

If the distinguishing facet of the joint work is fusion of effort into a unitary whole, whether by common design of collaborators, designation of a co-creator by an assignee of the co-authors or of an author, or unilateral fusion by a later author with the existing work of another author, then the principal characteristic of joint ownership is diffusion of ownership, whether of the work of a single author or the fused effort of two or more authors. The fact of fusion of effort is the merger of the respective contributions into a unitary whole. The work of a single author presupposes that it, too, is a unitary whole.

Again one must look to the nature of the work itself as a literary and artistic creation rather than to the copyright covering the same. Thus, for example, if A writes short stories that are published in book form, in all likelihood there will be a single copyright covering the book as a collection of short stories. However, the book would not be deemed a composite work if the theory of multi-authorship is the test of the composite work so that a work of a single author published in book form under a single copyright of the book could not be defined as a composite work.[1] Yet, a collection of short stories by dif-

---

[1] Judge Learned Hand in Shapiro, Bernstein & Co., Inc. v. Bryan, 123 F. 2d 697 (2d Cir. 1941) posits as to composite works, " . . . by which we understand those to which a number of authors have contributed distinguishable parts", at p. 699. Cf. Markham v. A. E. Borden Co., Inc., 206 F. 2d 199 (1st Cir. 1953), "There is nothing in the statute to indicate that the protection of component parts is limited to composite works whose parts are separately authored.", at p. 201.

ferent writers published in a single volume would without doubt constitute a composite work. Under any theory, the tests of distinguishable parts and separate authorship are met.

In this regard, proposed copyright revision defines a "collective work" but not a composite work. S. 543 states, "A 'collective work' is a work, such as a periodical issue, anthology, or encyclopedia, in which a number of contributions, constituting separate and independent works in themselves, are assembled into a collective whole." [2] The volume of short stories of separate authors would quite obviously qualify as collective works under this definition. In the case of the volume of short stories of a single author, greater difficulties are presented. Webster defines the adjective "anthological" as "Of or pertaining to an anthology; consisting of extracts from *different* authors, esp. the poets." [3] An encyclopedia, by its very nature, is a composite work of many authors. A periodical issue conceivably might consist of the contributions of a single author alone, but the likelihood of the same is remote and would be a rarity. In almost all instances, the nature of the periodical is the collection of works of many authors. Moreover, it is submitted that the sense of the definition is to cover periodicals as collective works and the reference to "periodical *issue*" is intended to pinpoint the fact that each issue of a periodical itself is a collective work, i.e., a work in and of itself as distinguished from other issues of the same periodical. It would appear that the phrase in the definition "such as a periodical issue, anthology or encyclopedia" is a qualifying phrase and that the doctrine of *ejusdem generis* would be applica-

[2] S. 543, 91st Cong., 1st Sess., January 22, 1969, Sec. 101.

[3] Webster's New International Dictionary, Second Ed., Unabridged (1961) at p. 114 (emphasis added).

ble thereto. Bouvier defines "*ejusdem generis*" as meaning "of the same kind" and adds, "In the construction of laws, wills, and other instruments, general words following an enumeration of specific things are usually restricted to things of the same (ejusdem generis) as those specifically enumerated." [4] It is submitted that the foregoing definition of "collective work" is to be qualified by categories of the same kind so that although short stories of a single writer collected into one volume may be published as separate and independent works in themselves, they are nonetheless not a collective work because the prerequisite of multi-authorship is absent. The fact that there may be "collected" works of a single author does not thereby transform the same into a composite work or a collective work.

It would seem therefore that in the area of joint authorship one is automatically within the scope of the fused work as a unitary whole, while in the case of the single author there is, of course, no fusion of effort. The work is to be deemed a unitary whole if, from a literary point of view, it is to be taken as a whole. From a copyright point of view, this may, in fact, become the irreducible minimum of originality capable of being copyrighted. But copyrights are not necessarily co-extensive with literary works. Thus a trilogy of an author might be copyrighted in a single volume or in three volumes. This depends upon the factor of publication form. Yet from a literary point of view, the author intends the three works to be a unitary whole and alternatively that each work stand on its own as a separate work. Webster defines "trilogy" as "A series of three dramas, or by extension, three literary or musical compositions, which, although each is in one sense com-

[4] 1 Bouvier's Law Dictionary (Rawle's 3rd Revision, 8th Ed., 1914) at p. 979.

plete, have a close mutual relation, and form one theme, historical, poetical, or the like, in nature; as Schiller's Wallenstein *trilogy*." [5]

Thus it may be seen that throughout the warp and woof of property formation of literary and artistic works, the personality of the author inheres. In the case of the trilogy, it is the author's intent at integration thematically, as to plot and characters, that projects an integrative character to the three works even though sometimes they are copyrighted as separate works and at other times as a single work. On occasion, a skein of continuity is provided by the author through the use of common characters in the course of many works.[6] Indeed, the Court in the *Sam Spade* case observes, " . . . historically and presently detective fiction writers have and do carry the leading characters with their names and individualisms from one story into succeeding stories. This was the practice of Edgar Allen Poe, Sir Arthur Conan Doyle, and others; and in the last two decades of S. S. Van Dine, Earle Stanley Gardner, and others." [7]

Copyright, in a sense, represents separation of the quantum of the collected works of an author of definable works of a unitary whole that are capable thereby of being denominated literary and artistic properties and thereby of entering into the mainstream of commerce. A qualification is in order here in the instance of the unfinished work. If an author dies before completion thereof,

---

[5] Webster, *op. cit., supra,* note 3, at 2712 (italics).

[6] See the Record on Appeal in Warner Bros. Pictures, Inc. v. Columbia Broadcasting System, Inc., 216 F. 2d 945 (9th Cir. 1954), for an enumeration of works of various writers where the same characters were used in different works of the same author or authors.

[7] *Idem* at p. 949.

it is nonetheless a unitary work, albeit one that was never finished, because the author intended the work to be a unitary one. The doctrine of copyright as irreducible minimum of originality qualifies the work for copyrightability even though it has not been completed. Viability of unfinished work or fragmental works subject to copyright, is essentially a matter of commerce. Franz Shubert's "Unfinished Symphony" can be marketed because people wish to listen to and perform the work, even though it was never completed, whereas incomplete or fragmental works of others may be less fortunate notwithstanding that such works are nonetheless property.

Sec. 10.2. Means of Creating Joint Ownership

What is true of the works of single authors is likewise true of works of joint authorship. The fusion of effort has the effect of making the works of co-authors into unitary wholes. Such works are likewise capable of being separated as literary and artistic properties. As to works under single authorship, they are capable of diffusion into joint ownership by a variety of means—by will, intestate succession, inter vivos transfer of a moiety and renewal. As to works that are fused efforts of two or more authors, there is an additional means of such diffusion, the fact of joint authorship itself. But in each instance, the work itself remains as a constant, the work itself continues to be a unitary whole regardless of the nature of original authorship, i.e., single author or two or more authors, and of the method of origin of joint ownership. Thus, the work as a literary property and also the copyright therein remain as constants even though for various reasons ownership may shift into assorted forms of joint ownership. The nature of the work does not change by reason of such changes in ownership. The literary and artistic property remains the same throughout all such transformations of ownership. Copyright therein continues to be a single copyright in whatever copyright there was originally in that particular work, subject, of course, to the new estate in the renewal copyright. But renewal may affect the nature of ownership and place the work in a renewal copyright; it does not transform a unitary whole into anything less upon renewal.[8]

Sec. 10.3. Undivided Ownership Interests in Jointly Created Works

Apart from the intrinsic nature of joint authorship in the creation of the joint work and the effect of joint authorship upon the renewal copyright, the principal facet of joint authorship, as such, in the creation of joint ownership of the work is that in the absence of prior agreement among the co-authors each becomes the owner of an equal undivided interest in the work. In *Sweet Music, Inc.* v. *Melrose Music Corp.*,[9] Milo A. Sweet and Glen Grant wrote the lyrics and the former, the music to "Fight On", the marching song of the University of Southern California. One of the issues in the case was the respective interests in the renewal copyright owned by the assignees of the renewal copyright. The Court proceeded to state the facts and rule thereon:

> ". . . defendants urge that they are entitled to a three-fourths interest in the renewal copyright, and that plaintiff is entitled to only a one-fourth interest. This claim of defendants rests upon the stipulation that: 'Milo A. Sweet and said Glen Grant were the joint

---

[8] See Chap. IX, *supra*.

[9] 189 F. Supp. 655 (S.D. Cal. 1960).

composers of said musical composition, Milo A. Sweet having written the music and Milo A. Sweet and said Glen Grant together having written the lyrics'. From this defendants appear to assume that Sweet wrote half the words and all the music, and that this assumed contribution entitled Sweet to three-fourths of the royalties.

"No facts are in evidence indicating that the ownership was intended as other than an undivided one-half interest for each of the co-authors. The 1939 assignment, providing for advance royalties to be paid to Sweet and Grant, states that these royalties are 'to be divided equally between them'. Moreover, looking to the analogy of tenants-in-common generally, the long-settled rule is that 'if their shares are not fixed in the deed or will creating the cotenancy, they take in equal shares'. 2 American Law of Property Section 6.5 (Casner ed. 1952)." [10]

Thus, in the absence of division by agreement among the co-authors, each becomes an equal co-owner of an undivided interest in the whole. The affects of this are far reaching from a practical point of view. Nimmer remarks:

"It is not necessary that the respective contributions of several authors to a single work be equal either

[10] *Idem* at p. 659. California Civil Code, Sec. 981 (a) provides: "Unless otherwise agreed, a composition in letters or art in the production of which several persons are jointly concerned, is owned by them as follows: 1. If the product is indivisible, in equal proportions. 2. If it is divisible, in proportion to the contribution of each." Nimmer is of the opinion that the statute has in mind divisibility in the legal sense of joint work and not in the sense of physical divisibility. Nimmer on Copyright (1969) Sec. 75, fn. 45, at p. 284.

> quantitatively or qualitatively in order to constitute such contributors as joint authors. It would seem, however, that each such contribution must, in any event, be more than *de minimis*. That is, more than a word or a line must be added by one who claims to be a joint author. But for this purpose the standard of *de minimis* is not necessarily the same as the standard for copyrightability." [11]

He illustrates this with the example of a collaboration of A's plot ideas and B's literary expression thereof, whereas A's ideas, standing alone, would not be copyrightable.[12]

Sec. 10.4. Standards of Joint Authorship and Joint Ownership

It is submitted, however, that there is a standard of *de minimis*. That is the same standard for such contributor were he in fact the sole author. He must, apart from contribution of plot ideas and the like which are not in and of themselves subject to copyright where not reduced to writing, contribute the irreducible minimum of originality in a writing that would earn him copyrightability in the absence of co-authorship. That is not to say that his actual contribution to the collaboration must necessarily be in that form. Nimmer is correct that words are not copyrightable, but the Regulations of the Copyright Office refer to "words and short phrases such as names, titles and slogans". [13] On the other hand, the Regulations proscribe "ideas . . . as distinguished from the particular

---

[11] Nimmer, *Idem* Sec. 74 at pp. 282-283.

[12] *Ibid.*

[13] Regulations of the Copyright Office, Sec. 202.1 (a).

manner in which they are expressed or described in a writing".[14]

Nimmer's conclusion as to inclusion of the idea man as a co-author when reduced to writing in a collaboration follows from the decision in *Maurel* v. *Smith*[15] where the plot, theme and characters of plaintiff scenarist were used by the defendant librettist and the plaintiff was held to be in co-authorship with the bookwriter, composer and lyricist. The doctrine of common design aside, presumably there is a fusion of effort which is, in part, elliptical. There is an ellipsis by one or more collaborators, where two or more are co-authors of writings in the literal sense of composition or creation in words and sentences. One form of collaboration may be reduction to writing by joint dictation reduced to writing, as opposed to writing of an initial draft by one or more collaborators, and then exchange and revision of drafts thereafter. The former method is basically initially oral with either a simultaneous reduction to writing by hand or typewriter, or subsequent reduction to written form after transcription from a tape recorder, cassette, dictation machine or other recording device. The oral method would include contributions of the idea man and also of the collaborator depending upon his co-authors to complete his elliptical word structures so that by a fusion of effort there is a collaborative writing. Therefore, one cannot automatically separate such oral contributions and apply standards of copyrightability to the oral contributions alone. One must imply completion of the word structure were such contributor creating alone and in the case of the idea man, reduction to writing. That is the nature of collaboration

---

[14] *Idem* Sec. 202.1 (b).
[15] 271 Fed. 211 (2d Cir. 1921).

in this method of co-authorship. One can readily imagine that collaborative scripts for screen, stage and television often take form in this manner. Therefore, as to the contribution of the words in elliptical form, one must assume the same as completed in written form. Then the standards of copyrightability of irreducible minimum of originality would be applicable thereto as though the same were standing alone to determine identification of the contributor as a co-author. A similar test would apply to the idea man's contributions where expression of his ideas are implied as though reduced to written form by him alone. This would then be measured against the test of irreducible minimum of originality.

This tentative, evanescent nature of some forms of contribution to co-authorship is basic to an understanding of the *gestalt* or overall construct of creation of a literary and artistic work and underlies many of the problems of creation, identification and limitation of authorship. The performing arts, in particular, are areas where this is markedly so.

Sec. 10.4(a). The Playwright

Webster defines a "playwright" as "a maker or writer of plays".[16] He defines a "wright" as "a constructive workman, an artificer".[17] Its derivation is from the Anglo-Saxon "wryhta" which is akin to the English "work".[18] The term "wrought" is a past tense and past participle of "work", hence an adjective. According to Webster, "wrought" means "worked into shape; fashioned; formed."[19]

---

[16] Webster, *op. cit., supra,* at p. 1887.
[17] *Idem* at p. 2958.
[18] *Ibid.*
[19] *Ibid.* at p. 2961.

A playwright, then, is a molder and fashioner of plays. This would appear to indicate that his writing is also tentative, to be revised and fashioned in the spotlight of rehearsals and previews to meet the exigencies of theatrical performance. Lines, scenes and even acts might very well be revised to conform to the real or imagined requirements and expediencies of performance. This plasticity arises not alone from the playwright's total absorption of the theatrical experience as he molds his play into an eventual fixation of final form. There are hints, suggestions—even words and lines—that are derived from the happenings of pre-fixation experience and may even emanate from actors, director, producer or other participants. Finally, there may be the play doctor or consultant to assist in fixation in final form. Such play doctoring may indeed be surgical. Yet, in each instance the construction of the play into final form partakes of methods not far removed from the oral method of collaboration.

Perhaps it is attributable to the custom of the theatre that such random contributors acknowledge the role of the playwright or co-playwrights as artificers and so do not ordinarily claim co-authorship. In a great many instances, conceivably their contribution might be insufficient as a matter of law anyway. In others, as in the case of the play doctor, presumably his status would be determined contractually as to whether or not he would be given the status of a co-author. Judging from the credits of authorship in the theatre and the musical theatre, it would appear that generally the play doctor does not assume that status.

Sec. 10.4(b). Film and Television Writer

If the author of a play for the stage is a molder of the play, *a fortiori* the same is true of the screenplay writer and the teleplay writer. But there one finds a fundamental distinction; the producer is deemed the creator of the film or tape. All artistic components engaged in the creation of the work, including the screenplay writer and teleplay writer are generally rendering services as employees for hire. Although the Screen Writers Guild may regulate the manner of attribution of credit to its writers by agreement,[20] first ownership in the copyright goes to the production company as employer for hire. Agreements of the production company with writers, directors and individual producers are therefore in the form of employment for hire. Moreover, such agreements generally provide that the fruit and proceeds of the services rendered, including any lines, dialogue, ideas, etc., belong to the employer.[21] Any such contribution would thereby be deemed fruits and services of employment from the inception, so that any claim of authorship or co-authorship in respect thereof would be automatically eliminated.

But not only forms of writing for performance are cases of the "wright at work", i.e., the molding into eventual final form. Attribution of authorship and elimination of same take many forms. Many books and articles are created by persons of note and personalities of the moment "as told to" an established author. There the latter often fashions tapes, conversations and other materials of the name person into literary form. Authorship may often be attributed to both the name person and the recipient of the material who fashions it into final form. At other times, the latter may agree to share in authorial royalties without taking credit as a co-author. It would appear that there is a true collaboration and that co-authorship is, in fact, in both.

---

[20] See Form No. 1A-5 in Volumes of Forms.

[21] See Form Nos. 1B-1 to 1B-4, inclusive, in Volumes of Forms.

Sec. 10.4(c). Ghost Writer

A much more difficult situation is that of the ghost writer who is not identified as a co-author in any manner. Presumably his status is intended to be governed by an employment for hire situation so that the fruits and proceeds belong to the person who has engaged him as a ghost writer. Let us assume that is the intent of the parties so that first ownership is in the former, notwithstanding that there may be no withholding from the employee for tax purposes. This is more consistent with the intent of the parties than an independent contractor relationship whereunder, in the event of the death of the ghost writer before the renewal period, the material would revert to his widow and children or other class under the statute, thereby divesting the owner in original term of any rights. This would be a harsh result as to the original owner which was never intended.

Ghost writing may then be deemed to be the result of an express or implied agreement whereby any and all attribution of authorship or co-authorship in the ghost writer is eliminated. One uses the term "co-authorship" here because two or more ghost writers may be writing the material together, or the ghost writer may in fact be collaborating with the person engaging his services who might be contributing the basic ideas for the ghost-written material or possibly revising the same to final form.

The elimination of attribution of credit of authorship may seem at first blush to be a denial of the right of personality of the ghost writer in and to his creations. Yet in the context of history there is a widespread and valid custom for writing by proxy. Not only in dramaturgy and opera does one find the inarticulate lover mouthing the creations of a Cyrano or a Figaro, but throughout most of recorded history, reading and writing were skills of the few. Illiteracy was widespread. The scribe and amanuensis were sometimes literalists taking dictation; at other times they were embellishers or composers of writings to order. Even today, illiteracy in the United States is far from eliminated and is widespread throughout the world. Moreover, standards of literacy in many places, including this country, can be less than one might deem desirable. Even where literacy is high, this does not preclude the use of the services of the scribe and amanuensis for improved composition as an adjunct of contemporary life, whether business, personal or otherwise.

Sec. 10.4(d). The Pseudo-Collaboration

A different situation is presented regarding the creation which becomes in whole or in part a pseudo-collaboration. A bandleader insists that the composer and lyricist include the former as a co-author of a song in order to play it. In the days of song-plugging when this was an important means of exposure of a tune, the power of the bandleader was great in this regard. Acquiescence to insistence upon attribution of co-authorship might be the only means of getting the tune off the ground. One decision involving such a "cut in" held that an ersatz co-author was to be without right of authorship in the renewal estate of that copyright, while another declined to grant a motion for summary judgment by reason of there being a question of whether or not plaintiff confirmed and ratified payments to defendant, Paul Whiteman, during the renewal period so as to create an estoppel that should be left for trial.[22] However, rights of authorship in the original term were not disturbed.

[22] Buck Ram v. Phil Levant, Illinois Circuit Ct., Cook Cty., (Unreported, no opinion) see Variety, Wed., June 10, 1964 as to first case; Heywood v. Robbins Music Corporation, 142 U.S.P.Q. 53 (N.Y. Sup. Ct., Spec. T., N.Y. Cty. 1964), as to second case.

Bogus authorship might originate from producers insisting upon authorial attribution so as to obtain ownership of a share of the copyright. This would, of course, be in a situation where the rights are acquired to use a song in a film, for example, where the composer and lyricist are not engaged as employees for hire. For in an employment situation the producer would own the copyright as employer for hire.

It is submitted that aggrieved true authors in situations of intrusion of a non-author may not be without remedy in the original term. If the inclusion of the non-author to authorial credit is a condition of performance, let us say, then the apparent agreement of the true author or authors to include the non-author as an author may be vitiated as an illegal tie-in or illegal restraint of trade under the antitrust laws.[23] The effect of any such adjudication might be to place the non-author in the position of an infringer if he has used or exploited the copyright under Sec. 101 of the Copyright Act,[24] possibly even subject to prosecution for a misdemeanor for willful infringement of copyright under Sec. 104 thereof[25] and/or to prosecution for a misdemeanor for fraudulent notice of copyright under Sec. 105 thereof.[26] Moreover, in due course, one might expect the various guilds representing authors and composers to institute procedures seeking to eliminate non-contributors from collaborative authorship for copyright purposes, whether along the lines of the Screen Writers Guild as to screenplay credit or otherwise.

---

[23] Sec. 1 of the Sherman Act; Sec. 3 of the Clayton Act; 15 U.S.C. 1 *et seq.;* see Taubman, Copyright and Antitrust (1960).

[24] 17 U.S.C. 101.

[25] 17. U.S.C. 104.

[26] 17 U.S.C. 105.

Sec. 10.4(e). Furnishing of Materials as Collaboration

Finally, one must distinguish collaboration from authorship where materials are furnished to another and conversations had with him. The function of the latter may be editorial and his credit may be that of an editor. He may or may not share in royalties of the author as a matter of agreement but not be deemed an author, nonetheless. This would follow in a situation where a person tapes his memoirs for publication as an autobiography or as his memoirs for transcription and editing by another. Conversely, the intent may be just the reverse. The other person is writing a biography and using the materials and interview method and even tape recordings of conversations as a means of creation of his own work. In that event, the supplier of the material and party being interviewed may be the subject of the work but not the author thereof.[27] Whatever right of property such party may have therein by agreeing to creation of a work out of these materials by another, he has, in effect, waived the right to be treated as co-author or as author of the resultant work by the other person.[28] It would appear that, in any event, where the latter has initiated the conversations and interviews, he is the owner thereof, much as the photog-

---

[27] See Hemingway v. Random House, Inc., 49 Misc. 2d 726, 268 N.Y.S. 2d 531 (Sup. Ct. N.Y. Cty. 1966); 53 Misc. 2d 462, 279 N.Y.S. 2d 51 (Sup. Ct. N.Y. Cty. 1967) relating to Hotchner's "Papa Hemingway". See Chap. XXV, *infra*.

[28] Cf. unauthorized appropriation of material prepared for oral delivery, as in King v. Mister Maestro, Inc., 224 F. Supp. 101 (S.D. N.Y. 1963). See also Williams v. Weisser, 153 U.S.P.Q. 866 (Cal. Super. 1967).

rapher owns the photograph taken by him not on commission of a customer.[29]

Thus, out of a variety of circumstances, under the doctrine of the *Sweet*[30] case, so long as a person has contributed the quantum of literary and artistic output to satisfy the legal requirements of co-authorship, in the absence of agreement among the parties specifying the manner of sharing, that person shares equally with his co-authors. That share remains constant into the renewal period as well, unless the parties, by agreement, change the method of sharing and without regard to the fact that the share itself may be subdivided in the course of time by will, gift, intestacy, or otherwise.

Sec. 10.5. Transmutation of Authorship Into Ownership

Assuming no agreement as to the method of sharing among co-authors, the status of co-authorship per se transmutes each contributor at the moment that the status has been fixed into the democracy of equal ownership. The fixation is two-fold. Each contributor must furnish the minimum necessary to satisfy the legal requirements of a fusion of effort into the work as a unitary whole and the work as so fused must have the form of a writing in the broadest sense which is capable of copyright. If A and B achieve a fusion of effort as a unitary whole in

---

[29] Nimmer, *op. cit., supra,* note 10, "Thus copyright in a photograph will belong to the photographer and not the subject and the work will not be regarded as commissioned if the photograph was taken at the request of and for the benefit of the photographer or where the photographer took the picture on his own initiative and at his own expense." Sec. 63, at p. 246.

[30] Note 9, *supra.*

the nature of ideas or even a format not reduced to writing, they may indeed be collaborators in the generic sense of laboring together, but they are not authors. Their fused effort has not achieved written form.

The legal designation of the status of equal ownership to co-authors is the analogue of the doctrine of irreducible minimum of originality in copyright law as a prerequisite for copyrightability. That doctrine enunciates the "cop out", censorship aside, of the law as a purveyor of the arts. The term "cop out" here is not intended to be used in a censorious way to suggest that the role and function of the law in copyright is to set qualitative standards of what is or is not meritorious as a literary or artistic work. Rather the term is used in the sense of a voluntary withdrawal by the law as a harbinger of taste. In short, the law deliberately withdraws from qualitative analysis except to the minimum extent necessary to determine standards for copyrightability.

Sec. 10.5(a). Sole Author

In the case of the single author, the grant of copyright upon compliance with such standards and, of course, the formalities of notice, etc., completes for the time being the function of the law as the instrumentality of permitting the property to seek its own way in the market. For, *ipso facto*, the sole author thereby has complete ownership. Here one is looking at the totality of our copyright jurisprudence, i.e., common law copyright and statutory copyright. The qualification of the work for copyright, be it under common law copyright or statutory copyright, is sufficient to bring the individual total ownership thereof into being at the instant of creation. Then, assuming the work is copyrightable under the statute and he does not dedicate it to the public domain by publication without notice of copyright, his total ownership inheres through the original term of copyright and, if he survives, into and through the renewal copyright.

Sec. 10.5(b). Co-Authors

With respect to co-authors, there is also a transmutation of authorship into ownership in like manner. But there is one difference. At this point, the law must determine respective shares of ownership among contributors. The law declines to become a critic of the arts and posits a merger of the efforts of all contributors into a unitary whole. This does not necessarily mean that the components of the unitary whole may not have aspects of physical attribution. If a song is deemed by the law to be a unitary whole of music of A and lyrics of B, it will not, in respect of the work as a unitary whole, i.e., as a song, go back and seek to assess the extent of the contribution of each. It will not sunder the merged work in any manner for the purpose of determining proportions of ownership. Thus, if A writes the book, B, the music and C and D, the lyrics, it will not attribute values of one-third each to book, music and lyrics so that C and D would each receive an undivided one-sixth (1/6) ownership interest. This would imply a qualitative judgment that book, music and lyrics are equal in merit and therefore should share in that proportion. This may in fact be the rationale of the collaborators. If so, they must secure that proportion by agreement. Rather, the law declines to make such literary judgments.

Instead, it concludes that the parties, having determined to work together, have decided to spread the benefits in like manner, absent some express arrangement to share otherwise. Thus, like the "one person, one vote" analogy in apportionment, the law imputes a division among co-authors by a head count, one co-author, one equal undivided share. Considering the myriad ways in which co-authorship may arise, the law is wise in not injecting itself needlessly into the mathematics of co-authorship.

Having said as much, the writer does not thereby mean to infer that the generic formula of the law is, in and of itself, fair to the particular co-authors. Suppose a song is composed by A, with lyrics by B, C and D. A may feel that he is entitled to 50% of the ownership of the tune. Yet under the doctrine of the *Sweet* case,[31] A, B, C, and D would each receive 25% of the undivided ownership. Practically speaking, A might have B, C and D agree that A receives 50% and the others 16⅔% each. In all likelihood this would not be reflected in a written agreement prior to the execution of a songwriter's agreement by A, B, C, and D with the music publisher, assigning the copyright and right to copyright to the latter and specifying therein the respective royalty shares of each.[32]

Sec. 10.6. Joint Ownership Combinations and Ownership Interests

Again the permutations and combinations of co-authorship are legion. In addition to the functional division by the nature of the contribution, e.g., book, music, lyrics, ideas, scripts, there may be more than one contributor in any given category and contributors may overlap in the categories in which they contribute to the work. In a great variety of situations, the equal sharing of ownership by head count might be deemed unfair by the creators themselves. It is therefore incumbent upon counsel, producers, managers, the parties themselves and others

---

[31] *Ibid.*

[32] Form Nos. 6B-1.1a-b in Volumes of Forms.

directly affected by the fact of co-authorship to ascertain the intent of the collaborators as to manner of sharing. Here one refers to producers, such as in the theatre, who would not normally own the work as employer for hire as in motion pictures and television. Thus, a music publisher acquiring the copyright in a song from co-authors would be well advised to insist upon a breakdown of shares of co-authors in writing. Otherwise the music publisher might find itself in a cross-fire of conflicting claims of ownership of shares of royalties. Of course, this happens anyway since the music publisher pays royalties respectively in accordance with the shares shown in the songwriter's agreement. But suppose, for some reason, the breakdown specified is 100% to A as lyricist and A and B as composers. This is the converse of the *Sweet* case[33] where A and B wrote the lyrics and A, the music. If the agreement provided that such 100% be turned over to the manager or agent for A and B, then perhaps the burden of determining division might be shifted to such manager or agent. Suppose, in the above illustration, the co-authors never actually determined the method of sharing and that each assumed different proportions as to the method of sharing. That is, A assumed he would receive 75% and B, 25%, whereas B assumed equal sharing. Until royalties are actually received, the assumptions of the respective co-authors might never be stated. Thus, upon the payment by the music publisher of the first monies to the manager or agent of A and B, without any contractual breakdown specified as among A and B as to their shares, a problem arises. Does the music publisher have a duty, as a matter of law, to specify the respective shares? Presumably he does not, since he might be deemed to have understandably relied on the decision in the *Sweet* case that, upon making its

[33] Note 9, *supra.*

distribution of 100% owed to the manager or agent, its obligation was discharged. Now suppose A and B fail to agree as to the manner of division and the manager or agent in his wisdom arbitrarily determines to distribute the proceeds—less his commission—in the way contended for by one or the other of the co-authors, such manager or agent either having eschewed the path of seeking a declaratory judgment as too expensive or, more likely, being unaware of the remedy, or dismissing the same as too cumbersome and too inefficacious in the premises. One of the co-authors thereby receives what he believes to be an unfair share. He seeks relief in the courts, joining his co-author and the manager or agent as co-defendants, and very likely the music publisher, in order to bind them by the hoped for determination of the court in his favor.

Since the songwriter's agreement provided for 100% distribution to the aggregate of the co-authors, specifying the nature of the contribution, but not the respective shares, the music publisher may well have earned for itself the headaches and expense of a lawsuit when it might have avoided all controversy by the simple expedient of setting forth the precise manner of division, i.e., equally or in some other proportion.

The advisability of prompt determination of the method of sharing among the parties cannot be overemphasized. This is eminently desirable because the law has determined upon a practical method of sharing by equal head-count as the most expedient way out of innumerable variants of co-authorship where the parties themselves have not reduced their collaboration to agreement as to method of sharing. The *Sweet* case,[34] which represents the application of the doctrine of co-tenancy to copyright insofar as

---

[34] *Ibid.*

method of sharing is concerned, is an invitation to co-authors to tend to their arrangement of interests *inter sese* if they do not intend to rely upon the common law formulation of undivided equal interests.

For the fact of the matter is that the common law regulates the incidents of co-authorship in the absence of agreement among the parties. As stated by the Court in *Ferrer* v. *Columbia Pictures Corporation,* "The fact that plaintiff and Davies may have collaborated without a so-called 'collaboration agreement' is of no consequence. The determination of whether a product is a 'joint work' is in no way dependent upon the existence of any expressed 'collaboration agreement'." [35]

What the creators in fact do is determinative of co-authorship with a legally permissible fusion of efforts into a unitary whole. Robert L. Sanders has written a cantata for narrator, soprano, chorus, brass instruments and percussion to the entire text of Walt Whitman's poem, "Song of Myself".[36] The copyright, of course, will inhere in the new material, but in fact composer Sanders has created a joint work consisting of music by Robert L. Sanders and text by Walt Whitman. If the joint work is assigned to a music publishing company, as is likely, then presumably the copyright in the cantata, i.e., the merged, unitary work will be in that company. Monies would be received by it for license of mechanicals, performances and for publication of the score and text assuming marketability of the work. Users would pay because the cantata is under copyright. Royalties would then be paid 100% to Sanders, the

---

[35] 149 U.S.P.Q. 236, 237 (Sup. Ct. Westch. Cty. 1966).

[36] Review by Peter G. Davis in New York Times, Tues., April 21, 1970, at p. 47, cols. 1 and 2 reports the same under headline, "Janus Chorale Gives Premiere of A Cantata to Whitman's Text."

composer. Although Walt Whitman is deemed a co-author and the poem is in the public domain, who is to gainsay the demand of the composer for 100% of the royalties and not 50% under the equal sharing formula among co-authors? If Walt Whitman had an heir alive, he could neither enjoin Sanders' creation of the cantata nor recover a 50% author's share since the Whitman text is in the public domain. The copyright inheres in the new material created by Sanders and so the heir is not entitled to share. The attribution of co-authorship to Whitman as author of the text, while Sanders receives 100% of the copyright royalties would represent a correct result.

The predicate of this is that ownership, rewards of ownership and control vest in the co-authors who contribute to that copyright material which is copyrightable. There is a divergence here of law and art. For literary and artistic purposes, Walt Whitman is acknowledged as the co-creator of the work in that a major part of it, to wit, his poem, was utilized as the text of the cantata. Indeed, it may be presumed that a principal reason for utilization of the text by Sanders is that Walt Whitman is a major American poet. The value of the cantata is correspondingly enhanced. As a literary and artistic work, the contribution of Whitman as creator of the text is given full credit. But in law the interest of the heirs of Walt Whitman, or of the state by escheat in the absence of heirs, is nil for the text is in the public domain.

Now let us take the text of a poet not in the public domain. Assume that composer A writes a cantata to text of a poem by poet B. Assume, too, that B is alive and the copyright in the poem is owned by him. Under one theory, if B, of course, authorizes the creation of the cantata by A, then A has a copyright in the new material added thereto, as a derivative work under Sec. 7 of the Copyright Law.[37] The work may be a derivative work insofar as the original poem of B is concerned. But it is submitted that the cantata is nonetheless a joint work between A and B. The result is the same as though a song were composed with music by A and lyrics by B and the parties intended to fuse their efforts into the creation of a song. Here, too, B authorized A to create the cantata. It is immaterial whether or not A and B worked together, A wrote the music to B's lyrics to create the song, or vice versa.

In respect of the cantata, it is conceivable that A or his music publisher obtained the rights from B or his book publisher to use the poem as the text of a cantata. If so, A or his music publisher either paid a flat sum or advanced a sum against royalties. The underlying agreement would be one between A and his music publisher providing for A's share of royalties, while another agreement would subsist between A or his music publisher and B or his publisher, specifying B's share as aforesaid. In A's contemplation and very likely in that of his music publisher, the work is primarily a work of music with copyright derived from A after the necessary rights were obtained to B's text.

As far as original term is concerned, it would make little difference how the work is viewed as long as the copyright interest is wholly owned by the music publisher. Control follows ownership, and as sole owner, the music publisher is in the identical position vis-à-vis original term of copyright as though the work were entirely created by A. Problems would arise on renewal if the creators were not living, or if only A were alive and had assigned the renewal copyright to his music publisher.

---

[37] 17 U.S.C. 7.

For the renewal term, being a new estate with a renewal copyright, is actually a further term of copyright in the *original* work with the rights of ownership therein determined by the statutory devolution under Sec. 24 of the Copyright Act[38] in respect of the undivided interests of each of the creators of the work. If B is to be deemed a co-author of the cantata and does not survive to the renewal term, then A's music publisher, assuming A's survival and assignment by A to his music publisher, does not automatically acquire B's interest in the renewal copyright. Per contra, A's music publisher would either have to acquire B's interest from the next succeeding class under the statute, e.g., widow and children—at a price—or else risk B's license of his undivided interest to another publisher. The result in that event would be the classic "split copyright". A's music publisher would acquire an undivided interest in the cantata and B's publisher would likewise.

As stated by the Court in the *Ferrer* case, "The law is settled that those in the position of 'collaborators' or 'joint authors' of a literary work stand in the position of tenants in common with respect to such work, and that either of the collaborators, without the consent of the other, may grant a license to use and deal with the work. The grantee or licensee from a joint author may not be considered an infringer and may not otherwise be prevented by any other alleged joint author from dealing with the work pursuant to the terms of the license."[39]

Where the creators have not specified by agreement their respective shares of ownership in the work, the law will impute that they share equally. Thus, if A and B were to

---

[38] 17 U.S.C. 24.

[39] Note 35, *supra*, at p. 236.

write a song without setting forth their respective interests, in the above illustration of a split copyright, A's music publisher would acquire an undivided one-half interest in the work and B's music publisher, a like interest.

In *Ferrer,* plaintiff Jose Ferrer sought to enjoin defendant, Columbia Pictures Corporation, from producing and distributing a film "The Long Ships" claiming that he had collaborated in the writing of the screen play with one Davies, claiming that the defendant was without right to use his material because it had failed to acquire rights from him. Since Ferrer claimed to be a co-author with Davies of the screenplay, the Court granted defendant's motion for summary judgment for the reasons stated above.[40]

The theory for the *Ferrer*[41] rationale is aptly stated in *Richmond* v. *Weiner*.[42] In that case, involving a dispute between erstwhile joint venturers, one of the issues was that of co-authorship. The Court stated, "Since that book and its parts were so jointly conceived, compiled and created by the joint efforts of both appellant and appellee and 'equity regards as done that which ought to be done' (19 Am. Jur. 316), appellant although having the copyrights registered in appellant's name only held the same in trust for the joint venture and appellant and appellee as its two members. Appellee, therefore, was and is at all material times in lawful right a joint owner with appellant of the copyrights covering the book Medical Practice Informant and its parts. Edward B. Marks Music Corp. v. Jerry Vogel Music Co., 2 Cir. 1955, 140 F. 2d 266, 268. As such owner appellee could not and did not infringe

---

40 *Ibid.*

41 Note 35, *supra.*

42 353 F. 2d 41 (9th Cir. 1965).

such copyrights, and we agree with the Trial Court in so ruling."[43]

Sec. 10.7. Rights of Joint Authors and Joint Owners

The rationale of this decision would appear to be that the co-author is deemed an author of the merged work as a unitary whole, regardless of the nature and extent of his contribution thereto, so long as he is a co-author. This would be so, too, irrespective of the extent of his undivided interest therein. In legal contemplation, he may do with the work whatever he wishes, use the work, license it, divest himself of his interest, and so on. Each co-author is in a like position. Each is deemed to be owner, limited only by the fact that others are similarly situated. This is not the operation of a legal fiction, but an acknowledgment of the realities of the actual legal position of each, predicated on the premise that as soon as co-authorship is established, the work for legal purposes is deemed the work of all regardless of the specific contribution of each. Thus, each co-author may license the work as he pleases,[44] or use it as he pleases,[45] short of destruction of the *res* by grossly unfair exploitation constituting waste,[46] absent any agreement requiring mutual consent therefor.[47] If he does not infringe, because as an owner he cannot infringe his own work, so his licensee does not infringe because his rights

---

[43] *Idem* at p. 46.

[44] Jerry Vogel Music Co., Inc. v. Miller Music, Inc., 272 App. Div. 571, 74 N.Y.S. 2d 425 (1st Dept. 1947).

[45] Note 42, *supra*.

[46] Brown v. Republic Productions, Inc., 26 Cal. 2d 867, 161 P. 2d 796 (1945), cf. Shapiro, Bernstein & Co., Inc. v. Jerry Vogel Music Co., Inc., 73 F. Supp. 165 (S.D.N.Y. 1947).

[47] Meredith v. Smith, 145 F. 2d 620 (9th Cir. 1944).

are derived from him as owner. So, too, he may assign his ownership interest and the assignee is free to use the work because an owner cannot infringe his own copyright.

Sec. 10.8. Accounting Among Joint Owners

The courts long ago abandoned the no accounting rule as to copyrights in the early Maine case of *Carter* v. *Bailey*.[48] In *Maurel* v. *Smith,* Judge Learned Hand stated, ". . . the plaintiff's rights arise from a constructive trust, created and cognizable only by a court of equity . . . The copyright is the resulting res, and by every equitable rule the defendants hold any legal rights they have upon trust in the same proportion." [49] A year later, the Court in *Klein* v. *Beach* stated, "Here both Beach and Klein became the owners of Klein's drama, and each could then do with it what he pleased, with the duty of accounting over. Beach could license Klein's dramatic version for the screen, and Klein could do the same thing; and, of course, they each could license others to produce the Klein play on the stage. But in all these instances one would be obliged to account to the other." [50]

Moreover, a failure to renew by one co-author is not fatal to his ownership in the renewal period. Thus, in *Edward B. Marks Music Corp.* v. *Jerry Vogel Music Co.,*

---

[48] 64 Me. 458 (1874). This decision followed the patent rule of no accounting among joint inventors, 1 Walker on Patents, Sec. 118 at p. 406 (Deller Ed. 1937). See Taubman, Joint Authorship and Co-Ownership in American Copyright Law. 31 N.Y.U.L. Rev. 1246 (1956).

[49] 220 Fed. 195, 201 (S.D.N.Y. 1915).

[50] 232 Fed. 240, 247 (S.D.N.Y. 1916), *aff'd,* 239 Fed. 108 (2d Cir. 1917).

Inc.,[51] lyricist Edward B. Marks renewed in 1920 but composer Loraine never renewed. Judge Learned Hand ruled as to their song "December and May" that " . . . when Marks took out the renewal of the song, he took it for the benefit of himself and Loraine, and that the legal title which he so acquired he held in trust for Loraine and Loraine's assignee. If so, he could not forbid that assignee from exploiting the subject matter of their right." [52] Ball has characterized this rule as follows: "The renewal copyright obtained by a co-author of a joint production embraces the whole work." [53]

The rule as to reciprocal accounting was stated by the Court of Appeals in *Shapiro, Bernstein & Co., Inc.* v. *Jerry Vogel Music, Inc.*[54] in effect providing that the proceeds of each co-owner of the copyright go into hotchpot for cross accounting over. Accounting is provided for license or use.[55] However, the licensee of co-owner A is accountable only to A and not to co-owner B where the license is from A only.[56]

The obligation to account is in a sense the corollary of ownership. If they are co-owners, A and B are entitled to share equally. Like the rules of joint tenancy as to real property, if a co-tenant receives more than his just share of the rents and profits he is required to account to his

---

[51] 140 F. 2d 266 (2d Cir. 1944), *aff'g* 47 F. Supp. 490 (S.D.N.Y. 1942).

[52] *Idem* at p. 268.

[53] Ball, Law of Copyright and Literary Property, Sec. 91, at pp. 202-203 (1944).

[54] 223 F. 2d 252 (2d Cir. 1955), modifying 221 F. 2d 569 (2d Cir. 1955).

[55] Nimmer, *op. cit., supra,* note 10, Sec. 79.

[56] Brown v. Republic Productions, Inc., note 46, *supra.*

co-tenants for the excess.[57] Thus, the rewards of copyright ownership are intended to be distributed fairly. This would accord with the intent of the constitutional clause,[58] to benefit the public and reward the authors.[59] As to this, Chief Justice Hughes stated, "Copyright is a right exercised by the owner during the term at his pleasure and exclusively for his own profit and forms the basis for extensive and profitable business enterprises."[60]

Thus, the accounting rules formulated by the courts are intended as an adjunct of fairness and reward to all of the co-authors and their assignees. The rationale is absolute freedom in each co-owner or assignee thereof to exploit the entire copyright in the joint work subject only to accounting over.[61]

Sec. 10.9. Destruction of the Work and Accounting

While there are conflicting views as to what might or might not constitute waste of a copyright,[62] it is an extremely difficult matter to apply with any certainty. Oil and gas are wasting assets; hence the rationale for the depletion allowance. But in copyright, new uses are constantly arising as to existing literary and artistic works. Consider, for example, new filmic uses of existing material in audio-visual cassettes, home television recorders and

---

[57] Walsh, Law of Property, Sec. 208 (2d Ed. 1934); New York Real Property Law, Sec. 532.

[58] Constitution of the United States, Art. I, Sec. 8, Clause 8.

[59] Fox Film Corp. v. Doyal, 286 U.S. 123 (1932).

[60] *Idem* at p. 130.

[61] Nimmer, *op cit., supra.* Sec. 77.3, underscores the desirability of all joint owners joining in the grant of a license in foreign jurisdictions, however.

[62] Note 46, *supra.*

cable TV. The history of television, in part, is the history of new uses of motion pictures made originally for exhibition in the theatre.[63] Of course, any given use affects possible other uses and may lessen its marketability. This has been well stated by Judge Bright:

> ". . . it seems reasonable that copyright business, in songs at least, indulged in by one co-owner, practically precludes the other from a like use. The use of one owner, by license or personally, in motion pictures, on the stage, by radio, in advertising, in bands or orchestras, can destroy, practically, the copyright so far as the other is concerned. It has been said that copyright, being an incorporeal right, cannot be destroyed. But its broad use by an active publisher can so far exhaust the popularity of a song, or any other musical composition, as to destroy its value after that use has ended. And the destruction of value of a copyright is, in effect, a destruction of the copyright."[64]

A contrary view has been expressed by Judge Schauer as follows:

> "Whether a destruction resulted was an issue of fact requiring proof by competent evidence. The use to which parts of the composition were put by defen-

---

[63] See, for example, U.S. v. T.C.-Fox Film Corp., 137 F. Supp. 78 (S.D. Cal. 1955) alleging a conspiracy in restraint of trade for failure to release films to television. Cohn, Old Licenses and New Uses, Motion Pictures and Television, 19 Law and Cont. Probs. 184 (1954); Silverberg, Televising Old Films—Some New Legal Questions About Performers and Proprietors' Rights 38 Va. L. Rev. 615 (1952).

[64] Shapiro, Bernstein & Co., Inc. v. Jerry Vogel Music Co., Inc., 73 F. Supp. 165 at p. 168 (S.D. N.Y. 1947).

dants does not by itself show destruction of the original composition or plaintiff's rights therein. Under the judgment plaintiff is to be recompensed for the rights in the rewritten composition. This, in itself, is in a measure inconsistent with the theory that he has been wholly deprived of his rights in and under the original literary property; his interest in and right under the revised composition necessarily derive only from his interest in and right under the original. Hence such rights are being recognized and given efficacy rather than being wholly destroyed." [65]

The contrast of the two positions indicates that there is a wide range between normal exploitation of a work which, by its very nature, might conceivably lessen interest in the work and the virtual termination of the market by reason of the particular license and exploitation thereof. The difficulty with literary and artistic works is that it is virtually impossible to prognosticate the actual success or failure of a work. *Ex post facto* post mortems are not the most reliable gauge. The vagaries of the market are considerable. One can only posit that the facts of each case must be considered *sui generis* as to destruction of the *res,* the copyright. One can only assert that the likelihood for destruction is small. Consider the facts in *Jerry Vogel Music Co., Inc.* v. *Miller Music, Inc.*[66] There Universal Pictures sought a license to use a tune, "I Love You California" in a film from the respective assignees of the co-authors. Obviously the tune was under split copyright. Universal was quoted a price of $1,000 by plaintiff and only $200 by defendant. Is this a normal gradual impair-

---

[65] Brown v. Republic Productions, Inc., 26 Cal. 2d 867, 869-870, 161 P. 2d 796, 798 (1945).

[66] 272 App. Div. 571, 74 N.Y.S. 2d 425 (1st Dept. 1947).

ment of the market so that plaintiff has to settle for its share of $200, 50% thereof, rather than for its share of $1,000? Who knows? If a film were a hit at the box-office, it might spark numerous mechanical licenses from co-owners of a split copyright. On the other hand, if the tune were commercially unsuccessful it might seriously affect the licensing of that tune for mechanicals. Of course, exclusive licensing of synchronization rights of particular music could exclude other licensing. One could go on and on in speculation without any firm conclusion.

Sec. 10.10. The Role of Renewals in Joint Authorship and Joint Ownership

It is to be noted that if the author does not survive to the 28th year, a member of the next succeeding class must so survive. The rule as to prior assignment of an expectancy by such a member is the same as that for an author. There must be survival to the 28th year in order for the right of renewal under the assignment of the expectancy by that member to be operative. As stated by the Court in *Cresci* v. *Music Publishers Holding Corp.*, "The rights of adult children of an author to assign their renewal expectancies do not differ from those of the author himself or of his widow who succeeds to the right of renewal only as a member of a class which includes the children." [67] Thus, if members of the second class fail to survive under the statutory rules of succession to renewals,[68] the executors would then have the right to renew personally as representatives of the legatees.[69] If however, the executors have been discharged in the interim, the

[67] 210 F. Supp. 253, 258 (S.D. N.Y. 1962).

[68] 17 U.S.C. 24.

[69] Miller Music Corp. v. Charles N. Daniels, Inc., 362 U.S. 373 (1960).

renewals would probably be vested in the next of kin rather than in an administrator.[70]

The renewal application must be taken in the name of the author, if living, or, if not, in the name of a member of the next class, if living, and not in the name of the assignee even if made by the assignee.[71] Assignments of renewal expectancies are deemed assignments under the recording statute,[72] and should be recorded within three months of execution within the United States and within six months of execution outside this country after renewal in order to defeat the claims of any subsequent purchaser for value without notice who has recorded his assignment.[73]

Bearing in mind that renewal copyright is principally a domestic phenomenon,[74] we can now draw the necessary conclusions of the immense practical importance of the

---

[70] Silverman v. Sunrise Pictures Corporation, 273 Fed. 909 (2d Cir. 1921), 290 Fed. 804 (2d Cir. 1923), cert. den. 262 U.S. 758 (1923), cf. Gibran v. National Committee of Gibran, 255 F. 2d 121 (2d Cir. 1958). In that case, no executor was named and the defendants were serving as administrators c.t.a.

[71] Regulations of the Copyright Office, Sec. 202.17(b) "Renewal claims may be registered only in the names of persons falling within one of the classes of renewal claimants specified in the copyright law." Sec. 24 of the Copyright Law, second proviso grants to the author the right of renewal "if still living, or the widow, widower or children of the author, if the author be not living, or if such author, widow, widower, or children be not living, then the author's executors, or in the absence of a will, his next of kin . . . "

[72] 17 U.S.C. 30.

[73] Rossiter v. Vogel, 134 F. 2d 908, 911 (2d Cir. 1943); see Bricker, Renewal and Extension of Copyright, 29 So. Cal. L. Rev. 23, 35 (1955).

[74] Renewal copyright is in effect only in the United States and the Philippines, which presumably followed the American experience when it adopted the renewal term.

operation of the principle of fission of ownership in the co-ownership. The fusion of effort of the joint authorship has the effect of merger of the contributions of two or more co-authors into a unitary whole with operative co-ownership at the instant of creation. Thus, apart from renewals, and the common law delineation of the formula of equal sharing among co-authors on the theory of co-tenancy, joint ownership principles are substantially the same whether the co-ownership originates out of co-authorship or subsequent division into undivided interests in a work of single authorship. Renewals merely sustain the principle of co-authorship into the new estate of the renewal term. The fusion of effort stays merged throughout the original term and the renewal term so that just as a co-author may copyright in his own name in trust for the benefit of his co-authors so the renewal copyright effects the same result.[75] A renewal by a co-author therefore constitutes a renewal in trust for the benefit of his co-author or the next succeeding class of his co-author if not living.

Thus, it may be seen that for all practical purposes the *res,* the work under copyright, stays the same as to its nature, whether singly or jointly created, but ownership thereof is subject to multiplication. The principle of fission of undivided ownership interests therein is operative from the inception of co-authorship by the fact of joint creation itself. Thereafter, it becomes in nature substantially like the work of the single author. Changes of ownership may originate in the same manner other ownership interests may arise—by assignment, transfer by will or the laws

---

[75] Assuming here no dissolution of a work, a song, for example, into its component parts by agreement, e.g., composer A and lyricist B subsequently agree to separate the music, which reverts to A, from the title and lyrics, which revert to B, so that the joint work no longer exists.

of intestate succession, gift, or operation of the renewal statute. Assignment, transfer by will or gift may transfer the entire copyright if there is a single author, but not necessarily so. There may be two or more assignees, legatees or donees who would then take undivided interests in the manner specified in the instrument effecting the transfer. In the absence of such specification, presumably they would take undivided equal interests as co-tenants. Whatever the single author does as to his copyright to assure single ownership may be thwarted as to the renewal estate by non-survival of the author to the renewal period. The same result might very well follow if the author should die without making a will providing for transfer of his copyrights. If there is no will, then one would look to the laws of intestate succession to ascertain who inherits. If the author is survived by a widow and children, they share ownership of the copyrights in undivided interests in the proportion set forth in the statutes as to descent and distribution of the particular state having jurisdiction.

But copyright under present law in the United States is measured by an original term, from date of publication if the work is published, and from date of registration if it is a statutory copyright in an unpublished work, with the renewal term following upon the expiration thereof. This means that each copyright has its own separate period to be measured, unlike copyright in Europe, for example, where term is measured by the life of the author plus a fixed number of years after his death, e.g., 50 years after death. The effect of this is that survivorship as a prerequisite of renewal and vesting of the expectancy has to be determined seriatim as to each copyright as it reaches its 28th year of original term. Thus, not only cannot one tell in advance whether an assignment of the author will ever become more than an expectancy by vesting due to his survivorship, but the same tests will be applicable to his widow and children long after his death. Thus, if an author dies and his widow and children assign their renewal interests thereafter, until each respective copyright goes into its 28th year, the assignee has only an expectancy as to the widow and each child. If the widow should die in the renewal period of some copyrights, these will have vested so that her rights therein belong to her estate. As to copyrights going into their 28th year of original term after her death, her rights therein will not have vested because as to her they were only an expectancy. She will have no renewal interest therein. Her assignee will not derive an undivided interest in such copyrights through her and her estate will have no rights therein. By rights therein after vesting, one refers to the royalty contract and rights to receive royalties which would go to the estate of the widow from the music publisher, by reason of the vesting of her expectancy by survival to the 28th year of the copyright, her husband having died prior thereto.

In respect of a co-authorship the principles of fission by renewal, death, or transfer inter vivos operate in the same manner as to the undivided interest of each co-author. Thus if A writes the music and B, the lyrics, and they are each 50% owners of an undivided interest in their song, each can treat his share, for purposes of fission, as though his co-owner did not exist. A can bequeath his 50% undivided interest, allow it to go by intestacy, transfer it by gift or assign it. B, independently of A, can do the same. The principle would be identical if there were three owners, A for music, B for lyrics and C for a book in a musical play. Each could do as he pleased as to his undivided interest; here it would be 33⅓% if there is no other agreed division. Now if four persons collaborate on a joint work, for example, book by A, music by B, and lyrics by C and D, they might, by their collaboration agreement, agree to share in the proportion of 33⅓% to each of A and B and one-half of 33⅓% to each of C and D. Again the principle of fission by each co-author as to his undivided interest would be operative.

Then, too, if some of the works have been written by the co-authors as employees for hire, e.g., for a music publisher on weekly salary, plus stipulated royalties, or for a motion picture producer by a composer and lyricist by way of flat sum plus royalties, then the renewal estate would not be in the co-authors, but in the employers for hire. Thus, in the event of the death of a co-author, as to such copyrights, the renewal term would not be in the widow and children of such author, but in the employer. That means that copyright royalties from such copyrights would be owned by the estate of the deceased co-author in the renewal period. By contrast, if the joint work were created not by way of employment for hire, then the renewal copyright would belong to the widow and children surviving into the 28th year of each such original term of copyright, the co-author from whom they derived such rights not surviving.

One must, therefore, determine the character of the copyright to ascertain the status of ownership thereof. Chain of title would follow therefrom, as well as the capacity in which the persons would take. Thus, the same widow and children might conceivably take as legatees under the will, by intestacy in the absence of a will, and by operation of the renewal statute, Sec. 24 of the Copyright Law.[76] The respective means of obtaining undivided interests must be ascertained in the course of tracing the devolution of ownership in each work. The ascertaining of the means of

---

[76] 17 U.S.C. 24.

achieving ownership, in turn, determines the method of division of ownership, but not in every instance. Since there are no decisions nor statutory guidance as to the class of women and children, the members of that class must first come to some agreement as to the method of sharing as members of that class.

Sec. 10.11. Joint Authorship, Joint Ownership, Renewals and Commerce

One must, therefore, conclude that copyright devolution in the possibilities of joint ownership, and even more so in works of joint authorship, are labyrinthian. Thus, at the point where rights are determined as an adjunct of commerce, principally in the form of ownership interests, be it of the entire copyright or of undivided interests therein, the legal facets alone of determination thereof are extraordinarily complex. The corollary is the elaboration of institutions dedicated to overcoming the problems—maintenance by large companies in the copyright industries of rights and permissions departments, title and copyright departments, specialized firms whose business it is to prepare title and copyright reports for a fee,[77] as well as copyright lawyers with the requisite expertise to evaluate not only such reports but to direct searches made at the Copyright Office.[78]

Thus, creativity in the performing arts, in terms of literary and artistic works, is not simply a matter of looking to the creator, as distinguished from the performer, to ascertain the starting point for bringing the work into com-

---

[77] E.g. Johnson & Tannenbaum in New York City, Seidel, Gonda and Goldhammer in Philadelphia and Fulton Brylawski in Washington, D.C.

[78] The Copyright Office will undertake a search as to any given copyright upon payment of specified fees therefor.

merce. Managers and administrators must take cognition of the fact that the other side of the coin of creation is ownership and that the facets of both are independently complex and are often inextricably interwoven in strands of further complexity, wherein it is often the role of the lawyer to unravel the same. Moreover, the interplay in depth is such that veritably estate planning may be involved for proper consideration of the creative output when viewed as a whole. Here, copyright expertise must join with broader considerations of tax planning, prognostication of devolution and marketing prospects over an extended period of time. Given the pervasiveness of joint authorship and the ramifications of co-ownership, the sequential roll must take into account that each co-owner can, in effect, institute his owner linear sequential roll as to his undivided interest in a work and the flow of derivative works stemming therefrom, subject to the ability of counsel, managers and administrators to channelize such fission by further fusion of ownership by assignment of a single assignee, coalescence of interests in a trustee or trustees, or otherwise by agreement of the co-owners.

Chapter XI

COPYRIGHT OWNERSHIP AND JURISDICTION

Sec. 11.1. Jurisdiction and Sovereignty

Thus far copyright has been treated principally as a domestic concern. The sequential roll has been viewed from the ambit of its effect principally in the United States. Moreover, authorship and co-authorship have been assumed to be American and perforce, co-ownership, American. However, to the complexities of the domestic scene must be added further complications as the international scene is examined from the perspective of ingress and egress. Authors are not only American; they may be foreign nationals residing abroad, resident aliens or stateless persons. Nationality and citizenship bring additional rules into play in the copyright arena in terms of the domestic scene. Similarly, they affect what happens in copyright in the foreign area.

Whoever expects to find neat categorization had better look elsewhere, for rules of law have developed in a context of national and international law. Moreover, what is denominated as national and international law are, in a sense, different jurisprudences. Each would appear to have its own theory as its basis for being. National law is a function of sovereignty; international law is based upon accord or convention of sovereign states. National law, in theory, may be based upon compact—consent of the governed. It may stem from force as the after-effect of dictatorship or absolute monarchy. It may claim legitimacy through history, as in the monarchical line going back generations or centuries. Its roots may be in religion, as in a theocracy. Whatever its basis, government enforces rules of law because the state is deemed to be sovereign. International law, on the other hand, is not based upon cession of power by the respective states to a supra-national authority of international law. Rather, the respective sovereign states enter into agreements bi-laterally or multi-laterally, by treaties, proclamation, and conventions. Internationalism is not a form of federalism, wherein the respective sovereign states have ceded a part of their power to the federal authority, which is paramount in the ceded area, and wherein cession is generally not permitted, as in the United States in respect of its Civil War and the recent attempt at secession by Biafra from Nigeria. International law is an attempt of the various sovereign states to govern their external relationships by various forms of agreement which, basically, do not cede the fundaments of power to international bodies that might be organized pursuant to treaties, conventions and assembly and from which cession is permissible in theory and in fact either at the expiration of a given period of time or at any time.

In this context, it may be seen that copyright is basically national in scope. This principle is aptly stated by the Court of Appeals in *American Code Co. (Inc.)* v. *Bensinger,* "If a British author, upon publication in England, copyrights his book in that country, the copyright protects him in that country; but, unless he has also copyrighted the work in the United States, his English copyright affords him no protection against any one who brings out in this country a piratical edition of the work. *The copyright laws of one country have no extraterritorial operation, unless otherwise provided.* (Ferris v. Frohman, 223 U.S. 424, 32 Sup. Ct. 263, 56 L. Ed. 492.)"[1]

[1] 282 Fed. 829, 833 (2d Cir. 1922) (emphasis added). Accord as to first recording of music, Beechwood Music Corporation v. Vee

In this regard, Nimmer has observed, "Copyright laws do not have any extraterritorial operation, and hence the only remedies available are under the law of the nation where the infringing acts occur."[2] However, a distinction must be made here between rights under copyright and determination of ownership. This was stated by the Court in *Brecht* v. *Bentley* as follows: "It by no means follows that because a proprietor under American Copyright Law is given no rights against an infringing foreign publication that his rights of ownership may not descend by the law of a foreign domicile."[3]

Sec. 11.2. Jurisdiction: Federal vs. State

Thus, ownership would be determined by the law of the owner's domicile. Presumably this would follow the rule that intangibles are to be construed under the laws of the domicile of the owner as the situs of the intangibles. Copyright, being an incorporeal hereditament,[4] is to be governed by the rules of the domicile of the owner as to descent and distribution. So, too, ownership of copyright is to be determined under local law rather than under federal law. In so holding in affirming a ruling of the District Court, the Court of Appeals stated in *T. B. Harms Co.* v. *Eliscu,* "Mindful of the hazards of formulation in this treacherous area, we think that an action 'arises under' the Copyright Act if and only if the complaint is for a

---

Jay Records, Inc., 328 F. 2d 728 (2d Cir. 1964). There recording abroad did not trigger compulsory license on mechanical reproduction in the United States. First use in the U.S. is a predicate to the compulsory license.

[2] Nimmer on Copyright (1969), Sec. 65.61 at p. 263.

[3] 185 F. Supp. 890 (S.D.N.Y. 1960) at p. 893.

[4] Silverman v. Sunrise Pictures Corp., 273 Fed. 909, 910 (2d Cir. 1921).

remedy expressly granted by the Act, e.g., a suit for infringement or for the statutory royalties for record reproduction, 17 U.S.C. Sec. 101, cf. Joy Music, Inc. v. Seeco Records, Inc., 166 F. Supp. 549 (S.D.N.Y. 1958), or asserts a claim requiring construction of the Act, as in De Sylva, or, at the very least and perhaps more doubtfully, presents a case where a distinctive policy of the Act requires that federal principles control the disposition of the claim. The general interest that copyrights, like all other forms of property, should be enjoyed by their true owner is not enough to meet this last test."[5]

Judge Weinfeld in his opinion[6] below cited *Danks* v. *Gordon,*[7] to the effect that a suit charging infringement and asking for injunctive relief and an accounting might in reality be a suit to enforce a contract between an author and a publisher. In *Danks,* the Court enunciated the principle as follows:

> "As respects jurisdiction the statute provides that the district courts shall have original jurisdiction of all suits at law or in equity arising under the copyright laws. If a suit to recover royalties agreed to be paid to an author out of the proceeds realized from the publication and sale of a copyrighted production is one which arises under the copyright laws, then the court not only had jurisdiction, but it had exclusive jurisdiction. (U.S. Compiled Statutes Ann. (1916), vol. 2, p. 1841, sec. 1233, par. 5.) In all such cases it is necessary to distinguish between the copyright and a contract of which the copyright is the subject matter. If

[5] 339 F. 2d 823, 828 (2d Cir. 1964), *aff'g* 226 F. Supp. 337 (S.D.N.Y. 1964), cert. den. 381 U.S. 915 (1965).

[6] 226 F. Supp. 337 (S.D.N.Y. 1964) at p. 340.

[7] 272 Fed. 821 (2d Cir. 1921).

> the suit is one brought to enforce a right based upon a contract which relates to a copyrighted production, the suit is one which arises out of the contract and is not one arising under the copyright statute, and the federal courts are without jurisdiction."[8]

Hence, in determining that the claim in *Eliscu*[9] did not involve infringement of copyright, the parties were therefore in a matter involving determination of ownership, as in construction of contracts, relegated to the state courts. Judge Weinfeld then concluded:

> "On the entire record here presented there is no evidence to support a claim of infringement, actual or threatened, of the four copyrights so as to vest this Court with jurisdiction under the Copyright Act, and accordingly the motion to dismiss for lack of jurisdiction is granted. The claim is one for declaration of ownership of the renewal interest based upon Eliscu's co-authorship of the four compositions—the very issue presented by the pending suit in the Supreme Court of the State of New York. That Court has jurisdiction of the question of title, and, if the facts warrant it, power to compel Eliscu to execute an assignment of his interest and a cancellation of the assignment filed in the copyright office." [10]

Yet, when one examines the determination in the State Court in *Eliscu*[11] as to ownership following the declination

---

[8] *Idem* at p. 827.

[9] Note 6, *supra.*

[10] *Idem* at p. 341.

[11] Eliscu v. T. B. Harms Co., 151 U.S.P.Q. 603 (Sup. Ct. Trial T., N.Y. Cty. 1966).

of jurisdiction by the federal court, one is struck by a certain ambience of the trial court. The trial court determined that the use of the phrase "we engage and employ you" which was found in the written instruments was insufficient to deny plaintiff his renewal right. Plaintiff was co-lyricist with Gus Kahn of four musical compositions for which the music was written by Vincent Youmans. The lyricists, by agreement, granted the motion picture rights to RKO Studios, Inc., and reserved mechanical and publishing rights. Defendant was the assignee of Max Dreyfus who had acquired publishing rights in original term. At the time of the writing of the lyrics, plaintiff was then in the employ of the film studio as a director and the engagement to write the lyrics was an additional assignment. The Court held that plaintiff, Eliscu, was neither an employee nor truly an independent contractor. It adverted to a clause in the agreement authorizing plaintiff to assign his publishing and small performing rights. It then concluded that plaintiff had neither surrendered nor lost his renewal right.

Sec. 11.3. Ownership of Copyright; Authorship; and Jurisdiction

The Court's ambience appears in the fact that ownership as to the renewal right goes back to a determination of ownership in the original term and then tracing the chain of title. In turn, ownership in original term, where there is more than one person involved, is often a function of authorship. Only at the inception of creation may one ascertain authorship and by so doing, ownership, for ownership then is derived by transmutation of authorship into ownership. Here joint authorship was involved. If the issue were purely one of ownership stemming from the interests of co-authors, one might conclude that the determination was entirely a matter of ownership under state law. But the fact is that the agreements probably intended to provide for a hybrid relationship which is not uncommon with composers and lyricists of note who thereby have sufficient leverage to obtain such a relationship even though normally an agreement between a film producer and composer is one of employment for hire.[12]

The film production company insists upon acquiring all rights from the composer in an employment for hire relationship just as it does from the actors, director and individual producer.[13] The purpose of this is to assure that the film is owned by the film production company as employer for hire, thereby enabling it to secure renewal copyright therein as the author and employer for hire.[14] The producer thereby assures copyright ownership will be renewed by it during the renewal term without having to acquire renewal rights from members of succeeding classes under the second proviso of Sec. 24 of the Copyright Law. If we assume that the non-surviving composer, for example, has contributed his music as an independent contractor and even assigns his renewal expectancy, more important even than the possible additional cost for such renewal rights is the risk that widow and children or other succeeding class acquiring the renewal right might decline to grant such renewal rights in any event. The potential danger might even encompass the inability to use the picture unless a brand new sound track were created therefor at considerable expense. Thus, sheer economics of film ownership by way of employment for hire underlie the nature of the form of agreement used.

---

[12] See Form Nos. 1B-6, 1B-6a-b, in Volumes of Forms.
[13] See Form Nos. 1B-1, 1B-1.4 and 1B-2 in Volumes of Forms.
[14] 17 U.S.C. 24, 26.

However, the composer, and where lyrics are involved, composer and lyricist in demand will often try to better the financial possibilities. For an incident of employment for hire relationship is that the publishing rights in such musical compositions will be vested in the motion picture production company. As such it will either exploit the publishing rights through its own music publishing company affiliate or, as is more likely, assign the rights to a music publishing company affiliate of the studio with which the producer is under agreement for financing and distribution of the film by the studio.[15] The composer and lyricist, assuming there are both, would then receive royalties from the music publishing company. But publishing is owned by others and renewal copyright, likewise.

Where, however, composer and lyricist are of sufficient stature to command a better deal in the negotiations leading to their agreement, they will sometimes adopt a hybrid form. The hybrid provides for composer and lyricist acting as employees for hire in respect of the synchronization and performing rights in the music and lyrics created by them for the film, but reserving publishing rights.[16] If the composer and lyricist then assign the publishing rights to their own music publishing company, they obtain additional benefits of ownership of publisher's share by reason of the interest in the music publishing company as well as their renewal copyright therein. Even if they should assign

---

[15] See Form No. 1E-1 in Volumes of Forms. The nature of rights and ownership of music for use in film and TV shows is now in litigation in an antitrust suit. See New York Times, Tues., Feb. 8, 1972, p. 26, cols. 1 and 2, entitled, Film and TV Music Writers File $300 Million Suit on Contracts.

[16] See Form No. 1B-6b in Volumes of Forms. It is a variant form in that the composer shares in publishing but does not acquire the complete music publishing interest.

the music publishing rights to a third party music publishing company so that they do not benefit from the publisher's share, they nevertheless are in a position to bargain for renewal rights upon expiration of the separate copyrights in the music and lyrics in original term, or at least, if they do not survive and have assigned their renewal expectancies therein, their widows and children may benefit therefrom in respect of the renewal term.

It would appear, therefore, that in *Eliscu*[17] the Court perforce had to determine the relationship of the parties as creators under the Copyright Act, specifically Sections 24 and 26.[18] If this is so, how does this differ from *De Sylva* v. *Ballentine*[19] wherein jurisdiction was assumed by the federal courts because the second proviso of Sec. 24 of the Copyright Law was being construed, to wit, the meaning of the phrase "widow, widower *or* children"?[20] In *De Sylva,*[21] the Supreme Court nevertheless resorted to state law, there California, to determine whether an illegitimate child could take as a member of the class. But, since a construction of Sec. 24 of the Copyright Law[22] was primarily at issue, there was jurisdiction in the federal courts.

Joy Music, Inc. v. *Seeco Records, Inc.,*[23] on the other hand, represents an implied construction of a section of the Copyright Law. In denying defendant's motion to dismiss, Judge Weinfeld stated, "Parties remain free to substitute private licensing agreements for the protections afforded them by

---

[17] Note 11, *supra.*
[18] Note 14, *supra.*
[19] 351 U.S. 570 (1956).
[20] 17 U.S.C. 24 (emphasis added).
[21] Note 19, *supra.*
[22] Note 20, *supra.*
[23] 166 F. Supp. 549 (S.D.N.Y. 1958).

section 1(e) of the Copyright Act, 17 U.S.C.A., section 1(e). Whether they have indeed done so is the question presented here. The parties have departed from the exact terms of the statute by varying the accounting period, lowering the royalties for several songs and dispensing with notice requirements. These mutually convenient variations, however, are not sufficient to support the contention that theirs was a private licensing agreement enforceable in state courts only. The letters relied upon by the defendant seem to indicate rather that the parties intended their relationship to be governed by the compulsory license provisions of section 1(e). Absent a clear showing to the contrary, it will not be presumed that this departure from the exact terms of the statute was intended as a waiver of its protection."[24]

Sec. 11.4. Origination of Ownership in Authorship and Jurisdiction

It is submitted that although the Trial Court correctly construed the nature of the relationship of plaintiff as a co-author in *Eliscu*,[25] nevertheless it ultimately had to deal with the nature of authorship as determinative of ownership. It had to determine whether or not Eliscu was a co-lyricist as employee for hire or not. Ownership of the renewal copyright followed from this determination. True, this was a factual determination of a relationship. But in *Joy*,[26] the Court was also making a factual determination as to whether or not the variances of the parties contractually had the effect of converting their relationship from one of reliance upon the statute, there Section 1(e),[27] as opposed

---

[24] *Idem* at p. 550.
[25] Note 11, *supra*.
[26] Note 23, *supra*.
[27] 17 U.S.C. 1(e).

to reliance upon their agreement cognizable under state law. Yet the Trial Court, in *Eliscu,*[28] seemed to be doing precisely the same thing. It found that the agreements of the parties were not in fact clear-cut. ". . . plaintiff was neither an employee, nor truly an independent contractor."[29] In effect, it was stating that the agreements between the parties were not so clear-cut that the status of the parties could be determined therefrom. Rather, it determined that a clear case of rights flowing from the employment for hire relationship had not been made out and that there were facts indicating an intent to enter into some other relationship. It is submitted, therefore, that had the matter of jurisdiction been considered from the point of view of authorship rather than ownership perhaps the result might have been different and federal jurisdiction entertained. There is a clear federal interest under the copyright statute for ascertaining the nature of authorship and the categories factually constituting the classification section of the Act even though, strictly speaking, there may not be a construction of any particular section itself. Thus, there may be a question as to whether a work constitutes a book, for example, copyrightable under Section 5[30] of the Act. Assume we are not concerned with an interpretation as to whether the work is a writing, but merely the particular form of the work. Inherent in any such determination would be the matter of copyrightability which clearly would be cognizable under federal jurisdiction as a federal question. So, too, it would appear that the nature of authorship, going as it does, to the heart of creativity, should be cognizable federally and not under local law. For the nature of authorship is a matter of determining what has

---

[28] Note 11, *supra.*

[29] *Idem* at p. 604.

[30] 17 U.S.C. 5.

been created, the manner of its creation, and the quantum of the work that is capable of protection under copyright. Of course, there is a confusion as between authorship and ownership at the moment of creation by transmutation of rights of authorship into rights of ownership. The transmutation effects a change from rights of personality of the author into property, literary and artistic property, to be sure, but property nonetheless. State law presumably is cognizable of property rights, including ownership. The nature of the copyright obviously is determined by the federal statute.[31] Apart from the scope there, as set forth in Sec. 1[32] of the Act, Sec. 27 thereof spells out the incorporeal nature of the copyright as follows:

> "The copyright is distinct from the property in the material object copyrighted, and the sale or conveyance, by gift or otherwise, of the material object shall not of itself constitute a transfer of the copyright, nor shall the assignment of the copyright constitute a transfer of the title to the material object; but nothing in this title shall be deemed to forbid, prevent, or restrict the transfer of any copy of a copyrighted work the possession of which has been lawfully obtained." [33]

The very statute which thereby spells out the incorporeal nature of the copyright at the same time recites that the fact of separability of copyright from the material object under copyright does not thereby affect the fact that both material object, as tangible property, and the intangible copyright are susceptible of transfer. Transfers, in turn, are cognizable under local law.

---

[31] For example, 17 U.S.C. 1, 27.

[32] 17 U.S.C. 1 which enumerates the various rights comprehending the copyright.

[33] 17 U.S.C. 27.

It is submitted that precisely because of the nature of copyright, ownership is initiated by creation, and that to the extent the nature of the creation is determinative of ownership, that is, that nature of authorship must be determined, then there is also an initial issue of creation of the literary and artistic work in which copyright is to subsist that is cognizable as a federal question. It is submitted further, that where this is so, there is sufficient federal interest to also determine the fact of ownership which usually follows ineluctably therefrom.

Sec. 11.5. Federal Copyright Pre-emption vs. State Ownership: Jurisdiction

In any event, it is to be noted that the Supreme Court decided *Sears*[34] and *Compco*[35] in 1964, and in 1965 denied *certiorari* in *Eliscu.*[36] In the 1964 decisions it preempted resort to rules of unfair competition as a remedy under local law where the parties might have obtained patent or copyright. The doctrine thereby enunciated was that patent and copyright were paramount under federal law, so that a failure to rely thereon barred relief by way of the alternative remedy of a suit for unfair competition under local law. Yet a year later, the Supreme Court was content to deny *certiorari* in a case in which the Court of Appeals had decided that the correct path was via local and not federal law! Thus, in *Sears*[37] and *Compco,*[38] the Supreme Court appeared to expand the scope of the federal ambit by denying resort to state remedy, while in

---

[34] Sears, Roebuck & Co. v. Stiffel Co., 376 U.S. 225 (1964).

[35] Compco Corp. v. Day-Brite Lighting, Inc., 376 U.S. 234 (1964).

[36] Note 5, *supra.*

[37] Note 34, *supra.*

[38] Note 35, *supra.*

Eliscu,[39] it declined to review the decision restricting federal jurisdiction in favor of local jurisdiction, by denying *certiorari.* It would seem that the purport of the 1964 decisions was that remedy follows the rights; the rights, having been granted by federal statute must be determined federally. There being no state right, there is no jurisdiction under local law to grant the remedy. Jurisdiction is vested in the federal courts since rights under federal statute are involved. The denial of *certiorari* would appear to represent the converse of that proposition. There being no rights to be construed under federal law and no issue of diversity of citizenship giving federal courts jurisdiction, and there being no federal common law, the matter is to be determined under local law by the state courts. No wonder, then, that the Court of Appeals in *Eliscu* bemoaned "the hazards of formulation in this treacherous area." [40]

Sec. 11.6. Works of Foreign Authors

If federal jurisdiction seems to be tacking and filling in the sails of esoterica vis-à-vis local law in respect of domestic authors, its zig-zagging appears to continue unabated in respect of foreign authors. The benign remark of Arpad Bogsch suggests smooth sailing when he states, "In the case of unpublished works protected by the common law, the nationality of the author has not in the past, and does not at present, have any significance. Works of alien authors have the same status as works of U.S. citizens under the common law." [41]

---

[39] Note 5, *supra.*

[40] *Ibid.* at p. 828.

[41] Bogsch, Arpad, Protection of Works of Foreign Origin, Study No. 32, in 1 Studies on Copyright 737, 739 (1963).

To appreciate this remark, ostensibly *simpliciter*, one must contrast it with the myriad rules affecting copyright where federal jurisdiction is involved. The Register's Report on general copyright revision states: "Common law protection extends to the published works of all authors, without regard to their nationality. Under the statute, however, the published or unregistered works of foreign authors are eligible for protection *only* when certain conditions are met.

"The provisions now governing the eligibility of foreign works for statutory copyright are found in section 9, which extends copyright protection to works by 'a citizen or subject of a foreign state or nation' only in the following cases:

(1) When the alien author is domiciled in the United States.

(2) When the author is a national of a country designated in a proclamation of the President.

(3) When the work is entitled to protection under the Universal Copyright Convention." [42]

But the problem of copyright protection of works of foreign authors is a part of the larger one of international copyright in which additional non-authorial factors complicate the situation.

Sec. 11.7. The Manufacturing Clause

The Register's Report then proceeds to describe them: "Before the International Copyright Act of 1891, the works of foreign authors had been freely and widely pirated

---

[42] Report of the Register of Copyrights on the General Revision of the U.S. Copyright Law, 2 Studies on Copyright 1199 (1963) at p. 1313 (emphasis added).

in the United States. The piratical printing of foreign works had become such a large part of the domestic industry that the printers opposed any extension of copyright to foreign works unless their interests were protected. They insisted upon requiring printing in the United States as a condition of U.S. copyright, not only for foreign works but for the works of U.S. authors as well.

"The result was the 'manufacturing clause' in the act of 1891 . . .

"The manufacturing clause was the price exacted by the printers for the establishment of international copyright protection in the United States." [43]

This has impelled one author to comment:

"A strange marriage of crafts is sheltered under the cloak of copyright. Copyright was constitutionally espoused to secure the rights of authors for the purpose of promoting the 'Progress of Science and Useful Arts.' Although the craft of printing is perhaps not one of the 'arts' contemplated by the Constitution, yet it is one on which authors depend for multiplication of copies of their works; and the printing trades, in order to protect themselves against foreign competition, have bound authors to a sort of servitude fixed in the copyright law many years ago." [44]

As to the manufacturing clause, the Register's Report states:

"The manufacturing clause is found in section 16 of the present statute, supplemented by sections 17, 18, 22, 23 and 107. The provisions of these sections are now an

---

[43] *Idem* at pp. 1319-1320.

[44] McCannon, Marjorie, The Manufacturing Clause of the U.S. Copyright Law, 2 Studies on Copyright 1123, 1125 (1963).

intricate and abstruse tangle of general requirements, exceptions, and special procedures." [45]

Efforts to alleviate the rigors of the manufacturing clause resulted in the adoption of the concept of the *ad interim* copyright permitting the publication abroad in English and importation of up to 1500 copies of such work within five years after such publication.[46] Proposed copyright revision would retain the manufacturing clause but limit to nondramatic literary material importation of up to 2000 copies of such work.[47]

Ironically, as Marjorie McCannon points out, "The import limitation, as well as the manufacturing requirement itself, were eliminated in 1955 for foreign works protected under the Universal Copyright Convention." [48] It is to be noted that the manufacturing clause excepts works of foreign origin "in a language or languages other than English".[49] Moreover, the further exception from the manufacturing clause to nationals of countries signatory to the Universal Copyright Convention would have the effect of excluding a significant part of foreign authors publishing in English since the United Kingdom and Canada are members of the UCC. Other countries where books often would be written and published in English that are signatories to this convention include India, Pakistan, Nigeria, and Israel, i.e., the British Commonwealth or formerly British Empire countries including, of course, Australia, New Zealand and

---

[45] Note 42, *supra,* at p. 1320.

[46] 17 U.S.C. 16, 22.

[47] S. 543, 91st Cong., 1st Sess., January 22, 1969, Sec. 601. See also Report No. 83, 90th Cong., 1st Sess. House of Representatives, dated March 8, 1967, re proposed Sec. 601 at pp. 131 *et seq.*

[48] Note 44, *supra* at p. 1188; see also 17 U.S.C. 9(c).

[49] 17 U.S.C. 16.

Ireland. Still other nations with strong publishing output that are signatories thereto are the Gereman Federal Republic, France, Italy, Spain, the Scandinavian countries, Greece, Austria, Switzerland, Holland and Belgium where authors might write in English or possibly publish in English translation for the English-speaking market.[50] Moreover, American authors have been able to obtain protection under the Berne Convention by the route of simultaneous publication which Nimmer characterizes as the "back door" method.[51] Also, major Latin American countries like Argentina, Brazil, Chile, Peru, Mexico, and Venezuela are signatories to the UCC.[52] Even some of the Iron Curtain countries are parties thereto.[53] It may be seen therefore, that by means of the Universal Copyright Convention, a substantial number of foreign authors is exempt from the manufacturing clause requirement, while through the device of simultaneous publication by an American author in a Berne Convention country, he can receive protection in countries signatory to that convention.[54] American authors, too, are beneficiaries of the Buenos Aires Convention[55] and a variety of bilateral conventions by Presidential proclamation.[56]

---

[50] See Nimmer, *op. cit., supra,* note 2, Appendix L, Universal Copyright Convention, List of Accessions and Ratifications (As of January 1, 1969), at p. 1002.

[51] *Idem,* Sec. 65.64 at pp. 265-266.1.

[52] Note 50, *supra.*

[53] *Ibid.*—Czechoslovakia, Yugoslavia.

[54] Note 51, *supra,* fn. 193 lists the signatories to the Berne Convention as of January 1, 1969.

[55] Nimmer, *op. cit., supra,* note 2, Appendix N, for a list of bilateral conventions and proclamations as well as the Buenos Aires Convention, the Mexico City Convention and the Universal Copyright Convention and the countries signatory thereto, at pp. 1009-1012.

[56] *Ibid.*

It is in this context that one should consider the remarks of Marjorie McCannon when she writes since the amendment to Sec. 9(c) in 1954, " . . . the limitation on importation applies only to books by U.S. authors and books by foreign authors not eligible for Universal Copyright Convention exemptions.

"United States citizens who write for publication in foreign books or periodicals are often shocked upon learning, perhaps too late, that their English-language works published abroad are not protected in the United States if they fail to make *ad interim* registration within six months, or fail to reprint and publish the work in the United States within five years. The shock is even greater when a U.S. citizen who writes in a foreign language learns that his work, having been printed and published abroad, cannot get any protection at all in the United States. Many persons are appalled that such a drastic penalty as copyright forfeiture is exacted against learned and influential Americans who write for a foreign market." [57]

Thus, by virtue of exemption under the Universal Copyright Convention, the manufacturing clause has had its principal impact upon writings of American authors writing in English. The clause has now come full circle to accomplish just the reverse. The original policy of nonrecognition of works of foreign authors for approximately one hundred years was to protect the domestic printer who could thereby bring the works of non-American authors to the American market without fear of sanctions. As a developing nation, America read and looked to the works of foreign authors for intellectual nourishment. But Emer-

---

[57] McCannon, Marjorie, *op. cit., supra,* note 44, at p. 1155.

son[58] and others[59] were successful in turning readers more and more to the works of American authors. Reasons for piracy became less compelling. The manufacturing clause from and after 1891 was enacted so as to protect the position of the American printer at a time when the principal source of works was indeed that of American authors. The effect of the Universal Copyright Convention exemption of foreign authors from the manufacturing clause was to underscore, once and for all, the inverted nature of the clause. Its restrictions are now primarily directed against American authors.

Sec. 11.8. Piracy and Jurisdiction

Perhaps there is something in the emotional context of words that transcends the factual circumstances to effect a tyranny of its own even where changes have eroded original facts and circumstances. The term "piracy" is a good example. A pirate is an outlaw on the high seas, a brigand, a freebooter, a buccaneer. The pirate is fair game upon capture to be imprisoned or hanged. The term is then adapted to copyright jurisprudence to refer to someone appropriating someone else's creative work, but not necessarily without attribution of credit to the creator, for purposes of avoiding payment of royalties and otherwise. It is a taking of literary and artistic property without claim of right.

Piracy in the arts refers to unfair playing of the rules of the game where there are in fact rules of the game. This refers to plagiarism of literary and artistic works without right or license and without payment of royalty and also

---

[58] Emerson, Ralph Waldo, Essays (1932).

[59] See Parrington, Vernon Louis, Main Currents in American Thought (1930).

unauthorized duplication of performances such as copying of performances on tapes and records without authority and license. Piracy in the arts, then, denotes some unauthorized taking contrary to law. Webster has this to say about this meaning, defining piracy as, "Any unauthorized appropriation and reproduction of another's production, invention or conception; literary or artistic theft; specif., 'Sometimes used in a quasi-figurative sense, of violation of copyright; but for this *infringement* is the correct and preferable term.' "[60] Yet, in its generic sense, piracy is something else again. Webster defines it thus, "In international law, in general, any act or practice of violence or depredation such as would be felonious if done ashore committed upon the high seas by one not acting under the authority of a politically established community, or such act or practice so committed upon unappropriated lands by a descent from the sea."[61]

Thus, the opprobrium visited upon the pirate historically as an outlaw to social organization is carried over principally in the fact that the same word is used in a somewhat different sense to refer to latter day artistic and literary piracy. A fundamental distinction arises in the factor of jurisdiction and absence of jurisdiction. The pirate upon the high seas was a usurper of authority, taking what he wished because jurisdiction was national. True, there might be a boarding of a ship of a given country, which claimed jurisdiction thereof on the high seas. But the buccaneer was beyond the jurisdiction physically of that country, after having illegally boarded its ship, except to the extent the armed forces of that country, in the absence of international

---

[60] Webster's New International Dictionary, Unabridged, Second Ed. (1961), at p. 1872 (italics).

[61] *Ibid.*

treaty or convention, exercised might and main to hunt down the pirates and capture and deal with them as criminals as though they were within the territorial jurisdiction of that country.

The problem with trans-national literary and artistic piracy is that it constitutes an authorized taking within a given jurisdiction because there is not only no law interdicting it but also the government of that country, in the absence of legislation to the contrary, would uphold the right of such otherwise unauthorized appropriation by the powers of the state. Thus, until 1891, American printers could copy works of foreign authors because they were denied copyright protection here. Without such protection, the taking of their work for such purposes was not unlawful. It was not, in terms of the jurisprudence of the United States, or any other country similarly situated, strictly speaking, piracy at all.

Sec. 11.9. Jurisdiction and Public Domain

The rationale is borne out by *Shostakovich* v. *Twentieth Century-Fox Film Corp.*[62] There Dmitry Shostakovich, Aram Khachaturian, Serge Prokofieff and Nicolai Miaskovsky sued Fox to enjoin use of their music in the film, "The Iron Curtain". Since the Soviet Union was not signatory to any convention or treaty with the United States, plaintiffs could not sue on copyright infringement. The Court denied the motion for injunctive relief which relied variously on the right of privacy under Sec. 51 of the Civil Rights Law of New York, injunctive power to enjoin publication of defamatory matter, deliberate infliction of injury without just cause and violation of plaintiffs' moral rights

[62] 196 Misc. 67, 80 N.Y.S. 2d 575 (Sup. Ct., Spec. T., N.Y. Cty. 1948), *aff'd* 275 App. Div. 692, 87 N.Y.S. 2d 430 (1st Dept. 1949).

as composers. Without stating its proposition directly, the Court obliquely referred to the fact that the work was in the public domain, stating, "No such implication exists, necessarily or otherwise, where the work of the composer is in the public domain and may be freely published, copied or compiled by others. . . . With reference to that which is in the public domain there arises a conflict between the moral right and the right of others to use such works . . ." [63]

Sec. 11.10. Federal Jurisdiction—Works of Foreign Authors

Jurisdiction, therefore, carries its own rules as to reciprocity. Works under copyright in the United States carry no protection in the Soviet Union. The *Shostakovich*[64] case in essence deprived that composer of any protection in the United States from copying. In effect his work was deemed to be in the public domain and could be copied freely. Yet different results followed in cases where this country had copyright relations with others. In *Heim* v. *Universal Pictures Co., Inc.*,[65] there was a subsisting copyright treaty with Hungary in 1935 and a copyright registration in the United States in 1936. Judge Frank observed, "The Hungarian publisher, the proprietor at the time of the copyright registration . . . was a citizen of a foreign country with which the United States has a treaty extending copyright protection to Hungarian citizens . . ." [66] The Court then held that absence of notice of copyright upon publication in Hungary was not a defect of notice of copyright upon subsequent publication here, stat-

[63] *Idem* 196 Misc. 67, 70, 80 N.Y.S. 2d 575, 578.

[64] Note 62, *supra*.

[65] 154 F. 2d 480 (2d Cir. 1946).

[66] *Idem* at p. 486.

ing, "We construe the statute, as to a publication in a foreign country by a foreign author . . . , not to require, as a condition of obtaining or maintaining a valid American copyright, that any notice be affixed to any copies whatever published in such foreign country, regardless of whether publication first occurred in that country or here, or whether it occurred before or after registration here."[67]

That is, in respect of nationals of a country with which this country has copyright relations, jurisdiction is extended to their works when published here. But as *Heim*[68] makes clear, upon taking jurisdiction under federal law, jurisdiction is then given a national configuration. The rules are given a construction consistent with a territorial application so that if copyright notice is required as a condition of publication in the United States, lack of such notice on publication of the work of a foreign national, consonant with the laws of his own state, without a notice of copyright will not work a forfeiture of the work so as to place it in the public domain.

Indeed, copyright will not be denied where the work is one of joint authorship of an American and a non-American, so that the American collaborator could protect the work here even though his co-author conceivably might not.[69]

Sec. 11.11. Works under Common Law Copyright and Jurisdiction

Moreover, our jurisprudence grants complete common law copyright protection without regard to nationality. In

---

[67] *Idem* at p. 486.

[68] *Idem.*

[69] Ricordi & Co., Inc. v. Columbia Graphophone Co., 258 Fed. 72 (1919).

Ferris v. *Frohman,*[70] there was a claim of common law copyright protection in the United States of a play by a British author and that this had not been divested by the fact that under British copyright law, performance was subsumed under copyright and that the U.S. and the U.K. had reciprocal copyright treaty relations. There was no printing or publication of the play. Chief Justice Hughes then held, "The deprivation of the common-law right, by force of the statute, was plainly limited by the territorial bounds within which the operation of the statute was confined."[71] British law did not have any extra-territorial effect on the prevailing rule here as to the common-law right of representation of the play in this country. The American common-law right was not lost.[72]

Thus, jurisdiction is not simply a matter of scope and ambit of federal law versus local law. It is also one of context of national law as opposed to international law. If the rule of *Ferris* v. *Frohman*[73] truly means what it says, then it stands for the proposition that our common law jurisprudence is open to all authors under local law regardless of the underlying nature of the work abroad, assuming there is no general publication of a divestive nature.[74] Assuming for the moment, no publication abroad, clearly under *Ferris*[75] even Dmitry Shostakovitch would have a cause of action here for infringement of his com-

---

[70] 223 U.S. 424 (1912).

[71] *Idem* at p. 434.

[72] Accord, Roberts v. Petrova, 213 N.Y. Supp. 434 (Sup. Ct., N.Y. Cty. 1925).

[73] Note 70, *supra*.

[74] Cf. Warner, Radio and Television Rights (1953), Sec. 203a, and Nimmer, *op. cit., supra,* note 2, Sec. 89.41. Warner disapproves of the *Heim* case whereas Nimmer believes the result to be correct.

[75] Note 70, *supra*.

mon law copyright. Yet, if that work had been published in the Soviet Union, it would be in the public domain under federal law. In any event, copyright being territorial, the foreign author or his assigns must register the copyright here to achieve protection under federal law, except insofar as modified by American adherence to the Universal Copyright Convention as provided by Sec. 9(c) of the Copyright Act.[76] It is true that the Universal Copyright Convention protects unpublished works of nationals reciprocally,[77] yet it would appear that as to its effect upon works of foreign nationals in the United States the rule is declaratory of what was the rule at common law, namely, that foreign authors can come in to protect their common law copyright in the United States.

Sec. 11.12. Factors in Ownership and Jurisdiction

If the norm of our copyright jurisprudence within the United States has been a jurisprudence of interests, that is, reconciliation and compromise of the variety of copyright interests, authors, publishers, users, etc., copyright, in its international relations, has been a function of politics. Whatever the cause of elaboration of rules, national and international, the results are an outgrowth of our federal jurisprudence in the relationship of federal law to local law with rationales that are not always easy to follow or reconcile, as well as of territorial concepts of international relations and of the conglomeration of treaties, conventions and bilateral treaty proclamations. The presumably unqualified recognition of creativity—before publication—in permitting

---

[76] See Nimmer, *op. cit., supra,* note 2, Appendix K, Universal Copyright Convention at p. 989; 17 U.S.C. 9(c), and Sec. 202.2(3), Regulations of the Copyright Office.

[77] Note 76, *supra,* Art. II, 2.

authors of all nationalities to avail themselves of our common law jurisprudence is affected by numerous qualifications and restrictions that are the outgrowth of our copyright jurisprudence as it affects foreign authorship.

Thus, in consideration of copyright ownership, four factors must be taken into consideration: (a) chain of authorship, including whether it is domestic or foreign, (b) chain of ownership, including whether it is in American or foreign hands, (c) domestic rights of implementation, copyright jurisprudence affecting it in the United States, and (d) foreign rights of implementation, copyright jurisprudence affecting it abroad.

The problems in this regard are not only legal, but also managerial and administrative. Analysis of these considerations ultimately must provide the determination of what rights are extant where, the chain of ownership therein, the territorial sequential roll of derivative rights therefrom, and so on. It may be said the complexities of copyright also thereby comprehend the complexities of international law and foreign relations and of a copyright jurisprudence within federalism.

Chapter XII

CONTRACTS

Sec. 12.1. Statutory Source of Rights

Whatever its vagaries as to jurisdiction, our copyright jurisprudence is not at all uncertain as to the source of origination of rights under copyright which, in turn, delineates the contractual scheme and its marketing mechanisms in respect of literary and artistic property. The source is to be found at the very inception of our Copyright Act in Sec. 1 thereof.[1] This section then proceeds to spell out a variety of exclusive rights granted under copyright, which can be characterized as the various publishing rights,[2] the transformation rights,[3] the performing rights, and the mechanical rights,[4] and, as of February 15, 1972, and prior to January 1, 1975, sound recording rights.[5] Thus, without further ado, our copyright jurisprudence becomes thereby our fundament for the copyright industries, almost, as it were, like a fast race horse off to a whirlwind start.[6]

The Copyright Act virtually completes its coverage in this respect in the very next section by relegating rights under common law copyright to the jurisdiction of local

---

[1] 17 U.S.C. 1.

[2] 17 U.S.C. 1(a).

[3] 17 U.S.C. 1(b).

[4] 17 U.S.C. 1(c), (d), and (e).

[5] 17 U.S.C. 1(f). See Secs. 5.4 and 6.3, *supra*.

[6] Cf. by contrast proposed copyright revision, S. 543, 91st Cong., 1st Sess., January 22, 1969, where the comparable section is Sec. 106, entitled, Exclusive rights in copyrighted works, and which follows an extensive section entitled, Definitions, Sec. 101 and sections dealing with the subject matter of copyright, Secs. 102-105.

law.[7] Although Sec. 2 of the Act does not thereby spell out the nature of the rights under common law copyright, it virtually completes the range of coverage. That is, the rights protected under Sec. 1 plus the rights reserved for protection to local law under Sec. 2 comprise substantially the range of rights protected under copyright. Warner distinguishes the two by reference to copyright before publication and copyright after publication.[8] His catalogue of rights protected under common law includes the exclusive rights of publication, transformation and performance.[9] Of course, the compulsory license for mechanical reproduction would be a material variance in the scope of the rights under statutory as compared to common law copyright.[10]

Proposed copyright revision would, however, pre-empt common law copyright and subsume it under federal statutory protection.[11] But the pre-emption so worked by S. 543, Sec. 301(a), is subject to the reservation of common law jurisdiction worked by Subdivision (b) thereof. Sec. 301(b) reads as follows:

> "(b) Nothing in this title annuls or limits any rights or remedies under the common law or statutes of any State with respect to:
>
> (1) unpublished material that does not come within the subject matter of copyright as specified by sections 102 and 103, including works of authorship not fixed in any tangible medium of expression;

---

[7] 17 U.S.C. 2.

[8] Warner, Radio and Television Rights (1953), Sec. 202, at p. 857.

[9] *Ibid.*

[10] 17 U.S.C. 1(e).

[11] S. 543, note 6, *supra,* Sec. 301.

(2) any cause of action arising from undertakings commenced before January 1, 1971;

(3) activities violating rights that are not equivalent to any of the exclusive rights within the general scope of copyright as specified by section 106, including breaches of contract, breaches of trust, invasion of privacy, defamation, and deceptive trade practices such as passing off and false representation." [12]

The reservation expressed in Sec. 301(b)(1) as to fixation of form is important. The House Report on Copyright Law Revision characterizes the meaning of this limitation in this manner:

> "Under the bill, the concept of fixation is important since it not only determines whether the provisions of the statute apply to a work, but it also represents the dividing line between common law and statutory protection . . . an unfixed work of authorship, such as an improvisation or an unrecorded choreographic work, performance, or broadcast, would continue to be subject to protection under State common law or statute, but would not be eligible for Federal statutory protection under section 102." [13]

Thus, pre-emption would not automatically comprehend the entire scope of exclusive rights afforded protection. There would still be a residue of creative works, which because of their form, i.e., their lack of fixation in a

---

[12] S. 543, note 6, *supra,* Sec. 301(b). The date has been changed to January 1, 1973 in Sec. 301(b)(2) of S. 644, 92d Cong.,1st Sess., February 8, 1971.

[13] Report No. 83, 90th Cong., 1st Sess., March 8, 1967, House of Representatives, at p. 15.

tangible medium of expression, would still not be subject to federal jurisdiction and would be reserved to common law protection under local law.

The reservation of Sec. 301(b)(3) as to contracts is likewise noteworthy. Breaches of contract not equivalent to violation of exclusive rights under copyright would continue to be reserved to common law jurisdiction. In this regard, the House Report states, "Nothing in the bill derogates from the rights of parties to contract with each other and to sue for breaches of contract;" [14] Actually, the reservation as to contracts continues the existing rule as expressed in *Danks* v. *Gordon,* "If the suit is one brought to enforce a right based upon a contract which relates to a copyrighted production, the suit is one which arises out of the contract and is not one arising under the copyright statute, and the federal courts are without jurisdiction." [15]

Thus it may be seen that only two sections of the present Copyright Act delineate the nature of the exclusive rights under copyright. The remainder of the Act relates to subject matter of copyright,[16] formalities of copyrighting,[17] nature and scope of protection of these rights,[18] authorship, ownership and renewal of copyright,[19] and copyright torts and remedies.[20] Essentially the renewal scheme of the statute purports to cover ownership in the renewal term.[21]

---

[14] *Idem* at pp. 99-100.

[15] 272 Fed. 821 (2d Cir. 1921), at p. 827.

[16] E.g. 17 U.S.C. 4, 5 covering writings of an author and classification of works under copyright.

[17] E.g., 17 U.S.C. 10-23, 28-32.

[18] E.g., 17 U.S.C. 4, 27.

[19] E.g., 17 U.S.C. 3, 9, 24, 26.

[20] E.g., 17 U.S.C. 101 *et seq.*

[21] 17 U.S.C. 24.

It does not, per se, delineate the nature of the exclusive rights under copyright although it may incidentally affect the fact of ownership therein by reason of the termination of the original term of copyright and the possible change of ownership effected by operation of the renewal statute. In other words, by affecting ownership, the renewal statute might thereby also affect contractual relationships extant as to the exclusive rights in the original term.

Sec. 12.2. Source of Rights and Copyright Industry Configurations

Sec. 1 of the present Copyright Act, then, is the key section in connection with delineation of rights and the legal, i.e., contractual and business ramifications of copyright industries. Indeed, it may be stated that publishing, motion pictures, television, theatre and music are structured, to an extent, by correlation to Sec 1. Each industry exists in our country because protections have been afforded under copyright so as to provide an overall umbrella of legal protection whereby economic incentives may be pursued in terms of rewards to be gained from exploitation in commerce of the literary and artistic works under copyright.

Thus, as to publishing, the basic rights of reproduction, i.e., publication, and of sale are set forth in Sec. 1(a) and are augmented by rights of translation and abridgment and other adaptation in Sec. 1(b). As to motion pictures and television, the basic performing right is contained in Sec. 1(d) as to a dramatic work along with the right to multiply copies contained in Sec. 1(a) and to make adaptations per Sec. 1(b). Also, the right to perform a musical composition publicly for profit is contained in Sec. 1(e) while Sec. 1(c) covers presentations of non-dramatic literary works. Thus the rights of exclusive performance, adaptation of literary material into screenplays and teleplays as the basis for such productions, and reproduction of prints and tapes for commercial exhibition form the basis of these audio-visual performing arts. As to music, the basis for formation of performing rights societies and of recording companies is inherent in Sec. 1(e). The exclusive right to perform the work publicly for profit granted in the section is the legal basis for the operation of the American Society of Composers, Authors and Publishers and of Broadcast Music, Inc.[22] The compulsory license provision of the same section enables record companies to reproduce musical compositions under compulsory license by payment of statutory royalties to the copyright proprietor. This has provided the ceiling for royalties payable for obtaining the mechanical license and has been the basis for record production of the same work in different recorded versions. If record companies, in fact, more often obtain a direct license with variances from the statute, e.g., possibly a lesser royalty rate or quarter or semi-annual accounting rather than monthly accounting, nevertheless this does not diminish the underlying existence of the compulsory license under the statute as the reason for the direct mechanical licenses. Of course, music publishing is based on the performing and

---

[22] See, Herbert v. Shanley, 242 U.S. 591 (1917), *rev'g,* 229 Fed. 340 (2d Cir. 1916) which had affirmed 222 Fed. 344 (S.D.N.Y. 1915), a suit brought by Victor Herbert to test the basis of the rights of the American Society of Composers, Authors and Publishers under Sec. 1(e) (17 U.S.C. 1(e)). Victor Herbert was one of the founders of ASCAP. The suit was a test case. Warner, *op. cit., supra,* note 8, remarks that "ASCAP . . . had financed this litigation for Victor Herbert", Sec. 131e at p. 339. He comments, "In *Herbert* v. *Shanley,* the Supreme Court interpreted the phrase 'for profit' and thereby furnished the judicial basis for the performing rights societies.", Sec. 131a, at p. 326. See Chaps. XXIII and XXIV, *infra.*

mechanical rights under Sec. 1(e). The copyright proprietor can thereby derive payments from the performing rights societies based on some logging formula of performances of the music in its catalogue used by the performing rights society of which it is a member. It also derives mechanical royalties from licensing the right to make recordings under compulsory license, as well as the license of the initial recording. Of course, the music publisher, as such, has the rights of publication in its music that are in common with any other type of publisher, that is, the broad range of publication rights granted by Sec. 1(a) as well as rights of arrangement and adaptation and translation under Sec. 1(b). Thus it may be seen that publishing, film, television and music as industries are largely based upon Sec. 1 of the Copyright Act. As for the theatre, to the extent the play is not published, its performance would be protected under common law copyright. If published, the source of rights therein would be Sec. 1(d) in the right of performance of a dramatic work with publication protected under Sec. 1(a) and adaptation under Sec. 1(b). Presumably musical components would also come under the protection of Sec. 1(e). As for the dance, there, too, protection might be sought under common law copyright for the choreography unless the same were embodied in notation, film or tape for protection under Sec. 1(d) as to performance of a dramatic work and under Sec. 1(c) as to performance of a non-dramatic work, and against multiplication of copies under Sec. 1(a) and against adaptation under Sec. 1(b).[23]

---

[23] See, Varmer, Borge, Copyright in Choreographic Works, Studies on Copyright, Study No. 28 (1963), at p. 103.

Sec. 12.3. Transmutation of Statutory Rights into Contract

If the source of rights is therefore Sec. 1 of the Copyright Act, how then does it become transmuted into contract? For example, A writes a novel which is published by B publishing company. Copyright in the book is in the name of A. The contract between author and publisher grants B exclusive book publishing rights. Motion picture rights are reserved therein to A. A film agreement is negotiated by A's literary agent, whereby exclusive rights to make a feature length motion picture based upon the novel are granted to C film production company.[24]

Sec. 12.3(a). Illustration—Motion Pictures

To begin with, one searches the statutory scheme for references to motion pictures. Alas, that is not very helpful. The present Copyright Act, when originally enacted in 1909,[25] did not even cover motion pictures. Perhaps it was felt that it was not necessary because film making was still in its infancy. Perhaps it was thought that it might be surplusage since the film had been held to be copyrightable under the category of photographs.[26] Whatever the reason, this was corrected three years later by the passage of the Townsend Act in 1912[27] classifying motion pictures as such

---

[24] In some instances, the book contract will appoint the book publisher to handle exploitation of subsidiary rights, such as motion pictures and television. In others, no such rights will be granted. The reserved rights will be handled by a literary agent on behalf of the author.

[25] Act of March 4, 1909, c. 320, 35 Stat. 1075 *et seq.*

[26] American Mutoscope & Biograph Co. v. Edison Mfg. Co., 137 Fed. 262 (C.C.D.N.J. 1905); Edison v. Lubin, 122 Fed. 240 (3d Cir. 1903).

[27] Act of Aug. 24, 1912, c. 356, 37 Stat. 488.

for copyright purposes. Sec. 5 of the Copyright Act therefore includes two categories relating thereto. Sec. 5(l) specifically covers "Motion-picture photoplays",[28] while Sec. 5(m) pertains to "Motion pictures other than photoplays".[29] The Regulations of the Copyright Office are terse in connection therewith, reading:

> "Sec. 202.15 Motion pictures (Classes L-M). A single application Form L-M is available for registration of works in Classes L (Motion Picture Photoplays) and M (Motion Pictures other than Photoplays).
>
> (a) Photoplays (Class L). This class includes published or unpublished motion pictures that are dramatic in character and tell a connected story, such as feature films, filmed television plays, short subjects and animated cartoons having a plot.
>
> (b) Other than photoplays (Class M). This class includes published or unpublished non-dramatic films such as newsreels, travelogs, training or promotional films, nature studies, and filmed television programs having no plot." [30]

Substantially the only other reference in the Copyright Act, as such, is in Sec. 12 which (apart from special damages for infringement under Sec. 101(b)) relates to works not reproduced for sale and provides for deposit of one print of a motion picture photoplay and of two prints of a motion picture other than a photoplay sought to be copyrighted as an unpublished work.[31] Thus, except for these skimpy references to the motion picture art, which has

---

[28] 17 U.S.C. 5(l).
[29] 17 U.S.C. 5(m).
[30] Regulations of the Copyright Office, Sec. 202.15.
[31] 17 U.S.C. 12.

grown into a billion dollar copyright industry in the decades since passage of the present Copyright Act, legislation now covering the same in the United States is virtually silent as to this major art and industry. Indeed, considering the outstanding contributions of this country to the birth and development of film making as a world-wide phenomenon, it might be said that the legislative coverage thereof in terms of its existence as an art is skimpy indeed. Consider, too, that the term "photoplay" is an archaism in that, if it is used at all in the industry today, it is done in legal documents as a synonym for film, or picture or feature.

Sec. 12.3(b). Film History and Statutory Source of Rights

It should be noted that the first film in this country which told a story was Edwin S. Porter's "The Great Train Robbery" which was produced in 1903. Arthur Knight observes, "What finally saved the movies was the introduction of narrative." [32] He refers to the films of George Méliès in France, commencing in 1900 and Porter's film.[33] Porter's picture was eight minutes in length. Knight remarks as to its success, "It established the single reel as the standard length for feature films (between eight and twelve minutes of film.)" [34]

To understand the context of the Townsend Act amendment in 1912, which referred to motion pictures, several other passages from Knight's work are illuminating. He states:

---

[32] Knight, Arthur, "The Liveliest Art" 23 (1957) (Mentor Book Edition).

[33] *Idem* at pp. 23-26. The author provides a subheading for this material, "Dawn of the Narrative Film: Méliès and Porter".

[34] *Idem* at p. 26.

> "In 1912 the great Sarah Bernhardt made a film version of her play *Queen Elizabeth* for Film d'Art in four reels. In Italy at the same time *Quo Vadis?* was being readied in eight reels—almost two hours on the screen. In America, on the other hand, film lengths had been arbitrarily frozen at one reel. It was the Motion Picture Patents Company that decided no audience would sit through a movie running longer than ten minutes, and thus established the single reel as the length for all its films. Composed of the largest producers and distributors in the United States, it sought to control through its pooling of patents every phase of the infant industry. And between 1909 and 1912 its word was law." [35]

But by 1912 by means of evasions the single reel story had given way to the two-reeler. As to this, Knight writes, "As early as May, 1911, Griffith had rebelled against the Trust's arbitrary single-reel restriction. When he made *Enoch Arden* in two reels, Biograph, which was one of the leading members of the Trust, insisted on releasing each reel separately. However, in response to audience demand, theater managers were soon showing the two parts together. And by 1912 the two-reeler had become accepted as the standard length for a serious story film." [36]

Actually the basis for the policy of the Motion Picture Patents Company was the tie of the supply of copyrighted films to its patents in the film equipment—the projectors, etc. This led to antitrust litigation and a few years later the Supreme Court in *Motion Picture Patents Co.* v. *Uni-*

---

[35] *Idem* at p. 30 (italics).
[36] *Idem* at p. 34 (italics).

versal[37] held that the tie was illegal in that it violated the antitrust laws.

It may be seen from the foregoing that the context for the term "photoplay" in 1912 was basically a one or two reel narrative film. Shortly thereafter, the feature length film came to assume a dominant position in film production and distribution. "The Birth of a Nation", for example, was produced in 1915. The combination of successful legal action to overcome the restraints on feature production, plus actual feature length production and public acceptance thereof, proclaimed the death knell of the short subject as the principal form of commercial film production, distribution and exhibition.

Thus, the language of the present Copyright Act as to motion pictures is archaic, in terms of film history, yet it represents the sum of copyright legislation directly in point thereon to date. This does not mean, of course, that Sec. 1, as a whole, is not relevant thereto; nor that other sections of the present Copyright Act cannot be utilized effectively for the purposes referred to in the respective sections even as they affect motion pictures. It does mean, however, that the language and context of motion pictures, a major copyright industry, is substantially absent from the

---

[37] 243 U.S. 502 (1917). For a discussion of this case see Taubman, Copyright and Antitrust (1960) at pp. 43-50. This is contained in Chap. II entitled, Contract, Copyright and Antitrust. The case is discussed in a section 1 thereof entitled, Copyrights and Patents. Upton Sinclair's biography of William Fox, published in 1933 entitled, Upton Sinclair Presents William Fox, is a most interesting account of efforts to overcome the patent pool by new film makers such as William Fox, many of whom ultimately went to Hollywood in this period in order to avoid the strictures on production of the patent pool, by producing longer pictures there.

present statute. Considering that films were in existence prior to the enactment of the 1909 Act, the present statute, and considering the tremendous growth and development of the film industry and technology since, the scant reference thereto underscores the problems of transmutation of rights provided by the present Copyright Act into contract and commercial norms. *A fortiori,* the problems are compounded as to television since the term "television" does not appear in Sec. 5 in any form.[38] Indeed, the statute appears not to refer to the term at all, nor to the most recent form of embodiment of the art therein, tapes.[39] However, the Regulations of the Copyright Office with respect to this term, Sec. 202.15, were amended effective as of May 14, 1971 by adding provisions for registration of videotape copies with respect to and as part of registration of "Motion Pictures (Classes L-M)" and includes "*filmed* television plays" [40] under "Photoplays (Class L)" and "*filmed* television programs having no plot" [41] under "Other Than Photoplays (Class M)". Thus, as far as the present statute itself is concerned, in terms of its draftsmanship, television does not exist, while the Regulations of the Copyright Office go no further than *filmed* television, and videotapes if otherwise qualified as a motion picture.

Moreover, it is to be noted that even in relation to motion pictures, the statute relates to classification for pur-

---

[38] 17 U.S.C. 5.

[39] The writer's perusal of 17 U.S.C. 1 *et seq.* does not appear to indicate any reference to the term "television" in our present Copyright Act. See the reference to "broadcast" in Sec. 1(c).

[40] Sec. 202.15(a), Regulations of the Copyright Office (emphasis added). Sec. 202.15(d) was added to cover videotape copies which otherwise qualify as a motion picture effective as of May 14, 1971. See 18 Bull. Cr. Soc. 438 (1971). See Chap. XXIII, note 82, *infra.*

[41] Sec. 202.15(b), Regulations of the Copyright Office (emphasis added).

poses of registration of copyright in the film itself. Consequently, it has practically no relevance to the matter of contract, i.e., how the rights granted by Sec. 1 of the Act are transmuted into contract.

Sec. 12.4. Copyright As a Source of Contractual Rights

Now let us examine actual forms used to ascertain how motion picture rights are granted by A to C film production company in the above example. We now proceed to analyze the rights granted in a form set forth by Harold S. Klein in his discussion of subsidiary rights and residuals in films.[42] The form is a typical form used by a major film studio in the acquisition of rights from an author. Article 1 thereof is generic, granting purchaser exclusively and forever, "the entire silent, sound, dialogue, talking and musical motion picture rights, televised motion picture rights, television rights, and dramatic rights". There follows an exception of stage rights, i.e., production of the spoken stage with living actors. The grant is in all languages and is world-wide. The clause provides that the owner, "grants, sells, assigns, transfers and sets over" to purchaser the aforesaid rights.

It is to be noted that the very first paragraph represents a departure from the language of the statute. Most of the rights granted do not appear *in haec verba* in the statute. That is, the statute does not carry the specific language of those rights, except possibly for the dramatic rights. As

---

[42] Klein, Harold S., Subsidiary Rights and Residuals in Motion Pictures, Chap. V, at pp. 33-65, in Subsidiary Rights and Residuals (1968), edited by Taubman, Joseph. The form appears at pp. 40 *et seq.* therein and is reproduced in Form No. 1A-2 in Volumes of Forms.

indicated above, there is no reference to motion pictures in Sec. 1 of the Copyright Act.[43] Thus, the contract introduces a congeries of rights in relation to motion pictures which are not expressly covered in the section of the Act which grants exclusive rights. Moreover, the grant in the agreement purports to break down these motion picture rights into various categories, to wit, silent, sound, dialogue, talking and musical. The species of motion picture rights are thereby detailed. Of course, the word "entire" preceding these purports to make the grant of each of these rights within their respective categories comprehensive.

The reasons for the inclusion of these terms in that form are best borne out by the cases. The Supreme Court, in *Kalem Co.* v. *Harper Bros.,*[44] determined that unauthorized exhibition of a film based upon the book, "Ben Hur" constituted a dramatization and infringement thereof. Justice Holmes stated in his opinion:

> "The subdivision of the question that has the most general importance is whether the public exhibition of these motion pictures infringed any rights under the copyright law. By Revised Statutes, section 4952, as amended by the act of March 3, 1891, c. 565, 26 Stat. 1106, authors have the exclusive right to dramatize any of their works. So, if the exhibition was or was founded on a dramatizing of Ben Hur this copyright was infringed. We are of opinion that Ben Hur was dramatized by what was done. Whether we consider the purpose of this clause of the statute, or the etymological history and present usages of language, drama may be achieved by action as well as by speech.

---

[43] 17 U.S.C. 1.

[44] 222 U.S. 55 (1911).

Action can tell a story, display all the most vivid relations between men, and depict every kind of human emotion without the aid of a word. It would be impossible to deny the title of drama to pantomime as played by masters of the art. *Daly* v. *Palmer,* 6 Blatchf. 256, 264. But if a pantomime of Ben Hur would be a dramatizing of Ben Hur, it would be none the less so that it was exhibited to the audience by reflection from a glass and not by direct vision of the figures—as sometimes has been done in order to produce ghostly or inexplicable effects. The essence of the matter in the case last supposed is not the mechanism employed but that we see the event or story lived. The moving pictures are only less vivid than reflections from a mirror. With the former as with the latter our visual impression—what we see—is caused by the real pantomime of real men through the medium of natural forces, although the machinery is different and more complex."[45]

This case indicates the basis for transmutation of the exclusive rights granted by the statute to contract. Although the context of the case was infringement, it stands for the proposition that motion picture story content based upon a work under copyright represents a dramatization thereof. In terms of the present statute, it would be subsumed under Sec. 1(d)[46] of the present Act as a performance of a dramatic work. The analogy to pantomime in the opinion is also illuminating. The Supreme Court predicated its opinion on the premise that there are various forms of dramatic works, not just the spoken form, but the silent form of dramatization. That is, story may be

---

[45] *Idem* at pp. 61-62.

[46] 17 U.S.C. 1(d).

dramatized without sound or dialogue. Since films at that time were silent, the analogy to pantomime was drawn upon to make the point and reach the conclusion of the opinion. In other words, the statutory grant of rights is generic, being stated in the broadest terms. At the time the statute under consideration was enacted, the motion picture was virtually unknown. At the time of decision, it was, of course, in existence. The opinion indicates that the technique for determination of infringement was to analyze the scope of the generic term and draw upon analogy to existing species thereunder to ascertain whether the new art infringed. By determining that it did, the Supreme Court, in effect, expanded the species comprehended by the generic term to include species not yet known or devised at the time of enactment of the statute based upon their similarity to existing species comprehended by the generic term.

The case founds the film right in the copyright as a dramatization thereof. Consequently, since production, distribution and exhibition of such film would constitute an infringement of copyright unless based upon some grant of right from the copyright proprietor, then in order to be able to make and exploit such film there must be some lawful permission, whether by assignment, license or otherwise enabling the filming and exploitation of the film to proceed. The basis for so proceeding is some form of agreement purporting to make the grant of right. *Kalem* makes clear, therefore, that the source of contract in and to various forms of literary and artistic property is the copyright therein.

Sec. 12.5. Sanction and Scope of Contracts

But sanction for contract and form and extent of contract are not necessarily the same thing. The sanction permits the form of the art to come into commerce but it does not per se determine the scope thereof in commerce. The scope thereof is differentiated by the parties in negotiations. The grantor of the rights, whether it be the proprietor of the copyright of the basic work or an assignee of rights therein, bargains with the other party as to the scope of the rights granted for a consideration. Presumably, if the author has conveyed his copyright to another as proprietor thereof, it was acquired by the latter in contemplation of exploitation of the various rights therein. Thus the reward to the author is derived immediately from his grantee of the copyright and possibly mediately from the exploitation thereof by such grantee. That is, the author may or may not share in the proceeds derived by his grantee from such exploitation and, if not, the consideration to the author directly from the grantee may or may not reflect the grantee's anticipated return therefrom.

The former Register of Copyrights has written, in characterizing copyright as a bundle of rights, "Copyright was no longer a single right, but had become an aggregation or bundle of rights, which might conveniently be referred to as 'copyright' but was in reality, many copyrights." [47] His reference was to the enumeration of exclusive rights in the statute growing by legislative enactment from the original publishing rights. Bundle of rights, therefore, refers to the generic categories constituting the rights under copyright in Sec. 1 of the present Act, subject, of course, to the compulsory license as to mechanicals.[48]

In practice, however, the statute is deemed to subsume all kinds of species which are the subject of contract, be-

---

[47] Kaminstein, Abraham L., Divisibility of Copyrights, Study No. 11, in Studies on Copyright (1963) 623, at p. 627.

[48] 17 U.S.C. 1(e).

cause judicial gloss comprehends the specific in the generic as in *Kalem.*[49] By contract, the parties set forth an enumeration of specific rights which are believed to be subsumed in the generic bundle of rights. Contract is therefore a principal means for the prismatic refraction of the bundle of generic rights denominated the copyright by the statute into the spectrum of specific rights.

Harper Bros. v. *Klaw,*[50] a later case involving the same basic work "Ben Hur" is a good example of this, only this time rights under contract were involved. There the author was also the copyright proprietor. With his permission, Harper Bros., publisher of his novel, granted by agreement in writing to Klaw & Erlanger, well-known theatre managers, i.e., producers, the right to employ writers to produce a dramatic version of the novel approved by author and publisher, and upon such approval, to make no further changes therein, with the sole right in the managers during life of copyright to produce on the stage or perform the dramatic version. Plaintiff sued to enjoin making of a movie by defendants and the latter counterclaimed to restrain violation of their contract.

The Court construed *Kalem*[51] to mean that the filmic presentation of the novel was a proper subject for grant of rights to make the same by contract, had the grant of the agreement been so extensive. It states, "If by the agreement of 1899 the defendants had been granted the exclusive right of dramatizing Ben Hur, or producing any play or plays that might be made out of Ben Hur, there would be no doubt at all as to their right to make a 'movie play,' as well as the kind of play that has heretofore been

---

[49] Note 44, *supra.*

[50] 232 Fed. 609 (S.D.N.Y. 1916).

[51] Note 44, *supra.*

produced."[52] The Court thereby reaffirmed that the sanction for contract is in the generic right granted the copyright proprietor to dramatize by the statute.

But the Court then proceeded to qualify the scope of the grant:

> "But the grant made by that agreement was far more limited. The right conferred was to produce one version only, and that in a particular manner, and in places limited to cities of a certain size. The contract prohibits any change in the manner of performance or text, and contains provisions as to royalties and their computation, confessedly incapable of application to any method of producing photoplays in commercial use or known to witnesses or counsel. It is unnecessary to expand this thought. The whole arrangement made between the parties in 1899 is not only inconsistent with, but repugnant to, the thought of making 'movies' out of Ben Hur."[53]

In other words, the Court construed the agreement between the parties as a limited grant for stage production purposes only. To that extent, the Court accepted the theory of the plaintiffs. The Court observed, "Plaintiffs do not rest upon the contract, nor bring their action to enforce the contract; they seek to restrain the commission of a tort, and leave the defendants to come in and prove, if they can, that the action complained of is not a tort, because it is justified by a contract."[54] This arose in a jurisdictional context because the Court could take jurisdiction of infringement of copyright under the

---

[52] Note 50, *supra,* at p. 612.

[53] *Ibid.* p. 612.

[54] *Idem* at p. 611.

statute whereas breach of contract would be relegated to the jurisdiction of local law. The plaintiffs' theory was based upon the notion of a limited grant of specific rights which were not co-extensive with the generic grant so that any claim of right by defendants in excess of the limited grant was unjustified and therefore tortious. Defendants' counterclaim was similarly couched in tort for jurisdictional purposes.

As to this, the Court stated,

> "Remembering that this is an action for infringement of copyright, the real theory of the counterclaim or cross suit is that plaintiffs threaten to infringe the rights of defendants, and in a very true sense should be considered as infringers themselves. This is exactly what may be and has been done in respect of patents. A patentee may be an infringer of his own patent, if after assignment thereof he does something that amounts to a violation of his contract with assignee. An ordinary action in equity for the infringement of patent rights may then be brought against the patentee himself. . . . The same remedy seems to me open to a similarly injured licensee." [55]

The Court therefore concluded that both the original action and the counterclaim were well brought. But the ratiocination was more than sophistries of jurisdiction, for the rationale of the Court posited the dialectical nature of contract in respect of copyright. A party claiming that his grant of rights by contract is less than co-extensive with the claimed grant has a remedy in tort, in infringement of copyright, while a party claiming rights by con-

[55] *Idem* at p. 612.

tract co-extensive with the claimed grant has a like remedy in tort against the grantor because the latter is without reservation of right in the claimed grant. Being without such reservation of right, the grantor infringes. Thus, in construction of the scope of the grant, the Court has jurisdiction because in each instance, claim and counterclaim, it is determining whether proprietary rights under copyright have been infringed.

Sec. 12.6. Art and Technology as a Source of Rights

It is to be noted that here, the grant of rights was claimed by plaintiffs to be specific whereas defendants in effect asserted them to be generic and co-extensive with the right to dramatize. Plaintiffs were asserting that they had granted stage rights but not motion picture rights. Considering that the grant had been made in 1899, preceding by many years any reference in the statute to motion pictures, it may be seen that plaintiffs' claim of limitation of the grant was based on the theory that the generic grant consisted of many specific rights which might be separately the subject of contract under the umbrella of the generic grant. The underlying premise, as sustained by the Court, is that contract transmutes the bundle of rights, denominated by statute as the copyright, into commerce because contract reflects subdivisions and combinations of the bundle of rights. From a commercial point of view, rights are as variegated as the uses to which the work may be put. Art and technology in this sense, from the point of view of commerce, likewise become a source of rights. Indeed, the source of rights in this regard is as broad as the spectrum of life itself, not only as it may be at the time the specific rights are enumerated in the agreement, but from time to time thereafter, as modified by new uses and technologies. The only condition is the principle of subsumption, that the specific rights that at any time may become the subject of contract must be capable of being subsumed within the statutory rights.

Sec. 12.7. The Principle of Subsumption

But the principle of subsumption contains within it a postscript that constitutes a modification of the tort/contract dialectic. The tort/contract dialectic may be stated as rights not granted under contract which are used under claim of contract are tortious infringement of copyright and that rights granted under contract may not be claimed as retained under contract and if used under reserved claim of contract constitute tortious infringement of copyright. Of course, the frame of reference here is the grant of exclusive right; obviously non-exclusive rights may be granted and also be the subject of reservation. The modification of the tort/contract dialectic is the negative covenant implied in the contractual grant of limited rights that the grantor's use thereof will not be made in such a way as to be to the detriment or destruction of the contractual grant.

Thus, the Court in *Harper* v. *Klaw* qualified its holding in favor of plaintiffs that the contractual grant to defendants was only a limited one by stating:

> "Plaintiffs assert, and almost assume, that since defendants cannot make a 'movie' out of Ben Hur, and such right must exist somewhere, it is in them, as being an unconveyed portion of the copyright estate wherefrom was carved defendants' limited license. In strictness of law I think this true; but it does not always follow that, because one owns a certain thing,

he may use it to the detriment of another, especially if the owner is under contractual obligations to such other. The 'movie' rights to Ben Hur undoubtedly existed in 1899, but in nubibus, or (what is frequently the same thing) in contemplation of law only. As a matter of fact they are an accretion or unearned increment conferred of late years upon the copyright owners by the ingenuity of many inventors and mechanicians.

"In my opinion there is implied a negative covenant on the part of the plaintiffs (the grantors of defendants' restricted license) not to use the ungranted portion of the copyright estate to the detriment, if not destruction, of the licensees' estate. Admittedly, if Harper Bros. (or Klaw & Erlanger, for the matter of that) permitted photo-plays of Ben Hur to infest the country, the market for the spoken play would be greatly impaired, if not destroyed. This being the fact, the law is analogous to that which implies, from a covenant to make a certain use of property, a covenant negative against doing anything else with it." [56]

Thus, the Court acknowledged a theory of existentialism as to copyright—copyright *in nubibus,* in contemplation of law. Movie rights existed in 1899 in some cloudy, misty form, more or less inchoate, but recognized as in being even if only in contemplation of law. *A fortiori,* one might say that broadcasting was likewise *in nubibus* at that time and in being in contemplation of law. If so, then the next step is to look to equities as to the unearned increment conferred by realization of the arts and technologies of new devices, processes and inventions. The

---

[56] *Idem* at p. 613.

Court is quite willing to reserve the increment to the grantor, *provided* the use of the reservation does not hurt the grantee of the limited right. Subject to this proviso, it is willing to enforce the tort/contract dialectic against a grantee on behalf of a grantor or vice versa. But the very qualification by means of such a proviso compels the Court to consider the facts of respective rights granted and reserved. That is, the Court must compare and evaluate the facts of use and potential use of the totality of the granted and reserved rights, in order to ascertain whether impairment or destruction of the granted rights might occur. The Court, in making the comparative analysis of actual and potential uses of such rights, is now in the arena of the factual context of copyright industries and uses. It must evaluate the nature and degree of actual and potential competition of arts media. It has, as it were, become concerned with the configuration of arts industries, in this instance, the competitive effects of performance of the same work in filmic form as opposed to a live stage presentation. The tort/contract dialectic is thereby qualified to correct distortions caused by the economics of competitive effect unduly affecting the rights granted or reserved. Subsumption, then, is subject to equitable considerations of elementary fairness.

But these equitable considerations are reciprocal, as the Supreme Court ruled in *Manners* v. *Morosco*.[57] There, plaintiff, dramatist of the play "Peg O' My Heart", sought to prevent defendant, Morosco, from representing the play in motion pictures in violation of plaintiff's copyright and from producing the play at all. Plaintiff claimed that its grant of right by an agreement of 1912 and a supplemental agreement of 1914 was for five years only. The

---

[57] 252 U.S. 317 (1920).

agreement granted the exclusive license to the defendant to produce, present and perform the play in the United States and Canada. It was to be performed, under the agreement, for at least 75 performances during the 1913-14 season and each season thereafter for a period of five years. It was to be presented in first class theatres with no alterations, eliminations or additions without the author's approval. The agreement provided for a release of the play to stock companies under certain conditions and a sharing of royalties therefrom. The Supreme Court agreed with the courts below that it was not a grant of rights to produce the play limited to a period of five years. Justice Holmes proceeded to analyze the specific language of the contracts and construed them as clearly indicating that no other form of production other than on the stage with live actors was contemplated. Justice Holmes observed, "The implied assumption of the contract seems to us to be that the play was to be produced only as a spoken drama, with respect for the author's natural susceptibility concerning a strict adhesion to the text." [58]

Sec. 12.8. The Principle of Reciprocity

The principle of reciprocity is expressed in two ways. In *Harper* v. *Klaw* it was expressed in terms of a double injunction, the Court stating, "The result is that plaintiffs may take the injunction prayed for against defendants, and the defendants may have the same relief against plaintiffs. The meaning of such double injunction is that as long as the contract of 1899 exists, neither party thereto can produce a photoplay of Ben Hur except by bargain

---

[58] *Idem* at p. 326.

with the other."[59] In *Manners* v. *Morosco,* the Supreme Court expressed its relief in terms of a single conditional injunction, stating, "The result is that the plaintiff is entitled to an injunction against the representation of the play in moving pictures, but upon the terms that the plaintiffs shall abstain from presenting or authorizing the presentation of the play in that form in Canada or the United States.

"*Decree reversed. Injunction to issue upon the condition that plaintiff shall neither represent nor authorize the representation of the play Peg O' My Heart in moving pictures while the contract with the defendant remains in force.*"[60] Presumably, there is no double injunction here because the defendant did not counterclaim for relief. Be that as it may, the basis for injunctive relief as to the plaintiff in each instance is founded on different grounds from that used to protect the defendants in each case. Plaintiff was entitled to injunctive relief in each instance because said party prevailed as to the scope of the grant made by contract. The grant was limited; therefore a use in excess thereof would constitute a tort because the grant was not co-extensive with the rights of the grantor prior to the grant as to the rights the grantee expected to utilize. Injunction was granted to plaintiff in each instance because such contemplated use by the grantee exceeded the grant and infringed the reserved right for such contemplated use which remained in the grantor. Injunction was granted to preserve the exclusive rights in the grantor remaining after the grant; source of rights in the statute was called upon to protect the position of the grantor who had granted less than the

---

[59] Note 50, *supra,* at p. 613.
[60] Note 57, *supra,* at p. 327.

grantee supposed he had received but which was more than the quantum of rights to which the grantee was actually entitled. But the prohibition on use as against the grantor in motion pictures, even though it was determined that the grantor had reserved and therefore owned these rights, was predicated on equitable considerations of fairness to the grantee. The reserved film right could not be used to compete with the grantee's stage rights to the detriment of the latter. Each determination did not go into any analysis as to the quantum of competition but appeared to hold that the possibility of competition in the same territory would constitute a potential impairment or destruction of the grant. In each instance, the implied negative covenant represents a condition read into the contract by the Court by implication to protect the actual, albeit limited rights, of the grantee. Thus the protection accorded the grantee of the limited right in the reciprocity of the double injunction or equivalent relief is effected by contract. That is, the facts of the respective competitive effects of the permitted and reserved uses are compared and the courts then proceed to protect the grantee against the grantor by implying a covenant not to compete to the impairment or destruction of the actual grant.

But contractual implication may be effectively negated by verbal excision of the source of implication. That is, implication is a form of judicial interpretation by reading something into an agreement that is not otherwise expressly stated. If the agreement were express on that point, there would be no basis for the courts to read anything into it. It is a cardinal principle of contracts that parties having contractual capacity, that is, who are not incompetent or are infants or subject to any disability in entering into an agreement, are bound by the terms of their agreement, assuming, of course, consideration and an agreement that is lawful, i.e., not contrary to public policy.[61] Hence, if the parties expressly provide language overriding the basis for implication of any negative covenant, there simply will be none implied.

Edward B. Colton remarks in this regard, "In order to negate such negative covenant, it is essential to provide in the contract that all rights not granted are reserved 'for use'. The words 'for use' should be added to make certain that not only are the rights not granted reserved (for this would follow even if there were no express reservation of rights), but that they can be used in competition with the rights granted." [62]

Indeed, where rights of third parties are involved as bona fide purchasers for value without notice, it would seem that the express reservation of rights in the grantor without more would protect the third party. In *Macloon* v. *Vitagraph, Inc.*,[63] Warner Bros. Pictures, Inc. had contracted for the acquisition of motion picture rights without notice or knowledge of appellant's contract as to exclusive stage rights. Appellant sought to enjoin the exhibition of a talking motion picture in competition with its living-stage production under the implied negative covenant doctrine.

The Court of Appeals for the Second Circuit declined to invoke this doctrine, stating:

---

[61] 2 Williston on Contracts, Third Ed. (1957), Sec. 222; 1 Restatement, Contracts (1932), Sec. 18(a).

[62] Colton, Edward B., Contracts in the Entertainment and Literary Fields, in 1953 Copyright Problems Analyzed 139, 145-146 (1953), edited by Kupferman, Theodore R., Fred B. Rothman & Co. reprint (1966).

[63] 30 F. 2d 634 (2d Cir. 1929).

> "But the parties contracted otherwise. By article XII of the contract, the appellant consented expressly that stock, motion picture, and all other rights, except the rights of a first-class stage production, limited to the territory granted her, remain in the owner. By express provision the parties have rendered inoperative the beneficial rights which the appellant might otherwise have gained from the implied negative covenant within the rule announced in the cited cases. The owner, reserving the rights to 'stock, motion pictures, and all other rights', assuredly intended that it may make use of them. . . . Such rights so reserved, were clear enough in expressing the intent of the owner that it was granting only the rights upon the living stage, and did not intend to embrace or carry with it the motion picture or the vitaphone rights. When asked, upon the argument, counsel for the appellant readily conceded that the term 'motion pictures' employed in article XII included the talking motion pictures herein referred to." [64]

The concession of appellant that the term "motion pictures" includes talking motion pictures is consistent with case law in this area. In the leading case of *L. C. Page & Co. (Inc.)* v. *Fox Film Corp.*,[65] the defendant, Fox Film Corp., had notice of the various grants made. Plaintiff was the successor in interest of the publisher of a novel entitled "Captain January" by Laura E. Richards, in whose name copyright of the work was taken. Plaintiff granted motion picture rights to Principal Pictures Corporation, not including versions with spoken words. When negotiations between Fox and plaintiff bogged down, defendant,

---

[64] *Idem* at pp. 635-636.
[65] 83 F. 2d. 196 (2d Cir. 1936).

Fox, being also dissatisfied with plaintiff's title to talking rights, obtained, through a subsidiary, a quitclaim deed from the author and copyright proprietor, Laura E. Richards, and acquired the silent rights from Principal Pictures Corporation. Plaintiff sought to enjoin Fox.

The Court reversed and granted a preliminary injunction. It stated that by agreement in 1923 plaintiff had obtained the "exclusive moving picture rights" from Mrs. Richards in exchange for stipulated royalties. The issue was whether this included talking as well as silent films based upon the novel.

Judge Swan stated,

> " 'Talkies' were not commercially known in 1923, but inventors had been experimenting with the idea for some years, and plainly the plaintiff contemplated the possibility of the commercial development of sound with motion pictures, for almost contemporaneously with obtaining the license from Mrs. Richards, it granted Principal Pictures Corporation the exclusive right to produce or sell or license motion picture versions of Captain January, with an express reservation of 'the right to use in connection with said motion picture versions any spoken words or words produced by sound of any kind.' It does not appear, however, that Mrs. Richards knew of this reservation or that sound motion pictures were within her contemplation when she executed the 1923 agreement. Nevertheless, we can entertain no doubt that the words used, 'the exclusive moving picture rights,' were sufficient to embrace not only motion pictures of the sort then known but also such technical improvements in motion pictures as might be developed during the term of the license, namely, the term of the copyright. The devel-

opment of mechanism making it possible to accompany the screen picture with the sound of spoken words was but an improvement in the motion picture art. As the plaintiff well says, 'talkies' are but a species of the genus motion pictures; they are employed by the same theaters, enjoyed by the same audiences, and nothing more than a forward step in the same art. Essentially the form and area of exploitation were the same. The mere fact that the species 'talkies' may have been unknown and not within the contemplation of the parties in their description of the generic 'moving pictures' does not prevent the latter from comprehending the former." [66]

Sec. 12.9. The Statute-Contract Syllogism

Thus far, in this opinion, the rationale would appear to follow the formulation of derivation syllogistically from *Kalem Co.* v. *Harper Bros.*[67] That is, the dramatization right is an exclusive right protected by the statute; a motion picture photoplay, i.e., feature, is a dramatization; and a talking motion picture is a species of generic term "motion pictures". It follows that a talking motion picture is a dramatization under the statute. The principle of subsumption would presumably so operate.

Indeed, Judge Leon R. Yankwich, then sitting as a state court judge, appears to adopt some such approach in the case of *M. Rosenberg & S. Lesser* v. *H. B. Wright.*[68] In that case, there was a grant of the "exclusive, universal, *motion-picture, dramatic and spoken-stage rights*". [69] Judge Yankwich assumed jurisdiction under the California Code of

[66] *Idem* at pp. 198-199.

[67] Note 44, *supra.*

[68] 20 C.O. Bull. 599 (Superior Ct., L.A. Cty, Cal. 1934).

[69] *Idem* at p. 601 (italics).

Civil Procedure, Sections 1060-1062 to construe the meaning of an agreement pursuant to which certain rights were transferred even though incidentally the Court might have to interpret rights under the law of copyright.

Judge Yankwich held that the quoted phrase included talking motion picture rights. In his opinion he stated:

> "A motion picture is essentially a dramatization of a subject, presenting characters in conflict, wherein the action is represented by means of a series of photographic stills, which, by means of projection upon a screen, are made to follow one another in such rapid succession as to create the impression of pictures in motion, or of a liquid-like flow of continuous action. The appeal is through the sense of sight, chiefly. This is the character of *all* motion pictures. The addition of sound *does not* change it. It merely makes audible the spoken words of the actors which, whether actually spoken or not, were conveyed formerly by subtitles printed upon the screen. In its essence, a talking picture *is a motion picture made audible,* appealing to the sense of hearing also, and not merely (as formerly) to the sense of sight. The chief appeal is still pictorial. Talking pictures have been thought of, and attempted, long before their successful commercial use began in 1926.
>
> "It seems to us that the words 'motion picture' used in a grant should be given their broad, generic meaning, and be made to include any dramatic representation by means of a series of photographic representations projected upon a screen, whether they are accompanied by sound or not." [70]

---

[70] *Idem* at pp. 601-602 (italics).

The Court then proceeded to find additional support for the same result in the words "dramatic" and "spoken-stage", citing *Kalem.*[71] The Yankwich opinion in effect followed the syllogism that dramatization encompasses genus, motion pictures, which encompasses species, talking motion pictures.

But the Court in *Page*[72] appears to go a bit further in terms of drawing sustenance from contract as it affects the syllogism. Judge Swan proceeded, stating:

> "In *Kalem Co.* v. *Harper Bros.,* 222 U.S. 55, 32 S. Ct. 20, 56 L. Ed. 92, Ann. Cas. 1913A, 1285, it was held that the words, 'exclusive right to dramatize' in the copyright statute, though used when motion pictures were unknown, included the right to produce by motion pictures when that mechanism was later developed; that is to say, the genus embraced the later developed species. In 1915 when the author and the plaintiff first employed the words 'motion picture rights' in the informal agreement evidenced by letters, there can be no doubt that 'talkies' were unknown; hence the analogy of the Kalem Case is perfect. The fact that there the words of a statute were being construed and here the words of a contract are involved does not make the case inapposite. The agreement of 1923 was an amendment of the earlier, less formal agreement and, like it, used the phrase 'moving picture rights.' Obviously the phrase should have the same meaning in each. Hence we think it beyond question that the plaintiff was given the exclusive right to sell or lease talking moving picture rights as well as silent motion picture rights." [73]

---

[71] *Ibid.*

[72] Note 65, *supra.*

[73] *Idem* at p. 199 (italics).

Judge Swan appears to be saying that if the term "motion pictures" was comprehended under the statutory generic term "dramatization" even when the art of the species, motion pictures, was unknown, it follows by analogy that if the genus, motion pictures, was set forth by agreement at a time when the art of talking motion pictures was unknown, that generic term comprehends the species, talking motion pictures. He uses statutory construction as the analogy for drawing the syllogism from contractual construction. The syllogism should therefore properly read that dramatization, as genus granted by statute as an exclusive right comprehends species, motion pictures, granted by contract which, itself, is genus as to various types of motion pictures and comprehends species, talking motion pictures.

Sec. 12.10. The Role of Contract in Transmutation of Rights

It is submitted that this formulation of Judge Swan suggests the manner whereby statutory rights are transmuted into contract. By equating contract to statute by analogy, contract, itself, is the means of transmutation. If the generic terms of the statute may be proliferated into a variety of species by contract, and by judicial gloss are analogized to statutory rights, then there is virtually no limit as to what may be done. For the means of statutory language are limited by the pertinent clauses which are relatively sparse. Contract, on the hand, may be as variegated as the draftsmen and the requirements of each deal allow. If the statute is the prism which refracts the spectrum of rights, then contract is the means by which the spectrum of rights is elucidated. Contract is to be viewed in this context from the perspective of the tort/contract dialectic. A dispute as to copyright infringement may resolve whether or not a right has been infringed. If there should be a determination of infringement, then the adjudication may become the basis for elaboration of a right by contract.

Judicial gloss, then, becomes a principal determinant of rights protectible under contract. Sometimes the lack of decisive determination may make it desirable to enumerate rights even though it is likely that the courts will sustain the grant without the enumeration, as in the cases referred to above regarding talking pictures. Nimmer, for example, observes, "It has generally been held that motion picture rights do include sound motion pictures, but this too has been qualified in some decisions." [74]

To avoid construction, draftsmen will specify, as in the form of agreement we are analyzing, "the entire silent, sound, dialogue, talking and musical motion picture rights . . ." [75] Explicitness has the virtue of elimination of construction, at least where the enumeration of species carries with it meanings of known forms of the generic term.

Contract, then, serves as the indispensable link between source of rights and the market. As such a medium, it is also the instrumentality for implementation of the role of rights in commerce. Contract, moreover, serves in a dual capacity. On the one hand, it is the connecting link between law and commerce, taking law in the sense of the source of rights and commerce, in the generic sense of the flow of rights into transactions, whether or not the same be for profit or non-profit. On the other hand, contract itself is one of the principal market mechanisms. It is a major instrumentality whereby production is realized and performance rendered.

---

[74] Nimmer on Copyright (1969), Sec. 125.3, at p. 543.

[75] Note 42, *supra*.

Contracts

Contract, in effect, becomes three dimensional. Analogized to statute, as in *Page*,[76] it becomes a source of rights along with the statute. Like a communications satellite, it is also the means of transference of rights, i.e., the transmutation of law into commerce. Finally, it is a mechanism of the market itself which is indispensable for carrying out virtually every facet of the arts.

---

[76] Note 65, *supra*.

Chapter XIII

CONTRACTUAL RIGHTS

Sec. 13.1. Rights: Film Art and Technology—Silent and Talking Pictures

It may be seen from the foregoing that disputes as to whether motion picture rights in the silent era embraced talkies, when not expressly granted, basically dealt with changes in technology in the same medium. The changes were of form. In the silent era, dialogue in feature films was represented as spoken, however exaggerated the representations of speech may have been. Superimposed titles conveyed the actual words represented as spoken. Sound accompaniment in the form of music was added, dehors the film, generally by means of live musicians in the pit of the theatre playing assorted musical compositions of their choosing. Sound, in the form of sound effects, was, of course, obviously not in the silent film just as the spoken words of the actors were not heard.

The technology of sound in the film permitted both dialogue and sound effects to be heard and also music and lyrics to be included in the film itself. The change in technology brought with it a change in the art of motion pictures. Thenceforth the medium was not only visual but audio-visual. The cases dealing with the audio-visual rights as to talking motion pictures were concerned with rights in the same medium—film, now catering to two senses, sight and sound, whereas the art of film making had carried with it, insofar as what was on the screen was concerned, only sight.

But the granting clause also included musical motion picture rights, televised motion picture rights, television rights and dramatic rights exclusive of dramatic stage rights with live actors.[1] Musical motion picture rights are still in the same medium, motion pictures, but represent yet another form thereof. Moreover, apart from the addition of music and lyrics as an integral part of the work, the musical form requires adaptation. The silent version of the work is naturally an adaptation of the underlying work of the author; any motion picture would constitute an adaptation thereof, if the basic literary and artistic property is a novel or a play. The scenario for a talking motion picture would be modified from its counterpart in the silent version because now the dialogue is intended to be heard rather than seen in the form of superimposed titles of the silent film. The writer of the screen play is now attuned to dialogue in the natural sense of sound. This may modify the form of the dialogue as written for the talking motion pitcure as compared to the silent version. The dialogue of the screen play writer therefore becomes more sophisticated in the sense that the *sound* of the spoken word is no longer imagined by the audience; it is actually heard. Whatever the theories of cinematography as to the nature of film making as *motion* pictures,[2] talking motion pictures formally are versions of movies where the sound is not just depicted, but heard. However, from a creative point of view, the sound version as an adaptation is close to the silent version as to the means

---

[1] Klein. Harold S., Subsidiary Rights and Residuals in Motion Pictures. Chap. V, of Subsidiary Rights and Residuals, Edited by Taubman. Joseph, (1968), at p. 33. The form granting the motion picture rights appears at p. 40 *et seq.* See also Form No. 1A-2 in Volumes of Forms (hereinafter Form No. 1A-2).

[2] See, for example, Eisenstein, Sergei, Film Form; Eisenstein, Sergei, The Film Sense, Meridian Books Ed. (1957) ; and Pudovkin, V. I., Film Technique and Film Acting, First Evergreen Ed. (1960).

of adaptation. In other words, the means of adaptation is the screen writing, principally the screen play, and very likely, along with it the preliminary outline and treatment. Story lines of the adaptation in each instance would be similar as would the screen play except for the actual dialogue of each. Therefore, of course, the dialogue written for the spoken word would be paramount in the approach of the scenarist for the talking motion picture.

The differing technologies of talkies and silents produce differing versions as art. Artistry of a silent film would consider somewhat different components from the talking film. Action carries all; dialogue is ancillary because it is not heard. That is, movement carries the art of the picture; dialogue is incidental, but not without its requirement of representation if dialogue is depicted. The point is that talking motion pictures represent a progression in the art of cinematography, if not always an improvement, as well as an advance in the technology of the film. But from a creative point of view, the basis for the film, the screen play of each version, sound and silent, is close. In a sense, they are species of the same genus, motion pictures, where the principal effort, at least in the feature, is to tell a story by the interplay of characters in a plot. The adaptive factors of the adaptation are therefore comparable.

The motion picture version of the same work with music represents a more fundamental shift in adaptation to fit the form. Whereas the silent version has sound added to the exhibition by the exhibitor, the talking motion picture version generally has a sound track added thereto as part of the picture. The sound included in the film consists of music and sound effects as well as dialogue. Composers are employed to create the music as part of the film by way of underscoring as background music for the film. On occasion, lyrics are combined with music to create one or more songs.

The collective bargaining agreement of the Composers and Lyricists Guild of America contains various definitions that are pertinent here. Article 1 of the Producer-Composers and Lyricists Guild of America Minimum Basic Agreement[3] is entitled "Definitions". Article 1(a) reads, "A 'composer' is a person who is employed by the Producer for the purpose of composing music and/or lyrics for use in the production of motion picture photoplays."[4] Article 1(c) defines "underscoring" as follows: "'Underscoring' is music composed or used to accompany dramatic action or visual images in motion pictures, but having no significance to the actors and of which the actor is not, as part of the story or plot, aware."[5] Finally the definition of "song" in Article 1(d) completes the picture in this respect. It reads, "'Song' is (i) the music and lyrics of any separate musical composition of which the actors in the motion picture are aware as part of the plot or story, or (ii) the music and lyrics of a separate musical composition intended to be heard by the audience."[6]

Underscoring, then, is incidental music. It may be intrinsic to the motion picture as a component thereof, but it is incidental to the story. Using the language of the definitions, the screen play writer creates the adaptation in literary and artistic form for purposes of being the basis

---

[3] See Spiegel, Irwin O., and Cooper, Jay L., Record and Music Publishing Forms of Agreement in Current Use, (1971), Form 13.6, at p. 621.

[4] *Idem* at p. 622.

[5] *Ibid.*

[6] *Ibid.*

of shooting the film therefrom. There may, of course, be last minute changes therein suggested by the facets of production itself, be it from the facts of the sets or locations, or the suggestions of director, producer, cast or others. The screen play, like the stage play, is wrought, rather than written in final form for shooting without change. It is constantly subject to revision in the course of shooting of the film. But, just as the stage play assumes a final form and is fixed in that form, so the screen play ultimately assumes a final form. If the dramatist should choose to revise his play thereafter, then his revision would constitute a revised version. But the screen play would be deemed fixed in final form, since it would be unlikely to be used again for that picture, except possibly for retakes. Whether or not the screen play as so fixed would be used again for production of the remake would depend upon the producer of the remake. The latter presumably would prefer to have a new screen play created for his remake version.

Thus, the underscoring is not part of the adaptive work, the screen play upon which the film is based. To the same effect would be a song as a separate musical composition intended to be heard by the audience but of which the actors are not aware. A title song opening the picture which is sung off the screen during the roll of the credits of the picture is a case in point. Such a song would likewise not be part of the adaptive work, although, as with the underscoring, it would be a component of the picture and would be judged accordingly by audience and critics alike. But underscoring and title songs may properly be part of a motion picture that is not a musical picture. It is indeed a rare feature motion picture without underscoring, be it composed for that picture, or library stock music selected for synchronization and performance with that picture.

Sec. 13.2. Rights: Film Art and Technology—Musical Motion Pictures

On the other hand, a musical motion picture is a species of motion picture in which the actors are aware of the music and lyrics as part of the story or plot. Musical composition is an integral part of the work as a literary and artistic property. Music becomes a third basic element of the film, in addition to sight and sound. The screen play as an adaptation must take into consideration musical and lyrical values even if the scenarist is not also the composer and/or lyricist. By values, one refers here to the musical compositions as an intrinsic part of the art form of the work and not to qualitative values as to the merit or lack of merit of the music and lyrics. Of course, a work may be largely a musical motion picture where music is part of the story or plot and the actors are aware thereof as such even if there are no lyrics. Thus, features about great composers in which their work is performed as part of the story or plot might be deemed musical motion pictures if the music is to be found therein in sufficient use, for example, for creation of a sound track album.

Thus, a musical motion picture based upon a novel, for instance, differs materially from the talking motion picture based thereon fundamentally in terms of the adaptation upon which the film is based. The silent and talking versions of the same picture may be said to be kindred in that the screen play of each is similar, apart from changes emanating from the technologies of each form. In respect of the musical motion picture, musical composition intrudes as an intrinsic part of the adaptation, whether or not the creator of the screen play is the creator of the musical composition. In short, because of the changes derived by reason of inclusion of the musical composition in the adaptation, the musical motion picture becomes a different genre, a different category of motion pictures caused by the addition of music or music and lyrics. Webster defines the term "genre" as, "A kind, sort, or description of anything; a species; a category;—applied esp. to works of literature or art as falling into distinctive groups with respect to style, form, purpose, etc."[7]

The musical motion picture, by making the music or music and lyrics an intrinsic part of the story or plot, changes the form of the work. This may be seen from the analogy of the musical play. There the composer and lyricist, along with the bookwriter, are denominated as authors, and copyright may be secured in the musical play as a whole by the three collaborators, assuming separate individuals as composer, lyricist and bookwriter respectively. In the absence of publication, common law copyright would be in the three creators as collaborators. They would be deemed joint authors whose work merged into a unitary whole.

The adaptive work for the musical motion picture corresponds except for the fact that the production company is the author of the film as the employer for hire of the screen play writer, composer and lyricist. But in terms of the basic components of the underlying work, adaptation is the means of bringing the novel, if that be the basic work, into literary and artistic form suitable for shooting of the picture. There is no necessary correspon-

---

[7] Webster's New International Dictionary, Second Ed., Unabridged, 1961, at p. 1046.

dence between form of copyright protection securing the component parts of the adaptation and the unitary nature of the work as a literary and artistic property. Thus, a production company may hire a screen play writer to create a script for a musical motion picture. The script may be under common law copyright, never having been published, or copyrighted as an unpublished work.[8] The music may be separately copyrighted by the music publishing company to which the production company assigns the same either as a published work[9] or as an unpublished work.[10] Thus, the adaptation creates the form for the film itself. One must distinguish here between the film itself as an adaptation from the intermediate literary and artistic material on which it is based. The intermediate material itself is a form of literary and artistic property adapted from the underlying material, on which the picture is ultimately based. The production company causes the material to be created, in some instances, after acquisition of rights to make a musical motion picture from the novel, for example. In other instances, it may acquire the intermediate material by assignment after the same has been created not as employee for hire by the creators thereof, or by assignment of the material from the employer for hire as the nominal author thereof.

Here we are concerned with the intermediate material as the adaptation from the underlying work. A genre creates its own requirements of intermediate material for

---

[8] 17 U.S.C. 12.

[9] 17 U.S.C. 5(e). However, if the screen play incorporated the music or music and lyrics, the work as a whole presumably would be copyrightable as a dramatico-musical composition under 17 U.S.C. 5(d).

[10] 17 U.S.C. 12.

adaptation from an underlying work. The musical motion picture is a different genre from the talking motion picture. Pantomime is a different genre from the spoken dramatic stage; both forms may co-exist with live actors. The scenarist for each creates a different adaptation if the respective dramatic works are adapted from the same underlying novel. But the pantomimist, unlike the silent picture with its dialogue being acted and with superimposed titles, performs without dialogue. Pantomime, in short, is a genre of the dramatic arts.

Sec. 13.3(a). Production Rights: Motion Picture Versions

The form of agreement considered by Harold S. Klein, in Article 2 thereof, proceeds to enumerate a congeries of rights.[11] Preceding the enumeration, the Article recites, "2. The Owner agrees that included among the rights so conveyed are the following:"[12] Subdivision (a) thereof reads as follows:

> "(a) The sole and exclusive right to make motion picture versions or adaptations of such Work or any part thereof, and to produce one or more silent, sound, talking, dialogue and/or musical motion picture photoplays of any type now known or hereafter to be known, based upon or adapted in whole or in part from the Work, or any part thereof, or any such versions or adaptations (all such photoplays, versions or adaptations being hereinafter included and embraced in the expression 'motion picture versions');"[13]

---

[11] Note 1, *supra,* at pp. 40-44. See also Form No. 1A-2.

[12] *Idem* at p. 40 and Form No. 1A-2.

[13] *Idem* at pp. 40-41 and Form No. 1A-2.

The clause purports to convey the broadest form of grant of motion picture versions, and is a major mechanism for correspondence of the grant to the market. Alternatively, the grant might have added that such versions might be in any and all languages or dialects. The silent film was international in scope in that meaning was conveyed by the portrayal of the actors. Action predominated. Dialogue was superimposed in titles. Here, however, language was a factor and translation presumably would be required for performance in the various linguistic markets. Talking pictures imposed a greater burden in terms of marketing because the spoken word may be understood only if the audience understands the particular language or dialect of the speaker. To meet this elementary problem of communication, films are often produced in multiple versions, i.e., produced in the language spoken by the cast during the shooting of the film, and then either dubbed into other languages and/or superimposed titles are added in other languages. Dubbing is the synchronization of the dialogue in some language other than that of the original production to the lip movements and action of the original production, usually by the voices of other persons dubbed into the sound track of the foreign language version. The superimposed version retains the sound track as produced and superimposes the dialogue by means of titles in the language or dialect of the audience. Marketing considerations as determined by the distributor govern the decisions as to use of dubbing and/or superimposed titles. Thus, in certain markets, features originally produced in English may be exhibited with superimposed titles, while in others, dubbed versions will be created.

In those countries or territories where the film is released with superimposed titles, for example, a Hollywood film in English released in Mexico with Spanish superimposed titles, for all practical purposes the version in release, insofar as the dialogue is concerned, is akin to the silent film, not so much in technique or technology of the film, but in that the spoken language as spoken is generally not understood by the audience. Rather, as in the silent film, dialogue is comprehended by means of the superimposed titles. Thus, there is an affinity of the talking motion picture to the silent motion picture through the means of superimposed titles where spoken language is a barrier and no dubbed version is presented.

The language of the clause as to motion picture versions is intended to correspond to the necessities of the market. Here the grant of rights enables the producer to make a variety of motion picture versions for distribution of the film in the various territorial and linguistic markets. If the grant of rights were limited to the making of only one talking motion picture from the basic work, the grant would still provide that the purchaser of the motion picture rights could make dubbed versions and versions with superimposed titles therefrom. If the right granted were to make only an English version motion picture, without more, with no right to make dubbed versions and/or superimposed versions, then the potential markets for the film would be seriously limited and the deal might not be made at all.

Sec. 13.3(b). Production Rights: Remakes

Presumably the right to make "motion picture versions" would carry with it the right to make remakes of the picture, i.e., the right to make later versions during the term of the grant, based upon the same underlying work. The essence of this right was expressed by the Court in *Edgar*

Rice Burroughs, Inc. v. *Metro-Goldwyn-Mayer, Inc.*[14] that inherent in the remake rights "there must be and is the right to update and modernize clothes, customs, dialogue, mood and tempo; to use current, modern techniques of color and camera; to adapt the story to the way people live and look at life in this and future generations, rather than in the generation in which the original photoplay was made." [15]

Again, the grantor may reserve the remake rights giving the purchaser only the right to make one basic feature version and dubbed versions thereof as well as superimposing titles on the basic feature version. The reservation of this right might originate from the feeling of the author or his agent that arms length bargaining has produced a satisfactory consideration for the basic feature version grant of rights and that the remake rights ought to be retained for further bargaining at a later date.

Sec. 13.3(c). Production Rights: Musical Motion Pictures

So, too, the author or his agent may restrict the grant to talking motion pictures and reserve the right to make musical motion pictures. This is particularly possible where the underlying property is a stage play. The dramatist might grant the production company the right to make a talking motion picture and motion picture versions thereof without granting and with reservation of musical motion picture rights. The dramatist may have in mind that he might ultimately license the making of a musical play from the work, wherein he might or might not be the bookwriter

---

[14] 15 Cal. Rptr. 611 (Superior Ct., L.A. Cty., Cal. 1961), *aff'd,* 23 Cal. Rptr. 14 (Dist. Ct. of App., 2d Dist. Div. 1, 1962).

[15] *Idem* at p. 614.

thereof. Assuming that a talking motion picture has been made from the play, the producer of the musical play will often endeavor to acquire such rights as the studio might have in the talking motion picture as copyright proprietor thereof, in respect of the musical play he wishes to produce. He would then have the plot, story, characters, etc., of the film to draw upon as well as the original stage play. He would also draw upon the residue of popularity of the talking motion picture version. The studio would consider granting the rights, provided it received some position as an author for purposes of sharing in the gross receipts in the play and the subsidiary rights therein. Equally important, it would obtain a right of first refusal to make a musical motion picture version of the musical play as a condition of its agreement granting the producer such rights. The producer of the musical play would presumably have a designated bookwriter, composer and lyricist enter into collateral agreements with the studio as proprietor of the talking motion picture.[16] Thus, the sequential roll begets derivative work after derivative work, with contract being the instrumentality for the development thereof.

Sec. 13.3(d). Production Rights: Adaptation Rights

Subdivision (b) of the form provides, in part:

> "(b) The sole and exclusive right to translate into all languages, to freely adapt, change, transpose, rearrange, add to and subtract from such Work, or any part thereof, and the title, theme, plot, sequences, incidents and characterizations thereof, to make interpolations in and substitutions for any part or parts

---

[16] See Form Nos. 3A-2.2b to 3B-1a, inclusive, in Volumes of Forms.

> thereof, to make sequels to and new versions or adaptations of the Work or any part thereof, to make serials of the Work, or any part thereof, of two or more episodes, to use any part or parts of such Work or of the theme thereof or any incidents, characters, character names, scenes, sequences or characterizations therein contained in conjunction with any other work or works, and to separately or cumulatively do any or all of the foregoing, to such extent as the Purchaser, in its sole discretion, may deem expedient in the exercise of any of the rights, licenses or privileges herein conveyed . . ." [17]

The first part of the clause makes explicit that the making of motion picture versions or adaptations of the underlying work may be translated into all languages. It merely spells out what is implicit, but by so doing, avoids a construction of the grant in subdivision (a) as to the scope of the grant of foreign language versions. The last part of the clause, not quoted above, includes the right to superimpose titles, subtitles, text and dialogue excerpted from the basic work or translations thereof. Together they form the basis for dubbing foreign language versions and superimposing titles. Foreign language versions in this context may include English. For example, if the picture is produced in France in a French language version in the original, then foreign language versions would include English.

The key to the next part of the quoted clause is "to freely adapt." Adaptation from one medium to another presupposes revision in material respects. That is, the very nature of the form of each necessitates change. If

---

[17] Note 1, *supra,* at p. 41 and Form No. 1A-2.

the basic work is a long novel, the film adaptation necessarily requires compression of the novel's incidents to manageable filmic form in feature length. A feature usually runs for ninety minutes, more or less. Even a feature of greater length of some two to three hours requires selection from a novel of any length. If compression were not intended to customary feature length, as in the two-part Russian motion picture version of Tolstoy's "War and Peace" of some six to seven hours' aggregate duration, the fact remains that the art of cinematography is not the art of the novel. Words of the narrative are replaced by images in motion, i.e. motion pictures. Dialogue is transformed from the inner ear of the reader, as he or she images it to be heard, to actual spoken words with all of the impact of speech. Adaptation from the written to the filmic form is a necessity, therefore, in any film in material respects as ingredients of the change of art forms. But the clause goes much further. The clause is intended to permit the film maker to change the basic work liberally, as to title, theme, plot, sequences, incidents and characterizations thereof. The film company, as purchaser of the motion picture rights, seeks virtually complete freedom of adaptation. Its approach is "free form", not in the sense that the film itself will be without form, for even the so-called plotless film has a form of its own derived from the editing and final cut of the film. Without form here means freedom to pull away in any manner from the novelist's form of theme, incidents, plot and characterizations in any manner or direction desired by the film maker as ultimately reproduced in the picture from the shooting script. In this respect, part of the clause not quoted above grants the purchaser the right to interpolate music and lyrics in the film and to market and exploit the same and to secure copyright therein as an incident thereof.

The foregoing rights are basically production rights to enable the producer to make the picture in the manner he wishes. The agreement grants the purchaser the right of assignment in Article 11 thereof. If the purchaser should be an independent production company, it probably will enter into a financing-distribution agreement with a studio.[18] Although some of the major film companies are currently divesting themselves of their studios, since the term "studio" has historically been used to denote major film companies engaged in production and distribution, it will continue to be used herein as synonymous with major distribution companies, since many of them continue to own studios and to make production possible. If they do not produce themselves, they certainly induce production by means of financing-distribution deals. The term is also intended to encompass United Artists Corp., which is only a distributor without studio facilities and which has not engaged in production itself, because its role in financing and distribution of films is comparable to the other majors.

An independent producer making a deal with a studio will normally be required by the latter in the financing-distribution agreement to allow the studio the final cut of the film,[19] unless the individual producer or the director employed by the independent production company has such stature in the industry as to command the leverage in the negotiations of the right to make the final cut. Thus, vis-à-vis the author of the basic work, the rights granted must be assumed to go beyond the purchaser thereof insofar as the various rights of production are concerned.

---

[18] See Form No. 1E-1 in Volumes of Forms.

[19] *Ibid.*

Sec. 13.4. Sequel Rights

The right to make sequels is of a different character. Sequels are follow-up motion pictures based upon some or all of the themes, plots, sequences, incidents and characterizations of the first motion picture. Sequels are not the same stories, substantially, in up-dated versions, but later films produced with enough identifying factors from the original film, be it characters, location, story line, incidents and the like, which are expected to carry over the good will and reputation of the original film into the sequel. Sequels represent further free adaptations, only this time from the original film. Economic motivation for making sequels is similar to that of reasons for adapting any other work, namely, it is hoped that recognition and approval of the original work will somehow inure to the sequel because the components utilized in the sequel version permit identification of the sequel version with the original.

Lindey, in his form book, utilized a clause which is tantamount to a definition of the sequel and reads as follows:

> "(b) The term 'sequel' as herein used shall mean a motion picture produced after the production of the initial Motion Picture hereunder or a remake thereof as above defined (1) that deals with substantially the same characters as those present in the original Motion Picture; (2) that has a substantially different plot, story-line and episodes; (3) that reveals the characters in substantially new and different situations; and (4) that represents a continuation of the original story, not a re-telling of it." [20]

---

[20] Lindey, Alexander, 1 Entertainment Publishing and the Arts —Agreements and the Law, Form 5: A-2.01, at p. 307.

Unlike the production rights in the clause, this is a right to make motion pictures in addition to the original which are based on some kind of follow-up development of characters, plot and sequences. An author of the underlying work with any leverage will normally insist upon additional compensation for the sequel rights, perhaps by way of writing the sequel story and payment therefor. Then again, the author with enough stature may decline to grant sequel rights altogether, as a valuable economic right which he would retain for the future. The author may wish to write new novels utilizing the same characters and continuing the original story and sell the motion picture rights *de novo* to the same purchaser or others. In that event, any subsequent picture made therefrom might not necessarily be a sequel. If the same producer were to make the picture, he would draw upon the original film, assuming he had the right to do so in his deal with the studio under a financing-distribution deal. That would then constitute a true sequel. But if another producer were to make a picture based upon a follow-up novel without any rights to draw upon the original picture, it would not be a sequel version of the original picture since the producer would not be able to draw upon that initial film except by way of infringement thereof.

Sec. 13.5. Serial Rights.

The reference to the right to make serials of the underlying work or any part thereof in two or more episodes refers to a form of production that is little utilized currently but which was of economic importance in the decades preceding television. The Saturday matinee in the neighborhood movies often included serials, that is, a film produced in episodic form with suspenseful endings in each episode that was shown weekly in succession for a series of weeks.

The serial was basically a very long feature shot in episodic form for exhibition of each episode weekly with the resolution of the problem ending each episode taking place in the serial the following week. The language of the clause was intended in this respect to grant the producer the right to make serials from the original or remake feature. Again, the intent was to enable the studio to exploit the goodwill and reputation of the feature by embodiment in serial form in a later version. The economic purpose is comparable to that of the sequel except that the serial was generally intended for a special market—children. The grant itself is broad enough so that the producer might make serials of the basic work without adapting serial versions from feature versions of the work.

Sec. 13.6. Character Rights

In this regard, it is an interesting question whether or not the clause grants exclusive character rights, sequels and serials aside. The clause grants the rights of production to freely adapt characterizations and to use characters, characters' names, characterizations in conjunction with any other work or works and to separately or cumulatively do any or all of the foregoing in the purchaser's sole discretion. It may be concluded from the clause that the purchaser has exclusive rights to use the characters to make sequels and serials. But if there were no grant of such sequel and serial rights, does the clause grant the purchaser exclusive character rights? Because the clause purports to grant the right to use the characters, character names and characterizations in connection with works other than the underlying work, it may be construed that the grant carried with it the right to use the characters in new pictures created by the producer or assigns which were not technically sequels.

By contrast, in the *Sam Spade* case, *Warner Bros. Pictures, Inc.* v. *Columbia Broadcasting System, Inc.,*[21] the Court of Appeals stated, "We are of the opinion that since the use of characters and character names are nowhere specifically mentioned in the agreements, but that other items, including the title, 'The Maltese Falcon', and their use are specifically mentioned as being granted, that the character rights with the names cannot be held to be within the grants, and that under the doctrine of *ejusdem generis,* general language cannot be held to include them." [22] In that case, Dashiell Hammett had granted, along with his book publisher, Alfred A. Knopf, Inc., motion picture rights to Warners and later granted radio serial rights to CBS. Warners was unsuccessful in its litigation against CBS based upon claim to the character rights in Sam Spade, the detective. The Court also adverted to the genre, namely, that authors of detective stories carried their leading characters, from one story into succeeding stories, e.g., Sir Arthur Conan Doyle—Sherlock Holmes; Earle Stanley Gardner—Perry Mason. The Court felt that the way to obviate this practice was not by using a general clause following specific grants.

A subsidiary question was whether characters were copyrightable under the copyright statute. The Court observed,

---

[21] 216 F. 2d 945 (9th Cir. 1954).

[22] *Idem* at p. 949. Cf. Columbia Broadcasting System, Inc. v. De Costa, 377 F. 2d 315 (1st Cir. 1967), cert. den. 389 U.S. 1007 (1967) wherein De Costa was held to have published the character of Paladin without notice. Basically the writing was his business card which read, "Have Gun, Will Travel, Wire Paladin, N. Court St. Cranston, R.I." See also Davis, Richard F., Sequel Rights: Federal Copyright Protection of Fictional Characters, 2 Perf. Arts Rev. 315 (1971) and Raskin, Kenneth, Copyright Protection for Fictional Characters, 2 Perf. Arts Rev. 587 (1972).

"It is conceivable that the character really constitutes the story being told, but if the character is only the chessman in the game of telling the story he is not within the area of the protection afforded by the copyright." [23] The Court then made its determination, "We conclude that even if the Owners assigned their complete rights in the copyright to the Falcon, such assignment did not prevent the author from using the characters used therein, in other stories. The characters were vehicles for the story told, and the vehicles did not go with the sale of the story." [24]

Nimmer criticizes this view, stating, "This seems to envisage a 'story' devoid of plot wherein character study constitutes all, or substantially all, of the work. There may be rare examples of such works, but for most practical purposes such a rule if followed would effectively exclude characters from the orbit of copyright protection. This is certainly not in accord with the principle suggested by Learned Hand . . ." [25]

The reference to Judge Hand is to his dictum in *Nichols v. Universal Pictures Corp.*[26] There Learned Hand stated,

> "But we do not doubt that two plays may correspond in plot closely enough for infringement. How far that correspondence must go is another matter. Nor need we hold that the same may not be true as to the characters, quite independently of the 'plot' proper, though, as far as we know, such a case has never arisen. If Twelfth Night were copyrighted, it is quite possible that a second comer might so closely imitate Sir Toby Belch or Malvolio as to infringe, but it would not be

[23] *Idem* at p. 950.
[24] *Ibid.*
[25] Nimmer on Copyright (1969), Sec. 30, at p. 135.
[26] 45 F. 2d 119 (2d Cir. 1930).

> enough that for one of his characters he cast a riotous knight who kept wassail to the discomfort of the household, or a vain and foppish steward who became amorous of his mistress. These would be no more than Shakespeare's 'ideas' in the play, as little capable of monopoly as Einstein's Doctrine of Relativity, or Darwin's theory of the Origin of Species. It follows that the less developed the characters, the less they can be copyrighted; that is the penalty an author must bear for marking them too indistinctly." [27]

In the recent case of *Goodis* v. *United Artists Television, Inc.*,[28] the Court of Appeals for the Second Circuit held that a notice of copyright on installments of a serialized novel, "Dark Passage" in the name of the periodical publisher and not in the name of the author inured to the latter's benefit and was not in the public domain. As to this, the Court stated, "We unanimously conclude that where a magazine has purchased the right of first publication under circumstances which show that the author has no intention to donate his work to the public, copyright notice in the magazine's name is sufficient to obtain a valid copyright on behalf of the beneficial owner, the author or proprietor." [29] Limiting the doctrine of indivisibility of contract to a procedural device, relating primarily to the prerequisite interest to bring an infringement action, the Court reversed the court below and declined to apply the doctrine as to the requisite interest of a party who may act to obtain copyright, particularly where the author is the plaintiff. In that case, a television series entitled "The Fugitive" had been produced by the defendant TV company based on a

---

[27] *Idem* at p. 121.

[28] 425 F. 2d 397 (2d Cir. 1970).

[29] *Idem* at p. 399.

claim of right derived from Warner Brothers to whom the author had granted the rights to make the motion picture "Dark Passage". The Court of Appeals reversed the court below, 2-1, as to the grant of motion for summary judgment on this point.[30] It held that the language of the agreement clearly did not permit production of "The Fugitive" so as to entitle the defendant to summary judgment. The Court indicated that the agreement clearly conveyed to Warner Brothers the right to make a movie and to show the same on TV. It also conveyed "the right to vary the plot and characters of *Dark Passage.*" [31] The Court posed the question as to whether or not the contract unambiguously placed any limits on the degree to which Warners could change or modify characters. The Court observed, "Viewed in the context of the entire contract, the 'additions' and 'alterations' clauses of Paragraph 17 could be read in a more restrictive manner to permit only those alterations necessary to adapt a written story to the medium of film. Similarly, use of the word 'unlimited' with respect to the rights to alter and supplement could have been intended only to prevent Goodis from protesting that his story had been distorted or mutilated." [32] Judge Waterman felt that a full inquiry was necessary because he did not wish the decision of the Court on appeal to affect the interpretation of other contracts where some divisible rights are conveyed which

---

[30] Judge Lumbard wrote the opinion, which was unanimous, that serialization in installments with notice of copyright by the publisher, but not in the name of the author, did not throw the work into the public domain. On the issue of what was contracted by plaintiff author, the opinion of Judge Waterman constituted the majority opinion, Judge Kaufman concurring; the opinion of Judge Lumbard in this regard becoming the dissenting opinion.

[31] *Idem,* opinion of Judge Waterman, at p. 405.

[32] *Idem* at pp. 405-406.

do not explicitly mention among the rights conveyed the right to make 'sequels', i.e., subsequent stories employing the same characters. The Court referred to this term "as such stories are called in the publishing industry." [33] He indicated that it was not crucial that the complaint below "used the term of art 'sequel' in referring to the television series." [34]

Sec. 13.7. Sequel Motion Pictures: Sequel Stories

The last reference of Judge Waterman indicates some of the difficulties inherent in the same term being used for different purposes. A sequel in film nomenclature has a specific meaning along the lines used in the clause quoted from Lindey.[35] The opinion of Judge Waterman also refers to sequel stories as so referred to in the publishing industry. There may therefore be sequels of the underlying work. Finally, one must distinguish between the nature of the rights from the nature of the sequels. Thus there may be television rights in sequels[36] which form the basis for television series rights.[37] Thus, a television sequel would be a second or subsequent TV work following an initial TV work. A TV series technically is a related group of TV shows, whether filmed, live or taped, with some common format or theme. The series may be viewed as a unitary whole, in which event no episode thereof could be a sequel, or as separate works in the series, one following another. As a term of art, a series is not a sequel, although technically it has many of the characteristics thereof.

---

[33] *Idem* at p. 406.
[34] *Idem* at p. 407.
[35] Note 20, *supra.*
[36] See Note 1, *supra,* Article 13(f) at p. 57 and Form No. 1A-2.
[37] *Idem,* Article 14 at pp. 57-60 and Form No. 1A-2.

Contractual Rights

The long form contract analyzed by Harold S. Klein contains option pages which define both "sequel motion picture" [38] and "sequel" in the sense of underlying work.[39] As to the former, the form provides,

> "The term 'sequel motion picture' as used herein shall mean any motion picture subsequent to the first motion picture based upon the Work:
>
> (a) in which the leading character or characters is or are taken from the Work; and
>
> (b) in which said character or characters are shown as participating for the most part in new or different events than those in which such characters participated in:
>
> (i) the Work, or
>
> (ii) the first picture or any remake thereof, or
>
> (iii) any earlier sequel or any remake thereof; and
>
> (c) in which the story is substantially different from that as set forth in:
>
> (i) the Work, or
>
> (ii) the first picture or any remake thereof, or
>
> (iii) any earlier sequel or any remake thereof." [40]

As to the latter, the form states,

> "the term 'sequel' as used in this Article 16 shall mean new material:

---

[38] *Idem,* Article 15, at pp. 60-61 and Form 1A-2.
[39] *Idem,* Article 16, at p. 61 and Form No. 1A-2.
[40] Note 38, *supra* and Form No. 1A-2.

(a) In which the leading character or characters are taken from the Work; and

(b) In which said character or characters are shown as participating, for the most part, in new and different events than those in which such character or characters participated in the Work; and

(c) In which the story of such new material is substantially different from that set forth in the Work." [41]

As *Goodis*[42] indicates, the grant of rights of free adaptation including characters, character names and characterizations may be limited to adaptation rights in respect of the film medium. Yet the very language of the grant may well be determinative as to whether the grant is so broad as to encompass certain subsidiary rights, here the right to create stories based upon the same characters, as the basis for a television series. Thus, in Subdivision (b) of the motion picture rights agreement quoted in part above, we find references to both production rights with respect to the making of motion picture versions and various spin-off production rights as to other types of film production, e.g., sequels and serials. The latter, in terms of the sequential roll of the producer, would ordinarily follow the production of the initial feature film some time thereafter. The spin-off rights are production rights in the same medium, however—film. But draftsmanship is merely a matter of form, which is basically what is in the eye of the beholder, the draftsman, as ultimately negotiated with his counterparts representing other parties to the agreement.[43] Conceiv-

---

[41] Note 39, *supra* and Form No. 1A-2.

[42] Note 28, *supra*.

[43] See, Taubman, Essentials of Professional Draftsmanship, The Lawyer's Encyclopedia (Prentice-Hall, 1963) at p. 161.

ably the same clause might contain so broad a grant that character rights, not only in motion picture sequels, but in story sequels, would be conveyed by the author as owner to the purchaser.

Sec. 13.8. Exploitation Rights

In a sense, the form of agreement under scrutiny contains a variety of clauses which overlap in some respects. Article 2(c)[44] continues the enumeration of grant of rights by granting the right to advertise and exploit the work and its title in relation to the film made based upon it. It is essentially a clause enabling the distributor to advertise and market the film and is primarily an advertising clause for advertising, publicizing and promoting the picture and the underlying work in relation thereto, that is, to advise the public that the film was based upon a given, well-known literary and artistic property.

Subdivision (d)[45] again is a comparable clause intended to promote the film on radio. Yet the language of the clause is broad enough to raise questions as to whether or not the entire film may be broadcast, not only on radio but also on television. The principal intent is to permit excerpts from the film recorded on electrical transcriptions or other sound recording to advertise the film. Yet, the clause may allow live broadcast thereof. Also, the exclusive right to "broadcast by radio, wire or any other means or method" might be deemed generic as to broadcasting and possibly include television, subject to construction as to whether the enumeration of radio, but not television, should be deemed an intent to exclude the latter under the *ejusdem generis* clause, to wit, that the enumeration of particulars excludes

---

[44] Note 1, *supra*, at p. 42 and Form No. 1A-2.

[45] *Idem* at p. 42 and Form 1A-2.

other categories that are not in the same category of those enumerated. Fortunately, construction is not necessary. Just as Subdivision (e)[46] enumerates various exploitation rights in motion picture versions, so Subdivision (f)[47] specifies various broadcasting rights in the motion picture versions, including television.

Subdivision (f) grants essentially a sound right in the underlying work, i.e., the right to make recordings in sound in synchronization with the motion picture versions and to reproduce the sound separately or in synchronization with the film. This is again an elaboration of the sound, dialogue and talking motion picture rights granted in Subdivision (a)[48] and also a method of detailing the various forms the sound rights may take.

Subdivision (h)[49] is the enumeration of a subsidiary right, the right to publish a novelization of each motion picture version, in order to advertise and exploit the picture. Thus, the film producer is thereby authorized to obtain a paper back publisher to publish a novelization of the film itself.

Subdivision (i)[50] is a broad grant of rights with respect to use of the title of the underlying work as the title of the film or of other films not based upon such work and as the title of musical compositions.

Subdivision (j)[51] is a grant of the right to secure copyright in the motion picture versions throughout the world.

---

[46] *Idem* at pp. 42-43 and Form No. 1A-2.
[47] *Idem* at p. 43 and Form No. 1A-2.
[48] *Idem* at pp. 40-41 and Form No. 1A-2.
[49] *Idem* at p. 44 and Form No. 1A-2.
[50] *Idem* at p. 44 and Form No. 1A-2.
[51] *Idem* at p. 44 and Form No. 1A-2.

This is buttressed by an elaboration of copyright benefits in the underlying work in Article 3[52] and further protective provisions as to future publication in Article 5[53] and renewal copyrights in the basic work in Article 6.[54] Further protection is granted the purchaser in Article 8 in the event of future publication, novelization or dramatization of the basic work.[55] Article 4 sets forth the owner's warranties and agreement of indemnification in the event of breach thereof.[56] Apart from the all-important, as to the author-owner, consideration clause, the remainder of the short form agreement is boiler plate except that Article 14[57] provides that nothing in the agreement will serve to derogate or impair any rights, licenses and privileges that the purchaser may have as a member of the public if the agreement were not in existence.

Sec. 13.9. Source of Rights in Contract

Thus the short form of agreement purports to spell out a variety of rights for production, distribution and exhibition of motion picture versions that the purchaser or assigns may make based upon the underlying work. The language of the clauses is far greater in scope than the language of the clause granting exclusive rights secured by copyright under Sec. 1 of the Copyright Act.[58] In terms of film rights, there is an enumeration and specification of rights that go on and on.

---

[52] *Idem* at p. 45 and Form No. 1A-2.
[53] *Idem* at p. 48 and Form No. 1A-2.
[54] *Idem* at pp. 48-49 and Form No. 1A-2.
[55] *Idem* at pp. 49-50 and Form No. 1A-2.
[56] *Idem* at pp. 45-48 and Form No. 1A-2.
[57] *Idem* at p. 52 and Form No. 1A-2.
[58] 17 U.S.C. 1.

This catalogue of rights granted, as so enumerated, emanates in the first instance from the facts and experiences of the motion picture industry. A major motion picture distributor is in the business of exploiting film versions in all sizes and gauges. Feature films will, ordinarily, be shot in 35mm for theatrical release; they may, in a big picture, be produced in 70mm. Prints will, in due course, be reduced to 16mm for exploitation by its 16mm department, directly or through licensees for non-theatrical release, e.g., ships, planes, hospitals, schools, and other institutions. Its television division or subsidiary or licensee will handle 16mm prints for release of the picture on television. It may also have an 8mm department for sale of short subjects, usually, but not of features. It probably also has music publishing and recording divisions or subsidiaries which will often exploit the musical copyrights in the underscoring and/or songs included in the film and which may release sound track albums of the picture. Its advertising and publicity departments will handle publicity, advertising and promotion, while its sales department will handle actual licensing of the picture for theatrical distribution.

The enumeration of clauses in such detail represents a specification of rights to back up felt needs of the various facets of the business of making and exploiting motion pictures in commerce. Most of the rights enumerated in the agreement can be translated into rights secured by the copyright statute. Article 7 of the agreement, however, grants the purchaser the right to publicize, advertise and use the name of the author in connection with the picture with a concomitant screen credit. This right is not based upon or secured by copyright but is a right of personality. In the absence of such a grant of right, the purchaser would be without right to so use the name of the author of the underlying work and might subject itself to a claim of violation of the rights of privacy of the author.[59]

Contract, with respect to a literary and artistic work in the arts, therefore, represents the grant of rights of all kinds and is not necessarily limited to rights secured by copyright. Contract contains its own bundle of rights which, as has been seen, may be far more detailed than the rights generically granted by statute. It is almost as if the purchaser of the rights were determined to obtain every conceivable protection by specification and enumeration of rights. Partly, this results from prior litigation where one or another party may have foundered for failure to specify or reserve a particular right. Contract represents an effort to correct such omissions. Partly, the form of the contract is dictated by a desire to avoid litigation, whether or not there has been prior litigation, by a particularization of rights.

In short, the cataloguing of rights is very often a function of the particular branch of the arts involved and its customs and practices, contract-wise. A right, in this regard, is then drafted as a sanction for particular industry behavior that is desired by the recipient thereof without regard, ultimately, to whether or not it is secured by copyright, privacy, or some other rule of law.

Contract, then, is the means whereby the grant of rights materializes. Consideration is the *quid pro quo* that the grantor receives from the grantee therefor. Rights take form by agreement, and the corollary, insofar as the grantor is concerned, is that he has obligated himself, that the rights granted are valid and subsisting. His obligation is expressed in his warranties and in his agreement to make

---

[59] See Civil Rights Law of New York, Sec. 51, for example.

good, in the event his grant of rights fails to hold up, by his agreement to indemnify, save and hold the grantee harmless for failure of the granted rights to stand up.

Contract, then, is the means of transference of rights from the proprietor thereof to other parties in order to set the commercial possibilities immanent therein in motion. Contract is then a prime market mechanism for the passage of rights in the copyright industries. The source of rights is in the market place itself as protected by the statute, or, alternatively, by common law where there has been no divestive publication. But it is only by contract that the source of rights can be translated into permissible commerce.

Contract, then, gives form to the copyright industries, reflects the practices of the copyright industries and is the basis for their extension into subsidiary activities and rights.

Chapter XIV

RIGHTS IN OTHER MEDIA

Sec. 14.1. Television Motion Picture Rights and Television Rights

Article 1 of the form of agreement we have been analyzing with respect to the grant of motion picture rights in a literary and artistic property grants:

> ". . . exclusively and forever, the entire silent, sound, dialogue, talking and musical motion picture rights, *televised motion picture rights, television rights* and dramatic rights (excepting only the right of production upon the spoken stage with living actors appearing and speaking in the immediate presence of the audience) in all languages and for the entire world, all such rights being hereinafter included and embraced in the expression 'motion picture rights'"[1]

Article 2 enumerates various rights of production and exploitation thereof.[2] Subdivision (g) thereof is a broad grant of broadcasting rights with respect thereto reading:

> "(g) The sole and exclusive right to transmit, broadcast, project and reproduce said Work and any adaptations or versions thereof and any motion picture versions, or any parts of any of the foregoing, and/or the sound, talking, singing, and other audible pictures

---

[1] Klein, Harold S., Subsidiary Rights and Residuals in Motion Pictures, Chap. V of Subsidiary Rights and Residuals (1968), edited by Taubman, Joseph, pp. 32-65 at p. 40 (emphasis added). See also Form No. 1A-2 in Volumes of Forms (hereinafter Form No. 1A-2).

[2] See Chap. XIII, *supra*.

thereof, through space for exhibition or reproduction at any and all places away from that wherein the same shall be projected or performed, with living persons or otherwise, by television, radio, electrical transcription, electricity, facsimile or in any other manner or by any other method whether now known or hereafter known, invented or devised." [3]

Insofar as the two clauses may be read together as a grant of television motion picture rights and the right to telecast the work, the result is clear. The language of the two rights as formulated in the preceding sentence is redundant. But then the generality of Article 1 and the enumeration of the rights included therein in Article 2 reflect a redundancy wherein the draftsman, out of an abundance of caution, first states the generic right—in Article 1—and then proceeds to enumerate species of the generic right—in Article 2.

Sec. 14.2. Non-Theatrical Rights and Television Rights

In part, this is an attempt to cope with the judicial gloss of case law. In *Weiss* v. *Hollywood Film Enterprises, Inc.*, plaintiff had granted to defendant the " 'exclusive right to make, sell, exploit, lease, license, rent and exhibit positive prints with sound in black and white in sixteen and eight millimeter sizes made from . . . described 35 millimeter size black and white negatives, non-theatrical only . . . owned by plaintiff.' " [4]

The Court granted an injunction against television use in 16 mm. or 8 mm. of the films. It considered the contract

---

[3] Note 1, *supra,* at p. 43 and Form No. 1A-2.

[4] 81 U.S.P.Q. 570, 571 (Superior Ct., L.A. Cty., Calif. 1949).

unambiguous except as to the term "non-theatrical". The Court then observed, "Accordingly, if, as claimed, these words have a trade meaning, parol evidence is admissible to show the trade meaning." [5] But whether or not parol evidence was actually adduced in this proceeding is not clear from the opinion.

The Court then proceeded to construe the clause against the defendant, stating,

> "The contract does not grant nor indeed does it speak of 'television' rights. What the defendant has is the right, as restricted by the phrase 'non-theatrical only,' to sell, lease, etc. the 16 and 8 positive prints *as such,* but without any additional rights. Plainly, the defendant may sell or license the 16 and 8 positives but he may not grant along therewith *to any one*—for theatrical or non-theatrical uses—television rights. Defendant does not have any such rights by the contract. The television productions are in the theatrical and not in the non-theatrical field must be obvious to everybody. As the defendant does not have any television rights, its endeavor to sell or lease such rights, is a violation of the property rights of plaintiff quite apart from any breach of the written contract in selling or leasing the positives for theatrical uses." [6]

It is submitted that the Court's conclusion is correct although for the wrong reason. The juxtaposition of theatrical uses versus non-theatrical uses originates from pre-television days. Film production on a commercial basis was principally for exhibition in theatres. The non-theatrical uses were mainly institutional, on ships, in

---

[5] *Ibid.*

[6] *Ibid.* (italics).

schools, hospitals and installations that were not primarily commercial. Moreover, such institutions generally used smaller auditoria or other facilities than the conventional motion picture theatre. Therefore, another distinguishing factor was generally the *gauge* of the print, with theatres using principally the larger 35mm. in which the feature was produced, and the non-theatrical institutions generally exhibiting in 16mm. reduction prints.

Thus "theatrical" and "non-theatrical" delineated different markets for the film. 8mm. film generally represented another market for short subjects which might be sold, rather than leased or licensed for exhibition, for home use. But, again, the context was non-theatrical in that its market was not the theatre, but facilities other than the theatre.

The non-theatrical market, however, represented a market of live projection, in the presence of an audience, just as did the theatrical market. In each instance, projection of the film and exhibition were simultaneous and within the same facilities in which the audience viewed the film.

Television superficially resembled the 16mm. non-theatrical market in that 16mm. reduction prints were also used. The Court was correct in its result because television motion picture exhibition is a different market from the 16mm. non-theatrical market. Television represents a *new* market that is distinct from the traditional 16mm. one. Television broadcasting constitutes a form of exhibition wherein projection is separated from exhibition and where there is no audience as such in the traditional sense. Television broadcasting is primarily for home viewing on the televison receiver, which is quite a different instrumentality from the silver screen in the theatre or the variety of institutional screens utilized. Television, too, is only superficially akin to home use of 8mm., or for that matter, 16mm. There is no simultaneous projection and exhibition within the same facility on television as compared to home viewing, theatrical or other non-theatrical exhibition.

Therefore, it is clear that the defendant did not receive the rights from the plaintiff. The term "non-theatrical" is a term of art in the motion picture industry which does not encompass television as such. However, the Court went too far in concluding that if television exhibition was not non-theatrical it must therefore be theatrical. The term "theatrical" in motion picture exhibition is likewise a term of art; it denotes exhibition in a motion picture theatre. The primary form of television exhibition is in the home and not in the theatre. There may be occasional closed-circuit television exhibition in the theatre, e.g., a championship prize fight telecast to selected motion picture theatres where the audience pays a price for admission. But this is a very special form of television and not the usual context for television motion picture rights. For film would be exhibited directly from a projector in the theatre and would not normally be telecast thereto. Even exceptional events, like a sporting event, as above, could not be shot in the medium of film for instantaneous transmission of the event as it occurs because film takes a period of time to develop. An audience would not normally pay for closed-circuit television exhibition in a theatre for delayed transmission, because the basis for its interest is in viewing the event as it takes place since the telecast is not otherwise available for immediate viewing.

Sec. 14.3. Television Motion Picture Rights

Shortly thereafter, the District Court had occasion to construe clauses as to television film rights in *Wexley* v.

KTTV, Inc.[7] There, John Wexley, author and copyright owner had granted film rights to his play "The Last Mile" in 1931. The picture was telecast over station KTTV in 1950.

The 1931 agreement granted broad motion picture rights but did not grant television motion picture rights in so many words. As to the character of the grant, the Court stated: "It will be observed that the owners grant '. . . the sole and exclusive right throughout the world to make . . . exhibit, . . . motion picture versions of the said dramatic composition . . . in any manner and method now or any time hereafter ever known or made available . . .'."[8] This was sufficient for the Court to conclude, "Television, being a presently known method of exhibiting motion pictures, the right to televise motion pictures is granted unless a limitation or reservation is expressly and clearly imposed."[9]

In fact, the 1931 agreement included four specific categories of rights reserved: "(a) production rights on the spoken stage with living actors, (b) publication rights, (c) television rights unaccompanied by a visual representation of the play, (d) the right to transmit or otherwise make available and visible performances of the said play, direct from living actors in a place other than that in which the actors are physically present."[10] The plaintiff had conceded that (d) referred to live television. The Court speculated that the parties might have had in mind recitals of the play in reservation (c) without the picture being tele-

---

[7] 108 F. Supp. 558 (S.D., Cal. 1952). See also Bartsch v. Metro-Goldwyn-Mayer, Inc., 391 F. 2d 150 (2d Cir. 1968).

[8] *Idem* at p. 559.

[9] *Ibid.*

[10] *Ibid.*

cast. There was a restriction of 15 years from the date of the agreement against the transmission of live television versions of the play reserved by the grantor. The Court then concluded, "It is quite obvious that the reason television rights *accompanied* by a visual representation of the play were not reserved was because such a reservation would conflict with the right granted by the purchaser to exhibit motion pictures in 'any manner or method now or any time hereafter ever known or made available'." [11]

The explanation of the nature of the restriction on live television tells us much about rights in other media. The Court opined, "The obvious reason for applying the fifteen year restriction 'to live television' *only,* was because *it was considered the most serious competition to the exhibition of motion pictures.*"[12]

The pattern goes something like this. The source of rights generically is in the Copyright Act or the common law if there has been no divestiture of common law copyright by publication. The rights secured by copyright, e.g., the right to perform and dramatize, are then granted with respect to any given medium. The historical pattern has been the grant of rights for the then established medium. Technology creates the basis for new media and therefore for new art forms. The presentation of the underlying work as adapted for each medium is generally deemed a performance of the same work as so adapted. Performance of the same works in different media in some kind of geographic propinquity may be potentially competitive. A presentation of a feature adapted from a play or performance of feature, as well as play, as adaptations from the same underlying novel in neighboring theatres

---

[11] *Idem* at p. 560 (italics).
[12] *Idem* at p. 560 (italics).

are considered competitive to each other. The populace drawn upon for audience may be the same in both cases. People with limited means may choose to see the one or the other. Also, a number of persons constituting potential audience may believe, without regard to their means, that it would be wasteful of time and money to see both versions and might choose one or the other. If the cost of the picture should be less than that of the play, economies of admission price might lead them to select the film. Soo, too, the availability of seeing the work on free television, whether it be the film version or a live or taped television version, might seem preferable to spending money to see the same work or the film adaptation of the same underlying work in the motion picture theatre.

Sec. 14.4. Competition Among Rights in Different Media

In short, the possibilities of exploitation of the same work, or different adaptations of the same underlying work, in various media render the respective rights of such exploitation potentially competitive with each other. Contract is a principal market mechanism for regulating such potential competition. The judicial doctrine of implied negative covenant that a grant of rights in one medium, which is potentially competitive with another without reservation of rights in the other medium, prevents the grantor from competing in the other medium to the detriment of the grantee in the granted medium is a principle of contract applied to the facts and circumstances of exploitation of rights secured by copyright.[13] At times, where there has been a refusal to deal, that is, a refusal

[13] See, Harper Bros. v. Klaw, 232 Fed. 609 (S.D.N.Y. 1916); Manners v. Morosco, 252 U.S. 317 (1920).

to enter into contractual relations, the antitrust laws will be invoked alleging that the failure to contract, i.e., refusal to deal, was a combination and conspiracy in restraint of trade under the antitrust laws. Thus, in 1952, the United States filed suit alleging such failure to release feature films for television broadcasting by the studios in favor of theatrical distribution, in *U.S.* v. *T.C.-Fox Film Corp.*[14] Judge Yankwich held such refusal to release to be reasonable since there was a direct relationship of the restraint to the protection of theatrical exhibition which had already been seriously affected by the growth of television. Also, the Court recognized that tentative, probing and experimental approaches to release of features to television had already taken place. Judge Yankwich opined, "It would be inequitable to force agreement, especially when reluctance, or even refusal to deal *(assuming that there was refusal)*, was not only the result of separate determination by each company, but was *temporary,* was dictated by the sound economics of the situation, the wish to make the most desirable arrangements consistent with a fair protection of their interests and the refusal of the lately-arrived customers,—the television industry,—to commit itself to definite guarantees."[15]

This case would tend to explain why certain contractual clauses might be prevalent at given times and not at others. If the studios, acting independently, believed that keeping their features off television tended to protect the theatrical market for the same pictures, then there would be no contract granting such right to television stations or networks or other TV users such as sponsors. This would imply an absence of contract with respect thereto. On the other

---

[14] 137 F. Supp. 78 (S.D. Cal. 1955).

[15] *Idem* at p. 115 (italics).

hand, if the studio licensed various rights to third parties, it might protect its position in this regard by providing, in some way, that television motion picture rights were not granted and were reserved.

Sec. 14.5. Draftsmanship and Rights in Other Media

But this presupposes that the studio had acquired the television motion picture rights in the first place with respect to the underlying work. The three cases referred to above, *Weiss, Wexley and T.C.-Fox Film Corp.*,[16] provide valuable insights into the progression of formulation of rights in other media, draftsmanship and the development of restrictive contractual devices to regulate competition of rights granted or reserved in the various media. Judicial gloss in interpretation of contractual clauses, as in the first two of these cases, becomes a catalyst for development of terms of art. In both *Weiss*[17] and *Wexley*,[18] the Courts had to construe language of each grant drafted at a time when television was not yet commercially viable. In a sense, the importance of such construction is not in the actual decision, important though each result may be in the development of the common law with respect to the scope of contractual grants involving film for television. In point of fact, litigation is intended as a determination of disputes among the parties thereto. The parties have resorted to the courts for resolution of imperfect language. Judicial determination has the effect of revealing to the world as a whole the imprecision involved in the cases at issue. To overcome occurrence of possibilities of litigation, draftsmen attempt to draw the necessary conclusions

---

[16] Notes 4, 7 and 14, *supra*.

[17] Note 4, *supra*.

[18] Note 7, *supra*.

from the results of litigation, be the decision in favor of one side rather than the other. Terms of art are developed that have greater clarity of meaning precisely because they are understood, being clearer than other language which might be used.

Thus the term "television motion picture rights" or words of similar import, such as "televised motion picture rights" as used in the form under analysis[19] will be used by draftsman in the sense of the right to telecast the film on television, either as a grant or reservation of such rights. But application of draftsmanship to take into account the lessons of judicial gloss is not the only explanation. Experience with the medium at issue is also involved. The grant of film rights to "The Last Mile" in 1931 in *Wexley*[20] only dimly perceived the patterns television would take at a later date. The draftsman, indeed, could not do otherwise because television was, at best, a technology on the horizon and not a present reality in 1931. The draftsman handles this problem of necessarily imperfect perception by imagination and improvisation. He tries to do the best he can with the inadequate factual tools of experience at his disposal.

The quality of *ad hoc* draftsmanship as to rights in new media is an ever present problem in a period of rapidly changing technologies of the arts. Thus, in a comparable situation today, a draftsman granting rights in television might consider possibilities of coverage of uses of audio-visual cassettes. Rights in home television use have yet to be developed as terms of art because the use of various forms of home television of such cassettes and other devices has barely begun. Until such usage assumes mini-

---

[19] Note 1, *supra,* at p. 40 and Form No. 1A-2.
[20] Note 7, *supra.*

mal importance in the market, the legal ramifications can be only dimly perceived and draftsmanship directed thereto will necessarily be imperfect even though such provisions might be as artful and sophisticated as they might be drafted in the premises. Experience, then, is a factor going to the nature and the form of the rights in new media and uses.

Sec. 14.6. Live Theatrical Television Rights

Sometimes industry precepts and practices furnish guidelines as to the nature and form of contractual provisions even where the types of uses under consideration may still be in their infancy. Thus, in the form under analysis, although live television is reserved to the owner in Article 13 of the long form contract,[21] certain types of television presentation are excluded from the live television rights reserved to owner. Thus, Article 13(b) provides:

> "(b) There are expressly excluded from the live television and dramatic rights herein reserved to the Owner the right to exercise same for transmission and projection through space for exhibition or reproduction at any theatre and/or place of public assembly away from that wherein the same shall be projected or performed, by television, electronically, or in any other manner or by any other method, whether now known or hereafter devised." [22]

This exclusion of telecast in a theatre of a live TV show, in theory, is directly competitive to the theatrical exhibi-

[21] Note 1, *supra* and Form No. 1A-2. The long form contract is set forth at pp. 54-65. Article 13 thereof appears at pp. 55-57.

[22] *Idem* at p. 55 and Form No. 1A-2.

tion of the motion picture of the same underlying work. That is, suppose there were no such exclusion. Based upon the reservation of such rights, to project and perform a live telecast at a theatre might enable a producer to present a closed circuit telecast with live actors which is transmitted and projected through space into a number of theatres where admission is charged. If a feature motion picture of the same underlying work is concurrently in theatrical exhibition, then it may be seen that the television adaptation with live actors could seriously affect the box office of the film, particularly if the live telecast were to take place in a number of first run markets.

In terms of actual experience with such a situation, the instances thereof are probably few and far between, if, in fact, the supposed instance has ever taken place. But the fact remains that producers have experimented with live telecast of dramatic works into theatres commercially. There have also been any number of closed circuit telecasts of sporting events into theatres as the events take place, particularly of boxing matches. It does not take the draftsman much to visualize the possible devastating impact of a competitive closed circuit theatrical telecast of reserved live television rights which has not been excluded. The clause, then, is derived from the *potential* imagined effects of such competition as conceived by the draftsman for the film company and reflects the fears of film distributors as to what might materialize, absent such a clause. Improvements in technology and/or the current vogue at any given time might very well cause the feared effects to materialize. For example, the recapturing of the events of the live outsized rock festival *à la* Woodstock and the commercial film made thereof could conceivably be sought in a closed circuit theatrical telecast live of the event rather than by film. A promoter of such a telecast could conceivably be very successful therewith. A failure to restrict such rights in a given situation, that is, to exclude them from the reservation of live television rights, might indeed prove disastrous to the purchaser of the motion picture rights. Of course, the nature of the underlying work and the proposed use of the motion picture rights will have a bearing as to the commercial possibilities of the closed circuit theatrical television rights. Thus, if a purchaser acquires rights to an underlying work of a certain theme, content and style, it might be anticipated that the motion picture adaptation will be the factor of commercial value and that a closed circuit theatrical telecast will have zero commercial value. This may indeed be true of the generality of literary and artistic properties wherein motion picture rights are granted, namely, that the fears of closed circuit theatrical telecast are ungrounded. Of course there are inhibiting factors. It probably will not be attempted in respect of works where the films based thereon are commercially unsuccessful. So, too, where the picture is a multi-million dollar production or embodies artistic production values it might be foolhardy for a promoter to attempt to compete therewith.

But draftsmanship in contract often covers not only what will, but what might be done. The sequential roll at times might seem to be self-propelling and self-generative of values. For example, "Pygmalion" by George Bernard Shaw, might start out as one of his better known plays. The film based thereon will add to its value as a known work. "My Fair Lady" by Alan J. Lerner and Fritz Loewe, as a musical play based thereon, then added to the lustre of the work substantially, while the film version thereof likewise won artistic and commercial acclaim. The sequential roll has enhanced the value of the basic work and the derivative works immeasurably. A reserved live television right might conceivably have tempted some promotor, foolhardy enough to try it in this context, to telecast a new version of "Pygmalion" by closed circuit theatrical television if such rights had been reserved and not excluded in relation to the grant of musical motion picture rights in the play. Normally, the failure to exclude the closed circuit theatrical television rights from reserved live television rights is therefore a risk the draftsman prefers not to take. Since the right, in the eyes of the grantor, at the time of the making of the deal with the film producer is at best minimal, he will generally accede to the exclusion of this right from reserved live television rights as being of little or no economic value. Yet, the exclusion is provided as a safeguard for the granted film rights and as a protection against conceived possibility of competition therewith.

Sec. 14.7. Pay TV and Live Television Rights

A more direct reason for exclusion is to be found in connection with the exclusion of pay TV from the reserved rights. Article 13(c) provides in this respect:

> "(c) Any and all rights herein reserved to the Owner do not include the right to exhibit or reproduce a performance of any kind by means of subscription television, whether the audience pays directly or indirectly or whether the payment may be made by means of cash, tokens or credit or in any other manner or by any other method, whether now known or hereafter known, invented or devised." [23]

Here the intent is not only to exclude the right from the reserved live television rights of the owner, but by reason

---

[23] *Idem* at pp. 55-56 and Form No. 1A-2.

thereof to vest the same in the purchaser. It will be recalled that Article 1 grants the purchaser "television rights and dramatic rights" excepting live stage rights.[24] Article 13(c) takes pay TV out of the reserved right of the owner. By reason of Article 1 and the exclusion of reservation by Article 13(c), pay TV would appear to be vested in the film producer.

This is the result precisely desired by the draftsman because film distributors consider pay TV to be an alternative form of film distribution to theatrical film distribution, the principal form for which features are produced for exploitation in the first place. The basis for theatrical exhibition of motion pictures is the admission price—the box office. Pay TV, by making payment for seeing a particular program the condition precedent to such viewing, accomplishes a like result in theory. Free television, by contrast, is not dependent upon payment for that specific program as a condition for seeing the same. A flick of the dial, without more, brings on the picture in free television. It may be argued that higher prices for products of television sponsors is an indirect subsidy since it results in recoupment of cost paid by the network, station or sponsor for the particular program. Philosophically, free television might indeed have an economic cost basis but in terms of tangible outlay, directly or indirectly, by the viewer, the relationship is too remote to be analogous. Payment for television here refers to either a direct outlay of moneys, such as putting coins into a device attached to the television set, or indirect outlay of some form of charge, registered electronically and/or mechanically, that becomes the basis either for billing for that program or

---

[24] *Idem* at p. 40 and Form No. 1A-2.

periodic charges for actual programs viewed or for contractual right to view stated programs or all programs in a given time interval.

Then, too, the film distributor knows from experience that free television usually will license features for telecast to commence after the same have first been exhibited in the theatre during a given period of time. The interval of time elapsing between theatrical exhibition and telecast of features has become less and less over the last two decades. The existence of television itself has materially affected viewing habits in the theatre and concomitantly, patterns of theatrical distribution. Television replaced motion picture theatres as the principal mass media of the visual arts. Production of motion pictures for the theatre was accordingly affected. The large number of features produced annually, including features known as program features which enabled film exhibition to run one or two changes weekly of single or double features in a sequence of runs at various theatres, gave way to more restricted and selective production with fewer runs and different patterns of distribution, such as multiple first runs at showcase theatres. At the same time, television motion picture rights, i.e., the license to telecast the same features, more and more assumed importance in terms of recoupment of negative cost, i.e., investment in cost of production of a picture. If television motion picture rights were, in the first decade of television, subsidiary rights in terms of motion picture production, by the advent of the second decade they could be deemed integral to such rights and, in an economic sense, not even subsidiary. In other words, economic recovery of investment was looked to from both theatrical exhibition and television on any sound, realistic projection of economic possibilities.

But the postulate of this is that the economic return could take place in two media, rather than in one. The producer and distibutor, in theory, might be made whole in two bites, as it were, by theatrical exhibition as the primary economic form of film distribution and by television distribution. For the converse of that proposition did not prove particularly viable, namely, the initial release of a film on television and the subsequent release thereof in the theatre. Viewers would not pay to see the film in the theatre if they were able to see it free on television. *A fortiori,* viewers paying for the right to see a film on television at home would certainly not pay to see the same film in the theatre in most instances. From the consumer point of view, pay TV represented a net subtraction from the market for the theatrical exhibition. It is this factor that has generated opposition of film exhibitors to pay TV.

Equally important, from the point of view of the distributors, pay TV appeared to be a virtual El Dorado which beckoned as the means of fortune making and as a superior future form of exhibition that might displace the theatres. Pay TV might, in theory, be the mass market for features in the future, so that telecast of features on pay TV might reap rich returns, literally with one telecast or possibly with a very limited number of telecasts, as compared to the policy of repeated exhibitions of the same picture during its run in the theatre. Moreover, the expenses of distribution might be reduced materially compared to the elaborate structure of film exchanges or branch offices in various parts of the country which are necessitated by theatrical exhibition in order to have ready access to the market.

In short, pay TV was conceived as the possible wave of the future in feature film exploitation. Moreover, pay

TV was actually tested over extended periods of time.[25] In order to be commercially feasible, pay TV either had to come up with events not otherwise programmed on free television or telecast films earlier than free television might license the same. For the license of films to pay TV, distributors assumed pay TV to be directly competitive with theatrical exhibition, and runs and clearances in any given area were set in such film licenses in terms of both the theatres in that geographical vicinity, as well as the pay TV facility. From the point of view of the market, pay TV was deemed to be prime competition to theatrical exhibition. This was so much so, indeed, that whereas features licensed to free television might be licensed by a subsidiary or affiliate of a studio, pay TV was licensed directly by the film distribution company itself.

For the foregoing reasons pay TV in a typical motion picture rights agreement, as per our agreement under analysis, was not included as part of the live television rights reserved to the owner. The purchaser obtains exclusive television motion picture rights in the agreement under analysis by means of Article 1[26] thereof. By Article 2(g) thereof, this includes the exclusive right to broadcast by television by any other manner or method now known or hereafter known, invented or devised.[27] Clearly the purchaser would have exclusive television motion picture rights on pay TV. The reservation of live TV rights might otherwise enable a competitive

---

[25] For example, the RKO General television station in Hartford, Conn. was authorized by the Federal Communications Commission to conduct experimental pay TV in collaboration with Zenith. There were other tests, both over the air and by cable, in various parts of the United States and Canada.

[26] Note 1, *supra,* at p. 40 and Form No. 1A-2.

[27] *Idem* at p. 43 and Form No. 1A-2.

adaptation under rights derived from the owner to be licensed on pay TV, but for the language of Article 13(c) excluding the same.[28] Thus, motion picture industry precepts and practices tend to explain why the exclusion is set forth therein, whether or not pay TV telecast live might be economically practical or feasible.

Sec. 14.8. CATV and Live Television Rights

The foregoing discussion as to closed circuit theatrical television and pay TV indicates the context in which contractual clauses might originate as to the newer form of CATV. As the possibility of program origination on community antenna facilities broadens, they, in turn, become a source of rights. Reserved rights as to live television, for example, in the form of agreement under analysis, might well consider a comparable exclusion of cable television.

Indeed, CATV is close in economic context to pay TV. CATV provides a service to its subscribers in the form of a community antenna which is a device to overcome logistic problems in rural areas or electrical interference in urban areas. In the course of so doing, it is able to bring in additional channels off the air over and above those received by the subscriber in the absence of the CATV facility. Subscribers pay an installation charge and a monthly service charge. Thus, unlike free television where costs are fully absorbed in the United States by sponsors or sustaining programs, the owner of the television receiver is attuned to paying the CATV operator for the use of the facility as a subscriber thereto. The essence of pay TV is payment for special programming—generally conceived of as free of advertising and free of

---

[28] *Idem* at pp. 55-56 and Form No. 1A-2.

commercial interruptions. Program origination on CATV would represent an additional service to the subscriber. Unless the CATV operator were to be recompensed out of advertising of programs, the economics of program origination would dictate some form of payment by the subscriber therefor. This might be on an overall subscription basis per week, per month or on some per program basis charged to the subscriber tuning in on the same.

The essence of the decision in *Fortnightly Corporation* v. *United Artist Television, Inc.*[29] is that CATV as such is little more than a transmission facility. Justice Stewart stated in the majority opinion, "The function of CATV systems has little in common with the function of broadcasters. CATV systems do not in fact broadcast or rebroadcast. *Broadcasters select the programs to be viewed;* CATV systems simply carry, without editing, whatever programs they receive. Broadcasters procure programs and propagate them to the public; CATV systems receive programs that have been released to the public and carry them by private channels to additional viewers. We hold that CATV operators, like viewers and unlike broadcasters, do not perform the programs that they receive and carry."[30]

Program origination would obviously constitute a selection of the programs going to the subscribers. Presumably the CATV system would then be procuring and propagating programs. Presumably, too, the failure to be licensed therefor would constitute an infringement of copyright of an exclusive right under Sec. 1 of the Copyright

---

[29] 392 U.S. 390 (1968).

[30] *Idem* at pp. 400-401 (emphasis added).

Act,[31] even though traditional CATV operation as a transmission facility without program origination would constitute a non-infringing use.[32]

Proposed copyright revision purports to regulate CATV, including provisions for a compulsory license under Sec. 111 of S. 543.[33] This, in turn, represents a revision of prior drafts.[34] As to this, speaking of a prior draft, the House Report observes, "Section 111 must necessarily be a complex provision."[35]

It is to be noted that Sec. 111(f)(C) contains a definition of a cable system, which reads:

> "(C) A 'cable system' is a facility operated for purposes of commercial advantage that receives signals transmitted by one or more television broadcast stations licensed by the Federal Communications Commission and simultaneously makes secondary transmissions of such signals by wires, cables, or other communications channels to subscribing members of the public who pay for such service."[36]

The House Report sets forth the industrial context of CATV, stating:

> "In general, 'community antenna systems' are commercial subscription services that pick up broadcasts of programs originated by others and retransmit them

---

[31] 17 U.S.C. 1.

[32] Note 29, *supra*.

[33] S. 543, 91st Cong., 1st Sess., Jan. 22, 1969, Dec. 10, 1969 Print.

[34] See, for example, S. 543, Jan. 22, 1969 Print, and Report No. 83, 90th Cong., 1st Sess., House of Representatives, Mar. 8, 1967, at pp. 48-59.

[35] *Idem.* at p. 52.

[36] Note 33, *supra*.

to paying subscribers. A typical system consists of a central antenna which receives and amplifies television signals, and a network of cables through which the signals are transmitted to the receiving sets of individual subscribers. In addition to an initial installation charge, the subscribers pay a monthly service charge averaging about $5 or $6. The number of CATV systems in the United States has grown very rapidly since their introduction in 1950, and now totals between 1,500 and 2,000 systems with more than 2 million subscribers and annual revenue of over $150 million.

"The CATV industry had its beginnings in areas where mountainous terrain or other conditions make satisfactory television reception impossible without a special antenna. In recent years, in addition to providing better reception of local stations, community antenna systems have been moving into larger communities and offering their subscribers a choice of more programs by bringing in signals from distant cities."[37]

Whatever the effect of program origination of cable systems as a form of pay TV on the liability of CATV under Sec. 111,[38] our concern here is with rights in literary and artistic properties utilized by CATV as a form of

---

[37] Note 34, *supra,* at pp. 48-49.

[38] The House Report, *idem* at p. 56, states, "The committee believes that if a transmitter operates as a 'pay-TV' service to any extent it should lose its special status as a secondary transmitter". It refers to Sec. 111(b)(3) imposing full liability if there were separate, direct charges for any particular transmission. Subdivision (b)(3) appears to be stricken in S. 543, Dec. 10, 1969 Print, note 33, *supra.*

pay TV. CATV, as such form of pay TV, would be subject to the exclusion of reserved live television rights referred to in Article 13(c) of the form under analysis.[39] The motion picture industry practice of treating pay TV as a medium directly competitive to theatrical exhibition in the licensing of features for exhibition would apply as much to cable systems as to pay TV of television broadcasting stations.

To the extent CATV enters into program origination, it becomes directly concerned with copyright protection in respect of such programs. Its status differs from its position under *Fortnightly.*[40] In that case, its position was that of permissible transmission because its function was not that of a copyright user in the traditional relationship to artist or creator. Artist here is used in the broadest generic sense of performer. It was neither adapting an underlying basic work nor acting in some entrepreneurial capacity with respect to performance. Like the theatrical manager presenting a touring production originating elsewhere, the broadcaster functions comparably, assuming responsibility for the programming of that station even though the program might be, and very often is, originated elsewhere. As a minimum, the broadcaster pays for the license to perform if he licenses the program directly. Thus, in syndication of a motion picture, for example, the broadcaster will enter into a licensing agreement providing for payment of a sum of money for telecast of the feature for the various runs licensed or possibly for unlimited use over a period of time.[41] Different arrangements are made if a program originates

---

[39] Note 1, *supra,* at pp. 55-56 and Form No. 1A-2.

[40] Note 29, *supra.*

[41] See Form Nos. 2E-1.1 to 2E-3, inclusive, in Volumes of Forms.

from the network to which the station is affiliated. Then the network may be the producer or co-producer of that program or else has acquired broadcasting rights thereto from a third party producer.[42] In such event, the relationship of the station to the program would be derived from its affiliation agreement with the network.[43] The station, as such, would not have licensed performing rights directly from the producer if the latter were an independent producer. The source of rights of the station, then, is a function of its status. If the television station itself were to produce programs, then its position is comparable to the purchaser of the motion picture rights in the agreement under analysis.[44] Its capacity would then become creative, as such producer. That is, it would acquire adaptation and production rights for the creation of a television program from the underlying work, as well as rights of distribution and exhibition.[45]

Consequently, it may be seen that the term "program origination" is susceptible of several meanings. Such meanings would be applicable to program origination of CATV as well. A particular cable system might originate its own programs by producing the same. Its status would be comparable to the local broadcasting station or group of stations engaging in production, or, indeed, to any other producer of television programming *qua* producer. As producer, the cable system would be concerned about the requisite grant of rights in and to the underlying work and its status as a creator of a derivative work

---

[42] See Form No. 2D-4 in Volumes of Forms.

[43] See Lindey, Alexander, Entertainment Publishing and the Arts —Agreements and the Law, Vol. 2, Form No. 6:E-2.01 at p. 631.

[44] Note 1, *supra*.

[45] See Form Nos. 2A-1 and 2A-1a-2.1a, inclusive, in Volumes of Forms.

or possibly creating new programs from original scripts written by telescript writers as employees for hire for the cable system as author. There would follow the enumeration of production, distribution and exhibition rights.

By contrast, the cable system may not be its own producer and nevertheless still be a program originator. There it would function like the television broadcasting station selecting and procuring programs from a variety of sources. The cable system might obtain programs specially prepared for performance over the cable systems by the studios and other producers of television programming. Various cable systems might combine in some sort of cable network so as to obtain programs from the cable network as affiliates thereof. Yet again, cable systems might license programs through some sort of group buyer for economies of purchasing. Market-wise, the cable system would be a user of programs, whereas as a producer the cable system would be not only a user of its own productions, but be involved in production and distribution as well. Thus, the concept of program origination as an economic form of operation of the cable system is not necessarily co-extensive with the manner of program origination. It is the manner of such origination which is co-extensive with contractual consequences. Thereby, economic activity is transformed into a source of rights by contract.

Sec. 14.9. Enumerated Rights and Generic Rights

Considering the variety of television rights, the grant of television rights exclusively in Article 1 of the agreement under analysis[46] requires elucidation. Article 2(g) sets forth a broad exclusive grant to transmit, broadcast,

---

[46] Note 1, *supra,* at p. 40 and Form No. 1A-2.

project and reproduce the underlying work and adaptations and film versions and with living persons or otherwise.[47] However, Article 13 of the long form contract commences, "With respect to the reserved right to televise the Work direct from living actors only." [48] Elsewhere in that article, there are references to the live television rights reserved to the owner and to the live and dramatic television rights reserved to the owner. Consequently, to be internally consistent, the grant of Article 1 of "television rights and dramatic rights (excepting only the right of production upon the spoken stage with living actors appearing and speaking in the immediate presence of the audience)" [49] must be deemed to constitute a reservation of both live stage rights and live television rights. Perhaps the agreement should contain an explicit reservation of live television rights at the inception in Article 1 because the reference to reservation of live television rights does not appear in the short form of this agreement.[50] The long form contains option pages purporting to govern the relationship of the parties as to the restrictions and uses in respect to the reserved rights and arrangements as to sequel rights in television and motion pictures.

Also confusing is the broad grant of exclusive right to broadcast, not only radio adaptations or versions of the motion picture version, but also of the underlying work itself, not only from sound records but with living persons or otherwise.[51] Yet Article 12 of the long form recites, "With respect to the radio broadcasting rights not herein granted

---

[47] *Idem* at p. 43 and Form No. 1A-2.
[48] *Idem* at p. 55 and Form No. 1A-2.
[49] *Idem* at p. 40 and Form No. 1A-2.
[50] *Idem* at pp. 40-53 and Form No. 1A-2.
[51] Article 2(d), *idem* at p. 42 and Form No. 1A-2.

to Purchaser." [52] One wonders what has not been granted to purchaser in the broad grant of radio rights made exclusively. Again, there is no other express reservation, which, perhaps, should appear early in the agreement.

The enumeration of rights in contract should be, above all, internally consistent and free from doubt and confusion as to what is intended, particularly when one is dealing with established media. The problem with the run-on enumeration of rights is that it has been drafted with an eye to maximizing the specification of rights of the user because the form has been prepared and printed by the user. Edward B. Colton has observed, "Incidentally, it is preferable not only in the reservation clause, but also in the grant clause, to use broad, general language rather than to enumerate the particular rights which are included." [53] Here the grant contains broad, general language in Article 1, but Article 2 not only enumerates particular rights which are included but a good deal of the language of Article 2 is likewise broad and general.[54]

Sec. 14.10. Restrictions and Reservation of Rights

In any event, the long form is interesting because the reservations of rights and the restrictions are explicit. These clauses constitute a virtual regimen or system of regulation between the parties of potentially competitive uses of reserved and granted rights. Thus Article 11 restricts owner from presenting the underlying work on the stage with live actors for a period of years

---

[52] *Idem* at p. 55 and Form No. 1A-2.

[53] Colton, Edward B., Contracts in the Entertainment and Literary Fields, in 1953 Copyright Problems Analyzed, edited by Kupferman, Theodore R., Fred Rothman & Co. reprint, (1966) at p. 146.

[54] Note 1, *supra,* at pp. 40-45 and Form 1A-2.

as agreed upon by the parties after the first general release of the film in the United States. The clause is a recognition of the potential competition between a film and a play based on the same subject matter, whether or not the underlying work was a story or the play, or whether or not the play may have been derived as an adaptation of a motion picture. The latter would arise where a musical play was based upon an adaptation of a feature film. In terms of a grant of rights to stage the musical play, the parties might also restrict the release of the feature film for a period of time. But that would depend on the relative strength of the parties in the course of bargaining and the importance of that film in release to the studio. Sometimes, as in the case of a grant of rights to make a musical motion picture from a musical play, the restriction may not be overall in the United States but may be limited to enumerated major cities constituting the key first run markets for the film or the cream of exhibition revenue-wise.

The restriction on radio is probably a lesser problem since radio has become far less competitive to the visual performing arts, such as motion pictures, since the advent of commercial television. Nevertheless, the writer is aware of an instance where a third party record company had recorded a television show of Elizabeth Taylor. In accordance with record company marketing practices, the album was released prior to the telecast.[55] A radio station in New York then proceeded to perform the entire album just immediately prior to the telecast. To the writer's knowledge, no action was taken by either the producer of the

---

[55] Colpix Records, then a label of Columbia Pictures Corporation, had released an album entitled, Elizabeth Taylor in London, which was substantially recorded from her television show.

television show or the network of the New York television affiliate against the radio station. Thus one cannot assume that a restrictive clause as to performance on radio might not be desirable in a given situation, even though the importance of radio as a broadcasting medium has been diluted by the primacy of television as the principal mass medium of broadcasting.

Sec. 14.11. Live Television and Ephemeral Recordings

A further restriction on broadcast of reserved live television is set forth in Article 13, containing a facet in subdivision (a) thereof so as to cover by such restriction supplemental broadcasts, or delayed transmission, within a period of 30 days after original broadcast on those stations not carrying the original where the live transmission is reproduced by kinescope or magnetic tape.[56] The clause is derived from the technology of television, whereby simultaneous transmission of live television by coaxial cable and/or microwave relay may be supplemented by other devices. The clause is intended to include, in the live television category reserved to the owner and subject to the restriction on release of live television, technological methods of recording of a live telecast which are transmitted shortly thereafter. For example, if a network wanted to schedule the same program at 9:00 P.M. Eastern Standard Time throughout the United States, the telecast would be seen in California at 6:00 P.M. The three hour time difference on a simultaneous telecast originating, for example, at 9:00 P.M. in New York would be seen out of prime time on the West Coast. Recording technologies, such as kinescope and tape, would allow delayed transmis-

---

[56] Note 1, *supra*, at p. 55 and Form No. 1A-2.

sion, to suit differences in time, program scheduling, addition or subtraction of affiliates for any given program from the network, and so on. Proposed copyright revision would grant a right to the broadcaster to make "ephemeral recordings" under Sec. 112 of S. 543.[57] The House Report defines the term as "copies or phono-records of a work made for purposes of later transmission by a broadcasting organization legally entitled to transmit the work." [58] It characterizes them as "mere technical adjuncts of broadcasting." [59] Sec. 112 would except ephemeral recordings from infringement.[60] However, the right of ephemeral recording is not granted in the case of motion pictures or other audio-visual works.[61] Sec. 101 defines "audiovisual works" as "works that consist of related images which are intrinsically intended to be shown by the use of machines or devices such as projectors, viewers, or electronic equipment, together with accompanying sounds, if any, regardless of the nature of the material objects, such as films or tapes, in which the works are embodied." [62] The definition excludes both film and tape from ephemeral recording. Thus it is clear that the purpose of the proposed statute is to preserve live telecasts in some form. Sec. 112 grants this right "to make no more than one copy or phonorecord of a particular transmission program embodying the performance or display, if

"(1) the copy or phonorecord is retained and used solely by the transmitting organization that made it, and no further copies or phonorecords are reproduced from it; and

---

[57] Note 33, *supra,* Sec. 112.

[58] Note 34, *supra,* at p. 59.

[59] *Idem* at p. 60.

[60] Note 33, *supra,* Sec. 112(a).

[61] *Ibid.*

[62] *Idem,* Sec. 101.

(2) the copy or phonorecord is used solely for the transmitting organization's own transmissions within its local service area, or for purposes of archival preservation or security; and

(3) unless preserved exclusively for archival purposes, the copy or phonorecord is destroyed within six months from the date the transmission program was first transmitted to the public." [63]

The House Report explains the scope of the term "organization" as used in the proposed statute. The Report states,

> "Some concern has been expressed by authors and publishers lest the term, 'organization' be construed to include a number of affiliated broadcasters who could exchange the recording without restrictions. The term is intended to cover a broadcasting network, or a local broadcaster or individual transmitter; but, under clauses (1) and (2) of the subsection, the ephemeral recording must be 'retained and used solely by the transmitting organization that made it,' and must be used solely for that organization's own transmission within its own area. Thus, an ephemeral recording made by one transmitter, whether it be a network or local broadcaster, could not be made available for use by any other transmitter." [64]

Sec. 14.12. Rights in Delayed Transmission: Kinescope and Tape

Thus, kinescopes and magnetic tapes of a live telecast would appear to come within the meaning of ephemeral re-

[63] *Idem,* Sec. 112(a).

[64] Note 34, *supra,* at pp. 60-61.

cordings in the proposed statute as qualified therein. Actually, kinescopes were a form of recording of a live television show by special film camera during the performance of the live show for purposes of delayed transmission and preceded the widespread utilization of audio-visual taping of television programs in point of time. Apart from transmission of film programs, television was live until kinescope recordings and later, taped programs were telecast.

The reference to magnetic tape as a means of delayed transmission carried with it certain ambiguities arising out of custom and practices of the industry. The best way to explain this is to refer to the jurisdiction of the two unions involved. Before television, the union covering screen actors was the Screen Actors Guild. The American Federation of Radio Artists had jurisdiction in radio and in recordings. Note that the one medium was audio-visual, while the other union covered the aural media. With the advent of commercial television, the Screen Actors Guild assumed jurisdiction of television performances on film while the other union, now the American Federation of Television and Radio Artists, assumed jurisdiction of live television. As tape technology came to be used, it was considered an alternative form of live television. The expression "live on tape" came to be used and aptly expresses this concept. Instead of a program being filmed for television transmission, the cast performed it live, often before a studio audience, for later transmission. The notion of "live on tape" indicates that the sources of tape television were in live television and that live television developed into tape television. Thus, the American Federation of Television and Radio Artists, having jurisdiction of live television, automatically assumed jurisdiction of television on tape as a natural progression therefrom, while the Screen Actors Guild continued its jurisdiction over film.

Thus the context of Article 13(a)[65], including kinescopes and magnetic tapes in delayed transmission of up to 30 days after live telecast origination as part of the reserved live television right, and subject to restriction for a period of years after release of the first motion picture based upon the underlying work, emanates from industry practices which arose at a given stage of television history. Even the period of 30 days for delayed transmission is a period stemming from industry practices and reflects what the draftsman considers to be a reasonable period. But time periods are negotiable, and, at times, periods of 45 days or 60 days have been used, such periods representing the periods as negotiated in the final draft of the parties, and as representing the conclusion of the parties that the actual contract number of days negotiated is reasonable, whether the same be 30, 45, 60, or some other number of days.

The problem with terms relating to technology is that often parties have an existing stage of the art or technology in mind, whereas material changes in the process may transform the art and technology and thereby bring into play questions of interpretation of the words of art used. Thus magnetic and optical tape describe differing tape processes. Yet until recently, the term "tape" as applied to aural recordings was substantially synonymous with what is now called "reel-to-reel tape" because the form of tape recorder and player principally used was in that form. Thus, the term "tape" was both genus and species insofar as aural tape was concerned. Today, however, with the proliferation of cassettes and 8-track cartridges as alternatives to reel-to-reel tape, the term "tape" may be said to be generic only and no longer

---

[65] Note 1, *supra,* at p. 55 and Form No. 1A-2.

describes what was the principal form of tape, reel-to-reel tape. Thus, the language used in drafting contracts today must be used with greater caution in respect of the term "tape" because technological advances have changed its meaning somewhat and its use must be made with greater care.

Sec. 14.13. Reserved Rights and Limited Grant of Rights

But Article 13 does not present a picture of simple reservation of rights subject to restriction in favor of release of the film for a period of time with the various exclusions and inclusions. It does more. Article 13(d)[66] gives the purchaser the right to use live actors on television for advertising purposes in order to promote the film for a stated period of time, not to exceed so many minutes in length. Usually the parties allow the purchaser to so promote the film on television for a period not to exceed 15 minutes in length. In all likelihood, the clause originated at a time when commercials on television were done live, preceding the present period when commercials are taped. But, again, the right might be valuable if, for any reason, live promotion on television is to be used by use of sketches, adaptations or excerpts with living actors.

Incidentally, the way the parties arrive at a time period, not to exceed 15 minutes in length, is interesting. The purchaser requires enough time for the commercials to be meaningful; this is measured in terms of seconds or minutes. The owner of the reserved live television rights does not wish to affect the potential television market for live performances. The shortest commercially viable time segment for a program is the half-hour show. The advertising exception granted the purchaser with live actors

---

[66] *Idem* at p. 56 and Form No. 1A-2.

normally would be granted for a time not to exceed 15 minutes because such a time period is deemed not to compete with the uses in point of time of programming reserved to the owner. *A fortiori*, hour or longer shows on live television reserved to the owner would be even less subject to competitive possibilities by the grant of Article 13(d).

Sec. 14.14. Reserved Rights and Rights of First Refusal

But the reserved live television rights are also subject to a right of first refusal in the purchaser to match a bona fide offer of a third party as set forth in Article 13(e).[67] Presumably the rationale here is that live television rights might conceivably have value by reason of the production and exploitation of the film. The purchaser would like to have an opportunity to acquire such rights at prevailing market prices, i.e., a bona fide offer of third parties, should it so elect without having to make up its mind prior thereto. The rationale here is that the parties, by reason of their contract, are already in some relationship purporting to govern the grant of various rights and the consideration therefor. The purchaser, therefore, believes that it should be given the edge over a third party in connection with those reserved rights because: (a) it has already acquired television rights from the owner; (b) it would be only fair for it to have an opportunity to acquire the remaining television rights; (c) the exercise of the right of first refusal would enable it to keep programs with live actors off television beyond the period of restriction, which is often negotiated at five or seven years, by acquiring such exclusive live television rights;

[67] *Idem* at pp. 56-57 and Form No. 1A-2.

and (d) it would pay no more than prevailing market price for such rights, which the purchaser itself might wish to exploit thereafter.

Sometimes the purchaser might negotiate a similar right of first refusal as to the living stage rights. But, in that event, the interest of the purchaser is probably directed not so much at the potential competition of the stage play. The restriction for a number of years probably would be more than enough to prevent competition with the theatrical release of the film and even television distribution thereof, at least for the most important commercial runs on television. That is, a film normally might be in release in the theatre for a year or two,—three years would be a long time for initial release. Thereafter the picture would be available for television, usually, in today's market, within about three years after initial theatrical release. Even with a five year stage restriction after initial theatrical release, a film would probably have had its run in the theatre and its important runs on television before the restrictive period were over. Rather, the purchaser would be interested in the first refusal rights because it wishes to obtain the stage production rights in order to present the play on stage with living actors, pure and simple. The primary reason for such a first refusal would be for stage performance purposes, without the purchaser having to commit itself unless and until the owner had a bona fide offer from third parties therefor.

Sec. 14.15. Television Series Rights

Article 14 adapts yet another technique in respect of television series rights.[68] Article 13(f)[69] distinguishes tele-

[68] *Idem* at pp. 57-60 and Form No. 1A-2.

[69] *Idem* at p. 57 and Form No. 1A-2.

vision broadcasts based upon the underlying work from television rights in sequels which is the subject of Article 14. That article begins with a definition, "The right to use the leading character or characters from the Work in substantially different stories in an episodic television series (live, tape, or filmed) and/or a serial type television program (live, tape, or filmed) is hereinafter referred to as the 'television series rights'. . ."[70] Article 14 vests the purchaser with those rights for a period of agreed number of years from the date of first release of the feature or other agreed years from date of agreement, whichever is to first expire. Often the latter is about two years longer than the former in order to allow for the production of the picture. Thus, if the rights after first release of the film are five years, then the rights after the date of agreement are seven years, whichever is the first to expire. The activation of these rights is that the purchaser had made or obtained a firm commitment for not less than 13 shows in the series. At such time, purchaser shall own the rights exclusively, and thereafter shall pay the owner an agreed price at the time of first broadcast of each episode and an agreed percentage thereof for the aggregate of the second through sixth runs thereof, which is the percentage payable by the Producer-Writers' Guild of America Television Film Agreement then in effect with respect to additional compensation to writers for reruns. In effect, the owner is given residual payments for such runs comparable to the formula worked out for the television writers under their collective bargaining agreement with the producers.[71]

---

[70] *Idem* at p. 57 and Form No. 1A-2.

[71] See Freund, Richard L., Residuals in Broadcasting, in Subsidiary Rights and Residuals, edited by Taubman, Joseph (1968),

If the purchaser fails to commence exploitation of the television series rights within the period of the grant, then said rights revert to the owner, subject to a right of first refusal after such reversion in the purchaser. Hence the original grant of rights is a grant subject to a condition subsequent to performance by the purchaser, failing which the right reverts to the owner. But even then, the reversion does not eliminate the possibilities of the purchaser for exploitation thereof because he continues to have a right of first refusal by matching a bona fide offer. The concept here is that the television series rights are close enough to the other granted rights so that the purchaser should be granted these rights absolutely for a period of time, subject to a commitment to produce the series during this period, and to production of a minimum of 13 segments of the series thereafter and to payment therefor. One might ask why should the owner grant this valuable right for a period of time without further consideration if the purchaser should choose not to exercise these rights? The answer is that the purchaser would insist upon a restriction against use by the owner thereof during the same period without further consideration coupled with the first refusal thereafter. From an economic point of view, the owner is no worse off since the period of vesting in the purchaser or the alternative restrictive period is dead time to the owner as far as exploitation is concerned. By contrast, the making or obtaining of a commitment by the purchaser within the vesting period may cause production of the television series to begin shortly thereafter so that the owner may realize the agreed upon royalties for the television series rights much sooner than

---

Chap. IX at pp. 91-114; Gilbert, Robert W., "Residual Rights" Established By Collective Bargaining in Television and Radio, 23 Law and Cont. Probs. 102 (1958).

he might otherwise. From the point of view of the purchaser, the clause enables him to produce the series or authorize production thereof at agreed royalties to the owner without having to be concerned with fluctuations of the market, particularly if the market prices should be rising.

Sec. 14.16. Sequel Rights in the Work and Sequel Motion Picture Rights

The balance of Article 14 is keyed in with yet another grant of rights, the sequel motion picture rights. Article 15 grants the purchaser the right to "write, produce and release sequel motion pictures made primarily for theatrical release and/or subscription or 'pay' television." [72] It is to be noted that the purchaser considers pay TV as the equivalent of theatrical release since the grant is limited only to these forms as the primary forms of distribution. Subscription TV, of course, is a form of pay TV where subscribers pay for programming on a periodic basis rather than directly or indirectly per program. The grant of the sequel motion picture right is to *write,* produce and release the sequel film. Feature films are generally produced from screen plays and from treatments and outlines preceding the script. The reference to writing here is to the writing of such material for the sequel motion picture. Lest there be any confusion as to what constitutes a sequel motion picture, the article proceeds to define the same. The article provides for payment of an agreed sum for each sequel motion picture upon the first general release thereof. Remakes are excluded from this article for the reason that the grant of rights to make motion picture versions includes remakes. The exclusion of remakes is

---

[72] Note 1, *supra,* p. 60 and Form No. 1A-2.

intended to clarify that the owner will not receive further compensation from the remakes as he would under the article for the production of sequels.

Article 16[73] reserves to the owner the right to create sequels of the underlying work subject to a first refusal in the purchaser to match a bona fide offer for production of a motion picture based upon the sequel work for theatrical exhibition or pay TV. Here, too, pay TV (including subscription TV) is placed in the same category as theatrical exhibition by the purchaser as an alternative economic form of exhibition. The right of the owner is further qualified in the article by a restriction against release of a motion picture based upon any such sequel work for a period of agreed number of years from the date of the agreement. Again, the intent here is to prevent a competitive film distributor from releasing a motion picture based upon the sequel work, which, by definition, contains the leading character or characters of the basic work and which may contain not only new events, but also events arising out of the story line of the basic work and the same locales. The purchaser would like to be free for a given agreed period of release of his basic motion picture from third party competition of features based upon such sequel works.

Thus, Article 15 grants the purchaser the right to make sequel films based upon the basic work and/or the first feature or remakes thereof based upon the underlying work for a stipulated price per sequel film payable to owner. This grant is non-exclusive because Article 16 reserves the right to write sequels of the work, from which motion pictures may be made, subject to a right of first refusal in the purchaser and a restriction for a period

---

[73] *Idem* at pp. 61-63 and Form No. 1A-2.

of time against release thereof. This may appear to be a semantic distinction because the pattern of each article is different. Sequel motion pictures are only those based upon the original work and/or the first film based thereon or remakes thereof. However, sequel works created by the author are new works, and features made based thereon are, in theory, new motion pictures and not sequel motion pictures, since the original films or remakes thereof based upon the sequel works are not based upon the underlying work or the first film or remake thereof made from the basic work.

Nevertheless, the writing of a sequel motion picture pursuant to the grant of Article 15 imports writing of dialogue, descriptive material, and other incidental writings necessary to make a sequel motion picture, in short, screen play, treatments, outlines, etc. Article 16, granting the right to write a sequel of the basic work, presumably implies a sequel written in comparable form. If the basic work were in novel form, the sequel presumably would be in like form. From an economic point of view, that is what the reservation of rights would make most desirable. But strictly speaking, it is not necessary that the sequel be in the identical form as the basic work. Thus sequels to a novel might be in the form of short stories. There is nothing in the definition of sequel, as set forth in the article, that sequel writing must be in the same or similar form as the basic work, provided the sequel writing adheres to the definition of sequel contained therein. Hence, there is nothing to prevent the owner, assuming the author is the owner, from writing new story lines in the form of treatments as sequels to his basic work, even though the underlying work was in the form of a novel.

Nonetheless, perhaps the language of Article 15 might be clarified as to the nature of the sequel motion picture rights, based upon the underlying work as to exclusivity. Certainly as to sequel films based upon the first picture or remakes thereof, since the purchaser or assigns would own the copyright therein, nobody else could make a sequel therefrom without a grant of right from the owner of the film. In effect, then, as to sequels made from the film, the rights are effectively exclusive. But the grant of rights to make sequel films from the underlying work is not in the same position. Article 1 grants the purchaser the exclusive right to make film versions of the basic work.[74] Article 15 grants sequel motion picture rights without the use of the term "exclusive". Juxtaposing the broad, exclusive grant as to the making of motion picture rights from the underlying work against the grant, which does not contain the term "exclusive", as to the sequel motion picture rights, it would seem that a court might indeed conclude that Article 15 represents a separate grant of right. If so, the failure to include the word "exclusive" might mean that conceivably sequel motion pictures, based upon the underlying work but not the first film made based thereon or remakes thereof, could be written and produced by third parties. Yet it is doubtful that the purchaser intends to open the door to such a possibility, particularly in the light of its right of first refusal as to the reserved right to make pictures based upon sequels of the underlying work. Perhaps Article 15 should be modified to vest the motion picture sequel rights for a period of time in the purchaser, in the fashion of Article 14 as to television series rights, subject to divestiture and reversion to owner upon non-exercise thereof by the purchaser. The reference here is to sequel films based upon the underlying work; as to sequels based upon the first film or remake thereof, there cannot be any reversion since the

---

[74] *Idem* at p. 40 and Form No. 1A-2.

copyright in the film, in no event, will be in the owner. There should be no limitation as to time in the purchaser for exercising its rights to make sequel films based upon its own first feature or remakes thereof.

Sec. 14.17. Rights Measuring Periods

In any event, Article 14[75] takes into consideration the operation of Articles 15 and 16 and tolls the reversion of television series rights to the owner in the event of exercise of sequel motion picture rights or production of a sequel film and making payment therefor, or the exercise of first refusal rights in respect of sequel works created by reservation thereof to the owner. Moreover, the rights vested in the purchaser as to the period within which it was to be committed for exploitation of television series rights would cover two respective periods, the first period being measured by release of the first picture, and the second period, by date of release of the film made pursuant to exercise of rights under Articles 15 and 16.

Article 17[76] represents the final substantive provision prior to the boiler plate in the long form. It provides that pictures produced "hereunder" for theatrical exhibition and/or pay TV may be released over free television, but that if owner exercises the television sequel rights, i.e., the television series rights, under Article 14, such exercise shall not be deemed to include theatrical exhibition and/or pay TV. From the context, the term "hereunder" is intended to refer to films produced pursuant to Articles 15 and 16, relating to sequel motion pictures and films produced from sequels of the basic work.

---

[75] *Idem* at pp. 57-60 and Form No. 1A-2.

[76] *Idem* at p. 63 and Form No. 1A-2.

Sec. 14.18. Rights Objectives and Negotiations

Hence the long form contract evidences a market approach, not only to a variety of film rights, but also to a variety of television rights, whether or not they be television film rights. The objective of the purchaser is threefold: (a) to tie up as many of these rights as it can for itself, by postponing additional consideration till such time as the economic possibilities therefrom can emanate from exercise of the rights and by scheduling provisions for payment as to such supplemental rights which the purchaser would not otherwise obtain without payment; (b) to provide restrictions as to exercise of competitive rights, whether in other media or the same media, for a period or periods long enough to enable the purchaser or assigns to have an opportunity for exploitation of its exclusive rights without such competition having the possibility of making inroads upon the market adverse to the purchaser's production; and (c) to give the purchaser a first refusal at such of the reserved rights as to which it is interested, but not prepared to undertake any contractual obligation as to consideration, at prevailing market prices at the time of exercise of the right of first refusal.

The objective of the owner is also threefold: (a) to reserve from the grant of rights to the purchaser as many rights of economic value that will not derogate or destroy the grant to the purchaser, lest the owner, who may be too reservation conscious without commensurate interest on the part of the purchaser, lose the deal altogether; (b) to maximize the economic potential from any of the rights granted for a period of time, subject to divestiture and reversion for non-exercise, in the hope that the purchaser or assigns will exercise such rights, as well as from reserved rights as to which the purchaser may have a right of first refusal; and (c) to accept restrictions on exploitation of the reserved rights of owner that are reasonably ancillary to the exploitation of the granted rights of the purchaser, but which are not so long as to impair the exploitation of the reserved rights by the owner or assigns thereafter.

Within this context, it may be seen that bargaining for rights in other media very often is a normal part of the *gestalt* or overall configuration of the negotiation. The *gestalt* can and does take into consideration rights in various media. Indeed, in the performing arts, the agreement, as in the long form contract hereinabove analyzed, may consider in detail exploitation of such rights in the various media. The objective of the parties determines the ultimate form of agreement. In the long form, it was clear that the purchaser was keenly interested in rights of exploitation in television as well as rights as to supplemental production of features derived from the same work, motion picture sequels, as well as features based on sequels to the basic work.

Contract takes form from the respective objectives of the parties. That, in turn, is dependent upon the respective strength of the parties, i.e., their bargaining positions. A well-known author, as owner, may limit the initial grant to a single motion picture plus its dubbed and superimposed versions and television motion picture rights. Such an author would probably ask for, in any event, a percentage of the net proceeds from the picture in addition to his base compensation.[77] The author, too, may very well enter into a collateral contract as employee for hire writing the screen play for the motion picture.[78] So, too, where a

---

[77] See Form Nos. 1A-2.1 and 1A-2.2 in Volumes of Forms.

[78] *Idem* Form No. 1A-2.2, and also Form No. 1A-2.3.

studio contracts to acquire musical motion picture rights from the authors—bookwriter, composer and lyricist of a musical play—it may also enter into additional contracts for the bookwriter to create the screen play as employee for hire, and for additional music and lyrics from the composer and lyricist.[79]

The purchaser, on the other hand, if it is strong enough and if the owner is anxious enough to make the deal, may enter into an "All Rights" agreement whereby all rights of whatsoever kind and nature in and to the literary and artistic property, including the copyright therein, are assigned to the purchaser.[80] Then, too, the purchaser, with great expectations as to a particular property, may pay large sums for very limited rights in only one medium, e.g., film or television, without any rights in other media whatsoever. Normally a television production is not the basis for a feature motion picture, although there are any number of films that have been made based upon dramatic television works, such as "Marty". However, the television producer does not normally require rights to distribute the television show theatrically or to make theatrical motion picture versions of the work as part of his economic incentives of production. Exceptions, however, are feature length films which are intended for initial release in television and which will be exploited theatrically in certain territories, where there is little or no television, or where it is hoped that the initial release in television will not destroy the market theatrically in areas where there is a television release.

The facts and circumstances of each deal will generally set the parameters of its negotiation as to rights in other

---

[79] See Form Nos. 2A-1 and 2A-1a in Volumes of Forms as to analogous television rights in a play.

[80] See Form No. 1A-1 in Volumes of Forms.

media. To the extent rights in other media materialize therefrom, they are to be considered as a continuum of the objectives of the purchaser and assigns. The market is not neatly compartmentalized by media. The market may be considered in several respects. The market generically is the market for rights in all media that may be the subject of a contract. On the other hand, the respective media may be seen as separate markets and separate industries. A production company may be entirely specialized in a single market, e.g., film production for theatrical exhibition, or production for television only. Yet that company may bargain for and obtain rights in other media, either for exploitation by that company directly by way of expansion into other media, or by assignment of those rights to third parties.

The existing business configuration of the purchaser is therefore not necessarily an indication of the scope of the rights sought from the owner. Prospective intentions or even expectations of the purchaser, therefore, may play a part in the type of negotiation intended. Conversely, the fact that the purchaser may be an integrated operation in various media, whether through divisions, subsidiaries or affiliates, does not necessarily imply that the purchaser in that particular instance seeks rights in other media, or, if it should seek the same, that the owner is prepared to grant those rights.

Then, too, regardless of the degree of knowledge or sophistication of the purchaser or owner, the parameters of the negotiation as to rights are sometimes circumscribed by their respective representatives, be they agents, managers, attorneys or other business advisers. The value of the printed form of the large user is that it includes a variety of rights that the purchaser ordinarily might consider, whether in the same or other media. It aids the negotiators, but, of course, does not thereby restrict them, in setting their own limits as to the scope of the negotiation.

Rights in other media as to literary and artistic properties may be deemed normative, and the inclusion or exclusion of the same, a function of the negotiation.

Chapter XV

RIGHTS AND PERFORMANCE

Sec. 15.1. Performance as a Stage Right

In considering contract in relation to copyright we have directed our attention to rights in any given literary and artistic property and development therefrom of other works. We have considered the manner in which the sequential roll takes place in the creation of derivative literary and artistic properties. In short, the focus of our concern was creativity.

But there is another predicate in our area of concern—performance. For a long time this was known as the "stage right." Brander Matthews wrote, in 1896, "Copyright and stage-right are wholly different and a dramatist is entitled to both."[1] He noted that France had granted the stage right in 1791 and the United Kingdom, in the first part of the 19th century.[2] It was not until 1856 that the stage right was granted in the United States.[3] According to Brander Matthews, the author thereby derived a double profit, ". . . controlling the publication by copyright and controlling performance by stage-right."[4]

The stage right granted in 1856 by the statute consisted of the sole right "to act, perform, or represent the same, or cause it to be acted, performed, or represented,

---

[1] Matthews, Brander, The Evolution of Copyright, reprinted from the Political Science Quarterly (November, 1890), in Putnam, George Haven, The Question of Copyright 2d Ed. (1896) at p. 342.

[2] *Idem* at p. 343.

[3] 34th Cong., 1st Sess., Chap. 169, Aug. 18, 1856, 11 Stat. 138 (1859).

[4] Note 1, *supra,* at p. 343.

on any stage or public place . . ." [5] On the other hand, Borge Varmer, in his study in 1958, used a different term, "The 'performing rights' to be considered in this study include not only the right to 'perform' dramatic or musical works, but also the corresponding rights to 'deliver' nondramatic literary works and to 'exhibit' motion pictures. All of these are commonly spoken of as the 'performing rights.' " [6] The progression from the stage right to performing rights is quite illuminating.

The Act of 1870[7] modified the language and added a concept thereto, providing a grant as follows: ". . . and in the case of a dramatic composition, of publicly performing or representing it, or causing it to be performed or represented by others; and authors may reserve the right to dramatize or to translate their own works." [8] In the intervening years between 1856 and 1870 there had been no significant transformation of the performing arts as to its technology. Consequently, the reference to public performance in 1870, as opposed to performance on any stage or public place in 1856, represented a shift in descriptive language referring to the same type of presentations. But the difference in language, however, represented a shift in terminology, from emphasis on a particular form of dramatic performance, on stage, to a more comprehensive term that encompassed the stage. It is true that the 1856 statute spoke of performance on any stage or public place, thereby accomplishing a substantially similar result. But the 1870 language represented a shift to generic termi-

---

[5] Note 3, *supra*.

[6] Varmer, Borge, Limitations on Performing Rights, Study No. 16, in 2 Studies on Copyright (1963) 835-875 at p. 837.

[7] 41st Cong., 2d Sess., Chap. 230, July 8, 1870, 16 Stat. 212 (1871).

[8] *Ibid*

nology, public performance of a dramatic composition. The additional language as to reservation of a right to dramatize the work was acknowledgment of a right of adaptation in the author of an underlying work in another form. That is, the author of a novel, for example, could reserve the right to create a dramatic adaptation therefrom, the right of dramatization. By the Act of 1891,[9] the reservation of such rights had become a further grant of an exclusive right of dramatization. The statute granted the right, ". . . in the case of a dramatic composition, of publicly performing or representing it, or causing it to be performed or represented by others; and authors or their assigns shall have exclusive rights to dramatize and translate any of their works for which copyright shall have been obtained under the laws of the United States."[10] It is to be noted that the Act of 1831 granted copyright in musical compositions.[11] In 1897, in a statute relating to damages for infringement, it was provided, "Any person publicly performing or representing any dramatic or musical composition for which a copyright has been obtained, without the consent of the proprietor of said dramatic or musical composition, or his heirs or assigns, shall be liable for damages therefor, . . ."[12] Borge Varmer remarks as to this, "In the act of January 6, 1897 the public performing rights were extended to musical works."[13] Such extension, however, was made in an involuted way. Instead of extending the grant of performing rights to musical compositions in the course of enumeration of the

---

[9] 51st Cong., 2d Sess., Chap. 565, Act of Mar. 3, 1891, 26 Stat. 1106 (1891).

[10] *Ibid.*

[11] 21st Cong., 2d Sess., Chap. 16, Feb. 3, 1831, 4 Stat. 436 (1846).

[12] 54th Cong., 2d Sess., Chap. 4, Jan. 6, 1897, 29 Stat. 481 (1897).

[13] Varmer, *op. cit., supra,* at p. 837.

bundle of rights in the copyright, the extension was made by tacking on performance of musical compositions to dramatic compositions as part of a damages amendment to the copyright statute.

Sec. 15.2. Right of Oral Delivery—Non-Dramatic

The present statute as passed in 1909[14] enumerated and categorized the bundle of rights constituting the copyright. The enumeration was made in Sec. 1 and the cataloguing, in Sec. 5 thereof.[15] Sec. 1(a)[16] set forth the traditional publishing rights and Sec. 1(b),[17] the rights of adaptation. Sec. 1(c) was new and contained a new performing right. It granted the exclusive right, "(c) To deliver or authorize the delivery of the copyrighted work in public for profit if it be a lecture, sermon, address, or similar production."[18]

It required, however, the passage of 25 years before the limitations of this exclusive right of oral delivery became apparent. Jimmie Durante had recited three poems written by Alfred Kreymborg in performances over radio and otherwise. The author had published a book of verse in 1917 and later incorporated three of the poems therefrom in a play. Kreymborg sued for infringement. In the original decision, *Kreymborg* v. *Durante*,[19] plaintiff contended that defendant Durante had infringed his copyright by dramatic performance under Sec. 1(d) of the statute. On rehearing,[20] it was contended that plaintiff had the exclusive right under Sec. 1(c). Judge Patterson de-

---

[14] 60th Cong., 2d Sess., Mar. 4, 1909, 35 Stat. 1075 (1909).
[15] *Idem,* Sec. 1 and Sec. 5.
[16] *Idem,* Sec. 1(a).
[17] *Idem,* Sec. 1(b).
[18] *Idem,* Sec. 1(c).
[19] 21 U.S.P.Q. 557 (S.D.N.Y. 1934).
[20] 22 U.S.P.Q. 248 (rehearing July 20, 1934).

clined to classify poetry, which was first published, as a category of production similar to lectures, sermons and addresses. In effect, he applied the doctrine of *ejusdem generis* in that the enumeration of particulars carried with it others of a like nature only. He stated:

> "In its mention of a production similar to or like a lecture, sermon, or address, Congress plainly meant a production likewise intended in the first instance for oral communication. A speech, argument, debate, interview, perhaps even an informal talk, would be a 'similar production.' There may be cases where a poem would be 'a lecture, sermon, address, or similar production.' If a poem were first spoken or rendered at a gathering, as in the case of some of Lowell's poems, it would be an address in poetry and if copyrighted would be secure against unauthorized delivery later on by others. But usually a poem nowadays is first made public in printed form, through book, magazine, or newspaper, and is in form to be read in the first instance, though of course it may later be recited or rendered vocally." [21]

Since the poems were not dramatic works and were not created for oral delivery, Kreymborg was without remedy. It meant that nondramatic works not prepared for oral delivery could be performed freely without license from or compensation to the creator or his assigns.

Finally, in 1952, the statute was amended to grant the performing right in such nondramatic works.[22] Sec. 1(c) was amended to its present form to read in pertinent part:

---

[21] *Idem* at p. 249.

[22] 82d Cong., 2d Sess., Chap. 923, 66 Stat. 752 (1952).

"(c) To deliver, authorize the delivery of, read, or present the copyrighted work for profit if it be a lecture, sermon, address or similar production, or other nondramatic literary work; to make or procure the making of any transcription or record thereof by or from which, in whole or in part, it may in any manner or by any method be exhibited, delivered, presented, produced, or reproduced; and to play or perform it in public for profit, and to exhibit, represent, produce, or reproduce it in any manner or by any method whatsoever." [23]

It is noteworthy that the legislative technique for covering the theretofore excluded category of public performance for profit of nondramatic works was to retain the enumeration of specific categories of works prepared for oral delivery including the language of *ejusdem generis*, i.e., works of similar production, and then to add thereto, "or other nondramatic literary work." Instead of a generic grant of the right, the statute in 1909 enumerated specific performance for profit in respect of nondramatic works. Thus the statute might have granted the right of public performance for profit in respect of nondramatic works prepared for oral delivery as a generic grant. Instead of this, it granted specific rights plus rights in productions similar to lectures, sermons, addresses. The effect of the *ejusdem generis* clause, when combined with the specific grants was to attempt to encompass the category of rights equivalent to what might have been covered by the generic grant of performing rights in respect of nondramatic works prepared for oral delivery. The 1952 addition of other nondramatic literary works is generic as to the

---

[23] *Ibid.*

category excluded by the *Kreymborg* case.[24] Together with the 1909 grant, the 1952 addition purports to represent a grant of rights in nondramatic literary works prepared for and/or delivered orally. The generic coverage is nondramatic literary works which are either prepared for oral delivery, such as sermons, lectures, addresses or other works so prepared, and in addition nondramatic, literary works not originally prepared for oral delivery but which nonetheless are so delivered, such as poetry written to be read. Nimmer is troubled by the scope of the 1952 amendment and observes, "The scope of the phrase 'nondramatic literary work' as used in Sec. 1(c) is not entirely clear. It would appear, at least, to include all works registrable as books, periodicals and scripts prepared for oral delivery." [25] He questions whether Sec. 1(c) would cover choreography and motion pictures other than photoplays.[26] Nevertheless, the 1952 amendment covered the hiatus in performance for profit of nondramatic literary works not prepared for oral delivery left by the *Kreymborg* decision.[27] Moreover, it is to be noted that the balance of the 1952 amendment, quoted above, grants the overall Sec. 1(c) right so as to cover any manner or by any method by which the work may be exhibited, delivered, presented, produced, or reproduced either from a record or transcription thereof, in whole or in part, or other play or performance thereof in public for profit. This language presumably is derived from the latter part of Sec. 1(d), relating to performance of dramatic works which was granted in 1909.[28] It is to be observed that the grant of dramatic

---

[24] Notes 19-20, *supra.*

[25] Nimmer on Copyright (1969), Sec. 107.1, at p. 399.

[26] *Ibid.*

[27] Notes 19-20, *supra.*

[28] Note 14, *supra,* Sec. 1(d).

performing rights prior to 1909 used language of "performing and representing." [29] The 1909 Act referred to the grant in terms of the work being "exhibited, performed, represented, produced, or reproduced." [30] The terms "exhibited, produced, or reproduced" are the language of motion pictures. That is, motion pictures were a medium of presentation in 1909 even though the statute did not list motion pictures as a category until the 1912 amendment[31] to Sec. 5 of the 1909 Act. Since the 1952 amendment to Sec. 1(c) was made while television was commercially extant, it may be concluded that the Congress felt that comparable language could apply as well to that newer medium.

In this respect, it is noteworthy that the language of proposed copyright revision appears to use different terminology. The term "exhibited, produced or reproduced" as now contained in Sec. 1(c) of the statute are not used in the proposed legislation. The definition of "motion pictures" in Sec. 101[32] of S. 543 refers to the same as audio-visual works in a series of related images *shown* in succession. The definition of "audio-visual works",[33] in turn, speaks in terms of a series of related images intended to be *shown* by means of machines or devices, such as projectors, viewers or electronic equipment. The terms "produced or reproduced" seem to have dropped out of usage altogether in the comparable context.

Moreover, Sec. 106(4) of S. 543 grants the exclusive performing right in copyrighted works, "in the case of

---

[29] Notes 3, 7 and 9, *supra*.

[30] Note 14, *supra*, Sec. 1(d).

[31] 62d Cong., 2d Sess., Aug. 24, 1912, 37 Stat. 488 (1913).

[32] S. 543, 91st Cong., 1st Sess., Jan. 22, 1969 (Dec. 10, 1969 Print), Sec. 101.

[33] *Ibid.*

literary, musical, dramatic, and choreographic works, pantomimes, motion pictures and other audiovisual works, and sound recordings, to perform the copyrighted work publicly."[34] By contrast Sec. 1(c) of the present Act grants the performing right with respect to sermons, lectures, addresses or similar productions and, as amended in 1952, to other nondramatic literary works. The term "literary works" as it appears in Sec. 1(c)[35] would therefore seem to be generic, encompassing both dramatic and nondramatic literary works since the section purports to cover only the latter category. Indeed, the very qualification, by means of the adjective "nondramatic" would suggest that there is another category of dramatic literary works. Elsewhere in Sec. 1,[36] light is shed on this. Sec. 1(b)[37] grants the right to translate and to make other versions if it be a literary work; to dramatize a nondramatic work; and to convert a novel or other nondramatic work into a drama. The context of this clause would seem to suggest that the term "literary" is generic and includes dramatic and nondramatic works. So, too, Sec. 1(d)[38] grants the performing right to a drama and refers to a dramatic work. The use of the term "dramatic work" there is consistent with its frame of reference in Sec. 1(b).[39] Nor is the scheme of Sec. 1 of the present Act at variance with the definition of "literary works" as contained in the proposed statute, in this regard, which defines the term as ". . . works other than audiovisual works, expressed in words, numbers, or other verbal or numerical symbols or indicia, regardless of the nature of the material objects, such as books, peri-

[34] *Idem*, Sec. 106(4).
[35] 17 U.S.C. 1(c).
[36] 17 U.S.C. 1.
[37] 17 U.S.C. 1(b).
[38] 17 U.S.C. 1(d).
[39] 17 U.S.C. 1(b).

odicals, manuscripts, phonorecords or film, in which they are embodied."[40] Since dramatic works are usually expressed in words, it follows that they may also be literary works. It follows, too, therefore, that Sec. 106[41] of S. 543, in granting the exclusive performing right to literary works, intends to cover both dramatic and nondramatic literary works thereby achieving substantially the same result as the grant of such rights by Secs. 1(c) and 1(d)[42] of the present Act even though the proposed statute refers to both literary and dramatic works. It may therefore be concluded that there is an overlap in meaning in the terms "literary works" and "dramatic works."

Sec. 15.3. Right of Dramatic Performance

The grant of the exclusive performing right by Sec. 1(d)[43], as enacted in 1909 and as embodied in the present law, goes much further than the stage right or right to perform or represent a dramatic work as contained in prior legislation from 1856 on. Sec. 1(d) reads as follows:

> "(d) To perform or represent the copyrighted work publicly if it be a drama or, if it be a dramatic work and not reproduced in copies for sale, to vend any manuscript or any record whatsoever thereof; to make or procure the making of any transcription or record thereof by or from which, in whole or in part, it may in any manner or by any method be exhibited, performed, represented, produced, or reproduced; and to exhibit, perform, represent, produce, or reproduce it in any manner or by any method whatsoever;"[44]

---

[40] Note 32, *supra*, Sec. 101.
[41] *Idem*, Sec. 106(4).
[42] 17 U.S.C. 1(c) and 1(d).
[43] 17 U.S.C. 1(d).
[44] *Ibid.*

The first part thereof, "To perform or represent the copyrighted work publicly if it be a drama . . ." is the language of the stage right embodied in varying forms in prior statutes from and after 1856. The remainder of the clause consists of three other rights, the right to vend the manuscript, the recording right and performance thereof, and the right to exhibit, produce or reproduce the work.

Sec. 15.3(a). Dramatic Performance and the Right to Vend

As to the vending right, the obvious frame of reference is the unpublished work. For the exclusive right of publication, reprinting, publishing, copying and vending the copyrighted work is granted by Sec. 1(a) of the statute.[45] It would appear to be a redundancy, therefore, to grant a right to vend a manuscript in the subdivision, Sec. 1(d),[46] dealing with exclusive right of performance of a dramatic work if the reference were to published works. However, Sec. 12 of the Copyright Act permits copyright of unpublished works of which copies are not reproduced for sale "if it be a lecture or similar production or a dramatic or musical composition;"[47] Since performance of a stage play does not constitute a publication thereof,[48] it may be seen that plays will continue to be under common law copyright protection unless the work has been published with notice of copyright or registered for copyright protection as an unpublished work. Since the performing right is one of the exclusive rights granted by the statute, being a recipient of the right under the statute presup-

[45] 17 U.S.C. 1(a).
[46] 17 U.S.C. 1(d).
[47] 17 U.S.C. 12.
[48] Ferris v. Frohman, 223 U.S. 424 (1912).

poses that the work is already under statutory copyright, otherwise there would be no such right exercisable under the statute.

Even so, one must ask why Sec. 1(d)[49] takes the peculiar form of protecting the vending of the *manuscript* of a play within the subdivision purporting to cover exclusive performing rights as dramatic works. One answer, from a structural point of view of the statute, is that Sec. 1(a) pertains to rights of *publication*,[50] whereas the right to vend a manuscript exclusively is a different right relating to unpublished works. This does not follow necessarily because the vending of manuscript copies might, under certain circumstances, constitute an unlimited publication requiring notice of copyright under Sec. 10[51] of the Act with registration and deposit to follow under Secs. 11[52] and 13.[53] Conceivably the vending of manuscripts for professional purposes only, i.e., to members of a cast as an incident to a license of performing rights in a play, might be a limited publication to a selected group provided the purchasers of the manuscript are prohibited from reproducing, distributing or selling copies thereof.[54]

Actually the hearings on copyright revision in 1908[55] tend to explain the origination of the additional three rights as part of the exclusive right of performance as enacted in 1909. The language as finally drafted was in-

---

[49] 17 U.S.C. 1(d).

[50] 17 U.S.C. 1(a).

[51] 17 U.S.C. 10.

[52] 17 U.S.C. 11.

[53] 17 U.S.C. 13.

[54] Nimmer, *op. cit., supra,* Sec. 58.12, at p. 226.

[55] Hearings on Revision of Copyright Laws Before the Committees on Patents of the Senate and House of Representatives, March 26, 27 and 28, 1908. See also Sec. 23.3, note 16, *infra.*

tended to protect the dramatist and his assigns against a variety of play pirates then in vogue. Thus, Mr. Harry P. Mawson, as a representative of the American Dramatists Club, testified as follows:

> "Now, the process of stealing a play is probably the most ingenious thing in the realm of the appropriation of copyrighted rights. An expert stenographer secretes himself somewhere in the theater and he takes down word for word everything that is spoken in the play. After he has gotten all the words in the play he then appropriates all the business of the play. That bit of business, as we call it, is derived from the motive assigned by the author for that particular action. It is a part of the dramatic composition. He steals that. After he has gotten all that, he takes down the makeup of the actor, everything he wears, the arrangement of the face, the beard or wig, if he wears one, the costume. Then he comes down to the scenery; the properties that are used. All of the play is stolen in that way. Now he has to find a market for that, and that market is in Chicago, and there it is sold. That property costs the manager from $10,000 to $25,000 to produce, and that entire play is sold for $5 a copy." [56]

Ligon Johnson filed a petition on behalf of the National Association of Theatrical Managers as its representative at the hearings. The petition recited:

> "Your petitioner shows that there are persons in the United States whose sole occupation is, in each instance of a successful play, to procure, by medium of stenographic notes taken during a performance or

[56] *Idem,* Statement of Mr. Harry P. Mawson, pp. 21-23, at p. 22.

in other surreptitious manner, a copy of the lines of a play which is supplied to any person seeking to pirate the play or reproduce the same through the medium of so-called 'talking pictures.'

"Your petitioner further shows that there is now being exploited in America a foreign-devised machine by which plays are mechanically reproduced through 'talking pictures' and without the permission of the authors at so-called picture theaters, such reproduction resulting in the utter destruction of the play so reproduced as a thing of dramatic value." [57]

The petition further recited:

"Petitioner seeks to prevent the unauthorized making of films or vending copies of plays.

"Petitioner respectfully requests that the following provisions as to dramatic work be in effect embodied in the copyright law of the land.

"That the copyright secured shall include the exclusive right 'to publicly perform or in any manner represent in whole or in part the copyrighted work; to make any transcription or other record whatsoever thereof or from which it may be reproduced, performed, or represented if it be a dramatic work.

"That the penalty shall apply to any person who 'shall for profit transcribe or procure the transcribing in whole or in part of any work not printed or reproduced for sale by the author or owner thereof or who shall vend any copy, in whole or in part, any work not printed or reproduced for sale by the author or

[57] *Idem,* Statement of Mr. Ligon Johnson, pp. 23-36. The petition appears at pp. 23-25. The quoted paragraphs are at p. 24.

owner thereof, or who shall willfully and for profit infringe, etc.' "[58]

In his oral testimony at the hearings, Ligon Johnson explained that the producers were powerless to remedy the abuses under existing law except by the medium of injunction. Under existing law, notice had to be given before curtain time. Mr. Johnson testified, "Unless that notice is given the court will not hold the performers. Usually a pirating company carries two plays, one for piracy purposes and the other to give as a substitute whenever notice is given."[59] He testified, too, that the organization of producers represented, directly and indirectly over $200,000,000 in actual investment in the United States.[60] In his oral testimony, he, too, referred to "the present so-called talking pictures."[61] Later on in the hearings he explained what is meant:

"So that before there can be any reproduction or any representation through the medium of any machine, he must first secure some person to go into the theater and endeavor by one means or another to secure the lines of the play. Then the next step is to get a company of actors to make up as nearly as possible along the lines of those who represent the play in the first instance. The pictures are then taken and the lines dictated into a machine, into a cameraphone or a photophone, or some other machine. In some instances pictures alone are taken and then somebody will stand back of the machine and imitate a phonograph speaking the lines. . . . When these acts

[58] *Idem* at p. 24.
[59] *Idem* at p. 33.
[60] *Idem* at p. 30.
[61] *Idem* at p. 31.

are once copied, it means that the photophone and instruments may be scattered broadcast throughout the land . . ." [62]

The testimony of a producer, William A. Brady, is also illuminating:

"In my play called Way Down East, it was necessary to run for seven months in New York City at a loss before it gained the universal public attention. It has lived for ten or fifteen years. That play is now being produced throughout the United States by the aid of moving pictures. They secured my play for the small sum of $5 from a man named Byers in Chicago and it is being produced by a member of this trust that Mr. Johnson just spoke about. They propose to go on further with it, by the aid of a phonographic attachment, and produce all the popular plays that are owned by private persons throughout the United States.

"My play, Way Down East, is now being printed on films at the rate of from 100 to 200 copies a week by a company which is a member of this trust in Chicago, and yesterday one of my companies, composed of 35 people, men and women, was forced off the road and sent back to New York. They never can play again, because in almost every one-night stand in this country Way Down East is being presented on every street corner, presented from a stolen manuscript by a man who went into one of our theatres and took down a copy of our play and sold it to

---

[62] *Idem,* Statement of Ligon Johnson, representing the National Association of Theatrical Producing Managers, and also the Dramatic Authors, of New York City, N.Y., pp. 173-179 at pp. 174-175.

this disreputable picture firm, who is now destroying my property. . . .

* * *

"What does it cost a man to make one of these reproductions. He takes a store and put a $400 front in it, has a sheet in the back part of the building, puts in a machine for $100, buys a film for $20 a week, deceives the people by stating that he is producing my play, and the people pay 5 cents to see it." [63]

The testimony of dramatist, Charles Klein, is also revealing:

"Representative Currier. Did the loss which you say you sustained arise out of the fact that your plays were surreptitiously obtained, and produced by traveling dramatic companies?

Mr. Klein. Yes, they were travelers.

Representative Currier. It was not because of the moving-picture business?

Mr. Klein. The moving-picture business was not in existence. It was not thought of then.

The Chairman. Your losses were caused by the theft of your plays by traveling companies?

Mr. Klein. Yes." [64]

Sec. 15.3(b). Dramatic Performance and the Right to Exhibit

The basis for the additional three rights in Sec. 1 (d)[65] over and above the stage right, i.e., performing right, now

---

[63] *Idem,* Statement of William A. Brady, pp. 180-183 at pp. 180-181.

[64] *Idem,* Statement of Charles Klein, pp. 186-188 at p. 187.

[65] 17 U.S.C. 1(d).

becomes clear. The balance of the section was an antipiracy statute aimed at the means of piracy of dramatic works and the performances thereof based upon the experiences extant at the time. The exclusive right to vend manuscripts was aimed at the source of piracy, stenographic piracy in the theatre itself. The exclusive recording right was aimed at the so-called talking pictures or devices which recorded pirated versions of the dramatic work taken originally by the pirating stenographer. The exclusive right to exhibit, produce or reproduce referred to the pirated film versions of the dramatic work. Indeed, the index to the hearings is revealing. The index does not list motion pictures or films as such. The category under which the above statements is indexed is "Talking Pictures." [66] This would also explain why Sec. 1(d)[67] includes terms of art relating to motion pictures, "exhibit, produce, reproduce" even though the 1909 Act does not otherwise refer to motion pictures.

Consequently, the District Court Judge in the first decision of *M.G.M.* v. *Bijou Theatre Co., Inc.* was factually in error in his contention that, "There is no provision in the statute concerning the scope or effect of the copyright of moving picture films. They were commercially unknown when section 1 of the current act was passed (1909) and are referred to only in the classification section of the statute, being brought in there by the amendment of 1912." [68] On remand after the decree was set aside by the Court of Appeals, District Court Judge McLellan stated:

---

[66] Hearings, note 55, *supra*, at p. 461.

[67] 17 U.S.C. 1(d).

[68] 50 F. 2d 908, 909 (D.C. Mass. 1931), decree set aside and remanded, 59 F. 2d 70 (1st Cir. 1932), motion to dismiss amended bill of complaint denied, 3 F. Supp. 66 (D.C. Mass. 1933).

> "The motion picture industry went through a period of rapid development during the years 1906 to 1909. In 1907 hundreds of thousands of persons daily attended exhibitions at thousands of theaters. During these years such trade publications as 'Views and Films Index', 'Moving Picture News', 'Moving Picture World', and 'Motography' were published. As early as 1905 the Commonwealth of Massachusetts began making laws affecting the use of motion-picture machines (St. 1905, c. 176; St. 1908, c. 565), while, according to the March 14, 1908 issue of the 'Moving Picture World', a Motion Picture Operators' Union was organized in the city of Boston in December, 1907.
>
> "It is clear that motion pictures were commercially known prior to the year 1909 . . ." [69]

It may be seen, therefore, that the 1909 Act was not silent as to motion pictures, but rather it was referred to negatively by way of a grant of an exclusive performing right which itself was a bundle of four rights. The rights included the exclusive right "to exhibit, perform, represent, produce, or reproduce it in any manner or by any method whatsoever." [70] This is the language of motion picture terms of art. It is not circular reasoning to suggest that the language is so used because it is in the statute. It is in the statute in the first place to grant exclusive performing rights not only by performing and representing the work under copyright itself but by copying, recording and exhibiting it. The language in the statute presumably was taken from terms of art then utilized in motion picture contracts to describe what was

---

[69] *Idem*, 3 F. Supp. 66 (D.C. Mass. 1933) at pp. 71-72.
[70] 17 U.S.C. 1(d).

being done, to wit, exhibit, produce and reproduce the same. The dramatic work, i.e., the original stage work, had to be produced in another medium, film, by the pirating producer. Prints made thereof were a means of reproducing the same. Exhibiting the prints was the means of performance and presentation of the pirated film version.

It follows, therefore, that Judge McLellan was also right in his conclusion that the 1909 Act afforded protection to motion picture films even if it were not founded upon an existing drama, scenario, or other literary work which was the subject of copyright. In the Court of Appeals prior to remand, Judge Morris made an unnecessary double ellipsis in his thinking to raise the question in the first place. In his opinion, Judge Morris stated, "As we understand the term 'motion picture photoplays', they are motion pictures founded upon existing drama or dramatizations of literary productions. In this respect they differ from 'motion pictures' under classification (m)." [71] He then states, "The bills of complaint do not allege that the copyrighted films are founded on *copyrighted* novels, dramas, scenarios, or other dramatic compositions. Neither do they say they are not. We are left in doubt." [72] This was the basis for remand. He continues, "If, from the above-mentioned allegations in the bills, we are to infer that the photoplays are founded upon *copyrighted* dramatic productions of which the plaintiffs are the sole proprietors, the bills should be amended so that nothing be left to inference." [73] The Court of Appeals' opinion then concludes:

---

[71] M.G.M. Corp. v. Bijou Theatre Co., Inc., 59 F. 2d 70 (1st Cir. 1932), at p. 76.

[72] *Idem* at pp. 76-77. (emphasis added.)

[73] *Idem* at p. 77. (emphasis added.)

> "By reference to the contracts it appears that we are dealing only with photoplays, which term connotes a moving picture founded upon a dramatic production.
>
> "We hold that films which are founded upon copyrighted dramas or other dramatic compositions are protected under the provisions of section 1(d) of the Copyright Act and their unlicensed exhibition is an infringement of the copyrighted dramatic composition.
>
> "We are not called upon to decide whether the unlicensed exhibition of a motion picture other than a photoplay would constitute an infringement of the copyrighted film of such a picture." [74]

Evidently the Court of Appeals was troubled by the nature of a film not based upon a copyrighted dramatic work, or dramatization. Sec. 1(d) grants the exclusive performing right to a drama or a dramatic work.[75] This Court's thesis seems to be that if the film were not based upon a dramatic work, the film presumably could not be a motion picture photoplay and, therefore, must be a motion picture other than a photoplay. If it were founded upon a dramatic production, then, *ipso facto,* in order to receive the protection of the exclusive performing right as to the *film,* it had to be based upon a copyrighted dramatic production of some kind.

Actually neither is a requirement for classification of a motion picture photoplay. The Copyright Regulations, in referring to motion picture photoplays, recite, "This class includes published or unpublished motion pictures that are dramatic in character and tell a connected story, such as feature films, filmed television plays, short sub-

---

[74] *Idem* at p. 77.
[75] 17 U.S.C. 1(d).

jects and animated cartoons having a plot."[76] The reference to unpublished works also occurs in the very next paragraph of the Regulations pertaining to motion pictures other than photoplays, "This class includes published or unpublished nondramatic films such as newsreels, travelogs, training or promotional films, nature studies, and filmed television programs having no plot."[77] It is conceded that the 1909 Act contained no reference to copyrighting of unpublished motion pictures and that the same did not appear in the statute until 1912.[78] Thus, as of the 1909 Act per the Judge Morris opinion, there was no statutory basis for copyrighting a motion picture as an unpublished work. Clearly, then, his references were to copyrighted films, i.e., films as to which there was a notice of copyright thereon and a registration of copyright of the film.

Sec. 15.4. Dramatic Performance and Statutory Classification

Yet, even within his frame of reference, it is submitted that Judge Morris makes a double ellipsis not required by the art and technology of motion pictures or, for that matter, the copyright statute. Sec. 5[79] of the present Act is a classification scheme for registration of works under copyright. Since 1912, it has included motion picture photoplays under Class L and motion pictures other than photoplays in Class M thereof.[80] The last paragraph of

---

[76] Regulations of the Copyright Office, Sec. 202.15(a).

[77] *Idem,* Sec. 202.15(b).

[78] 17 U.S.C. 12, July 30, 1947, Chap. 391, 61 Stat. 656, as amended by Act of Aug. 24, 1912, 37 Stat. 488 (1913).

[79] 17 U.S.C. 5.

[80] Act of August 24, 1912, 62d Cong., 2d Sess., 37 Stat. 488 (1913). See also Sec. 23.12, *infra.*

the section provides, "The above specifications shall not be held to limit the subject matter of copyright as defined in section 4 of this title . . ." [81] Since motion pictures had been classified as photographs prior to the 1912 amendment and even prior to the enactment of the 1909 Act,[82] it may be concluded that the source of copyright is derived essentially from Sec. 4 of the Act which states, "The works of copyright may be secured under this title shall include all the writings of an author." [83] This, in turn, is derived from the Constitution of the United States which provides power in Congress ". . . by securing for limited times . . . to Authors . . . the exclusive Right to their respective Writings . . ." [84]

Judge McLellan on remand, after noting that Sec. 5(d) consisted of the category of "Dramatic or dramatico-musical compositions", then stated, "Section 5, supra, by its very terms is a nonexclusive definition of works subject to copyright; refers to a classification made for the convenience of the Patent Office; and is merely administrative." [85] He cites *Tiffany Productions, Inc.* v. *Dewing*.[86] There Judge Coleman remarked, "To the contention that, since section 5 has separate classifications for dramatic or dramatico-musical compositions and for motion picture photoplays, therefore section 1(d) is not to be interpreted as embracing the latter, it is sufficient to point out that the classification of section 5 is merely for the convenience

---

[81] 17 U.S.C. 5.

[82] American Mutoscope & Biograph Co. v. Edison Mfg. Co., 137 Fed. 262 (C.C.D. N.J. 1905); Edison v. Lubin, 122 Fed. 240 (3d Cir. 1903).

[83] 17 U.S.C. 4.

[84] Art. 1, Sec. 8, Clause 8.

[85] 17 U.S.C. 5(d), 3 F. Supp. 66 (D. Mass. 1933) at p. 73.

[86] 50 F. 2d 911 (D. Md. 1931).

of the copyright office and of applicants for copyrights. Such interpretation is strengthened by the last paragraph of section 5." [87]

Conceivably this classification scheme of the section may have also troubled Judge Morris in writing the opinion for the Court of Appeals. Perhaps he felt that by founding the film upon a copyrighted dramatic production he could overcome the fact of separate reference in Sec. 5(d) to dramatic compositions from Sec. 5(l) to motion picture photoplays. Judge Morris makes the bridge by predicate number 1, to wit, that a film is necessarily based upon an underlying work—his first ellipsis; and by predicate number 2, to wit, that the underlying work is necessarily a copyrighted work,—his second ellipsis.

Sec. 15.4(a). Film Making and Classification

In fact, it does not follow in the art and technology of film making that there be a scenario or any other underlying work, or that if there is a scenario or other underlying work that the same be copyrighted. D. W. Griffiths produced his famous "The Birth of a Nation" at a cost of some $110,000 in 1914 for release in 1915 at a running time of three hours basing his film on the novel, "The Clansman" by Thomas Dixon and parts of another novel, "The Leopard's Spots" by the same author.[88] Richard Schickel makes this most interesting observation, "But perhaps the most miraculous were not the financial difficulties *Griffith* overcame to produce his movie, but the fact that he *shot the entire three-hour film* 'off the cuff' that is, *without a script.* Somehow he managed to keep the entire, detailed concep-

---

[87] *Idem* at p. 915.

[88] Schickel, Richard, Movies, The History of an Art and an Institution (1964) at pp. 47-48.

tion in his own mind, and nowhere else, from the initial idea to the final editing, . . ."[89] Shickel notes that the film was released at the then unheard of price of two dollars a ticket and made a fortune for Griffith and his backers.[90] Thus, a film, which was presumably released on a roadshow, hard ticket basis, which Schickel characterizes as a "masterpiece",[91] and which all and sundry film critics hail as a seminal work of cinematography[92] was produced without a script.

Thus, if a landmark film such as "The Birth of a Nation" could be produced without the aid of a script, it may be concluded that screen plays, as such, are not necessarily an indispensable ingredient of film making. Indeed, the current vogue of "Now" film production in the United States also includes a genre of "Follow Me" type of cinematography. A noted performer in the arts goes about his business, on tour and at home, while the film makers follow him or her and photograph and record sequences which are later edited into a feature length motion picture. Some of these, for example, the film "Carry It On" is based upon the story of Joan Baez and her draft resisting husband, David Harris. The film was likewise made without the use of a screen play or script.

It is submitted films are often produced as original works without their being a derivative work at all, as in the case of "Carry It On." Moreover, the entire category

---

[89] *Idem* at p. 50. (emphasis added.)

[90] *Ibid.*

[91] *Idem* at p. 49.

[92]-See, for example, Rotha, Paul, The Film Till Now, (Spring Ed., 1967) at p. 151, in referring to "The Birth of a Nation", wherein he states, "Nevertheless, the importance of the film lay in its achievement of attracting the notice of serious-minded people to the expressive power of the cinema."

of films which are not adaptations are based either upon original screen plays or shot without scripts. As to such original works based upon scripts, there is no necessity for copyrighting the script or scenario, any more than there is for copyrighting the screen play based upon a novel or play. Analysis will indicate that the screen play, in terms of literary and artistic property, assumes two forms, either it is an adaptation of another work or an original work. If the former, the screen play itself is a derivative work, and perforce so is the motion picture produced therefrom. If the screen play is an original work, then in terms of copyright, the film is a derivative work in that it is derived from a work which itself is capable of being copyrighted, although in intrinsic terms the film is an original work in that its story is not derived from any other work but contains a story written solely for that film. With respect to films produced without any scripting therefor, the motion picture is not a derivative in any sense, whether in copyright terms or in a literary sense. Moreover, where a film production company employs a script writer to create a script as an original screen play, it is likely that the screen play will not be copyrighted. The film production company, as employer for hire, is then the common law copyright proprietor thereof. It may decide not to register the work for copyright as an unpublished work because it does not wish to deposit a copy thereof in the Copyright Office where it would be a public record. The producer might feel that it is better not to allow the contents of his forthcoming feature film to be a public record for fear that others might come out with competitive elements based upon the disclosure. The fear is less of copying since the registration of the screen play as an unpublished work presumably would afford the proprietor the remedies of the copyright statute against infringing copiers. Rather, the inhibition against deposit might stem from concern that the deposit of the script might indicate the nature, style, period and contents of the forthcoming film. Thus, if a producer feels that his forthcoming film has something fresh and original to say—perhaps even its genre may be an innovation—he would avoid premature disclosure like the plague, including copyrighting the screen play as an unpublished work. Conversely, where screen writers prepare a script as independent contractors for possible sale to producers, they will very likely consider copyrighting the same as an unpublished work. The copyright will be prima facie evidence of authorship and ownership.[93] Since such copies will be circulated for consideration by prospective producers, the creators of the screen play will have the benefit of the rule in proving prior authorship and origination in the event of a defense of independent origination as opposed to a claim of access and infringement of copyright by copying.

Thus it may be seen that motion pictures are writings subject to copyright under the statute and that their classification thereunder is purely for administrative convenience. As such copyrightable subject matter, it is surely irrelevant whether such films are based upon works under statutory or common law copyright, material in the public domain, or indeed are original. The fact of the matter is that the statute makes the film copyrightable, regardless of the source of the material in the film. Moreover, as has been seen, one of the rights comprehended by the exclusive right, if the copyrighted work be a drama, is the right to exhibit, produce or reproduce the same. Although the reason for inclusion of this right was to protect stage plays against film piracy, the technique em-

---

[93] 17 U.S.C. 209.

ployed to accomplish such protection was to grant the rights of production, reproduction and exhibition—as well as performance and representation—to the dramatic work. In effect, the statute grants the film right—to use an analogy to the stage right—to the copyright proprietor. Then one must ask, copyright proprietor of what? The answer must be, to the proprietor of works in dramatic form, no matter whether presented on stage or otherwise, so long as it is for public performance. Writers have interpolated this right as a "stage right." [94] This is so because the principal place for dramatic performances was on the stage of a theatre, hence the stage right. Yet from the very inception of the grant of the dramatic performance right by Congress in 1856, the right granted has been *in haec verba* broader than the right of dramatic performance on the stage. The 1856 Act speaks of "the sole right also to act, perform, or represent the same, or cause it to be acted, performed, or represented, *on any stage or public place* during the whole period for which the copyright is obtained;" [95] The Act of 1870 states that "in the case of a dramatic composition," there is a grant of the sole liberty "of publicly performing or representing it, or causing it to be performed or represented by others." [96] The language of the 1873 Revised Statutes is to the same effect,[97] as is the Act of 1891.[98] Thus, from 1856 on, the right granted was the *dramatic* right of public performance, and not just the stage right. In addition, the

---

[94] E.g., Matthews, Brander, *op. cit., supra,* note 1.

[95] Act of Aug. 18, 1856, 34th Cong., 1st Sess., c. 169, 11 Stat. 138 (1859). (emphasis added).

[96] Act of July 8, 1870, 41st Cong., 2d Sess., c. 230, 16 Stat. 212 (1871).

[97] Act of Dec. 1, 1873, Revision, 41st Cong., 1st Sess.

[98] Act of Mar. 3, 1891, 51st Cong., 2d Sess., c. 565, 26 Stat. 1106 (1893).

present statute, as enacted in 1909, provided in Sec. 1(d) thereof, that the copyright proprietor was to receive the exclusive right to publicly perform the drama or dramatic work "and to exhibit, perform, represent, produce, or reproduce it in any manner or by any method whatsoever." [99] The section speaks of right of performance of the copyrighted *work*, be it a drama or dramatic work. Presumably the thought of the Court of Appeals in *M.G.M.* v. *Bijou Theatre Corp.*[100] was that there had to be a subsisting copyrighted work to trigger invocation of the exclusive performing right in respect of the motion picture. But the section states that the exclusive performing right is granted, "To perform or represent the copyrighted work publicly *if it be a drama, or it be a dramatic work . . .*" [101] But Judge Morris in his opinion refers to "copyrighted films . . . founded on copyrighted *novels,* dramas, scenarios, or other dramatic compositions." [102] But a novel is not a dramatic composition. This is clear from Sec. 1(b) of the present Act which grants the exclusive right "to convert it into a novel *or other nondramatic work* if it be a drama." [103] Thus, on the face of the statute, a novel is not deemed a category of dramatic work. In literary terms, the statute is entirely correct since a dramatic work is written to be acted, played or in some manner performed whether with living actors or otherwise. Therefore, the Court of Appeals' opinion must be deemed not to mean that the sequence of copyrighted novels, dramas, scenarios, or other dramatic compositions was *ejusdem generis* because novels are not dramatic works. Thus the

---

[99] 17 U.S.C. 1(d).

[100] Note 71, *supra.*

[101] 17 U.S.C. 1(d). (emphasis added.)

[102] Note 71, *supra,* at pp. 76-77. (emphasis added.)

[103] 17 U.S.C. 1(b). (emphasis added.)

underlying notion of the Court of Appeals could not have been the language of Sec. 1(d) itself.

Sec. 15.4(b). Dramatic Performance and Film Exhibition

It follows, therefore, from the language of that section and from the history of the section as developed in the hearings as to the reason for the inclusion of the language that dramatic works could be exclusively publicly performed as film presentations, because the grant of this right was so provided to protect dramatic works against film piracy. If dramatic works could be in film form in terms of such protection, it follows that such dramatic works actually in film form are necessarily dramatic works. Since films are copyrightable as writings under the statute, they are copyrighted works assuming compliance with copyright formalities, etc.; being dramatic works in film form, they are themselves capable of the exclusive performing right. Hence, it follows that films in dramatic form are the subject of the exclusive performing right if the films themselves are copyrighted motion pictures under the statute. Thus, without more, under Sec. 1(d) an unlicensed performance of a copyrighted motion picture is an infringement of the exclusive right of public performance whether or not the film is based: (a) on a copyrighted work of any kind; (b) upon a dramatic work of any kind; (c) upon a dramatic work not under statutory copyright; and (d) upon any scripting of any kind whatsoever. The conclusion of the Courts in *Tiffany*[104] and in *Bijou*[105] to the effect that the films at issue, i.e., motion picture photoplays, were protected under Sec. 1(d) without regard to any other

---

[104] Note 86, *supra.*

[105] Note 69, *supra.*

factor because they are dramatic works is in accord with the internal construction of the statute.

In making this point, Judge Coleman in *Tiffany,* stated:

> "We find nothing in the congressional debates which indicate a different legislative intent. In fact, the question appears not to have been discussed when sections 5, 11, and 25 were amended in 1912. The debates that occurred with respect to prohibiting and penalizing the unauthorized exhibition, through moving pictures, of copyrighted plays and books are obviously not apposite to the precise point. Since, then, a motion-picture photoplay is to be considered as embraced within the term 'dramatic work', as used in section 1(d), and since, if copyrighted, it is an infringement for one without permission, 'to exhibit, perform, represent, produce, or reproduce it in any manner or by any method whatsoever', projecting it upon the screen is of course within the prohibition. The fact that the construction of the statute here adopted excludes motion pictures other than photoplays may produce an undesirable or even inequitable result. But that is a practical, not a legal objection, properly to be addressed to the lawmakers, not to the courts. Only photoplays are here involved." [106]

In support of this position, the Court, in *Universal Pictures Co., Inc.* v. *Harold Lloyd Corp.* extrapolated:

> "The Bijou case was remanded to the district court, 3 F. Supp. 66, and the court was of the opinion that the circuit court did not require, in its opinion, a holding that an unlicensed exhibition of a print of a copy-

---

[106] Note 86, *supra,* at p. 915.

> righted motion-picture photoplay infringes the copyright only if the film is based on a copyrighted novel or dramatic composition. The court held that an unlicensed exhibition of a motion-picture print of a motion-picture photoplay film, duly copyrighted, constituted an infringement, even though the film was not founded on a copyrighted novel or dramatic composition. The court, at page 73, states: 'Motion picture photoplay films are either dramatic works entitled to protection under subdivision (d) of section 1, supra, whose unauthorized performance is an infringement of the performing rights given to dramatic works, or they are nondramatic works entitled to protection under subdivision (b). It would seem that they are the former. The decision in Tiffany Productions, Inc. v. Dewing, et al., supra, which the Circuit Court of Appeals commends, decides that motion picture photoplay films are dramatic works entitled to protection under subdivision (d)." [107]

In *Harold Lloyd*, the claim was infringement by taking certain comedy routines embodied in Harold Lloyd's "Girl Crazy" which were reproduced in a sequence of some 57 scenes allegedly used in defendant's film, "So's Your Uncle". After finding that the gag scenes were a proper subject of copyright, the Court observed, "We agree with the trial court that the appellee's photoplay is a dramatic work and within the meaning of Section 1(d) of the Copyright Act." [108] Thus, infringement may occur by violation of the exclusive right of public performance by exhibition of part of a work by unauthorized copying of only part thereof and performing the same. It can also take place

---

[107] 162 F. 2d 354, 367 (9th Cir. 1947).

[108] *Idem* at p. 359.

by unauthorized performance of the whole of the infringed work itself even when the latter is under license to the defendant where, as in *Tiffany*[109] and *Bijou*,[110] the exhibitors exceed the terms of their licenses and exhibit the licensed film after the expiration of such respective terms.

Sec. 15.5. Film Exhibition as a Dramatization

But it is the next two sentences immediately following the part quoted by the Court in *Harold Lloyd*[111] from *Bijou*[112] on remand that are most revealing. The District Court in *Bijou* on remand went on to state, after considering that motion picture photoplays are either dramatic works under Sec. 1(d)[113] or nondramatic works under Sec. 1(b)[114] and concluding that they were dramatic works, "If they are not dramatic works, the exhibition of the photoplays by the defendant constitutes a dramatization of a nondramatic work, and constitutes an infringement of the rights secured by subdivision (b), supra. This subdivision secures the exclusive right 'to dramatize it (the copyrighted work) if it be a nondramatic work.' "[115]

The concession here, *arguendo*, by the Court, that it might not be a dramatic work presumably relates to the fact that motion picture photoplays are not classified as dramatic compositions under Sec. 5 of the Act, but have a *sui generis* classification in that section.[116] The Court

---

[109] Note 86, *supra*.
[110] Note 68, *supra*.
[111] Note 108, *supra*.
[112] Note 71, *supra*.
[113] 17 U.S.C. 1(d).
[114] 17 U.S.C. 1(b).
[115] Note 68, *supra*, 3 F. Supp. 66 at p. 73.
[116] 17 U.S.C. 5(d), 5(l).

takes this alternative position nevertheless, in holding on the authority of *Kalem Company* v. *Harper Bros.*[117] that exhibition of unauthorized film based upon scenes from the novel "Ben Hur" had infringed upon the exclusive rights of the copyright owner of the novel to dramatize the same, stating, "Upon the authority of this case, the plaintiff is entitled to protection against an unauthorized exhibition, either because the moving picture photoplay constituted a dramatic work, or because the unlicensed exhibition constituted a dramatization of a nondramatic work." [118]

But *Kalem*[119] dealt with infringement by dramatizing a novel whereas the remarks of the District Court on remand in *Bijou*[120] pertained to the character of the right in the motion picture photoplay itself. The District Court's reliance on *Kalem*[121] leads to the conclusion that a corollary of infringement, that, but for the infringement, the act purporting to constitute an exercise of the alleged right would not be wrongful, and conceivably may be a right protected by copyright itself. Dramatizing a novel in the form of a motion picture infringed the exclusive right to dramatize the novel in *Kalem*[122], whereas in *Bijou*[123], the exhibition of the film itself was deemed to constitute the dramatization of the same motion picture as a non-dramatic work. Applying the corollary doctrine, if motion picture photoplays are nondramatic works, then the proprietor has the exclusive right to protect unlawful

---

[117] 222 U.S. 55 (1911).
[118] Note 68, *supra,* 3 F. Supp. 66 at p. 73.
[119] Note 117, *supra.*
[120] Notes 108, 118, *supra.*
[121] Note 117, *supra.*
[122] *Ibid.*
[123] Notes 108, 118, *supra.*

exhibition thereof because exhibition itself is a right under copyright, the right to dramatize. The argument is ingenious, yet not without validity. Sec. 1(b) grants the exclusive right to dramatize a work "if it be a nondramatic work; to convert it into a novel or other nondramatic work if it be a drama." [124] The term for the adapted work subject to dramatization is generic, i.e., the term "nondramatic" is not limited to any particular genre of nondramatic works. So, too, while the word "novel" in the converse construct is specific, the reference to "other nondramatic work" is likewise generic excepting only the "novel". Together they are generic as in the dramatization part of the clause.

But the presupposition that a motion picture photoplay is a nondramatic work renders it the equivalent of a motion picture other than photoplay in this regard. Both would therefore be nondramatic works. If so, then it follows that an exhibition of a motion picture other than a photoplay is likewise a dramatization of a nondramatic work, unless the term "photoplay" has some intrinsic meaning of dramatic upon exhibition thereof that is not also applicable to the term "other than photoplay" where both categories of motion pictures are deemed to be nondramatic works for purposes of Sec. 1(d).[125] Assuming exhibition of a motion picture photoplay is a dramatization of a nondramatic work under Sec. 1(b),[126] presumably the photoplay is nondramatic because either Sec. 5 uses different language in subdivisions (d) as to dramatic compositions and in (1) as to motion picture photoplays,[127] or else Sec. 1(d) was intended to be a stage right literally, to apply to the right of public

---

[124] 17 U.S.C. 1(b).
[125] 17 U.S.C. 1(d).
[126] 17 U.S.C. 1(b).
[127] 17 U.S.C. 5(d) and (1).

performance live of dramatic works.[128] But the term "dramatize" means to put into dramatic form.[129] If Sec. 1(d)[130] were limited to the stage right, then the term "dramatize" in Sec. 1(b)[131] would have a broader meaning since a motion picture exhibition would constitute a dramatization under that section. On the other hand, if dramatization rendered a work dramatic, then its showing here, the exhibition, should also be a performance. As a performance of a dramatic work it ought to come under Sec. 1(d).[132] If so, then Sec. 5[133] of the act has been effectively disregarded to make the elision because a motion picture photoplay is deemed non-dramatic for purposes of Sec. 1(b),[134] without regard to the photo*play* aspect of the differentiation of motion picture photoplays in Sec. 5(1)[135] and motion pictures other than photoplays in Sec. 5(m).[136] If not so, then Sec. 5 still has been disregarded because the "play" root in photoplay has been disregarded for purposes of Sec. 1(d)[137] and even for Sec. 1(b)[138] because it is not the equivalent for purposes of the exclusive dramatic right of public performance and is deemed a nondramatic work for adaptation purposes excepting, possibly, upon exhibition thereof.

---

128 17 U.S.C. 1(d).

129 See Webster's New International Dictionary, Unabridged, Second Ed. (1961), at p. 782.

130 17 U.S.C. 1(d).

131 17 U.S.C. 1(b).

132 17 U.S.C. 1(d).

133 17 U.S.C. 5.

134 17 U.S.C. 1(b).

135 17 U.S.C. 5(l).

136 17 U.S.C. 5(m).

137 17 U.S.C. 1(d).

138 17 U.S.C. 1(b).

Sec. 15.6. The Doctrine of Corollary Right

But if Sec. 5[139] is truly a classification scheme, might not the categories "motion-picture photoplays" and "motion pictures other than photoplays" apply for all purposes in the delineation of rights under Sec. 1?[140] Under the corollary doctrine enunciated above, an infringing exhibition by a film would be an infringement of the right of dramatic performance of a stage play under Sec. 1(d).[141] The section literally applies thereto. A corollary of that is that since the section was intended to protect public performance of stage plays against film piracy, it follows that a non-infringing film thereof is a dramatic work which is the subject of the exclusive right of public performance. If the classification of films into photoplays and other than photoplays under Sec. 5[142] is for administrative conveniences only for the Copyright Office and copyright applicants, then perhaps the differentiation of categories in that section and in the Regulations of the Copyright Office thereunder[143] may likewise be disregarded for purposes of delineation of rights under Sec. 1.[144]

On the one hand, *Tiffany*[145] and *Bijou*[146] would disregard Sec. 5[147] in terms of granting the exclusive right of public performance to motion pictures under Sec. 1(d).[148] Yet, the differentiation of Sec. 5[149] as between Classes L

[139] 17 U.S.C. 5.
[140] 17 U.S.C. 1.
[141] 17 U.S.C. 1(d).
[142] 17 U.S.C. 5.
[143] Regulations of the Copyright Office, Sec. 202.15(a) and (b).
[144] 17 U.S.C. 1.
[145] Note 86, *supra.*
[146] Note 69, *supra.*
[147] 17 U.S.C. 5.
[148] 17 U.S.C. 1(d).
[149] 17 U.S.C. 5(l) and (m).

and M are not disregarded when it comes to such analysis. Effect is given to the terms "motion-picture photoplays" and "motion pictures other than photoplays" and to the Regulations thereunder, over and above that section.

Sec. 15.7. Films as Dramatic Works

It is submitted that perhaps the distinction between the two categories might be disregarded under Sec. 1 in that *all* motion pictures *be* deemed dramatic works thereunder for purposes of the exclusive right of public performance. If, as in *Bijou,*[150] the section may be disregarded to accord motion picture photoplays an equivalence to motion pictures other than photoplays, and despite the language of the Regulations, as non-dramatic works, then conceivably the section may also be disregarded so as to characterize them as dramatic works.

At first blush this may seem outlandish. Not only is there a clear differentiation in dramatic content in the categories under the section, but the Regulations are explicit. Photoplays thereunder include, "published or unpublished motion pictures that are dramatic in character and tell a connected story, such as feature films, filmed television plays, short subjects and animated cartoons having a plot." [151] On the other hand, motion pictures other than photoplays thereunder include, "published or unpublished non-dramatic films such as newsreels, travelogs, training or promotional films, nature studies and filmed television programs having no plot." [152] Moreover, it is also clear from the history of motion pictures that

---

[150] Note 69, *supra*. See Sec. 23.12(a), *infra*.

[151] Regulations of the Copyright Office, Sec. 202.15(a).

[152] *Idem*, Sec. 202.15(b).

the term "photoplay" was adopted to describe a dramatic work in film form.

Yet, it is submitted, the differentiation for other than classification purposes may be more apparent than real. The stage right is spoken of as a dramatic right, but the essence of the right is performance on stage or other public place. The stage right does not set forth the various genres comprising the stage right. Thus in the theatre, one may find many different types of works performed: comedy, tragedy, melodrama, revues, burlesque, variety, puppetry, marionettes, operetta, musical comedy, opera, mixed media and otherwise. The test for protection of any kind is copyrightability generally of that work. In order to obtain statutory protection there must, in the first instance, be a work which is capable of being copyrighted. If it is the subject of copyright, then the next question is whether it be a drama or dramatic work, in respect of the protection accorded in terms of the exclusive right of public performance. It may be assumed that comedy, tragedy and melodrama are intrinsically dramatic works. So, too, with some of the other forms. The question really is whether the right of dramatic performance publicly relates exclusively to dramatic forms, e.g., plays, operas, that tell a story with characters portraying the action of a plot. Yet characters need not be fictional. There may be plays dramatizing events in real life, such as "Sunrise at Campobello" and "In the Matter of J. Robert Oppenheimer". News events and actualities may be dramatized, as in the case of the Living Newspaper Project of the Works Progress Administration in the 1930's.[153] The Theatre of the Absurd would denigrate plot and story in

[153] See Taubman, Howard, The Making of the American Theatre, (1965) at pp. 230-231.

their traditional senses. To encompass the scope and breadth of the theatre, one must use the term in its broadest sense in application to drama or dramatic work. Otherwise, statutory norms would be delimited by forms and traditions in effect when the present Act was passed in 1909 and the then known sense of what is drama or the dramatic. The mere fact of the genre itself, the theatre, creates, almost by assimilation, as it were, the drama and dramatic work. Thus, in the case of the Living Newspaper, Howard Taubman wrote, "The Living Newspaper was not strictly objective. It editorialized as well as reported".[154] Even if it had not editorialized and were only to report—assuming that could be done—the very act of selection and presentation on the stage was a dramatic rendition, i.e., rendering the work in theatrical terms. By so doing, the work automatically assumes a theatrical form which generically might be deemed dramatic. Of course, one-man shows consisting of readings, *à la* Hal Holbrook as Mark Twain, might be deemed dramatic performances, even though the script might be read rather than enacted, if the intent is to convey the sense of drama in the work by way of theatrical performance. The same might be true of readings by two or more persons, particularly noted actors and actresses, who are, in effect, dramatizing the respective works by theatrical performance. So, too, a concert version of an opera might be a dramatico-musical performance even though there are no scenery, costumes, chorus or corps de ballet. The performance is primarily a version which emphasizes the musical elements of the opera, but it might be a dramatico-musical performance, nonetheless, because the soloists enact their roles by their singing parts, gestures and expressions.

---

[154] *Idem* at p. 230.

Indeed, in *Rice* v. *American Program Bureau,* the Court of Appeals for the Second Circuit had occasion to review whether the rendition of the rock opera "Jesus Christ Superstar", given in concert version, constituted a dramatico-musical version thereof. The Court first set forth the basis for the dramatic from the non-dramatic musical rights with respect thereto, stating, " . . . we conclude that appellants cannot perform the overall opera *Jesus Christ Superstar* nor advertise that their program consists of that opera or any adaptation thereof. Appellants can present separate songs, fragments of songs, or excerpts from the opera including the lyrics from the original works but cannot accompany such songs or excerpts with words, pantomime, dance, costumes, or scenery that will lend a visual representation of the work from which the music is taken." [154a] The fact that the ASCAP license did not extend to dramatico-musical works begged the question, to wit, whether or not the presentation of the separate songs therein without more, as authorized by the license, constituted a dramatico-musical performance. The Court then indicated in response to this query, ". . . the presentation of all of the songs from the opera *Jesus Christ Superstar* without costumes, words, or scenery, but in sequence could arguably develop the overall plot of the opera, and thus it might be 'dramatic' or a presentation of the opera in its 'entirety'. But we have no proof of this here and until there is proof, we cannot so hold." [154b]

The readings comparably emphasize dramatic content of the voice, possibly gestures and expressions. The readings are made for dramatic content of the renditions rather than the fact that there is an oral delivery of a non-

---

[154a] 446 F.2d 685, 689 (2d Cir. 1971). See Sec. 24.6(b), *infra*.
[154b] *Idem* at p. 690.

dramatic work. In the latter, the sermon, lecture or address is important because of the character in real life of the person delivering the same, e.g., the minister delivering the sermon, the professor giving the lecture, or the distinguished citizen making his after-dinner address. The Regulations of the Copyright Office also specify, in addition to lectures, sermons, and addresses, "monologs, panel discussions and variety programs prepared for radio and television." [155] But the specification refers to scripts thereof for purposes of registration under Sec. 5(c) which classifies, "Lectures, sermons, addresses (prepared for oral delivery)." [156]

Sec. 15.7(a). The Nature of Motion Pictures

If a work prepared for theatrical performance or adapted therefor may be classified generically as a dramatic work for purposes of the exclusive right of public performance, i.e., the stage right, by reason of the nature of the theatre, then one must look to the nature of motion pictures to determine the character of film for the same purposes.

Feature films, for example, are not limited to the fictional. There are any number of biographical films purporting to tell the story of the lives or aspects thereof of actual persons, e.g., "The Jolson Story", "The Sound of Music", "Disraeli", "A Song To Remember" and many, many others. Yet those are clearly dramatic works. Then, too, the Theatre of the Absurd has its counterpart in the cinema in films which de-emphasize plot and story line. In some respects the telling of a story has virtually disappeared, and the plot with it. Characters and events are almost disembodied or the locus is placed in happenings which

---

[155] Regulations of the Copyright Office, Sec. 202.6.

[156] 17 U.S.C. 5(c).

have little or no apparent continuity as in "Elvira Madigan" and "Easy Rider". Experimental film makers may at times eschew narrative in the film altogether. There is a whole genre of short subject production having a vogue among college student audiences which emphasizes impressionism, abstraction and the unreal. Given the category of photoplays, are these films to be deemed photoplays? There is also in vogue today a type of documentary feature, such as "Woodstock." "Don't Look Back" is a "Follow Me" type of film about Bob Dylan that would be difficult to characterize as photoplay in the traditional sense. The sense of these is the recreation of an actuality or happening. Finally, there is a genre of film which combines story and actuality, such as the Canadian film "Prologue" which has a story line and fictional components, yet was produced in part on location at the scene of the Chicago riots at the time of the National Democratic Convention in 1968 in which actualities, current events as they happened, were integrated into the plot.

It is submitted that the term "photoplay" was embodied in the statute in 1912, when Sec. 5 was amended, because it was a term of art.[157] There was a progression in film production in its infancy from shooting of events to staging. Lewis Jacobs writes, "So movie subjects began to evolve from bits of passing movement toward simple-real-life scenes, from staged scenes toward drama. By 1903 movie makers were staging events and soon were to acquire the ability to tell stories of their own making." [158] Prior to the Act of 1909 and the 1912 amendment, the theatre was the principal form of mass entertainment. Since plays were staged in the theatre, motion picture exhibitors, in

---

[157] Act of Aug. 24, 1912, 62d Cong., 2d Sess., 37 Stat. 488 (1913).

[158] Jacobs, Lewis, The Rise of the American Film (1967) at p. 11.

due course, added the word "photo" to "plays" to create a new term "photoplays". Plays being a mass form of entertainment, it was felt desirable to appeal to playgoers by incorporating a term which carried the sense of drama in film terms, hence, "photoplays". Indeed, the principal length of photoplays in 1912 was not at all the feature, so that the term referred to something which was not even the time equivalent of the stage play. Jacobs writes, "DeMille was one of the first to produce feature-length pictures: . . . In 1913-14 he did *The Squaw Man* . . ." [159] Arthur Knight notes, "One further effect of these ambitious Film d'Art productions was to help push the motion picture in this country beyond its single-reel length. In 1912 the great Sarah Bernhardt made a film version of her play *Queen Elizabeth* for Film d'Art in four reels. In Italy at the same time *Quo Vadis* was being readied in eight reels—almost two hours on the screen. In America, on the other hand, film lengths had been arbitrarily frozen at one reel." [160] Richard Schickel writes, "By 1912 Griffith had broken down most of the commercial and artistic restraints under which the American movie makers had been operating. But the powers remained adamant on the subject of length, claiming that the audience . . . would never sit through a film of more than one reel in length. Early in 1912 Griffith attempted a two-reel version of Tennyson's long poem, *Enoch Arden,* which Biograph released one reel at a time until audiences demanded to see both reels on the same program." [161] Thus, the context of the term "photoplays" as enacted by Congress was the

---

[159] *Idem* at p. 336. (italics)

[160] Knight, Arthur, The Liveliest Art (Mentor Book Ed., 1957) at p. 30. (italics)

[161] Schickel, Richard, Movies, The History of an Art and an Institution, (1964) at p. 45. (italics).

film genre now known as the short subject, particularly, the one-reeler. The progression in length to 1912 was from odd lengths such as 50 seconds, measured in number of feet film, to the basic one reel length. Jacobs, in discussing the first American story films, remarks that they were "... never longer than one reel".[162]

In this regard, Fulton notes:

> "The growth of the motion pictures as a business was greater than their growth as an art. The film companies were still turning out short-one-reel pictures hardly more indicative of what the art was to become than *The Great Train Robbery.* Even though short stories, epic poems, plays, and operas were now being adapted to the screen, the scope of the adaptations was limited to the length of a reel of film, that is, to about one thousand feet, or twelve minutes' running time. Furthermore, the producers were making money with one-reel films, and they saw no reason to change an established and profitable practice. In 1909, J. Stuart Blackton directed a five-reel film, *The Life of Moses,* for Vitagraph, but the company released it a reel at a time, one reel a week, beginning in January, 1910. Later in 1910, Vitagraph produced a three-reel version of *Uncle Tom's Cabin,* but it too was released in single reels. However, the next year, when Griffith made a two-reel adaptation of Tennyson's *Enoch Arden* and the film was released in separate reels, popular demand of the nickelodeon patrons resulted in the two reels' being screened in one showing. *Enoch Arden* is thus the first American film longer than one reel." [163]

---

[162] Jacobs, *op. cit., supra,* note 158, at p. 68.

[163] Fulton, A. R., Motion Pictures, The Development of an Art from Silent Films to the Age of Television (1960) at pp. 61-62. (italics).

Fulton also observes that the American premiere of the four-reel import from France, "Queen Elizabeth," starring Sarah Bernhardt, took place on July 12, 1912.[164]

Thus, it may be seen that the term "photoplay", as used by exhibitors in nickelodeons and elsewhere prior to the 1912 amendment (approved August 24, 1912) of the 1909 Copyright Act was hardly referring to the prototype of the latter day feature length dramatic film, which was only imported in 1912 ("Queen Elizabeth", starring Sarah Bernhardt) by Adolph Zukor. Feature length or, for that matter, films in a length of only four reels, were made after the 1912 amendment. Thus, the reference to the term "photoplays" when enacted, in the context of the times, is not to be taken to be the feature length equivalent of full-length stage dramas.

Sec. 15.7(b). Theatre and the Motion Picture Art

Rather, it might be well to look at the influences of the theatre on motion picture techniques and the nature of the film esthetically as a dramatic work, instead of focusing on the terminology which was embodied in the statute regarding film classification in 1912. A.R. Fulton quotes from the New York Times of April 14, 1896 with respect to the exhibition of the vitascope invented by Thomas A. Edison at Koster & Bial's Music Hall as follows:

"The vitascope projects upon a large area of canvas groups that appear to stand forth from the canvas, and move with great facility and agility, as though actuated by separate impulses. *In this way the bare canvas before the audience becomes instantly a stage upon which living*

---

[164] *Idem* at p. 73.

beings move about."[165] Knight observes, "The importance of this theatrical tradition has too often been ignored in tracing the pre-screen history of the film."[166] Fulton remarks, "Méliès noticed that the fading of the scene made a more effective transition—like the slow closing of a theatre curtain at the end of a scene—rather than an abrupt cut. It was a fade-out, which gave him the idea of introducing the scene with a fade-in."[167] Finally, Rotha makes this point, "Again it is found that the reproduction of dialogue demands almost stationary action in the accompanying visual image, which prevents freedom in the development of the action during any sequence. Thus action has to progress step by step, destroying, as it jerks forward, both rhythmic continuity and harmony. It is no longer a film. *It has returned to the early photo-play of theatrical tradition."*[168]

It is indeed the early photoplay of theatrical tradition that the 1912 amendment was referring to in classifying motion picture photoplays. However, although the norm was the one-reeler prior to enactment of that act, longer length films were not unknown at the time. Moreover, the fact that the history of the film prior thereto was one of production of motion pictures in varying lengths served to indicate to the Congress that there was no optimum length of a film or, indeed, any ceiling on the length thereof.

---

[165] *Idem* at p. 15. (emphasis added.) The author notes at p. 18, "Whether the invention may be called Mr. Edison's is as the records show—open to question."

[166] Knight, *op. cit., supra,* note 160 at p. 19.

[167] Fulton, *op. cit., supra,* note 165, at p. 25.

[168] Rotha, *op. cit., supra,* note 92, at p. 407. (emphasis added).

It is therefore fair to extrapolate that the statutory reference to photoplays was not intended as a fixed rooting of the term in the trade practices prevalent at the time. For, if this were so, the statute would have been a fairly meaningless exercise in legislation. Within a very short time after passage of the Townsend Act in 1912, feature length films became the dominant form of motion picture exhibition. The 1912 amendment was unchanged by Congress in the face of such transformation of industry patterns. Indeed, motion pictures became the mass art form in the decade thereafter so that its growth and its problems scarcely would have escaped the attention of Congress. Neither did the courts nor the Copyright Office assume otherwise.

Sec. 15.7(c). The Film Art

But film art is not merely a quantitative change of length of film measured by the equivalence by analogy to the theatre or not, as the case may be, in terms of the motion picture photoplay or the motion picture other than the photoplay. Rotha defines a film differently. He states:

> "A film is primarily a dynamic pattern or rhythm (achieved by the editing and cutting) imposed on nature (the material taken, preferably the reality). It is governed pictorially by the use of light and movement in the creation of visual images, and mentally by psychology in the creation of mental images. Music and synchronized sound, used in counterpoint and contrapuntally, heighten the emotions of the spectator aurally and subconsciously. This dynamic mental pictorialism is, I claim, the most powerful form of expression available to-day to a creative artist." [169]

---

[169] *Idem* at p. 336.

Note that Rotha was referring to *film,* not solely *photoplay.* And the principal ingredients of film making are the camera and editing. As to the camera, George Bluestone has written:

> ". . . . Whatever the standards of the future, however, it is highly probably that the film's basic materials will remain more mechanically fixed than those of the more traditional arts.
>
> "Beyond these limitations, however, the camera is free to use almost endless visual variations. It is at this point that the camera, its reel of sensitized film sprocketed in place, announces itself as an artistic instrument. The camera can go anywhere, see anything, in the natural world. . . . Even immobilized, the camera makes space pliable.
>
> "More significantly, however, the camera can move, and its mobility has enabled it to achieve unprecedented visual effects. At this point, the film declares its historical independence from the theater." [170]

Rotha adds the observation, "The capabilities of the camera as an instrument of expression are almost unlimited." [171] Bluestone notes, "Bound by its respect for physical reality, but unbound by the vision of any *one* spectator, the lens becomes an ideal, unrealistic eye; unbound by natural observation, the eye of the spectator becomes omniscient. It took several years for film-makers to understand that the film's angle of vision was non-naturalistic; that being non-naturalistic, yet bound by optical and mechanical laws, the film had found its formative power." [172]

---

[170] Bluestone, George, Novels Into Film (1966) at p. 15.

[171] Rotha, *op. cit., supra,* note 92, at p. 366.

[172] Bluestone, *op. cit., supra,* note 170, at p. 17. (italics).

Bluestone then describes the role of editing. "Once film technicians discovered that the scripts of celluloid were their real raw material, and once directors interrupted the camera's natural eye to join the film in ways contrary to nature, the mode of transition from one shot to the next became all important. Spatial transition, the core of editing, becomes in Raymond Spottiswoode's phrase, 'the grammar of the film.' "[173] Rotha remarks in this respect, "In the case of the film, we are now able to grasp fully the fact that the material is on the strips of film and the composing is the act of editing, . . ."[174] Moreover, "The power of editing in the hands of a capable director is unlimited."[175]

But camera and editing are the artistic and technical means of implementing a presupposition—a theme, i.e., what the film maker sets out to produce in the first instance. Rotha describes the theme as follows:

> "A film demands that a theme—either personal, impersonal or inanimate—shall be presented to the mind through the eye by the flowing relation and interrelation of a succession of visual images projected on a screen. It further requries the theme to be emphasized by the full range of cinematic resources; by the use of the intimate to reinforce the general at a similar moment or in development; by the instantaneous pictorial vision of more than one idea at the same time; by symbolism and suggestion; by the association of ideas and shapes; by the varying high and low tensions caused by rhythmic cutting; by variation in the intensities of light; by the contrast

[173] *Idem* at p. 18.
[174] Rotha, *op. cit., supra,* note 92, at p. 389.
[175] *Idem* at p. 388.

> and similarity of sounds; by all the intrinsic properties peculiar to the medium of the film. The film possesses the power of expanding and contracting the centre of interest, and of comparison by rapid change of the relationship of the trivial to essential. By these means may the audience be compelled to accept the *dramatic* meaning of the theme and to realise its continually developing content."[176]

It is to be noted that Rotha uses the term "dramatic" in this context. The portions quoted above as to camera, editing and theme, have deliberately been selected so as to exemplify concepts which would be equally applicable to both films that purport to tell a story, i.e., motion picture photoplays, and all other categories of film. In other words, the principles of selection of theme, the artistic roles of the camera and of editing are generic to motion pictures and are not limited to films of any particular kind or category. It is to the generic term "motion pictures" that Rotha is referring when he comments on the *dramatic* meaning of the theme. In effect, he is observing that the film art is inherently dramatic regardless of its particular form. If the films are inherently dramatic, then it follows that a work in film form may properly be categorized as a dramatic work.

Sec. 15.8. Dramatization: Stage Right; Film Right

In this regard, as early as 1914, Judge Learned Hand recognized a distinction between the stage right and the film right in *Photo Drama Motion Picture Co.* v. *Social Uplift Film Corp.*[177] After stating, ". . . to the present time the only right to protect moving pictures arises from the

---

[176] *Idem* at p. 338. (emphasis added.)
[177] 213 Fed. 374 (S.D.N.Y. 1914).

words 'dramatic' or 'drama' "[178] Judge Hand went on to say:

> "A man having general statutory dramatic rights like Kauffman might make a play and perform it under his common-law rights without publication, or he might copyright the play, and he would still not have copyrighted or published his moving picture rights. If he wrote such a scenario and made his film, he could get a separate copyright upon that. Of course, he could sell his statutory or common-law copyright of the play and keep the moving picture copyright, or he could sell each.
>
> "It seems to me clear that, if he could do this, he could sell separately the right to dramatize and the right to make a moving picture play, dividing his statutory dramatizing rights, and giving each assignee the right, when he has exercised these rights, to get his own copyright for a drama or for a moving picture show." [179]

Thus, insofar as the right to dramatize is concerned, Judge Hand distinguishes between the stage play and the film play. Dramatization is not a matter of a particular form and may be separable into various rights of dramatization, depending upon the form. Elsewhere in the opinion, Judge Hand states, "Thus, the statutory right to protect against the making of a moving picture scenario *from a book* still arises from section 1, subd. 'b', and the statutory right to protect against infringement of the scenario arises from section 1, subd. 'd.' "[180] Basically, the

---

[178] *Idem* at p. 377.
[180] *Ibid.* (emphasis added.)
[179] *Ibid.*

right under Sec. 1(b)[181] is a right of adaptation, in this context, from a novel or other non-dramatic work to a film. The adaptation in this respect is the transference of expression of various aspects of the adapted work to another medium, here film.[182] Unless the court, in any given matter, is to set itself up as some kind of literary and dramatic critic as to the end result of a film adaptation telling or not telling the *story* of the underlying work, as the case may be, it must assume that the film form is dramatic by nature so that a film adaptation of any literary work is *ipso facto* a dramatization. *A fortiori,* if the film adaptation, the film itself, is a dramatization, then, as Judge McLellan held in *Bijou,*[183] its exhibition, i.e., the means by which the film is perceived, is also a dramatization. A motion picture consists of exposed film, edited in some sequence and continuity to a given length in the form of a negative, from which positive prints are manufactured, for a projection on a screen and exhibition thereof.

Sec. 15.9. Exclusive Right of Performance and Classification of Rights

But exhibition is also performance, as Sec. 1(d) specifies.[184] A film theme will be a dramatization if made from any other material of a literary nature. Since the medium, by its very nature, is dramatic in form, exhibition of the film would constitute performance of a dramatic work. One should not look to subdivisions (d) dramatic or dramatico-musical compositions, (l) motion-picture photo-

---

[181] 17 U.S.C. 1(b).

[182] See, for example, the discussion of the inherent limitations in such transference from novel into film in Bluestone, *op. cit. supra,* note 170.

[183] Note 69, *supra.*

[184] 17 U.S.C. 1(d).

plays and (m) motion pictures other than photoplays of Sec. 5[185] for an exegesis as to whether or not motion pictures of both categories are dramatic works. It is to be noted that Sec. 1(a) of the statute grants rights of publication.[186] Yet there is no correspondence between that section and subdivision (a) of Sec. 5 alone.[187] Indeed, the specification of literary categories, in the broadest sense, is encompassed by both subdivisions (a) and (b) of Sec. 5,[188] covering: (a) "Books, including composite and cyclopedic works, directories, gazetteers, and other compilations"; and (b) "Periodicals, including newspapers." [189] If there is no necessary correspondence as between publication rights under Sec. 1(a)[190] and classification of the media of publication in Sec. 5,[191] which, in any event, is broader since motion pictures also may be published—for example, by sale of prints thereof—it follows that there is no necessary correspondence between adaptation rights, including dramatization rights, as set forth in Section 1(b),[192] as well as performance of dramatic rights in Sec. 1(d),[193] with the category of dramatic composition of Sec. 5(d) alone.[194] Of course, one can refer to the coincidence of subdivision headings of Section 5(e).[195] Musical compositions, with the coverage of music in Sec. 1(e)[196] and of the classification of

---

185 17 U.S.C. 5.
186 17 U.S.C. 1(a).
187 17 U.S.C. 5(a).
188 17 U.S.C. 5(a) and (b).
189 Notes 187-188, *supra.*
190 17 U.S.C. 1(a).
191 17 U.S.C. 5.
192 17 U.S.C. 1(b).
193 17 U.S.C. 1(d).
194 17 U.S.C. 5(d).
195 17 U.S.C. 5(e).
196 17 U.S.C. 1(e).

lectures, sermons, etc. prepared for oral delivery in Sec. 5(c)[197] with the exclusive right of performance granted works of this nature in Sec. 1(c).[198] Then how does one explain Sec. 5(f) and (j)[199] relating respectively to maps and photographs, cognizable under the exclusive publication rights of Sec. 1(a)[200] and the hybrid dramatico-musical compositions under Sec. 5(d)?[201] These presumably refer to works both dramatic and musical in nature and whose performance would otherwise be cognizable under Sec. 1(d)[202] were it solely a dramatic work or under Sec. 1(e)[203] were it solely a musical work.

It may thereby be seen that Sec. 5,[204] concededly a section drawn for administrative convenience, should not be the yardstick for determination of rights under Sec. 1.[205] Nor should interpretation be based narrowly on the prevalent trade practices in effect at the time of the enactment of the pertinent legislation. Moreover, one would have to ignore the effect of judicial gloss being read into legislation, as in the classification of motion pictures as copyrightable as photographs even prior to the passage of the present statute in 1909.[206] Otherwise, one reaches the bizarre result that the Congress, being aware of the art of motion pictures in the hearings and passage of the 1909 legislation and of the judicial gloss purporting to include

---

[197] 17 U.S.C. 5(c).
[198] 17 U.S.C. 1(c).
[199] 17 U.S.C. 5(f) and (j).
[200] 17 U.S.C. 1(a).
[201] 17 U.S.C. 5(d).
[202] 17 U.S.C. 1(d).
[203] 17 U.S.C. 1(e).
[204] 17 U.S.C. 5.
[205] 17 U.S.C. 1.
[206] Note 82, *supra*.

motion pictures as the subject of copyright prior thereto, intended to permit a hiatus in protection as to motion pictures, in the unlawful performance, i.e., exhibition thereof, and that when it had a second chance to review the situation, upon enactment of specific legislation relating to motion pictures in 1912, it blithely omitted such protection once again, at least with respect to motion pictures other than photoplays. Since motion pictures other than photoplays were shown in nickelodeons and elsewhere publicly before the 1912 amendment, along with motion picture photoplays, it would be difficult to see why the legislature would discriminate in favor of the one as against the other, or that it would protect only the motion picture photoplay as to the grant of dramatic rights and possibly the film as a dramatization of other works, but not the performance of motion pictures other than photoplays.

Sec. 15.10. The Film Right; Exclusive Right of Public Performance

It may therefore be fairly contended that the film is an art form, dramatic in form, by the very nature of its art and technology, that, regardless of its classification for purposes of copyright application, it is and was intended to be the subject of the exclusive right of public performance as a dramatic work under the statute as enacted in 1909.

In this regard the observation of Borge Varmer is apt·

> "It may be desirable in a general revision of the law, as was one in a number of the previous general revision bills, to make specific for the right to exhibit motion pictures. If that is done, consideration will need to be given to the question of whether this right should extend to all exhibitions or only to public exhibitions.

"It might be observed first that insofar as exhibition rights are concerned, no reason is apparent for making any distinction between photoplays and other motion pictures. For both alike, their chief commercial value lies in their exhibition; and the methods of distribution, licensing and exhibition are the same. Both are also alike in regard to the premise that people having seen the motion picture at one exhibition are not likely to pay to see it again. In all of the previous general revision bills which provided for exhibition rights in motion pictures, the rights pertained to all motion pictures without distinction between photoplays and others." [207]

There being no apparent reason for making this distinction, it is submitted that a fair interpretation of present law is that Congress did not make this distinction in the grant of exclusive rights even though it classified film into photoplays and other than photoplays for purposes of administrative convenience.

---

[207] Varmer, Borge, Limitations On Performing Rights, Study No. 16, Studies on Copyright (1963) 835 *et. seq.* at p. 873.

Chapter XVI

RIGHTS IN PERFORMANCE: MUSICAL

Sec. 16.1. The Right of Performance in Music

The third major exclusive performing category granted by the present Copyright Act is that of public performance of music for profit. Subject to certain qualifications, limitations and exemptions, Sec. 1(e) grants three basic rights in pertinent part as follows:

> "(e) To perform the copyrighted work publicly for profit if it be a musical composition; and for the purpose of public performance for profit, and for the purposes of subsection (a) hereof, to make any arrangement or setting of it or of the melody of it in any system of notation or any form of record in which the thought of an author may be recorded and from which it may be read or reproduced:" [1]

The rights embodied therein are the performing right, the arranging right and the recording right.

Thus it may be seen that the grant of the non-dramatic performing right of oral delivery in Sec. 1(c),[2] the grant of the dramatic performing right in Sec. 1(d)[3] and the music rights per above all have common attributes of public performance, the right to record and perform the recording. However, the recording right in respect of non-dramatic performances for oral delivery originated in 1952,[4] whereas

---

[1] 17 U.S.C. 1(e).

[2] 17 U.S.C. 1(c).

[3] 17 U.S.C. 1(d).

[4] Act of July 17, 1952, 82nd Cong. 2d Sess., 66 Stat. 752 (1952).

the dramatic and musical recording rights were included in 1909.[5] Nimmer opines, "Apparently these various forms are interchangeable and all refer to what is here termed the right to record." [6]

The musical recording right, unlike the fears as to piracy by recording as to the dramatic performing right,[7] stemmed from monopoly considerations. William M. Blaisdell refers to the antitrust antecedents with respect to the reasons for concern as to the right to record. "From the 1909 House committee report it is clear that the committee, in its recommendation to include the compulsory license provision, was chiefly concerned with the possibility that one recording company might obtain a monopoly of the recording rights in popular music." [8] As a hedge against an adverse decision in pending litigation, a mechanical reproducing establishment had entered into mechanical reproduction agreements with 80 leading music publishing companies for long terms. The contingency never came into effect because the contention was successfully made that piano player rolls were not "copies" and therefore did not infringe copyright.[9] Blaisdell remarks in this regard, "However, to the committee the fact that such contracts had been made meant the strong probability of a monopoly in the music recording business if the mechanical recording right was provided

---

[5] Act of Mar. 4, 1909, 60th Cong. 2d Sess., 35 Stat. 1075 (1909).

[6] Nimmer on Copyright (1969), Sec. 108.1, fn. 237, pp. 418-419, at p. 419.

[7] See Chap. XV, *supra*.

[8] Blaisdell, William M., Economic Aspects of the Compulsory License, Study No. 6, in Studies on Copyright (1963), pp. 937-961, at p. 958.

[9] White-Smith Music Publishing Co. v. Apollo Co., 209 U.S. 1 (1908).

for without some restriction such as the compulsory license."[10]

The fears of monopoly may explain the provision for the compulsory license in the 1909 statute, but they do not tend to give the rationale as to the form of the grant of the rights, with respect to which the compulsory license was only a limitation. For example, this does not explain the nature of the grant of the performing right in music as enacted in the 1909 Act. In this regard, Borge Varmer writes, "In the act of January 6, 1897 the public performing rights were extended to musical works."[11] Yet all that act did was to amend Sec. 4966 of the Revised Statutes to provide in pertinent part: "Sec. 4966. Any person publicly performing or representing any dramatic or musical composition for which a copyright has been obtained, without the consent of the proprietor of said dramatic or musical composition, or his heirs or assigns, shall be liable for damages therefor . . ."[12] The amendment substantially changed that section by adding "musical compositions" to dramatic composition for which damages would be accorded for infringement for public performance thereof without consent of the proprietor of the copyright or his heirs and assigns.

What is peculiar about this is that the amendment did not purport to refer to Sec. 4952 of the Revised Statutes[13]

---

[10] Blaisdell, *op. cit., supra,* note 8, at p. 959.

[11] Varmer, Borge, Limitations on Performing Rights, Study No. 16, in Studies on Copyright (1963), pp. 835-875, at p. 837.

[12] Act of Jan. 6, 1897, 54th Cong. 2d Sess., c. 4, 29 Stat. 481 (1897) as set forth in Copyright Enactment Laws Passed in the United States Since 1783 Relating To Copyright, Copyright Office, Bulletin No. 3 (Revised), 1963, at pp. 56-57.

[13] Revised Statutes, Sec. 4952, Dec. 1, 1873 Revision, Sec. 4952. See Copyright Enactments, *idem* at p. 44.

which granted the exclusive public performing rights in dramatic compositions, and did not refer to the musical performance right. Indeed, the Act of March 3, 1905, which amended Sec. 4952 of the Revised Statutes with respect to books printed abroad in a foreign language, modified the grant of rights clause somewhat in respect of translation and dramatization, but substantially retained the exclusive right of dramatic public performance without reference to any right of public performance for profit.[14] Thus, the 1897 amendment appears to be anomalous in having amended the damages provision to include the exclusive right of public performance of music without at the same time having amended the section granting the right of public performance. Then when that section was amended, it was only done so with respect to other matters and the hiatus therein as to the grant of right in musical public performance continued.

The 1909 Act corrected this by providing expressly for an exclusive grant of right of public performance in music[15] and adding a "for profit" limitation thereto.[16] Thus the exclusive right of public performance clearly came into its own with the 1909 Act by reason of Sec. 1(e) thereof, even though it was limited to public performance of musical compositions for profit.[17] Hence, instead of the backdoor approach through the damages provision, the exclusive right of musical performance was expressly set forth in the grant of rights which were part of the bundle of rights constituting the copyright. The grant continues in substantially the

---

[14] Act of Mar. 3, 1905, 58th Cong. 3d Sess., c. 1432, 33 Stat. 1000 (1905). See Copyright Enactments, *idem* at p. 62.

[15] Act of Mar. 4, 1909, 60th Cong. 2d Sess., 35 Stat. 1075 (1909).

[16] Varmer, *op. cit., supra,* note 11, at p. 838.

[17] Act of Mar. 4, 1909, note 15, *supra,* Sec. 1(e).

same form in the present Act.[18] The 1909 Act had the virtue of comprehensive consideration of the problem of public performance of music and the reflection thereof in the statute.

Sec. 16.2. The Compulsory License

This was done by the additional rights granted by Sec. 1(e),[19] to wit, the arranging right and the recording right. Of course, the exclusive right to record is a divestible right, insofar as exclusivity is concerned, because the first recording of a musical composition under the statute renders the right to record non-exclusive by means of the compulsory license. The fact that the right to record is thereafter non-exclusive does not defeat its quality as a right. What is transformed thereby is the nature of the right. The monopoly or exclusivity is gone; it is replaced by the compulsory license—or contractual substitute—but the recording right nonetheless continues in effect. Thus, unlike the publication which divests the common law copyright and renders it nugatory, the first recording of a musical composition does not serve to terminate or destroy the right. It merely changes the quality of the right from complete control of its exercise through the monopoly nature of exclusivity to qualified control by means of the compulsory license in lieu thereof. The owner of the copyright, in effect, is transformed from someone vested with the power to create, which can be assigned in respect of the first recording or be exercised by the owner thereof, into the beneficiary of the broadcasting—not in a technological sense but in the sense of spreading out, such as the farmer broadcasting his seed—of the recording right after the initial recording.

---

[18] 17 U.S.C. 1(e).

[19] *Ibid.*

The compulsory license serves to transform the copyright proprietor, vis-à-vis the recording right, into an administrator of the broadcast recording right. His functions are transformed from the creative role of enabling a work to be created by means of the exercise of the power to create, as embodied in the exclusive right to first recording, into the accounting, ministerial and legal functions of administering the compulsory license. After the first recording, the proprietor of the copyright has lost effective control over the creative manifestations of the recording right, exercisable prior thereto in the designation of the party to whom the right of first recording is granted. Thereafter, the copyright proprietor has the option of accepting the statutory ceiling of two cents a side for the copyright recorded or negotiating a lesser rate or the statutory rate by contract. The remaining functions of the copyright proprietor are to police the license so granted by means of the accounting function of accepting and possibly auditing payments and statements, and, in an extreme situation, by means of the legal function, i.e., either to institute litigation for an accounting and/or to attempt to revoke or rescind the license so granted for failure to make payments.

The compulsory license, then, represents a transference of the market function by legal fiat from creator and assigns to the user. In the ordinary situation the investiture of the exclusive rights in the copyright in the copyright proprietor serves as the lever for operation of the market mechanisms. The grant of the exclusive right serves as the means for the owner thereof to command a price for the exercise of the particular right by the user thereof. The rights are so obtained in negotiations, either at arms length subject to the economics of supply and demand of the market, or to the distortions thereof by reason of the market strength and/or the monopolistic or restrictive position of the owner or the user of the right, as the case may be.

Sec. 16.3. The Arrangement Right and Mechanical Reproduction

The compulsory license eliminates the market mechanisms of supply and demand and the distortions thereof in the reality of the market place and superimposes thereon a form of trade regulation and price fixing. After the first recording, recordings are not free to be exclusively licensed but automatically become subject to the regulatory devices of the compulsory license or the contractual substitute. The freedom of the owner of the copyright is taken from him in this regard and a payment schedule is set up on a ceiling or maximum basis in the statute under which the copyright owner must operate. Congress has thereby provided that the proprietor may not receive more than this amount as the consideration for the grant of the license. Realistically speaking, the user will never pay more than this ceiling, and should a mechanical license agreement be entered into between proprietor and user for a royalty in excess thereof, it would contravene the statutory rate and, in all likelihood, be void as a violation and evasion of the statute and of the public policy embodied therein.

One attempt to enlarge the thrust of the license agreement by reading the arrangement right out of it was made in *Edward B. Marks Music Corporation* v. *Foullon.*[20] There the plaintiff was the owner of the copyrighted song, "Malaguena." Defendant, United Masters, Inc., evidently had received a contractual license to record the work which had been recorded by it as a substitute for the compulsory

[20] 79 F. Supp. 664 (S.D.N.Y. 1948), *aff'd* 171 F. 2d 905 (2d Cir. 1949). See also Sec. 6.3(c), *supra.*

license. At issue was the nature of an arrangement that the defendants had made which they had embodied in the recording. The plaintiff contended that the alleged license, relied on as a defense, was not a separate and distinct contract but was merely a memorandum of defendant, United Masters, Inc., of its use under the compulsory license provision. The plaintiff further contended that the compulsory license does not comprehend the right to make a version and arrangement of the work. Consequently, the arrangement for commercial purposes exceeded the grant of rights under either the compulsory license or contractual license and the pressing of a record embodying the arrangement constituted an infringement of copyright.

Judge Goddard in the District Court construed the statute as not granting to the copyright owner control over the arrangement in mechanical reproduction thereof stating, "To hold that the separate and distinct right to make a version and arrangement also existed in connection with the right to mechanical reproduction, would be to rewrite the section so as to add to subsection (a) the right to mechanical reproduction. This the Congress has steadfastly refused to do on the ground that to grant to the copyright owner the right to control the arrangement and version of the mechanical reproduction would be to create an opportunity for the birth of mechanical trusts." [21]

It appears that the defendant, United Masters, Inc., never filed a notice of intention to use under then Sec. 25(e) of the Copyright Act, now Sec. 101(e).[22] The statutory pro-

---

[21] *Idem* at p. 666.

[22] 17 U.S.C. 101(e) sets forth the damages for recording which is unauthorized and therefore infringing. The statute provides that the same shall not be a criminal act, i.e., no criminal action shall be brought but plaintiff may recover the Sec. 1(e) royalty and the

vision for such notice appears in the section of the statute specifying damages for infringing recording, i.e., recording unauthorized by absence of a license agreement or by failure to serve notice of intention to use pursuant to the statute. The statute thus characterizes the defense as procedural. Actually, the service of the notice of intent to use also partakes of substantive attributes. Vis-à-vis the copyright proprietor, the invocation of the notice of intention of use procedure may be a condition precedent to avoidance of liability, but it is, at the same time, the means for the would-be user to invoke the compulsory license free of liability as an infringer. The notice of intention to use is the catalyst for inception of the license. It is, indeed, the instrumentality for commencement of use, free of damages and injunctive relief. In effect, the license is a limited, i.e., non-exclusive right, to use the copyrighted material for the creation of a mechanical reproduction thereof at prescribed statutory rates and accounting procedures, e.g., monthly, and subject to payment thereof and accounting therefor. Thus, the notice of intention to use has substantive attributes since, without service thereof pursuant to the statute, the compulsory license will not become effective because the user will then be subject to the statutory damages and injunction. In effect, the user would then be in the position of an infringing user.

The notice of intention to use was important in this case because the second count of plaintiff's complaint was based upon an alleged failure to file a notice of intention to use

---

court may also award a further sum not exceeding three times such amount and issue a temporary injunction until the award is paid. A defense is accorded a party who does not have a license agreement by service of a notice of intent to use, i.e., record, pursuant to the statute, upon copyright proprietor by registered mail, copy to the Copyright Office. See Sec. 26.3, *infra*.

by the defendants. Therefore, it was incumbent upon the plaintiff to vitiate the effect of the mechanical license agreement and make the defendants infringing parties by failure to comply with the statutory requirements of filing the notice of intention to use required of licensees under the compulsory license. Judge Learned Hand then went on to note:

> "The plaintiff's position is that the 'Mechanical License agreement' must be taken, not as a contract or consensual license substituted for the compulsory license of Sec. 1(e), but only as a recognition—a mere acknowledgment, as it were—that Sec. 1(e) and Sec. 25(e) did in fact govern the parties' rights and obligations. Turning to these sections, the plaintiff then argues that, although they gave United Masters a compulsory license, which allowed it to make records, those were only records of the copyrighted composition as it was, and did not authorize any 'arrangement'. The 'arrangement' for the group of performers was therefore itself an infringement under Sec. 1(e), and the manufacture of the records was a second infringement. In both aspects United Masters exposed itself to the remedies provided in Sec. 25 as a tortfeasor." [23]

It appears that the defendant, United Masters, Inc., had already made the arrangement when it requested the mechanical license agreement which it obtained. Judge Hand asserted that this defendant chose to rely upon the license agreement because it felt it needed express consent to the arrangement by means of the license agreement and that seeking a compulsory license by service of the notice of intention to use might subject it to a claim as a bare

---

[23] Note 20, *supra,* 171 F. 2d 905, at p. 907.

infringer.[24] Presumably the arrangement had been made prior to the date of the request for a mechanical license agreement and was already in being, so that the existence of the arrangement might technically be an infringement of Sec. 1(e),[25] which granted the right of arrangement for performance and copying or publication purposes to the copyright proprietor.[26] Judge Hand then held that the agreement between the parties was contractual by reason of their mechanical license agreement, even though it incorporated some of the terms of the statute granting the compulsory license[26a] and that the agreement served to release the defendant, United Masters, Inc., from any infringing consequences of arranging the song and acted as a consent to the manufacture thereof.[27] The decision thereby eliminated the possibility of any claim of infringement by failure to file the prescribed notice of intention to use as a predicate to the compulsory license under the statute and simultaneously found a sanction for the use of the arrangement in the recording and manufacture of records therefrom.

Judge Goddard, in his decision below, made this point:

> "It is also to be noted that the requirement that a 'compulsory license' be limited in its use in mechanical reproduction to the use originally made or granted by the plaintiff in the initial mechanical reproduction, has been liberally construed. This requirement has

---

[24] *Idem* at p. 907.

[25] 17 U.S.C. 1(e).

[26] Cf. Joy Music, Inc. v. Seeco Records, Inc. 166 F. Supp. 549 (S.D.N.Y. 1958).

[26a] Note 23, *supra,* at p. 908.

[27] *Ibid.* See also, Leo Feist, Inc. v. Apollo Records, 300 F. Supp. 32 (S.D.N.Y. 1969), *aff'd per curiam,* 164 U.S.P.Q. 481 (2d Cir. 1969). See Sec. 26.3, *infra.*

been said to mean that the reproduction need not be identical, but that some latitude must be allowed to each manufacturer to prepare an individual instrumental or vocal arrangement of the composition. . . .

* * *

"Certainly the plaintiff realized that defendant United Masters, Inc. was not just going to use words and music without making some arrangement of both the words and music." [28]

This would seem to indicate that arrangement for mechanical recording purposes is an incident thereof, whether the same be deemed granted by way of consent in the mechanical license agreement or as an implied adjunct of the compulsory license. As Judge Goddard correctly observes, the significance of mechanical reproduction is in the right to control the arrangement thereof. Failing this concomitant right in the user, the right of mechanical reproduction, in effect, would become a nullity because the importation of the arrangement right as a separate right to be licensed from the owner of the copyright would be under the exclusive control of the latter. Such proprietor would then have the substantial equivalent of the exclusive recording right—except conceivably in the precise form the original recording was made, as to which the user might have a right of mechanical reproduction without arrangement. Such exclusive control would tend to vitiate the compulsory license. Moreover, if such consent to arrangement were not read into the mechanical license agreement, the latter really becomes a *nudum pactum,* a virtual nullity as an agreement because the user could not effectively exercise the same.

Thus the importance of arrangement in recording becomes manifest, and the relationship of the right of ar-

[28] Note 20, *supra,* 79 F. Supp. 664, at p. 667.

rangement granted in Sec. 1(e), meaningful in respect of the right of recording and the compulsory license. For arrangement is the means whereby the style and sound of the performer become distinguishing factors in the rendition of the musical composition. If all mechanical reproductions were licensed under the compulsory license for the arrangement as embodied in the original recording only, then music would indeed become monotonous. Talent evaluations by audience, critics and professional musicians alike would be limited to considerations solely of pitch, timbre, nuances, and the like. The interpretations would have a mechanical quality because of the limitations imposed on the creative aspect of the musical composition, i.e., the form in which it is conceived for performance. On the other hand, arrangement for performance for mechanical reproduction allows a variety of interpretations based upon something other than quality of voice or instrument, and over and above the literal transposition of musical notation into musical sound. To limit the performer in arrangement is to negate performance because the arrangement expresses an amplification of the possibilities of the performer to present an individual style, through arrangement of the musical composition, and with it, to create the distinctive "sound" that becomes the characteristic expression of the talent of the performer.

Sec. 16.4. The Nature of Arrangement and The Arrangement Rights

Arrangement, then, is the decisive ingredient for effecting the bridge between the creator—the composer—and the performer—the interpreter. It is the means for effectuation of the visual into the aural in musical terms, i.e., of musical notation into melody, harmony and musical sound generally. Arrangement, then, is the means of relating the literary and artistic property, the musical composition, to performance, for arrangement sets the form of the interpretation by the performer. Arrangement thereby also becomes the means for transition from the right of performance as embodied in the copyright statute to the right of the performer, and also of the manufacturer, in the mechanical reproduction embodying the particular performance, as in the phonograph recording.

If arrangement for mechanical reproduction cannot be denied to the licensee either under the mechanical license agreement or under the compulsory license because it is integral to any meaningful recording, then what, in fact, is the function of the right of arrangement accorded by Sec. 1(e)? It is to be noted that the ingredients of mechanical reproduction are performance and reproduction of that performance. The arrangement for recordings, then, is utilized in two forms: first, in the performance which is recorded and then in the form as mechanically reproduced. The statute,[29] in setting forth the provisions as to the compulsory license, provides, "The payment of the royalty provided for by this section shall free the articles or devices for which such royalty has been paid from further contribution to the copyright except in case of public performance for profit." [30] This means that if a phonograph recording, for example, were performed over radio or television, it would be comprehended by the license of the performing rights society for the performance of the musical compositions embodied therein and would be logged accordingly for credits to the authors and composers thereof, on the one hand, and the respective music publishing company proprietors thereof, on the other, which

---

[29] 17 U.S.C. 1(e).
[30] *Ibid.*

have licensed their musical compositions to that performing rights society. Indeed, a principal form of air play of musical compositions on radio is precisely in the form of performance of discs or tapes embodying the tunes. Yet each such performance is a performance of the arrangement as embodied in the recording. It follows that if the copyright proprietor of a musical composition cannot control the arrangement of a musical composition for recording purposes, it cannot control the public performance thereof for profit—apart from being the recipient of payment for performance by reason of license thereof for performance.

It is submitted that Sec. 1(e) in pertinent part should be paraphrased to read as follows:

> "(e) To perform the copyrighted work publicly for profit if it be a musical composition; and for the purpose of public performance for profit, and for the purposes set forth in subsection (a) hereof, to make any arrangement or setting of it or of the melody of it in a system of notation *or any form of record in which the thought of an author may be recorded and from which it may be read*; and to make any form or record in which the thought of an author may be recorded and from which it may be reproduced."[31]

The problem with the statute is that it uses the term "record" in two senses. The dictionary defines the term "notation" as an "Act, process, or system of recording music or musical details by means of notes and symbols; also, musical notes and symbols collectively."[32] This conveys the sense of the term "record" as a form of writing.

---

[31] Cf., 17 U.S.C. 1(e). (words in italics added.)

[32] Webster's New International Dictionary, Second Ed., Unabridged, (1961) at p. 1668.

On the other hand, another meaning of the term is that it is the generic term for mechanical forms of reproduction, e.g., disc, tape, etc., embodying speech and/or music and/or other sounds.

What the statute therefore provides is that performers and producers of sound recordings may indeed utilize arrangements specially created for purposes of the recording, whether the arrangement itself has been reduced to writing or is an aural form of arrangement embodied in the recording, either from memory or by way of improvisation, but that in no event may such users or any one on their behalf, such as the actual arranger for the recording, utilize the arrangement for the purposes of Sec. 1(a), i.e., to print, reprint, publish, copy and vend the copyrighted work.[33] In other words, the users of the work for recording purposes may not market or otherwise turn the arrangement to commercial account. For that matter, nor may they make other versions of the musical composition as derivative works and then proceed to copyright such arrangements as derivative works because the exclusive right to make arrangements and other versions as derivative works belongs to the copyright proprietor of the basic musical composition under Sec. 1(b)[34] of the statute.

Sec. 16.5. The Right of Arrangement and Performance

As for users of the basic work in a performance which is not a rendition of a performance by mechanical reproduction, a parallel situation is reached by a somewhat different route. In theory, the copyright proprietor can control the form of arrangement utilized in live performance because

[33] 17 U.S.C. 1(a).
[34] 17 U.S.C. 1(b).

there is no compulsory license for a live performance, for example, whereunder the licensee can pay the statutory rate and perform, as in a phonograph recording. In theory, the copyright proprietor can insist upon performance of his arrangement simply by the device of refusal to sell as a corollary of the right of a seller to select his customers absent monopolization or contract, combination or conspiracy in restraint of trade.[35] However, if the would-be user can show that the real reason for refusal to sell was not selection of customers or failure to arrive at a mutually satisfactory price for the arrangement, then there might be a question of possible violation of Sec. 3 of the Clayton Act[36] by way of illegal conditioning or tie-in of performance to the specific arrangement of the copyright proprietor. But if the transaction were couched in the form of a license rather than a sale, then the same contention might be made under Sec. 1 of the Sherman Act[37] since the language of Sec. 3 of the Clayton Act does not cover licenses.[38] In the event of allegation of illegal conditioning, the copyright proprietor might argue along the lines of *Cardinal Films Inc.* v. *Republic Pictures Corp.*[39] that the license or sale of the arrangement was reasonably ancillary and necessary to the performance of the work so that there was no illegal tie. In that case it was alleged that distribution of films on television by Cardinal of pictures produced by Republic

---

[35] See, for example, U.S. v. T.C.-Fox Film Corp., 137 F. Supp. 78, 115 (S.D.Cal. 1955) where the Court sustained a refusal to sell feature motion pictures by various film suppliers to television. See also, Secs. 1 and 2 of the Sherman Act, 26 Stat. 209 (1890), Secs. 1 and 2, 15 U.S.C. 1 and 2, as amended; 50 Stat. 693 (1937).

[36] 38 Stat. 731, Sec. 3 (1914); 15 U.S.C. 14.

[37] 26 Stat. 209, Sec. 1 (1890), 15 U.S.C. 1 as amended.

[38] Note 36, *supra*. See, Taubman, Copyright and Antitrust 53-54 (1960).

[39] 148 F. Supp. 156 (S.D.N.Y. 1957).

was illegally conditioned on the requirement to acquire prints of the films from Republic. The Court rejected this contention, stating, "It follows that the licensor may properly condition the right of his licensee to purchase only from the licensor the services necessary to bring the licensed use to fruition. The provision of the licensing agreement requiring plaintiff to order all prints exclusively from the defendant is not within the 'tie-in' prohibition of the Clayton Act."[40]

It is submitted that the copyright proprietor would have greater difficulty than Republic Pictures in refutation of such a contention for other reasons. A print of a motion picture is presumably a fixation in form of the negative and represents the form in which it will be perceived. In other words, the studio will insist upon distribution thereof in the form of the final cut, theatrically, and even where it has the right to release the same for television, subject to its contractual express or implied rights to insert commercials along accepted lines in conformity with industry practice and limitations imposed by the Federal Communications Commission.[41] The purpose of insistence by a studio upon use of prints manufactured by it or through its affiliate is to assure a form of quality control, to wit, that the prints actually utilized in exhibition conform to the standards the studio itself maintains in respect of such prints. The norm, then, is the requirement of minimum standards of quality with regard to a work that has a fixed form, subject, of

---

[40] *Idem* at p. 158.

[41] See, Preminger v. Columbia Pictures Corp., 49 Misc. 2d 363, 267 N.Y.S. 2d 594, (Sup. Ct., Spec. and Trial T., N.Y. Cty 1966), *aff'd* 25 App. Div. 2d 830 (1st Dept. 1966), *aff'd,* 150 U.S.P.Q. 829 (Ct. App. N.Y. 1966); Stevens v. National Broadcasting Company, 148 U.S.P.Q. 755 (Sup. Ct., L.A. Cty., Cal. 1966), and 150 U.S.P.Q. 572 (Sup. Ct., L.A. Cty., Cal. 1966).

course, to variations in the way of other versions, dubbed and superimposed foreign language versions, and the commerical requirements in the manner of exhibition on television.

Performance of musical compositions live, on the other hand, is the antithesis of fixation of form. Judge Yankwich has aptly described what a performer does in his rendition, "The introduction of additional bars of music, additional notes in the recording of a song, as a part of its interpretation, is a practice to which probably every known singer resorts. It gives individuality to the particular interpretation of the song." [42] What gives performance its singularity is interpretation of the performer. In this respect, the same is true whether or not performance is live, embodied in some form of aural recording or in an audio-visual recording. Judge Yankwich had to consider the problem of a claim of unfair competition in that case, *Supreme Records, Inc.* v. *Decca Records, Inc.*, by way of the alleged appropriation of Supreme's arrangement as embodied in its recording of the song "A Little Bird Told Me" in the Decca recording thereof. Supreme Records was not the copyright proprietor of the song, nor did it claim common law rights therein. The Court held that Supreme had no property right therein which was capable of protection. As a second point, assuming, *arguendo,* that such a right were otherwise recognizable in equity, Judge Yankwich nevertheless held that the arrangement of Supreme did not combine unique elements in a finished form with a distinctive existence of its own. On the contrary, the Decca record was itself distinctive so that the ordinary listener could not confuse the two.

---

[42] Supreme Records, Inc. v. Decca Records, Inc., 90 F. Supp. 904 (S.D. Cal. 1950) at p. 911.

The doctrine of lack of property right in the sound of performance was later reinforced in *Miller* v. *Universal Pictures Co.*[43] There Mrs. Glenn Miller had entered into an agreement with Universal Pictures granting it the rights to make a movie "The Glenn Miller Story". RCA Records then had exclusive recording rights to performances by Glenn Miller and his orchestra. Universal granted Decca Records, its record affiliate, the right to make a sound track album from the motion picture in the style of Glenn Miller. The court below held for Miller's widow but was reversed on appeal as to the proprietary interest of the widow in the Glenn Miller sound. The Appellate Division reversed stating, "Plaintiff never had, and certainly does not now have, any property interests in the Glenn Miller 'sound'. Indeed, in the absence of palming off or confusion, even while Glenn Miller was alive, others might have meticulously duplicated or imitated his renditions . . ." [44] The Court then cited *Supreme* and made the further observation, "The authorities relied on by plaintiffs are distinguishable because in those cases the offending parties did not provide their own performances . . ." [45] The Appellate Division felt, however, that the sound track was part of the film and since the transfer by Universal to Decca was not at arms length, Universal should include the sound track album for purposes of computing royalties to Mrs. Miller.[46]

Thus performance, which is not copying in the sense of reproduction of the actual sound produced by another, as in the cases of *Metropolitan Opera Ass'n, Inc.* v. *Wagner-*

---

[43] 11 App. Div. 2d 47, 201 N.Y.S. 2d 632 (1st Dept. 1960), *rev'g* 18 Misc. 2d 626, 188 N.Y.S. 386 (1959), *amended,* 13 App. Div. 2d 473, 214 N.Y.S. 2d 645 (1st Dept. 1961), *aff'd* 10 N.Y. 2d 972 (1961).

[44] *Idem,* 11 App. Div. 2d at p. 49, 201 N.Y.S. 2d 632 at p. 634.

[45] *Idem,* 11 App. Div. 2d at p. 49, 201 N.Y.S. 2d at pp. 634-635.

[46] *Idem,* 11 App. Div. 2d at p. 50, 201 N.Y.S. 2d at p. 635.

Nichols Recorder Corp.,[47] and *Gieseking* v. *Urania Records, Inc.*,[48] is not the source of a property right that can make the competitive performance a tortious infringement thereof per se. It is conceivable that a competitive performance can combine with it the distinctive attributes of another so as to give rise to a claim of unfair competition, either by passing off of visual attributes[49] or the unique calls of another.[50] But unlike either, music as a distinctively aural phenomenon is intended to convey an appreciation of the sound itself in its various performances. Thus if a copyright proprietor were to license a performance of a complete score by an orchestra, and the same were then played by other performers, it must be evident, that depending upon a minimum of professional competence, the same sound will be heard, i.e. the same music will sound alike subject to the variations induced by interpretation. Thus, a function of musical performance is similarity where the same work is performed more than once. The variations come in style, in interpretation derived from the skill and qualities of performer, whether in voice or instrument, or both, and the further variations induced by the particular form that takes, i.e., the arrangement.

Sec. 16.6. The Arrangement Right and the Right to Market

Hence it may be seen that what the statute, Sec. 1(e)[51] does, insofar as the right of arrangement is concerned, is

---

[47] 101 N.Y.S. 2d 483 (Sup. Ct. N.Y. Cty. 1950), *aff'd* 279 App. Div. 632, 108 N.Y.S. 2d 977 (1st Dept. 1951).

[48] 17 Misc. 2d 1034, 155 N.Y.S. 2d 171 (Sup. Ct., Spec. T., N.Y. Cty. 1956).

[49] Chaplin v. Amador, 93 Cal. App. 358 (1928).

[50] See, Warner, Harry P., Radio and Television Rights (1953), Sec. 236 at pp. 1026-1027.

[51] 17 U.S.C. 1(e).

to preserve the market for original acquisition by the performer and for the various publication rights since the copyright proprietor already has the right of arrangement as a derivative right under Sec. 1(b).[52] Thus a performer, for live or recordation purposes, needs music to perform. This is either purchased or licensed from the music publisher, his selling agent or his dealer. On a purchase, the purchaser will own the physical property[53] and, subject to right of license for performance or of the mechanical license, can use the music for such purposes. On the other hand, there is an implied right in such licensee of the limited right to perform to create his own arrangement for purposes of such performance only, whether the same be for a live performance or a recording. Otherwise the license is rendered musically meaningless.

The net effect of Sec. 1(e)[54] as to arrangements is to vest the market for sale and rental of music of the creator in the latter and his assigns and not in the user, insofar as performance is concerned. This would emanate from the sale or rental of a score of a particular composer insofar as such performance or performances are concerned. Generally when one speaks of a rental in this respect, one refers to a form of rental agreement providing for the right to use the scores for a stipulated period of time at a given rental fee and the return thereof at the expiration of such period. Thus, for example, rental of parts of symphonic pieces in the classical repertory might be the means that is most economical for a symphony orchestra to obtain the parts from the music publisher where it does not perform the composition often enough to purchase the score and parts. The music publisher, in turn, is able to make

---

[52] 17 U.S.C. 1(b).
[53] 17 U.S.C. 27.
[54] 17 U.S.C. 1(e).

copies of the work available for performance without having to go to the expense of publication and sale of copies which might indeed be uneconomical because of the limited market for the work. Then again, the music publisher might actually have a given work published in parts for sale in various versions or arrangements, e.g., band, orchestral. The purchaser as a user would then acquire the parts for performance by outright purchase for use. In neither instance could the party renting or purchasing the parts set itself up in business to make arrangements of the works for publication, vending, printing and reprinting thereof. The copyright proprietor presumably cannot prevent the user from disposing of the particular score and parts purchased by it as a physical property, including resale thereof as second-hand music, any more than Bobbs-Merrill could impose restrictions on R. H. Macy in the sale of its books.[55] Here the reference is to control of the use of the physical property in the absence of a valid fair trade contract prescribing minimum prices for resale when lawful under local law under the Miller-Tydings Act.[56] As for the user under a rental agreement, it may be assumed that it would be the essence of any such agreement that the user could not dispose of the music in violation thereof by sale or unauthorized use by third parties or use by the user itself in excess of the permitted uses, such as use after the expiration of the rental period.

From the point of view of the user purchasing parts for purposes of performance, it often makes many changes in

---

[55] Bobbs-Merrill v. Straus, 210 U.S. 339 (1908). See also Straus v. American Publishers Association, 231 U.S. 222 (1913).

[56] Act of 1937, 50 Stat. 693, amending Sec. 1 of the Sherman Act, 26 Stat. 209 (1890), 15 U.S.C. 1. But see, Schwegemann Brothers v. Calvert, 341 U.S. 384 (1951) to the effect that fair trading could not bind non-signers.

the music which are in the nature of arrangements. Thus, in the case of a band or orchestra, its conductor may eliminate repeats, prescribe that the first desk only play certain parts rather than the entire section, particularly where difficulty is anticipated or certain effects are desired, emphasize or de-emphasize certain dynamics in the score, and so on. These are all matters going to interpretation of the work based upon the nature of the instrumentation at hand, the ability and number of the performers, as well as the musical effects the conductor is seeking. Where music is performed from the written score, necessarily such changes are made in the score and parts so that the work as so modified by the changes may be read by the performer, and, hopefully, accordingly performed.

Sec. 16.7. Copyright of Musical Compositions and Arrangements

Moreover, in practice the relationship of copy to performance may be far more rudimentary than the foregoing. A musical composition, whether rock, folk, pop, rhythm and blues, country and western, or other songwriting, however classified, is generally copyrighted as an unpublished work by submission of a "lead sheet" [57] as the best copy of the work available for such registration.[58] The lead sheet is generally the means whereby the music and lyrics assume form as a complete copy of the manuscript of the tune. Therefore, it is the form of the work which is submitted for deposit to the Copyright Office along

[57] See Form E, Class E, Application for Registration of a Claim to Copyright and Certificate—Registration of a Claim to Copyright.

[58] The form of application requires that one complete copy of the musical composition be submitted; see also, Circular 50 of the Copyright Office, Copyright for Musical Compositions, which sets forth the same requirement.

with the application. Later, where the work is published, two copies of the work as published are then submitted for deposit. These, of course, will be the printed copies of the work placed on sale as sheet music of the tune. Generally the sheet music will contain the lyrics, or at least the initial stanzas of verse and chorus, or whatever other form the song may take.

Sec. 16.8. Performing Rights Societies and Licenses

The lead sheet is also the form submitted to the performing rights society by publisher and writer members with respect to tunes of composers and lyricists who have assigned the particular works to such publisher. This, in turn, is the basis for indexing of the catalogue of the respective composers, lyricists and music publisher members and the logging of the performances with respect thereto.

Although the lead sheet is musically rudimentary in form in that it is the minimal basis for notation of the music and lyrics of a tune, nevertheless the performing rights societies will issue blanket licenses of all their works to licensees,[59] including those with the skimpy lead sheets. The source of the licenses are the agreements entered into between the performing rights societies and the respective music publisher and composer-author members.[60] These agreements represent a form of spin-off of the "small rights", that

---

[59] See, for example, Warner, Harry P., Radio and Television Rights (1953), Chap. XIII, The Music Industry—The ASCAP Story, at pp. 323-455; Finkelstein, Herman, Public Performance Rights in Music and Performance Right Societies, 7 Copyright Problems Analyzed 69 (1957), edited by Kupferman, Theodore R., Fred B. Rothman & Co. reprint (1966); Arrow, Allen, Performing Rights Societies, Chap. XI of The Business and Law of Music 95 (1965) edited by Taubman, Joseph.

[60] See Forms Nos. 6C-4.1a-b in Volumes of Forms.

is, the musical performing rights in works as opposed to the "grand rights", that is, the dramatic rights in works which are generally reserved and not contracted to the performing rights society for the period of the agreement. The performing rights society thus acts as an instrumentality for mass licensing of musical compositions for performance to users thereof where blanket licensing is utilized, so that separate licenses for use of particular tunes do not have to be obtained.

The performing rights societies thereby function in a manner analogous to the compulsory license for mechanical reproduction insofar as they become the means for readily making the music available under license for performance. The difference is that performance is made free of infringement by means of the blanket license from the performing rights societies, whereas the mechanical license agreement as the contractual alternative to the statutory license is the means utilized directly by the music publisher as copyright proprietor or one degree removed through its agent, the Harry Fox Agency, or other duly authorized agency. In each instance, concern for the form of arrangement of the musical work is secondary to the fact of the license itself authorizing the infringement-free performance or recording, as the case may be. Quite often the compositions are performed and recorded by the creators thereof. In this regard the statute operates as the strongest incentive to generate composition because the creators are thereby entitled to all of the copyright rewards as composers and lyricists, whether through songwriting agreements specifying the respective shares of the music publisher's revenues from the work, through writer's credits and payments from the performing rights societies and possibly through an equity interest in the music publishing company itself. In this regard, the statute itself acts as a catalyst in the generation of creation by performers. The statute thereby serves as a very real incentive in providing economic rewards for creation. It also tends thereby to restore the traditional role of the artist and creator—performer and composer—as an integrated one, such as it has so often been historically in the musical creation and performance of songs by assorted bards, troubadors, folk singers, and the like.

But the performing rights society is basically a permission granting society—for a fee—and not the music publisher. Its concern is performances *en masse* and not the nature of the arrangement of particular music for specific performances. A jazz band would use its own arranger for this purpose to obtain the particular sound that the leader felt would be characteristic of the group, whether or not the materials obtained as an incident to the license were lead sheet, purchase of score and parts or the rental thereof from the music publisher. Small combos, solo vocalists and/or instrumentalists might prefer to compose their own arrangements for performance purposes, either in some form of chordal progression, whether in actual musical notation, or guitar or other representation of chords, and perform the same, or else the performance and/or recording might be entirely improvised around the basic tune.

Sec. 16.9. Market Control of Arrangements and the Implied Right to Arrange

From a practical point of view, therefore, it may be seen that the copyright proprietor, its performing right society licensee or its agent for grant of the mechanical recording license might indeed have very little to offer in terms of arrangements for performance and/or recording other than the "bare bones" lead sheet. This would serve to reinforce the conceptual conclusion that the statutory grant of the right of arrangement in Sec. 1(e)[61] is consistent with market control of the right of sale and rental and other facets of the Sec. 1(a)[62] rights, to copy, vend, print, reprint and publish the work. Thus, the copyright proprietor may publish and sell to potential performers all kinds of versions—piano, ensemble, band, orchestra, choral, and so forth—for purposes of public performance for profit, in addition to the sale thereof for other performances, whether the same be private or public non-profit performances. The copyright proprietor has this exclusive right of arrangement for sale and other marketing thereof in relation to *all* performances but such exclusive right does not limit or affect the implied right under the statute of the licensee for performance, i.e. the user, to create his own arrangement for performance, whether it be live or recorded. Thus, the performer's arrangement is a qualified, limited right implied from the fact and nature of performance, which is co-extensive with the performance itself. This does not mean that the performer's arrangement is destroyed upon performance or reverts to the copyright proprietor. If the arrangement so created for a live performance is in written form, its implied authorized use terminates with the performance. Thereafter, it is only archival in the hands of the user. Any other use would be unauthorized and an infringement of copyright. Of course, if the user should thereafter choose to perform the work again as so arranged, the arrangement would be resurrected from the archives for this purpose under the new performing license, or the general authority of the blanket license, as the case may be.

In the case of the mechanical recording, the fact of performance results in the existence of an aural form of the

---

[61] 17 U.S.C. 1(e).
[62] 17 U.S.C. 1(a).

work, whether or not a written arrangement for recording purposes was ever made. It is possible for an arranger to reduce the aural recording to written form and so to a form of written arrangement. If this is done or there is an extant written arrangement prepared for recording purposes, neither may be marketed by the user, the person reducing the same to written form or any other party other than the copyright proprietor and its authorized arrangers. Any such written form might be retained for archival purposes and for subsequent use under a new performing license or mechanical recording license but may not be sold, licensed, leased or otherwise marketed for a consideration because those exclusive rights are vested in the copyright proprietor under the statute.

The differentiation of the nature of the arranger is well-expressed by Shemel and Krasilovsky as follows:

> "Arrangers for record company sessions rarely have any relationship to the music publisher and achieve no copyright status; they receive compensation solely from the record company or artists.
>
> "Some arrangers work directly for or with music publishers, and copyrights are obtained on their arrangements. These are the musically knowledgeable and trained persons who prepare songs for printing in sheet music, orchestration, or folio form. They are customarily employed on a weekly salary or assignment basis, with no right to royalties, and, although their names may sometimes appear on the printed edition, as employees for hire they have no copyright or renewal copyright status." [63]

---

[63] Shemel, Sidney and Krasilovsky, M. William, This Business of Music 131 (1964).

Thus, although the forms of recording have been transformed greatly, what with cassettes, cartridges, reel-to-reel tape recording, stereophonic hi-fidelity recording etc., as compared to the cylinders and bands in use prior to the enactment of the present statute in 1909, it may be seen that the principles of arrangement for recording purposes, in terms of copyright status, have not changed in any significant respect. The changes in the nature of the art and technology of recording, however all-embracing they may be and might become, do not materially change the nature of arrangement for recording purposes as an embodiment of interpretation that is the implied right of the performer and/or his designee to make. The same is true as to arrangement for performance, whether the performance was live before an audience prior to the passage of the statute in 1909 or is embodied in some electronic form such as live radio or television, whether or not there is a studio or other audience on hand. Thus the context of arrangement for performance, live or recorded, has not changed conceptually since the statute was passed even though the art of such arrangement may have undergone changes over the years.

Thus arrangement may be seen as a duality, arrangement by or on behalf of the copyright proprietor with all the emoluments of the copyright available thereto, and arrangement as an implied right which is an incident of the live or recorded performance.

Chapter XVII

RIGHTS OF PERFORMERS

Sec. 17.1. The Evanescent Performance vs. Preserved Performance

The right of performance originated as a stage right in 1856,[1] many years before the invention of the phonograph record, motion pictures, radio and television. What was granted was the right of public performance with respect to a work under copyright. The right of performance, then, was an additional right given exclusively to the creator of the literary and artistic work, subject to the statutory limitations and exceptions, as enacted in the various statutes to date, particularly the 1909 Act.[2] But the distinguishing fact of the right of performance as originally enacted was that the subject matter of copyright, the literary and artistic property, had a different form from its performance. The subject matter of the copyright in respect of the stage right was the written play. The work being performed was a writing in the form of a text which was performed by live actors "on any stage or in public".[3] The play, as copyrighted, was fixed in the form of its submission for copyright; its performance was the substantial representation of the form of fixation in a manner calculated to develop the plot and characterization together with the dramatic content of the work. In the live dramatic performance, no part of the performance pertained to creation of the

---

[1] Aug. 18, 1856, 34th Cong., 1st Sess., Chap. 169, 11 Stat. 138 (1859).

[2] See Chaps. XV and XVI, *supra*.

[3] Note 1, *supra*.

work but to its recreation, except to the extent that the dramatist rewrote lines in rehearsal or in preview performances before the play was fixed in form. But insofar as creation and performance were concerned, they were separable and clearly identifiable parts of the theatre arts. Moreover, performance was impermanent, indeed, evanescent. Performance represented the artist as a function of time; once the particular performance was over, it disappeared forever. Only the writing remained, the play, for presentation at a later date. Since nothing remained of the artist's creation, there was nothing left to protect legally. Rights in artists could not arise so long as performance was evanescent.

But performance, in due course, assumed a different character with the development of technology capable of freezing performance into a fixed form. The motion picture photoplay is both the fixation of performance thereof in filmic form—celluloid—as well as the subject matter of copyright itself. The work as embodied in tangible form is the performance itself. What is protected as a writing is the performance embodied in the print and negative. Exhibition of the print is also its performance by way of projection of the print by means of a motion picture projector upon a screen or other surface. The original performance of the actors engaged in embodying the story line, characterization, effects and dialogue in the edited and exposed film is the means of fixation of the work in final form as the creative work which is the subject of copyright. Film production, then, is the performance of the actors, live, necessary to create the work in fixed form. Performance is a creative component in film production, whereas on the live stage, performance does not create the work, but only reproduces the work. Performance of a film, on the other hand, is a representation, however evanescent,[4] of the original performance as frozen in the embodied film.

Like film, audio-visual tape serves the same function in respect of television. Discs and tapes, in turn, are the means of preserving aural performances in fixed form, but the principle is not quite the same. That is, original performance of a musical composition, for example, embodies the work in fixed form. The subsequent performance of the work is by reproduction of the work as originally performed mechanically so that the listener hears only the work in frozen form. Here, too, performance is an element of creation. Moreover, the performance, unlike in the theatre, is not evanescent, but embodied in fixed form. Like the motion picture exhibition, the performance that is ultimately rendered for the market is that of playing of the recording, i.e., the reproduction of the original performance in fixed form of the recording.

Sec. 17.2. Performance in Audio vs. Audio-Visual Forms

But there is a fundamental distinction as between audio-visual and audio original performance. In the former, the work subject to copyright only assumes fixed form by reason of the performance. In the latter, there is the pre-existing work which is the subject of copyright. In respect of motion pictures, there can be no copyright separate and apart from the film itself. Of course, screen plays may be the subject of copyright, but the copyright of the screen play would not preserve the film from the public domain if the prints of the picture were sold

[4] Nimmer on Copyright (1969), Sec. 101.4, pp. 379-380; Patterson v. Century Productions, Inc., 93 F. 2d 489 (2d Cir. 1937).

without notice of copyright thereon. Whether the film be deemed a derivative work taken mediately from another medium by adaptation into a screen play or immediately from an original screen play, the end result is the same. The film itself is the subject of a new copyright, whether as a derivative work or not. The same would be true of performances embodied on audio-visual tape.

However, the phonograph or other aural recording differed in this respect because the recording was not deemed a writing that could be the subject of copyright prior to the enactment of Public Law 92-140 which became law October 15, 1971.[5] Indeed, the Regulations of the Copyright Office stated, "A phonograph record or other sound recording is not considered a 'copy' of the compositions recorded on it, and is not acceptable for copyright registration. Likewise, the Copyright Office does not register claims to exclusive rights in mechanical recordings themselves, or to the performances they reproduce."[6] Indeed, the Court in *Capitol Records, Inc.* v. *Mercury Records Corp.*[7] went further. It not only expressed this position, stating, "From the foregoing it appears, first, that Congress, before the 1909 amendment, intended that one who performed a public-domain musical composition should not be able to obtain copyright protection for a phonographic record thereof, and, second, that nothing in the

[5] White-Smith Music Publishing Co. v. Apollo Co., 209 U.S. 1 (1908); Regulations of the Copyright Office, Sec. 202.8(b). Public Law 92-140, 92nd Cong., S. 646, granted a copyright in sound recordings published, fixed and copyrighted from and after February 15, 1972 and before January 1, 1975. See Secs. 5.4 and 6.3, *supra* and 23.7, *infra*.

[6] *Idem* Sec. 202.8(b).

[7] 221 F. 2d 657 (2d Cir. 1955), opinion of Dimock, J., dissenting opinion, Learned Hand, J.

1909 amendment indicated any change in that intention," [8] but it also asserted, "There can be no doubt that, under the Constitution, Congress could give to one who performs a public domain musical composition the exclusive right to make and vend phonograph records of that rendition." [9] That case first determined whether phonograph records of certain musical compositions in the public domain were susceptible of statutory copyright in the United States. The majority opinion decided that they were not, so that a virtuoso's rendition as embodied in the mechanical recording was not the subject of statutory copyright. Even Judge Learned Hand, in dissenting, agreed with the majority opinion of Judge Dimock. The majority, after determining that federal copyright was not at issue since recordings could not be copyrighted under the statute, then proceeded to analyze the quantum of protection of the recordings against sale of copies thereof under the common law, in this instance, the laws of New York. The majority granted this protection. Judge Hand, in his dissent, felt that the sale of the records was a divestive publication by application of federal criteria of publication, as opposed to the unlimited monopoly available to the plaintiff under the common law.

Whatever the effect of constitutional permissibility of protection of phonograph recordings as writings, the fact of lack of Congressional authorization therefor rendered such recordings outside the pale of statutory coverage as to performances embodied in aural recordings. This meant that, apart from whatever rights there might be as common law property, the recording as a performance embodying the musical composition in fixed form was

---

[8] *Idem* at p. 661.

[9] *Idem* at p. 660. See Public Law 92-140, note 5, *supra*.

not protectible under principles of copyright. The rationale was the phrase employed by Judge Hand in his opinion, *casus omissus*[10]—omission from the statute. Thus, the cause was not technology per se, namely, that a subject of copyright had to be perceived, i.e., in visual form, whereas the aural recording could only be heard.

Sec. 17.3. Copyright in Sound Recordings

Apart from the interim legislation of Public Law 92-140, it remained for proposed copyright revision to make the necessary transition between constitutional scope of writings and Congressional authorization. Sec. 102(7) of S. 543[11] makes "sound recordings" the subject of copyright. Sec. 101 thereof proceeds to define the term, stating, " 'Sound recordings' are works that result from the fixation of a series of musical, spoken, or other sounds, but not including the sounds accompanying a motion picture or other audiovisual work; regardless of the nature of the material objects, such as disks, tapes, or other phonorecords, in which they are embodied."[12] Sec. 101 also defines the term "phonorecords", stating, " 'Phonorecords' are material objects in which sounds other than those accompanying a motion picture or other audiovisual work, are fixed by any method now known or later developed, and from which the sounds can be perceived, reproduced, or otherwise communicated, either directly or with the aid of a machine or device. The term 'phonorecords' includes the material object in which the sounds

---

[10] *Idem* at p. 667.

[11] See note 5, *supra*. S. 543, Dec. 10, 1969 Print, 91st Cong., 1st Sess., Jan. 22, 1969.

[12] *Idem* Sec. 101. 17 U.S.C. 26 was amended by Public Law, 92-140 to include the same definition.

are first fixed."[13] However, Sec. 114[14] of S. 543 limits the scope of rights in sound recordings to only certain of the rights granted by Sec. 106 (1) (3) and (4)[15] thereof, to wit, the rights to reproduce, distribute and publicly perform the sound recording. Sec. 114 further differentiates the scope of the right in the sound recording, providing:

"Sec. 114. Scope of exclusive rights in sound recordings.

(a) Limitations on Exclusive Rights.—The exclusive rights of the owner of copyright in a sound recording are limited to the rights specified by clauses (1), (3), and (4) of section 106. The exclusive rights of the owner of copyright in a sound recording to reproduce and perform it are limited to the rights to duplicate the sound recording in the form of phonorecords that directly or indirectly recapture the actual sounds fixed in the recording, and to perform those actual sounds. These rights do not extend to the making or duplication of another sound recording that is an independent fixation of other sounds, or to the performance of other sounds, even though such sounds imitate or simulate those in the copyrighted sound recording.

(b) Performance Rights Distinct.—The exclusive right to perform publicly, by means of a phonorecord, a copyrighted literary, musical, or dramatic work, and the exclusive right to perform publicly a copyrighted sound recording, are separate and independent rights under this title."[16]

---

[13] *Ibid.* This definition is not contained in Public Law 92-140.

[14] *Idem* Sec. 114.

[15] *Idem* Sec. 106.

[16] *Idem* Sec. 114. Cf. 17 U.S.C. (f) as added by Public Law 92-140.

In connection with the earlier House version of the bill, H.R. 4347, the House Report asserts, "Enactment of H.R. 4347 will mark the first recognition in American copyright law of sound recordings as copyrightable works."[17] It, too, believed that sound recordings were capable of copyright protection as writings, stating, "The committee believes that, as a class of subject matter, sound recordings are clearly within the scope of the 'writings of an author' capable of protection under the Constitution, and that the extension of limited statutory protection to them is overdue."[18]

Two observations in the House Report go far to explain the nature of the copyright in the sound recording. In connection with the right of performance thereof, the Report states:

> "Subsections (b) of section 114 makes clear that statutory protection for sound recordings extends only to the particular sounds of which the recording consists, and would not prevent a separate record of another performance in which those sounds are imitated. Thus, infringement takes place whenever the actual sounds that go to make up a copyrighted sound recording are reproduced in phono-records by repressing, transcribing, recapturing off the air, or any other method. Mere imitation of a recorded performance would not constitute a copyright infringement even where one performer deliberately sets out to simulate another's performance as exactly as possible." [19]

---

[17] Report No. 83, 90th Cong., 1st Sess., House of Representatives, Mar. 8, 1967, at p. 17. See Sec. 17.4 and 18.6, *infra.*

[18] *Idem* at p. 18.

[19] *Idem* at pp. 65-66.

The second observation relates to the nature of the ownership in the sound recording. As to this, the House Report remarks:

> "The copyrightable elements in a sound recording will usually, though not always, involve 'authorship' both on the part of the performers whose performance is captured and on the part of the record producer responsible for setting up the recording session, capturing and electronically processing the sounds, and compiling and editing them to make the final sound recording. There may be cases where the record producer's contribution is so minimal that the performance is the only copyrightable element in the work, and there may be cases (for example, recordings of birdcalls, sounds of racing cars, et cetera) where only the record producer's contribution is copyrightable. As in the case of motion pictures, the bill does not fix the authorship, or the resulting ownership, of sound recordings, but leaves these matters to the employment relationship and bargaining among the interests involved."[20]

By extending copyright to sound recordings as within the penumbra of writings of an author, proposed copyright revision—and the present Act as revised by Public Law 92-140—adds a new dimension to copyright conceptions. Not only the visual and audio-visual but also the purely aural may receive copyright protection, provided the aural is embodied in some fixed form. The proposed legislation and Public Law 92-140 are an acknowledgment that writings generically are no longer limited to literary and other visual or audio-visual forms but may be embodied in technological

---

[20] *Idem* at p. 18. This element of ownership for performance purposes was not contained in Public Law 92-140.

forms which render the work intelligible by means other than perception, i.e., hearing. Aural media in fixed form are therefore capable of reducing a work to a form that may be the subject of copyright. Like the motion picture, which is a derivative work to the extent it is derived from the screen play, the sound recording is likewise a derivative form of copyright in that it is derived from a basic work, most often, a musical composition.

Sec. 17.4. Rights in Sound Recordings

But the analogy substantially ends there. What is protected in the visual or audio-visual work is the expression of ideas as reduced to writing. That is, it is the form of those ideas that is protected against copying. The protection accorded by the statute is not only against Chinese copying, i.e., exact reproduction, but even more importantly, *other infringement* thereof. By other infringement one means a more limited appropriation of the expression of the ideas as reduced to fixed form of writing or other visual expression in addition to the aforesaid complete appropriation. The copyright protects against taking of the content of the expression, whether the same be done by exact reproduction or by paraphrase. Copying by paraphrase is a form of copying by simulation. Thus, the statute protects against both exact and simulated reproduction of the expression of ideas.

However, the right of copyright in sound recordings represents a grant of copyright protection to the expression of such ideas as embodied in some mechanical reproduction thereof, but only in the precise form in which those ideas are so embodied and grants protection only against exact copying thereof but not against simulation thereof. Protection, therefore, is granted to the *specific* performance as fixed in aural recording and then only against unauthorized reproduction thereof. What is protected is the distinctive "sound" so achieved as embodied in the sound recording but only against exact copying, and not imitation. This means that certain rights in copyright, i.e., the sound recording, would be protected against counterfeiting, by attempting to market the sound recording of another as the work of someone else. It is also an anti-piracy statute in that, even where performance is properly attributed, it may not be reproduced without authorization from the copyright proprietor of the sound recording. Thus, the unlawful appropriation of the performance of another as embodied in fixed aural form could be prevented under copyright with uniform federal application throughout the country and accordingly enjoined without concern about the vagaries of disparate treatment by the respective states. Here the reference is to the source of rights in the copyright proprietor of the sound recordings as contrasted with the rights of the copyright proprietor of the musical composition which has been performed without benefit of the mechanical license and without payment of copyright royalties by the record pirate.

It may be seen, therefore, that, whereas the copyright in audio-visual and literary works is intended to protect against copying or other simulation of the expression of ideas embodied in the concrete form, the copyright in sound recordings encourages the expression of the same ideas in the form of phonorecords and the like. The distinction arises because what the copyright in sound recordings accords is protection in specific interpretations. The motion picture copyright is the source of protection of the copyright proprietor thereof against unauthorized reproduction and performances thereof because what is generally performed is substantially the same print or version except as the same might be edited for various purposes. This, in turn, follows from the requirements of the market. Generally large sums of money will have been expended for production of the film. Unless the copyright proprietors were able to control exhibitions thereof exclusively, they could not recoup the negative cost of production and the film industry would literally whither away. There may, of course, be infringement of a motion picture by copying copyrighted components thereof by an independently produced work.

By contrast, the phonograph recording generally represents a far smaller investment in terms of production costs. What is valued is the particular rendition, that is, the interpretation or "sound" of that recording. Mechanical reproduction as an industry is built on the premise of free accessibility to the market of musical compositions by means of the compulsory license or contractual mechanical license equivalent. The proposed statutory revision does not change the marketing concept in that respect. The compulsory license continues to be a feature thereof.[21] The principal effect of the copyright in the sound recording, then, is to furnish the added protections to the specific recording after such compulsory or contractual mechanical license has been obtained. The market in recordings of the same work will not thereby be changed; nor will the industrial practice of certain artists making "cover" records in the attempt of labels to partake of the proceeds of popularity of somebody else's recording by a, hopefully, marketable cover record of the, perhaps, more well-known artist on the label recording the cover record.

---

[21] S. 543, note 11, *supra,* Sec. 114(c); House Report, note 17, *supra,* at p. 66. See Sec. 17.3, *supra,* and Secs. 18.6, and 24.1, *infra.*

Sec. 17.5. Performance and Authorship

Thus it would seem that the predicates of performance in relation to copyright differ with the medium utilized for reducing the performance to concrete form for copyright purposes. But this does not give us all of the facets of the nature of performance. One must also consider the nature of authorship in this regard. In motion pictures, it is generally the film production company which is the author of the picture. Here authorship proceeds from the premise that film making is a collective effort requiring the contributions of many persons,—e.g., actors, directors, editors, cameramen, individual producer, screen writer, and so on. The rationale of authorship is that the producer is the creator, i.e., author, by putting the film together and therefore is entitled to the copyright. There are so many individuals involved in film making that no single one is entitled to be deemed author of the film so that the copyright is to go to the production company as author thereof. Another facet of this is that the production company arrives at the same position as employer for hire. In the course of production the artistic components and even the literary and musical components, to the fullest extent possible, render services in the making of the film in the capacity of employees for hire. Thus, the actors, screen writers and composers, directors, editors, crew, and individual producer will render services in an employment relationship. This will have the effect of giving the production company all rights, in the course of production, to the production company so as to give the latter the position of author of the film as employer for hire.[22] Of course,

[22] The producer is not deemed the author in continental Europe; the writers, directors and composers are deemed the author. But the producer obtains an assignment of their respective rights to perfect its title in the film.

where existing music is acquired for the film, the synchronization and performance rights are granted. Even if granted for the duration of copyright, the film producer is faced with the problem of survival of the composer as to the latter's right of renewal. Indeed, to avoid cutting the protection accorded the film by copyright by loss of various components attributable to the right of renewal as a new estate, it is deemed desirable by the film production company to take all rights, if possible, as employer for hire.

The nature of film production, then, is the instrumentality for vesting copyright in the film production company as employer for hire. Other forms of audio-visual production generally follow suit, such as television taped productions. Artistically, the director of a film may believe that he, above all, furnishes the principal creative components to the film. Film esthetics do, in fact, attribute creativity of film making to the director. But legal and artistic conceptions are not necessarily co-extensive, as in the case of the motion picture.

Sound recordings, though, are on a different level as to rationales of authorship. The essence of the right protected in the phonorecord or other sound recording is the specific rendition. The right emanates from interpretation, from performance itself as embodied in the phonorecord. It is the singularity thereof that is the basis for protection. Hence, the artist as performer figures more prominently therein. What is distinctive is the "sound" of the virtuoso performance. It may be anticipated that artists with any discernible negotiating position vis-à-vis the record manufacturer would insist upon a position of authorship in copyright in the sound recording. Then, too, since artists record under a collective bargaining agreement of the

American Federation of Musicians, as to instrumentalists, and of the American Federation of Television and Recording Artists, as to vocalists, provisions as to copyright position might emanate on their behalf in collective bargaining agreements. Of course, the recording by large numbers of artists in a single recording, such as by symphony orchestras, might raise serious problems of attribution of authorship to large bodies of performers. But then their collective bargaining organizations might seek to administer their copyright interests in some manner akin to handling of residuals.

Nor is the position of the record manufacturer necessarily simple even with respect to the latter's ownership of the copyright. Some record companies employ their own individual producers, their "a & r" (artists and repertoire) men. In such event, whatever position the record manufacturer would have in negotiation vis-à-vis the performer would presumably not include the "a & r" men since the latter would be only employees for hire. But a more complex situation is present where the "a & r" man is an independent producer. If he has his own independent production company, he probably would seek a copyright interest for his company jointly with the record manufacturer. On the other hand, if he were strong enough in the market, he might command the entire copyright in the sound recording, whether or not he also had a separate label with that record manufacturer.

Thus performance may be seen to consist of a variety of shifting contexts, many of which are determined by the state of the particular art and technology at the time, as well as the scope of the protection accorded by statute. Something of the variety of constructions emanating therefrom may be seen in the definition of the term "perform" in S. 543, which reads, "To 'perform' a work means to recite, render, play, dance, or act it, either directly or by means of any device or process or, in the case of a motion picture or other audiovisual work, to show its images in any sequence or to make the sounds accompanying it audible, and, in the case of a sound recording, to make audible the sounds fixed in it." [23] This is further elaborated by the statement in the House Report, "A performance may be accomplished 'either directly or by means of any device or process,' including all kinds of equipment for reproducing or amplifying sounds or visual images, any sort of transmitting apparatus, any type of electronic retrieval system, and any other techniques and systems not yet in use or even invented." [24] Thus, from the relatively simple stage right, as right of exclusive performance of a dramatic production, the combination of development of the performing arts and technologies, as well as statutory elaboration, have resulted in a complex set of relationships and rights, both under present law and under proposed copyright revision.

Sec. 17.6. Performers' Equitable Servitudes

But the lack of recognition of rights of performers and manufacturers of phonograph records, i.e., rights of interpretation, has not prevented efforts to obtain protection therefor dehors statutory copyright. In *Fred Waring* v. *WDAS Broadcasting Station, Inc.*,[25] the orchestra leader had the legend "Not licensed for Radio Broadcast" placed on certain records recorded by Fred Waring and His Pennsylvanians. Notwithstanding this restriction, radio station WDAS played the records and the litigation ensued. At

---

[23] Note 11, *supra*, Sec. 101.

[24] Note 17, *supra*, p. 27.

[25] 327 Pa. 433, 194 A. 631 (1937).

that time, Fred Waring's Pennsylvanians, Inc., the corporation operating the orchestra, of which Fred Waring was sole shareholder except for two qualifying shares, also had a contract with the Ford Motor Company for lucrative weekly radio broadcasts one night a week. Judge Stern, in his opinion, spoke of a right of the performers—the orchestra and the conductor—in the performances embodied in the phonograph records which somehow for litigation purposes resided in plaintiff, Fred Waring, as alter ego and sole stockholder of the orchestra organization at common law, since such property rights were not the subject of protection under statutory copyright. He queried, "Does the performer's interpretation of a musical composition constitute a product of such novel and artistic creation as to invest him with a property right therein?" [26] He found such property rights in plaintiff and granted protection, after concluding that there was no divestive publication that would terminate the common law right. Judge Maxey, in a concurring opinion, agreed in the result on the theory of invasion of a right of privacy, rather than a right of property.

Judge Stern also found that the parties were in competition and stated, "On the facts in the present case, therefore, and having in mind the many unique factors which enter into its consideration, we are of opinion that on the ground of unfair competition, apart from any other theory of equitable relief, plaintiff is entitled to the injunction which the court below awarded." [27] As to this ground, Judge Maxey disagreed in his concurring opinion.

Waring,[28] then, in both opinions, affirmed the restriction contained in the legend on the phonograph record on

---

[26] *Idem,* 327 Pa. at p. 440, 194 A. at p. 634.
[27] *Idem,* 327 Pa. at pp. 455-456, 194 A. at pp. 641-642.
[28] Note 25, *supra.*

varying grounds of a performer's right as a property right, unfair competition and right of privacy.

In another case decided a few years later, Paul Whiteman and his orchestra had recorded for RCA Victor Company and a legend had been placed on the label, "Not Licensed for Radio Broadcast". Litigation ensued when radio station WNEW broadcast the same, in *RCA Manufacturing Co., Inc.* v. *Whiteman.*[29] Judge Learned Hand, in his opinion, took a contrary view. He indicated that performance was a publication which dedicated the common law right to the public domain. Judge Hand noted:

> "Nevertheless, even if Whiteman's 'common-law property' in his performances survived the sale of the records on which they were inscribed it would be very difficult to see how he, or a fortiori the maker of the records, could impose valid restrictions upon their resale. Concededly that could not be done (regardless of the present statutory prohibition) if the restriction went to the resale price Bobbs-Merrill Co. v. Straus, 210 U.S. 339, 28 S.Ct. 722, 52 L.Ed. 1086. It would also have been impossible if the restriction forbade the buyer to use the article except with other articles bought of the record maker. Motion Picture Patents Co. v. Universal Film Co., 243 U.S. 502, 37 S.Ct. 416, 61 L.Ed. 871, L.R.A. 1917E, 1817 Ann. Cas. 1918A, 959. We do not, however, have that question to decide, for we think that the 'common-law property' in these performances ended with the sale of the records and that the restriction did not save it; and that if it did, the records themselves could not be clogged with a servitude." [30]

---

[29] 114 F. 2d 86 (2d Cir. 1940), *rev'g* 28 F. Supp. 787 (S.D.N.Y. 1939).

[30] *Idem* at p. 88.

Essentially, Judge Hand applied antitrust notions that had been made applicable by the Supreme Court to copyrighted books, in *Bobbs-Merrill*[31] when he stated, "Retrictions upon the uses of chattels once absolutely sold are at least prima facie invalid; they must be justified for some exceptional reason, normally they are 'repugnant' to the transfer of title." [32] He analogized the common law property in the rendition to the sale of a musical score as a publication that could not preserve the right to copy by notice of restrictions. Like books, there would be a dedication under statutory copyright by reason thereof which the purported restriction could not save. Therefore, as to the rendition, "That being true, we see no reason why the same acts that unconditionally dedicate the common-law copyright in works copyrightable under the act, should not do the same in the case of works not copyrightable. Otherwise it would be possible, at least pro tanto, to have the advantage of dissemination of the work at large, and to retain a perpetual though partial, monopoly in it. That is contrary to the whole policy of the Copyright Act and of the Constitution. Any relief which justice demands must be found in extending statutory copyright to such works, not in recognizing perpetual monopolies, however limited their scope." [33] Judge Hand, in his opinion, also narrowed the scope of *International News Service* v. *Associated Press*,[34] relied upon by Judge Stern for his finding of unfair competition in *Waring*[35], by limiting that decision to its

---

[31] 210 U.S. 339 (1908).
[32] Note 29, *supra,* at p. 89.
[33] *Idem* at p. 89.
[34] 248 U.S. 215 (1918).
[35] Note 25, *supra*.

facts.[36] Nor did Judge Hand give much credence to Judge Maxey's application of the right of privacy.[37]

Basically, Judge Hand declined to impose an equitable servitude, i.e., a restriction, in favor of rights of performers when no such rights would be available in respect of property under statutory copyright. Resale of a book could not be restricted in respect of a copyrighted work under the statute because the copyright is separate from the property itself. The rights under the statute are those enumerated in Sec. 1 of the Copyright Act.[38] Upon sale of a book, the copyright proprietor or his licensee has exercised the exclusive right "to vend" the work. Of course, the purchaser may not use the work to create a dramatization therefrom or to perform the work because these are exclusive rights granted to the copyright proprietor, except that in respect of musical compositions, the exclusivity is a right of first recording, after which the right is non-exclusive and subject to the compulsory license or contractual substitute.

Judge Hand made the point that the performer's right should not be enlarged when the rights under statutory copyright could not be enlarged. Judge Stern noted in *Waring*, "Having purchased one of the records made by plaintiff's orchestra, and having obtained a license to broadcast the songs from the American Society of Composers, Authors and Publishers, to which both the publishers and the composers had assigned *the exclusive right of public performance under the copyright*, defendant broadcast the

---

[36] Note 29, *supra*, at p. 90.

[37] *Ibid.*

[38] 17 U.S.C. 1.

records as a part of its sustaining program." [39] The radio station was therefore a valid licensee of the right of performance under the copyright with respect to the musical works performed. But the reference in both cases is to the exercise of the right of performance in performers as embodied in a phonograph recording. Proposed copyright revision would grant protection under statutory copyright to the copyright proprietors of sound recordings,[40] proprietorship being worked out contractually as between the performer and the record manufacturer.[41] Therefore, the presupposition is that there must be some *res* embodying the performer's interpretation as to which there is protection. Moreover, as to this *res*, exclusivity is limited by Sec. 114 of the proposed statute to rights of reproduction, distribution and performance and, as to the latter, the right of performance of the sound recording being distinct from the exclusive right of performance of the underlying work embodied therein.[42] It is clear, however, that under proposed copyright revision the right of performance of the sound recording is co-extensive in a number of respects with the right of performance of the musical composition under copyright. Moreover, although the reference is to distinctive rights of performance, the fact remains that the reference, insofar as sound recordings are concerned, is that each performance of the sound recording constitutes a performance of the musical composition embodied therein. The only difference to the user is the source from which the license to use the sound recording emanates, it being in the performing rights society as to the musical copyright and presum-

---

[39] Note 25, *supra,* 327 Pa. at p. 437, 194 A. at p. 633 (emphasis added.)

[40] Note 11, *supra,* S. 543, Sec. 102.

[41] Notes 17, 20, *supra.*

[42] Notes 17, 14-16, *supra.*

ably in some licensee or agent for the copyright proprietor of the sound recording, if not in the latter. The sound recording may indeed be deemed a derivative work under copyright in respect of the musical composition, but the public performance of the sound recording is necessarily such performance of the musical composition embodied therein. This means that vis-à-vis the musical composition, if the sale of the phonorecord were to constitute a publication, comparable to the sale of sheet music or other printed forms of the work, then *a fortiori*, vis-à-vis the sound recording, such sale of the phonorecord would likewise constitute a publication. Otherwise, there would be an enlargement of the monopoly under statutory copyright as to the sound recording as compared to that of the musical composition. Since the musical composition after first recording does not control subsequent recordation, subject to payment of statutory royalties or contractual substitute therefor, and since the right of exclusive performance, for all practical purposes, has been made generally available through license to the performing rights society under blanket license to broadcasting stations, subject to payment of royalties under the blanket license, it would appear that the intent of proposed copyright revision is to grant performers and record manufacturers limited rights in sound recordings, including right of performance thereof, but without foreclosing the rights of performance in the musical composition. The performer no longer need be concerned under the proposed statute about restrictions imposed in phonorecords because the sound recording copyright proprietor would presumably license performance rights through some sound recording performing rights agency along the lines of the blanket licenses of the performing rights agencies. In short, the rights of exclusive performance as distinct rights presuppose some harmonious relationship between the owners of the respective rights, i.e., in the musical compositions and in the sound recordings, because use of the latter automatically embodies use of the former in public performance. Restrictions permissible to the copyright proprietor of the sound recordings under the proposed copyright revision, by virtue of the exclusive right of public performance, should not be permitted to the detriment of the rights of the copyright proprietor of the musical compositions as to his right of public performance. That would explain why Sec. 114(c) of S. 543[43] provides for a compulsory license for public performance of sound recordings. Proposed copyright revision thereby provides a break upon the possibility of enlargement of the restriction in favor of the restrictive possibilities in the exclusive right of public performance of sound recordings by rendering them non-exclusive, after first distribution thereof.[44] The compulsory license, in effect, puts the right of exclusive performance of the musical composition in *pari materia* with the exclusive right of public performance of the sound recording, to the extent the former is embodied in the latter, by means of a new compulsory license. Thus, proposed statutory revision would treat the performer's rights in the manner indicated by Judge Hand in his opinion in *Whiteman*,[45] that is, granting the protection to performers in their recordings by legislation along the rationale of that decision, that property rights of performers do not represent an enlargement of rights otherwise given under copyright. In other words, Judge Hand's opinion was predicated upon antitrust and trade regulation principles, and proposed copyright revision, through the compulsory license in sound recordings,

---

[43] Note 11, *supra*, Sec. 114(c).
[44] *Idem*, Sec. 114(c)(1).
[45] Note 29, *supra*.

is an expression of due concern therefor and for overcoming of the antitrust and trade regulation objections.

Sec. 17.7. Sale of a Record and Copying

In this regard, *Capitol Records, Inc.* v. *Mercury Records Corp.*[46] may be distinguished because the rights of performers were not at issue. There the litigation involved rights to sell records under separate licenses of the original masters. Plaintiff derived its title from Telefunkenplatte, G.m.b.h. of Berlin, Germany, whereas the defendant derived its claim to ownership from the alien property custodian in Czechoslovakia. Telefunken was the original owner of the masters which came from Czechoslovakia. Thus the issue involved chain of title and which party had a superior claim to ownership. While it is true that Judge Hand wrote the dissenting opinion, which was consistent with his views as to divestiture upon sale of the records, there being no statutory copyright in the records, rights of performers were not involved. What the majority held was that rights in the common law copyright did not end with the sale of the records so that anybody could copy them and use them as he saw fit. To that extent, *Whiteman*[47] was modified and overruled. In a note to this decision, Stanley Rothenberg remarks, "Further the Court does not distinguish between the right to broadcast a record and the right to copy it, the former being in issue in *Whiteman* and the latter in *Metropolitan Opera*".[48] Nimmer observes

---

[46] Note 7, *supra.*

[47] Note 29, *supra.*

[48] Rothenberg, Stanley, Copyright Law, Basic and Related Materials (1956) at p. 738 (italics).

that neither *Waring*[49] *nor Capitol Records*[50] was concerned with the rights in the composition recorded.[51]

The issue as to rights of performers differs from the result of the sale of a record as to its effect on the copyright in the musical composition recorded. In *Yacoubian* v. *Carroll*[52] it was held that the sale of a record of a musical composition registered under then Sec. 11 of the Copyright Act as an unpublished work did not terminate its copyright protection. Per contra, Judge Igoe in *Shapiro, Bernstein & Co., Inc.* v. *Miracle Record Co., Inc.,* by way of dictum, stated, "I might also add that the evidence is that Lewis abandoned his rights, if any, to a copyright by permitting his composition to be produced on phonograph records and sold some time before copyright. It seems to me that production and sale of a phonograph record is fully as much a publication as production and sale of sheet music. I can see no practical distinction between the two. If one constitutes an abandonment, so should the other." [53] In the decision on the motion for a new trial, Judge Igoe reiterated his position and stated, "It seems to me that publication is a practical question and does not rest on any technical definition of the word 'copy'. Nor do the notice and registration provisions of the Copyright Act Sec. 1 *et seq.,* 17 U.S.C. Sec. 1 et seq., determine the issue here. Modern recording has made possible the preservation and reproduction of sound which theretofore had disappeared immediately upon its creation. When phonograph records of a musical composition are available for purchase in every city, town and hamlet, certainly the dissemination of

[49] Note 25, *supra.*
[50] Note 7, *supra.*
[51] Nimmer, *op. cit., supra,* note 4, Sec. 51.1, p. 204.
[52] 74 U.S.P.Q. 257 (S.D. Cal. 1947).
[53] 91 F. Supp. 473, 475 (N.D. Ill. 1950).

the composition to the public is complete, and is as complete as by sale of a sheet music reproduction of the composition." [54] Judge Igoe cited *Whiteman*[55] in support of his position. But *Whiteman* was overruled on this point by *Capitol Records*.[56]

Sec. 17.8. Antitrust and Equitable Servitudes

Although so overruled, query, what remains of *Whiteman* in respect of the antitrust notions therein asserted by Judge Learned Hand? Judge Hand discussed the problem of common law property there in the manner of assuming, *arguendo,* a common law property which would be divested upon sale of the records. But it would seem that *Capitol Records* was not discussing the problem of equitable servitudes in respect of performance of the records and so did not address itself to the problem of restraints and monopoly under antitrust notions inherent in the restriction. It would seem, therefore, that the antitrust notions in Judge Hand's opinion were and remain good law and would tend to override copyright considerations. That is, as between the monopoly of the copyright, whether limited in time by statutory copyright or perpetual under common law copyright, and antitrust doctrine, that the latter overrides the former so that no matter what the source of the monopoly of the copyright, if its use results in a contract, combination or conspiracy in restraint of trade, monopolization or tie-in, such use is very likely to run afoul of the antitrust laws. By reason of that alone, such use would therefore be impermissible.

---

[54] *Ibid.*

[55] Note 29, *supra.*

[56] Note 7, *supra.*

Rights of Performers

If antitrust considerations override copyright considerations and, by analogy, rights in property in the nature of copyright, such as performers' rights in phonograph records, which, but for the lack of Congressional authorization might be deemed "writings" constitutionally, then it would follow that the same antitrust considerations would apply thereto as to works under statutory copyright. In other words, assuming, *arguendo,* that rights of performers were validly the subject of common law copyright, as found in *Waring,*[57] then it would follow that station WDAS might properly have a valid antitrust defense against the restriction in the phonograph record on the grounds that the equitable servitude therein was an unlawful restraint and a tie-in. The latter is more problematical in that there must be a tying and tied product. But it might be contended that the license by WDAS and ASCAP was now tied to another license from plaintiff, Fred Waring, by reason of the restriction imposed on the phonograph record. If the two may be seen as tying and tied products, then regardless of the fact that Waring was found to have a common law property in performance in Pennsylvania, there was the basis for allegation of violation of the antitrust laws on the grounds stated above, and as set forth by Judge Hand.

The result thereof would be that safeguarding of rights of performers, even assuming their existence at common law, runs the risk of effective counterattack under the antitrust laws to the extent such rights are sought to be protected by equitable servitudes. Barbara Ringer has asserted, "It appears settled that the contributions of performing artists to a sound recording constitute an original intellectual creation, and are therefore eligible for common law copyright protection. There are no decisions denying

---

[57] Note 25, *supra.*

this proposition, and it has been strongly reiterated in recent cases."[58] Nevertheless, it may be seen that antitrust considerations may effectively limit the impact of the equitable servitude. This may explain Zechariah Chafee's conclusion in his article on equitable servitudes which also considered antitrust factors, "At the close of my inquiry it must be admitted that I am much less convinced of the desirability of equitable servitudes on chattels than when I began."[59]

[58] Ringer, Barbara A., The Unauthorized Duplication of Sound Recordings, Study No. 26, in Studies on Copyright 117 (1963) at p. 130.

[59] Chafee, Zechariah, Jr., Equitable Servitudes on Chattels, 41 Harv. L. Rev. 945, 1013 (1928).

Chapter XVIII

PERFORMERS' RIGHTS: PERFORMANCE RIGHTS

Sec. 18.1. Authorship, Group Creation and Performance

Because motion pictures are a group creation and the production company is the instrumentality—on paper at least[1]—for putting the group components together, it assumes the position of author as employer for hire and thereby derives a position as copyright proprietor. However attenuated that position may ultimately become, in that ownership interests in the picture, to the extent they are divided with the studio putting up monies in consideration for its entering into the production-distribution deal, other non-distributing financing, possibly strong talent, such as name stars or directors, deal makers or what-have-you, from a formal point of view the production company is the owner of the picture as copyright proprietor thereof, and others holding ownership interests therein are holders of profit participations therein. From a practical point of view, the various agreements entered into by the production company with the studio, talent, director, other financing, author or publisher of the underlying work on which the film is based, and others purport to define the scope

---

[1] Components are often, in fact, put together in a variety of ways —from the stable of actors and other talent under contract to the studio when the latter had long term contracts, by talent agencies as packagers, particularly with talent under contract to the agencies; by a strong director hired by the producer; by a male or female lead currently "hot" at the box office whom the producer wishes to please, by the parties putting up financing seeking to obtain protection for the film in the real or fancied ability or box office draw of suggested components.

of the rights being granted and the manner and means of their transfer and exercise. Nevertheless, under the statute, rights in performance of the film are vested in the first instance in the production company as copyright proprietor.[2]

Moreover, as copyright proprietor, subject, of course, to contractual "spread" of the rights whereby the film may be released in distribution and exhibited theatrically, non-theatrically, on television and otherwise, in a variety of versions and gauges, the production company is the owner of the film. The group components, as respective contributors to the film, do not thereby acquire any position of ownership, as such, in relation to the film similar to the manner in which performers might acquire a copyright in sound recordings.[3] By virtue of the fact of film agreements being in the form of employment agreements, talent and directorial components, for example, have no opportunity to stake out proprietory claims in the film, unless they happen to control the production company, or if the production be a joint venture, to control one of the production companies as a co-adventurer. Their rights are governed by contract with the production company, unless the talent is already under contract to a studio which makes the agreement with the production company to lend the services of that particular actor or actress for the production under a lending agreement.[4]

---

[2] 17 U.S.C. 1.

[3] S. 543, 91st Cong., 1st Sess., Dec. 10, 1969 print, Jan. 22, 1969, Secs. 102, 114.

[4] See Form No. 1B-1.5, as to form of lending agreement in Volumes of Forms.

Sec. 18.2. Ownership of Spin-Offs from Group Creations

One is referring here to the film itself and proprietary rights, i.e., rights of ownership as copyright proprietor in the film itself, and not in various literary and artistic properties which may be spun off from the film. Thus, for example, it is possible for the composer and lyricist who compose and write the music and lyrics for a picture to be engaged as employees for hire in respect of the picture and yet to reserve the music publishing rights which they might thereupon assign to their own music publishing company.[5] Alternatively, the film production company might, as part of the deal, be given the music publishing rights under an agreement to assign the same to the music publishing company owned, controlled or otherwise designated by the composer and lyricist. The differences here are merely formal as to the means of vesting the copyright in the musical compositions separate and apart from the film. In practice, however, music publishing rights are important to the studio and generally it will insist upon a transfer of these rights, and correspondingly, of the copyrights in the musical compositions from the production company.

So, too, the studio may have a recording subsidiary which will manufacture and release a sound track album. Under proposed copyright revision, the performers and the record manufacturer would have a position by reason of having bargained with each other as to the rights of authorship. The performers would, no doubt, be the same as in the film, if the picture is a musical motion picture, since, by definition, the sound track album is the track

---

[5] See Forms Nos. 1B-5-6b, inclusive, in Volume of Forms.

taken from the film. But there the performers will have entered into agreement as to their position as performing artists in the sound recording as to their copyright status therein. This is different from their status as employees in the picture because that will not vest any proprietary interest in the film, as such, in them by reason of being performers in the film.

Sec. 18.3. Protection of Performers by Contract and Collective Bargaining Agreements

Being without a proprietary position in the film because there are no performers' rights, as such, in the film, in the nature of a proprietary interest, as in the sound recording, then the talent is relegated to contract and collective bargaining to stake out rights and interests of various kinds. Talent and production company will enter into detailed agreements specifying the rights granted and the services being rendered.[6] From the point of view of the latter, in relation to the agreement, the perspective, above all, is to obtain the body of rights of performance of the talent in the film as employee for hire, so as to perfect title of the production company as owner of the copyright, and concomitantly, all of the rights of reproduction, distribution and exhibition so as to enable the film company to market the film. From the point of view of the talent, the agreement seeks to delimit the rights necessary to the producer for the production and marketing of the film and rights allied thereto, unless the rights under agreement are part of a multi-faceted deal under which film rights are only one part of the contract. Thus, contractual arrangements between talent and producer are not necessarily

---

[6] See Forms Nos. 1A-4.1, 1B-1-1.2b, inclusive, and 1B-2 in Volumes of Forms.

limited to the particular medium under agreement, such as motion pictures, television, recording or otherwise. It may not only have a time sequence of duration and involve utilization of the talent in a number of film or other productions in the same medium, but it may also cut across various media. Thus, a particular talent may be under contract for performance in films, television and recordings, or there may be firm commitments contractually as to one or more media and options as to others. The permutations and combinations are as varied as the parties may lawfully make them.

But regardless of the scope of the particular agreement, the fact remains that, as to the rights of talent in films, because of the absence of any proprietary position, the recourse of talent is to contract for carving out any special position. Often this may be in the form of a restriction against certain uses of the performance of the talent or by way of affirmative obligation, such as in the form of credits. At times, there is a question of interpretation, as to whether or not the agreement granted certain rights where there was no express restriction or reservation of rights by the talent. As Judge Bone stated in *Republic Pictures Corp.* v. *Rogers,* "But express restrictions upon the producer in his use of any particular right cannot by subsequent implication be read into separate and distinct rights as a restriction upon them."[7] That case and its companion case of *Autry* v. *Republic Productions, Inc.*[8] presented varying problems of interpretation of performers' agreements with film companies. In the latter, actor, Gene Autry, sought to enjoin Republic from editing pictures in which he appeared, from feature

---

[7] 213 F.2d 662, 666 (9th Cir. 1954).

[8] 213 F. 2d 667 (9th Cir. 1954).

length (presumably of varying lengths in excess of one hour, but generally in the neighborhood of 90 minutes), to 53 to 53½ minutes, so that they might be telecast along with some 7 minutes of advertising in an hour television program. Judge Bone conceded that Autry might have a claim if his performance were emasculated beyond recognition, stating, "Although appellees unquestionably have the right to cut and edit the motion pictures, and to license others to do the same, we can conceive that some such cutting and editing could result in emasculating the motion pictures so that they would no longer contain substantially the same motion and dynamic and dramatic qualities which it was the purpose of the artist's employment to produce." [9] However, the Court of Appeals held that the appellees "should not be enjoined from cutting the appellant's performances to approximately 53 minutes, and showing them in connection with commercial advertising over television, pursuant to a License Agreement such as that above quoted." [10] The license agreement quoted was the standard clause granting the film production company rights to photograph and reproduce the "acts, poses, plays and appearances of the artist", to record his voice, reproduce and transmit the same with his acts, poses, etc., as well as in connection with the advertising and exploitation of the picture and to use his name and likeness for the purpose of advertising, exploiting and/or publicizing the picture.[11] The rights granted are basically terms of art which the production company requires in order to embody the performance of the talent in the film and to market the same. Roy

---

[9] *Idem* at p. 669.
[10] *Idem* at p. 669.
[11] *Idem* at p. 668.

Rogers granted similar rights in his agreement with Republic.[12] There, Judge Bone differentiated two distinct sets of rights, stating:

> ". . . the parties contracted with respect to a number of different and separate rights, using separate and distinct phrases which apparently seemed apt to the parties at the time, to separately designate those rights. The subject matter of those rights was (1) photography and reproduction of the artist's 'acts, poses, plays and appearances'; (2) ownership of the products of that photography; (3) use of the 'name, voice and likeness' of the artist in advertising and exploiting the products of the photography; and (4) use of the 'name, voice and likeness' of the artist in advertising commercial products other than the products of the photography. Each of these matters is separately provided for, and the terminology, as above indicated, is consistently used so as to maintain the distinction. Taking the instruments as a whole, it seems clear to us that 'acts, poses, plays and appearances' has reference to the activities of the artist in connection with the motion pictures which it was the main purpose of these agreements to facilitate; whereas 'name, voice and likeness' has reference to non-motion picture reproductions of characteristics of the artist, which last said reproductions themselves are valuable because of the notoriety of the artist and his great public following." [13]

Having differentiated the two rights, the Court then reached its conclusion and decision, stating:

---

[12] Note 7, *supra,* at pp. 663-664.
[13] *Idem* at pp. 665-666.

"We are not called upon to delineate the nature of the restrictions upon appellants' use of the artist's 'name, voice and likeness' (according to the meaning herein indicated) in commercial advertising. Those limitations are not in dispute once we distinguish the subject matter to which they apply from appellants' rights to the artist's 'acts, poses, plays and appearances'. We are called upon to settle the uses, at least in part, which appellants may make of the motion pictures containing appearances of the artist, which are owned by appellants. Appellee, the artist, was paid full measure for his services in creating these films, and has specifically relinquished 'all rights of every kind and character whatsoever in and to the same . . . perpetually.' We are bound to give effect to the meaning of that agreement, that grant, and are bound not to cut it down by implication from another grant unless it is necessary to the effective operation of the contract. . . . We therefore hold that appellants may exercise their ownership and rights to the product of artist's employment, whether or not such exercise involves exhibition of the subject motion pictures in connection with commercial advertising." [14]

Herbert T. Silverberg interprets these decisions as follows:

"The decisions of the Ninth Circuit Court in the *Rogers* and *Autry* cases did not deny or affirm the performers' property rights in their performances; but by interpreting a general clause in the respective contracts as assignments of television rights, they effectively excluded the performers from participation in the profitable televising of old motion pictures.

[14] *Idem* at p. 666.

> "Both Autry and Rogers argued that licensing the motion pictures for television without their consent constituted unfair competition, and in both cases, the court held that contractual consent to any use of the film included such exhibition and precluded a claim of unfair competition." [15]

From a practical point of view, the cases are tantamount to negation of any property rights of performers in their performances, even if there were such rights, because they have effectively granted such rights to the film production company by contract so that attacks upon such uses under various theories fail to stand up. This has impelled Robert W. Gilbert to opine, "Efforts by individual screen actors to halt the televising of motion pictures originally produced for theatrical purposes, on the theory that this was a different use of their services than contemplated by the terms of their initial engagement, have largely met with defeat in the courts." [16]

The upshot of these decisions was that the talent guilds sought effective coverage for their members by means of collective bargaining agreements through formulae for re-use payments as so-called residual payments.[17] At times it took the form of contractual restrictions in collective bargaining agreements on release of motion pictures, for

---

[15] Silverberg, Herbert T., Authors' and Performers' Rights, 23 Law and Cont. Probs., Radio and Television, Part II, (Winter, 1958) 125, at p. 152.

[16] Gilbert, Robert W., "Residual Rights" Established by Collective Bargaining in Television and Radio, 23 Law & Cont. Probs., Radio and Television, Part II, (Winter, 1958) 102, at p. 117.

[17] *Ibid;* Freund, Richard L., Residuals in Broadcasting, Chap. IX of Subsidiary Rights and Residuals, edited by Taubman, Joseph, pp. 101-114 (1968).

example, to television without the consent of the talent guild as in the 1948 agreement of the American Federation of Musicians.[18] The Screen Actors Guild provided for various interim or "stop-gap" measures on releases of film to television in the period 1948 to 1958 in its agreement enabling it to cancel its contract with the producer who released theatrical films to television.[19] Thus arose the distinction in the release of pre-1948 feature films and post-1948 feature films produced originally for theatrical release as to availability for television. Gilbert concludes in this respect, "The underlying theory advanced by the talent guilds in restricting the right of the producer to use recorded and filmed material for several different uses appears to have been based upon the idea that the talent employee should, as a matter of fairness, receive additional compensation for additional uses of the results of his services. Where agreement has been reached on a formula for payment of additional compensation for a subsidiary use or different type of use, the talent guilds have consistently agreed to removal of the restrictions previously imposed by the contract." [20]

Collective bargaining agreements at least have the effect of simplifying and clarifying the issues in that they become and are resolved as purely economic ones. The questions become two-fold: (a) should the performers represented by that particular talent guild receive additional compensation in the form of residual or re-use payments for services rendered in one medium for re-use of the same fruits and proceeds of such services in the same or another medium? and (b) if so, how much, i.e., under what formula

---

[18] Gilbert, *idem* at p. 117.
[19] *Idem* at pp. 117-118.
[20] *Idem* at p. 118.

for compensation? This writer has characterized residuals by stating that they ". . . do not add any present rights, but are merely rights to receive payments for subsequent uses of *past* rights granted or *past* services rendered." [21]

By contrast, the efforts of individual performers to stake out positions as to their rights probably have mixed motivations, both economic and artistic. The economic resolution hoped for, in turn, is dependent upon the artistic resolution. By artistic, one means here the right of the defendant in each case to make the further use of the fruits and proceeds of the services of the performer without new permissions, consents or approvals of the artist. Thus, in cases involving showing of feature films on television, the contention would be made that there is no right of contract in the distributor, or that the given new use "emasculates" the proceeds of artist's employment—upon some theory of *droit moral*—or that such use is unfair competition, and so on. Whatever the route employed in terms of causes of action articulated by the particular plaintiff, the intent is to stop the re-use in that form, either to make the projected re-use subject to agreement for compensation to the performer or else to modify the form of re-use so as to comply with the sought for norms of performance of the work to protect the integrity of the artist in that work. In other words, the motivation of the performer is generally mixed.

---

[21] Taubman, Subsidiary Rights and Residuals: Some Definitions, Chap. II of Subsidiary Rights and Residuals, edited by Taubman, Joseph, pp. 5-8 at p. 8 (1968).

Sec. 18.4. Moral Rights in Production and Performance

On occasion, the intent is to eliminate the particular use sought altogether. The question arose in *Granz* v. *Harris*[22] as to the right to manufacture and release phonograph records of Norman Granz's "Jazz at the Philharmonic" in various forms. Granz was the producer of the program and had also recorded one of the concerts presented by him under that name. He entered into an agreement providing for the right to manufacture and release phonograph recordings of "How High the Moon" and "Lady Be Good" which he had recorded. The court below granted judgment on the merits to defendant. On appeal, the Court of Appeals agreed that the defendant could manufacture and sell ten-inch 33⅓ rpm records and those records singly instead of as part of an album. It remanded, however, on the manufacture and sale of ten-inch 78 rpm records. Judge Swan, in his opinion, felt that there was a breach of contract in such manufacture and that plaintiff could enjoin, but remanded for determination as to whether plaintiff's conduct constituted a waiver. Judge Frank, in a concurring opinion, noted, "I agree, of course, that, whether by way of contract or tort, plaintiff (absent his consent to the contrary) is entitled to prevention of the publication, as his, of a garbled version of his uncopyrighted product . . . Whether the work is copyrighted or not, the established rule is that, even if the contract with the artist expressly authorizes modifications . . . , it is an actionable wrong to hold out the artist as author of a version which substantially departs from the original. Under the authorities, the defendant's con-

[22] 198 F.2d 585 (2d Cir. 1952), modifying 98 F. Supp. 906 (S.D. N.Y. 1951) and remanding.

duct here, as my colleagues say, may also be considered a kind of 'unfair competition' or 'passing off'."[23] The defendant had failed to include the contractual provisions requiring a credit line "Presented by Norman Granz". Without rejecting the doctrine of "moral right", Judge Frank opined that he would, if the evidence favored the plaintiff on remand, grant injunctive relief on contract rather than on some theory of moral right because he was uncertain as to the meaning and scope of such a broad generalization.[24]

The problem came up again in relation to television in respect of two directors whose feature films were released to television. It is to be noted that Judge Frank had extended the notion of emasculation from authors of literary works to a record producer in his discussion of moral rights. But the moral rights are rights generally of authors. Nimmer writes, "Certain European countries, and other Berne Convention countries have long recognized rights which are personal to *authors,* and as such viable separate and apart from copyright. Those rights are known as *droit moral,* or moral rights."[25] In this regard, it is noteworthy that the title of the well-known article by William S. Strauss in his study for the Copyright Office is "The Moral Right of the *Author.*"[26]

One might therefore assume that Norman Granz was able to make his contention as record producer because,

---

[23] *Idem* at p. 589.

[24] *Idem* at pp. 590-591.

[25] Nimmer on Copyright, (1969), Sec. 110 at pp. 442-443. (emphasis added as to *authors; droit moral* in italics).

[26] Strauss, William S., The Moral Right of the Author, Study No. 4, in Studies on Copyright, (1963) pp. 963-992. (emphasis added).

although records are not writings under the statute, they are not excluded from the scope of the term constitutionally, so that the record producer is akin to the author of a literary work in terms of moral rights. By extension, one might contend that esthetically films are the creation of film directors, and writers on film often discuss motion pictures in terms of the work of the film directors. Moreover, in continental European jurisprudence, the film director is deemed to be one of the authors of a film. By analogy, the director is somehow entitled to claim the benefits of moral rights in this country. But a better explanation is offered by Harry P. Warner. He writes:

> "The moral right concept where recognized, has been expanded by legislation, judicial decision and collective bargaining agreements to furnish protection to the interpretive rights of performers. The theoretical basis for protecting the interests of performers is premised on the notion of work done. This theory of labor rights rejects the view that performers' rights are based on literary and artistic property; the latter is the prerogative of creators and authors. The concept of work done considers artists as a category of producers whose product possesses an economic value which varies according to the conditions under which it is utilized." [27]

Under this theory, Norman Granz would be considered a category of producer—record producer, while Gene Autry would qualify as a performer. That is why Judge Bone could write as to his performances, "Although appellees unquestionably have the right to cut and edit the

---

[27] Warner, Harry P., Radio and Television Rights, Sec. 215, at p. 952 (1953).

motion pictures, and to license others to do the same, we can conceive that some such cutting and editing could result in emasculating the motion pictures so that they would no longer contain substantially the same motion and dynamic and dramatic qualities which it was the purpose of the artist's employment to produce." [28]

Sec. 18.5. Rights of Film Directors

As to the film director, however, he is not a performer, as such, yet the fruits and proceeds of his directorial services are embodied in the film production which is essentially a representation of various performances, live, as shot by the camera under the supervision of the director and as cut and edited by him. The director, in a sense, straddles performance and literary and artistic works in that his is the creative force that puts the film together in production and substantially in the form it is finally fixed, subject to the rights contractually of the studio to the final cut or fixation of form. The final cut in the studio, however, is rationalized as a marketing device that it requires for a film with the requisite box-office appeal. Of course, the right to the final cut is generally an outgrowth of the strength of the studio in relation to the director. Where the film director has sufficient stature, he might command the right to the final cut contractually. Otto Preminger had such right as director of "Anatomy of a Murder" which his film production company produced for distribution by Columbia Pictures under a production-distribution agreement. Preminger was the individual producer and also director of the film. He sought to enjoin release of the film for television because of the deletions

---

[28] Autry v. Republic Productions, Inc., 213 F. 2d 667, (9th Cir. 1954), at p. 669.

made in the film in the shortened television version which was subject to interposition of TV commercials.[29]

Plaintiff, Preminger, lost because the right of the final cut, which he had contractually, related to preparation of the film for theatrical release and did not extend to television. Moreover, he had had a right of approval for cutting and editing of certain film produced and directed by him earlier for United Artists, but no such clause appeared in his agreement with Columbia Pictures. Accordingly, the Court held that Preminger was aware of existing industry practices which the Court felt should be applicable, namely, interspersing of television commercials in theatrical films presented on television which have been cut and edited to conform to the time requirements of that medium. As to the prevalence of such practices, the Court observed, "The plaintiffs, as well as any independent producer or director, could have obviated this problem by specifically prohibiting such cuts or interruptions by contract." [30] The standard, in the absence of contractual limitation, was then spelled out by the Court as, "The criterion for the determination of what the defendants were likely to do with respect to interrupting and cutting the subject film, in the absence of a specific contractual arrangement, was not what plaintiffs might disapprove of or dislike but, rather, what was the normal custom and practice in the industry." [31] Earlier in the opinion, the Court referred to the fact that "guidelines have been established in the

---

[29] Preminger v. Columbia Pictures Corp., 49 Misc. 2d 363, 267 N.Y.S. 2d 594, (Sup. Ct., Spec. and Trial Term, N.Y. Cty. 1966), *aff'd* per curiam, 25 App. Div. 2d 830, 269 N.Y.S. 2d 913 (1st Dept. 1966), *aff'd* without opinion, 18 N.Y. 2d 659, 273 N.Y.S. 2d 80 (1966).

[30] *Idem,* 49 Misc. 2d at p. 371, 267 N.Y.S. 2d at p. 603.

[31] *Ibid.*

television industry as to the maximum number of commercials regarded as acceptable in a given time period." [32] Presumably the reference is to the limitations imposed by the Federal Communications Commission as to the time and number of television commercials authorized within each broadcast hour that might be permissible.

Judge Rabin, in his dissenting opinion on appeal in the Appellate Division, believed that the right to cut, which the plaintiff had, could be construed as covering television cuts as well. The difficulty with that position is that it does not conform to the nature of theatrical film production. The primary purpose of such film production is the presentation of the picture in the motion picture theatre, that is, the traditional "movies." Television exhibition in relation to the same is subsidiary thereto, although it is an important allied right and often determines whether a film produced for the theatre recoups its negative cost or not. Nevertheless, the director's cutting of a theatrical feature relates to fixation of form for that medium. The work assumes form by reason of either the final cut in the director or as the same may be made under right of contract by the studio. Television cutting for presentation in given time requirements of that medium interwoven with intercutting of commercials is basically a marketing requirement of that medium. The purpose of the production-distribution agreement is to provide detailed rules governing the creation of the work and, after completion, its distribution. Whatever one may consider the esthetics of television exhibition of feature films in shortened versions with commercials interrupting the continuity of viewing as compared to uninterrupted viewing in the theatre, the practice has indeed become standardized and, for better or for worse, accepted as such.

---

[32] *Idem,* 49 Misc. 2d at p. 370, 267 N.Y.S. 2d at p. 602.

The safest way, therefore, for a director to protect his creative work from cutting for television distribution is contractually. But even there, commercial imperatives are operative. If undue restrictions are placed on television cutting so that the ability to market the film for television exhibition is jeopardized, then the studio might consider that its uncertain right of television distribution by reason of the possible veto of the director might be tantamount to no final right of television distribution and assess its willingness to make the production-distribution deal accordingly. Judge Arthur Klein very realistically pointed out in his opinion in *Preminger* v. *Columbia Pictures Corp.*, "This, of course, might have had an adverse effect on the extent of television distribution—an eventuality which most producers would not welcome." [33]

Even where there was no cutting and editing clause as to television, no evidence that the director had any knowledge of television customs and practices, such as Otto Preminger had, and the Court was more sympathetic to the dangers of emasculation of works by truncation, there is no assurance that the result might not be the same. Thus, in *Stevens* v. *National Broadcasting Company,*[34] director George Stevens had produced and directed "A Place in the Sun". The Court in that case, on the motion for preliminary injunction on grounds of unfair competition, granted plaintiff a limited form of relief as follows:

> "I think that the ruling of this court specifically states it so there wouldn't be any misunderstanding. It permits the defendant to insert commercials; however, the commercials must not be inserted so as to

---

[33] *Idem,* 49 Misc. 2d at p. 371, 267 N.Y.S. 2d at p. 603.

[34] 148 U.S.P.Q. 755 (Sup. Ct., L.A. Cty., Cal. 1966).

> alter or adversely affect or emasculate the artistic or pictorial quality of the film, or destroy or distort materially or subsequently the mood, effect or the continuity of the film. In other words, the defendants in inserting commercials must give primary consideration as to whether the insertion of the commercials will substantially or materially distort the mood, effect or continuity of the film." [35]

A subsequent show cause order for contempt in the implementation of the cutting permitted thereunder did not prevail. The Court proceeded to analyze the nature, timing, location and content of the interruptions by the commercials on the telecast by the defendant and then stated, "It is true that the effect of the commercial interruptions was to lessen, to decrease, to disturb, to interrupt, and to weaken the mood, effect or continuity, and the audience involvement; and, therefore, some of the artistry of the film. But I do not think they substantially or materially *destroyed* or *distorted* such elements, and, as stated above, the words of the injunction must be strictly construed." [36]

One may therefore anticipate that, as in the case of actors, probably the most efficacious way of protecting directors from the consequences of undue television changes in exercise of motion picture television rights, i.e., exhibition of the feature motion picture on television, will be by some sort of specification as to permissible changes, within given wide latitudes, in collective bargaining agreements. Judicial intercession might permit gross revisions, as in the early days of television, when any product was in demand

---

[35] *Idem* at p. 758.

[36] Stevens v. National Broadcasting Company, 150 U.S.P.Q. 572 (Sup. Ct., L.A. Cty, Cal. 1966), at p. 573 (italics).

and feature length westerns were on occasion edited to half-hour lengths. But the cases, absent specific contractual governance of cutting of feature films for television, will probably sanction customary cutting of films for television and insertion of commercials, excepting only instances where such editing for commercials is grossly crude, insensitive and incompetent so as to make the film a series of interruptions of commercials.

It is noteworthy that formal copyright ownership is not the determinative factor as such. Judge Benjamin J. Rabin makes this observation in his dissenting opinion in the Appellate Division in *Preminger*, "The defendants are not the owners of the picture to do with it as they will. Ownership still lies with plaintiffs. The defendants have only those rights—broad as they are—as are given to them by the contract, subject, however, to whatever limitations the contract contains." [37] Judge Rabin is thereby noting the legal consequence of the marketing effect of film production-distribution agreements. Copyright is an institutional system, i.e., of our judicial and legislative system, whereby rights of ownership may be so denominated and utilized for reward. The sum total reward is the aggregate of uses which may be realized within the copyright term and any renewals and extensions thereof that are presently known, plus those which may be invented and/or devised thereafter during the term, as well as any derivative copyrights from that work which may come into existence during the same period. The process of utilization is analogous to slicing of the pie; there is a given, finite amount comprehended by the copyright that may be so utilized and which creates the aggregate rewards therefrom. Rights and licenses are peeled off from the copyright, like so many

---

[37] Note 29, *supra,* 25 App. Div. 2d 830, 269 N.Y.S. 2d 913.

slices of the pie, representing possibilities for utilization for which the copyright proprietor (and presumably through him, the author) and the users share in some agreed manner in the benefits and rewards of the work. The copyright, through use, is thereby brought into the market and its economics. Like ownership of real property, which can be encumbered by enfeoffment, life estates, trusts, tenancies and a variety of other devices for holding land, the copyright can be made subject to all kinds of limitations, restrictions and transfers until the copyright proprietor, like the owner of realty who rents his land for a ground rent for annual rents reserved in leases for 99 years, renewable forever,[38] may be left with the bare shell of ownership, but not the rights and emoluments of which such proprietorship has effectively been divested as a matter of law. Judge Rabin's remarks are an acknowledgment that the production-distribution agreements in motion pictures may result in the transfer of marketing rights so completely by contract that, assuming no material breach of contract that might give rise to a right to rescind the agreement, then, for all practical purposes, copyright proprietorship becomes a status, not of ownership as dominion, but a relatively inactive one, like the grantor of the ground rent lease, as the recipient of statements and payments, if any, under the contract. The same would be true even if the production-distribution agreement were for a relatively short term, like seven years, except that there the copyright proprietor would have reserved distribution rights, *in futuro,* after the expiration of the term of contract, which it might be able to implement by a further contract by negotiations during the original term of contract. What is most significant, then, is where the im-

[38] Taubman, Note, The Land Trust Taxable as Association, 8 Tax L. Rev. 103 (1952) at pp. 106-107.

portant market uses, actual and potential, are vested by license or assignment of rights in the copyright relating thereto.

Sec. 18.6. Performers and Producers of Sound Recordings

This may not prevent certain anomalies from arising, however. The House Report on Copyright Law Revision would leave the performers and record producers to negotiate their relationship as to ownership of the copyright in the sound recording.[39] But the norm today of the recording artist's agreement is the *employment* of the recording artist.[40] Such agreements may actually specify that the record company employs the artist. Generally, however, that relationship is derived from a perusal of the four corners of the agreement. Thus, a typical form of agreement might commence as follows: "We hereby engage you to render your exclusive personal services to us as a skilled vocalist for a period of . . ."[41] The same agreement recites, "18. AFTRA: Nothing herein contained shall require you to do or refrain from doing anything that would violate any rule or regulation of the American Federation of Tele-

---

[39] Report No. 83, 90th Cong., 1st Sess., House of Representatives, Mar. 8, 1967, at p. 18. See Secs. 17.3 and 17.4, *supra*.

[40] See Form 12, Shemel, Sidney and Krasilovsky, M. William, This Business of Music (1964) at p. 401, which is a form of agreement between record company and record artist and the first paragraph thereof reads:

> "1. This contract for your personal services is made between Record Company as the employer and you. We hereby employ you to render personal services for us or in our behalf for the purpose of recording and making phonograph records."

[41] 2 Lindey, Alexander, Entertainment Publishing and the Arts (1963), Form 8: B-1.01 at p. 740.

vision and Radio Artists."[42] Still other agreements recite that artist is either a member in good standing of the American Federation of Television and Radio Artists and/or the American Federation of Musicians or will become such (whichever is applicable—AFTRA as to vocalists; AFM as to instrumentalists) within 30 days after entering into the agreement, that the recording artist's agreement incorporates the terms and provisions of the existing collective bargaining agreement with such unions and that, in the event of any inconsistency between the recording artist's agreement and the collective bargaining agreement, the latter shall prevail.[43] Agreements as to instrumentalists generally also provide that the recording artist's agreement shall not become effective unless and until approved in writing by the American Federation of Musicians.[44]

The form of the recording artist's agreement originates in this respect from the divergent attempts of record company and artist to achieve different objectives. The record manufacturer is desirous of obtaining the entire results and proceeds of the artist's performances as embodied in the recording by reason of the employment relationship so that the artist might not thereafter claim some property right in his performances that was not granted by the artist to the record producer. In other words, the motivation of the latter is completeness of its title, i.e., ownership of the masters without encumbrances. The language as to the unions stems, on the other hand, from the fact that open shop trade unions are the norms and that the clauses in-

---

[42] *Idem* at p. 749. See Sec. 1.5, *supra*.

[43] See Form Nos. 5A-1 to 5A-2.4, inclusive, in Volumes of Forms. See also Form 12, Shemel and Krasilovsky, Note 40, *supra*.

[44] *Ibid.*

cluded in the agreement are designed to protect the position of the particular union vis-à-vis the record manufacturer.

But the fact of the recording artist rendering his services in an employment relationship would appear to create certain anomalies in relation to ownership of the sound recordings if, as is proposed, the performer is to share the copyright therein with the record manufacturer. As the House Report indicates as to proposed copyright revision, "As in the case of motion pictures, the bill does not fix the authorship, or the resulting ownership, of sound recordings, but leaves these matters to the employment relationship and bargaining among the interests involved." [45] This follows from the language of the proposed statute, which substantially retains present concepts. Thus, Sec. 201(b) of S. 543 reads, "(b) Works Made for Hire.—In the case of a work made for hire, the employer or other person for whom the work was prepared is considered the author for purposes of this title, and, unless the parties have expressly agreed otherwise in a written instrument signed by them, owns all of the rights comprised in the copyright." [46] In commenting on the analogous section in respect of the House Bill, H.R. 2512, the House Report remarks, "The presumption that initial ownership rights vest in the employer for hire is well established in American copyright law. . ." [47]

Nevertheless, it would seem that the way to preserve the copyright interest in the sound recording might be by the very artist's recording agreement. The House Report observes, "The committee has also accepted a proposal, advanced by various author and publisher organizations and

---

[45] Note 39, *supra,* at p. 18.
[46] Note 3, *supra,* Sec. 201(b).
[47] Note 39, *supra,* at p. 86.

concurred in by representatives of motion picture producers, that any agreement under which the employee is to own rights should be in writing and signed by the parties, and has amended the subsection accordingly." [48]

Perhaps this might require consideration of revision of existing contracts to reflect this possibility. Some agreements, after stating that the recordings shall be the property of the record manufacturer, proceed to enumerate specific rights in the company granted by the artist, including "the sole and exclusive right, if Company so desires, to publicly perform the records, or to permit the public performance thereof, by means of radio broadcast or otherwise;".[49] Sometimes there is a reference to inclusion of performance fees received by the record company abroad in the proceeds included for computation of royalties. This would follow in countries where there is either a copyright in recordings or phonograph record manufacturers are allowed to collect the same under the notion of neighboring rights.[50] A recent artist's recording agreement of a British-based record company enumerates among the grant of rights that the record company shall have, "The copyright throughout the world in all sound recordings made by the Company of performances of musical works by the Artist." [51] Since there is a copyright in sound recordings in the United

---

[48] *Idem* at p. 85.

[49] The language is quoted from a recent printed form prepared by Atlantic Recording Corporation.

[50] See Ringer, Barbara A., The Unauthorized Duplication of Sound Recordings, Study No. 26, in Studies on Copyright 117 (1963) at pp. 156-164; Nimmer, *op. cit., supra,* note 25, Sec. 35, p. 145.2, fn. 652.

[51] Paragraph 6(i) of form of Transatlantic Records Limited recording artist's agreement. See Form No. 5A-4 in Volumes of Forms as to a British recording artist's agreement.

Kingdom,[52] the reference thereto in a British recording artist's agreement is readily understandable. On the other hand, a form of agreement utilized by Columbia Records in 1961 contains this language, "Nothing herein contained shall deprive the musicians of any rights which may hereafter be created in their favor in or in connection with the use in public performances of recordings made hereunder." [53]

It would seem, therefore, that notwithstanding the employment for hire relationship, whether spelled out by use of the term "employs" or from examination of the entire agreement, that under the proposed statute the artist might nevertheless reserve an interest in the copyright in the sound recording, however anamolous and inconsistent it might otherwise be to the employer for hire as author status. Alternatively, the recording artist might acknowledge in the agreement that the copyright in the sound recordings vests in the record producer but the royalty provisions provide for the artist sharing in the performance fees derived by the record company by reason of the copyright in the sound recording. One might therefore assume that copyrights in sound recordings will be negotiated, as among

---

[52] Ringer, *op. cit., supra,* note 50, at pp. 158-160.

[53] Set forth in Paragraph 4, at the end thereof after stating that the recordings shall be entirely the property of Columbia Records. There follows an enumeration of specific rights which the record company shall have and sentence quoted in the text. The Columbia clause avoids using the term "grant" in this clause, from the artist and so makes the clause consistent with the employment status. Other usage of the term "grant" in this context might lead to the contention, in the absence of language using the phrase expressly that "company employs artist", that artist is rendering services exclusively in some free-lance capacity as an independent contractor and not as an employee for hire.

artist, independent record producer and record manufacturer, in accordance with the relative strength of the respective parties and the meaning of ownership of the copyright therein. As with motion picture copyrights, if the record manufacturer effectively is vested with all rights of distribution during the period of release, which may be perpetual or for a term, then ownership of the copyright in the sound recording in the name of the performing artist will have little meaning except in respect of any period after the expiration of the term. A term of distribution, rather than perpetual rights, sometimes is utilized for masters where there is a strong independent producer who wishes to obtain a reversion of rights after the expiration of the term, say, of 7 years. Alternate forms of marketing might be, as is sometimes done now, by lease of the masters and reversion after the expiration of the term.[54] It is conceivable that a strong performing artist might insist upon copyright ownership of the sound recording, lease of the masters for a term to the record manufacturer, and reversion after the term, with some formula for sharing copyright performance royalties in the sound recordings. Thus, instead of a hybrid form of agreement being grafted onto the employment for hire relationship in the recording artist's agreement pursuant to the provisions of Sec. 201(b) of S. 543,[55] the strong artist might virtually become an independent producer as to his recordings, by reason of the advantages to be derived from the additional potential revenues from the copyright performing fees in sound recordings, combined with a lease of the masters and a reversion after the expiration of the term.

---

[54] Cf. Form No. 5C-1 Lease of Master Agreement with Form Nos. 5C-2-5C-4, inclusive, which are Master Purchase Agreements in Volumes of Forms.

[55] Note 46, *supra*.

Chapter XIX

CLEARANCES AND SUBSIDIARY RIGHTS

Sec. 19.1. Performance as Fixation of Work in Final Form

Performance, then, occupies a dual position in relation to copyright. In connection with certain types of literary and artistic works, there is no literary and artistic property unless and until there is performance fixed in form. Such is the nature of motion pictures, for example. In connection with audio-visual works embodied in film, tape and other processes, production, i.e., performance edited into some fixed final form, is the means of creation of the work subject to copyright, whether the same be registered under statutory copyright or maintained under common law copyright.

Such works, however, have this in common with literary and artistic properties which do not require performance in order to be copyrightable, such as the stage play. The drama is a literary work which can be conceived and expressed in writing, subject to copyright without any performance whatsoever thereof, in order to secure and maintain copyright. Yet the drama does not embody performance in the fixation of its form in order to be copyrighted or protected under common law copyright. In each instance, however, the translation, figuratively speaking, of the fixation of form to the primary purpose of the creation of the work is its performance. In the case of the film, it is performed by its projection through a projector upon a screen or other surface; in the case of a stage play, it is performed live. Of course, there are differences. The stage play may be read and not performed. Also, the stage play is generally directly performed; that is, the stage play may be original and not an adaptation of another work, so that the play itself would not be deemed a derivative work, whereas other plays may be adaptations of other works and, hence, derivative works. On the other hand, films are generally derivative works in that they are mostly based upon screen plays which may be original or adaptations of other works. Some types of films may be made without the use of screen plays, such as newsreels and possibly short subjects, so that such films would be deemed originals.

By and large, however, the performance which begets production, that is, creates the work under copyright in the form of film, tape or other process carries within it the seeds of property. Thus an actor's acts, plays, poses and appearances in the film are photographed. In order for the production company to have rights of ownership in and to such footage there must be either a grant of rights by the actor to the production company to the embodiment of such acts, poses, plays and appearances in the film, or a release of such rights to the production company and a waiver of claim of right with respect thereto. Hence, the perfection of title in the production company imports the proper coverage of the passage of rights from the actor to the producer. The dramatist, as copyright proprietor, does not have this problem vis-à-vis the actor in order to perfect title to his work because the stage play is dependent upon no performance to perfect title in the work. The stage play is complete when written in some fixed form that the dramatist wishes to protect under statutory or common law copyright.

What has been said about actors here is also true of the contributions of all others as to the group's creation, whether their contributions to the film or tape be "above the line", commonly known as the artistic components, or "below the line", the technical components. Actually the expressions so used in production are not entirely exact to depict the respective elements going into the creative side of production. The cameraman, for example, is a "below the line" component whose work is highly creative and who makes the production take the particular form by reason of the shots photographed by him. So, too, the film editor or cutter is the one who makes the production take final fixed form by reason of his competence in selection of various takes.

Then, too, the director's services are of a quality where his contributions are not directly perceived as such. He makes suggestions to the actors in the course of production. His contributions take final form only through the implementation of his ideas through the acts, poses, plays and appearance of the actors, set construction, decoration and costume designs, and the cutting of the film by the editor. His ideas may be so expressed by what is visually perceived through the direct participation of others. Nevertheless, to perfect title, the film production company will obtain a like grant of rights from the director so that, to the extent that what he does is embodied in the film, there will be a grant of rights thereto from director to film production company. The same is done with the individual producer. As to the below the line components, the fruits and proceeds of the services are obtained by employment for hire so that the film production company will have title thereto as author.

Sec. 19.2. The Film as Group Creation

The objective of the film production company is to gather all of the separate elements of group creation into valid title in the production company so that upon completion of the production, all right, title and interest therein vests in the company as producer. Only then can it be said that the property is marketable. Again, contract and collective bargaining arrangements are the means whereby this is achieved.

Co-ordinately, since the film must be exhibited, various rights of performance, i.e., distribution and release of the film in various gauges, processes and versions and in various media, are obtained from the artistic components. The male and female leads will enter into agreements with the producer which will specify the various rights that the latter has in connection with the acts, poses, plays and appearances insofar as marketing of the film is concerned. The same is true of agreements with the director and individual producer.

The purpose of the grant of these rights is to enable the production company to exercise its right of performance, that is, distribution and exhibition of the film, once production has been completed.

In turn, the production company will have secured not only the rights to embody the performances constituting the production, that is, the making of the literary and artistic property, which might then be the subject of property, from the parties involved in the group creation, but also, even prior thereto, production rights from the proprietor of the underlying work, if the film is a derivative work, and from the creator of the screen play on which the film is based. Likewise, the producer will obtain rights from such persons or entities with respect to the marketing of the film, i.e., the distribution and exhibition rights.

This explains the enumeration of rights in film and television agreements. It also sets forth the parameters of clearances with respect to film and television production. Even then, the breakdown is not complete. Music and lyrics embodied in such filmed or taped works are similarly subject to embodiment of rights. To perfect title, the producer must have received the rights to synchronize the music and lyrics with the action and dialogue of the film and then to perform the same. Generally, the film producer will obtain such rights in an employment for hire relationship in order to make the rights coterminous with the rights of ownership of the film. This can be done because the composition of music and lyrics for the film will be original and will inhere in the producer as employer for hire. At the same time, this will vitiate the possibility of a claim as to renewal rights if the composer and/or a lyricist die prior to the vesting of the renewal right, assuming that the producer obtained the rights thereto from the composer and/or lyricist.

Sec. 19.3. Term of Rights in Group Creations

A different problem is presented where the music and lyrics are obtained under license with respect to an existing composition. There, the license of synchronization and performing rights as embodied in the film cannot extend the copyright in the music and lyrics beyond its original term and any renewals and extensions thereof. Thus, if the license should grant such rights for duration of copyright and renewals and extensions thereof, the grant of rights therein—subject to rights of renewals vesting in third parties, such as widow and children if the author and composer fail to survive—in the film is dependent upon the balance of the term of copyright in the composition. Thus a film will take on a new copyright upon production thereof. But necessarily, if existing music under copyright is embodied in the film, and rights thereto are obtained for the duration of copyright in that composition, plus renewals and extensions thereof, it is clear that such rights will expire prior to the expiration of copyright in the film, plus renewals and extensions thereof. If the rights so acquired should be exclusive synchronization rights, then upon the composition entering into the public domain, anybody else could embody the music in another film freely. The same would be true if the license were non-exclusive, but for a like duration, except that during term of copyright, renewals and extensions of the music, others could be licensed to embody the music in other films.

If music were embodied in the film for a period of time less than the duration of copyright, that is, if a producer accepted rights for 15 or 20 years, then upon the expiration of such term, the licensor, assuming the music were still under copyright, could compel removal of such music from the picture upon penalty of infringement of copyright.

A fortiori, if the producer were to obtain rights to adapt and produce film versions of underlying works for a period of less than the copyright, then a like problem would arise as to the underlying rights of the producer. Thus, if the producer accepted rights for a period of 15 years, at the end of 15 years it would have lost its rights to embody the underlying work in the film unless it obtained an extension of time, presumably for an additional consideration. Of course, the film based upon an underlying work cannot be co-extensive in copyright. The pre-existing underlying work necessarily will have an expiration of copyright in the same country or territory prior in time to that of the film based thereon. Thus, even if the copyright proprietor of an underlying work grants exclusive film production, distribution and exhibition rights to a producer, the copyright in the underlying work will enter into the public domain some time prior to the expiration of the copyright in the hands of the film proprietor. The film producer will thereafter have perpetual film rights in the underlying public domain material by reason of the expiration of the copyright in the underlying work, but such rights will be non-exclusive. Upon entry of the underlying work into the public domain, anybody would be free to copy the underlying work and, perforce, adapt the same for the making of motion pictures, albeit, such new motion pictures could not copy the original film still under copyright.

Sec. 19.4. Territorial Nature of Rights

Finally, the copyright being national, i.e., territorial, and a function of the laws of the respective sovereign states, as the same might be modified by international treaty or convention, the element of duration of respective copyrights must be ascertained under the laws of the respective countries and territories involved. Thus, one must consider in terms of clearance of rights the laws of the particular country as to duration. In the United States, one would be concerned with the concept of renewal copyright,[1] whether the same be under employment for hire or otherwise, although the rules as to devolution of statutory ownership differ in each instance. In Europe, one would be concerned with the fact that the author of the film is deemed to be the director, writer and composer. Also one might be concerned with rights of termination after a given number of years. Then, too, one should consider the impact of shifting concepts in the event proposed copyright revision is adopted. For example, one must evaluate the effect of the adoption of the concept of ter-

---

[1] 17 U.S.C. 24.

mination interests with respect to works made other than for hire as a substitute for renewal interests.[2] Thus, termination interests would be of concern with respect to underlying works where the author is the copyright proprietor or has assigned his copyright to a third party. The same would be true as to music and lyrics embodied in a film not composed and written under employment for hire.

Moreover, the territorial nature of copyright also requires investigation for purposes of analyzing where ownership and marketing rights vest. Thus, a film production company may have obtained copyright in the film but may have granted marketing rights for various territories and/or for various media as part of its method of financing of production of its film in the first place. Thus, the producer may have granted European film rights to A, or possibly such rights for particular countries in Europe and Western Hemisphere rights to B, and the distribution rights for the rest of the world to C.[3] Such rights might be only theatrical and possibly non-theatrical, not including television. As to television, there may be again a grant of world television rights or of territorial rights.

Sec. 19.5. Chain of Title—Clearances

By contrast, the film production company may vest world distribution and exhibition rights in the studio finan-

---

[2] S. 543, Dec. 10, 1969 print, 91st Cong., 1st Sess., Jan. 22, 1969, Sec. 203; House Report No. 83, 90th Cong., 1st Sess., House of Representatives, Mar. 8, 1967, at pp. 90-95.

[3] See Form Nos. 1E-4 and 1E-5 in Volumes of Forms. The agreement granting the rights may specify the territory in the body of the agreement or enumerate the countries and territories in a schedule attached thereto.

cing the film so that the tracing of the chain of title may end with the one film studio which is the recipient of those rights, vis-à-vis the producer. However, this does not prevent the studio from, in turn, parceling its distribution rights territorially, particularly in countries and territories where it may not have any distribution facilities.

Then, too, the basis of exhibition, whether in the theatre, non-theatrically, or on television, generally is the license of film to an exhibitor, be it a theatre operator, a non-theatrical institution or a television network or station. In general, one would not be concerned with licenses of this nature in connection with the usual copyright report tracing clearances and ownership of title to a film or television property. But if particular uses under license were at issue, then, of course, such license agreements would have to be considered as well.[4]

But what is explicit in the chain of title is not the only matter of cognizance in clearance. Thus, suppose a film is made based upon an underlying work which has been published in periodicals and also in book form. This might be true of a novel as to which a periodical had serial rights, and the book publisher, other publishing rights. The copyright in the work may be found to be in the name of the author, as is indeed customary in recent decades. Perfection of the chain of title would require a quitclaim from the periodical and from the publisher as to the motion picture rights.[5] The publisher, in each instance, received no motion picture rights and has no interest therein. The film producer, therefore, obtains such quitclaim so as to avoid the possibility at a later date of

---

[4] See Form Nos. 1E-7–1F-1, inclusive, in Volumes of Forms.

[5] See Form No. 1A-2.3a in Volumes of Forms as to form of quitclaim.

some claim of rights in and to the film and allied rights allegedly obtained from the author by such periodical and/or book publisher.

Sec. 19.6. Subsidiary Rights and Copyright Reports

But clearance reports may not be considered separate and apart from the question of subsidiary rights. Subsidiary rights are additional rights presently granted, whether in the same or other media over and above the basic right for which the contract was entered into in the first instance. Original contractual purposes determine which are the basic rights and which are the rights subsidiary thereto. Thus, a hard cover book contract may provide for rights to publish in paperback form as subsidiary rights to the basic hard cover publishing rights. So, too, the film rights to a stage play may be subsidiary thereto. The basic purpose determines what rights are granted as subsidiary rights thereto.[6]

But the denomination of basic rights and subsidiary rights may have effect only in terms of a time sequence, the principal rights—the basic purpose of the contract—very often being implemented before the rights subsidiary thereto. From a contract point of view, they are all rights under contract regardless of when those rights might be implemented. The effect of this is to make subsidiary rights significant only as a function of marketing time sequence. Legally, there is no material effect in the differentiation as between the basic rights and the subsidiary rights.

The net result is that, from a clearance point of view, one must peruse the entire agreement as to the *scope* of the

---

[6] See Taubman, Subsidiary Rights and Residuals (1968), edited by Taubman, Joseph, Some Definitions, Chap. II of Subsidiary Rights and Residuals, at pp. 5-8.

rights under contract, however denominated, whether as the basic purpose or in respect of subsidiary rights. This means that from a negotiating viewpoint, there is no necessary relationship between contractual content and the scope of the agreement of the parties. Absent restrictions and limitations imposed by statute, judicial decisions and public policy, e.g., the effect of prohibitions against price fixing, tie-ins and other restraints, the parties are free to negotiate as broad or as narrow an agreement as they desire. The net result may be an agreement limited only to the basic purpose, such as a grant of film rights with no subsidiary rights of any consequence. On the other hand, the parties may determine upon an entire course of contractual relations covering a multitude of uses and media. Contract is neutral as to whether it ought to be comprehensive or narrow in scope. The net result will be determined by the parties themselves.

This being so, then analysis of clearances knows no preconceptions as to what might be anticipated to be covered in any given agreements. A performing artist might enter into a recording artist's agreement in customary form,[7] or the agreement might also include a screen test and option term agreement,[8] as well as an option agreement for a television series. So, too, the independent film production company might conceivably enter into a production-distribution agreement for a single picture or for a multi-picture deal.[9]

---

[7] See Form Nos. 5A-1–5A-2.4, inclusive, in Volumes of Forms. Actually there are a number of varieties of such agreements depending upon the particular record company and variations within the same from time to time. The forms are not as standardized as the limited partnership agreements in the theatre, for example, although many clauses similar in form and content recur in the recording artist's agreements used.

[8] See Form No. 1B-1 in Volumes of Forms.

[9] See Form No. 1E-1 to Volumes of Forms.

Then again, there is nothing to prevent the same agreement covering television production as well, or even independent record production. The scope of the agreement will be determined, in the last analysis, by the intent of the parties.

Sec. 19.7. Assignments

The question then arises as to how clearances are ascertained. The two principal tools are the copyright search and the title search. As to the former, one may proceed directly through utilization of the services of the Copyright Office[10] for a fee, or through a number of private agencies, rendering such services.[11] The report as to copyright status should reveal what copyrights, with respect to the work, have been registered, whether in unpublished or in published form, as well as any versions thereof. In music, for example, arrangements under copyright will also be covered. Thus a music publisher might copyright a musical composition as an unpublished work in the form of a lead sheet. Upon publication thereof, it would then copyright the published work and deposit copies of the printed sheet music. Should there be a piano version, band or orchestral arrangements, these might also be copyrighted. The copyright report would cover the various copyrights with respect to the basic work and arrangements thereof.

Then, too, all documents filed in the form of assignments or licenses in Washington for recording purposes should be picked up by the report. In connection with literary works, one might be able to ascertain the chain of title and

---

[10] See Circular 22, Copyright Office, How To Investigate the Copyright Status of a Work.

[11] Johnson & Tannenbaum in New York City, Fulton Brylawski in Washington, D.C. and Seidel, Gonda & Goldhammer in Philadelphia, Pa.

various interests relating thereto. The Copyright Office has this to say about filing of documents with respect to assignments and related documents:

> "The law also provides that assignments of copyright should be recorded in the Copyright Office. This requirement apparently does not apply to other types of transfers, but many persons believe that there are advantages in having documents pertaining to their copyrights appear in the records of the Copyright Office. Thus, in addition to assignments, the Copyright Office will record papers such as licenses, contracts, mortgages, powers of attorney, certificates of corporate title, wills, decrees of distribution, and the like." [12]

Since there is no requirement as to transfers, other than assignments, that the same be recorded, the records of the Copyright Office in this respect must be deemed informational only—apart from assignments—and by no means definitive in the search for clearances. Sometimes counsel will record agreements relating to grant of rights other than assignments, at other times not. Still other counsel will not do so at all.

As for the obligation to record, Sec. 30 of the Copyright Act provides:

> "Every assignment of copyright shall be recorded in the copyright office within three calendar months after its execution in the United States or within six calendar months after its execution without the limits of the United States, in default of which it shall be void as against any subsequent purchaser or mortgagee for a

[12] Circular 10, Copyright Office, Assignments and Related Documents.

valuable consideration, without notice, whose assignment has been duly recorded." [13]

With respect to transfers of exclusive rights under Copyright, Justice Frankfurter has remarked, "Moreover, the Copyright Office will record these partial assignments, thus protecting the transferee and thereby increasing the marketability of the separate rights." [14] Moreover, in a case where the plaintiff claimed title to the copyright, having reserved the right of magazine publication, the Court observed, "... it may be noted that the instrument apparently is deemed sufficient as an assignment by the copyright office, as it was regularly registered therein as an assignment." [15]

In *Vidor* v. *Serlin*,[16] there was a grant of exclusive motion picture, television, radio and allied rights to producer Charles Vidor by Romola Nijinsky, widow of the ballet dancer, Vaslav Nijinsky. She gave him a separate instrument of assignment of these rights which he recorded in the Copyright Office. The Court of Appeals stated:

> "No one doubts that Vidor's assignment was recordable and properly recorded. Appellants, nevertheless, say that the recording act did not give Vidor priority over Bass, since, so they argue, the Nijinsky-Bass document was at most a license, not an 'assignment' of the sort described in section 30 of title 17 of the United States Code. Their submission is that such a nonrecordable license loses nothing by the statute and

---

[13] 17 U.S.C. 30.

[14] Commissioner of Internal Revenue v. Wodehouse, 337 U.S. 369 (1949), dissenting opinion of Justice Frankfurter, at p. 422.

[15] Witwer v. Harold Lloyd Corp., 46 F. 2d 792 (S.D. Cal. 1930), at p. 795, *rev'd*, on other grounds, 65 F. 2d 1 (9th Cir. 1933).

[16] 7 N.Y. 2d 502, 199 N.Y.S. 2d 669 (Ct. App. 1960).

> that its priority in time gives it priority in rank. The first answer is in the Nijinsky-Bass contract itself since in terms it 'assigns' to Bass 'any and all rights' of Mrs. Nijinsky. A more complete answer is in the controlling case of *Photo-Drama Motion Picture Co.* v. *Social Uplift Film Corp.*, (2 Cir., 220 F. 448, 449, 450, [C.C.A. 2d]) which says that a separate conveyance of motion-picture rights 'must be recorded to avail of the constructive notice which the section contemplates.'"[17]

Since Charles Vidor was found to have no actual or implied notice of the claims of defendant, Serlin, Vidor was held to be a bona fide purchaser for value.

In Photo-Drama Motion Picture Co. Inc. v. *Social Uplift Film Corporation,*[18] Judge Learned Hand considered the facts of a playwright assigning his copyright to a book publisher who copyrighted the play and then reassigned dramatic and motion picture rights. The author purported to grant dramatic rights to one, Totten, by letter. The latter never filed any assignment or claim of assignment in the Copyright Office. The dramatist then assigned motion picture rights to the complainant. Totten had assigned whatever rights he possessed to defendant, Social Uplift Film Corporation. Judge Hand held that motion picture rights were separable and different rights from the right to dramatize, giving each assignee the right to obtain his own copyright. Moreover, notice of dramatic rights is not necessarily notice of motion picture rights, so that one, Kingsley, who had obtained the motion picture rights, presumably from the dramatist, Reginald Wright Kauffman, was found to be a bona fide purchaser without notice. The grant of exclusive dramatic rights, including moving picture rights in the

---

[17] *Idem,* 7 N.Y. 2d at p. 509, 199 N.Y.S. 2d at p. 672 (italics).
[18] 213 Fed. 374 (S.D.N.Y. 1914).

contract by the author, as well as the exclusive leasing of the play, binding upon the heirs, executors and assigns of the parties, was held clearly to be an assignment. The Court stated, "I cannot think that there is any doubt of the intention of this language to create an assignment of all the dramatic rights which Kauffman had." [19] The assignment, however, was held not to affect the rights of a subsequent purchaser without notice, where not recorded within three months under the statute.

Nimmer has stated in this regard, "It appears, however, that the courts are inclined to view the recording of a purported assignment or license of exclusive rights in a given medium (e.g., 'motion picture rights') as constituting constructive notice under Sec. 30 even if the recorded instrument is not an 'assignment' in the strictest sense under the doctrine of indivisibility." [20] Although he believes the question is not entirely settled, he remarks, "It is, then, advisable to record the initial disposition of rights regardless of whether it may be regarded as an assignment or license. If such recordation does not constitute constructive notice as to subsequent assignees, it may well establish actual notice as to persons making a title search of the Copyright Office records." [21]

In this regard, Judge Desmond noted, "There is testimony of an 'invariable custom' whereby one who acquires motion-picture rights files an assignment in the Copyright Office." [22] While such is no doubt the custom, it would seem that the custom is not necessarily invariably followed, some

---

[19] *Idem* at pp. 376-7.

[20] Nimmer on Copyright (1969), Sec. 119.33, at pp. 521-522.

[21] *Idem* Sec. 123.2 at p. 535.

[22] Vidor v. Serlin, note 16, *supra,* 7 N.Y. 2d at pp. 509-510, 199 N.Y.S. 2d at p. 673.

assignees, for whatever reasons, simply not recording the instrument whereby motion picture rights are acquired.

It would seem, however, that the judicial tendency is in the right direction. Justice Frankfurter, moreover, noted that this is in accord with the statutory scheme. He states, "The scheme and details of the Copyright legislation manifest a separate treatment of the various exclusive rights conferred by the statute. 61 Stat. 652, 17 U.S.C. Sec. 1 *et seq.* It segregates these rights into separately numbered paragraphs. In each paragraph there is listed, in the alternative, a more detailed subdivision of the various rights." [23]

Sec. 19.8. Transfers of Ownership

Proposed copyright revision goes further. It expressly authorizes transfers of exclusive rights as transfers of ownership. Sec. 101 of S. 543 defines transfers of copyright ownership. "A 'transfer of copyright ownership' is an assignment, mortgage, exclusive license, or any other conveyance, alienation, or hypothecation of a copyright or of any of the exclusive rights comprised in a copyright, whether or not it is limited in time or place of effect, but not including a nonexclusive license." [24] Sec. 201(d) of S. 543 then spells out the nature of transfer of ownership and provides:

"(d) Transfer of Ownership.—

(1) The ownership of a copyright may be transferred in whole or in part by any means of conveyance or by

---

[23] Note 14, at pp. 420-421. Judge Frankfurter's dissent also sets forth the language of Sec. 1 of the Copyright Act as footnote 15 thereto.

[24] Note 2, *supra,* Sec. 101.

operation of law, and may be bequeathed by will or pass as personal property by the applicable laws of intestate succession.

(2) Any of the exclusive rights comprised in a copyright, including any subdivision of any of the rights specified by section 106, may be transferred as provided by clause (1) and owned separately. The owner of any particular exclusive right is entitled, to the extent of that right, to all of the protection and remedies accorded to the copyright owner by this title."[25]

Sec. 205 of S. 543 is the recordation statute. Subdivision (a) thereof provides:

"(a) Conditions for Recordation.—Any transfer of copyright ownership or other document pertaining to a copyright may be recorded in the Copyright Office if the document filed for recordation bears the actual signature of the person who executed it, or it is accompanied by a sworn or official certification that it is a true copy of the original, signed document."[26]

It would seem, however, that the reference to document in the statute is to one evidencing a transfer of ownership as defined in the statute because Sec. 205(c) sets forth the effect of recordation as constructive notice. This subdivision reads:

"(c) Recordation as Constructive Notice.—Recordation of a document in the Copyright Office gives all persons constructive notice of the facts stated in the recorded instrument, but only if:

---

[25] *Idem* Sec. 201(d).
[26] *Idem* Sec. 205(a).

(1) the document, or material attached to it, specifically identifies the work to which it pertains so that after the document is indexed by the Register of Copyrights, it would be revealed by a reasonable search under the title or registration number of the work; and

(2) registration has been made for the work." [27]

Since the definition of a transfer of ownership excludes non-exclusive licenses, it would seem that constructive notice would be limited to documents pertaining to transfers of ownership. Indeed, Sec. 205 not only retains the substance of the present statute as to unrecorded assignments later made, but in the broader context of transfers as defined in the statute, although reducing the time for recordation from three months to one month after execution of the document in the United States and from six months to two months outside the U.S.A. in subdivision (e),[28] it also grants priority to non-exclusive licenses, whether recorded or not, if the license was evidenced by a written instrument signed by the owner of the licensed rights or his duly authorized agent and if the license preceded the transfer, or was taken in good faith before recordation of the transfer and without notice of it.[29] It would seem that the limitations of statutory time to record must be read into the taking of the license before recordation. That is, in respect of conflicting transfers provided for in Sec. 205(e),[30] the first transferee has one month within which to record in the United States and two months without this country. Otherwise a later transfer first recorded,

---

[27] *Idem* Sec. 205(c).
[28] *Idem* Sec. 205(e).
[29] *Idem* Sec. 205(f).
[30] *Idem* Sec. 205(e).

if taken in good faith for a valuable consideration and without notice, prevails. The later transfer, therefore, is conditioned upon the right of the first transferee to record timely. It is submitted that this limitation is also to be read into Sec. 205(f)[31] as to prior unrecorded transfers vis-à-vis a later non-exclusive license, even though not expressly stated in the statute, otherwise such a license without notice could conceivably defeat the transfer even prior to the expiration of the period allowed by the statute for recordation.

It would seem, too, that the reference to recordation of non-exclusive licenses does not mean that recordation thereof, which obviously would be permissible as evidenced by such reference, would constitute constructive notice under Sec. 205(c). Otherwise, the effect of the permissibility to record non-exclusive licenses would be to extend the effect of such recordation beyond transfers of ownership, when the intent of the statute is to govern recordation of transfers of ownership as defined so as not to include non-exclusive licenses. Rather the intent seems to be to indicate by statute that the Copyright Office will accept any instrument for recordation, including non-exclusive licenses, even though such instruments may not, by such filing, constitute constructive notice. Perhaps the Regulations of the Copyright Office might cover this in the event proposed copyright revision should become law.

Sec. 19.9. Recordation of Documents—Scope

Indeed, Nimmer observes, "Assignments and other such papers will be recorded even if the copyright which is the subject thereof has never been registered."[32] One might

---

[31] *Idem* Sec. 205(f).

[32] Nimmer, *op. cit., supra,* note 20, Sec. 123.2, fn. 151, at p. 535.

assume that the Copyright Office, even under proposed copyright revision, would continue to accept such documents for filing, whether or not the same has been registered. Moreover, under present law, some of this material may continue in unregistered form under common law copyright because of the prevailing doctrine that performance is not a publication. Joseph A. McDonald, in referring to broadcast literary material, observed, ". . . it is rarely copyrighted. In view of the fact that the broadcasting of the material is not a dedication, the practice is not to copyright this material unless it is intended to be distributed in written form." [33] Mr. McDonald was then treasurer of the National Broadcasting Company, Inc.[34] With respect to the material as telecast, he remarked, "On our network programs we do not copyright these films. . ." [35] In this regard, Harry P. Warner has written, "It is believed that the great bulk of radio programs other than a few network shows have not been copyrighted. . . In all probability the great bulk of 'live' television programs which will be presented only once or twice will not be copyrighted . . ." [36]

Whatever the effect of recordation as to copyrighted works, it would seem that if many forms of literary and artistic properties are not placed under statutory copyright, then it is unlikely that documents relating thereto will be filed in the Copyright Office, and to the extent such docu-

---

[33] McDonald, Joseph A., The Law of Broadcasting, in 7 Copyright Problems Analyzed (1951), edited by Kupferman, Theodore R., Fred B. Rothman & Co., reprint (1966), 31 at p. 47.

[34] *Idem* credit line at p. 31.

[35] *Idem* at p. 47. The credit line at p. 31 points out that Mr. McDonald had formerly been Vice President and General Attorney for American Broadcasting Company, Inc. Indeed, the late Mr. McDonald was a distinguished copyright lawyer.

[36] Warner, Harry P., Radio and Television Rights (1953), Sec. 200, at pp. 842-833.

ments are filed, that they are necessarily complete. This means that the search in terms of title clearance does not begin or end at the Copyright Office, whether or not undertaken directly by the Copyright Office or by one of the agencies regularly engaged in such activities, and who may have on hand facilities prepared by the Copyright Office, such as catalogs of copyright entries.[37]

Sec. 19.10. Titles and Title Clearances

More importantly, title clearance is not co-terminous with copyright searches. The term "title clearance" has at least three meanings. First, it may mean examination of ownership in its broadest sense. Clearance of rights to a motion picture, for example, includes not only examination of the chain of title to the antecedent copyrights in the underlying work, but also ascertaining that the film producer has appropriate rights and releases to use the acts, poses, plays and appearances of the actors, director, etc. These documents would not normally be filed in the Copyright Office because they are not documents relating to ownership interests in the film; they are neither assignments nor exclusive licenses of rights going from copyright proprietor to the user. Second, the term "title clearance" might be used synonymously with the copyright search to refer to the chain of title in the underlying work so that a derivative motion picture or teleplay might be adapted therefrom. In this sense, it is co-terminous with the copyright search and, hopefully, the information will be embodied in the copyright report. Third, the term "title clearance" may refer to the process of clearing the proposed title to the work in production by obtaining and analyzing a title report. Again, the agencies engaged

---

[37] See note 11, *supra* and 17 U.S.C. Secs. 210-211; Regulations of the Copyright Office, Sec. 201.3 Catalog of Copyrights Entries.

in rendering copyright reports will furnish title reports.[38] There the concern is with doctrines of unfair competition, whether a title currently or in prior use has acquired secondary meaning so that use of the same or substantially similar title will constitute unfair competition. In this regard, the Court, in *Johnston* v. *Twentieth Century-Fox Film Corp.*,[39] in affirming an oral contract for the sale of the title "Queen of the Flat Tops" for film and other uses, but reserving the right to use the title for book publication purposes without any sale of rights in and to the underlying work, stated:

> "A title alone is not copyrightable. *Patten* v. *Superior Talking Pictures,* D.C., 8 F. Supp. 196, 197. Upon publication of the book with the title the owners ceased to have an exclusive common right to use of the title. *Little et al.* v. *Hall et al.,* 18 How. 165, 15 L. Ed. 328; *Keene* v. *Kimball,* 16 Gray, (Mass.) 545, 550, [77 Am. Dec. 426]; *Palmer* v. *DeWitt,* 47 N.Y. 532, 539, [7 Am. Rep. 480]). While an author may not have any property interest in the use of a title under his common law right after publication, it does not follow that he does not have a property interest in the title and in its use as against a competitor. (*International News Service* v. *Associated Press,* 248 U.S. 215, [39 S. Ct. 68, 63 L. Ed. 211, 219, 2 A.L.R. 293].) To protect the author in his property right to the title and its use after publication of the work, the courts have developed the doctrine of secondary meaning." [40]

Warner observes, in this respect, "The courts have uniformly held that the title of a work cannot be the subject-

---

[38] See note 11, *supra.*

[39] 82 Cal. App. 2d 796, 187 P. 2d 474 (1947).

[40] *Idem,* 82 Cal. App. 2d at p. 810, 187 P. 2d at p. 483. (italics).

matter of copyright and that the copyright of the work does not cover its title." [41] Indeed, the Regulation of the Copyright Office lists titles among the items not subject to copyright.[42] Nimmer has stated in this regard, "As a matter of first impression it might well be argued that fanciful original titles should be regarded as a form of literary expression protectible under the copyright laws. Moreover, nothing in the Copyright Clause of the Constitution, or in the Copyright Act itself expressly precludes such protection. It is nevertheless clear, as a matter of statutory construction by the courts (as well as Copyright Office Regulations) that titles may not claim statutory copyright. It is almost equally clear that titles may not be protected under principles of common law copyright." [43] However, concern as to whether or not *Sears*[44] and *Compco*[45] have affected protection of titles under doctrines of unfair competition has prompted one writer to espouse coverage of titles under statutory copyright and by protection thereunder against title infringement.[46]

Rudolph Callmann has noted that the title, like the trademark, is an intangible and incorporeal property right which should be similarly protected.[47] He states, "The title of a publication, while it partakes of some of the essential attributes of a name and a trademark, differs materially

---

[41] Warner, *op. cit., supra,* note 36, Sec. 231a at p. 999.

[42] Regulations of the Copyright Office, Sec. 202.1(a).

[43] Nimmer, *op. cit., supra,* note 20, Sec. 34, at p. 140.

[44] Sears, Roebuck & Co. v. Stiffel Co., 376 U.S. 225 (1964).

[45] Compco Corp. v. Day-Brite Lighting Inc., 376 U.S. 234 (1964).

[46] Messinger, Barry William, A Nice Dilemma: The Protection of Literary Titles, 1 Perf. Arts Rev. 585 (1970); see also Nimmer, note 43, as to his expression of concern as to the impact of *Sears* and *Compco.*

[47] 3 Callmann, The Law of Unfair Competition Trademarks and Monopolies, Third Ed. (1969), Sec. 83.2 at pp. 882-883.

from both."[48] Titles serve to identify the work but the identification continues even after copyright has expired and even if there has been no copyright.[49]

In the absence of copyright protection for titles, the parties concerned are relegated to judicial protection or internal industrial regulation. In terms of the former, the ultimate result may not be necessarily satisfactory to either side of the dispute. Thus, in *Warner Bros. Pictures, Inc.* v. *Majestic Pictures Corp.*,[50] Warners had obtained motion picture rights to "Gold Diggers" and obtained rights based upon a play by Avery Hopwood, entitled the "Gold Diggers". It then produced motion pictures under titles "Gold Diggers of 1933" and "Gold Diggers of Broadway". It sought to enjoin Majestic Pictures' use of the title "Gold Diggers of Paris". Judge Augustus Hand, in his opinion, reversed the denial of preliminary injunction below and granted an injunction *pendente lite* because the title "Gold Diggers", without regard to continuity of plot or composition in Warners' films using the title or even the play by Hopwood, had acquired a meaning in connection with origin and certain standards of competence and achievement that could be protected against defendant's use of the title "Gold Diggers" in its motion pictures likely to compete with Warners. But note the form in which the protection was granted by Judge Augustus Hand:

> "An injunction pendente lite should issue restraining the defendants from using the words 'Gold Diggers' in connection with the motion picture 'Gold Diggers of Paris' unless they place upon every piece of advertising used in connection with the picture and

[48] *Idem* at pp. 880-881.
[49] *Idem* at p. 882.
[50] 70 F. 2d 310 (2d Cir. 1934).

upon the motion picture film also, the words, in type as large as 'Gold Diggers': 'A production of Majestic Pictures Corporation, not based on Avery Hopwood's play or on the motion pictures of Warner Bros. Pictures, Inc.', or some equivalent words of differentiation which may be settled by the District Court after hearing the respective parties. In view of the fact that the words 'Gold Diggers' are in themselves terms of general description, it is but to limit their use only so far as may be necessary to prevent unfair competition, and we think that may be done along the general lines which we have indicated." [51]

Indeed, the Court in *Johnston* stated that the evidence showed, "that titles are of such value in the industry that Motion Picture Producers and Distributors of America maintains an elaborate system for their registration;" [52] It is submitted that the institution of the Title Registration Bureau of this organization, now known as the Motion Picture Association of America, was deemed to be as much a matter of necessity because the resolution of cases like *Majestic* was thought to be unsatisfactory as a matter of desirability for orderly coverage of use of titles among its registrants. For title registration is not limited to members of the Motion Picture Association of America. Non-members may become registrants in its Title Registration Bureau upon agreeing to abide by its procedures, which include methods of internal resolution of disputed use of titles —prior to use thereof—by the device of a register of titles

---

[51] *Idem* at pp. 312-13.

[52] Note 39, *supra,* 82 Cal. App. 2d at p. 804, 187 P. 2d at p. 480. See Forms used by the Motion Picture Association of America in operation of its Title Registration Bureau, Form No. 1C-8 in Volumes of Forms.

that the respective parties wish to use and notice thereof to registrants.

Thus it may be seen that copyright will not be the means of title clearance as used in this third sense. The Copyright Office catalog of entries may indicate which titles have been used for what literary and artistic properties over the years and as such are an aid to determination of title clearance. However, because performance is not publication, plays and other works, such as television shows, are often not registered for copyright because the copyright proprietor prefers common law copyright and the status of perpetual copyright thereunder. Thus, the sources of determination of use of titles will be in actual use thereof, not only as to published works, as to which the sources of the Copyright Office would be helpful, but also actual performances of unpublished works under given titles.

Sec. 19.11. Clearance Procedures

Clearance policies and procedures take a variety of forms in the market, depending upon the purposes of the user. Thus book publishing companies often have permissions and rights departments or agents or other instrumentalities for the same purpose to grant, very often for a fee, permission to use parts or all of a work in a variety of places, such as anthologies, periodicals and in other media. This is to be distinguished from the negotiation for the rights to adapt the work for other media and to create a derivative copyright with respect thereto by the sale of motion picture and television rights in and to a given literary property.

Motion picture and television companies will often maintain separate copyright and title departments to keep records in detail of each work under copyright or exclusive rights or licenses in the inventory of that company. These departments will maintain abstracts of the principal rights under copyright, duration of copyright, territorial coverage, source of rights therefor if the film or television show is a derivative work, and separately copyrightable source of ingredients that may be in the film or TV work, such as music and lyrics.

But ultimately, clearance procedures become a function of lawyers in respect of the production of motion picture or television works. Counsel's interest therein is much broader than even the concern of the copyright and title departments, which are basically administrative operations. Counsel must adjudge the quantum and quality of the documents necessary to render an opinion as to whether there is title clearance in the broadest sense. Thus production-distribution agreements in film deals will often provide that the independent production company must submit all of its production agreements with talent and others for review and approval by the studio so that the latter may be assured of a proper chain of title. This function is undertaken by the lawyers. Counsel must determine, from what has been done, that the production company has acquired suitable and adequate title of ownership in the film, since the rights of distribution granted to the studio are based upon proper title in the production company. It is here that counsel must be an adept in the tort/contract dialectic. Thus the production company must furnish a proper actor's agreement evidencing rights in the production company and to the use thereof in performance.[53] Similar transfer of rights, all within the context of employment for hire relationship, must be produced in duly executed form as to the writer of the screen

[53] See Form Nos. 1B-1 to 1B-1.2a, inclusive, in Volumes of Forms.

play, director and other artistic "above the line" components. Similarly, appropriate releases and quitclaim documents may have to be produced as to various persons and places appearing in the film or show. For the lack of right may presuppose the possibility of claim of tort and possibly suit to enjoin release of the picture or show. Thus a claim may be based upon invasion of privacy where no release has been obtained from a person appearing recognizably in a picture.[54] Counsel must be able to evaluate the tort consequences of the absence of contract with respect to the numerous factors utilized in the production of that particular film. He must also be able to evaluate the sufficiency of the scope of contractual grants for the purposes intended so as to be able to advise as to the rights of his client with respect thereto and the legal position of others who may pursue a certain course of action that may or may not affect his client's claim of right, if any. A good example is the construction of the scope of the grant of rights to Warners in the *Sam Spade* case,[55] as to whether the grant of rights to make the picture, the "Maltese Falcon", included character rights in Sam Spade and other characters therein. The Court there held that the author and publisher had reserved such rights. Of course, there it took judicial construction to reach that conclusion, but only after counsel for Warners had first concluded that Warners had been granted such rights.

Counsel, then, in connection with production, must evaluate the source of rights and the possibilities of a hiatus in the chain of title. On occasion, his task is to close such gaps by arranging for execution of missing documents,

---

[54] See Hofstadter, Samuel H., The Development of the Right of Privacy in New York (1954).

[55] Warner Bros. Pictures, Inc. v. Columbia Broadcasting System, Inc., 216 F. 2d 945 (9th Cir. 1954).

after the fact, as to pertinent grants of rights and releases. Sometimes the hiatus cannot be cured by after-procurement of documents either because of their unavailability, the impracticability of obtaining the same, or what-have-you. At such time, counsel must determine whether or not it is a "fair risk" to proceed with the deal in the absence of such documentation. Fair risk implies that the likelihood of claim or litigation is remote or, alternatively, that the contemplated risks, damage-wise, are exceedingly small in relation to the overall expenditures of the client and its expectations, market-wise, in relation thereto.

In this regard, the scope of errors and omissions insurance covering tort liability from Lloyd's or other carrier must be considered, whether under a blanket policy or policy written for that particular production. Even with such coverage that is obtained to cover the hiatus, counsel and management cannot be cavalier about seeking protection thereunder by way of the doctrine of fair risk because, if too many claims should materialize under the policy, the rates upon expiration of the existing policy might soar or else the policy might not even be renewed. In some instances, the hiatus might even affect the possibility of obtaining such coverage, in the first instance, if the carrier should feel that the gaps contain a potential risk beyond its willingness to assume.

It is evident, therefore, that with respect to the performing arts, where performance inheres in the constitution of the work under copyright, as in motion pictures and videotapes, that the problems of clearances are of considerable importance. The primary function of clearances is to determine whether the right, (i.e., the ownership as to the particular aspect of production, distribution and exhibition is there. The rights involved are rights under copyright and rights of all kinds constituting the performance embodied in a fixed form—such as celluloid or tape—that is ultimately the subject of copyright. The basis for determination thereof is principally analysis of contracts, plus, of course, the results of the copyright and title searches. Back of this must be consideration of the nature and scope of such rights and whether they are sufficient for the purposes required by the client and the tort consequences—be they violation of right of privacy, unfair competition, infringement of copyright, or otherwise, if somehow there is a defect of some material kind in the chain of title.

Thus it may be seen that copyright and contract considerations, as interpreted through clearance procedures, determine the parameters in a given context of market factors in the copyright industries.

Chapter XX

THEORY OF RIGHTS

Sec. 20.1. Statutory Grant of "Sole Liberty" of Copyright—State

A most interesting facet of American copyright development has been that while mandating and constitutional sanction for copyright has been stated in terms of "exclusive right", enabling legislation, until the present Act of 1909, it has been stated more in terms of "sole liberty" than in terms of "exclusive right".

Thus the Resolution of the Continental Congress of May 2, 1783[1] recommended to the several states that they secure to authors and publishers the copy right for a term of fourteen years plus a renewal right of like term. The Resolution then refers to "such copy or *exclusive right* of printing, publishing and vending" [2] new books.

However, three states had passed laws with respect to copyright containing varying provisions in 1783, even prior to the date of the Resolution of the Continental Congress. Thus, in January, 1783, Connecticut passed an act granting authors "the *sole liberty* of printing, publishing and vending".[3] Massachusetts passed its act on March 17,

---

[1] Resolution of the Continental Congress, May 2, 1783, in Copyright Enactments Laws Passed in the United States Since 1783, Relating to Copyright, Copyright Office, Bulletin No. 3, (Revised) (1963) at p. 1.

[2] *Ibid.* (emphasis added).

[3] State of Connecticut, Act of Jan., 1783, Sess., Copyright Enactments, note 1, *supra,* at pp. 2-4. The statute also incorporated a form of trade regulation by granting the judiciary powers to regulate publication of sufficient numbers of the work secured by copy-

1783[4] providing that books, treatises and literary works "shall be the *sole property*"[5] of the authors whose names were printed in such works. Massachusetts provided for an original term of 21 years with no right of renewal.[6] Connecticut, on the other hand, provided for an original term of 14 years with a right of renewal of a further 14 years. As to the renewal, it provided that "the *sole right* of printing and disposing of any such book, pamphlet, map or chart in this State, shall return to the author thereof, if then living, and his heirs and assigns, for the term of 14 years more."[7] Maryland, on the other hand, passed its statute on April 21, 1783[8] providing authors with the "*sole liberty* of printing such book or books, writing or writings, for the term of fourteen years" with a right of renewal. Thus none of the three states which had enacted copyright statutes prior to the Resolution of the Continental Congress spoke in terms of a grant of exclusive rights.

After the passage of the Resolution, the other states which passed such statutes did so with even greater variety. Thus New Jersey, the first state to act after the Resolu-

---

right at a reasonable price, and if the author or proprietor neglected or failed to do so, to license a complainant to reprint sufficient numbers of the work at a reasonable price. One is mindful of the regulatory powers of the federal courts, with respect to consent decrees covering the performing rights societies (ASCAP and BMI) following disposition of antitrust suits brought by the government to hear and determine scope and reasonableness of license fees of users as an incident of such consent decrees.

[4] Commonwealth of Massachusetts, Act of Mar. 17, 1783, Copyright Enactments, note 1, *supra,* at pp. 4-5.

[5] *Idem* at p. 4 (emphasis added).

[6] Note 4, *supra,* at p. 4.

[7] Note 3, *supra,* at p. 2. (emphasis added).

[8] State of Maryland, Act of April 21, 1783, Copyright Enactments, note 1, *supra,* at pp. 5-6. (emphasis added).

tion, provided by its Act of May 27, 1783[9] that the author of any book or pamphlet not yet printed "shall have the *exclusive right* of printing, publishing and vending the same"[10] for a term of 14 years with the exclusive right in a renewal term of 14 years. New Hampshire followed the pattern of Massachusetts in its Act of November 7, 1783[11] by providing that books, treatises, and other literary works "shall be the *sole property* of the author or authors"[12] for a single term of 20 years, as contrasted with the 21 years in Massachusetts. Rhode Island, by its Act of December, 1783,[13] followed Massachusetts in granting authors "the *sole property*"[14] in books, treatises and other literary productions for a term of 21 years. Pennsylvania, however, by its act of March 15, 1784,[15] granted authors "the *exclusive right* of printing, publishing and vending"[16] for a term of 14 years with a renewal term of 14 years. South Carolina, by its act of March 26, 1784,[17] provided that the authors shall have "the *sole right and liberty* of printing"[18] books for a term of 14 years with a like renewal term. The provision as to the renewal term provides that "the *sole right* of printing

---

[9] State of New Jersey, Act of May 27, 1783, Copyright Enactments, note 1, *supra,* at pp. 6-7.

[10] *Idem* at p. 7. (emphasis added).

[11] State of New Hampshire, Act of Nov. 7, 1783, Copyright Enactments, note 1, *supra,* at pp. 8-9.

[12] *Idem* at p. 8. (emphasis added).

[13] State of Rhode Island, Act of Dec. Sess., 1783, Copyright Enactments, note 1, *supra,* at p. 9.

[14] *Ibid.*

[15] Commonwealth of Pennsylvania, Act of Mar. 15, 1784, Copyright Enactments, note 1, *supra,* at pp. 10-11.

[16] *Idem* at p. 10.

[17] State of South Carolina, Act of Mar. 26, 1784, Copyright Enactments, note 1, *supra,* at pp. 11-14. Like Connecticut, here, too, there was provision for judicial regulation.

[18] *Idem* at p. 12 (emphasis added).

and disposing copies"[19] shall return to the author for the renewal term. Virginia, on the other hand, provided in its Act of October, 1785,[20] for authors to have the "*exclusive right*"[21] for a term of 21 years, with respect to printing and reprinting of books and pamphlets. North Carolina granted authors, by its Act of November 19, 1785,[22] "the *sole liberty* of printing, publishing, and vending"[23] books, maps or charts for a single term of 14 years. Georgia, by its Act of February 3, 1786,[24] provided for authors "the *sole liberty* of printing, publishing and vending"[25] books and pamphlets for a term of 14 years with a like renewal term as to which, "the *sole right* of printing and disposing of any such book, pamphlet, map or chart . . . , shall return to the author."[26] New York, by its Act of April 29, 1786,[27] provided that authors "shall have the *sole liberty* of printing, publishing or vending"[28] any book or pamphlet for a term of 14 years with a renewal term of 14 years, as to which "the *sole right* of printing and disposing of any such book"[29] shall return

---

[19] *Idem* at p. 14. (emphasis added).

[20] Commonwealth of Virginia, Act of Oct., 1785, Copyright Enactments, note 1, *supra,* at pp. 14-15.

[21] *Idem* at p. 24. (emphasis added).

[22] State of North Carolina, Act of Nov. 19, 1785, Copyright Enactments, note 1, *supra,* at pp. 15-17.

[23] *Idem* at p. 15 (emphasis added). North Carolina's statute provided for judicial regulation of prices, but not of quantity of works printed, unlike Connecticut and South Carolina whose statutes provided for judicial regulation of both.

[24] State of Georgia, Act of Feb. 3, 1786, Copyright Enactments, note 1, *supra,* at pp. 17-19.

[25] *Idem* at p. 17.

[26] *Ibid.*

[27] State of New York, Act of Apr. 29, 1786. Copyright Enactments, note 1, *supra,* at pp. 19-21.

[28] *Idem* at p. 19. (emphasis added).

[29] *Idem* at p. 20. (emphasis added).

to the author. Delaware enacted no copyright statute.[30] Most of the states included reciprocity provisions as to authors of other states, but only Massachusetts, New Hampshire and Rhode Island included in their reciprocity statutes language, in the event of passage of similar laws in other states, that authors of such other states shall have "the exclusive right and benefit" reciprocally in the enacting state.[31]

Thus it would appear that the states continued to use various forms of expression as to the nature of the grant secured by copyright, notwithstanding the language embodied in the Resolution of the Continental Congress, without any particular pattern being evident regionally or in respect of inclusion of renewal terms and other provisions.

Sec. 20.2. Federal Grant of "Sole Liberty" of Copyright

One would expect a more uniform code of coverage after the adoption of the Constitution of the United States of September 17, 1787, which provided in Article I, Section 8, Clause 8 that Congress shall have the power "To promote the progress of science and useful arts, by securing, for limited times, to authors and inventors, the *exclusive right* to their writings and discoveries." [32] After all, thereafter, there would be uniform coverage by Congress rather than separate legislation by the several states. Only one legis-

---

[30] Copyright Enactments, note 1, *supra,* at p. 21.

[31] Note 4, *supra,* as to Massachusetts, at p. 5; note 11, *supra,* at p. 8, as to New Hampshire; and Rhode Island at note 13, *supra,* at p. 9.

[32] Constitution of the United States, Art. 1, Sec 8, Clause 8. See, Copyright Enactments, note 1, *supra* at p. 21. (emphasis added).

lative body, the Congress of the United States, consisting of the Senate and House of Representatives, would thenceforth enact legislation, rather than the lawmaking bodies of the separate states.

Nevertheless, the history of such federal legislation reveals that until the passage of the present Act of 1909, substantially all of such Congressional legislation varied in language from the authorization of the Constitution. Indeed, the very first Act of May 31, 1790,[33] following adoption of the Constitution in 1789, provided that authors, for an original term of 14 years and a renewal term of like years, shall have "the *sole right and liberty* of printing, reprinting, publishing and vending" [34] books, maps and charts, language which, oddly enough, is substantially the very language employed by South Carolina![35] When the copyright was extended to prints and engravings by the Act of April 29, 1802,[36] substantially the same language was used. However, the Act of February 15, 1819,[37] extended jurisdiction to the circuit courts of the United States "under any law of the United States, granting or confirming to authors or inventors the *exclusive right* to their respective writings, inventions, and discoveries;".[38] This language, of course, is reminiscent of the language of the Constitution. The next reference is the revision by the Act of February 3,

---

[33] Act of May 31, 1790, 1st Cong., 2d Sess., Chap. 15, 1 Stat. 124 (1845). Copyright Enactments, note 1, *supra,* at pp. 22-24.

[34] *Idem* at p. 22.

[35] Note 18, *supra.*

[36] Act of Apr. 29, 1802, 7th Cong., 1st Sess., Chap. 36, 2 Stat. 171 (1845), Copyright Enactments, note 1, *supra,* at pp. 24-26.

[37] Act of Feb. 15, 1819, 15th Cong., 2d Sess., Chap. 19, 3 Stat. 481 (1846), Copyright Enactments, note 1, *supra,* at pp. 26-27.

[38] *Idem* at p. 26.

1831,[39] which included music, and continued to provide that the author "shall have the *sole right and liberty*" [40] with respect to the enumeration of books, maps, charts, prints, engravings and musical compositions, for a term of 28 years. A variation is provided in respect of the renewal term of 14 years in that the author shall have "the *same exclusive right*" [41] for a further term of 14 years. When the right of public dramatic performance to the copyright was added by the Act of August 18, 1856,[42] the reference there was to "the *sole right*" [43] to print, publish and perform the dramatic composition. The Act of July 8, 1870[44] revision continues the formulation used in the 1831 statute both as to original term and renewal term. The same is true of the revision by the Act of December 1, 1873.[45] It is to be noted that each revision simply continued the enumeration of the separate matters which became the subject of copyright in the intervening years, such as the right of dramatic performance[46] and photographs.[47] The Act of March 3, 1891[48] likewise contained the 1831 formulation. Just before the pas-

---

[39] Act of Feb. 3, 1831 (Revision), 21st Cong., 2d Sess., Chap. 16, 4 Stat. 436 (1846), Copyright Enactments, note 1, *supra,* at pp. 27-31.

[40] *Idem* at p. 27. (emphasis added).

[41] *Idem* at p. 27. (emphasis added).

[42] Act of Aug. 18, 1856, 34th Cong., 1st Sess., Chap. 169, 11 Stat. 138 (1859), Copyright Enactments, note 1, *supra,* at p. 33.

[43] *Ibid.*

[44] Act of July 8, 1870, 41st Cong., 2d Sess., Chap. 230, 16 Stat. 212 (1871), Copyright Enactments, note 1, *supra,* at pp. 36-41.

[45] Dec. 1, 1873, 43rd Cong., 1st Sess., Copyright Enactments, note 1, *supra,* at pp. 43-47.

[46] Note 42, *supra.*

[47] Act of Mar. 3, 1865, 38th Cong., 2d Sess., Chap. 126, 13 Stat. 540 (1866).

[48] Act of Mar. 3, 1891, 51st Cong., 2d Sess., Chap. 565, 26 Stat. 1106 (1891), Copyright Enactments, note 1, *supra,* at pp. 49-54.

sage of the present Act, the Act of January 7, 1904,[49] with respect to works published abroad intended for exhibition at the Louisiana Purchase Exposition, provided that such authors shall have "the *sole liberty* of printing, reprinting, publishing, copying and vending"[50] the same within the United States. The Act of March 3, 1905[51] likewise retained this language in amending Sec. 4952 of the Revised Statutes in respect of deposit of works of authors in a foreign language.

Sec. 20.3. The "Exclusive Right" of Copyright

It is only with the passage of the present statute, Act of March 4, 1909[52] that we find the grant is made to persons who "shall have the *exclusive right*"[53] followed by the enumeration of rights under copyright in Sec. 1 thereof. Title 17, which codified the 1909 Act in 1947 added a heading to Sec. 1 in addition to substantially the same introductory paragraph of Sec. 1, as follows: "Sec. 1. *Exclusive Rights* as to Copyrighted Works.—Any person entitled thereto, upon complying with the provisions of this title, shall have the *exclusive right*:"[54] The enumeration of the section follows. Proposed copyright revision would continue this concept. Sec. 106 of S. 543 provides in part ". . . the owner of copyright under this title has the *exclu-*

---

[49] Act of Jan. 7, 1904, 58th Cong., 2d Sess., Chap. 2, 33 Stat. 4 (1905), Copyright Enactments, note 1, *supra,* at pp. 60-61.

[50] *Idem* at p. 60.

[51] Act of Mar. 3, 1905, 58th Cong., 3rd Sess., Chap. 1432, 33 Stat. 1000 (1905), Copyright Enactments, note 1, *supra,* at pp. 62.

[52] Act of Mar. 4, 1909, 63d Cong., 2d Sess., 38 Stat. 311 (1915). Copyright Enactments, note 1, *supra,* at pp. 64-92.

[53] *Idem* at p. 64. (emphasis added).

[54] Pub. Law 281, 80th Cong., 1st Sess., Chap. 391, being Title 17, of the United States Code, approved July 17, 1947, Copyright Enactments, note 1, *supra,* pp. 102-121 at p. 103. (emphasis added).

sive rights to do and authorize any of the following:"[55] There follows the section's own enumeration of rights.

Sec. 20.3(a). "Sole Property" Distinguished

It is to be noted that the term "sole property" was not used in federal legislation after the adoption of the Constitution. Its use by Massachusetts, New Hampshire and Rhode Island pursuant to implementing the Resolution of the Continental Congress apparently did not go further thereafter because of federal pre-emption of copyright after passage of the first federal statute in 1790. Moreover, there is an inherent ambiguity in the term which can best be explained by reference to the first sentence of Sec. 27 of the present Act, which reads, "The copyright is distinct from the property in the material object copyrighted . . ." Therefore to refer to the "sole property" as the nature of the copyright is to confuse concepts by use of the term "property" for both the copyright and the material object copyrighted. To add the word "sole" implies that the property in the copyright is the property only of the author or assigns. It implies the sense of the entire property in the copyright being so owned. Again this causes confusion because of the duality of the conception of property in the copyright and in the material object. The term "sole property" therefore gave way to the others used by the states and later the Congress.

Sec. 20.3(b). "Sole Liberty" Distinguished

One is struck, in this regard, by the virtually uninterrupted use of the term "sole liberty" from the very first statute in 1790 through 1905 and thereafter the shift in

---

[55] S. 543, Dec. 10, 1969 print, 91st Cong., 1st Sess., Jan. 22, 1969, Sec. 106 (emphasis added).

terminology to the term "exclusive right". Moreover, one wonders at the continuous usage of the first term for so long, notwithstanding the expression of the latter term in the Constitution granting Congress the power to legislate with respect thereto. There are three conceivable explanations as to the usage of such draftsmanship in the manner Congress actually made thereof, as exemplified by the statutes. The first is that the terms "sole property", "sole liberty", "sole right" or "exclusive right" are interchangeable so that speculation as to differentiation in use is an aimless exercise in semantics. The second is that the terms did have different meanings, however slight and variable they might be, so that Congressional draftsmanship incorporated a certain amount of sloppy, careless use of language, thereby rendering such legislation somewhat inexact but, nonetheless, sufficiently clear to be utilized. The third is that the terms were all terms of art with precise meanings which were, in fact, used artistically and that different terms were utilized only when there was a change of circumstances necessitating use of such different language.

At first blush, one is tempted to believe that the draftsmen used the terms "sole liberty" and "exclusive right" interchangeably because the statute enacted in 1831 uses the term "sole liberty" as to the original term and then refers to the grant as to renewal term of the "same exclusive right" which language was carried over to successive statutes of 1870, 1873 and 1891. This might tend to suggest either that the terms were not substantially different or that the draftsmen fudged whatever differences there might have been originally so as to equate the two.

It is submitted, however, that the two terms were and are terms of art and that only a change of circumstances dictated the abandonment of the concept of "sole liberty".

Otherwise, one is puzzled why the Congress so consistently went out of its way to employ this term from a period of within months after adoption of the Constitution, which utilized the other term, until the enactment of the present Act in 1909. The consistency of Congress in this regard would tend to imply a rather high regard for the use of the prior term as a term of art, rather than an unthinking carry-over of the term, as used originally in 1790, into subsequent legislation. Also, one might wonder why the departure from the term in 1909 after more than a century of uninterrupted usage. The change cannot be attributed solely to the enumeration of additional rights to the copyright since the history of copyright in the 19th Century in the United States is one of inclusion of new rights under copyright, over and above the traditional right of copy. The legislation in 1909 did not really affect either a qualitative or quantitative change in the rights under copyright to warrant such a change, excepting only for the notion of the compulsory license as to mechanical reproduction of musical compositions.

It would appear that the Congress employed the term "sole liberty" with respect to the exclusive rights under copyright because the term expressed the means of securing to authors for limited times the exclusive right to their writings, as Congress was so empowered by the Constitution. Congress, in its legislation from 1790 to 1909, granted authors the "sole liberty" with respect to the various rights of copy as extended from time to time. The expression is almost a contradiction in terms, yet it effectively captures the sense of the grant of a monopoly for a limited period of time. The root of the term "liberty" is *liber,* derived from the Latin, meaning "free".[56] Conse-

[56] Ford, Celia, First Latin Book (1931), Latin-English vocabulary at p. xvii, "liber, -era, -erum, free".

quently, the meaning of the noun would be expressed by the term "freedom". However, the term "sole liberty" by denoting freedom only for the author, appears to denote a contradiction in terms, to wit, the relative lack of freedom if only one, i.e., the author, or assigns, has the sole liberty or freedom. Yet it is precisely this that the Congress wanted to provide, the freedom in the author or assigns, i.e., the copyright proprietor, alone, as the means for securing to the author the rewards of his intellectual creations. Rather than a grant of a monopoly by means of letters patent on special grant, there was a grant of the sole liberty to the author by general applicability of the statute to all who might qualify thereunder as authors. This is analogous to general acts of incorporation whereby any parties qualifying under the general provisions thereof might incorporate, as opposed to special acts of incorporation of a legislature.

Sec. 20.4. Rights and Liberties

But the term "liberty" imports more than "freedom". George H. Smith indicates that the terms "liberty" and "power" have substantially the same meaning.[57] He refers to liberty as denoting the absence of restraint and connoting the ability to act, whereas power denotes the ability to act and connotes the absence of restraint. Power implies control over others, while liberty is the absence of impediment of that which a man wills to do. He states, "The term 'liberty' as used in jurisprudence therefore denotes merely the absence of restraint of others upon the free performance of volition . . . "[58] He defines a right as " . . . the jural or rightful power or liberty to act in a particular

---

[57] Smith, George H., Elements of Right and of the Law (1887) at p. 33.

[58] *Idem* at p. 34.

case or class of cases." [59] As to the right, he remarks, "There is implied in every right the liberty or power of acting freely with reference to the object of the right, and it is this which constitutes the essence of the right." [60]

Perhaps Congress wished to emphasize the affirmative nature of the grant in that copyright, being a right of copy and other rights, was affirmative and not negative. Copinger and Skone James have stated the latter point of view in asserting, "Copyright is, in fact, only a negative right to prevent the appropriations of an author by another".[61] The affirmative nature of rights and powers are well stated by Hohfeld, in his assertion, "A right is one's affirmative claim against another, and a privilege is one's freedom from the claim of another. Similarly, a power is one's affirmative 'control' over a given legal relation as against another; whereas an immunity is one's freedom from the legal power or 'control' of another as regards some legal relation." [62] If rights and powers are affirmative, then the copyright cannot be a negative right if it is a species of the genus "right". Moreover, Congressional prescription by copyright legislation as an incident to the constitutional powers of Congress appears to be a consistent application of positive law as expressed by Austin, "Every legal right is a creature of positive law. A man is no more able to confer a right upon himself, than he is able to impose on himself a law or duty." [63] In turn, the

[59] *Idem* at p. 33.

[60] *Idem* at p. 31.

[61] Copinger and Skone James, Law of Copyright 2 (8th Ed. 1948).

[62] Hohfeld, Wesley Newcomb, Fundamental Legal Conceptions (1923) at p. 60. See his construct of jural opposites and jural correlatives as to rights, privileges, powers and immunities at p. 36.

[63] 1 Austin, John, Lectures on Jurisprudence, 2 Vols. (1875), Sec. 264, at p. 166.

doctrine of Austin as to positive law, in terms of the implementation of Congressional powers, was strongly reinforced by the Supreme Court in 1834, when it held in *Wheaton* v. *Peters*, "Congress, then, by this act, instead of sanctioning an existing right, as contended for, created it." [64]

Perhaps what Copinger and Skone James had in mind, in terms of the negative right of copyright to prevent appropriation by another, is inherent in the nature of all rights. William Edward Hearn has observed that a right has no independent existence; it is essentially a function of, that is, draws its force from the violation of the right or its infringement and what it really means is the duty in respect of which a right exists insofar as it affects the donee of the right.[65] He remarked, "A right, therefore, is a relation which arises in a series of commands." [66] A right, then, is a command given for the benefit of some definite person other than on whom a duty is imposed, upon whom the state imposes a duty, i.e., some act or forbearance, for the benefit of a third party.[67]

The nature of the right can be seen as the investiture by means of positive law by the state of power in a party which such party can enforce against breaches thereof by imposing a duty to act or forbearance upon others for the benefit of the recipient of the right. As explained by George H. Smith, " . . . wherever there is a right there shall be an

---

[64] 8 Peters 591, 660-661 (1834). Whicher, John F., The Creative Arts & The Judicial Process, (1965) appears to believe that this is dictum, see pp. 189-190. See also his interesting discussion of the case at pp. 186-206.

[65] Hearn, William Edward, The Theory of Legal Duties and Rights, Chap. VIII, The Theory of Legal Rights (1883) at p. 153.

[66] *Idem* at p. 141.

[67] *Idem* at pp. 145, 153.

action" [68], so that the law of private rights is a resultant body of law relating to both rights and actions.[69]

The legislation of Congress, in granting the "sole liberty" of the copyright, was, in effect, granting power to the author and assigns. The exercise thereof would be the claim of right in the copyright. Since the nature of the power was that of monopoly, it took the form of expression of "sole liberty" or power to enforce those rights under copyright. The grant so made was made in the original term of copyright. The renewal term, although it might be a new estate in the copyright, was, in effect, a reaffirmation of the right to exercise the power which was granted with respect to the original term. The reaffirmation took place by the party rightfully entitled to the "same exclusive right" as that obtained by reason of the power vested in the copyright proprietor—be he author or assignee—by the original grant of power in respect of the original term. Renewal put the proprietor of the renewal copyright in the same position vis-à-vis the Congress as the original term. Although it was a new estate insofar as the copyright was concerned, it was indeed a new estate in the same copyright. Therefore, draftsmanship did not require statement in the form of repetition of the grant of the "sole liberty" to the author or assigns because such repetition would be needless. The powers so vested in the original term automatically carried over to the renewal term to the party entitled to renew. It was sufficient that, upon compliance with the formalities of renewal, such party, as the donee of the right, was characterized to have the "same

[68] Smith, George H., The Law of Private Right (1890) at p. 1.

[69] *Idem* at p. 2. For a history of the relationship of writs and rights, i.e., the development of causes of action to provide a remedy for wrongs in the common law, see Plucknett, Theodore, A Concise History of the Common Law (Fourth Ed. 1948).

exclusive right" that could be exercised in respect of the power already vested by Congress by virtue of the grant of the copyright in respect of the original term.

This would tend to explain the usage of both terms so consistently from 1790 to 1909. The only reason for modification of the original concept from and after 1909 would appear to be the fact that the institution of the compulsory license as to mechanical reproduction of music virtually nullified the fact that as to that right there was a "sole" liberty after the first mechanical reproduction. The language simply no longer fit, due to change of circumstances, and so the draftsmen reverted to the original language of the Constitution as to "exclusive right" as the generative source of the statutory copyright.

Paul G. Kauper[70] provides a distinction between "liberties" and "rights" in the context of "civil liberties" and "civil rights". He writes:

> "The term 'civil liberties' is here used in a very broad sense to refer to basic rights of the person that are in some ways secured to him under the Constitution or the laws of the United States and which are enforceable either against the state or individual persons or both." [71]

He then proceeds to distinguish the two terms, stating:

> "A distinction that may be observed is that between the term 'civil liberties' to characterize liberties or freedoms that may be asserted as against the exercise of governmental power, and the term 'civil rights' to connote the rights and privileges that a person may assert

[70] Kauper, Paul G., Civil Liberties and the Constitution (1962).
[71] *Idem* at p. 169.

against other persons. The whole mass of private rights recognized in the law of torts, contract, and property and protected also by the criminal law, as well as rights created by legislation fall into this category." [72]

Liberties, then, were an affirmative grant from the sovereign which decreed specific freedoms whether, in gross, that is for all the subjects or citizens of the state, or for particular categories thereof. Such a grant, for example, was made in a document called "The Liberties of the Massachusetts Colony in New England" which confirmed specific "rites, liberties and privileges." [73] In turn, liberties are broken down into various categories. George H. Smith refers to jural liberty, actual liberty, moral liberty.[74] Webster's dictionary specifies still other categories in defining "liberty":

"The sum of the rights and immunities of all the citizens of an organized civil community concurrent with the guaranteed protection against interference with such rights and privileges (civil liberty), or the state or condition of those who are invested with the right effectually to share in framing and conducting the government under which they are politically organized (political liberty), or of those who are free from external restraint in the exercise of the rights that are considered as within the province of the government to control (individual liberty). Individual liberty under modern constitutional governments in general in-

---

[72] *Idem* at p. 170.

[73] See Civil Rights and the American Negro A Documentary History, edited by Bloustein, Albert P., and Zangrando, Robert L. (1968), at pp. 7-8.

[74] Smith, George H., *op. cit., supra,* note 57 at p. 34.

> volves freedom of the person in going and coming (personal liberty), equality before the courts, security of private property, freedom of opinion and its expression, and freedom of conscience." [75]

The grant of the "sole liberty" of copyright to authors by Congress from 1790 to 1909 represented a grant of the freedom to do certain things as specified in the respective statutes with the implied condition that the state would stand behind this freedom to enforce it if in jeopardy. Along with the affirmative grant of the liberty, then, went an implied covenant that the recipient of the grant was empowered to exercise it. Since it was a grant "sole", necessarily it was a grant to the exclusion of all others. The grant "sole" of the liberty of copyright, in order to be meaningful, imposed the duty of forbearance by command of the state upon all others for the benefit of the grantee. The jural correlative[76] of such duty imposed on others was that the grant of the sole liberty by the state at the same time invested the author with the right to enforce such duty, by means of the courts, for the benefit of the author.

Thus it may be seen that Congress, until the enactment of the present Act in 1909, chose to implement its Constitutional powers of furnishing rewards to authors for limited times by securing to them the exclusive right to their writings by the instrumentality of the "sole liberty" as the means of securing such exclusive right. Such liberties only came into effect upon the general, as contrasted with the limited publication, of the work which had the simultaneous effect of investing the author with the sole liberty therein upon compliance with copyright formalities and of divest-

---

[75] Webster's New International Dictionary, Second Ed., unabridged (1961), at pp. 1424-1425.

[76] Hohfeld, *op. cit., supra,* note 62 at p. 36.

ing him of his common law copyright therein. Publication triggered the time factor of when the instrumentality came into effect, but the grant of the sole liberty was immanent in all literary and artistic properties of authors that could be availed of *eo instante* publication.

Sec. 20.5. The Right in Positive Law and Natural Law

Thus it would seem that the statutory copyright, whether a grant of the "sole liberty" or of the "exclusive right", would appear to be a classic illustration of the operation of positive law whereby rights are vested by statute as the command of the sovereign. Alternatively, one might conclude that the statutory copyright as the precept of positive law co-exists with the common law copyright as the inalienable right of the author as creator to the fruits of his intellectual labors as a dual system of jurisprudence, not necessarily in relation to the same copyright because publication of a general nature is the means of ending the one and beginning the other. But the co-existence weaves in and out in a more complex way even in relation to the same copyright. When one considers the nature of derivative copyrights, the nature of production of films and television, the market for the performing arts and the sequential roll, it may be seen that the same underlying work may be adapted into a variety of creative forms in the various media, some of which might be under common law copyright, while others will become the subject of statutory copyright.

One might contend, moreover, that although couched in positive law, the constitutional authorization as to copyright and the legislative implementation thereof is, in reality, a recognition of natural rights of creators and therefore of natural law. This result would be achieved by tracing the source of rights of governance, in the first place, in American history, from statutes to the Constitution and back thereof to the Declaration of Independence, which opens with assertion of the right of independence based upon the "Laws of Nature" and then proceeds, "We hold these truths to be self-evident, that all men are created equal, that they are endowed by their Creator with certain inalienable rights, that among these are Life, *Liberty* and the pursuit of Happiness. That to secure these rights, Governments are instituted among Men, deriving their just powers from the consent of the governed." [77] The preamble of the Constitution of the United States speaks of ordaining and establishing the Constitution "in Order to . . . secure the Blessings of *Liberty* to ourselves and our Posterity . . ." [78] There follows not only the grant of power to Congress to enact copyright legislation to secure the exclusive right to authors in their writings for limited times,[79] but also, the First Amendment which recites, "Congress shall make no law . . . abridging the freedom of speech, or of the press . . ." [80] In this view, statutory copyright is merely the legislative means of protecting the natural rights and liberties of authors to create and avail themselves of the fruits and proceeds of their creation.

Lawrence H. Leder has written of Colonial America, "Americans handled the discussion of jury trials and taxation with ease and clarity of purpose, but not so their discussion of other liberties and rights." [81] One reason for

---

[77] Declaration of Independence, as set forth in 6 Collier's Encyclopedia (1961) at p. 137. (emphasis added).

[78] Constitution of the United States, 5 Collier's Encylopedia (1961) at p. 489. (emphasis added).

[79] *Idem* at p. 490.

[80] *Idem* at p. 492.

[81] Leder, Lawrence H., Liberty and Authority (1968) at p. 125.

this was that "Americans had no need to define their liberties with precision."[82] They relied on the rights of Englishmen that liberty was absolute and God-given, requiring no definition, whereas power was human and required limitation. This, in turn, constituted a reliance on the concept of John Locke of creation of government, that gave birth to power, which forced the British in a very practical way to make the definitions and so shifted the burden to them.[83] In effect, he avers, "Americans never sought a full and comprehensive philosophy of government, rather specific justifications of *a posteriori* positions."[84]

Speaking of natural law, Edmond N. Cahn remarked, "Positive law was considered to be merely derivative. It drew its force from the principles of the higher constitutive code of natural law[85] . . . In the United States, the position has been substantially affected by the adoption of a written Constitution. So long as that document was considered the engraved tablet of natural law—elemental and eternal—judges must turn to nature to find the exposition and gloss to the written phrases of the Constitution."[86] He pointed out that it was only a step from natural law to seeking justice under "the aegis of sovereign constraint" by accepting "power as the substance of legality."[87] This, in turn, was weakened by the "search for the unique source of the command".[88] Oliver Wendell Holmes, Jr. stated, "But for legal purposes a right is only the hypostasis of a prophecy—the imagination of a substance supporting the fact

---

[82] *Idem* at p. 127.
[83] *Idem* at p. 144.
[84] *Idem* at p. 79 (italics).
[85] Cahn, Edmund N., The Sense of Injustice, (1949) at p. 4.
[86] *Idem* at p. 5.
[87] *Idem* at p. 7.
[88] *Idem* at p. 9.

that the public force will be brought to bear upon those who do things said to contravene it— . . . No doubt behind these legal rights is the fighting will of the subject to maintain them, and the spread of his emotions to the general rules by which they are maintained; but that does not seem to me the same thing as the supposed *a priori* discernment of a duty or the assertion of a preexisting right."[89]

Sec. 20.6. The Judicial Process and Conflicting Interests

This skepticism as to the nature of the sovereign command was further weakened by another jurist who went one step away from the legal practitioner's projection of the natural rights—Holmes' "hypostasis of a prophecy" to the realities of the nature of the judicial process. Jerome Frank wrote in this regard, ". . . for court purposes, a substantive legal right does not depend on (1) substantive legal rules plus (2) the procedural rules plus (3) the actual facts. It depends on (a) those rules, and (b) the court's guess about the facts. And that guess usually depends, among other things, upon the personalities of the trial judge or jury in reacting to the conflicting oral testimony." [90]

This, in turn, evidences a development away from analysis of general legal concepts as the source of legal rules, as adumbrated by the historical school of jurisprudence.[91] Philipp Heck remarks in this respect,

---

[89] Holmes, Natural Law, 32 Harv. Law. Rev. 40 (1918) as reprinted in Hall, Jerome, Readings in Jurisprudence (1938) at pp. 260-261 (italics).

[90] Frank, Jerome, Courts on Trial (1950) at p. 106.

[91] Heck, Philipp, The Jurisprudence of Interests An Outline, in The Jurisprudence of Interests, translated from the German and edited by Schoch, M. Magdalena, (1948) pp. 31-48. Heck states at

> "The traditional school of jurisprudence placed the emphasis on general concepts. It regarded concepts as the basis of legal rules, and hence as the main object of legal research. This school has been superseded by more modern views, whose common characteristic is the greater stress which they put on the study of the effects of law on actual life. Various terms have been applied to the new school of thought. It is referred to as the Teleological School, or Realistic or Sociological Jurisprudence or Jurisprudence of Interests." [92]

Max Rümelin looks to the close association created thereby between legal science and economics.[93] He asserts, "Sociological Jurisprudence necessarily leads the jurist to factual research. Thus a bridge is erected between legal science and economic research." [94] Lon Fuller traces the departure by this means from reliance on *stare decisis* and precedent, from the Langdell view of ". . . a peculiar geometric brand of legal reasoning that made every conclusion the inevitable consequences of an assumed necessity of juristic thought . . . a gapless system of pre-existing law, from which a solution for every new case could be obtained by deduction." [95]

If the methodology of ratiocination has been attentuated by the instrumentalism of the conflict and resolution of

---

p. 34, "This theory of the causality of general concepts had come into power through the Historical School of jurisprudence. . . . These general concepts were regarded as the source of legal rules."

[92] *Idem* at pp. 31-32.

[93] Rümelin, Max, Developments in Legal Theory and Teaching During My Lifetime, in The Jurisprudence of Interests, note 91, *supra,* pp. 3-27 at p. 26.

[94] *Idem* at p. 27.

[95] *Idem* Fuller, Lon, Introduction, The Jurisprudence of Interests, note 91, *supra,* pp. xvii-xxv, at p. xix.

interests, then the process of resolution of interests takes the form in respect of copyright in some such manner as described by the writer in 1964.

> "Indeed, if copyright revision is effectuated, it will be because the Register of Copyrights has been so adept in the jurisprudence of interests. For the past year, more or less, periodic meetings have been held in Washington and elsewhere by the Copyright Office, to which the interested copyright public has been invited to discuss and review seriatim, sections of legislation to be embodied in a new bill to be proposed to Congress by the Copyright Office. Various proposals and alternative proposals indicate that the recommendations in the Register's Report are not rigid and inflexible formulae but were also intended to be exposed to the scrutiny of the copyright public for consideration in advance of submission of a general copyright revision bill to Congress. What may or may not eventuate in the proposed new bill must first be sifted through the sieve of compromise and conciliation of copyright interests, e.g., authors, publishers, motion picture producers, broadcasters, etc." [96]

Indeed, the House Report[97] accompanying H.R. 2512, dated Mar. 8, 1967 has this to say, "*The bill now reported* reflects the intricate network of relationships among the many groups and industries dependent for their existence upon works created by authors, and *represents an effort to reconcile conflicting interests* as fairly and construc-

[96] Taubman, Review of Studies on Copyright: Arthur Fisher Memorial Edition, 32 Ford. L. Rev. 875 (1964) at p. 877.

[97] House Report No. 83, 90th Cong., 1st Sess., House of Representatives, to accompany H.R. 2512, dated Mar. 8, 1967.

tively as possible." [98] S. 543, Dec. 10, 1969 print, represents further efforts to reconcile the conflicting points of view of broadcasting interests, CATV interests, librarians, motion picture producers, programmers, and so forth.[99] Title II thereof establishes a National Commission on New Technological Uses of Copyrighted Works to make recommendations in the copyright law and procedures made necessary by changes in technology.[100] No doubt that such a commission will anticipate and investigate such inventions and uses for legislative revision in the same context of resolution of conflicting interests of all sorts that have swirled around proposed copyright revision in its myriad facets.[101]

---

[98] *Idem* at p. 3. (emphasis added).

[99] S. 543, Dec. 10, 1969 print, 91st Cong., 1st Sess., Jan. 22, 1969. Title II.

[100] *Idem,* Title II—National Commission on New Technological Uses of Copyrighted Works, Secs. 201-208 of Title II.

[101] The trade papers during the period of proposed copyright revision contain reports from time to time as to the various interests of the contending parties. Thus, an article by Mildred Hall, entitled, "Easing of CATV Rules Seen Speeding Copyright," Billboard, July 4, 1970, pp. 3, 10, refers to the controversial CATV issue, the controversial new performance royalty for performances, i.e., the recording copyright, among others. For details of the conflicting positions see Copyright Law Revision, Hearings before the Subcommittee on Patents, Trademarks and Copyrights of the Committee on the Judiciary, United States Senate, 90th Cong., 1st Sess., Parts 1-4, held in March and April, 1967, with respect to S. 597; Hearings of the Subcommittee on CATV held in August, 1966, 89th Cong., 2d Sess., with respect to S. 1006; Hearings before Subcommittee No. 3 of the Committee on the Judiciary, House of Representatives, on H.R. 4347, H.R. 5680, H.R. 6831, and H.R. 6835. Parts 1-3, held May to September, 1965. Comparable testimony of various interests is reflected in the hearings held prior to enactment of the 1909 Act.

Sec. 20.7. Legal Theory and Practice

The problem with legal theory is that each theory is presented by its proponent from the perspective of the completeness of its explanation of the legal phenomena theorized, while at the same time critics thereof can "strike the jugular" of the weakness of that theory. The alternatives to conceptualization are eclecticism and relativism. Eclecticism is a kind of free style borrowing or use of any and all theories without proposing any single theory by way of explanation. Relativism would see phenomena only in relation of one matter to another and finds significance principally in contexts—i.e., relations of one thing to another. Theoretical principles are thereby virtually made dependent upon relationships. It is a theory of "now" in that significances are made dependent upon relationships which, in turn, become significant because they are in some meaningful connection. It is a form of pragmatism since the only meaningful relationships are those which have consequences, meaningful consequences arising out of the experience of the relationship. The alternative of no conceptualism in the sense of no concern with theoretical formulations is more apparent than real since a complete "how-to" approach of the practitioner postulates acceptance of given theoretical premises of the way things happen and is basically an approach of pragmatism, of concern with effects of experience rather than the meanings and underlying causes of such effects. In any event, given the complexities of copyright theory and practice, at the risk of being characterized as eclectic and relativistic, the writer will essay some views on copyright conceptions.

One can readily assess that many of the criticisms of the aforementioned theoretical postulates can be utilized in cancelling out the underlying premises of others. For example, it is difficult to find complete sustenance in a theory of natural law as to the rights of creators when the history of statutory copyright legislation, as reinforced and interpreted by *Wheaton* v. *Peters,*[102] confirms that statutory copyright arises only by the grace of Congress, which immediately extinguishes the common law copyright upon effectuation of the incidence of general publication. But positive law, in turn, as a series of commands of the sovereign for the benefit of the author, as the third party beneficiary of the rights inherent in the statutory grant of copyright against the rest of society under the jurisdiction of the sovereign, upon whom is imposed the duty of forbearance as to the exclusive rights granted by the sovereign to the author and his assigns, postulates an omniscience and omnipotence of law, whether legislative or judicial, in regulation of the commands in behalf of the third party beneficiary. What we find, instead, is a legislative process effecting legislation through the pulling and tugging of conflicting interests and in legislation, at least, a sovereign striving mightily to effect expression of legislative policy through obeisance to the resolution of the various interests seeking redress or complaining of being aggrieved by one point or another of the proposed legislation. What we find, too, is a judicial system, federal in nature, almost esoteric as to the province of the respective state and federal judiciaries as to the legitimate concern of each, where results are elucidated in the course of judicial battles engaged in by competing counsel as legal gladiators in the fight theory of litigation as the means of eliciting truth and legal decision.[103]

---

[102] 8 Peters 891 (1834).

[103] Frank, Jerome, *op. cit., supra,* note 90.

On the other hand, one might asseverate, as to each theory, that common law copyright emanates out of the labors of the author as a natural right. Positive legislation is an expression thereof since the sanction therefor is the consent of the governed. As to positive law, the means of arriving at legislation by compromise and conciliation of conflicting interests in no material manner dilutes the force and effect of the resultant legislation being the command of the sovereign enforceable ultimately by the full power and resources of the state. Or, one can contend, that commands are not self-fulfilling since they require the projection by counsel and clients of the expected results of legislative and judicial rule-making by way of the "hypostasis of a prophecy" [104] to make sense of the so-called "command" of the sovereign. But even the rationalism of hypostasis in that rules are projected as prophecies on some orderly, sequential, meaningful basis becomes severely attentuated if the process is reduced to the musings of judge and jury as the outgrowth of legal gladiatorial combat of the trial system for ascertaining judgment. Again, the jury system can be rationalized as epitomizing a legal system of consent of the governed.

Sec. 20.8. The Jurisprudence of Flexible Concepts

Perhaps a way out of this epistemology of circular reasoning might be found in a theory oriented to the perspective of the legal practitioner in a jurisprudence of flexible concepts. Perhaps the nature of the rights under copyright might be better analyzed and understood from the point of view of a system structured upon what lawyers do and how they behave in any given context.

---

[104] Holmes, Oliver Wendell, Jr., *op. cit., supra,* note 89.

The starting point is the fact of the constitutional grant of the exclusive right for limited times to authors as among the powers vested by the people in the Congress by that charter of government. The Constitution represents a compact of government whereby the natural rights of the people are transformed thereby into legislated rights. Thereafter, the organs of government respond as the sources of sovereign power, subject, in a democracy, to renewal by replacement through the electoral process. The uninterrupted grant by Congress from 1790 to 1909 of the "sole liberty" of the copyright to authors and assigns as the measure of the scope of the rights under copyright represented a grant, which, though couched in the language of liberty and freedom, was not only reminiscent of grants of other sovereigns of such powers, but by the grant of the *sole* liberty constituted, in effect, a grant of rights tantamount to a monopoly because all others were excluded from this liberty. The grant of the sole liberty imported that the owner thereof could enforce his rights against the entire world, subject to the jurisdiction of the sovereign, by means of all of the paraphernalia of its power to enforce its commands and process.

Legal practitioners respond to the grant of the exclusive right of copyright, whether entirely a sole liberty, or, as the exclusive rights have been modified from and after 1909 by the compulsory license, into a non-exclusive right as to mechanical reproduction after the first recording, but exclusive, nevertheless, as to rewards of all recordings.[105] The judicial system is utilized in this respect in that the judicial gloss of court construction and interpretation is read into the statutory grant. Legal rules are

---

[105] 17 U.S.C. 1(e).

accorded their due as a matter of systematization and order of conceptions, and the rules of *stare decisis* and precedent are taken into consideration in the lawyer's own predictions thereon, his hypostasis of a prophecy, as to the meaning and interpretation of legal doctrine as adumbrated from the statute and cases.

But the lawyer's extrapolation of rationality and order, however circuitous and illogical the development of particular legal doctrines may be, out of the legislative and judicial systems is not made *in vacuo* of law disembodied from the purposes of law. The copyright is the basis for the formation of the market in literary and artistic property and so sets the organizational structure of the market, in the form of the legal norms utilized for business and non-profit forms of the market. The copyright jurisprudence, in a sense, structures the economy of copyright exploitation. Copyright does not represent thereby a merger of law into economics or absorption of legal doctrine into economic doctrine of the market. Rather statutory and judicial rules serve as the framework for the exploitation of the copyright. The rules do not disappear into the fundaments of the business of exploitation of the copyright, rather they serve as the framework therefor.

But the statutory rules in and of themselves are meager. The "sole liberty" of copyright was embodied substantially in one paragraph from 1790 to 1909, even as the scope of the rights under copyright expanded in the various revisions of the statute. The present statute, by contrast, is extensive in language by comparison, yet, upon analysis, the enumeration of the "exclusive rights" is bare bone. It takes judicial gloss to put flesh and meat on these rights as the practical meaning of the concepts is verified in the refinery of judicial battle and decision. The practitioner does look upon the statutory grant as the embodiment of commands for the benefit of the author or other copyright proprietor, and the copyright industries are structured accordingly. But the commands are taken as refined by litigation so that the legal practitioner, computer-like, intuitively rewires his memory bank to take into account the permutations and combinations of judicial decision, whatever the intrinsic rationality of rule making by the judicial process. The legal practitioner, therefore, responds flexibly to the commands of the sovereign as embodied in the numerous modifications and variegations of judicial decision. Counsel is required to assess and re-assess the meaning of the various rules as so formulated from time to time. Whatever counsel might do as a legal gladiator in trial to achieve a desired result in terms of the proffer of witnesses and evidence, and whatever counsel might do as a protagonist or antagonist to a given point of view of one or more of the interests involved in the structure of the market, whether institutional, individual or interstitial, the legal practitioner, as counsel, will respond to the legal system of copyright in terms of rights granted by Congress, *stare decisis* and precedent.

But counsel does not presuppose that the sum of the rights is expressed by the statutory grant or even the residuary common law copyright. The nature, scope and extent of the rights under copyright have a living, mutational experience as expressed by counsel on behalf of the market in terms of contract. One wonders how the rather limited exposition of rights granted by statute, denominated exclusive copyright, can be translated into so many permutations and combinations of specific rights. Indeed, the command of the sovereign as to the basis of the exclusive right is pre-emptive and complete. Only Congess can create such rights in implementation of the constitutional vesting of powers. Where Congress was held not to have done so as yet, as in the case of sound recordings, there were no such rights under copyright as to sound recordings. But within the scope of the legislation of Congress, as construed and interpreted by the courts, counsel extrapolates a variety of circumstances and details for exercise of such rights. Moreover, counsel deals with the manifestations of creativity comprising the ultimate fixation of form of the literary and artistic property which is the subject of copyright, for example, the motion picture. In constituting a chain of title of ownership in and to the film, the industry is structured so that the film producer will obtain clear title for purposes of distribution and exhibition, however the picture may be otherwise encumbered for reasons of financing by priorities as to recoupment extended to persons furnishing the financing or perhaps by means of parceling out of the rights on a territorial or media basis. The copyright may be seen as the crown jewel in the various measures taken to assure a clear chain of title because the copyright is symbolic and, indeed, prima facie evidence of ownership.[106]

The legal practitioner reflects the translation of legal rights accorded by statute and the judiciary into rights of contract. The commands of the sovereign per se as to copyright are inadequate tools for the commerce of the market in copyright. The legal norms of the exclusive copyright, e.g., the various publishing and performing rights specified in Sec. 1(e)[107] are inadequate in and of themselves to govern the course of commerce therein. Rather the practitioner and perforce, the market, draw

---

[106] 17 U.S.C. 209.
[107] 17 U.S.C. 1(e).

upon all of the tools of the law, all of its rules and norms as to contract, torts, and other legal notions, to break down the exclusive rights concretely into details of particular uses of any given right. As between the parties thereto, contract serves as its own regimen of control and a means of fission of rights under statutory copyright to the specific grant of rights under contract. So long as the parties abide by the provisions of the agreement, the extrapolation of species of rights out of the statutory genus of rights will govern their relations. Where the parties differ and resort to the courts or arbitration, then they are resorting to extra-party decision as to the meaning and interpretation of their market arrangement as to fission of rights.

Judicial determination, ultimately, is the means of classification of the generic rights under statutory copyright and represents a method of sanctioned ordering of the fissioned genus of statutory, exclusive rights into what is permissible and impermissible within the meaning and scope of the statutory bundle of rights. Such structuring is not necessarily limited to the actual language of the contract. The agreement may well be silent as to the new rights claimed as implied in the grant or reservation of rights. The judiciary will construe the ordination of the bundle of rights in the context of the market use thereof, as incorporated in contract or as failed to be included therein, in terms of the specifics of the market as utilized in contract. The prime mover of contract origination of specific rights as the fissionable rights of the generic bundle of statutory rights would be the legal practitioner who embodies the language of fissionable specific rights into contract and who also litigates its construction and interpretation. But contract is not, of course, solely the work product of the lawyer. Contracts of all sorts, oral, informal, even formal written documents, are entered into by parties without benefit of counsel. To that extent, whatever is said herein about the nature of contract as the source of fissionable rights, i.e., specific rights arising out of the bundle of rights in the copyright, would be true of contracts of all kinds, whether or not drafted by counsel. But it is the distinctive function of counsel to set the pace for the norms of the copyright industries both by legal draftsmanship and by advice of counsel as to the nature and meaning of the rules of the market by responding regularly and periodically to judicial interpretation as to the correct manner and nature of such contractual fission of the exclusive rights under copyright. This provides the basis for elaboration of the variety of forms employed in the various copyright industries and for modification thereof. Also, because copyright is not separate from other aspects of rights, e.g., the obtaining of a release from an actor in a film so as to perfect title thereto and to the copyright therein, failing which there might well be a violation of the actor's right of privacy, rights utilization as a practical matter is not always separately handled from the copyright aspects of creation and exploitation of literary and artistic property. Performance sometimes creates the copyright as in the production of the motion picture. Performance also creates one of the principal means of exploitation of copyright. The predicate of performance would seem to be the tracing of proper title in a work created by such performance, such as a motion picture, so that the copyright represents not only the sum total of the exclusive rights accorded by statute as interpreted by the courts but also, in the course of production thereof, a freedom from rights of others whether in respect of copyright or other rights. Thus, clear title means that there is a valid derivation of copyright in the basic work. It also means that no personal rights of others have been violated sufficient to constitute a violation of the right of privacy, a libel, slander or other tort with respect thereto.

In other words, fissionable rights in copyright are created in practice to account for permissible uses that would not be enjoined and/or be the subject of damages. The activities of creators—authors—and of interpreters—performers—give rise to the particular milieu in which the fissionable rights arise and are exercised. Legal practitioners, in particular, are instrumental in setting the environment for the exercise thereof by creating the forms for utilization thereof and by construing the legal norms, as pronounced by the courts and, from time to time, by the legislature. These and the pronouncements of administrative bodies, such as the rulings and regulations of the Copyright Office, have the force of law and are the basis for the arrangement of conceptions of the market as interpreted in the first instance by the legal practitioners. But counsel will attune thereto as legal decisions are handed down varying the context of interpretation by resort not only to those whose expressions of opinion are ultimately embodied in legal rules, the judiciary. Counsel will deem the congressional, judicial and administrative rules truly as authorities for abidance, i.e., governance in extrapolation of fissionable rights to be embodied in contract and, in general, in advice to clients as to the existing state of the law. Counsel will look to reports of these bodies, as shedding light on the meaning of the legal norms, where not otherwise explicit in the statute or decisions, as quasi-authoritative, such as committee reports of the Congress in connection with proposed legislation, or the reports of the Register of Copyrights with respect thereto.

Finally, counsel will rely upon the interpretations of various writers of law review articles, textbooks and treatises as oracular constructions of the meanings of the particular uses of fissionable rights, the proper fusion thereof into the legal system of protection of the bundle of exclusive rights ordained by statute, the consequences of the judicial rationalization thereof, and the desirable sequences of systematization by *stare decisis* and precedent.

Counsel might, in the course of such interplay, strive for the development of new rights as a judicial and possibly statutory expression of the natural rights of the citizenry, such as the right of privacy.[108] At other times, he might find that protection by tort as to rights might be circumscribed by existing rights, such as the pre-emption of copyright norms over unfair competition in certain circumstances by *Sears*[109] and *Compco.*[110]

Sec. 20.9. Rights in Copyright and the Market

Copyright, then, is the means for structuring the market for the arts. The actions and reactions of the market, taken in their broadest sense of the interplay of creation and performance with commerce, including the dissemination of derivative works in the same and other media, interact with legal norms at innumerable points of contracts and torts, in particular, to set the basis for anal-

---

[108] See Warren, Samuel D., and Brandeis, Louis D., The Right To Privacy, 4 Harv. L. Rev. 193 (1890) as reprinted in Hofstadter, Samuel H., The Development of the Right of Privacy in New York (1954); see Mayer, Michael F., Rights of Privacy (1972).

[109] Sears, Roebuck & Co. v. Stiffel Co., 376 U.S. 225 (1964).

[110] Compco Corp. v. Day-Brite Lighting, Inc., 376 U.S. 234 (1964).

ysis and evaluation of rights, both in gross, i.e., as a bundle of statutory rights denominated the exclusive rights comprising the copyright and, in particular, as fissioned into specific rights and uses. It is the role of the market, as developed through the instrumentality of the language and concepts of its legal practitioners, to provide the materials for creative development, exploitation and use thereof in reflection of the given state of jurisprudence at the time and as the materials for further systematization thereof by the judiciary and legislature.

The jurisprudence of flexible concepts is teleological in that it posits legal rules as purposeful and meaningful because they induce social relations which react upon and call into existence constant modifications of the legal norms as a response to the operation of the market which the legislation and judicial decisions brought into operation in the first place. The legal practitioner in this context, by responding rationally to legal norms and ordering the same for purposes of market operations as to the true value of the rights granted, i.e., the creation of fissionable rights and uses with respect thereto, acts both as a mechanism for flexible operation of the market and also as its barometer as to the judicial weather for change because of his or her constant interpretation and re-interpretation of the meaning of rights under copyright and the permissible limits of uses thereof as applied to the warp and woof of a rapidly changing technology of the arts. Thereby the creative manifestations of the market in its perorations of rights in detail, as they reflect creators, performers and users, are, by means of the jurisprudence of flexible concepts, converted into meaningful legal norms, however one or more of the interested parties in the market may disagree with the resultant legal construction.

The jurisprudence of flexible concepts is, then, both a description of the legal and economic processes of interaction as applied to copyright and the market, and a thesis of the attributes and sources of copyright and contract in respect of literary and artistic creation and performance.

PERFORMING ARTS MANAGEMENT AND LAW

by

JOSEPH TAUBMAN
Doctor Juridical Science
Member of New York Bar

Introduction by Jed Harris

VOLUME II

LAW-ARTS PUBLISHERS, INC.
New York, New York
1972

Library of Congress Cataloging in Publication Data

Taubman, Joseph.

Performing arts management and law.

1. Copyright—United States. 2. Performing arts—United States. I. Title.

KF4290.T35 344'.73'097 74-189328

ISBN 0-88238-055-9

Library of Congress Catalog Card No. 74-189328

Printed in the United States of America by
MEILEN PRESS INC., NEW YORK, N. Y.

By JOSEPH TAUBMAN

Author

Copyright and Antitrust (1960)

The Joint Venture and Tax Classification (1957)

Separate Stations (Poems) with Liffy Taubman (1963)

Editor

Subsidiary Rights and Residuals (1968)

The Business and Law of Music (1965)

Financing A Theatrical Production (1964)

Antitrust Bulletin (1962-1966)

Performing Arts Review (1969—)

To Liffy

With Gratitude

For Encouragement and Assistance

From Perception to Realization

TABLE OF CONTENTS

VOLUME II

Part III. Torts and Crimes

Part III

TORTS AND CRIMES

Chapter XXI

RIGHTS AND REMEDIES

Sec. 21.1. Rights and the Market

The essence of copyright is the creation of property, literary and artistic property, to be sure, but nonetheless property. This is accomplished by the independent origination of a work by the creator which is more than trivia. It is the irreducible minimum of the creator in this regard.[2] Statutory copyright is the recognition by the state of the right to protection therein in the creator and his assigns. Such protection is secured under the Constitution[3] by a grant of exclusivity in the work to the author and his assigns for limited periods of time, as provided in the present Copyright Act.[4] Whatever the ultimate nature of right therein at common law, i.e., whether or not the copyright is a right of property, natural right, right of personality or otherwise, the statutory right, as interpreted by the Supreme Court,[5] is substantially the investiture of a right of property in such creations of originality.

Property, by its very nature, has two attributes, the physical *res* that is the tangible form of the property and

---

[1] Alfred Bell & Co. Ltd. v. Catalda Fine Arts, Inc., 191 F. 2d 99 (2d Cir. 1951).

[2] Bleistein v. Donaldson Lithographing Co., 188 U.S. 239, 250 (1903).

[3] Constitution of the United States, Art. I, Sec. 8, Clause 8.

[4] 17 U.S.C. 1 *et seq.*

[5] Wheaton v. Peters, 8 Peters 591 (1834).

the bundle of rights characterizing ownership thereof.[6] The Copyright Act acknowledges the incorporeal nature of copyright, by differentiating the same from the tangible *res* in which it is embodied[7] and then provides for alienation by grant, assignment, mortgage and bequest by will,[8] as well as its method of devolution as to the renewal term.[9] It has been characterized as a branch of the law of intellectual property.[10] What is protected is the form of fixation of ideas—"writings", as it were, to use the constitutional term.[11] As Judge Mandelbaum stated, "It is well-settled law that an author has no property right in his ideas unless the same are given embodiment in a tangible form. It is the means of expressing these ideas rather than the ideas themselves which warrant protection."[12] It is this tangible form of expression which is protected by the enumerated exclusive rights granted to the author and his assigns under the statute,[13] against the world subject to the jurisdic-

---

[6] Sec. 6.1, *supra*. See Burdick, William L. Principles of Roman Law and Their Relation to Modern Law (1938), Chaps. XI-XIII, entitled, The Law of Property, at pp. 298-385. Referring to modern usage, Burdick states, ". . . we employ the word 'property' to designate both the subject matter, whether corporeal or incorporeal, of ownership, such as lands, tenements, hereditaments, goods, chattels, patent-rights, and rights of user, and also to designate any other valuable right or interest that one may possess or to which he has a legal claim." at p. 299.

[7] 17 U.S.C. 27.

[8] 17 U.S.C. 28.

[9] 17 U.S.C. 24.

[10] Fox, Monopolies and Patents 4 (1947).

[11] Note 3, *supra*. See Chap. V, *supra*.

[12] O'Brien v. RKO Radio Pictures, Inc., 69 U.S.P.Q. 367 (S.D. N.Y. 1946), at p. 368.

[13] 17 U.S.C. 1 *et seq.*

tion of our courts and compliance with the copyright formalities[14] and the exempted non-infringing fair use.[15]

Indeed, it may therefore be said that the statute invests the author, and, through him, the proprietor of the copyright, with affirmative rights of ownership in his original creations upon such compliance, the sum total of said rights, as set forth in the statute, constituting the copyright in the work. More exactly, the statute transforms the bundle of rights denominating the ownership in such creation under common law copyright into the bundle of rights denominating the ownership of copyright under the statute.[16] Perhaps, therefore, it is imprecise to refer to copyright as "only a negative right to prevent the appropriations of an author by another".[17] Judge Frank adverted to a somewhat comparable view, "For a copyright confers the exclusive right to copy the copyrighted work—a right not to have others copy it."[18] Judge Learned Hand was also impressed by the negative pregnant of the copyright when he states, "Copyright in any form, whether statutory or at common law, is a monopoly; it consists only in the power to prevent others from reproducing the copyrighted work."[19]

---

[14] 17 U.S.C. 10-14.

[15] See Latman, Alan, Fair Use of Copyrighted Works, Study No. 14, in Studies on Copyright (1963) at pp. 781-812 and Chap. XXV, *infra.*

[16] See 17 U.S.C. 2.

[17] Copinger and Skone James, Law of Copyright 2 (8th Ed. 1948).

[18] Note 1, *supra,* at p. 105.

[19] RCA Manufacturing Co., Inc. v. Whiteman, 114 F. 2d 86 (2d Cir. 1940), at p. 88.

It is submitted that the so-called negative right or right to prevent appropriation, copying or reproduction is the result of focussing on an attribute of the nature of the exclusive right generally, i.e., the correlative duty of forbearance on the part of third parties, since the nature of the right, at least in statutory form, is the investiture of a position by the state for the benefit of the recipient of the right in respect of the various attributes of ownership granted by the right.[20] Moreover, the grant of the copyright by statute may be generic in form, as in Sec. 1 of the Copyright Act, i.e., rights of copying, publishing, dramatization and performance.[21] Such rights may be deemed rights in gross which are then reduced to specifics in a variety of sub-rights subsumed under the generic rights by contract, custom and practice of the copyright industries.[22] In principle, the exclusive rights might be exercised without benefit of contract, for example, where the author as copyright proprietor publishes, dramatizes and performs by himself. Theoretically, too, if the creator as user were to make a first recording of music by himself even that would not necessarily effect entry into contracts. For in that event, even if there were no mechanical reproduction license or if the creator-proprietor were to refuse to give one, the user, after such first recording, could avail himself of the compulsory license under the statute[23] without resort to contract. For

---

[20] See Austin, John, Lectures on Jurisprudence, Third Ed. (1869) in Hall, Jerome, Readings in Jurisprudence (1938), at pp. 442-456.

[21] 17 U.S.C. 1.

[22] See Griswold v. Conn., 381 U.S. 479 (1965) where statutory rights are considered in relation to the principle of subsumption of specific rights under the statutory generic rights at p. 482.

[23] 17 U.S.C. 1(e).

all practical purposes, however, it is precisely by contract that market mechanisms are able to be created in respect of copyright and to operate within the structure of business organization deemed most advisable for operation within the legal and economic norms of the copyright industries.

But contract in respect of copyright posits a theory of rights, that is, of ability to trace a proper chain of title regarding ownership of the rights and licenses emanating from ownership of the copyright. Contract presupposes ability to delineate the scope of rights: (a) under the statute and at common law, as the case may be; and (b) with respect to uses and marketing possibilities, to delineate specific uses of the generic statutory rights by subsumption. The processes are legal and business functions. By tracing the scope of the rights and delineating the range of such uses, whether by undertaking systematic clearance procedures or otherwise, counsel enables copyright creators, proprietors and users to materialize a market with respect to literary and artistic properties. Contract is the means of materializing the market. The instrumentality therefor is the negotiation of agreements with respect to utilization, i.e., exploitation, of the various rights under copyright. Negotiation is the method utilized by enterprise for this purpose. But negotiation alone is generally insufficient; there is an interaction between such business negotiation and the lawyer's function in reducing the negotiations to contract. That is, legal form is the means of realization of the negotiations, both in a mediate sense of drafts which are revised as to legal formulation and deal points by the negotiators and counsel, and, in an ultimate sense, in the agreement of the parties reduced to final form of the contract entered into in writing by the parties. Of course, at times negotiations may lead to oral agreement, whether or not sanctified by the traditional handshake and whether or not counsel is involved at any point in relation thereto. But the norm of market utilization of the copyright is, by and large, the meshing of business negotiation and legal participation which is ultimately embodied in a written form of agreement that is largely the product of legal draftsmanship.[24]

Sec. 21.2. Rights: Duty of Forbearance: Remedies

The operation of the market mechanisms in this manner is possible because the law has specified the nature of the duty of forbearance by others with respect to the exclusive rights under copyright and the resultant remedies both in the owner of the copyright and in the state to right the wrongs caused by violation of this duty of forbearance. In short, the Congress has detailed a series of remedies to right the wrongs so caused and thereby to secure to the recipient of the copyright the benefits of the rewards for limited times of his proprietorship thereof.

Congress has so legislated to remedy wrongs by use of substantially a single term to describe the wrong. Chapter 2 of Title 17 of the United States Code is entitled "Infringement Proceedings".[25] The principal section thereof is Sec. 101[26] which is entitled "Infringement". This section begins, "Sec. 101. Infringement.—If any person shall infringe the copyright in any work protected under the copyright laws of the United States such person shall be liable".[27] The relief for such infringement is

[24] See Taubman, Essentials of Professional Draftsmanship, Chap. 9 of Lawyer's Encyclopedia (Prentice-Hall, 1963), at p. 161.

[25] 17 U.S.C. Chap. 2, covering Secs. 101-116.

[26] 17 U.S.C. 101.

[27] *Ibid.*

then set forth in subdivisions (a)-(e) thereof, as stated in the headings of each subdivision, to wit:

> "(a) Injunction.
>
> (b) Damages and profits : amount : other remedies.
>
> (c) Impounding during action.
>
> (d) Destruction of infringing copies and plates.
>
> (e) Royalties for use of mechanical reproduction of musical works." [28]

Sec. 104 then provides that willful infringement for profit is a misdemeanor subjecting the party guilty thereof to a possible jail term of one year, a fine of not less than $100 nor more than $1,000, or both, in the discretion of the court.[29] The remaining sections thereof specifying wrongs are not couched in terms of infringement as such. Thus, Sec. 105 provides that fraudulent notice of copyright, or removal or alteration thereof is a misdemeanor punishable by a fine of not less than $100 nor more than $1,000.[30] Secs. 106-109 relate to prohibition of importation of articles bearing false notice or piratical copies of copyrighted work and the forfeiture and destruction of articles prohibited importation.[31] But the critical fact as to these sections is that Chapter 2, which embraces all of these sections, is entitled "Infringement Proceedings".

---

[28] *Ibid.*

[29] 17 U.S.C. 104.

[30] 17 U.S.C. 105; Cf. Strauss, William S., Remedies Other Than Damages for Copyright Infringement, Study No. 24, in Studies on Copyright (1963), pp. 1029-1044, fn. 6, at p. 1031, that fraudulent notice does not relate to infringement.

[31] 17 U.S.C. 106-109.

Sec. 21.3. The Tort of Infringement

In other words, the gravamen of the wrong in each instance is the term "infringement" which is not otherwise defined in the Act, nor at common law.[32]

Webster's Dictionary defines the term "fringe" as an edge, border, margin.[33] The prefix "in" denotes within so that to infringe is to come within the edge, border or margin. Infringement is the act or process of coming within the edge, border or margin and the fact of having done so. Infringement of copyright would therefore denote the act or process of coming within the scope of the copyright, i.e., of the bundle of rights comprehended thereby, by transgressing the edge, border or margin of the rights of the holder thereof without leave of the owner of the right and without valid claim of right in the person transgressing such edge, border or margin. Webster therefore defines "infringement" as, "An encroachment or trespass on a right or privilege; a trespass, specif: The unlawful manufacture, use or sale of a patented or copyrighted article. Such an infringement is a tort in nature of a trespass on the case." [34]

In this regard, Plucknett has written, "The field of tort was by no means extensive until the last century." [35] Trespass is defined by Webster as a transgression, and the verb as exceeding the bounds of what is right or lawful.[36] Plucknett states in this regard, "As forms became

---

[32] Warner, Harry P., Radio and Television Rights (1953), Sec. 154, at p. 563.

[33] Webster's New International Dictionary, Second Ed., Unabridged, (1961), at p. 1010, "fringe".

[34] *Idem* at p. 1277, "infringement".

[35] Plucknett, Theodore, A Concise History of the Common Law, (Fourth Ed. 1948) at p. 432.

[36] Webster, *op. cit., supra,* note 33, at p. 2704.

settled, it was evident that writs of trespass for assault, breach of close, and asportation were practically common form; the others were an unclassified mass of instances where the writ had to be specially drafted so as to include a good deal of narrative matter. Such writs were said to be 'upon the case'—an expression constantly used of writs (and also of pleadings) which set out particular circumstances in unusual detail." [37] Plucknett points out that trespass was a violation of possession,[38] whereas damage, less direct, or caused by means less personal was case.[39] He points out that ". . . just after the middle of the fourteenth century it was not considered vital to distinguish the three forms of trespass, case and *assumpsit.* That task was left for the reign of Richard II, and more particularly to the fifteenth century, which seems to have felt a special vocation for establishing logical distinctions. As a result of that development, *assumpsit* became in effect contractual; and so we are left with trespass on the case." [40]

Infringement expresses this tortious nature in that the invasion or transgression of the copyright of another is for the purpose of wrongful taking of that right. Although copyright is not tangible, nevertheless infringement conveys the possessory nature of trespass in the wrongful taking, not of possession, because an intangible cannot, by definition, be possessed, but, by extension, of the incidents of the right. If ownership of tangible property, real and personal, in a legal sense, is the incidence of lawful relationship of the bundle of rights

---

[37] Plucknett, *op. cit., supra,* note 35, at p. 353.

[38] *Idem* at p. 441.

[39] *Idem* at pp. 440-441.

[40] *Idem* at pp. 442-443. (italics).

comprising ownership in a proprietary sense, then, by analogy, incorporeal hereditaments, such as copyrights, may also be deemed to be in a similar relationship. If trespass is an unlawful posession of chattels or an unlawful invasion of the rights of the person of another, as in an assault, then infringement is a form of trespass, in that there is an unlawful taking of possession of the fruits and proceeds of the rights of ownership of another and an invasion of the rights of ownership thereof. Thus, infringement, like trespass, denotes a wrongful crossing of the possessory scope of another, sanctified by law as the rights of another, without right in the infringer, which unlawfully exceeds the bounds of what the transgressor may do.

As stated by the Court in *American Code Co. Inc.* v. *Bensinger,* "The joinder of these parties as defendants proceeds upon the theory that infringement of a copyright is a tort, and that all persons concerned therein are jointly and severally liable." [41] The Court therein cited *Gross* v. *Van Dyk Gravure Co.* wherein it was stated in affirming the decree below, "This action is to recover damages for infringement against the appellant and the other defendant as joint and several tort-feasors." [42] Then the Court concluded in that case, "Therefore, as all united in infringing, all are responsible for the damages resulting from the infringement." [43]

Thus it may be seen that the characterization of infringement of copyright as a tort is judicial since the expression "tort" does not appear to be used in the Copyright Act to classify the nature of infringement.

---

[41] 282 Fed. 829 (2d Cir. 1922), at p. 834.

[42] 230 Fed. 412 (2d Cir. 1916), at p. 414.

[43] *Idem* at p. 414.

Indeed, the Court of Appeals, in denying that the Court of Claims had jurisdiction to hear actions against the United States for infringement of copyright, reaffirmed the tortious nature of infringement, stating, in *Turton* v. *United States,* "An action for damages by reason of infringement of a patent is one sounding in tort . . . We are of the opinion that an action for damages by reason of infringement of a copyright is likewise one sounding in tort." [44]

The decisions have impelled Harry P. Warner to conclude, " . . . copyright infringement is a tort".[45] Alan Latman and William S. Tager observe in this regard, "Copyright infringement consists of interference with any of a variety of rights and justifies resort to a number of remedies. Such interference may be intentional, negligent or accidental.

"The law of torts, from which these terms are borrowed . . ." [46]

By the same token, the Copyright Act does not specify that Sec. 104[47] thereof provides a criminal penalty, as such. The fact that willful infringement for profit is a crime is deduced from the statutory designation thereof as a misdeameanor. Since a misdemeanor, by definition, is a lesser crime than a felony, it may be said that having specified a category of crime, the statute does, in fact, set forth that it deals with criminal sanctions.

---

[44] 212 F. 2d 354 (6th Cir. 1954), at p. 355.

[45] Warner, Harry P., *op. cit., supra,* Sec. 156, at p. 608.

[46] Latman, Alan and Tager, William S., Liability of Innocent Infringers of Copyrights, Study No. 25, in Studies on Copyright (1963), pp. 1045-1066 at p. 1047.

[47] 17 U.S.C. 104.

Sec. 21.4. Civil and Criminal Remedies

Nevertheless the integration of remedies and sanctions of all kinds, tort and criminal, in Chapter 2 of the Copyright Act indicates that the purpose of the legislation is to provide a panoply of remedies and sanctions in respect of copyright from the two-fold view of the copyright proprietor as the recipient of the statutory rights as against third parties and the interest of the state to protect such recipient in those instances where the deterrent effect of action by the state might be required to implement the relief available to the copyright proprietor for infringement. For example, Webster defines the term "plagiarize" as, "To steal or purloin and pass off as one's own (the ideas, words, artistic productions, etc. of another)..." [48] As to plagiarism, the Court in *Cloth* v. *Hyman* noted, "To charge an author with wilfully infringing a copyright by plagiarism is to charge him with a crime. 17 U.S.C.A. Sec. 104".[49] While plagiarism is only one form of infringement, for example, an infringer might not purport to take credit as author of someone else's work by either claiming a right that is subsequently proven not to exist or that the proprietor's right is not founded in law because the work is in the public domain, nevertheless it indicates that willful infringement may be hydra-headed, sounding both in tort and in crime. But the dual quality as to willfulness is an instrumentality of the state in policing copyrights so as to enable the Copyright Act to be implemented generally and at the same time provide a further coercive measure, the might of the sovereign power, in giving the copyright proprietor the assistance of an additional possible remedy, as a specter

---

[48] Webster, *op. cit., spura,* note 33, at p. 1878, "plagiarize".

[49] 146 F. Supp. 185 (S.D.N.Y. 1956), at p. 192.

to assist the proprietor by means of the full force and effect of the sovereign power, over and above the civil process, in bringing the malefactor willful infringer the realization of the criminal as well as civil risks entailed. Speaking of the criminal sanctions of Sec. 104[50] as to willful infringement of copyright, William S. Strauss has observed, "This section has been rarely invoked. The infrequency of its use, however, does not disapprove of its efficacy as a deterrent to willful and reckless infringements." [51]

Perhaps the deterrent effect of the civil side of infringement proceedings may also be operative to inhibit litigation by reason of compliance with the Copyright Act. Joseph D. Karp has commented on the relative paucity of copyright litigation, "In a sense, copyright litigation is limited. The number of litigated actions which are actually tried throughout the United States is small compared to other actions—probably 25 or 30 in any one year. . . .

"The paucity of copyright litigation is somewhat surprising when it is considered that an average of 200,000 works of art are deposited each year in the Copyright Office in Washington for the purpose of copyright registration. They include books and plays and musical compositions and lectures and even statues." [52]

Although Karp attributes the reluctance to litigate to hesitancy to incur the expense of litigation unless the would-be litigant believes that the financial success of

---

[50] 17 U.S.C. 104.

[51] Strauss, William S., *op. cit., supra,* note 30 at p. 1040.

[52] Karp, Joseph D., Copyright Litigation, in 7 Copyright Problems Analyzed 1951, reprinted in Copyright Problems Analyzed, Fred B. Rothman & Co. (1966), pp. 143-184, at p. 143.

the work at issue provides the overriding incentive,[53] it would appear that the array of remedies available against infringers would also serve to act as a deterrent to infringement, and thereby diminish proceedings against infringers.

Sec. 21.5. Actions: State and Federal in American History

What is noteworthy in the history of American copyright legislation is that the term "infringement" was not used by the states which passed copyright statutes before Congress enacted such legislation and thereafter was not used by Congress prior to 1870!

The Resolution of the Continental Congress of May 2, 1783,[54] recommending that the several states enact copyright legislation, was silent as to penalties that might be incurred in violation of such statutes. Such state legislation, whether adopted before or after the Resolution was promulgated, used several concepts as to liability and damages, but not infringement.

Connecticut, for example, provided that any person engaging in the enumerated publishing rights granted to authors under its statute without the consent of the proprietor forfeit and pay double the value thereof to the proprietor.[55] It is to be noted that Connecticut passed its statute as early as January, 1783.[56] Another remedy in

---

[53] *Ibid.*

[54] Resolution of May 2, 1783, Continental Congress, See Copyright Enactments Laws Passed in the United States Since 1783 Relating to Copyright, Copyright Bulletin No. 3 (Revised) (1963) at p. 1.

[55] Act of Jan. 1783, sess., State of Connecticut; Copyright Enactments, *Idem* at pp. 1-4.

[56] *Ibid.*

this statute was to provide that a publisher of an unpublished manuscript without consent of the author or proprietor, who lived in the United States, was liable to such author or proprietor for his just damages.[57]

Massachusetts, by its Act of Mar. 17, 1783,[58] provided a similar concept of printing and publishing without consent of the author or proprietor except that the wrongdoer was required to forfeit and pay to the author or assigns a sum not exceeding 3,000 pounds nor less than 5 pounds. Such sum was to be recovered "by an action of debt". There was no provision as to unpublished manuscripts.

Maryland, the third state to enact its own statute before the Resolution of the Continental Congress, also adopted a publication without consent clause, only without consent of the proprietor. Its statute of Apr. 21, 1783[59] provided for forfeiture to the copyright proprietor of such books and writings so published without consent as well as a forfeiture of two pence per sheet. The statute provided that all actions and information for any offense had to commence within 12 months after the offense was committed.[60]

New Jersey, by its Act of May 27, 1783,[61] followed the Connecticut concept of publication without consent sub-

---

[57] *Idem* at p. 3. Cf., 17 U.S.C. 2. Common law copyright being reserved to the states under Sec. 2, unpublished manuscripts not registered for copyright under Sec. 12 of the Act, 17 U.S.C. 12 presumably could be similarly covered by state legislation today.

[58] Act of Mar. 17, 1783, Commonwealth of Massachusetts; Copyright Enactments, *Idem* at pp. 4-5.

[59] Act of Apr. 21, 1783, State of Maryland; Copyright Enactments, *Idem* at pp. 5-6.

[60] *Idem* at p. 6.

[61] Act of May 27, 1783, State of New Jersey; Copyright Enactments, *Idem* at pp. 6-7.

jecting the offender to forfeit and pay double the value recovered by the author or copyright proprietor. On the other hand, New Hampshire[62] and Rhode Island[63] followed the Massachusetts formula except that the former set limits for the recovery in an action of debt of 5 pounds to 1,000 pounds, whereas the latter used the same ceiling as Massachusetts of 3,000 pounds.

Pennsylvania,[64] like New Jersey, followed the Connecticut concept of forfeiting and payment of double the value by publication without consent. The reference to publication without consent in this context is a short cut for stating that the publication of the enumerated publishing rights, i.e., printing, publication, sale without consent, carried the forfeiture and payment consequences.

South Carolina[65] modified the Maryland concept in that it not only provided for forfeiture of the offending sheets published, etc., without consent of the copyright proprietor, to the proprietor for destruction but that the offender also surrender one shilling per sheet, one moiety thereof going to the state and the other to the person bringing suit. Its statute awarded costs to the prevailing defendant[66] and included a short statute of limitations for bringing suit, after the offense was committed, of three months.[67]

---

[62] Act of Nov. 7, 1783, State of New Hampshire; Copyright Enactments, *Idem* at pp. 8-9.

[63] Dec. 1783, Sess. State of Rhode Island; Copyright Enactments, *Idem* at pp. 9-10.

[64] Act of Mar. 15, 1784, Commonwealth of Pennsylvania; Copyright Enactments, *Idem* at pp. 10-11.

[65] Act of Mar. 26, 1784, State of South Carolina; Copyright Enactments, *Idem* at pp. 11-14.

[66] *Idem* at p. 14.

[67] *Idem* at p. 14.

Virginia,[68] on the other hand, followed Connecticut in providing for forfeiture and payment of double the value, whereas North Carolina[69] followed a variation of the Connecticut and South Carolina formulations in providing for surrender of offending books to the proprietor plus double the value of offending books imported, one moiety thereof to go to the state, the other, to the injured party.

Georgia[70] followed Connecticut in providing that the offender forfeit and pay double the value to the proprietor with a comparable provision that publication of an unpublished manuscript without consent of the author or proprietor subjected the offender to an action for just damages. New York[71] followed the formulation of Connecticut and Georgia in both respects.

It is noteworthy that three states appeared to exclude from copyright protection censorable works as therein defined; Connecticut,[72] Georgia[73] and New York[74] all excluded works that might be "prophane, treasonable, defamatory, or injurious to government, morals or religion".

As might be anticipated, the Constitution of the United States[75] was silent as to remedies for violation of the exclusive rights of authors. The first copyright statute, the

---

[68] Act of Oct., 1785, Commonwealth of Virginia; Copyright Enactments, *Idem* at pp. 14-15.

[69] Act of Nov. 19, 1785, State of North Carolina; Copyright Enactments, *Idem* at pp. 15-17.

[70] Act of Feb. 3, 1786, State of Georgia; Copyright Enactments, *Idem* at pp. 17-19.

[71] Act of Apr. 29, 1786, State of New York; Copyright Enactments, *Idem* at pp. 19-21.

[72] Note 55, *supra,* at p. 3.

[73] Note 70, *supra,* at p. 19.

[74] Note 71, *supra,* at p. 21.

[75] Art. I, Sec. 8, Clause 8.

Act of May 31, 1790[76] adopted the basic formulation common to all of the states which enacted copyright legislation, to wit, the requirement of obtaining consent of the copyright owner, failing which the enumerated rights of publication subjected the offender to liability. The first federal formulation followed that of South Carolina in providing for a forfeiture of offending books, maps and charts to the author or proprietor for destruction plus a forfeiture and payment of fifty cents per sheet, to be shared one moiety by the United States, the other by the author or proprietor, to be recovered by an action of debt. Sec. 6 thereof provided however, that the publication of any manuscript without the prior consent of the author or proprietor, (being a citizen or resident of the United States) shall subject such offender to all damages caused by such injury, "to be recovered by a *special action on the case*".[77] It is noteworthy in this respect that Massachusetts, New Hampshire and Rhode Island specified that forfeiture of double the value in the event of publication without consent was likewise cognizable by an action of debt[78] while the statutes of Connecticut, Georgia and New York as to the right of action for damages for publication of an unpublished manuscript did not specify the nature of the action brought thereon.[79]

It would seem that the federal reference to a special action on the case represents a shift from notions of action of debt, from an action sounding in contract to one sounding in tort. Plucknett refers to the nature of the action of debt at common law as follows:

[76] Act of May 31, 1790, 1 Stat. 124 (1845); Copyright Enactments, *Idem* at pp. 22-24.

[77] *Idem* at p. 24. (emphasis added).

[78] Notes 58, 62-63, *supra.*

[79] Notes 55-56, 70-71, *supra.*

> "The oldest and most important was the action of debt which lay for formal contract ('obligations') under seal if they specified a sum certain, and for a number of real contracts, that is to say, contracts where a *res* had passed between the parties. Debt could thus be used to recover the price of goods sold and delivered, to recover money lent, and to recover the rent on a lease even although the lease was not written. It could also be used for certain special purposes such as the recovery of statutory penalties and for the enforcement of obligations arising out of suretyship." [80]

It is in the recovery of statutory penalties that the action of debt becomes pertinent to the statutes. One must surmise that the theory enabling such recovery of statutory penalties, which is not, in fact, a real obligation, with other forms of the action of debt lies in a legal fiction. The law assumes by a legal fiction that the defendant is indebted to the plaintiff, i.e., obligated to him, by reason of his breach of his duty of forbearance in the amount of the penalties imposed by the statute. And so the claim of the plaintiff for recovery of statutory penalties is analogized to the action of debt in the form of true obligations by an assumption.

By contrast, the action on the case was a progenitor sounding in tort. Plucknett states, "For many centuries it would have been impossible to state the common law otherwise than in the form of a list of various torts which have been remedied by various forms of action . . . It was

---

[80] Plucknett, *op. cit., supra,* note 35, at p. 597 (italics); see also, 1 Williston on Contracts, Sec. 11, Revised Ed. (1936), at pp. 16-17 entitled, Debt.

the action of case which first evolved a principle sufficiently wide to cover many of the constantly recurring forms of tort. This principle was negligence . . ." [81] At first blush, one wonders how negligence relates to an action founded on the case relating to publication of a manuscript without the consent of the author. Plucknett observes, ". . . case was available where the defendant had 'neglected' to do his duty (such as enclose, or repair, his property). Hence the combination of negligent action and passive inaction covers a fairly large part of the ground included in 'case'." [82] If case was available where the defendant neglected to do his duty, it might be paraphrased that the defendant had failed to abide, in the case of the federal statute, by his duty of forbearance from publication without the consent of the copyright proprietor of the manuscript. If the author of the manuscript had the copyright therein at common law, then its publication without his consent constituted a neglect by the party so publishing the same of that party's duty of forbearance from publication without such consent. Hence, the statute provided for recovery of damages by a special action on the case by the aggrieved author. The first copyright statute therefore provided a remedy which sounded in tort, in allowing such an action on the case.

Sec. 21.6. The Crime of Fraudulent Notice or Removal or Alteration of Notice

By contrast, the analogous fraudulent notice of copyright under Sec. 105[83] of the present Act is a criminal statute in that the same and various other acts are characterized as a misdemeanor punishable by fine of not less

---

[81] Plucknett, *Idem* at p. 434.
[82] Plucknett, *Idem* at p. 443.
[83] 17 U.S.C. 105.

than $100 nor more than $1,000. One might question whether publication without consent of the author or proprietor is analogous to imposition of fraudulent notice of copyright. In the instance of publication without consent, the party wrongfully publishing the same might publish the same with or without notice. Publication without notice in the instance of such publication by the author or copyright proprietor would place the work in the public domain,[84] but not so publication without authority of the proprietor.[85] Nimmer states the proposition thus, ". . . generally notice constitutes a *sine qua non* to copyright. It is to be noted, however, that the notice requirement is applicable only with respect to *authorized* publications. Therefore a publication devoid of notice will not invalidate the copyright unless it is shown that such publication occurred by or under the authority of the copyright proprietor." [86]

However, a publication without the consent of the author or copyright proprietor might be made by a third party in the mistaken belief of color of right to do so. It would not constitute fraudulent intent if in such instance the party also affixed a notice of copyright. On the other hand, an unauthorized willful omission of notice of copyright by a party presumably would not come under Sec. 105 since there would be neither insertion nor impression of any copyright notice nor removal or alteration thereof,

---

[84] 17 U.S.C. 10, 21. Circular 3 of the Copyright Office cautions readers of the circular, entitled, Copyright Notice, "NOTE: Once a work has been published without the required copyright notice, copyright protection is *lost permanently* and cannot be regained." (italics in bold type).

[85] Gerlach-Barklow Co. v. Morris and Bendien, Inc., 23 F. 2d 159 (2d Cir. 1927).

[86] Nimmer on Copyright (1970), Sec. 82, at p. 302. (italics).

there being none in the first instance.[87] Thus, there must be a state of facts of some affirmative act of affixing copyright notice or alteration or removal of same in order for the section to apply even though the omission of notice might be fraudulent. Since the statute is intended to cover fraudulent acts, i.e., affirmative acts with intent to deceive without authority of the copyright proprietor, it would follow that such fraudulent affirmative acts would no more affect the copyright status of the author or proprietor than unauthorized omission of notice.

Note that the affirmative acts of the statute relate to affixation, impression, alteration or removal with respect to an "uncopyrighted article." [88] In discussing this section, Nimmer remarks that it means, ". . . without statutory copyright in the United States. A work is therefore 'uncopyrighted' even if it commands either common law copyright or the copyright protection of a foreign nation." [89] Technically, therefore, the criminal liability does not relate to infringement of copyright because the uncopyrighted article is not protected by statutory copyright. That is, the unauthorized fraudulent affirmative act does not have any legal effect on the author or proprietor of the work. If the uncopyrighted article were a literary work under common law copyright, it would continue to remain so and the rights of the author or proprietor thereof would not be affected or impaired by the fraudulent notice because the publication must be an authorized one, whereas the insertion or impression of a fraudulent notice would obviously have been done without authority. Thus the rights of the author or proprietor are preserved

---

[87] See 17 U.S.C. 105.

[88] *Ibid.*

[89] Nimmer, *op. cit., supra,* Sec. 163, at p. 709.

as an unpublished work under Sec. 2 of the Copyright Act, which reads:

> "Sec. 2. Rights of Author or Proprietor of Unpublished Work.—Nothing in this title shall be construed to annul or limit the right of the author or proprietor of any unpublished work, at common law or in equity, to prevent the copying, publication, or use of such unpublished work without his consent, and to obtain damages therefor." [90]

The affirmative acts being done with fraudulent intent perforce are in violation of the rights of the author or proprietor in the unpublished work without consent. Therefore such author or proprietor is relegated to his remedies at common law for damages. Thus the claim would ordinarily be for common law infringement of copyright.[91]

However, in *Scarves By Vera, Inc.* v. *American Handbags, Inc.*,[92] plaintiff sought a preliminary injunction restraining defendant from removing plaintiff's copyright notice from linens and towels embodying plaintiff's copyright marks. The Court held, " . . . injunctive relief expressly provided for in the case of false use of copyright notice was deleted in 1909 when criminal sanctions were written into the law for the false removal of a copyright notice. Moreover, 17 U.S.C. Sec. 105, which plaintiff relies on, has apparently never been used to

---

[90] 17 U.S.C. 2.

[91] Warner, *op. cit., supra,* note 32, Sec. 150, at p. 522 refers to infringement of common law copyright. His footnote 1 thereto indicates that he prefers to use the terms "piracy", "plagiarism " and "infringement" interchangeably in his Chap. XV entitled, Infringement of Copyright, at pp. 522-624.

[92] 188 F. Supp. 255 (S.D.N.Y. 1960).

support injunctive relief. In view of the above and the general rule that equity will not enjoin the commission of crimes, I do not think this court has the power to issue an injunction restraining defendant from removing plaintiff's copyright notices." [93] The plaintiff also sought to show that the violation was of a specific property right, although the same was also a crime because the defendant's removal of copyright notice destroyed plaintiff's copyright and placed it in the public domain. This the Court indicated, the defendant could not do by its own actions without authority of the plaintiff.[94]

Nimmer cites this case as authority for the proposition that removal or alteration of notice does not give rise to civil liability for copyright infringement.[95] At the same time, he has indicated that neither does insertion or impression of a notice.[96] But the reference to the common effect of no civil liability therefor proceeds from differing ambits. In the case of wrongful insertion or impression, there is no civil liability for infringement because the wrongful insertion with fraudulent intent upon an uncopyrighted article leaves the uncopyrighted article in *status quo ante,* that is, under common law copyright. The wrongful insertion or impression does not convert the work from one under common law copyright to one under statutory copyright. Its status remains as it was before the wrongful purported change of status of the copyright. Since the remedies available for common law copyright are not covered by the statute, which relate only to infringement proceedings under statutory copyright, the complaining author or proprietor must seek his

---

[93] *Idem* at p. 257.
[94] *Idem* at pp. 257-8.
[95] Nimmer, *op. cit., supra,* Sec. 163, at p. 710.
[96] *Idem* at pp. 709-710.

remedies at common law. Not so the aggrieved owner of the work where there has been an alteration or removal of notice of copyright with fraudulent intent. Here there is an existing notice in being, presumably one rightfully inserted by the author or proprietor. This presupposition of publication and affixation of notice implies that the work is already covered by statutory copyright. This being so, the owner necessarily must rely upon his remedies under the statute as to infringement.

In each instance, however, whether the wrongful act be insertion or impression, on the one hand, or alteration or removal, on the other, the wrongful act does not affect the copyright status because such act was unauthorized by the author or proprietor. Therefore, one looks for infringement purposes to the status of the work prior to the wrongful act in order to determine its status for infringement, and, concomitantly, what other acts were undertaken by the party committing the crime under Sec. 105.[97] The Copyright Act, being pre-emptive, would supersede state law as to the acts declared to be a crime thereunder. Thus, presumably there would be no claim for damages as an infringement of common law copyright for affixing a notice with fraudulent intent. However, if the same act were also accompanied by actual publication, i.e., offering copies of the work for sale, without authority of the copyright owner, then the publication without consent would subject the party wrongfully publishing the work to damages under common law, pursuant to the reservation of such matters to the states under Sec. 2 of the Copyright Act.[98]

---

[97] 17 U.S.C. 105.

[98] 17 U.S.C. 2.

Similarly, if the wrongdoer who altered a copyright notice also undertook to exploit one or more of the exclusive rights under the statutory copyright carried by the original notice rightfully contained thereon, then such party would be subject to the array of remedies that the copyright owner might resort to under the statute by way of civil infringement proceedings.

Thus, Sec. 105 of the present Act,[99] a criminal statute, and Sec. 6 of the Act of 1790,[100] a civil liability statute, both purport to cover the consequences of certain wrongful acts which, by reason of the wrong committed, if it were to stand, might conceivably have the effect of converting a work from one covered by common law copyright to one secured by statutory copyright protection. In each instance federal jurisdiction is asserted to prevent the consequences of wrongful cross-over from state coverage to purported federal protection.

Sec. 21.7. Forfeitures and Penalties in Federal Legislation

But it did not take Congress long to differentiate the penalty consequences of addition of new rights and/or categories subject to statutory copyright to the bundle of rights constituting the statutory copyright. The Act of 1802[101] added prints and engravings to the items secured by copyright. Sec. 2[102] thereof secured copyright in prints and engravings, in addition to the books, maps

---

[99] 17 U.S.C. 105.

[100] Act of May 31, 1790, 1st Cong., 2d Sess., Chap. 15, 1 Stat. 145 (1845). Copyright Enactments, note 54, *supra,* at pp. 22-24.

[101] Act of Apr. 29, 1802, 7th Cong., 1st Sess., Chap. 36, 2 Stat. 171 (1845). Copyright Enactments, *Idem,* at pp. 24-26.

[102] *Idem,* Sec. 2. Copyright Enactments, *Idem,* at p. 25.

and charts covered by the Act of 1790.[103] Sec. 3[104] of the Act of 1802 provided for forfeiture of the plates of the printer or engraver publishing, etc., without consent of the copyright owner for destruction thereof and forfeiture of one dollar per print, one moiety thereof to go to the party bringing the action, the other to the United States. Since there was no reference therein to books, maps and charts nor to the nature of the action, it must be presumed that the provisions of Sec. 2 of the Act of 1790,[105] providing for forfeiture of 50 cents per sheet continued in effect and that the reference to bringing of an action on debt, set forth therein, would be deemed extended to prints and engravings under Sec. 3 of the Act of 1802.[106] Thus, a different rate of forfeitures governed prints and engravings from books. Congress no doubt took into consideration differing values of the respective items as well as differing economic effects. Indeed, the same is true in the present Act with respect to the varying subjects under copyright, e.g., $10 for every infringing copy of a painting, statue, or sculpture; $1 for infringing copy of other works; infringing newspaper reproduction of copyrighted photographs ranging from $50-$200.[107]

Sec. 4 of the Act of 1802[108] set forth a 2 year statute of limitations and also provided a civil liability for inser-

---

[103] Act of 1790, note 100, *supra.* Copyright Enactments, *Idem* at pp. 22-24.

[104] Act of 1802, note 101, *supra,* Sec. 3, Copyright Enactments, *Idem,* at pp. 25-26.

[105] Act of 1790, note 100, *supra,* Sec. 2, Copyright Enactments, *Idem,* at pp. 22-23.

[106] Act of 1802, note 101, *supra,* Sec. 3, Copyright Enactments, *Idem* at pp. 25.

[107] 17 U.S.C. 101(b).

[108] Act of 1802, note 101, *supra,* Sec. 4, Copyright Enactments, note 54, *supra,* at p. 26.

tion of impression of copyright without legally having acquired the same of $100, payable one moiety to the person suing and the other moiety to the United States, recoverable by an action of debt. This statute may be said to be the progenitor of Sec. 105 of the present Act[109] except that it imposed civil rather than criminal liability.

The Act of 1819[110] extended injunctive relief by providing that the circuit courts would have cognizance in equity as well as in law with authority to grant injunctions with respect to copyrights and patents with a writ of error or appeal from all judgment and decrees going to the Supreme Court of the United States.

The Act of 1831[111] extended statutory copyright to musical compositions as part of its general revision of copyright legislation. However, it transposed maps and charts to the $1 per print forfeiture provisions applicable to prints and engraving, along with musical compositions, while it retained the 50 cent per sheet clause as to books. Sec. 6 of the Act of 1831[112] specified that the forfeiture as to books shall be recoverable by an action of debt. Curiously, Sec. 7[113] which related to the forfeitures as to prints, etc., failed to specify the nature of the action to be brought for such recovery. But since the forfeiture was substantially the same as for books, it must be presumed that the draftsman felt the reference to the nature of the action would be surplusage.

---

[109] 17 U.S.C. 105.

[110] Act of Feb. 15, 1819, 15th Cong., 2d Sess., Chap. 19, 3 Stat. 481 (1846). Copyright Enactments, note 54, *supra,* at pp. 26-27.

[111] Act of Feb. 3, 1831 (Revision), Copyright Enactments, *Idem* at pp. 27-31.

[112] *Idem,* Sec. 6, Copyright Enactments, *Idem,* at pp. 28-29.

[113] *Idem,* Sec. 7, Copyright Enactments, *Idem,* at p. 29.

The statute contained provisions as to wrongful insertion or impression of copyright at the same forfeiture of $100 by an action of debt, and as to wrongful publication of a manuscript, recovery of damages by special action on the case, injunctive relief and a two year statute of limitations. This is so because the prior acts were repealed by this statute. Sec. 10 of the Act of 1831[114] added a provision allowing full costs upon any recovery.

The Act of 1856[115] was the first statute which extended the copyright to dramatic performance. In so doing, it provided for damages for performance without the consent of the author or proprietor "to be sued for and recovered by action on the case or other equivalent remedy" [116] at the rate of $100 for the first performance and $50 for every subsequent performance with costs. Thus, the first statute which granted exclusive rights beyond the traditional publishing rights continued the formulation of remedies in terms of the nature of the action to be pleaded. The statute purported to preserve process in equity, presumably including injunctive relief as one of the most important equitable processes. The clause making the statute prospective read as follows: "*Provided, nevertheless,* That nothing herein enacted shall impair any right to act, perform, or represent a dramatic composition as aforesaid, which right may have been acquired, or shall in future be acquired by any manager, actor, or other person previous to the securing of the copyright for the said composition, . . ." [117] The first part of the proviso was intended to make the operation of the statute prospective so as not

---

[114] *Idem,* Sec. 10, Copyright Enactments, *Idem,* at p. 30.

[115] Act of Aug. 18, 1856, 34th Cong., 1st Sess., Chap. 169, 11 Stat. 138 (1859), Copyright Enactments, *Idem,* at p. 33.

[116] *Ibid.*

[117] *Ibid.* (italics).

to impair existing obligations of contract. However, the reference to future acquisition of rights of performance prior to securing copyright would indicate that the stage right, as granted by the statute, was an incident of the bundle of rights secured by copyright and that the stage right under the statute would not exist unless copyright were secured, and whatever performing rights were secured prior to statutory copyright would not be impaired. Presumably, if statutory copyright had not been secured, the remedy would be at common law in respect of the common law copyright regarding such rights and obligations so that the parties would have to seek redress in the state courts.

The Act of 1861 provided that writs of error or appeal would lie to the Supreme Court of the United States in respect of the copyright statute without regard to the value or sum in controversy in the action.[118]

The Act of March 3, 1865[119] extended the copyright to photographs and stated that the provisions applicable (under the Act of 1831)[120] as to books, on the one hand, and the remaining enumerated subjects of copyright, prints, etc., should apply to photographs, upon the same conditions as were applicable to prints and engravings.

In many respects, the Act of July 8, 1870[121] was the progenitor of the present Act. The Act repealed the prior

---

118 Act of Feb. 18, 1861, 36th Cong., 2d Sess., Chap. 37, 12 Stat. 130 (1863), Copyright Enactments, *Idem,* at p. 34.

119 Act of Mar. 3, 1865, 38th Cong., 2d Sess., Chap. 126, 13 Stat. 540 (1876), Copyright Enactments, *Idem,* at pp. 34-35.

120 Act of Feb. 3, 1831 (Revision), 21st Cong., 2d Sess., Chap. 16, Copyright Enactments, *Idem,* at pp. 27-31.

121 Act of July 8, 1870, 41st Cong., 2d Sess., Chap. 230, Copyright Enactments, *Idem,* at pp. 36-41.

legislation in effect and therefore purported to be comprehensive in scope. For the first time, Congress used the term "infringement" in its copyright legislation. Sec. 97 thereof reads in part, "*And be it further enacted,* That no person shall maintain an action for infringement of his copyright unless he shall give notice thereof . . ." [122] There followed language containing the notice provisions of the statute. This was the only reference therein to infringement. However, the specification of actions was materially modified. Sec. 98 covered wrongful insertion or impression of copyright. Although it retained the same forfeiture provisions as the previous legislation in effect, $100, one moiety to the aggrieved party, the other, to the United States, it no longer specified recovery by the form of the action. It simply provided for recovery by action, rather than by action of debt as theretofore.[122a] Moreover, the offending party publishing without consent of the author or proprietor under Sec. 99[123] not only forfeited books, but the proprietor was authorized to sue for damages, without specification of any rate, in a civil action, without detailing the nature of the action. On the other hand, by Sec. 100, as to the remaining matters which were the subject of copyright and additional items made subject of copyright under that Act,—statues, statuary, models or designs intended to be perfected and executed as works of fine arts—there was a forfeiture of the plates, etc., to the copyright owner with statutory damages of $1 per sheet continued, except that as to a painting, statue, or statuary, it was $10 per copy. The moiety principle continued in effect. Recovery was by action, without specification of the nature thereof,

---

[122] *Idem,* Sec. 97, Copyright Enactments, *Idem,* at p. 38. (italics).
[122a] *Idem,* Sec. 98, Copyright Enactments, *Idem,* at pp. 38-39.
[123] *Idem,* Sec. 99, Copyright Enactments, *Idem,* at p. 39.

in any court of competent jurisdiction.[124] The public performance without consent of the copyright proprietor continued to be subject to the same rate of damages by Sec. 101[125] to be recovered by action, without any longer specifying the nature of the action. Congress, in granting the stage right by the Act of 1856,[126] had provided for recovery of damages by an action on the case or other equivalent remedy. Yet Congress, by the Act of 1870, in eliminating reference to the nature of the action as to dramatic performance without consent, in the very next section, Sec. 102,[127] relating to publication without consent of a manuscript, retained provisions for recovery of damages by action on the case. The provisions of prior statutes as to injunctive relief, appeals, costs and statute of limitations were carried over from prior statutes and embodied in the Act of 1870.

Thus, for the first time, specific reference to the action of debt as a remedy for recovery of forfeitures was eliminated while the same statute embodied the first reference to infringement. By retaining the one reference to action on the case, while eliminating reference to action of debt and mentioning infringement for the first time, it would seem that Congress was moving in the direction of comprehending civil liability under statutory copyright by actions sounding in tort. However, this cannot be said as to the penalty of the author or proprietor for failure to make the requisite deposit. The Act of 1867[128] provided

---

[124] *Idem,* Sec. 100, Copyright Enactments, *Idem,* at p. 39.

[125] *Idem,* Sec. 101, Copyright Enactments, *Idem,* at p. 39.

[126] Act of Aug. 18, 1856, note 115, *supra,* Copyright Enactments, *Idem,* at p. 33.

[127] Act of July 8, 1870, Sec. 102, note 121, *supra,* Copyright Enactments, *Idem,* at pp. 39-40.

[128] Act of Feb. 18, 1867, 39th Cong., 2d Sess., Chap. 43, 14 Stat. 395 (1868), Copyright Enactments, *Idem,* at pp. 36-37.

for a penalty of $25 for failure of the proprietor to make the requisite deposit within one month after publication. But that Act failed to specify the nature of the action. Nevertheless, Sec. 94[129] of the Act of July 8, 1870 specified that such penalty shall be collected in an action of debt. However, the recovery was to be made by the Librarian of Congress, unlike prior legislation specifying action of debt brought by the author or proprietor. The differences are two-fold; the Librarian of Congress is an instrumentality of the United States. The recovery, therefore, was presumably made in the sovereign capacity of the state. Moreover, the recovery was of a penalty for failure to make timely deposit. Presumably the penalty was due and owing upon failure to make timely deposit so that its recovery sounded in debt because upon such failure, there accrued a penalty for such default which was in the nature of an obligation which is deemed due and owing to the sovereign recoverable by the action of debt.

In 1873, Congress provided that jurisdiction of the courts of the United States shall be exclusive of the courts of the several states " . . . of all cases arising under the patent-rights or copyright laws of the United States." [130] However, the Act of Dec. 1, 1873,[131] (Revision) which revised the copyright statutes, restated the substance of the prior Act of 1870;[132] any revisions as to the nature of the actions

---

[129] Act of July 8, 1870, Sec. 94, note 121, *supra*, Copyright Enactments, *Idem* at p. 38.

[130] Act of Dec. 1, 1873, Revision, 43rd Cong., 1st Sess., Revised Statutes, Title 13, The Judiciary, Sec. 711 (Rev. Stat. 1878, pp. 134, 135), Copyright Enactments, *Idem*, pp. 42-43, at p. 42.

[131] Act of Dec. 1, 1873 (Revision), Revised Statutes, Title 60, Patents, Trade-Marks and Copyrights, 43rd Cong., 1st Sess., Copyright Enactments, *Idem*, at pp. 43-47.

[132] Act of July 8, 1870, note 121, *supra*, Copyright Enactments, *Idem*, at pp. 36-41.

being minor language revisions which did not affect the substance of the remedies provided earlier, e.g., the default per Sec. 4960 of the Revised Statutes of 1873 provided for recovery of the penalty of $25 for failure to deposit to be recovered by an action in the nature of debt,[133] rather than by the action of debt as set forth in the Act of 1870.[134]

The principal effect of the Act of March 3, 1891[135] was two-fold in terms of remedies. Both the Acts of 1870[136] and 1873[137] had provided that authors might reserve the right to dramatize and translate their own works. The Act of 1891 amended Sec. 4952 of the Revised Statutes to grant to authors the exclusive right to dramatize and translate their works for which copyright had been obtained.[138] Sec. 4964 was therefore correspondingly amended to provide for forfeiture and damages with respect, not only to works published, etc., without consent, but, in addition, to such dramatizations and translations made without consent.[139] Sec. 4964 related to books. Sec. 4965 was also amended to refer to dramatizations and translations.[140] This section related to all of the remaining enumerated subjects of copyright other than books.

---

[133] Act of Dec. 1, 1873 (Revision), note 131, *supra,* Sec. 4960, Copyright Enactments, *Idem,* at p. 45.

[134] Act of July 8, 1870, note 121, *supra.*

[135] Act of Mar. 3, 1891, 51st Cong., 2d Sess., Chap. 565, 27 Stat. 743 (1893), Copyright Enactments, *Idem,* at pp. 49-55.

[136] Note 121, *supra.*

[137] Note 130, *supra.*

[138] Act of Mar. 3, 1891, note 135, *supra,* Sec. 4952, Copyright Enactments, note 54, *supra,* at pp. 49-50.

[139] Act of Mar. 3, 1891, *Idem,* Sec. 4964, Copyright Enactments, *Idem,* at p. 52.

[140] Act of Mar. 3, 1891, *Idem,* Sec. 4965, Copyright Enactments, *Idem* at p. 53.

The second material change in this regard by the Act of 1891 was to extend copyright protection to non-citizens of the United States, albeit on a basis of reciprocity, by Sec. 13 of that act.[141] Consequently, the damage provisions in favor of authors and proprietors were to be deemed extended as to such non-citizen authors and proprietors. To the extent the statute prior to amendment in 1891 secured copyright to authors and proprietors and then provided for remedies where publishing, etc., was effected without consent of the author or proprietor, no change in language was required to give effect to Sec. 13. However, where the statute, prior to revision, qualified relief in terms of citizenship, the statute was accordingly amended. Thus, Sec. 4967 of the Revised Statutes, prior to revision, granted damages for publication of a manuscript without consent of the author or proprietor, "if such author or proprietor is a citizen of the United States, or resident therein, . . . "[142] This section was amended by deletion of the qualification, quoted above, as to citizenship and residence.[143]

The Act of Feb. 9, 1893,[144] which established a Court of Appeals for the District of Columbia, provided for writ

---

[141] *Idem,* Sec. 13, Copyright Enactments, *Idem,* at pp. 53-54; McCannon, Marjorie, The Manufacturing Clause of the U.S. Copyright Law, Study No. 35, in Studies on Copyright (1963), pp. 1123-1197 states at p. 1131, "The Act of March 3, 1891 provided that the citizens of any foreign country in whose favor a copyright proclamation had been made could obtain copyright in the United States. Fourteen such proclamations had been issued by the time of the Register's Report for the fiscal year 1903-1904."

[142] Act of Dec. 1, 1873 (Revision), Revised Statutes, Title 60, Patents, Trade-Marks and Copyrights, note 130, *supra,* Sec. 4967, Copyright Enactments, *Idem,* at p. 47.

[143] Act of Mar. 3, 1891, note 135, *supra,* Sec. 4967, Copyright Enactments, *Idem,* at p. 53.

[144] Act of Feb. 9, 1893, 52nd Cong., 2d Sess., Chap. 74, 27 Stat. 436 (1893), Copyright Enactments, *Idem,* at p. 54.

of error or appeal to the Supreme Court of the United States without regard to sum or value of the matter in dispute where the validity of patents and copyrights was involved.

Sec. 21.8. Copyright Legislation and Actions for Infringement

It was not until the Act of Mar. 2, 1895[145] that the reference in federal legislation to "infringement", first introduced by Congress in 1870 in terms of the notice clause, to wit, that no action for infringement of copyright could be maintained unless there was compliance with the notice provisions,[146] was extended to refer to specific remedies. Sec. 4965 of the Revised Statutes was amended in 1895 to modify statutory damage provisions with respect to the enumerated subjects of copyright. Theretofore the section had provided for forfeiture of $1 per sheet, published, etc., without consent and $10 per copy of a painting, statue, or a statuary, one-half thereof to go to the person bringing the action for recovery, the other half to the United States.[147] The Act of 1895 modified the section by adding two provisos: "*Provided, however,* That in case of any such infringement of the copyright of a photograph made from any object not a work of fine arts, the sum to be recovered in any action brought under the provisions of this section shall be not less than one hundred dollars, nor more than

---

[145] Act of Mar. 2, 1895, 53rd Cong., 3d Sess., Chap. 194, 28 Stat. 965 (1895), Copyright Enactments, *Idem,* at pp. 55-56.

[146] Act of July 8, 1870, note 121, *supra,* Sec. 97, Copyright Enactments, *Idem,* at p. 38; See also Act of Dec. 1, 1873 (Revision), note 131, *supra,* Sec. 4962, Copyright Enactments, *Idem,* at p. 46.

[147] Sec. 4965, Revised Statutes, Title 60, Patents, Trade-Marks and Copyrights, as amended, by Sec. 8, of Act of Mar. 3, 1891, note 142, *supra,* Copyright Enactments, *Idem,* at p. 53.

five thousand dollars, and *Provided, further,* That in case of any such infringement of the copyright of a painting, drawing, statue, engraving, etching, print, or model or design for a work of the fine arts or of a photograph of a work of the fine arts, the sum to be recovered in any action brought through the provisions of this section shall not be less than two hundred and fifty dollars, and not more than ten thousand dollars." [148]

The section as amended also provided for the usual one-half of the recovery going to the copyright proprietor, the other one-half to the United States, except that the reference thereto as amended was to "the foregoing penalties".[149]

Thus, for the first time, actions for recovery of damages for publication, etc., without consent of the copyright proprietor were characterized specifically in the copyright legislation as actions for infringement. The amendment here related to the enumerated subjects of copyright other than books. Since the section as to publication of books without such consent was comparable in formulation (other than as to the measure of damages), it may be said that the two sections were in *pari materia.* Consequently, the provisos, quoted above, insofar as they modified the measure of damages as to the matters covered by the respective provisos, also referred to "in the case of any such infringement of copyright",[150] to wit, the publication without consent as to the enumerated subjects of copyright. Since the section as to books was comparable in formulation, except as to the measure of damages, then it must be presumed that if there were a similar proviso as to books, that such a pro-

---

[148] Act of Mar. 2, 1895, note 145, *supra,* Copyright Enactments, *Idem,* at p. 56. (italics).

[149] *Ibid.*

[150] Note 148, *supra.*

viso would likewise refer to that section as a case of infringement of copyright. In other words, for the first time, the damage provisions for the doing of any of the acts under exclusive copyright could now be designated as relating to provisions for recovery brought under actions for infringement because the statute now directly, in part, and by logical application thereof, as to the remainder, so provided. Prior thereto, it could not be said with complete assurance, solely from a reading of the statute, exactly what was comprehended by an action for infringement of copyright.

The Act of Jan. 6, 1897 extended copyright protection to musical performance and amended Sec. 4966[151] of the Revised Statutes to apply the damage provisions applicable to dramatic performance thereto, i.e., public performance without consent was actionable in damages of $100 for the first such performance and $50 for every subsequent one. The section was also amended to make such dramatic or musical public performance that was willful and for profit a misdemeanor, punishable by imprisonment not to exceed one year. In addition, injunctive relief was provided to specifically restrain any performance of music or drama under the section, enforceable by punishment for contempt; there was also provision for motions to dissolve and set aside such injunction.[152] Thus, for the first time, copyright legislation by Congress added criminal sanctions to civil liability for violation thereof.

The Act of Mar. 3, 1897[153] amended Sec. 4963 of the Revised Statutes to prohibit importation of the enumerated

[151] Act of Jan. 6, 1897, 54th Cong., 2d Sess., Chap. 4, 29 Stat. 481 (1897), Copyright Enactments, *Idem,* at pp. 56-57.

[152] *Ibid.*

[153] Act of Mar. 3, 1897, 5th Cong., 2d Sess., Chap. 392, 29 Stat. 694 (1897), Copyright Enactments, *Idem,* at pp. 58-59.

subjects of copyright bearing a notice of copyright inserted or impressed thereon where no copyright thereon in fact had been obtained and extended the penalty of $100 thereto, in an action brought by the author or proprietor, one-half thereof recoverable by the person suing, the other half by the United States.

Sec. 21.9. The Act of 1909 and Infringement

But it was not until the passage of the present Copyright Act in 1909[154] that infringement was clarified as to the relationship of infringement to the exclusive rights under copyright. Sec. 24 thereof specifies the relief and remedies "if any person shall infringe the copyright in any work protected under the copyright laws of the United States". Unlike prior statutes, Sec. 25 no longer referred to enumerated subjects of copyright being published, etc., (the "etc." being the enumerated exclusive rights) without the consent of the copyright proprietor. The entire section, indeed the entire Act was cast in language of infringement. The section referred to "infringer", "infringing copies", as well as "infringement". The essential scheme of prior legislation was retained, however redrafted, in that damages are specified by statute for various types of infringement, many of the damage provisions of prior acts being carried over without change as to the measure of damages. What was new in terms of the concept of infringement, apart from generic use of infringement, as the term for which there was recovery for civil liability, was the addition of reference in Sec. 25, Third to "infringing delivery" and in Sec. 25, Fourth to "infringing performance".[155]

---

[154] Act of Mar. 4, 1909, 60th Cong., 2d Sess., 35 Stat. 1075 (1909), Copyright Enactments, *Idem,* at pp. 64-86.

[155] *Idem,* Sec. 25, Copyright Enactments, *Idem,* at pp. 74-76.

Conceivably the use of the generic term "infringement" was deemed advisable because Sec. 5[156] of the Act specified the separate classes for application for copyright. In other words, the classification system embodied therein made it possible for generic use of the term as a matter of draftsmanship. However, Sec. 1[157] of the Act purported to enumerate the exclusive rights under copyright, that is, the bundle of rights constituting the copyright, yet there was only a limited correspondence thereto in Sec. 25 in terms of "infringing delivery" and "infringing performance" as it related to the respective exclusive rights.

It remained for the codification of the Act in 1947[158] to indicate more precisely the nature of Sec. 25 of the 1909 Act,[159] as amended.[160] Title 17 of the United States Code, as enacted in 1947, embodied three chapters. Chapter 1 related to registration of copyright. Chapter 2 thereof was entitled "Infringement Proceedings" and covered Secs. 101-116, inclusive. Sec. 101 thereof was entitled, "Infringement" and contained 6 subdivisions, as follows:

"(a) Injunction.

(b) Damages and profits; amounts; other remedies.

(c) Impounding during action.

(d) Destruction of infringing copies and plates.

(e) Royalties for use of mechanical reproduction of musical works.

---

[156] *Idem,* Sec. 5, Copyright Enactments, *Idem,* at pp. 66-67.

[157] *Idem,* Sec. 1, Copyright Enactments, *Idem,* at pp. 64-66.

[158] Public Law 281, 80th Cong., 1st Sess., chap. 391, approved July 30, 1947, Copyright Enactments, *Idem,* at pp. 102-121.

[159] Note 154, *supra.*

[160] Act of Aug. 24, 1912, 62d Cong., 2d Sess., 37 Stat. 488, Copyright Enactments, *Idem,* at pp. 87-90.

(f) Rules of Procedure." [161]

Clearly, then, the editorial revision of the 1909 statute as now embodied in Title 17 indicates that violation of copyright is actionable in infringement proceedings, i.e., actions for infringement of copyright, and the remedies applicable in respect of such violation pertain to the same in actions for infringement.

Proposed copyright revision goes even further by including a general statement as to the nature of infringement. Sec. 501(a) of S. 543 reads, "Anyone who violates any of the exclusive rights of the copyright owner as provided by sections 106 through 117, or who imports copies or phonorecords into the United States in violation of section 602, is an infringer of the copyright." [162] The House Report, in this regard, remarks, "The bill, *unlike the present law,* contains a general statement of what constitutes infringement of copyright." [163] But subdivisions Third and Fourth of Sec. 101 of Title 17 do specify damages for violation of certain of the exclusive rights, to wit, exclusive delivery, and exclusive performance, respectively.[164] The sense of proposed Sec. 501 of S. 543 may be said to carry the concept of Sec. 101, Third and Fourth, to its logical conclusion and to apply the same to *all* of the exclusive rights. Indeed, it may be contended that Sec. 501 in this regard is merely spelling out generically what is implicit in the language of Sec. 101, Third and Fourth.

---

[161] 17 U.S.C. Chap. 2, Copyright Enactments, *Idem,* at p. 111.

[162] S. 543(a), Dec. 10, 1969 Print, 91st Cong., 1st Sess., Jan. 22, 1969.

[163] Report No. 83, House of Representatives, 90th Cong., 1st Sess., Mar. 8, 1967, Copyright Law Revision, at p. 126 (emphasis added).

[164] See note 154, *supra,* now 17 U.S.C. 101 and note 161, *supra.*

It may be concluded, then, that infringement, even under the present Act, is a generic term for tortious acts which relate to the enumerated rights specified in Sec. 1 of the present Act.[165] That is, for the violation of each of the rights granted to the copyright proprietor under Sec. 1 of the present Act, there is a corresponding tort. Each of the bundle of rights constituting the statutory copyright carries with it the duty of forbearance with respect thereto. The violation of each right gives rise to a corresponding action for infringement. This is explicit in proposed copyright revision and set forth in the present Act as to infringing delivery and infringing performance. There are, then, as many torts, i.e., violations of the duty of forbearance, as there are rights either exclusively under copyright or as modified by compulsory licenses.

Thus the legislative scheme as to infringement, which was initiated in 1870, only received a suitable expression of correspondence of tort to right in the present Act of 1909. Unlike the common law, where originally there had to be a writ that was acceptable before there could be a remedy,[166] the Copyright Act by means of the term "infringement" has provided for a correspondence between right and violation thereof in that, although the term "infringement" is generic, the violation of the respective exclusive rights imports a corresponding tort and remedy, be it for infringing delivery, infringing performance, or for any of the other infringed rights, such as infringing copying, infringing publication, infringing vending, infringing dramatization, etc. If the copyright consists of a bundle of rights constituting the copyright, then it may be said that infringement of copyright is a tort in respect of each and any of

---

[165] 17 U.S.C. 1.

[166] Plucknett, *op. cit., supra,* note 35 at p. 336.

the rights constituting the bundle so that the tort of copyright infringement refers generically to a variety of infringement actions corresponding to the respective rights under copyright.

Chapter XXII

THE CONCEPT OF INFRINGEMENT

Sec. 22.1. Piracy and Plagiarism

The concept originally was one of literary freebootery. In the beginning there were creators, pirates and plagiarists. The literary hack was on the lower order of creativity, turning out works of little originality and even less creativity, almost by formula as it were. But the lowest order, by far, in the literary world were the literary thieves, the wretches who could not or would not create but stole from another.

The world of the literary thieves consisted of two classes of purloiners of the creations of others,—pirates and plagiarists. The pirates would take the work of another and dispose of it as a freebooter, as a plunderer, as it were, as though might is main. The pirate, however, generally plundered on the principle of attribution of authorship. The piracy had value precisely because the taker, without color of legal right or authority, was able to market the work as that of the creator. The author lost compensation but not necessarily attribution of authorship; indeed, the fact of piracy might have enhanced the attribution. The pirate thought enough of the work of the author so as to tout the attribution of authorship in the illegal marts where the pirate sought to turn a sale and profit thereon.

Not so the plagiarist. The literary thief who sought to purloin the works of another as his own was indeed the literary devil. He was the lowest of the low in the literary order. The plagiarist, like the pirate, stole in order to turn the work to his economic advantage. But the plagiarist went further. He was, in a sense, the great emasculator. He sought to deny the real creator the fruits of his labors, not only economically, but more importantly, attribution-wise. The plagiarist would steal not only the literary labors of another, and perforce the fruits of such labors, but indeed that very identification of authorship of the work by passing the work off as his own. The plagiarist might be a literalist, stealing word for word, or a colorist, taking the thoughts and expression of another and after coloring the same by paraphrase, palming it off as his own. The plagiarist was anti-creator because he stole the work of the creator and sought to deny the personality of the creator, as creator, by obliterating the same and by substituting his own imprimatur as creator when, in fact, he had not created. The plagiarist was lower than the literary hack who, at least, aspired to creativity and who, in his own way, had created a work he could truly call his own, however lacking it might be in literary merit or true creativity.

Indeed, Webster defines the term "plagiarize" as, "To steal or purloin and pass off as one's own (the ideas, words, artistic productions, etc., of another); to use without due credit the ideas, expressions, or productions of (another)." [1] Harry P. Warner would equate "plagiarize" with "infringement". His opening chapter on infringement of copyright reads, "Plagiarism or infringement of common law and statutory copyright is not a modern *sin*." [2] Moreover, Warner would go even further. His footnote thereto begins, "Although there is a good deal of disagreement

[1] Webster's New International Dictionary, Second Ed., Unabridged (1961), at p. 1878, "plagiarism".

[2] Warner, Harry P., Radio and Television Rights, Chap. XV, entitled, Infringement of Copyright, Sec. 150, at p. 522 (1953) (emphasis added).

as to the proper definitions of the terms, 'plagiarism', 'piracy' and 'infringement', they will be used interchangeably throughout this chapter." [3]

Without adjudging the necessary identity or overlap of the three terms, one can state categorically that "infringement" *ipso facto* comprehends the fact of the other two. Infringement is a legal term of art to denote the unlawful taking of the work of another by violating or invading the rightful borders of ownership and possession secured to such proprietor as the owner of such right. In the case of literary works, infringement covers such unlawful taking against the person rightfully entitled thereto as author or proprietor because his right has been secured by copyright, be it under common law prior to publication or by statute. Piracy and plagiarism are perforce unlawful means of such appropriation.

But Warner's use of the term "sin" conveys the context of the problem. Sin, according to Webster, is used primarily in terms of its religious denotation of failure under the deity; but it also denotes "moral failure".[4] As a religious failing, the term would not be apposite as applied to literature. It must therefore be deemed to apply in a moral sense. Plagiarism therefore is a moral wrong.[5] To equate plagiarism and infringement as a modern sin, even though done in the context of indicating that literary borrowing by the greatest of creators has proceeded from time immemorial, Warner nevertheless is alluding to the ethical overtones inherent in both. Warner has indeed done this by first equating the two terms. After having made such

---

[3] *Idem,* fn. 1, at p. 522.

[4] Webster, *op. cit., supra,* note 1, at p. 2342, "sin".

[5] Warner, *op. cit., supra,* note 2. The Warner footnote indeed quotes Philip Wittenberg to the effect that it is a moral wrong.

equation, he has then, in effect, extrapolated that the ethical norm inherent in the opprobrium directed against the plagiarist is somehow carried over into the legal context of abhorrence of the infringer of copyright.

Indeed, the legal norms lend color to the view that infringement of copyright, that is, non-innocent infringement, at least, might be less than honorable and carries with it the stigma of moral obloquy. The detestation of the *literati* for the plagiarist is rendered by the legal norms to make of infringement of copyright a kind of badge of infamy, of literary moral turpitude.[6] Consider the remedies provided by Congress in the present Act under Chapter 2 of Title 17 of the United States Code, entitled, "Infringement Proceedings".[7]

Sec. 101(c) thereof permits the court to impound all allegedly infringing articles in its discretion.[8] Sec. 101(d) is a more permanent and more drastic resolution. The court may order destruction thereunder of all infringing "plates, molds, matrices or other means for making such infringing copies".[9] In addition to confiscating and ultimately destroying the means of infringement, the court is authorized to enjoin acts of infringement by Sec. 101(a).[10] All of the force inherent in sovereignty to implement judgments and decrees of the judicial system is behind enjoining acts of infringement. Violation thereof by the party under injunction conjures possibilities of apprehen-

[6] See the discussion in "infamia" in Roman law, "infamy" and "moral turpitude" in modern law in Burdick, William L., Principles of Roman Law and Their Relation to Modern Law (1938) at pp. 209-211.

[7] 17 U.S.C. Chap. 2—Secs. 101-116.

[8] 17 U.S.C. 101(c).

[9] 17 U.S.C. 101(d).

[10] 17 U.S.C. 101(a).

sion of the violator for contempt of court and punishment by incarceration and/or fine for continued violation. Then, too, Sec. 104[11] makes willful infringement of copyright for profit a crime—a misdemeanor punishable by imprisonment of up to a year, a fine, or both, in the discretion of the Court. The legislation of such a crime automatically brings into play the investigatorial resources of the federal government through the Federal Bureau of Investigation to ascertain detection of the commission of a crime. Perhaps even more importantly, the statute arrays the prosecutorial forces of the federal government against the indicted, alleged offender, so that the latter is also faced by all of the resources of the state seeking his punishment for the offense of willful infringement for profit. As though these purgative measures were not enough, the infringer risks further deterioration of his position by way of damages. Not only might the infringer be prevented from continuing his acts of infringement while his infringing *res* or property is destroyed, within the context of a possible risk of incarceration by the sovereign, but he also faces possible severe economic dislocation in his pocketbook in order to make good the wrong done to the proprietor of the copyright. Under Sec. 101(b)[12] the infringer faces risk of damages as well as possible loss of profits. Schedules of statutory damages are detailed therein. Moreover, in the event of actual notice given to an alleged infringer, statutory exceptions, i.e., formulae for damages, in certain instances give way so that recovery might be had without such limitation.

Congress has, indeed, aligned a veritable array of remedies to uphold the integrity of creativity against assorted

---

[11] 17 U.S.C. 104.
[12] 17 U.S.C. 101(b).

pirates and plagiarists denominated infringers of copyright secured by statute! Congressional concern for securing exclusive rights to authors in their writings for limited times, while at the same time promoting the progress of science and the useful arts, has been set forth in the statute as an implementation of the constitutional mandate.[13] Moreover, proposed copyright revision continues this preceptual concern for the creator in S. 543, Chap. 5 entitled, "Copyright Infringement and Remedies" in substantially comparable ways.[14] True, the concepts might vary somewhat and the limits of statutory damages might be pushed upward to take into consideration the effects of an inflationary period. Thus, willful infringement for commercial advantage or private financial gain is denominated "Criminal Infringement" in Sec. 506(a) of S. 543.[15] Also, in assessing damages for willful infringement, pursuant to S. 543, Sec. 504(c), the court in its discretion might exceed the limits of $250 to $10,000 otherwise applicable and award a sum of up to $50,000.[16] At the same time, the court is authorized thereunder to reduce the award of statutory damages to not less than $100 "In a case where the infringer sustains the burden of proving, and the court finds, that he

---

[13] Constitution of the United States, Art. I, Sec. 8, Clause 8.

[14] S. 543, Dec. 10, 1969 print, 91st Cong., 1st Sess., Jan. 22, 1969, Chap. 5, Secs. 501-508. See also, House Report 83, 90th Cong., 1st Sess., House of Representatives, March 8, 1967, re Copyright Law Revision at pp. 126-131.

[15] S. 543, *Idem,* Sec. 506(a). The limits of criminal penalties by way of a fine are increased therein, from $2,500 to $10,000 after the first offense. In the present Act, 17 U.S.C. 104, provides for criminal fines of $100 to $1,000. There is no floor in S. 543, Sec. 506(a).

[16] S. 543, *Idem,* Sec. 504(c).

was not aware and had no reason to believe that his acts constituted an infringement of copyright . . ." [17]

Sec. 22.2. Innocent Infringement

This is but a spelling out of the notion of innocent infringement. Indeed, Sec. 21 of the present Act specifies that in cases of accidental or mistaken omission of notice of copyright, where the proprietor has sought to comply with the act, copyright will not be invalidated, nor shall recovery for infringement be prevented thereby with respect to someone who has actual notice of copyright and then infringes. But such omission ". . . shall prevent recovery against an innocent infringer who has been misled by the omission of the notice; and in a suit for infringement no permanent injunction shall be had unless the copyright proprietor shall reimburse to the innocent infringer his reasonable outlay innocently incurred if the court, in its discretion, shall so direct." [18]

Alan Latman and William S. Tager define the term "innocent infringer" as follows, "A possible general definition of the innocent infringer is one who invades the rights of the copyright owner without intending to do so and without having any reason to suspect that he is doing so."[19] In alluding to the nature of innocent infringement, they aver that it is not a unitary concept, and add, "As broadly understood, the term encompasses a number of factual situations in which infringement is not intended, for example: (1) use of material on which notice has been

---

[17] S. 543, *Idem,* Sec. 504(c)(2). Cf, 17 U.S.C. 1(c) which limits damages for innocent infringement by broadcasting to $100.

[18] 17 U.S.C. 21.

[19] Latman, Alan and Tager, William S., Liability of Innocent Infringers of Copyrights, Study No. 25 in Studies on Copyright (1963) pp. 1045-1066 at p. 1063.

omitted; (2) belief that certain material in a copyrighted publication is in the public domain; and (3) a variety of secondary infringements where infringing material has been received for reproduction or distribution with the reasonable assumption of its originality." [20]

Whatever the factual basis for innocent infringement and whatever the treatment thereof for purposes of damages,[21] for purposes of determination of infringement, intention is not the test of liability of the tort of infringement. Justice Brandeis indicated as much in *Buck v. Jewell-La-Salle Realty Co.,* by his observation there, "Intention to infringe is not essential under the act." [22]

In holding defendant Hearst Magazines, Inc. liable for publishing excerpts from an infringing biography of the life of Clara Barton, Judge Clark in the Court of Appeals for the First Circuit remarked in *De Acosta* v. *Brown,* a case involving infringement of common law copyright, "It is suggested that recovery is contrary to the general doctrine of torts, apparently on the view that liability and damage should be limited to such as can be foreseen and avoided. But 'torts' is a broad field of law; and while the doctrine may apply to negligence, it does not apply to conversion or appropriation. Cf. Restatement, Torts, 1934, secs. 222, 244, with Sec. 289. Here the analogy of the cases has always been that of the conversion of literary property; and, as in the American Press case cited above, that analogy here is complete to justify recovery as against even an innocent copier." [23]

---

[20] *Ibid.*

[21] *Ibid.*

[22] 283 U.S. 191, 198 (1931).

[23] 146 F. 2d 408 (2d Cir. 1944), Learned Hand, J., dissenting, cert. den. 325 U.S. 862 (1945) at p. 412.

Thus the gravamen of infringement is the taking of the property of another without right. Copyright, being an intangible, cannot, of course, be possessed in the sense that real property or chattels can be physically possessed. It is the unlawful use that invades the borders of the configuration of ownership of the copyright proprietor. It is this invasion that is tortious, whether or not the same be done with intent to invade or under a mistaken belief as to ownership of the configuration, e.g., that it is in the public domain, or in all innocence of intent because the invasion is one degree removed and without knowledge of the nature of ownership of the configuration. The infringement occurs when there has been such an invasion without regard to the color of right of the invader. The predicate of infringement is ownership of the right under copyright in another which has been utilized in some form, i.e., invaded, without right or license from such owner. As soon as rightful ownership and lack of right or permission for use are determined, there is, without more, infringement, both under the statute and at common law. Thereafter, even the vendor of the infringing material is liable without regard to the degree of innocence, that is lack of knowledge of such seller, as F. W. Woolworth found out as to copyrighted statuary which was reproduced without right and as so reproduced sold by Woolworth,[24] and as Sam Goody experienced as to phonograph recordings which it sold that had been pirated.[25] In this regard, Latman and Tager have stated, "The rule is

---

[24] F.W. Woolworth Co. v. Contemporary Arts, Inc., 193 F. 2d 162 (1st Cir. 1951), *aff'd,* 344 U.S. 228 (1952). In a dissent, Justice Black states at p. 236, "We accept the Court of Appeals' appraisal of the consequences of the judge's remarks on the factual issue of copyright infringement." The dissent was concurred in by Justice Frankfurter, p. 234.

[25] Shapiro, Bernstein v. Goody, 248 F. 2d 260 (2d Cir. 1957), *rev'g* sub. nom. Miller v. Goody, 139 F. Supp. 176 (S.D.N.Y. 1956).

well established that lack of intention to infringe is generally no defense to an action for infringement." [26]

If, then, innocent infringers are also held accountable, albeit with possibly differing approaches as to measure of damages,[27] along with pirates and plagiarists, then what is the rationale therefor? One line of reasoning is suggested by Judge Clark in *De Acosta* v. *Brown,* after setting forth the rule as to liability of innocent copiers for infringement, "This case well illustrates the dangers to authors if a different rule were to be established. For the finding of innocence of Hearst is based upon two factors only, namely, that Brown the infringer assured the Cosmopolitan editor of the research that she had done on the matter, and that the reputation of Brown was known to the editor—a reputation, however, distinctly other than in the field of historical research. And if it be suggested that other more effective means of inquiry are not conveniently available to publishers, then that seems an additional reason for not depriving authors so easily of the fruits of their labors." [28]

Judge Clark seems to suggest that as to the fact of infringement, in weighing the equities, as between the author (and assigns) and the alleged innocent infringer, the former should be protected in terms of determination of liability because a contrary result would defeat the purpose of copyright by depriving the creator of the fruits of his labor. Moreover, determination of intent is subjective, whether the user knew or could have known the facts as to ownership in the proprietor and of lack of right in the party with whom the user was in privity upon further investigation. It requires a reading of the state of mind of the user

---

[26] Note 19 *supra* at p. 1052.
[27] *Idem;* 17 U.S.C. 21.
[28] Note 23, *supra,* at p. 412.

and also an analysis of the safeguards the user might have employed to ascertain ownership before it truly could be determined that it might have known the identity of the proprietor before such infringing use. The purport of Judge Clark's rationale was that this burden would not be shifted, for purposes of determining liability, from the user to the proprietor. Presumably this is inherent in the nature of copyright and in the effect of copyright registration under the statute as prima facie evidence of proprietorship.[29]

The user, then, must seek his protection from freedom from infringement by a variety of ways. He might employ the technique of copyright clearance. That is, he might undertake a copyright search, either of his own, or with the aid of one or another of the agencies specializing in making searches and preparing reports thereon.[30] Then again, he might arrange for warranties from the party authorizing his use as to the rights of proprietorship of the warrantor with concomitant indemnification for breach of such warranties.[31] Finally, as in film and television production, the user might have an errors and omissions policy, whether in blanket form to cover all production of the user, or for that particular production, for insurance against infringement of copyright by reason of the wrongful use of the property in that proprietorship is not in the party purporting to grant the rights of use to the user.

Sec. 22.3. Infringement: Piracy: Plagiarism

The tort of infringement, then, is in the wrongful taking. Innocence of intent may be a mitigating factor as to

---

[29] 17 U.S.C. 209.

[30] See Sec. 19.7, *supra*.

[31] See, for example, Form Nos. 1A-2 and 2A-1a in Volumes of Forms.

damages, but it does not affect the determination of liability. Publishers might be seen to be innocent infringers often, particularly where the infringed work is paraphrased, rather than literally copied. Certainly the publisher is more likely to be put on notice where a work is pirated in the sense of literally appropriated because there the form of infringement is based upon attribution of authorship. In such event, the publisher may be lending itself to publication of a pirated edition and the fact of attribution may be notice enough to put the publisher on guard to investigate proprietorship.

Plagiarism imposes a different burden on the publisher. There the expression of ideas of another is appropriated in violation of copyright without attribution of credit to the author. The editorial staff of the publisher may be sufficiently knowledgeable in that literary genre to spot literal appropriation of the work of another whereas it might find it more difficult to detect skillful paraphrase thereof. Of course, if the source of literal appropriation is obscure, even the publisher might not be able to discover that variety of plagiarism.

Thus it may be seen that the traditional right of copy, comprehending the so-called publishing rights, necessarily would involve the possibility of innocent wrongful publication because the publisher could not reasonably detect plagiarism simply by editorial inspection, not being aware of the character of the infringement, i.e., the identity of plagiarized material with the original from which it was taken. Meaningful protection of the right of copy necessarily had to include a monopoly of the copyright in a work which secured the right of copy not only against pirates and plagiarists but those lending themselves, however innocently or unwittingly, to the implementation of the denial of the fruits and proceeds of the copyright monopoly. In terms of the scope of the security afforded the proprietor of the copyright, his possessory interest (fair use and other copyright defenses aside) gave him absolute protection in determination of liability, regardless of the degree of innocence of the infringer.[32] A contrary resolution might well nullify the protection intended to be accorded the copyright proprietor. For the holding accountable of an impecunious pirate or plagiarist might avail the proprietor little if the harm had been done in the sense that the innocent publisher or other user had widely disseminated the infringing work and there were no recourse as against such disseminator. All of the drastic remedies of injunctive relief, impounding and destruction of the infringing articles and imprisonment of the willful infringer for profit would scarcely be of much solace to the copyright proprietor if his work had been effectively circulated without recompense therefor. The result would be to place a premium upon innocent invasion of the possessory configuration of the copyright proprietor and seriously impair the economic value of his ownership.

Thus, in order to protect the proprietor, the target of the sovereign's protection of the monopoly in the copyright is necessarily extended to cover not only the pirate and plagiarist, the larcenous at heart, with intent to steal the fruits and labors of another, but also the entire sequential roll from such ill-begotten piracy and plagiarism. If the work is tainted by infringement, all and sundry acquiring

---

[32] See, for example, the exceptions as to the damages provision of 17 U.S.C. 101(b), providing for damages and loss of profits limiting statutory damages to innocent infringers of undramatized or non-dramatic works by means of motion pictures to $100 and of copyrighted dramatic or dramatico-musical works by such means to not more than $5,000 nor less than $250. See, Latman and Tager, *op. cit., supra,* note 19, at pp. 1050-1051.

any claim or color of right thereto, must likewise bear the burdens thereof. A logical corollary thereof is that if the wrong is in the taking without possessory right or license to do so, then there need not even be any intent to pirate or plagiarize for a user to bear the attaint of infringement. There need not even be an unlawful sequential roll emanating from a pirate or plagiarist to be wrongful. The sequential roll derived initially from an innocent infringer, for example, in the mistaken belief that the underlying work being adapted is in the public domain, will likewise result in lack of right in the infringed material even though the claim of right might originate in all innocence. Motivation in granting the monopoly of the copyright might have been the protection of creators against the ravages of pirates and plagiarists. Nevertheless, the umbrella of such protection broadly covers all and sundry who might invade the borders of such protection by infringement of copyright.

Sec. 22.4. Creation of Literary Property and Ideas

For it is the creative process that may be seen to be the generative arena for infringement. Creation is both process and rest; dynamics and motion, on the one hand, and rest, on the other. Creation at rest is the determination that a work has been fixed at some point in the creative process and so the fixation becomes the point at which copyright may be secured. For the creator has determined that at that point, his work has taken some definitive form with sufficient finality for obtaining a copyright therein.

Copyright is said to inhere in the expression of the creator and not in abstract ideas. Lindey has characterized this by his remark, ". . . copyright resides in *form.*"[33] Fixation of thought in the creator's formulation is deemed to be protected but not the ideas themselves. It is by apparent separation of form and content that copyright doctrine proceeds to provide continuity of scholarship and learning that is not throttled by monopolistic restriction and control of ideas while at the same time securing rewards to creators—and assigns—for limited times.

But because the separation of form and content, the particular from the abstract, may be more metaphysical and philosophically ambiguous, and because creation is primarily process rather than rest, the inherent contradictions of the nature of creation in the context of the literary and artistic media employed for creation almost define the contours of infringement. To begin with, the term "ideas" has a variety of meanings. Webster defines the term as follows:

> "1 A concept, a representation, or a presentation of a sense; also, sometimes, the object of a concept. The word has various special meanings with different philosophers and schools; specif: a. . . . With Plato, an archetype . . . ; a transcendant universal . . . b with Aristotle, the form or form-giving cause, c With Berkeley, an impression of sense or imagination; esp. a percept. d With Hume, representation or construct of memory and association, as distinguished from a direct impression of sense. e With Kant, a transcendant but nonempirical concept of reason; a noumenon. f With Hegel, the highest category; the complete and final product of reason; also, its realization and embodiment.

---

[33] Lindey, Alexander, Plagiarism and Originality (1952) at p. 12.

"2 A conception or standard of any perfection; an ideal, as, to fall below the *idea* of human nature; hence, a conception or design; a preliminary plan; now more often, a plan or purpose for action; project; . . .

* * *

"5 Broadly, any object of the mind existing in apprehension, conception, or thought; a notion, thought, or mental impression; . . .

"6 A product of reflection or mental concentration; a formulated thought or opinion; as, to have *ideas* on a subject; clearly defined *ideas*.

"7 Whatever is known, believed, or supposed regarding any object; . . .

"8 The central or key meaning or the chief end of a particular action or situation; . . .

"10 *Music* A theme, phrase, or figure, as first conceived.

"11 *Psychol.* In recent usage, any thought or conception of an object not actually present to the senses." [34]

Collier's Encyclopedia notes that the term is derived from the Greek and the related verb in Greek means to see.[35] It observes,

"Psychologically, idea refers to the mental product or result of experience or thinking, and is usually the synonym of concept. It may also refer to a plan or a purpose or a general meaning. The meaning of a sensation (sight or hearing, for example) is known as a percept. Perception refers to one's understanding of a particular act, or object. Thus a car, or the car, is a

---

[34] Webster's New International Dictionary, Unabridged, Second Ed. (1961) at p. 1236 "idea" (italics).

[35] 9 Collier's Encyclopedia, "idea", at p. 715 (1961).

> percept derived from awareness of the simple object car. If one refers to several cars in general as means of transportation, the idea of car is used. An idea, therefore, may be an abstraction of the qualities of many closely similar objects or acts. It may also be a theory or interpretation, as an ideology, which is the teaching or promulgation of a dominant idea of life, of government, or of society." [36]

In terms of philosophy, ideas are identified with a variety of philosophic schools.[37] Indeed, the use of the term assumes different meanings depending upon the philosopher and philosophic school. But rather than the variable sense in the meaning of the term as used by philosophers, perhaps the sense as used in psychology is most relevant in our context. In this regard, Collier's Encyclopedia states:

> "It should be noted, also, that most psychologists hold that ideas are related to some type of mental imagery. A mental image is regarded as the impression from a particular sense experience, such as sight. Hence, the visual image is the foundation of an idea whose content is mainly visual, such as the moon. In music, ideas are mainly auditory. The tea taster employs taste ideas. Such ideas as goodness, truth, beauty, and freedom, however, invoke a content that transcends mere sensory experience, and may be viewed as abstracts of many kinds of interpretations of these concepts. It is highly probable that abstract ideas of this kind originally were derived from some form of sensory experience." [38]

---

[36] *Ibid.*
[37] *Idem* at p. 716.
[38] *Ibid.*

One might emend this observation in relation to music in that musical ideas are not necessarily entirely auditory. Of course, music requires performance in order to be heard. But music, unless it is being performed in improvisation, also has attributes of the visual. Musical notation is the visual representation of music and is the principle means for the expression of musical ideas. Indeed, a musician who has lost his hearing, like Beethoven, can reconstruct the sound of music in his mind from notation—or memory—even though he cannot hear musical performance.

Thus, if expression of ideas is somehow different from the abstract ideas contained therein, ideas per se have no existence apart from their expression. In other words, ideas can only be expressed in terms of means of communication, language, art, music, and so on. There is an underlying literary and artistic base, using the term generically, to all ideas. Ideas are unable to be adduced unless there is a finite means of their articulation. The principal medium for this is language. Words are a primary means for expression of ideas. Meaning of ideas is articulated in terms of the meaning of the words available in language. Symbols, for example, the language of mathematics, are another means of expression of ideas. Art is another form for creation of ideas. Art may also serve as the handmaiden of symbol creation, such as in traffic signs and other directional ideas. Art itself may become the basis of language as in hieroglyphics and ideographs.[39] Indeed, each medium presents possibilities of expression of ideas not necessarily available by other

---

[39] See Lindsay, Vachel, The Art of the Moving Picture (1922), revision of work first published in 1915, in 1970 reprint with Introduction by Stanley Kauffmann, who perceived the ideational affinity of ideographs of ancient Egypt with the sensory experiences projected cinematographically by motion pictures.

media in terms of the nature of that medium. That is why one can speak of musical ideas, artistic ideas, filmic ideas, etc. There is a quantum of ideas that can arise through any given medium of communication while, at the same time, the limitations of that particular medium impose a contour or outside limit of possible idea configurations that may be conceived within it.

Thus it may be seen that ideas, themselves, originate only through some tangible means of communication and therefore have within them some fixation of expression. Hence, to speak of rights in ideas and the law of ideas in the sense that ideas are free unless reduced to concrete form or unless otherwise protected upon some theory of contract, implied contract or quasi-contract,[40] is wide of the mark as to the nature of ideas. Even oral articulation of ideas constitutes ideas expressed in language or symbols. Philip Wittenberg has remarked in this regard, "The earliest works of man passed by mouth. It was only when copies could be physically made that one could in any way control the communication of ideas from man to man." [41] Oral communication, then, is nevertheless a means of expression of ideas; what changes with written communication is that expression could now be preserved and repeated in some concrete form. The reference to control in this context refers to generic control, in terms of reproduction of the expression and not to the exercise of restraints on expression because of censorship. For censorship could also attempt to control oral expression as well as writings, be it for sedition, defamation, blasphemy, social control or otherwise. The point is that only reduction of ideas

---

[40] See Nimmer on Copyright, Chap. 15, The Law of Ideas (1970).

[41] Wittenberg, Philip, The Protection and Marketing of Literary Property (1937) at p. 4.

to concrete form provided for a fixation of the ideas in some form of expression.

If, therefore, the nature of infringement of copyright is considered to be metaphysical,[42] it is because the copyright is considered to protect the expression of ideas rather than the ideas themselves. Yet, in order to do this, one must differentiate the particular expression of the ideas, which are the peculiar product of the labors of the creator, from the generic possibilities of expression of that idea. For however abstract an idea may be, it can only be articulated through expression. Even the oral rendition is such; the difference is that the oral articulation has not been captured by reduction to concrete form. Speaking of the nature of a right of first publication in *Millar* v. *Taylor,* Judge Yates observed, "Ideas are free. But while the author confines them to his study, they are like birds in a cage, which none but he can have a right to let fly: for, till he thinks proper to emancipate them, they are under his dominion." [43] Some philosophers have noted that ideas, words, concepts, etc. already exist; what we call invention or creation is really discovery. Everything is immanent. Knowledge, information and, perforce, creation are merely facets of discovery of what already exist. In effect, they are facets of formulation, of application.[44]

---

[42] See Folsom v. Marsh, 9 Fed. Cas. 342 (No. 4901), (C.C. D. Mass. 1841) at p. 344, where Justice Story referred to copyright as being metaphysical.

[43] 4 Burr. 2303, 2378 (1769).

[44] The late Professor Edmond N. Cahn made similar observations in his course in jurisprudence without necessarily espousing such views as his own, but merely as epistemological observations.

Sec. 22.5. Protection of Intellectual Creation

But the philosophy of copyright is antithetical to this notion because it is posited in the affirmative nature of creation. The latter is not so much discovery as a process of articulation originating in the psyche of the creator out of the experiences and imagination of the creator and articulating whatever emotive and cognitive expressions that may be stated by means of that particular medium of communication. It is this process with its consequent articulations in concrete form that Drone characterizes as "intellectual creation". He writes:

> "There can, then, be no property in a production of the mind unless it is expressed in a definite order of words. But the property is not in the mere words alone,—nor alone in the one form of expression chosen by the author. It is in the intellectual creation, which language is merely a means of expressing and communicating. The words of a literary composition may be changed by substituting others of synonymous meaning; but the intellectual creation will remain substantially the same. The truth is judicially recognized in the established principle, that the property of the author is violated by an unauthorized use of his composition, with a colorable change of words; the test of piracy being not whether the identical language, the same words, are used, but whether the substance of the production is unlawfully appropriated. So an intellectual production may be expressed in any number of different languages. The thing itself is always the same; only the means of communication are different. The plot, the characters, the sentiments, the thoughts, which constitute a work of fiction, form an immaterial creation, which may be communicated by

a hundred different tongues,—by labial or sign language of the mute, the raised letters of the blind, the comprehensive characters of stenography. The means of communication are manifold; but the invisible, intangible, incorporeal creation of the author's brain never loses its identity." [45]

It is intellectual creation, according to Drone, which therefore gives rise to literary property and ownership thereof by preoccupancy, i.e., by first possession, by creation—through first production.[46]

Writing a few years before Drone, Morgan referred to two classes of intellectual labor,[47] corresponding roughly to the authorial and editorial functions. Morgan also felt that title to literary property was by first occupancy.[48] In terms of infringement, Morgan noted that the doctrine

---

[45] Drone, Eaton S., A Treatise on the Law of Property in Intellectual Productions in Great Britain and the United States (1879) at p. 97. See Chap. V, *supra*.

[46] *Idem* at pp. 2-6.

[47] Morgan, James Appleton, The Law of Literature (1875), 2 vols. At vol. 1, p. 320, he states, "The law can recognize but two classes of intellectual labor, viz., original labor and secondary labor. An original work alone has, properly speaking, an author. The producer of a secondary work, that is, a work consisting of parts, passages, or matters collected, condensed, or amplified from various sources is a compiler, editor, arranger, or abridger, as the case may be."

[48] *Idem,* Vol. 1, at p. 312. ". . . title to literary property is a title by occupancy" . . . the . . . "idea is first occupied and possessed by the arranger and adapter, the law will give him his proprietorship therein . . ." Note the emphasis therein on possession and occupancy of the idea. This seems to reflect the discovery nature of literary property as compared to the notion posited by Drone of creation.

of literary equivalents was being utilized by way of analogy to the doctrine of mechanical equivalents of patent law.[49]

Indeed, the analogy to the doctrine was invoked by a party claiming infringement of copyrighted operas by publication of an infringing booklet entitled "Opera Stories", in *G. Ricordi & Co.* v. *Mason,* in its motion for a preliminary injunction.[50] In denial of this motion, Judge Coxe remarked,

> "It is said that the same rule should be applied to a copyright as to a patent for a machine. If this proposition be granted, it does not aid the complainant.
>
> "No one, for instance, infringes a claim for a machine unless he uses a similar machine operating in substantially the same manner and producing a like result by the same or equivalent means. A model of a machine incapable of producing any practical result does not infringe any more than the brief synopsis of an opera infringes the author's copyright. In the one case the property protected is the right to make, use, and vend the machine; in the other it is the right to publish, reproduce in other forms and sell the opera. Neither the model of the machine nor the synopsis of the opera interferes with any of these rights." [51]

Indeed, the quotation from Drone, above, as to the rendition of a production in many different languages, by sign

---

[49] *Idem,* vol. 2, at p. 322.

[50] 201 Fed. 182 (C.C. S.D.N.Y. 1911). After trial on the merits, there was a decision dismissing the complaint, 201 Fed. 184 (S.D. N.Y. 1912). The plaintiff was thus denied his motion for preliminary injunction and relief on the merits. The decisions below were *aff'd per curiam,* 210 Fed. 277 (2d Cir. 1913).

[51] *Idem,* 201 Fed. 182 at p. 183.

language, raised letters of the blind and stenography is a good illustration of literary equivalents. It indicates that what is protected by copyright includes transformations of the work insofar as they are correlative to capturing the sense of the sentiments, thoughts, expressions and ideas of the original work regardless of the linguistic identity of the language utilized. It is obvious that translation into numerous linguistic versions must "bend" to the exigencies of the particular language employed. Comparative philology reveals that different languages have a variety of attributes—differing abundance of vocabulary, word building capabilities, as in German, and indeed in our legal vocabulary, with its "hereinaboves" and "hereinafters", nuances in meaning in translation, figurative as opposed to literal translation, and so on. Linguistic versions of a work, therefore, are really transformations of the original. They are not literal reproductions, in the sense that copies are, when that work in its original form is reproduced word for word. Translations are forms of literary equivalents but not copies in the literal sense. So, too, the transformation of a two-dimensional comic cartoon race horse called "Spark Plug" into a three-dimensional horse doll,[52] is not literally a copy in the literal sense. In that case, the Court noted, "We do not think it avoids the infringement of the copyright to take the substance or idea, and produce it through a different medium, and picturing in shape and details in sufficient imitation to make it a true copy of the character thought of by the appellant's employee." [53] Note that the Court uses both the terms "imitation" and "copy".

---

[52] King Features Syndicate v. Fleischer, 299 Fed. 533 (2d Cir. 1924).

[53] *Idem* at p. 535.

Sec. 22.6. Copying: Literal and Non-Literal

The term "copy" in this sense must be seen to be used generically, rather than literally. There is a range of different types of copying. Webster defines the term as imitation, transcript or reproduction of an original work.[54] It is derived from the Latin word *copia* meaning "abundance, supply".[55] An exact reproduction of a work is called a Chinese copy being identical in all respects insofar as reproduction of the text and other pertinent material are concerned. Xerox copies and other comparable copying devices of the art of reprography generally produce Chinese copies, substantially identical in all respects to the material copied. Transcription is closely allied to the exact reproduction to the extent it is a printed or typed reproduction of the original. In the literal sense of being written over, transcription generally is intended to be an exact reproduction of the contents of the original without the mechanical means of identity. A handwritten copy of a document would be an exact reproduction of the text thereof but it would not be an identical reproduction in the manner that prints of photographs and of motion pictures are, in effect, Chinese copies of the negative. On the other hand, transcription of stenographic notes is a form of transposition of shorthand into English or other language. It is a form of transcription, but not, in a literal sense, copying.

Imitation, like transcription, may have this dual sense of meaning. A painting may be reproduced by imitation. The imitator purports to make an exact reproduction of the original. To the extent he succeeds, it becomes a Chinese

---

[54] Webster, *op. cit., supra,* note 34, at p. 589, "copy".

[55] Ford, Celia, First Latin Book (1931), Latin-English Vocabulary, at p. vii.

copy thereof, artistic considerations aside. The result is comparable to print reproductions of paintings and other devices for making Chinese copies of originals. Imitation may not be complete or exact for both technological and artistic reasons. The imitation may be stylistic, trying to capture the particular style of another without necessarily copying his content. Imitation denotes simulation, be it conscious or unconscious. Thus, Judge Learned Hand, in *Fred Fisher, Inc.* v. *Dillingham,* held that Jerome Kern had taken an ostinato accompaniment from the copyrighted musical composition "Dardanella" owned by plaintiff in Kern's vocal number "Kalua" in the light opera "Good Morning, Dearie".[56] Judge Hand noted, "Mr. Kern swears that he was quite unconscious of any plagiarism, and on the whole I am disposed to give him the benefit of the doubt."[57]

Media transposition similarly gives rise to inherent differentiation in the nature of the imitation. Stephen Ladas has stated, ". . . a performance of a dramatic work is not a copy of the work, and that that fact of presentation by its nature, does not constitute a communication of a copy of the work to the public."[58] Thus, performance, per se, unless it also constitutes a publication, is not literally a copy of a work. That does not mean that performance may not infringe. Performance infringes when it appropriates material and substantial elements of a work under copyright without right or license. Similarly, there could be a mechanical infringement even though the unlawful reproduction of a musical composition by player piano

---

[56] 298 Fed. 145 (S.D.N.Y. 1924).

[57] *Idem* at p. 147.

[58] Ladas, Stephen, 2 The International Protection of Literary and Artistic Property (2 vols.) (1938), at p. 693.

roll[59] or by a phonograph record[60] was not deemed a copy thereof. Mechanical infringement may arise if a party purports to release a first recording of a musical composition without authorization or by failure to obtain a compulsory license after first use or contractual equivalent.[61] But technical rules as to the nature of copying for purposes of invoking statutory copyright aside, infringement, generically, covers both common law and statutory copyright. Copying has an analogous generic meaning for infringement purposes, regardless of whether or not there is a copying upon performance, and therefore a publication, or whether or not the particular material and/or use may be the subject of property. For infringement purposes, media differentiation is nonetheless conceivably within the scope of infringement whether or not performance is a copy.[62] For performance purports to be a presentation of a given work. The production is of a property as an underlying work, unless, as in rare cases, the

---

[59] White-Smith Music Publishing Co. v. Apollo Co., 209 U.S. 1 (1908).

[60] Regulations of the Copyright Office, Sec. 202.8(b).

> "A phonograph record or other sound recording is not considered a 'copy' of the compositions recorded on it, and is not acceptable for registration. Likewise, the Copyright Office does not register claims to exclusive rights in mechanical recordings themselves, or in the performances they reproduce."

But cf., Public Law 92-140, 92d Cong., S. 646, which became law October 15, 1971, Sec. 2 amending 17 U.S.C. 1(e) to make interchangeable parts, such as discs and tapes, copies of the work reproduced mechanically for purposes of remedies under 17 U.S.C. 101, 106 and 109.

[61] 17 U.S.C. 1(e); 101(e).

[62] See Patterson v. Century Productions, Inc., 93 F. 2d 489 (2d Cir. 1937), for example, as to motion pictures, and Shapiro, Bernstein & Co. v. Miracle Record Co., 91 F. Supp. 473 (N.D. Ill. 1952) as to phonograph records.

performance is improvised or is done without adaptation from a basic underlying work or from a scenario prepared for the performance. Whatever the source of the literary and artistic material, if the performance represents a substantial and material appropriation of the work of another and that work consists of protectible property, then there is a direct infringement of that work even though the underlying work which the performance purportedly is based upon may also infringe the work of the other. For the tort of infringement consists in the wrongful taking of the property of another. Judge Woolsey stated this well in *Lowenfels* v. *Nathan,* "The approved inquiry which must be answered by trier of the facts in every copyright case . . ." (citing cases) ". . . is:

> "(1) What was appropriated by the defendant from the plaintiff, and (2) if anything was appropriated, whether such appropriation was of copyrightable matter, and, if so, (3) whether it was a substantial appropriation." [63]

Not every transposition from one medium to another is capable of appropriation by reason of the very nature of the medium. Thus, literary works might be said to "inspire" musical compositions (without lyrics or other text), but such music cannot be said to infringe literary text because there is no equivalent transposition of the visual to the purely musical. The converse proposition is also true. To attempt to characterize sound, i.e., musical sound, by words falls short of any real representation of the sound and so cannot infringe. Of course, this is not true of musical notation since there a copy is made in musically understandable equivalents and if the copy

---

[63] 2 F. Supp. 73, 79 (S.D.N.Y. 1932).

were to infringe copyrighted music, then there would be infringement of copyright.

But equivalence by transposition is not necessarily on a work infringing work basis as in the linguistic versions in the Drone illustration. As Judge Noyes pointed out in *Dam* v. *Kirke La Shelle Co.*, ". . . the adaptation of a story to the stage must necessitate changes and additions. Few short stories could be transformed into dramatic compositions without the addition of many new incidents."[64] Literary genres as well as media thus play an important part in the nature of the infringed work in relation to the infringing work. A short story may consist of only several thousand words yet it may be infringed by another work even when new incidents and scenes have been added to the infringing work. So, too, a large novel may be condensed pictorially into a relative handful of the scenes and incidents therefrom in creating a motion picture based thereon. Again, infringement is not measured by total equivalence of infringing to infringed work.

Sec. 22.7. The Ingredients of the Tort of Infringement

The ingredient of infringement, then, is the taking of the literary and artistic property of another which is secured by statutory or common law copyright in a material and substantial way without right or permission from such other and as to which there are no defenses, as a matter of law or fact. This taking, or wrongful appropriation, is the gravamen of the tort. As stated by the Court in *Shipman* v. *R.K.O. Radio Pictures, Inc.*, "Thus piracy, hitherto defined as deliberate use, is now defined

[64] 175 Fed. 902, 907 (2d Cir. 1910).

to include both deliberate and unintentional use."[65] Judge Learned Hand had earlier expounded on the nature of infringement in this regard without using the term "piracy", stating:

> "The author's copyright is an absolute right to prevent others from copying his original collocation of words or notes, and does not depend upon the infringer's good faith. Once it appears that another has in fact used the copyright as the source of his production, he has invaded the author's rights. It is no excuse that in so doing his memory has played him a trick. In an indictment under Copyright Act, section 28 (Comp. St. sec. 9549), the excuse might be a defense, since the infringement would not be willful; but it is seldom that a tort, as this is, depends upon the purpose of the wrongdoer."[66]

The tort, then, is in the taking, regardless of intent. It would seem desirable therefore to confine the term "piracy" to its traditional meaning of deliberate or intentional taking of the literary and artistic property of another, whether or not authorship is attributed to the true creator or the piracy also consists of plagiarism. Since plagiarism is not the only form of appropriation and also has attributes of willful taking, it would seem better to use only the term "infringement" to characterize the tort.

If the essence of the tort of copyright infringement, or, of the infringement of exclusive rights under copyright, such as performance infringement, mechanical infringement, delivery infringement, are species of the generic term "copyright infringement", and if the essence of copy-

---

[65] 100 F. 2d 533, 537 (2d Cir. 1938).

[66] Fisher v. Dillingham, *supra,* note 56, at p. 148.

right is intellectual creation, then it would appear that the nature of copyright infringement consists in determination of creation. The claim of infringement of copyright is the first real test of validity of the copyright in the alleged infringed literary and artistic property. Whether the claim originates in the first instance in the summons and complaint of litigation or in the preliminary notice of infringement of copyright, the fact of claim of infringement is the first real test of such validity. Prior thereto, the certificate of copyright will be only prima facie evidence of the facts therein stated as to authorship and ownership.[67] Reliance may also be had on contractual warranties as to authorship and proprietorship, on the results of a search and copyright report, and on errors and omissions insurance. But warranties are no more than contractual clauses, the breach of which might result in indemnification and like safeguards but in no sense do they constitute a determination, as a matter of law, of authorship. The presumed creator or assignee warrants and represents that the person designated as author is the originator. The recipient of the warranty enters into the agreement in reliance thereon. Warranties therefore constitute a substitute for determination of creation. A copyright search and report are primarily means of ascertaining prima facie authorship as evidenced by registrations in the Copyright Office and the chain of title emanating therefrom. They are means of a generalized informational study as to the presumed origination of a particular work and its chain of title of ownership, but do not necessarily stem from an investigation undertaken in respect of a claim or suit for infringement. Search and report may be preliminary as part of the way of acquisition of rights in and to literary and artistic property and part of the mechanisms

---

[67] 17 U.S.C. 209.

for marketing the same. Once there is a contest involving determination of creation, whether in the claim stage or in litigation, the search and report may be an adjunct to ascertaining facts in relation to the contest but the search and report have no other intrinsic validity in respect thereto, apart from being able to trace and adduce facts that might be uncovered thereby. Errors and omissions insurance is the very abnegation of personal commitment to determination of creation. The insured simply turns over the claim or the suit to the insurer to defend, and if the limits of liability are sufficient and there is a compromise or an adverse determination in litigation, to pay off. That does not mean lack of personal involvement on the part of the insured because the insured is nevertheless a party defendant and its rights, such as they may be following such determination, may well be at stake in the contest.

None of these, in the final analysis, is a substitute for the contest invoked by claim of infringement. At times the contest may be in a stage where the rule making determination of the courts is never realized, as in the case of a claim prior to litigation or of a claim in litigation settled prior to determination by the judicial process.

Defenses aside, there is a comparison of the relative claims as to intellectual creation in the infringed work and in the infringing work. This is underscored by former Rule 2 of the Rules of the Supreme Court of the United States with respect to copyright infringement cases, which reads: "A copy of the alleged infringement of copyright, if actually made, and a copy of the work alleged to be infringed, should accompany the petition, or its absence be explained; except in cases of alleged infringement by the public performance of dramatic and dramatico-musical compositions, the delivery of lectures, sermons, addresses, and so forth, the infringement of copyright upon sculptures and other similar works and in any case where it is not feasible." [68]

The basis for an infringement action is that the defendant appropriated protectible literary and artistic property created by the plaintiff without right or permission. This presupposes that the party defendant directly infringing, as contrasted to the contributory infringer: (a) had an opportunity to avail himself of the infringed work; (b) did so; (c) appropriated substantial and material portions of the same; (d) such infringed work was protectible under copyright in such respects and could itself not be deemed a copy of the work of a third party because it had the irreducible modicum of originality; (e) the infringed work continued under copyright protection when the cause of action accrued; and (f) in no event was the appropriation fairly used.

Sec. 22.8. Access

Access is a determination that the directly infringing defendant had available a copy of the infringed work. Such a determination might be made by proof of actual sending of such copy to said defendant or by a presumption of access from the facts and circumstances. Then again, where there is no proof of actual access, access might be assumed by the substantial similarity of infringing and infringed works. In *Alexander* v. *Irving Trust Co.,*[69] plaintiff claimed infringement of her two-page article "Oliver Wendell

---

[68] Rules Adopted by the Supreme Court of the United States for Practice and Procedure Under Section 25 of an Act to Amend and Consolidate the Acts Respecting Copyright, Approved March 4, 1909, in Nimmer, *op. cit., supra,* note 40, Appendix G., at p. 938. Fn. 3 thereto indicates that Rule 2 was rescinded effective July 1, 1966.

[69] 132 F. Supp. 364 (S.D.N.Y. 1955).

Holmes—Psychiatrist" by defendant author, Clarence P. Oberndorf, who wrote a book entitled, "The Psychiatric Novels of Oliver Wendell Holmes". The book was first published in 1943 and revised in 1946. The article was published in 1939 in a medical journal which had ceased publication some time thereafter. Plaintiff claimed access should be inferred from the similarities. The Court held there was no access and no appropriation of any substantial part of plaintiff's article and that she had failed to sustain her burden of proof of access. Nor could a plaintiff sustain his burden of proof of access when he left a song entitled, "The Russian Gypsy Valse" with one, Gilbert, in defendant's employ, who urged revisions and remitted to Gilbert who later rejected and returned the song. Plaintiff failed to prove access by the composer of the alleged infringing tune. Judge Learned Hand indicated in this respect, "Really, the only tenable theory for the plaintiff is therefore that Altman himself pirated the song and brought it to Deutsch, and that theory depends upon the wholly unproven assumption that Altman got a copy of the song from some undisclosed third person." [70]

In *Wilkie* v. *Santly Bros.,*[71] plaintiff had composed a song in 1927 and 1928. His song "Confessing" had never been published but had been privately performed. Defendant, Bernice Petkere, composed her song "Starlight" in 1931. The District Court stated, "There is no direct evidence in the case that the defendants had access to the plaintiff's song, but access may be inferred from circumstances in the same way that any other fact is proved; and, although in a common-law copyright the range of contacts is necessarily

---

[70] Arnstein v. Edward B. Marks Music Corp., 82 F. 2d 275 (2d Cir. 1936), *aff'g* 11 F. Supp. 535 (S.D.N.Y. 1935).

[71] 13 F. Supp. 136 (S.D.N.Y. 1935), *aff'd* 91 F. 2d 978 (2d Cir. 1937).

restricted, I cannot say that it is entirely improbable that at some time prior to 1931, Miss Petkere may have had access to the melody of "Confessing." [72]

In *Lowenfels* v. *Nathan*[73] and *Caruthers* v. *R.K.O. Radio Pictures,*[74] Judge Woolsey employed the device of determining substantial similarity on a motion to dismiss based upon an assumption of access for purposes of the motion. The purpose was to determine preliminarily whether or not there was such great dissimilarity, so that as a matter of law, there was no case that might be tried as a matter of fact as to the nature of the similarities sufficient to determine whether appropriation had occurred. This practice was criticized by Judge Manton in *Shipman* v. *R.K.O. Radio Pictures, Inc.,* who remarked:

> "The instant case was decided on a motion to dismiss the bill, the result of a recent practice formulated below . . ." (citing *Lowenfels* and *Caruthers*) ". . . The judge dismissed the complaint on motion without taking testimony but upon a reading of the play and viewing an exhibition of the motion picture. Such a test by motion admits access and use. It admits what is tantamount to a presumption of piracy and a denial of good faith for, with access admitted, similarity of incident rests upon a high degree of probability of copying and a low degree of probability of independent creation. Such a practice puts a defendant in a dangerous position." [75]

It would seem that access might be inferred, in any event, where the alleged infringed work has been published. By

---

[72] *Idem,* at p. 136.
[73] 2 F. Supp. 73 (S.D.N.Y. 1932).
[74] 20 F. Supp. 906 (S.D.N.Y. 1937).
[75] 100 F. 2d 533, 538 (2d Cir. 1938).

publication here, one refers to the actual placing of copies on sale or making them generally available to the public or at least the relevant market of potential users. It is not necessarily used in the strict, technical sense of what constitutes publication for purposes of statutory copyright. For under that test, copies of a work may, in fact, be published, but copies available might really be sold regionally or in such few numbers as to fail to come to the attention of an alleged infringer. However, in the generality of matters, such as publication of books, periodicals and newspapers, certainly of national scope and distribution, it might fairly be said that in such situations access might conceivably be inferred from the fact of general availability, unless there is credible evidence from the alleged infringer that he was unaware of the same.

It should be stated here that, from a legal point of view, access should not and does not necessarily have the overtones of larcenous taking, like the burglar who is caught with the goods. Access in the case of placing of copies for sale is an ordinary and accepted concomitant of dissemination of literary and artistic works.[75a] In this sense, access is meaningless where an alleged infringer has possibilities of access open to him in the same manner as all other readers. If a work is readily obtainable at a public library, a newsstand, or a bookstore, the issue of access is almost

---

[75a] Echevarria v. Warner Bros. Pictures, Inc., 12 F. Supp. 632 (S.D. Cal. 1935), Yankwich, J., at p. 638, "Ordinarily, of course, after a literary work is published, it is accessible to every one. And if there be actual infringement, mere priority is sufficient. Even in those instances, however, the similarity may be the fortuitous similarity of conception. Access becomes important where, as here, the publication in which the synopsis appeared is not one in general circulation, accessible to any one who pays the price. It was evidently not for sale to the general public and was sent to a selected list only."

irrelevant. No weight should be given to it either way where the plaintiff did not also provide the alleged infringer with a copy of the work, directly call it to his attention, or otherwise prove access by credible evidence.

A more difficult problem is the matter of copyright registration of a musical composition or other literary material able to be so registered, as an unpublished work.[76] Thus, a song might be unpublished but nevertheless performed as an unpublished work. If such a work is readily available for examination, e.g., in the form of lead sheets, or professional copies for performance purposes, then no inference might be drawn as to access and it conceivably might be deemed an attribute of operation of a music publishing company,[76a] inferable from its general availability to the profession and deniable by the alleged infringer if unaware thereof.

On the other hand, if the unpublished song is not disseminated, for example, because it is unpublished by the composer and left in his files, then the burden of proof of access would be his to prove availability to the defendant. Of course, in theory, it is conceivable that by reason of deposit of a copy of the work in the Copyright Office,[77] access might be deemed *ipso facto* available therefrom. Ordinarily, there would be no reason for a party to seek such copy from the Copyright Office unless it were already involved in a

---

[76] 17 U.S.C. 12.

[76a] In Hirsch v. Paramount Pictures, Inc., 17 F. Supp. 816 (S.D. Cal. 1937), plaintiff had registered an unpublished song for copyright. Judge Yankwich stated at p. 818, "Nor, even if we accepted her version as to the defendants' access to her song and chorus—through her humming it to Revel in a Hollywood Restaurant—does her case fare better, on the issue of similarity. . . . Access assumed, similarity becomes all-important."

[77] *Idem,* note 75, *supra.*

claim of infringement with respect thereto. This being unlikely, the fact of request of such a copy from the Copyright Office would then be proof of access.

With respect to unpublished works, the greatest problems of access are likely to arise. The market operates, in part, by submission of works to prospective users by authors or their representatives. In some instances there is a regular channel of communication as to consideration of such properties by staff readers, publishers, producers or otherwise. In such event, there is no issue as to access, only as to whether the same was used. But where there is widespread performance of an unpublished work, there is a greater likelihood of awareness thereof as an ordinary observer over and above any cognizance of literary and artistic works through limited publication for marketing purposes. In such event, there arises the question of access through having seen the performance and the quality and nature of the access in the capacity of viewer—or in the case of a concert—listener, without having access to the physical manuscript or score.

In other instances, users will even refuse to look at works where they are not received through their regular channels for fear of claim of use without right and therefore infringement. Seymour Bricker has indicated that Universal Pictures would not even look at unsolicited material and would return it to the sender unopened.[78]

However, access often turns on the issue of credibility, as to whether judge or jury will believe any particular witness. For example, Judge Learned Hand had this observation after referring to some vague testimony, "Although we should have to hold all four of these witnesses deliberate

[78] Bricker, Seymour, ABA Copyright Symposium, Dallas, Texas, Aug. 25, 1956, on Motion Pictures.

perjurers, willing to forge documents to back up their testimony, that is sometimes the only possible conclusion when the piracy is close enough . . . As we have said, Arnstein at the beginning of his testimony tried to fasten possession of a copy of his song upon Altman and retracted later. Altman might have got hold of one of the supposed thirty copies from someone else, but there has been no suggestion of this, and it is not very likely, since the song fell flat." [79]

By whatever method, whether or not in issue because access is acknowledged by the defendant, or assumed for purposes of a motion to dismiss, or presumed from the fact of publication and sale of copies, or even from substantial similarity, there must be a determination that there is a comparative copy of an allegedly infringed work available to the alleged infringer, to wit, access.

The issue of access is a predicate for the statement of opportunity to use. Mere opportunity is of no account without the determination of the fact of such use. This, of course, is the gravamen of the claim for infringement. A corollary thereto is that the use was in fact substantial and material. Where there is literal equivalent use, then there must be a determination that plaintiff's creation is prior in time, was original and that the appropriation was substantial and material and not a fair use. In *Boosey* v. *Empire Music Co.,*[80] the Court granted a motion for a temporary injunction since the words "I hear you calling me" and the music accompanying these words were practically identical in both tunes. However the Court took market realities into consideration by suspending the injunction upon defendant's posting a bond in the sum of

---

[79] Arnstein v. Edward B. Marks Music Corp., note 70, *supra,* at p. 276.

[80] 224 Fed. 646 (S.D.N.Y. 1915).

$3,000 pending final hearing. Indeed, a single performance of the chorus of Victor Herbert's "Kiss Me Again" was held to constitute an infringement when performed by an organist in a motion picture theatre providing musical accompaniment for silent motion pictures.[81]

Sec. 22.9. Quality and Quantity of Copying

Even literal copying is not necessarily infringing. Where ten of eighteen lines of a song were printed in Collier's National Weekly from plaintiff's song "You Can't Stop Me From Lovin' You" such use was held to be a fair use because the music was not reproduced, only snatches of the lyrics were used which could not be pieced together and the use was not a subterfuge for presenting the song to the public. In the course of this decision, in *Shapiro, Bernstein & Co.* v. *P. F. Collier,* Judge Goddard laid down the test for fair use, stating:

> "Without attempting to lay down any hard and fast rule for determining what constitutes a 'fair use' of a copyrighted matter, the following are generally considered as some of the tests to be applied: The extent and relative value of the extracts; the purpose and whether the quoted portions might be used as a substitute for the original work; the effect upon the distribution and objects of the original work."[82]

There is a progression, then, in terms of comparison of alleged infringing and infringed works, that pertains to the nature of the copying and the quality of the copying. From literal reproduction, the next type of copying is one

---

[81] M. Witmark and Sons v. Pastime Amusement Company, 298 Fed. 470 (E.D. S. Car. 1924).

[82] U.S. P. Q. 40, 43 (S.D.N.Y. 1924). See Chap. XXV, *infra.*

with immaterial variation. The infringement does not consist of an exact reproduction but of immaterial revisions, paraphrases, and transpositions. In finding infringement, in *Haas* v. *Leo Feist, Inc.,*[83] Judge Learned Hand remarked, "Nevertheless, between the two choruses in question there is a parallelism which seems to my ear to pass the bounds of mere accident. If the choruses be transposed into the same key and played in the same time, their similarities become at once apparent. . . . The case is not of the mere suggestion of a bar common to each, but of a continuously suggestive melodic parallelism, except at the end. Identity was not to be expected, but derivation seems to me proved." [84]

In a sense, the quantum and quality of infringement are inseparable from the character of the infringement. One must start from a determination other than of copying versus no copying whatsoever, in ascertaining infringement or not, as the case may be. Of course, such polarity will end the matter, one way or the other. But there may be in-between stages which dispose of the matter. Thus, the doctrine of *de minimis* has relevance. If a single bar of a tune is in common and does not convey any material aspect of the tune, melodically, rhythmically or harmonically, it might be said to be of such minimal account, that even if it were found to be taking, it would be such an immaterial taking as to be unworthy of legal consideration.

A second area of appropriation that would not be cognizable as infringement, even if there were a use of the work of another—is under the doctrine of fair use. Saul

---

[83] 234 Fed. 105 (S.D.N.Y. 1916).
[84] *Idem* at p. 107.

Cohen has characterized fair use as the excision or elimination by such use from the quality of infringement, stating, " . . . it seems incorrect somehow to say a fair use is an infringement which is permitted; if it is permitted, it is not an infringement."[85] Fair use, then, is exempt use so that any such use means that, by virtue thereof, there can be no infringement.

Thus, in both cases of *de minimis* and fair use, it is immaterial whether the appropriation has been by literal copying, immaterial variation or other type of appropriation. In either event, there is no infringement. A third type of exemption relates to the taking of non-protectible components. Sec. 3 of the present Copyright Act provides in part: "The copyright provided by this title shall protect all the copyrightable components of the work copyrighted, and all matter therein in which copyright is already subsisting. . . ."[86] In *Seltzer* v. *Sunbrock*,[87] plaintiff had registered for copyright two books on roller derby races in the form of dramatic compositions and then sued defendants for infringement by printing programs as copies thereof and for running roller derby contests as infringements by performance without right or license from plaintiff. The Court held, "What Seltzer really composed was a description of a system for conducting races on roller skates. A system, as such, can never be copyrighted."[88]

---

[85] Cohen, Saul, Fair Use in the Law of Copyright, 6 Copyright Law Symposium 43 (1955) at p. 48.

[86] 17 U.S.C. 3.

[87] 22 F. Supp. 621 (S.D. Cal. 1938); cf. Seltzer v. Corem, 26 F. Supp. 892 (N.D. Ind. 1939), *rev'd,* however, in 107 F. 2d 75 (7th Cir. 1939) which dismissed the complaint on the merits while noting the want of good faith in bringing the action as a friendly suit between the parties.

[88] *Idem* at p. 630.

In holding that there was nothing copyrightable in plaintiff's pamphlet about General Pershing, Judge Hough remarked in *Eggers* v. *Sun Sales Corporation,*

> "What is registered is a 'claim to copyright.' (Act March 4, 1909, c. 320, sec. 10 (Comp. St. sec. 9531). There is no provision for examination, as in the case of patents, and probably for that reason the act (section 3 [Comp. St. sec. 9519]) declares that protection is extended to 'all the copyrightable component parts of the work copyrighted.' The inference is that there may be in that for which claim is made much to which the protection of the act cannot extend." [89]

Again Judge Hough construed the phrase in the statute, "all the copyrightable component parts of the work copyrighted" in *Dymow* v. *Bolton*, observing that said ". . . phrase presupposes that there may be much in what is popularly called a copyrighted work as to which the statute affords no protection." [90]

Sec. 22.10. Protectible Components

But it remained for Judge Manton to interpret the meaning of the section so as to give it application to a literary work and thereby indicate the context for the acting out of the elements of a determination of creation in infringement proceedings. In *King Features Syndicate* v. *Fleischer*, he remarked that Sec. 3 " . . . provides protection for all the copyrightable component parts of the thing copy-

---

[89] 263 Fed. 373, 374 (2d Cir. 1920).
[90] 11 F. 2d 690, 691 (2d Cir. 1926).

righted, and the proprietor has all the rights in respect thereto which he would have, if each part were individually copyrighted under the act. The courts have given this meaning to this section. Da Prato Statuary Co. v. Guiliani Co. (C.C.) 189 Fed. 90; Mail and Express Co. v. Life Pub. Co., 192 Fed. 899, 113 C.C.A. 377. Copying is not confined to a literary repetition, but includes various modes in which the matter of any publication may be adopted, imitated, or transferred with more or less colorable alteration. The disguise of the source from which the material was derived does not defeat the protection of the copyright, nor does taking a part of the work constitute an evasion of the copyright. Lawrence v. Dana, Fed. Cas. No. 8, 136, 4 Cliff. 80. The appellees did not take all of the copyrighted matter, or all its principal characters, but took one, the idea of the horse 'Sparky'." [91] But *Da Prato*[92] involved the taking of 18 copyrighted cuts of plaintiff's for use in defendant's infringing catalogue, the balance of the cuts out of a total of 117 so utilized by plaintiff being uncopyrighted. Since plaintiff's catalogue constituted a publication of all of the cuts, he was limited to claim for infringement as to the copyrighted components, the 18 cuts under copyright. *Mail & Express Co.*[93] likewise covered copyrighted pictures, so held by reason of the copyright of the periodical in which the pictures were contained. In both cases, there was a clear separability of the material into component parts each of which is susceptible of copyright. The House Report on Sec. 3 of the 1909 Act says very little about the application thereof on this point except to point out, " . . . nor do we intend to

---

[91] 299 Fed. 533, 535 (2d Cir. 1924).
[92] 189 Fed. 90 (C.C. D. Minn. 1911).
[93] 192 Fed. 899 (2d Cir. 1912).

make copyrightable anything which has fallen into the public domain." [94]

It is submitted that such an interpretation of the section has the effect of providing the context for the third type of appropriation, the first being literal copying, the second being paraphrase and immaterial variation. It has been held that mere paraphrase is actionable infringement.[95] Judge Learned Hand has expressed this in terms of immaterial variations, stating, "It is of course essential to any protection of literary property, whether at common law or under the statute, that the right cannot be limited literally to the text, else a plagiarist would escape by immaterial variations." [96]

Sec. 22.11. Abstractions Test

Mere paraphrase and immaterial variation are but one degree removed from literal copying. Presumably, in a true case of infringement, the purpose is to provide colorable imitation and at the same time evade claim of copying. Of course, the paraphrase or immaterial variation may be made with impunity as a fair use if the use is otherwise fair. Independent origination may also be claimed therefor by the alleged infringer as well as the claim of lack of origination thereof by the plaintiff, or possibly that the material allegedly appropriated does not consist truly of a copyrightable component.

However, it is but an extension, a matter of degree, to go from mere paraphrase and immaterial variation to

---

[94] Report No. 2222, House of Representatives, 60th Cong., 2d Sess., Feb. 22, 1909, as reprinted in Nimmer on Copyright (1970), Appendix I, p. 959 at p. 971.

[95] West Publishing Co. v. Edward Thompson Co., 169 Fed. 833, 834 (C.C. E.D.N.Y. 1909), *mod. and aff'd,* 176 Fed. 833 (2d Cir. 1910).

[96] Nichols v. Universal Pictures Corporation, 45 F. 2d 119, 121 (2d Cir. 1930).

colorable imitation and the abstractions test of Judge Hand which he articulated in the same case. Note the manner in which he proceeds in this respect from the one to the other after rejecting the test of literal copying as the sole test. Judge Hand stated in *Nichols*:

> "It is of course essential to any protection of literary property, whether at common law or under the statute, that the right cannot be limited literally to the text, else a plagiarist would escape by immaterial variations. That has never been the law, but, as soon as literal appropriation ceases to be the test, the whole matter is necessarily at large, so that, as was recently well said by a distinguished judge, the decisions cannot help much in a new case. Fendler v. Morosco, 253 N.Y. 281, 292, 171 N.E. 56. When plays are concerned, the plagiarist may excise a separate scene [Daly v. Webster, 56 F. 483 (C.C.A. 2); Chappell v. Fields, 210 F. 864 (C.C.A. 2); Chatterton v. Cave, L.R. 3 App. Cas. 483]; or he may appropriate part of the dialogue (Warne v. Seebohm, L.R. 39 Ch. D. 73). Then the question is whether the part so taken is 'substantial', and therefore not a 'fair use' of the copyrighted work; it is the same question as arises in the case of any other copyrighted work. Marks v. Feist, 290 F. 959 (C.C.A. 2); Emerson v. Davies, Fed. Cas. No. 4436, 3 Story 768, 795-797. But when the plagiarist does not take out a block in situ, but an abstract of the whole, decision is more troublesome. Upon any work, and especially upon a play, a great number of patterns of increasing generality will fit equally well, as more and more of the incident is left out. The last may perhaps be no more than the most general statement of what the play is about, and at times consist only of its title; but there is a point in

this series of abstractions where they are no longer protected, since otherwise the playwright could prevent the use of his 'ideas', to which, apart from their expression, his property is never extended. Holmes v. Hurst, 714 U.S. 82, 86, 19 S. Ct. 606, 43 L. Ed. 904; Guthrie v. Curlett, 36 F. (2d) 694 (C.C.A. 2). Nobody has ever been able to fix that boundary, and nobody ever can." [96a]

Judge Hand appears to be developing a kind of ripple theory. If a stone were thrown into a more or less placid body of water, it would generate ripples as waves moved further and further away from the stone. Those closest to the stone would clearly be seen as the direct consequence of the impact of the stone. As the ripples spread farther and farther from the point of impact, they become broader and broader and less and less formulated as stemming from the impact until they merge almost imperceptibly into the surrounding body of water and disappear. Like the ripples, the alleged infringing work is seen as becoming less and less identifiable in terms of exact relation to the point of impact, the alleged infringed work, and more and more generalized in respect thereto. Non-literal copying, then, is a progression from the paraphrase or immaterial variation to the less and less specifically identifiable to the more and more generally identifiable and, finally, to the non-protectible only abstractly identifiable, if at all. Others have characterized this phenomenon in other terms; Chafee, as the pattern of events;[97] Libott, as tracking;[98]

[96a] *Ibid.*

[97] Chafee, Zechariah, Jr., Reflections on the Law of Copyright, 45 Col. L. Rev. 503, 513 (1945).

[98] Libott, Robert Yale, Round The Prickly Pear: The Idea-Expression Fallacy in a Mass Communication World, 16 Copyright Law Symposium 41 (1968).

Spring, as treatment copying;[99] Nimmer, as comprehensive literal or nonliteral similarity.[100] Chafee adverts to the line between the idea and the precise form of its expression and that protection covers the work's pattern, its sequence of events and development of character interplay. Libott refers to the degree to which the unauthorized appropriator had tracked substantial portions of the language of the alleged infringing work. Spring notes that copying can consist of treatment and development and larger items of creative expression of another—ideas, plots, character, conflict, situation, surprise, narrative suspense and plot manipulation.[101] Nimmer considers comprehensive nonliteral similarity as operative "where the fundamental essence or structure of one work is duplicated in another."[102]

It is precisely in this area that the metaphysics of comparison of works is operative. Spring has remarked, "This process of exclusion or elimination of similarities of material is difficult, because it involves an artificial distinction between material and expression."[103] The difficulties have impelled Shafter to observe, "Infringement, or plagiarism, is the most important consideration in any discussion of copyright. . . .[104] The determination of infringement is one of the most difficult of all legal questions. . . ."[105]

---

[99] Spring, Samuel, Risks and Rights 213-214 (1952).

[100] Nimmer on Copyright (1970), Secs. 143.1 and 143.11 at p. 620.

[101] Spring, *op. cit., supra,* note 99, at p. 117.

[102] Nimmer, *op. cit., supra,* note 100, Sec. 143.11 at p. 620.

[103] Spring, *op. cit., supra,* note 99, at p. 218. Parenthetically, he believes that the issue of access is not too important realistically, at p. 216.

[104] Shafter, Alfred M., Musical Copyright, Second Ed. (1939) at p. 189.

[105] *Idem* at p. 192.

The Concept of Infringement

Whether the determination of the point at which it is found that there is copying or not, as the case may be, because the relationship is or is not too abstract to constitute appropriation or protectible similarity, be done by the ordinary observer in the audience test or by the expert, is probably more a matter of philosophic predilection. In either event, as Nicholson notes, "It is not always immediately apparent whether there has been infringement or not."[106] As a result, in cases where there is non-literal appropriation, the observation of Birmingham is apt, "What constitutes a copy is a question involving a value judgment."[107] There must be a judgment that the alleged infringed work has or has not protectible copyrightable components, because it has or has not appropriated its materials from a prior work and/or it is or is not a system, plan, idea that is not the subject of copyright. This is the gravamen of the test for originality, which Dworkin concludes, ". . . has resolved itself to little more than an absence of copying. . . ."[108] There must be a second judgment that the alleged infringing work has or has not appropriated substantial or material portions of the alleged infringed work in a manner that does not constitute an exempted fair use thereof. Inherent in this judgment is the determination of the source of defendant's origination. The alleged infringer might have independently created the alleged infringing material. This would have greater theoretical possibility in areas like photography where innumerable originals may be indepen-

---

[106] Nicholson, A Manual of Copyright Practice, Second Ed. (1956) at p. 97.

[107] Birmingham, William T., A Critical Analysis of the Infringement of Ideas, 5 Copyright Law Symposium 107 (1954) at p. 125.

[108] Dworkin, Alan T., Originality in the Law of Copyright, 11 Copyright Law Symposium 60 (1962) at p. 81.

dently created of the same subject matter by taking the photograph from the same angle and position. The likelihood of linguistic parallelism of this kind is far less, but even there, if the particular area of concern is technical, for example, with a limited vocabulary and therefore limited means of expression, the possibility of independent creation would appear to be greater than in literary creation generally.

Sec. 22.12. Ordinary Observer Test

In any event, the perspective for making such judgments is generally that of the ordinary observer, although, on occasion, experts are used. Judge Hough expressed this in *Dymow* v. *Bolton,* stating: " . . . the copyright, like all statutes, is made for plain people, and that copying which is infringement must be something 'which ordinary observation would cause to be recognized as having been taken from' the work of another. King Syndicate v. Fleischer (C.C.A.), 299 F. 533. It requires dissection rather than observation to discern any resemblance here."[109] In *King Features,* the Court observed, "The artist's concept of humor was embodied in the copyrightable form, was addressed to the contemplation of the observer and the reader; . . ."[110]

Indeed, in the very case where Judge Hand articulated his abstractions test, he also expressed his displeasure with the use of experts, stating:

> "We cannot approve the length of the record, which was due chiefly to the use of expert witnesses. Argument is argument, whether in the box or at the bar,

[109] 11 Fed. 2d 690, 692 (2d Cir. 1926) (italics).

[110] King Features Syndicate v. Fleischer, 299 Fed. 533, 538 (2d Cir. 1924).

> and its proper place is the last. The testimony of an expert upon such issues, especially his cross-examination, greatly extends the trial and contributes nothing which cannot be better heard after the evidence is all submitted. It ought not to be allowed at all; and while its admission is not a ground for reversal, it cumbers the case and tends to confusion, for the more the court is led into the intracacies of dramatic craftsmanship, the less likely it is to stand upon the firmer, if more naive, ground of its considered impressions upon its own perusal. We hope that in this class of cases such evidence may in the future be entirely excluded; and the case confined to the actual issues; that is, whether the copyrighted work was original, and whether the defendant copied it, so far as the supposed infringement is identical." [111]

Judge Yankwich qualified this distaste for the expert in *Hirsch* v. *Paramount Pictures, Inc.,* stating, "Expert testimony is helpful, especially in matters involving musical composition. But, in the end, the test—as pointed out by the Second Circuit in Arnstein v. Edward B. Marks Music Corp., supra—is resemblance noticeable to the average hearer." [112]

Actually, there appear to be two variants of the ordinary recipient test in the performing arts: the ordinary spectator in the theatre and other visual arts, and the ordinary listener as to music. The spectator test was set forth by Judge Blatchford in *Daly* v. *Palmer*[113] in terms of rec-

---

[111] Nichols v. Universal Pictures Corporation, note 96, *supra,* at p. 123.

[112] 17 F. Supp. 816, 818 (S.D. Cal. 1937).

[113] 6 Fed. Cas. 1132, Case No. 3552, 6 Blatch. 256 (C.C. S.D.N.Y. 1868).

ognition by the spectator—the audience—of the test set forth by the Court. He stated, "The true test of whether there is piracy or not, is to ascertain whether there is a servile or evasive imitation of the plaintiff's work, or whether there is a bona fide original compilation, made up from common materials, and common sources, with resemblances which are merely accidental, or result from the nature of the subject. Emerson v. Davies (Case No. 4,436)." [114]

Sec. 22.13. Criteria of Dramatic Composition

Judge Blatchford had to determine in that case whether a rescue from a railroad scene in plaintiff's play, "Under the Gaslight" had been infringed by Dion Boucicault's play "Railroad Scene". The claim as to infringement pertained to this scene only as being the subject of unlawful appropriation. The case is important because it sets forth the nature of a dramatic composition and criteria for ascertaining infringement.

After stating that a dramatic composition is a written or literary work set in order, the Court stated:

> "A dramatic composition is such a work in which the narrative is not related but is represented by dialogue and action. When a dramatic composition is represented, in dialogue and action, by persons who represent it as real, by performing or going through with the various parts or characters assigned to them severally, the composition is acted, performed, or represented; and, if the representation is in public, it is a public representation. To act, in the sense of the statute, is to represent as real, by countenance,

---

[114] *Idem* at p. 1138 (italics).

voice or gesture, that which is not real. A character in a play who goes through with a series of events on the stage without speaking, if such be his part in the play, is none the less an actor in it than one who, in addition to motions and gestures, uses his voice. A pantomime is a species of theatrical entertainment, in which the whole action is represented by gesticulation, without the use of words. A written work, consisting wholly of directions, set in order for conveying the ideas of the author on a stage or public place, by means of characters who represent the narrative wholly by action, is as much a dramatic composition designed or suited for public representation, as if language or dialogue were used in it to convey some of the ideas." [115]

Defendant, the manager of Niblo's Garden, who was to perform the Boucicault play, sought to show that the elements of the railroad scene were common property and therefore not protectible. The Court held it was plaintiff's invention as to the manner in which set forth in his play, "Under the Gaslight". Although there were different characters and language in the two plays, "The action, the narrative, the dramatic effect and impression, and the series of events in the two scenes, are identical." [116] The Court then articulated the spectator test. "All that is substantial and material in the plaintiff's 'railroad scene' has been used by Boucicault, in the same order and sequence of events, and in a manner to convey the same sensations and impressions to those who see it represented, as in the plaintiff's play." [117]

The Court's test as to the unlawful appropriation seems to be that the taking of a scene central to plaintiff's play

---

[115] *Idem* at pp. 1135-36. See Sec. 23.3, ***infra.***
[116] *Idem* at p. 1136.
[117] *Idem* at p. 1138.

in elements of its story line—action and narrative—,as developed—order and sequence of events—,projecting comparable dramatic effect—same sensations and impressions—, was a substantial and material appropriation which was unlawful because it was a taking of protectible property. In short, the plaintiff had composed a dramatic composition, telling of a story by means of actors, whether with dialogue or by pantomime, which necessarily carried its own sequence or order of events, and which, as drama, sought to convey certain sensations, impressions and ideas. Ideas in the latter sense might be two-fold. Ideas might refer to the theme of the dramatic composition, its story line, the thought behind the work, the point the dramatist was trying to make in dramatic terms. Then again, ideas might be such as are more or less extrinsic to the story line itself, for example, the projection of a particular ideology, the deliberate espousing of a particular point of view, whether by way of propaganda or, as in the morality play, in terms of the moral purpose to be derived from the drama.

In those terms, ideas are projections or expressions of sentiments and thoughts of the dramatist himself, generally as viewed from the perspective of the playwright in terms of dramatic creation. But there is yet another development of ideas of dramaturgy; those seen from the perspective of dramatic criticism. The critic, essentially any third party analyst of the work, finds certain ideas in a work, sometimes in terms of characterization, sometimes in the nature of dramatic development. These are third party conclusions as to the nature of the thoughts immanent in the work which may not have been consciously articulated by the dramatist either by way of story line—theme—, or overt ideological approach. Ideas so adumbrated critically may have important pedagogic value in terms of understanding of the theatre, but inasmuch as they are not the ideas as seen by the dramatist himself and as intended to be projected by him, they would seem not to have legal significance in terms of tests of dramatic composition for infringement purposes.

What Judge Blatchford sought then to protect was the configuration of dramatic composition. As stated by the Court in *Fuller* v. *Bemis* in discussing dramatic composition, "It is essential to such a composition that it should tell some story. The plot may be simple. It may be but the narrative or representation of a single transaction, but it must repeat or mimic some action, speech, emotion, passion, or character, real or imaginary. And when it does, it is the ideas thus expressed which become subject of copyright." [118] In granting a perpetual injunction with respect to the infringing railroad scene at issue in *Daly* v. *Palmer,*[119] the Court, in *Daly* v. *Webster,* restated the elements of a dramatic composition, "There must be a series of events, dramatically represented, in a certain sequence or order. In other words, there must be a 'composition', i.e. a work invented and set in order—a work of various parts and characters, which, when put upon the stage, is developed in a series of circumstances." [120]

The Court then showed a profound awareness of the mechanics of creation as it relates to the problem of determining what is creation, and by a determination of infringement, what is copying, and therefore not creation. It observed in this respect, "It is plain that the author of such a work, where various incidents, in themselves, common literary property, are grouped to form a particular story,

---

[118] 50 Fed. 926, 929 (C.C. S.D.N.Y. 1892).
[119] Note 113, *supra.*
[120] 56 Fed. 483, 487 (2d Cir. 1892).

must be confined, in his claim to copyright, closely to the story he has thus composed, and that another author, who by materially varying the incidents, materially changes the story, should not be held to be an infringer." [121] The Court thereby proposed to look at two things, the elements of protectible property in dramatic composition, i.e., what the dramatist really does that is susceptible to protection under copyright and perforce capable of being infringed, which pertains to the creative process of the creator of the alleged infringed work, and then at the creative process of the alleged infringer to determine what he has really done.

For the creative process is a dialectical construct of creation of originality out of literary materials that are so common that Judge Story was impelled to observe that without borrowing by writers much of the great literature would simply not have been created.[122] The test to him was whether or not the imitation was close enough to constitute an evasion of copyright even if such closeness were not in the form of literal copying.[123]

Sec. 22.13(a). Borrowing and Rearrangement

But literary borrowing and refashioning to create original works, many of them masterpieces, are generally considered in the context of sufficient change of essential elements so that, in effect, the later work is essentially a new work that is deemed the creation of that writer. The reference of Judge Story to literary borrowing of this sort over the centuries would, in all likelihood, have little legal application under copyright because, by the passage of time,

---

[121] *Ibid.*

[122] Emerson v. Davies, 8 Fed. Cas. 615, Case No. 4,436 (C.C. D. Mass. 1845), Story, J. at p. 619.

[123] *Idem* at p. 625.

the prior works very likely would have been in the public domain anyway at the time the later writer created his work, so that in any event he would have been spared the possibility of claim of infringement. But if a defense to a claim of borrowing close enough to constitute infringement is the fact of non-copying, then a writer might, in a given situation, attempt to create a non-infringing work by deliberate change from essential elements of the work of another in the course of creation by the writer so as to vitiate any claim of infringement. Just as there may be unconscious infringement,[124] such as a taking from memory where there was access and originality in the infringed work, so, too, there may be conscious variation with an intent to avoid infringement. This should be seen as part of the creative process as observed by the Court in *Daly* v. *Webster*.[125] As pointed out by the Supreme Court in *Holmes* v. *Hurst*, "The right thus secured by the copyright act is not a right to the use of certain words, because they are the common property of the human race, and are as little susceptible of private appropriation as air or sunlight; nor is it the right to ideas alone, since in the absence of means of communicating them they are of value to no one by the author. But the right is to that arrangement of words which the author has selected to express his ideas." [126]

Arrangement, then, can be negated by legally permissible rearrangement by sufficient variation of incidents and story so that the result is deemed to be a creative work and not an infringement. Of course, the result does not always mate-

---

[124] Fred Fisher, Inc. v. Dillingham, 298 Fed. 145 (S.D.N.Y. 1924), L. Hand, J.

[125] Note 120, *supra*.

[126] 174 U.S. 82, 86 (1899).

rialize in that the changes made are not material and substantial so that there is substantial and material incorporation of protectible elements of the work of another. This was the case in *Davis* v. *DuPont de Nemours & Co.,* where the Court observed,

> "Defendants further contend that even if they copied the Davis play through the Deutsch screenplay, they did not make substantial use of the Davis play in the actual television program. After Misses Babbin and Gellen had completed their adaptation from the Deutsch screenplay, they were informed of the existence of the Davis play and the possible infringement liability. They then proceeded to do what in defendants' opinion was necessary *to 'unDavis' the T.V. script.*
>
> "Defendants urge the court to remember, in ruling on whether they were successful in this endeavor, that they had contractual rights to use the novel and the Deutsch screenplay. They argue that 'anything in the Deutsch scenario which can be found in or attributed to the Wharton novel, that is the independent creation of Deutsch, or which are merely elements which are inherent in the particular theme, environment, background or setting of 'ETHAN FROME' were fairly at the disposal of defendant Talent.'
>
> * * *
>
> "Plaintiff's contentions are consistent with this analysis. He does not question Talent's right to adapt Mrs. Wharton's novel for television; he does assert that Talent had no right to copy his dramatization of the novel." [127]

---

[127] 240 F. Supp. 612 (S.D.N.Y. 1965) (emphasis added), pp. 620-621.

The Concept of Infringement

The phrase "to 'unDavis' the TV script" in the context of other rights to adapt and create from the novel and the Helen Deutsch screenplay, without use of the Davis play in its protectible elements, indicates that creation, in a proper case, might consciously skirt infringement by variation of elements found in a protected work as to which there is no right or authority for use for adaptation or other creation, but there are other rights and permissions. Copying, *simpliciter,* should not be determined then solely in terms of an alleged infringing work and an alleged infringed work. The contours of the market with respect to the literary and artistic work must be ascertained and defined. The bundle of exclusive rights constituting the copyright for any given work should be determined as to the uses made thereof in the market. The sequential roll of the property has to be developed as to both works, to determine what has been granted and what has been reserved in terms of the work. The copyright report might be the initial step in this regard. The review of contractual clauses granting rights in the bundle of rights should also be explored. Often these might include various permissions and quitclaims. Only after the legally permissible has been separated from the legally impermissible can a comparison be made of the alleged infringing work and the alleged infringed work, because only then can one ascertain what has been copied from the latter as opposed to use of permissible sources for adaptation. Whether or not there is a contention of permissible use in the sequential roll, the presumptive creator of the variant work may also have relied on borrowing of permissible elements, be it common property in the public domain not susceptible of protection by copyright, or be it elements which, by their very nature, are not protectible as dramatic composition without regard to commonality of such elements as public property. In theory, these are not the plaintiff's creation so that claim of infringement cannot cover these elements. Even if copied, these elements are not protectible so that the defendant cannot possibly have invaded the copyright of the plaintiff because there has been no invasion of the area of protectible rights of the proprietor.

Sec. 22.13(b). Choreography

Fuller v. *Bemis*[128] involved a claim of infringement of a copyrighted, written description entitled "Serpentine Dance", by Marie Louise Fuller, each part of which was characterized as a "tableau". A motion for a preliminary injunction based upon the authority of *Daly* v. *Palmer*[129] was denied on the theory that the work was not a dramatic composition.

The Court stated:

> "It is essential to such a composition that it should tell some story. The plot may be simple. It may be but the narrative or representation of a single transaction; but it must repeat or mimic some action, speech, emotion, passion, or character, real or imaginary. And when it does, it is the ideas thus expressed which become subject of copyright. An examination of the description of complainant's dance, as filed for copyright, shows that the end sought for and accomplished was solely the devising of a series of graceful movements, combined with an attractive arrangement of drapery, lights, and shadows, telling no story, portraying no character, depicting no emotion. The merely mechanical movements by which effects are produced on the stage are not subjects of copyright where they

---

[128] 50 Fed. 926 (C.C. S.D.N.Y. 1892).

[129] Note 113, *supra*.

> convey no ideas whose arrangement make up a dramatic composition." [130]

It will be recalled that, in *Daly* v. *Palmer,* the Court had included pantomime, as action by gesticulation and written words conveying the ideas of the author as to narrative action, among dramatic compositions.[131] It would seem that the description did not qualify as sufficiently detailed and descriptive of dramatic content to qualify as a dramatic composition. Borge Varmer's language is apt in respect thereto. "Even a textual description of a dance would not seem to constitute a dramatic work of choreography if the description is so general and lacking in detail that the dance could not be performed therefrom." [132] Indeed, Copyright Office Circular 41 requires detailed written form for registration of a choreographic work as a dramatic composition in verbal description, dance notation, pictorial or graphic diagram or a combination thereof. "The dance must convey a dramatic concept or idea, and must be complete enough for performance without further development." [133] Per contra, the Circular provides, "It is not possible to secure copyright protection for a mere dance step or variation as such, apart from a developed choreographic work in which it appears. Ballroom, social, and folk dance steps are not considered copyrightable material." [134] The Court, in *Fuller*, characterized the tableaux as conveying ". . . no other idea than that a comely woman . . . illustrating the poetry of motion in a singularly graceful fashion." [135] There are

---

[130] Fuller v. Bemis, note 128, *supra,* at p. 929.

[131] Note 115, *supra.*

[132] Varmer, Borge, Copyright in Choreographic Works, Study No. 28, in Studies on Copyright (1963), pp. 103-116 at p. 109.

[133] Copyright Office Circular 41, "Choreographic Works".

[134] *Ibid.*

[135] Note 128, *supra,* at p. 929.

distinctions between choreography as dramatic performance, and as something other than the dramatic performance, on the one hand, and choreography generally and mere social steps which are unprotectible under copyright as general ideas, on the other. Varmer observes, "It may not be feasible to define precisely those dances that are proper subject matter for copyright protection. But this is not unique to choreographic works; . . . Perhaps this much can be said in broad terms: that to qualify for copyright protection (as regards performance), a choreographic work should constitute an original creation of dance movements to be performed for an audience, conveying some story, theme, or emotional concept.

"Choreographic works of this character are typified by ballets. But many 'modern' dances, as distinguished from traditional ballets, are no doubt creative works of authorship; and although no 'story' may be readily evident in a dance of the 'modern' variety, the dance movements are expected to convey some thematic or emotional concept to the audience." [136]

Even if the tableaux were somehow more than the vaudevillian's dance routine or general patterns of graceful movement, the written descriptions might nonetheless fail to make the dances copyrightable if the written, i.e., verbal description, conveyed insufficient detail as to the actual choreography necessary to describe the work. Notation, such as Labanotation, and filmic reproduction of a choreog-

---

[136] Varmer, *op. cit., supra,* note 132, at p. 113. For a discussion as to categories under which choreographic works might be classified for registration of copyright under Sec. 5 (17 U.S.C. 5), it not being separately mentioned in the Section, and as to the applicability of Sec. 1(c) (17 U.S.C. 1(c)) to performance of non-dramatic choreographic works under statutory copyright, see Nimmer on Copyright (1970), Sec. 128. See Sec. 24.5, *infra.*

raphic work, spell out the work in sufficient detail so that there is a description or depiction of the work that can be protected against copying. Narrative alone, i.e., verbal description, sustains a far greater burden in this respect because the specific schemata of the choreographic work that are embraced by notation and film (or videotape) are much more difficult to achieve by verbalization of movement in great detail.

Sec. 22.13(c). Theatrical Architectonics

The decision in *Fuller* is also interesting in that it suggests that the architectonics of the theatre are not copyrightable. The opinion refers to arrangement of drapery, lights and shadows as well as merely mechanical movements as not being the subject of copyright, insofar as they do not tell a story or make up a dramatic composition.[137] This is also the rationale of *Serrana* v. *Jefferson*,[138] where a claim of copyright infringement was rejected on grounds of copying of immersion in water scenes. The Court distinguished the railroad scene of *Daly* v. *Palmer*[139] where there was a novel series of events, an extended chain of incidents, character and action, stating, "The decisions which extend the definition of 'dramatic composition' so as to include situations and 'scenic' effects, do not cover the mere mechanical instrumentalities by which such effects or situations are produced." [140]

In *Barnes* v. *Miner*,[141] a case which is the forerunner of our modern mixed media, the plaintiff wrote and copy-

---

137 Note 128, *supra*, at p. 929.
138 33 Fed. 347 (C.C. S.D.N.Y. 1888).
139 Note 113, *supra*.
140 Note 138, *supra*, at p. 348.
141 122 Fed. 480 (C.C. S.D.N.Y. 1903).

righted a sketch setting forth her act of quick costume changes. She used prefatory dialogue therein. She had a film made showing her in rehearsal of her act and copyrighted the film. The film was used in her act in between costume changes. She sued for copyright infringement, claiming that defendant, Zink, had copied her material under copyright. After stating that only the general plan or plot of showing rapid changes of costume was the same, the Court remarked, ". . . assuming that the plaintiff's copyright is valid, what does it cover and protect? Clearly not the setting or production of this performance on a stage with drop curtains, screens and lights turned up or down, for all this is old, and common property." [142] The Court also indicated that it did not cover the mere fact of use of photographic films, songs not owned by plaintiff, impersonation, or prefatory dialogue not imitated, plagiarized or infringed. Here there was no play, nor any use of the same order or sequence to convey the same sensations and impressions. Nothing substantial or material was used except the mere idea of rapid clothing change.[143]

Again, the Court had adverted there to theatrical architectonics—drop curtains, screens and lights. By architectonics, one means here the physical accoutrements that are attributes of theatre generally, in respect of its stagecraft. Just as a theatre's appointments, seating, lobby facilities, structural "hang", carpeting, lounges, etc. would not be copyrightable as elements of common property in the theatre, so its stagecraft, generically, would be common property and not the subject of copyright.

But theatrical architectonics are not limited to nonhuman stagecraft. It relates also to acting and what hap-

---

[142] *Idem* at p. 491.
[143] *Ibid.*

pens on stage generally. These, too, are common property. In *Savage* v. *Hoffmann*,[144] plaintiff claimed that he had the exclusive right to produce Franz Lehar's "Merry Widow" in the United States and Canada and that defendant infringed by imitating the characters in the title role. The Court stated, ". . . the complainant has no literary property in the manner in which Barbanell and Brian dance or posture. They, if any one, have the right to complain. The manner and method of every dancer and actor is individual, and utterly unlike the railroad scene, which was held the subject of literary property in Daly v. Palmer . . ." [145] Thus impersonation, it would seem, does not violate a property right under copyright where the material used is incidental to a take off by the impersonator and does not constitute an attempt to evade the copyright by performance thereof.[146] In *Bloom & Hamlin* v. *Nixon*, the Court held, "It is the personality imitated that is the subject of Miss Templeton's act, modified, of course, by her own individuality, and it seems to me that the chorus of the song is a mere vehicle for carrying the imitation along." [147] It would seem, therefore, that the rationale of parody or burlesque as a fair use is along comparable lines.[148]

---

[144] 159 Fed. 584 (C.C. S.D.N.Y. 1908).

[145] *Idem* at p. 585.

[146] Bloom & Hamlin v. Nixon, 125 Fed. 977 (C.C. E.D. Pa. 1903); Green v. Minzensheimer, 177 Fed. 286 (C.C. S.D.N.Y. 1909); cf., Green v. Luby, 177 Fed. 287 (C.C. S.D.N.Y. 1909).

[147] *Idem* at p. 978. Cf. Chaplin v. Amador, 93 Cal. App. 358, 269 Pac. 544 (1928), imitation of Charlie Chaplin as unfair competition.

[148] Columbia Pictures Corporation v. National Broadcasting Co., 137 F. Supp. 348 (S.D. Cal. 1955); cf. Loew's Inc. v. Columbia Broadcasting System, Inc., 131 F. Supp. 165 (S.D. Cal. 1955), *aff'd, sub nom.* Benny v. Loew's Incorporated, 239 F. 2d 532 (9th Cir. 1956), *aff'd per curiam,* equally divided court, 356 U.S. 43 (1958).

Moreover, in addition to lack of literary quality in voice, motions and postures of actors, mere stage business may be imitated for like reason.[149] Thus it may be seen that direction as well as acting are generally not subjects of copyright because they are parts of the common property of stagecraft, in effect, part of the theatre's architectonics. So, too, gags as such would be common property if they are well known and in any event are not dramatic composition per se.[150]

As has been seen, stage props, being part of stagecraft, are common property; being part of theatrical architectonics, they are not protectible under copyright. Scenery would appear to present a more difficult matter because there, infringement of copyright might occur from another direction. If the scenic artist were to copyright his designs or sketches, he would have a copyright therein as works of fine art. Even without statutory copyright, since performance does not constitute publication, the scenic artist would still have his copyright therein under common law copyright.[151] Therefore, scenery might infringe the copyright of the scenic artist if it were held to be a copy of a work copyrightable as artistic property.[152]

---

[149] Chappell & Co., Ltd. v. Fields, 210 Fed. 864 (2d Cir. 1914); see also, Harold Lloyd Corporation v. Witwer, 65 F. 2d 1 (9th Cir. 1933).

[150] Hoffman v. Le Traunik, 209 Fed. 375 (N.D.N.Y. 1913). In Universal Pictures Co., Inc. v. Harold Lloyd Corp., 162 F. 2d 354 (9th Cir. 1947), Universal sought unsuccessfully to defend against infringement on the ground that gags were used which have no dramatic quality. The Court affirmed a finding below of infringement of 57 scenes of Harold Lloyd's "Movie Crazy" by Universal's "So's Your Uncle".

[151] Ferris v. Frohman, 223 U.S. 424 (1912).

[152] 17 U.S.C. 5(g); Regulations of the Copyright Office, Sec. 202.10. It is submitted that scenery as painted by the scenic artist

On the other hand, if the costume designer were to make drawings of the costumes for a show and copyrighted them, he could not prevail against an infringer for making costumes as copies thereof. In a case involving a dress copied from a drawing of a dress, Judge Goddard stated, "A dress is not copyrightable. A picture of a dress is; and the statute expressly includes sculpture. To give an author or designer an exclusive right to manufacture the art described in the certificate of copyright registration, when no official examination of its novelty has ever been made, would unjustly create a monopoly and moreover would usurp the functions of letters-patent."[153] Nimmer observes, "Thus copyright in a dress design may protect against the duplication of such design on a paper to be used as an instructional sheet for an unauthorized designer, but it will not protect against the embodying of the design in competitive garments."[154]

But scenery as indicia of locale would not be protectible property. In other words, to the extent the alleged infringing scenery is not literal copying or copying with immaterial variations, it approximates the type of simulation that may be comparable to similarity of locale. In referring to similarity of locale on a claim of infringement of a scenario by a motion picture, Judge Yankwich stated, "Locale is not the subject of copyright protection, or to common law protection as literary property."[155]

---

would satisfy the tests of originality and separability of its artistic quality from utilitarian function as stage scenery to qualify for copyright under Mazer v. Stein, 347 U.S. 201 (1954).

[153] J. Adelman, Inc. v. Sonner's and Gordon, Inc., 112 F. Supp. 187 (S.D.N.Y. 1934), pp. 189-190.

[154] Nimmer on Copyright (1970), Sec. 27.3, at p. 122.

[155] Schwarz v. Universal Pictures Co., Inc., 85 F. Supp. 270 (S.D. Cal. 1945) at p. 276. The scenario and film related to the Philip-

Scenery, generally, is a means of stagecraft to establish locale and in that respect, apart from the problem of copying a work of art, would not be protectible property.

Sec. 22.13(d). Plot

But locale is simply the place or places where the plot unfolds. Webster defines "plot" as, "The plan or main story of a literary composition, as a play, novel, romance, or poem, comprising a complication, or causally connected series, of motived incidents which are gradually unfolded, sometimes by unexpected means; also, a similar subordinate complication." [156]

Judge Hough had this observation as to plot in *Dymow* v. *Bolton,*

> "If one compares two dramatic compositions, whether in forms suitable for the stage or for the library, what has been called the 'fundamental plot', the 'same old plot', or an 'old story', can assume any author's dressing or adornment; that author can devise and use his own way of expressing that plot, and he will not infringe. This general proposition is illustrated in London v. Biograph Co., 231 F. 696, 145 C.C.A. 582; Eichel v. Marcin (D.C.) 241 F. 404; Stodart v. Mutual Corp. (D.C.) 249 F. 507.
>
> * * *

pines, in Echevarria v. Warner Bros. Pictures, Inc., 12 F. Supp. 632 (S.D. Cal.), opinion of Yankwich, J.; Underhill v. Belasco, 254 Fed. 838 (S.D.N.Y. 1918) (convent locales in alleged infringing and infringed plays); Simonton v. Gordon, 297 Fed. 625 (S.D.N.Y. 1924) (African locales).

[156] Webster's New International Dictionary, Unabridged, Second Ed. (1961), p. 1892, "plot".

> "Admitting, now, that a plot, the mere concept of a situation around which to build and develop literary adornment, is not copyrightable, . . ."[157]

In *London* v. *Biograph,* the Court compared the plots of plaintiff, Jack London, in his short story "Just Meat" with defendant's plot in its motion picture "Love of Gold". The Court noted that the fundamental idea common to both of mutual poisoning of criminals, who thus die by their own hands, was an old one, going back to Chaucer and earlier. The Court reversed the decision below because the resemblances in minor incidents were unimportant, stating, "The copyright cannot protect the fundamental plot, which was common property long before the story was written; it will protect the embellishments with which the author added elements of literary value to the old plot, but it will not operate to prohibit the presentation by some one else of the same old plot without the particular embellishments."[158]

Eichel v. *Marcin*[159] involved a claim of infringement of plaintiffs' play "Wedding Presents" by defandants' "Cheating Cheaters". Again the Court traced the fundamental plot to plays prior to both as to the hijinks of a band of thieves and indicated similarities of minor incidence. Judge Manton then remarked, "The resemblances between the two dramatic compositions, I am of the opinion, are minor instances and are not important. The copyright cannot protect the fundamental plot, which is common property, as was pointed out above, long before the story was written. It will, of course, protect the

---

[157] 11 F. 2d 690 (2d Cir. 1926) (italics), pp. 691-692.
[158] 231 Fed. 696 (2d Cir. 1916) at pp. 698-699.
[159] 241 Fed. 404 (S.D.N.Y. 1917).

author, who adds elements of literary value to the old plot; but it will not prohibit the presentation by someone else of the same old plot without the particular embellishments. London v. Biograph, 231 Fed. 696, 145 C.C.A. 582." [160]

In *Stodart* v. *Mutual Film Corp.*,[161] the Court compared the plot found sufficient similarity with respect to plaintiff's play "The Woodsman" and defendants' film "The Strength of Donald Mackenzie" to constitute infringement. He noted insofar as plots were concerned, "A man may take an old story and work it over, and if another copies, not only what is old, but what the author has added to it when he worked it up, the copyright is infringed. It cannot be a good copyright, in the broader sense that all features of the plot or the bare outlines of the plot can be protected; but it is a good copyright in so far as the embellishments and additions to the plot are new and have been contributed by the copyright. That is this case." [162]

But it was Judge Yankwich's analysis that extended the nature of plot in two directions. He not only looked at the plots in relation to one another and at their relationship to prior plots as common property, he also sought to comprehend the nature of dramaturgy in terms of the commonality of dramatic situations. He stated in *Echevarria* v. *Warner Bros. Pictures, Inc.*, "The dramatic situations which form the stuff of drama are few. The entire dramatic literature of the world can be reduced to some three dozen situations. In fact, an ingenious Frenchman has written a book in which, after analyzing the entire

---

[160] *Idem* at p. 411.

[161] 249 Fed. 507 (S.D.N.Y. 1917), *aff'd without opinion,* 249 Fed. 513 (2d Cir. 1918).

[162] *Idem* at p. 510.

dramatic literature from the time of the Greek and Hindu dramas to the present time, he concludes that all these dramatic works present, in variant form, the few situations which he has analyzed." [163]

Later, in *Schwarz* v. *Universal Pictures Co., Inc.,* Judge Yankwich observed, "Dramatic situations are few. It is common knowledge that many of Shakespeare's plots were chosen from novelletas—short stories current in Italy at the time. But he took an ordinary love story, and made the thing of great beauty which is Romeo and Juliet. He took a common story of accession to a throne through murder, from Scottish annals, and gave us the brilliant tragedy of Macbeth. It would be daring, indeed, to deny originality to that great creator.

"Originality consists in the development of a theme."[164]

Thus it would appear that he uses the terms "plot", "dramatic situation" and "theme" almost interchangeably. Judge Hough, too, appears to approximate such usage in *Dymow* v. *Bolton* where he remarked, "Admitting, now, that a plot, the mere concept of a situation around which to build and develop literary adornment, is not copyrightable, it is insisted that the court below was right in holding that Bolton had appropriated the 'theme' of Dymow's work. 'Theme' is not a word of art, and an examination of the cases will show that where it has been used in decision writing, it means a great deal more than the jealousy motif on which the fabric of Othello is hung, or, to go to the other extreme of composition, the theorem of a proposition of Euclid[165] . . . . And it will be

---

[163] 12 F. Supp. 632, 634 (S.D. Cal. 1935).
[164] 85 F. Supp. 270, 278 (S.D. Cal. 1945).
[165] 11 F. 2d 690, 692 (2d Cir. 1926).

quite plain that no mere plot or so-called theme was protected by these decisions." [166]

Sec. 22.13(e). Scenes and Characters

Judge Yankwich did not leave it, however, to statement of ideas, theme, plot, or dramatic situation, as being stock, but he went further, stating, in *Schwarz,*

> "An English case which deals with the problem is Bagge v. Miller, MacGillivaray, Copyright Cases, page 178, in which the works involved the fundamental idea of compulsory truth-telling by means of a bet. The court held that that idea was stock, and that there could be no infringement of it.
>
> "The French use a very expressive phrase in dramatic literature: 'scènes à faire'; that is, scenes which 'must' be done. For instance, the 'scène à faire' in the present script is called for by the scene in which the girl burned her hand on a cigarette. Something had to be done with that burn, and the author uses it as a means of identification. In an old play in which Adolphe Menjou appeared, in the days before talking pictures, he came in, spilled some red ink; then took a handkerchief and wiped the ink off his hand with it. That was the beginning. Ultimately there had to be a scene explaining the red spot.
>
> So in all dramatic works we find that situations which are identical call for scenes which are similar."[167]

Judge Yankwich carried this observation to the conclusion that, in effect, stock ideas carry with them stock scenes.

---

[166] *Idem* at p. 692.

[167] Note 164, *supra,* at p. 275.

In the same case, he remarked in this respect, "In sum, the first fundamental to be deduced from these cases is, that once we deal with a particular situation which is not original with any one, it calls for certain sequences in the methods of treatment, which cannot be avoided, because they are, in the very nature of the development of the theme, and are used by every writer who knows his craft."[168]

Just as scenes may be stock, so, too, there may be no copyrightable property in incidents. In *Eichel* v. *Marcin,* Judge Manton stated, "A copyright does not give a monopoly in any incident in a play. Other authors have a right to exploit the facts, experiences, field of thought, and general ideas, provided they do not substantially copy a concrete form, in which the circumstances and ideas have been developed . . ."[169] Judge Yankwich made a similar observation in *Echevarria,* "One cannot build a story around a historical incident and then claim exclusive right to the use of the incident. If originality can be claimed in opposing Aguinaldo to Funston, as the plaintiff claimed in open court, then all the novels, short stories, and dramas written about the Civil War, opposing Grant and Lee, might never have been written after the first one because the author of the first one could have claimed exclusive right to the product."[170]

Thus plot, theme, scene and incident may all be non-protectible as common property. Emotions, per se, may similarly be non-protectible. Judge Goddard observed below in *Nichols,* "That two productions display the same trend of emotions is not enough to show plagiarism. Emo-

---

[168] *Idem* at p. 276.
[169] Note 159, *supra,* at p. 409.
[170] Note 163, at p. 638.

tions, like mere ideas, are not subject to preemption; they are common property." [171]

Even characters and some similar phraseology may be common property. In *Echevarria,* Judge Yankwich stated,

> "Even though there are characters in both plays having similarity and some instances of similar phraseology, when the theory of the two plays is entirely different, there is no infringement. Vernon v. Sam S. & Lee Shubert, Inc. (D.C. N.Y. 1915), 220 F. 694. The connection between the two works must be obvious to the ordinary reader or observer. Bachman v. Belasco (C.C.A. 2d Cir. 1915), 224 F. 817; Roe-Lawton v. Hal E. Roach Studios (D.C. Cal. 1927), 18 F. (2d) 126." [172]

Vernon v. *Sam S. & Lee Shubert, Inc.* involved a claim of infringement of plaintiff's play "At Bay" by the play "Thread of Destiny", written by a Mr. Scarborough and Augustus Thomas. The complaint was dismissed when insufficient similarities could be established and independent creation determined. The Court noted, "Of course, as so happens, there are some characters in both plays having a similarity, and there are here and there some instances of similar phraseology. But that is a very old story in playwriting, because, after all, there are not so many themes around which a play may be plotted." [173]

In *Bachman* v. *Belasco,* Judge Lacombe, in his opinion affirming dismissal of a claim for infringement of plaintiff's play "Etelle" by the play "A Case of Becky" stated:

---

[171] Nichols v. Universal Pictures Corp., 34 F. 2d 145 (S.D.N.Y. 1929) at p. 147, *aff'd,* 45 F. 2d 119 (2d Cir. 1930), L. Hand, J.

[172] Note 163, *supra,* at p. 635 (italics).

[173] 220 Fed. 694, 696 (S.D.N.Y. 1915).

> "The parallel columns in the brief of appellant are not only unpersuasive, but in many parts silly. For instance, the statements that the action of both plays begins 'in the morning' with 'one man on the stage'; that in one play the leading lady says to her fiancé, 'I'm so glad to see you', in the other, 'I am so pleased to see you'; that in one play a physician says of the heroine, 'She is in a highly nervous condition', in the other a similar character says of the villain, 'He will probably be in a highly nervous state'; that in the one play a comic character says, 'Ain't it awful, sir?' and in the other a serious character says, 'Oh, it is awful.' The first of these phrases, changing merely the last word to 'Mabel', was common property here when both plays were written. There are several pages of these inconsequential similarities." [174]

In rejecting a claim for infringement in *Roe-Lawton* v. *Hal E. Roach Studios* by reason of alleged motion picture infringement of plaintiff's copyrighted wild horse stories published in a weekly journal, the Court stated, "If it could be said in this case that the Roach Studios, using the underlying theme of plaintiff's stories, had adapted characters and incidents closely resembling those used by the plaintiff in the exposition thereof, infringement would be shown. There are a few incidents in the films which are quite strikingly similar to those which the stories describe, but they all belong to the character of natural and expected happenings, considering the normal action of animals and persons placed as the characters are in the environment which we find them." [175]

---

[174] 224 Fed. 817, 818 (2d Cir. 1915).
[175] 18 F. 2d 126, 127 (S.D. Cal. 1927).

Finally, with the remark of Judge Woolsey in *Park* v. *Warner Bros.* with respect to a song, one completes the ambit of common property, "Neither ideas nor phrases nor ordinary English idioms or words are protected by copyright."[176]

Thus it may be seen from the foregoing, that practically every component of dramaturgy—plot, theme, ideas, characters, scenes, incidents, locale, words and phrases, scenery, costumes, props, gestures, motions, countenances—may be found, if considered separately, to be common property.

Sec. 22.14. The Inseparable Unity of the Creative Work

But it was Judge Learned Hand who recognized the dead end of this notion of commonality by abstraction into separable components of unprotectible property. In *Sheldon* v. *Metro-Goldwyn Pictures Corp.*, he articulated his objection to this technique of abstraction, stating, after referring to a number of these separable components—scenes, incidents, scenic tricks—"The play is the sequence of the confluents of all these means, bound together in an inseparable unity; . . ." [177]

At this point one must differentiate between techniques for determining infringement, the "how" of infringement

---

[176] 8 F. Supp. 37 (S.D.N.Y. 1934) at p. 39; see also, Lowenfels v. Nathan, 2 F. Supp. 73 (S.D.N.Y. 1932) and Lewys v. O'Neill, 49 F. 2d 603 (S.D.N.Y. 1931).

[177] 81 F. 2d 49, 55-56 (2d Cir. 1936), which found infringement, reversed the court below, 7 F. Supp. 837 (S.D.N.Y. 1934), and directed an accounting. The final decree in 26 F. Supp. 134 (S.D.N.Y. 1934) was reversed in 106 F. 2d 45 (2d Cir. 1939) and the Court of Appeals was affirmed by the Supreme Court in 309 U.S. 390 (1940).

from the substance of infringement, the "what" of such unlawful appropriation. The first relates to the means of arriving at a determination, the second, to the content of the result arrived at by using any given means. Thus the so-called ordinary observer or audience test is a means of looking at alleged infringing and infringed works for the purpose of arriving at a determination. Expert testimony and "dissection"—i.e. detailed analysis—are other means of coming to a conclusion. A third approach is the "common materials and common sources" test.[178] Judge Learned Hand's abstractions test, articulated in *Nichols*,[179] is not really a test of means at arriving at a determination of infringement. It is a test purporting to describe the line of infringement, that is, at what point similarity ceases to be infringement. So, too, the separable components test suggested by the language of Sec. 3[180] of the present Act, insofar as it refers to copyright protection which is accorded in all the copyrightable components of the work, is not a test of means of determining infringement, but one of just what has been infringed.

Sec. 22.14(a). Abstractions and Protectible Components

Judge Hand's abstractions test does not tell us what is or is not too abstract to constitute non-infringement. It cannot serve as a means test because it is merely a conclusion, after a determination has been made of what has been infringed or not, as the case may be. But even when Judge Learned Hand had articulated his abstractions test,

---

178 This phrase is used by Judge Manton in Shipman v. R.K.O. Radio Pictures, Inc., 100 F. 2d 533 (2d Cir. 1938).

179 45 F. 2d 119 (2d Cir. 1930).

180 17 U.S.C. 3.

he was aware of the problems posed by the abstraction of separable components of dramaturgy as a descriptive conclusion of the results of a determination of infringement or not. It must be seen that the common materials and common sources test as mentioned by Judge Manton in *Shipman*[181] is different from the separable components or commonality test. The former is a means test for comparison of the alleged infringing work and the alleged infringed work with the prior art to determine to what extent the plaintiff's work was original and/or the defendant's was independently created. It is a creation test. It is an actual issues test, ". . . whether the copyrighted work was original, and whether the defendant copied it, so far as the supposed infringement is identical." [182] One might amend Judge Hand's use of the word "identical" to "substantially similar." The whole point here is that the references are to determination of non-literal copying which, by definition, cannot be identical precisely because they are not literal copies. Per contra, the commonality of abstractions is a test of exclusion or not of particular matter after it has been determined that the separate components are, by reason of the abstraction, unprotectible, common property. In fact, there is a prior determination of lack of originality in the plaintiff's work and/or lack of substantial similarity in the defendant's work that enables the abstraction to be made into separable components. Judge Learned Hand's abstractions test differs from this in that it is grounded in specifics of determination of originality and similarity and the resultant conclusion is the basis for decision of remoteness or not from the critical line of infringement. The commonality of protectible components is really the articulation, *a posteriori,*

---

[181] Note 178, *supra.*

[182] L. Hand, J., note 179, *supra,* at p. 123.

of the various abstract components of dramaturgy by way of explanation of a result that must be posited upon a determination of creation of the compared works.

In pulling away from the abstract components test in *Nichols,*[183] long before his articulation of the unity of the work as a whole in *Sheldon,*[184] Judge Hand recognized the limitations of the components test. Thus he took issue with the separation of plot into an abstraction in *Nichols,* stating:

> "We did not in Dymow v. Bolton, 11 F. (2d) 690, hold that a plagiarist was never liable for stealing a plot; that would have been flatly against our rulings in Dam v. Kirk La Shelle Co., 175 F. 902, 41 L.R.A. (N.S.) 1002, 20 Ann. Cas. 1173, and Stodart v. Mutual Film Co., 249 F. 513, affirming my decision in (D.C.) 249 F. 507; neither of which we meant to overrule. We found the plot of the second play was too different to infringe, because the most detailed pattern, common to both, eliminated so much from each that its content went into the public domain; and for this reason we said, 'this mere subsection of a plot was not susceptible of copyright.' But we do not doubt that two plays may correspond in plot closely enough for infringement. How far that correspondence must go is another matter." [185]

If there is any doubt on this point, Judge Learned Hand continued to make his point in the balance of the very same paragraph of *Nichols,* only this time with respect to characters, stating:

---

[183] *Idem,* note 179, *supra.*

[184] Note 177, *supra.*

[185] Note 179, *supra,* at p. 121.

"Nor need we hold that the same may not be true as to the characters, quite independently of the 'plot' proper, though, as far as we know, such a case has never arisen. If Twelfth Night were copyrighted, it is quite possible that a second comer might so closely imitate Sir Toby Belch or Malvolio as to infringe, but it would not be enough that for one of his characters he cast a riotous knight who kept wassail to the discomfort of the household, or a vain and foppish steward who became amorous of his mistress. These would be no more than Shakespeare's 'ideas' in the play, as little capable of monopoly as Einstein's Doctrine of Relativity, or Darwin's theory of the Origin of Species. It follows that the less developed the characters, the less they can be copyrighted; that is the penalty an author must bear for marking them too indistinctly." [186]

The analytic approach of the commonality of respective components, if carried to its logical conclusion, does injustice to the very precepts of copyright. Judge Yankwich in *Echevarria*, in his paragraph which refers to the paucity of dramatic situations, went on to state therein, "A rule, therefore, which would place originality *not in the manner of treatment of a theme,* but *in the theme,* would place the 'hack writer' upon the same footing with the genius." [187]

Sec. 22.14(b). Copyrightability and Infringement

It is submitted that the reference to the paucity of dramatic situations is, itself, a device of critical analysis

---

[186] *Idem* at p. 121.

[187] Note 163, *supra,* at p. 634 (italics).

rather than going to the nature of creation and may give rise to elitist determinations of originality because hack writers might conceivably be abstracted out of manner of treatment into separable components. The genius of American copyright law is its preceptual approach of irreducible minimum of originality and fixation of writings. It is a democratic approach which eschews critical criteria in seeking a lowest common denominator of copyrightability. So long as there is fixation in some concrete form so that the limits and nature of any given work may be determined for copyright classification purposes, the barest minimum of originality will sustain copyright. The legislative scheme is to remove the legal framework, to the maximum extent possible, from the arenas of literary and artistic criticism as to what is meritorious and what is dross. The legislative scheme is to seek criteria of copyrightability at the barest minimum so that the act of copyrighting rarely has to become an act of prejudgment as to artistry embodied in the work.

A theory of abstractions into separable components would appear to negate this approach. For by differentiation into common property components which are unprotectible, the work of the hack and of the non-genius is disadvantaged.[188] Such work is deemed to be unoriginal by neat compartmentalization into abstract components and therefore runs the risk of less likelihood of being sustained in infringement proceedings.

It is submitted that such an approach misconceives the nature of literary and artistic property. Just as Learned Hand perceived that a play is not a whole of separable components but an "inseparable unity", so it may be said

---

[188] Note 178, *supra*.

that each work, regardless of its form as literary and artistic property, is similarly an inseparable unity. Theme, plot, ideas, characters, scenes, incidents, etc., are merely abstractions for critical characterization of various components of a work. The nature of creation of literary and artistic property generally is analogous to creation by a playwright in the sense that plays are not written so much as wrought or molded. Indeed, writing generally, as creation, is comparable "wroughtsmanship", the molding of words and phrases into a literary work. Writing consists of the tentative use or rejection of a variety of approaches to any given subject, changes in text and context thereof, until there is a fixation of form by the author so as to be deemed a work. At that point there is simultaneously a literary and artistic property. Fixation may arise at times by extrinsic means beyond the control of the writer, such as by death or disability of the creator. This objective fixation may likewise characterize literary and artistic property if there has been sufficient creation to meet the standards of irreducible minimum and sufficient fixation of form to constitute a work. Thus mere notes and bare outlines for a work might not constitute literary property because they might not constitute the irreducible minimum of originality of writings. On the other hand, an uncompleted work might have both originality on the irreducible minimum test and fixation of form to qualify for copyrightability.

Sec. 22.14(c). "Wroughtsmanship"

Indeed, the quality of "wroughtsmanship" is characteristic of all creation of literary and artistic property in its broadest sense of writings, be it of films or television tapes, as well as strictly literary works. The problem of writing, in this regard, involves determination of the creator. In film production, the creative components may be actually seen in production creating the picture, so, too, with a television production. There are objective ways of determining who did what in film production because, in most instances, the documents reflecting chain of title specify the various creative components. Indeed, most of them can be seen at work in the process of production, e.g., director, cameramen, individual producer, film editor. Thus physical presence at production can verify who did what in most respects of film and television production.

Writing, on the other hand, is a private craft. Even the painter or sculptor's work may be verified as to creator thereof by physical presence in observation of the artist at work. The writer's art, however, is mainly a private one. This is true of most forms of writing, although independent verification might be obtained as to joint authorship where the collaborators actually worked together in the presence of each other. So, too, this would be true where script writers collaborated in this manner. At times revisions might be made publicly, such as by a playwright in rehearsal or by a screen play writer during production.

By and large, however, creation is done by writers out of sight of others. To that extent, verification of authorship is an article of faith because the putative author so acknowledges, whether under oath or otherwise. The observations as to writers would appear to apply to composers working alone. Composers collaborating with lyricists and bookwriters might obtain independent verification by means of testimony of their collaborators as to proof of actual creation.

Thus, when an author mails a manuscript to himself by certified or registered mail to establish date of creation of a manuscript, as a precaution in the event of a contest determining priority of his creation, such an author is not really verifying authorship thereby. The mailing is self-serving in this regard. Ultimately, the affirmation of authorship in a given person is based upon his statement under oath that he is the creator of the work. If the claim of authorship, whether under oath or not, is not disputed, or there is no credible evidence to the contrary, then that person is accorded the attributes of authorship.

Sec. 22.15. Creation as Specific Constructs

But whether or not there may be objective determination of authorship, the basis for protection in the present Act is in the writing, used in its broadest sense, to include film and other visual materials. What the creator thereof creates is a work as a whole, not separable components of plots, ideas, characters, etc. What is copyrighted is the work as a whole, although copyrighted protection may be accorded only to the copyrightable components therein. It is an abstraction by extraction of separate components, for analytical purposes, that one speaks of such separable elements. The playwright or screen writer may, indeed, develop his work from the general to the particular by blocking plot, theme, characters, etc. as aids in construction of his work. The novelist or short story writer may do the same thing. But such instrumentalities, which may or may not correspond to critical criteria, do not per se constitute the work. Each work stands on its own in its own construct.

It is the specific construct that carries with it the basic situation of that work, its characters, scenes and incidents. Each work, then, carries with it its own dramatic situation, characters, etc.

The Concept of Infringement

In *Golding* v. *R.K.O. Pictures, Inc.,*[189] the Supreme Court of California affirmed a determination below as to infringement by defendant's movie "Ghost Ship" of plaintiffs' play "The Man and His Shadow". The Court opined that the ordinary observer rule was an oversimplification. It felt as to that rule, "The rule of law stated is correct insofar as the issue of *similarity* is concerned, but it has no application to the preliminary issue of *originality* or a plaintiff's protectible property interest." [190]

The Court then proceeded to spell out its theory of dissection, stating:

> "It is essential from the nature of the inquiry as to originality to first dissect the play to determine wherein, if at all, plaintiffs have any protectible property right. Assuming this is established, then comparison may be made between the two works *as to the original and protectible portion only.* If, as may often be the case, plaintiff's rights extend to the entire play, then the trier of fact should compare the one with the other . . . But where, as in the present case, the plaintiffs' property rights extend only to the dramatic core, a portion of the play, the issue of similarity is accordingly limited to a comparison on the basis of an overage observer looking to that part of the literary work which can properly be protected from infringement. Otherwise stated, dissection may be necessary to define the existence and extent of a plaintiff's property interest, and on the issue of similarity the test is always that of the average observer comparing such property interest with the alleged copy made by the defendant." [191]

---

[189] 35 Cal. 2d 690, 221 P. 2d 95 (Sup. Ct. Cal. 1950).

[190] *Idem,* 35 Cal. 2d at p. 700, 221 P. 2d at p. 100 (italics).

[191] *Idem,* 35 Cal. 2d at p. 700, 221 P. 2d at pp. 100-101 (italics).

Sec. 22.15(a). Dissection and Protectible Components

It is ironic that the majority opinion should carry its theory of dissection to separable components this far because it correctly perceived, "Literary property in the fruits of a writer's creative endeavor extend to the full scope of his inventiveness. This may well include, in the case of a stage play or moving picture scenario, the entire plot, the unique dialogue, the fundamental emotional appeal of theme of the story, or merely certain novel sequences or combinations of otherwise hackneyed elements." [192] But it applied the dissection test to protectible property in terms of the plaintiffs' own indication of value. "The plaintiffs do not claim that their entire play, or any particular sequence or dialogue, was directly or totally pirated. Their insistence throughout has been that the thing of value in their play is the central dramatic situation and interplay of the dominant and secondary characters upon each other. All other characterizations and dialogue are admittedly nothing more than hackneyed filler which could be added or subtracted without affecting the value or substance of the plaintiffs' literary property." [193] In applying this test, the Court then stated, "According to this evidence, the real value of a story or play may have little to do with specific dialogues or sequence of scenes or locale and there is ample evidence tending to prove that the basic dramatic core of the plaintiffs' play constitutes the truly original and valuable feature of it. . . . Nor was it a mere abstract idea. It had been reduced to the form of a full stage play. Its creators

---

[192] *Idem,* 35 Cal. 2d at pp. 694-695, 221 P. 2d at p. 97.

[193] *Idem,* 35 Cal. 2d at p. 696, 221 P. 2d at p. 98.

had embellished it with much of the trappings that give form, if not substance, to such literary work."[194]

But the reference to value is almost a carry-over of a theory of damages to liability. Damages are a different issue from liability for infringement, so that the reference to the value of what was appropriated tends to inject an element that is a consequence of liability but not its cause. In affirming the Court of Appeals, (opinion of Judge Learned Hand), the Supreme Court stated in *Sheldon* v. *Metro-Goldwyn Pictures Corp.*, "As the Court of Appeals found, respondents in producing the motion picture in question worked over old material; 'the general skeleton was already in the public demesne. A wanton girl kills her lover to free herself for a better match; she is brought to trial for the murder and escapes.' But not content with the mere use of that basic plot, respondents resorted to petitioners' copyrighted play. They were not innocent offenders. *From comparison and analysis*, the Court of Appeals concluded that they had 'deliberately lifted the play'; their 'borrowing was a deliberate plagiarism.' "[195]

"Basic dramatice core" and "central dramatic situation" as characterized by the California Supreme Court in *Golding*[196] and "basic plot" by the Supreme Court of the United States in *Sheldon*[197] can nevertheless be derived without abstraction of dramatic works into a few dramatic plots, as Judge Yankwich did in *Echevarria.*[198] Commonality of specific components is so derived by abstraction into generalized common elements, plot, characters, scenes, in-

---

[194] *Idem,* 35 Cal. 2d at p. 697, 221 P. 2d at pp. 98-99.

[195] 309 U.S. 390 (1940) at p. 397 (emphasis added).

[196] Note 189, *supra,* 35 Cal. 2d at pp. 696-697, 221 P. 2d at p. 97.

[197] Note 195, *supra.*

[198] Note 163, *supra.*

cidents, etc., precisely by reconstruction in the ways of the *literati*. The differentiation should, on the contrary, be very specific, in terms solely of the determination of originality. The comparison should be made in terms of the specific plots as part of the entire work and not by means of abstraction of separate components.

Sec. 22.16. Analysis: Ordinary Observer and Experts

It is submitted that part of the difficulty arises from the differentiation into ordinary observer and dissection by experts tests. In point of fact, the ordinary observer test is an oversimplification of what is actually done in terms of comparison of the determination of creation. The judge and jury are not simply observing and making comparisons as an audience would. They are contrasting and comparing. A concomitant thereof is analysis.

So, too, experts engage in the same function of comparing and contrasting. The breakdown by so-called dissection is merely a more intense analysis. The role of the expert is to assist in determination of originality. In music, the expert might be a musicologist who can trace derivations from prior art, or at least be someone conversant therewith. The expert in dramaturgy serves a like purpose. But as Judge Yankwich stated in *Schwarz*, "The court's opinion must be arrived at after a comparison; not by reducing the play to an abstraction, but by weighing the work in the light of the final composition and its manifest developments." [199]

Weighing the work, however, ought to be done by evaluating it as a whole because each work is a construct of literary and artistic development. There are no plots, ideas, themes, etc. in the abstract, only those that are

---

[199] Note 164, *supra*, at p. 279.

embodied therein. The same is true of musical composition as well. The approach in each instance is not to work inward from outer common elements to the core of originality. Rather the need is to view each work as a real construct and to assess it in terms of comparison of other constructs of prior art and the work with which it is compared for purposes of determination of infringement.[200]

In this regard, Edward Silber would overcome the objection to use of experts of the parties by use of court experts or alternatively " . . . by placing the jurisdiction of infringement actions in a Copyright Court." [201] This view would merely displace experts of the parties by those of the courts or a particular court. But experts proffered by the parties serve a purpose in bringing to the fore and classifying material. Their function is an aid to judge and jury in understanding.

Sec. 22.17. Creative Peerage and Infringement

It is submitted that the pendulum has swung between the lay ordinary observer and the expert as though the entire range of determination were encompassed within such polarity. There is yet another approach. Perhaps creation, as such, should be determined by the peers of the creator. In other words, writing has professional attributes, whether done by the professional or the amateur. Just as the Screen Writers Guild has devised its own criteria for determining attribution of credits for authorship of screen plays in situations of multiple creation and

---

[200] See Nimmer on Copyright (1970), Sec. 143.53 at pp. 641-643, entitled, Judicial Modification of the Audience Test.

[201] Silber, Edward, Use of Experts in Literary Piracy A Proposal, 9 Copyright Law Symposium 149 (1958) at p. 174.

revision of scenarios, so, too, it would appear that writers should be the best guides as to determining originality of creation of various constructs of literary and artistic property. Where films are involved, the film makers would be such peers—directors, screen writers and producers. If infringement were to be considered in different media in a given case, then peers would be drawn from both media. Perhaps panels of peers in terms of infringement of literary and artistic works in the performing arts and literature could be constructed. They might, in the beginning, be advisory panels to the court for advisory opinions as to originality. The entire work would be so compared for determination of creation as to the alleged infringing and infringed work. This would not necessarily eliminate experts as to derivations in the prior art, finding and analyzing what was done earlier of a similar nature. If the ultimate judgment is to be made by the trial judge or jury as to the issue of substantial appropriation, at least the court will have been aided by the panel of peers who will have reviewed the two works and other comparable works of prior art as professionals.

Literature and art are not so much concretization of abstract ideas, clothed in plot, scene, characters, etc., but specific works with their own intrinsic reality—to the extent they are not ultimately determined to be copies—but, on the contrary, abstract ideas are themselves verbalized articulations, whether or not reduced to writings, of generalizations from the concrete to the general. Literature and art may perceive of such abstractions as creative tools in preparation of works, of critical means and of the stuff of linguistic and other communication.

But the essence of infringement is the comparison of concrete works claimed by the respective parties to be *sui generis*, albeit of a particular genre or medium. Necessarily, each case must stand on its own facts because a comparison is being made of concrete literary works, which, if they are not copied, are *sui generis*. As stated by Judge Learned Hand in *Peter Pan Fabrics, Inc.* v. *Martin Weiner Corp.*, "The test for infringement of a copyright is of necessity vague. In the case of verbal 'works' it is well settled that although the proprietor's monopoly extends beyond the exact reproduction of the works, there can be no copyright in the 'ideas' disclosed but only in their 'expression'. Obviously, no principle can be stated as to when an imitator has gone beyond copying the 'idea,' and has borrowed its 'expression.' Decisions must therefore inevitably be *ad hoc.*"[202] Each case not only stands on its own facts, but upon the respective constructs of literary and artistic expression, for the whole of literature and art are in the elaboration, i.e., the specific creations of the author thereof as creator.

---

[202] 274 F. 2d 487 (2d Cir. 1960) at p. 489 (italics).

Chapter XXIII

PERFORMANCE INFRINGEMENT

Sec. 23.1. Performance and Litigation

"The Copyright Act does not give a copyright holder control over all uses of his copyrighted work. Instead, Sec. 1 of the Act enumerates several 'rights' that are made 'exclusive' to the holder of the copyright. If a person, without authorization from the copyright holder, puts a copyrighted work to a use within the scope of one of these 'exclusive rights,' he infringes the copyright. If he puts the work to a use not enumerated in Sec. 1, he does not infringe."[1] This remark of Justice Stewart in the majority opinion of *Fortnightly Corp.* v. *United Artists Television, Inc.*,[2] taken alone, might be unexceptionable. But when it is in an opinion of the Supreme Court of the United States, pertaining to a decision as to whether cable television constitutes infringing performance, which qualified a prior landmark ruling of the same Court, *Buck* v. *Jewell-LaSalle Realty Co.*,[3] and limits that decision to its own facts,[4] then perhaps it is necessary to take a close look at the nature of the grant of the right of performance and the correlative effect of litigation and resultant decisions with respect to infringement of that right. Taken literally, the emphasis on litigation might lead to the kind of orientation expounded by Tom Arnold in his remark, "The law is only what a court will do on a given record on a given

---

[1] Fortnightly Corporation v. United Artists Television, Inc., 392 U.S. 390 (1968) at pp. 393-395.

[2] *Ibid.*

[3] 283 U.S. 191 (1931).

[4] Note 1, *supra,* fn. 18 at pp. 396-397.

day." [5] In this view legal certainties in terms of precedent and *stare decisis* as guidelines for legal counseling are minimized because the only verities are judicial decisions. On the other hand, the quotation of Justice Stewart might be taken in yet another sense, namely, that the parameters of rights are determined by torts in the decisional framework and the scope of the specific right is invested with dimension by judicial interpretation. The exclusive performance right assumes form and shape only as it is molded by judicial decision. It is this malleation by the courts with respect to the performance right that probably made Harry P. Warner refer to "The Judicial Basis of the Performing Rights Societies".[6]

Of course the courts are the ultimate umpires whose decisions mold and set the course of doctrine. But it would be a supererogation to attribute verities of doctrine exclusively to the judiciary—which it, of course, does not claim—or to invert the law into discrete decision making, a kind of chancellor's foot justice dependent upon the decision of the day. Rather the law must be seen as an interaction of a variety of parameters over and above the gladiatorial norm of trial by counsel with its panoply of record making amidst a welter of procedural and evidentiary rules for the attaining of a result in the given case. Legal norms are set by statute, where applicable. Legislative interpretation is often found in committee reports and hearings. Statutory purpose is a presumed objective goal of judicial interpretation. Then, too, the

---

[5] Arnold, Tom, Product Simulation and Trade Secret Law, What's Happened Since Sears and Compco, 1966 Patent Law Annual, 61 at p. 63.

[6] Warner, Harry P., Radio and Television Rights (1953), Sec. 131e is entitled, The Judicial Basis of the Performing Rights Societies, at p. 336.

administrative overlay in which the statute functions assumes significance. The nature, purpose and function of the governmental agency involved assumes importance in the *gestalt* of overall structure of the problem. Then, too, the marketing mechanisms involved in implementation of the statute and its administration are of significance because they define the social forces operative in the particular problem. The judiciary, whether sitting in trial by court or as beneficent legal lodestar to a jury, must take into account specific facts, of course, but must deal with specificities in a context of broader overall significance, to wit, the nature of the contending parties and the meaning of decision in that given case to the course of judicial doctrine in that particular field. Courts must interpret and reinterpret the nature of legal precedent and binding authority within the jurisdictional boundaries of the particular court structure involved. In addition, the judiciary, in reaching its opinions, will look beyond the prevailing wisdom of the cases to the thoughts and opinions of other writers on the subject. In particular, it is the views of the law review and treatise authors as well as those of the encyclopedists and quasi-authoritative restatements and the like that are perused. Judicial decision may or may not cite such doctrinal scrutiny but it is an ever-present part of decision making. So, too, counsel in litigation may or may not cite such works as authority in trial briefs and memoranda but such views are constantly examined. Finally, lawyers giving counsel outside of litigation base their opinions upon their analysis and interpretation drawn from statutory purpose and analysis, administrative patterns, *stare decisis* and precedent, the structure and mechanisms of the market, the views of the writers on the subject and their own experience. Legal doctrine is a living interaction of these various elements and the practical implementation thereof is the arena in which the jurisprudence of flexible concepts takes place. The nature of the performance right and of performance infringement is a good example of its operation.

The present Act,[7] with slight revisions, embodies the doctrines and language of the 1909 legislation[8] as to performance and performance infringement. It is to be noted at the outset that the statute, as amended, in fact articulates a number of concepts which, when viewed comprehensively, are held to constitute the performance right.

Sec. 23.2. Sec. 1(c) Performance

Thus Sec. 1(c) as amended in 1952,[9] has several components. It granted the exclusive right to the copyright proprietor to deliver, authorize delivery, read, or present copyrighted lectures, sermons, addresses or similar productions or other non-dramatic literary works which are copyrighted works in public for profit. The subsection also provides for the right to make a transcription or recording thereof by which it might in any manner or by any method be exhibited, delivered, presented, produced, or reproduced. As to such transcription or record, there was likewise the exclusive right to play or perform it in public for profit and to exhibit, represent, produce or reproduce it in any manner or by any method. The performance right as to non-dramatic works, generically speaking,

---

[7] 17 U.S.C. 1 *et seq.*

[8] Act of Mar. 4, 1909, 35 Stat. 1075, 60th Cong., 2d Sess., Chap. 320, see Copyright Enactments Laws Passed in the United States since 1783 Relating to Copyright, Copyright Office Bulletin No. 3 (Revised) 1963 at pp. 64-86.

[9] 17 U.S.C. 1(c), as amended, by Pub. Law 575, 82nd Cong., 2d Sess., Chap. 923, approved July 17, 1952, effective Jan. 1, 1953, see Copyright Enactments, *idem* at p. 127.

thereby comprehended not only live performance but forms of reproduction which fixed the live performance by embodying it in some form, such as transcription of recording, be it aural only or aural and visual, and the performance of the reproductions. Finally, instead of including the amendatory provision as to innocent infringement by broadcasters in Chapter 2 of Title 17 which is entitled, "Infringement Proceedings",[10] for whatever reason, the drafters of the amendment, in their wisdom, provided that damages for innocent infringement by broadcasters would not exceed $100 and should be part of the substantive provisions of Sec. 1(c)[11] rather than in the damages provisions of Sec. 101.[12]

The exclusive right of performance therefore takes a variety of forms in the subsection—delivery, reading and presenting the copyrighted work; playing or performing recordings and transcriptions thereof, and exhibiting, representing, producing or reproducing such recordings and transcriptions in any manner or by any method whatsoever. One might asseverate that the additional language represents contemporary terminology, taking into consideration modern technology, with phonograph and tape recordings, motion pictures, radio and television in mind, because Sec. 1(c), as passed in 1909,[13] granted only the bare exclusive right to deliver or authorize delivery of a copyrighted lecture, sermon, address or similar production.

---

[10] Chap. 2 of Title 17 includes Secs. 101-116 and is entitled, Infringement Proceedings.

[11] 17 U.S.C. 1(c).

[12] 17 U.S.C. 101.

[13] Act of Mar. 4, 1909, note 8, *supra,* Sec. 1(c), see Copyright Enactments, note 8, *supra,* at p. 64.

Sec. 23.3. Sec. 1(d) Performance

However, examination of Sec. 1(d) of the 1909 Act[14] indicates that it is embodied in substantially the identical form in the present Act.[15] Thus, in 1909, the statute prevented the exclusive right to perform or represent the copyrighted work publicly. If copies were not reproduced for sale there was a vending right. This, plus the right to make a recording or transcription thereof, was included from which it could be exhibited, performed, represented, produced, or reproduced as well as the right to exhibit, perform, represent, produce, or reproduce such recording or transcription in any manner or by any method whatsoever. The hearings prior to enactment of the 1909 Act indicate that theatrical managers and dramatists were concerned about play piracy by the use of stenographers who wrote down the dialogue of a play as it was being performed and then transcribed and reproduced copies in manuscript form for performance of the work by play pirates, whether as a dramatic work on the stage or as a truncated one-reel motion picture.[16] Note that the statute in 1909 granted the exclusive right to perform or represent the work, with respect to dramatic works. Legal literature prior thereto

---

[14] Act of Mar. 4, 1909, *idem,* Sec. 1(d), Copyright Enactments, *idem.*

[15] 17 U.S.C. 1(d). See Chap. XV, *supra.*

[16] "It has sometimes happened that upon the first production of a dramatic work a stenographer would be present and would take all the words down and would then turn the manuscript over to some one who had hired him to do the work or sell it to outside parties. This manuscript would then be duplicated and sold to persons who, without any authority whatever from the author, would give public performances of the work.", Report No. 2222, House of Representatives, 60th Cong., 2d Sess., Feb. 22, 1909, to accompany H.R. 28192, as reprinted in Nimmer on Copyright (1970), Appendix I, pp. 959-986, at p. 963. See Sec. 15.3, *supra.*

was careful to indicate that the nature of performance was in large measure by representation. Thus, in *Daly* v. *Palmer,* decided in 1868 in defining dramatic composition and actor, Judge Blatchford stated:

> "A dramatic composition is such a work in which the narrative is not related, but is *represented* by dialogue and action. When a dramatic composition is represented in dialogue and action, by persons who *represent* it as real, by performing or going through with the various parts or characters assigned to them severally, the composition is acted, performed, or *represented;* and, if the *representation* is in public, it is a public *representation.* To act, in the sense of the statute, is to *represent* as real, by countenance, voice, or gesture, that which is not real." [17]

There the Court was construing the Act of 1856 which first granted the stage right and extended the copyright to include " . . . the sole right also to act, perform, or *represent* the same, or cause it to be acted, performed, or represented, on any stage or public place" [18] during the period of copyright. The 1909 statute went further. In its concern to protect theatrical performance of copyrighted works against piracy, it set forth in Sec. 1(d) that the right to make recordings of the dramatic work was in the copyright proprietor and covered any exhibition, performance, representation, production, or reproduction thereof in any manner or by any method whatsoever. In other words, the copyright proprietor had the exclusive right to vend manuscript or recordings of the

---

[17] 6 Fed. Cas. 1132, Case No. 3552 (C.C. S.D.N.Y. 1868) at p. 1135. (emphasis added). See Sec. 22.13, *supra.*

[18] Act of Aug. 18, 1856, 34th Cong., 1st Sess., Chap. 169, 11 Stat. 138 (1859) (emphasis added).

work where copies were not reproduced for sale. This was intended to prevent pirates from selling stenographic and other recordings of the work taken surreptitiously in the theatre during an authorized performance of the play. So, too, the making of such pirated versions was prohibited without authorization by making such recordings and transcriptions part of the exclusive right of the copyright proprietor. Such recordings and transcriptions were so prohibited where the play could be in any manner or by any method exhibited, performed, represented, produced, or reproduced. The reference to "exhibited" connoted performance in some other media, in this context, motion picture exhibition. Such exhibition required a production of a photoplay, and its reproduction in the form of prints. The performance thereof would take place as in the live theatre by representation by actors portraying characters. Not only was the means of such piracy, recording and transcription, for the aforesaid enumerated purposes prescribed in the statute by granting the exclusive rights to the copyright proprietor, but the use of the fruits of the transcription or recording was likewise prohibited to contributory parties drawing upon the pirated recordings and transcriptions for performance thereof in whatever medium or form it was to be presented. This was important because it could not be necessarily assumed that the party so using the transcription or recording was necessarily a willful infringer for profit, thereby subjecting himself to criminal sanctions of the statute.[19] Whatever the criminal consequences of such piracy, the legislature proposed to grant the right of performance of such reproductions and recordings of dramatic works, no matter how made, to the copyright

---

[19] Act of Mar. 4, 1909, Sec. 28, note 8, *supra;* Copyright Enactments, *idem,* at p. 28 (now Sec. 104 of 17 U.S.C.).

proprietor so that any exhibition, performance, representation, production or reproduction thereof without authorization would constitute the tort of copyright infringement. Congress, then, wishing to correct a particular type of piracy then extant, granted broad rights to the copyright proprietor covering a variety of means of performance and presentation, including recordings and transcriptions of the dramatic work and production and reproduction of the dramatic work from the recordings and the exhibition thereof. Hence, because the performance right so granted was comprehensive, infringement thereof could similarly take place in a variety of ways of invasion of the borders of the comprehensive right.

Sec. 23.4. Sec. 1(e) Performance

By contrast, Congress utilized the simple language of performance when it came to music. It is to be noted that the musical performance right was a late-comer, originating in 1897, by revision of Sec. 4966 of the Revised Statutes to provide for damages by any person publicly performing or representing any dramatic or musical composition without consent of the copyright proprietor.[20] Sec. 1(e) of the 1909 Act granted the exclusive right of public performance for profit of copyrighted musical compositions and contained no language in terms of representing such music.[21] One must conclude that the draftsmen felt that the term was apposite in 1897, when the clause

---

[20] Act of Jan. 6, 1897, 54th Cong., 2d Sess., Chap. 4, 29 Stat. 481 (1897); Copyright Enactments, note 8, *supra,* at pp. 56-57.

[21] Act of Mar. 4, 1909, note 8, *supra,* Sec. 1(e), Copyright Enactments, *idem,* at pp. 65-66. Cf., the slight grammatical revision effected by punctuation in the present Act, 17 U.S.C. 1(e), see Pub. Law 281—80th Cong., 1st Sess., Chap. 39, Sec. 1(e); Copyright Enactments, *idem,* at pp. 103-104.

referred to both dramatic and musical composition, because of the continued intent to cover dramatic representation and the terms, dramatic and musical composition, were linked conjunctively. When separated into different paragraphs in the 1909 legislation, there was no necessity to include representation because the phrase was not particularly apt as to it. Music is performed. That is, notation is translated into music, the "collocation of sounds",[22] performed by memory or *extempore* by improvisation. Program music is not, strictly speaking, representation by music in a literal sense; it is merely the characterization by program notes or other description by the composer of what the particular composition is supposed to represent. Of course, true representation might be made musically in the form of dramatico-musical composition. The classification scheme of the statute, Sec. 5 thereof, takes cognizance of this differentiation by classifying dramatico-musical compositions along with dramatic compositions in Subdivision (d) thereof and separately classifying musical compositions in Subdivision (e) thereof.[23]

Sec. 1(e) goes much further, of course. It provides for the compulsory license as to mechanical reproductions. However, it is nonetheless still rooted in performance because it provides, "The payment of the royalty provided for by this section"—that is, the royalty for the compulsory license—"shall free the articles or devices for which such royalty has been paid from further contribution to the copyright except in case of *public performance for profit...*"[24] It would appear that Congress thereby intended to separate public performance for profit from other per-

---

[22] White-Smith Music Publishing Co. v. Apollo Co., 209 U.S. 1 (1908), Holmes, J., concurring opinion, at p. 20.

[23] 17 U.S.C. 5(d) and (e).

[24] 17 U.S.C. 1(e) (emphasis added).

formance since it is obvious that the purpose of mechanical recording is performance of the musical compositions embodied in the recording. Sec. 1(e) does, however, qualify its nature to some extent by additional language, apart from language relating to mechanical reproduction, in its so-called "jukebox" exemption. Sec. 1(e) contains a concluding paragraph:

> "The reproduction or rendition of a musical composition by or upon coin-operated machines shall not be deemed a public performance for profit unless a fee is charged for admission to the place where such reproduction or rendition occurs." [25]

Here the statute purports to deal with a particular form of mechanical reproduction, coin-operated machines. It seeks to cover the nature of the embodiment of the copyrighted musical composition and/or its rendition. Since the same is not to be deemed a public performance for profit, other language is sought to characterize what is done other than the term "performance", for clarity and to differentiate the exemption from public performance for profit where no admission fee is charged in connection with reproduction or rendition by or upon coin-operated machines.

Sec. 23.5. Performance and Damages

Having thereby set forth the performance provisions of the statute as to rights, Congress also included a number of clauses as to damages and an exculpatory clause in one of the criminal provisions. Sec. 101(b), Fourth sets forth a scale of statutory damages for infringement as follows: "In the case of a dramatic or dramatico-musical

---

[25] *Ibid.*

or a choral or orchestral composition, $100 for the first and $50 for every subsequent infringing performance; in the case of other musical compositions $10 for every infringing performance." [26] But note that Sec. 101(b) also sets forth statutory damages for innocent infringement of undramatized or non-dramatic works by means of motion pictures not to exceed $100; and for innocent infringement by motion picture makers or their distribution agencies of a copyrighted dramatic or dramatico-musical work statutory damages not to exceed $5,000 nor less than $250.[27] Immediately thereafter the statute provides, "and such damages shall in no other case exceed the sum of $5,000 nor be less than the sum of $250, and shall not be regarded as a penalty." [28] It would appear from the context of this paragraph that "such damages" here refers to in lieu damages from infringement generally, and refers to a like clause at the opening of the paragraph which reads:

> "(b) Damages and Profits; Amount; Other Remedies. To pay to the copyright proprietor such damages as the copyright proprietor may have suffered due to the infringement, . . ." [29]

Although Sec. 101(b), Third provides for statutory damages of $50 for every infringing delivery of a lecture, sermon, or address,[30] this clause is not to be read alone

---

[26] 17 U.S.C. 101(b), Fourth.

[27] See Report No. 756, 62d Cong., 2d Sess., House of Representatives, Statute in Relation to Copyrights, May 24, 1912, to accompany H.R. 24224 at pp. 3-4, and Townsend Copyright Amendment Complete File of Arguments Before the Committee on Patents, House of Representatives on H.R. 15263 and H.R. 20596 Commencing January 24, 1912.

[28] 17 U.S.C. 101(b).

[29] *Ibid.*

[30] 17 U.S.C. 101(b), Third.

because Sec. 1(c) adds a proviso that innocent infringement by broadcast shall not exceed $100 in statutory damages.[31] The damages provision for mechanical reproduction of music is interesting in that it is intended to supplement the compulsory license provision. Under Sec. 1(e) the record manufacturer is accorded a compulsory license at the rate of two cents a side and upon failure to pay therefor within thirty days after demand—accounting and payment being made monthly under the statute—the court may award the amount due and a sum not exceeding three times the amount due, as royalty as well as taxable costs and a reasonable counsel fee.[32] Sec. 101(e) provides in this regard that in respect of unauthorized mechanical reproduction no criminal action shall be brought but by civil action an injunction might be granted and in lieu of profits and damages the plaintiff might recover the Sec. 1(e) royalty.[33] The section goes on to provide that in absence of a license agreement, a party should file a notice of intent to use, failing which, the court might award a complainant a further sum, in its discretion, by way of damages, not to exceed three times the amount provided by Sec. 1(e).[34]

It is to be borne in mind that Sec. 104 of the present Act makes willful infringement for profit a misdemeanor punishable by up to a year in prison, a fine of from $100 to $1,000, or both.[35] *A fortiori* this would cover willful

---

[31] 17 U.S.C. 1(c) as amended by Public Law 575, 82d Cong., 2d Sess., Chap. 923, approved July 17, 1952, effective January 1, 1953.

[32] 17 U.S.C. 1(e).

[33] 17 U.S.C. 101(e).

[34] *Ibid.* See the discussion in Nimmer, note 16, *supra,* Sec. 155, at pp. 695-697.

[35] 17 U.S.C. 104.

infringing performance for profit. There is a proviso in Sec. 104 which reads:

> "*Provided, however,* That nothing in this title shall be so construed to prevent the performance of religious or secular works such as oratorios, cantatas, masses, or octave choruses by public schools, church choirs, or vocal societies, rented, borrowed, or obtained from some public library, public school, church choir, school choir, or vocal society, provided the performance is given for charitable or educational purposes and not for profit." [36]

In discussing this provision prior to enactment of the 1909 Act, the House Report states:

> "The existing law provides that any person publicly performing a dramatic or musical composition without the consent of the proprietor of the copyright shall be liable for damages of not less than $100 for the first and $50 for every subsequent performance, and this prohibition covers cases of public performances where the performance is not for profit. We have provided in this section that where the public performance is given by public schools, etc., for educational or charitable purposes and not for profit it may be done without subjecting those who give the performance to any suit for damages, and we further provide that the music used for the performance may be rented, borrowed, or obtained from public libraries or other public schools, etc." [37]

---

[36] *Ibid* (italics).

[37] Report No. 2222, House of Representatives, 60th Cong., 2d Sess., Feb. 22, 1909, to accompany H.R. 28192, as reprinted in Nimmer, note 6, *supra,* Appendix I, pp. 959-986, at p. 980. See

Performance Infringement

It would seem that the reference to damages for non-profit public performance in the above quote would refer to musical performance, since the exclusive right given as to musical composition is public performance for profit.[38]

Thus the statutory scheme appears to be comprehensive in its provision for exclusive rights of performance and correlative provisions as to damages and criminal penalties for infringement thereof. The statutory scheme also spells out certain norms by virtue of the limitations as to exclusivity of the right.

Sec. 23.6. Public Performance: For Profit

In respect of all performance, be it dramatic, non-dramatic, or musical, the same must be public; in respect of all non-dramatic and musical performance, it must also be non-profit. It is to be noted as to dramatic performance that when the stage right was granted in 1856, the statute provided for the right to act, perform or represent the copyrighted dramatic composition, "on any stage or public place." [39] At that time, there was only live performance. The reference to public place was intended to comprehend alternatives to performance in theatres on stage, such as performances out of doors at fairs, festivals, and elsewhere. It should be remembered that the theatre has had a long tradition of performance in courts of inns, and of mysteries and passion plays in churches, church courts and public squares. The reference to public place was

---

Sec. 28, Act of Mar. 4, 1909, Copyright Enactments, note 8, *supra,* at p. 76.

[38] Sec. 1(e), Act of Mar. 4, 1909, Copyright Enactments, note 8, *supra,* at p. 65, and as embodied in 17 U.S.C. 1(e).

[39] Act of Aug. 18, 1856, note 18, *supra,* Copyright Enactments, *idem* at p. 33.

intended to comprehend such alternatives generically. By the Act of 1870, however, the reference to performance "on any stage" had been deleted in favor of language of "publicly performing or representing" a dramatic composition.[40] Thereafter to date, the reference to "on any stage" no longer appeared and the language used was in terms of public performance. But there, i.e., live theatre, used generically as dramatic or dramatico-musical performance is almost always public. Its very nature is performance of the dramatic or dramatico-musical composition in the presence of an audience. Private performance may have been the prerogative of royalty and nobility in prior centuries in other countries, as characterized by the players' scene in Shakespeare's "Hamlet", but the tradition and history of American theatre has been largely that of public performance.[41] Private performance of live theatre in the sense of theatre in the home is a rarity. Moreover, the designation of various clubs as "private" but which are open to the public by membership have generally been held to be public.[42] The licensing of performance rights to plays to public schools by the Dramatists Play Service, Inc., Samuel French, Inc. and others would tend to suggest that performance before the audience of the schools, students, faculty, possibly parents, is not deemed private

---

[40] Act of July 8, 1870, 41 Cong., 2d Sess., Chap. 230, 16 Stat. 212 (1871), Sec. 86, Copyright Enactments, note 8, *supra,* pp. 36-41 at p. 36.

[41] See, for example, Taubman, Howard, The Making of the American Theatre (1965).

[42] Lerner v. Club Wander In, Inc., 174 F. Supp. 731 (D. Mass. 1959); Witmark, M. & Sons v. Tremont Social and Athletic Club, 188 F. Supp. 787 (D. Mass. 1960); Lerner v. Schectman, 228 F. Supp. 354 (D. Minn. 1964); cf. Metro-Goldwyn-Mayer Distributing Corporation v. Wyatt, and Maryland Yacht Club, 21 C.O. Bull. 203 D. Md. 1932). See Secs. 24.9 and 24.12, *infra.*

but rather restricted segments of the public, whether or not there be an admission charge therefor. The same would follow as to performances in institutions which may be for members of that institution, e.g., churches, temples, fraternal and benevolent organizations, and/or for members and friends. Theatre benefits partake of the characteristics of limited segments of the public. One would be hard put to classify such performances as private, even though the entire house may have been bought out for a particular organization and even if every seat for such performances may have been sold only to members of such organization. In short, public constituencies are not to be characterized as private because limitations are placed upon membership in such constituencies. This seems to be the rationale in the so-called private club cases. In this regard, it is submitted that the ruling in *Metro-Goldwyn-Mayer Distr. Corp.* v. *Wyatt,*[43] the Maryland Yacht Club case, which held exhibition of a film in that club not to be a public performance, should be seen as pertaining to motion pictures and not a live theatrical production. In this regard, Judge Coleman stated:

> "Of course, as has been pointed out by counsel for plaintiff, this is a question of degree in the last analysis. No hard and fast lines can be drawn. It is true that the fact that a club is a social club does not mean that a public performance could not be held there, and the nature of it would not necessarily be determined by whether tickets were sold. But I do fail to see that there is any substantial difference between the showing in the present case at the Maryland Yacht Club and a showing in a private home. We cannot measure the question by numbers of persons. The public is not ad-

---

[43] *Idem,* 21 C.O. Bull. 203.

> mitted to a social club of this kind, as we understand the term 'public.' The members enjoy these privileges and have the right to bring in their friends. No one profits financially. That is substantially what takes place when one of those same members has an entertainment at home and asks friends to come to his house.
>
> "Of course, it may be argued that all these forms of entertainment increase the membership of the club and therefore, in a sense, are appeals to the public. But I am not impressed with that argument in the face of the limitations which I believe have been placed upon the copyright law with relation to the interpretation of the phrase 'public performance.'" [44]

The Court there evidently dealt with a situation within the tort/contract dialectic. Apparently there was a contract between the parties and unauthorized use of certain of the films contrary to the contract, giving rise to a claim of infringing performance. Presumably these were exhibitions of 16mm. prints which are not normally sold but rather licensed for exhibition by distributors. The film probably was obtained rightfully under contract but the claim of infringement arose by reason of assertions of unauthorized use thereof.

Sec. 23.7. Performance and Fixation of Form for Copyright

But a distinguishing factor between live theatre and motion pictures is the availability of the analogy of home entertainment in films which the Court referred to, not normally present in live theatre. In this regard, Judge Herlands in his "in-depth" opinion on CATV as a per-

---

[44] *Idem* at p. 206. See Sec. 24.12, *infra.*

formance, in *United Artists Television, Inc.,* v. *Fortnightly Corp.,* states:

> "In determining whether to do that which defendant does is 'to perform,' the court must ascertain the content of the word 'perform' as it is used in the statute.
>
> "Perhaps the paradigm image of a performance, i.e., something which all would agree is exemplary of what the word performance is used to connote, occurs when Sir Laurence Olivier delivers Hamlet's soliloquy from the stage of a theatre at which there is an audience in attendance. All of the classic elements of a performance, as that word is used in common parlance, are then and there present: (1) an actor; (2) a work to be acted; and (3) an audience present to immediately see and hear the actor. From the time of the ancient Greeks, these triune elements indubitably would be said to constitute a performance of the playwright's work." [45]

Judge Herlands was faced with a physical separation of these triune elements in CATV. This is also true of film but not of the theatre. That is, performance perceived by an audience for a film is a reproduction of the original performance creating the work as embodied in a print so that necessarily there is a separation of performers rendering their performance and ultimate audience, a factor not present in live theatre. There, by contrast, there is a rendition directly in the presence of its purveyors, the audience.

There is, indeed, a further differentiation of live theatre from media representation. In the live theatre the creative,

---

[45] 255 F. Supp. 177 (S.D.N.Y. 1966) at p. 203, *aff'd,* 377 F. 2d 872 (2d Cir. 1967), *rev'd,* 392 U.S. 390 (1968).

copyrighted work is the play itself. Performance is a representation of the copyrighted work. Performance, in a sense, is a derivative of literary creation. In motion pictures, on the other hand, *performance creates the copyrighted work.* A feature film may be a visual representation of a screen play, true; but it is much more. Film production is the creation of a new literary and artistic property, the motion picture, which is itself the subject of copyright.[46] Performance in production by actors, live, before a camera is not performance of the film at all, since the picture is in the process of production and, at the time of such performance, the representations of the actors have not yet been embodied in filmic form. This would also be true of the various takes of a scene. Each take is a separate embodiment of a live performance by actors before a camera. It is the fixation of form of the film as finally cut that is the subject of copyright. The edited version then becomes the subject of copyright. The film as so fixed is reproduced into prints from the composite negative of film, dialogue, music and sound effects tracks. What is performed before an audience is the exhibition of such prints. Thus, unlike the live theatre, where all performance is a representation of the copyrighted work, in film it is not the fully cut and edited version. For in motion pictures there is no work until it is created by performance, whereas in live theatre, the play is created not by performance but by the writing of a play by a playwright. Television partakes of the characteristics of each, depending upon the form of rendition. If a teleplay is performed live, it is a representation of a script. The teleplay is then the copyrighted work which is the subject of the exclusive right of performance. If the teleplay is not represented live on

---

[46] 17 U.S.C. 5(l) motion-picture photoplays and 17 U.S.C. 5(m) motion pictures other than photoplays.

television, but is taped, filmed or otherwise reproduced, it is the reproduction that is the subject of copyright, not the telescript which formed the basis of the performance that was reproduced in fixed form. Performance of the reproduction, then, is the basis of the performance right. Of course, it is assumed that the producer in each instance, be it of the film or television reproduction, has acquired the necessary rights in respect of the screen play or teleplay, and any underlying work on which the same might be based, to produce and perform the film or television reproduction. A radio play would be somewhat different in that a transcription thereof would be aural only and not visual. Therefore, it could not be the subject of copyright as a sound recording prior to enactment of Public Law 92-140 on October 15, 1971 and fixation, registration and publication of such a transcription thereunder from and after February 15, 1972 and prior to January 1, 1975.[47] There the performance on the transcription would be a reproduction that could not qualify as a writing as a copyrighted work prior to such enactment. Hence there would be no exclusive right of performance of the transcription as a copyrighted dramatic work. The exclusive right of performance would reside only in the radio play, as it would analogously in the stage play. Any transcription or other recording of either, if played publicly, would be a per-

---

[47] Regulations of the Copyright Office, Sec. 202.8(b). But see Public Law 92-140, 92d Cong., S. 646, 85 Stat. 391, which provides for a copyright in sound recordings effective four months after date of enactment by notice by a P in a circle, Ⓟ. The Act became law October 15, 1971 and covers sound recordings, fixed, published and copyrighted from and after February 15, 1972 and prior to January, 1975. The Act amends 17 U.S.C. 26 to define sound recordings as works resulting from fixation of musical, spoken and other sounds, not accompanying a motion picture. The definition would encompass radio transcriptions.

formance subject to the exclusive right of performance of the radio play or stage play under copyright.

Sec. 23.8. Home Use as Performance

Since an exhibition of a film is a performance thereof, it may be seen that any running of a film on a projector would constitute a performance thereof. Thus, if a person should project a feature film on a 16mm. projector at home, that *ipso facto* would constitute a performance of the film. But the home exhibition of the film would not constitute a public performance since the very nature of a home is a private place which precludes entry of the public. Of course, the matter, even in the home, can become one of degree, for example, where admission is charged, such as in benefit exhibitions to aid a pet charity, or perhaps even to defray the rental of the film. Then the notion of relative publics might come into play. Presumably entrée would be limited to invited friends and relatives, thereby retaining the private character. But if the home performance were advertised generally to the public or were thrown open to friends of friends or even strangers without limitation, it might be said that the performance might be deemed more public than private. Ownership of premises is not determinative because most premises operating for profit, i.e., open to the public subject to an admission charge, are privately owned, be it by individuals, partnerships or closely or publicly held corporations. Nor is the character of the premises, architecturally, determinative. Dramatic public performances have been given in converted barns, garages, homes, apartments, basements and countless other places which originally were built for some other purpose and then utilized as theatres.[48]

[48] For example, the Yale Repertory Theatre under the direction of Dean Robert Brustein performed Molière's "Don Juan in Hell"

Performance Infringement

Be that as it may, one can speak of home use of films, as indeed of audio and videotape recordings, but for all practical purposes there is no home performance of live theatre, which is not, normatively speaking, a home entertainment as such. Thus, the ready analogy available in the *Maryland Yacht Club* case[49] as to films as home entertainment is not necessarily apposite as to live theatre which is not normally a home entertainment. Conceivably the Court in that case might have reconsidered its views if it had to decide upon a live theatrical performance at the same premises because the analogy to home entertainment would not hold up as to live theatre.

Per contra, musical performance can and does take place in the home. The third element of audience is not necessary in musical performance. Professionals as well as amateurs perform the copyrighted works just by playing, and perform even in practice and rehearsal performances, at which time the presence of an audience is neither required nor generally found. In other words, live theatre without an audience of any kind, whether present in person or in some kind of remote radio, television or recording audience, is simply not theatre. Actors and other artistic components of the theatre may mount productions simply for the joy and love of working in the theatre but always there is a presupposition of an audience of some kind, direct or remote, to perceive and/or hear. Music, on the other hand, can be its own reward to the performer, economics aside. It can thrive in the home and does not necessarily require an audience to react thereto in terms of what the performer does. It is not unknown, therefore,

---

in a former church adjacent to the campus which made very effective use of the church architecture in its performance of the play given in the spring of 1970.

[49] Notes 42-44, *supra*.

for performers to engage in rehearsal orchestras and ensembles without compensation and without any expectation thereof for the sheer sake of playing different works or in various combinations as opposed to their ordinary, routine occupation as musicians.

Sec. 23.9. Musical Performance and Dramatic Performance

Audience factor has a certain corollary in music and the theatre. Music attracts not only for novelty but also for repetition. Cover records released competitively by record companies to take advantage of a song that has been released as a hit record or is rapidly moving in that direction attest to the popularity of a variety of versions of works. Thus it was Louis Armstrong's cover song rendition of "Hello Dolly" which ascended in chart ratings as compared to Carol Channing's original stage performance as recorded. Latterly, of course, there is the Barbra Streisand version and many others. The same is true of "Fiddler on the Roof" tunes and many, many pop tunes, whether or not derived from the musical theatre. Part of the interest is attributable to the performer's rendition and the arrangement being performed. Comparably, one might say that in the live theatre, too, artistic interpretations are important. Audiences will compare and, from time to time, go to see different renditions of "Hamlet" as performed by Richard Burton, Laurence Olivier, Christopher Plummer, or Maurice Evans, not to mention a number of others. But, in the main, apart from the sophisticated *cognoscenti* in the theatre, ordinarily performance satiation within a period of several years after viewing the same is generally reached by the average theatregoer with respect to that particular play after one viewing of the same. This is generally true of motion pictures in the theatre too.

Audiences do not, in most instances, return to see a play or film a second or third time within a period of weeks, months or several years after first viewing the same. The norm of theatrical and motion picture performance is based upon presentation of fresh productions for which an audience is to be found. Of course there are exceptions both as to particular plays, especially musical plays, and films that happen to strike a responsive chord from a sector of the audience sufficient to spark a desire for repeat viewing.

But in music, the norm differs. Audience-wise, music in all forms—pops, classical, rock, blues, country, etc.—bears repetition as far as the public is concerned. The particular publics for the various genres of music will accept repeated performances and constitute audiences therefor, direct or remote, until, as with pop tunes, a point of satiety is reached with the public and the tune falls off in popularity and repetition.

Perhaps this differentiation is true because of the nature of the spoken word, be it dramatic or non-dramatic, as contrasted to music. An audience for selected readings by a noted performer would not be likely to return to listen to a second or third noted performer read the same material within an interval comparable to return for viewing a live dramatic production or a film exhibition.

Economics play a part in such decisions. One might hazard a guess that the incidence of viewing of repeat performances of dramatic works or of non-dramatic, non-musical performances on television is far greater than in the theatre or in theatrical motion picture exhibition because repeat television is free to the viewer. Even then, however, the fall-off of repeat viewing from original viewing of the same performance, no doubt, is considerable.

On the other hand, repeat musical shows on television probably attract more repeat viewing than non-musical shows on the same notion that musical repetition is of greater interest to the audience, be it on television or in the live theatre, in the motion picture theatre, on recordings or on radio.

In this regard, Nimmer has observed with respect to the statutory distinctions as to profit limitations in music and non-dramatic works on the one hand, and dramatic works on the other:

> "Why this distinction? It is reasoned that if a dramatic work is performed, even on a non-profit basis, those who view such performance are not likely to thereafter attend a performance for profit of the same work. Thereafter any performance of a dramatic work in some degree diminishes the potential revenue to be obtained from performances for profit. It is thought that this is not true of performances of musical compositions and nondramatic literary works. That is, so the argument goes, one who attends a non-profit performance of such a work rather than being sated with it is more likely thereafter to wish to see a professional (for profit) performance of the same work." [50]

Nimmer questions the applicability of repeat interest as to non-dramatic works—and correctly so—but adds a second explanation and justification, "It is thought that to prohibit unlicensed non-profit performances of musical and nondramatic literary works in such public places as schools and churches would constitute an undue restriction on the benefits which should be available to the public." [51]

---

[50] Nimmer, *op. cit., supra,* note 16, Sec. 107.31, at p. 402.

[51] *Idem* at p. 403.

Performance Infringement

The differentiation, as determined by Congress, appears to reflect in good measure market realities of the particular arts and a balancing of public interest and economic rewards to the creator and assigns. The reality of the theatre is that its principal economic basis is in theatrical performance and derivative performances, and not otherwise. Plays are largely intended to be seen rather than read and play viewing is of much greater scope and value economically than play publishing. Of course, classical plays are read as literature and taught in the schools and therefore large numbers of the classical plays are bought and read. But in terms of what is produced in the live theatre annually and the proportion thereof published and read as literature, it is clear that plays are written to be performed rather than to be read as closet plays and the public so reacts. Theatre is a performing art and the subsidiary right of play publishing is of relatively small account therein. The subsidiary rights emanating therefrom that are economically important, and even artistically important, are subsidiary theatrical performing rights and derivative production and performing rights—motion pictures, television and cast albums.[52] In other words, the economic basis of dramatic works is in performance in various media. Given a rapid fall-off in audience satiety within the same medium, normatively speaking, a nonprofit limitation could be detrimental to the marketing of such works. Of course performance of adaptations of dramatic works in different media compete, to an extent, with each other, particularly if performed concurrently, but such derivative works are characterized by the forms of the artistic media employed. A filmed "My Fair Lady"

---

[52] See Weissberger, Arnold L., Subsidiary Rights in the Theatre, Chap. X of Subsidiary Rights and Residuals, edited by Taubman, Joseph (1968), pp. 115-184.

is of quite a different character technically, artistically and possibly even emotionally in terms of audience reaction from a live stage version thereof. Similarly, the television show "The Last Angry Man" was different from its later motion picture version. Adaptations for different media provide variants of the work in many ways that tend to overcome the satiety factor and induce audience interest in seeing the derivative work as performed in other media. Even then, time lapse is important. The market takes cognizance of this fact in often providing for contractual clearances as between a work still in performance and an adaptation thereof for performance in another medium.

Given the generally public nature of live theatre and the satiety factor accounting for the lack of a non-profit limitation, it may be said that the market is substantially coextensive with theatrical possibilities and that Congress has wisely inhibited inroads thereon that might otherwise have arisen by non-profit limitations.

Non-dramatic literary works are in a different category. On the one hand, commercial possibilities are extant in publication—books, newspapers and periodicals—which are not normally an important segment of the economic possibilities for dramatic works. Moreover, non-dramatic works do not ordinarily have the economic possibilities, market-wise, of dramatic works. Therefore, the preservation of performance impact theory, applicable to dramatic works, does not have as much relevance in relation to non-dramatic works. On the contrary, the value of dramatic works is principally in performance; the experiential factor of seeing the work performed is what is effective in relation to the dramatic work. Non-dramatic literary works may be equally or even more rewarding when read as opposed to being seen or heard. This would also apply to lectures, sermons and addresses unless, of course, the person happens to be unusually effective as a speaker, such as Winston Churchill, Franklin Delano Roosevelt or Martin Luther King, Jr. More importantly, lectures, sermons, addresses and non-dramatic literary works generally are a good part of the warp and woof of education. They are the substance and means of educational transmission of learning. Given the overriding and abiding social interest in this and the relative economic importance of performance of such works, be it for profit or not for profit, again the legislature has wisely balanced the equities of creators and audience.

Music, in turn, has its own parameters of function, market and purpose. Musical performance, be it by bands, choruses, orchestras and music appreciation courses generally, is an integral and important part of the educational scene. If performance fees were payable for educational uses, assuming there were no non-profit limitation, then copyright proprietors might find that the schools would gravitate to public domain works. Considering the vast number of musical compositions, including many of the greatest masterpieces in all genre, royalties for performance in education might have the effect of drying up performance revenues from education because of the ready availability of royalty-free music in the public domain of major stature. Then, too, the audience interest in musical composition with its facet of interest in identification of an artist or group with particular musical compositions and in differing renditions provides a large market for performances for profit in recordings, radio, motion pictures and television, as well as live or transcribed performances at night clubs, cabarets, restaurants and other places. Even recordings serve a dual purpose of public performance over radio and elsewhere, as well as private home use.

Thus musical performance does not *ipso facto* face material diminution by reason of the non-profit limitation. Although the principal non-profit users are in education, it is submitted that the balance of the non-profit uses does not materially have an adverse impact on performance royalties since non-profit performance is largely in education.

Music may face other problems in terms of economic impact, market-wise, such as the nature and scope of fair use in reproduction of parts and scores by reprography as part of the increasing availability of reproduction devices. The market enjoyed by music publishers in education in terms of sales of copies of music may be affected by reproduction which exceeds fair use in terms of the extent of xerox or other copying made, but that is a different problem from the market possibilities of musical performance in non-profit, particularly educational, institutions.

Sec. 23.10. The Juke-Box Exemption

It is with respect to the juke-box, however, and the outright exemption accorded thereto that one finds a limitation which has been outlived by Congressional expectations, even though the exemption was broader than one limited to non-profit performance, assuming no admission was charged where such coin-operated machines were emplaced. The irony of the performance exemption accorded the half-billion dollar grossing industry is to be found in the reasons propounded for the exemption in the House Report prior to the enactment of the 1909 Act, which reads:

> "The exception regarding the public performance of a musical composition upon coin-operated machines in a place where an admission fee is not charged is understood to be satisfactory to the composers and proprietors of musical copyrights. A representative of one of the largest music publishing houses in the

> country stated that the publisher finds the so-called 'penny parlor' of first assistance as an advertising medium." [53]

Indeed, the House Report on current copyright revision has observed in this regard, "No provision of the present law has attracted more heated denunciation and controversy than the so-called jukebox exemption of section 1(e).

* * *

"Efforts to repeal the clause have been going on for more than 40 years . . ." [54]

In this regard, proposed copyright revision, S. 543, Sec. 116, is a statute designed to provide a juke-box compulsory license to be administered by the Copyright Office. Here proposed copyright revision represents a recognition that changed circumstances of juke-box use, primarily commercial in nature, do affect the market for performance with no real countervailing reason to retain the exemption, whatever might have been the original motivation therefor so that some legislative action is desirable to correct the imbalance.[55]

Sec. 23.11. Scope of Performance

Whatever the impact of limitations on performance as expressed legislatively and as embodied in market norms,

---

[53] House Report 2222, note 8, *supra,* as reprinted in Nimmer, *idem,* at p. 970.

[54] Report No. 83, House of Representatives, 90th Cong., 1st Sess., Mar. 8, 1967, to accompany H.R. 2512, at p. 75. The House Report weighs the pros and cons for repeal at pp. 75-84.

[55] S. 543, Sec. 116, Dec. 10, 1969 Print, 91st Cong., 1st Sess., Jan. 22, 1969. House Report 83, *idem,* had proposed a compromise juke-box compulsory license as an alternative to outright repeal or retention of the juke-box exemption.

the present Act on its face purports to grant the performing right to three basic categories—dramatic works, music and non-dramatic literary works. As to dramatic and musical compositions, it is clear that the essence of protection of the copyright is in performance. Plays are intended to be seen, music is meant to be played. One does not buy sheet music to read the score silently but to perform it. In other words, the principal attribute of dramatic and musical works, in terms of their abiding social value, is in performance. Therefore, the right of performance accorded under copyright therein is of primary importance; concomitantly, infringement thereof by performance. Non-dramatic literary works have less claim to this status except for the fact that the statute as originally enacted in 1909[56] related solely to lectures, sermons and addresses whose primary function was to be orally delivered. Oral delivery perforce constitutes a type of performance in that the lecture, sermon or address is rendered as a principal means of communication thereof. The 1952 amendment of Sec. 1(c)[57] to cover nondramatic literary works generally in performance and to overturn legislatively the decision of *Kreymborg* v. *Durante*[58] wherein a rendition by Jimmy Durante of Alfred Kreymborg's poem on radio was held to constitute a non-infringing performance, was intended to expand the category of nondramatic works in performance to nondramatic literary works generically. Thus, performance even here related to *literary* works.

---

[56] Act of Mar. 4, 1909, Sec. 1(c), 60th Cong., 2d Sess., 35 Stat. 1075, Copyright Enactments, note 8, *supra,* at p. 64.

[57] 17 U.S.C. 1(c) as amended, Public Law 575, 82d Cong., 2d Sess., Chap. 923, 66 Stat. 752, approved July 17, 1952, effective January 1, 1953.

[58] 21 U.S.P.Q. 557 (S.D.N.Y. 1934), and on rehearing, 22 U.S.P.Q. 248 (S.D.N.Y. 1934). See Sec. 15.2, *supra.*

Performance Infringement

Thus the scope of coverage granted by the statute to performance is the exclusive right of performance in what are commonly known as the performing arts which are the subject of copyright. Correspondingly, if there is infringement, it is likewise within the same scope of the infringed work.

Sec. 23.11(a). Sporting Events as Performance

In this respect, the scope of the performing arts cannot be artificially extended so as to protect something else in the guise of relief from infringing performance. In *Seltzer v. Sunbrock,*[59] plaintiff, Leo A. Seltzer, evidently copyrighted two works as dramatic compositions which related to roller derbies. He granted an exclusive license to stage this event, which involved competition, to plaintiff, Transcontinental Roller Derby Association, Inc. Defendants were sued for alleged infringement by copying the works in their books and by unauthorized performance of plaintiff's copyrighted works. After disposing of the copying issue adversely to plaintiffs on the principle that there was no copying, the Court then directed itself to the issue of alleged infringing performance. As to this, the Court stated, regarding the nature of plaintiff Seltzer's books as dramatic compositions, "All we have here is a set of regulations for running a race." [60] The elements necessary to constitute a dramatic composition were, upon analysis, lacking. But the Court went further. Conceivably a work lacking in qualification as a dramatic composition could be a nondramatic literary composition as to which protection could still be accorded unauthorized performance by infringing delivery after 1952 in public for

---

[59] 22 F. Supp. 621 (S.D. Cal. 1938).
[60] *Idem* at p. 630.

profit.[61] This follows from the language at the end of Sec. 5, the classification section, ". . . nor shall any error in classification invalidate or impair the copyright protection secured under this title." [62] However, the Court demolished this possibility by stating,

"What Seltzer really composed was a description of a system for conducting races on roller skates. A system, as such, can never be copyrighted. If it finds any protection, it must come from the patent laws." [63] The Court went even further in disposing of the contention of plaintiffs. "Even if plaintiffs' books be held to describe a game or sporting event, the rules thereof, as ideas, are not copyrightable. Whist Club v. Foster, D.C. 42 F.2d 482; Russell v. Northeastern Pub. Co., D.C., 7 F. Supp. 571. Nor is the system of staging a game or spectacle covered." [64] The Court was quick to point out that dramatic expression could relate to sports and games and in the telling of such a story, the expression thereof could be protected. This would not give the creator thereof any exclusive right to performance of the sporting event or game so described by reason of the copyright in the composition. The Court concluded that the plaintiffs could have no relief under the Copyright Act as to Seltzer's "so-called drama".

The case at least involved a genuine controversy. The lengths to which protection against infringing performance was sought in the guise of performance of dramatic composition appears from the Court of Appeals' reversal[65] of the

---

[61] 17 U.S.C. 1(c) as amended, see note 57, *supra.*

[62] 17 U.S.C. 5.

[63] Note 59, *supra,* at p. 630.

[64] *Ibid.*

[65] Seltzer v. Corem, 107 F.(2d) 75 (7th Cir. 1939), *rev'g* 26 F. Supp. 892 (D. N.D. Ind. 1939).

District Court decision in *Seltzer* v. *Corem.* Plaintiff, Seltzer, brought an action on the same books which he had copyrighted and the District Court held that the copyrights covered a dramatic composition which had been infringed by the defendant. The Court of Appeals for the Seventh Circuit reversed and dismissed the complaint. The Court of Appeals observed, "This is an exceedingly friendly suit. Indeed it is so much so that our suspicion is somewhat aroused." [66] After reviewing the procedural steps taken by the parties which aroused the appellate court's suspicions, it stated, "These facts of themselves are perhaps not sufficient to warrant notice on our part, but we are interested, of course, in knowing whether there is a good faith controversy between these parties, and whether appellant has really committed the acts which he has admitted in his stipulation." [67] The Seventh Circuit adverted to *Seltzer* v. *Sunbrock*[68] and reversed in reliance thereon. After pointing out that appellee was the plaintiff in both the prior California case and the Indiana case before it on appeal, the Court of Appeals remarked, "A significant fact is that neither appellant nor appellee in this case called our attention to that case, and we assume that the District Court's attention was not called to it." [69]

If there were, in fact, no real controversy between the parties, one can only speculate why the defendant appealed when the plaintiff already had the benefit of a favorable decision in the court below. Perhaps, on further speculation, this might have arisen because a decision in a Court of Appeals might have carried more weight as authority throughout the United States other than in the district

---

[66] *Idem* at p. 76.
[67] *Ibid.*
[68] Note 59, *supra.*
[69] Note 65, *supra,* at p. 77.

where *Sunbrock*[70] was decided than a co-ordinate District Court decision elsewhere. The Southern District of California handles a great many copyright decisions and would probably be accorded greater weight as authority than a District Court decision in Indiana. Thus, if the Court of Appeals' own speculations as to the reasons for the friendliness of the suit had any substance in fact, it would indicate the extreme lengths to which the advantages of designation of a work for copyright registration were sought in terms of characterization thereof for classification purposes as a dramatic composition with a concomitant claim of infringement thereof by performance of the copyrighted work, a right exclusively given to the creator and assigns of the dramatic composition. *A fortiori,* the performing right benefit might be sought in delivery infringement after 1952 if the alleged infringing performance took place with respect to a non-dramatic literary work. But these cases were brought long before the amendment to Sec. 1(c)[71] and the right of exclusive delivery under that section prior to 1953 was then limited to lectures, sermons and addresses.[72]

This much is clear. The plaintiff in both suits thought enough of the advantage of protecting his roller derby against competitive events by copyright that he sought to extend the monopoly of the copyright to cover roller derby performance as alleged infringing performance of his works. Roller skating derby partakes of both athletic event and game in that it has rules and competition. Superficially there is a resemblance between athletics and the

---

[70] Note 59, *supra.*

[71] Act of Mar. 4, 1909, 17 U.S.C. 1(c); notes 56-57, *supra.*

[72] Kreymborg v. Durante, 21 U.S.P.Q. 557 (S.D.N.Y. 1934), rehearing 22 U.S.P.Q. 248 (S.D.N.Y. 1934).

performing arts in that the essence of athletics is also performance. The difference, from a copyright point of view, is that an athletic event as such is not a representation of a story, where the work is dramatic, or a delivery of some kind of literary non-dramatic production. The nature of athletic performance is in the fact of contest wherein the athlete performs in some kind of competition, be it against others directly or indirectly, as in certain athletic events, such as figure skating. Competitors may or may not be visible during the competitive performance, depending upon whether the outcome is measured by judging performers in action contemporaneously or whether performance is to be judged individually, whether against the clock, or by other yardsticks of merit. The same would be true if no humans were involved in sporting events, as in greyhound races.

This does not exclude the possibility of athletics being the subject of a literary or dramatic work thereby giving rise to a right of dramatization and to dramatic performance thereof and of derivative works. But that is quite different from protecting performance of sporting and athletic events under copyright. If a writing is tantamount only to being a description of the rules of the game, then it is not the subject of copyright, because what is really expressed is the idea and ideas as such are not subject to copyright.[73]

Sec. 23.11(b). Games as Performance

The same principle is true of games generally, whether or not the same be an athletic or sporting event. Thus, in *Whist Club* v. *Foster*[74] a claim for infringement of a work,

---

[73] Baker v. Selden, 101 U.S. 99 (1879).
[74] 42 F. 2d 782 (S.D.N.Y. 1929).

"Laws for Auction Bridge-1926" by publication of "Foster's Simplified Auction Bridge (with the New Law)" was dismissed by the Court. Judge Thacher rendered his opinion as follows:

> "In the conventional laws or rules of a game, as distinguished from the forms or modes of expression in which they may be stated, there can be no literary property susceptible of copyright. The defendant has not infringed, because he has not copied the literary composition of the plaintiff's publication, but, in language quite distinctly his own, has restated the same set of conventional precepts. This under all the authorities he was entitled to do, and neither the general acceptance of the rules as official, nor, if it were true, their rejection as officious, could have any bearing on this controversy." [75]

It would follow then that if the defendant simply stated the rules of the game by restating the same set of conventional precepts, then playing the game of auction bridge, i.e., performance thereof, would likewise not constitute performing infringement. In this regard, in connection with a claim of infringement by a newspaper of plaintiff's work, "Rapid Contract Bridge", the Court, in *Russell* v. *Northeastern Pub. Co.,* stated,

> "The page from complainant's book, described in his bill, presents a problem illustrating a principle of play rather than of bidding without revealing the author's solution of that problem. It is extremely doubtful whether the page contains any matter whatever which can be said to be properly the subject of copyright. However that may be, it is clear on the authorities

---

[75] *Ibid.*

> that the complainant can acquire no exclusive rights in the particular distribution of the fifty-two cards, in the problem of play, or the principles of contract bridge applicable to its solution. The most that can be claimed is protection against the language used in presenting the problem." [76]

Thus, playing of the game according to its rules would not constitute an infringing performance since rules of the game are not the subject of copyright. So, too, following the plan of "Bank Night" by a "Parlay Cash Night" under principles of unfair competition in *Affiliated Enterprises, Inc.* v. *Meyer Gruber, Inc.*[77] was held not protectible. By way of dictum, the Court indicated that the game could not be copyrighted because it was in no sense a writing under the Constitution or the statute.[78]

By contrast, the performing arts are not contests of events, games or performances of rules. There is either a writing which is performed as a dramatic or musical work or a nondramatic literary work, or some combination thereof, as in a dramatico-musical composition which is the subject of copyright, assuming originality. In that event, performance is representation, the following of some fixation of form as the abiding means of rendering that work. Alternatively, there is improvisation where no prior writing serves as the basis for interpretation by the artist. Absent a writing, there is constitutionally no basis for copyright and so improvised performance, that is not captured in some fixed form which is the subject of copyright, cannot be copyrighted. Where the improvisation is captured in

---

[76] 7 F. Supp. 571, 572 (D. Mass. 1934).
[77] 86 F. 2d 958 (1st Cir. 1936).
[78] *Idem* at p. 961.

fixed form, as in film or videotape, then the fixation of form, assuming originality, may provide the subject of copyright because it is the fixation of performance which renders the same into a tangible form of writing that is the subject of copyright.

This may also happen with music where, for example, a group improvises in a recording session and a lead sheet or score is drawn from the recording. In that case, the fixation requires two steps. The first is the recording as a fixation in audio form only, which was not copyrightable prior to enactment of Public Law 92-140.[79] Second, the recording is then transcribed into score form which is a visual fixation of form that is copyrightable under the statute, assuming originality. Thus even improvisation is not necessarily excluded from copyrightability provided it is captured in visual form and is original.

Thus sporting events and games would appear not to be copyrightable matter. As stated by Judge Bright, "And it is very doubtful if rules of a game can, in any event, be copyrightable subject matter." [80] It requires something more in the way of a writing for copyrightability. There must be expression of a story content in a writing. If there is, only that particular expression may then be copyrightable. For example, the musical play "Damn Yankees" protects the copyrightable components in the work, but not baseball. The particular story line and characters therein as expressed by the work are the subject of protection, not the story of the New York Yankees factually or historically. So, too, if athletic events are embodied in photographs or athletes are reproduced in sport

---

[79] Regulations of the Copyright Office, Sec. 202.8(b).

[80] Chamberlin v. Uris Sales Corporation, 56 F. Supp. 987, 988 (S.D.N.Y. 1944), *aff'd,* 150 F. 2d 512 (2d Cir. 1945).

in painting and sculpture, then the particular scenes, or artistic works,[81] assuming originality, are the subject of copyright. Then, too, Dostoyevsky's story, "White Night" about gambling at Monte Carlo, assuming copyright of the work, protects against infringement of his story and not against the games played at the casinos there. Finally, football, baseball and countless other athletic events are reproduced on television in some fixed form, be it film, videotape or other process. The fixation creates the embodiment in a form of writing. If the event is part of a story, it is a dramatic work; if not, it is a nondramatic work.[82]

---

[81] Bleistein v. Donaldson Lithographing Co., 188 U.S. 239 (1903); Mazer v. Stein, 347 U.S. 201 (1954); Alfred Bell & Co. Ltd. v. Catalda Fine Arts, Inc., 191 F.2d 99 (2d Cir. 1951).

[82] By letter dated April 28, 1961 of Richard Colby to Professor Walter J. Derenberg, the Copyright Society was advised that on April 19, 1961, the Copyright Office had accepted a videotape of Gian Carlo Menotti's "The Consul" from International Telemeter Corp., a division of Paramount Pictures Corporation. The letter is set forth in 8 Bull. Cr. Soc. 205 (1961) and a photograph of the acceptance, showing the Register of Copyright receiving the magnetic video tape from Fulton Brylawski, on behalf of Paramount. The Certificate of Registration thereof is set forth in pertinent part at p. 207. Note, however, that Circular 47 of the Copyright Office, which is entitled "Radio and Television Programs" refers to copyrighting of "Filmed Television Programs" under Classes L-M. The Certificate of Registration of the videotape was on Form L-M. Nimmer remarks in this regard, "The Copyright Office regards magnetic video tape as a form of motion picture for purposes of registration under Secs. 5(1) and (m)." *op. cit., supra,* note 16, Sec. 25.3 at p. 117. See Fritch, Bruce E., Some Copyright implications of Videotapes, 37 U.S.C. L. Rev. 214 (1964), at p. 219, however, "It seems, therefore, that the Copyright Act as it currently exists does not with reasonable certainty answer questions about the copyright status of videotapes." See Regulations of the Copyright Office, Sec. 202.15(d), effective as of May 14, 1971, and Sec. 12.3, *supra;* Latman, Howell's Copyright Law, Revised Ed. (1962).

In either event, copyrightability inheres in the particular expression, and not in the fact of the particular sport itself. Even photographs of sporting events are copyrightable,[83] assuming a modicum of originality therein. But what is copyrightable is the particular representation in that photograph, and what is infringement is copying that photograph, not the reproduction of the original event. Thus, two photographs might have the same events in the picture. Independently created, there is no infringement. The gravamen of the complaint is copying unless there is a fair use.[84]

Sec. 23.12. Performance Correlation: Sec. 1 and Sec. 5

At this point one must ask whether or not there is a correlation between the exclusive performance rights given by Sec. 1(c), (d) and (e)[85] of the statute and Sec. 5 of the Act.[86] In other words, is exclusivity limited to the classes referred to in Sec. 5(c)—Lectures, sermons, addresses prepared for oral delivery, vis-à-vis Sec. 1(c); Sec. 5(d)—Dramatic or dramatico-musical compositions, in respect of Sec. 1(d); and Sec. 5(e)—Musical compositions, in regard to Sec. 1(e)?[87] Obviously, there is such a correspondence so that the copyrights registered under those classes qualify for the exclusive performance rights. But the relationship should not be left at that because it is incomplete.

---

[83] Burrow-Giles Lithographic Co. v. Sarony, 111 U.S. 53 (1884).

[84] Time, Inc. v. Bernard Geis Associates, 293 F. Supp. 130 (S.D. N.Y. 1968) held that charcoal sketches copied from certain frames of the Zapruder film of the John F. Kennedy assassination owned by Life Magazine, embodied in defendant's book constituted a fair use. See Chap. XXV, *infra*.

[85] 17 U.S.C. 1(c), (d) and (e).

[86] 17 U.S.C. 5.

[87] 17 U.S.C. 5(c), (d) and (e).

Performance Infringement

The Supreme Court held in *Kalem Co.* v. *Harper Bros.*[88] that the unauthorized adaptation into a film of the novel "Ben Hur" constituted an infringing dramatization thereof. Although decided under the statute in effect prior to the enactment of the present Act, the exclusive right to dramatize is also to be found in the 1909 Act, Sec. 1(b).[89] If the infringing film constituted an unauthorized dramatization, *a fortiori* such adaptation would be classified as a dramatic work. Dramatic works are accorded exclusive right of performance under Sec. 1(d).[90] It follows that when the Townsend Act was enacted in 1912[91] amending Sec. 5 of the 1909 Act so as to classify films into "Motion-picture photoplays" under Sec. 5(l) and "Motion pictures other than photoplays" under Sec. 5(m) that all photoplays would qualify thereunder as dramatic works. Moreover, the Regulations of the Copyright Office refer squarely to the dramatic nature of photoplays. Sec. 202.15(a) of the Regulations reads:

"Photoplays (Class L) This class included published or unpublished motion pictures that are dramatic in character and tell a connected story, such as feature films, filmed television plays, short subjects and animated cartoons having a plot." [92] By contrast, Sec. 202.15(b) categorizes motion pictures other than photoplays as "nondramatic films." [93] Indeed, one of the bills introduced in the House of Representatives, H.R. 21295 March 4, 1912 by Congressman Moon of Pennsylvania proposed to amend Sec. 5 by changing subdivisions 5(d) and (j) as follows:

---

[88] 222 U.S. 55 (1911).
[89] Now 17 U.S.C. 1(b).
[90] 17 U.S.C. 1(d).
[91] Act of Aug. 24, 1912, 62d Cong., 2d Sess., 37 Stat. 488 (1913).
[92] Regulations of the Copyright Office, Sec. 202.15(a).
[93] Idem, Sec. 202.15(b).

"(d) Dramatic or dramatico-musical compositions or motion-picture photoplays;

* * *

"(j) Photographs or motion pictures (other than photoplays);" [94]

There would seem little doubt, therefore, that motion pictures telling a story and with a plot would be classified as dramatic works for purposes of Sec. 1(d). Indeed, Sec. 1(d), without explicitly mentioning films, grants the exclusive right of performance to recordings and transcriptions of a dramatic work including the right to "exhibit, perform, represent, produce, or reproduce it in any manner or by any method whatsoever".[95] Considering that this section was enacted in this form to cover piracy by motion pictures and live theatre by recording by stenographers of copyrighted stage plays and then performing the pirated work,[96] it may be concluded that Sec. 1(d), from the time of its enactment in 1909, even prior to the 1912 amendment to specifically cover motion pictures, intended to comprehend motion picture photoplays as dramatic works.[97]

The question was squarely determined by Judge Coleman in *Tiffany Productions, Inc.* v. *Dewing,* that a motion picture photoplay was a dramatic work.[98] In *Metro-Goldwyn-Mayer Distributing Corporation* v. *Bijou Theatre Co.,* the Court of Appeals for the First Circuit stated,

---

[94] H.R. 21295, Introduced March 4, 1912 by Congressman Moon of Pennsylvania to amend Sec. 5 of the 1909 Act.

[95] 17 U.S.C. 1(d). See Chap. XV, *supra.*

[96] Report No. 2222, House of Representatives, note 16, *supra,* Nimmer, *idem,* at pp. 963-4.

[97] See also Photo-Drama Motion Picture Co., Inc. v. Social Uplift Film Corp., 220 Fed. 448 (2d Cir. 1915) which referred to separate stage and film dramatization rights after the 1912 amendment.

[98] 50 F. 2d 911 (D. Md. 1931).

"We hold that films which are founded upon copyrighted dramas or other dramatic compositions are protected under the provisions of section 1(d) of the Copyright Act and their unlicensed exhibition is an infringement of the copyrighted dramatic composition." [99] Clearly the rationale that Sec. 1(d) of the Act covers motion picture photoplays as dramatic works has been accepted by the cases even though motion picture photoplays are separately classified under Section 5.

Sec. 23.12(a). Motion Pictures Other Than Photoplays: Performance Right

Whatever problem may have been created by the nature of motion pictures other than photoplays appears to have been resolved by the amendment to Sec. 1(c). The dictum of Judge Coleman in *Tiffany Productions, Inc.* v. *Dewing*[100] to the effect that there was a hiatus as to coverage of motion pictures other than photoplays appears to be dispelled by the 1952 amendment to Sec. 1(c). At that time, the exclusive performing right was extended not only to delivery of nondramatic literary works, in addition to lectures, sermons, addresses and like productions, but recordings and transcriptions thereof were protected as well as the right in respect thereof "to exhibit, represent, produce, or reproduce it in any manner or by any method whatsoever." [101] The language and conception follows almost precisely the formulation of Sec. 1(d) in respect of recordings and transcriptions. Motion pictures other than photoplays would therefore seem to be accorded the right

---

[99] 59 F. 2d 70, 77 (1st Cir. 1932). See also 3 F. Supp. 66 (D. Mass. 1933).

[100] Note 98, *supra*.

[101] Note 57, *supra*.

of public performance for profit thereunder, certainly to the extent they are adaptations of non-dramatic literary works.

In this regard, it is to be noted that Judge Herlands' first ruling in *Fortnightly* is as follows:

"1. With respect to plaintiff's copyrighted motion pictures other than photoplays, defendant has infringed upon plaintiff's copyrights by performing plaintiff's said copyrighted motion pictures in public for profit. 17 U.S.C. Sec. 1(c) (1964)."[102] What is noteworthy here is that the defendant apparently did not set forth any affirmative defense in his answer with respect thereto.[103] Conceivably the point was felt to be unimportant to the defendant since the bulk of motion pictures carried by defendant would have been feature motion pictures characterized as motion picture photoplays as to which the law is well settled that exhibition thereof would constitute infringing performance if there were no other valid defenses thereto. This, of course, meant that the District Court held motion picture photoplays to infringe Sec. 1(d) in its second conclusion in the opinion.[104] The Court of Appeals[105] affirmed the District Court decision which was then reversed by the Supreme Court on other grounds without any comment on the classification of motion pictures as photoplays or other than photoplays for infringement purposes.[106]

One might suggest that perhaps motion pictures other than photoplays require antecedently a scenario to constitute the non-dramatic literary work to be recorded under

[102] 255 F. Supp. 177, 215 (S.D.N.Y. 1966).
[103] *Idem* at pp. 181-182.
[104] *Idem* at p. 215.
[105] 377 F2d 872 (2d Cir. 1967).
[106] 392 U.S. 390 (1968).

Sec. 1(c) before such a film may be said to be an exhibition, etc., of such recording. In other words, it might be contended that if a motion picture other than photoplay be shot without the use of an underlying script upon which it is based, there is nothing to record and therefore Sec. 1(c) does not apply. In such event, it might be argued under *Patterson* v. *Century Productions, Inc.*[107] that the film itself is the nondramatic literary work and that its projection constitutes a recording thereof so that the exhibition constitutes a performance of the work. True, that case suggested that exhibition of a film was a copy but a recording which may be perceived visually would constitute a copy and so the performance right under Sec. 1(c) could be given effect even where there is no script. Nimmer[108] raises the question as to whether a motion picture other than a photoplay might be a nondramatic literary work. He endeavors to qualify it as such by statutory reference to notice requirements and classification. One might argue, too, that the scope of copyright is literary and artistic property, together comprehended by the constitutional and Congressional requirements that they be writings. In other words, statutory copyright is intended to cover the fine arts in their broadest sense and literature. The performing arts are renditions of literature, either by adaptations into motion pictures, television, choreography or performances of musical literature. Literature comprehends non-fiction as well as fiction. Literary works include both. Although originally classified as photographs, motion pictures are like the theatre, representational, in that they are depictions of scenes, locales, and constitute concrete expressions of ideas, pictorial, by dialogue, sound

---

[107] 93 F.2d 489 (2d Cir. 1937).

[108] Nimmer, *op. cit., supra,* note 16, Sec. 28.

effects, and by combination thereof. It may be said, then, that motion pictures include attributes of both literary and artistic property. Therefore, partaking as they do of the character of literary works in part, they may be deemed to qualify as literary works in their broadest sense.

Judge McLellan, on rehearing in *Bijou,* suggested by way of dictum that a motion picture other than a photoplay might be deemed a dramatization under Sec. 1(b) of the Act.[109] He opined, "If they are not dramatic works, the exhibition of the photoplays by the defendant constitutes a dramatization of a nondramatic work, and constitutes an infringement of the rights secured by subdivision (b) . . ." [110]

It has been suggested earlier by the writer[111] that all motion pictures might be deemed photoplays or dramatic works by their very nature notwithstanding the classification of Sec. 5 (l) and (m) which has been so adopted for the convenience of the Copyright Office and copyright applicants, i.e., for administrative convenience.[112] Vachel Lindsay has commented on the dramatic qualities of the camera, in speaking of news films, as follows:

> "Any picture of a sea-gull flying so close to the camera that it becomes as large as a flying machine, or any flying machine made by man and photographed in epic flight captures the eye because it is architecture in motion, motion which is the mysterious fourth dimension of its grace and glory. So likewise, and in kind, any picture of a tossing ship." [113]

---

[109] 3 F. Supp. 66 (D. Mass. 1933).

[110] *Idem* at p. 73.

[111] Sec. 15.7 *et seq., supra.*

[112] Note 98 *supra.*

[113] Lindsay, Vachel, The Art of the Moving Picture, with an introduction by Stanley Kauffmann (1970), the 1922 revision of the

Performance Infringement

Finally, it is to be noted that the Townsend Act amended the 1909 Act in 1912 to provide special damages for infringing performance by films of both dramatic and nondramatic works. The hearings are replete with references to the reasons for the special damages rules as to infringing performance by film and the reasons for differentiating damages as to the nature of the work infringed.[114] If copyright infringement is seen as the analogue of the grant of a right, by reason of the reference to infringement by motion pictures in the Townsend Act, amending Sec. 25 of the Act of 1909,[115] to specify statutory damages for infringement by motion pictures in terms of dramatic works and nondramatic works, then it may be concluded that Congress evidenced by its actions that there was, in fact, an exclusive right of motion picture performance granted by statute in the 1909 Act.

It follows, therefore, that there is protection, both as to motion picture photoplays under Sec. 1(d) as to the exclusive right of performance, and under a variety of theories as to motion pictures other than photoplays, and as to the latter, that there is an exclusive right of public performance under two of those theories, under Sec. 1(c) with the for profit limitation and Sec. 1(d) without such restriction.

---

book first published in 1915, at p. 12. Lindsay also uses similar language at p. 63 and at p. 189 with respect to the photoplay, but the use of the camera as a means of dramaturgy might be deemed applicable to all film, whether or not photoplays.

[114] Townsend Copyright Amendment Complete File of Arguments Before the Committee on Patents, House of Representatives on H.R. 15263 and H.R. 20596, commencing January 24, 1912.

[115] Act of Aug. 4, 1912, 62d Cong., 2d Sess., 37 Stat. 488 (1913).

Sec. 23.12(b). Books and Plays

Thus far, the performance right has been seen to have been directly granted by Congress under the statute either in *haec verba* as in the case of Classes C, D and E of Sec. 5[116] or by deductive inference from all the surrounding circumstances, as in the case of Classes (L) and (M) thereof. These are the categories that are structured by their very nature for performance and correspond roughly to the performing arts. Two other categories, Class A, the book classification, and Class B, periodicals, including newspapers, are classes of literary works as to which there may be a right of performance under Class C if they are non-dramatic in form. Thus, if a book or a newspaper or periodical contains sermons, lectures, addresses or poetry, stories or even non-fiction material capable of being delivered orally as nondramatic literary material, then, to that extent, there is an exclusive performing right under Sec. 1(c) with respect thereto. As for Class D, although the Regulations of the Copyright Office refer to inclusion therein of published dramatic works such as acting versions of plays, etc.,[117] it is clear that dramatic works may also be published as anthologies in book form, as textbook editions for student study, in paperback editions for general reading purposes, and so forth. So, too, newspapers and periodicals may publish dramatic works under the copyright of the newspaper or periodical so as to protect the component parts thereof.[118] Similarly, although Class E covers musical compositions and the Copyright Regulations provide for copyright of published musical

---

[116] 17 U.S.C. 5.

[117] Regulations of the Copyright Office, Sec. 202.7.

[118] 17 U.S.C. 3.

compositions thereunder,[119] music may be published in book form or in newspapers and periodicals much the way dramatic works may be published therein. To the extent performance is attempted of such dramatic or musical works from a published book, newspaper or periodical, the right of exclusive performance is not diminished by reason of such classification.

However, among the adaptation rights granted by Sec. 1(b) is the right of dramatization, i.e. the right to adapt a work into dramatic form. Classes A and B being principally applicable to literary works, it would follow that literary works covered by publication are thereby capable of being adapted into dramatic form and, upon copyright of the work in such dramatic form, there would then be a right of exclusive performance therein under Sec. 1(d) as a dramatic work.

Sec. 23.12(c). Music

Music is somewhat different. A literary work cannot be adapted into music; the parameters of transformation are too remote. Literary works may "inspire" musical works and vice versa. So, too, artistic works may "inspire" musical works, such as Mussorgsky's "Pictures at an Exhibition". But the music is in no sense an adaptation of the literary or artistic work, using literary in the sense of word form and artistic in the sense of fine art.

But music embodied in a book or periodical may be performed. If the work of music is under statutory copyright, it would follow that there is a right of public performance for profit therein in the copyright proprietor regardless of the derivation of the copyright classification,

---

[119] Regulations of the Copyright Office, Sec. 202.8(a).

e.g., in the book or periodical, and that the performance right follows from the nature of the work, in this instance, as music. The statute, Sec. 1,[120] enumerated the bundle of rights under copyright, including publication and performing rights. The placing of works under copyright in various categories under Sec. 5[121] was intended to be for administrative convenience of the Copyright Office and the public.

But it is clear from Sec. 1 that Congress intended to extend the exclusive rights of performance to the performing arts because the scope of the latter corresponds, in the main, with the scope of the coverage granted by the statute. Performance of dramatic works and music takes place in the theatre, concert hall, films, and on radio and television. To the extent the dance is choreographed in a fixed form capable of copyright protection, choreography is similarly protected. Finally, exclusive public performance for profit is extended to nondramatic literary works under copyright that are delivered orally, e.g., public readings of poetry and other literary works, as well as rendition of sermons, lectures and addresses.

Sec. 23.13. Architecture as Performance

Congress has thereby expressed an intention to assist the performing arts by providing recognition of creation in the performing arts in the form of economic rewards through the control extended to the creator and assigns in the form of exclusive performance rights.

Performance rights have not, in the main, been so extended to other categories of works that are copyrightable.

[120] 17 U.S.C. 1.

[121] 17 U.S.C. 5. See Chap. XVI, *supra,* as to rights of performance in music generally.

For example, architectural plans are copyrightable under subsection i of Sec. 5 which covers "Drawings or plastic works of a scientific or technical character." [122] In *DeSilva Construction Corp.* v. *Herrald*[123], certain drawings of architectural plans by plaintiff's predecessor in interest were registered in the Copyright Office under Class I. Plaintiff brought this action for infringement of copyright and unfair competition without success. The Court disposed of a claim of performance right in the plans as follows:

> "Another contention of the plaintiff is that an infringement took place when the defendants filed their competing building plans with the City of Sarasota after March 30, 1961, the alleged date of acquisition of the statutory copyright, and that it is immaterial that the actual mechanical copying took place prior to the acquisition of the statutory copyright, and that, therefore, the defendants are guilty of infringement of the statutory copyright. This contention is also without merit. This argument assumes, without any legal basis, that the architect is entitled, in addition to the right of author specified in the Copyright Act, to per-

---

[122] 17 U.S.C. 5(i). Note that the Copyright Office structures its application forms for copyright in terms of the statute. Such categories are capitalized but do not carry a precise identity with Sec. 5. For example, forms of application relating to Sec. 5(a) are currently Form A. Class A, for books manufactured in the U.S.A.; Form A-B Ad Interim, Class A for books and periodicals in English manufactured and first published outside the U.S.A.; and Form A-B Foreign, Class A, for books and periodicals manufactured outside the U.S.A. other than those subject to ad interim copyright. In other words, Copyright Office classifications represent further refinements of copyright classification and also cover matters not even appearing in Sec. 5, e.g., Form R, Renewal copyright and Form U, Notice of use of copyrighted music on mechanical instruments.

[123] 213 F. Supp. 184 (D. M.D. Fla. 1962).

> formance or execution rights granted to authors of musical compositions and dramatic works. Case law is clearly contrary to the proposition urged."[124]

The Court then proceeded to adduce the case law thereon which consists of precedent and analogy. As to these, the Court observed, "These holdings are in accord with the view previously expressed that the only monopoly which the copyright gave the author was the exclusive right to reproduce the design in an artistic figure. (Fulmer v. United States, 103 F. Supp. 1021, 122 Ct. Cl. 195 (1952))."[125]

The conclusion of the Court therefrom was that there was no performing right in architectural plans. The Court stated in this regard, "This Court is not willing to read into the current copyright laws that which is not present; and until Congress decides to extend the protection afforded to architects, there is no basis in law to grant such an extension."[126] In other words, the case represents a square holding on this point that there is no performing right in architectural plans. That is, that the erection of structures in accordance with plans will not infringe because there is no performing right therein. The Court noted that the "architectural plans of the plaintiff were copyrightable and valid."[127] In other words, in a given case, not here, it is possible for there to be an infringement by copying of copyrighted plans by means of making a copy of such plans. Performance, therefore, does not infringe by the making of the architectural structure, i.e., building origination by architectural plans. If such plans are copies of copyrighted plans, then such plans infringe the copyright

---

124 *Idem* at p. 198.
125 *Ibid.*
126 *Ibid.*
127 *Ibid.*

under Class I even though the completed structure does not.[128]

Sec. 23.14. Designs and Drawings, Plans as Performance

The Court relied principally on *Muller* v. *Triborough Bridge Authority*[129] for its precedental value. There the plaintiff claimed infringement in copying his drawings copyrighted under Class I of designs and plans for access to bridge which allegedly was infringed by the designing, planning and construction of defendant's Broad Channel Bridge over Jamaica Bay to Rockaway Beach in Queens, New York. The Court found independent conception and execution and therefore no appropriation from plaintiff despite similarities as between the plaintiff's copyrighted drawing and the defendant's design. With respect to the construction of the bridge approach, assuming use of plaintiff's drawing by the defendant, the Court noted that plaintiff would be without remedy, stating, "In the case at bar plaintiff's copyright of a drawing, showing a novel bridge approach to unsnarl traffic congestion, does not prevent any one from using and applying the system of traffic separation therein set forth."[130] Although dictum, because the Court had already held that there was no copying, the Court nevertheless pointedly noted the limitations of Class I coverage in that construction, i.e., use or performance, of the bridge approach, an engineering structure, did not, by such use, infringe copyright in drawings of a scientific or technical character copyrightable under Class I.

---

[128] See Strauss, William S., Copyright in Architectural Works, Study No. 27, in Studies on Copyright (1963), at pp. 67-79.

[129] 43 F. Supp. 298 (S.D.N.Y. 1942).

[130] *Idem* at p. 300.

The only difference was that *Herrald*[131] dealt with architecture whereas *Triborough Bridge*[132] pertained to engineering. But in both cases there was use by construction, performance by rendering the drawing into construction finality. But the Court in *Herrald,* not only applied the rule of the engineering construction suit to architecture, but stated the holding in doctrinal terms, "The underlying rationale of the Triborough Bridge case seems to be that a copyright in a drawing or picture of a non-artistic object of utility does not preclude others from making the three-dimensional object portrayed in the drawing or picture." [133] The Court, in *Herrald,* then drew upon the analogy of a trade catalog protected by copyright which depicted ladies' garments.[134]

The dress cases relate to items separately copyrightable under Class K as prints and pictorial illustrations.[135] In overruling a demurrer in *National Cloak & Suit Co.* v. *Kaufman,*[136] the Court found the requisite minimum art in plaintiff's illustrations of dress garments embodied in a book. It distinguished cases involving no copyrightability at all, stating, "This case has nothing to do with cases involving attempts to copyright mere catalogues or price lists, or labels, sometimes containing pictures, reproduced by photographic or other mechanical processes, of articles intended for sale, but which obviously have no artistic merit or originality." [137] Thus, there is a differentiation between the no copyrightability contexts where there is nothing at all that may be the subject of copyright and other situations

---

[131] Note 123, *supra.*
[132] Note 129, *supra.*
[133] Note 123, at p. 198.
[134] *Ibid.*
[135] 17 U.S.C. 5(k).
[136] 189 Fed. 215 (C.C.M.D. Pa. 1911).
[137] *Idem* at p. 219.

where there is a subject of copyright but the protection afforded thereon is limited. The Court then proceeded to explain this distinction:

> "The fallacy in the argument that the complaint cannot copyright 'productions of the industrial arts' lies in the confusion of the pictures with the things they depict in a particular way; that is, the wearing apparel which appears in the illustrations as part of the pictures. As said by Mr. Justice Bradley in Baker v. Selden, supra:
>
> > 'There is a clear distinction between the book as such and the article which it is intended to illustrate. The object of the one is illustration; of the other it is the use thereof. The former may be secured by copyright, the latter by patent.'
>
> "The complainant does not claim to monopolize the manufacture and sale of the wearing apparel depicted by reason of its copyright. It does, however, claim the right thereby to prevent others from copying and appropriating its exclusive property in such pictures and to this it is entitled by reason of its copyright which appears to be valid." [138]

By way of dictum the Court differentiated the protectible from the unprotectible. Performance equivalent in use of the illustrations by manufacture and sale is not the subject of protection. The source of protection, as stated by the Supreme Court in *Baker* v. *Selden,*[139] is in patent, for the industrial or useful arts, and not in copyright. That is, the copyright system is not even designed to cover and

---

[138] *Ibid.*
[139] 101 U.S. 99 (1879).

protect against uses arising from the nature and utility of the plan or system. This is the province of patent covering the uses of invention, the claimed utility or uses that may be *devised* from a particular discovery or invention. Performance in copyright notions is of a different nature. Protectible performance of work under copyright relates to an arts orientation. Performing rights are granted in dramatic and musical works and in non-dramatic literary works without regard to any notions of utility or function at all. Performing rights inhere in such rights because they have qualified for copyright as works with minimal criteria of literary and artistic merit necessary for copyrighting the works. Practical questions of utility or the uses the works may be put to, of a utilitarian nature, are immaterial and irrelevant to the grant of performing rights under the statute.

Judge Lacombe stated the parameters of coverage in utilitarian uses in another suit brought by the same plaintiff. Overruling a demurrer in *National Cloak & Suit Co.* v. *Standard Mail Order Co.,* he stated:

> "I am entirely in accord with defendant in the proposition that a manufacturer of unpatented articles cannot practically monopolize their sale by copyrighting a catalogue containing illustrations of them. From a comparison of the illustrations upon which complainant relies, the fair inference would seem to be that defendant makes some garments which are identical with complainant's and offers them for sale. If this be so, he cannot be deprived of the right to issue a catalogue of the garments he offers, with illustrations showing what they look like, provided that his illustrations are drawn from the garments themselves, and not copied from complainant's copyrighted catalogue. The difficulty with undertaking to decide the case on demurrer

> is that we can not be sure how defendant's illustrations were produced. Complainant might be able to show that they were in fact copied from its own, and not drawn with the garments as models."[140]

In other words, use by manufacture and sale does not infringe, whereas a drawing utilized for such manufacture, if copied from a work under copyright, would infringe. The use is dehors copyright protection because it is a use of the industrial arts subject to protection by patent.

Sec. 23.15. Utility and Performance

It is here that the terms "use" and "performance" must be distinguished in respect of copyright and patent. The terms are used commonly both in copyright and patent to describe differing phenomena. A work under copyright may be used or performed within the ambit of the performing right in the sense of rendition of the dramatic, musical or nondramatic literary work, whether or not there is otherwise any utility whatsoever therein by reason of such performance. The control given the creator and assigns through the right of exclusive performance relates directly to the rewards of creation. Performance is the instrumentality for a principal form of exposition of the work of the creator. But it is a protection granted under copyright, *viz.*, the performing right, based upon the ultimate merit of the work under copyright in the market. It is the means for providing a form of economic equivalence in the market by exploitation and authorization of exploitation of the performing right in the work of the creator.

The status of works that can be used or rendered useful in the functional or utilitarian sense is on a different level.

---

[140] 191 Fed. 528 (C.C. S.D.N.Y. 1911).

There the inventor may or may not be the same person as the one claiming copyright. The illustrator claiming copyright or the author of the descriptive language of a book expounding a plan or system is not necessarily the designer or inventor. There is a separable claim for protection in respect of claimed uses of a work under patent from the claim of protection under copyright. The fact that the authorship and invention may reside in the same person should not thereby provide a circumstantial means of overriding the patent laws by granting patent protection to such a person without availing himself of the patent laws just because he is also the creator with certain protections under copyright.

Accordingly, it may be seen that there are four areas of incidence operative here: (a) where there is no copyright whatsoever because there are no copyrightable elements to which copyright protection can be accorded, e.g., ideas, plans, methods, systems;[141] (b) where, however, there is sufficient individual expression in connection therewith, a modicum of protection is accorded under copyright to such expression;[142] (c) full protection is accorded to performing rights in dramatic, musical and nondramatic literary works to the extent of copyrightable elements therein subject to statutory exemptions (juke-box) and limitations (public performance and as to music and nondramatic literary works, for profit) and the doctrine of fair use; and (d) pro-

---

[141] See Regulations of the Copyright Office, Sec. 202.1.

[142] Thus, Copyright Office Circular 31 reads in part:

> "A description, explanation, or illustration of an idea can be copyrighted, assuming the requirements of the copyright law are met. Copyright in such case protects the particular literary or pictorial form in which an author chooses to express himself. However, it gives the copyright owner no exclusive rights in the ideas, plan, method, or system involved."

tection for other types of performances and uses other than under (c) are to be sought under the patent laws.

Thus there may be no protection at all under copyright, or, given qualifying expression, only limited protection in the expression, with a further limitation that infringement thereof cannot occur by use because such use is utilitarian encompassed by patent protection, if at all, and not by copyright, and finally, literary and artistic property protectible against infringing performance of the copyrightable components thereof.[143]

Sec. 23.16. Works of Art and Performance

There remains then the question as to whether there can be performance of works of art, that is, whether the statute under present law grants such works the exclusive right of performance. The categories which may be encompassed thereby are: Sec. 5(g)—Works of art; models or designs for works of art; Sec. 5(h)—Reproductions of a work of art; Sec. (i)—Drawings or plastic works of a scientific or technical character; Sec. (j)—Photographs; and Sec. (k)—Prints and pictorial illustrations including prints or labels used for articles of merchandise.[144] In the main, what they have in common is that the categories relate in the aggregate to two or three dimensional objects in the fine and/or applied arts and that they are static in character. By static, one means here that they are at rest and do not assume form through motion as in the case of motion pictures. The common characteristic of such forms as art is that the copyright is in the art work, be it two or three dimensional, rather than in words. Art as "writings" is thereby given copyright protection. These classes of the

---

[143] 17 U.S.C. 3.
[144] 17 U.S.C. 5.

statute constitute what might be called artistic property as opposed to the notion of literary property where originality is embodied in the use of words and language as protectible creations. In art, it is the modicum of originality embodied in the representation, as in the case of photography, which is basically an art of reproduction by means of utilization of the still camera, or in the use of materials in the case of the two or three dimensional fine arts. Maps, Class F[145] have a common attribute of pictorial quality, whether the map be two or three dimensional. But maps necessarily must rely on words, at least in the form of names of geographical places, in order for them to have any validity as maps although conceivably there may be use of maps on occasion with no verbal accompaniment whatsoever. But, in the main, maps may be considered as a separate category by reason of their purpose.

Sec. 23.16(a). Notice Provisions Differential

However, it would seem that the notice provision of the statute as enacted in 1909 categorizes the above classes, Sec. 5(f)-(k), as not being literary, musical or dramatic works. Sec. 18 of the 1909 Act reads in pertinent part:

> "Sec. 18. That the notice of copyright required by section nine of this Act shall consist either of the word 'Copyright' or the abbreviation 'Copr.', accompanied by the name of the copyright proprietor, and if the work be a printed literary, musical, or dramatic work, the notice shall include also the year in which the copyright was secured by publication. In the case, however, of copies of works specified in subsections (f) to (k), inclusive, of section five of this Act, the notice may consist of the letter C enclosed within a circle,

[145] 17 U.S.C. 5(f).

> thus: ©, accompanied by the initials, monogram, mark, or symbol of the copyright proprietor: *Provided,* That on some accessible portion of such copies or of the margin, back, permanent base, or pedestal, or of the substance on which such copies shall be mounted, his name shall appear."[146]

Significantly, when the Townsend Act was passed in 1912[147] to include motion pictures as among Sec. 5 classes, as Sec. 5(l) "Motion-picture photoplays" and Sec. 5(m) as "Motion pictures other than photoplays", Sec. 18 remained unchanged. Prior to the enactment of the Townsend Act, motion pictures had been classified as photographs.[148] However, even prior thereto, the Supreme Court, in *Kalem Co.* v. *Harper Bros.*[149] had effectively disposed of the argument that motion pictures do not infringe a copyrighted story. Counsel for appellant had relied on the proposition that it did not infringe, among other reasons, because it was a picture and photographs cannot infringe a copyrighted book. In other words, there was no equivalence in story-telling and in pictorial presentation. Justice Holmes disposed of this argument in determining in his opinion that motion pictures of "Ben Hur" constituted an infringing dramatization of the work when made without authorization. He stated, ". . . drama may be achieved by action as well as by speech. Action can tell a story . . ."[150]

---

146 Act of Mar. 4, 1909, Sec. 18, note 8, *supra,* Copyright Enactments, *idem,* at pp. 71-72. (italics).

147 Act of Aug. 24, 1912, 62d Cong., 2d Sess., 37 Stat. 488, Copyright Enactments, note 8, *supra,* at pp. 87-90.

148 American Mutoscope & Biograph Co. v. Edison Mfg. Co., 137 Fed. 262 (C.C. D.N.J. 1905); Edison v. Lubin, 122 Fed. 240 (3rd Cir. 1903).

149 222 U.S. 55 (1911).

150 *Idem* at p. 61.

That is, the projection of motion pictures dramatized the story. Any question as to the nature of the right under the 1909 Act, that case having been decided under the prior statute, was disposed of by the determination in *Photo Drama Motion Picture Co.* v. *Social Uplift Film Corp.*[151] that there was a separate motion picture right of dramatization. Thus it may be seen that Congress, in enacting the 1912 amendment to Sec. 5, very likely considered that Sec. 5(l) and 5(m) might be deemed literary, or dramatic works, and if with music, dramatico-musical works. Indeed, the enactment of Title 17 of the United States Code in 1947,[152] substantially incorporated Sec. 18, now renumbered as Sec. 19, as did the amendment to Sec. 19 of Title 17 in 1954,[153] providing for the addition of © as the form of notice for literary, musical or dramatic works, in order to conform to the Universal Copyright Convention.[154]

The House Report, prior to the enactment of the 1909 Act, explained why Sec. 18 included a statement of the year of publication with respect to books, and not as to works of art, stating:

> "Your committee felt that in case of books or printed publications, including dramatic and musical works, the year in which the copyright began should be stated in the notice, and we have provided for the insertion of the date in the notice in all such works. Your commit-

---

[151] 220 Fed. 448 (2d Cir. 1915), *aff'g,* 213 Fed. 374 (S.D.N.Y. 1914).

[152] Public Law 281, 80th Cong., 1st Sess., Sec. 19, Copyright Enactments, note 8, *supra,* at pp. 108-109.

[153] Public Law 743—83d Cong., 2d Sess., Chap. 1161, approved Aug. 31, 1954, Sec. 19, Copyright Enactments, note 8, *supra,* at p. 131.

[154] See Universal Copyright Convention Analyzed, edited by Kupferman, Theodore R. and Foner, Matthew (1955).

> tee did not feel that it was necessary to have the date printed on works of art, etc. Artists have always objected to the copyright notice which they were obliged to put on the pictures, because it was considered a disfigurement, and we have retained substantially the provision of the original bill regarding the notice in such cases. The original bill provided that when the rights of public performance were desired the notice should include the statement 'rights of public performance reserved.' Since the right of public performance is as incidental to the general right as is the right of translation or dramatization and is so treated in the bill, specific notice of it seems as little requisite as in the case of other subsidiary rights." [155]

The reference in this paragraph to right of public performance after works of art, at first blush, would seem out of place since by the structure of Sec. 18, (now renumbered Sec. 19) there would be no exclusive right of performance in works of art as such. However, the Report contains several paragraphs as to the notice provisions of the proposed legislation, and the reference to the reasons for elimination of the reservation of public performance in the notice provision is to be seen merely as a run-on paragraph which happened to cover the point.

Sec. 23.16(b). Cartoons

Any question as to the relationship of the notice provision to classification in this respect would appear to be dispelled by Judge Manton's opinion in *Fleischer Studios, Inc.* v. *Freundlich, Inc.*[156] This case involved a claim of infringe-

---

[155] House Report 2222, note 16, *supra,* reprinted in Nimmer, *idem* pp. 959-986 at p. 975.

[156] 73 F. 2d 276 (2d Cir. 1934).

ment in the manufacture of dolls which allegedly copied the book of cartoons picturing the character "Betty Boop". Evidently, one of the defenses asserted below was that of defective notice under Sec. 18 in failing to affix the year of publication to the bound leaf of cartoons. Judge Manton disposed of this objection stating:

> "As to the notice of date required by the statute, section 18 of the Copyright Law (17 U.S.C.A., sec. 18) provides that the year in which the copyright was secured by publication shall be inserted in the notice if it be a printed literary, musical, or dramatic work. This section does not require notice of the year in other copyrightable articles. What was copyrighted here did not come within the statutory classification. The cartoon characters displayed in bound leaf form constitute neither a printed literary, musical, nor dramatic work. To say that the appellees' article is a book and as such is a literary work would be incorrect. The copyright (act) of April 29, 1802 (chap. 36, 2 Stat. 171), specifically mentioned a book. Section 18 of the present law does not. U.S.C.A., title 17, sec. 18. A book is one of the classifications of the present law and is copyrightable as such. U.S.C.A., title 17, sec. 5(a). This book of cartoons depicting a series of unconnected poses is without story or continuity, and may not be said to be a printed literary work as referred to in section 18." [157]

Judge Manton also noted that "Betty Boop" had also been popularized on the motion picture screen.[158] Probably

---

[157] *Idem* at p. 278. Note the reference to Title 17, U.S.C.A. therein. Cf. the preamble to the 1947 Act, "That title 17 of the United States Code entitled 'Copyrights' is codified and enacted into positive law and may be cited as Title 17, U.S.C., Sec. ——".

[158] *Idem* at p. 277.

that would have been classified under Sec. 5(l) as a motion picture photoplay because it told a story and utilized dialogue in so doing. Indeed, in the comic strip infringement cases involving "Superman" and others, the District Court referred to ". . . unfair use by the defendant of the plaintiff's copyrighted pictures and unfair paraphrase of the plaintiff's text accompanying its pictures." [159]

It is not clear from the *Betty Boop* opinion[160] whether or not the cartoons carried any accompanying text or written dialogue. However, in *National Comics Publications, Inc.* v. *Fawcett Publications, Inc.*[161] the comic strips at issue again involved "Superman" and other cartoons. There, however, Republic Pictures was named as a party defendant for allegedly having infringed by making a motion picture serial from defendant Fawcett's comic strip "Captain Marvel" which in turn was alleged to have infringed plaintiff's "Superman". The District Court took the view that the comic strip was copyrightable as a book, stating:

> "I think that Section 18 required that each 'Superman' strip, as published in the newspapers, should be copyrighted as a book. Each strip was a printed literary work, and the word 'book' is not to be limited to a bound volume but includes 'any species of publication which the author selects to embody his literary product.' *Holmes* v. *Hurst,* 174 U.S. 82, 89, 19 S. Ct. 606, 609, 43 L. Ed. 904.

---

[159] Detective Comics, Inc. v. Bruns Publications, Inc., 28 F. Supp. 399, 400 (S.D.N.Y. 1939), *aff'd,* 111 F. 2d 432 (2d Cir. 1940). See also, Detective Comics, Inc. v. Fox Publications, Inc., 46 F. Supp. 872 (S.D.N.Y. 1942).

[160] Note 156, *supra.*

[161] National Comics Publications, Inc. v. Fawcett Publications, Inc., 93 F. Supp. 349 (S.D.N.Y. 1950), *rev'd,* 191 F. 2d 594 (2d Cir. 1951).

"It is not correct to say that these 'Superman' strips are prints or pictorial illustrations. A single panel might be called a print. But each strip consists of a number of panels, comprising a continuous sequence of events, with accompanying explanatory text. The panels are not used merely to illustrate the text, as the illustrations in a novel or other literary work do; rather, the panels themselves, together with the explanatory text, constitute the literary work—the story intended to be depicted. As the strips were not prints or pictorial illustrations, the use of the letter 'C' in a circle as the form of copyright notice did not result in obtaining valid copyrights. Advertisers Exchange v. Anderson, 8 Cir. 144 F. 2d 907." [162]

The Court of Appeals reversed on this point. In doing so, it referred to the pertinent section, as renumbered, Sec. 19. By way of dictum it distinguished the strict construction and loss of copyright by use of the letter "C", rather than the term, "Copyright" or the abbreviation, "Copr." as decided in *Advertisers Exchange* v. *Anderson*[163] in the Eighth Circuit, and *Deward & Rich* v. *Bristol Savings & Loan Corp.* in the Fourth Circuit[164], and determined that the comic strips at issue were pictorial illustrations within Sec. 5(k).[165] Therefore, since the letter "C" had been used, there was no loss of copyright under the statute by reason of the character of the notice. Since the amendment of Sec. 19 in 1954, providing for the use of © for notice as to both categories of that section, the problem would not arise today with respect to loss of copyright by reason of use of

[162] *Idem* at p. 357.

[163] 144 F. 2d 907 (8th Cir. 1944).

[164] 120 F. 2d 537 (4th Cir. 1941), *aff'g*, 34 F. Supp. 345 (W.D. Va. 1940).

[165] Note 161, *supra*, 191 F. 2d 594 at p. 602.

such copyright symbol. No doubt the Court of Appeals was motivated by a desire to protect the copyright proprietor from forfeiture by reason of a technicality or imperfect designation of notice of copyright. It would seem, however, that if the comic strips were classifiable as pictorial illustrations that there would be no right of performance with respect thereto. The Court of Appeals remanded to determine whether Republic Pictures did infringe any valid copyrights, stating, "In so far as 'Republic' copied the details of these 'strips' which 'Fawcett' had copied from 'Action Comics' or 'Superman', it infringed;" [166] But the nature of the infringement, it would appear, if the comic strips were pictorial illustrations, would be in copying and dramatizing the comic strips. If the strips were Sec. 5(k) pictorial illustrations, they would not perforce qualify as literary, dramatic or musical works as to which there is an exclusive right of public performance. Consequently, it would appear that the infringement would not be in the form of infringing performance but in that the serial motion picture prints and negatives constituted copies of the comic strips under Sec. 1(a), and the films, dramatizations thereof, under Sec. 1(b).[167]

It is to be noted that the District Court, in holding the strips to be literary works, distinguished illustrations in a novel or other literary work. It is to be noted that in *Anderson*[168] what was originally copyrighted in book form contained certain illustrations and applicable text material for advertisements for beauty parlors. The plaintiff then furnished certain matrices which did not contain the form of notice for books but contained the letter "C" in a circle. The Court in *Anderson* observed, "But plaintiff had not

---

[166] *Idem* at p. 603.

[167] 17 U.S.C. 1.

[168] Note 163, *supra.*

copyrighted any of its illustrations and their text material as a work of art or as a print and pictorial illustrations, but only as a component part of a book." [169] The Court of Appeals therefore affirmed the District Court in holding that the improper notice constituted a forfeiture or dedication to the public so that there was no infringement.[170]

It is submitted that both *Fleischer Studios, Inc.* v. *Freundlich, Inc.*[171] and *National Comics Publications, Inc.* v. *Fawcett Publications, Inc.*[172] pulled away from a harsh result of forfeiture of copyright on the technicalities of notice, in the first case as to the inclusion of year of publication in the notice, and in the second case as to the substitution of a symbol of "C" in a circle for the word "copyright" or its abbreviation. But the nature of comic strips is to be determined by its content as a comic strip. This content normally consists of both illustrations and accompanying text. Indeed, comic strips in books, newspapers and periodicals are precisely intended to have story and continuity. The text is intended to act as dialogue. Every facet of storytelling is present—story line, plot, continuity, locale, characters, and so on. Probably they are to be characterized as literary works for there is the requisite story telling with textual dialogue. Such works are capable of oral delivery. Therefore, they are entitled to the protection of Sec. 1(c) as nondramatic literary works capable of being delivered orally if they are not otherwise protectible as dramatic works. It would be tautological to say that they cannot be categorized as Sec. 1(c) works as non-dramatic literary works because they are dramatic works in that they are dramatic in character, and then conclude that they are not

---

[169] *Idem* at p. 908.
[170] 52 F. Supp. 809 (S.D. Iowa 1943).
[171] Note 156, *supra.*
[172] Note 161, *supra.*

classifiable as dramatic for the reason that they are not actable as such in that form, and therefore do not qualify under Sec. 5(d) as a dramatic composition. The Regulations of the Copyright Office state as to Class C, "When published with notice as prescribed by law, such works may be considered for registration as 'books' in Class A."[173] So, too, the Regulations include in Class D published versions of dramatic works such as "acting versions for plays for the stage, motion pictures, radio, television and the like, operas, operettas, musical comedies and similar productions and pantomimes."[174] *A fortiori,* this would not preclude the inclusion in Class A as books of textbook editions of the same works intended to be read in class and not acted, other annotated editions, anthologies inclusive of such plays, and the like. Nor would the fact of such inclusion under Class A, presumably as the class correlative to Sec. 5(a) of the statute, preclude the same work from also being a dramatic work for purposes of the exclusive right of dramatic public performance of the work. The same result would follow as to Class B works to the extent the play was included in a periodical and the copyright of the periodical protected the play as a component part thereof.[175]

We therefore have a situation where the comic strip with dialogue that is contained in books, newspapers or periodicals tells a story. The same work as adapted for the screen would constitute a dramatization so that the exclusive right of performance would be available to protect performances of the motion picture under Sec. 1(d) of the statute. Yet, if the comic strip were presented by means of actors directly from the comic strip, it would appear that the strips

---

[173] Regulations of the Copyright Office, Sec. 202.6.
[174] *Idem,* Sec. 202.7.
[175] 17 U.S.C. 3.

would be entitled to protection as dramatic works. However, this is unlikely without adaptation into a stage play, just as in the case of a motion picture an adaptation would be made. Therefore, oral delivery as readings without costumes, scenery and props would be deemed nondramatic and so such readings, verbatim, of comic strips should be entitled to the protection of Sec. 1(c).

Sec. 23.16(c). Illustrations

One may go further, in terms of illustrations, even where there is no accompanying text or dialogue. Just as acting without dialogue, pantomime, choreography and silent motion pictures, even without subtitles may be dramatic,[176] so it would seem that illustrations, even without words, provided that there is continuity and they tell a story, can be considered as literary. They are also artistic because if the creators desired, the separate pictorial illustrations could be copyrighted as such under Class K. Indeed, Circular 55 of the Copyright Office sets forth a variety of classifications relating thereto. Thus, film strips embodying cartoons are copyrightable as photographs under Form J; animated cartoons as motion pictures, under Form L-M. The foregoing relate to both published and unpublished works. As to published works only, individual cartoons and comic strips separately published with notice of copyright are covered under Prints and Pictorial Illustrations (Form K); Newspaper or magazine comic strips with their own notice of copyright are protectible under Form BB as Contributions to Periodicals; cartoons and comic strips used in advertisements warrant Form KK relating to Commercial

---

[176] Daly v. Palmer, 6 Fed. Cas. 1132, No. 3552 (C.C. S.D.N.Y. 1868). See Sec. 22.13(a), *supra;* Kalem Co. v. Harper Bros., 222 U.S. 55 (1911).

Prints or Labels; Form B is used for "comic books" published at regular intervals under a general title or where so distributed by feature syndicates; and finally, Form A is used for comic books and syndicate books not published at regular intervals.[177]

It would seem that there is little difference in the nature of the protection of comic strips which have both text and illustrations, and illustrations in a book under copyright consisting of separate text and illustrations. In such a book it is not unusual for there to be separate copyright in the text of the book by the author thereof and yet another copyright in the illustrations in the book in the illustrator thereof. Presumably the purpose there is to enable the illustrator to own the reproduction rights in and to his illustrations without having the author of the text share therein. The fact remains, however, that the illustrations under separate copyright must be viewed independently of the text to ascertain if the illustrations are to be deemed literary in character. If the illustrations include dialogue or other text of their own, then the combined matter under copyright of the illustrator or assigns might be deemed literary in character if the combined matter has its own continuity and story line. Where there is a single copyright covering both text of the book and illustrations, *a fortiori* it would appear that the work is to be considered as a whole and would be deemed literary. Where, however, there are illustrations under separate copyright and no text or dialogue, it would seem that the illustrations might nonetheless be a literary work in that the same might, independently of the text of the book, tell a story and have the requisite continuity to tell the story. Yet, there being no text thereto,

---

[177] Copyright Office, Circular 55, Cartoons and Comic Strips, subdivision 5 thereof, which is entitled, Classification.

it would seem that such illustrations could not qualify under Sec. 1(c) because the nature of that subdivision is to provide exclusivity for public performance for profit for delivery. It would seem that delivery of lectures, sermons and addresses are mainly in the form of oral delivery. However, Sec. 1(c) as amended included exhibition of recordings thereof. Presumably motion pictures other than photoplays are protected thereunder. If so, if there should be a film including superimposed poems which are to be read silently by the viewer rather than read out loud in the film, then the same would nevertheless constitute a form of delivery under Sec. 1(c). So, too, it would seem, if there were projection of film strips embodying such poetry or other literary work or slides. But these would be classifiable under Form J,[178] as photographs. On the other hand, Circular 67,[179] provides that for poems published separately, as with a leaflet, folder, or card, Form A is to be used, and Form BB, for inclusion in a periodical.

It would seem, therefore, that in terms of copyrighting, the forms utilized for literary works should correspond to Subdivisions (a)-(e) and (l)-(m) rather than to subdivisions (f)-(k) of Sec. 5.[180]

Sec. 23.17. Display as Performance

But this does not quite dispose of the problem of display as performance. As has been seen, Sec. 1(d) grants the exclusive right of public performance of dramatic works to the copyright proprietor and the exclusive right to ex-

[178] Copyright Office, Circular 70, entitled, Copyright Information About Pictorial, Graphic and Sculptural Works, subdivision 5, relates to Class J, Photographs, and covers in addition to photographic prints, filmstrips, slide films and individual slides.

[179] Copyright Office, Circular 67 entitled, Poems and Song Lyrics.

[180] 17 U.S.C. 5.

hibit recordings thereof.[181] This was the language, too, of the 1909 Act.[182] Similar language was embodied in the 1952 amendment to Sec. 1(c)[183] which grants the exclusive right of public performance for profit in respect of lectures, addresses, sermons and similar productions and, as amended in 1952, to non-dramatic literary works. As amended, the section was extended to recordings and the exclusive right granted to exhibitions thereof along the lines of the language already in Sec. 1(d).

In discussing Sec. 1(c) in 1909, the House report adverted that the section was new, wise and needed no explanation.[184] William S. Strauss relies on Bowker to explain what was intended by Sec. 1(c), stating, "The drafters of the 1909 Act therefore thought of an unpublished work in terms of a work capable of and 'intended for oral delivery before it is printed in a book or periodical' and proposed that such a work 'might be registered and protected for oral delivery before publication.' This innovation was further motivated by the knowledge that the 'courts seemed disposed to protect a lecturer on the common law ground that the lecture read is not published by reading, and can be controlled by manuscript.' Even then, lectures, performances and exhibitions were presented to a limited audience, and the works involved could be controlled through possession of the manuscript, which was essential to the reproduction or performance of the work." [185]

---

[181] 17 U.S.C. 1(d).

[182] Note 8, *supra.*

[183] Note 9, *supra.*

[184] Note 16, *supra,* Nimmer, *idem* at p. 963.

[185] Strauss, William S., Protection of Unpublished Works, Study No. 29, in 1 Studies on Copyright, 2 vols. (1963), pp. 189-227, at pp. 215-216. The Strauss quotes are from Bowker, Copyright, Its History and Its Law, at p. 59 for the first quote and at p. 90 for the second and third quotes. See fns. 215-219 in Strauss article.

Note that Strauss refers to the term "exhibition". Obviously lectures and addresses can be accompanied by exhibitions. Indeed, a literal reading of Sec. 1(c) as amended would indicate that delivery need not be live and may be performed by exhibitions of recordings. Such delivery and exhibition may be made by use of film and tape. Nor is there any reason why such recording or indeed the original delivery need necessarily be oral. Delivery may be made of a lecture or address by running lines on cards, screen or television tube in visual form without sound so that delivery is not oral. Although the drafters may have intended to cover oral delivery, the language of the statute speaks of "delivery" and not "oral delivery". Moreover, an essential ingredient of certain types of lectures, sermons and addresses might be exhibition of material. *A fortiori,* this would apply to the broadened language of the statute as amended.

It follows, therefore, that a right of public performance for profit by display might conceivably be an attribute of the statute. If the materials displayed could be copyrightable and they consisted of nondramatic literary works, it would seem that if copyrighted, and displayed publicly for profit, that this right would be exclusive and the unauthorized display thereof might be an infringement of copyright as an infringing delivery. It is true that a sale of a work divests the further right of use of the copy in terms of control thereof by the proprietor.[186] Indeed, this has been codified in Sec. 27 of the Copyright Act, ". . . nothing in this title shall be deemed to forbid, prevent, or restrict the transfer of any copy of a copyright work the possession of which has been lawfully obtained." [187] But the same section provides that the copyright is distinct from the material

[186] Bobbs-Merrill Co. v. Straus, 210 U.S. 339 (1908).
[187] 17 U.S.C. 27.

object. The fact of alienability of a tangible copy after sale thereof does not affect the exclusive right of the copyright proprietor to make copies thereof. The same is true of the other exclusive rights under copyright. Thus a purchaser of a copy of a book of poems could not deliver them publicly for profit merely because he bought a copy of the book. The right of such public performance for profit resides in the copyight proprietor of the nondramatic literary work under Sec. 1(c).

Thus it would seem that the right of display might therefore, under certain circumstances, be deemed protectible under copyright. However, the right of exhibition of works of art appears to be a more difficult problem. Amdur states in this regard, "The right of exclusive performance (exhibition) is given by the statute to the owners only of dramatic, musical and dramatico-musical compositions. . . No equivalent rights are given to the owner of copyrighted works of art, such as paintings and statues (nor to the owners of copyrighted books, etc.). The only right given to owners of such copyrights is that of exclusively multiplying copies." [188] Presumably one would have to modify his observation as to copyrighted books which are non-dramatic literary works or dramatic or musical works which by means of the display constitute a protectible performance under copyright pursuant to Sec. 1 of the Copyright Act.

Amdur makes the further point, "Since the statute fails to provide the owner of a copyrighted work of art with the exclusive right of exhibition, exhibition of the work for special purposes does not divest the owner of his rights, i.e., it does not amount to a general publication."[189]

---

[188] Amdur, Leon H., Copyright Law and Practice (1936), Sec. 33, at p. 387.

[189] *Ibid.*

The art cases attest to Kaplan's observation in this regard that the courts have tended to require more by way of divestive publication of the common law copyright so as to prevent harsh rules of forfeiture.[190] Thus, the Supreme Court held that exhibition of a painting where there was a reservation of copyright and restrictions on copying constituted a limited publication which did not divest common law copyright and stated, in *American Tobacco Company* v. *Werckmeister,* ". . . the paintings are expressly entered at the gallery with copyrights reserved. There is no permission to copy; on the other hand, officers are present who rigidly enforce the requirements of the society that no copying shall take place." [191] Warner observes, in his discussion of the case, "Although the painting was for sale, the by-laws of the Royal Academy precluded any person from copying works on exhibition." [192]

Yet, in *Atlantic Monthly Co.* v. *Post Publishing Co.*[193] three copies of an article were printed from galleys, one was sold outright for ten cents and the other two registered for copyright. The Court stated in this regard:

> "It seems to me quite inadvisable to introduce into the law of copyright refinements between so-called 'colorable' sales—whatever they may mean—and bona fide ones. It will be better, I think, to take the law simply and directly, and to hold that an absolute and unrestricted sale of a printed copy, especially where accompanied by filing similar copies with the Register,

---

[190] Kaplan, Publications in Copyright Law: The Question of Phonograph Records, 103 U. of Pa. L. Rev. 469 (1955).

[191] 207 U.S. 284, 300 (1907).

[192] Warner, Harry P., Radio and Television Rights (1953), Sec. 61a at p. 165.

[193] 27 F. 2d 556 (D. Mass. 1928).

> amounts to publication under the act; and I think the decisions support this view." [194]

The Court also opined that it did not see anything to the contrary in *American Tobacco Co.* v. *Werckmeister*[195] to the cases cited in support of its view.

Note, however, that Sec. 26 of the Copyright Act defines publication as the earliest date when copies are placed on sale, sold or publicly distributed.[196] This relates to the date when copies are placed on sale. It does not purport to refer to the date when the original is placed on sale. Presumably the placing on sale appears to be synonymous with the offer of sale. Thus, Sec. 101 of S. 543, the proposed copyright revision statute, defines "Publication" as ". . . the distribution of copies or phonorecords of a work to the public by sale or other transfer of ownership, or by rental, lease, or lending. The offering to distribute copies or phonorecords to a group of persons for purposes of further distribution, public performance, or public display, constitutes publication." [197]

Thus, publication does not per se take place by offer of sale of the original. Mere exhibition thereof is not a general publication because the rights protected under copyright with respect to paintings and other works of fine art are those against copying and not against exhibition.[198] Presumably the rationale is that offer for sale of a work of art does not per se constitute a publication because such original might be offered for sale under common law copyright,

---

[194] *Idem* at p. 558.

[195] *Ibid.*

[196] 17 U.S.C. 26.

[197] Note 55, *supra,* Sec. 101.

[198] Werckmeister v. American Lithographic Co., 134 Fed. 321 (2d Cir. 1904).

as in the case of a private sale by an artist with no exhibition thereof in any gallery. In that event, it would seem that the problem of what constitutes divestive publication nonetheless remains as to the owner of the painting who is no longer the creator thereof. Thus if the purchaser of a painting should acquire reproduction rights therein, he cannot permit free copying thereof without losing his common law copyrights as a publication.[199] That is, the common law copyright might be divested by permitting public reproduction thereof.

In *Carns* v. *Keefe Bros.*,[200] plaintiffs, at a celebration on a city street to which the public was invited, erected a structure including a monstrous elk to which it attached a notice: "Copyrighted. Infringers beware." Defendants bought and sold post-card reproductions of the structure. The Court held that it could not be copyrighted and therefore could not claim infringement, stating:

> "If, however, the production is intended for or bound to be given free and unrestricted public exhibition—to attract the public to come and enjoy without price—and, if it is so displayed, there is publication of the thing and dedication to the public, again in analogy to patents, defeating copyright. For this display inevitably exposes the production to copy, and so is in-

[199] See Pushman v. New York Graphic Society, Inc., 287 N.Y. 302 (1942) where the Court of Appeals held that the failure to reserve reproduction rights by the artist upon sale of his painting vested those rights in the purchaser where the painting was held under common law copyright and had not been under statutory copyright. The rule was later changed by statute; see Gen. Bus. Law, N. Y., Sec. 224, which was added in 1966. Under the statute upon a sale, the right to reproduce is expressly reserved to the grantor unless expressly transferred.

[200] Carns v. Keefe Bros., 242 Fed. 745 (D. Mont. 1917).

consistent with claim of copyright; and the latter can not be preserved by any notice thereof hung upon the exhibit." [201]

The rationale here is the fact of freedom of copying. Although the Court speaks of free public exhibition, there are many museums and art galleries that are open to the public without admission charge. Yet, the gravamen of the fact of publication or not would appear to rest not on cost of entry or not, as the case may be, but whether copying is allowed freely.

In a more recent case, two enlisted men had created a statue while in military service in the Army at Fort Dix, New Jersey. The defendant subsequently reproduced the same by agreement with the Army. The Court held that there was a divestive publication and in any event ownership vested in the Government because the statue was basically created under the "works for hire" rule, that is, they were employees for hire under the statute,[202] so that the copyright vested in the Government as employer for hire. The defendants also contended that the statue constituted a Government publication under the statute,[203] so that in any event there was no copyright therein. Summary judgment was entered in favor of the defendants. The Court felt that that section related to printed works. However, the nature of the display was such as to invalidate common law copyright. The Court stated, therefore, (in *Scherr* v. *Universal Match Corp.*),

"Since its unveiling, 'The Ultimate Weapon' has at all times been, and is today, on view at Infantry Park, a

---

[201] *Idem* at p. 746.
[202] 17 U.S.C. 26.
[203] 17 U.S.C. 8.

> site open to the public. During this time there has never been any restriction, posted or otherwise, on the copying or photographing of the statue. Because the statue was displayed without restriction as to either persons or purpose and without adequate notice, it is concluded that there was a divestive publication under an invalid copyright such as to place 'The Ultimate Weapon' in the public domain." [204]

Thus display of works of art might be subject to the vagaries of the exhibition forum. In that regard, indoor exhibition is far more likely to have the means of restricting and enforcing restrictions on copying. Cameras may be checked at the door. Permission for copying by another artist may be refused.[205] On the other hand, it is anticipated that sculpture placed in the open at a World's Fair, for example, is not likely to be readily subject to comparable regulation. There copying may be prevented, subject to supervision insofar as it relates to copying by fellow sculptors physically sketching or drawing a replica for subsequent sculpting. But fair grounds are generally fairly available to patrons who are also camera enthusiasts to click away happily. Indeed, a piece of sculpture out of doors is often used as a backdrop for photography of nearest and dearest as well as part of panoramic shots of the grounds. But there is no intrinsic reason for the application of a

---

[204] 297 F. Supp. 107, 112 (S.D.N.Y. 1967). On appeal, the case was affirmed on the ground that if any copyright existed it was the exclusive property of the United States. Hence it did not have to decide whether the notice was adequate and whether the statute was not a Government publication, 417 F. 2d 497 (2d Cir. 1969).

[205] It is submitted that special permission given to art classes or to artists on request to copy a work would not constitute divestive publication because the purpose is limited to art study and is not made available generally to the public.

rule on controlability dependent upon the facility of enclosure per se. Perhaps, after all, the matter of control of copying is one of degree and so long as there are any restrictions imposable under present law, then there should be no dedication. That is, so long as sculpture so placed can be regulated as to reproduction in whatever small way by a requirement of prior permission by artists and sculptors as to copying, then there should be no dedication of a common law copyright.

Nimmer has construed *Werckmeister* v. *American Lithographic Co.*[206] as going somewhat further than *American Tobacco Co.* v. *Werckmeister*[207] ". . . in that it suggests (although it does not so rule) that exhibition does not constitute publication even in the absence of such restriction."[208] It is submitted that the fair ground illustration as to a work of sculpture might be deemed an example of the application of this "somewhat further" rule.

It would seem that, absent any enclosure, such as in fair grounds, one might still have a degree of supervision and restriction even in an outdoor display or exhibition, for example, in outdoor art exhibitions and temporary exhibits and displays. It would seem that the "somewhat further" rule there would encompass implied restrictions against copying. For example, painters and sculptors participate in outdoor exhibitions all over the country. The artists or their representatives normally are to be found within a short distance of their respective works. Generally no sign or any other notice containing any restriction is posted. More often than not, there are no adequate facilities for posting any because the outdoor exhibition is being held

---

[206] Note 198, *supra.*
[207] Note 191, *supra.*
[208] Nimmer, note 16, *supra,* Sec. 54, at p. 213.

on the sidewalk near some school or park or actually on the grounds of some institution or in a public park or facility. It would seem that the works are physically within the control of the artist or representative and notice might be implied from the fact of physical supervision as an indication of control.

It is only where a statue or other work of sculpture is placed with a degree of permanence in a public place, such as in city squares, parks, plazas and other adornments of a municipality or other outdoor area, where there is no attempt or reasonable possibility at supervision that the doctrine of divestive common law publication should be invoked to deny an artist or assigns ownership of the fruits and proceeds of his reproduction rights. If there are express or implied restrictions against copying, then there should be no general publication tag imposable thereon. Perhaps the test as to copying should be copying in the nature of reproduction for commercial purposes, as in the case of post-card reproduction in *Carns*[209] for purposes of sale or in the case of copying by one artist from another, as alleged without success by one sculptor against another in *Fitzgerald* v. *Hopkins*.[210] Photography by the casual

---

[209] Note 200, *supra*.

[210] 144 U.S.P.Q. 771 (Wash. Superior Ct., King Cty. 1965), *modified*, 70 Wash. 2d 924, 425 P. 2d 920 (Supreme Ct., En Banc 1967). The plaintiff could not only sustain his claim of copying, but on appeal, damages of $15,000 which had been awarded the defendant as damages for defamatory remarks of plaintiff were reduced to $7,500 by a 4 to 3 decision, and if the defendant declined to accept the same upon remittitur, the trial court was authorized to grant a new trial limited to the damages on the counterclaim of the defendant for defamation. The Appellate Court construed the negative finding of the trial court that there was no conscious copying and felt that there was a finding by the trial court that there was no copying.

amateur picture taker might be deemed a fair use in relation to works of sculpture. A two-dimensional photograph by such an amateur is not a commercial representation of a three-dimensional object. This notion of the amateur photography fan should not denigrate the ruling of *King Features Syndicate* v. *Fleischer*[211] that a three-dimensional reproduction of the cartoon character of "Spark Plug" infringes—or vice versa—except as to what constitutes a fair use. Of course, a more difficult problem would arise if the amateur photographer were to then copyright his photographs and seek to exploit the same commercially by means of reproduction thereof. It would seem, however, that then the work of sculpture as so utilized would be in commerce and be subject to the same rule governing other commercial use as infringement.

The fact of widespread dissemination of a copyrighted work in book form, where a great many copies are sold and circulated, does not, nevertheless, impair in any manner the fact that the right of copy therein is in the copyright proprietor, who, by reason thereof, can police the multiplying of copies by unauthorized third parties, even though the sale of authorized copies to the public is widespread. So, too, by analogy, on a doctrine of fair use, the right of reproduction in enclosed public areas, such as fair grounds, and even military reservations,[212] can be preserved to the creator or assigns. Of course, this is complicated in the case of commission and/or sales of the work depending upon whether or not there has been a reservation of the right

---

[211] 299 Fed. 533 (2d Cir. 1924).

[212] Cf., Scherr v. Universal Match Corp., note 204, *supra*. Even there the defendant purported to obtain rights of reproduction from the military authorities presumably because it felt that the Army had proprietorship of the work of sculpture on display at Fort Dix, N.J.

of reproduction in the work. In *Morton* v. *Raphael*,[213] a mural painter lost out in a claim of infringement of her work under common law copyright because she had painted the mural for display at a hotel without reservation of rights of reproduction. She was denied relief because the display in the hotel was held to be public so that the common law copyright was lost. In any event, she was deemed to have conveyed her rights to the mural by reason of the commission and to have created the same under hire. There the plaintiff claimed that defendants' advertisement showing photographic views of the newly decorated room, including the murals, as published in a nationally circulated magazine, constituted common law infringement of copyright. The Court affirmed the ruling below that there was no infringement. It treated the Great Lakes Room of the Knickerbocker Hotel in Chicago, where the murals had been painted and were on display, as a public place. Again, it would seem, assuming no question of ownership as between the hotel and the artist, that there was an implied restriction against copying. One would think that if another artist sought to sketch or draw a copy of the mural in that room, such artist might be evicted by the hotel as a trespasser just as the military authorities might prohibit someone from sketching or drawing a reproduction of the work of sculpture on display on the military reservation as a trespasser.

Alternatively, the painter or sculptor might affix a proper notice of copyright pursuant to Secs. 10 and 19 of the Copyright Act,[214] in compliance with the formalities of copyright

---

[213] 334 Ill. App. 399, 79 N.E. 2d 522 (App. Ct., 1st Dist, 2d Div. 1948). See also The Letter Edged in Black Press, Inc. v. Public Building Commission of Chicago, 168 U.S.P.Q. 559 (N.D. Ill. 1970).

[214] 17 U.S.C. 10 relates to requirement of notice on publication; 17 U.S.C. 19 pertains to form of such notice.

registration. But the deposit requirements of the statute would then require the making of a determination by the registration applicant as to whether or not the display constituted publication. It would appear that as to original works of fine art, published works might be registered under Class G[215] as works of art and photographs thereof deposited. But then works of art might be registered under Sec. 12 as unpublished works.[216] Therefore, the applicant must determine whether his registration under Class G is for an unpublished or published work. Since registration would protect the work under statutory copyright and errors of classification will not invalidate or impair copyright protection, then the applicant should not be prejudiced if he determines, upon registration, that the particular display constitutes publication and therefore files his application for a registration as a published work, or he determines that the display does not constitute a publication and files the same as an unpublished work. But it would seem that the same criteria would be applicable here as divestive publication and investive publication. In other words, if the display were to be sufficiently public so as to constitute a publication divesting common law copyright, then the same facts should give rise to publication sufficient to qualify the work as a publication for statutory copyright.

It is to be noted that proposed copyright revision would pre-empt common law copyright and subsume the latter un-

---

[215] Regulations of the Copyright Office, Sec. 202.10; Copyright Office Circular 70, and Chart 70 set forth classifications of pictorial, graphic and sculptural works; cf., Class H which is available for registration of reproductions of works of fine art but only if published.

[216] 17 U.S.C. 12.

der statutory copyright.[217] Automatically this would create problems in terms of existing terminology because of the uncertainty as to the scope of performance. In this regard, the House Report states,

> "*Right to public display.*—Clause (5) of section 106 represents the first explicit statutory recognition in American copyright law of an exclusive right to show a copyrighted work, or an image of it, to the public. The existence or extent of this right under the present statute is uncertain and subject to challenge. The bill would give the owners of copyright in 'literary, musical, dramatic, and choreographic works, pantomimes, and pictorial, graphic, or sculptoral works' the exclusive right 'to display the copyrighted work publicly.' " [218]

S. 543 provides in Sec. 102(5) thereof that such category as a subject matter of copyright is called "pictorial, graphic, and sculptural works".[219] Sec. 101 thereof includes "public display" within the definition of "publication".[220] The term "to perform" as defined in that section[221] does not include any reference to display. More importantly, Sec. 106 thereof, which sets forth the grant of exclusive rights in copyrighted works, provides in subdivision (4) thereof, "in the case of literary, musical, dramatic, and choreographic works, pantomimes, motion pictures and audiovisual works, and sound recordings, to perform the copyrighted work publicly;" [222] Sec. 106(5) then sets forth

---

[217] S. 543, Dec. 10, 1969 print, 91st Cong., 1st Sess., Jan. 22, 1969, Secs. 301, 303.

[218] Report No. 83, House of Representatives, 90th Cong., 1st Sess., Copyright Law Revision, Mar. 8, 1967, at p. 26 (italics).

[219] Note 217, *supra,* Sec. 102(5).

[220] *Idem,* Sec. 101.

[221] *Ibid.,* Sec. 101.

[222] *Idem,* Sec. 106(4).

the scope of the right of display, "in the case of literary, dramatic and choreographic works, pantomimes, and pictorial, graphic, or sculptural works, including the individual images of a motion picture or other audiovisual work, to display the copyrighted work publicly." [223]

The House Report spells out in some detail the scope of this right of display, as follows:

> "With the growing use of projection equipment, closed and open circuit television, and computers for displaying images of textual and graphic material to 'audiences' or 'readers', this right is certain to assume great importance to copyright owners. A recognition of this potentiality is reflected in the proposal of book publishers and producers of audiovisual works which, in effect, would equate 'display' with 'reproduction' where the showing is 'for use in lieu of a copy.' The committee is aware that in the future electronic images may take the place of printed copies in some situations, and has dealt with the problem by amendments in sections 109 and 110, and without mixing the separate concepts of 'reproduction' and 'display'. No provision of the bill would make a purely private display of a work a copyright infringement.
>
> "In H.R. 4347 as introduced, the operative word in clause (5) was 'exhibit.' This term proved confusing and objectionable because of its common usage in referring to performance of motion pictures. As recommended by the Register of Copyrights, therefore, the committee has substituted the word 'display' here and throughout the bill." [224]

---

[223] *Idem,* Sec. 106(5).
[224] Note 218, *supra,* at pp. 26-27.

After differentiating motion picture or other audio-visual performance, where images are shown in sequences or to make accompanying sounds audible, from the filmstrip, where images are not shown in sequence, the House Report then goes on:

> "Since 'copies' are defined as including the material object 'in which the work is first fixed,' the right of public display applies to original works of art as well as to reproduction of them. With respect to motion pictures and other audiovisual works, it is a 'display' (rather than a 'performance') to show their 'individual images nonsequentially.' In addition to the direct showings of a copy of a work, 'display' would include the projection of an image on a screen or other surface by any method, the transmission of an image by electronic or other means, and the showing of an image on a cathode ray tube or similar viewing apparatus connected with any sort of information storage and retrieval system." [225]

Thus, by recognition of the uncertainties and ambiguities of the gray area encompassed by the term "exhibit" which has application in the scope of exclusive right of performance under the present Act, by attempting to protect and extend the right of display to works of fine arts once statutory copyright pre-empts common law copyright, and by seeking to extend protection to both areas in relation to technological change which is about to assume commercial significance on a large scale, proposed copyright revision has proffered the right of display as one of the exclusive rights under copyright. It would appear that the scope of this proposed right would encompass some of the exhibi-

---

[225] *Idem* at p. 28.

tion rights of performance now permissible under the term "exhibition", particularly those covered by Sec. 1(c) of the Act as amended and also areas as to which there are presently no protectible rights of exhibition. For example, widespread public exhibition of works of art out of doors or in hotels and other public places where there is no attempt to regulate public copying probably would result in divestiture of common law copyright as a publication. The same display under statutory copyright protection would not be deemed a performance so that the only rights protected under statutory copyright would be the rights of reproduction. The advent of the age of presentation by display amidst the variety of existing and predictable technological inventions, the so-called "hardware" for learning and other presentation, as to which the matter displayed are deemed the so-called "software", has revolutionized the possibilities market-wise. It therefore calls for the adoption of some such new right of display which cuts across and corrects the lacunae of the present Copyright Act, gaps as to the scope of exhibition as performance under Sec. 1(c) and the corresponding nature of infringement, if any, thereof, and gaps as to the scope of the protection accorded to creators and assigns in the fine arts trapped in the common law copyright publication syndrome and the limited protections accorded under statutory copyright. Just as technological uses in terms of performance by radio, motion pictures and television have been the means of bringing the rewards of creation to the creator of literary works and of literary and artistic works and to their assigns, so, too, the opportunities of the new technology may bring the constitutional promise of rewards to the artistic creators and assigns to fruition because the fine arts represent a fertile source of the "software" for the new means of widespread dissemination by means of display.

Chapter XXIV

INFRINGEMENT AND PUBLIC PERFORMANCE FOR PROFIT

Sec. 24.1. Litigation and Performance

Warner has stated, "Today the performing rights are the most significant and important rights conferred by the Copyright Code; they furnish the chief source of revenue to the copyright proprietor."[1] This remark should be taken in the context that the rights have taken on meaning in the crucible of litigation for copyright infringement thereof and that litigation, perforce, has been, and is a principal market mechanism for the policing of performing rights and, by reason thereof, of the structuring of performing rights institutions, the performing rights societies. Nowhere is this truer than in the area of public performance for profit and the law made by the American Society of Composers, Authors and Publishers, (ASCAP), in particular, in its efforts to enforce the performing right.

Sec. 1 of the Copyright Act[2] serves as the source of rights constituting the bundle of rights under copyright. Sec. 1(a) grants the right of copy, broadly, the publishing rights.[3] Performance rights follow, almost, as it were, as adjuncts: (a) of rights of oral delivery, (Sec. 1(c)),[4] where there is a right of public performance for profit; (b) of dramatic rights, (Sec. 1(d)),[5] where there is a right

---

[1] Warner, Harry P., Radio and Television Rights, Chap. XII, Performing Rights (1953) at p. 301.

[2] 17 U.S.C. 1.

[3] 17 U.S.C. 1(a).

[4] 17 U.S.C. 1(c).

[5] 17 U.S.C. 1(d).

of public performance without any for profit limitation; and (c) of the right of musical performance and mechanical reproduction under compulsory license (Sec. 1(e)),[6] where there is a right of public performance for profit. Embodied in the last subsection, is an exemption of right of public performance for coin-operated machines where there is no admission charge.[7] Damages are provided for infringement of the right of performance under Sec. 101 of the Act.[8]

The parameters of the right in litigation are never far removed from broader problems of the nature of copyright. Thus, in *Blanc* v. *Lantz,*[9] plaintiff sued for infringement of his common law property of a musical laugh as used in the Woody, the Woodpecker, motion picture animated cartoons. The Court felt that either there was a performance sufficient to constitute a dedication or abandonment to the public domain thereby divesting the plaintiff of his common law property by publication without statutory copyright,

---

[6] 17 U.S.C. 1(e). One must distinguish between the performing right in non-dramatic, dramatic, and musical material embodied in sound recordings, as to which Secs. 1(c), (d) and (e) grant performing rights in such material, and Sec. 1(f). Public Law 92-140, 92d Cong., S. 646, grants exclusive rights to reproduce and distribute sound recordings fixed, published and copyrighted from and after February 15, 1972 and prior to January 1, 1975 in Sec. 1(f). No performing rights were given to the owners of the sound recordings—e.g., record manufacturers, performers, independent record producers in this interim legislation. See S. 543, Dec. 10, 1969 Print, 91st Cong., 1st Sess., Jan. 22, 1969, Secs. 101, 102(7), 106 and 114. By Sec. 114 of S. 543 the exclusive rights therein are limited to the rights to reproduce, distribute and publicly perform, i.e., Sec. 106(1), (3) and (4). See Secs. 17.3, 17.4 and 18.6, *supra.*

[7] *Ibid.*

[8] 17 U.S.C. 101.

[9] 83 U.S.P.Q. 137 (Superior Ct., Cal., L.A. Cty., 1949).

or else the exhibition of the films was so widespread as to constitute publication, with the same result. In either event, there was not a limited publication. Thus a claim for infringement of common law copyright ran afoul of the notion that, in that instance, performance without statutory copyright dedicates.[10]

The same rationale appears to underly the performance of phonograph records. Concededly, Judge Igoe in *Shapiro, Bernstein & Co., Inc.* v. *Miracle Record Co., Inc.*[11] held that common law copyright in a musical composition did not survive the *sale* of phonograph records embodying the tune. In this regard, Nimmer adverts, ". . . the relatively few courts which have considered the question have almost unanimously determined that public sale *or other distribution* of phonograph records *does* constitute a publication and hence a divestment of common law rights in the works recorded." [12] It is submitted that, in this context, widespread performance might be deemed a publication under this rationale, regardless of the technical nature of the distribution. Thus, air plays by disc jockeys, as performances of a new phonograph recording as part of the effort of the record manufacturer or his record distributor to "break" the record in the particular market or markets, might be deemed a form of other distribution in the Nimmer sense, even if the distribution is gratuitous as such distributions usually are. One might go even further and rely on the distribution per se, whether or not in fact there are concomitant performances of the complimentary record, as constituting such widespread dissemination as

---

[10] See, Nimmer on Copyright (1970), Sec. 109.4, The Right To Exhibit Motion Pictures, at pp. 435-439.

[11] 91 F. Supp. 473 (N.D. Ill. E.D. 1960).

[12] Nimmer, *op. cit., supra,* note 10, Sec. 50.2, pp. 198-199 (emphasis added), as to words, "or other distribution".

to constitute a publication and, perforce, divestiture of common law copyright. This would follow even if the record "bombed" and there were few or virtually no performances.

Thus tangibility of the object which creates the performance, as contrasted with the live performance, carries with it the risk that a claim for infringement of common law copyright by unauthorized performance cannot be maintained because the performance dedicates. Hence, live performance appears to be longer lived in respect of the protection under common law copyright whether directly in front of an audience or by means of conveyance to a scattered audience through some medium of communication.[13]

---

[13] See, Ferris v. Frohman, 223 U.S. 424 (1912) (theatre); Uproar Co. v. NBC, 8 F. Supp. 358 (D. Mass. 1934) (radio); McCarthy & Fischer v. White, 259 Fed. 364 (S.D.N.Y. 1919) (music); Nutt v. National Institute, Inc., 31 F. 2d 236 (2 Cir. 1929) (lectures). Cf. DeMille v. Casey, 121 Misc. 78, 201 N.Y.S. 20 (1923) (motion pictures), which extended the protection of performances under common law copyright as to the theatre to films, and Patterson v. Century Productions, Inc., 93 F. 2d 489 (2d Cir. 1937) at pp. 492-493 cert. den. 303 U.S. 655 (1938) with the views of the court in Blanc v. Lantz, note 9, *supra*. See, Amdur, Copyright Law and Practice, Chap. XI, Performance (1936). But see, Szekely v. Eagle Lion Films, Inc., 242 F. 2d 266 (2d Cir. 1957) where plaintiff owned common law literary property in a screen play for security purposes. Defendant was held to infringe by releasing the film without consent. The opinion recited that appellant "published the film," *Idem* at p. 268. Presumably the Court intended to denote, without actually so stating, that appellant, Eagle Lion had taken out a statutory copyright on the film in which it presumably indicated that date of release constituted date of publication. Hence, appellant "published the film." For neither the trade nor the motion picture copyright bar uses the expression in that sense. Date of release may be taken as distribution date for copyright purposes under the statute, but the film is nevertheless considered released or distributed, not published,

Infringement and Public Performance for Profit

When one moves into statutory copyright in the area of infringing performance, one must also be able to separate the right of performance from other rights under Sec. 1 of the Act since, on occasion, efforts are made to link the same inextricably for the purpose of the particular litigation. Thus, in *Interstate Hotel Co. of Nebraska* v. *Remick Music Corp.*,[14] the Court of Appeals rejected appellants' argument that Sec. 1 conferred a choice on the copyright proprietor between the rights under Sec. 1(a), the so-called publishing rights, and Sec. 1(e), the right of musical performance, and having availed themselves of the former, the copyright owners waived the rights of public performance for profit. The Court correctly pointed out that the rights are separable, stating:

> "The right to publish and sell copies of the copyrighted musical work and the right publicly to perform the work for profit are separate and distinct rights separately granted by the Copyright Act. The separate

---

in the motion picture industry. Many films are copyrighted under the statute to avoid the possibility of dedication, but the release of such films is not taken to mean that such films are published, in the sense that a book is published. By using the term "published" interchangeably with released or distributed, even in a context of statutory copyright, there is an implication that all films, even those under common law copyright, upon release and distribution, may also be deemed "published." If so, absent statutory copyright, *i.e.*, notice of copyright and registration and deposit, the latter conceivably thereafter, might result in a dedication to the public domain because distribution published the film. It is noteworthy that copyright application Form L-M, page 4, contains a subheading under "Information concerning copyright in motion pictures" which is called "Published motion pictures." See Sussman, Jerome J., Copyright Publication, The Motion Picture Distributor and The Copyright Revision Bill, 15 Bull. Cr. Soc. 373 (1968).

[14] 157 F. 2d 744 (8th Cir. 1946).

> rights thus exclusively granted by the copyright owners are distinct in character and differ widely in value. There is nothing in the Act which makes the exercise of one right dependent upon the abandonment of the other. The copyright owner may exercise either right or both as its interest may dictate."[15]

The Court took pains to explain a remark of the Court of Appeals in *Church* v. *Hilliard*, "When the copyright proprietor of a musical composition sells printed copies of it to the public, the performing right goes with them".[16] That opinion, it correctly noted, also differentiated the separate right of performance, although the decision was that it was not a public performance for profit, its decision being a reversal of the determination below[17] that was later reversed by the Supreme Court, *sub nom. Herbert* v. *Shanley*.[18]

It would seem, therefore, that the remark of Circuit Judge Ward in the Court of Appeals in *Hilliard* was dictum in the form of an extrapolation on Sec. 27 of the Copyright Act which reads:

> "The copyright is distinct from the property in the material object copyrighted, and the sale or conveyance, by gift or otherwise, of the material object shall not of itself constitute a transfer of the copyright, nor shall the assignment of the copyright constitute a transfer of the title to the material object; but nothing in this title shall be deemed to forbid, prevent, or re-

---

[15] *Id.* at p. 745; see also, Buck v. Swanson, 33 F. Supp. 377 (D. Neb. 1939).

[16] 221 Fed. 229, 230 (2d Cir. 1915).

[17] *Ibid.*

[18] 242 U.S. 591 (1917); Holmes, J.

> strict the transfer of any copy of a copyrighted work the possession of which has been lawfully obtained."[19]

This was essentially a codification of the decision in the Supreme Court in *Bobbs-Merrill Co.* v. *Straus,*[20] to the effect that a sale of a copyrighted article, in that case, books, by the book publisher resulted in a termination of any rights of control as to use of the physical property thereafter so that such publisher could not impose any price limitations or restrictions on the subsequent disposition of such books. Explaining the meaning of its decision in *Bobbs-Merrill,* the Supreme Court later had occasion to remark in *Straus* v. *American Publishers Association*:

> "This court, in the case of Bobbs-Merrill Co. v. Straus, supra, held that the copyright act did not grant the right to fix a limitation upon prices of books at subsequent sales to purchasers from retailers by notice of price limitation inscribed upon the books, and, construing the copyright act, held that, in conferring the right to vend a book, it did not intend to confer upon the holder of the copyright any further right after he had exercised the right to vend secured to him by the act."[21]

Sec. 24.2. Performance and Jus Disponendi

Actually this absolute right of ownership after sale is an expression of the *jus disponendi* of Roman law. Burdick has written in this respect, "The owner, or dominus of the thing owned, is entitled to its use, to its products, or its entire consumption. He has also the right to dispose of it

---

[19] 17 U.S.C. 27.
[20] 210 U.S. 339 (1908).
[21] 231 U.S. 222, 234 (1913).

absolutely (jus disponendi)."[22] A sale is an absolute divestiture of right, title and interest of the seller upon transfer to the buyer. Thereafter, the *jus disponendi,* the right of disposition of the property sold is vested absolutely in the buyer. The remark of Circuit Judge Ward in *Hilliard,* was intended to convey the same notion that the sale of the copy carried with it all rights of ownership including the performing right. He hastened to add, however, in the very next sentence that the statute gave the copyright proprietor the performing right in Sec. 1(e).[23] His remark may be then seen to mean that the sale of copy, in that case of sheet music, carries with it the rights in the copy as proprietor of the copy, except such rights as are reserved to the copyright proprietor under the statute. To have said that the sale of the copy carries all rights except the copyright does not quite meet the issue in the context. It would not have explained specifically what the buyer could have done with the copy in the light of the reservation of the copyright contained in the statute, as distinct from the physical object that might embody the same. Judge Ward correctly pointed out that the buyer could perform the work embodied in the copy, which he immediately qualified by adverting to the right of public performance for profit reserved to the copyright proprietor. The Court of Appeals, in effect, was saying that a sale of the copy carried with it all rights of performance not reserved to the copyright proprietor under the statute. The vendee of the copy could perform the work to his heart's content provided that the same did not constitute a public performance for profit. The vendee, or any transferee, licensee or even mere user of his copy, could per-

[22] Burdick, William L., The Principles of Roman Law and Their Relation to Modern Law, 325 (1938).

[23] 17 U.S.C. 1(e).

form the work freely, privately, and publicly not for profit. These were incidents of ownership that followed the purchase of the copy by the buyer and constituted his *jus disponendi,* or right of disposition, without further attribution to the seller of the copy, subject only to the reserved rights of public performance for profit. In other words, Sec. 27 of the Copyright Act, by separating the rights of ownership of the physical property from the rights of ownership in the copyright, effectively annexes a statutory reservation as to rights of copyright ownership to any sale of copy so that the *jus disponendi,* or the right of disposition of the copy, may be absolute insofar as the material object is concerned, but qualified in respect of the rights of copyright inhering therein which are reserved to the copyright proprietor. Dominion over the tangible may be absolute in the buyer, qualified only to the extent that it may not carry with it any rights of exploitation or uses reserved in the owner of the intangible copyright embodied in the text of the copy.

Sec. 24.3. Performance: Dramatico-Musical or Musical?

Thus the attempt to subsume the performing right into the publishing right in *Hilliard* failed. An even more interesting attempt to achieve the hoped for result by subsumption was tried and failed in *Herbert* v. *Shanley.*[24] Although the defendant in that case also claimed the right to perform by reason of purchase of the sheet music, in *Shanley* there was an additional factor. The claimed infringement was the performance of the waltz song "Sweethearts" by Victor Herbert which was taken from his comic opera of the same name. The operetta had been copy-

---

[24] 229 Fed. 340 (2d Cir. 1916), *aff'g* 222 Fed. 344 (S.D.N.Y. 1915), L. Hand, J., *rev'd,* 242 U.S. 591 (1917), Holmes, J.

righted as a dramatico-musical composition. A separate copyright had been taken out on the tune. Circuit Judge Rogers stated as to this,

> "This second copyright is upon words and music, which are a component part of the previously copyrighted dramatico-musical composition similarly entitled. It is alleged to be the leading vocal number of the composition, and the success and popularity of that opera is said to be largely due to this particular vocal number." [25]

The plaintiff sought to avail himself of the performing right under Sec. 1(d),[26] which gives the copyright proprietor a right of public performance to his dramatic compositions, by reason of the correspondence of Section 5(d)[27] to Sec. 1(d). Sec. 5(d) covers both dramatic and dramatico-musical compositions.[28] Ergo, the right of public performance is not subject to any for profit limitation thereunder. It is to be noted that the issue in the case was whether or not the performance of the song "Sweethearts" by an orchestra at defendant's restaurant infringed plaintiff's copyright. If it were a public performance for profit of a musical composition, then the issue would have been whether the performance was for profit since no admission was charged separately for the performance, the only charge to the patrons being for the price of their food. If it were a public performance of a dramatico-musical composition, then the issue would have been whether this constituted a public performance. Since public patronage was obviously invited by the defendant, it was clear that

[25] *Idem,* 229 Fed. at p. 341.
[26] 17 U.S.C. 1(d).
[27] 17 U.S.C. 5(d).
[28] *Ibid.*

there was no real issue as to whether or not the performance was a public one. It is not clear from *Hilliard*[29] when the action was brought in relation to the commencement of *Shanley*.[30] Both the District Court and Court of Appeals in *Shanley* relied on the Court of Appeals' decision in *Hilliard,* dated February 9, 1915, to the effect that the performance of "Sweethearts" in *Shanley* by the restaurant orchestra did not constitute a public performance for profit, the decision of the District Court in *Shanley,* being dated May 1, 1915. Plaintiff, in *Shanley,* sought to avail itself of the argument that the defendant had also infringed plaintiff's dramatico-musical composition by public performance thereof without permission. Circuit Judge Rogers in his opinion in *Shanley,* dated January 11, 1916, had the benefit of the precedent of *Hilliard,* holding that a comparable performance of a musical composition by an orchestra in a hotel where there was no separate admission charge did not constitute a public performance for profit. Even though Circuit Judge Rogers came to the same conclusion in reliance on the precedent in *Hilliard,* he took great pains to treat the problem of the nature of the rights of performance of the tune "Sweethearts" as a dramatico-musical composition seriously.

Thus, after differentiating the nature of the respective performance rights under the statute as between a dramatic or dramatico-musical composition, on the one hand, and a musical composition, on the other, he then stated:

> "The distinction, therefore, exists that in the case of the dramatico-musical composition the act secures to the author the sole right to publicly perform it without reference to whether it is performed for profit.

---

[29] Church v. Hilliard, 221 Fed. 229 (2d Cir. 1915).

[30] Note 24, *supra.*

> But in the case of the musical composition, so far as performance is concerned, the act restricts the author's exclusive right to public performance for profit." [31]

However, the determination of the Court of Appeals on this point went off on technical grounds. Following the precedent in *Hilliard,* the Court of Appeals felt it ". . . unnecessary to inquire whether a subsequent copyright can be obtained upon a portion of a previously copyrighted work" [32], and declined to express an opinion on that question. Judge Rogers apparently refined Judge Learned Hand's opinion below on the technical ground of lack of notice of the earlier copyright in the dramatico-musical composition being embodied in the copyright of the musical composition, stating:

> "This brings us to inquire whether the complainants can claim protection for this song under their prior copyright of the dramatico-musical composition from which it has been taken. The copyright of a dramatico-musical composition secures to the proprietor, as already stated, the exclusive right of performance, and it makes no difference whether the performance is or is not for profit. Did the complainants by publishing and copyrighting the song separately and apart from the previously copyrighted dramatico-musical composition of which it was a part, lose as to the part so published the benefit of its copyright as a dramatico-musical composition? There can be no doubt that they have lost that right as to the republished part, for the reason that in republishing they failed to state that the comic opera from which the song was taken was itself copyrighted. We have failed to find any such announcement

---

[31] 229 Fed. at p. 343.

[32] *Ibid.*

> printed on the music sheets of the song. In its absence the complainants can not claim the benefit of the prior copyright. Whether, if they had inserted a notice of the previous copyright, they could have retained the advantages of it as to the republished song, we need not now consider." [33]

It is regrettable that Judge Learned Hand's opinion below was so terse in this regard because the resulting confusion makes it difficult to ascertain just what he meant and exactly what Circuit Judge Rogers had in mind by his determination per above on technical grounds. In part, the decision stemmed from the fact that it was one denying plaintiffs' motion for an injunction on the theory that the performance infringed the copyright of the dramatico-musical composition.

It would be useful here to reproduce Judge Learned Hand's opinion following his recital of the facts since they consist of only three short paragraphs:

> "Learned Hand, *District Judge* (after stating the facts as above). That the opera was a dramatico-musical composition seems to me to admit of no question; a performance need not, therefore, be 'for profit' to infringe, under the rule in Church Co. v. Hilliard 221 Fed. 229, 136 C.C.A. 639, decided by the Circuit Court of Appeals for the Second Circuit February 9, 1915. Furthermore, a performance in words and music alone infringed the dramatico-musical copyright, for words and music alone may constitute a dramatic performance (Russell v. Smith, 12 Q.B. 217), and it did not matter that the performance was only of a scene or part of a scene (Brady v. Daly, 83 Fed. 1007, 28 C.C.A. 253). So far the case is all with the plaintiffs.

---

[33] *Ibid.*

"However, the authors took out a copyright upon the song separately as a musical composition, and in so doing they necessarily gave into the public domain all musical rights, except as they were covered by the resulting copyright. Whatever be the minimum of musical rights, it includes the right to perform the music publicly without any unnecessary accessories. Singing the words to the music, accompanied by the orchestra, is therefore within the musical rights so dedicated. On the other hand, we now have it, on the authority of Church Co. v. Hilliard, supra, that a public performance of this kind is not within the statutory copyright, which the plaintiffs received as consideration for their dedication. It seems necessarily to follow that the performance did not infringe.

"This result no doubt involves the abandonment of some rights, secured by the dramatico-musical copyright, but that is because the plaintiffs wished a double protection. There can be no justice in preserving their dramatic rights at the expense of the public's rights arising from taking out a musical copyright. Had they wished to retain a complete dramatic monopoly, they had it in their power to do so. As it is, that monopoly remains to their complete protection, except so far as its limitation is necessary to give full scope to the musical copyright. For instance, if the performance here had been anything beyond the least essentials to a musical reproduction of the copyrighted song, it would be protected; but it was not. The plaintiffs are really trying to eat their cake and have it; they would get the full benefit of a musical copyright, while they prevent the public from enjoying the corresponding rights." [34]

---

[34] 222 Fed. 344, 345 (S.D.N.Y. 1915).

It is submitted that by focusing almost exclusively on the dichotomy between the dramatico-musical composition, on the one hand, and the musical composition, on the other, Judge Learned Hand was so intent upon the consequences of each respectively that he overstated the differentiation in his sentence, "Singing the words to the music, accompanied by the orchestra, is therefore within the musical rights so dedicated." [35] Indeed, the headnote of his decision purports to recite his holding as follows: "Authors of a comic opera, who take out a copyright on a song with orchestral accompaniment, dedicate to the public the right to sing the words to the music, accompanied by an orchestra." [36]

But the various copyright statutes enacted since protection was extended to music in 1831 refer to copyright in "musical compositions".[37] Indeed, the Regulations of the Copyright Office in this regard read as follows:

> "Sec. 202.8 Musical compositions (Class E). (a) This class includes published or unpublished musical compositions in the form of visible notation (other than dramatico-musical compositions), *with or without* words, as well as new versions of musical compositions. . ." [38]

In this regard, Circular 67 of the Copyright Office, entitled, "Poems and Song Lyrics" states that poems or song lyrics without music cannot be registered for copyright in un-

---

[35] *Idem* at p. 345.

[36] *Idem* at p. 344.

[37] See Copyright Enactments, Laws Passed in the United States since 1783 Relating to Copyright, Copyright Office, Bulletin No. 3 (Revised) (1963).

[38] Sec. 202.8(a), Regulations of the Copyright Office (emphasis added).

published form but might be registered as books under Form A, where published, or, if published in a periodical, under Form BB, as contributions to a periodical. As to settings of same to music, the Circular states,

> "Poems set to music. When words have been set to music, the resulting work may be registered as a 'musical composition' in either published or unpublished form. Form E should be used in either case. The *composition* deposited should be written in some form of legible musical notation and if possible the words should be written above or below the notes to which they are sung." [39]

It is clear beyond peradventure of doubt that musical compositions necessarily include musical works with textual accompaniment, whether in the form of poems set to music, lyrics, or just plain prose text. Not only is this in accord with the history of copyright and the nature and history of musical art, but it may be seen that the present Act as enacted in 1909 embodied this concept. Sec. 1(e) thereof, in setting forth the rights in respect of music and the compulsory license provides that the same ". . . shall not include the works of a foreign *author* or composer. . ." unless there is reciprocity.[40] By using the two words "author" as well as "composer" in the phrase, the statute automatically differentiates writers of words from composers. In this sense, the former expression is used as a species of genus "author", as used in the Constitution.[41] The use in this manner in the statute makes both terms species of the generic term.

---

[39] Circular 67, Copyright Office (emphasis added).

[40] 35 Stat. 1075, Act of Mar. 4, 1909, 60th Cong., 2d Sess. (emphasis added).

[41] Constitution of the United States, Art. 1, Sec. 8, Clause 8.

Infringement and Public Performance for Profit

It is to be noted that the same section provides for the right to perform the copyrighted work publicly for profit. Significantly, Sec. 28 of the 1909 Act contains a proviso excepting certain types of performance from willful infringement of copyright for profit from constituting a misdemeanor. This section expressly exempts from criminal conduct the following:

> "*Provided, however,* That nothing in this Act shall be so construed as to prevent the performance of religious secular works, such as oratorios, cantatas, masses or octavo choruses by public schools, church choirs or vocal societies, rented, borrowed, or obtained from some public library, public school, church choir, or vocal society, provided the performance is given for charitable or education purposes and not for profit." [42]

All of the uses referred to in the proviso are vocal uses and presuppose use of words as part of the musical compositions referred to therein. It is clear from the context thereof that public performance not for profit of such music would not constitute the crime of willful infringement of copyright otherwise covered by the section.

Consequently, it may be assumed that Judge Learned Hand, an eminently knowledgeable jurist in matters relating to literary and artistic property, must have had a narrow meaning for his remark as to the public domain nature of the words accompanying the music as rendered by the orchestra. He could not have meant by that remark that the lyrics went into the public domain as part of the copyright of the musical copyright by mere performance thereof. For to do so would vitiate the copyright in the work as a

---

[42] Note 40, *supra,* Sec. 28 (italics). Now renumbered 17 U.S.C. 104.

musical composition. Rather he meant that whatever the quality of the lyrics as dramatic composition or dramatico-musical composition by reason of their being part of the overall comic opera, subsequent copyrighting of the music and lyrics as a musical composition did not serve to grant any public performance rights in the musical composition by the fact that the words were later embodied in a musical composition. The headnote in respect thereto merely parrots the judge's remarks and in a sense compounds the possibility of misinterpretation.

In this regard, Circuit Judge Rogers seemed to suggest in his opinion the possibility that insertion of notice of prior copyright of the dramatico-musical composition in the copyright of the musical composition might have preserved the benefits for the plaintiffs but felt that the court need not consider the question as part of its determination.

Thus the rationale of the Learned Hand opinion appears to be confusing. This confusion is compounded by Nimmer's comment:

> "Is it necessary to claim a separate musical composition copyright in order to protect the music thus published? In an early decision Learned Hand implied that such an additional copyright may be necessary in order to prevent others from copying the music minus the dramatic elements." [43]

Nimmer is correct to the extent that he equates words in the separately copyrighted song with dramatic elements but, as noted above, Learned Hand in *Shanley* referred to words of the song as dedicated, presumably as the public performance elements, without differentiating between words as part of a musical composition and words of the

[43] Nimmer, *op. cit., supra,* note 10, Sec. 16.4 at p. 71.

same composition as elements of a dramatico-musical composition.

Nimmer is correct in concluding that Learned Hand's conclusion is incorrect. Nimmer makes the point that:

> ". . . since the proprietor's rights in a composite work (e.g., a dramatico-musical composition) are with respect to a component part thereof (e.g., a particular song from such composition) the same as if the component part had been individually copyrighted, it follows that the proprietor may claim as against one who copies only the component part, and not the entire composition, only such rights as would have been available if the part were separately copyrighted." [44]

Nimmer then suggests that if only a single song were infringed that the performance for profit test of a musical copyright would apply, whereas if all or a part of the entire dramatico-musical composition were infringed, then the for profit test would not obtain.[45]

The functional nature of the dramatico-musical composition in that it combines elements of dramatic composition and musical composition is such that the copyright on the whole work, i.e., the dramatico-musical composition, protects against infringement, but the nature of the infringement does not necessarily have an equivalence in form. If only musical composition is infringed, then the copyright in the dramatico-musical composition should protect *pro tanto* as an infringement of a musical work. But musical composition must be understood to include words and music. In the ordinary sense, the mere performance of a tune—music and lyrics—without dramatic elements of scenery,

---

[44] *Idem* at pp. 71-72.
[45] *Idem* at p. 72.

costumes and continuity of story line, constitutes infringement of the musical element of the copyright in the dramatico-musical composition. Where there is a separate musical copyright, it would, of course, infringe that copyright.

Sec. 24.4. Composition—Composite or Component?

Judge Learned Hand therefore erred in making such a drastic differentiation among copyright of the dramatico-musical composition, the musical composition and the elements protected thereby. Nimmer states, "A copyright in a dramatico-musical composition will not only protect against unauthorized appropriation of the entire composition, but will also serve to protect against unauthorized appropriation of a particular component part of the composition such as a single song." [46] The delineation of the character of separate works into categories is for administrative convenience in copyright classification[47], and also to determine the quantum of rights covered under the copyright in respect to that category under the Copyright Act. It is clear, for example, that a map, registrable for copyright under Sec. 5(f)[48] would not carry with it any performing right because the right of performance is only accorded under Sec. 1(c), (d) or (e) thereto.[49] Such performing rights are limited under the latter section to dramatic works,[50] dramatico-musical works,[51] musical works[52]

[46] *Idem* at pp. 70-71.
[47] 17 U.S.C. 5.
[48] 17 U.S.C. 5(f).
[49] 17 U.S.C. 1.
[50] 17 U.S.C. 1(d).
[51] *Ibid.*
[52] 17 U.S.C. 1(e).

and works intended for oral delivery.[53] But a copyright in a work subsumes all of the rights under copyright accorded by the statute subject only to specific statutory limitations as aforesaid. Thus, a dramatico-musical composition may be infringed by copying under Sec. 1(a).[54] Nor may it be translated or novelized under Sec. 1(b) without authority from the copyright proprietor since the same would constitute an infringement.[55] As Warner has indicated, "The nature and subject matter of the work determines its classification." [56] But classification does not mean that infringement necessarily comes from the same class, nor that a reclassification by separate copyright of a part of a work, such as a musical composition, dedicates dramatic elements covered by the dramatico-musical composition. Nimmer's explanation of separability into component parts is one explanation of the means of protecting the work against infringement.[57] The copyright proprietor with his overall copyright in the dramatico-musical composition is limited to the protection he would have had, had he separately copyrighted the component parts. If he had taken out a separate copyright on a musical composition which was part of the dramatico-musical composition he would have had only a right of infringement of a musical composition if that were not performed dramatically.[58]

Nevertheless, the writer is troubled by the Nimmer formulation for other reasons. Nimmer relies on the second sentence of Sec. 3 of the Act,[59] in order to rationalize

---

[53] 17 U.S.C. 1(c).

[54] 17 U.S.C. 1(a).

[55] 17 U.S.C. 1(b).

[56] Warner, *op. cit., supra,* note 1, Sec. 136, p. 419.

[57] Nimmer, *op. cit., supra,* note 10, Sec. 16.4, at pp. 71-72.

[58] *Ibid.*

[59] 17 U.S.C. 3.

his conclusion. This sentence reads: "The copyright upon composite works or periodicals shall give to the proprietor thereof all the rights in respect thereto which he would have if each part were individually copyrighted under this title."[60] Nimmer arrives at this from his conclusion, "It should be noted, however, that a dramatico-musical composition will almost certainly constitute a composite work."[61]

This writer cannot agree. Paul Sherman has written: " . . . the musical theatre is a collaborative effort on a major scale. The cornerstone of this collaboration is the bookwriter, composer and lyricist. . . . One of the first steps is the Collaboration Agreement.. . . The Dramatists Guild of the Authors League of America has prepared a general form of collaboration agreement."[62] Clearly, if A writes music and B, lyrics, intending to unite them, there is a joint work.[63] Even the music publisher can act as a catalyst to a collaborative work as copyright proprietor of one of the elements, e.g., the music, by having a writer create lyrics therefor.[64] In either event, the unitary concept for joint authorship resides in the fact that the fusion of effort, regardless of the time sequence thereof, has resulted in a unitary work.

So, too, A and B might collaborate as joint authors of a dramatic work. So long as they contribute to the work, the respective contributions fuse into a unitary whole, the play. Respective contributions for purposes of co-owner-

---

[60] *Ibid.*

[61] Nimmer, *op. cit., supra,* note 10, Sec. 16.3, at p. 69.

[62] Sherman, Paul, Tin Pan Alley to Shubert Alley, Chap. VI, of The Business and Law of Music, Edited by Taubman, Joseph (1965), at p. 42.

[63] See Chaps. IX-X, Sec. 9.1, *supra.*

[64] *Idem,* Sec. 9.2, *supra.*

ship are thereafter deemed fused so that each contributor is deemed a co-author and joint owner, assuming this is not written by them as employees for hire.

Immediately, there is a distinction as between the musical work, where music and lyrics might be separated, and the play where there is no element of separability. Separability in the tune is an objective facet of its component parts, the music and lyrics, not of the quantum of contribution of each collaborator. Thus, A and B might jointly contribute to each component part, yet there would still be separability. That is, although it is unlikely, A and B, as contributors to the music and as joint writers of the lyrics, might decide for some reason to separate music and lyrics. They would then remain collaborators as to the music and likewise as to the lyrics. But if A wrote the music and B, the lyrics and a separation occurred by agreement, then separation of the component parts would carry with such process the respective authorships.

Yet, it is submitted, that the process of fission, or separability of joint authorship, does not make the tune, absent such separation, any less a joint work. Fusion of separable elements as collaboration and fission of such work does not change the character of the fused efforts as a joint work. In a non-legal sense, music and lyrics of the tune would be component parts thereof. It is therefore unfortunate that Sec. 3[65] of the Act might seem to imply that the term "component parts" might have some necessary correlation to composite works exclusively by reason of the juxtaposition of the two sentences of the section. The first sentence thereof provides for copyright protection in the component parts of a work; the second sentence thereof gives to the proprietor of composite works all the

---

[65] 17 U.S.C. 3.

rights in respect thereto which he would have if they were separately copyrighted.[66] Yet it would seem that component parts of a copyrighted work mean exactly what they say, namely, the various elements constituting the work. Thus music and lyrics are component parts of a copyrighted work even though the same work is a collaborative work, the musical composition.

Perhaps Nimmer is troubled by the variegated nature of the musical theatre in reaching his conclusion that dramatico-musical compositions are composite works.[67]

Musical theatre usually consists of a number of tunes with music and lyrics plus a dramatic text of dialogue. This is characteristic of operetta as well. By contrast, opera as music drama generally consists of dramatic text, whether in prose or verse form, that is sung. However, in many operas there is also "recitative", or dramatic speaking or declamation of lines, rather than singing of same, usually to musical accompaniment. Very often, the quantum of music and lyrics and their juxtaposition to the show, as well as the intent of the creators of the component parts, will determine whether or not the work is a joint work.[68] Even where there is a collaboration resulting in a joint work, there is an interplay of objective criteria and copyright. Suppose A, B and C create a musical play, A composing the music, B writing the lyrics, and C writing the book. The collaboration agreement among them might spell out that if the book is published without music and lyrics, copyright therein will be in C alone. But if the book is published with lyrics, the copyright will belong to B and C. In a parallel manner, the agreement will, in

---

[66] *Ibid.*

[67] Nimmer, *op. cit., supra,* note 10, Sec. 16.3.

[68] See Secs. 9.8-9.10, *supra.*

all likelihood, exclude C from any interest in the music and lyrics separate and apart from the musical play. A and B will have the right to copyright the music and lyrics separately, and to convey the copyrights therein or right to copyright the same to a music publisher.

Conceivably, A, B and C might copyright the musical play, i.e., music, lyrics and book as a dramatico-musical composition under Sec. 5(d),[69] either as an unpublished or published work.[70] Circular 48 of the Copyright Office states, "A dramatico-musical work can be registered for copyright in unpublished form, either as a complete entity or, alternatively, in separate parts consisting of the script for the dramatic portions and the score for the music." [71] At first blush, this would seem to lend credence to Nimmer's view that the dramatico-musical work is composite in nature because even the Copyright Office provides for separability of copyright thereof alternatively.

Nevertheless, were the work not copyrighted at all under the statute, i.e., reliance were had upon common law copyright, the work would be deemed a collaboration and a joint work. There is a fusion of effort into a single work, the dramatico-musical composition intending to create a joint work. True, the market is not neat. Thus composers like Jerome Kern used to write fillers, that is, individual songs that were included in a musical play of others. Howard Taubman writes, "Jerome Kern and Irving Berlin, who were to figure prominently in the transformation of the musical theatre, began to contribute to a musical comedy here or a revue there. Kern did his first complete

---

[69] 17 U.S.C. 5(d).

[70] Circular 48, Copyright Office, "Dramatico-Musical Works".

[71] *Ibid.*

score for *The Red Petticoat* in 1912." [72] Such filler rights in a musical comedy probably were acquired from Kern by contract without making him a joint author since the single tune as a filler constituted a musical interpolation in the music, lyrics and books of others.

There is a range, then, in the musical theatre from the musical revue, which may be truly composite, in that there are separate works by separate authors and composers, to the joint creation, whether the same be opera or musical play. Dramatico-musical composition may take a variety of forms. Even a single song may be performed in such a way as to be a rendition of a dramatico-musical performance. Thus, in *Green* v. *Luby*,[73] a preliminary injunction was granted against performance of the copyrighted song "I'm Bringing up the Family", written as a number of a copyrighted dramatic sketch entitled, "The Queen of the Vaudeville".

After conceding that the song was a musical composition and not a dramatic composition, the Court then stated, however:

> "The work is essentially a series of recitations and songs to be recited or sung by the same person dressed in different costumes. The action and dialogue in addition thereto are hardly sufficient to make a dramatic composition. Still the work is something more than a mere musical composition. The singer dresses in costumes to represent the different characters. There is very little dialogue or 'patter'—the latter being, apparently, the professional term. There is also a very little action. The singer gets out of a cradle. There is

---

[72] Taubman, Howard, The Making of the American Theatre 143 (1965) (italics).

[73] 177 Fed. 287 (C.C. S.D.N.Y. 1909).

scenery, and lights are thrown upon the singer. I think the sketch may fairly be classified as a 'dramatico-musical composition' within the meaning of the copyright act." [74]

The Court pointed out that the fact that the sketch was improperly classified as a dramatic composition would not affect or impair its validity as a dramatico-musical composition. Here the song was copyrighted by complainant, Feist, prior to copyright of the sketch. The Court noted that no question had been raised as to the validity of such copyright. This is the converse of the proposition raised by Judge Learned Hand in *Shanley*[75] in that musical copyright preceded the copyright in the dramatic composition, which was found by the Court to be a dramatico-musical composition, whereas in *Shanley* the copyright of the dramatico-musical composition preceded the separate copyright of the musical composition. Significantly, the Court, in *Luby*, concluded that the complainants had the exclusive right to perform the sketch as a dramatic composition under Sec. 1(d) and the song as a musical composition under Sec. 1(e). The defense of burlesque was not countenanced because the Court felt it was not necessary to sing the entire song.[76] Thus, it may be seen that Judge Noyes, in *Luby*, avoided the pitfalls of over-differentiation as between dramatico-musical compositions and separate musical compositions included therein that Judge Learned Hand fell into.

---

[74] *Idem* at pp. 287-288.

[75] Note 24, *supra*.

[76] Note 73, *supra,* p. 288, cf. Bloom & Hamlin v. Nixon, 125 Fed. 977 (C.C. E.D. Pa. 1903) where there was held to be good faith mimicry and the singing of a chorus of a song was held to be incidental.

Carried to its logical conclusion, if loss of words in separate copyrighting meant loss of protection, then separate copyrighting might simply not be undertaken. Then there might be the temptation by writers and composers to claim that the separate tunes would not be subject to compulsory license, assuming a first recording of a cast album, by reason of the fact that the whole work is a dramatico-musical composition. Nimmer fears that this would encourage circumvention by writers and composers and is not within the spirit and intent of the copyright laws.[77]

But the separability of copyright in dramatico-musical compositions does not thereby convert a collaborative or joint work into a composite work, any more than an integrated music drama by Richard Wagner would make his operas into composite works because the component parts might be separable. If the work is integrated with only a single creator, it remains nonetheless integrated if there are multiple creators without regard to the nature of their creation, provided that they or their assigns intend to put the components together into a joint work. Thus, in a collaboration, artistically there may be an integrated work if the filler tune of a Jerome Kern is included, but it may be excluded by reason of the intent of the principal creators to subsume rights in the filler as a separate, composite work for ownership and copyright purposes. Then again, the principals might treat the creator of the filler tune as a co-author of the dramatico-musical composition for all purposes and in that event the entire work would be a collaborative work.

The fact that the Minimum Basic Production Contract in respect of Dramatico-Musical Productions of the Dramatists Guild denominates composer, lyricist and bookwriter

---

[77] Nimmer, *op. cit., supra,* note 10, Sec. 16.4 at p. 72.

as author would appear to signify an intent to treat all of these creators of the dramatico-musical work as creators of a collaborative or joint work. It is true that a film studio licensing rights to make a derivative dramatico-musical work for the stage out of a motion picture that is not a musical motion picture will probably insist upon a status as author vis-à-vis the producer for purposes of sharing in the subsidiary rights as an author, but it is doubtful that this will constitute the film studio as an author in the true sense of the word as a collaborator in the creation of the dramatico-musical work. Rather it may be seen as an attempt to give the creator or proprietor of the film from which the musical play will be derived a stance to obtain the benefits of the author of the musical play. In other words, the film is basically the underlying work drawn on for adaptation into the derivative work of the musical play.

Sec. 24.5. Choreography as an Integer of the Integrated Work

The musical play collaboration is further complicated in that the choreographer of the work is not deemed to be in collaboration in a joint work with the composer, lyricist and bookwriter. If the choreographer has reduced his work to copyrightable form, such as Labanotation, then he may have a separate copyright therein.[78] Hence one might say that the musical play with a ballet therein is composite in respect of the choreography, but collaborative in respect of the other components—books, music and lyrics. One might contend that this is absurd because from an audience point

---

[78] Circular 41, Copyright Office, "Choreographic Works", provides for a registration of such works as dramatic or dramatico-musical compositions in Class D where conveying a dramatic concept and the movements are fixed in dance notation or other legible written form. See Sec. 22.13(b), *supra*.

of view there is only one show, only one work. One can only conclude that custom and practice in the creation of literary and artistic properties, as well as particular technologies relative thereto, play an important role in the determination of market and legal conceptions.

A case in point is provided by the choreographic work that is not part of a musical play. Note that Circular 41 of the Copyright Office entitled, "Choreographic Works" states that choreography meeting the requisite tests of dramatic conception and legible written form can be registered as a "dramatic or *dramatico-musical* composition."[79] Yet invariably, choreography will be treated separately from the music that might be commissioned for the very work being choreographed. The composer will have his separate copyright in the music, and the choreographer, in the dance, if he so chooses, by reduction to some legible written form, be it film, diagrams, written words, or dance notation.[80]

On the face of it, this might lend strong support to the Nimmer view that the respective elements of dramatico-musical composition are composite. This follows at the present time as to music and choreography because that has been the custom and practice and almost always choreographer and composer are different individuals. Yet, Circular 41 permits copyrighting of choreography as a dramatico-musical composition. This presupposes that the dance may be set to music in some form of composition or work. Now suppose a single person were to compose music and choreography and attempt to register the combined elements as a dramatico-musical composition. It is submitted that the work could be so registrable under a

---

[79] *Ibid.* (emphasis added).

[80] *Ibid.*

single copyright pursuant to Circular 41. The theoretical underpinnings therefor would be the fact that the work is conceived of as an integrated work of music and dance in dramatic conception. Presumably, as a dramatico-musical composition, the resultant work could also be separately registrable for copyright as a musical composition and as a dramatic composition.[81] If it were the work of a single creator who insisted that his work was not a composite work, then who is to gainsay the intent of the creator thereof? On the other hand, if he chose to separate at times music from dance for various purposes, such as performances, it would seem that concert performances of the music might be protected under his copyright under Class D as a dramatico-musical composition even though he never separately copyrighted the music. And if he did separately copyright the music, such separation should in no way render the dramatico-musical composition any less an integrated work subject to protection under copyright without falling into the public domain under the Learned Hand view, or being rendered into a composite work thereby under the Nimmer view.

In other words, existing conventions play a large part in the determination of what is to be deemed a collaborative work or not. It is entirely conceivable that choreographers might some day insist upon the status of authors by reason of their contributions to the musical theatre and join in collaboration agreements with respect to their works with bookwriters, composers and lyricists. The fact that it has not been done as a matter of custom and practice does not mean that such choreographers might not be able to do so. If such be the case, then their work would be part of the integrated work and part of a collaborative or joint

[81] Notes 70-71, *supra*.

work. So, too, the composers of incidental music for dramatic works in the theatre might insist, because of the quantum and quality of their contributions, that they are, indeed, co-authors of dramatico-musical compositions entitled to the emoluments of joint authorship and co-ownership in the work. Again, custom and practice might be varied by changes in time, technology and contract.

Sec. 24.6. Fusion, Collaboration, Composite Work and Composition

Just as fusion of seemingly disparate elements might be made into joint creations in the legal sense of co-authorship and collaboration as integrated works, so the fact of fission or separability should not in any manner derogate from the fact of fusion of the fused work. If a music drama by a single author and composer, such as Richard Wagner, might be deemed an integrated work because this is what he intended and created, so the separation of his fused music drama into separate elements of music and accompanying words, as musical compositions, and text, as a dramatic composition should not by reason of such separability render the music drama into a composite work. *A fortiori*, fusion of efforts by two or more persons should not thereby render composite a musical play created by them, without regard to the character or quality of their respective contributions (apart from *de minimis*, which would presumably disqualify the contributor from co-authorship, anyway). Thus, if co-authors jointly write book, or music, or lyrics, this should not affect the result any more than if they severally write book, music and lyrics. The fact of separate copyrightability of the components does not *ipso facto* derogate from the nature of the joint work as a colloboration or co-authorship. In other words, the same result would apply regardless of the form of collaboration; the contents determine separability rather than the medium. Thus a book with illustrations may be separately copyrighted as to text and lyrics. This would constitute a composite work. There is no intent to create a joint work. On the other hand, the parties may decide to create a joint work and take out a single copyright thereon. This may be hydra-headed, in fact, because the parties may intend to collaborate in manuscript and nonetheless, upon publication, change to separate copyrights. Where there is a fusion of dramatico-musical elements into a composition, in most instances there is an intent to create a joint work. That is the nature of the meaning of the term "composition" which Webster defines as the "Formation of a whole or integral by placing together and connecting different things, parts, or ingredients." [82] That is the nature of writing as composition and the constitutional basis for the copyright.[83] Copyright is a function of composition, i.e., is derived from composition, from the putting together of different things, parts or ingredients, into an integral whole constituting the creative work because it has the requisite modicum of originality. A dramatico-musical composition is nonetheless a composition because it combines dramatic and musical elements into the mixed media form denominated dramatico-musical. The integral whole of the composition is the basis for copyright, assuming requisite originality. Separability merely means that other configurations may be made from the materials embodied therein which themselves constitute integral wholes as writings with requisite originality and therefore are likewise capable of copyright. If derivation may be made from underlying works in new copyrights or from the public domain, then separable compositions

[82] Webster's New International Dictionary, Second Ed., unabridged (1961), at p. 548.

[83] Constitution of the United States, Art. I, Sec. 8, Clause 8.

may arise by separability, whether or not the same be technically denominated as derivative works.

Sec. 24.6(a). Fission and Composition

Separability of composition is inherent, then, in the nature of copyright without regard to the nature of the basic configuration constituting the copyright. The fact of separability, therefore, no more affects the nature of the basic work as a composition, whether contributions thereto be joint or the work of a single person, than the fact that separable components or elements may be fused into a joint work. The analogy of books and periodicals is not completely in point. Books per se are not necessarily written compositions entitling the creator to copyright the same as integral works as opposed to composite works. Books may be single compositions under a single copyright of an integral whole as a writing or they may be literary or editorial composites. That is, they may be composite works of separate authors or editorial compilations of material not necessarily subject to copyright except for the format of compilation. Books, generically, are not necessarily synonymous with literary compositions entitling the creator to copyright of an integral whole. If they are literary compositions, then separability depends upon the viability of the separated material as separate compositions for copyright purposes. The same is true of dramatico-musical compositions.

It would seem, therefore, that the term "composition" is crucial in determining the nature of the work for copyright purposes and that the dramatico-musical composition is generally a work of co-authorship, whether or not the component parts may be separable for copyright purposes, where the requisite intent is present to create integral works by the collaborators. Where this intent is not present, when, for example, revues are created, utilizing disparate works of the same or different creators that might be readily replaced, then there may be truly composite works of a number of dramatico-musical compositions and if there should be a single copyright thereon, it is essentially a copyright of composite works.

Sec. 24.6(b). Dramatico-Musical Composition: Separability and Integration

It is noteworthy in this regard that Circular 48, entitled, "Dramatico-Musical Works" explains under its subtitle, "What Is A 'Dramatico-Musical Composition' ":

> "Operas, music dramas, musical comedies, musical plays for television, and other productions in which music and drama are *integrated* with each other are classified as 'dramatico-musical compositions' registrable in Class D." [84]

It is submitted that separate numbers in a musical play are integrated when the creators of the work determine to treat such numbers as integral parts of the work. There is an element of fixation or finality in the inclusion of the separate numbers. Integration here does not necessarily mean that the separate numbers are organically part of the whole work, as in later musical comedies and musical plays from "Oklahoma" on, where the story line is advanced through the separate musical and lyrical numbers and integrated therewith. The cohesion of integration is not tested in such a critical sense, i.e., by the norms of the dramatic critic, as to approximation to story line for integration. The norms of the musical theatre in the United States have allowed for other types of musical integration which preceded such organic fusion of music and drama and probably

---

[84] Circular 48, note 70, *supra* (emphasis added).

will continue to do so hereafter. That is, normatively, there have been many musical comedies which have integrated musical numbers with only the flimsiest relationship to the story. It was felt that a ballad belonged here, a production number there, and so on. It would seem that if the creators of the show deemed that the numbers belonged in the show and were continued after opening night or whenever finally fixed in the show, that those numbers were an integral part of the show, provided that authorial credit were accorded thereto. If occasional numbers were fixed in the show by third parties who were not deemed authors of the show, then presumably rights to include the fillers were acquired contractually and integrated by contract rather than by the mechanics of collaboration. In collaboration there would be an intent to fuse efforts into co-authorship by creators or assigns and thereby create a joint work. Thus the musical play could be created by one individual, or by collaborative effort combining respective contributions to authorship. In either event there would be an integration of music and drama because the creators intended to combine music and lyrics, whether or not the separate numbers particularly advanced the story line. There is a correlation of authorship and the work created. If the filler tune were not authored by the creators of the balance of the show and they declined to include him as an author, then the addition of the filler tune with some separate credit therefor would make of the show a composite work consisting of the show minus the filler tune as one integration of music and drama and, to that extent, a dramatico-musical composition, plus the addition of the filler tune, as a separate work. The combination, i.e., the show as a whole, would really constitute a composite work.

If, on the other hand, the entire show, inclusive of filler, were to be copyrighted as a dramatico-musical composition showing the composer of the filler tune as one of the authors, that would evidence an intention to include him as a joint author for copyright purposes while his share as joint owner would be regulated by agreement, probably to accord him less than an undivided equal share of the whole.

In this context, it may be seen that the determination of what is a dramatico-musical composition and the separability of individual numbers and the separate copyright thereof may be seen to be complex, arising out of the practices of creators in putting shows together in an interplay of copyright rules and practices. In this regard, the Copyright Act is not too helpful. Sec. 1[85] thereof does not refer to dramatico-musical compositions. Rights are spelled out in terms of dramatic works or the drama in Secs. 1(b) and 1(d), while Sec. 1(e) refers to rights in a musical composition.[86] Sec. 5, however, classifies in the same subdivision, Sec. 5(d), both dramatic and dramatico-musical compositions.[87] Sec. 12 allows copyright in unpublished works in dramatic, musical or dramatico-musical compositions.[88] Sec. 101(b), Fourth differentiates damages for infringement as follows:

> "In the case of a dramatic or dramatico-musical or a choral or orchestral composition, $100 for the first and $50 for every subsequent infringing performance; in the case of other musical compositions $10 for every infringing performance;"[89]

Rule 2 of the Rules of Copyright Practice of the Supreme Court was in effect until its rescission as of July 1, 1966.

---

[85] 17 U.S.C. 1.
[86] 17 U.S.C. 1(b), (d) and (e).
[87] 17 U.S.C. 5(d).
[88] 17 U.S.C. 12.
[89] 17 U.S.C. 101(b), Fourth.

The Rule provided that a copy of the alleged infringing work as well as of the alleged infringed work had to accompany the petition; "except in cases of alleged infringement by the public performance of dramatic and dramatico-musical compositions." [90]

In this regard, in *April Productions, Inc.* v. *Strand Enterprises, Inc.,*[91] plaintiff brought an action for infringement of copyright in musical play "The Student Prince". Defendant claimed that the complaint was insufficient as a matter of law for failure to comply with Rule 2 by annexing the requisite copies of alleged infringing and infringed works. The Court cited Rule 9 of the Rules of the Copyright Office, 17 U.S.C.A.[92] and Amdur[93] and then held, "The musical play alleged to be infringed is sufficiently set forth and described as a dramatico-musical composition and comes within the exception in Rule 2, supra." [94] Indeed, the present Regulations of the Copyright Office, Sec. 202.7, entitled, "Dramatic and Dramatico-Musical Compositions (Class D)" provide in pertinent part:

> "This class includes published or unpublished works dramatic in character such as the acting version of plays for the stage, motion pictures, radio, television

[90] Rules Adopted by the Supreme Court . . . Respecting Copyright, see Nimmer, *op. cit., supra,* note 10, Appendix G at p. 938.

[91] 79 F. Supp. 515 (S.D.N.Y. 1948).

[92] Rule 9, Copyright Office, 17 U.S.C.

[93] Amdur, Copyright Law and Practice, Sec. 20, p. 127 (1938) reads, "Dramatico-musical compositions differ from dramatic compositions in that, besides a plot, characters and acting, there is present musical and/or vocal accompaniment. Operas, operettas and musical comedies are the most usual form of dramatico-musical compositions."

[94] Note 91, *supra,* at p. 516.

> and the like, operas, operettas, musical comedies and similar productions, and pantomimes."[94a]

It is to be noted that in affirming the decree below in *Herbert* v. *Shanley*, i.e., of Judge Learned Hand in the District Court, Circuit Judge Rogers set forth two conclusions:

> "(1) That complainants can not claim the benefit of the copyright of the dramatico-musical composition for that portion of the composition which they republished separately and without notice of the copyright previously obtained.
>
> "(2) That the copyright of the song 'Sweethearts' as a separate musical composition, even if valid, is not infringed by its being rendered in a public restaurant where no admission fee is charged, although the performer is privately paid for rendering it by the proprietor of the resort."[95]

Sec. 24.7. Infringement: Public Performance for Profit

In the Supreme Court, both *Hilliard*[96] *and Shanley*[97] were heard together on writs of *certiorari* to review the respective decrees affirming decrees in the District Court below dismissing the respective bills or complaints. Again, as in the opinions below, decision was terse. Justice Holmes, after reciting the facts of each case in single paragraphs for each, disposed of the issue by reversing the decree in a single paragraph which reads:

[94a] Regulations of the Copyright Office, Sec. 202.7. See Sec. 15.7, *supra*.

[95] 229 Fed. 340, 344 (2d Cir. 1916), *aff'g* 222 Fed. 344 (S.D.N.Y. 1915).

[96] 221 Fed. 229 (2d Cir. 1915).

[97] 229 Fed. 340 (2d Cir. 1916).

> "If the rights under the copyright are infringed only by a performance where money is taken at the door, they are very imperfectly protected. Performances not different in kind from those of the defendants could be given that might compete with and even destroy the success of the monopoly that the law intends the plaintiffs to have. It is enough to say that there is no need to construe the statute so narrowly. The defendants' performances are not eleemosynary. They are part of a total for which the public pays, and the fact that the price of the whole is attributed to a particular item which those present are expected to order is not important. It is true that the music is not the sole object, but neither is the food, which probably could be got cheaper elsewhere. The object is a repast in surroundings that to people having limited powers of conversation or disliking the rival noise give a luxurious pleasure not to be had from eating a silent meal. If music did not pay, it would be given up. If it pays, it pays out of the public's pocket. Whether it pays or not, the purpose of employing it is profit, and that is enough." [98]

Significantly, the Supreme Court did not consider the validity of the later separate copyright for "Sweethearts", mentioned by Circuit Judge Rogers in his conclusions in his opinion, and simply reversed. Nimmer footnotes his comments on the Learned Hand opinion and the affirmance thereof in the Court of Appeals by noting that the decision below in *Shanley* was reversed on other grounds and that "The Supreme Court expressly declined to rule on this issue." [99] The Supreme Court had indeed stated that the

---

[98] 242 U.S. 591, 594-595 (1917).

[99] Nimmer, *op. cit., supra,* Sec. 16.4, fn. 218, at p. 71.

District Court had held that plaintiffs' rights in *Shanley* were limited to those conferred by the separate copyright, "a matter that it will not be necessary to discuss." [100]

What is interesting in this regard is that the matter seems not to have arisen again, that is, the validity of the separable copyright, as the basis for copyright infringement, or its relationship to the copyright in the dramatico-musical composition, of which it was a part even though numerous cases were decided in relation to public performance for profit both in the lower courts and the Supreme Court. Perhaps the reason this, in a sense, became moot was the very determination of the Supreme Court in *Shanley* that performance by an orchestra at a public place of a musical composition, which was a part of a dramatico-musical composition, where no admission was separately charged but there was a charge for food, constituted a public performance for profit. Bear in mind that Sec. 1(d) of the Copyright Act grants the right of public performance as to dramatic works and Sec. 1(e) thereof provides for the right of public performance for profit as to musical compositions. An orchestra plays music, whether or not words are also sung to the tune in a vocal version of the musical composition.

Sec. 24.7(a). Performing Rights Societies: The ASCAP Test Suits

Warner observes that the *Shanley* litigation was financed by ASCAP.[101] Herman Finkelstein, General Attorney for ASCAP, has indicated that Victor Herbert and eight

---

[100] Note 98, *supra,* at p. 594.

[101] Warner, *op. cit., supra,* note 1, Sec. 131e, at p. 339. See Chap. XIII of his book, at pp. 323-455. The chapter is entitled, The Music Industry-The ASCAP Story. See also, Rothenberg, Stanley, Copyright and the Public Performance of Music (1954).

other outstanding writers formed ASCAP in 1914 to solve the difficulties of administering and protecting rights of public performance given by the 1909 Act.[102] Allen Arrow has written in this regard that ASCAP upon formation, had no rights other than the performing non-dramatic rights granted by its members and that, "The Society attempted immediately to solve the problems of clearance of rights by users and to form a sort of nation-wide police organization through which proprietors could have their rights enforced. So the case of *Herbert* v. *Shanley* was initiated against Shanley's Restaurant." [103]

Warner notes that *Shanley* became the judicial prop for ASCAP, and, indeed, of performing rights societies generally. He observes:

> "The *Shanley* case was of tremendous significance to ASCAP and the music industry. It recognized separate and distinct performing rights in a musical composition derived from a dramatico-musical composition. Furthermore, the incidental or secondary use of music, whether in a restaurant, dance hall, motion picture theatre or radio station would require a license from the copyright proprietor. Obviously, authors, composers and publishers could protect and exploit the economic worth of their performing rights by banding together in an organization which could deal effectively

---

[102] Finkelstein, Herman, Public Performance Rights in Music and Performing Right Societies, in 7 Copyright Problems Analyzed 69 (1951) as reprinted by Fred B. Rothman & Co., with 1953 Copyright Problems Analyzed *sub nomine* Copyright Problems Analyzed (1966) at p. 73.

[103] Arrow, Allen, Chapter XI Performing Rights Societies, in The Business and Law of Music (1965), edited by Taubman, Joseph, at pp. 95-100 at p. 96.

> with the many users of music. The decision furnished the judicial prop for ASCAP's operations." [104]

Finkelstein has refined this by indicating the two-fold purpose of ASCAP. He writes:

> "The purpose of the organization was two-fold; on the one hand, to provide a clearing house through which users of musical works would be able to obtain licenses to use the copyrighted works of all of the members on the payment of a single fee without accounting separately for each work performed; and, on the other, to provide composers and publishers with a central means through which they could license performances of their works, and at the same time enable them to detect any infringements of such works occurring simultaneously in thousands of places throughout the country." [105]

Shanley then may be said to have opened the floodgates to a variety of test suits and enforcement suits which determined the parameters of the performing rights societies and their operations. It is to be noted in this regard that Sec. 1(e)[106] as embodied in the 1909 Act and continued to date has two concepts, public performance for profit and, in respect of coin-operated machines, i.e., the juke-box exemption, the notion of admission charge. The last paragraph of the subsection ties in both notions, and reads:

> "The reproduction or rendition of a musical composition by or upon coin-operated machines shall not be deemed a public performance for profit unless a fee

---

[104] Warner, *op. cit., supra,* note 101, Sec. 131e at p. 340. Sec. 131e is entitled, The Judicial Basis of the Performing Rights Societies.

[105] Finkelstein, *op. cit., supra,* note 102, at p. 73.

[106] 17 U.S.C. 1(e).

is charged for admission to the place where such reproduction or rendition occurs." [107]

Sec. 24.7(b). For Profit Test: The Conditioned Indirect Charge

Evidently, the defendants in *Hilliard* and *Shanley* sought to rely on this rationale as embodied in the statute in respect of coin-operated machines, to wit, that there had to be a separate admission charge for the service in order to have a public performance for profit. That is, unless there were a separate charge for hearing the orchestra, there was not public performance for profit because no payment was being made for this service, i.e., musical performance, and since there was no payment, there could not be any profit flowing therefrom. Of course, Justice Holmes cut through this essentially weak rationale by treating the entire transaction as one for this purpose. Overall commercial benefit, however derived, was enough to satisfy the for profit test of the statute. It matters not that there was no separate charge for the service, here musical performance. The restaurant in *Shanley* and the hotel in *Hilliard* were in the business of serving dining patrons for profit; musical performance was incidental thereto. Orchestral performance was ancillary thereto. A condition for entering the dining room was to order food and pay therefor. Musical entertainment furnished was tied in with it for the enjoyment of the patrons. Presumably one could not have the music without ordering food and paying for the repast. The tie of music with dining was reasonably ancillary to dining and therefore permissible. Yet its very fact of permissibility did not eliminate the economic incidents of operation of these dining rooms as places where patrons were in fact

[107] *Ibid.*

charged. If there was not any admission charge at the door, there was nevertheless an indirect charge as embodied in the enhanced cost of the food. The musical performers were privately paid for their performances. Elementary economics would dictate that there was a charge, be it an indirect one, and that the motivation for rendering the performances was the profit of the proprietor. Here the relationship of freedom of charge for the musical service was not so far removed in terms of proximate cause of the overall charge for the food as to raise a semantic problem of whether in fact the musical service was indeed free or not. Such might be the case with so-called free television where it might be contended that the service to the viewer is not really free because the cost factor is included in the increased prices charged to the consumer to pay for the costs of advertising by the advertiser via such medium and the particular program thereon. But the particular viewer of that program on free television may not in fact ever be utilizing the products of that advertiser so that there is a question as to whether there is indeed a charge to him, whereas the patron of the restaurant who listens to the orchestra almost always pays for the musical service by paying for the enhanced price of the food being served in that dining hall.

Sec. 24.7(c). Coin-Operated Machines and the Juke-Box Exemption

It should be noted that the concept of conditioned service by musical performance being for profit as ancillary to a charge for food and drink has not found its counterpart in connection with the exemption for coin-operated machines. In *Irving Berlin* v. *Anziano*,[108] one of a number of test cases

[108] 62 U.S.P.Q. 146 (S.D.N.Y. 1944).

brought by ASCAP to test the juke-box exemption, plaintiff had alleged in its complaint that the purchase of food and beverage was tantamount to an admission charge. It also complained that the juke-boxes were different from coin-operated machines in use when the statute was passed. Also, the complaint averred that the public did not have free and unrestricted access to the juke-box, but could operate the same only if food or beverage were purchased. Therefore, the performance was for profit and not exempt. As to this case and two other test cases brought at the time, Warner states, "This case and two which were similar, were concerned with technical issues of pleading. It is believed ASCAP abandoned this litigation." [109] Indeed, the Court itself, in determination of defendant's motion to strike allegations from the complaint or alternatively for a bill of particulars, referred to the action as one of three test cases.

In an earlier suit testing the juke-box exemption, no admission charges had been made to the dance hall in which the coin-operated machine in question had operated. There the issue was whether or not coins had been placed in the machine. The ASCAP investigator testified that nobody put money into the machine. Evidently, the machines could be operated by removal of wires leading to them and thus controlled without the use of coins. The Court declined to accept the testimony of the investigator as conclusive that he kept all machines under observation or that he even knew where they all were. Defendant had testified that the machine was at all times controlled by coins. The Court dismissed the complaint because the plaintiff had not sustained his burden of proof and upon all of the evidence the Court was not satisfied that the machine was not coin-operated.[110]

---

[109] Warner, *op. cit., supra,* note 1, Sec. 124, fn. 9 at pp. 318-319.

[110] Buck v. Kelly, 7 U.S.P.Q. 164 (D. Mass. 1930). See Warner, *ibid.* at pp. 319-320 for a discussion of the case.

It is noteworthy that in *Kelly* there was no admission charge to the dance hall in conformity with the statutory requirement. Presumably the basis of the complaint, apart from the contention that the machines were not in fact coin-operated, was that food and beverage were served there and that no coins were required because the proprietor wanted its patrons to have that as a further inducement for purchase of food and beverages. This is a variant of the contention of plaintiffs in *Shanley* and indeed of the later *Anziano* case predicated upon the equation of admission charge with indirect charge through service of food and beverage and charge therefor. That is, by elimination of coin operation from the machine, then *Shanley* would apply. In *Anziano* a more direct attack on the juke-box exemption took place in that indirect admission charge was the basis of the test case in the context of conceded coin operation.

The House Report on Copyright Law Revision does not in so many words refer to the conspicuous lack of success of making judicial inroads on the juke-box exemption, but states, "Efforts to repeal the class have been going on for more than 40 years, . . ." [111] It recommended repeal of the juke-box exemption and the substitution of a compulsory license therefor.[112]

Although the arena of proposed copyright revision in relation to the juke-box exemption is repeal and operation of coin-operated machines under a compulsory license,[113] it

---

[111] Report No. 83, House of Representatives, 90th Cong., 1st Sess., March 8, 1967, "Copyright Law Revision" at p. 75.

[112] *Idem* at pp. 75-84. See S. 543, December 10, 1969 Print, 91st Cong., 1st Sess., Jan. 22, 1969, Sec. 116 which provides a limitation upon the exclusive public performance of musical works by coin-operated phonorecord players in the form of the compulsory license thereon, to be administered by the Copyright Office.

[113] *Idem.*

would appear that attempts to limit or overturn the jukebox exemption judicially have long since been abandoned as not being efficacious. One reason for the difficulty in equating the *Shanley* rule of indirect charge in service for food and beverage is the fact that coin operation per se constitutes a form of charge for the music in the machine. It is difficult to speak of a tie or conditioning of music with other services for which a charge is made to the patron when, in fact, there is a separate charge for the music by deposit of a coin in the machine for its operation. Since coin operation is generally standardized, that is, coin charges for operation do not usually fluctuate wildly from location to location, it can be fairly contended that the coin charge for operation is set at prevailing rates. Such a defense is difficult to overcome.

Given, moreover, the statutory mandate that the exemption is applicable where there is no admission charge, it may be argued that the statute contemplates only a direct admission charge at the door as a condition for gaining entrance to the premises because the statute speaks of a separate charge for the music in the form of coin operation. Thus, the fact of additional charges for food and beverage are immaterial so long as there is no door charge. Since coin operation posits separate charge for the music, the setting of a rule of admission charge by indirection, i.e., by charging for food and beverage, might have the effect of nullifying the statute since there is nothing in the statute that suggests or implies a limitation as to the places where coin-operated music might be performed. The fact that the House Report on the 1909 Act in its reference to the coin-operated machines' exemption referred to "penny parlors" as the places where they were located and the usefulness of the same as an advertising medium for composers and publishers[114] does not mean that the application Congress then had in mind precluded broader applications and uses when later circumstances made them feasible.

Sec. 24.7(d). Performing Rights Societies: Small Rights

By contrast, whereas ASCAP was less than successful in its attempts to overcome the juke-box exemption, it and other performing rights societies were able to achieve a substantial measure of success in their efforts to police the performing right, at least until antitrust considerations were finally successfully interposed several decades later.[115] Thus, in *Harms* v. *Cohen,*[116] an organist at defendant's Model Theatre played "Tulip Time" from the "Ziegfeld Follies, 1919". Only short excerpts were played. The defenses interposed included the fact that the organist was an independent contractor and that the defendant had no control over what the organist played. The Court disposed of these defenses stating:

> "He who employs a musician to perform in an exhibition for profit, under a contract by which the musician has authority to play whatever compositions are in accordance with her judgment appropriate and fitting must be held responsible for all that is done by the musician. By giving her that authority the employer acquiesces and ratifies whatever she does. If under his

---

[114] Report No. 2222, House of Representatives, 60th Cong., 2d Sess., Feb. 22, 1909, to accompany H.R. 28192, reprinted in Nimmer, *op. cit., supra,* pp. 959-986 at p. 970.

[115] Alden-Rochelle, Inc. v. American Society of Composers, Authors and Publishers, 80 F. Supp. 888 (S.D.N.Y. 1948); M. Witmark & Sons v. Jensen, 80 F. Supp. 843 (D. Minn. 1948).

[116] 279 Fed. 276 (E.D. Pa. 1922).

> contract he has parted with the right to exercise this control over her actions, without making inquiry as to what she intends to play, he yet must be deemed to have taken part, and to have given her general authority to perform copyright compositions." [117]

The Court thereby disposed of the defense of independent contractor. Other defenses likewise got short shrift. The Court rejected the defense of no charge for performance of the music by analogizing the admission charge to the theatre to the separate charge for food and beverage in the restaurant in *Shanley.* Ordinary rules of infringement of copyright applied so that the fact of playing short excerpts was no defense. Likewise, the fact that professional copies had been given did not constitute a license to perform.

In *M. Witmark & Sons.* v. *Pastime Amusement Company,*[118] the organist played part of "Kiss Me Again" by Victor Herbert by ear in defendant's Princess Theatre. She had no score. The evidence as to infringement was that she played the chorus only once or twice during the same performance or twice on the same day during different performances but on no other day. Defense of insubstantiality of the infringement did not stand up. Defense of no specific charge for the music was overruled on authority of *Shanley.* The independent contractor defense was likewise overruled on authority of *Harms* v. *Cohen.*[118a]

---

[117] *Idem* at p. 278. To the same effect, see also, Dreamland Ball Room, Inc. v. Shapiro, Bernstein & Company, 36 F. 2d 354 (7th Cir. 1929) where the owner of the hall was held liable even though the orchestra was an independent contractor.

[118] 298 Fed. 470 (E.D. S. Car. 1924).

[118a] Note 117, *supra.*

A defense was raised of capacity to sue as copyright proprietor because of the assignment by plaintiff to the performing rights society (ASCAP). Plaintiff had reserved dramatic rights. The Court therefore held that the grant to the society was a mere license so that the right to sue remained in plaintiff. Conceding that the song was not a dramatic song, the Court observed it might be dramatized and that the plaintiff did not part with this right.

In effect, the Court spelled out the nature of the rights obtained by performing rights societies in obtaining the right to perform nondramatically. The Court averred, in holding that the plaintiff was the proper party to bring the suit and not the performing rights society:

> "It is clear that the plaintiff did not by assignment part with all interest in the copyright. The copyright is only partially assigned, the assignment being limited both as to time and as to particular rights and privileges.
>
> "In relation to the right to sue for an infringement, a copyright is an indivisible thing, and can not be split up and partially assigned as to time, place, or particular rights or privileges, less than the sum of all the rights comprehended in the copyright. Certainly the statute authorizing assignments of copyrights contains no recognition of such partial assignments. Of course, such exclusive rights may be granted, limited as to time, place, or extent of privileges which the grantee may enjoy; but the better view is that such limited grants operate merely as licenses and not as technical assignments, although often spoken of as assignments."[119]

---

[119] Note 118, *supra,* at pp. 474-475.

Thus, the grant of the exclusive performing right to ASCAP would not be deemed a divestiture of the bundle of rights reserved to the music publisher as copyright proprietor. However, within the procedural point there inheres an important substantive one going to the nature of the performing right.

The so-called "small rights" of performance are transferred exclusively to the performing rights society while the proprietor retains the so-called "grand rights" or dramatic rights. Rights are granted to the performing rights society for policing because the separate tunes are deemed playable over and over so that the grant of a license by the individual proprietor becomes difficult and time-consuming, particularly where music is performed in quantity, be it at a dance hall, a restaurant, or over radio or television. By aggregating small rights in numerous tunes, the performing rights society, vis-à-vis the user, can license its catalogue in a blanket license although per program and per piece licenses are also available. The fact of mass consumption of music by users and the ability to license performances *en masse* through control of exclusive rights of musical performance, enable the performing rights societies to become a market mechanism for administration of musical performance through exploitation of the single right of public performance for profit out of the bundle of rights under Sec. 1(e). This means that subject to satisfying the limitation contained in the statute that the public performance must be for profit, a limitation that is not present with respect to the exercise of the exclusive dramatic right of performance, the performing rights societies may effectively and viably operate in the market. Therefore, the defense asserted as to the proper party to sue as plaintiff had significance only in the context of the particular litigation, it being the province of the litigator for the defendant to assert as many defenses, technical, i.e., procedural, as well as substantive, that he could dream up with any possible substance of validity. Had the defendant prevailed on this defense, presumably a new action would have been brought on the same infringement, assuming the statute of limitations had not run, in the name of the performing rights society.

Thus, in each instance, assuming a grant of the exclusive musical performing rights to the performing rights society, a key determinant, once infringing performance had been ascertained, is whether or not there is a valid defense that the performance is not for profit.

Sec. 24.7(e). Performance and Notice

At the same time, the fact that this right is set forth in Sec. 1(e), which also comprehends the right of mechanical reproduction, subject to the compulsory license, does not mean that criteria of that subsection relating to mechanical reproduction are to be superimposed on the test of public performance for profit. Thus, in a case where defendant ran a dance hall and in a companion case, another defendant operated a theatre, it was contended by way of defense that plaintiff had failed to file a notice of use where the infringments occurred by performance by means of phonograph records. The Court held for the plaintiff, stating, "We conclude that the provision in question does not have the effect of making a failure to file the notice referred to a defense to a suit for infringement of the right to perform a copyrighted work publicly for profit." [120] Similarly, the requirements as to notice under

---

[120] Irving Berlin, Inc. v. Daigle, Same v. Russo, 31 F. 2d 832 (5th Cir. 1929), at p. 834, *rev'g* 26 F. 2d 150 (E.D. La 1928) *sub. nom.* Irving Berlin, Inc. v. Russo.

other sections would not affect the enforcement of the right of public performance for profit. Thus infringement by performance on a record player in a restaurant of a phonograph record could not be defended by allegation of no notice of copyright on the record.[121] Notice of copyright was not affixed to the record and the defendant had no notice thereof. The Court held that this was no defense. It would seem, therefore, that the exclusive right of public performance casts the burden on the user to ascertain the source of music to be performed in order to avoid infringement. Where the nature of the performance is such that there is no tangible copy of the work under copyright on hand that would evidence the notice of copyright, the user must perforce undertake clearance procedures to ascertain whether or not the particular work may be freely used because it is in the public domain, or whether a license to perform the same is required because it is copyrighted. Even the tangible copy might not necessarily evince ownership if the work is under common law copyright and there has been no publication. Thus, a musical composition might be available in copies for performance without being sold or otherwise published without loss of common law copyright. If the work should indicate the names of the composer and lyricist, if any, there probably still would not be any notice of copyright thereon. Indeed, the work might have been assigned under common law to a third party, or transferred by gift or devise, without the copy being performed indicating ownership.

Thus the burden in respect of performance is on the defendant to investigate and clear title. Performing rights societies have been conceived of as aids to users by eliminating this burden in great measure by making vast

---

[121] Buck v. Heritis, 24 F. 2d 876 (E.D. S. Car. 1928).

catalogues of music available under blanket license. Thus, if a user should be licensed by ASCAP and BMI, the major American performing rights societies, and also by SESAC, the risk of infringing performance borne by the user would appear to be minimal. Thus the market function of user protection against innocent infringement by reason of license from the performing rights societies is not to be underestimated.

Sec. 24.8. For Profit Limitation and Commercial Motivations

However, the determination, in the foregoing cases that the performance is for profit, where no admission is charged at the door, but is an ancillary factor of indirect charge for the musical service included in the enhanced price of food and beverage, is primarily economic. Implicit in the application of the doctrine is that the principal operation, service of food and beverage, is comercially oriented, i.e., for profit. Two steps are basically undertaken in analysis of each situation: one, a search for the tie of the indirect charge for the musical service and, two, the commercial purpose of the principal operation.

Thus, in *Secunda* v. *Goldstein,*[122] there was a collection taken up from the guests at the defendant's hotel on behalf of the producer of the performance who employed the singer of certain Jewish tunes. The action was brought by the plaintiff as President of the Society of Jewish Composers, Publishers and Song Writers. The Court held that the proceeds of the collection were not for charitable uses. The Court stated, "We find as a fact that the entertainment was commercial and the defendants were commercially interested in it and procured or allowed it for

[122] 68 U.S.P.Q. 258 (S.D.N.Y. 1946).

purposes that to them were profitable."[123] Here there was a commercial profit motive of the defendant in operating the hotel. The collection was apparently the means of compensating the performers. It was a form of charge for the musical service but only a voluntary one and, as to non-contributors, the principle of indirect charge for hotel service, inclusive of food and beverage, would still be applicable. The fact of a collection in no way derogated from the essential nature of the musical performance as incidental to service of food and beverage at mealtime at the hotel, so that the basic purpose of the musical performance was to entertain the guests so as to get them to continue to patronize the hotel for the greater profit of the proprietor. The dominant aspect of the notion of public performance for profit in respect of what is or is not for profit would therefore appear to be the motivation of the entrepreneur who provides the musical service.

Ordinarily, this can be gathered from the nature of the enterprise of such person. If the entrepreneur operates a hotel or restaurant, there is the strongest likelihood that commercial motive will be found and the for profit label applies. This doctrine has been stated by the Court in *Harms, Inc.* v. *Sansom House Enterprises, Inc.*:

> "In construing Section 1(e) of the Copyright Law, the courts have uniformly adopted the view that any performance at a restaurant to which the public is admitted and where food and beverages are sold, is given for the purpose of profit and, if unauthorized, is an infringement of the right granted by this section."[124]

---

[123] *Idem* at p. 259.

[124] 162 F. Supp. 129, 133 (E.D.Pa. 1958).

It is noteworthy that the restaurant employed yet another means of provision of musical service, performance on transcription discs transmitted by leased telephone wires to the defendants who purchased such musical service and amplified the music on loudspeakers.

Sec. 24.9. Private vs. Public Tests—The "Private Club"

Indeed, the later cases involving service of food and beverage have sought to vitiate the impact of this rule by the defense that the enterprise was private rather than public. If the operation were not, as a matter of fact, open to the public, i.e., were not a *public* performance for profit, then the fact of service of food and beverage would be immaterial. This defense arose in a line of cases involving the so-called "private club" or private operation which is really quasi-private and essentially of a public character.

Thus, in *Alan Jay Lerner* v. *Club Wander In, Inc.,*[125] the defense to infringement was that the club was private and not for profit. There were no stockholders and no profits. Dues originally were $1 a year. Later this was increased to $2 a year. The only paid employees were the entertainers. A sign on the premises stated that this was for members and guests. However, strangers were allowed entry when the club was not crowded. The Court felt that it did not have to reach the question whether a performance limited strictly to members would be public; here, in fact, performances were open to the general public. The right to exclude did not necessarily make the club private when, in fact, it was really not exercised.

[125] 174 F. Supp. 731 (D. Mass. 1959).

M. Witmark & Sons v. *Tremont Social and Athletic Club*[126] reached a similar conclusion. There were no shareholders in the social and athletic club. Drinks were sold on the premises. There were no written membership forms. No inquiry was made of plaintiff's investigator as to his membership. The musical performance was held to be a public performance for profit without authorization.

Yet another variant of the membership club was considered by the Court in *Alan Jay Lerner* v. *Schectman.*[127] There defendant claimed he was operating a membership club which was not the equivalent of a common key club. However, membership was open to anyone who sent in $10; company membership was available for $50. Gift certificates were also available as a means of providing memberships. The Court held that the club was public in character. Its purpose was personal profit. It was more of a commercial night club with no meaningful qualifications for membership.

Finally, the Court in *Porter* v. *Marriott Motor Hotels*[128] held that the operation of the Sirloin & Saddle Club in the defendant's hotel was publicly operated for profit in the hotel.

It may be deduced from the foregoing cases that denomination of private in club operation must be truly so in fact. Attention must be given to the formalities. There must be meaningful qualifications for membership. The qualifications must be observed. Then, too, the club must be truly private in character. If membership is observed in the sense that only members and guests are admitted, but

---

[126] 188 F. Supp. 787 (D. Mass. 1960).
[127] 228 F. Supp. 354 (D. Minn. 1964).
[128] 137 U.S.P.Q. 473 (N.D. Tex. 1962).

the membership is quasi-public, open to the public at large without any qualification other than payment of membership dues or fees without any other considerations, then the facility is treated by the courts for what it really is, a public operation in club form for reasons of status and prestige, meeting technical provisions of liquor laws, and so forth. This would comprehend the so-called key clubs where membership is open to the public generally, the separate facilities provided to deluxe or first class air passengers at various terminals by some airlines, the so-called bottle clubs which permit entry to members for drinking liquor on the premises from bottles brought by the members where state law otherwise prohibits sale of drinks on the premises, and the entertainment equivalent of book clubs and record clubs open to the public generally whether by payment of dues, membership fees or other nominal qualification, but where essentially the attribution of the term "club" is intended for prestige and status purposes.

It would appear, therefore, that the principal motivation of the enterprise, operation of the so-called "club" for profit, also has considerable significance in the ultimate determination as to the character of the operation as public or private. Assume as a predicate of all such operations that there is no separate charge for the musical service. Then for profit performance is attributed thereto under the general rule if the principal motive of the operation is sale of food and/or beverage and/or accommodations to the patrons. Commercial motivation inheres in the latter and for profit teleology permeates the character of the enterprise. Enterprise directed to segments of the public characterized by profit motivation almost necessarily induces a public character to the operation even though the qualifications for entry thereto may be limited to particular segments of the public for status or other reasons. It would appear, therefore, that profit motivation would be a strong element in determining the fact of public character of the enterprise.

Sec. 24.10. Mixed Operations and the Eleemosynary Motivation

Indeed, profit form of the enterprise may be enough to reach such a conclusion by the courts even where other motivations, including the non-profit, may be strong. This was precisely the issue in *Associated Music Publishers, Inc.* v. *Debs Memorial Radio Fund, Inc.*[129] There the defense to suit for infringing performance on station WEVD was that this was not a public performance for profit. The defendant was a New York stock corporation wherein the nominal stock outstanding was held by nominees of Forward Associates, Inc., a New York membership corporation. Under the by-laws of the corporation, it was to be conducted as a non-profit sharing corporation. Profits, if any, were to be used for improvement of facilities and programming. There was limited revenue from advertisers; only about one-third of the time was devoted to commercial broadcasts. Public donations were asked to make up the deficit in the earlier years, and after 1931, Forward Associates, Inc. made advances and donations to the corporation.

The District Court was doubtful that the corporation had lost its character as a stock corporation and held that,

[129] 46 F. Supp. 829 (S.D.N.Y. 1942), *aff'd,* 141 F.2d 852 (2d Cir. 1944). See also, Gershwin Publishing Corp. v. Columbia Artists Management, Inc., 312 F. Supp. 581 (S.D.N.Y. 1970) where defendant was held liable for minimum statutory fees and damages where it helped organize local community concert associations to whom it furnished artists.

although the infringing performance was on a sustaining program, the performance was for profit. Sustaining programs could not be distinguished from the rest of the operations. Even though sustaining programs do not bring in direct revenue, they build up listener appeal and therefore serve as inducements to advertisers.

Judge Augustus Hand, in his opinion in the Court of Appeals, noted that although the ultimate objectives were philanthropic and educational, the station sought immediate commercial profit. He stated:

> "It can make no difference that the ultimate purposes of the corporate defendant were charitable or educational. Both in the advertising and sustaining programs Debs was engaged in an enterprise which resulted in profit to the advertisers and to an increment to its own treasury whereby it might repay its indebtedness to Forward Association and avoid an annual deficit. . . . there was . . . an immediate profit from advertising programs both to the advertisers and to the corporate defendant. . . . It is unimportant whether a profit went to Debs or to its employes or to the advertisers. The performance was for profit and the owner had the statutory right to preclude each and all of them from reaping where they had not sown."[130]

He also noted that the station manager, who was personally paid for managing the station and who selected the program to be broadcast, was also responsible as an infringer or as a contributory infringer.

The Court of Appeals, in affirming, seemed to reinforce the view of the District Court that the nature of the

---

[130] *Idem,* 141 F. 2d 852 at p. 855.

defendant was not particularly relevant to the ultimate result. The District Court had stated in this regard:

> ". . . it is at least doubtful whether it has lost its character as a stock corporation. I do not, however, deem it necessary to decide that point, for regardless whether the corporation in its general structure is a profit sharing corporation or not, I still think that the broadcast was a performance for profit within the meaning of the Copyright Act." [131]

It must be assumed, nevertheless, that the District Court gave weight to the formal commercial character of the defendant corporation as a stock corporation. By its very nature it was organized as a business corporation. The fact that by its by-laws and operations it sought to become a hybrid non-profit operation was not enough. Ultimate philanthropic and educational objectives were insufficient to save the venture from infringing performance. Formally it was a business corporation and, by revision of its by-laws, it would have all of the attributes of operation for profit. The fact that it chose not to was not enough; by its charter and the inherent nature of a stock corporation its very purposes were institutionally for profit. This was buttressed by the character of its station operations. A little commercial operation, here the not insubstantial extent of one-third of its programming, was on sponsored programming paid for by advertisers. Like a little pregnancy, it tainted the entire operation and made the Court, both below and on appeal, look to the integrated nature of all programming, both sponsored and sustaining, as part of the whole where the without charge programming was really sustained by the fact of charge for sponsored programming. Thus, like the conditioning of no

---

[131] *Idem,* 46 F. Supp. 829, at p. 830.

separate charge for musical service in hotels and restaurants upon the charge for food and beverage and other facilities in a unitary view of for profit motivation, so here, the important fact of commercial broadcast, to the extent of a third of all programming, together with sustaining programs and without charge programs accorded other institutions (a variant of the sustaining program), rendered the whole tainted by the for profit activities.

Motivation as to profits need not therefore be ultimate. The courts will look to the immediate or present motivation in arriving at a for profit conclusion. Nor will the fact of lack of profits make for a different result if the motivation is for profit. In *Debs*, the defendant had recurring deficits, yet its motivation was held to be for profit. The Court in *Debs* noted, too, that the test of for profit motivation is not to be limited to the motivations of the principal entrepreneur. The latter may indeed be only a conduit for personal gain in some other form. Thus, if an allegedly non-profit enterprise were used by a promoter as a means of extracting profits therefrom as lessee of the premises to the non-profit lessor, the for profit motivation might be extended to the lessee on the rationale of *Debs,* which found for profit motivations also in employees and the advertisers. Economic benefit to the advertisers was likewise motivated by for profit considerations. In effect, the Court in *Debs* was saying that even the maintenance of an alleged non-profit facility might result in performance for profit where the facility was regularly maintained for profit purposes of others. Thus, by analogy, if a trade show were put on which were completely non-profit but which was intended as a vehicle to serve the advertisers therein, then presumably, under the *Debs* rationale, the performance would be deemed to be for profit.

One is more troubled by the reference to payment of employees in *Debs.* The rationale of the limitation of public performance of music for profit in the statute is to lift restrictions on musical education and comparable edification of the community. One cannot quarrel with a result of public performance for profit where an educational facility, such as a college or university, operates a concert hall open to the public, whether by admission charges at the door or by subscription, and collects money therefrom to pay performers and defray expenses. It would seem that such operation might be characterized as public performance for profit for copyright purposes in that proceeds are used to defray expenses of payment of compensation of talent as well as for administration of the public presentations and maintenance of the facilities. This seems to be implicit in the holding in *Debs.* Indeed, schools are deemed a prime market for certain types of talent, such as rock performers who command important fees for their performances. *Debs* is correct in the respect that the nature of the facility should not be determinative where other facets of the operation result in profitability.

However, the fact of payment of employees should be carefully analyzed in its context in determining whether the *Debs* rationale should be applicable thereto. The analogy of the theatre benefit or film benefit might be applied to it. Usually a benefit for a charity performance at a legitimate or motion picture theatre consists of two price components, the regular admission price and the donation over the regular price. Such a performance, as in *Debs,* includes a major facet of profitability to the exhibitor, distributor and producer, to wit, the regular admission charge. Therefore, if comparable yardsticks were to be applied to a musical performance, the resultant concert would be a public performance for profit. Thus, if a charity were to run a concert and pay prevailing rates for talent, then its break-even point might include a factor of ticket sales attributable to for profit operation on the rationale of *Debs*. This should be modified in situations where talent cannot be secured by reason of union regulations, for example, that an orchestra be paid union scale. Then again, if the condition for giving the concert is payment to an orchestra of its prevailing rates, as for example, with a symphony ochestra, and there is little or no "give" as to allowances from such rates, then such payment should not be a factor in determining whether the performance is for profit. Of course, the tickets for the benefit have to be scaled so that there is a real possibility of realizing proceeds in excess of house expenses for the concert. The same rationale should apply to payment of customary cost of house rental for the concert. The fact that there is a charge for house rental for the benefit should not make it a for profit concert. Concert halls, whether the same are operated for profit or not, rarely make their facilities available to third parties for benefits without charge—and usually at their customary rates—therefor. So, too, if soloists scale down their customary charges to nominal sums or sums to cover expenses or charge expenses only, then the fact of payment thereof should not, under the *Debs* rule, serve to convert concerts by talent under such circumstances into for profit performances, even though overall expenses of hall rental and such artists' expenses may be rather large in the aggregate.

Sec. 24.11. The Crime of Willful Infringement for Profit

The not for profit nature of such benefits should therefore be construed liberally in favor of the charity. Take the proviso which excludes certain performances from the effect of Sec. 104 and exempts them from the possibility of commission of the crime of willful infringement for profit, which reads:

> "That nothing in this title shall be so construed as to prevent the performance of religious or secular works such as oratorios, cantatas, masses, or octavo choruses by public schools, church choirs, or vocal societies, rented, borrowed, or obtained from some public library, public school, church choir, school choir, or vocal society, provided the performance is given for charitable or education purposes and not for profit." [132]

Borge Varmer has written as to this provision:

> "It is not clear why this provision was included in the 1909 act. Inasmuch as it also contains the 'for profit' limitation, it would seem that the particular activities mentioned therein are already protected by the general 'for profit' limitation in section 1. At most, the provision is evidence to the effect that the activities mentioned therein are those which Congress found most deserving of an exemption from the author's performing rights." [133]

The section certainly reflects an intent to protect the right of civic, educational and religious institutions to publicly perform for "charitable or educational purposes". Therefore, the standards for judgment should be liberal, not only in respect of criminal liability, but also the tort of infringement. If public policy, as expressed by Congress in the section is to protect such activities from liability, it would seem that it is also an expression of intent, not only to shield them from imprisonment and criminal penalty but

---

[132] 17 U.S.C. 104.

[133] Varmer, Borge, Limitations on Performing Rights, Study No. 16, in Studies on Copyright (1963) pp. 835-875 at p. 840.

also from tortious infringement in respect of the for profit limitation. The statute has a predicate of willful infringement for profit as the gravamen of the crime, but the proviso would seem to make excluded performances under the provision at most innocent infringement. The statute purports to except such exempted activity from the crime of willful infringement for profit. But implicit in a liberal provision to save certain constituencies from commission of such crime is that the for profit clause should be construed liberally in their favor. Otherwise, such groups might be found to be tortious infringers subject to the penalties of Sec. 101[134] in spite of the liberal application of the for profit provision in the context of willful infringement for profit under Sec. 104[135] as read together with Sec. 1(e).[136] It would seem that the latter two sections should be read together and that each draws sustenance from the other, insofar as one is dealing not only with the particular groups enumerated in Section 104 but, by the doctrine of *ejusdem generis*, the reading together should encompass comparable groups in the categories. Thus, if a school symphony orchestra were to publicly perform a symphonic work publicly not for profit, not only should Sec. 1(e) be applicable thereto as to tortious infringement but also the exemption of Sec. 104 should apply thereto even though the enumeration of categories does not, in so many words, refer to symphonic music and symphony orchestras.

Thus it would seem that the original purposes of the statute, to foster educational and like performances of music where not for profit, would be furthered by a liberal construction of the for profit limitation as a limiting factor upon the application of *Debs*. Hence the *Debs* test of pay-

---

[134] 17 U.S.C. 101.
[135] 17 U.S.C. 104.
[136] 17 U.S.C. 1(e).

ment of employees should not apply to otherwise non-profit performance of educational institutions. Therefore, the fact that the performers are on the staff of the school should not thereby mean invocation of the *Debs* rule. It is submitted that faculty performance per se should not disqualify the school from the non-profit limitation merely by the fact that such performers are employees and are paid salaries by the school. The same would apply to musicians in residence who perform in a similar manner.

Sec. 24.12. Maryland Yacht Club: The Truly Private Club

Likewise, where there is a truly private club in the accepted sense of the term, then the fact that the club has paid employees should not cause an extension of the *Debs* rationale thereto. This apparently was the nature of the Maryland Yacht Club. It is not entirely clear from the opinion in *Metro-Goldwyn-Mayer Distributing Corporation* v. *Wyatt and Maryland Yacht Club*[137] how the cause of action arose. Judge Coleman refers to the fact that, "the films . . . are admitted to have been released under the contract, and to have been performed at the Yacht Club contrary to the provisions of the contract." [138] There, the claim was for copyright infringement. The Court relied upon his prior decision in *Tiffany Productions, Inc.* v. *Dewing*[139] to the effect that an infringing exhibition of a motion picture was an infringement of a dramatic work under Sec. 1(d)[140] of the Copyright Act. Therefore, the issue became whether this was a public performance. The Court adverted that the same test would apply as to the meaning of the term

---

[137] 21 C. O. Bull. 203 (D. Md. 1932).

[138] *Idem* at p. 203.

[139] 50 F. 2d 911 (D. Md. 1931).

[140] 17 U.S.C. 1(d).

"public" under Sec. 1(d) as under Sec. 1(e)[141] which pertained to public performance for profit. The Court rejected the contention that the exhibition of the film constituted a duplication or copy thereof within the meaning of Sec. 1(a)[142] where no test of public performance would be applicable. The Court dismissed the bill, stating:

> "... this is a question of degree in the last analysis. No hard and fast lines can be drawn. It is true that the fact that a club is a social club does not mean that a public performance could not be held there, and the nature of it would not necessarily be determined by whether tickets were sold. But I do fail to see that there is any substantial difference between the showing in the present case at the Maryland Yacht Club and a showing in a private home. We cannot measure the question by numbers of persons. The public is not admitted to a social club of this kind, as we understand the term 'public'. The members enjoy these privileges and have the right to bring in their friends. No one profits financially. That is substantially what takes place when one of those same members has an entertainment at home and asks friends to come to his house." [143]

The rationale of the opinion appears to be predicated upon the exclusivity of the club and the fact that no one profits from it. Yet the for profit test is not applicable in respect of dramatic works. Rather the reference thereto is brought in to point out the exclusivity of the club and that lack of profit motivation is an indication that it is not public. Presumably the Court excluded the plaintiff's profit

---

[141] 17 U.S.C. 1(e).
[142] 17 U.S.C. 1(a).
[143] Note 137, *supra*, at p. 206.

expected to be derived from film rental to the club as a factor of profitability. Thus incidental profit to those furnishing services to the club, such as suppliers of food and beverages and even entertainment, are not deemed to be tests of profitability. However, it is submitted that profit to performers might indeed, in certain instances, be deemed a test of profitability. Thus, if an exclusive membership club otherwise similar to the Maryland Yacht Club were to serve as a showcase for big time entertainment at enormous salaries or other compensation (as independent contractors), then it would seem that the *Debs* case might apply as to profitability even though the club itself might not be run for profit. In effect, it would then be maintained for the profit of the entertainers. But the rental of films by the Maryland Yacht Club apparently was incidental to its operations as a private club.

Nevertheless, the opinion is upsetting because the plaintiff was apparently left without remedy in the context of the tort/contract dialectic. The films being allegedly exhibited dehors the contract, their projection then presumably became an infringement of copyright except for the ruling in that case that there was no such right in the plaintiff because the alleged wrongful performances were not public. One must assume that the films were classifiable as motion picture photoplays in order for them to be categorized by the Court as dramatic works.

The result is anomalous in a sense. One assumes that the Club may have also raised questions as to claim of right to exhibit the films under the contract, although that is not discussed in the opinion. Assuming this were so, then there has been no willful infringement for profit within the meaning of Sec. 104[144] which makes such act a

---

[144] 17 U.S.C. 104.

crime. Moreover, the Club might have defended that in any event the exhibitions were not for profit. Thus the Club presumably would not be subject to criminal prosecution and the plaintiff would be without remedy for copyright infringement. Conversely, if a defendant had no contract and there were only a question of infringement by wrongful appropriation that might perhaps be deemed willful, then a club might attempt to rely on the for profit limitation as to criminal conduct, if, in fact, the club could qualify as a non profit operation and, in particular, if it did not charge admission for the viewings. So, too, a home viewer under this doctrine would not be viewing for profit and so escape the impact of Sec. 104. In either event, there would be a performance which was not public so that the copyright proprietor could not recover under this doctrine on a theory of copyright infringement.

It is submitted that the owner of films wrongfully appropriated is not without remedy in such instances. If there were no contract *ab initio*, then the wrongful appropriation might be a trespass[145] and if there were a contract which had expired and there were unauthorized exhibitions, then there might have been a breach of contract.[146] In such event, the measure of damages might be what film rental could be earned by the distributor in comparable situations. Comparability might then be determined by the contract film rental charged the very same club under the lapsed agreement, if there were a license *ab initio*, and, if there were none, what the distributor was charging in comparable situations for such exhibitions. This would be the application of a contract measure of damages to the tort. Presum-

---

[145] Metro-Goldwyn-Mayer Distributing Corporation v. Bijou Theatre Co., 3 F. Supp. 66, 74 (D. Mass. 1933).

[146] *Ibid.*

ably statutory damages for copyright infringement would be inapposite because such measure of damages are arbitrarily set by statute precisely because they are deemed to be in effect in lieu of calculation of damages, almost by Congressional fiat. Of course, Sec. 101[147] provides that upon notice, actual damages may be recoverable for copyright infringement.

Conceivably, then, the plaintiff might have an election of remedies with the attendant risk that having elected to sue in tort for trespass, or breach of contract, as the case may be, then he may have lost his right to sue for copyright infringement.[148] In dealing with film exhibitions at exclusive clubs, unless a copyright proprietor can obtain relief under the doctrine that an exhibition is a copy of the film[149] in that jurisdiction, then presumably the distributor is better off relying on his rights under the contract, i.e., for breach of the film license agreement.

Sec. 24.13. Public Performance for Profit: The Radio Cases

But it is to be noted that *Maryland Yacht Club* cited *Shanley*[150] and *Buck* v. *Jewell-LaSalle Realty Co.*,[151] in the Supreme Court, as to hotel operations as public performance for profit in order to make the point that the same tests apply with respect to what is public under Sec. 1(d) as to dramatic performance, as under Sec. 1(e) regarding musical performance. In *Jewell-LaSalle*, defendant's hotel

---

[147] 17 U.S.C. 101(b).

[148] Note 145, *supra*.

[149] See Patterson v. Century Productions, Inc., 93 F. 2d 489 (2d Cir. 1937).

[150] Herbert v. Shanley, 242 U.S. 591 (1917).

[151] 283 U.S. 191 (1931), Brandeis, J.

had set up a master receiving set wired to private rooms in the hotel. But the determination there can best be understood, not only in terms of *Shanley*, but two earlier broadcasting cases involving claims of copyright infringement of musical performance under Sec. 1(e).

In *M. Witmark and Sons* v. *L. Bamberger and Co.*,[152] defendant operated a department store in Newark, New Jersey, where it sold radio equipment. It also operated radio station WOR. Plaintiff alleged infringement of copyright by performance of copyrighted song, "Mother Machree" on WOR without authorization. Defendant claimed that the performance was not a public performance for profit because no charge was made to listeners. The Court rejected this contention and stated:

> ". . . the defendant is not 'an eleemosynary institution'. A department store is conducted for profit, which leads us to the very significant fact that the cost of broadcasting was charged against the *general expenses of the business*. It was made a part of the business system."[153]

Moreover, the fact that the radio department might, at times, show losses rather than profits did not change the result; the intent was still to operate at a profit. The Court felt that the carrying of the cost of WOR was an indirect charge comparable to the indirect charge for music as in *Shanley*. Again, the attaint of business opportunity was sufficient to embrace radio in its early days, apparently before sponsored commercial programming had been adopted, so that the musical service, this time via radio, was conditioned upon profitability, not of particular items,

---

[152] 291 Fed. 776 (D. N.J. 1923).

[153] *Idem* at p. 779. (italics).

e.g., food, beverage, accommodations, but upon business operations generally of the department store. Losses in related fields of sales of radio equipment would not change the picture, assuming that musical service on radio were conditioned upon profitability in the radio equipment department. Operations for profit are not to be equated with the fact of profit; if losses occur, the operation is nonetheless for profit. This is exactly the teaching of *Debs*.

Indeed, the Court in *Bamberger* anticipated *Debs* by its reference to the fact that defendant was not an eleemosynary institution. Like Lincoln's aphorism that a nation cannot be half slave and half free, WEVD, in *Debs*, could not be half (there a third) commercial in terms of sale of time to sponsors and half, non-commercial. Had it been all non-commercial, assuming it were not also a stock corporation and had valid non-business forms of organization, it might have then been an eleemosynary institution within the meaning of the term as used by the Court in *Bamberger*.

The later case of *Remick & Co.* v. *American Automobile Accessories Co.*,[154] equated eleemosynary with philanthropic, stating in respect of *Shanley*:

> "It suffices, as there held, that the purpose of the performance be for profit, and not eleemosynary; it is against a commercial, as distinguished from a *purely philanthropic*, public use of another's composition, that the statute is directed." [155]

Note that the opinion stresses the totality view; in order to qualify as non-profit, it must be *purely*, i.e. wholly

---

[154] 5 F. 2d 411 (6th Cir. 1925), *rev'g* 298 Fed. 628 (S.D. Ohio 1924).

[155] *Idem* at p. 412 (emphasis added).

philanthropic. Any attaint of commercial advantage, including general commercial advantage, would eliminate the not for profit exemption. In *American Automobile Accessories,* the alleged infringement was by radio station WLW. The defendant manufactured and sold radio products. The operation of the radio broadcasting service was charged on the books of defendant to its advertising and publicity account. Thus, as in *Bamberger,* a facility promoting the good-will of the corporation, even when operated without separate charge therefor, was part of the configuration of business operation and so done for profit as part of the general commercial advantage.

Sec. 24.13(a). The Nature of Public Performance

But just as the nature of "public" is entwined with the character of for profit operations in many respects, so, too, the categorization of what is "public" may be taken from the nature of the term "performance". In effect, the defendant contended in *American Automobile Accessories* that because this was a performance over radio it could not be public because reception was private. As to this argument, the Court remarked:

> "A performance, in our judgment, is no less public because the listeners are unable to communicate with one another, or are not assembled within an enclosure, or gathered together in some open stadium or park or other public place. Nor can a performance, in our judgment, be deemed private because each listener may enjoy it alone in the privacy of his home. Radio broadcasting is intended to, and in fact does, reach a very much larger number of the public at the moment of the rendition than any other medium of performance. The artist is consciously addressing a great, though unseen and widely scattered, audience,

and is therefore participating in a public performance." [156]

Performance of a public nature accordingly does not require physical propinquity. Nor does it, in fact, necessarily require a large audience, or, indeed, any audience, however scattered. Like the notion of publication, it is the act of broadcasting in the literal sense of trying to reach a *broad* audience that is determinative, just as the fact of placing copies on sale or offering of same constitutes a publication even though few or no copies may actually be sold. Thus, if a radio or television program is broadcast that is so bad as to attract little or no audience, it is nonetheless a public performance even though the audience be miniscule or even non-existent. Objectively, it is the possibility of reception that creates the public performance, the ability to turn the program on, whether or not it is actually done.

Sec. 24.13(b). Broadcasting Reception as Performance

Indeed, the fact of "picking up" the program by turning on a receiving set by a member of such an audience not only is incidental to constitution of the public making up the audience, but is also ancillary to performance and does not constitute a performance. In *Buck* v. *Debaum*,[157] plaintiff sought without success to hold an operator of a café for infringement of copyright by reason of installation of a radio receiving set on its premises which played music broadcast over a station licensed by ASCAP. Turning on a receiving set was held not to constitute a performance.

---

[156] *Ibid.*

[157] 40 F. 2d 734 (S.D. Cal. 1929).

The licensed broadcast occurred at the studio. Performance was completed there. "The action, play, and use of the copyrighted composition has been completed within the studio." [158] Moreover, when plaintiffs licensed the station, ". . . they impliedly sanctioned and consented to any 'pick up' out of the air that was possible in radio reception." [159]

It is submitted that the fact of license of the station was merely additional argument as to the validity of the reception by implied license from the station to the persons tuning in. If reception per se is not a performance, it follows that mere reception cannot infringe public performance for profit. It would seem, therefore, that the views of the Court might be *obiter dictum*, rendered in passing, but not necessary to sustain the position of the ordinary owner of a receiving set, whether it be at home or in a restaurant, because turning on the set does not constitute a performance. The case, then, stands for the proposition that ordinary reception does not constitute performance. Moreover, where the station broadcasting the performance is licensed, there is an implied consent thereto. Thus, the ordinary operator of a receiving set is exempt from infringement: (a) because of the overall exemption from the tort since there is no act which gives rise to the tort; and (b) because the act of reception in any event is authorized. The party turning on the receiving set is deemed a third party beneficiary of the license between the performing rights society and the station, to the extent that the benefits of the license, insofar as reception of performance is concerned, inure to the listener, in the case of radio, and to the viewer, in the case of television. The license serves to insulate the public tuning in

---

[158] *Idem* at p. 735.
[159] *Ibid.*

because the licensor has acquiesced in the consequences of performance, i.e., reception thereof.

In *Jewell-LaSalle*, however, there was a different set of facts in two respects. There were two actions brought in the District Court, tried together, *Buck* v. *Duncan. Same* v. *Jewell-LaSalle Realty Co.*[160] The action against Duncan related to infringement by performance over a radio station without a license. Defendant admitted his infringement. In *Jewell-LaSalle*, the Court of Appeals for the Eighth Circuit had certified to the Supreme Court whether the installation and operation of a master set by the defendant hotel, wired to the public and private rooms, constituted a performance. Among the programs thereby picked up were the unlicensed programs originating on Duncan's radio station.

Justice Brandeis distinguished *Debaum* on its facts by a somewhat different theory. Separate modulation and amplification constitute reproduction, i.e., performance, as opposed to mere acoustical hearing of the original program. Justice Brandeis stated:

> "The modulation of the radio waves in the transmitting apparatus, by the audible sound waves is comparable to the manner in which the wax phonograph record is impressed by these same waves through the medium of a recording stylus. The transmitted radio waves require a receiving set for their detection and translation into audible sound waves, just as the record requires another mechanism for the reproduction of the recorded composition. In neither case is the original program heard; and, in the former, complicated electrical instrumentalities are necessary for its ade-

[160] 32 F. 2d 366 (W.D. Mo. 1929).

> quate reception and distribution. . . . In addition, the ordinary receiving set, and the distributing apparatus here employed by the hotel company are equipped to amplify the broadcast program after it has been received. Such acts clearly are more than the use of mere mechanical acoustic devices for the better hearing of the original program. The guests of the hotel hear a reproduction brought about by the acts of the hotel in (1) installing, (2) supplying electric current to, and (3) operating the radio receiving set and loud-speakers. There is no difference in substance between the case where a hotel engages an orchestra to furnish the music and that where, by means of the radio set and loud-speakers here employed, it furnishes the same music for the same purpose. In each the music is produced by instrumentalities under its control." [161]

Since the question of performance for profit had not been certified, the Supreme Court did not feel impelled to decide the question. But it was almost a foregone conclusion that the precedent of *Shanley* would apply on remand and the Court of Appeals duly cited this and other cases, in holding that the performance was for profit.[162]

Again, there appear two grounds for the decision of the Supreme Court. One was that the original broadcast was unauthorized, therefore the reproduction by the de-

---

[161] Buck v. Jewell-LaSalle Realty Co., 283 U.S. 191 (1931) at pp. 200-201.

[162] *Idem,* 51 F. 2d 726 (8th Cir. 1931).

fendant, Jewell-LaSalle, was not permissible. The now famous dictum[163] of Justice Brandeis reads, in this regard:

> "If the copyrighted composition had been broadcast by Duncan with plaintiffs' consent, a license for its commercial reception and distribution by the hotel company might possibly have been implied. Compare *Buck* v. *Debaum* D.C. 40 F. (2d) 734. But Duncan was not licensed; and the position of the hotel company is not unlike that of one who publicly performs for profit by the use of an unlicensed phonograph **record.**" [164]

Basically the theory here is one of innocent infringement. As to this, Justice Brandeis observed:

> "Intention to infringe is not essential under the act . . . And knowledge of the particular selection to be played or received is immaterial. One who hires an orchestra for a public performance for profit is not relieved from a charge of infringement merely because he does not select the particular program to be played. Similarly, when he tunes in on a broadcasting station, for his own commercial purposes, he necessarily assumes the risk that in so doing he may infringe the performing rights of another. . . . It may be that proper control over broadcasting programs would automatically secure to the copyright owner sufficient protection from unauthorized public performances by use of a radio receiving set, and that this might justify legislation denying relief against those who in using the

[163] See Fortnightly Corporation v. United Artists Television, Inc., 392 U.S. 390 (1968).

[164] Note 161, *supra,* fn. 5, at p. 199. (italics).

receiving set innocently invade the copyright, but the existing statute makes no such exception." [165]

Sec. 24.13(c). Plural or Multiple Performance

The second ground is what Warner calls the doctrine of "plural performance"[166] and Nimmer, "multiple performance".[167] Here Justice Brandeis resorted to radio technology and engineering to adduce that modulation of radio waves in transmission and amplification thereof in reception make the former a performance and the latter, a reproduction thereof. The conclusion results in a kind of circularity of reasoning which brings us back full circle to the first ground. It is an infringement because Duncan was unlicensed by ASCAP for his radio station so that there was no implied license in the hotel. Therefore, the mere tuning in by the hotel, however innocent, constituted an infringement because the receiving apparatus was under the control of the hotel, the reception constituted a reproduction of the performance and so was also a performance. Warner, in this regard, refers to the theory of reproduction as performance as a conclusion " . . . based on a scientific explanation of how radio works." [168]

Nimmer, on the other hand, makes the point that if the Court conclusion is carried out logically, then multiple performance means that one cannot mechanically attribute characteristics of the first performance to the later performances. He notes that, on remand, the Court of Appeals in *Jewell-LaSalle*[169] referred to the hotel pick up of the station broadcast as public performance for profit pre-

---

[165] *Idem* at pp. 198-199.

[166] Warner, *op. cit., supra,* note 1, Sec. 133a, at p. 356.

[167] Nimmer, *op. cit., supra,* note 10, Sec. 107.4, pp. 407-414.

[168] Warner, note 166, *supra,* at p. 355.

[169] 51 F. 2d 726 (8th Cir. 1931).

sumably because that was the character of the station broadcast. Yet, if the same reception took place in a private home, it would still be a new performance, although not a *public* performance, because it occurred in the privacy of the home. Nimmer indicates that the hotel there nevertheless engaged in a public performance because it was done by the hotel for the benefit of its guests, whereas the same acts would not transform the same performance into a public one if it were done by a private individual for his own benefit.[170] He notes from the Brandeis opinion that the guests of the hotel hear a reproduction induced by the hotel by installing, supplying electric current and operating the receiving set and loud speakers.

Indeed, Justice Brandeis had remarked: "Reproduction in both cases amounts to a performance" [171] and had referred to reproduction by radio waves and a phonograph recording. Immediately thereafter he stated, "Compare *Buck* v. *Heretis* D.C. 24 F. (2d) 876; *Irving Berlin, Inc.* v. *Daigle* 31 F. (2d) 832, 833." [172] But these are phonograph record cases in which the unauthorized performance of copyrighted music on a phonograph record in a café and motion picture theatre, respectively, constituted performance infringement. Nimmer finds authority for this in the express statutory language of Sec. 1(e) to the effect that the compulsory license for mechanical reproduction frees the same, upon payment thereof, from contribution to the copyright "except in case of public performance for profit." [173] He notes that the sanction as to phonograph recordings is in the statute. The analogy is not apt because playing or performing a record within the

---

[170] Nimmer, note 167, *supra,* at pp. 411-412.

[171] Note 161, *supra,* at p. 201.

[172] *Ibid.* (italics).

[173] 17 U.S.C. 1(e), Nimmer, *idem,* at pp. 409-410.

express language of the statute is not comparable, within the intent and meaning of such language, to reception of radio or television broadcasts. Moreover, there is a further difference in kind in that phonograph records are heard at different points of time from original performance, whereas radio sound waves are usually heard simultaneously.[174]

Notwithstanding the difference, Nimmer seems to feel that the Supreme Court went very far in equating reception with performance in its doctrine of multiple performance.[175] Indeed, he notes, " . . . the multiple performance theory seems open to criticism on a policy level both because it goes too far and because it does not go far enough. It is submitted that it goes too far when it renders an infringer any restaurant or bar which plays a radio or television set for its customers." [176]

Yet, *Buck* v. *Debaum*[177] held to the contrary insofar as operation of a receiving set in a café was concerned. There the Court stated:

> "One who manually or by human agency merely actuates electrical instrumentalities, whereby inaudible elements that are omnipresent in the air are made audible to persons who are within hearing, does not 'perform' within the meaning of the Copyright Law. The performance in such case takes place in the studio of the broadcasting station, and the operator of the receiving set in effect does nothing more than one would do who opened a window and permitted the strains of music of a passing band to come within the inclosure in which

---

[174] Nimmer, *ibid.*

[175] *Idem,* Sec. 107.42, at pp. 411-412.

[176] *Idem,* Sec. 107.45, at p. 415.

[177] Note 157, *supra.*

he was located. It is true that it is the voluntary act of the person turning on the dial on the receiving set that enables electricity to animate the mechanism so as to make audible within hearing distance of the receiving set that which is disseminated from the broadcasting station and which is 'on the air' by reason of the broadcast, but such voluntary action in my opinion is far from 'performing' the copyrighted work. The performance, which is licensed as just stated, occurs entirely in the studio of the broadcasting station where the copyrighted musical composition is lawfully used, and the action occurring at the receiving set is simultaneous therewith, and is in no sense a reproduction of the musical composition that is being lawfully performed at the broadcasting studio. The action, play, and use of the copyrighted composition has been completed within the studio." [178]

Sec. 24.13(d). Authorized Broadcasts and Implied Consent to Receive

As indicated above,[179] had the Court been content to stop there, that would have been the end of it; for absent performance, there is obviously no infringing performance. But the same opinion went on to develop the theory that by licensing of the broadcasting station, ASCAP impliedly sanctioned and consented to the reception. At this point the confusion is compounded because the conclusion there was basically *obiter dictum*, and while not directly inconsistent with the notion that reception was not performance, the doctrine of implied license should have had no relevance in the context. Nevertheless, Justice Brandeis seized upon this

[178] *Idem* at p. 735.

[179] Sec. 24.13(c), *supra*.

in his footnote[180] in order to distinguish the implied license in *Debaum*, by reason of the license granted the radio station there, whereas Duncan in *Jewell-LaSalle* had performed the infringing compositions without a license. A literal reading of the Brandeis opinion might seem to equate reception in radio broadcasting with performance by reason of the fact that reception constitutes a form of reproduction, as in the analogy to phonograph recordings. If so, then *Debaum* implicitly was overruled by *Jewell-LaSalle* in instances where there is no implied license to the person operating the receiving set because reception is to be deemed equated with reproduction as performance.

This could become a real problem where, as in *Society of European Stage Authors and Composers, Inc.* v. *New York Hotel Statler Co., Inc.*, the Court noted in respect of the license from SESAC:

> "The license before me contained a limitation—set forth in full in the agreed statement of facts—which precluded the National Broadcasting Company, by sublicense, express or implied, from granting to others the right publicly to perform the plaintiff's copyrighted musical compositions for profit." [181]

Warner notes in this regard that after the *Debaum* decision, "In order to forestall any implication of an implied license, ASCAP changed the terms of their licenses and forbid broadcast stations to grant performing licenses to others." [182]

If reception equals reproduction equals performance in the broadest interpretation of the Brandeis opinion, then

---

[180] Note 164, *supra*.

[181] 34 U.S.P.Q. 6, 11 (S.D.N.Y. 1937).

[182] Warner, *op. cit., supra*, note 1, Sec. 133e, at p. 355.

the contractual limitation against sub licensing would effectively eliminate the implied license, whether implied in law, as Nimmer suggests,[183] or implied in fact. Reception in private homes would still not be affected because the equation of reception to performance would still not constitute a *public* performance as a later plural or multiple performance of the original broadcast performance; nor would it be one for profit. But bar and restaurant reception of radio or television would meet the tests of public performance for profit and so the proprietors, under this theory, would be subject to licensing by the performing rights societies solely by reason of having a radio or television receiving set on the premises, the possibility of which Nimmer implies under the multiple performance doctrine and contrary to the ruling of *Debaum* as to the nature of radio reception.

Sec. 24.13(e). The "Doing More" Test of Justice Brandeis

It is submitted, however, that despite the confusion in *Debaum* as to its theoretical premises and in the Supreme Court in *Jewell-LaSalle* as to its disposition of *Debaum* in the footnote and broad language as to the nature of reproduction as performance, the Supreme Court appeared to express the view that the hotel did more than mere tuning in, as in ordinary reception, as the rationale of its decision. Justice Brandeis stated:

> "In addition, the ordinary receiving set, and the distributing apparatus here employed by the hotel company are equipped to amplify the broadcast program *after it has been received.* Such acts clearly are *more* than the use of the mere mechanical acoustic devices for the

[183] Nimmer, *op. cit., supra,* note 10, Sec. 107.43, pp. 413-414.

better hearing of the original program. The guests of the hotel hear a reproduction brought about by the acts of the hotel in (1) installing, (2) supplying electric current to, and (3) operating the radio receiving set and loud-speakers." [184]

This notion of doing *more* is decisive. In *Hotel Statler,* the master receiving set enabled guests to tune in on their radio sets in their private rooms; there was no such reproduction in the public rooms of the hotel. The hotel at issue was called the Hotel Pennsylvania. The Court noted:

> ". . . I regard as without significance the differences between the physical arrangements in the LaSalle Hotel and the Hotel Pennsylvania, and, accordingly, I find that when the owner of an hotel does as much as is done in the Hotel Pennsylvania to promote the reproduction and transmission within its walls of a broadcast program received by it, it must be considered as giving a performance thereof within the principle laid down by the Supreme Court in the LaSalle Hotel case." [185]

Here, too, the doing of *more* is emphasized by the Court referring to "as much as is done" by the hotel. Degree of activity is paramount when juxtaposed to the language of the Court in the two sentences immediately preceding this quoted portion, where the Court stated:

> "For the reception of a broadcast program by one who listens to it is not any part of the performance thereof. Indeed, both physically and mentally it is about as far removed from performance as can well be imagined." [186]

---

[184] Note 161, *supra,* at p. 201 (emphasis added).
[185] Note 181, *supra,* at p. 10.
[186] *Ibid.*

This principle of doing more than ordinary reception was also adopted by the Court in *Harms, Inc.* v. *Sansom House Enterprises, Inc.*[187] The District Court followed both *Jewell-LaSalle* and *Hotel Statler* in concluding that the playing of transcription discs by defendants, transmitted by leased telephone wires, as customers purchasing such musical service constituted public performance for profit. The fact that the patron had to exercise his option to make the music audible by turning on the loudspeaker did not make the performance private as contended by defendants. The case actually involved a consolidation of two suits with a common defendant. An appeal was taken in the case denominated *Leo Feist, Inc.* v. *Lew Tendler Tavern, Inc.* and the Court of Appeals for the Third Circuit affirmed.[188] The Court of Appeals appeared to accept the distinction between ordinary reception and the concept of doing more, here the "piping" in of the music by defendant, Muse-Art Corporation, stating:

> "Point was made that it was not proved that on the night in question the music may not have come from Muse-Art, but may have come through the restaurant's loudspeaker from a radio. But there was no evidence one way or the other that there were musical facilities other than Muse-Art available in Tendler's and there was positive testimony that there were not such pauses in the music program either by or for commercials as are found in radio programs. There was sufficient support for the trial court's conclusion that the compositions heard in Tendler's came from music 'piped' in by Muse-Art." [189]

---

[187] 162 F. Supp. 129 (E.D. Pa. 1958).
[188] 267 F. 2d 494 (3d Cir. 1959).
[189] *Idem* at p. 495.

By discussing this defense, both below and on appeal, the Courts gave credence to the view set forth explicitly in *Hotel Statler* that ordinary reception does not constitute a performance and that the addition of something more makes the difference.

Sec. 24.14. Fortnightly and CATV: The Television Test of Performance

It remained for the majority opinion in *Fortnightly Corp.* v. *United Artists Television, Inc.,* the test case involving CATV as public performance for profit, to set forth the sharp distinction between broadcasting as performance, and ordinary reception as viewing and other than performance. Justice Stewart, writing for the majority, stated:

> "Television viewing results from combined activity by broadcasters and viewers. Both play active and indispensable roles in the process; neither is wholly passive. The broadcaster selects and procures the program to be viewed. He may produce it himself, whether 'live' or with film or tape, or he may obtain it from a network or some other source. He then converts the visible images and audible sounds of the program into electronic signals, and broadcasts the signals at radio frequency for public reception. Members of the public, by means of television sets and antennas that they themselves provide, receive the broadcaster's signals and reconvert them into the visible images and audible sounds of the program. The effective range of the broadcast is determined by the combined contribution of the equipment employed by the broadcaster and that supplied by the viewer.
>
> "The television broadcaster in one sense does less than the exhibitor of a motion picture or stage play;

he supplies his audience not with visible images but only with electronic signals. The viewer conversely does more than a member of a theater audience; he provides the equipment to convert electronic signals into audible sound and visible images. Despite these deviations from the conventional situation contemplated by the framers of the Copyright Act, broadcasters have been judicially treated as exhibitors, and viewers as members of a theater audience. Broadcasters perform. Viewers do not perform. Thus, while both broadcaster and viewer play crucial roles in the total television process, a line is drawn between them. One is treated as active performer; the other, as passive beneficiary." [190]

Thus far, the analysis would not appear to be objectionable even to Justice Fortas, although he referred to it as disarmingly simple for allowing CATV to fall on the viewer side of the line.[191] The majority, to this extent, propounded a practical view with a clearcut differentiation between performance and viewing, as opposed to the emphasis on viewing as a form of reproduction and therefore, at some stage thereof, conceivably a performance, as in the Brandeis view. Scientific doctrine was backstaged in the interest of clarity of the distinction.

But the majority in *Fortnightly* in the Supreme Court did not, by such analysis alone, meet the stumbling block of *Jewell-LaSalle* which had propounded the "something more" doctrine. The majority resolved its dilemma by limiting, in another by now famous footnote, that case to its facts and indicating by way of dictum therein that the result might have been different if the original broad-

---

[190] 392 U.S. 390 (1968) at pp. 398-399.

[191] *Idem* at p. 405.

cast, as in *Fortnightly*, had been authorized.[192] The doctrine of implied license was thereby again invoked.

But note the rationale of the decision. The majority held that CATV "falls on the viewers side of the line".[193] The opinion went on:

> "Essentially a CATV system no more than enhances the viewer's capacity to receive the broadcaster's signals; it provides a well-located antenna with an efficient connection to the viewer's television set. It is true that a CATV system plays an 'active' role in making reception possible in a given area, but so do ordinary television sets and antennas. CATV equipment is powerful and sophisticated, but the basic function that equipment serves is little different from that served by the equipment generally furnished by a television viewer. If an individual erected an antenna on a hill, strung a cable to his house, and installed the necessary amplifying equipment, he would not be 'performing' the programs he received on his television set. The result would be no different if several people combined to erect a cooperative antenna for the same purpose. The only difference in the case of CATV is that the antenna system is erected and owned not by its users but by an entrepreneur.
>
> "The function of CATV systems has little in common with the function of broadcasters. CATV systems do not in fact broadcast or rebroadcast. Broadcasters select the programs to be viewed; CATV systems simply carry, without editing, whatever programs they receive. Broadcasters procure programs and propagate them to the public; CATV systems receive pro-

---

[192] *Idem* fn. 18 at p. 397.
[193] *Idem* at p. 399.

grams that have been released to the public and carry them by private channels to additional viewers. We hold that CATV operators, like viewers and unlike broadcasters, do not perform the programs that they receive and carry." [194]

Once again one is faced with the relationship of a determination of non-performance, here as to CATV, and implied licenses. If, in fact, the CATV operation does not constitute a performance, then why the reference in the footnote to the fact that had the station in *Jewell-La Salle* been licensed, the hotel's transmission would have been authorized as implied under the doctrine of *Debaum*? But with a comparable determination that there was no performance, it would seem that the reference to implied license had no relevance if the reception by the hotel did not constitute a performance. Again, both rationales are relied upon even where they do not appear to be internally consistent because the determination of non-performance renders the second argument moot, if not altogether contradictory.

The dissent of Justice Fortas expressed the view that *Jewell-LaSalle* as a precedent has been effectively overruled by its limitation to its facts. He found difficulty distinguishing the function of CATV as an aid to the viewer from the function of the hotel in aiding reception in that case. He did not accept the latter decision as an ideal gloss

[194] *Idem* at pp. 399-401. Cf. Walt Disney Productions v. Alaska Television Networks, Inc., 164 U.S.P.Q. 211 (W.D. Wash. N. Div. 1969) where the Court distinguished *Fortnightly,* where the time lapse between broadcast and reception was essentially simultaneous, as compared to a week's time lapse between recording and playing. Whether or not this equalled performance was held to be immaterial. Both the preparation of the videotapes and their transmission over cable were held to infringe.

on the meaning of the term "perform", the vague functional test being unsatisfactory. The television camera is analogous to the eye of the spectator in transmission. Even if CATV served as a community antenna to improve reception, that is not the sole function of CATV. He averred:

> "But such a description will not suffice for the case in which a CATV has picked up the signals of a licensed broadcaster and carried them beyond the area—however that area be defined—which the broadcaster normally serves. In such a case the CATV *is* performing a function different from a simple antenna for, by hypothesis, the antenna could not pick up the signals of the licensed broadcaster and enable CATV patrons to receive them in their homes." [195]

Indeed, the reference to distant signals by the dissent was not an isolated abstraction. Although the House of Representatives had passed H.R. 2512 on April 11, 1967,[196] as a copyright revision bill, and had deleted Sec. 111 from the bill, H.R. 2512, pertaining to CATV, prior to the passage thereof, the context of such proposed legislation was to provide a scheme for award of statutory damages for secondary transmission of distant signals where the court

---

[195] *Idem* at p. 407. (italics). See also, Hearings before the Committee on Patents, Trademarks and Copyrights of the Committee on the Judiciary, U.S. Senate, 89th Cong., 2d Sess., on S. 1006, "Copyright Law Revision-CATV", held Aug. 2, 3, 4 and 25, 1966; S. 543, Dec. 10, 1969 print, 91st Cong., 1st Sess., Sec. 111.

[196] H.R. 2512, 90th Cong., 1st Sess., an Act, dated April 12, 1967. Congressman Celler who introduced the bill bearing the same number, H.R. 2512, notes, "The measure failed of enactment in the Senate." See his article, "Whither Copyright?" in N.Y. L. J., Monday, Oct. 26, 1970, p. 1, cols. 3-4, in col. 4.

found that the infringer had refused or failed to accept an offer for a reasonable fee.[197]

Sec. 24.15. Proposed Copyright Revisions and Exempt Secondary Transmissions

Sec. 111(a) of the bill, H.R. 2512, contained a number of exemptions. Sec. 111(a)(1)(A) exempted secondary transmissions consisting of relays of primary transmissions to private rooms of hotels where there was no direct charge to the occupants of such rooms.[198] Sec. 111(a)(3) thereof provides:

> "Subject to the provisions of subsections (b) and (c), the secondary transmission to the public of a primary transmission embodying a performance or display of a work is not an infringement of copyright if the secondary transmission is made for reception solely within the limits of the area normally encompassed by the primary transmission."[199]

Sec. 111(a)(3) almost anticipates the result of the majority decision in the Supreme Court, albeit on opposite grounds, and the consequences of the rationale of the dissent as to liability for distant signals, by exempting secondary transmissions from copyright liability within the area of the primary transmission. Only the approach differs for achieving what are ultimately comparable results. The rationale of the subsection is that the classical function of CATV as community antenna to provide better reception in the area of the primary transmission should not have copyright consequences by reason thereof. The

---

[197] See H.R. 2512, 90th Cong., 1st Sess., a Bill, Jan. 17, 1967, Sec. 111(c)(2)(A).

[198] *Idem,* Sec. 111(a)(1)(A).

[199] *Idem,* Sec. 111(a)(3).

technique is to exclude such consequences by first characterizing the same as a performance and then exempting this type of performance. Per contra, the majority in the Supreme Court excluded all CATV that does not originate or charge directly for performance because the reception does not constitute a performance.

The formulation is accomplished, in part, by the definition of Sec. 101 of said bill, specifically, with reference to the terms "to perform" and "to transmit". Sec. 101 of the bill H.R. 2512 provides in this regard:

> "To 'perform' a work means to recite, render, play, dance, or act it, directly or by means of any device or process or, in the case of a motion picture or other audiovisual work, to show the images in sequence or to make the sounds accompanying it audible." [200]
>
> • • • • •
>
> "To 'transmit' a performance or display is to communicate it by any device or process whereby images or sounds are received beyond the place from which they are sent." [201]

Speaking of the 1965 copyright revision bills,[202] which were substantially identical in regard to said definitions, the Register of Copyrights, in his Supplementary Report of May, 1965, stated, "On balance, however, we believe that what community antenna operators are doing represents a performance to the public of a copyright owner's work." [203]

---

[200] *Idem,* Sec. 101.

[201] *Ibid.*

[202] H.R. 4347, 89th Cong., 1st Sess., Feb. 4, 1965, Sec. 101, 109.

[203] Supplementary Report of the Register of Copyrights on the General Revision of the U.S. Copyright Bill, 1965 Revision Bill (May, 1965), at p. 42.

The Register concluded in this respect, "For these reasons, we have not included an exemption for commercial community antenna systems in the bill." [204] On the other hand, he would exempt non-profit operation or installation of a " . . . 'translator,' 'booster' or similar equipment which merely amplifies broadcast signals and retransmits them to everyone in an area for free reception." [205] It is to be noted, however, that the October 12, 1966 print of H. R. 4347[206] deletes Sec. 109 of the prior print of the bill and sets CATV provisions in Sec. 111 thereof, including in subsection (a)(3) thereof the language contained in H. R. 2512,[207] the bill before the House in 1967 from which the CATV provisions were deleted when the bill was passed by the House.[208]

In the same Supplementary Report, the Register, in discussing *Jewell-LaSalle*, stated, "Since the audience represented by the occupants of private rooms is ordinarily limited to a relatively small number of separate individuals, we have felt that an exemption in this situation is justified, if the broadcast program is piped into the private rooms without change and the occupants are not charged for this service." [209] The Register reiterated and confirmed his

---

[204] *Ibid.*

[205] *Idem* at pp. 42-43. The Register then quotes H.R. 4347, note 202, *supra,* Sec. 109(5).

[206] H.R. 4347, 89th Cong., 2d Sess., Union Calendar No. 999, Report No. 2237, introduced Feb. 4, 1965, October 12, 1966 print.

[207] Note 197, *supra.*

[208] Note 196, *supra.* See the comparative tables and outlines from the Alternative Draft Provisions on Secondary Transmission of the Copyright Office as reproduced in 16 Bull. Cr. Soc. 109 (1968).

[209] Note 203, *supra,* at p. 43.

views[210] as stated in his original Report.[211] There the Register stated:

> "Although the *Jewell-LaSalle* case involved a retransmission, the effect of this decision may be that any business establishment that operates a radio or television receiving set for the entertainment of its patrons—including hotels, restaurants, taverns, barber shops, etc.—could be required to procure performing licenses for all copyrighted works in the broadcast it receives.
>
> "As a practical matter this problem has been confined so far to broadcasts of music, though it could conceivably arise also as to broadcasts of dramatic and literary works and even of motion pictures. We understand that the two principal organizations controlling the performing rights in music (ASCAP and BMI) have generally followed the policy of confining their demands for license fees to those establishments, such as the hotel in the *Jewell-LaSalle* case, that retransmit broadcasts to their various rooms. Other similar organizations, however, may not have the same policy. And there have been complaints from some small establishments that they were asked to obtain performing licenses for the mere operation of receiving sets. In any event, the free use of receiving sets should not be left to the grace or forbearance of the performing rights organizations or other copyright owners." [212]

Note that the Register articulated the uncertainty as to mere reception by a radio or television set in a business

---

[210] *Idem* at p. 44.

[211] Report of the Register of Copyrights on the General Revision of the U.S. Copyright Law, as reprinted in Studies on Copyright (1963), pp. 1199-1346. The Report was published in 1961 originally.

[212] *Ibid.* at pp. 1230-1231 (italics).

establishment by indicating that the effect of *Jewell-La Salle may be* that performing licenses could be required therefor. The exemption was therefore proposed to eliminate such uncertainty by eliminating the rule of that case to the extent it pertained to private rooms, in effect by legislative repeal of the holding of *Hotel Statler* which was limited by its facts to retransmission to private rooms without direct charge therefor.

Sec. 24.16. Fortnightly, Debaum, Jewell-LaSalle and Implied Licenses

Indeed, the need for legislative direction is underscored by the interpretation of *Debaum* by Judge Herlands in the District Court in *Fortnightly*.[213] There the District Court, in discussing *Jewell-LaSalle* in the Supreme Court, stated:

> "Perhaps the most fruitful way to analyze the Supreme Court's reference to the *Debaum* case is to recognize that the District Court in *Debaum* rested its finding of no infringement on two theories—one of which the Supreme Court overruled and the other of which it did not find necessary or appropriate to consider on the facts then before it. The *Debaum* court's conclusion that the reception of a broadcast of a copyrighted work for commercial purposes cannot constitute a performance because the only performance in such a case takes place in the studio of the broadcasting station was clearly overruled by the Supreme Court. However, the court in *Debaum* also rested its decision on the ground that, when the copyright proprietors 'licensed the broadcasting station to disseminate the * * * [copyrighted song,] they impliedly sanctioned

[213] 255 F. Supp. 177 (S.D.N.Y. 1966), *aff'd* 377 F. 2d 872 (2d Cir. 1967), *rev'd* 392 U.S. 390 (1968).

> and consented to any 'pick up' out of the air that was possible in radio reception.'" [214]

Chief Judge Lumbard in the Court of Appeals, in discussing the defendants' contention as a defense in ***Fortnightly***, that there was an implied license in law by reason of the grant of the license to the broadcasting stations originating the transmission, simply reiterated the position of Judge Herlands as to the first ground raised in ***Debaum*** that "this ground was overruled by *Jewell-LaSalle*".[215] Although the Court of Appeals agreed with the District Court that the defense of a license implied in law could not be sustained, the Supreme Court did not consider the question. There the matter was disposed of by a footnote which simply mentioned that the result might have been different in *Jewell-LaSalle* if the original broadcast by Duncan's station had been authorized. In any event, *Jewell-LaSalle* was limited to its facts in that footnote.[216]

There is a thread of continuity, however, in the various cases. In ***Debaum*** the Court had stated:

> "The owner of a copyrighted musical composition can fully protect himself against any unauthorized invasion of his property right by refusing to license the broadcasting station to perform his musical composition; but, when he expressly licenses and consents to a radio broadcast of his copyrighted composition, he must be held to have acquiesced in the utilization of all forces of nature that are resultant from the licensed broadcast of his copyrighted musical composition." [217]

---

[214] 255 F. Supp. 177, *idem* at p. 211 (italics).
[215] 377 F. 2d 872, *idem* at p. 881 (italics).
[216] 392 U.S. 390 (1968), fn. 18, at p. 396-397.
[217] 40 F. 2d 734 (S.D. Cal. 1929) at p. 736.

Judge Lumbard, in discussing the limitations placed by performing rights societies on sublicensing retransmissions, noted Judge Woolsey's assumption in *Hotel Statler* that the limitation was a redundancy but that in any case it exorcised implied sublicenses. Judge Lumbard remarked, "Judge Woolsey clearly assumed that Judge Brandeis had meant a license implied in fact." [218] Judge Lumbard then quoted the above sentence from *Debaum* and remarked in respect thereto, "The district court's statement that a copyright holder could protect himself by refusing to license broadcasts strongly suggests that it believed that any attempted limitation upon a license would be invalid." [219]

It is noteworthy that although the Brandeis footnote cited *Debaum* in its comment that had Duncan been licensed in *Jewell-LaSalle* a license might have been implied, the comparable footnote of the majority of the Supreme Court in *Fortnightly*, even though it cited *Hotel Statler* in the same footnote as supporting the prevailing test of *Jewell-LaSalle,*[220] failed to mention the limitation imposed on sublicenses of SESAC, the plaintiff performing rights society. The majority[221] simply reiterated the conclusion of Justice Brandeis in his footnote in *Jewell-LaSalle* that the result might have been different had the original broadcast been authorized.

Thus, in both cases, the effect of *Debaum* in the Supreme Court, at least as a dictum, would seem to be that there might be an implied license. Yet, if it were subject to limitations, as *Hotel Statler* held, then this was because it was a license implied in fact, and by appropriate contrac-

---

[218] Note 213, *supra,* 377 F. 2d at p. 881.
[219] *Ibid.*
[220] 283 U.S. 191 (1931) fn. 5, at p. 199.
[221] Note 216, *supra.*

tual limitation, or perhaps by grant of the license with its own countervailing statement of limitation on any sublicense, there could be no factual implication thereof. On the other hand, if the grant of a license to a station serves to impart the resultant forces of nature unleashed thereby, then the law implies a grant for the benefit of recipients much in the manner of real estate covenants running with the land.

Yet the Supreme Court decision in *Jewell-LaSalle* must be seen to rest on the ground that what the defendant hotel did constituted a performance. Otherwise, we have the anomaly that ASCAP picked as a test case one which was strong on its specific facts but of little practical application generally. That is, the station in *Jewell-LaSalle* was not authorized. Therefore there was no possibility of the question of implied license arising. On the other hand, the resulting favorable decision might not necessarily be a guide to similar situations in the future if there were truly a license implied in law upon consent because broadcasting stations were generally subject to license in the period following the decision. Thus, if the lower courts were correct in *Fortnightly* that *Debaum* was overruled by Justice Brandeis in *Jewell-LaSalle* and there is no license implied in law, then there is nothing left of *Debaum*. If so, then why the dictum of Justice Brandeis as to implied licenses, had there been a consent, in his footnote and his reference to *Debaum* in that footnote? Also, why the failure of the majority of the Supreme Court in *Fortnightly* to do other than substantially restate what Justice Brandeis had said in his footnote in which *Jewell-LaSalle* was restricted to its facts.

It is submitted that despite the observation of Judge Herlands and the affirmation by Judge Lumbard that *Debaum* was overruled by *Jewell-LaSalle* as to the nature of reception as performance, that although Justice Brandeis concededly took a position, which, if read literally, would support the Herlands-Lumbard view, nevertheless, the Brandeis opinion must be read in the context of his statement immediately following in the same paragraph where he stated:

> "In addition, the ordinary receiving set, and the distributing apparatus here employed by the hotel company are equipped to amplify the broadcast program after it has been received. Such acts clearly are more than the use of mere mechanical acoustic devices for the better hearing of the original program. The guests of the hotel hear a reproduction brought about by the acts of the hotel in (1) installing, (2) supplying electric current to, and (3) operating the radio receiving set and loud-speakers. There is no difference in substance between the case where a hotel engages an orchestra to furnish the music and that where, by means of the radio set and loud-speakers here employed, it furnishes the same music for the same purpose. In each the music is produced by instrumentalities under its control." [222]

Query, would the result have been the same in *Jewell-La Salle* in the Supreme Court had the facts been on all fours with *Debaum,* namely, merely having a radio set in the rooms of the hotel, as in the café in *Debaum,* without more, assuming an authorized broadcast? It is to be noted that Justice Brandeis did not state in *haec verba* that *Debaum* was overruled. Nor, for that matter, did he indicate any limitation thereof to its facts, as the majority in *Fortnightly* did with *Jewell-LaSalle.* It is therefore arguable that the entire paragraph of Justice Brandeis must be read as a

[222] Buck v. Jewell-LaSalle Realty Co., 283 U.S. 191, 201 (1931).

whole, to wit, that when something more is added to ordinary reception, the addition has the effect of putting the party making such addition in *pari materia* with the party engaging an orchestra in a hotel or restaurant, as in *Shanley*. Otherwise, the analogy to the facts of *Shanley* by Justice Brandeis, and also the reference to the acts of doing more by the hotel in *Jewell-LaSalle,* would have been superfluous and unnecessary. Moreover, the footnote of the majority in *Fortnightly,* limiting *Jewell-LaSalle* to its facts in the context of the decision of the majority that CATV did not constitute a performance, would have been only a very restricted limitation if *Debaum* had been overruled by *Jewell-LaSalle* as contended by Judge Herlands. On the contrary, the majority seemed to have reinforced the rationale of *Debaum* by its holding that CATV transmission did not constitute performance in the absence of origination, direct charge, or editing. If Judge Herlands should be correct in his analysis, then it would follow that *Debaum* was restored as good law by the majority of the Supreme Court by virtue of the effective overruling of *Jewell-LaSalle* by *Fortnightly* in limiting the case to its facts.

Sec. 24.17. Proposed Copyright Revision and the "Something More" Test

A more plausible explanation is provided by the views of the Register in this maze of parsimonious parsing. In view of the uncertainty of reception in bars, restaurants, taverns, etc., as performance where nothing is added by the proprietor, he would treat all reception on radio and television as performance and exempt private reception or the *Hotel Statler* type of reception in hotels where reception is obtained in private rooms by the guest turning on the receiving set. This basic approach has been embodied in proposed copyright revision, including the more recent revisions with respect to CATV as embodied in Sec. 111 of S. 543,[223] and the definitions of "to perform" and "to transmit" in Sec. 101 thereof.[224] Sec. 111 provides its own schemata of exemptions and limitations within the context of a compulsory license for CATV but continues the exemption for secondary transmission by hotels, apartment houses and the like to private lodgings or residents thereof.[225]

Thus the rationale of proposed copyrighted revision may be seen to be the legislative repeal of *Jewell-LaSalle* to the extent of reception in private, as contrasted to public rooms, within a context that under Sec. 106(4)[226] of S. 543 there is a right of *public* performance only. Literally speaking, the definitions of Sec. 101 in respect to "to perform" and "to transmit" would have the effect of making reception on radio and television a performance, providing exemption for private reception at home by means of Sec. 106(4) which grants the exclusive right under copyright only with respect to public performance and with respect to private room reception in public places, like hotels, etc., by means of the exemption of Sec. 111(a)(1).

Thus the rationale of performance appears to have come full circle. *Jewell-LaSalle* seems to have developed the doctrine of "something more", to wit, that some addition was

---

[223] S. 543, 91st Cong., 1st Sess., Dec. 10, 1969 print, Sec. 111. See also Senate Report No. 91-1219, 91st Cong., 2d Sess., dated Sept. 22, 1970, Report of the Committee on the Judiciary, by the Subcommittee on Patents, Trademarks, and Copyrights, at pp. 12-13.

[224] S. 543, *supra,* Sec. 101. The additional language in the definition of "to perform" added by S. 543 relates to sound recordings and does not affect the definition in any pertinent way as compared to the definition quoted from H.R. 2512, note, 200, *supra.*

[225] *Idem,* Sec. 111(a)(1).

[226] *Idem,* Sec. 106(4).

necessary to make a performance. This rule was evidently followed by subsequent lower court cases. The majority in *Fortnightly* carried this rule to its logical conclusion by drawing the line between broadcasting as performance and reception as not. CATV in this view fell on the receiver side and so did not constitute a performance. Proposed copyright revision would deem all reception on radio and television as performance but control the use thereof by exemptions, such as home reception and private reception in hotels, etc.

The approach may be pragmatically correct as opposed to line-drawing between performance and reception. However, in the event Congress sets up a National Commission on New Technological Uses of Copyrighted Works dehors copyright revision,[227] such a commission should explore the nature of performance and reception in the light of the new technologies. The approach of proposed copyright revision takes the view of science and engineering as to the nature of performance and reception, viz., that reception requires amplification to achieve reproduction, ergo, performance. This is the basic approach used in *Jewell-LaSalle* as applied to what the hotel was doing. Stated in its broadest terms, reception is performance. Multiple performance, as in that case, arises by reason of the doctrine of doing more than ordinary reception to subject the party doing something more to copyright liability for public performance, and in the case of music, to the for profit limitation. Multiple performance is eliminated by *Fortnightly* by means of CATV falling on the recipient side of the line. In effect, *Fortnightly* pulled away from the science-engineering approach by looking at the functions of broad-

[227] Such a commission was appended as Title II of the December 10, 1969 print of S. 543 in Secs. 201-208.

caster and recipient. Proposed copyright revision would eliminate the distinction in terms of cause and effect as to the nature of performance but would effectively regulate the same by limitations and exemptions. In effect, unless there are such limitations and exemptions applicable, multiple performance would presumably still be operative except in eliminated cases such as reception in private rooms of hotels and the like.

The problems arise from line-drawing in a practical, common sense approach of the traditional view, carried to the point where CATV becomes exempt, as in *Fortnightly*, or by an alternative route of treating broadcasting at both ends, transmission and receiving as performance and then excluding. Pragmatic exemption under the approach of proposed copyright revision is workable so long as the phenomena at issue are reasonably predictable.

Sec. 24.18. The Public/Private Dichotomy, New Technologies and Proposed Copyright Revision

This approach will hold as long as the distinction between public and private can reasonably hold, e.g., as between home use and general non-home use, that might be denominated public use. But *Maryland Yacht Club* serves as a constant reminder that the lines as between public and private will not always hold in clear-cut, logical manner. Even assuming, *arguendo*, that the case were overruled and factually deemed public, there remains nevertheless a lingering doubt so that the nature of performance should be thoroughly explored in respect of the new technologies before the approach of proposed copyright revision is applied thereto. That approach to the public-private dichotomy is to eliminate the performance factor in broadcasting and to base results upon the exclusion of the private from the public. Essentially this follows from the present Copyright Act, too, the problems of what constitutes a performance aside. But at least under present law, distinctions might be made by utilization of the nature of the occurrence in terms of performance doctrine, i.e., the phenomenon does or does not constitute a performance. Under proposed copyright revision, only the public/private dichotomy remains, subject to certain exceptions, as in the case of hotels with private reception only. But if the new technologies were somehow to cast doubt on the relationship involved, whether the same were private or public, then the mere fact of reception would *ipso facto* result in copyright liability under proposed copyright revision because the phenomenon has been defined so as to constitute a performance. Perhaps there is a residual usefulness of current rules in analysis of new technology in respect of the performance or not test.

It is to be remembered that the overall issue as to performance does not, in the first instance, involve, in terms of liability, the fact of performance itself. In other words, generally speaking, the concern is not with the fact that something is being rendered, so much as responsibility for the origination of the phenomenon. Thus the hotel or restaurant will be held liable for copyright infringement when an orchestra plays because, as proprietor, each is responsible for the origination of the event taking place. It is a kind of *respondeat superior* as applied to copyright. This does not mean that others may not be liable as contributory infringers, including the performers without license or authorization. But ultimately copyright proprietors look to principals who control the performance or initiate the same. As applied to broadcasting, the doctrine is extended to cover responsibility for various acts of initiation of an entrepreneurial or proprietary nature. If the principal permits loudspeakers and other amplification to occur within its control, it becomes an originator. If it collects a direct charge for the performance, it is treated as a quasi-originator. Thus, the doctrine of origination is not necessarily a literal, scientific approach. Instigation under present law by doing something more may subject the doer to copyright liability for performance, unless somehow, as in the case of classical CATV, the doing falls on the recipient side of the line, under *Fortnighlty*. Thus editing of programs, deletion of commercials and comparable change of programs might subject the proprietor to liability. Performance in this regard becomes a kind of induction by production. Changes are such as to vest the proprietor with a kind of producing, albeit editorial, function, and so the doctrine of origination is invoked for liability. The merits of this approach under present law in approximating performance lose their flexibility when applied to technological situations of stasis, i.e., where the doer arguably is doing nothing approaching origination, as in the majority view in *Fortnightly*. Apparent technological stasis then results in effective exemption comparable to the statutory juke-box exemption, unless cable systems are otherwise affected by Federal Communications Commission regulation.[228]

It is therefore submitted that the new technologies be studied in their various manifestations to determine what the results would be under proposed copyright revision, as to whether new uses would be deemed public or private, and if public, whether there should be additional exemptions granted with respect thereto. The study should consider the same under existing law as to whether the occur-

---

[228] See, Botein, Michael, CATV Regulation: A Jumble of Jurisdictions, 45 N.Y.U. L. Rev. 816 (1970), and Ozro, William Childs IV, The FCC's Proposed CATV Regulations, 21 Stan. L. Rev. 1685 (1967).

rences should be considered performances by reason of origination or passive excepted reception and whether these criteria are properly applicable thereto.[229]

Judge Herlands has written a veritable essay on the nature of performance by reason of the impact of broadcasting, in his opinion in *Fortnightly.* Further study should follow with respect to the revolution which may be around the corner in respect of the new technologies in audio-visual works, whether alone or in combination with broadcasting, cable systems, computers, and what-have-you.

---

[229] See, for example, Smith, Ralph Lee, The Wired Nation, A Special Issue of The Nation, dated May 18, 1970. Smith enumerates under his proposal for an electronic highway various functions cable might perform—home library services, facsimile data service, delivery of mail, crime detection and prevention, conferences and documentation by videophone in lieu of travel, p. 603. Add to this various audio-visual technologies, EVR, cassettes, discs, tapes, laser devices, and so on, which are not mentioned in the article, as well as computer innovations, and there is much to study. Indeed, will two-way communications so envisaged affect notions of performances under present law. Might the transaction of business by cable not turn the privacy of the home into an electronic office so that under proposed copyright revision reception as performance might also have enough non-profit characteristics, albeit in the home, so as to make such electronic devices in reception public performances susceptible of copyright liability.

Chapter XXV

FAIR USE AND INFRINGEMENT

Sec. 25.1. Fair Use and the First Amendment

Claims of infringement are met in a variety of ways, both procedural and substantive, as defenses thereto. The former pertain to legal and equitable considerations, be they defenses of statute of limitations, misjoinder of parties, improper party plaintiff, unclean hands and laches. The latter go to the merits of the claim, disputing, for example, the originality of claimant's copyrighted work, the fact of copying, i.e., alleging as a defense, taking of material from the public domain and not from the plaintiff's work, or that the asserted copyright is invalid by reason of failure to comply with the formalities of notice, etc.

Among the substantive defenses is an issue which is most difficult of articulation. The Court of Appeals for the Second Circuit has referred to the issue of fair use as " . . . the most troublesome in the whole law of copyright".[1] Nimmer has observed, "The scope and limits of this judge-made rule of reason are most obscure . . ."[2] The Register of Copyrights, in his first report on copy-

---

[1] Dellar v. Samuel Goldwyn, Inc., 104 F. 2d 661 (2d Cir. 1939), per curiam; Marvin Worth Productions v. Superior Film Corporation, 168 U.S.P.Q. 693, 697 (S.D.N.Y. 1970) refers to the "quicksilver concept of 'fair use.' "

[2] Nimmer on Copyright, Sec. 145, The Defense of Fair Use, at p. 643 (1970).

right revision in 1961, remarked, "The term eludes precise definition . . ." [3]

It is submitted that the doctrine of fair use represents such a limitation on the right inhering in the creator and assigns as to merit further exploration of its conceptual underpinnings. In this regard, Judge Wyatt recently referred to the doctrine of fair use as " . . . entirely equitable" and ". . . so flexible as virtually to defy definition." [4] Nimmer, on the other hand, refers to the "statutory privilege known as fair use".[5] According to him, "The scope and extent of fair use falls within the discretion of the Congress." [6]

Indeed, recent expressions of judicial concern as to the nature of the relationship of First Amendment guarantees of freedom of speech and press[7] were later examined in an overall context of the relationship of copyright to the First Amendment by Professor Nimmer.[8] Thus Judge Lumbard, in his concurring opinion in *Rosemont Enterprises, Inc.* v. *Random House, Inc.*[9], remarked as to plaintiff's attempt to

---

[3] Report of the Register of Copyrights on the General Revision of the U.S. Copyright Law in 2 Studies on Copyright pp. 1199-1346 at p. 1224 (1963).

[4] Time, Inc. v. Bernard Geis Associates, 293 F. Supp. 130, 144 (S.D.N.Y. 1968).

[5] Nimmer, Copyright vs The First Amendment, 17 Bull. Cr. Soc. 255, 275 (1970).

[6] *Ibid.*

[7] Concurring opinion of Chief Judge Lumbard, concurred in by Circuit Judge Hays in Rosemont Enterprises, Inc. v. Random House, Inc., 366 F. 2d 303 (2d Cir. 1966), *rev'g,* 256 F. Supp. 55 (S.D.N.Y. 1966), cert. den. 385 U.S. 1009 (1967); Hemingway v. Random House, Inc., 53 Misc. 2d 462, 279 N.Y.S. 2d 51 (Spec. T., N.Y. City, Pt. 1, 1967).

[8] Nimmer, *op. cit., supra,* note 5.

[9] Note 7, *supra.*

acquire the Look Magazine copyright in order to prevent publication of the Random House biography of Howard Hughes,

> "It would be contrary to the public interest to permit any man to buy up the copyright to anything written about himself and to use his copyright ownership to restrain others from publishing biographical material concerning him.
>
> "The *spirit* of the First Amendment applies to the copyright laws *at least* to the extent that the courts should not tolerate any attempted interference with the public's right to be informed regarding matters of general interest when anyone seeks to use the copyrighted statute which was designed to protect interests of quite a different nature."[10]

Again, the Court, in *Hemingway* v. *Random House, Inc.*[11], considered the constitutional impact of common law copyright in conversations, stating:

> "The effect on the freedom of speech and press would be revolutionary. It is a basic tradition of our society that, subject to certain limits not here pertinent, what any man says or does may be reported, quoted or written about in the interest of maintaining the *freedom of access* to all kinds of information which may be of legitimate interest. It is generally left to writers and publishers to determine what is of such interest. Only in rare cases does the law interfere with the freedom and then only to protect some paramount interest, such as the national security, or the individual's right to be free from malicious falsehood or invasion of privacy.

---

[10] *Idem* at p. 311 (emphasis added).

[11] Note 7, *supra.*

> The limitation drawn to protect such interests have generally been as narrow as the courts could make them."[12]

Indeed, Justice Schweitzer, in the same opinion, went even further. He remarks:

> "The justification for the privilege of fair use derives from the original rationale for copyright protection, as set forth in the Federal Constitution, (Art. 1, sec. 8), 'To promote the Progress of Science and useful Arts', including literature."[13]

Nimmer, in his address exploring the parameters of copyright in relation to the First Amendment, considered the even broader point, "If one adopts Justice Black's absolutist approach to the first amendment it is difficult to show how any copyright law can be regarded as constitutional."[14] Nimmer was referring to the literal language of the First Amendment, to wit, "Congress shall make no law . . . abridging the freedom of speech, or of the press . . ."[15] Nimmer noted that the existence of the copyright clause in the Constitution of the United States does not, *ipso facto,* sanctify it as an exception to the force of the First Amendment. He stated in this regard:

> "There are several reasons why refuge for copyright may not be found in this manner. First, if a completely

---

[12] *Idem* at p. 53 Misc. 2d at p. 470, 279 N.Y.S. 2d at p. 60 (emphasis added).

[13] *Idem* at p. 53 Misc. 2d at pp. 466-467, 279 N.Y.S. 2d at p. 57.

[14] Nimmer, *op. cit., supra,* note 5 at p. 256. The occasion for his address was the delivery of the Inaugural Donald C. Bruce Memorial Lecture on Copyright Law, delivered on March 16, 1970 in New York City, sponsored by the Copyright Society of the U.S.A.

[15] 5 Collier's Encyclopedia, Constitution of the United States, pp. 489-494, at p. 492 (1961).

> literal reading of the first amendment is to be made, then we must likewise recognize that the first amendment is an amendment, and hence supersedes anything inconsistent with it which may be found in the main body of the Constitution. This, of course, includes the copyright clause. In any event, even if the original Constitution and the Bill of Rights are viewed as a single instrument, the copyright clause may not be read as independent of and uncontrolled by the first amendment. Because Congress is granted authority to legislate in a given field, it does not follow that such a grant immunizes Congress from the limitations of the Bill of Rights, including the first amendment." [16]

Nimmer found his way out of this absolutist dilemma by pointing out, ". . . no one can responsibly adhere to the position that the first amendment must be literally construed so as to invalidate all laws which in any degree abridge speech." [17] Indeed, one might go further by way of the historical sequence of adoption of the Constitution, the first Copyright Act by Congress,[18] and the ratification of the Bill of Rights.

The Constitution was submitted to the several states for ratification in September, 1787. New Hampshire was the ninth state to ratify on June 21, 1788. The First Congress convened in April, 1789.[19] Opposition had arisen to ratifica-

---

[16] Nimmer, *op. cit., supra,* note 5, at p. 257.

[17] *Idem* at p. 258.

[18] Public Act of May 31, 1790, 1st Cong., 1st Sess. Chap. 15, set forth in Copyright Enactments, Laws Passed in the United States Since 1783 Relating to Copyright, Copyright Office, Bulletin No. 3 (Revised) (1963), at pp. 22-24.

[19] See, Heritage of Freedom, The History and Significance of the Basic Documents of American Liberty, by Frank Monaghan (1948) at p. 53; Bowen, Catherine Drinker, Miracle at Philadelphia, The

tion of the Constitution because it did not contain a Bill of Rights. Indeed, George Mason of Virginia had drafted a Proposed Declaration of Rights for the Constitution in 1788, Article 16 of which reads as follows:

> "That the people have a right to Freedom of Speech, and of Writing and publishing their Sentiments; that the Freedom of Press is one of the great bulwarks of Liberty, and ought not to be violated." [20]

Justice William O. Douglas pointed out, in a book written in 1954, "our most famous Bill of Rights goes back to June 12, 1776, the date Virginia adopted a *Declaration of Rights* drafted by George Mason. It guaranteed freedom of press and religion." [21] Indeed, Article 12 of the Virginia Bill of Rights of June 12, 1776 reads: "That the freedom of the press is one of the great bulwarks of liberty, and can never be restrained by despotick governments." [22]

It was James Madison who proposed amendments to the Constitution in the House of Representatives. On June 8, 1789, seventeen amendments were reported out by the House, which were then reduced to twelve by the Senate. These were adopted by a Joint Resolution of September 25, 1789. Ten of the twelve, but not the first two, were adopted by three-fourths of the states and became law as the Bill of Rights on December 15, 1791.[23]

Story of the Constitutional Convention, May to September 1787 (1966); The Federalist Papers #84, Mentor Book Ed., Introduction by Clinton Rossiter (1961); 3 Collier's Encyclopedia, Bill of Rights 317-321 (1960).

[20] Heritage of Freedom, *ibid.* Document 58, pp. 56-58 at p. 58.

[21] Douglas, William O., An Almanac of Liberty 361 (1954) (italics).

[22] Commager, Henry Steele, Documents of American History 103, 7th Ed. (1963).

[23] Note 19, *supra.*

It is to be noted that the amendatory process of the Bill of Rights straddled the passage of the first Copyright Act in point of time. Congress had passed the twelve amendments which were inclusive of the ten that became the Bill of Rights on September 25, 1789. This preceded the enactment of the first Copyright Act of May 31, 1790. The subsequent ratification in 1791 by the requisite number of states merely related to the date when the Bill of Rights became law as constitutional amendments. That is, Congress had expressed its intent as to the language of the Bill of Rights *prior* to the passage of the first Copyright Act. The Congress, therefore, had before it both the constitutional clause as to copyright and the passage of the Bill of Rights in the process of ratification when it considered the drafting of legislation relating to copyrights. Hence, it knew that copyright legislation would relate to the constitutional ambit of "exclusive rights to writings". The Constitutional Convention of 1787 included a great many of the principal figures in the fight for independence of the nation. They knew first-hand of abridgements of freedoms of speech and press prior to the American Revolution, and indeed, the reference in the Declaration of Independence of 1776 had this very much in mind. Mitchell and Louis Pearson Broadus aver, "Most of the state constitutions, formed during the war, were prefaced or accompanied by a bill of rights." [24] It is true, as they point out, "The convention busied itself to replace the feckless Confederation with a competent government; concern was with giving powers, not denying them. The framers at Philadelphia conceived their mandate to be political, not ethical." [25] After all, the Articles of Confederation had

[24] Broadus, Mitchell and Broadus, Louis Parsons, A Biography of the Constitution of the United States 190 (1964).

[25] *Idem* at pp. 188-189.

contained no such protection. But the proponents of the Bill of Rights would not be denied and prevailed.

The Bill of Rights may therefore be seen as a reaffirmation of profoundly political doctrine of freedoms wrought in the crucible of experience, notwithstanding the asservations of Alexander Hamilton in The Federalist that a Bill of Rights was unnecessary.[26] He stated there:

> "It has been several times truly remarked that bills of rights are, in their origin, stipulations between kings and their subjects, abridgements of prerogative in favor of privilege, reservations of rights not surrendered to the prince.
>
> • • •
>
> "It is evident, therefore, that, according to their primitive signification, they have no application to constitutions, professed upon the power of the people and executed by their immediate representatives and servants. Here, in strictness, the people surrender nothing; and as they retain everything they have no need of particular reservations." [27]

But it was the will of the Republic, probably in expression of safeguards against sovereign power, even in a democracy, that freedom of speech and press be expressly safeguarded and not merely reserved by implication. A phrase used by Diamond, Fisk and Garfinkel aptly expresses both concepts, to wit, "freedom of expression".[28] It encompasses both the aural as well as the visual, speech and press. Press may be equated in its broadest significance to writings. Thus, the

---

[26] The Federalist Papers, note 19, *supra.*

[27] *Idem* at pp. 512-513.

[28] Diamond, Martin, Fisk, Winston Mills, and Garfinkel, Herbert, The Democratic Republic, An Introduction to American National Government 434 (1966).

First Amendment was broader in its scope than the copyright clause of the Constitution[29] because it covered all kinds of expression, oral as well as written.

Sec. 25.2. Fair Comment

Nevertheless, the ambit of the First Amendment was political. It constituted a guarantee of political freedom constitutionally, viz., freedom of speech and press. There was to be liberty to speak and write as basic rights of the individual without encroachment by the sovereign, or, in terms of the democratic credo, by the organs of government entrusted with governance of the people. Milton R. Konvitz articulated the substance of this right when he wrote:

> "In addition to qualified privilege, newspapers have the right of fair comment, and may use this right as a defense to a charge of libelous defamation. Without the right of fair comment, there would be no freedom of the press. This right is enjoyed by any individual; it is not restricted to newspapers; and is available whether the statement is oral or written. The defense of fair comment must possess the following elements: The comment must be founded on facts, or what to a reasonable man would be acceptable as facts; it must be fair; it must not be made out of malice, but must be the result of honest opinion; the comment must be upon a subject of public interest. If the comment possesses these elements, it may be severe, caustic, bitter and even intemperate, for the comment does not purport to report objective facts but to be a subjective reaction to facts. The comment must be on a matter of public interest; it may not invade the privacy of a person under the guise of a comment on public affairs. The sub-

[29] Art. I, Sec. 8, Clause 8.

> ject of the comment may be candidates for public office, public officials, books, dramas, concerts, or any other public presentation." [30]

The substance of fair comment, then, is the right to speak out, orally or in writing, about any matter, upon a subject of public interest. Note that the last sentence in the quote referring to the scope of the right of commentary is very broad indeed, encompassing as it does, books, dramas, concerts and any other public presentation. Note, too, that the reference to the term "fair" therein is not to the sense of reasonable, but rather to the motivation of freedom from malice. In short, subject to individual safeguards against invasion of privacy, defamation, and presumably, the interest of the state in its own survival, i.e., safeguards against treason and sedition, it may be seen that fair comment is absolute. No law is to be made abridging this right to speak or write what one pleases within these limitations. Fair comment in this respect is not simply, via the First Amendment, the upholding of the right of the people to speak out, a kind of affirmation of the democratic ethic, reduced to the ultimate in the right to be cantankerous. Fair comment goes further. William O. Douglas has written, "But the most important aspect of freedom of speech is freedom to learn. . ." [31] The First Amendment in this regard provides a forum for learning in that, by permitting fair comment, it allows for freedom in the market place of ideas. The state may not legislate permissible thinking because the Bill of Rights, via the First Amendment, prohibits infringements of the freedoms of the populace in this respect to select and arrange its thoughts as it sees fit. By thus out-

[30] Konvitz, Milton R. Fundamental Liberties of a Free People: Religion, Speech, Press, Assembly (1957), at pp. 143-4.

[31] Douglas, *op. cit., supra,* note 21, at p. 363.

lawing proscribed thinking and writing, the First Amendment permits the learning process to thrive because fair comment denotes freedom of discussion, freedom of expression.

Indeed, it is in the mechanics of fair comment that the rationale for fair use may be seen to originate. Fair comment means the right to discuss the sayings and writings of others. In order to do this, one must be able to refer thereto. It is submitted in this regard that Judge Learned Hand's definition, set forth in a context of stories, fiction and dramatic works, is not apposite. He stated in *Sheldon* v. *Metro-Goldwyn Pictures Corp.* as to fair use, ". . . but it is convenient to define such a use by saying that others may 'copy' the 'theme', or 'ideas', or the like, of a work, though not its 'expression'." [32]

But fair comment imports the right to refer to the speech and writings of others. It imports the right to discuss and criticize. In order to do this, it must be able to deal with specifics, the text of others. Essentially Judge Learned Hand posits the permissible beyond the line of his abstractions test for determining infringement.[33] But the viewpoint of fair comment is concern with the specific writing or speech at issue. Fair comment implies the right to be able to discuss the expression of the particular subject or commentary. This, in turn, implies the right to reproduce the expression in order to be able to discuss it. Criticism, then, as an off-shoot of fair comment, carries with it the right of quotation, paraphrase, or both. Freedom to consider is thus constitutionally guaranteed and would seem to be the fundamental basis underlying the doctrine of fair use.

[32] 81 F. 2d 49, 54 (2d Cir. 1936).

[33] See Nichols v. Universal Pictures Corp., 45 F. 2d 119 (2d Cir. 1930), L. Hand, *J.*

Sec. 25.3. Uses and Fair Use

To cast the concept of fair use as a notion of equity, pure and simple,[34] would seem to fly in the face of the Constitution, granting authors exclusive rights in their writings. Judge Wyatt, in *Time, Inc.* v. *Bernard Geiss Associates*[35], would differentiate the exclusive rights granted by statutory copyright from the exclusive right to use such work. He states, "Unlike the owner of a patent (35 U.S.C. Sec. 154), the owner of a copyright is not given by statute (17 U.S.C. Sec. 1) any exclusive rights to use the work. The word 'use' does not appear in the statute." [36] But just how does one use a work? Indeed, differing uses of the work are what copyright is all about. The statute accords copyright in other versions and arrangements.[37] By the process of subsumption, the generic exclusive rights of Sec. 1 of the Copyright Act[38] comprehend specific uses that are not spelled out in the statute, e.g., synchronization rights, motion picture rights, television rights. These are all uses, but are species of production and performing rights.

Of course, a distinction must be made between the uses in respect of the physical property and the copyright therein. Thus, under Sec. 27[39] of the Copyright Act, the physical property is separate and distinct from the copyright. Therefore, the copyright proprietor of a book cannot control its resale by imposing limitations thereon.[40] But the copyright proprietor can prevent other uses by the purchaser of the book that are exclusively in the creator and assigns. He

---

[34] Time, Inc. v. Bernard Geis Associates, note 4, *supra.*

[35] *Idem* at p. 144.

[36] *Ibid.*

[37] 17 U.S.C. 1(b), 7.

[38] 17 U.S.C. 1.

[39] 17 U.S.C. 27.

[40] Bobbs-Merrill Co. v. Straus, 210 U.S. 339 (1908).

can prevent, in addition to copying, the making of other versions, i.e., derivative works, as well as public performance thereof if the book be dramatic, and public performance for profit, if the work be non-dramatic. If the book is under copyright, the purchaser of a copy may not adapt a film or TV show, a play therefrom or even read the book publicly for profit if it be nondramatic. It would seem, therefore, that the section does not convey an exclusive right of use, per se, does not mean that, in fact, the Copyright Act does not cover a great many exclusive uses.

Equity draws its sustenance, in the face of exclusivity as enunciated in the statute—and, indeed, the Constitution—when the same use, media-wise, is contemplated, because there is some underlying ground of recognition of the reasonableness of the use notwithstanding the statutory grant. One court seeks to draw this rationale from the very constitutional clause which gives the Congress power to grant rights of copyright, namely, Article I, Section 8, "To promote the Progress of Science and useful Arts."[41] It is submitted that this clause is modified immediately thereafter by the phrase, "by securing, for limited times, to authors . . . , the exclusive right to their . . . writings . . ."[42] The clause must be read as a whole. Promotion of learning, as expressed in the first part, cannot be cut off from the instrumental portion of the clause, which sets forth the means of implementation thereof, to wit, by exclusive right of copyright. Otherwise, one arrives at a conclusion that appears to be a contradiction in terms. Promotion of science and the useful arts sanctions fair use which is antithetical to the very exclusivity of copyright granted for achieving such promotion. Of course, it can be argued under one theory that fair use is technically infringement because it

---

[41] Hemingway v. Random House, Inc., note 7, *supra*.

[42] Constitution of the United States, Art. I, Sec. 8, Clause 8.

flies in the face of the exclusive right, but that the infringement is so small as to be *de minimis* and therefore not worthy of legal consideration.[43]

Sec. 25.4. Substantiality Test: The Patent Rule

Variants of this appear to be the theme or idea vs. expression test of Judge Learned Hand[44] or the substantiality test.[45] The Hand test would come about by taking non-copyrightable components[46] of a work, to wit, its theme or idea, and therefore such taking is not copying because the theme or idea is in the public domain and not per se protectible. Inherent in this theory is probably the notion of *de minimis.* If incidental, small references are taken, their very minimality excludes infringement.

The Hand definition is probably also a variant of the substantiality test. This, it appears, draws sustenance from the law of patents. In *G. Ricordi & Co.* v. *Mason,* the Court stated:

> "No one, for instance, infringes a claim for a machine unless he uses a similar machine operating in substantially the same manner and producing a like result by the same or equivalent means. A model of a machine incapable of producing any practical result does not

---

[43] See Needham, Roger, Tape Recording, Photocopying and Fair Use, 10 Copyright Law Symposium 75 (1959); Shapiro, Bernstein v. P. F. Collier & Son, Co., 26 U.S.P.Q. 40 (S.D.N.Y. 1934); Nimmer, *op. cit., supra,* note 2, Sec. 145.

[44] Sheldon v. Metro-Goldwyn Pictures Corp., note 32, *supra.* See also Shipman v. RKO Radio Pictures, Inc., 100 F. 2d 533 (2d Cir. 1938), where Judge Manton referred to *Sheldon* and stated that "Fair use is defined as copying the theme or ideas rather than their expression.", at p. 537.

[45] G. Ricordi & Co. v. Mason, 201 Fed. 184 (S.D.N.Y. 1912).

[46] 17 U.S.C. 3.

> infringe any more than the brief synopsis of an opera infringes the author's copyright."[47]

The Court had in mind a practicality test. In patents, it is by means of engineering that the doctrine of equivalence comes about, i.e., similar machines operating in substantially the same manner and producing like results. In that case, it was held that, practically speaking, the opera synopsis did not perform the same function and therefore was not a version of the opera, so that it did not infringe.

But the mechanical test of equivalents of patent law runs into conceptual difficulties when translated into copyright norms. Functionalism as a test of fair use inevitably leads to economic and market tests as in *Mason.* This appears from *Hill* v. *Whalen & Martell, Inc.*,[48] the so-called Mutt and Jeff case. Plaintiff was the proprietor of the Mutt and Jeff cartoons. Defendant performed dramatically by use of characters named "Nutt" and "Giff". The Court rejected a defense of parody or burlesque, stating,

> "One test which, when applicable, would seem to be ordinarily decisive, is whether or not so much as has been reproduced as will materially reduce the demand for the original. If it has, the rights of the owner of the copyright have been injuriously affected . . . The reduction in demand, to be a ground of complaint, must result from the partial satisfaction of that demand by the alleged infringing production. A criticism of the original work, which lessened its money value by showing that

---

[47] G. Ricordi & Co. v. Mason, 201 Fed. 182, 183 (C.C. S.D.N.Y. 1911). This opinion related to denial of a motion for a preliminary injunction. The opinion in note 45, *supra,* was on the merits.

[48] 220 Fed. 359 (S.D.N.Y. 1914).

> it was not worth seeing or hearing, could not give any right of action for infringement of copyright."[49]

The defendant was held to have infringed.

Judge Goddard has articulated the economic test inherent therein in the oft-quoted passage from *Shapiro, Bernstein* v. *P.F. Collier & Son Co.* wherein he stated,

> "Without attempting to lay down any hard and fast rule for determining what constitutes a 'fair use' of a copyrighted matter, the following are generally considered as some of the tests to be applied. The extent and relative value of the extracts; the purpose and whether the quoted portions might be used as a substitute for the original work; the effect upon the distribution and objects of the original work."[50]

There the quotation of part of the lyrics was held to be incidental and background and, therefore, a fair use.

Purpose of use and economic results thereof are taken into consideration. Thus, a teacher preparing memoranda or outlines from Taussig's "Principles of Economics" could not escape the publisher's complaint of infringement because the use was injurious.[51] Exploitation of three sentences from a scientific work for use for cigarette ads was held to advance a commercial purpose not contemplated by the author.[52] Quotation of lyrics as part of a eulogy in the New Yorker was held to be fair use upon a comparison of

---

[49] *Idem* at p. 360.

[50] Note 43, *supra,* at p. 43.

[51] Macmillan Co. v. King, 223 Fed. 862 (D. Mass. 1914).

[52] Holt & Co., Inc. v. Liggett and Myers Tobacco Co., 23 F. Supp. 302 (E.D. Pa. 1938).

purpose. The resulting quotation in the context was incidental and called fair comment.[53]

Sec. 25.5. Music and Fair Use

But as soon as music enters the picture, fair use appear to be severely restricted. Thus in *Associated Music Publishers, Inc.* v. *Debs,*[54] the use of one entire part of a four part composition, for some six minutes, one third of the entire work, was held not to be a fair use. Indeed, substantial copying was held to have taken place where two bars of music were used which were identical with two of four bars of plaintiff's key melody. Two other bars of defendant were strikingly similar to plaintiff's key melodic phrase. The result was held to be substantial copying.[55] Contrast this use of music with lyrical uses without music. In *Karll* v. *Curtis Publishing Company,*[56] eight lines of plaintiff's copyrighted song entitled "Go! You Packers, Go!" were embodied in an article in the Saturday Evening Post on the Green Bay Packers football team. The result was held to be a fair use. No music was reproduced. The material was not competitive. The reference to the chorus of the song was incidental and no sale or individual use of the chorus was involved. The article was unrelated to musical endeavor.

Sec. 25.6. The Research Test

At the other extreme is the degree of latitude allowed where knowledge—processes, directories, law books, history, etc.—as distinct from literary works, is concerned. A re-

---

[53] Broadway Music Corporation v. P.R. Publishing Corporation, 31 F. Supp. 817 (S.D.N.Y. 1940).

[54] 46 F. Supp. 829 (S.D.N.Y. 1942).

[55] Robertson v. Batten, Barton, Durstine & Osborn, Inc., 146 F. Supp. 795 (S.D. Cal. 1956).

[56] 39 F. Supp. 836 (E.D. Wis. 1941).

search test is adumbrated. As stated by the Court of Appeals for the Second Circuit in *Nutt* v. *National Institute, Inc.,*[57] ". . . the test is whether the one charged with the infringement has made an independent production, or made a substantial and unfair use of the complainant's work." There plaintiff's copyrighted lectures on how to improve memory were held to have been infringed. Again, in *College Entrance Book Co., Inc.* v. *Amsco Book Co., Inc.,*[58] copying of less than 15% of printed matter in the copying of lists from plaintiff's book of French preparation for Regents' exams was held to constitute infringement. The Court stated, "Both plaintiff's and defendant's books met exactly the same demand on the same market, and defendant's copying was unquestionably to avoid the trouble or expense of independent work. This is an unfair use." [59]

A later work on the law of eminent domain was held to have infringed an earlier work and the author of the later work was held to have done little more than edit and bring the plaintiff's work up to date.[60] There the Court said, "Appropriation of the fruits of another's labor and skill in order to publish a rival work without the expenditure of the time and effort required for independently arrived at results is copyright infringement." [61]

Here, too, the research test requires the requisite digging independently. Where a second biographer failed to go to her own sources, in connection with the life of Hans Christian Andersen, but unduly relied on plaintiff's work, there

---

[57] 31 F. 2d 236, 237 (2d Cir. 1929), *aff'g* 28 F. 2d 132 (D. Conn. 1928). See also, W. H. Anderson v. Baldwin Law Pub. Co., 27 F. 2d 82 (6th Cir. 1928).

[58] 119 F. 2d 874 (2d Cir. 1941).

[59] *Idem* at p. 876.

[60] Orgel v. Clark Boardman Co., 301 F. 2d 119 (2d Cir. 1962), cert. den. 371 U.S. 817 (1962).

[61] *Idem* at p. 120.

was held to be infringement thereof.[62] The Court cited the test in *Nutt*, "... whether one charged with the infringement has made an independent production, or made a substantial and unfair use of the complainant's work." [63] But the matter of such independent digging ultimately is decided as a question of fact. Concomitantly, fair use is a question of fact.[64] Consequently, the courts are reluctant to determine questions of fair use on the pleadings. The Court of Appeals for the Second Circuit, in *MacDonald* v. *Du Maurier*,[65] reversed and remanded a motion for judgment on the pleadings which was granted dismissing the complaint. Although it held it was not necessary to go to trial, it felt that on a motion for summary judgment, under Rule 56 of the Federal Rules of Civil Procedure, there would have to be affidavits setting forth the facts. In *Thompson* v. *Gernsback*,[66] the Court denied a motion for summary judgment even though it did not believe that defendant's magazine was a scientific document or a work of science. Since the defendant may possibly have raised triable issues by way of defense of fair use, and other pleaded defenses, the motion was denied. To like effect, a motion for summary judgment was denied in *New York Tribune, Inc.* v. *Otis & Co.*, the Court stating, "On the whole, I am persuaded that the determination of the 'fair use' should not be resolved on affidavits but is best left to the trial judge." [67] It would seem that the courts are concerned about short cuts to determination of fair use.

---

[62] Toksvig v. Bruce Pub. Co., 181 F. 2d 664 (7th Cir. 1950).

[63] *Idem* at p. 667.

[64] See Eisenschiml v. Fawcett Publications, Inc., 246 F. 2d 598 (7th Cir. 1957), cert. den. 355 U.S. 907 (1957); Greenbie v. Noble, 151 F. Supp. 45 (S.D.N.Y. 1957); Holdredge v. Knight Publishing Corporation, 214 F. Supp. 921 (S.D. Cal. 1963).

[65] 144 F. 2d 696 (2d Cir. 1944).

[66] 94 F. Supp. 453 (S.D.N.Y. 1950).

[67] 39 F. Supp. 67, 68 (S.D.N.Y. 1941).

In *Collins* v. *Metro-Goldwyn Pictures Corp.,*[68] the lower court had compared a cutting continuity—scenario—to determine whether or not a film had infringed plaintiff's book. The court below held there was no infringement, but it never saw the film. The court, on appeal, reversed and remanded because there first had to be a determination that the cutting continuity correctly represented the film if it were to be used without the judge seeing the film. Justice Augustus N. Hand stated, for the Second Circuit, "We are not, however, satisfied that the parties ever agreed that the continuity is a fair representation of the film . . . For this reason we think that the decree must be reversed and the cause remanded . . . If upon the new hearing the judge should determine that the continuity is a fair representation of the motion picture, he should dismiss the complaint. A view of the picture may be the best means of reaching a satisfactory conclusion." [69]

This would appear to follow because the research test, in effect, is a restatement of the law of infringement as applied to the defense of fair use. In *Matthews Conveyor Company* v. *Palmer-Bee Company*[70] the Court concluded that sketches of defendant did not infringe copyrighted photographs of bearings. The Court set forth the criteria of infringement, stating:

> "From numerous cases it may be concluded that in order to sustain an action for infringement of copyright, a substantial copy of the whole, or a material part, must be reproduced . . . On the principal of de minimis non curat lex, it is necessary that a substantial part of the copyrighted work be taken . . . Among criteria for as-

---

[68] 106 F. 2d 83 (2d Cir. 1939).

[69] *Idem* at p. 87. See Dellar v. Samuel Goldwyn,Inc., note 1, *supra,* at p. 662.

[70] 135 F. 2d 73 (6th Cir. 1943).

certaining infringement, which have been mentioned by the courts, are whether so much has been taken as would sensibly diminish the value of the original; and whether the labors of the party entitled to copyright are substantially to an injurious extent appropriated by another." [71]

At this point the Court presented a parallelism. It continued:

"Like rules are applicable to the so-called fair use which may be made of copyrighted material, based upon the principle that subsequent workers in the same field are not deprived of all use thereof, as, otherwise, the progress of science and the useful arts would be unduly obstructed. Fair use is to be determined by a consideration of all the evidence, and among other elements entering into the determination of the issue, are the extent and relative value of copyrighted material, and the effect upon the distribution of objects of the original work. . . . Whether a particular use of a copyrighted article, without permission of the owner is a fair use, depends upon the circumstances of the particular case, and the court must look to the nature and objects of the selections made, the quantity and value of material used, and the degree in which the use may prejudice the sale, diminish the profits, or supersede the objects of the original work." [72]

Sec. 25.7. The De Minimis Test

The quoted excerpts are most interesting. For one thing, the language suggests the possibility that fair use is merely the obverse of infringement, i.e., insubstantial taking. If

---

[71] *Idem* at pp. 84-85.
[72] *Idem* at p. 85.

fair use is no more than a rule of *de minimis,* then it would seem not to be much more than a restatement of non-infringement by reason of insubstantial taking. Secondly, the langage provides strong support for not deciding the defense of infringement upon pleadings. If the defense is to be determined upon all the evidence, then the defendant is entitled to the opportunity to present sufficient facts which might throw the balance his way. Trial to sort the facts, possibly stipulation of facts, or at least, minimally, affidavits setting forth purported statements of facts may be necessary for a determination. Thirdly, the language emphasizes the strong nature of the economic or market tests in determining fair use.

Most importantly, the language seems to adumbrate a sort of constitutional conveyor belt of copyright theory. To the extent fair use may comprehend uses over and above *de minimis,* which are not deemed infringements, then the rationale for use is in the constitutional power in Congress to promote the progress of science and the useful arts. Fair use is justified under this view permissibly in tandem with the instrumental part of the clause, because fair use would enable the fair users to have copyright in their works. Subsequently acquired copyright in B is justified in his fair use of A's earlier copyright because it is permitted as promotion of the later copyright. So, too, D might come along in fair use of C's work in promotion of D's copyright thereafter. The power of Congress is deemed the source of fair use under this theory and a limitation on the instrumental clause, the securing of copyright, i.e., exclusive rights, to writers in their writings for limited terms.

Sec. 25.8. Fair Use and Common Law Copyright

But what about common law copyright? It is patent that Congress can pre-empt the entire copyright field and subsume both types of copyright under the Constitution. Proposed copyright revision seeks to place control of both published and unpublished works under the federal law.[73] Under present law, Sec. 2 of the Copyright Act relegates protection of unpublished works to the proprietor under local law.[74] If fair use stemmed inexorably from the constitutional power of Congress to promote the progress of the science and the useful arts, should it then be applicable comparably in terms of common law copyright? Yet the California state court has stated in *Golding* v. *RKO Radio Pictures, Inc.*:

> "A dispute exists between the parties as to whether the test to be applied here—a case of alleged piracy of unpublished copyrighted material—is the same as that applied in cases of alleged piracy of copyrighted material. The test for determining whether there is piracy is the same in both cases. The only distinction between the two classes of cases is that the law permits 'fair use' of copyrighted material. It does not permit 'fair use' of unpublished, uncopyrighted material . . . The privilege of 'fair use' accorded in statutory copyrighted cases is not accorded by the common law in the case of unpublished works and the author has exclusive control of his work." [75]

Contrariwise, the Court in *Hemingway* v. *Random House, Inc.*[76], in discussing the use of letters by the recipient, apparently pulled away from the rule insofar as use was concerned. The writer of a letter can prevent verbatim

[73] See S. 543, 91st Cong., 1st Sess., Jan. 22, 1969, Dec. 10, 1969 print, Sec. 301.

[74] 17 U.S.C. 2.

[75] 193 P. 2d 153 (Dist. Co. App., 2nd Dist., Div. 3, Calif. 1948), at pp. 162-163, *aff'd* 208 P2d 1 (Supreme Ct., Cal. 1949).

[76] 53 Misc. 2d 462, 279 N.Y.S. 2d 51 (Spec. T., N.Y. Cty., Pt. I, 1967).

copying but his control does not extend to contents not amounting to copying. Thus, the bounds of fair use have been extended to include, presumably, reference thereto without copying. This rule would seem to be in accord with the use of primary material of a similar nature, i.e., letters and other communications, given as archives to a library by the recipient thereof. Presumably the sender or author of the epistles could not prevent reference thereto by the scholar as a fair use.

It would seem, too, that the doctrine that fair use is inapplicable to common law copyright would be eroded by the line of cases holding that common law copyright is not lost by mere performance because performance per se does not constitute a publication.[77] This would mean that a drama critic could not quote from a play that he has reviewed but which was never copyrighted. The result is obviously untenable on its face—on constitutional grounds. The First Amendment grants this right. As Judge Goddard has stated, "Dramatic criticism is one of the most common forms of 'fair use' ".[78] The source of the right would not be in the copyright, which, hypothetically, is common law. It would appear that the rationale therefor is in the First Amendment, in the right of fair comment. The illogic of the situation may appear from the juxtaposition of *Mura* v. *Columbia Broadcasting System, Inc.*[79] with our hypothetical situation. In *Mura,* the use of plaintiff's copyrighted puppets on defendant's Captain Kangaroo Show was held to be evanescent and not a copy, an incidental fair use. But if the puppets were uncopyrighted, the

---

[77] Ferris v. Frohman, 223 U.S. 424 (1912). See Nimmer, *op. cit., supra,* note 2, Sec. 53.

[78] Shapiro, Bernstein v. P. F. Collier & Son Co., 26 U.S.P.Q. 40 (S.D.N.Y. 1934), at p. 42.

[79] 245 F. Supp. 587 (S.D.N.Y. 1965).

defense of fair use could not apply because of the doctrine that fair use is inapplicable to common law copyright. One suspects that the defendants in such a suit would dispense with the defense of fair use and simply state that the use was evanescent, did not constitute a copy and was *de minimis*. In short, the same result would be sought to be achieved without characterizing the defense as fair use.

Sec. 25.9. Mimicry and Parody

In *Collier,* Judge Goddard also adverted, "Mimicry, editorial comment, and parodies are other varieties or instances of 'fair use'." [80] But it was in connection with parodies that Judge Carter drew out the inherent contradiction between the rationale of fair use and copyright exclusivity. In the case in which Jack Benny sought unsuccessfully to parody the film "Gaslight", *Loew's, Incorporated* v. *Columbia Broadcasting System, Inc.,*[81] Judge Carter stated:

> "The mere absence of competition or injurious affect upon the copyrighted work will not make a use fair. The right of a copyright proprietor to exclude others is absolute and if it has been violated the fact that the infringement will not affect the sale or exploitation of the work or pecuniarily damage him is immaterial." [82]

Notwithstanding this observation, Judge Carter determined the result upon the degree of use. Broader use is permitted

---

[80] Note 78, *supra,* at p. 42.

[81] 131 F. Supp. 165 (S.D. Cal. 1955), *aff'd* 239 F. 2d 532 (9th Cir. 1956), *aff'd per curiam* 356 U.S. 43 (1958) by an equally divided court.

[82] *Idem* at p. 184.

as to scientific and learned works. He noted, however, "As we draw further away from the fields of science or pure or fine arts, and enter the fields where business competition exists we find the scope of *fair use* is narrowed but still exists." [83] He observed that one could take an incident, a character, a theme, or bare plot and create new burlesque so long as one didn't take a substantial part. In effect, he followed the rationale of *Green* v. *Luby*.[84] There defendant sang plaintiff's copyrighted song on stage purporting to mimic the complainant. The Court there held for the plaintiff, stating:

> "The mimicry is said to be the important thing; the particular song, the mere incident. But I am not satisfied that, in order to imitate a singer, it is necessary to sing the whole of a copyrighted song." [85]

Indeed, the Ninth Circuit, in affirming the *Jack Benny* case, picturesquely described parody as substantial copying, by stating:

> "The fact that a serious dramatic work is copied practically verbatim, and then presented with actors walking on their hands or with other grotesqueries, does not avoid infringement of the copyright." [86]

By contrast, Judge Carter, in *Columbia Pictures Corp.* v. *National Broadcasting Co.*,[87] held that the parody of the film, "From Here To Eternity" by a television sketch, "From Here To Obscurity" was fair use because the taking was

---

[83] *Idem* at p. 175. (italics).
[84] 177 Fed. 287 (C.C. S.D.N.Y. 1909).
[85] *Idem* at p. 288.
[86] 239 F. 2d 532, 536 (9th Cir. 1956).
[87] 137 F. Supp. 348 (S.D. Cal. 1955).

insubstantial. The Judge set forth a pattern for judgment, as follows: (a) Serious work from other serious work, the line is drawn more strictly than farce or comedy or burlesque from serious work or vice versa; (b) In historical burlesques, a part of the content is used to conjure up at least the general image of the original. "Some limited taking should be permitted under the doctrine of fair use, in the case of burlesque, to bring about this recalling or conjuring up of the original.";[88] (c) Burlesque may take locale, theme, a setting, or a situation and even bare basic plot without infringement, since the same is ordinarily not protectible; (d) "The doctrine of fair use permits burlesque to go somewhat farther so long as the taking is not substantial. It may take an incident of the copyrighted story, a developed character (subject to the limited right of an author in certain situations), . . . a title (subject to right of protection under unfair competition), . . . some small part of the development of the story, possibly some small amount of the dialogue.":[89] (e) When one takes more, one runs the risk of substantial taking; and (f) The defense of burlesque per se is not a defense.

The *Jack Benny* case had the unforeseen effect of confusing its result of infringement with the means employed by the infringer, i.e., parody. Thus, in the *Mad Magazine* case, *Berlin* v. *E.C. Publications, Inc.*,[90] Judge Metzner cited the *Jack Benny* case as well as the *Mutt and Jeff* case, *Hill* v. *Whalen & Martell,* stating, "It is clear that a parody of a copyrighted work is an infringement of the copyright."[91] Judge Metzner, however, felt that the use of lyrics

[88] *Idem* at p. 350.
[89] *Ibid.*
[90] 219 F. Supp. 911 (S.D.N.Y. 1963).
[91] *Idem* at p. 913.

in Mad Magazine in a take off on Irving Berlin's tunes was not such as to permit granting of plaintiff's motion for summary judgment. He contrasted lyrical paraphrase in *Leo Feist, Inc.* v. *Song Parodies, Inc.*[92] (where, incidentally, the parodies were competing for the same market), and mere satire. To reach his result, he distinguished satire from parody, stating, "Defendants have not parodied plaintiffs' lyrics. Rather, they have satirized, in original words and thought, several aspects of modern life."[93]

The broad scope attributed to the ruling in the *Jack Benny* case evidently troubled Judge Irving Kaufman on appeal in the *Mad Magazine* case. He indicated that the extent the parodist may borrow is unsettled. He referred to the substantiality test of the *Jack Benny* case and criticized the holding and dictum there that parody could not be justified as fair use, stating:

> ". . . where, as here, it is clear that the parody has neither the intent nor the effect of fulfilling the demand for the original, and where the parodist does not appropriate a greater amount of the original work than is necessary to 'recall or conjure up' the object of his satire, a finding of infringement would be improper."[94]

One suspects that the taking of exception may have been due to the fact of the formulation of the result rather than possibly to the result itself. Had the *Jack Benny* case held simply that the taking was so substantial as to constitute infringement, then the fact of copying, without more, would have determined the result. The means of infringement,

---

[92] 146 F. 2d 400 (2d Cir. 1944).
[93] Note 90, *supra* at p. 914.
[94] 329 F. 2d 541, 545 (2d Cir. 1964).

in any event, is by substantial copying. How the defending party chooses to characterize what he has done as a defense is ultimately immaterial if such a result is determined. It is immaterial that an infringing defendant calls his taking parody, burlesque, mimicry, scholarship, learning, or any other category of alleged fair use. Upon a determination of infringement, the character of the alleged defense becomes immaterial, because, whatever the term used for the purported defense, the judicial determination is otherwise. This does not mean that in a given case the asserted term used as a defense could not be properly used. The breakdown of the various facets of parody and burlesque by Judge Carter in *Columbia Pictures Corp.* v. *National Broadcasting Co.*[95] would indicate the contrary. Rather it indicates that courts will not be content with labels, but go behind them to the substance of the use.

Sec. 25.10. Television

Indeed, Judge Carter's reference to the absolute right of the copyright proprietor to exclude others goes to the heart of the matter. In *Mura*, the use of plaintiff's copyrighted puppets on the Captain Kangaroo Show on television was held to be an incidental, fair use. But puppets presumably perform. Jack Benny's parody of "Gaslight" was also a performance. Under Sec. 1 of the Copyright Act,[96] it was held to be an infringing performance. Of course, in *Mura,* there was the additional contention that the projection of the puppet on television was not a copy because it was evanescent. That defense pertained, however, only to Sec. 1(a),[97] in respect of the exclusive right to

[95] Note 87, *supra.*
[96] 17 U.S.C. 1.
[97] 17 U.S.C. 1(a).

make copy, one of the so-called publishing rights. But infringing performance, be it non-dramatic under Sec. 1(c)[98] or dramatic under Section 1(d)[99], where as to both there is public performance and as to the former also for profit performance, is also an infringement of the exclusive rights and a form of copying in the generic sense in that the copyrighted work is allegedly performed, i.e., utilized by way of representation, without authorization. Copying in this sense refers to the substantial taking of the copyrighted material by any means which is a violation of the exclusive rights, be it by copying in the sense of reproduction in the form of copies, or performing or making other versions.

The *Mura* case appears to follow the rationale espoused by Warner, who stated:

> ". . . it is believed that the doctrine of fair use should be invoked by the courts particularly if the reproductions occasionally appear throughout the live telecast. It is believed that the doctrine of fair use should apply even if the reproductions are more than occasional reproductions. This is premised on the philosophy that transitory images cannot compete or interfere with the rights secured by Section 1(a) of the Copyright Code . . .
>
> • • •
>
> "But if the unauthorized exhibition of a film does not infringe the printing, publishing and vending rights, because it is not a copy, it follows that the reproductions of copyrighted works viewed in the television

[98] 17 U.S.C. 1(c).
[99] 17 U.S.C. 1(d).

home receiver is not a copy. The same argument can be made, viz., that the transitory images from a televised film do not compete with the original work. Thus a television station could make a persuasive argument that the reproductions in a receiver from a televised film are not copies, or if they are copies, they constitute a fair and not an infringing use of the copyrighted work." [100]

The difficulty with such an approach is that the ultimate result would be that television could not infringe unless the performance were embodied in concrete form, e.g., film or tape, and even then, under the second portion of the quote above, there would only be transitory images. The same could be said about film projection in a theatre, viz., that the performance is transitory. *A fortiori*, the live, legitimate theatre production could not be more transitory. It is seen and then is gone. It is submitted that in each instance use by performance by substantial taking would be infringing performance, otherwise the grant of exclusive performance rights in the statute would be rendered a nullity. It is one thing to consider the scope of infringement by copying, i.e., the making of a copy. It is another to consider that the statute provides other exclusive rights, such as the right of performance. It is true that the decision in *White-Smith Publishing Co.* v. *Apollo Co.*[101] held that a piano roll did not constitute a copy and that until recently the Copyright Office would not register phonograph records for copyright.[102] But, Sec.

---

[100] Warner, Harry P., Radio and Television Rights, Sec. 153 at p. 623 (1953).

[101] 209 U.S. 1 (1909).

[102] Regulations of the Copyright Office, Sec. 202.8(b). Cf. Public Law 92-140, 92d Cong., S. 646, which authorizes copyright in sound recordings from and after February 15, 1972 and prior to January 1, 1975.

1(e)[103] grants the exclusive right of mechanical reproduction in music in the first such use, after which the work is subject to the compulsory license. Moreover, there is no compulsory license with respect to reproduction by mechanical means as to dramatic works.[104]

This is not to say that an incidental use on television might not in fact be a fair use if it is non-competitive, background and without commercial significance. The test is basically the same as elsewhere, whether the copyright has been invaded to the point that liability should be imposed. While this may sound circular in that it tells us nothing about what is fair use as opposed to infringement, it indicates that possibly infringement and fair use are proceeding from two separate norms rather than the single norm of infringement modified, somehow, by judicial considerations of equity. The latter rule posits the notion that the copyright statute granting exclusivity may sometimes be unduly harsh to the point of contravening other norms of public policy and interest, e.g., learning and scholarship, or perhaps even the carrying on of orderly governmental and judicial proceedings by the ability to introduce copyrighted matter into evidence as exhibits.

Sec. 25.11. Fair Use and Consent

Equity as a source for the rationale draws upon a legal fiction at times to reach its result. Rights in others are presumed to fairly use the material. As stated in *Holt & Co., Inc.* v. *Liggett and Myers Tobacco Co.,* "It is true that the law permits those working in a field of science or art to make use of ideas, opinions, or theories, and in

[103] 17 U.S.C. 1(e).
[104] 17 U.S.C. 1(d).

certain cases even the exact words contained in a copyrighted book in that field . . . This is permitted in order . . . 'that the world may not be deprived of improvements, nor the progress of the arts be retarded.' In such cases the law implies the consent of the copyright owner to a fair use of his publication for the advancement of the science or art."[105] The notion of implied consent was carried even further in *Towle* v. *Ross* where the Court said, "There is no fair or non-competing use of copyright material unless by consent."[106] The Court footnoted that quote as follows:

> "The doctrine of 'fair usage' means that the matter which was under copyright was neither copied nor adopted, but that the underlying uncopyrightable idea was used. 'A theme or idea is of course not copyrightable.' Shipman v. R.K.O. Radio Pictures, Inc., D.C. 20 F. Supp. 249, 250. Again 'fair usage' may apply to works for the advancement of science, where 'to a certain extent by common consent, including the implied consent of the first publisher, others interested in advancing the same art or science may commence where the prior author stopped.' Sampson & Murdock v. Seaver-Radford Co., 1 Cir., 240 F. 539, 541."[107]

In *Towle,* a map was held to have been infringed by a photographic reproduction thereof.

It would seem that, in fact, the proprietor does not expressly consent, as such, to fair use. If a publisher were to be asked whether he would permit quotes for purposes of learning and scholarship, he might agree to grant per-

---

[105] 23 F. Supp. 302, 304 (E.D. Pa. 1938).
[106] 32 F. Supp. 125, 127 (D. Ore. 1940).
[107] *Idem,* fn. 4 at p. 127.

mission provided credit is accorded in the quoting work to the effect that permission was granted. The fear of the publisher is that a free policy of quotation without such credit might otherwise impair the copyright as a form of dedication to the public domain of the work quoted. Neither, would it seem, is there an implied consent, in fact, by the publisher to the quotation as a fair use except possibly in instances of form books where the work is intended to be used by copying. Thus it was held in *The American Institute of Architects* v. *Fenichel,*[108] that it was fair use for the defendant to copy the largest and most important form of architect agreements from the plaintiff's copyrighted form books. The Court stated in this regard:

> ". . . but fair use is not determined by quantity alone. When the plaintiff put on the general market a book of forms, he implied the right of others to their private use. This conclusion follows from the nature of a book of forms. No one reads them as literature; their sole value is their usability. To constrict the defendant to mere reading of the forms in the bound volume would unjustly enrich the plaintiff whose very publication of a form implies its usability." [109]

The Court referred to this as an "outright invitation to use its contents." [110] In effect, if the forms may be copied as fair use, then what the copyright covers is the editorial content and compilation of the work. The form per se arguably is not the subject of copyright.[111] If it were and the entire form were subject to fair use, then we would

---

[108] 41 F. Supp. 146 (S.D. N.Y. 1941).

[109] *Idem* at p. 147.

[110] *Ibid.*

[111] *Cf.* Amdur, Copyright Law and Practice, Sec. 8, at pp. 102-103 and Nimmer, note 2, *supra,* Sec. 37.

have an anomalous situation, a right to copyright that could not be protected from infringement because it could be fairly used. However, one must distinguish between utilitarian works which are not copyrightable[112] and copyrightable matter with respect to which there is a limitation on the copyright by reason of fair use. Amdur observes, "Nor are legal or commercial forms and coupons copyrightable (the textual matter therein may, however, be copyrighted.)" [113] Thus, if the legal form is common in language to forms used generally, in effect, it is in the public domain. However, to the extent it contains original copyrightable matter it would be protectible, subject, however, to the doctrine of fair use. As to this, Amdur states, "The purchaser of the form or book of forms may copy and use the form for his personal needs but may not copy the forms for the purpose of publishing a similar work." [114] This means, as in *Fenichel,* that fair use denotes private use, but one could not publish a similar form book. Actually, this is close to the *Baker* v. *Selden*[115] doctrine that where the art embodied in a work cannot be used without employing the material embodied in the book, e.g., methods and diagrams, there bookkeeping ledgers, then the work is not copyrightable. But strictly utilitarian works aside, where the description of the work embodies the use thereof, although, as Nimmer points out[116], there may be infringement in the explanation as opposed to use thereof, Sec. 3 of the Copyright Act protects copyrightable components and composite works. Legal form books, it would seem, would not be denied copyrightability because the limita-

---

[112] *Ibid.* See also, Regulations of the Copyright Office, Sec. 202.1.

[113] Amdur, *Ibid.* at p. 102.

[114] *Idem* at p. 103.

[115] 101 U.S. 99 (1879). See Nimmer's criticism of the case, note 111, *supra.*

[116] Nimmer, *Ibid.* Sec. 37.2 at p. 151 and Sec. 37.21 at p. 152.

tion is as to use, private use would be fair use. The research test would apply as to publication. The same would be true as to copying from the headnotes of copyrighted law reports.[117]

Research tests attempt to apply a kind of rule of thumb as to methods of working and when improper research constitutes infringement.[118] The cases make much of independent research. Here we are dealing with the use of independent sources. But the reference to independent research or sources may be confusing. It implies to the scholar possibly the use of primary materials. Yet not all material is so set out that scholarship and research is to be pursued from primary sources. One cannot expect a historian to go to the National Archives to peruse the original documents when he can use copies set forth in textbooks compiling them.[119] However, the scholar will utilize primary sources for his research in preference to secondary sources as a means of authentication of his scholarship wherever possible. That is, the scholar prefers to avail himself of original sources as opposed to derivative sources.[120] But that does not mean eschewing use of copies of documents in favor of original documents

---

[117] West Publishing Co. v. Edward Thompson Co., 169 Fed. 833 (C.C. E.D.N.Y. 1909).

[118] W. H. Anderson v. Baldwin Law Pub. Co., 27 F 2.d 82 (6th Cir. 1928); Orgel v. Clark Boardman Co., 301 F. 2d 119 (2d Cir. 1962).

[119] See Toksvig v. Bruce Pub. Co., 181 F. 2d 664 (7th Cir. 1950) where the Court made much of the undue reliance on the English translation of the plaintiff's work and plaintiff's use of Danish sources as opposed to the reliance by defendant on English sources, i.e., the defendant author, Margaret Ann Hubbard.

[120] See, for example, Commager, Henry Steele, Documents of American History, 7th Ed. (1963).

unless, of course, the original has some intrinsic significance to the research, as in archeology.

Sec. 25.12. Fair Use and Fair Comment

But the nature of independent research goes further. The fact that the defendant biographer in *Toksvig* v. *Bruce Pub. Co.*[121] chose to rely on English sources as opposed to Danish sources for her research into the life of Hans Christian Andersen should not per se be a factor in the fact of independent research or not. The quality of the research should not be determined by scholarship norms of the academic community as a legal norm. The test, pure and simple, is infringement. Did a defendant rely unduly on a plaintiff's work so as to constitute copying? That is the question. A student researcher using entirely derivative sources with a very low quality of verification in his work and with poor conclusions is nonetheless doing independent research, notwithstanding what may otherwise be below par work from an academic point of view, so long as he is not "cribbing," i.e., copying somebody else's work.

Even then the legal norms are quite different because of the doctrine of fair use. A researcher may fairly use materials of others for his scholarship. This imports criticism and, as a part thereof, the ability to refer to such material and even quote therefrom. Research very often requires exposition. The work of others must be expressed in order to be dealt with to make the researcher's point in the course of advancing the latter's own exposition. The fact of the matter is that the researcher, in this context, is dealing not so much in abstract ideas but the expression of others. The researcher must be in a position to set forth

---

[121] Note 119, *supra*.

the point of view of others; he does this by expressing the ideas of others, either by quotation, paraphrase, or both. After having done so, the researcher is then in a position to advance his own thesis by assent, dissent or some intermediate view. With all due respect to the abstractions test of Judge Learned Hand, as expressed in *Nichols* v. *Universal Pictures Corp.*,[122] and his concomitant notion that fair use is the right to copy theme or ideas but not its expression, as set forth in *Sheldon* v. *Metro-Goldwyn Pictures Corp.*,[123] research is concerned with expression of others. Moreover, the fair use is made in relation thereto by quote or paraphrase of such expression of others.

It would seem that the research parameters of fair use can best be explained by the notion of fair comment. In order to be able to comment fairly on the position of others, the researcher must be able, in the first instance, to set forth such position. The researcher reviews the contention of others by explaining the same. He must first be able to set the same forth, in order to draw conclusions with respect thereto. He sets it forth by extract, either in the form of quotes or summary paraphrase. In order for the paraphrase to be valid as such, the researcher attempts to catch the essence of the position of the party being paraphrased; the essence thereof is to be able to set forth in slightly revised language the position of the other. In short, the aim is fidelity of expression. Fair comment in this regard allows the researcher to do this to the extent reasonably necessary for the researcher to make his point. The researcher, in effect, works like an extruder. He extracts the essence of the thoughts of others as expressed by them in order to comment thereon. The researcher intrudes his own thoughts in the course thereof.

---

[122] 45 F. 2d 119 (2d Cir. 1930).

[123] 81 F. 2d 49 (2d Cir. 1936).

These are his comments. Scholarship, then, becomes a process of combining extrusion and intrusion, advancing learning by expression of the insights of the scholar gained in the course of consideration of the work of others. How much quotation and/or paraphrase may a scholar make from a single work of another in the process? The answer must be, as much as the scholar reasonably requires to make his point. If the scholar should somehow unduly extrude and minimally intrude, he may be exceeding the limits of fair comment to the point where he may be doing little more than copying. The result would be infringement.

If what the scholar does is descriptive of the learning process in general, then it may be seen that the research test, as based on the notion of independent production, may be somewhat wide of the mark. It seems to emphasize going away from the source of the work allegedly infringed to other sources when actually scholarship may be operative by going to that source and extracting quotation and paraphrase, i.e., expression, as a necessary adjunct of research. All materials and sources are fairly the scope of the researcher. The legal test should not depend on the effectiveness of the researcher in utilization of sources *qua* researcher. Just as the law does not sit in judgment as to the literary quality of a work in determination of its right to copyrightability over and above the barest minimal criteria of originality and expression that are more than mere words, short phrases, titles and slogans,[124] so, too, it should not apply the qualitative test of the researcher as to independent sources or independent production in a mechanical sense. A researcher need not be a scholar, in legal contemplation. Nor need he be good at research or seek other sources if he chooses not to.

---

[124] Regulations of the Copyright Office, Sec. 202.1(a).

Here we are talking about substantive expression. A somewhat different situation is at hand where one is dealing with compilations, directories, fact sources and the like. There the fruits and proceeds of the original research are in the editorial process of editing and compilation. Short-circuiting the investigation process, the second researcher simply avails himself of existing materials to come up with a like work. In effect the latter has extruded without intrusion. He has added little of his own comment and taken too much from the original researcher's work. This is the basis for allegation of infringement.[125]

Sec. 25.13. The Privilege Test

Subject to the nature of the materials one is discussing, it would seem that the basis for expression is fair comment. *Toksvig* refers to this as a *privilege,* stating, "Fair use has been defined as a privilege in others than the owner of a copyright to use the copyrighted material in a reasonable manner without his consent, notwithstanding the monopoly granted to the owner of the copyright."[126] Unlike the implied consent theory, the source of fair use is dehors the author or proprietor of the work subject to fair use. Hence, it is not a matter of consent by implication. Consent is immaterial. As a limitation upon the exclusive right of the proprietor, it is a privilege, in this argument. It is a form of immunity from infringement because it is permissible.

However, the reference to privilege in this context is troublesome because it seems to fly in the face of exclusivity, the monopoly granted to the copyright owner. Conceivably it may be a rule of reason developed by equity to

---

[125] See discussion in W. H. Anderson v. Baldwin Law Pub. Co., 27 F. 2d 82 (6th Cir. 1928).

[126] Note 119, *supra,* at p. 666.

mitigate the severity of the absolute effects of exclusivity. Yet, in *Hemingway* v. *Random House, Inc.*, the Court placed the source of the privilege elsewhere, stating, "The justification for the privilege of fair use derives from the original rationale for copyright protection, as set forth in the Federal Constitution, (art I, sec. 8), 'To promote the Progress of Science and the useful Arts, . . .' "[127] The source, in this contention, for the privilege of fair use is in the enabling clause of the Constitution relating to the power of Congress to promote learning. The Court, in effect, links the instrumental clause of the Constitution which follows, as to the exclusive copyright in writings for limited times, by validating it as to the fair user and his right to exclusivity in his writings. The substantive part of the clause as to the power to promote learning is made absolute and the instrumental clause immediately following, secondary. The latter clause is subjected to a qualifying limitation of fair use in this interpretation, so as to preserve the absoluteness of the substantive clause, the power to promote learning. In this view, the source of the limitation on the copyright is inherently constitutional and so the privilege of fair use is to be found in the power of Congress to promote learning. The immunity from infringement by fair use follows therefrom in this contention. Basically, this approach is an enclave theory. Protection is carved out of the copyrighted work for the fair user as a privilege. The limitation approach permits a qualified use. Fair use in this regard imports a countervailing use that is permissible because it promotes learning. It is not surprising that such an argument should arise in a case involving biography. For the courts must decide in such cases whether to foster works about the

---

[127] 53 Misc. 2d 462, 466-467, 279 N.Y.S.2d 51, 57 (Spec. T., N.Y. Cty., Pt I, 1967).

lives of others when the authors thereof may be inhibited by possibility of other legal impediments—invasion of privacy, access to documents that may be under common law copyright, etc. Sources of materials are a further complicating factor, as in *Hemingway,* where conversations were at issue. To what extent could A.E. Hotchner rely upon the many talks he had with Ernest Hemingway for his biography?

And yet, somehow the enclave theory of privilege and immunity for fair use, even though couched in constitutional sanction, does not appear to be an adequate explanation of the theoretical underpinnings of the fair use doctrine. True, it extracts immunity from exclusivity for the fair user, but only as a privilege. In its own way as a kind of rule of reason as to the monopoly of the copyright, i.e., exclusive rights granted to the author and assigns, it nevertheless pays homage to the paramountcy of the exclusive rights. The privilege is available because the rights under copyright are there in the first place, subject to the qualified use or uses under the privilege.

Sec. 25.14. A Theory of Fair Use

It is submitted that fair use proceeds from the constitutional ambit of the First Amendment out of the unqualified right of freedom of speech and press. The basis for fair use is in the right of free expression, i.e., fair comment. Consequently, the objective of the courts has been one of reconciliation of sometimes competing rights of the copyright proprietor under Article I, Section 8, Clause 8 of the Constitution with the rights of others drawing on the work under copyright as fair commentary under the First Amendment. Fair comment generically is much broader than the right of the press to comment upon matters of public interest fairly, i.e., without malice. In the *Jack Benny* case,[128] the Court of Appeals for the Ninth Circuit discounted the defense of dramatic or literary criticism as an alternative contention as a parody on the meaning of criticism.

It is submitted that fair commentary is a generic term which encompasses all kinds of criticism, including dramatic and literary criticism. It also comprehends parody of all kinds—burlesque, mimicry, satire, parody, and so on. However, merely calling material by one of these names does not isolate usage from infringement if, in fact, the use is unfair and infringing. This would apply to genus "fair comment" as well. Nor is fair use limited to scholarly works. In *Rosemont Enterprises, Inc.* v. *Random House, Inc.,* the District Court sought to define fair use in those terms, stating, "In general 'fair use' is limited to cases where copyrighted material is used for purposes of criticism or comment or in scholarly works of scientific or educational value." [129] This was reversed by the Court of Appeals[130] as unjustifiably restricting fair use to scholarly works. Motivation for writing of biographies, in this case the biography of Howard Hughes, arose from a variety of sources, according to this opinion. The Court stated:

> "Biographies, of course, are fundamentally personal histories and it is both reasonable and customary for biographers to refer to and utilize earlier works dealing with the subject of the work and occasionally to quote directly from such works.
>
> • • •

---

[128] Benny v. Loew's, Inc., 239 F. 2d 532 (9th Cir. 1956), *aff'd* 356 U.S. 43 (1958).

[129] 256 F. Supp. 55, 66 (S.D.N.Y. 1966).

[130] 366 F. 2d 303 (2d Cir. 1966), cert. den., 385 U.S. 1009 (1967).

"Whether an author or publisher reaps economic benefits from the sale of a biographical work, or whether its publication is motivated in part by a desire for commercial gain, or whether it is designed for the popular market, i.e. the average citizen rather than the college professor, has no bearing on whether a public benefit may be derived from such a work. Moreover, the district court in emphasizing the commercial aspects of the Hughes biography failed to recognize that [a]ll publications presumably are operated for profit. . .' Koussevitsky v. Allen, Towne & Heath, 188 Misc. 479, 483, 68 N.Y.S. 2d 779, 783, aff'd 272 App. Div. 759, 69 N.Y.S. 2d 432 (1st Dept. 1947), and that 'both commercial and artistic elements are involved in almost every [work] * * *' Note, 56 Colum. L. Rev. supra at 597. Thus, we conclude that whether an author or publisher has a commercial motive or writes in a popular style is irrelevant to a determination of whether a particular use of copyrighted material in a work which offers some benefit to the public constitutes a fair use." [131]

The opinion also refers to the fair use *privilege* as being applied to a variety of publications where the obvious motivation was, in part, a desire for economic gain, citing, articles in popular magazines, a popular biographical novel, commercial television and a history study outline. The opinion tries to reconcile these with the *Jack Benny* case and the *Liggett & Myers* case involving, respectively, findings of infringement in a parody of a motion picture and in the

---

[131] *Idem* at p. 307.

taking of three sentences from a scientific work for a pamphlet on cigarettes.[132]

Although the opinion considers fair use to be a privilege, it goes far in spelling out that purpose of fair use is mainly irrelevant. Implicit in this view necessarily is the addition of the notion that purpose other than to use the copyrighted work unduly, i.e., to copy and thereby infringe, is meant thereby. By definition, infringement and fair use are mutually exclusive. Infringement other than technical infringement or *de minimis* would be actionable and so, of course, not a fair use. Conversely, a fair use would not be actionable as an infringing use. Thus the opinion takes a broad view that so long as the use is a permissible, non-infringing use, then it is a fair use and the motivation therefor, be it scholarship, learning, economic gain, ego, or whatever, is immaterial. This is consistent with the notion of fair comment in its broadest sense of free expression under the First Amendment.

If teleology or purpose of use is irrelevant, excepting only for the non-fair use purpose of infringing, then it follows that purpose of use should not be a criterion other than the very limited one of determining whether it was intended to copy so much as to constitute infringement. As free comment, such fair use ought to be permitted under any circumstance, no matter how subjective or even inarticulate the purpose. Conversely, the scope of the copyrighted work should not be limited by a use denominated fair without consideration of the parameters of permissible uses under the Copyright Act under genus, exclusive rights. The history of the 1909 Act has been the subsumption of many new uses

---

[132] See the criticism of *Jack Benny* in Berlin v. E. C. Publications, Inc., 329 F. 2d 541 (2d Cir. 1964), Kaufman, *J.*, and of *Liggett & Myers* in Nimmer, *op. cit.,* supra, note 2, Sec. 145.

as species of generic exclusive rights without reference to the fact that the legislative scheme remained the same while technology has changed considerably. For example, puppets, as such, perform. Generally they tell a story in the course of performance. Unless they were displayed as inanimate puppets in *Mura* on television, it would seem that their use on the Captain Kangaroo Show was by dramatic performance under Sec. 1(d).[133]

It would seem, then, that courts are faced with the problem of weighing countervailing constitutional mandates, protection of authors and assigns in their exclusive rights under copyright as promotion of learning as against free comment. Each, in theory, is allowed the broadest mandate, but at some point each may intrude upon the other. A nice dilemma! Each needs the fullest protection, in theory, to flourish. Yet, upon inspection of particular matters in some instances, public policy clearly bends in one direction or another.

The Register of Copyrights, in his First Report, set forth a number of permissible fair uses as follows:

"1. Quotation of excerpts in a review or criticism for purposes of illustration or comment.

2. Quotation of short passages in a scholarly or technical work, for illustration or clarification of the author's observations.

3. Use in a parody of some of the content of the work parodied.

4. Summary of an address or article, with brief quotations, in a news report.

5. Reproduction by a library of a portion of a work to replace part of a damaged copy.

---

[133] 17 U.S.C. 1(d).

6. Reproduction by a teacher or student of a small part of a work to illustrate a lesson.

7. Reproduction of a work in legislative or judicial proceedings or reports." [134]

It would seem clear that uses set forth in items 1, 2 and 4 are necessary to free comment and protectible under the First Amendment, in the generality of instances. A difficult matter is presented with respect to music where the proprietor will argue that it constitutes reproduction of a substantial part of the basic melody and the commentator, free comment. It would seem that the test should be whether the quote can be used commerically. Reproduction of two bars from a four bar melody in a scholarly work or review should be permitted as a fair use. It is unlikely that the reader would use the two bar quote as a substitute for the real thing. It is concededly a copy and a substantial part of the tune. But in reality it has no utility except as fair comment. To compel the scholar to get permissions—at a price and subject to all kinds of limitations, conditions and inconveniences—inhibits free comment and the promotion of learning. Perhaps the notion of reasonable interchangeability should be included, whether the quote would serve as a substitute for the copyrighted four bars in the context of likelihood of use of the two bar quote for any reasonable purpose other than scholarship.

Then, too, it would seem that item 7 should have the broadest application in favor of free comment. In part, this is already expressed in the last sentence of Sec. 8 of the Copyright Act:

---

[134] Report of the Register of Copyrights on the General Revision of the U.S. Copyright Law in Studies on Copyright, Vol. 2 (1963) at p. 1224; see also, Latman, Alan, Fair Use of Copyrighted Works, Study No. 14, *idem* at p. 781.

> "The publication or republication by the Government, either separately or in a public document, of any material in which copyright is subsisting shall not be taken to cause any abridgement or annulment of the copyright or to authorize any use or appropriation of such copyright material without the consent of the copyright proprietor." [135]

That, of course, refers to publication. Nevertheless, in order for the processes of government to be able to function in an orderly manner, material under copyright may be used in legislative, judicial and executive proceedings of all kinds as exhibits and can be fairly reproduced as an incident thereof. Copyright cannot and should not be used to thwart operations of government in an orderly manner by withholding matters under copyright from reproduction as part of proceedings. Here free comment is taken in the broader sense of communication. Free comment is necessary, regardless of who seeks it or, indeed, whether any litigant seeks it, if the presiding judge or other person officiating at the proceeding deems the reproduction of the document or documents necessary. Free comment in this sense means communication and the processes of communication, of which due process in this respect is a part.

Item 3 should have the broadest application as fair comment subject to the limitation that substantial appropriation, i.e., copying, cannot be undertaken in the guise of parody. Free comment comprehends any kind of comment, not necessarily only serious comment. Some of the sharpest commentary has been made in the form of satire, burlesque, parody and fun-poking in general. What is permissible

---

[135] 17 U.S.C. 8.

without a smile should be permissible with a smile. Free comment is not truly free under the First Amendment if the jester cannot have his say. The limits, indeed, are similar both as to scholarship and parody. In each instance, the line is drawn at copying, taking someone else's work as opposed to origination of one's own. Great latitude is permitted both in scholarship and in parody as separate aspects of free comment.

Items 5 and 6 highlight the problems of the educator *qua* librarian and teacher versus those of the author, be he educator or otherwise, *qua* creator. *Macmillan* v. *King*[136] highlights the dilemma as to how far the teacher may go. There the teacher preparing outlines lost out to the publisher of the book. Yet the Register would allow a teacher or student of a small part of a work to illustrate a lesson. The development of xerography and other forms of reproduction has both heightened the controversy[137] as between conflicting aims and indicated the path for resolution thereof. Proposed copyright revision seeks to resolve specific dilemmas by legislation. Thus, Sec. 108 of S. 543[138] purports to grant limited rights of reproduction to libraries and archives, and Sec. 110 thereof[139], certain exemptions to teachers and students. In this regard, Amdur notes that prior to the enactment of the present Act in 1909, abridg-

---

[136] 223 Fed. 862 (D. Mass. 1914).

[137] See Supplementary Report of the Register of Copyrights on the General Revision of the U.S. Copyright Law, 89th Cong., 1st Sess., Fair Use, at pp. 25-28; Senate Report No. 64, National Commission on New Technological Uses of Copyrighted Works, 90th Cong., 1st Sess., Oct. 11, 1967, to accompany S. 2216; S. 543, 91st Cong., 1st Sess., Jan. 22, 1969, Dec. 10, 1969 print, Title II—National Commission on New Technological Uses of Copyrighted Works.

[138] S. 543, *idem,* Sec. 108.

[139] *Idem,* Sec. 110.

ments embodying intellectual labor and judgment and not mere selection or rearrangement of the copyrighted work were instances of fair use.[140] Then in 1909 Congress swung in the other direction, as it should have, to protect the creator and assigns in the exclusive right to create other versions. Now proposed copyright revision hopes to inject some semblance of clarification by specification of permitted fair uses in education. Conceivably the proposed reforms may not satisfy either educators, on the one hand, or authors and publishers, on the other. But clearly, guidelines of some kind are in order in the face of the onrush of technology before both groups are overwhelmed by the lack thereof in judicial application of the general notion of fair use.

It would seem that literature, particularly story-telling of all kinds, is the place where, apart from accommodations of teaching to utilize literature, that proscriptions favor the creator as against the would-be fair user. That is why the notion of Learned Hand that fair use is permissible use of themes and ideas, but not the expression, is apt in regard to literary works. He is saying, in effect, that in literature, copying of expression is *verboten* as an unfair use except possibly to the minimal extent necessary to be able to state the theme or idea. That is, themes and ideas are in the public domain. Use thereof is fair. But then again, if they are in the public domain, there can be no infringing copying. The two notions appear to be mutually exclusive. But Judge Learned Hand seems to imply that one can work outward to the abstractions, past the limits of expression, by shedding the expression, and taking the abstraction. Yet a certain amount of language may be common to the theme or idea and to the expression thereof. It may be

140 Amdur, Copyright Law and Practice, Chap. XXII, Fair Use, Sec. 5, Instances of Fair Use: Abridgements (Former Law), at pp. 762-764.

necessary to utilize certain language to set forth the theme or idea in any event, even if the same should also be in the expression thereof. To that extent, the use thereof is fair. In short, when it comes to literature, fair comment denotes the right to use ideas and themes of all kinds but it would severely limit the right of commentary so that the expression thereof is not taken. Again, the notion is independent origin as opposed to availing one's self of the fruits and labors of others. But there is a stronger aspect, here, that tends to weigh in favor of the copyrighted work. All the creator has to offer is his expression, his style, his manner of putting together the various elements that go into his literary work—setting, characters, locale, and ability to convey thoughts and emotions in language. Take that away and the exclusive rights under copyright become a virtual nullity. The constitutional clause, willy-nilly, in protecting the creator and assigns, protects the fabric of our arts, our culture, in the finest sense of the word. The fair user does not require to draw on the resources of the *littérateur* to create his own art, unless he himself is a parodist, and then he must see that fair comment does not degenerate into substantial appropriation. In literature, the balance shifts in favor of the creator. *A fortiori,* to the extent the performing arts are derivatives of literature, the same notion should be applicable. Where story-telling literary works are involved, performance thereof is only an exercise of the exclusive performing rights therein, subject to the compulsory license in the case of music. Thus the same rules should be applicable in the performing arts as to literature where the underlying work is literary, especially of a story-telling nature.

But there is a middle area in literature which is the nonfiction area where the emphasis should, arguably, shift to free comment. Biography is a good example. The right of the people to know, and of the commentator freely to bring this knowledge to their attention, is sufficient to give greater latitude in the direction of fair use. But even there, expression, as the stock in trade of the creator of the work being subject to fair use, should be respected. The creator is a professional in the sense that his stock in trade is style or manner of expression. He may, in fact, be an amateur, and the notion of fair comment covers all of us, whether those who are paid to create or not, but the point is that the aspect of style or manner of expression should be respected as an attribute of writing, whether done for gain or not. The attribute is professional, although the creator need not be. Thus the Court of Appeals for the Seventh Circuit correctly saw that even taking of news could infringe because journalists, too, were entitled to and did have their own style and manner of expression. In *Chicago Record-Herald Co.* v. *Tribune Association,* it stated:

> "But if the whole of it were considered as stating news or facts, yet the arrangement and manner of statement plainly discloses a distinct literary flavor and individuality of expression peculiar to authorship, bringing the article within the purview and protection of the Copyright Law." [141]

Finally, it is to be noted that proposed copyright revision in S. 543, Sec. 107, purports to set up guidelines by embodying the same in a fair use section of the statute for the first time, as follows:

"(1) the purpose and character of the use;

(2) the nature of the copyrighted work;

(3) the amount and substantiality of the portion used in relation to the copyrighted work as a whole; and

---

[141] 275 Fed. 797, 799 (7th Cir. 1921).

(4) the effect of the use upon the potential market for or value of the copyrighted work." [142]

These guidelines substantially embody the criteria proposed by the Register in his original Report.[143] In turn, they are a paraphrase of Judge Goddard's criteria as set forth in *Shapiro, Bernstein* v. *P. F. Collier & Son Co.*[144] Legislative guidelines would be an improvement over common law yardsticks insofar as they presumably would have a common application, whereas courts in other jurisdictions are free to develop their own criteria in the absence of the highest court of the land enunciating its own rules. Nevertheless, they are only guidelines. Interpretation thereof in specific contexts would nevertheless require analysis of the various constitutional ambits to be served, the specific types of use and the relative priorities to be accorded each within the respective constitutional ambits (protection of the creator's exclusive right; free comment). Analysis should help in pointing the direction of emphasis as to the applicability of the respective doctrines. Where new uses and new purported fair uses arise out of our technology or otherwise, perhaps the proposed National Commission on New Technological Uses should be operative as a permanent body to weigh and evalute the same. True, judicial hindsight often tells us more on this point than threshold projections of use. Yet it would seem, as in the case of the dawning era of audio-visual cassette technology of all kinds, that the courts would welcome the professionalism of such a Commission to aid it in its determinations by suggesting tentative guidelines in the light of its own research and studies.

---

[142] S. 543, note 137, *supra,* Sec. 107.

[143] Note 134, *supra.*

[144] 26 U.S.P.Q. 40 (S.D.N.Y. 1934).

Chapter XXVI

INFRINGEMENT: DAMAGES AND OTHER REMEDIES

Sec. 26.1. Justice, Rights, Remedies, Damages

With all due respect to the Goddess of Justice and her scales, justice, as the end goal and embodiment of law, is neuter, but never neutral. Justice, in this sense, is not so much the end result of being overseen by the sweet, well-groomed, equable mythological deity, but the terminal point of the arc of the compass of man-made laws. If such laws are harsh, such as providing hanging or life imprisonment for stealing a loaf of bread, then the justice of such laws may be questionable. Conversely, if commission of murder as a crime of honor would allow the murderer to go scot-free, then under such jurisprudence, the leniency of such justice may raise questions. Justice, as such, is therefore not necessarily synonymous with law. The swing of the arc of the laws is too broad to equate justice with law in any mechanical sense. Justice may have sex appeal as the attribute of the Goddess in mythology, but in practice it is a resultant, neither feminine nor masculine, but neuter. The factor of being common to both sexes does not mean that it is a dead-center concept. Rather it is a determination of efficacious application of right results in the premises. Justice is rooted in pragmatism in a social context. Its predicate is a fair result enabling society to resolve the particular dispute without an undue residue of harshness to any of the disputants or society as a whole and to enable society to go on to resolve other disputes on a like, equable basis.

Justice, then, in relation to rights and remedies, is tripartite. In order for there to be a righting of a wrong, there must first be recognition of a right which can be wronged. Unless there is right, there can be no wrong thereto. The means of setting the wrong right is the remedy. But redress by way of remedy only makes sense if there is some reasonable relationship between right and remedy. The reasonable relationship is one of efficacy as to whether or not the intended relief comports with the violation of the right so as to provide redress by way of compensation and, if possible, restoration of the *status quo ante,* and by discouraging future violations of such right. Thus, justice is never neutral. Laws which do not grant the right thereby allow for no wrong thereto, there being no right. This is an expression, either way, by granting or not granting the right, of the philosophy of the society at any given time. Justice, in this regard, then, becomes an expression of philosophical predilection of the need and desirability of granting the right at any given time. Laws which grant the right are only just if the granting of the right also includes a grant of a remedy for violation of the right. Without remedy, a right which is without manifest means of enforcement is essentially a right without the sanctions of society, i.e., of the state, to enforce the right, and so the right is virtually naked without means of realization. Justice has been thwarted where the right gives rise to no remedy. In the same category is the right without commensurate remedy. In order for justice to prevail, there must be a direct relationship between the grant of the right and the efficacy of the remedy. A grant of the right presupposes reasonable compensation and deterrence of future wrong-doing so that the malefactor will have restored to the holder of the right the gains wrongfully realized therefrom, while malefaction or wrongdoing in the context will have been discouraged. If the right can only be protected by perpetual and endless litigation, it is not much of a right. The holder of such right cannot be truly said to enjoy the exercise of the right; in effect, he has become little more than a policeman *cum* litigator. Justice, in this regard, presupposes that the penalties for malefaction, the deliberate wrongdoing, will encourage abidance by the rules of respect for the exercise of the right in the market, so that its exercise, perforce, becomes meaningful because the majority of mankind in that jurisprudence subject to the right respects its exercise as opposed to its violation.

Justice presupposes that deliberate malefaction or even litigation or instigation of litigation as tactical maneuvers for market position, such as the instituton of patent litigation for jockeying in the market, or to wear down a competitior economically, has only limited efficacy because justice will provide reasonable safeguards in the judicial process so that the latter may become normative, i.e., as the means for suitable resolution of bona fide disputes rather than a bad faith forum for maneuvering to thwart good faith ownership of rights. Justice is therefore concerned with the nature of the judicial process as the mechanism for good faith resolution of disputes.

It is in this context that we review the nature of the remedies accorded for infringement of copyright. Damages, for example, may be seen as the ultimate of pragmatism, in that practical consequences of violation of rights are paid for by award of damages. Yet damages, as the mundane application of relief to a determination of liability, are not necessarily in and of themselves practical if unrelated to the wrong to the holder of the right. The quality of efficaciousness of the result must also be considered in determining its practicality. The result must be just, within reasonable limits, if it may be said that there is an equation of the prosaic area of determination of damages with practicality. An illustration of this is

Shapiro, Bernstein & Co. v. *4636 S. Vermont Ave., Inc.*[1] There a "fake" song book had utilized 19 tunes of plaintiff's out of a thousand. The term "fake" here means that the harmony would be "faked" by vocalists or instrumentalists, the folio including only melody. The Court of Appeals held that no damages had been determined and that profits were *de minimis* and also agreed with the court below that it was not required to apply the provisions as to statutory damages. Also, there was no error below in withholding injunction since there was little likelihood that the defendant would infringe again. On such a result, the holder of the right is effectively without a remedy so that the practicality of the relief as an instrumentality of justice is questionable.

A swing in the other direction is shown by *Whitman Publishing Company* v. *Writesel.*[2] There the defendant sold 10,600 copies at $1 each but submitted no evidence concerning cost. The Court allowed plaintiff to recover for infringement, $10,600 profits and $250 for infringement of copyright, plus $1,500 in attorney's fees. Presumably the recovery of $250 constituted in lieu rather than actual damages under the statute.[3] It is true that Sec. 101(b) provides for grant of infringer's profits to the copyright proprietor as a remedy and "in proving profits the plaintiff shall be required to prove sales only, and the defendant shall be required to prove every element of cost which he claims, . . ."[4] The statute thereby shifts the burden of proof to the defendant. The Court handled the situation by literal application of the statute where the defendant failed to meet this burden. Yet it is submitted that the

---

[1] 367 F. 2d 236 (9th Cir. 1966).

[2] 83 U.S.P.Q. 535 (S.D. Ohio 1949).

[3] 17 U.S.C. 101.

[4] 17 U.S.C. 101(b).

result on its face is unjust. The plaintiff, by this decision, in all likelihood realized a windfall because the literal application of the rule embodied in the statute produced a harsh result. Assuming defendant had some cost of production, it would seem that the Court might have elicited the same upon examination of defendant's witnesses. Alternatively, the Court might have taken judicial notice of the minimum cost of production of such infringing copies and set the profits at the difference between sales price and such minimum cost of production. Whatever the reason for the defendant's failure to proffer proof of cost, assuming such copies were indeed manufactured rather than stolen, the copies had some minimal cost, by any standard of commerce. Here, it would seem, the Court leaned in the other direction in relating relief to infringement of the right. If such a defendant were an innocent, not of wrongdoing but of understanding the nature of his act, and if his counsel were completely without experience in litigation and copyright and thereby failed to submit proof of cost, it would seem that justice ought to take such circumstances into consideration in determination of profits and, perforce, recovery thereof.

Sec. 26.2. Section 101 Remedies

It may be seen that Section 101[5] granted broad powers to the judiciary to do justice in the area of remedies. Equity, historically, represented a parallel development in the common law in order to do justice where the rigidities of law might result in injustice. A variety of remedies was developed by equity to achieve such results by giving the chancellor in equity the flexibility of efficacious relief. This is well expressed as applied to copyright in-

---

[5] 17 U.S.C. 101.

fringement by the Court in *Lundberg* v. *Welles*[6] where it stated:

> "Traditionally in an action at law for infringement, damages only can be recovered. However, inasmuch as infringements could be enjoined in equity, and in order to avoid a multiplicity of suits, the infringer was considered a trustee as to his profits for the benefit of the owner of an infringed work. Thus, an accounting of profits is an equitable remedy . . ." [7]

Thus it may be seen that Sec. 101 of the Copyright Act abounds with equitable remedies of all kinds, injunctive relief,[8] recovery of profits,[9] impounding allegedly infringing articles during pendency of the action,[10] and destruction of infringing copies.[11] Apart from the extraordinary remedies of injunction, impounding and destruction, the very formulation of the damage provisions as embodied in Sec. 101(b) and (e) would indicate an intent to do justice.

Sec. 101(b) provides that the infringer " . . . pay to the copyright proprietor such damages as the copyright proprietor may have suffered due to the infringement, as well as all the profits which the infringer shall have made from such infringement, . . . " [12] Thus far the theme is restitution for actual injuries suffered plus, as between the wrongdoer and the aggrieved party, payment to the latter of the illegal gains of the former on the theory of unjust

[6] 93 F. Supp. 359 (S.D.N.Y. 1950).
[7] *Id.* at p. 361.
[8] 17 U.S.C. 101(a).
[9] 17 U.S.C. 101(b).
[10] 17 U.S.C. 101(c).
[11] 17 U.S.C. 101(d).
[12] 17 U.S.C. 101(b).

enrichment. Not only does the statute shift the burden to the infringer in respect of profits as to deductibility of costs, leaving the plaintiff only with the obligation of proving sales, but the statute goes a fundamental step further. There may be allowed, " . . . in lieu of actual damages and profits, such damages as to the court shall appear to be just, . . . "[13] After enumerating in lieu damages for newspaper reproduction of a copyrighted photograph and for motion picture infringement, the section provides, " . . . and such damages shall in no other case exceed $5,000 nor be less than the sum of $250 and shall not be regarded as a penalty."[14] The limitations as to in lieu or statutory damages do not prevail, however, in respect of recovery for infringements where there has been actual notice, either by service of process, or other written notice to a defendant.

The balance of Sec. 101(b) contains what are known as statutory yardsticks which set forth varying rates for infringement, e.g., for painting, $10 per infringing copy,[15] for books, $1 per copy,[16] for infringing lectures, $50,[17] and $100 for the first dramatic, or dramatico-musical infringing performance and $50 for each subsequent performance, with $10 for other infringing musical performance other than of a choral or orchestral composition which has the $100/$50 rate.[18] As to these yardsticks, District Judge Feinberg remarked in *Davis* v. *E.I. DuPont de Nemours & Co.*, "The cases abound with statements that the yardstick amounts are discretionary and need not be

---

[13] *Ibid.*

[14] *Ibid.*

[15] 17 U.S.C. 101(b), First.

[16] 17 U.S.C. 101(b), Second.

[17] 17 U.S.C. 101(b), Third.

[18] 17 U.S.C. 101(b), Fourth.

followed by the courts. However, these have generally been made in the context of an award where the statutory minimum of $250 and maximum of $5,000 both applied." [19]

It is noteworthy that performance is covered by Sec. 101(b) both by limitation—as to motion pictures—and by statutory yardsticks as to infringing delivery of lectures, dramatic or dramatico-musical works and music. Innocent infringement of non-dramatic or of undramatized works by means of motion pictures carries with it a $100 limitation, while innocent infringement of copyrighted dramatic or dramatico-musical work by means of motion pictures is subject to a total recovery of damages of not more than $5,000, nor less than $250. This was the contribution of the Townsend Act of 1912, apart from the classification of motion pictures in Section 5 of the Copyright Act of 1909.[20] Interestingly, the language as to the motion picture limitation does not use the word "performance" while the statutory yardstick as to infringing lectures, etc., likewise does not use this expression. All of these may, however, be denominated as damages for infringing performance.

Sec. 26.3. Section 101(e) and Section 1(e) Damages and Remedies

Sec. 101(e), on the other hand, establishes a criterion of an engineering nature, to wit, mechanical reproduction. The purpose of mechanical reproduction is embodiment of original performance, or derivatives thereof, in forms—

---

[19] 249 F. Supp. 329 (S.D.N.Y. 1966).

[20] Act of Aug. 24, 1912, 62d Cong., 2d Sess., 37 Stat. 488 (1913), which amended Sec. 5 of the Copyright Act of 1909 as to classification of motion pictures and also Sec. 25(b) thereof (now renumbered as Sec. 101(b), 17 U.S.C. 101(b)).

discs, rolls, tapes—for performance of the reproduction. By reason of the tests of public performance under Sec. 1(d)[21] as to dramatic works, of public performance for profit as to non-dramatic works under Sec. 1(c),[22] and as to musical works under Sec. 1(e),[23] most of the mechanical reproductions would not be subject to copyright infringement as performances, since they are reproduced primarily for home use. Thus, although the purpose of mechanical reproduction ultimately is performance and in given situations performance may infringe, Sec. 101(e) is not a damages statute related to performance, but rather to the fact of mechanical reproduction for purposes of performance. Hence, Sec. 101(e) could be infringed by reason of the engineering facet of reproduction, whether or not there were any performances, or such performances were otherwise exempt from infringement.

The significance of Sec. 101(e), rather, is derived from its nature as spelled out in Sec. 1(e). Under the latter section, after the first use by the copyright proprietor or authorization for such use, there is a compulsory license available to subsequent users at a royalty of two cents a side. Sec. 1(e) also provides for monthly statements and payments thereof. There is a confusion of rights and remedies within Secs. 1(e) and 101(e) in that Sec. 1(e) provides that the copyright proprietor is required to file a notice of use upon the first use thereof, whereas Sec. 101(e) sets forth that compulsory licensees file a notice of intent to use. Both are procedural and both trigger damage consequences or possible damage consequences. Sec. 1(e) effectively provides a bar for failure to file a statement of

---

[21] 17 U.S.C. 1(d).
[22] 17 U.S.C. 1(c).
[23] 17 U.S.C. 1(e).

notice of use by the copyright proprietor, stating, "... any failure to file such notice shall be a complete defense to any suit, action, or proceeding for any infringement of such copyright."[24] Thus, where recording of plaintiff's song took place in August, 1952 and the notice of use was filed in January, 1954, the failure to file the notice of use was held to be a complete bar to the action in *Stasny Music Corp.* v. *Santly-Joy, Inc.*[25] But this was later construed in *Norbay Music, Inc.* v. *King Records, Inc.*[26] as a bar only as to infringements prior to the filing of the notice of use. Apparently the first use took place in October, 1956 but the notice of use was not filed until November, 1957. The Court of Appeals reversed the decision below construing the late filing as a bar and stated, "We therefore hold that the plaintiff's failure to file a timely notice of use bars suit for acts of infringement occurring prior to the time notice was filed, but not for acts occurring afterwards."[27] The Court of Appeals explained that the failure to file in *Stasny* constituted a complete bar there because all of the acts of infringement took place prior to the filing of notice of use.

The Court of Appeals also showed the interrelationship of Sec. 1(e) and Sec. 101(e) in that, although the defense language as to failure to file a notice of use is in Sec. 1(e), which relates to royalties, whereas Sec. 101(e) relates to infringement, the change in nomenclature could have no affect on the result. The Court stated, "We conclude, therefore, that the 'complete defense' provision, in barring ac-

---

[24] *Ibid.*

[25] 156 F. Supp. 795 (S.D.N.Y. 1957), *aff'd per curiam,* 249 F. 2d 957 (2d Cir. 1957).

[26] 290 F. 2d 617 (2d Cir. 1961).

[27] *Idem* at p. 619.

tions for infringement, applies to all actions for unpaid statutory royalties, however they may be named." [28]

Sec. 101(e), moreover, provides not only actual consequences where there is a failure to file on the part of the defendant, i.e., the notice of intent to use, but possible treble damages in the discretion of the court. The Court of Appeals, in *Norbay,* declined to make this provision applicable to infringement prior to the filing of the notice of use by the plaintiff, and remanded for the trial court to determine whether or not it might, in its discretion, award, for the period after plaintiff's filing of notice of use, an amount not to exceed three times the statutory royalty of two cents a side in addition thereto, i.e. up to eight cents a side.[29]

There is, nevertheless, a logical relationship between the two sections, each of which carries provisions for discretionary trebling after the basic rate of two cents a side. The trebling in Sec. 1(e) relates to failure to pay within 30 days after demand in writing and relates, in effect, to willful non-payment by a compulsory licensee. The trebling in Sec. 101(e) relates to an infringer who has failed to file a notice of intent to use. Thus there are three types of provision for compensation for mechanical reproduction. The first is extra-statutory but based on the statute. This is reproduction under a license agreement, i.e., contractual.

---

[28] *Idem* at p. 620.

[29] Nimmer speculates that theoretically it is conceivable that a failure to pay the statutory royalty within 30 days under Sec. 1(e) might make the 2¢ a side royalty plus its trebling, or 8¢ a side, the basis for further trebling under Sec. 101(e) to 24¢ plus the 2¢ royalty under Sec. 101(e) to bring the damages to 26¢ a side. Nimmer on Copyright, Sec. 155, at pp. 697-8 (1970). At the same time he recognizes that such compounding would, in all likelihood, not be approved.

But the measure of royalty almost invariably is the ceiling imposed by the statute, to wit, two cents a side. Most mechanical reproduction in practice is made pursuant to such licensing with the statutory rate as the highest royalty unless a lower rate is negotiated. Note that the expression invariably was qualified. Presumably a licensee could contract to pay more than two cents a side, as a matter of contract, but it would seem that the excess over two cents a side could not be collected as unenforceable, being against public policy as expressed by the compulsory license at two cents a side. For all practical purposes, then, the royalty by contract would not exceed the compulsory license rate of two cents a side, whether or not the contractual license provision in excess thereof were set forth out of ignorance of both parties, one of the parties or otherwise.

The determinative, of course, is the statutory rate of two cents a side as set forth in Sec. 1(e). This is based on the compulsory license therein accorded without regard to the wishes or intent of the copyright proprietor. Sec. 101(e) may be seen, then, as a kind of alter ego of Sec. 1(e), to accord the same compensation to those users who are technically infringers because they have not complied with the formalities of obtaining the compulsory license, to wit, the filing of a notice of intent to use. Thus, since the copyright proprietor, by virtue of the compulsory license has been deprived of the right to grant or withhold permission for subsequent recording, after the first use, infringement is not a derivative of copying by reason of lack of grant, license or permission from the copyright proprietor. In all instances outside of mechanical reproduction, fair use aside, there must be privity with the copyright proprietor as a condition precedent of copying of the material under copyright by some form of authorization which takes the use out of the realm of infringement. Under the compulsory license, after the first use, the matter of privity becomes irrelevant and immaterial. The state becomes the source of the grant of authority and the only nexus to the copyright proprietor is the facet of rendering statements and payment of royalties thereon. It is true, as a practical matter, that the compulsory license serves to induce users to seek privity with the copyright proprietor anyway, by means of contractual license, in order to eliminate the necessity of compliance with the more onerous statutory formalities of the compulsory license, to wit, the monthly filings of statements and payments as well as the filing of notice of intention to use. Nevertheless, the compulsory license takes the play away from the copyright proprietor; license is no longer a matter of largesse at the whim, caprice or discretion of the copyright proprietor. The latter no longer has a say as to the fact of licensing. Thus statutory licensing may be seen as a form of automatic licensing. This being so, it can be readily seen that the rationale of Sec. 101(e) is to restore the copyright proprietor substantially to the position he would be in as to royalty and discretionary damages had the technical infringer obtained his notice of intent to use and abided by the formalities of the statutory license. Thus Sec. 1(e) and Sec. 101(e) are to be seen as being substantially in *pari materia*, to give the copyright proprietor automatic royalties; in the first instance, where there is a license imposed by the state, the compulsory license, and in the second instance, by a form of *de facto* compulsory license, where there is no license under the statute because the statutory formalities have not been complied with, that would otherwise give the user the protection of the compulsory license.

Therefore, infringement of mechanical reproduction is *sui generis* and so concomitantly carries its own rules as to damages without regard to the other damage provisions.

In holding a retailer of phonograph recordings liable for infringement, the Court of Appeals for the Second Circuit stated in *Shapiro, Bernstein & Co.* v. *Goody,* "We conclude, . . . that under the statutory scheme the general damage provisions of Sec. 101(b) are not applicable to the infringement of a musical copyright by mechanical reproduction. . . . For the royalty under the compulsory license, provided by Sec. 1(e), which Congress set arbitrarily at 2¢ per record, was a form of statutory compensation which by its very nature measured the damages resulting from its non-payment."[30] Consequently, no problem of proof would arise as to actual damages or profits under Sec. 101(b) and therefore the in lieu damages limitations of that subsection would not apply. Hence, Sec. 101(e) would control. In effect the Court was saying that the rate of the compulsory license as set forth in Sec. 1(e) was the absolute yardstick for measuring damages and that Sec. 101(e) was to be read in conjunction therewith, but not with the general damages provision. Thus the provisions as to damages for infringement by mechanical reproduction may be seen as special provisions within the broad general scheme covering infringement which carry their own scheme of compensation for damages that are inextricably correlated with the compulsory license.

Sec. 26.4. Substantive and Procedural Predicates to Remedies

It should be noted in this respect that substantive and procedural provisions of the Copyright Act are constantly

[30] 248 F. 2d 260, 265 (2d Cir. 1957), cert. den. sub nom., Goody v. Shapiro, Bernstein & Co., 355 U.S. 952 (1958). Nor would a plaintiff be granted a preliminary injunction where first use has already been authorized (American Metropolitan Enterprises of New York, Inc. v. Warner Bros. Records, Inc., 389 F.2d 903 (2d Cir. 1968)).

entwined with remedies and that one cannot limit one's investigation as to remedies to the provisions of Sec. 101. Just as Sec. 1(e) and its language as to the failure to file a notice of use serve as a complete defense, and by judicial gloss, as seen above,[31] to infringements prior to filing of such notice of use, so other provisions may have an affect. Thus, Sec. 13[32] provides for *prompt* deposit of copies in the Copyright Office after publication. The Supreme Court had occasion to construe this language in *Washingtonian Publishing Company* v. *Pearson*.[33] There some fourteen months had elapsed between the time of publication and deposit. The Court construed the statute (then numbered Sec. 12) as not providing for forfeiture of copyright by reason of failure to deposit. The statutory requirement was for notice of copyright, not for deposit insofar as liability was concerned. However, no action could be brought for infringement of copyright before deposit.[34]

Thus certain formalities may be seen as substantive, i.e., notice of copyright, going to the matter of liability. If

---

[31] Norbay Music, Inc. v. King Records, Inc., note 26, *supra*.

[32] 17 U.S.C. 13.

[33] 306 U.S. 30 (1939).

[34] 17 U.S.C. 13 recites in the last sentence thereof, "No action or proceeding shall be maintained for infringement of copyright in any work until the provisions of this title with respect to the deposit of copies and registration of such work shall have been complied with." Of course, the Register of Copyrights can pursue the matter of deposit by making a demand for deposit pursuant to Sec. 14 (17 U.S.C. 14) and in default thereof subject the copyright proprietor to a fine of $100 and payment of twice the retail price of the best edition, and as part of such penalty, void the copyright. But that consequence will only arise by reason of affirmative steps taken by the Register of Copyrights to assure compliance. Mere delay in deposit, without regard to the length of delay, will presumably not otherwise cause a forfeiture of copyright under the rationale of the Supreme Court.

there were a failure of affixation of notice of copyright altogether, assuming no accidental omission of notice subject to the provisions of Sec. 21,[35] there would be a forfeiture of copyright.[36] Hence, failure on the part of the copyright proprietor to affix notice of copyright pursuant to the statute has the effect of placing the work in the public domain. It would seem that the objective fact of failure to affix such notice is determinative of elimination of the possibility of liability, regardless of the reason for such total failure of notice. Ignorance of the law would presumably be no excuse or saving factor in elimination of the copyright. Where the copyright proprietor intends to publish completely without notice, whether or not he intended to dedicate the work to the public domain or proceeded without the advice of persons knowledgeable in copyright, be they lawyers or otherwise and does so, he has forfeited his copyright. The savings clause, as provided by Sec. 21 of the Copyright Act, only becomes operative as follows: "Where the copyright proprietor has sought to comply with the provisions of this title with respect to notice, the omission by accident or mistake of the prescribed notice from a particular copy or copies shall not invalidate the copyright or prevent recovery for infringement against any person who, after actual notice of the copyright, begins an undertaking to infringe it, but shall prevent the recovery of damages against an innocent infringer who has been misled by the omission of the

[35] 17 U.S.C. 21.

[36] Report No. 2222, House of Representatives, 60th Cong., 2d Sess., to accompany H.R. 28192, February 22, 1909, as reprinted in Nimmer, *op. cit., supra,* note 29, Appendix I, 959 at p. 972. Nimmer states in Sec. 81, at p. 301, with respect to notice, ". . . the failure to affix a copyright notice in proper form and in the proper place on published copies of the work may prove fatal either to a claim of copyright or its maintenance."

notice; and in a suit for infringement no permanent injunction shall be had unless the copyright proprietor shall reimburse to the innocent infringer his reasonable outlay innocently incurred if the court, in its discretion, shall so direct." [37]

In the requirement for notice and the savings clause, we find the undulations of policy as expressed by the Congress both as to the right and the remedy. The broad grant of rights given to the creator and assigns by Sec. 1[38] in respect of protection of all of the writings of the author by Sec. 4[39] are accorded copyright protection as to their copyrightable components by Sec. 3,[40] and their derivatives under Secs. 1 and 7[41] are, in many respects, liberal and in accordance with constitutional mandate.[42] But the liberality of the rights is effectively qualified by procedural obligations of the copyright proprietor as conditions precedent to the effective realization of the rights. Assuming a valid copyright otherwise available in a writing under the Copyright Act, a condition precedent to obtaining statutory copyright is the affixation of notice of copyright. The common law copyright is lost upon publication in any event.[43] Thenceforth, there may be the grant of rights under statutory copyright, "upon complying with the pro-

---

[37] 17 U.S.C. 21.

[38] 17 U.S.C. 1.

[39] 17 U.S.C. 4.

[40] 17 U.S.C. 3.

[41] 17 U.S.C. 1(b) and 7.

[42] Constitution of the United States, Art. I, Sec. 8, Clause 8:

"The Congress shall have power:

"To promote the progress of science and useful arts, by securing, for limited times, to authors and inventors, the exclusive right to their respective writings and discoveries."

[43] Wheaton v. Peters, 8 Peters 591 (1834), 17 U.S.C. 2.

visions of this title." [44] The failure to affix notice, absent any savings clause, would constitute a failure to comply with the procedural requirements for obtaining statutory copyright. Thus the obligation to affix notice of copyright upon publication invests the omission with substantive consequences, the elimination of the possibility of obtaining the right. Concomitantly, the failure to obtain the right eliminates all remedies inhering in the right under statutory copyright.

The harshness of the rule is mitigated in respect of accidental omission or mistaken notice in a particular copy or copies where the copyright proprietor seeks to comply with the notice provisions.[45] Thus all of the liberality of the grant of rights must go through the right procedures as to formalities of notice in order to be protectible, relaxed only somewhat by the mitigating factors of the savings clause. Having so set the ground rules for the copyright formalities, Congress has again expressed concern for fairness and reasonableness in the operation of the savings clause as to remedies. Thus, having set the ground rules of public policy as to when the broad rules of according rights to the creator might be exercisable upon publication, i.e., upon compliance with the formalities of notice, Congress has seen fit to adopt rules of fairness as to the consequences of the remedies once the rights are saved by the mitigating effects of the savings clause. There shall be no recovery of damages against an innocent infringer misled by the accidental omission of the notice of copyright. The savings clause also allows for recovery of damages after actual notice of copyright. If the copyright proprietor, in a suit for infringement, wishes to obtain a

[44] 17 U.S.C. 1.

[45] See House Report, No. 2222, note 36, *supra,* Appendix I, Nimmer, at p. 975.

permanent injunction, the court has the discretion to order the copyright proprietor to reimburse the innocent infringer for his reasonable outlay before granting any such permanent injunction.[46]

Sec. 26.5. Rights and Remedies: Trial by Jury

But the interplay of right and remedy with the Constitution of the United States, as seen above in connection with notice and formalities, also is immanent in respect of the various remedies and trial by judge or jury. Amendment VII to the Constitution preserves the right to trial by jury in suits at common law.[47] But, as noted above, the remedy at common law was recovery of damages; the other relief provided by the statute, including recovery of profits, was equitable.[48] This, of course, raises the question of trial of law issues in an action which includes equitable issues. As to issues cognizable at common law, there is the right to trial by jury, but not as to equitable issues which historically were determined by the court sitting as a court of equity.

The resolution of this problem was expressed by the Court of Appeals for the Ninth Circuit in *Bruckman* v. *Hollzer*,[49] where it observed that the Federal Rules of Civil Procedure give a party having a claim triable by jury at common law the power to preserve that right when the

---

[46] 17 U.S.C. 21.

[47] Constitution of the United States, Amendment VII:

"In Suits at common law, where the value in controversy shall exceed twenty dollars, the right of trial by jury shall be preserved, and no fact tried by a jury, shall be otherwise reexamined in any Court of the United States, than according to the rules of the common law."

[48] Notes, 5-11, *supra*.

[49] 152 F. 2d 730 (9th Cir. 1946).

claim is joined with other equitable claims by trying common law issues before the others. Speaking of this procedure, Joseph D. Karp has remarked, "The present tendency in most districts is for the Court to hold that the right to trial by jury is 'preserved' under Rule 38 Federal Rules of Civil Procedure, when a law cause is joined with one in equity. The procedure is for the trial by jury on the law issues to be brought on before the equitable issues are tried before a Judge without a Jury." [50]

In this regard, an interesting question arises as to the handling of in lieu or statutory damages in a trial by jury, such damages not being actual damages but statutory substitutes. The Court of Appeals for the Second Circuit considered this question in *Mail & Express Co.* v. *Life Pub. Co.*[51] There the defendant contended it was error for the court to charge the jury that it must award at least $250 damages. The defendant said that the trial court could have taken the question of damage away from the jury and himself awarded stated damages but he could not direct such an award. Judge Noyes stated for the Court of Appeals, " . . . we do not think that by the use of the word 'court' it is required that the judge acting by himself shall assess the damages when a case is presented calling for an award under the minimum damage clause." [52] He felt that the better view is that the court can direct the jury, but in any event the defendant was not harmed.

---

[50] Karp, Joseph D., Copyright Litigation, 7 Copyright Problems Analyzed, 1951, reprinted in Fred B. Rothman & Co. edition with 1953 Copyright Problems Analyzed sub. nom. Copyright Problems Analyzed (1966), pp. 143-184 at p. 171.

[51] 192 Fed. 899 (2d Cir. 1912).

[52] *Idem* at p. 901.

Sec. 26.6. Proof of Damages: Actual Damages

It is in this context that we can best assess the nature and meaning of the cornerstone of the remedies provided by the statute, Sec. 101(b) (formerly Sec. 25(b)),[53] which tied in statutory or in lieu damages with actual damages and recovery of profits. Judicial expressions spell out the nature and purpose of the statute in this respect.

In an early case, *Gross* v. *Van Dyk Gravure Co.*, Judge Learned Hand had remarked below:

> "This is, as I understand the duty laid upon the court by section 25b: In place of the old penalties the court is to estimate damages, but to estimate them within the sums given, without the limitation of usual legal proof. I think the whole course of copyright law shows a recognition of the difficulty of making legal proof of damages, and that, in substituting for rigid penalties the discretionary power of the judge, we must assume that a plaintiff should not fail for lack of proof." [54]

Judge Hough, speaking for the Court of Appeals for the Second Circuit in *S. E. Hendricks Co., Inc.* v. *Thomas Publishing Co.*,[55] had these observations:

> " . . . the language of this section is a growth of years, resulting from the efforts of Congress to avoid that strictness of construction which historically attaches to any statute inflicting penalties, and to confer upon an injured party some pecuniary solace even when the

---

[53] 17 U.S.C. 101(b), numbered Sec. 25(b) in the Copyright Act of 1909.

[54] 230 Fed. 412, 413 (2d Cir. 1916). See note 86, *infra*.

[55] 242 Fed. 37 (2d Cir. 1917).

rules of law render it difficult, if not impossible (as it often is) to prove damages or discover profits.[56]

* * * * *

"That assessment of damages or ascertainment of profits under the facts hereinabove recited would be not only difficult but expensive is similarly obvious. We entertain no doubt that it was the intention of Congress (1) to preserve the right of a plaintiff to pursue damages and profits by the historic methods of equity if he chooses to do so; and (2) to give the new right of application to the court for such damages as shall 'appear to be just' in lieu of actual damages." [57]

Justice Van Devanter, speaking for the Supreme Court, in *L. A. Westermann* v. *Dispatch Printing Co.*, referred to the Copyright Act of 1856 and Sec. 4966 of the Revised Statutes and stated:

"In 1909, when the copyright statutes were revised, these provisions, and others without present bearing, were brought together in the 'in lieu' provision now under consideration. True, they were broadened so as to include other copyrights and the limitations were changed in amount, but the principle on which they proceeded—that of committing the amount of damages to be recovered to the court's discretion and sense of justice, subject to prescribed limitations—was retained." [58]

Justice Brandeis observed in *Jewell-LaSalle Realty Co.* v. *Buck*:

---

[56] *Idem* at p. 41.
[57] *Idem* at pp. 41-42.
[58] 249 U.S. 100, 107 (1919).

"... the primary purpose of section 25 was to incorporate in one section all of the civil remedies theretofore given, including statutory damages where actual proof was lacking. . . . We are of opinion that the maximum and minimum provisions were intended to be applicable alike to all types of infringement except those for which the section makes other specific provision." [59]

Justice Roberts remarked in *Douglas* v. *Cunningham*:

"The phraseology of the section was adopted to avoid the strictness of construction incident to a law imposing penalties, and to give the owner of a copyright some recompense for injury done him, in a case where the rules of law render difficult or impossible proof of damages or discovery of profits. In this respect the old law was unsatisfactory. In many cases plaintiffs, though proving infringement, were able to recover only nominal damages, in spite of the fact that preparation and trial of the case imposed substantial expense and inconvenience. The ineffectiveness of the remedy imposed wilful and deliberate infringement." [60]

It was Circuit Judge Hough who purported to define the terms "actual" and "in lieu" in relation to damages, stating in *Hendricks*, "These words present no difficulty in interpretation. 'Actual' means 'real', as opposed to 'nominal' . . . It means 'existent', without precluding the thought of change . . . 'In lieu' means in place of the thing modified by the quoted phrase." [61] Actual damages, then, are proven damages that judge or jury have found a copyright proprietor to have sustained by reason of the infringement.

[59] 283 U.S. 202 (1931), at pp. 206-207.
[60] 294 U.S. 207, 209 (1935).
[61] Note 55, *supra*, at p. 42.

Actual damages and their ambit have variant applications so that in and of themselves they may or may not adequately serve as a means of restitution. In *Douglas* v. *Cunningham*,[62] plaintiff wrote a story in the American Mercury and the copyright in the story was duly assigned to him. The defendant wrote an infringing story in the Boston Post which had sold 384,000 copies of that issue. At the close of trial, plaintiff stated that he was unable to prove actual damages. Presumably plaintiff had intended to prove actual damages had he been able to do so. In *Davis* v. *E.I. DuPont de Nemours & Co.*,[63] plaintiff did not claim actual damages, relying instead on a claim of in lieu damages. Then, too, even if claimed, there is always the possibility of a determination of no actual damages. Thus, in *Warren* v. *Whyte & Wyckoff Mfg. Co.*[64] plaintiff had written a book selling for $6. Defendant had printed a calendar appropriating two pages of the book. The court felt that there were no actual damages and the same could not be proven. In a case involving infringement of auto maps, *General Drafting Co., Inc.* v. *Andrews*,[65] the Court held that plaintiff's business had not been materially injured.

Moreover, in certain circumstances, actual damages might be a sum which an infringer would be glad to settle for, such amount being no more than the license fee that the complainant would have accepted anyway for a license from the defendant were he not infringing. This argument was actually advanced by infringing defendant without success in *Widenski* v. *Shapiro, Bernstein & Company, Inc.*[66] in a typical suit by ASCAP for violation of plaintiff's perform-

---

[62] Note 60, *supra*.
[63] 249 F. Supp. 329 (S.D.N.Y. 1966).
[64] 39 F. 2d 922 (S.D.N.Y. 1930).
[65] 37 F. 2d 54 (2d Cir. 1930).
[66] 147 F. 2d 909 (1st Cir. 1945).

ing rights in a musical composition. ASCAP had tried to license the café operated by defendant for an annual rental of $90 or monthly rental of $10. Defendant could not avoid in lieu damages of $250 by his contention that actual damages were only $10, the amount ASCAP had been willing to take for a license fee.

If a defendant cannot necessarily rely on the nominality of actual damages in order to extricate himself from the culpability of infringement, neither ought a plaintiff rely on the possibility of punitive damages. In *Smith* v. *Little, Brown & Co.*,[67] a case involving common law copyright, plaintiff alleged plagiarism of his book and asked for actual compensatory damages, punitive damages and loss of profits. The Court had this to say, as to punitive damages:

> "The courts have been reluctant to grant punitive damages. This is especially true in copyright cases.
>
> * * *
>
> "Punitive damages are of course a pure windfall to a plaintiff. They amount to a penalty against a defendant."[68]

Thus it may be seen that the results of efforts to ascertain actual damages are indeed quite variable, and in given situations ascertainment thereof may provide little or no solace to a plaintiff, or become an escape valve for an infringing defendant seeking to rely on small license fees as actual damages, were the courts to accept such formulations as the measure of damages. Even if one concedes, *arguendo,* that ". . . in appropriate cases techniques are

---

[67] 273 F. Supp. 870 (S.D.N.Y. 1967), *aff'd,* 396 F. 2d 150 (2d Cir. 1968).

[68] *Idem* at pp. 873-874.

available for determining actual damages",[69] it would seem that nevertheless the availability of such techniques does not necessarily assure the justice of applying the results thereof. Brown has set forth some of these techniques as follows:

> "One shortcoming of actual damages as a remedy in copyright cases, it has long been considered, is the supposed difficulty of computing them. Since works subject to copyright are by and large differentiated from each other, it is difficult to establish values. If the values of the work before the infringement and its diminished value afterward are sought, in accordance with one approved technique of damage law, two valuations are necessary. Or, if the plaintiff's lost profits are proposed as a measure of his damages, there is the problem of establishing with reasonable certainty what they would have been.
>
> "On the other hand, it is suggested that where valuations are called for, expert testimony is admissible, in line with the admissibility of such testimony in cases where profits have to be apportioned. As for lost profits, the trend in damage law in recent decades has been to relax the requirements of exactness. Once the fact of damage has been established, some freedom is left to the trier to estimate the amount." [70]

Nimmer has also set forth some of these techniques, stating:

---

[69] Brown, Ralph S., Jr., The Operation of the Damages Provisions of the Copyright Law: An Exploratory Study, Study No. 23, of 2 Studies On Copyright, pp. 1067-1098 at p. 1077 (1963).

[70] *Idem* at p. 1075.

> "Monetary recovery for common law copyright infringement is subject to the same principles as are applicable in connection with injury to other forms of personal property. The plaintiff may claim damages in the same manner as in the misappropriation or conversion of tangible peronalty, i.e. measured by the exchange or market value of the plaintiff's work at the time of infringement. If the infringement has entirely destroyed the value of the work, the damages then equal the full such value. If the special value of the work to the plaintiff is greater than its market value, he may claim such greater measure. In determining such special value to the plaintiff the court may look to the nature of the work itself, its particular utility to the plaintiff, and to whether or not it can be reproduced. The fact that such damages are difficult to ascertain will not prevent a substantial recovery." [71]

In certain types of cases, such as those involving motion pictures, it would appear that the effect of infringement is to impair or destroy the plaintiff's literary and artistic property. Here the rationale would appear to be comparable to the refusal to accord an exception of a for profit limitation to dramatic or dramatico-musical works in Sec. 1(d)[72] of the Copyright Act, in granting exclusive rights as to public performance, as compared to musical works in Sec. 1(e).[73] The public is not likely to go to another dramatic or dramatico-musical performance, whereas music can be heard over and over again without impairment. Thus, in *Universal Pictures Co., Inc.* v. *Harold*

---

[71] Nimmer, *op. cit., supra,* note 29, Sec. 150, at p. 666.
[72] 17 U.S.C. 1(d).
[73] 17 U.S.C. 1(e).

Lloyd Corp.,[74] the Court of Appeals for the Ninth Circuit affirmed a lower court ruling of $40,000 actual damages for appropriation of 57 scenes from Harold Lloyd's "Movie Crazy" in appellant's film, "So's Your Uncle". The Court stated, "We are of the opinion that there is substantial evidence in the case to show that property rights and present existing intrinsic property values have been impaired or destroyed. The testimony of the expert witnesses clearly establishes that the picture's value has been lessened by the appropriation of an important sequence by the appellant, and it is common knowledge that the repeated use of comedy, detracts from its force as amusement." [75]

It is submitted that market considerations as to extent of impairment must have been taken into account. In *Golding* v. *RKO Pictures, Inc.*,[76] a case involving infringement of common law copyright, plaintiff authors testified that the value of their work was between $25,000 and $50,000. The court below was affirmed on a judgment of $25,000, since the authors themselves could testify as to value of their literary property even though they introduced no experts. The Court of Appeals for the Second Circuit spelled out this rationale of impairment in *Szekely* v. *Eagle Lion Films, Inc.*[77] There plaintiff had contracted to write a screenplay adaptation of the novel "Christ in Concrete" for $35,000. He received $10,000 with a security title until he received $35,000. Rod E. Geiger Productions, Inc., the other

---

[74] 162 F. 2d 354 (9th Cir. 1947).

[75] *Idem* at p. 369.

[76] 35 Cal. 2d 690, 221 P. 2d 95 (1950).

[77] 242 F. 2d 266 (2d Cir. 1957). See also Smith v. Little, Brown & Company, 396 F. 2d 150 (2d Cir. 1968), *aff'g* 273 F. Supp. 870 (S.D.N.Y. 1967) awarding $650.11, amount found to be defendant's profits and denying punitive damages.

party to the agreement, began to run into many problems. It used another writer to complete the screenplay and did not pay plaintiff the balance. It then granted defendant, Eagle Lion, Western hemisphere distribution rights in the film. The latter grossed $46,719.84 and Geiger received $29,758.04 as producer's share. The Court held that the market value was at least $25,000 at the time of the conversion of the literary property. It stated that compensatory damages for the conversion was equal to the exchange value, or a different value where necessary, to give just compensation. The market had ended for plaintiff upon the sale to defendant, Eagle Lion. The lower court determination of $25,000 in actual damages was affirmed. The Court indicated that it should not allow the difficulty in ascertaining precise value of the thing destroyed from a computation of actual damages where the difficulty was created largely to allow the infringer to escape without compensation. Damages were at least $25,000 from the conversion.

In *Szekely,* the Court, in effect, looked to the balance of the contract price and its loss as the measure of actual damages, since the conversion represented a total impairment or destruction of the ability of the plaintiff to follow through. Again, the infringement had effectively denied plaintiff any ability to utilize his work in the market since the public would not go to see the same story, substantially, in another movie. What plaintiff really had lost was his contract price, and although Eagle Lion was not privy to the contract between the writer of the screenplay, plaintiff, and the production company, Rod E. Geiger Productions, Inc., the Court made the plaintiff whole as though he had performed, which he was unable to do by reason of the infringement and conversion. Thus damages were transported from impossibility of performance by reason of breach of contract, i.e., the contract price of $25,000, to become the measure of damages for tortious conversion and infringement of common law copyright.

But films represent, in a sense, a separate market and separate means of ascertainment of values. Writers have their price for literary and artistic works. Box office receipts are available as to the infringed work, as in the Harold Lloyd film, as well as in the infringing film. Projections of receipts are constantly being made in the film industry, particularly by the sales accounting departments of the studios, to estimate what remakes and re-issues of any given picture might gross based upon comparability of the box office of initial release of that picture with box office receipts of other pictures of like nature and the remake and re-issue thereof, and so forth. Projection, in the sense of sales estimation is an established technique of motion picture distribution and so, just as actual damages may be sought on the creative side for converted writings, so infringing use of filmic material may similarly be sought in the market.

In book publication, a more precise method of computation of actual damages may be used where the infringement arises by a substantial copying of the infringed work. In *Ziegelheim* v. *Flohr*,[78] plaintiff's sales of his copyrighted Hebrew prayer book were as follows:

Year	*Copies*
1950	1232
1951	1532
1952	1355
1953	150

[78] 119 F. Supp. 324 (E.D.N.Y. 1954).

As to these, the Court noted:

> "Defendant's book was published in June 1952. Plaintiff's sales on order do not appear to have been substantially affected in 1952 by the appearance of defendant's book on the market, because plaintiff sold 703 books during the first half of 1952 and 652 books during the second half of 1952, while his average sales for the second half of 1950 and 1951 appears to have been 678 copies.
>
> "However, plaintiff's average sales on order for 1950 and 1951 amounted to 1,382 copies, which approximates his sales of 1,355 in 1952, and his sales on order in 1953 were only 150 copies, so that plaintiff lost 1,232 sales on order in 1953 when compared with his average sales on order in 1951 and 1952. Plaintiff also testified to a loss of sales over the counter in 1953 of approximately 450 copies. Thus plaintiff's total loss of sales in 1953 were approximately 1,682 copies at 75 cents per copy, or a total of approximately $1,261.50."[79]

The Court awarded total damages of $1,700 as reasonable and just on a printing by defendant of 4,000 copies after concluding that defendant's profits were substantially less than the $901.60 computed by plaintiff. It should be noted that the damages computed as to decrease in sales would approximate the classic method of showing actual damages attributable to the infringing copy of defendant.

It would appear from the foregoing, that while ascertainment of actual damages may be invaluable methods of ascertaining recovery by a wronged copyright proprietor in a variety of circumstances, actual damages alone would not produce justice and would thwart the purpose of copy-

---

[79] *Idem* at p. 329.

right. The damages provisions of the Copyright Act not only serve as a means of recompense to an aggrieved plaintiff, they also serve as mechanisms for policing plagiarism, piracy and assorted types of infringement. The judicial process provided such plaintiffs is a principal means of achieving the Congressional grant of rights to creators and assigns and thereby of implementing the constitutional mandate. The judicial process, by according the facilities for private parties to police infringement, thereby enables contracts to function in the market by enabling marketing agencies and their counsel to rely on prognostications of the effects of infringement of copyright, by reason of such policing, so as to avoid the same, by proper license or assignment of rights.

Although it has been stated by one Court, ". . . there is no necessary connection . . ." between damages and profits,[80] the judiciary does not always categorize actual damages, profits and statutory damages into neat, separate compartments. In *Twentieth Century-Fox Film Corporation* v. *Stonesifer*, the Court of Appeals for the Ninth Circuit stated:

> "Appellant finally contends that there is no evidence whatsoever to sustain the findings of damages or the conclusion based thereon. The record reveals that considerable trial time in the court below was consumed in the determination of the film's approximate total cost. It appears that this, including costs of production, prints and distribution, amounted to $842,400, and that the film rentals amounted to $862,200, or a net profit of $19,800. From this the trial court assessed damages for the infringement of $3,960, or one-fifth of the net profits.

[80] Lundberg v. Welles, 93 F. Supp. 359, 361 (S.D.N.Y. 1950).

"It is now settled that where a portion of the profits of an infringing work is attributable to the appropriated work, to avoid an unjust course by giving the originator all profits where the infringer's labor and artistry have also to an extent contributed to the ultimate result, there may be a reasonable approximation and apportionment by the court of the profits derived therefrom. We find no reason to disturb the award of damages or the allowance of attorney's fees in the court below." [81]

In *Silver* v. *Television City, Inc.*[82] the court affirmed a lower court submission to the jury of the question of damages on infringement of common law copyright by use of plaintiff's script on television and the jury's award of $7,500 in damages. The Court concluded its affirming opinion by stating, "We are of the opinion that sufficient proof was offered in the present case and we cannot say that the jury's finding of $7,500 or approximately $200 per broadcast for the use of plaintiff's program is so unreasonable as to shock our conscience, justifying a new trial on that basis." [83]

Stonesifer apparently used net profits as the measure of damages, whereas *Silver* approximated notions of multiple performance in fixing damages at a dollar amount per broadcast. In *Advertisers Exchange, Inc.* v. *Hinckley*,[84] the Court declined to apply the statutory yardstick of $1 a copy as suggested by plaintiff where the latter's service of annual subscription to an exclusive advertising book at

---

[81] 140 F. 2d 579, 583-584 (9th Cir. 1944).

[82] 207 Pa. Super 150, 215 A. 2d 335 (Superior Ct. Pa. 1965).

[83] *Idem* at 207 Pa. Super at pp. 158-159, p. 215 A. 2d at p. 339.

[84] 101 F. Supp. 801 (W.D. Mo. 1951), *aff'd,* 199 F. 2d 313 (8th Cir. 1952), cert. den. 344 U.S. 921 (1953).

$156 a year was infringed, there being actual notice of infringement by defendant in placing ads after cancellation of his subscription. There were no actual damages nor loss of profits. The infringing use took place in 29 publications, each of which had a run of 3,261 copies. Plaintiff sought $94,569, or 29 times $3,261, at the rate of the statutory yardstick of $1 a copy. The Court felt this was a ridiculous amount. Instead, the court below used the contract subscription rate of $156 as the measure of in lieu damages and awarded $312 in damages. The Court of Appeals affirmed. In effect, the Court applied the rule comparable to the relationship of the compulsory license for recordings under Sec. 1(e) to infringement thereof under Sec. 101(e). If all the plaintiff could have gotten under contract was $156 a year, the contract price, similar to the two cents a side under the compulsory license, then the damages for infringement were the contract price times the number of years during which the infringement occurred. The difference is that Sec. 101(e) explicitly sets forth damages for infringement at the same rate as for the compulsory license under Sec. 1(e), to wit, two cents a side (plus the discretionary trebling, in each instance).

Indeed, in *Gross* v. *Van Dyk Gravure Co.*, Circuit Judge Lacombe had this to say:

> "The District Judge made a careful calculation to determine how many sales of the copyrighted photographs were lost to plaintiff, because of sales of the infringing photograph to persons who would otherwise have bought the copyrighted one. He then calculated what net profit plaintiff would have realized on the sales which he would have made, had not the infringing photograph prevented his making such sales. These *lost profits* of the *plaintiff* he found to be the measure of plaintiff's damages. We find nothing wrong about

the calculation; indeed, the judge's figures are not attacked." [85]

The District Judge in *Gross* was Learned Hand. Judge Hand had stated below that he would not take the number of infringing photographs printed as the measure of damages " . . . as I can not think it has any relation to actual damages. I shall rather try to estimate Gross's actual damages without observing the rules of evidence, as though the issue had to be proved like other such issues and allowing myself considerable latitude in speculation." [86] Judge Hand then took 20% of plaintiff's gross sales of $3,850 or $770 plus expenses or a total of $1100 as measure of damages, and remarked, "Of course, it is a mere speculation; but if I am right, the statute requires me to make as fair a speculation as I can." [87]

Sec. 26.7. Profits and Allocation

Although Learned Hand took plaintiff's lost profits as the measure of damages in *Gross,* unlike the Court in *Stonesifer,* which took the defendant's profits as the measure of damages, yet the approach of Judge Hand, in taking a percentage of profits foreshadowed his later approach as to allocation and apportionment in *Sheldon* v. *Metro Goldwyn Pictures Corp.*[88] There the District Court had followed the earlier case of *Dam* v. *Kirk La Shelle Co.*[89] and given all of profits on infringement by defendant by use of plaintiffs'

---

[85] 230 Fed. 412, 414 (2d Cir. 1916) (italics).

[86] The opinion of the District Court is reproduced in 230 Fed. 412 immediately prior to the opinion of Judge Lacombe. The quoted portion appears at p. 413.

[87] *Idem* at p. 413.

[88] 106 F. 2d 45 (2d Cir. 1939), Hand, L., *J.; aff'd,* 309 U.S. 390 (1940), Hughes, *C.J.*

[89] 175 Fed. 902 (2d Cir. 1910).

play even though it thought an allocation of 25% of the profits to the plaintiff to be just. The special master appointed by the District Court had given all of the profits to the plaintiff. Circuit Judge Hand overruled the *Dam* case and awarded 20% of the net profits to plaintiff. The burden for separation is on the defendants, so that by meeting the same, an allocation can be made. Judge Hand stated in this regard:

> "The difficulties of separation have generally prevented infringers from attempting any apportionment; they have contented themselves with getting down the net profits as low as possible. That was the case in Callaghan v. Meyers, supra; and in Belford, Clarke & Co. v. Scribner 144 U.S. 488, 508, 12 S. Ct. 734, 36 L. Ed. 514; and for this reason the general language there used is not to be taken as holding that the infringer must always be unsuccessful, no matter what evidence he may bring forward. They hold no more than when he makes no effort to discharge the duty resting upon him, he will be cast for the whole profit." [90]

As indicated in the earlier decision[91] as to liability, the defendants had negotiated with the plaintiff and sought to acquire rights in plaintiff's play after inducing him to get up a scenario at a negotiated price of $30,000. The negotiations aborted because of possible censorship problems involving the Will Hays office, the association of motion picture producers.

In the later decision as to damages, Judge Hand discarded the agreed price of the play because of various uncertainties involving its application in the premises. In-

---

[90] Note 88, *supra,* at p. 49.

[91] 81 F. 2d 49 (2d Cir. 1936), Hand, L., *J.*

stead, the percentage of apportionment of net profits of defendant evolved. Various factors were taken into consideration including that ". . . the plaintiffs worked over old material, the general skeleton was already in the public demesne." [92] Also, defendants' standing and reputation in the industry could not be counted because they were not innocent offenders. Judge Hand adverted, "It follows that they can be credited only with such factors as they bought and paid for; the actors, the scenery, the producers, the directors and the general overhead . . . a plagiarist may not charge for his labor in exploiting what he has taken. A fortiori he should not be allowed for the currency which his reputation may have given to the combined product." [93] He then determined an allocation of net profits attributable to plaintiffs at 20%, applying the patent rule of apportionment in justification of following the rule in copyrights.

Chief Justice Hughes, in affirming, stated, "We agree with petitioners that the 'in lieu' clause is not applicable here, as the profits have been proved, and the only question is as to their apportionment." [94] He then construed the language of the statute as to recovery of all of the profits and related the same to the cognate clause of damages attributable to the infringement, stating:

> "Petitioners stress the provisions for recovery of 'all' the profits, but this is plainly qualified by the words 'which the infringer shall have made from such infringement.' This provision in purpose is cognate to that for the recovery of '. . . such damages as the copyright proprietor may have suffered due to the infringement.' . . . The purpose is thus to provide just compen-

---

[92] Note 88, *supra,* at p. 50.

[93] *Idem* at p. 51.

[94] 309 U.S. 390, 399 (1940).

> sation for the wrong, not to impose a penalty by giving to the copyright proprietor profits which are not attributable to the infringement." [95]

Chief Justice Hughes appeared to set up a proportion. If damages are by statute allocable to those suffered by the copyright proprietor, i.e., are limited to those approximately caused by the infringement of the defendants, then the term "all" immediately thereafter as modifying the term "profits" is to be taken to have a like meaning, to wit, all of the profits attributable to the infringement.

Justice Hughes buttressed his decision by pointing out that, prior to the 1909 Copyright Act, there had been no provision for recovery of profits, but that the same had been allowed in equity in both patent and copyright cases to prevent unjust enrichment. He noted that statutory provision for recovery of profits in patent cases had been enacted in 1870. He remarked, "In passing the Copyright Act, the apparent intention of Congress was to assimilate the remedy with respect to the recovery of profits to that already recognized in patent cases." [96] He then adverted to the House Report with respect to Sec. 25(b) of the 1909 Act which he quoted in part as follows:

> " 'Section 25 deals with the matter of civil remedies for infringement of a copyright . . . The provision that the copyright proprietor may have such damages as well as the profits which the infringer shall have made is substantially the same provision found in section 4921 of the Revised Statutes relating to remedies for the infringement of patents. The courts have usually construed that to mean that the owner of the patent might have one or the other, whichever was the greater.

---

[95] *Ibid.*

[96] *Idem* at p. 400.

> As such a provision was found both in the trade-mark and patent laws, the committee felt that it might be properly included in the copyright laws.' "[97]

Thereupon, the Supreme Court distinguished prior decisions[98] where it was not possible to separate profits attributable to the infringement from other profits and awarded all to the plaintiffs. The test is evidentiary. Where the evidence supports allocation, the courts will make the apportionment. Further analogy was made to the patent rules. In 1922, Congress had passed a statute permitting allocation in patent cases; the fact that the Copyright Act was not similarly amended was no reason for equity not to apply the same rule.

The Supreme Court effectively supported Judge Learned Hand in its opinion of affirmance. In doing so, it not only reiterated the statutory following of the patent rule for recovery of profits in copyright, but also set forth the judicial determination of apportionment in copyright by analogy to the statutory rule of allocation in patents as the doctrine of the highest court of the land.

But the affirmance of the rule enunciated by Judge Learned Hand represented a shift in thinking. Chief Justice Hughes had stated as to patents, "The analogy found in cases of patent infringement is persuasive. There are many cases in which the plaintiff's patent covers only a part of a machine and creates only a part of the profits. The patented invention may have been used in combination with additions or valuable improvements made

---

[97] *Idem* at pp. 400-401. The entire House Report No. 2222 is set forth in Appendix I of Nimmer on Copyright, note 36, *supra.*

[98] Callaghan v. Myers, 128 U.S. 617 (1888) and Belford, Clarke & Co. v. Scribner, 144 U.S. 488 (1892).

by the infringer and each may have contributed to the profits." [99] The shift to the Supreme Court's sanctioning of the apportionment rule in literary and artistic property based on the analogy to mechanics—the realm of patents—is most interesting.

One can contend that support for this view might also be found, in addition to the patent analogy, in the Copyright Act itself, to wit, Sec. 3[100] thereof, which accords protection to the copyrightable components of literary and artistic properties. Protection is accorded thereby only to the original contribution of the creator and assigns and not to material which is in the public domain which may be embodied in the work. One might argue, by analogy to the substantive effect of Sec. 3, that essentially the rule in *Sheldon* represents an attribution of profits by application of the rule as to liability. That is, the defendants used only so much of the work of the plaintiffs in the course of making the infringing film.

But the analogy is not thereby complete. In *Orgel* v. *Clark Boardman Co.*,[101] defendant's infringing book on valuation used plaintiff's material to the extent of 35% of the defendant's book. The District Court had allocated all of profits of $12,849.32 to plaintiff on the theory that there was no evidence of allocation to the non-infringing part of the defendant's book written by one, Jahr. The Court of Appeals determined, "The very existence of the remaining sixty-five percent in the infringing work is convincing evidence that some part of the commercial value of the whole is attributable thereto. We are not persuaded that

---

[99] Note 94, *supra,* at p. 402.

[100] 17 U.S.C. 3.

[101] 301 F. 2d 119 (2d Cir. 1962), *modifying* 128 U.S.P.Q. 531 (S.D.N.Y. 1960), cert. den. 371 U.S. 817 (1962).

the principle of apportionment, announced in Sheldon, must be limited to cases in which experts have testified with respect to the relative contributions of the plagiarized and original portions." [102] The Court of Appeals then allocated 50% of the profits to the plaintiff on the theory that valuation was the most important part of the defendant's book even though it constituted only 35% of the material.

Thus, quantum of material appropriated, i.e., the copyrightable components under Sec. 3, is not necessarily the test for apportionment. The respective contributions of infringed work and the infringer, in adding other factors with a cost basis which contribute to the value of the new work, are to be weighed. It is submitted that here, too, Judge Learned Hand probably determined his 20% apportionment to plaintiff in *Sheldon* on the basis of relative importance of story to film in terms of market, i.e., box office results, rather than actual prices paid for literary and artistic works in the market, as the basis for adaptation into films. The result is a variable in each instance, depending upon the reputation and drawing power of the underlying novel or play and its author at that given time, but, in most instances, studios do not pay 20% of cost of production for a literary work unless the titles have already been proven as extraordinary drawing cards in sales as novels, or at the box office, as plays. Rather the technique adopted by Judge Learned Hand was to weigh the contribution of the underlying work, discarding its possible contract price, to the overall box office value. This is difficult to do at best because the result is derived, as in the *Gross* case, where Judge Hand speculated as to the plaintiff's lost profits, by speculation, after testimony of experts and

---

[102] *Idem* at p. 121.

other evidence, as to the attribution of profits to the plaintiffs' play.

But once such a yardstick is adduced by such speculation, it tends to be adopted as a measure in other situations. Although denominated damages in *Stonesifer*, the same 20% of net profits of the defendant was allocated to the plaintiff's infringed work.[103] The same 20% factor was deemed to be a fair allocation with respect to the infringement of 57 sequences, or 20%, of the film, "Movie Crazy" made by Harold Lloyd by the infringing film, "So's Your Uncle".[104] In that case, profits were found to exceed $20,000 and despite the 20% allocation to plaintiff, actual damages of $40,000 were awarded as being in excess thereof, and profits as such were not allowed.

Again, judicial nomenclature as to the award must be scrutinized, as in *Neal* v. *Thomas Organ Co.*[105] There the defendant had sold courses for its organ with attached records which infringed plaintiffs' material written for such courses. The Court held that the attached phonograph records served no purpose when separated from the instruction manual and that only the course as a whole had substantial value. Accordingly, on sales by defendant of 5,578 courses grossing $57,026.34 with direct costs of $24,131.67 and indirect costs of 14.7% or $8,382.67, net profits amounted to $24,511.80. Plaintiffs were awarded *damages* of $24,511.80. Again, plaintiffs had had a course of prior dealing with defendant in connection with the material

---

[103] Cf. Smith v. Little Brown Co., 273 F. Supp. 870 (S.D.N.Y. 1967), *aff'd,* 396 F. 2d 150 (2d Cir. 1968), where it was held that defendant's book as a whole infringed and no allocation could be made so that plaintiff received all of the $650.11 profits.

[104] Universal Pictures Co., Inc. v. Harold Lloyd Corporation, 162 F.2d 354 (9th Cir. 1947).

[105] 241 F. Supp. 1020 (S.D. Cal. 1965).

plaintiffs had prepared. Any approximation to contractual arrangements prior to infringement would have brought plaintiffs far less than the award of total net profits as damages. What the parties did before the infringement, in effect, was discarded in favor of the award of total net profits as damages. The decision does not spell out the use of the term "damages" in this context. It could be conceivably an award of total net profits of the defendant as the measure of plaintiffs' damages, or it could be the use of the term "damages" generically to describe any sort of recovery under the statute, be it actual damages, net profits or statutory damages.

However, different rules are applicable as to allocation where there are plural defendants. In *Sammons* v. *Colonial Press, Inc.*,[106] defendant, Colonial Press, as a contract printer, had agreed to print 3,000 copies of an infringing work on behalf of defendant, Larkin. Larkin had net profits of $7,236.50. The court below had awarded net profits of $7,236.50 against Larkin and in lieu damages of $250 against Colonial. The Court of Appeals affirmed the application of the lower court of the patent rule of several accountability for profits where the co-infringers are not partners, stating, "Accountability for profits is therefore peculiarly personal, as equity acts on the conscience of the infringer." [107] The appellate court asked the lower court on remand to ascertain whether Colonial had net profits and if it did, then in lieu damages could not be assessed against it.

The rule is stated in *Alfred Bell & Co. Ltd.* v. *Catalda Fine Arts, Inc.* as follows:

---

[106] 126 F. 2d 341 (1st Cir. 1942).
[107] *Idem* at p. 345.

> "Had the plaintiff attempted to prove damages, it is clear that the defendants, as indicated in the earlier ruling, would be jointly and severally liable for the damages resulting therefrom. Gross et al. v. Van Dyke Gravure Co., 2 Cir. 1916, 230 F. 412. But the plaintiff here has proved only profits. Originating in equity, accountability for profits is peculiarly personal, the presupposition being that the infringer has gotten something which it is unreasonable for him to keep. The defendants here are not jointly accountable but individually accountable for the profits which each received, not being held for the profits which may have been received by a co-infringer. Sammons et al. v. Colonial Press, Inc. et al., 1 Cir. 1942, 126 F. 2d 341. The responsibility for costs and attorneys' fees under the statute is, however, joint as well as several." [108]

One suspects that the rationale for personal liability for profits as opposed to damages is derived from two sources. Damages are based on a theory of restitution, to make the wronged party whole. Regardless of the technique of ascertaining the measure of damages that is used by any given court, the purpose is to make the plaintiff whole for losses he is found to have suffered—where actual damages are ascertained—or presumed to have been sustained without regard to actual loss by application of the legal fiction of statutory damages. Tortfeasors are therefore deemed joint so as to make a joint contribution thereto to make the plaintiff party whole. But profits are predicated on unjust enrichment; the party making the profits should not enjoy them at the expense of the wronged plaintiff. Such a de-

---

[108] 86 F. Supp. 399 (S.D.N.Y. 1949), *aff'd,* 191 F. 2d 99 (2d Cir. 1951) Frank, *J.* at p. 403. Accord, The Washingtonian Publishing Co., Inc. v. Pearson, 140 F. 2d 465 (C.C.A. D.C. 1944), Edgerton, *J.*

fendant therefore is deemed to hold the profits as constructive trustee on behalf of the plaintiff. Only the party making the profits presumably has them to hold as constructive trustee. Hence such party is liable therefor. The liability for profits consequently would be seen to be several.

Accordingly, plaintiffs seeking to hold tortfeasors jointly should seek to prove profits as damages and to take the net profits as a measure of damages, rather than as profits. Defendants not making profits, conversely, should make sure that an award, should there be one, is denominated profits and not damages so as to avoid joint liability for something never received or earned by such tortfeasor. Of course, where there is only a single defendant, the designation would seem to be immaterial.

It should be noted that, in computing profits, the courts have devised their own yardsticks in the ascertainment of net profits. Thus, in *Sheldon,* the Court used the master's theory of ascertaining distribution cost by dividing the number of pictures distributed in proportion to total gross receipts. Louis B. Mayer's percentage participation in profits was allowed to be deducted. Foreign profits were includable, as were profits of subsidiaries since they were actually real tortfeasors. Overhead was allocated as a function of the cost of production of each picture, not in terms of the total number of pictures produced. A continuity reserve for losses was disallowed. There was no warrant for excluding interest on the loan which had been excluded by the master. The Court disagreed with the master who had allowed a credit for income taxes. Idle time of the stars was allowed as a credit where they were contract players. Charges of the Motion Picture Association of America were allowed. The test for application of overhead was whether it assisted in the production of the picture. Interest on overhead on the plant (realty) was allowed, on a basis of use, of cost of production of the picture in proportion to all costs for the year, rather than by a percentage of the proportion of the property used. Exhibition losses were not allowed as a credit, except for foreign. A credit was allowed for scrapped continuities. A complex computation was allowed for export of negatives manufactured by the defendants. In sum, special rules were devised by the Court for allowances or disallowances of credits in computing net profits.

It would seem, therefore, that in computation of profits, plaintiffs would have to use experts and/or accountants conversant with the industrial pattern of the infringing profit maker to be able to formulate theories of allocation of charges and credits in ascertaining profits. In *Sheldon* situations, the computations would involve a knowledge of the motion picture industry as it existed at the time when defendant, Metro-Goldwyn Pictures Corp., was part of an integrated operation which included production, distribution and exhibition. In *Sammons,* there was a remand to ascertain the overhead expense of Colonial Press in order to determine whether it had sustained net profits. The book industry has its own configuration of expenses that might or might not be charges against net profits. In *Catalda*, the special master had determined separate net profit figures as to each of three defendants. A deduction was sought there as to cost of unsold prints. The Court remarked in respect thereto:

> "Equity allows the plaintiff here to recover profits only on the infringing prints which were actually sold by the infringers, and similarly it limits the credits or deductions allowable to the infringer from costs, to those costs which can be properly allocated to these infringing prints actually sold. It would be manifestly

> unjust to allow the defendant Catalda Company to reduce the amount of the plaintiff's recovery by permitting Catalda Company to deduct the total cost to it of all the infringing prints, including those unsold and under Court order, from the total sales price realized by Catalda Company from the infringing prints in fact sold on the market."[109]

Sales discounts, freight and cartage outward, salesmen's salaries and commissions, commissions to dealers and shipping and packing were allowed. Rent was allowed as a general item of overhead subject to apportionment as with other items of overhead. The Court in *Catalda* referred to general accounting usage. Thus it would seem that ascertainment of profits would require the application not only of general accounting principles in ascertaining profits but also those accounting doctrines relative to the particular industry at hand.

The application of such principles may have some relationship to the ascertainment of the infringing components embodied in the infringing work, as in *Sheldon,* where the respective infringing and non-infringing contributions had to be assessed in order to find the percentage of profits to be apportioned. Apportionment aside, ascertainment of net profits partakes of the attributes of an accounting proceeding in equity, once the right to an accounting has been granted, with a direct application of accounting principles to the particular defendant accounting in the context of his pertinent operations in the specific industry involved.

Sec. 26.8. In Lieu Damages (Statutory Damages)

But all of this takes place in the guise of judicial consideration of a segue from one type of recovery into an-

---

[109] 86 F. Supp. at pp. 411-412.

other, depending upon the adequacy and justice of the given type of recovery as in *F. W. Woolworth Co.* v. *Contemporary Arts, Inc.*[110] There respondent had made small sculptures and figurines. Petitioner had bought 127 dozen cocker spaniel statuettes from a different supplier and distributed them through a number of Woolworth stores. These had been copied from respondent, although unbeknown to petitioner, and so the latter had infringed. The cost to petitioner was 60 cents each and they were sold for $1.19 each at a gross profit of $899.16. The infringer did not assume the burden of proving other costs pursuant to Sec. 101(b). The petitioner could not show actual damages. It had had $35,000 gross annual income, eight employees and had sold its statuettes for $4, $9 and $15. The lower court had not allowed it to prove complaints from Woolworth sales competition, decline in its own sales and abandonment of the line with unsalable stock. The lower court had indicated that statutory damages rendered proof of actual damages unnecessary. In this regard, Justice Jackson stated, "It might have been better practice to have received the evidence, even if it fell short of establishing the measure of liability; for when recovery may be awarded without establishing any injury, it cannot hurt and may aid the exercise of discretion to hear any evidence on the subject that has probative value."[111] But petitioner could not complain because the exclusion was in response to its objections.

By this remark of the Supreme Court, it may be seen that the discretion of the trial court to award in lieu damages is broad enough to supersede examination of actual damages and award statutory damages. In other words,

---

[110] 344 U.S. 228 (1952).

[111] *Idem* at pp. 230-231.

the discretion to award in lieu damages is complete and not merely a substitute for actual damages where no actual damages are shown, after at least an attempt to prove actual damage. Since the award by statutory damages does not constitute a fixed amount, the dictum of the Supreme Court would indicate that even such evidence would tend to assist the trial court in determining the amount of statutory damages.

The Supreme Court pointed out the capriciousness of the petitioner's position. "It has admitted gross profits, which make no deduction for sales costs, overheads or taxes and, hence, may appear substantial on this particular record. But gross profits is not what a copyright owner is entitled to recover, but only such profits as remain after the defendant reduces them, as it may, by proof of allowable elements of cost. If we sustain petitioner's contention that profits may be the sole measure of liability as matter of law, such profits could be diminished even to the vanishing point."[112]

Apparently Woolworth was willing to settle for recovery of all of the gross profits of $899.16 as the total recovery by the plaintiff. It may have feared that the dilution of this figure by deduction of costs to a figure of net profits would have impelled the trial court, in any event, to award statutory damages, there being no proof of actual damages. The Supreme Court declined to accept this approach. It pointed out,

> "Net profits realized by a far-flung distributing enterprise like Woolworth's upon sales of a given item in a few of its many stores can be calculated only by a process of allocating overheads, sales expenses, taxes,

---

[112] *Idem* at p. 233.

> and a host of items. A plaintiff in the position of the present one could hardly verify or contest such apportionments unless it should audit the whole Woolworth business." [113]

In effect, the Supreme Court was asserting that the literal application of the statute (17 U.S.C. 101(b)) to wit, "... and in proving profits the plaintiff shall be required to prove sales only, and the defendant shall be required to prove every element of cost which he claims, ..." would mean that the failure of the defendant to prove costs automatically would mean an imposition of gross profits as the measure of recovery of profits, in a context where it constituted the entire award, if such a result were to thwart a just recovery by the plaintiff. Here it was apparent that the gross profits were small and, if reduced to net profits, might have become miniscule. Woolworth preferred to argue on a take-it-or-leave-it basis that the small gross profits should constitute the entire recovery. The Supreme Court's approach would tend to indicate that the result in *Whitman Publishing Company* v. *Writesel*[114] might have been different had the trial court chosen to take the position that even where defendant submitted no evidence of cost, a sale by the infringer of $10,600 at $1 a copy should not have resulted in literal application of the statute to bring about a recovery of profits of $10,600 as representing a windfall to the plaintiff. Just as the Woolworth effort, in precisely the same failure of submission of proof of costs, resulted in a modification of the rule so as to avoid the harshness of literal application—there against the plaintiff—so, in *Writesel,* the Court might have done the same to mitigate the harshness of the rule, at least to reduce the recovery

---

[113] *Ibid.*

[114] See note 2, *supra.*

to gross profits by reducing the total sales figure of $10,600 by the cost to defendant per copy, either on the theory that the Court, in its discretion, as a matter of public policy, could do so, or on the theory that the total amount of sales was not even the equivalent of gross profits and at least the cost per copy to the defendant ought to be subtracted.

But the Supreme Court went further. It affirmed a recovery of statutory damages in the sum of $5,000, stating:

> "Moreover, a rule of liability which merely takes away the profits from an infringement would offer little discouragement to infringers. It would fall short of an effective sanction for enforcement of the copyright policy. The statutory rule, formulated after long experience, not merely compels restitution of profit and reparation for injury but also is designed to discourage wrongful conduct. The discretion of the court is wide enough to permit a resort to statutory damages for such purposes. Even for uninjurious and unprofitable invasions of copyright the court may, if it deems it just, impose a liability within statutory limits to sanction and vindicate the statutory policy." [115]

The principles adumbrated in *Woolworth* have been interpreted by Circuit Judge Barnes as follows:

> "First, we disagree with the trial judge's conclusion of law 4 that if either profits *or* damages are ascertainable, the minimum provided for in the 'in lieu' provision need not be resorted to, citing Sheldon v. Metro-Goldwyn Corp., 309 U.S. 390, 60 S. Ct. 681 (1940). The *Sheldon* case did make reference to and relied upon a report of the House Committee on the Copyright

---

[115] Note 110, *supra*, at p. 233.

Act (309 U.S. at 400, 60 S. Ct. 681), which said that where both profits *and* damages had been ascertained the court could award the greater amount but not both. But that statement was superseded by the majority opinion in F. W. Woolworth Co. v. Contemporary Arts, 344 U.S. 228, 73 S. Ct. 222 (1952). This distinguished the *Sheldon* case specifically, holding that the only question before the court in *Sheldon* had been apportionment of profits from an infringing motion picture, and that the case did not stand for the proposition that where profits were established the 'in lieu' provision did not come into play. Further support for the view that *Sheldon* does not stand for the point cited by the district court is the dissenting opinion in *Woolworth* which quotes the same provision from the House Committee report which was rejected in the majority opinion. We conclude that *Sheldon* is not authority for the rule stated in conclusion of law 4, and that, since the opinion in *Woolworth*, *Sheldon* does not stand for the proposition that where both profits and damages can be ascertained the court should award the higher but not both and should decline to resort to the 'in lieu' provision.

"Second, while we can agree that the *Woolworth* case stands for the proposition stated in conclusion of law 6, it is important to emphasize that the judicial discretion to be employed in choosing between proven profits and damages on the one hand and the statutory limits on the other only comes into play when profits *and* damages have actually been proved, and unless they have, the court *must* apply the statutory standard. Westermann Co. v. Dispatch Co., 249 U.S. 100, 39 S. Ct. 194, 63 L. Ed. 499 (1919); Jewell-LaSalle Realty Co. v. Buck, 283 U.S. 202, 51 S. Ct. 407, 75 L. Ed. 978

> (1931); Douglas v. Cunningham, 294 U.S. 207, 55 S. Ct. 365 (1935). We do not believe that the references in *Woolworth, supra,* to the court's discretion in any way conflict with the rule stated in these three older cases. The *Woolworth* case merely held that the trial court has discretion to choose between actual damages and profits on the one hand and statutory damages on the other where actual damages and profits *have been proved.* Where such damages and profits have not been proved the statutory limits must be applied and the trial court's only discretion lies in determining the amount (between a minimum of $250 and a maximum of $5,000) per infringement to be awarded." [116]

It would seem, therefore, that the supersession of in lieu damages for profits is discretionary for the purpose of doing justice. Such alternative route for determining amount of recovery by a wronged party has a subsidiary purpose of discouraging infringement, as pointed out by the majority in *Woolworth.* This purpose partakes of using the remedial provisions of the statute as an instrumentality for policing the copyright laws. Justice Black contended, in his dissenting opinion in *Woolworth,* that the effect of

---

[116] Shapiro, Bernstein & Co. v. 4636 S. Vermont Ave., Inc., 367 F. 2d 236 (9th Cir. 1966) at p. 240 (italics). Conclusions of law 4 reads, "If either profits or damages are ascertainable, the minimum provided for in the 'in lieu' provision need not be resorted to. Sheldon v. Metro-Goldwyn Corp., 309 U.S. 390 [60 S. Ct. 681, 84 L. Ed. 825] (1940)." at p. 239.

Conclusion of law 6 reads, "It is a matter of judicial discretion as to whether or not it is more just that recovery be based upon proven profits of the defendant and damages to the plaintiff, or be within the statutory limits. F. W. Woolworth Co. v. Contemporary Arts, Inc., 344 U.S. 288 [73 S. Ct. 222, 97 L. Ed. 276] (1952)." at p. 240.

the majority decision was tantamount to inflicting a penalty rather than recompense for injury.[117] It would seem that discouragement of infringement by the very economics of low net profits is not inconsistent with a just discretionary determination even if the in lieu award might seem to be out of line with the sum shown to be the amount of profits. The trial court in *Woolworth* evidently felt that the operations of the plaintiff had been seriously damaged by the infringement even though it chose not to calibrate them in terms of actual damages—perhaps for the very reason of the difficulty of showing relationship of cause and effect on plaintiff in terms of actual damages—and that an award of statutory damages of $5,000 was not such a sum that was so out of line as to be punitive. Damages as a penalty are those intended primarily as punishment for wrongdoing, *ipso facto,* without regard to the loss suffered by plaintiff or the gain received by the defendant. The fact that in lieu damages in a given situation may exceed profits by a substantial amount or even possible actual damages is no reason for not using statutory damages in a given situation to do justice. In *Stodart* v. *Mutual Film Corp.,*[118] Judge Learned Hand, in a supplemental opinion, reduced damages to $500 because of the trifling character of the infringed play. There Stodart had given Smith, a play broker, his play and told him not to sell the film rights for less than $500. Defendants had infringed with film. Judge Hand in effect accepted the plaintiff's own figure of $500. But Judge Hand apparently did not think much of the plaintiff's work. If he had, he might have determined far greater actual damages, or assuming he chose to disregard the same in his discretion, under the rationale of *Woolworth,* he might have awarded far greater in lieu damages on the

[117] Note 110, *supra,* at p. 235.
[118] 249 Fed. 507 (S.D.N.Y. 1917), Hand, L., *J.*

theory of policing the copyright, deterrence and possible effect on the plaintiff's work for film purposes, without the same being deemed punitive.

It must be remembered that in *Woolworth* the award of statutory damages of $5,000 exceeded the profits of the defendant by a substantial amount. The decision characterized the entire award as one of in lieu damages. *Peter Pan Fabrics* v. *Jobela Fabrics, Inc.*[119] is noteworthy in this respect. There the master's report determined a recovery of net profits of $6,464.00. The master also founded damages to plaintiff in the sum of $8,683.65 on the basis that plaintiff's sales would have increased by the amount of defendant's infringing sales at the price charged by plaintiff. The District Court disallowed this amount since there was no proof to justify this award, but did not consider the propriety of awarding in lieu damages.

On appeal, Circuit Judge Leonard P. Moore stated as follows:

> "The language of Sec. 101(b) is reasonably plain. As a practical matter it may be divided into two related parts: the first proviso permits the recovery of proven damages and profits; the second, or 'in lieu of' clause, allows 'the owner of a copyright some recompense for injury done him, in a case where the rules of law render difficult or impossible proof of damages or discovery of profits.' Douglas v. Cunningham, 294 U.S. 207, 209, 55 S. Ct. 365, 366, 79 L. Ed. 862 (1935).
>
> "The statutory language 'damages . . . as well as all the profits which the infringer shall have made,' would seem to contemplate a 'cumulative' recovery. However, confusion has been engendered by the House Report

[119] 329 F. 2d 194 (2d Cir. 1964).

accompanying the bill which indicated that the drafters envisioned recovery in the alternative in a manner similar to that under the Patent Statute. Although this theory has met with judicial approval, the Supreme Court in F. W. Woolworth Co. v. Contemporary Arts, Inc, 344 U.S. 228, 73 S. Ct. 222, 97 L. Ed. 276 (1952), holding that the Trial Court had discretion to grant recovery under the 'in lieu of' clause, where plaintiff had shown the amount of the infringer's profits, stated:

> '[A] rule of liability which merely takes away the profits from an infringement would offer little discouragement to infringers. It would fall short of an effective sanction for enforcement of the copyright policy. The statutory rule, formulated after long experience, not merely compels restitution of profit and reparation for injury but also is designed to discourage wrongful conduct.' 344 U.S. at 233, 73 S. Ct. at 225, 97 L. Ed. 276.

"The 'cumulative' recovery and not the 'alternative' would therefore seem to be appropriate under Sec. 101(b)." [120]

The Court of Appeals therefore remanded so that the District Court might consider whether there should be an award of in lieu damages, particularly where the assumption of identical sales by the plaintiff, as had by the defendant, was not permissible as a basis for award of actual damages.

Under this theory of cumulative damages, in effect, it might be contended that the result in *Woolworth* spelled

[120] *Idem* at pp. 195-196. See also Thomas Wilson & Company, Inc. v. Irving Dorfman & Company, Inc., 167 U.S.P.Q. 417 (2d Cir. 1970) which applied cumulative damages.

out a cumulative award of the profits plus the difference between the profits and $5,000 as actual damages. However, the result was one of a single award of statutory damages. Similarly, in *Universal Pictures Co., Inc.* v. *Harold Lloyd Corp.*[120a] actual damages of $40,000 exceeded net profits and the award was a single one of actual damages. This, of course, is in accord with the House Report with respect to the proposed 1909 Copyright Act[121] which suggested award of damages or profits, whichever was greater. Nevertheless, in a given situation the theory of alternative damages might, in respect of statutory damages, be cast in the form of cumulative damages without doing material harm to the end result in terms of recovery, dollar-wise. Thus, in *Woolworth*, there was a total recovery of $5,000 as statutory damages. On the application of *Peter Pan* of cumulative recovery of profits and actual damages the same dollar result might have been arrived at by a finding of loss of profits of $899.16 and actual damages of $4,100.84 as a cumulative recovery, to reach the identical figure of $5,000 recovery. Actual damages, even where determined upon estimation and some speculation as stated by Judge Learned Hand in *Gross* v. *Van Dyk Gravure Co.*,[122] are presumed to be a determination of real injury to the wronged party, whereas statutory damages are awardable in the court's discretion in lieu of actual damages or even when none may be determined. Thus the arithmetic of a recovery, as in *Woolworth,* may be flexible enough to achieve the identical dollar result on an alternative theory of award of statutory damages or a cumulative theory of loss of profits and actual damages. Of course, the predicates of such arithmetic are in the limitations of statutory damages, to wit, the limits—a

[120a] Note 74, *supra.*

[121] Note 36, *supra.*

[122] 230 Fed. 412 (2d Cir. 1916). See note 86, *supra.*

maximum of $5,000 and a minimum of $250 for each infringement, unless notice has been given. Thus, the statutory damages that could be awardable on a single infringement in *Peter Pan* on remand could not, in any event, come up to the rejected figure awarded by the special master for actual damages—$8,683.65—rejected by the District Court and on appeal for lack of proof.

But the principal attribute of statutory damage, nonetheless, is its flexibility of application. In *L.A. Westermann Co.* v. *Dispatch Printing Co.,*[123] the Supreme Court affirmed the determination of the Court of Appeals that statutory damages by infringement of 7 pictorial illustrations constituted one infringement subject to minimum statutory damages of $250 and not to nominal damages of 7 infringements times $10, or $70 as found by the trial court. The Supreme Court stated:

> "The fact that these damages are to be 'in lieu of actual damages' shows that something other than actual damages is intended—that another measure is to be applied in making the assessment. There is no uncertainty as to what that measure is or as to its limitations. The statute says, first, that the damages are to be such as to the court shall appear to be just; next, that the court may, in its discretion, allow the amounts named in the appended schedule, and finally, that in no case shall they be more than $5,000 nor less than $250, except that for a newspaper reproduction of a copyrighted photograph they shall not be more than $200 nor less than $50. In other words, the court's conception of what is just in the particular case, considering the nature of the copyright, the circumstances of the infringement

---

[123] 249 U.S. 100 (1919).

> and the like, is made the measure of the damages to be paid, but with the express qualification that in every case the assessment must be within the prescribed limitations, that is to say, neither more than the maximum nor less than the minimum. Within these limitations the court's discretion and sense of justice are controlling, but it has no discretion when proceeding under this provision to go outside of them." [124]

The discretionary aspect of statutory damages, the "may" part of the judicial award, has, however, its interplay with the "must" part thereof as applied to the limitations. This was brought out by the Supreme Court in *Jewell-LaSalle Realty Co.* v. *Buck,*[125] which also confirmed the applicability of in lieu damages to performance. Justice Brandeis stated in his opinion there, "An unbroken line of decisions in the lower courts has since held that the rule declared in the *Westermann* case is applicable also to infringement of the monopoly of giving performances." [126]

Sec. 26.9. Minimum Statutory Damages

In *Jewell-LaSalle,* the defendant had contended that the statutory damages for infringing radio broadcast were $10 whereas the plaintiff, in that ASCAP test case, had contended that they were $250, the $10 figure being the yardstick amount set forth in the statute as applicable to infringing musical performance. Justice Brandeis stated with respect thereto:

> "It is urged, however, that under such interpretation the suggested measure of ten dollars a performance,

[124] *Idem* at pp. 106-107.

[125] 283 U.S. 202 (1931). (italics).

[126] *Idem* at p. 205.

scheduled in the fourth subdivision of section 25, would not be applicable unless more than twenty-five infringing performances were proved. This appears to be the meaning of the section read as a whole, particularly since the amounts in the scheduled subdivisions appear to have been inserted merely as an aid to the court in awarding such damages as 'shall appear to be just'. The definite specification of a maximum and minimum in every case is not contradicted in any way by these legislative suggestions as to what may be deemed reasonable allowances in cases falling within the prescribed limitations." [127]

Justice Brandeis therefore concluded that, subject to the application of the minimum of $250 in statutory damages, the yardstick figure of $10 per performance might then be multiplied by the number of performances and the excess over twenty-five could then be applied as further statutory damages within the minimum of $250 and the maximum of $5,000. He stated in this regard:

"Where more than twenty-five infringing performances are proved, and there is no showing as to actual loss, the court must allow the statutory minimum, and may, in its sound discretion, employ the scheduled ten dollars a performance as a basis for assessing additional damages." [128]

Thus the formula for application of statutory damages appears to be as follows: Whether or not the court will apply in lieu damages is in its discretion. The court "may"

---

[127] *Idem* at p. 207.
[128] *Idem* at p. 208.

do so. But once it does, it "must" grant at least the minimum of $250. It "may" use the statutory yardsticks to increase the amount of recovery above the minimum as a measure of damages—in *Jewell-LaSalle* at the rate of $10 per infringing musical performance—up to the ceiling of $5,000. The court "must" not exceed the maximum of $5,000 in the absence of actual notice of claim of infringement.

The *Jewell-LaSalle* determination of $250 in lieu damages was applied to non-broadcasting infringements in *Irving Berlin, Inc.* v. *Daigle; Same* v. *Russo,*[129] both ASCAP cases. *Daigle* involved infringement by performance by an orchestra; *Russo*, musical performance in a motion picture theatre by accompanying phonograph record. The $250 minimum was applied in both instances. Circuit Judge Walker in *Russo* concluded that liability as to public performance by use of a phonograph record is governed by Sec. 25, other than subdivision (e) thereof.[130] The award of minimum damages of $250 as in lieu damages for infringement of musical copyright has had wide application. Indeed, it might be said that the application of the rule has enabled the performing rights societies to police the infringement of musical copyright in the course of their efforts to license

---

[129] 31 F. 2d 832 (5th Cir. 1929).

[130] Sec. 25(e) (now Sec. 101(e)) provided for a royalty of 2 cents a side, plus discretionary trebling, for infringement by mechanical reproduction. Circuit Judge Foster concurred in the decision except as to the measure of damages as to infringement by use of phonograph recordings in *Russo*. Since Sec. 1(e) provides that the royalty of 2 cents a side frees the reproduction except from further contribution for public performance for profit, the result was correct in awarding damages under Sec. 25 other than subdivision (e) thereof in order for this provision as to damages for public performance for profit to have any meaning.

musical performance.[131] Had the defendant prevailed in *Widenski* v. *Shapiro, Bernstein & Co.*,[132] that the ASCAP license fee of $10 to café operators like the defendant was the measure of actual damages, instead of $250 minimum in lieu damages, the performing rights societies might have had much greater difficulty policing cafés, restaurants, dance halls and other places where live music was performed.

Sec. 26.10. Minimum Damages and Separate Infringements

But infringement in respect of in lieu damages is not always a simple matter of a single unauthorized performance where the $250 minimum damages rule is the starting point—and often the terminal point—for award of damages. There are complications of multiple performance and determinations of how many infringements there are with respect to any given situation. In *Law* v. *National Broadcasting Co., Inc.*,[133] infringement of only a single tune was the basis for the award of damages. But there the song "On Iowa" was performed three times over varying line-ups of radio stations in the NBC network. The Court stated, "Plaintiff's composition was performed on three occasions by the NBC with chain hook-ups of 67, 66 and 85 stations, in all 218. Damages should be awarded on the theory that there were 218 performances, not three." (citing *Jewell-LaSalle*)[134] The Court then awarded damages of $2,180. This represented the application of statutory yardstick

[131] See, for example, Buck v. Bilkie, 63 F. 2d 447 (9th Cir. 1933); Edward B. Marks Music Corp. v. Borst Music Pub. Co., 110 F. Supp. 913 (D.N.J. 1953).

[132] 147 F. 2d 909 (1st Cir. 1945).

[133] 51 F. Supp. 798 (S.D.N.Y. 1943).

[134] *Idem* at p. 799.

damages of $10 per infringing musical performance. The result was within the minimum and maximum limitations.

In *Select Theatres Corporation* v. *The Ronzoni Macaroni Co.,*[135] there was a more complex situation. There plaintiff, Casella, had written a play. Defendant, Caimi, was found to have infringed parts thereof in his own play. Defendant, Ronzoni, arranged for radio broadcast of the Ciami play over the International Broadcasting Corp. station, which was piped to the station of the William Penn Broadcasting Corporation. Judge Bondy stated:

> "The unauthorized performance of a single scene from one act of a copyrighted play with very little dialogue constitutes infringement. . . ." (citing cases) "There therefore can not be any reason why each unauthorized performance or broadcast of a different scene of a play on different occasions should not be considered an infringement merely because the different scenes are reproduced from the same play." (citing cases)[136]

The parties had stipulated that if there was a finding of infringement, then there were three episodes containing infringements from the Casella play and seventeen episodes containing infringments from the Ferris version, an English adaptation of the Casella play. The Court accordingly granted plaintiff, Casella, judgment of $750 against Ronzoni, Ciami and International Broadcasting, jointly and severally, $750 against William Penn Broadcasting, and $750 against Caimi for the stage productions. Plaintiff, Select Theatres, as owner of the rights in the Ferris version, was awarded $4,250 against Caimi, Ronzoni and International

---

[135] 59 U.S.P.Q. 288 (S.D.N.Y. 1943), Bondy, *J.*

[136] *Idem* at p. 291.

Broadcasting, jointly and severally, $4,250 against William Penn Broadcasting, and $750 against Caimi.

In his opinion, Judge Bondy stated:

> "No decisive authority has been cited or found as to whether the publication or broadcast of different episodes of a copyrighted play serially at different times constitutes more than one infringement, and not, as defendants claim, collectively only one infringement of the copyright.
>
> "Each unauthorized publication of the same copyrighted matter at different times has been held to constitute a separate infringement. All the component parts of a copyrighted work are protected by the copyright of the work." [137]

The award of damages represented a multiplication of minimum statutory damages of $250 each for the three episodes of the Casella play to reach the sum of $750 and of $250 times seventeen episodes to reach the result of $4,250 in respect of the Ferris version. Had the court applied this approach in *Law*, i.e., had it found 218 infringements, then the result would have been 218 infringements times $250, or $54,500. This would have been within the statutory limits since each infringement has its own limits of $250 minimum to $5,000 maximum, where in lieu damages are awarded. Instead, in *Law*, the 218 performances on three different occasions only resulted in the application of the $10 yardstick damages for musical performance within the minimum and maximum limits. Although the Court in *Law* did not spell out the manner of reaching its award other than referring to 218 performances and a resultant award of $2,180, it is to be noted that the result is the same

[137] *Ibid.*

as if the *Ronzoni* rule had been applied, at least to the extent of considering each occasion as a separate infringement, "On Iowa" having been broadcast on three separate occasions. On the first occasion, 67 stations carried the tune. If this constituted a single infringement, then the result would have been damages of $670 therefor. This figure would be based on $10 per infringing performance for 67 stations predicated on a minimum of $250 for the infringement. Applying this method to the second occasion, we get damages of $660 or 66 times $10 for the second infringement. Similarly, we reach $850 as damages for the third occasion. The sum of the damages for the three occasions is identical to the judicial determination of 218 performances times $10, or $2,180. It is noteworthy that Judge Bondy's decision was handed down September 30, 1943 in *Ronzoni*, and *Law*, July 10 of the same year. Both cases were decided in the District Court for the Southern District of New York, yet the Bondy decision did not refer to *Law* in his opinion.

In *Davis* v. *E. I. DuPont de Nemours & Co.*,[138] there was an infringing telecast and actual notice. Plaintiffs did not claim actual damages. The issue there, on a simultaneous telecast by 162 stations, was whether minimum damages should be $250 for one infringement or $40,500, i.e., $250 times 162. Also, if the former, were the limits of $250-$5,000 applicable where there was actual notice? Judge Feinberg in his decision reviewed the pertinent cases. He noted that *Jewell-LaSalle* resulted in multiple performance and therefore multiple infringement. That is, the radio station had infringed. The transmission by the hotel was also a public performance for profit so that it, too, had infringed. He also considered the question of whether a

---

[138] Note 19, *supra*.

later publication constituted a continuation or repetition of the first infringement, as in *Westermann*, thereby requiring invoking of yardstick amounts as opposed to separate infringements. Judge Feinberg then determined that a review of the cases indicated no binding precedent in point and that the legislative history was inconclusive even with the 1912 amendment setting limits as to motion picture damages and the 1952 amendment limiting damages for infringing broadcast of lectures.

District Judge Feinberg then proceeded to hold that the simultaneous broadcast over 162 stations constituted a single infringement, stating, "On balance, it seems preferable, for the purpose of applying the statutory damage provisions, to regard the simultaneous network telecast here as one infringement by the network and these co-defendants, rather than many. This preserves flexibility, avoids the possibility of a ridiculous and injurious award in other cases and is the result at least suggested by the cases and the statute." [138a]

Sec. 26.11. Maximum Damages

Had the Court then applied the yardstick amounts under Sec. 101(b), Fourth,[139] this being an infringement of a dramatic composition, then in lieu damages, absent notice, would have exceeded the maximum of $5,000 and been limited thereto. That is, under the yardstick formula, there would have been an award of $100 for the first infringing performance and $50 for each succeeding performance. Thus there would have been 161 infringing performances at $50 each, or $8,050 plus $100 for the first infringing performance, or a total of $8,150. This sum

---

[138a] *Idem* at pp. 342-343.

[139] 17 U.S.C. 101(b), Fourth.

exceeding the maximum, damages, absent notice, would have automatically been reduced to $5,000. But the Court declined to apply the yardstick rule. The Court then reviewed the cases in order to determine whether or not the yardstick amounts had to be applied in the event of actual notice and observed, "Research discloses no case where the statutory damage award for one infringement was over $5,000 and exceeded the yardstick amount." [140] The Court then decided that it had discretion to depart from the yardstick amounts when they exceeded $5,000 as well as where they were below that figure. He felt that such discretion should be used sparingly and only where the yardstick amounts would produce an inadequate award. The Court then, in effect, speculated as to what the market value might be, and after reviewing various facts with respect thereto, found the in lieu damages to be $25,000.

Sec. 26.12. Proposed Revision: Remedies and Damages

The Supplementary Report of the Register of Copyrights, discussing Sec. 101 of the Copyright Act, states, "In a detailed section having a remarkable and pervasive impact on the entire operation of the copyright law, it is remarkable how many of the most practical questions the statute leaves equivocal or unanswered." [141] Various preliminary studies[142] and the two reports of the Register of Copy-

---

[140] Note 19, *supra,* at p. 347.

[141] Supplementary Report of the Register of Copyrights on the General Revision of the U.S. Copyright Law: 1965 Revision Bill (1965) at p. 134.

[142] See, Strauss, William S., The Damage Provisions of the Copyright Law, Study No. 22, in 2 Studies on Copyright, pp. 995- 1028; and Study No. 23, Professor Ralph S. Brown, Jr., The Operation of the Damage Provisions of the Copyright Law: An Exploratory Study, *idem* at pp. 1067-1098.

rights[143] explored proposed copyright revision with respect thereto.

The original Register's Report of 1961 made various recommendations. It proposed that damages and profits not be made cumulative, the present mandatory minimum in respect of an innocent infringer be made discretionary, statutory damages within the minimum and maximum limits to be the total award for all the infringements for which the defendant is liable, damages in excess of the maximum might be awarded, not based on actual notice, but on willful infringement or, possibly, to a raised maximum of $10,000 or $20,000, and that the maximum be raised to $10,000 because of the depreciated value of the dollar.[144] In substance, this Report would retain existing provisions as to injunctive relief, the extraordinary remedies of impounding and destruction of infringing articles, allowance of costs and discretionary attorney's fees.

The Supplementary Report adverts to the modification of proposed copyright revision to allow cumulative recovery in certain circumstances and to the right of the copyright owner to elect as between actual profits and damages, on the one hand, and statutory damages, on the other. Sec. 504 of S. 644 reads in part as follows:

> "(b) Actual Damages and Profits.—The copyright owner is entitled to recover actual damages suffered by him as a result of the infringement, and any profits of the infringer that are attributable to the infringe-

---

[143] Report of the Register of Copyrights on the General Revision of the U.S. Copyright Law, in 2 Studies on Copyright, pp. 1199-1346, Chap. IX, Remedies For Infringement, at pp. 1301-1309; Supplementary Report of the Register, note 141, *supra,* Chap. 7, Copyright Infringement and Remedies at pp. 131-140.

[144] Register's Report, *idem* at pp. 1302-1306.

ment and are not taken into account in computing the actual damages. In establishing the infringer's profits, the copyright owner is required to present proof only of the infringer's gross revenue, and the infringer is required to prove his deductible expense and elements of profit attributable to factors other than the copyrighted work."[145]

The first sentence thereof purports to incorporate the prevailing case law of *Sheldon* as to apportionment and at the same time avoid a double recovery by reason of loss of profits being used as the measure of damage. The Register explains this in his Supplementary Report as follows:

> "An award of damages basically serves a different purpose from an award of profits. Damages are awarded to compensate the copyright owner for all of the losses caused him by the infringement, while an award of profits is intended to prevent the infringer from unjustly benefiting from his wrongful act. Profits are often used as a measure of the copyright owner's damages and, where they coincide in this way, it would be appropriate to award either damages or profits, whichever is greater. In that situation it would be unfair to award damages and profits 'cumulatively,' since in effect it would mean that the plaintiff would be recovering the same amount twice. On the other hand, there are cases in which the plaintiff has suffered losses not reflected in the defendant's profits, and the defendant has enjoyed profits that are attributable to his use of the plaintiff's work but are not considered in assessing damages."[146]

---

[145] S.644, 92d Cong., 1st Sess., Feb. 8, 1971, Sec. 504 (b). S.644 was introduced by Senator McClellan.

[146] Supplementary Report, note 141, *supra,* at p. 135.

S. 644, Sec. 504(c) provides for a right of election of statutory damages in the copyright owner as follows:

"(c) Statutory Damages.—

(1) Except as provided by clause (2) of this subsection, the copyright owner may elect, at any time before final judgment is rendered, to recover, instead of actual damages and profits, an award of statutory damages for all infringements involved in the action, with respect to any one work, for which any one infringer is liable individually, or for which any two or more infringers are liable jointly and severally, in a sum of not less than $250 or more than $10,000 as the court considers just. For the purposes of this subsection, all the parts of a compilation or derivative work constitute one work." [147]

The House Report indicates that there is *de facto* already a right of election in the plaintiff, stating, ". . . as under the present law, the plaintiff in an infringement suit is not obliged to submit proof of damages and profits if he chooses to rely on the provision for minimum statutory damages." [148] The Supplementary Report of the Register comments with respect to the infringement of any one work:

"This marks a change from the 1961 *Report*'s recommendations, which would have provided a single recovery of statutory damages for all infringements for which the infringer is liable. Under the bill, where separate works are involved, separate awards of statutory damages could be made. However, the bill makes clear that, although they may constitute separate works

---

[147] S. 644, note 145, *supra,* Sec. 504(c).

[148] House Report No. 83, House of Representatives, 90th Cong., 1st Sess., Mar. 8, 1967, Report to accompany H.R. 2512 at p. 128.

> for other purposes, '[f]or the purposes of this subsection, all the parts of a compilation or derivative work constitute one work.' Note that the criterion here is the number of distinct 'works' infringed, and not the number of copyrights, exclusive rights, owners, or registrations involved." [149]

Subdivision (2) of Sec. 504(c)[150] grants the court discretion to increase statutory damages to not more than $50,000 for willful infringement. It also permits the court, in its discretion, to reduce damages of an innocent infringer to a sum not less than $100. Moreover, with respect to good faith belief by an instructor, librarian or archivist of a non-profit institution, library or archives, that a use is a fair use under Sec. 107, the court, in its discretion, might remit statutory damages in whole or in part.[151]

The subsection thereby raises the amount of the statutory limits, set as $250 and $10,000 in Sec. 504(c)(1), to a substantial sum in excess thereof in the case of willful infringement, in the discretion of the court. Thus the present removal of the ceiling of $5,000 in cases of actual notice would be superseded by a new ceiling for willful infringement with the provisions as to actual notice eliminated. Moreover, the Register had shifted from discretionary award of minimum damages to a floor of $100 in his Supplementary Report.[152] The possible exception carved out in the subsection as to innocent reproduction by librarians, etc., in the belief that such use is a fair use no doubt was intended to reduce the perils of education and scholarship in relation

---

[149] Supplementary Report, note 141, *supra,* at p. 136 (italics).

[150] S. 644, note 145, *supra,* Sec. 504(c)(2).

[151] S. 644, *idem,* Sec. 107, which defines fair use.

[152] Supplementary Report, note 141, *supra,* at p. 137.

to use of copyrighted materials where even innocent infringement might otherwise bring mandatory minimum award of damages. The subsection, in effect, purports to strike a balance between the needs of protection of the copyright proprietor against erosion of his copyright by the inroads of possible mass innocent infringement and the notion that education and scholarship should be pursued in good faith without fear of monetary liability for what may be essentially a bona fide mistaken application of fair use when, in fact, there is infringement.

The House Report makes this comment as to what is covered by the award of statutory damages:

> "2. Although, as explained below, an award of minimum statutory damages may be multiplied if separate works and separately liable infringers are involved in the suit, a single award in the \$250 to \$10,000 range is made 'for all infringements involved in the action.' A single infringer of a single work is liable for a single amount between \$250 and \$10,000, no matter how many acts of infringement are involved in the action and regardless of whether the acts were separate, isolated, or occurred in a related series."[153]

It is to be noted that the statutory yardstick amounts now contained in the present Copyright Act are eliminated in proposed copyright revision and the provisions of Sec. 504(c) purport to set a single amount of recovery "for all the infringements involved in the action" without reference to the type of infringement and the enumeration of the rate of recovery proposed in the yardstick as under present law.

---

[153] House Report, note 148, *supra,* at p. 129.

Infringement, Damages and Other Remedies

In accordance with the Supplementary Report of the Register,[154] proposed copyright revision in Sec. 506 of S. 644 would increase penalties for criminal infringement to not more than $2,500 fine for the first offense or imprisonment of one year, or both, to not more than $10,000 fine or imprisonment of one year, or both, for any subsequent offense.[155] Fines for fraudulent copyright notice, fraudulent removal of copyright notice and false representation are increased to not more than $2,500.[156] Present criminal penalties provide for fines of not less than $100 nor more than $1,000 or imprisonment not exceeding one year, or both, for criminal infringement[157] and fines of not less than $100 nor more than $1,000 for fraudulent notice of copyright or removal or alteration of notice.[158] These are explained by the Supplementary Report as follows:

> "The extensive and spirited discussions of the criminal infringement provision reflect the importance many copyright owners attach to the criminal provisions as an effective sanction against infringement. Among the main points stressed were that the present penalties—a fine of $100 to $1,000 and imprisonment of up to one year—are not adequate to deter infringement, and that difficulties are sometimes encountered in inducing Federal prosecutors to bring criminal action because the relative weakness of the penalties makes them feel the offense is not very serious." [159]

---

[154] Supplementary Report, note 141, *supra,* at p. 139.

[155] S. 644, note 145, *supra,* Sec. 506(a).

[156] *Idem,* Sec. 506(b), (c) and (d).

[157] 17 U.S.C. 104.

[158] 17 U.S.C. 105.

[159] Supplementary Report, note 141, *supra,* at p. 139.

Existing three year statute of limitations as set forth in Sec. 115[160] is left unchanged in proposed copyright revision (Sec. 507 of S. 644)[161] because the present rule as to limitations was enacted as recently as 1957[162] and in itself represents a reconciliation of views which had best be left unaltered.[163]

Sec. 26.13. Costs and Attorney's Fees

As for costs and attorney's fees, Sec. 116 of the present Copyright Act reads as follows:

> "In all actions, suits, or proceedings under this title, except when brought by or against the United States or any officer thereof, full costs shall be allowed, and the court may award to the prevailing party a reasonable attorney's fee as part of the costs." [164]

The Register's Report of 1961 states in this regard:

> "The language of section 116 indicates that the allowance of 'full costs' is mandatory, and some courts have so held, but others have treated the allowance of costs as discretionary. Section 116 should be clarified in this respect. We believe that the allowance of costs, like the award of attorney's fees, should be left to the discretion of the court." [165]

---

[160] 17 U.S.C. 115.

[161] S. 644, note 145, *supra,* Sec. 507.

[162] Public Law 85-313, 85th Cong., H.R. 277, Sept. 7, 1957, 71 Stat. 633 effective one year after enactment.

[163] Supplementary Report, note 141, *supra,* at pp. 139-140; House Report, note 148, *supra,* at p. 131.

[164] 17 U.S.C. 116.

[165] Register's Report, note 143, *supra,* at p. 1309.

Sec. 505 of S. 644 follows this precept and provides:

> "In any civil action under this title, the court in its discretion may allow the recovery of full costs by or against any party other than the United States or an officer thereof. Except as otherwise provided by this title, the court may also award a reasonable attorney's fee to the prevailing part as part of the costs." [166]

The area of discretionary award of attorney's fees is noteworthy in a number or respects. The Study as to the operation of the damage provisions is illuminating in several ways.[167] The Study notes that award of attorney's fees is not unique. It refers to a variety of awards on varying bases in private treble damage antitrust cases and in such more limited instances in patents and trademarks.[168] The Study explains the operative role of attorney's fees as follows:

> "The Copyright Act differs from all these neighboring fields in that the allowance to the prevailing party is entirely a matter of judicial discretion—a discretion that is, however, reviewable by the courts of appeals (in contrast to the supposed impregnability of statutory damage awards). That discretion may be exercised to withhold an allowance altogether if the courts consider the statutory damage award adequate—or excessive. On the other hand, a liberal allowance may be made that has the effect of substantially enhancing any other form of recovery." [169]

---

[166] S. 644, note 145, *supra,* Sec. 505.

[167] Brown, Ralph S., Jr. Study No. 23, The Operation of the Damage Provisions of the Copyright Law, note 142, *supra,* at pp. 1090-1092.

[168] *Idem* at p. 1090.

[169] *Idem* at pp. 1090-1091; see also Nimmer on Copyright, Sec. 161 (1970).

The Study contains an accompanying Table B[170] which sets forth the award of attorney's fees in a number of cases referred to therein beside the amount of damages or profits recovered. The Study makes observations with respect to Table B as follows:

> "Treated as an enhancement of damages, some of the amounts listed are substantial, at least when they are contrasted to the usual American civil practice of making no provision for the successful party's legal expenses. But if their purpose is to provide for the *actual* reasonable expenses of prosecuting or defending an infringement, the prevailing opinion among lawyers interviewed was that fee allowances rarely are sufficient. For one thing, they are likely to be scaled roughly in proportion to the amount recovered by successful plaintiffs; and though this approach may not be inconsistent with lawyers' own habits in billing clients, it may bear little relation to the time and energy expended on a case." [171]

For these reasons, the Study believes that attorney's fees "should always be taken into account in appraising the substantiality of recovery in a copyright case . . ." [172] and yet, according to the interview sources of the Study, the likelihood of a fee allowance " . . . is not a factor they will count on in deciding whether to settle or litigate." [173]

Several conclusions may be drawn therefrom and from a reading of the cases as to award of attorney's fees. Such award tends to be primarily related to the amount of re-

---

[170] Study No. 23, *idem* at p. 1097.

[171] *Idem* at p. 1091 (italics).

[172] *Idem* at p. 1090.

[173] *Idem* at p. 1091.

covery, and in a great many instances well below normal billing rates of attorneys to clients. Also there is a sufficient element of uncertainty as to the discretionary grant thereof so as to make the statutory discretionary allowance a relatively hazardous basis for taking a copyright case on the basis of recovery of attorney's fees or not.[174]

The Study points to the fact that allowance of attorney's fees has not shown any discernible trend to adjustment of such allowances to take into account postwar inflation.[175] Perhaps proposed copyright revision should take this factor into account, as well as the effect of the financial ability of putative successful plaintiffs or even defendants to sustain copyright litigation in an inflationary period. The existing statute as to damages, with all of its shortcomings as borne out by the cases, strives to provide a vehicle for the courts to do justice. Proposed copyright revision seeks to correct some of the shortcomings and make the scheme of copyright as to damages and other relief even more in line with the precepts of justice. Perhaps it is time to consider the economics of doing justice in this context.

---

[174] Handling copyright litigation on a contingency basis would, in all likelihood, be based on a percentage of the amounts recovered by the plaintiff with the grant of discretionary award of attorney's fees not being deemed significant enough in advance assessment of source of attorney's compensation. By contrast, the award of attorney's fees in successful antitrust litigation is more likely to be substantial. Consequently, counsel is more likely to consider this as a potential source of compensation in antitrust matters as compared to copyright. Indeed, the application of attorney's fees against contingency percentage awarded to the successful client in antitrust litigation may amount to a substantial portion of the contingent compensation of counsel and could conceivably even exceed the total recovery of the client.

[175] Study No. 23, note 142, at p. 1091.

APPENDICES

APPENDIX A

The Copyright Law of the United States of America

United States Code

Title 17—Copyrights

Chapter I

REGISTRATION OF COPYRIGHTS

§ 1. Exclusive Rights as to Copyrighted Works

Any person entitled thereto, upon complying with the provisions of this title, shall have the exclusive right:

(a) To print, reprint, publish, copy, and vend the copyrighted work;

(b) To translate the copyrighted work into other languages or dialects, or make any other version thereof, if it be a literary work; to dramatize it if it be a nondramatic work; to convert it into a novel or other nondramatic work if it be a drama; to arrange or adapt it if it be a musical work; to complete, execute, and finish it if it be a model or design for a work of art;

(c) To deliver, authorize the delivery of, read, or present the copyrighted work in public for profit if it be a lecture, sermon, address or similar production, or other nondramatic literary work; to make or procure the making of any transcription or record thereof by or from which, in whole or in part, it may in any manner or by any method be exhibited, delivered, presented, produced, or reproduced; and to play or perform it in public for profit, and to exhibit, represent, produce, or reproduce it in any manner or by any method whatsoever. The damages for the infringement by broadcast of any work referred to in this subsection shall not exceed the sum of $100 where the infringing broadcaster shows that he was not aware that he was infringing and that such infringement could not have been reasonably foreseen; and

(d) To perform or represent the copyrighted work publicly if it be a drama or, if it be a dramatic work and not reproduced in copies for sale, to vend any manuscript or any record whatsoever thereof; to make or to procure the making of any transcription or record thereof by or from which, in whole or in part, it may in any manner or by any method be exhibited, performed, represented, produced, or reproduced; and to exhibit, perform, represent, produce, or reproduce it in any manner or by any method whatsoever; and

(e) To perform the copyrighted work publicly for profit if it be a musical composition; and for the purpose of public performance for profit, and for the purposes set forth in subsection (a) hereof, to make any arrangement or setting of it or of the melody of it in any system of notation or any form of record in which the thought of an author may be recorded and from which it may be read or reproduced: *Provided,* That the provisions of this title, so far as they secure copyright controlling the parts of instruments serving to reproduce mechanically the musical work, shall include only compositions published and copyrighted after July 1, 1909, and shall not include the works of a foreign author or composer unless the foreign state or nation of which such author or composer is a citizen or subject grants, either by treaty, convention, agreement, or law, to citizens of the United States similar rights. And as a condition of extending the copyright control to such mechanical reproductions, that whenever the owner of a musical copyright has used or permitted or knowingly acquiesced in the use of the copyrighted work upon the parts of instruments serving to reproduce mechanically the musical work, any other person may make similar use of the copyrighted work upon the payment to the copyright proprietor of a royalty of 2 cents on each such part manufactured, to be paid by the manufacturer thereof; and the copyright proprietor may require, and if so the manufacturer shall furnish, a report under oath on the 20th day of each month on the number of parts of instruments manufactured during the previous month serving to reproduce mechanically said musical work, and royalties shall be due on the parts manufactured during any month upon the 20th of the next succeeding month. The payment of the royalty provided for by this section shall free the articles or devices for which such royalty has been paid from further contribution to the copyright except in case of public performance for profit. It shall be the duty of the copyright owner, if he uses the musical composition himself for the manufacture of parts of instruments serving to reproduce mechanically the musical work, or licenses others to do so, to file notice thereof, accompanied by a recording fee, in the copyright office, and any failure to file such notice shall be a complete defense to any suit, action, or proceeding for any infringement of such copyright.

In case of failure of such manufacturer to pay to the copyright proprietor within thirty days after demand in writing the full sum of royalties due at said rate at the date of such demand, the court may award taxable costs to the plaintiff and a reasonable counsel fee, and the court may, in its discretion, enter judgment therein for any sum in addition over the amount found to be due as royalty in accordance with the terms of this title, not exceeding three times such amount.

The reproduction or rendition of a musical composition by or upon coin-operated machines shall not be deemed a public performance for profit unless a fee is charged for admission to the place where such reproduction or rendition occurs.

§ 2. Rights of Author or Proprietor of Unpublished Work

Nothing in this title shall be construed to annul or limit the right of the author or proprietor of an unpublished work, at common law or in equity, to prevent the copying, publication, or use of such unpublished work without his consent, and to obtain damages therefor.

§ 3. Protection of Component Parts of Work Copyrighted; Composite Works or Periodicals

The copyright provided by this title shall protect all the copyrightable component parts of the work copyrighted, and all matter therein in which copyright is already subsisting, but without extending the duration or scope of such copyright. The copyright upon composite works or periodicals shall give to the proprietor thereof all the rights in respect thereto which he would have if each part were individually copyrighted under this title.

§ 4. All Writings of Author Included

The works for which copyright may be secured under this title shall include all the writings of an author.

§ 5. Classification of Works for Registration

The application for registration shall specify to which of the following classes the work in which copyright is claimed belongs:

(a) Books, including composite and cyclopedic works, directories, gazetteers, and other compilations.

(b) Periodicals, including newspapers.

(c) Lectures, sermons, addresses (prepared for oral delivery).

(d) Dramatic or dramatico-musical compositions.

(e) Musical compositions.

(f) Maps.

(g) Works of art; models or designs for works of art.

(h) Reproductions of a work of art.

(i) Drawings or plastic works of a scientific or technical character.

(j) Photographs.

(k) Prints and pictorial illustrations including prints or labels used for articles of merchandise.

(l) Motion-picture photoplays.

(m) Motion pictures other than photoplays.

The above specifications shall not be held to limit the subject matter of copyright as defined in section 4 of this title, nor shall any error in classification invalidate or impair the copyright protection secured under this title.

§ 6. Registration of Prints and Labels

Commencing July 1, 1940, the Register of Copyrights is charged with the registration of claims to copyright properly presented, in all prints and labels published in connection with the sale or advertisement of articles of merchandise, including all claims to copyright in prints and labels pending in the Patent Office and uncleared at the close of business June 30, 1940. There shall be paid for registering a claim of copyright in any print or label not a trademark $6, which sum shall cover the expense of furnishing a certificate of such registration, under the seal of the Copyright Office, to the claimant of copyright.

§ 7. Copyright on Compilations of Works in Public Domain or of Copyrighted Works; Subsisting Copyrights Not Affected

Compilations or abridgements, adaptat ons, arrangements, dramatizations, translations, or other versions of works in the public domain or of copyrighted works when produced with the consent of the proprietor of the copyright in such works, or works republished with new matter, shall be regarded as new works subject to copyright under the provisions of this title; but the publication of any such new works shall not affect the force or validity of any subsisting copyright upon the matter employed or any part thereof, or be construed to imply an exclusive right to such use of the original works, or to secure or extend copyright in such original works.

§ 8. Copyright Not to Subsist in Works in Public Domain, or Published Prior to July 1, 1909, and not Already Copyrighted, or Government Publications; Publication by Government of Copyrighted Material

No copyright shall subsist in the original text of any work which is in the public domain, or in any work which was published in this country or any foreign country prior to July 1, 1909, and has not been already copyrighted in the United States, or in any publication of the United States Government, or any reprint, in whole or in part, thereof: except that the Postmaster General may secure copyright on behalf of the United States in the whole or any part of the publications authorized by section 2506 of title 39.

The publication or republication by the Government, either separately or in a public document, of any material in which copyright is subsisting shall not be taken to cause any abridgment or annulment of the copyright or to authorize any use or appropriation of such copyright material without the consent of the copyright proprietor.

§ 9. Authors or Proprietors, Entitled: Aliens

The author or proprietor of any work made the subject of copyright by this title, or his executors, administrators, or assigns, shall have copyright for such work under the conditions and for the terms specified in this title: *Provided, however,* That the copyright secured by this title shall extend to the work of an author or proprietor who is a citizen or subject of a foreign state or nation only under the conditions described in subsections (a), (b), or (c) below:

(a) When an alien author or proprietor shall be domiciled within the United States at the time of the first publication of his work; or

(b) When the foreign state or nation of which such author or proprietor is a citizen or subject grants, either by treaty, convention, agreement, or law, to citizens of the United States the benefit of copyright on substantially the same basis as to its own citizens, or copyright protection, substantially equal to the protection secured to such foreign author under this title or by treaty; or when such foreign state or nation is a party to an international agreement which provides for reciprocity in the granting of copyright, by the terms of which agreement the United States may, at its pleasure, become a party thereto.

The existence of the reciprocal conditions aforesaid shall be determined by the President of the United States, by proclamation made from time to time, as the purposes of this title may require: *Provided,* That whenever the President shall find that the authors, copyright owners, or proprietors of works first produced or published abroad and subject to copyright or to renewal of copyright under the laws of the United States, including works subject to ad interim copyright, are or may have been temporarily unable to comply with the conditions and formalities prescribed with respect to such works by the copyright laws of the United States, because of the disruption or suspension of facilities essential for such compliance, he may by proclamation grant such extension of time as he may deem appropriate for the fulfillment of such conditions or formalities by authors, copyright owners, or proprietors who are citizens of the United States or who are nationals of countries which accord substantially equal treatment in this respect to authors, copyright owners, or proprietors who are citizens of the United States: *Provided further,* That no liability shall attach under this title for lawful uses made or acts done prior to the effective date of such proclamation in connection with such works, or in respect to the continuance for one year subsequent to such date of any business undertaking or enterprise lawfully undertaken prior to such date involving expenditure or contractual obligation in connection with the exploitation, production, reproduction, circulation, or performance of any such work.

The President may at any time terminate any proclamation authorized herein or any part thereof or suspend or extend its operation for such period or periods of time as in his judgment the interests of the United States may require.

(c) When the Universal Copyright Convention, signed at Geneva on September 6, 1952, shall be in force between the United States of America and the foreign state or nation of which such author is a citizen or subject, or in which the work was first published. Any work to which copyright is extended pursuant to this subsection shall be exempt from the following provisions of this title: (1) The requirement in section 1 (e) that a foreign state or nation must grant to United States citizens mechanical reproduction rights similar to those specified therein; (2) the obligatory deposit requirements of the first sentence of section 13; (3) the provisions of sections 14, 16, 17, and 18; (4) the import prohibitions of section 107, to the extent that they are related to the manufacturing requirements of section 16;

and (5) the requirements of section 19 and 20: *Provided, however*, That such exemptions shall apply only if from the time of first publication all the copies of the work published with the authority of the author or other copyright proprietor shall bear the symbol © accompanied by the name of the copyright proprietor and the year of first publication placed in such manner and location as to give reasonable notice of claim of copyright.

Upon the coming into force of the Universal Copyright Convention in a foreign state or nation as hereinbefore provided, every book or periodical of a citizen or subject thereof in which ad interim copyright was subsisting on the effective date of said coming into force shall have copyright for twenty-eight years from the date of first publication abroad without the necessity of complying with the further formalities specified in section 23 of this title.

The provisions of this subsection shall not be extended to works of an author who is a citizen of, or domiciled in the United States of America regardless of place of first publication, or to works first published in the United States.

§ 10. Publication of Work With Notice

Any person entitled thereto by this title may secure copyright for his work by publication thereof with the notice of copyright required by this title; and such notice shall be affixed to each copy thereof published or offered for sale in the United States by authority of the copyright proprietor, except in the case of books seeking ad interim protection under section 22 of this title.

§ 11. Registration of Claim and Issuance of Certificate

Such person may obtain registration of his claim to copyright by complying with the provisions of this title, including the deposit of copies, and upon such compliance the Register of Copyrights shall issue to him the certificates provided for in section 209 of this title.

§ 12. Works Not Reproduced for Sale

Copyright may also be had of the works of an author, of which copies are not reproduced for sale, by the deposit, with claim of copyright, of one complete copy of such work if it be a lecture or similar production or a dramatic, musical, or dramatico-musical composition; of a title and description, with one print taken from each scene or act, if the work be a motion-picture photoplay; of a photographic print if the work be a photograph; of a title and description, with not less than two prints taken from diffent sections of a complete motion picture, if the work be a motion picture other than a photoplay; or of a photograph or other identifying reproduction thereof, if it be a work of art or a plastic work or drawing. But the privilege of registration of copyright secured hereunder shall not exempt the copyright proprietor from the deposit of copies, under sections 13 and 14 of this title, where the work is later reproduced in copies for sale.

§ 13. Deposit of Copies After Publication; Action or Proceeding for Infringement

After copyright has been secured by publication of the work with the notice of copyright as provided in section 10 of this title, there shall be promptly deposited in the Copyright Office or in the mail addressed to the Register of Copyrights, Washington, District of Columbia, two complete copies of the best edition thereof then published, or if the work is by an author who is a citizen or subject of a foreign state or nation and has been published in a foreign country, one complete copy of the best edition then published in such foreign country, which copies or copy, if the work be a book or periodical, shall have been produced in accordance with the manufacturing provisions specified in section 16 of this title; or if such work be a contribution to a periodical, for which contribution special registration is requested, one copy of the issue or issues containing such contribution; or if the work belongs to a class specified in subsections (g), (h), (i) or (k) of section 5 of this title, and if the Register of Copyrights determines that it is impracticable to deposit copies because of their size, weight, fragility, or monetary value he may permit the deposit of photographs or other identifying reproductions in lieu of copies of the work as published under such rules and regulations as he may prescribe with the approval of the Librarian of Congress; or if the work is not reproduced in copies for sale there shall be deposited the copy, print, photograph, or other identifying reproduction provided by section 12 of this title, such copies or copy, print, photograph, or other reproduction to be accompanied in each case by a claim of copyright. No action or proceeding shall be maintained for infringement of copyright in any work until the provisions of this title with respect to the deposit of copies and registration of such work shall have been complied with.

§ 14. Same; Failure to Deposit; Demand; Penalty

Should the copies called for by section 13 of this title not be promptly deposited as provided in this title, the Register of Copyrights may at any time after the publication of the work, upon actual notice, require the proprietor of the copyright to deposit them, and after the said demand shall have been made, in default of the deposit of copies of the work within three months from any part of the United States, except an outlying territorial possession of the United States, or within six months from any outlying territorial possession of the United States, or from any foreign country, the proprietor of the copyright shall be liable to a fine of $100 and to pay to the Library of Congress twice the amount of the retail price of the best edition of the work, and the copyright shall become void.

§ 15. Same; Postmaster's Receipt; Transmission by Mail Without Cost

The postmaster to whom are delivered the articles deposited as provided in sections 12 and 13 of this title shall, if requested, give a receipt therefor and shall mail them to their destination without cost to the copyright claimant.

§ 16. Mechanical Work To Be Done in United States

Of the printed book or periodical specified in section 5, subsections (a) and (b), of this title, except the original text of a book or periodical of foreign origin in a language or languages other than English, the text of all copies accorded protection under this title, except as below provided, shall be printed from type set within the limits of the United States, either by hand or by the aid of any kind of typesetting machine, or from plates made within the limits of the United States from type set therein, or, if the text be produced by lithographic process, or photoengraving process, then by a process wholly performed within the limits of the United States, and the printing of the text and binding of the said book shall be performed within the limits of the United States; which requirements shall extend also to the illustrations within a book consisting of printed text and illustrations produced by lithographic process, or photoengraving process, and also to separate lithographs or photoengravings, except where in either case the subjects represented are located in a foreign country and illustrate a scientific work or reproduce a work of art: *Provided, however,* That said requirements shall not apply to works in raised characters for the use of the blind, or to books or periodicals of foreign origin in a language or languages other than English, or to works printed or produced in the United States by any other process than those above specified in this section, or to copies of books or periodicals, first published abroad in the English language, imported into the United States within five years after first publication in a foreign state or nation up to the number of fifteen hundred copies of each such book or periodical if said copies shall contain notice of copyright in accordance with sections 10, 19, and 20 of this title and if ad interim copyright in said work shall have been obtained pursuant to section 22 of this title prior to the importation into the United States of any copy except those permitted by the provisions of section 107 of this title: *Provided further,* That the provisions of this section shall not affect the right of importation under the provisions of section 107 of this title.

§ 17. Affidavit to Accompany Copies

In the case of the book the copies so deposited shall be accompanied by an affidavit under the official seal of any officer authorized to administer oaths within the United States, duly made by the person claiming copyright or by his duly authorized agent or representative residing in the United States, or by the printer who has printed the book, setting forth that the copies deposited have been printed from type set within the limits of the United States or from plates made within the limits of the United States from type set therein; or, if the text be produced by the lithographic process, or photoengraving process, that such process was wholly performed within the limits of the United States and that the printing of the text and binding of the said book have also been performed within the limits of the United States. Such affidavit shall state also the place where and the establishment or establishments in which such type was set or plates were made or lithographic process, or photoengraving process or printing and binding were performed and the date of the completion of the printing of the book or the date of publication.

§ 18. Making False Affidavit

Any person who, for the purpose of obtaining registration of a claim to copyright, shall knowingly make a false affidavit as to his having complied with the above conditions shall be deemed guilty of a misdemeanor, and upon conviction thereof shall be punished by a fine of not more than $1,000, and all of his rights and privileges under said copyright shall thereafter be forfeited.

§ 19. Notice; Form

The notice of copyright required by section 10 of this title shall consist either of the word "Copyright," the abbreviation "Copr.," or the symbol ©, accompanied by the name of the copyright proprietor, and if the work be a printed literary, musical, or dramatic work, the notice shall include also the year in which the copyright was secured by publication. In the case, however, of copies of works specified in subsections (f) to (k), inclusive, of section 5 of this title, the notice may consist of the letter C enclosed within a circle, thus ©, accompanied by the initials, monogram, mark, or symbol of the copyright proprietor: *Provided,* That on some accessible portion of such copies or of the margin, back, permanent base, or pedestal, or of the substance on which such copies shall be mounted, his name shall appear. But in the case of works in which copyright was subsisting on July 1, 1909, the notice of copyright may be either in one of the forms prescribed herein or may consist of the following words: "Entered according to Act of Congress, in the year , by A. B., in the office of the Librarian of Congress, at Washington, D. C.," or, at his option, the word "Copyright," together with the year the copyright was entered and the name of the party by whom it was taken out; thus, "Copyright, 19—, by A. B."

§ 20. Same; Place of Application of; One Notice in Each Volume or Number of Newspaper or Periodical

The notice of copyright shall be applied, in the case of a book or other printed publication, upon its title page or the page immediately following, or if a periodical either upon the title page or upon the first page of text of each separate number or under the title heading, or if a musical work either upon its title page or the first page of music. One notice of copyright in each volume or in each number of a newspaper or periodical published shall suffice.

§ 21. Same; Effect of Accidental Omission from Copy or Copies

Where the copyright proprietor has sought to comply with the provisions of this title with respect to notice, the omission by accident or mistake of the prescribed notice from a particular copy or copies shall not invalidate the copyright or prevent recovery for infringement against any person who, after actual notice of the copyright, begins an undertaking to infringe it, but shall prevent the recovery of damages against an innocent infringer who has been misled by the omission of the notice; and in a suit for infringement no permanent injunction shall be had unless the copyright proprietor shall reimburse to the innocent infringer his reasonable outlay innocently incurred if the court, in its discretion, shall so direct.

§ 22. Ad Interim Protection of Book or Periodical Published Abroad

In the case of a book or periodical first published abroad in the English language, the deposit in the Copyright Office, not later than six months after its publication abroad, of one complete copy of the foreign edition, with a request for the reservation of the copyright and a statement of the name and nationality of the author and of the copyright proprietor and of the date of publication of the said book or periodical, shall secure to the author or proprietor an ad interim copyright therein, which shall have all the force and effect given to copyright by this title, and shall endure until the expiration of five years after the date of first publication abroad.

§ 23. Same; Extension to Full Term

Whenever within the period of such ad interim protection an authorized edition of such books or periodicals shall be published within the United States, in accordance with the manufacturing provisions specified in section 16 of this title, and whenever the provisions of this title as to deposit of copies, registration, filing of affidavits, and the printing of the copyright notice shall have been duly complied with, the copyright shall be extended to endure in such book or periodical for the term provided in this title.

§ 24. Duration; Renewal and Extension

The copyright secured by this title shall endure for twenty-eight years from the date of first publication, whether the copyrighted work bears the author's true name or is published anonymously or under an assumed name: *Provided,* That in the case of any posthumous work or of any periodical, cyclopedic, or other composite work upon which the copyright was originally secured by the proprietor thereof, or of any work copyrighted by a corporate body (otherwise than as assignee or licensee of the individual author) or by an employer for whom such work is made for hire, the proprietor of such copyright shall be entitled to a renewal and extension of the copyright in such work for the further term of twenty-eight years when application for such renewal and extension shall have been made to the copyright office and duly registered therein within one year prior to the expiration of the original term of copyright: *And provided further,* That in the case of any other copyrighted work, including a contribution by an individual author to a periodical or to a cyclopedic or other composite work, the author of such work, if still living, or the widow, widower, or children of the author, if the author be not living, or if such author, widow, widower, or children be not living, then the author's executors, or in the absence of a will, his next of kin shall be entitled to a renewal and extension of the copyright in such work for a further term of twenty-eight years when application for such renewal and extension shall have been made to the copyright office and duly registered therein within one year prior to the expiration of the original term of copyright: *And provided further,* That in default of the registration of such application for renewal and extension, the copyright in any work shall determine at the expiration of twenty-eight years from first publication.

§ 25. Renewal of Copyrights Registered in Patent Office Under Repealed Law

Subsisting copyrights originally registered in the Patent Office prior to July 1, 1940, under section 3 of the act of June 18, 1874, shall be subject to renewal in behalf of the proprietor upon application made to the Register of Copyrights within one year prior to the expiration of the original term of twenty-eight years.

§ 26. Terms Defined

In the interpretation and construction of this title "the date of publication" shall in the case of a work of which copies are reproduced for sale or distribution be held to be the earliest date when copies of the first authorized edition were placed on sale, sold, or publicly distributed by the proprietor of the copyright or under his authority, and the word "author" shall include an employer in the case of works made for hire.

§ 27. Copyright Distinct from Property in Object Copyrighted; Effect of Sale of Object, and of Assignment of Copyright

The copyright is distinct from the property in the material object copyrighted, and the sale or conveyance, by gift or otherwise, of the material object shall not of itself constitute a transfer of the copyright, nor shall the assignment of the copyright constitute a transfer of the title to the material object; but nothing in this title shall be deemed or forbid, prevent, or restrict the transfer of any copy of a copyrighted work the possession of which has been lawfully obtained.

§ 28. Assignments and Bequests

Copyright secured under this title or previous copyright laws of the United States may be assigned, granted, or mortgaged by an instrument in writing signed by the proprietor of the copyright, or mav be bequeathed by will.

§ 29. Same; Executed in Foreign Country; Acknowledgment and Certificate

Every assignment of copyright executed in a foreign country shall be acknowledged by the assignor before a consular officer or secretary of legation of the United States authorized by law to administer oaths or perform notarial acts. The certificate of such acknowledgment under the hand and official seal of such consular officer or secretary of legation shall be prima facie evidence of the execution of the instrument.

§ 30. Same; Record

Every assignment of copyright shall be recorded in the copyright office within three calendar months after its execution in the United States or within six calendar months after its execution without the limits of the United States, in default of which it shall be void as against any subsequent purchaser or mortgagee for a valuable consideration, without notice, whose assignment has been duly recorded.

§ 31. Same; Certificate of Record

The Register of Copyrights shall, upon payment of the prescribed fee, record such assignment, and shall return it to the sender with a certificate of record attached under seal of the copyright office, and upon the payment of the fee prescribed by this title he shall furnish to any person requesting the same a certified copy thereof under the said seal.

§ 32. Same; Use of Name of Assignee in Notice

When an assignment of the copyright in a specified book or other work has been recorded the assignee may substitute his name for that of the assignor in the statutory notice of copyright prescribed by this title.

Chapter 2

INFRINGEMENT PROCEEDINGS

§ 101. Infringement

If any person shall infringe the copyright in any work protected under the copyright laws of the United States such person shall be liable:

(a) Injunction—To an injunction restraining such infringement:

(b) Damages and Profits; Amount; Other Remedies—To pay to the copyright proprietor such damages as the copyright proprietor may have suffered due to the infringement, as well as all the profits which the infringer shall have made from such infringement, and in proving profits the plaintiff shall be required to prove sales only, and the defendant shall be required to prove every element of cost which he claims, or in lieu of actual damages and profits, such damages as to the court shall appear to be just, and in assessing such damages the court may, in its discretion, allow the amounts as hereinafter stated, but in case of a newspaper reproduction of a copyrighted photograph, such damages shall not exceed the sum of $200 nor be less than the sum of $50, and in the case of the infringement of an undramatized or nondramatic work by means of motion pictures, where the infringer shall show that he was not aware that he was infringing, and that such infringement could not have been reasonably foreseen, such damages shall not exceed the sum of $100; and in the case of an infringement of a copyrighted dramatic or dramatico-musical work by a maker of motion pictures and his agencies for distribution thereof to exhibitors, where such infringer shows that he was not aware that he was infringing a copyrighted work, and that such infringements could not reasonably have been foreseen, the entire sum of such damages recoverable by the copyright proprietor from such infringing maker and his agencies for the distribution to exhibitors of such infringing motion picture shall not exceed the sum of $5,000 nor be less than $250, and such damages shall in no other case exceed the sum of $5,000 nor be less that the sum of $250, and shall not be regarded as a penalty. But the foregoing exceptions shall not deprive the copyright proprietor of any other remedy given him under this law, nor shall the limitation as to the amount of recovery apply to infringements occurring after the actual notice to a defendant, either by service of process in a suit or other written notice served upon him.

First. In the case of a painting, statue, or sculpture, $10 for every infringing copy made or sold by or found in the possession of the infringer or his agents or employees;

Second. In the case of any work enumerated in section 5 of this title, except a painting, statue, or sculpture, $1 for every infringing copy made or sold by or found in the possession of the infringer or his agents or employees;

Third. In the case of a lecture, sermon, or address, $50 for every infringing delivery;

Fourth. In the case of a dramatic or dramatico-musical or a choral or orchestral composition, $100 for the first and $50 for every subsequent infringing performance; in the case of other musical compositions $10 for every infringing performance;

(c) Impounding During Action—To deliver up on oath, to be impounded during the pendency of the action, upon such terms and conditions as the court may prescribe, all articles alleged to infringe a copyright;

(d) Destruction of Infringing Copies and Plates—To deliver up on oath for destruction all the infringing copies or devices, as well as all plates, molds, matrices, or other means for making such infringing copies as the court may order.

(e) Royalties for Use of Mechanical Reproduction of Musical Works—Whenever the owner of a musical copyright has used or permitted the use of the copyrighted work upon the parts of musical instruments serving to reproduce mechanically the musical work, then in case of infringement of such copyright by the unauthorized manufacture, use, or sale of interchangeable parts, such as disks, rolls, bands, or cylinders for use in mechanical music-producing machines adapted to reproduce the copyrighted music, no criminal action shall be brought, but in a civil action an injunction may be granted upon such terms as the court may impose, and the plaintiff shall be entitled to recover in lieu of profits and damages a royalty as provided in section 1, subsection (e), of this title: *Provided also,* That whenever any person, in the absence of a license agreement, intends to use a copyrighted musical composition upon the parts of instruments serving to reproduce mechanically the musical work, relying upon the compulsory license provision of this title, he shall serve notice of such intention, by registered mail, upon the copyright proprietor at his last address disclosed by the records of the copyright office, sending to the copyright office a duplicate of such notice; and in case of his failure so to do the court may, in its discretion, in addition to sums hereinabove mentioned, award the complainant a further sum, not to exceed three times the amount provided by section 1, subsection (e), of this title, by way of damages, and not as a penalty, and also a temporary injunction until the full award is paid.

§ 104. Willful Infringement for Profit

Any person who willfully and for profit shall infringe any copyright secured by this title, or who shall knowingly and willfully aid or abet such infringement, shall be deemed guilty of a misdemeanor, and upon conviction thereof shall be punished by imprisonment for not exceeding one year or by a fine of not less than $100 nor more than $1,000, or both, in the discretion of the court: *Provided, however,* That nothing in this title shall be so construed as to prevent the performance of religious or secular works such as oratorios, cantatas, masses, or octavo choruses by public schools, church choirs, or vocal societies, rented, borrowed, or obtained from some public library, public school, church choir, school choir, or vocal society, provided the performance is given for charitable or educational purposes and not for profit.

§ 105. Fraudulent Notice of Copyright, or Removal or Alteration of Notice

Any person who, with fraudulent intent, shall insert or impress any notice of copyright required by this title, or words of the same purport, in or upon any uncopyrighted article, or with fraudulent intent shall remove or alter the copyright notice upon any article duly copyrighted shall be guilty of a misdemeanor, punishable by a fine of not less than $100 and not more than $1,000. Any person who shall knowingly issue or sell any article bearing a notice of United States copyright which has not been copyrighted in this country, or who shall knowingly import any article bearing such notice or words of the same purport, which has not been copyrighted in this country, shall be liable to a fine of $100.

§ 106. Importation of Article Bearing False Notice or Piratical Copies of Copyrighted Work

The importation into the United States of any article bearing a false notice of copyright when there is no existing copyright thereon in the United States, or of any piratical copies of any work copyrighted in the United States, is prohibited.

§ 107. Importation, During Existence of Copyright, of Piratical Copies, or of Copies Not Produced in Accordance With Section 16 of This Title

During the existence of the American copyright in any book the importation into the United States of any piratical copies thereof or of any copies thereof (although authorized by the author or proprietor) which have not been produced in accordance with the manufacturing provisions specified in section 16 of this title, or any plates of the same not made from type set within the limits of the United States, or any copies thereof produced by lithographic or photograving process not performed within the limits of the United States, in accordance with the provisions of section 16 of this title, is prohibited: *Provided, however,* That, except as regards piratical copies, such prohibition shall not apply:

(a) To works in raised characters for the use of the blind.

(b) To a foreign newspaper or magazine, although containing matter copyrighted in the United States printed or reprinted by authority of the copyright proprietor, unless such newspaper or magazine contains also copyright matter printed or reprinted without such authorization.

(c) To the authorized edition of a book in a foreign language or languages of which only a translation into English has been copyrighted in this country.

(d) To any book published abroad with the authorization of the author or copyright proprietor when imported under the circumstances stated in one of the four subdivisions following, that is to say:

First. When imported, not more than one copy at one time, for individual use and not for sale; but such privilege of importation shall not extend to a foreign reprint of a book by an American author copyrighted in the United States.

Second. When imported by the authority or for the use of the United States.

Third. When imported, for use and not for sale, not more than one copy of any such book in any one invoice, in good faith by or for any society or institution incorporated for educational, literary, philosophical, scientific or religious purposes, or for the encouragement of the fine arts, or for any college, academy, school, or seminary of learning, or for any State, school, college, university, or free public library in the United States.

Fourth. When such books form parts of libraries or collections purchased en bloc for the use of societies, institutions, or libraries designated in the foregoing paragraph, or form parts of the libraries or personal baggage belonging to persons or families arriving from foreign countries and are not intended for sale: *Provided,* That copies imported as above may not lawfully be used in any way to violate the rights of the proprietor of the American copyright or annul or limit the copyright protection secured by this title, and such unlawful use shall be deemed an infringement of copyright.

§ 108. Forfeiture and Destruction of Articles Prohibited Importation

Any and all articles prohibited importation by this title which are brought into the United States from any foreign country (except in the mails) shall be seized and forfeited by like proceedings as those provided by law for the seizure and condemnation of property imported into the United States in violation of the customs revenue laws. Such articles when forfeited shall be destroyed in such manner as the Secretary of the Treasury or the court, as the case may be, shall direct: *Provided, however,* That all copies of authorized editions of copyright books imported in the mails or otherwise in violation of the provisions of this title may be exported and returned to the country of export whenever it is shown to the satisfaction of the Secretary of the Treasury, in a written application, that such importation does not involve willful negligence or fraud.

§ 109. Importation of Prohibited Articles; Regulations; Proof of Deposit of Copies by Complainants

The Secretary of the Treasury and the Postmaster General are hereby empowered and required to make and enforce individually or jointly such rules and regulations as shall prevent the importation into the United States of articles prohibited importation by this title, and may require, as conditions precedent to exclusion of any work in which copyright is claimed, the copyright proprietor or any person claiming actual or potential injury by reason of actual or contemplated importations of copies of such work to file with the Post Office Department or the Treasury Department a certificate of the Register of Copyrights that the provisions of section 13 of this title have been fully complied with, and to give notice of such compliance to postmasters or to customs officers at the ports of entry in the United States in such form and accompanied by such exhibits as may be deemed necessary for the practical and efficient administration and enforcement of the provisions of sections 106 and 107 of this title.

§ 112. Injunctions; Service and Enforcement

Any court mentioned in section 1338 of Title 28 or judge thereof shall have power, upon complaint filed by any party aggrieved, to grant injunctions to prevent and restrain the violation of any right secured by this title, according to the course and principles of courts of equity, on such terms as said court or judge may deem reasonable. Any injunction that may be granted restraining and enjoining the doing of anything forbidden by this title may be served on the parties against whom such injunction may be granted anywhere in the United States, and shall be operative throughout the United States and be enforceable by proceedings in contempt or otherwise by any other court or judge possessing jurisdiction of the defendants.

§ 113. Transmission of Certified Copies of Papers for Enforcement of Injunction by Other Court

The clerk of the court or judge granting the injunction, shall, when required so to do by the court hearing the application to enforce said injunction, transmit without delay to said court a certified copy of all the papers in said cause that are on file in his office.

§ 114. Review of Orders, Judgments, or Decrees

The orders, judgments, or decrees of any court mentioned in section 1338 of Title 28 arising under the copyright laws of the United States may be reviewed on appeal in the manner and to the extent now provided by law for the review of cases determined in said courts, respectively.

§ 115. Limitations

(a) Criminal Proceedings—No criminal proceedings shall be maintained under the provisions of this title unless the same is commenced within three years after the cause of action arose.

(b) Civil Actions—No civil action shall be maintained under the provisions of this title unless the same is commenced within three years after the claim accrued.

§ 116. Costs; Attoney's Fees

In all actions, suits, or proceedings under this title, except when brought by or against the United States or any officer thereof, full costs shall be allowed, and the court may award to the prevailing party a reasonable attorney's fee as part of the costs.

Chapter 3

COPYRIGHT OFFICE

§ 201. Copyright Office; Preservation of Records

All records and other things relating to copyrights required by law to be preserved shall be kept and preserved in the copyright office, Library of Congress, District of Columbia, and shall be under the control of the register of copyrights, who shall, under the direction and supervision of the Librarian of Congress, perform all the duties relating to the registration of copyrights.

§ 202. Register, Assistant Register, and Subordinates

There shall be appointed by the Librarian of Congress a Register of Copyrights, and one Assistant Register of Copyrights, who shall have authority during the absence of the Register of Copyrights to attach the copyright office seal to all papers issued from the said office and to sign such certificates and other papers as may be necessary. There shall also be appointed by the Librarian such subordinate assistants to the register as may from time to time be authorized by law.

§ 203. Same; Deposit of Moneys Received; Reports

The Register of Copyrights shall make daily deposits in some bank in the District of Columbia, designated for this purpose by the Secretary of the Treasury as a national depository, of all moneys received to be applied as copyright fees, and shall make weekly deposits with the Secretary of the Treasury, in such manner as the latter shall direct, of all copyright fees actually applied under the provisions of this title, and annual deposits of sums received which it has not been possible to apply as copyright fees or to return to the remitters, and shall also make monthly reports to the Secretary of the Treasury and to the Librarian of Congress of the applied copyright fees for each calendar month, together with a statement of all remittances received, trust funds on hand, moneys refunded, and unapplied balances.

§ 204. Same; Bond

The Register of Copyrights shall give bond to the United States in the sum of $20,000, in form to be approved by the General Counsel for the Department of the Treasury and with sureties satisfactory to the Secretary of the Treasury, for the faithful discharge of his duties.

§ 205. Same; Annual Report

The Register of Copyrights shall make an annual report to the Librarian of Congress, to be printed in the annual report on the Library of Congress, of all copyright business for the previous fiscal year, including the number and kind of works which have been deposited in the copyright office during the fiscal year, under the provisions of this title.

§ 206. Seal of Copyright Office

The seal used in the copyright office on July 1, 1909, shall be the seal of the copyright office, and by it all papers issued from the copyright office requiring authentication shall be authenticated.

§ 207. Rules for Registration of Claims

Subject to the approval of the Librarian of Congress, the Register of Copyrights shall be authorized to make rules and regulations for the registration of claims to copyright as provided by this title.

§ 208. Record Books in Copyright Office

The Register of Copyrights shall provide and keep such record books in the copyright office as are required to carry out the provisions of this title, and whenever deposit has been made in the copyright office of a copy of any work under the provisions of this title he shall make entry thereof.

§ 209. Certificate of Registration; Effect as Evidence; Receipt for Copies Deposited

In the case of each entry the person recorded as the claimant of the copyright shall be entitled to a certificate of registration under seal of the copyright office, to contain the name and address of said claimant, the name of the country of which the author of the work is a citizen or subject, and when an alien author domiciled in the United States at the time of said registration, then a statement of that fact, including his place of domicile, the name of the author (when the records of the copyright office shall show the same), the title of the work which is registered for which copyright is claimed, the date of the deposit of the copies of such work, the date of publication if the work has been reproduced in copies for sale, or publicly distributed, and such marks as to class designation and entry number as shall fully identify the entry. In the case of a book, the certificate shall also state the receipt of the affidavit, as provided by section 17 of this title, and the date of the completion of the printing, or the date of the publication of the book, as stated in the said affidavit. The Register of Copyrights shall prepare a printed form for the said certificate, to be filled out in each case as above provided for in the case of all registrations made after July 1, 1909, and in the case of all previous registrations so far as the copyright office record books shall show such facts, which certificate, sealed with the seal of the copyright office, shall, upon payment of the prescribed fee, be given to any person making application for the same. Said certificate shall be admitted in any court as prima facie evidence of the facts stated therein. In addition to such certificate the register of copyrights shall furnish, upon request, without additional fee, a receipt for the copies of the work deposited to complete the registration.

§ 210. Catalog of Copyright Entries; Effect as Evidence

The Register of Copyrights shall fully index all copyright registrations and assignments and shall print at periodic intervals a catalog of the titles of articles deposited and registered for copyright, together with suitable indexes, and at stated intervals shall print complete and indexed catalog for each class of copyright entries, and may thereupon, if expedient, destroy the original manuscript catalog cards containing the titles included in such printed volumes and representing the entries made during such intervals. The current catalog of copyright entries and the index volumes herein provided for shall be admitted in any court as prima facie evidence of the facts stated therein as regards any copyright registration.

§ 211. Same; Distribution and Sale; Disposal of Proceeds

The said printed current catalogs as they are issued shall be promptly distributed by the Superintendent of Documents to the collectors of customs of the United States and to the postmasters of all exchange offices of receipt of foreign mails, in accordance with revised list of such collectors of customs and postmasters prepared by the Secretary of the Treasury and the Postmaster General, and they shall also be furnished in whole or in part to all parties desiring them at a price to be determined by the Register of Copyrights for each part of the catalog not exceeding $75 for the complete yearly catalog of copyright entries. The consolidated catalogs and indexes shall also be supplied to all persons ordering them at such prices as may be fixed by the Register of Copyrights, and all subscriptions for the catalogs shall be received by the Superintendent of Documents, who shall forward the said publications; and the moneys thus received shall be paid into the Treasury of the United States and accounted for under such laws and Treasury regulations as shall be in force at the time.

§ 212. Records and Works Deposited in Copyright Office Open to Public Inspection; Taking Copies of Entries

The record books of the copyright office, together with the indexes to such record books, and all works deposited and retained in the copyright office, shall be open to public inspection; and copies may be taken of the copyright entries actually made in such record books, subject to such safeguards and regulations as shall be prescribed by the Register of Copyrights and approved by the Librarian of Congress.

§ 213. Disposition of Articles Deposited in Office

Of the articles deposited in the copyright office under the provisions of the copyright laws of the United States, the Librarian of Congress shall determine what books and other articles shall be transferred to the permanent collections of the Library of Congress, including the law library, and what other books or articles shall be placed in the reserve collections of the Library of Congress for sale or exchange, or be transferred to other governmental libraries in the District of Columbia for use therein.

§ 214. Destruction of Articles Deposited in Office Remaining Undisposed of; Removal of by Author or Proprietor; Manuscripts of Unpublished Works

Of any articles undisposed of as above provided, together with all titles and correspondence relating thereto, the Librarian of Congress and the Register of Copyrights jointly shall, at suitable intervals, determine what of these received during any period of years it is desirable or useful to preserve in the permanent files of the copyright office, and, after due notice as hereinafter provided, may within their discretion cause the remaining articles and other things to be destroyed: *Provided,* That there shall be printed in the Catalog of Copyright Entries from February to November, inclusive, a statement of the years of receipt of such articles and a notice to permit any author, copyright proprietor, or other lawful claimant to claim and remove before the expiration of the month of December of that year anything found which relates to any of his productions deposited or registered for copyright within the period of years stated, not reserved or disposed of as provided for in this title. No manuscript of an unpublished work shall be destroyed during its term of copyright without specific notice to the copyright proprietor of record, permitting him to claim and remove it.

§ 215. Fees

The Register of Copyrights shall receive, and the persons to whom the services designated are rendered shall pay, the following fees:

For the registration of a claim to copyright in any work, including a print or label used for articles of merchandise, $6; for the registration of a claim to renewal of copyright, $4; which fees shall include a certificate for each registration: *Provided,* That only one registration fee shall be required in the case of several volumes of the same book published and deposited at the same time: *And provided further,* That with respect to works of foreign origin, in lieu of payment of the copyright fee of $6 together with one copy of the work and application, the foreign author or proprietor may at any time within six months from the date of first publication abroad deposit in the Copyright Office an application for registration and two copies of the work which shall be accompanied by a catalog card in form and content satisfactory to the Register of Copyrights.

For recording the renewal of copyright and issuance of certificate therefor, $4.

For every additional certificate of registration, $2.

For certifying a copy of an application for registration of copyright, and for all other certifications, $3.

For recording every assignment, agreement, power of attorney, or other paper not exceeding six pages, $5; for each additional page or less, 50 cents; for each title over one in the paper recorded, 50 cents additional.

For recording a notice of use, or notice of intention to use, $3, for each notice of not more than five titles; and 50 cents for each additional title.

For any requested search of Copyright Office records, or weeks deposited, or services rendered in connection therewith, $5 for each hour of time consumed.

§ 216. When the Day for Taking Action Falls on Saturday, Sunday, or a Holiday

When the last day for making any deposit or application, or for paying any fee, or for delivering any other material to the Copyright Office falls on Saturday, Sunday, or a holiday within the District of Columbia, such action may be taken on the next succeeding business day.

APPENDIX B

Acts Extending the Duration of Copyright Protection in Certain Cases

Public Law 87-668
87th Congress, H. J. Res. 627
September 19, 1962
76 STAT. 555.

Resolved by the Senate and House of Representatives of the United States of America in Congress assembled, That in any case in which the renewal term of copyright subsisting in any work on the date of approval of this resolution would expire prior to December 31, 1965, such term is hereby continued until December 31, 1965.

Approved September 19, 1962.

Public Law 89-142
89th Congress, H. J. Res. 431
August 28, 1965
79 STAT. 581.

Resolved by the Senate and House of Representatives of the United States of America in Congress assembled, That in any case in which the renewal term of copyright subsisting in any work on the date of approval of this resolution, or the term thereof as extended by Public Law 87-668, would expire prior to December 31, 1967, such term is hereby continued until December 31, 1967.

Approved August 28, 1965.

Public Law 90-141
90th Congress, S. J. Res. 114
November 16, 1967
81 STAT. 464.

Resolved by the Senate and House of Representatives of the United States of America in Congress assembled, That in any case in which the renewal term of copyright subsisting in any work on the date of approval of this resolution, or the term thereof as extended by Public Law 87-668, or by Public Law 89-142 (or by either or both of said laws), would expire prior to December 31, 1968, such term is hereby continued until December 31, 1968.

Approved November 16, 1967.

Public Law 90-416
90th Congress, S. J. Res. 172
July 23, 1968
82 STAT. 397.

Resolved by the Senate and House of Representatives of the United States of America in Congress assembled, That in any case in which the renewal term of copyright subsisting in any work on the date of approval of this resolution, or the term thereof as extended by Public Law 87-668, by Public Law 89-142, or by Public Law 90-141 (or by all or certain of said laws), would expire prior to December 31, 1969, such term is hereby continued until December 31, 1969.

Approved July 23, 1968.

Public Law 91-147
91st Congress, S. J. Res. 143
December 16, 1969

JOINT RESOLUTION

Extending the duration of copyright protection in certain cases.

Resolved by the Senate and House of Representatives of the United States of America in Congress assembled, That in any case in which the renewal term of copyright subsisting in any work on the date of the approval of this resolution, or the term thereof as extended by Public Law 87-668, by Public Law 89-142, by Public Law 90-141, or by Public Law 90-416 (or by all or certain of said laws), would expire prior to December 31, 1970, such term is hereby continued until December 31, 1970.

Approved December 16, 1969.

Public Law 91-555
91st Congress, S. J. Res. 230
December 17, 1970

JOINT RESOLUTION

Extending the duration of copyright protection in certain cases.

Resolved by the Senate and House of Representatives of the United States of America in Congress assembled, That in any case in which the renewal term of copyright subsisting in any work on the date of approval of this resolution, or the term thereof as extended by Public Law 87-668, by Public Law 89-442, by Public Law 90-141, by Public Law 90-416, or by Public Law 91-147 (or by all or certain of said laws), would expire prior to December 31, 1971, such term is hereby continued until December 31, 1971.

Approved December 17, 1970.

Public Law 92-170
92nd Congress, S.J. Res. 132
November 24, 1971

JOINT RESOLUTION

Extending the duration of copyright protection in certain cases.

Resolved by the Senate and House of Representatives of the United States of America in Congress assembled, That in any case in which the renewal term of copyright subsisting in any work on the date of approval of this resolution, or the term thereof as extended by Public Law 87-668, by Public Law 89-142, by Public Law 90-141, by Public Law 90-416, by Public Law 91-147, or by Public Law 91-555 (or by all or certain of said laws), would expire prior to December 31, 1972, such term is hereby continued until December 31, 1972.

Approved November 24, 1971.

APPENDIX C

Anti-Piracy Act in Sound Recordings

Public Law 92-140
92nd Congress, S. 646
October 15, 1971
AN ACT

To amend title 17 of the United States Code to provide for the creation of a limited copyright in sound recordings for the purpose of protecting against unauthorized duplication and piracy of sound recording, and for other purposes.

Be it enacted by the Senate and House of Representatives of the United States of America in Congress assembled, That title 17 of the United States Code is amended in the following respects:

(a) In section 1, title 17, of the United States Code, add a subsection (f) to read:

"To reproduce and distribute to the public by sale or other transfer of ownership, or by rental, lease, or lending, reproductions of the copyrighted work if it be a sound recording: *Provided,* That the exclusive right of the owner of a copyright in a sound recording to reproduce it is limited to the right to duplicate the sound recording in a tangible form that directly or indirectly recaptures the actual sounds fixed in the recording: *Provided further,* That this right does not extend to the making or duplication of another sound recording that is an independent fixation of other sounds, even though such sounds imitate or simulate those in the copyrighted sound recording; or to reproductions made by transmitting organizations exclusively for their own use."

(b) In section 5, title 17, of the United States Code, add a subsection (n) to read:

"Sound recordings."

(c) In section 19, title 17, of the United States Code, add the following at the end of the section: "In the case of reproductions of works specified in subsection (n) of section 5 of this title, the notice shall consist of the symbol Ⓟ (the letter P in a circle), the year of first publication of the sound recording, and the name of the owner of copyright in the sound recording, or an abbreviation by which the name can be recognized, or a generally known alternative designation of the owner: *Provided,* That if the producer of the sound recording is named on the labels or containers of the reproduction, and if no other name appears in conjunction with the notice, his name shall be considered a part of the notice."

(d) In section 20, title 17, of the United States Code, amend the first sentence to read: "The notice of copyright shall be applied, in the case of a book or other printed publication, upon its title page or the page immediately following, or if a periodical either upon the title page or upon the first page of text of each separate number or under the title heading, or if a musical work either upon its title page or the first page of music, or if a sound recording on the surface of reproductions thereof or on the label or container in such manner and location as to give reasonable notice of the claim of copyright."

(e) In section 26, title 17, of the United States Code, add the following at the end of the section: "For the purposes of this section and sections 10, 11, 13, 14, 21, 101, 106, 109, 209, 215 but not for any other purpose a reproduction of a work described in subsection 5(n) shall be considered to be a copy thereof. 'Sound recordings' are works that result from the fixation of a series of musical, spoken, or other sounds, but not including the sounds accompanying a motion picture. 'Reproductions of sound recordings' are material objects in which sounds other than those accompanying a motion picture are fixed by any method now known or later developed, and from which the sounds can be perceived, reproduced, or otherwise communicated, either directly or with the aid of a machine or device, and include the 'parts of instruments serving to reproduce mechanically the musical work', 'mechanical reproductions', and 'interchangeable parts, such as discs or tapes for use in mechanical music-producing machines' referred to in sections 1(e) and 101(e) of this title."

SEC. 2. That title 17 of the United States Code is further amended in the following respect:

In section 101, title 17 of the United States Code, delete subsection (e) in its entirety and substitute the following:

"(e) INTERCHANGEABLE PARTS FOR USE IN MECHANICAL MUSIC-PRODUCING MACHINES.—Interchangeable parts, such as discs or tapes for use in mechanical music-producing machines adapted to reproduce copyrighted musical works, shall be considered copies of the copyrighted musical works which they serve to reproduce mechanically for the purposes of this section 101 and sections 106 and 109 of this title, and the unauthorized manufacture, use, or sale of such interchangeable parts shall constitute an infringement of the copyrighted work rendering the infringer liable in accordance with all provisions of this title dealing with infringements of copyright and, in a case of willful infringement for profit, to criminal prosecution pursuant to section 104 of this title. Whenever any person, in the absence of a license agreement, intends to use a copyrighted musical composition upon the parts of instruments serving to reproduce mechanically the musical work, relying upon the compulsory license provision of this title, he shall serve notice of such intention, by registered mail, upon the copyright proprietor at his last address disclosed by the records of the copyright office, sending to the copyright office a duplicate of such notice."

SEC. 3. This Act shall take effect four months after its enactment except that section 2 of this Act shall take effect immediately upon its enactment. The provisions of title 17, United States Code, as amended by section 1 of this Act, shall apply only to sound recordings fixed, published, and copyrighted on and after the effective date of this Act and before January 1, 1975, and nothing in title 17, United States Code, as amended by section 1 of this Act, shall be applied retroactively or be construed as affecting in any way any rights with respect to sound recordings fixed before the effective date of this Act.

Approved October 15, 1971.

APPENDIX D

Title 28 Judicial Copyright Procedure

Pertinent Sections of
Title 28, United States Code

§ 1338. Patents, Copyrights, Trade-Marks, and Unfair Competition.

(a) The district courts shall have original jurisdiction of any civil action arising under any Act of Congress relating to patents, copyrights and trade-marks. Such jurisdiction shall be exclusive of the courts of the states in patent and copyright cases.

(b) The district courts shall have original jurisdiction of any civil action asserting a claim of unfair competition when joined with a substantial and related claim under the copyright, patent or trade-mark laws.

§ 1400. Patents and Copyrights.

(a) Civil actions, suits, or proceedings arising under any Act of Congress relating to copyrights may be instituted in the district in which the defendant or his agent resides or may be found.

(b) Any civil action for patent infringement may be brought in the judicial district where the defendant resides, or where the defendant has committed acts of infringement and has a regular and established place of business.

§ 1498. Patent and Copyright Cases.

. . . .

(b) Hereafter, whenever the copyright in any work protected under the copyright laws of the United States shall be infringed by the United States, by a corporation owned or controlled by the United States, or by a contractor, subcontractor, or any person, firm, or corporation acting for the Government and with the authorization or consent of the Government, the exclusive remedy of the owner of such copyright shall be by action against the United States in the Court of Claims for the recovery of his reasonable and entire compensation as damages for such infringement, including the minimum statutory damages as set forth in section 101(b) of title 17, United States Code: *Provided,* That a Government employee shall have a right of action against the Government under this subsection except where he was in a position to order, influence, or induce use of the copyrighted work by the Government: *Provided, however,* That this subsection shall not confer a right of action on any copyright owner or any assignee of such owner with respect to any copyrighted work prepared by a person while in the employment or service of the United States, where the copyrighted work was prepared as a part of the official functions of the employee, or in the preparation of which Government time, material, or facilities were used: *And provided further,* That before such action against the United States has been instituted the appropriate corporation owned or controlled by the United States or the head of the appropriate department or agency of the Government, as the case may be, is authorized to enter into an agreement with the copyright owner in full settlement and compromise for the damages accruing to him by reason of such infringement and to settle the claim administratively out of available appropriations.

Except as otherwise provided by law, no recovery shall be had for any infringement of a copyright covered by this subsection committed more than three years prior to the filing of the complaint or counter-claim for infringement in the action, except that the period between the date of receipt of a written claim for compensation by the department or agency of the Government or corporation owned or controlled by the United States, as the case may be, having authority to settle such claim and the date of mailing by the Government of a notice to the claimant that his claim has been denied shall not be counted as a part of the three years, unless suit is brought before the last-mentioned date.

(c) The provisions of this section shall not apply to any claim arising in a foreign country.

§ 2072. RULES OF CIVIL PROCEDURE FOR DISTRICT COURTS.

The Supreme Court shall have the power to prescribe, by general rules, the forms of process, writs, pleadings, and motions, and the practice and procedure of the district courts of the United States in civil actions.

Such rules shall not abridge, enlarge or modify any substantive right and shall preserve the right of trial by jury as at common law and as declared by the Seventh Amendment to the Constitution.

Such rules shall not take effect until they have been reported to Congress by the Chief Justice at or after the beginning of a regular session thereof but not later than the first day of May, and until the expiration of ninety days after they have been thus reported.

All laws in conflict with such rules shall be of no further force or effect after such rules have taken effect. Nothing in this title, anything therein to the contrary notwithstanding, shall in any way limit, supersede, or repeal any such rules heretofore prescribed by the Supreme Court.

APPENDIX E

Rules Adopted by the Supreme Court of the United States[1] for Practice and Procedures Under Section 25[2] of an Act to Amend and Consolidate the Acts Respecting Copyright, Approved March 4,1909

1.

Proceedings in actions brought under section 25[2] of the Act of March 4, 1909, entitled "An Act to amend and consolidate the acts respecting copyright," including proceedings relating to the perfecting of appeals, shall be governed by the Rules of Civil Procedure, insofar as they are not inconsistent with these rules.

[2.[3]]

3.

Upon the institution of any action, suit or proceeding, or at any time thereafter, and before the entry of final judgment or decree therein, the plaintiff or complainant, or his authorized agent or attorney, may file with the clerk of any court given jurisdiction under section 34[2] of the Act of March 4, 1909, an affidavit stating upon the best

---

[1] 214 U. S. 533 (1909), as amended by 307 U. S. 652 (1939).

[2] Historical note: Sections 25 and 34 of the Act of March 4, 1909, as amended, later became sections 101 and 110, respectively, of Title 17 of the United States Code by the Act of July 30, 1947 (61 Stat. 652). Sections 101 (f) and 110 were repealed by the Act of June 25, 1948 (62 Stat. 869). However, see section 2072 of Title 28, United States Code, on page 1233, *supra*.

[3] By amendment to the Rules of Civil Procedure for the United States District Courts, prescribed by the Supreme Court of the United States on February 28, 1966, pursuant to Title 28, U.S.C., Sec. 2072, Rule 2 was rescinded by the Court's order, effective July 1, 1966, 383 U. S. 1031.

of his knowledge, information and belief, the number and location, as near as may be, of the alleged infringing copies, records, plates, molds, matrices, etc., or other means for making the copies alleged to infringe the copyright, and the value of the same, and with such affidavit shall file with the clerk a bond executed by at least two sureties and approved by the court or a commissioner thereof.

4.

Such bond shall bind the sureties in a specified sum, to be fixed by the court, but not less than twice the reasonable value of such infringing copies, plates, records, molds, matrices, or other means for making such infringing copies, and be conditioned for the prompt prosecution of the action, suit or proceeding; for the return of said articles to the defendant, if they or any of them are adjudged not to be infringements, or if the action abates, or is discontinued before they are returned to the defendant; and for the payment to the defendant of any damages which the court may award to him against the plaintiff or complainant. Upon the filing of said affidavit and bond, and the approval of said bond, the clerk shall issue a writ directed to the marshal of the district where the said infringing copies, plates, records, molds, matrices, etc., or other means of making such infringing copies shall be stated in said affidavit to be located, and generally to any marshal of the United States, directing the said marshal to forthwith seize and hold the same subject to the order of the court issuing said writ, or of the court of the district in which the seizure shall be made.

5.

The marshal shall seize said articles or any smaller or larger part thereof he may then or thereafter find, using such force as may be reasonably necessary in the premises, and serve on the defendant a copy of the affidavit, writ and bond by delivering the same to him personally, if he can be found within the district, or if he cannot be found, to his agent, if any, or to the person from whose possession the articles are taken, or if the owner, agent, or such person be found within the district, by leaving said copy at the usual place of abode of such owner or agent, with a person of suitable age and discretion, or at the place where said articles are found, and shall make immediate return of such seizure, or attempted seizure, to the court. He shall also attach to said articles a tag or label stating the fact of such seizure and warning all persons from in any manner interfering therewith.

6.

A marshal who has seized alleged infringing articles, shall retain them in his possession, keeping them in a secure place, subject to the order of the court.

7.

Within three days the articles are seized, and a copy of the affidavit, writ and bond are served as hereinbefore provided, the defendant shall serve upon the clerk a notice that he excepts to the amount of the penalty of the bond, or to the sureties of the plaintiff or complainant, or both, otherwise he shall be deemed to have waived all objection to the amount of the penalty of the bond and the sufficiency of the sureties thereon. If the court sustain the exceptions it may order a new bond to be executed by the plaintiff or complainant, or in default thereof within a time to be named by the court, the property to be returned to the defendant.

8.

Within ten days after service of such notice, the attorney of the plaintiff or complainant shall serve upon the defendant or his attorney a notice of the justification of the sureties, and said sureties shall justify before the court or a judge thereof at the time within stated.

9.

The defendant, if he does not except to the amount of the penalty of the bond or the sufficiency of the sureties of the plaintiff or complainant, may make application to the court for the return to him of the articles seized, upon filing an affidavit stating all material facts and circumstances tending to show that the articles seized are not infringing copies, records, plates, molds, matrices, or means for making the copies alleged to infringe the copyright.

10.

Thereupon the court in its discretion, after such hearing as it may direct, may order such return upon the filing by the defendant of a bond executed by at least two sureties, binding them in a specified sum to be fixed in the discretion of the court, and conditioned for the delivery of said specified articles to abide the order of the court. The plaintiff or complainant may require such sureties to justify within ten days of the filing of such bond.

11.

Upon the granting of such application and the justification of the sureties on the bond, the marshal shall immediately deliver the articles seized to the defendant.

12.

Any service required to be performed by any marshal may be performed by any deputy of such marshal.

13.

For services in cases arising under this section, the marshal shall be entitled to the same fees as are allowed for similar services in other cases.

APPENDIX F

Universal Copyright Convention[1] Text

The Contracting States,

Moved by the desire to assure in all countries copyright protection of literary, scientific and artistic works,

Convinced that a system of copyright protection appropriate to all nations of the world and expressed in a universal convention, additional to, and without impairing international systems already in force, will ensure respect for the rights of the individual and encourage the development of literature, the sciences and the arts,

Persuaded that such a universal copyright system will facilitate a wider dissemination of works of the human mind and increase international understanding,

Have agreed as follows:

ARTICLE I

Each Contracting State undertakes to provide for the adequate and effective protection of the rights of authors and other copyright proprietors in literary, scientific and

[1] The most recent convention to which the United States is a party is the Universal Copyright Convention, which came into force on September 16, 1955, following ratification on November 5, 1954. This Convention is considered to be in force in the Panama Canal Zone, Puerto Rico, the Virgin Islands, and Guam, and in many territories or possessions of the foreign member countries.

The United Staes is also a member of the Buenos Aires Copyright Convention of 1910.

The United States has never joined the International Union for the Protection of Literary and Artistic Works, better known as the Berne Union.

Some foreign states have copyright relations with the United States solely on the basis of a bilateral agreement. In certain cases, bilateral agreements also exist as to countries that have copyright relations with the United States under the Universal Copyright Convention or the Buenos Aires Convention.

artistic works, including writings, musical, dramatic and cinematographic works, and paintings, engravings and sculpture.

ARTICLE II

1. Published works of nationals of any Contracting State and works first published in that State shall enjoy in each other Contracting State the same protection as that other State accords to works of its nationals first published in its own territory.

2. Unpublished works of nationals of each Contracting State shall enjoy in each other Contracting State the same protection as that other State accords to unpublished works of its own nationals.

3. For the purpose of this Convention any Contracting State may, by domestic legislation, assimilate to its own nationals any person domiciled in that State.

ARTICLE III

1. Any Contracting State which, under its domestic law, requires as a condition of copyright, compliance with formalities such as deposit, registration, notice, notarial certificates, payment of fees or manufacture or publication in that Contracting State, shall regard these requirements as satisfied with respect to all works protected in accordance with this Convention and first published outside its territory and the author of which is not one of its nationals, if from the time of the first publication all the copies of the work published with the authority of the author or other copyright proprietor bear the symbol © accompanied by the name of the copyright proprietor and the year of first publication placed in such manner and location as to give reasonable notice of claim of copyright.

2. The provisions of paragraph 1 of this article shall not preclude any Contracting State from requiring formali-

ties or other conditions for the acquisition and enjoyment of copyright in respect of works first published in its territory or works of its nationals wherever published.

3. The provisions of paragraph 1 of this article shall not preclude any Contracting State from providing that a person seeking judicial relief must, in bringing the action, comply with procedural requirements, such as that the complainant must appear through domestic counsel or that the complainant must deposit with the court or an administrative office, or both, a copy of the work involved in the litigation; provided that failure to comply with such requirements shall not affect the validity of the copyright, nor shall any such requirement be imposed upon a national of another Contracting State if such requirement is not imposed on nationals of the State in which protection is claimed.

4. In each Contracting State there shall be legal means of protecting without formalities the unpublished works of nationals of other Contracting States.

5. If a Contracting State grants protection for more than one term of copyright and the first term is for a period longer than one of the minimum periods prescribed in article IV, such State shall not be required to comply with the provisions of paragraph 1 of this article III in respect of the second or any subsequent term of copyright.

ARTICLE IV

1. The duration of protection of a work shall be governed, in accordance with the provisions of article II and this article, by the law of the Contracting State in which protection is claimed.

2. The term of protection for works protected under this Convention shall not be less than the life of the author and 25 years after his death.

However, any Contracting State which, on the effective date of this Convention in that State, has limited this term for certain classes of works to a period computed from the first publication of the work, shall be entitled to maintain these exceptions and to extend them to other classes of works. For all these classes the term of protection shall not be less than 25 years from the date of first publication.

Any Contracting State which, upon the effective date of this Convention in that State, does not compute the term of protection upon the basis of the life of the author, shall be entitled to compute the term of protection from the date of the first publication of the work or from its registration prior to publication, as the case may be, provided the term of protection shall not be less than 25 years from the date of first publication or from its registration prior to publication, as the case may be.

If the legislation of a Contracting State grants two or more successive terms of protection, the duration of the first term shall not be less than one of the minimum periods specified above.

3. The provisions of paragraph 2 of this article shall not apply to photographic works or to works of applied art; provided, however, that the term of protection in those Contracting States which protect photographic works, or works of applied art in so far as they are protected as artistic works, shall not be less than ten years for each of said classes of works.

4. No Contracting State shall be obliged to grant protection to a work for a period longer than that fixed for the class of works to which the work in question belongs, in the case of unpublished works by the law of the Contracting State of which the author is a national, and in the case of published works by the law of the Contracting State in which the work has been first published.

For the purposes of the application of the preceding provision, if the law of any Contracting State grants two or more successive terms of protection, the period of protection of that State shall be considered to be the aggregate of those terms. However, if a specified work is not protected by such State during the second or any subsequent term for any reason, the other Contracting States shall not be obliged to protect it during the second or any subsequent term.

5. For the purposes of the application of paragraph 4 of this article, the work of a national of a Contracting State, first published in a non-Contracting State, shall be treated as though first published in the Contracting State of which the author is a national.

6. For the purposes of the application of paragraph 4 of this article, in case of simultaneous publication in two or more Contracting States, the work shall be treated as though first published in the State which affords the shortest term; any work published in two or more Contracting States within thirty days of its first publication shall be considered as having been published simultaneously in said Contracting States.

ARTICLE V

1. Copyright shall include the exclusive right of the author to make, publish, and authorize the making and publication of translations of works protected under this Convention.

2. However, any Contracting State may, by its domestic legislation, restrict the right of translation of writings, but only subject to the following provisions:

If, after the expiration of a period of seven years from the date of the first publication of a writing, a translation of such writing has not been published in the national language or languages, as the case may be, of the Contracting State, by the owner of the right of translation or with his authorization, any national of such Contracting State may obtain a non-exclusive license from the competent authority thereof to translate the work and publish the work so translated in any of the national languages in which it has not been published; provided that such national, in accordance with the procedure of the State concerned, establishes either that he has requested, and been denied, authorization by the proprietor of the right to make and publish the translation, or that, after due diligence on his part, he was unable to find the owner of the right. A license may also be granted on the same conditions if all previous editions of a translation in such language are out of print.

If the owner of the right of translation cannot be found, then the applicant for a license shall send copies of his application to the publisher whose name appears on the work and, if the nationality of the owner of the right of translation is known, to the diplomatic or consular representative of the State of which such owner is a national, or to the organization which may have been designated by the government of that State. The license shall not be granted before the expiration of a period of two months from the date of the dispatch of the copies of the application.

Due provision shall be made by domestic legislation to assure to the owner of the right of translation a compensation which is just and conforms to international standards, to assure payment and transmittal of such compensation, and to assure a correct translation of the work.

The original title and the name of the author of the work shall be printed on all copies of the published translation. The license shall be valid only for publication of the translation in the territory of the Contracting State where it has been applied for. Copies so published may be imported and sold in another Contracting State if one of the national languages of such other State is the same language as that into which the work has been so translated, and if the domestic law in such other State makes provision for such licenses and does not prohibit such importation and sale. Where the foregoing conditions do not exist, the importation and sale of such copies in a Contracting State shall be governed by its domestic law and its agreements. The license shall not be transferred by the licensee.

The license shall not be granted when the author has withdrawn from circulation all copies of the work.

ARTICLE VI

"Publication," as used in this Convention, means the reproduction in tangible form and the general distribution to the public of copies of a work from which it can be read or otherwise visually perceived.

ARTICLE VII

This Convention shall not apply to works or rights in works which, at the effective date of the Convention in a Contracting State where protection is claimed, are permanently in the public domain in the said Contracting State.

ARTICLE VIII

1. This Convention, which shall bear the date of September 6, 1952, shall be deposited with the Director-General of the United Nations Educational, Scientific and Cultural Organization and shall remain open for signature by all States for a period of 120 days after that date. It shall be subject to ratification or acceptance by the signatory States.

2. Any State which has not signed this Convention may accede thereto.

3. Ratification, acceptance or accession shall be effected by the deposit of an instrument to that effect with the Director-General of the United Nations Educational, Scientific and Cultural Organization.

ARTICLE IX

1. This Convention shall come into force three months after the deposit of twelve instruments of ratification, acceptance or accession, among which there shall be those of four States which are not members of the International Union for the Protection of Literary and Artistic Works.

2. Subsequently, this Convention shall come into force in respect of each State three months after that State has deposited its instrument of ratification, acceptance or accession.

ARTICLE X

1. Each State party to this Convention undertakes to adopt, in accordance with its Constitution, such measures as are necessary to ensure the application of this Convention.

2. It is understood, however, that at the time an instrument of ratification, acceptance or accession is deposited on behalf of any State, such State must be in a position under its domestic law to give effect to the terms of this Convention.

ARTICLE XI

1. An Intergovernmental Committee is hereby established with the following duties:

(a) to study the problems concerning the application and operation of this Convention;

(b) to make preparation for periodic revisions of this Convention;

(c) to study any other problems concerning this international protection of copyright, in co-operation with the various interested international organizations, such as the United Nations Educational, Scientific and Cultural Organization, the International Union for the Protection of Literary and Artistic Works and the Organization of American States;

(d) to inform the Contracting States as to its activities.

2. The Committee shall consist of the representatives of twelve Contracting States to be selected with due consideration to fair geographical representation and in conformity with the Resolution relating to this article, annexed to this Convention.

The Director-General of the United Nations Educational, Scientific and Cultural Organization, the Director of the Bureau of the International Union for the Protection of Literary and Artistic Works and the Secretary-General of the Organization of American States, or their representatives, may attend meetings of the Committee in an advisory capacity.

ARTICLE XII

The Intergovernmental Committee shall convene a conference for revision of this Convention whenever it deems necessary, or at the request of at least ten Contracting States, or of a majority of the Contracting States if there are less than twenty Contracting States.

ARTICLE XIII

Any Contracting State may, at the time of deposit of its instrument of ratification, acceptance or accession, or at any time thereafter, declare by notification addressed to the Director-General of the United Nations Educational, Scientific and Cultural Organization that this Convention shall apply to all or any of the countries or territories for the international relations of which it is responsible and this Convention shall thereupon apply to the countries or territories named in such notification after the expiration of the term of three months provided for in article IX. In the absence of such notification, this Convention shall not apply to any such country or territory.

ARTICLE XIV

1. Any Contracting State may denounce this Convention in its own name or on behalf of all or any of the countries or territories as to which a notification has been given under article XIII. The denunciation shall be made by notification addressed to the Director-General of the United Nations Educational, Scientific and Cultural Organization.

2. Such denunciation shall operate only in respect of the State or of the country or territory on whose behalf it was made and shall not take effect until twelve months after the date of receipt of the notification.

ARTICLE XV

A dispute between two or more Contracting States concerning the interpretation or application of this Convention, not settled by negotiation, shall, unless the States concerned agree on some other method of settlement, be brought before the International Court of Justice for determination by it.

ARTICLE XVI

1. This Convention shall be established in English, French and Spanish. The three texts shall be signed and shall be equally authoritative.

2. Official texts of this Convention shall be established in German, Italian and Portuguese.

Any Contracting State of group of Contracting States shall be entitled to have established by the Director-General of the United Nations Educational, Scientific and Cultural Organization other texts in the language of its choice by arrangement with the Director-General.

All such texts shall be annexed to the signed texts of this Convention.

ARTICLE XVII

1. This Convention shall not in any way affect the provisions of the Berne Convention for the Protection of Literary and Artistic Works or membership in the Union created by that Convention.

2. In application of the foregoing paragraph, a Declaration has been annexed to the present article. This Declaration is an integral part of this Convention for the States bound by the Berne Convention on January 1, 1951, or which have or may become bound to it at a later date. The signature of this Convention by such States shall also constitute signature of the said Declaration, and ratification, acceptance or accession by such States shall include the Declaration as well as the Convention.

ARTICLE XVIII

This Convention shall not abrogate multilateral or bilateral copyright conventions or arrangements that are or may be in effect exclusively between two or more American Republics. In the event of any difference either between the provisions of such existing conventions or arrangements and the provisions of this Convention, or between the provisions of this Convention and those of any new convention or arrangement which may be formulated between two or more American Republics after this Convention comes into force, the convention or arrangement most recently formulated shall prevail between the parties thereto. Rights in work acquired in any Contracting State under existing conventions or arrangements before the date this Convention comes into force in such State shall not be affected.

ARTICLE XIX

This Convention shall not abrogate multilateral or bilateral conventions or arrangements in effect between two or more Contracting States. In the event of any difference between the provisions of such existing conventions or arrangements and the provisions of this Convention, the provisions of this Convention shall prevail. Rights in works acquired in any Contracting State under existing conventions or arrangements before the date on which this Convention comes into force in such State shall not be affected. Nothing in this article shall affect the provisions of articles XVII and XVIII of this Convention.

ARTICLE XX

Reservations to this Convention shall not be permitted.

ARTICLE XXI

The Director-General of the United Nations Educational, Scientific and Cultural Organization shall send duly certified copies of this Convention to the States interested, to the Swiss Federal Council and to the Secretary-General of the United Nations for registration by him.

He shall also inform all interested States of the ratifications, acceptances and accessions which have been deposited, the date on which this Convention comes into force, the notifications under Article XIII of this Convention, and denunciations under Article XIV.

APPENDIX DECLARATIONS
relating to Article XVII

The States which are members of the International Union for the Protection of Literary and Artistic Works, and which are signatories to the Universal Copyright Convention,

Desiring to reinforce their mutual relations on the basis of the said Union and to avoid any conflict which might result from the co-existence of the Convention of Berne and the Universal Convention,

Have, by common agreement, accepted the terms of the following declaration:

(a) Works which, according to the Berne Convention, have as their country of origin a country which has withdrawn from the International Union created by the said Convention, after January 1, 1951, shall not be protected by the Universal Copyright Convention in the countries of the Berne Union;

(b) The Universal Copyright Convention shall not be applicable to the relationships among countries of the Berne Union insofar as it relates to the protection of works having as their country of origin, within the meaning of the Berne Convention, a country of the International Union created by the said Convention.

RESOLUTION CONCERNING ARTICLE XI

The Intergovernmental Copyright Conference

Having considered the problems relating to the Intergovernmental Committee provided for in Article XI of the Universal Copyright Convention

resolves

1. The first members of the Committee shall be representatives of the following twelve States, each of those States designating one representative and an alternate: Argentine, Brazil, France, Germany, India, Italy, Japan, Mexico, Spain, Switzerland, United Kingdom, and United States of America.

2. The Committee shall be constituted as soon as the Convention comes into force in accordance with article XI of this Convention;

3. The Committee shall elect its Chairman and one Vice-Chairman. It shall establish its rules of procedure having regard to the following principles:

(a) the normal duration of the term of office of the representatives shall be six years; with one third retiring every two years;

(b) before the expiration of the term of office of any members, the Committee shall decide which States shall cease to be represented on it and which States shall be called upon to designate representatives; the representatives of those States which have not ratified, accepted or acceded shall be the first to retire;

(c) the different parts of the world shall be fairly represented;

and expresses the wish

that the United Nations Educational, Scientific, and Cultural Organization provide its Secretariat.

In faith whereof the undersigned, having deposited their respective full powers, have signed this Convention.

Done at Geneva, this sixth day of September, 1952 in a single copy.

Protocol 1 to the Universal Copyright Convention concerning the application of that Convention to the works of stateless persons and refugees

The States parties hereto, being also parties to the Universal Copyright Convention (hereinafter referred to as the "Convention") have accepted the following provisions:

1. Stateless persons and refugees who have their habitual residence in a State party to this Protocol shall, for the purposes of the Convention, be assimilated to the nationals of that State.

2. (a) This Protocol shall be signed and shall be subject to ratification or acceptance, or may be acceded to, as if the provisions of article VIII of the Convention applied hereto.

(b) This Protocol shall enter into force in respect of each State, on the date of deposit of the instrument of ratification, acceptance or accession of the State concerned or on the date of entry into force of the Convention with respect to such State, whichever is the later.

In faith whereof the undersigned, being duly authorized thereto, have signed this Protocol.

Done at Geneva this sixth day of September, 1952, in the English, French and Spanish languages, the three texts being equally authoritative, in a single copy which shall be deposited with the Director-General of Unesco. The Director-General shall send certified copies to the signatory States, to the Swiss Federal Council and to the Secretary-General of the United Nations for registration.

Protocol 2 annexed to the Universal Copyright Convention, concerning the application of that Convention to the works of certain international organisations

The State parties hereto, being also parties to the Universal Copyright Convention (hereinafter referred to as the "Convention"),

Have accepted the following provisions:

1. (a) The protection provided for in article II (1) of the Convention shall apply to works published for the first time by the United Nations, by the Specialized Agencies in relationship therewith, or by the Organisation of American States;

(b) Similarly, Article II (2) of the Convention shall apply to the said organisation or agencies.

2. (a) This Protocol shall be signed and shall be subject to ratification or acceptance, or may be acceded to, as if the provisions of article VIII of the Convention applied hereto.

(b) This Protocol shall enter into force for each State on the date of deposit of the instrument of ratification, acceptance or accession of the State concerned or on the date of entry into force of the Convention with respect to such State, whichever is the later.

In faith whereof the undersigned, being duly authorised thereto, have signed this Protocol.

Done at Geneva, this sixth day of September, 1952, in the English, French and Spanish languages, the three texts being equally authoritative, in a single copy which shall be deposited with the Director-General of the Unesco.

The Director-General shall send certified copies to the signatory States, to the Swiss Federal Council, and to the Secretary-General of the United Nations for registration.

Protocol 3 annexed to the Universal Copyright Convention concerning the effective date of instruments of ratification or acceptance of or accession to that Convention

States parties hereto,

Recognizing that the application of the Universal Copyright Convention (hereinafter referred to as the "Convention") to States participating in all the international copyright systems already in force will contribute greatly to the value of the Convention;

Have agreed as follows:

1. Any State party hereto may, on depositing its instrument of ratification or acceptance of or accession to the Convention, notify the Director-General of the United Nations Educational, Scientific and Cultural Organization (hereinafter referred to as "Director-General") that that instrument shall not take effect for the purposes of Article IX of the Convention until any other State named in such notification shall have deposited its instrument.

2. The notification referred to in paragraph 1 above shall accompany the instrument to which it relates.

3. The Director-General shall inform all States signatory or which have then acceded to the Convention of any notifications received in accordance with this Protocol.

4. This Protocol shall bear the same date and shall remain open for signature for the same period as the Convention.

5. It shall be subject to ratification or acceptance by the signatory States. Any State which has not signed this Protocol may accede thereto.

6. (a) Ratification or acceptance or accession shall be effected by the deposit of an instrument to that effect with the Director-General.

(b) This Protocol shall enter into force on the date of deposit of not less than four instruments of ratification or acceptance or accession. The Director-General shall inform all interested States of this date. Instruments deposited after such date shall take effect on the date of their deposit.

In faith whereof the undersigned, being duly authorised thereto, have signed this Protocol.

Done at Geneva, the sixth day of September 1952, in the English, French and the Spanish languages, the three texts being equally authoritative, in a single copy which shall be annexed to the original copy of the Convention. The Director-General shall send certified copies to the signatory States, to the Swiss Federal Council, and to the Secretary-General of the United Nations for registration.

APPENDIX G

Standard Reference Data Act

Public Law 90-396
90th Congress, H. R. 6279
July 11, 1968

An Act To provide for the collection, compilation, critical evaluation, publication, and sale of standard reference data.

Be it enacted by the Senate and House of Representatives of the United States of America in Congress assembled,

DECLARATION OF POLICY

Section 1. The Congress hereby finds and declares that reliable standardized scientific and technical reference data are of vital importance to the progress of the Nation's science and technology. It is therefore the policy of the Congress to make critically evaluated reference data readily available to scientists, engineers, and the general public. It is the purpose of this Act to strengthen and enhance this policy.

DEFINITIONS

Sec. 2. For the purposes of this Act—

(a) The term "standard reference data" means quantitative information, related to a measurable physical or chemical property of a substance or system of substances of known composition and structure, which is critically evaluated as to its reliability under section 3 of this Act.

(b) The term "Secretary" means the Secretary of Commerce.

Sec. 3. The Secretary is authorized and directed to provide or arrange for the collection, compilation, critical evaluation, publication, and dissemination of standard reference data. In carrying out this program, the Secretary shall, to the maximum extent practicable, utilize the reference data services and facilities of other agencies and instrumentalities of the Federal Government and of State and local governments, persons, firms, institutions, and associations, with their consent and in such a manner as to avoid duplication of those services and facilities. All agencies and instrumentalities of the Federal Government are encouraged to exercise their duties and functions in such manner as will assist in carrying out the purpose of this Act. This section shall be deemed complementary to existing authority, and nothing herein is intended to repeal, supersede, or diminish existing authority or responsibility of any agency or instrumentality of the Federal Government.

SEC. 4. To provide for more effective integration and coordination of standard reference data activities, the Secretary, in consultation with other interested Federal agencies, shall prescribe and publish in the Federal Register such standards, criteria, and procedures for the preparation and publication of standard reference data as may be necessary to carry out the provisions of this Act.

SEC. 5. Standard reference data conforming to standards established by the Secretary may be made available and sold by the Secretary or by a person or agency designated by him. To the extent practicable and appropriate, the prices established for such data may reflect the cost of collection, compilation, evaluation, publication, and dissemination of the data, including administrative expenses; and the amounts received shall be subject to the Act of March 3, 1901, as amended (15 U.S.C. 271-278e).

Sec. 6. (a) Notwithstanding the limitations contained in section 8 of title 17 of the United States Code, the Secretary may secure copyright and renewal thereof on behalf of the United States as author or proprietor in all or any part of any standard reference data which he prepares or makes available under this Act, and may authorize the reproduction and publication thereof by others.

(b) The publication or republication by the Government under this Act, either separately or in a public document, of any material in which copyright is subsisting shall not be taken to cause any abridgment or annulment of the copyright or to authorize any use or appropriation of such material without the consent of the copyright proprietor.

Sec. 7. There are authorized to be appropriated to carry out this Act, $1.86 million for the fiscal year ending June 30, 1969. Notwithstanding the provisions of any other law, no appropriations for any fiscal year may be made for the purpose of this Act after fiscal year 1969 unless previously authorized by legislation hereafter enacted by the Congress.

Sec. 8. This Act may be cited as the "Standard Reference Data Act."

Approved July 11, 1968.

APPENDIX H(a)

Regulations of the Copyright Office

Part 201—General Provisions

Part 202—Registration of Claims to Copyright

PART 201

GENERAL PROVISIONS

§ 201.1. Communications With the Copyright Office

Mail and other communications shall be addressed to the Register of Copyrights, Library of Congress, Washington, D.C. 20540.

§ 201.2. Information Given by the Copyright Office

(a) In General (1) Information relative to the operations of the Copyright Office is supplied without charge. A search of the records, indexes and deposits will be made for such information as they may contain relative to copyright claims upon application and payment of the statutory fee. The Copyright Office, however, does not undertake the making of comparisons of copyright deposits to determine similarity between works, nor does it give legal opinions or advice on such matters as:

(i) The validity or status of any copyright other than the facts shown in the records of the Office;

(ii) The rights of persons, whether in connection with cases of alleged copyright infringement, contracts between authors and publishers or other matters of a similar nature;

(iii) The scope and extent of protection of works in foreign countries or interpretation of foreign copyright laws or court opinions;

(iv) The sufficiency, extent or scope of compliance with the copyright law.

(2) In addition, the Office cannot undertake to furnish the names of copyright attorneys, publishers, agents, or other similar information.

(b) Inspection and Copying of Records (1) Inspection and copyright of completed records and indexes relating to a registration or a recorded document, and inspection of copies deposited in connection with a completed copyright registration, may be undertaken at such times as will not result in interference with or delay in the work of the Copyright Office.

(2) The copying from the Copyright Office records of names and addresses for the purpose of compiling mailing lists and other similar uses is expressly prohibited.

(3) The Copyright Office maintains an administrative staff manual, referred to as its "Compendium of Office Practices," and an index to the manual, for the general guidance of its staff in making registrations and recording documents. The manual and index, as amended and supplemented from time to time, are available in the Copyright Office for public inspection and copying.

(c) Correspondence (1) Official correspondence, including preliminary applications, between copyright claimants or their agents and the Copyright Office, and directly relating to a completed registration or to a recorded document, is made available for public inspection. Requests for photocopies of the correspondence shall be made pursuant to paragraph (d) of this section.

(2) (i) Correspondence, application forms and any accompanying material forming a part of a pending or rejected application are not records which are open to public inspection under paragraph (b) of this section.

(ii) Inspection of such files may be afforded upon presentation of written authorization of the claimant or his agent, or upon submission to the Register of Copyrights, Library of Congress, Washington, D.C. 20540, of a written request which is deemed by him to show good cause for such access and which establishes that the person making the request is one properly and directly concerned.

(iii) Where such access is authorized and photocopies of the official file are subsequently requested, the conditions and procedures of paragraph (d) of this section are controlling.

(3\` Correspondence, memoranda, reports, opinions, and similar material relating to internal matters of personnel and procedures, office administration, security matters, and internal consideration of policy and decisional matters, including the work product of an attorney, are not open to public inspection.

(4) The Copyright Office will return unanswered any abusive or scurrilous correspondence.

(d) Requests for Copies (1) Requests for additional certificates of registration should be sent to the Copyright Office, and the accompanying fees should be made payable to the Register of Copyrights.

(2) Requests for photocopies of copyright deposits, official correspondence, and Copyright Office records (other

than additional certificates of registration) should be sent to the Chief, Photoduplication Service, Library of Congress, Washington, D.C. 20540, the accompanying fees in payment of such services being made payable to that official. When the photocopy is to be certified by the Copyright Office, the additional certification fee should be made payable to the Register of Copyrights and both remittances together with the transmittal letter are to be sent to the Copyright Office.

(3) Requests for photocopies of official correspondence shall identify the specific material desired and shall contain a statement enabling the Copyright Office to determine if the writer is properly and directly concerned.

(4) Requests for photocopies of copyright deposits will be granted when one or more of the following conditions are fulfilled:

(i) Authorization by Owner. When authorized in writing by the copyright owner or his designated agent.

(ii) Request by Attorney. When required in connection with litigation, actual or prospective, in which the copyrighted work is involved; but in all such cases the attorney representing the actual or prospective plaintiff or defendant for whom the request is made shall give in writing (*a*) The names of the parties and the nature of the controversy; (*b*) the name of the court where the action is pending, or, in the case of a prospective proceeding, a full statement of the facts of the controversy in which the copyrighted work is involved; and (*c*) satisfactory assurances that the requested copy will be used only in connection with the specified litigation.

(iii) Court Order. When an order to have the copy made is issued by a court having jurisdiction of a case in which the copy is to be submitted as evidence.

§ 201.3. Catalog of Copyright Entries

The current subscription price for all parts of the complete yearly Catalog of Copyright Entries is $50.00. Each part of the Catalog is published in two semiannual numbers covering, respectively, the periods January-June and July-December. The prices given in the list below are for each semiannual number. The Catalog may be obtained, upon payment of the established price, from the Register of Copyrights, Library of Congress, Washington, D.C. 20540, to whom requests for copies should be addressed and to whom the remittance should be made payable.

Part 1—Books and Pamphlets Including Serials and Contributions to Periodicals, $7.50.
Part 2—Periodicals, $2.50.
Parts 3-4—Dramas and Works Prepared for Oral Delivery, $2.50.
Part 5—Music, $7.50.
Part 6—Maps and Atlases, $2.50.
Parts 7-11A—Works of Art, Reproductions of Works of Art, Scientific and Technical Drawings, Photographic Works, Prints and Pictorial Illustrations, $2.50.
Part 11B—Commercial Prints and Labels, $2.50.
Parts 12-13—Motion Pictures and Filmstrips, $2.50.

§ 201.4. Assignments of Copyright and Other Papers

Assignments of copyright and other papers relative to copyrights will be recorded in the Copyright Office upon payment of the statutory fee. Examples of such papers include powers of attorney, licenses to use a copyrighted work, agreements between authors and publishers covering a particular work or works and rights thereto, mortgages, certificates of change of corporate title, wills, and decrees of distribution. The original, signed instrument should be submitted for recordation, and is returned to the sender with a certificate of record. Where the original instrument is not available, a certified or other copy might be submitted, but it shall be accompanied by a statement that the original is not available.

§ 201.5. Amendments to Completed Copyright Office Registrations and Other Records

(a) No Cancellations No correction or cancellation of a Copyright Office registration or other record will be made (other than a registration or record provisional upon receipt of fee as provided in § 201.6) after it has been completed if the facts therein stated agree with those supplied the Office for the purpose of making such record. However, it shall be within the discretion of the Register of Copyrights to determine if any particular case justifies the placing of an annotation upon any record for the purpose of clarification, explanation, or indication that there exists elsewhere in the records, indexes or correspondence files of the Office, information which has reference to the facts as stated in such record.

(b) Correction By New Registration In exceptional cases, where an applicant desires to correct, amend or amplify a registration previously made in accordance with information furnished by a claimant or his agent, a new application indicating its amendatory purpose shall be filed, accompanied by the statutory fee and the same number of copies required for a new application. Where it is satisfactorily established that copies of the original work cannot be obtained for submission, photostat or microfilm copies of the original may be submitted.

§ 201.6. Payment and Refund of Copyright Office Fees

(a) In General All fees sent to the Copyright Office should be in the form of a money order, check or bank draft payable to the Register of Copyrights. Coin or currency sent to the Office in letters or packages will be at the remitter's risk. Remittances from foreign countries should be in the form of an International Money Order or Bank Draft payable and immediately negotiable in the United States for the full amount of the fee required. Uncertified checks are accepted subject to collection. Where the statutory fee is submitted in the form of a check, the registration of the copyright claim or other record made by the Office is provisional until payment in money is received. In the event the fee is not paid, the registration or other record shall be expunged.

(b) Deposit Accounts Persons or firms having a considerable amount of business with the Copyright Office may, for their own convenience, prepay copyright expenses by establishing a Deposit Account.

(c) Refunds Money paid for applications which are rejected or payments made in excess of the statutory fee will be refunded, but amounts of twenty-five cents or less will not be returned unless specifically requested and such sums may be refunded in postage stamps. All larger amounts will be refunded by check.

(d) Return of Deposit Copies Copies of works deposited in the Copyright Office pursuant to law are either retained in the Copyright Office, transferred for the permanent collections or other uses of the Library of Congress, or disposed of according to law. When an application is rejected, the Copyright Office reserves the right to retain the deposited copies.

§ 201.7. Preparation of Catalog Card

The catalog card which may accompany a work of foreign origin, as provided in section 215 of title 17, U.S. Code, as amended, may be a catalog card supplied by a library in the country of publication. In lieu of such a card the applicant may prepare his own card, or may fill out the form supplied by the Copyright Office. The catalog card should contain the full name of the author of the original work, title and description from the title page, paging, copyright claimant, the city and year of publication, and the names of all other authors, editors, etc., whom the applicant considers of sufficient importance to record. When available, the year of birth of each author named should be given. If the form furnished by the Office is not used, the size of the card should preferably be 5 inches wide by 3 inches deep or 12.5 centimeters wide by 7.5 centimeters deep. The Register of Copyrights reserves the right to accept catalog cards not complying with the above requirements.

§ 201.8. Import Statements

(a) The Copyright Office will issue statements for books and periodicals first published abroad in the English language which are to be imported under the provisions of section 16 of title 17, U.S. Code, as amended. A statement for the importation of 1,500 copies will be issued to the person named in the application for ad interim copyright registration. The holder of this statement shall present it to the customs officer in charge of the port of entry. Upon receipt of a statement from the customs officer, showing importation of less than 1,500 copies, a new statement will be issued for the balance.

(b) The provisions in the Customs Regulations covering the use of the import statement (Copyright Office Form C-85) are found in 19 CPR 11.21 (21 F.R. 2517).

PART 202

REGISTRATION OF CLAIMS TO COPYRIGHT

§ 202.1. Material Not Subject to Copyright

The following are examples of works not subject to copyright and applications for registration of such works cannot be entertained:

(a) Words and short phrases such as names, titles, and slogans; familiar symbols or designs; mere variations of typographic ornamentation, lettering or coloring; mere listing of ingredients or contents;

(b) Ideas, plans, methods, systems, or devices, as distinguished from the particular manner in which they are expressed or described in a writing;

(c) Works designed for recording information which do not in themselves convey information, such as time cards, graph paper, account books, diaries, bank checks, score cards, address books, report forms, order forms and the like;

(d) Works consisting entirely of information, that is common property containing no original authorship, such as, for example: Standard calendars, height and weight charts, tape measures and rulers, schedules of sporting events, and lists or tables taken from public documents or other common sources.

§ 202.2. Copyright Notice

(a) General (1) With respect to a published work, copyright is secured, or the right to secure it is lost, at the date of publication, i.e., the date on which copies are first placed on sale, sold, or publicly distributed, depending upon the adequacy of the notice of copyright on the work at that time.

(2) If publication occurs by distribution of copies or in some other manner, without the statutory notice or with an inadequate notice, the right to secure copyright is lost. In such cases, copyright cannot be secured by adding the notice to copies distributed at a later date.

(3) Works first published abroad, other than works eligible for ad interim registration, must bear an adequate copyright notice at the time of their first publication in order to secure copyright under the law of the United States.

(b) Defects In Notice Where the copyright notice does not meet the requirements of the law, the Copyright Office will reject an application for copyright registration. Common defects in the notice include, among others, the following:

(1) The notice lacks one or more of the necessary elements (i.e., the word "Copyright," the abbreviation "Copr.,"

or the symbol ©; the name of the copyright proprietor; or, when required, the year date of publication);

(2) The elements of the notice are dispersed;

(3) The notice is not in one of the positions prescribed by law;

(4) The notice is in a foreign language;

(5) The name in the notice is that of someone who had no authority to secure copyright in his name;

(6) The year date in the copyright notice is later than the date of the year in which copyright was actually secured, including the following cases:

(i) Where the year date in the notice is later than the date of actual publication;

(ii) Where copyright was first secured by registration of a work in unpublished form, and copies of the same work as later published without change in substance bear a copyright notice containing a year date later than the year of unpublished registration;

(iii) Where a book or periodical published abroad, for which ad interim copyright has been obtained, is later published in the United States without change in substance and contains a year date in the copyright notice later than the year of first publication abroad: *Provided, however,* That in each of the three foregoing types of cases, if the copyright was actually secured not more than one year earlier than the year date in the notice, registration may be considered as a doubtful case.

(7) A notice is permanently covered so that it cannot be seen without tearing the work apart;

(8) A notice is illegible or so small that it cannot be read without the aid of a magnifying glass: *Provided, however,*

That where the work itself requires magnification for its ordinary use (e.g., a microfilm, microcard or motion picture) a notice which will be readable when so magnified, will not constitute a reason for rejection of the claim;

(9) A notice is on a detachable tag and will eventually be detached and discarded when the work is put in use;

(10) A notice is on the wrapper or container which is not a part of the work and which will eventually be removed and discarded when the work is put in use;

(11) The notice is restricted or limited exclusively to an uncopyrightable element, either by virtue of its position on the work, by the use of asterisks, or by other means.

§ 202.3. Application Forms

(a) In General Section 5 of Title 17 of the U.S. Code provides thirteen classes (Class A through Class M) of works in which copyright may be claimed. Examples of certain works falling within these classes are given in §§ 202.4 to 202.15 inclusive, for the purpose of assisting persons who desire to obtain registration of a claim to copyright, to select the correct application form.

(b) Claims of Copyright (1) All works deposited for registration shall be accompanied by a "claim of copyright" in the form of a properly executed application, together with the statutory registration fee. The Office reserves the right to refuse to accept any application that is a carbon copy, illegible, defaced, or otherwise not in an acceptable condition for examination and recording.

(2) Where these separate elements are not received simultaneously, the Copyright Office holds the submitted elements for a reasonable time and, in default of the receipt of the missing element or elements after a request made

therefor, the submitted item or items may be returned to the sender. Such action does not constitute a waiver of the right of the Register of Copyrights pursuant to section 14, title 17, U.S. Code, to demand compliance with the deposit provisions of that title.

(3) Applications for copyright registration covering published works should reflect the facts existing at the time of first publication, and should not include information concerning changes that have occurred between the time of publication and registration. The name given as copyright claimant in the application should agree with the name appearing in the copyright notice.

(4) Applications should be submitted by the copyright claimant, or by someone acting under his authority.

(5) All information requested by the Copyright Office application form should be given in the appropriate spaces provided. There should not be attached to the application any slips of paper or extra pages containing additional information, or a continuation of requested information.

(c) Forms The Copyright Office supplies without charge following forms for use when applying for the registration of a claim to copyright in a work and for the filing of a notice of use of musical compositions on mechanical instruments.

Form A—Published book manufactured in the United States of America (Class A).

Form A-B Ad Interim—Book of periodical in the English language manufactured and first published outside the United States of America (Classes A-B).

Form A-B Foreign—Book or periodical manufactured outside the United States of America (except work subject to the ad interim provisions of the copyright law) (Classes A-B).

Form B—Periodical manufactured in the United States of America (Class B).

Form BB—Contribution to a periodical manufactured in the United States of America (Class B).

Form C—Lecture or similar production prepared for oral delivery (Class C).

Form D—Dramatic or dramatico-musical composition (Class D).

Form E—Musical composition the author of which is a citizen or domiciliary of the United States of America or which was published in the United States of America (Class E).

Form E Foreign—Musical composition the author of which is not a citizen or domiciliary of the United States of America and which was not first published in the United States of America (Class E).

Form F—Map (Class F).

Form G—Work of art or a model or design for a work of art (Class G).

Form H—Reproduction of a work of art (Class H).

Form I—Drawing or plastic work of a scientific or technical character (Class I).

Form J—Photograph (Class J).

Form K—Print or pictorial illustration (Class K).

Form KK—Print or label used for an article of merchandise (Class K).

Form L-M—Motion picture (Classes L-M).

Form R—Renewal copyright.

Form U—Notice of use of copyrighted music on mechanical instruments.

§ 202.4. Books (Class A)

(a) Subject Matter and Forms This class includes such published works as fiction and nonfiction, poems, compilations, composite works, directories, catalogs, annual publications, information in tabular form, and similar text matter, with or without illustrations, as books, either bound or in loose-leaf form, pamphlets, leaflets, cards, single pages or the like. Applications for registration of claims to copyright in published books manufactured in the United States of America are made on Form A; in books manufactured outside of the United States of America, except those subject to ad interim provisions of the copyright law, on Form

A-B Foreign; and in books in the English language manufactured and first published outside the United States of America, and subject to the ad interim provisions of the copyright law, on Form A-B Ad Interim.

(b) Ad Interim Registrations (1) An American edition of an English-language book or periodical identical in substance to that first published abroad will not be registered unless an ad interim registration is first made.

(2) When a book or periodical has been registered under the ad interim provisions, an American edition of the same work, to be registrable, must be manufactured and published in the United States within five years after the date of first publication abroad.

(3) Since by law ad interim copyright expires at the end of the ad interim term unless an American edition is published during the term, a renewal application covering a work registered only under the ad interim provisions will be rejected. Where both an ad interim and an American edition have been registered, the registrability of the renewal application is governed by the date of the first publication abroad.

§ 202.5. Periodicals (Class B)

This class includes such works as newspapers, magazines, reviews, bulletins, and serial publications, published at intervals of less than a year. Applications for registration of claims to copyright in published periodicals manufactured in the United States of America are made on Form B; in periodicals, or in contributions thereto, manufactured outside the United States of America, except those subject to the ad interim provision of the copyright law, on Form A-B Foreign; and in periodicals, or in contributions thereto, in the English language manufactured and first published outside of the United States of America, and subject to the ad interim provisions of the copyright law, on Form A-B Ad Interim. Applications for registration of claims to copyright in contributions to periodicals manufactured in the United States of America are made on Form BB. Application for registration of claims to copyright in contributions to periodicals, which contributions are prints published in connection with the sale or advertisement of an article or articles of merchandise, are made on Form KK.

§ 202.6. Lectures or Similar Productions Prepared for Oral Delivery (Class C)

This class includes the scripts of unpublished works prepared in the first instance for oral delivery, such as lectures, sermons, addresses, monologs, panel discussions, and variety programs prepared for radio or television. The script submitted for registration in Class C should consist of the actual text of the works to be presented orally. Formats, outlines, brochures, synopses, or general description of radio and television programs are not registrable in unpublished form. When published with notice as prescribed by law, such works may be considered for registration as "books" in Class A.

§ 202.7. Dramatic and Dramatico-Musical Compositions (Class D)

This class includes published or unpublished works dramatic in character such as the acting version of plays for the stage, motion pictures, radio, television and the like, operas, operettas, musical comedies and similar productions, and pantomimes. Choreographic works of a dramatic character, whether the story or theme be expressed by music and action combined or by actions alone, are subject to registration in Class D. However, descriptions of dance steps and other physical gestures, including ballroom and social dances or choreographic works which do not tell a story, develop a character or emotion, or otherwise convey a dramatic concept or idea, are not subject to registration in Class D.

§ 202.8. Musical Compositions (Class E)

(a) This class includes published or unpublished musical compositions in the form of visible notation (other than dramatico-musical compositions), with or without words, as well as new versions of musical compositions, such as adaptations or arrangements, and editing when such editing is the writing of an author. The words of a song, when unaccompanied by music, are not registrable in Class E.

(b) A phonograph record or other sound recording is not considered a "copy" of the compositions recorded on it, and is not acceptable for copyright registration. Likewise, the Copyright Office does not register claims to exclusive rights in mechanical recordings themselves, or in the performances they reproduce.

§ 202.9. Maps (Class F)

This class includes all published cartographic representations of area, such as terrestrial maps and atlases, marine charts, celestial maps and such three-dimensional works as globes and relief models.

§ 202.10. Works of Art (Class G)

(a) General This class includes published or unpublished works of artistic craftsmanship, insofar as their form but not their mechanical or utilitarian aspects are concerned, such as artistic jewelry, enamels, glassware, and tapestries, as well as works belonging to the fine arts, such as paintings, drawings and sculpture.

(b) In order to be acceptable as a work of art, the work must embody some creative authorship in its delineation or form. The registrability of a work of art is not affected by the intention of the author as to the use of the work, the number of copies reproduced, or the fact that it appears on a textile material or textile product. The potential availability of protection under the design patent law will not affect the registrability of a work of art, but a copyright claim in a patented design or in the drawings or photographs in a patent application will not be registered after the patent has been issued.

(c) If the sole intrinsic function of an article is its utility, the fact that the article is unique and attractively shaped will not qualify it as a work of art. However, if the shape of a utilitarian article incorporates features, such as artistic sculpture, carving, or pictorial representation, which can be identified separately and are capable of existing independently as a work of art, such features will be eligible for registration.

§ 202.11. Reproductions of Works of Art (Class H)

This class includes published reproductions of existing works of art in the same or a different medium, such as a lithograph, photoengraving, etching or drawing of a painting, sculpture or other work of art.

§ 202.12. Drawings or Plastic Works of a Scientific or Technical Character (Class I)

(a) This class includes published or unpublished two-dimensional drawings and three-dimensional plastic works which have been designed for a scientific or technical use and which contain copyrightable graphic, pictorial, or sculptured material. Works registrable in Class I include diagrams or models illustrating scientific or technical works or formulating scientific or technical information in linear or plastic form, such as, for example: a mechanical drawing, an astronomical chart, an architect's blueprint, an anatomical model, or an engineering diagram.

(b) A work is not eligible for registration as a "plastic" work in Class I merely because it is formed from one of the commonly known synthetic chemical derivatives such as styrenes, vinyl compounds, or acrylic resins. The term "plastic work" as used in this context refers to a three-dimensional work giving the effect of that which is molded or sculptured. Examples of such works include statues of animals or plants used for scientific or educational purposes, and engineers' scale models.

(c) A claim to copyright in a scientific or technical drawing, otherwise registrable in Class I, will not be refused registration solely by reason of the fact that it is known to form a part of a pending patent application. Where the patent has been issued, however, the claim to copyright in the drawing will be denied copyright registration.

§ 202.13. Photographs (Class J)

This class includes published or unpublished photographic prints and filmstrips, slide films and individual slides. Photoengravings and other photomechanical reproductions of photographs are registered in Class K on Form K.

§ 202.14. Prints, Pictorial Illustrations and Commercial Prints or Labels (Class K)

(a) This class includes prints or pictorial illustrations, greeting cards, picture postcards and similar prints, produced by means of lithography, photoengraving or other methods of reproduction. These works when published are registered on Form K.

(b) A print or label, not a trademark, containing copyrightable pictorial matter, text, or both, published in connection with the sale or advertisement of an article or articles of merchandise is also registered in this class on Form KK. In the case of a print which is published in a periodical, use Form KK if the print is used in connection with the sale or advertisement of an article of merchandise, Form BB if it is not. Multipage works are more appropriately classified in Class A than in Class K.

(c) A claim to copyright cannot be registered in a print or label consisting solely of trademark subject matter and lacking copyrightable matter. While the Copyright Office will not investigate whether the matter has been or can be registered at the Patent Office, it will register a properly filed copyright claim in a print or label that contains the requisite qualifications for copyright even though there is a trademark on it. However, registration of a claim to copyright does not give the claimant rights available by trademark registrations at the Patent Office.

§ 202.15. Motion Pictures (Classes L-M)

A single application Form L-M is available for registration of works in Classes L (Motion Picture Photoplays) and M (Motion Pictures other than Photoplays).

(a) Photoplays (Class L) This class includes published or unpublished motion pictures that are dramatic in character and tell a connected story, such as feature films, filmed television plays, short subjects and animated cartoons having a plot.

(b) Other Than Photoplays (Class M) This class includes published or unpublished nondramatic films such as newsreels, travelogs, training or promotional films, nature studies, and filmed television programs having no plot.

§ 202.16. Deposit of Photographs or Other Identifying Reproductions In Lieu of Copies

(a) Availability of Option In the case of a published photograph which is reproduced in copies for sale, classified in Classes (g), (h), (i), and (k) of section 5, title 17, U.S. Code, copies of which are considered by the Register of Copyrights to be impracticable of deposit because of their size, weight, fragility, or monetary value, photographs or other identifying reproductions may be deposited in lieu of copies as provided by section 13, title 17, U.S. Code. The deposit of such photographs or reproductions shall be made in accordance with the following criteria:

(1) The number of sets of photographs or of reproductions to be submitted shall be the same as the number of copies provided by said section 13; duplicate sets shall be deposited unless the work is by a foreign author and has been published in a foreign country. Each set shall consist of as many photographs or reproductions in black and white, or in color, as are necessary to identify the work.

(2) All photographs or reproductions shall be of equal size, not less than 5 x 7 inches, and not exceeding 9 x 12 inches, but preferably 8 x 10 inches. The image of the work shown in all photographs or reproduction shall either be lifesize or larger, or if less than lifesize shall be at least 4 inches in its greatest dimension. The exact measurement of at least one dimension of the work shall be indicated on at least one corresponding photograph or reproduction in each set.

(3) The copyright notice and its position on the work must be clearly shown on at least one corresponding photograph or reproduction in each set. If, because of the size or location of the copyright notice, a photographic repro-

duction cannot be prepared, a drawing may be included in each set, of the same size as the photographs or reproductions, showing the exact appearance of the notice, its dimensions, and its specific position on the work.

(4) The title of the work shall appear on the front or back of each photograph or reproduction.

(5) A copy shall be considered to be impracticable of deposit if, because of its size, weight, fragility or monetary value, it is unsuited to the filing procedures of the Copyright Office.

(b) Exceptions The provisions of this section, permitting the deposit of photographs in lieu of copies in certain cases, shall not apply to fine prints and two-dimensional art reproductions. The Register of Copyrights reserves the right in any other particular case to require as a condition precedent to registration, the deposit of copies of the work as published.

§ 202.17. Renewals

(a) Claims to renewal copyright must be registered within the last (28th) year of the original copyright term. The original term for a published work is computed from the date of first publication; the term for a work originally registered in unpublished form is computed from the date of registration in the Copyright Office. Unless the required application and fee are received in the Copyright Office during the prescribed period before the first term of copyright expires, copyright protection is lost permanently and the work enters the public domain. The Copyright Office has no discretion to extend the renewal time limits.

(b) Renewal claims may be registered only in the names of persons falling within one of the classes of renewal claimants specified in the copyright law. If the work was a new version of a previous work, renewal may be claimed only in the new matter.

§ 202.18. Notices of Use

Notices of use of copyrighted musical compositions on mechanical instruments, required by section 1(e) of title 17, U.S. Code, will be recorded upon receipt of a properly executed Form U and upon payment of the prescribed fees. Notices of intention to use will be received pursuant to section 101(e) of title 17, U.S. Code; no special form is provided therefor.

APPENDIX H(b)

Change in Copyright Office Regulations re Section 202.17

Section 202.17 of the Regulations of the Copyright Office (Chapter II of Title 37 of the *Code of Federal Regulations*), which relates to renewal applications, has been amended by the following provison which appeared in the April 1, 1970, issue of the *FEDERAL REGISTER,* Vol. 35, No. 63, at page 5402.

Title 37—PATENTS, TRADEMARKS, AND COPYRIGHTS

Chapter II—Copyright Office, Library of Congress

PART 202—REGISTRATION OF CLAIMS TO COPYRIGHT

Renewal Applications

In confirmation of a procedure heretofore authorized and given effect by the Register of Copyrights in a number of cases, § 202.17 of Chapter II of Title 37 of the Code of Federal Regulations is amended by adding a new paragraph (c) reading as follows:

§ 202.17 Renewals.

* * * * *

(c) Whenever a renewal applicant has cause to believe that a formal application for renewal (form R), if sent to the Copyright Office by mail, might not be received in the Copyright Office before the expiration of the time limits provided by 17 U.S.C. section 24, he may apply for renewal registration by means of a telephone call, telegram, or other method of telecommunication. An application made by this method will be accepted if: (1) The message is received in the Copyright Office within the specified time limits; (2) the applicant adequately identifies the work involved, the date of first publication or original registration, the name and address of the renewal claimant, and the statutory basis of the renewal claim; and (3) the fee for renewal registration, if not already on deposit, is received in the Copyright Office before the time for renewal registration has expired.

(Sec. 207. 61 Stat. 666; 17 U.S.C. 207)

Dated: March 27, 1970.

ABRAHAM L. KAMINSTEIN
Register of Copyrights

Approved:

L. QUINCY MUMFORD
Librarian of Congress

APPENDIX H(c)

Changes in Copyright Office Regulations re Section 202.15

Section 202.15 of the Regulations of the Copyright Office (Chapter II of Title 37 of the Code of Federal Regulations), which relates to the registration of motion pictures, has been amended by adding the following provisions, which appeared in the May 14, 1971, issue of the FEDERAL REGISTER, Volume 36, Number 94, at page 8869.

Title 37—PATENTS, TRADEMARKS,
AND COPYRIGHTS

Chapter II—Copyright Office,
Library of Congress

PART 202—REGISTRATION OF
CLAIMS TO COPYRIGHT

Deposit for Registration of Motion Pictures

Section 202.15 of Chapter II of Title 37 of the Code of Federal Regulations is amended by adding new paragraphs (c) and (d) reading as follows:

§ 202.15 Motion pictures (Classes L-M).

* * * * *

(c) *Deposit copies of motion pictures.* In the case of published motion pictures submitted for registration in Classes L or M, the requirement for deposit of "two complete copies of the best edition thereof then publishd" will be satisfied by the deposit of identical copies of that edition of the motion picture, from among any two or more editions in existence, that in the opinion of the Register of Copyrights most closely conforms to the established criteria of the Library of Congress with respect to the acquisition and retention of copies of motion pictures for its collections, as expressed in the Library of Congress acquisitions policy statement in effect at the time of the deposit. The Copyright Office will furnish to any person concerned, upon request, a copy of the pertinent Library of Congress acquisitions policy statement then in effect.

(d) *Videotape copies.* If otherwise qualified as a motion picture, a work published in the form of videotape copies may be registered in Class L or M. If a motion picture is published in both videotape and film copies, the requirement for deposit of "two complete copies of the best edition thereof then published" will be satisfied by the deposit of two identical film copies in accordance with paragraph (c) of this section. If a motion picture is published solely in the form of videotape copies, the deposit requirement will be satisfied by the deposit of two identical videotape copies accompanied by a set of photographic reproductions of portions of the videotape copies showing the title of the work, the copyright notice, the production, performance and other creativity credits, and two or more scenes from different sections of the work.

(Sec. 207, 61 Stat. 666; 17 U.S.C. 207)

Effective date. This amendment shall become effective on the date of its publication in the FEDERAL REGISTER (5-14-71).

ABRAHAM L. KAMINSTEIN,
Register of Copyrights.

Approved:

L. QUINCY MUMFORD,
Librarian of Congress.

APPENDIX H(d)

Changes in Copyright Office Regulations re Sound Recordings

Part 202 of Chapter II of Title 37 of the Code of Federal Regulations has been amended effective February 15, 1972, to provide rules for the registration of claims to copyright in sound recordings, pursuant to Public Law 92-140 relating to sound recordings. The amendments to the Regulations of the Copyright Office were published in the February 11, 1972 issue of the FEDERAL REGISTER, Volume 37, Number 29.

Title 37—PATENTS, TRADEMARKS, AND COPYRIGHTS

Chapter II—Copyright Office, *Library of Congress*

PART 202—REGISTRATION OF CLAIMS TO COPYRIGHT

Registration for Sound Recordings

Effective February 15, 1972, Part 202 Of Chapter II of Title 37 of the Code of Federal Regulations is amended as follows:

1. In § 202.2, paragraph (b) is amended by revising subparagraphs (1), (2), and (10) to read as follows:

§ 202.2. Copyright notice.

* * * * *

(b) *Defects in notice.* Where the copyright notice does not meet the requirements of the law, the Copyright Office will reject an application for copyright registration. Common defects in the notice include, among others, the following:

(1) The notice lacks one or more of the necessary elements (i.e., the word "Copyright," the abbreviation "Copr.", or the symbol ©, or, in the case of a sound recording, the symbol ℗; the name of the copyright proprietor, or, in the case of a sound recording, the name, a recognizable abbreviation of the name, or a generally known alternative designation, of the copyright owner; and, when required, the year date of publication);

(2) The elements of the notice are so dispersed that a necessary element is not identified as a part of the notice; in the case of a sound recording, however, if the producer is named on the label or container, and if no other name appears in conjunction with the notice, his name will be considered a part of the notice;

* * * * *

(10) A notice is on the wrapper or container which is not a part of the work and which will eventually be removed and discarded when the work is put to use; the notice may be on a container which is designed and can be expected to remain with the work;

* * * * *

2. Section 202.3 is revised as follows:

a. Paragraph (a) is revised to read as set forth below.

b. In paragraph (c) of § 202.3, the list of application forms for the registration of claims to copyright is amended by inserting, after the item "Form L-M—Motion picture (Classes L-M)," the new item "Form N—Sound recording (Class N)."

§ 202.3 Application forms.

(a) *In general.* Section 5 of title 17 of the United States Code provides fourteen classes (Class A through Class N) of works in which copyright may be claimed. Examples of certain works falling within these classes are given in §§ 202.4 to 202.15a inclusive, for the purpose of assisting persons who desire to obtain registration of a claim to copyright, to select the correct application form.

* * * * *

3. In § 202.8, paragraph (b) is revised to read as follows:

§ 202.8 Musical compositions (Class E).

* * * * *

(b) A phonorecord, such as a disc, tape, or other reproduction of a sound recording, is not considered a "copy" of the musical composition or the literary or dramatic work recorded on it, and is not acceptable as a deposit copy for copyright registration of the musical composition or the literary or dramatic work. Concerning the registration of copyright claims in sound recordings as works in themselves (as distinct from the musical compositions or the literary or dramatic works recorded), see § 202.15a.

4. Part 202 is amended by adding a new § 202.15a, reading as follows:

§ 202.15a Sound recordings (Class N).

(a) This class includes published sound recordings, i.e., works that result from the fixation of a series of musical, spoken, or other sounds. Common examples include recordings of music, drama, narration, or other sounds, as published in the form of phonorecords such as discs, tapes, cartridges, cassettes, player piano rolls, or similar material objects from which the sounds can be reproduced either directly or with the aid of a machine or device. Registration for sound recordings is made in Class N.

(b) Only those sound recordings fixed and published on or after February 15, 1972, are eligible for registration. A sound recording is "fixed" when the complete series of sounds constituting the work is first produced on a final master recording that is later reproduced in published copies.

(c) Sound recordings registrable in Class N do not include a sound track that is an integrated part of a motion picture. Registration for motion pictures, of which a sound track may be an integrated part, is made in Class L or M; see § 202.15.

(d) Registration for a sound recording in Class N does not cover the musical composition or the literary or dramatic work of which a rendition is recorded. A claim of copyright in the recorded musical composition is to be registered separately in Class E; see § 202.8. A claim of copyright in the recorded literary or dramatic work is to be registered separately in Class A, B, C, or D, whichever is appropriate; see §§ 202.4, 202.5, 202.6, and 202.7.

(Sec. 207.61 Stat. 666; 17 U.S.C. 207)

Dated: February 8, 1972.

GEORGE D. CARY,
Register of Copyrights.

Approved:

L. QUINCY MUMFORD,
Librarian of Congress.

BIBLIOGRAPHY

BOOKS

Amdur, Leon H. *Copyright Law and Practice.* New York: Clark Boardman Co., Ltd., 1936.

Austin, John. *Lectures on Jurisprudence* (2 Vols.). Jersey City, F. D. Linn & Co., 1875.

Ball, H. G. *Law of Copyright and Literary Property.* New York: Matthew Bender & Co., Inc., 1944.

Barnouw, Erik. *A History of Broadcasting in the U.S.* (3 Vols.): Vol. 1: *A Tower in Babel: to 1933* (1966). Vol. 2: *The Golden Web: 1933 to 1953* (1968). Vol. 3: *The Image Empire* (1970). New York: Oxford University Press, 1966, 1968 and 1970.

Baumol, William J. and Bowen, William G. *Performing Arts: The Economic Dilemma.* New York: Twentieth Century Fund, 1966.

Bernheim, Alfred L. *The Business of The Theatre, An Economic History of the American Theatre, 1750-1932.* New York: Benjamin Blom, Inc., 1932.

Birrell, Augustine. *Seven Lectures on Law and History of Copyright.* New York: G. P. Putnam & Sons, 1899.

Bloustein, Albert P. & Zangrando, Robert L. *Civil Rights and the American Negro, A Documentary History.* New York: Washington Square Press, 1968.

Bluestone, George. *Novels Into Film.* Berkeley: University of California Press, 1966.

Bouvier, John. *Bouvier's Law Dictionary & Concise Encyclopedia* (Rawle's 3rd Revision, 8th Ed.). Westport: Greenwood Press, 1914.

Bowen, Catherine Drinker. *Miracle at Philadelphia, The Story of the Constitutional Convention, May to September, 1787.* Boston: Little, Brown & Co., 1966.

Bowker, Richard Rogers. *Copyright, Its History and Its Law.* Boston: Houghton, 1912.

Brackett, Albert. *Theatrical Law, The Legal Right of Manager, Artist, Author and Public,* Boston, C.M. Clark Publishing Co., 1907.

Briffault, Robert. *The Troubadours.* Bloomington: Indiana University Press, 1965.

Broadus, Mitchell & Broadus, Louis Parsons. *A Biography of the Constitution of the U.S.* New York: Oxford University Press, 1964.

Burdick, William L. *Principles of Roman Law and Their Relation to Modern Law.* New York: The Lawyers Cooperative Publishing Co., 1938.

Cahn, Edmund N. *The Sense of Injustice.* New York: New York University Press, 1949.

Callmann, Rudolf. *The Law of Unfair Competition, Trademarks, and Monopolies (3rd Ed.).* Chicago: Callaghan & Co., 1969.

Chambers, E. K. *The Mediaeval State* (2 Vols.). New York: Oxford University Press, 1903.

Clabault, James M. & Burton, J. F. *Sherman Act Indictments, 1955-1965, A Legal and Economic Analysis.* New York: Federal Legal Publications, Inc., 1966.

Code Civil of France, Paris: Librairie Dalloz, 1953.

Code de Commerce of France, Paris: Librairie Dalloz, 1954.

Collier, P. F., *Collier's Encyclopedia.* New York: P. F. Collier & Son Corp., 1960.

Commager, Henry Steele. *Documents of American History, 7th Ed.* (2 Vols.). New York: Appleton-Century, 1963.

Copinger, W. A. & Skone, James. *Law of Copyright* (8th Ed.). Toronto: Carswell Co., Ltd., 1948.

Curtis, George Ticknor. *Treatise on the Law of Copyright.* Boston: C. C. Little and J. Brown, 1847.

Curtis, Natalie (edited & recorded by). *The Indians' Book: Songs and Legends of the American Indians.* Gloucester, Mass.: Peter Smith, 1950.

Dalrymple, Jean. *Careers and Opportunities in the Theatre.* New York: E. P. Dutton & Co., 1969.

Diamond, Martin; Fisk, Winston Mills; & Garfinkel, Herbert. *The Democratic Republic, An Introduction to American National Government.* Chicago: Rand-McNally & Co., 1966.

Dichter, Harry & Shapiro, Elliott. *Early American Sheet Music, Its Lure and Its Lore, 1768-1889.* New York: R. R. Bowker Co., 1941.

Douglas, William O. *An Almanac of Liberty.* Garden City, N.Y.: Doubleday, 1954.

Dorian, Frederick. *Commitment to Culture Arts Patronage in Europe—Its Significance for America.* Pittsburgh: University of Pittsburgh Press, 1964.

Drone, Eaton S. *A Treatise on the Law of Property in Intellectual Productions in Great Britain & the U.S.* (also titled *The Law of Copyright and Playwright*). Boston: Little, Brown & Co., 1879.

Eisenstein, Sergei. *Film Form.* New York: Harcourt Brace Jovanovich, Inc., 1957.

Eisenstein, Sergei. *The Film Sense.* New York: Harcourt Brace Jovanovich, Inc., 1957.

Emerson, Ralph Waldo. *Essays.* New York: Macmillan, Inc., 1932.

Farber, Donald C. *Producing on Broadway, A Comprehensive Guide.* New York: Drama Book Specialists Publishers, 1969.

Ford, Celia. *First Latin Book.* New York: Holt, Rinehart & Winston, Inc., 1931.

Fox, Harold George. *Monopolies and Patents.* Toronto: University of Toronto Studies 1947.

Frank, Jerome. *Courts on Trial.* Princeton: Princeton University Press, 1950.

Friedman, Albert B. *The Viking Book of Folk Ballads of the English-Speaking World.* New York: Viking Press, Inc.. 1956.

Fulton, A. R. *Motion Pictures, The Development of an Art from Silent Films to the Age of Television.* Norman: University of Oklahoma Press, 1960.

Goldin, Milton. *The Music Merchants.* New York: Macmillan Co., 1969.

Goldron, Romain. *Ancient and Oriental Music.* Garden City, New York: Doubleday & Co., Inc., 1968.

Gray, John Chipman. *The Nature and Sources of the Law* (2nd Ed.). Gloucester, Mass.: Peter Smith, 1921.

Hall, Jerome. *Readings in Jurisprudence.* Indianapolis: The Bobbs-Merrill Co., 1938.

Hamilton, Alexander, et al. *The Federalist.* Westminster, Md.: Modern Library, Inc., 1937.

Hearn, William Edward. *The Theory of Legal Duties and Rights.* Melbourne: J. Ferres, Government Printer, 1883.

Hoffmann, Malcolm A. (edited by). *Hoffmann's Antitrust Law and Techniques.* (3 Vols.). Albany: Matthew Bender & Co., 1963.

Hofstadter, Samuel H. *The Development of the Right of Privacy in New York.* New York: Grosby Press, 1954.

Hohfeld, Wesley Newcomb. *Fundamental Legal Conceptions as Applied in Judicial Reasoning.* New Haven: Yale University Press, 1923. (Introduction of Walter Wheeler Cook.)

Howell, Herbert Allen, Revised Ed. by Latman, Alan, *Copyright Law.* Washington: Bureau of National Affairs, 1962.

Jacobs, Lewis. *The Rise of the American Film.* New York: Teachers College Press, Columbia University, 1967.

Jacobs, Milton Cecil. *Outline of Theatre Law.* M. C. Jacobs, 1949.

Jacobson, Howard Boone (editor). *A Mass Communications Dictionary.* Westport: Greenwood Press, Inc., 1961.

Kaplan, Benjamin. *An Unhurried View of Copyright.* New York: Columbia University Press, 1967.

Kauper, Paul G. *Civil Liberties and the Constitution.* Ann Arbor: University of Michigan Press, 1962.

Knight, Arthur. *The Liveliest Art.* New York: New American Library, 1957.

Kohlmeier, Louis, Jr. *The Regulators Watchdog Agencies and the Public Interest.* New York: Harper & Row Publishers, Inc., 1969.

Konvitz, Milton R. *Fundamental Liberties of a Free People: Religion, Speech, Press, Assembly.* Ithaca: Cornell University Press, 1957.

Kupferman, Theodore R. (edited by). *Copyright Problems Analyzed* (1953). South Hackensack: Fred Rothman & Co., reprint (1966).

Kupferman, Theodore R. & Foner, Matthew (edited by). *Universal Copyright Convention Analyzed.* New York: Federal Legal Publications, Inc., 1955.

Ladas, Stephen P. *International Protection of Literary and Artistic Property* (2 Vols.). New York: Macmillan Co., 1938.

Leach, MacEdward. *The Ballad Book.* Cranbury: A. S. Barnes & Co., 1955.

Leder, Lawrence H. *Liberty and Authority.* Cleveland: Quadrangle Books, Inc., 1968.

Levy, Alan. *The Culture Vultures.* New York: G. P. Putnam's Sons, 1968.

Lindey, Alexander. *Lindey Entertainment Publishing and the Arts* (2 Vols.). New York: Clark Boardman Co., Ltd., 1963.

Lindey, Alexander. *Plagiarism and Originality.* New York: Harper & Row Publishers, 1952.

Lindsay, Vachel. *The Art of the Moving Picture.* New York: Liveright, 1922 Ed. (Introduction by Stanley Kauffmann.)

Lomax, Alan (edited by). *The 111 Best American Ballads, Folk Songs, U.S.A.,* collected, adapted, and arranged by Lomax, John A. & Lomax, Alan. New York: Duell, 1948.

Lomax, John A. & Lomax, Alan. *Cowboy Songs and Other Frontier Ballads,* collected by Lomax, John A. & Lomax, Alan. New York: Macmillan Co., 1948.

McLuhan, Marshall. *Understanding Media, The Extension of Man.* New York: New American Library, 1964.

Maltfield, Julius. *Variety Music Cavalcade, New & Enlarged Ed.* Englewood Cliffs: Prentice-Hall, 1962.

Mayer, Michael F. *Rights of Privacy.* New York: Law-Arts Publishers, Inc., 1972.

Middleton, George. *The Dramatists Guild* (5th Ed.). New York: The Dramatists Guild, 1966.

Monaghan, Frank. *Heritage of Freedom, The History and Significance of the Basic Documents of American Liberty.* Princeton: Princeton University Press, 1948.

Morgan, James Appleton. *The Law of Literature* (2 Vols.). New York: J. Cockcroft & Co., 1875.

Morison, Bradley & Fliehr, Kay. *In Search of An Audience.* New York: Pitman Publishing Co., 1968.

Nicholson, Margaret. *Manual of Copyright Practice for Writers, Publishers and Agents* (2nd Ed.). New York: Oxford, 1956.

Nimmer, Melville B. *Nimmer on Coppyright.* New York: Clark Boardman Co., Ltd., Matthew Bender & Co., 1972.

Orsingher, Roger. *Banks of the World.* New York: Macmillan Co., 1967.

Parrington, Vernon Louis. *Main Currents in American Thought.* New York: Harcourt Brace Jovanovich, Inc., 1930.

Plucknett, Theodore F. T. *A Concise History of the Common Law* (4th Ed.). London: Butterworth & Co., Ltd., 1948.

Poggi, Jack. *Theater in America, The Impact of Economic Forces, 1870-1967.* Ithaca: Cornell University Press, 1968.

Pudovkin, V. I. *Film Technique and Film Acting.* New York: Grove Press, Inc., 1960.

Putnam, George Haven. *The Question of Copyright* (2nd Ed.). New York: G. P. Putnam's Sons (2nd Ed.), 1896.

Restatement, Contracts (2 Vols.). St. Paul: American Law Institute, 1932.

Rich, Alan. *Music, Mirror of the Arts.* New York: Praeger Publishers, 1969.

Rockefeller Brothers Fund. *The Performing Arts: Problems and Proposals.* New York: McGraw-Hill, 1965.

Rotha, Paul & Griffith, Richard. *The Film Till Now.* New York: Twayne Publishers, 1967.

Rothenberg, Stanley. *Copyright Law; Basic and Related Materials.* New York: Clark Boardman Co., Ltd., 1956. (Introduction by Morris Ebenstein.)

Rothenberg, Stanley. *Copyright and Public Performance of Music.* The Hague, Netherlands: Nijhoff, 1954.

Schickel, Richard. *Movies, The History of an Art and an Institution.* New York: Basic Books, Inc., 1964.

Schlesinger, Rudolf B. *Comparative Law Cases and Materials.* Brooklyn, N.Y.: The Foundation Press, Inc., 1950.

Schoch, M. Magdalena (translated & edited by). *The Jurisprudence of Interests.* (Introduction by Lon L. Fuller.) Cambridge, Mass.: Harvard University Press, 1948.

Shafter, Alfred Martin. *Musical Copyright* (2nd Ed.). Chicago: Callaghan & Co., 1939.

Shakespeare, William. *The Complete Works of Shakespeare* (The Cambridge Ed. Text.) Garden City, N.Y.: Doubleday & Co., 1936.

Shemel, Sidney & Krasilovsky, M. William. *This Business of Music.* New York: Billboard Publishing Co., 1964.

Sinclair, Upton. *Upton Sinclair Presents William Fox.* New York: Arno Press, 1933.

Smith, George H. *Elements of Right and of the Law.* Chicago: Callaghan & Co., 1887.

Smith, George H. *The Law of Private Right.* New York: The Humboldt Publishing Co., 1890.

Spiegel, Irwin O. and Cooper, Jay L. *Record and Music Publishing Forms of Agreement.* New York: Law-Arts Publishers, Inc., 1971.

Spring, Samuel. *Risks and Rights in Publishing, Television, Radio, Motion Pictures, Advertising and the Theater.* New York: W. W. Norton & Co., Inc., 1952.

Steinberg, Charles S. (edited by). *Mass Media and Communication.* New York: Hastings House Publishers, Inc., 1965. (Introduction by William A. Bluem.)

Stocking, George W. & Watkins, Myron W. *Monopoly and Free Enterprise.* Westport: Greenwood Press, Inc., 1951.

Taubman, Howard. *The Making of the American Theatre.* New York: Coward McCann, Inc., 1965.

Taubman, Joseph (edited by). *The Business and Law of Music.* New York: Federal Legal Publications, Inc., 1965.

Taubman, Joseph. *Copyright and Antitrust.* New York: Federal Legal Publications, Inc., 1960.

Taubman, Joseph (edited by). *Financing a Theatrical Production.* New York: Federal Legal Publications, Inc., 1964.

Taubman, Joseph. *The Joint Venture and Tax Classification.* New York: Federal Legal Publications, Inc., 1957.

Taubman, Joseph (edited by). *Subsidiary Rights and Residuals.* New York: Federal Legal Publications, Inc., 1968.

Timberlake, E. Compton. *Federal Treble Damage Antitrust Actions.* Chicago: Callaghan & Co., 1965.

Walker, Albert Henry. *Walker on Patents* (Deller Ed.). New York: Baker, Voorhis & Co., 1937.

Walsh, William F. *Law of Property* (2nd Ed.). New York: Baker, Voorhis & Co., 1934.

Warner, Harry P. *Radio and Television Rights.* New York: Matthew Bender & Co., Inc., 1953.

Weber, Max. *General Economic History.* (Knight translation.) New York: Collier Books, 1961.

Webster, Noah. *Webster's New International Dictionary, 2nd Ed., Unabridged.* Cambridge, Mass: The Riverside Press, 1961.

Webster, Hutton & Wolf, John B. *History of Civilization.* Indianapolis: D. C. Heath & Co., 1947.

Wechsberg, Joseph. *The Merchant Bankers.* Boston: Little, Brown & Co., 1966.

Whicher, John F. *The Creative Arts and The Judicial Process.* New York: Federal Legal Publications, Inc., 1965.

Williston, Samuel. *Williston on Contracts.* Revised Ed. (8 Vols.). New York: Baker, Voorhis & Co., 1936, also 3rd Ed. (1957).

Wittenberg, Philip. *The Protection and Marketing of Literary Property.* Boston: Writer, Inc., 1937.

Wolff, Hans J. *Roman Law, An Historical Introduction.* Norman: University of Oklahoma Press, 1951.

PERIODICALS, ARTICLES AND BOOK REVIEWS

Arnold, Tom. "Product Simulation and Trade Secret Law; What's Happened Since 'Sears' and 'Compco'." 1966 *Patent Law Annual* 61.

Arrow, Allen. "Performing Rights Societies" in *The Business and Law of Music,* edited by Taubman, Joseph (1965).

Austin, John. "Lectures on Jurisprudence"; 3rd Ed. (1869) in *Readings in Jurisprudence,* Hall, Jerome (1938).

Bergstrom, Robert W. "The Businessman Deals with Copyright". 3 *Copyright Law Symposium* 249 (1940).

Birmingham, William T. "A Critical Analysis of the Infringement of Ideas". 5 *Copyright Law Symposium* 107 (1954).

Blaisdell, William M. "Size of the Copyright Industries"; Study No. 2 of General Revision of the Copyright Law of the Copyright Office (1959), in *Studies on Copyright* 3 (1963), (2 Vols.), Arthur Fisher Memorial Edition.

Blaisdell, William M. "Economic Aspects of the Compulsory License", Study No. 6, in *Studies on Copyright* (1963).

Bogsch, Arpad. "Protection of Works of Foreign Origin", Study No. 32, in *Studies on Copyright* 737 (1963).

Botein, Michael. "CATV Regulation: A Jumble of Jurisdictions". 45 *N.Y.U. L. Rev.* 816 (1970)

Bricker, Seymour M. *ABA Copyright Symposium,* Dallas, Texas, Aug. 25, 1956, on "Motion Pictures".

Bricker, Seymour M. "Renewal and Extension of Copyright". 29 *So. Cal. L. Rev.* 23 (1955).

Brown, Ralph S., Jr. "The Operation of the Damages Provisions of the Copyright Law: An Exploratory Study", Study No. 23, in *Studies on Copyright* 1067 (1963).

"California Arts Commission Resume of Activities, 1965-1968". 1 *Perf. Arts Rev.* 177 (1969).

Cary, George D. "Joint Ownership of Copyrights", Study No. 12, in *Studies on Copyright* 689 (1963).

Celler, Emanuel, Cong. "Whither Copyright?", *N.Y. L.J.*, Monday, Oct. 26, 1970, p. 1, cols. 3-4.

Chafee, Zechariah, Jr. "Equitable Servitudes on Chattels". 41 *Harv. L. Rev.* 945 (1928).

Chafee, Zechariah, Jr. "Reflections on the Law of Copyright", reprinted in *Copyright and Related Topics,* ed. by the L.A. Copyright Society and the UCLA School of Law, 1964, also 45 *Col. L. Rev.* 503, 719 (1945).

Cohen, Saul. "Fair Use in the Law of Copyright", 6 *Copyright Law Symposium* 43 (1955).

Cohn, Morris E. "Old Licenses and New Uses, Motion Pictures and Television", 19 *Law and Cont. Probs.* 184 (1954).

Colton, Edward B. "Contracts in the Entertainment and Literary Fields" (1953) in *Copyright Problems Analyzed* 145-6, edited by Kupferman, Theodore R., Fred B. Rothman & Co. reprint (1966).

Colton, Edward B. "Theatrical Limited Partnerships and Joint Ventures" in *Financing a Theatrical Production* 375, edited by Taubman, Joseph (1964).

Davis, Richard F. "Sequel Rights: Federal Copyright Protection of Fictional Characters", 2 *Perf. Arts Rev.* 315 (1971).

Dworkin, Alan T. "Originality in the Law of Copyright". 11 *Copyright Law Symposium* 60 (1962).

Fenning, Karl. "The Origin of the Patent and Copyright Clause of the Constitution". 17 *Geo. L.J.* 109 (1929).

Finkelstein, Herman. "Public Performance Rights in Music and Performance Rights Societies". 7 *Copyright Problems Analyzed* (1951), as reprinted in *Copyright Problems Analyzed* (1966).

Finkelstein, Herman. "The Copyright Law—A Reappraisal". 104 *U. Pa. L. Rev.* 1025 (1956).

Freund, Richard L. "Residuals in Broadcasting" in *Subsidiary Rights and Residuals* 101, edited by Taubman, Joseph (1968).

Fritch, Bruce E. "Some Copyright Implications of Videotapes", 37 *U.S.C. L. Rev.* 214 (1964).

Gilbert, Robert W. "Residual Rights Established by Collective Bargaining in Television and Radio". 23 *Law and Cont. Probs.* 102 (1958).

Heck, Philipp. "The Jurisprudence of Interests, An Outline", in *The Jurisprudence of Interests,* translated and edited by Schoch, Magdalena M. (1948).

Henn, Harry. "Rights Magazine, A Division of Indivisible Copyright". 40 *Corn. L.Q.* 411 (1955).

Holmes, Oliver Wendell, Jr. "Natural Law". 32 *Harv. L.R.* 40 (1918), as reprinted in *Readings in Jurisprudence* 260, Hall, Jerome (1938).

Kaminstein, Abraham L. "Divisibility of Copyrights", Study No. 11, in *Studies on Copyright* 623 (1963).

Kaplan, Benjamin. "Publications in Copyright Law: The Question of Phonograph Records". 103 *U. of Pa. L. Rev.* 469 (1955).

Karp, Joseph D. "Copyright Litigation", 7 *Copyright Problems Analyzed* 1951, reprinted in Fred B. Rothman & Co. with 1953 *Copyright Problems Analyzed, sub. nom.,* Copyright Problems Analyzed 143 (1966).

Katz, Arthur S. "The Doctrine of Moral Right and American Copyright Law: A Proposal". 4 *Copyright Law Symposium* 79 (1952).

John F. Kennedy Center for the Performing Arts, 1 *Perf. Arts. Rev.* 341 (1969).

Klein, Harold S. "S.O.S., Subsidy for Our Screen, An Examination of Subsidy Abroad". 1 *Perf. Arts Rev.* 19 (1969).

Klein, Harold S. *"Subsidiary Rights and Residuals in Motion Pictures"*, in *Subsidiary Rights and Residuals* 33, edited by Taubman, Joseph (1968).

Latman, Alan. "Fair Use of Copyrighted Works", Study No. 14, in *Studies on Copyright* 781 (1963).

Latman, Alan & Tager, William S. "Liability of Innocent Infringers of Copyrights", Study No. 25, in *Studies on Copyright* 1045 (1963).

Libbott, Robert Yale. "Round The Prickly Pear: The Idea-Expression Fallacy in a Mass Communication World", 16 *Copyright Law Symposium* 41 (1968).

Loevinger, Lee. "Private Practice—The Strongest Pillar of Antitrust" in *Hoffmann's Antitrust Law and Techniques* 373 (1963).

Lyon, Milton. "The Professional Actor at the University". 1 *Perf. Arts Rev.* 219 (1969).

McCannon, Marjorie. "The Manufacturing Clause of the U.S. Copyright Law", Study No. 35, in *Studies on Copyright* 1123 (1963).

McDonald, Joseph A. "The Law of Broadcasting", in 7 *Copyright Problems Analyzed,* 1951; edited by Kupferman, Theodore R., Fred B. Rothman & Co. reprint, 31 (1966).

Matthews, Brander. "The Evolution of Copyright", reprinted from *The Political Science Quarterly,* Nov. 1890, in *The Question of Copyright,* Putnam, George Haven (2nd Ed. 1896).

Messinger, Barry William. "A Nice Dilemma: The Protection of Literary Titles". 1 *Perf. Arts Rev.* 585 (1970).

Needham, Roger. "Tape Recording, Photocopying, and Fair Use". 10 *Copyright Law Symposium* 75 (1959).

Nimmer, Melville. "Copyright v. The First Amendment", 17 *Bull. Cr. Soc.* 255 (1970).

Ozro, William Childs IV. "The FCC's Proposed CATV Regulations". 21 *Stan. L. Rev.* 1685 (1967).

Peaslee, Richard. "Notes on Composing the Marat/Sade". 1 *Perf. Arts Rev.* 113 (1969).

Raskin, Kenneth. "Copyright Protection for Fictional Characters", 2 *Perf. Arts Rev.* 587 (1972).

Redleaf, Gilbert T. "Co-Ownership of Copyright". 119 *N.Y. L.J.* 760, 782, 802, 821 (1948).

Ringer, Barbara A. "Renewal of Copyright", Study No. 31, in *Studies on Copyright* 539 (1963).

Ringer, Barbara A. "The Unauthorized Duplication of Sound Recordings", Study No. 26, in *Studies on Copyright* 117 (1963).

Rümelin, Max. "Developments in Legal Theory and Teaching During My Lifetime", in *The Jurisprudence of Interests,* translated and edited by Schoch, Magdalena M. (1948).

Sherman, Paul. "Tin an Alley to Shubert Alley" in *The Business and Law of Music* 41, edited by Taubman, Joseph (1965).

Silber, Edward. "Use of Experts in Literary Piracy". 9 *Copyright Law Symposium* 149 (1958).

Silverberg, Herbert T. "Authors' and Performers' Rights", 23 *Law and Cont. Probs.*, Radio and Television, Part II, 125 (Winter, 1958).

Silverberg, Herbert T. "Televising Old Films—Some New Legal Questions About Performers and Proprietors' Rights". 38 *Va. L. Rev.* 615 (1952).

Smith, George Alan. "Arts Administrator Need and Potential in New York State", 1 *Perf. Arts Rev.* 127 (1969).

Smith, Ralph Lee. "The Wired Nation", in *The Nation,* Special Issue, May 18, 1970.

Steinberg, Charles S. "Public Relations and Mass Communication" in *Mass Media and Communication* 401, edited by Steinberg, Charles S. (1966).

Stevenson, Arthur L., Jr. "Moral Right and the Common Law: A Proposal", 6 *Copyright Law Symposium* 89 (1955).

Strauss, William S. "Copyright in Architectural Works", Study No. 27, in *Studies on Copyright* 67 (1963).

Strauss, William S. "The Damage Provisions of the Copyright Law", Study No. 22, in *Studies on Copyright* 995 (1963).

Strauss, William S. "The Meaning of 'Writings' in the Copyright Clause of the Constitution", Study No. 3, in *Studies on Copyright* 67 (1963).

Strauss, William S. "The Moral Right of the Author", Study No. 4, in *Studies on Copyright* 963 (1963).

Strauss, William S. "Protection of Unpublished Works", Study No. 29, in *Studies on Copyright* 189 (1963).

Strauss, William S. "Remedies Oother Than Damages for Copyright Infringement", Study No. 24, in *Studies on Copyright* 1029 (1963).

Taubman, Joseph. "Creation, Copyright and the Constitutional Clause", 6 *Bull. Cr. Soc.* 153 (1959).

Taubman, Joseph. "Essentials of Professional Draftsmanship", *The Lawyers Encyclopedia* 161 (Prentice-Hall, 1963).

Taubman, Joseph. "Joint Authorship and Co-Ownership", 31 *N.Y.U. L. Rev.* 1246 (1956).

Taubman, Joseph. "Law and Sociology in the Control of Small Groups", 13 *U. of Toronto L.J.* 23 (1959).

Taubman, Joseph. "Limited Partnerships". 3 *Corporate Practice Commentator* 15 (1962).

Taubman, Joseph. "Subsidiary Rights and Residuals: Some Definitions", Chap. II of *Subsidiary Rights and Residuals,* edited by Taubman, Joseph (1968).

Taubman, Joseph. "Theatrical Limited Partnerships", 37 *Taxes* 979 (1959).

Taubman, Joseph. Review of "Movies, Censorship, and the Law", by Ira H. Carmen, 41 *Tulane L. Rev.* 976 (1967).

Taubman, Joseph. Review of "Performing Arts: The Economic Dilemma", by Baumol, William J. and Bowen, William G., 43 *Tulane L. Rev.* 184 (1968).

Taubman, Joseph. Review of "Studies on Copyright", Arthur Fisher Memorial Ed., 32 *Ford. L. Rev.* 875 (1964).

Tournier, Jean-Loup. "The French Law of March 11, 1957, on Literary and Artistic Property", 6 *Bull. Cr. Soc.* 1 (1958).

Varmer, Borge. "Copyright in Choreographic Works", Study No. 28, in *Studies on Copyright* 103 (1963).

Varmer, Borge. "Limitations on Performing Rights", Study No. 16, in *Studies on Copyright* 835 (1963).

Varmer Borge. "Works Made for Hire and On Commission", Study No. 13, in *Studies on Copyright* 717 (1963).

Warren, Samuel D. & Brandeis, Louis D. "The Right to Privacy", 4 *Harv. L. Rev.* 193 (1890) as reprinted in Hofstadter, Samuel, *The Development of the Right of Privacy in New York* (1954).

Weissberger, Arnold L. "Subsidiary Rights in the Theatre" in *Subsidiary Rights and Residuals* 115, edited by Taubman, Joseph (1968).

Wittenberg, Philip. "Subsidiary Rights" in *Subsidiary Rights and Residuals* 9, edited by Taubman, Joseph (1968).

NOTES AND COMMENTS

Copyright Renewals—"Rights of Widow and Children of Deceased Author". 31 *N.Y.U. L.Rev.* 1319 (1956).

Kupferman, Theodore R., Note: *"Renewal of Copyright, Sec. 23 of the Copyright Act of 1909"*. 44 *Col. L.Rev.* 712 (1944).

The Meaning of "Writings" in the Copyright Clause of the Constitution, 31 *N.Y.U. L.Rev.* 1263 (1956); also, Study No. 3, in *Studies on Copyright 43* (1963).

Taubman, Joseph, Note: "The Land Trust Taxable as Association". 8 *Tax L.Rev.* 103 (1952).

MISCELLANEOUS

Davis, Peter G. "Janus Chorale Gives Premiere of A Cantata to Whitman's Text", *N.Y. Times,* Apr. 21, 1970, p. 47, cols. 1-2.

Dubin, Joseph. "Chart: Duration of Copyright in Different Countries and Territories of the World".

"Film and TV Music Writers File $300 Million Suit on Contracts", *N.Y. Times,* Feb. 8, 1972, p. 26, cols. 1-2.

Hall, Mildred. "Historical Booklet Out on Copyright", in *Billboard,* Dec. 18, 1971, p. 1, col. 5.

Television Code, National Association of Broadcasters.

Variety, Feb. 11, 1970, p. 4, cols. 1-2.

OFFICIAL DOCUMENTS

ACTS

Administrative Procedure Act, 5 USC 551, *et seq.,* 60 Stat. 237.

Clayton Antitrust Act, 15 USC 12, *et seq.,* 38 Stat. 730.

Communications Act of 1934: 47 USC 151, *et seq.,* 48 Stat. 1064.

Copyright Act, 17 USC 1, *et seq.,* 61 Stat. 652.

Copyright Enactments, Laws Passed in the U.S. Since 1783 Relating to Copyright; Copyright Office Bulletin No. 3 (revised) (1963).

Federal Trade Commission Act, 15 USC 41, *et seq.,* 52 Stat. 111.

Public Law 42-190, 92nd Cong., S. 646, Oct. 15, 1971—Record Piracy Act.

Sherman Antitrust Act, 15 USC 1, *et seq.,* 26 Stat. 209.

BILLS

H.R. 21295, Introduced Mar. 4, 1912 by Congressman Moon of Pa., to amend Sec. 5 of the 1909 Act.

H.R. 4347, 89th Cong., 1st Sess., Feb. 4, 1965.

H.R. 4347, 89th Cong., 2d Sess., Union Calendar No. 999, Report No. 2237, introduced Feb. 4, 1965; Oct. 12, 1966 print.

H.R. 2512, 90th Cong., 1st Sess., a Bill, dated Jan. 17, 1967.

H.R. 2512, 90th Cong., 1st Sess., an Act, dated Apr. 12, 1967.

S. 543, 91st Cong., 1st Sess., Jan. 22, 1969.

S. 543, 91st Cong., 1st Sess., Jan. 22, 1969, Dec. 10, 1969 print, including Title II, National Commission on New Technological Uses of Copyright Works.

S. 644, 92nd Cong., 1st Sess., Feb. 8, 1971.

HEARINGS

Hearings on Revision of Copyright Laws Before the Committees on Patents of the Senate and House of Representatives, Mar. 26, 27, 28, 1908.

Townsend Copyright Amendment Complete File of Arguments Before the Committee on Patents, House of Representatives, on H.R. 15263 and H.R. 20596, commencing Jan. 24, 1912.

Hearings before Subcommittee #3 of the Comm. on the Judiciary, House of Representatives, on H.R. 4347, H.R. 5680, H.R. 6831, and H.R. 6835, held May to Sept., 1965.

Hearings before the Subcommittee on Patents, Trademarks, and Copyrights of the Comm. on the Judiciary, U.S. Senate, 89th Cong., 2nd Sess., on S. 1006, "Copyright Law Revision—CATV", held Aug. 2, 3, 4, and 5, 1966.

Hearings on Copyright Law Revision before the Subcommittee on Patents, Trademarks and Copyrights, 90th Cong., 1st Sess., Mar. 15, 16, 17, 20, 21, 1967, and Apr. 4, 6, 11, 12, and 28, 1967.

REPORTS

House Report No. 2222, House of Representatives, 60th Cong., 2d Sess., Feb. 22, 1909, to accompany H.R. 28192.

House Report No. 756, 62nd Cong., 2d Sess., House of Representatives, Statute in Relation to Copyrights, May 24, 1912, to accompany H.R. 24224.

House Report No. 83, 90th Cong., 1st Sess., re Copyright Law Revision, Mar. 8, 1967, to accompany H.R. 2512.

Senate Report No. 64, National Commission on New Technological Uses of Copyrighted Works, 90th Cong., 1st Sess., Oct. 11, 1967, to accompany S. 2216.

Senate Report No. 91-1219, 91st Cong., 2d Sess., dated Sept. 22, 1970. Report of the Comm. on the Judiciary by the Subcommittee on Patents, Trademarks, and Copyrights.

Report of the Register of Copyrights on the General Revision of the U.S. Copyright Law (1961), reprinted in *Studies on Copyright* 1199 (1963).

Supplementary Report of the Register of Copyrights on the General Revision of the U.S. Copyright Law: 1965 Revision Bill (1965).

RULES AND REGULATIONS

Regulations of the Copyright Office.

Rules Adopted by the Supreme Court of the U.S. for Practice and Procedure Under Sec. 25 of an Act to Amend and Consolidate the Acts Respecting Copyright, Approved Mar. 4, 1909.

TABLE OF CASES

A

B

C

D

E

F

G

H

M

P

R

S

Shapiro, Bernstein & Co. v. Miracle Record Co., Inc., 91 F. Supp. 473 (N.D. Ill. 1950), pp. 607, 608, 781, 941.

Shapiro, Bernstein & Co. v. 4636 S. Vermont Ave., Inc., 367 F. 2d 236 (9th Cir. 1966), pp. 1106, 1155.

Shapiro, Bernstein & Co., Inc. v. Jerry Vogel Music Co., Inc., 161 F. 2d 406 (2d Cir. 1946), on remand 73 F. Supp. 165 (S.D.N.Y. 1947), *cert. den.* 331 U.S. 820 (1947), pp. 225, 274, 336.

Shapiro, Bernstein & Co., Inc. v. Jerry Vogel Music Co., Inc., 221 F. 2d 569 (2d Cir. 1955), modified on rehearing, 223 F. 2d 252 (2d Cir. 1955), *rev'g* 115 F. Supp. 754 (S.D.N.Y. 1953), pp. 275, 276, 287, 334.

Sheldon v. Metro-Goldwyn Pictures Corp., 81 F. 2d 49 (2d Cir. 1936); *rev'g* 7 F. Supp. 837 (S.D.N.Y. 1934); final decree: 26 F. Supp. 134 (S.D.N.Y. 1934), *rev'd,* 106 F. 2d 45 (2d Cir. 1939), *aff'd,* 309 U.S. 390 (1940), pp. 830, 833, 841, 1059, 1062, 1086, 1137, 1138, 1139, 1140, 1141.

Shipman v. RKO Radio Pictures, Inc., 100 F. 2d 533 (2d Cir. 1938), pp. 784, 789, 831, 832, 835, 1062.

Shostakovich v. Twentieth Century-Fox Film Corp., 196 Misc. 67, 80 N.Y.S. 2d 575 (Sup. Ct., Spec. T., N.Y. Cty. 1948), *aff'd,* 275 App. Div. 692, 87 N.Y.S. 2d 430 (1st Dept. 1949), pp. 368, 369.

Silver v. Television City, Inc., 207 Pa. Super. 150, 215 A. 2d 335 (Superior Ct. Pa. 1965), p. 1135.

Silverman v. Sunrise Pictures Corp., 273 Fed. 909 (2d Cir. 1921), *modified,* 290 Fed. 804 (2d Cir. 1923), *cert. den.* 262 U.S. 758 (1923), pp. 248, 252, 256, 339, 349.

Simonton v. Gordon, 297 Fed. 625 (S.D.N.Y. 1924), p. 822.

Smith v. Little, Brown Co., 273 F. Supp. 870 (S.D.N.Y. 1967), *aff'd,* 396 F. 2d 150 (2d Cir. 1968), pp. 1127, 1130, 1144.

Society of European Stage Authors and Composers, Inc. v. N.Y. Hotel Statler Co., Inc., 34 U.S.P.Q. 6 (S.D.N.Y. 1937), pp. 1023, 1025.

Stasny Music Corp. v. Santly-Joy, Inc., 156 F. Supp. 795 (S.D.N.Y. 1957), *aff'd per curiam,* 249 F. 2d 957 (2d Cir. 1957), p. 1112.

Stevens v. National Broadcasting Co., 148 U.S.P.Q. 755 (Sup. Ct., L.A. Cty., Cal. 1966); 150 U.S.P.Q. 572 (Sup. Ct., L.A. Cty., Cal. 1966), pp. 570, 628, 629.

Stodart v. Mutual Film Corp., 249 Fed. 507 (S.D.N.Y. 1917), *aff'd without opinion,* 249 Fed. 513 (2d Cir. 1918), pp. 824, 1156.

Straus v. American Publishers Assn., 231 U.S. 222 (1913), pp. 575, 945.

Supreme Records, Inc. v. Decca Records, Inc., 90 F. Supp. 904 (S.D. Cal. 1950), p. 571.

Sweet Music, Inc. v. Melrose Music Corp., 189 F. Supp. 655 (S.D. Cal. 1960), pp. 255, 310, 321, 324, 325, 326.

Szekely v. Eagle Lion Films, Inc., 242 F. 2d 266 (2d Cir. 1957), pp. 942, 1130.

T

U

V

W

INDEX TO COPYRIGHT ACT

A

B

C

D

E

F

M

N

O

P

R

S

T

U

GENERAL SUBJECT INDEX

(All References are to Sections)

A

B

D

E

J

P

S

T

U